wwnorton.com/nawr

The StudySpace site that accompanies *The Norton Anthology of World Religions* is FREE, but you will need the code below to register for a password that will allow you to access the copyrighted materials on the site.

WRLD—RLGN

THE NORTON ANTHOLOGY OF

WORLD
RELIGIONS

DAOISM

THE NORTON ANTHOLOGY OF

WORLD
RELIGIONS

DAOISM

James Robson

PROFESSOR OF EAST ASIAN LANGUAGES AND CIVILIZATIONS

HARVARD UNIVERSITY

JACK MILES, *General Editor*

DISTINGUISHED PROFESSOR OF ENGLISH AND
RELIGIOUS STUDIES,
UNIVERSITY OF CALIFORNIA, IRVINE

W · W · NORTON & COMPANY

NEW YORK · LONDON

W. W. Norton & Company has been independent since its founding in 1923, when William Warder Norton and Mary D. Herter Norton first published lectures delivered at the People's Institute, the adult education division of New York City's Cooper Union. The firm soon expanded its program beyond the Institute, publishing books by celebrated academics from America and abroad. By midcentury, the two major pillars of Norton's publishing program—trade books and college texts—were firmly established. In the 1950s, the Norton family transferred control of the company to its employees, and today—with a staff of four hundred and a comparable number of trade, college, and professional titles published each year—W. W. Norton & Company stands as the largest and oldest publishing house owned wholly by its employees.

Manufacturing by RRDonnelley Crawfordsville
Composition by Westchester Book
Book design by Jo Anne Metsch
Production Manager: Sean Mintus

LIBRARY OF CONGRESS CATALOGING-IN-PUBLICATION DATA

The Norton anthology of world religions / Jack Miles, General Editor, Distinguished Professor of English and Religious Studies, University of California, Irvine; Wendy Doniger, Hinduism; Donald S. Lopez, Jr., Buddhism; James Robson, Daoism. — First Edition.
    volumes cm
    Includes bibliographical references and index.
    ISBN 978-0-393-91897-7 (hardcover)
    1. Religions. 2. Religions—History—Sources. I. Miles, Jack, 1942– editor.
II. Doniger, Wendy, editor. III. Lopez, Donald S., 1952– editor. IV. Robson, James, 1965 December 1– editor.
    BL74.N67 2014
    208—dc23
                                                                            2014030756

**Daoism (978-0-393-91897-7): Jack Miles, General Editor;
James Robson, Editor**

W. W. Norton & Company, Inc.
500 Fifth Avenue
New York NY 10110
wwnorton.com

W. W. Norton & Company Ltd.
Castle House, 75/76 Wells Street, London W1T 3QT

1 2 3 4 5 6 7 8 9 0

Contents

LIST OF MAPS AND ILLUSTRATIONS   xvii

PREFACE   xix

ACKNOWLEDGMENTS   xxxi

GENERAL INTRODUCTION
How the West Learned to Compare Religions   3

JACK MILES

DAOISM   43
Introduction: Daoism Lost and Found   45

JAMES ROBSON

CHRONOLOGY   69

The Dawn of Daoism: From the Zhou Dynasty (1046–256 B.C.E.) through the Qin Dynasty (221–206 B.C.E.)   77

THE BOOK OF MASTER MO (Mozi)   83
    From Against the Confucians   83

THE SCRIPTURE OF THE WAY AND ITS VIRTUE
(Daode jing, *or* Laozi)   85
    From Book One   87
    From Book Two   93

THE BOOK OF MASTER ZHUANG (Zhuangzi)   97
    Free and Easy Wandering   98
    The Secret of Caring for Life   102
    In the World of Men   103
    Mastering Life   110

MASTER OF HUAINAN (Huainan-zi)   117
    From One. Originating in the Way   118
    From Two. Activating the Genuine   125

FROM INWARD TRAINING (Neiye)   128

FROM THE SEAL OF THE UNITY OF THE THREE, IN ACCORDANCE
WITH THE BOOK OF CHANGES (Zhouyi cantong qi)   133

THE BOOK OF MASTER HAN FEI (Han Feizi)   142
    From Explaining the *Laozi* (Jielao)   143

THE OLD MAN BY THE RIVER COMMENTARY (Heshang gong)   152
    Chapter 3. How to Pacify the People   153

Sima Tan • *FROM* ESSENTIAL POINTS ON THE SIX LINEAGES OF
THOUGHT (Lun liujia yaozhi)   154

Classical Daoism Takes Shape: From the Han Dynasty (202 B.C.E.–220 C.E.) through the Six Dynasties Period (220–589 C.E.)

                                                 159

THE SCRIPTURE OF GREAT PEACE (Taiping jing)   169
    Section 41. How to Distinguish between Poor and Rich   170

THE LAOZI INSCRIPTION (Laozi ming)   177

SCRIPTURE ON LAOZI'S TRANSFORMATIONS (Laozi bianhua jing)   181

Cao Zhi • TWO POEMS ON TAISHAN   184
    [Urge on the Carriage]   184
    [In the Morn I Wandered]   186

Xiang Kai • *FROM* MEMORIAL TO EMPEROR HUAN
CONCERNING BUDDHISM AND DAOISM   186

Wang Fu • THE CONVERSION OF THE BARBARIANS   188

FROM THE XIANG'ER COMMENTARY ON THE LAOZI
(Laozi xiang'er zhu)   193

FROM COMMANDS AND ADMONITIONS FOR THE FAMILY OF
THE GREAT DAO (Dadao jia lingjie)   202

REGULATIONS OF THE DARK CAPITAL (Xuandu lüwen)   207
    Regulations for Petitioning   208

THE MOST HIGH JADE SCRIPTURE ON THE INTERNAL
VIEW OF THE YELLOW COURT (Taishang huangting neijing yujing)   210

THE ARRAY OF THE FIVE NUMINOUS TREASURE TALISMANS
OF THE MOST HIGH (Taishang lingbao wufu xu)   215
    Absorption of Solar and Lunar Essences   215

INSTRUCTIONS ON THE SCRIPTURE OF THE DIVINE ELIXIRS
OF THE NINE TRIPODS OF THE YELLOW EMPEROR
(Huangdi jiuding shendan jing)   218

Ge Hong • THE INNER CHAPTERS OF THE BOOK OF THE
MASTER WHO EMBRACES SIMPLICITY (Baopu zi neipian)   223
    Climbing [Mountains] and Fording [Rivers]   224
    Talismans for Entering Mountains   233

TRADITIONS OF DIVINE TRANSCENDENTS (Shenxian zhuan)   234
    Li Changzai   235
    Mozi   236
    Zhang Ling   236

FROM THE DEMON STATUTES OF LADY BLUE (Nüqing guilü)   240

FROM THE RECORD OF THE TEN CONTINENTS (Shizhou ji)   243

THE 180 PRECEPTS SPOKEN BY LORD LAO
(Laojun shuo yibai bashi jie)   247

FROM THE SPIRIT SPELLS OF THE ABYSS (Dongyuan shenzhou jing)   256

THE DECLARATIONS OF THE PERFECTED (Zhen'gao)   261
    The Diffusion of the Corpus   262
    Betrothal   273
    Marriage   276

MASTER ZHOU'S RECORDS OF HIS COMMUNICATIONS
WITH THE UNSEEN (Zhoushi mingtong ji)   280
    From Tao Hongjing's Preface   281
    From Zhou's Records, Annotated by Tao Hongjing   286

THE MARVELOUS SCRIPTURE IN PURPLE CHARACTERS
OF THE LORD EMPEROR OF THE GOLD PORTAL
(Huangtian shangqing jinque dijun lingshu ziwen shangjing)   292
    Ingesting Solar and Lunar Pneumas   293

SCRIPTURE OF THE THREE PRIMORDIAL PERFECTED
ONES, BY THE IMPERIAL LORD OF THE GOLDEN PORTAL
(Jinque dijun sanyuan zhenyi jing)   298

FROM THE WONDROUS SCRIPTURE OF THE UPPER CHAPTERS OF LIMITLESS SALVATION (Lingbao wuliang duren shangpin miaojing) — 305

PURIFICATION RITE OF LUMINOUS PERFECTED (Mingzhen zhai) — 314

Lu Xiujing • THE ABRIDGED CODES OF MASTER LU FOR THE DAOIST COMMUNITY (Lu xiansheng daomen kelüe) — 321

Lu Xiujing • THE FIVE SENTIMENTS OF GRATITUDE (Dongxuan lingbao wugan wen) — 330

SCRIPTURE OF THE OPENING OF HEAVEN BY THE MOST HIGH LORD LAO (Taishang laojun kaitian jing) — 332

FROM BIOGRAPHIES OF STUDENTS OF THE DAO (Daoxue zhuan) — 336

FROM THE SCRIPTURE OF THE INNER EXPLANATIONS OF THE THREE HEAVENS (Santian neijie jing) — 340

THE GREAT PETITION FOR SEPULCHRAL PLAINTS (Dazhong songzhang) — 343

Liu Yiqing • A NEW ACCOUNT OF TALES OF THE WORLD (Shishuo xinyu) — 348
[A Buddhist Critique of Daoist Talismans] — 349

Zhen Luan • THE ESSAY TO RIDICULE THE DAO (Xiaodao lun) — 349
Preface — 350
Revival of the Dead through Fivefold Purification — 352
Laozi Became the Buddha — 353
Taking Cinnabar Brings a Golden Complexion — 354
Plagiarizing Buddhist Sutras for Daoist Scriptures — 355

The Consolidation and Expansion of Daoism: From the Sui Dynasty (581–618 C.E.) through the Tang Dynasty (618–907 C.E.)

359

FROM THE ESSENTIALS OF THE PRACTICE OF PERFECTION FROM THE ONE AND ORTHODOX RITUAL CANON (Zhengyi fawen xiuzhen zhiyao) — 367

SCRIPTURAL INSTRUCTIONS OF THE PRIMORDIAL PERFECTED FROM THE HALL OF LIGHT OF HIGHEST CLARITY (Shangqing mingtang yuanzhen jingjue) — 372
The Technique of the Mystic Realized One — 373

Zhang Wanfu • *FROM* THE SHORT EXPOSITION ON THE
TRANSMISSION OF THE SCRIPTURES, RULES, AND
REGISTERS OF THE THREE CAVERNS
(Chuanshou sandong jingjie falu lüeshuo)   375

FROM THE SCRIPTURE AND CHART FOR THE MYSTERIOUS
CONTEMPLATION OF MAN-BIRD MOUNTAIN
(Xuanlan renniao shan jingtu)   380

THE REGULATIONS FOR THE ACCEPTANCE AND
CULTIVATION OF DAOISM ACCORDING TO THE DONGXUAN,
LINGBAO, AND SANDONG SCRIPTURES
(Dongxuan lingbao sandong fengdao kejie yingshi)   382
   Crimes as Conditions for Retribution   383
   Good Deeds as Conditions for Retribution   384
   The Creation of Icons   385
   The Daoist's Clothes   389

SCRIPTURE ON INNER OBSERVATION BY THE MOST HIGH
LORD LAO (Taishang laojun neiguan jing)   391

Shitou Xiqian • THE SEAL OF THE UNITY OF THE THREE
(Cantong qi)   395

Yan Zhenqing • STELE INSCRIPTION FOR THE ALTAR OF
THE TRANSCENDENT LADY WEI OF THE JIN DYNASTY,
THE LADY OF THE SOUTHERN PEAK, PRIMAL WORTHY OF THE
PURPLE VOID, CONCURRENTLY SUPREME TRUE MISTRESS OF
DESTINY (Jin zixu yuanjun ling shangzhen siming nanyue furen
xiantan beiming)   396

Wu Yun • CANTOS ON PACING THE VOID (Buxu ci)   398

SELECTED POEMS   403
   Li Bo   404
   The Ascent of Mount Tai   404
   The Lady of the Supreme Primordial   407
   Flying Dragon Conductus   408
   Bo Juyi   409
   Composed in Response to "Sending Daoist Master Liu
     Off to Wander on Heavenly Platform Mountain"   409

Li Ao • *FROM* THE BOOK OF RETURNING TO ONE'S
TRUE NATURE (Fuxing shu)   410

Guifeng Zongmi • THE INQUIRY INTO THE ORIGIN
OF HUMANITY (Yuanren lun)   415
   Exposing Deluded Attachments   415

Du Guangting • RECORDS OF THE ASSEMBLED
TRANSCENDENTS OF THE FORTIFIED WALLED CITY
(Yongcheng jixian lu)   418
    Wang Fajin   419
    Ms. Wang   422
    Mao Ying   423

Du Guangting • BIOGRAPHIES OF PERSONS WHO HAD
CONTACTS AND ENCOUNTERS WITH SUPERNATURAL
BEINGS AND IMMORTALS (Shenxian ganyu zhuan)   426
    Biography of Li Quan   426

Du Guangting • RECORD OF MIRACLES IN SUPPORT OF
DAOISM (Daojiao lingyan ji)   428
    An Examination of the Altar of the Transcendent Lady
      Wei of Nanyue   429

THE SUTRA OF THE THREE KITCHENS, PREACHED BY THE
BUDDHA (Foshuo sanchu jing)   429

Du Guangting • FROM RECORDED FOR THE RITUAL OF MERIT
AND VIRTUE FOR REPAIRING THE VARIOUS OBSERVATORIES
OF QINGCHENG MOUNTAIN (Xiu qingcheng shan zhuguan
gongde ji)   432

THE COLLECTION OF BOOKS NEW AND OLD ON THE
ABSORPTION OF BREATH GATHERED BY THE MASTER OF
YANLING (Yanling xiansheng ji xinjiu fuqi jing)   434
    Formula for the Use of Breath by Perfect Men of Mysterious
      Simplicity, Expounded by the Master of Great Respect 435

YU XUANJI'S LIFE AND POEMS   437
    From Minor Writings from Shanshui by Huangfu Mei   437
    POEMS
    Feelings in the Last Month of Spring; Sent to a Friend   439
    On the Assigned Topic of Willows by the River   440
    Early Autumn   440
    Selling Wilted Peonies   440
    During a Visit to the Southern Tower of the Veneration
      of Truth Monastery I Saw the New Examination
      Graduates Writing Their Names on the Wall   440

THE CHRONICLES OF JAPAN (Nihongi)   441
    [Corpse Liberation]   441

POEMS COMPOSED BY KAKINOMOTO NO ASOMI HITOMARO
WHEN THE SOVEREIGN WENT ON AN EXCURSION TO THE
PALACE AT YOSHINO   442
    [Where our Sovereign reigns]   442
    [Our great Sovereign]   443

Kukai • INDICATIONS OF THE GOALS OF THE THREE
TEACHINGS (Sango shiki)   444
   Preface   445
   Part Two: The Argument of Kyobu [Daoist]   446

Sŏl Ch'ong • INSCRIPTION ON AN IMAGE AT KAMSAN
MONASTERY   451

The Resurgence and Diversification of Daoism: The Song (960–1279 C.E.) and Yuan (1260–1368 C.E.) Dynasties   455

FROM THE SCRIPTURE ON THE GOLDEN ELIXIR OF THE
DRAGON AND TIGER (Jindan longhu jing)   465

Zhang Boduan • AWAKENING TO REALITY (Wuzhen pian)   468

Zhang Boduan • A SONG FOR LIU, A COMRADE OF THE
DAO, OF WHITE TIGER CAVE (Zeng bailongdong Liu daoren ge)   474

Zhou Dunyi • EXPLANATION OF THE DIAGRAM OF THE
SUPREME POLARITY (Taijitu shuo)   476

Shao Yong • BIOGRAPHY OF THE GENTLEMAN WITH NO
NAME (Wuming jun zhuan)   479

Yuan Miaozong • FROM SECRET ESSENTIALS OF THE MOST
HIGH PRINCIPAL ZHENREN ASSISTING THE COUNTRY AND
SAVING THE PEOPLE (Taishang zhuguo jiumin zongzhen biyao)   483

Hong Mai • FROM HEARD AND WRITTEN BY YIJIAN (Yijian zhi)   487

ESOTERIC BIOGRAPHY OF QINGHE (Qinghe neizhuan)   493

THE CORPUS OF DAOIST RITUAL (Daofa huiyuan)   495
   Song of the Dark Pearl   496

PRIVATE TUTOR OF THE NINE SPONTANEOUSLY GENERATING
LINGBAO HEAVENS OF PRIMORDIAL COMMENCEMENT:
ON LATENT REFINEMENT FOR TRANSCENDENT SALVATION
AND VITALIZING TRANSFORMATION (Yuanshi lingbao ziran
jiutian shenghua chaodu yinlian bijue)   501

Bai Yuchan • FROM A VERMILION PETITION MEMORIALIZING
THE THUNDER COURT ON THE MATTER OF DELIBERATING
MERIT TITLES (Leifu zou shiyi xun danzhang)   505

Wang Qizhen • THE GREAT LINGBAO METHOD OF THE
SHANGQING HEAVEN (Shangqing lingbao dafa)   510

FROM TRACT OF THE MOST EXALTED ON ACTION AND
RESPONSE (Taishang ganying pian)   514

Wang Zhe • *FROM* REDOUBLED YANG'S FIFTEEN
DISCOURSES FOR THE ESTABLISHMENT OF THE DOCTRINE
(Chongyang lijiao shiwu lun)   519

Li Zhichang • *FROM* THE RECORD OF PERFECTED PERPETUAL
SPRING'S TRAVELS TO THE WEST (Changchun zhenren xiyou ji)   523

INSCRIPTIONS FROM THE PALACE OF ETERNAL JOY   529
    Yuan Congyi • *From* A Record of the Tang Dynasty Shrine
        to Perfected Man Lü of Purified Yang (You Tang
        Chunyang lü zhenren citang ji)   530
    Wang E • *From* A Stele on the Reconstruction of the Great
        Palace of Purified Yang and Limitless Longevity [during]
        Our Great Dynasty (Dachao chongjian Chunyang
        wanshou gong zhi bei)   531
    A Stele of an Imperial Decree [Issued to] the Palace of
        Purified Yang and Limitless Longevity (Chunyang
        wanshou gong shengzhi bei)   532

Wang Daoyuan • ESSAY ON THE SECRET ESSENTIALS OF
THE RECYCLED ELIXIR (Huandan biyao lun)   533

ZHONGLI OF THE HAN LEADS LAN CAIHE TO ENLIGHTENMENT
(Han Zhong Li dutuo Lan Caihe)   537

MEMORABILIA OF THE THREE KINGDOMS (Samguk yusa)   552
    Podŏk (Koguryŏ)   553

RECORDS OF THE THREE KINGDOMS (Samguk sagi)   554
    Yŏn Kaesomun (Koguryŏ)   554

The New Standardization and Unification of Daoism: From the Ming Dynasty (1368–1644 C.E.) through the Qing Dynasty (1644–1912 C.E.)   557

JOURNEY TO THE WEST (Xiyou ji)   573
    At the Three Pure Ones Temple the Great Sage Leaves
        His Name; At the Cart Slow Kingdom the Monkey King
        Reveals His Power   573

JOURNEY TO THE NORTH (Beiyou ji)   587
    The Dark Emperor Descends Once More into the Mortal
        World to Save the People from Misery   587

A RECORD OF THE LAND OF THE BLESSED (Sanshan fudi zhi)   591

Hanshan Deqing • COMMENTARIES ON THE *LAOZI* AND
ZHUANGZI   595

A TASTE OF IMMORTALITY   599

Matteo Ricci • *FROM* RELIGIOUS SECTS AMONG THE CHINESE   604

SELECTED QING DYNASTY EDICTS   608
    On Private Founding of Monastic Buildings, and Private
        Ordinations of Buddhist and Daoist Monks   608
    Regulation of the Clergy   610

THE DAOIST PRIEST OF THE LAO MOUNTAINS   611

FROM THE SECRET OF THE GOLDEN FLOWER
(Taiyi jinhua zongzhi)   614

Fu Shan • CUTTING THE RED DRAGON
(Duan Honglong)   619

He Longxiang • COMBINED COLLECTION OF FEMALE
ALCHEMY (Nüdan hebian)   620
    From The Preface   621
    Awaiting Salvation   622

Zhang Sanfeng • *FROM* SECRET PRINCIPLES OF GATHERING
THE TRUE ESSENCE (Caizhen jiyao)   623

Min Yide • TRANSMISSION OF THE MIND-LAMP FROM
MOUNT JIN'GAI (Jin'gai xindeng)   626
    Biography of Zhao Daojian (1163–1221), the First Patriarch   627
    Biography of Wang Changyue (?–1680)   628

THE HERMITS OF HUASHAN   629

IMMORTAL'S CERTIFICATE   629

A SHAMANISTIC EXORCISM   631

BIOGRAPHICAL STELE INSCRIPTION FOR THE DAOIST WANG
(Wang daoren daoxing bei)   632

Modern Chinese History and the Remaking of Daoism: From the Republican Era (1912–1949) to the Early Twenty-First Century

                                       637

THE DAO AMONG THE YAO OF SOUTHEAST ASIA:
SELECTED TEXTS   651

Alfred, Lord Tennyson • *FROM* THE ANCIENT SAGE   654

Oscar Wilde • A CHINESE SAGE   657

TAOISM: A PRIZE ESSAY   663

Martin Buber • *FROM* COMMENTARY ON "TALKS AND
PARABLES OF CHUANG TZU"   667

Carl Gustav Jung • FOREWORD TO "THE SECRET OF THE
GOLDEN FLOWER"   673

Chen Yingning • *FROM* EXPLORATIONS IN ORAL SECRETS
(Koujue gouxuan lu)   675

Fangnei Sanren • A BALLAD ON LOOKING FOR THE WAY   677

FROM THE COMPLETE PERFORMANCE OF SU (Dachu su)   679

Yoshitoyo Yoshioka • *FROM* DAOIST MONASTIC LIFE   687

Paul Shih-yi Hsiao • *FROM* HEIDEGGER AND OUR
TRANSLATION OF THE *DAODE JING*   700

Xu Jianguo • WHY MUST WE PROHIBIT THE REACTIONARY
DAOIST CULTS?   707

BUDDHISTS AND DAOISTS AT MOUNT NANYUE WELCOME
THE PEOPLE'S COMMUNES   711

George Harrison • THE INNER LIGHT   713

Fritjof Capra • THE TAO OF PHYSICS: AN EXPLORATION
OF THE PARALLELS BETWEEN MODERN PHYSICS AND
EASTERN MYSTICISM   714
    From Beyond the World of Opposites   716

Qian Zhongshu • LIMITED VIEWS: ESSAYS ON IDEAS AND
LETTERS (Guanzhui bian)   721
    The Insights and Myopia of Mystical Philosophies   722

TWO RITUAL DOCUMENTS   727
    Memorial for a Communal Ritual   727
    Announcement for a Communal Ritual   730

A DAOIST ORDINATION CERTIFICATE FROM PUTIAN, FUJIAN   732

TWO PRAYERS TO THE DEIFIED LAOZI FROM
PENANG, MALAYSIA   736
    Limitless Longevity   737
    Lord Lao's Spirit Medium   738

Ursula K. Le Guin • INTRODUCTION TO THE *TAO TE CHING* and EPILOGUE: DAO SONG   740

RZA • THE WU-TANG MANUAL   745
   Look to the East   746
   The "Three Ways": Taoism, Buddhism, Confucianism   746

Zhang Jiyu • A DECLARATION OF THE CHINESE DAOIST ASSOCIATION ON GLOBAL ECOLOGY   748

Glossary   A3

Selected Bibliography   A9

Permissions Acknowledgments   A15

Index   A23

Maps and Illustrations

MAP
Daoist Sites and Sacred Mountains   74

ILLUSTRATIONS
Talisman from a Tang dynasty manuscript   53
Porcelain vase Ming dynasty   61
Detail from the Mawangdui Silk Texts   76
Painting of Laozi   86
Bronze statue of the deified Laozi   158
Detail from *The Kangxi Emperor's Southern Inspection
   Tour* by Wang Hui   185
Talisman for protection when entering mountains   233
A portion of *The Wondrous Scripture of the Upper Chapters
   of Limitless Salvation* in esoteric script   314
Tang dynasty star map   358
Wu Zetian   361
Yuan dynasty illustration of the Lord of Nine Heavens
   with thunder gods and other attendants   454
Illustrations of the human body from a text on internal
   alchemy   460
Diagram of the Supreme Polarity   478
Illustration of the Pace of Yu   487
Ming dynasty painting of the God of Literature (Wenchang)   493
Song dynasty painting depicting the descent of a Daoist
   deity and attendants to liberate a soul from
   the netherworld (Liang Kai)   502
Zhongli Quan holding a gourd (Zhao Qi)   537
Detail from *Spring Dawn at the Cinnabar Terrace* (Lu Guang)   556
Qing dynasty portrait of a Daoist priest   564
Diagram of the Chinese concepts concerned with the
   development of the Golden Flower   617
Illustration of Marriage of the Dragon and Tiger (woodblock)   623
Female Daoist priest talking on her mobile phone   636
Propaganda poster from the Cultural Revolution   645
The White Cloud Temple in Beijing on New Year's Day, 2011   646
The dynamic unity of polar opposites   717
A transition from two to three dimensions   719
Coat of arms devised by Niels Bohr   720

Preface

Welcome to *The Norton Anthology of World Religions*. The work offered to you here is large and complex, but it responds to a simple desire—namely, the desire that six major, living, international world religions should be allowed to speak to you in their own words rather than only through the words of others about them. Virtually all of the religious texts assembled here are primary texts. Practitioners of Hinduism, Buddhism, Daoism, Judaism, Christianity, and Islam have written and preserved these texts over the centuries for their own use and their own purposes. What is it like to read them, gathered as they are here like works of religious art in a secular museum?

For practitioners of any of these six religions, who number in the hundreds of millions, this anthology is likely to provide some of the surprise and fascination of a very large family album: some of one's religious ancestors trigger an immediate flash of recognition, while others look very distant and perhaps even comical. For an army of outsiders—those whose religion is not anthologized here, those who practice no religion, those who are "spiritual but not religious," and those who count themselves critics or antagonists of religion—the experience will be rewarding in different ways. No propaganda intrudes here on behalf either of any given religion or of religion in general. The goal at every point is not conversion, but exploration. The only assumptions made are that the most populous and influential of the world's religions are here to stay, that they reward study best when speaking to you in their own words, and that their contemporary words make best sense when heard against the panoramic background of the words they have remembered and preserved from their storied pasts.

Many of the texts gathered here have been translated from foreign languages, for the religions of the world have spoken many different languages over the course of their long histories. A few of the works—the *Bhagavad Gita*, the *Daode jing*, the Bible, the Qur'an—are readily available. Many more are available only in the libraries of a few major research universities or, though physically available, have not been intellectually available without detailed guidance that was impossible for the lay reader to come by. Bibliographic information is always provided for previously published translations, and a number of translations have been made especially for this anthology. A central concern throughout has been that the anthologized texts should be not just translated but also framed by enough editorial explanation to make them audible and intelligible across the barriers of time and space even if you are coming to them for the first time. When those explanations require the use of words in a foreign language with a non-Roman writing system, standard academic modes of transliteration have sometimes been simplified to enhance user-friendliness.

Globalization, including international migration in all its forms, has brought about a large-scale and largely involuntary mingling of once-separate religious communities, and this historic change has created an urgent occasion for a deeply grounded effort at interreligious understanding. Yes, most of the world's Hindus still live in India, yet the Hindu Diaspora is enormous and influential. Yes, many Jews have migrated to Israel, but half of the world's Jews still live in deeply rooted Diaspora communities around the world. Conventionally, Islam is thought of as a Middle Eastern religion, yet the largest Muslim populations are in South and Southeast Asia, while the Muslim minority in Europe is growing rapidly. By the same token, Christianity is not thought of as an African religion, yet the Christian population of sub-Saharan Africa is growing even more rapidly than the Muslim population of Europe. In a bygone era, the six religions treated here might have been divided geographically into an "Eastern" and a "Western" trio, but we do not so divide them, for in our era they are all everywhere, and none is a majority. Religiously, we live and in all likelihood will continue to live in a world of large and mingling minorities.

This involuntary mingling has created a state of affairs that can be violently disruptive. Terrorism in the name of religion, more often within national borders than across them, has turned many minds against religion in all forms. And yet, paradoxically, religious violence during the twenty-first century has persuaded many that, contrary to innumerable past predictions, religion is by no means fading from modern life. And though the threat of religious violence is a dark challenge of one sort, the bright new opportunities for cross-cultural and interreligious learning present an unprecedented challenge of a different and, in the end, a more consequential sort. On the one hand, whatever some of us might have wished, religious violence has made religion a subject that cannot be avoided. On the other, for those who engage the subject in depth, the study of religion across cultural and political borders builds a uniquely deep and subtle form of cosmopolitan sophistication.

In all its formal features—the format of its tables of contents; its use of maps and illustrations; its handling of headnotes, footnotes, glossaries, and bibliographies; its forty-eight pages of color illustration in six inserts—*The Norton Anthology of World Religions* announces its membership in the venerable family of Norton anthologies. As was true of *The Norton Anthology of English Literature* upon its first publication more than half a century ago, this anthology is both larger and more rigorously realized than any prior anthology published in English for use by the general reader or the college undergraduate. It opens with a generous introduction addressing a set of basic questions not linked to any single tradition but affecting all of them. Each of the six religious traditions is then presented chronologically from its origins to the present (the Buddhism volume also uses a geographical organizing principle). Each presentation begins with a substantial overview of the tradition being anthologized. Each is also punctuated by period introductions tracing the history of the tradition in question. And yet this work is not a history merely enlivened by the inclusion of original texts. No, history here is simply the stage. The texts themselves are the performance, displaying as only they can the perennial and subversive power of religious literature. The difference might be compared to the difference between English history with a bit of Shakespeare and Shakespeare with a bit of English history. The histories come and go, but Shakespeare is irreplaceable. Shakespeare is, to use a term that originated in the church, *canonical*.

Derived from the Greek word for a ruler or measuring rod, *canon* came to mean a rule or criterion of any kind. By extension, the same word came to mean the church rule or "canon" law governing the contents of the Bible: which books were to be included and which excluded. And by yet a further extension, canon came to refer to the understood list of acknowledged masterpieces in English or some other literature. So, the Bible has a canon. English literature has a canon (however endlessly contested). But what works of religious literature constitute the world religious canon?

Aye, dear reader, there was the rub as plans were laid for this anthology. In 2006, when the editorial team began work in earnest, no canons existed for the literatures of the world's major religions. There were limited canons within that vast expanse of written material, the Bible itself being the paradigmatic example. But the literature of Christianity is larger than the Bible, and the situation grows only more complicated as one ranges farther afield into traditions whose concentric canons are more implicit than explicit. Even though more than one canon of the Bible exists, Bible scholars can easily handle that limited variety and still quite literally *know what they are talking about*: they can deal with a clearly delimited body of material within which evidence-based historical interpretation can go forward. But what canon of religious texts exists to help define the entire field of religious studies for religion scholars? The field has never had an agreed-upon answer to that question, and some of the most sweeping theoretical statements about religion turn out, as a result, to rest on an astonishingly small and vague empirical base.

Granted that no master canon in the original religious sense of that term can ever be devised for the religions of the world, the lack of a limited but large and serious study collection of texts is one major indication that the study of religion remains at an early stage of its development as a discipline. For the religions of Asia, especially, it has been as if the Elizabethan theater were being studied without ready access by students to the plays of Shakespeare or with, at most, access to *Hamlet* alone. This lack has been particularly glaring in the United States for reasons that deserve a brief review. Until the early 1960s, the study of religion was largely confined to private colleges and universities, where, thanks to the country's Protestant intellectual heritage, it consisted overwhelmingly of biblical studies and Christian theology. Often, the department of religion was a department of philosophy and religion. Often, too, there was a close relationship between such departments and the college chaplaincy. In public colleges and universities, meanwhile, the situation was quite different. There, the traditional constitutional separation of church and state was understood to preclude the formal study of religion, perhaps especially of the very religions that the student body and the faculty might turn out to be practicing.

But then several events, occurring at nearly the same moment in both the public and the private spheres, created a new climate for the study of religion, and "religious studies" emerged as a new academic discipline distinct from philosophy or theology, on the one hand, and even more distinct from the chaplaincy, on the other. We are still reckoning with the consequences of this shift.

In 1963, Associate Justice Arthur Goldberg wrote for the Supreme Court of the United States in a concurring opinion in *Abington v. Schempp* (374 U.S. 203, 306): "It seems clear to me . . . that the Court would recognize the propriety of . . . the teaching *about* religion, as distinguished from the teaching *of* religion, in the public schools," language that seemed to clear a path for the study of religion in tax-supported schools. Significantly, Goldberg was a Jew; just three years earlier, Americans had elected John F. Kennedy as their first Roman Catholic president. American religious pluralism was becoming increasingly inescapable at the highest levels in American public life; and as it came to be understood that university-level religious studies was to be the study of various religions at once, including but by no means confined to the religions of the United States, the Founding Fathers' fear of an imposed, national religion began to recede from the national consciousness. American pluralism was now as powerful a factor in American religious life as the Constitution itself.

This anthology is published on the fiftieth anniversary of an event little noticed in the cultural ferment of the 1960s but of great importance for the study of religion—namely, the 1964 reincorporation of the National Association of Biblical Instructors (NABI), the principal association of college professors teaching these subjects, as the American Academy of Religion (AAR), whose current mission statement focuses pointedly on "the understanding of religious traditions, issues, questions, and values"—all in the plural. The formal incorporation of the AAR was intended first as a quiet but magnanimous gesture of invitation by a Protestant academic establishment toward the scholars of America's Catholic and Jewish communities, but this was just the beginning. Others would soon be drawn into a conversation whose animating academic conviction is well captured in a dictum of the great nineteenth-century scholar Max Müller: "He who knows one religion knows none."

Catholics and Jews had had their own seminaries and their own institutions of higher learning, but scholarship produced in them tended to remain in them—partly, to be sure, because of Protestant indifference but also because of defensive or reactively triumphalist habits of mind among the residually embattled minorities themselves. But this was already changing. Optimism and openness in the Roman Catholic community had been much assisted in the earlier 1960s by the Second Vatican Council, whose byword was the Italian *aggiornamento*—roughly, "updating"—as employed by the benignly bold Pope John XXIII. American Jews, meanwhile, profoundly traumatized as they had been during and after World War II by the Shoah, or Holocaust, Nazi Germany's attempted genocide, breathed a collective (if premature) sigh of relief in 1967 after Israel's stunning victory over its Arab opponents in the Six-Day War. During the same period, the Reverend Dr. Martin Luther King, Jr., had spearheaded a revolution in American race relations, as segregation ended and the social integration began that would lead to the election of a black president, Barack Obama, in 2008. In short, the mood in the early 1960s was in every way one of barred doors swung open, locked windows flung up, and common cause undertaken in moral enterprises like the interfaith campaign to end the war in Vietnam.

One influential scholar saw the shift occurring in the study of religion as cause for academic jubilation. Writing in 1971 in the *Journal of the American Academy of Religion* (which had been, until 1966, *The Journal of Bible and*

Religion), Wilfred Cantwell Smith clearly welcomed the change that was taking place:

> Perhaps what is happening can be summed up most pithily by saying that the transition has been from the teaching of religion to the study of religion. Where men used to instruct, they now inquire. They once attempted to impart what they themselves knew, and what they hoped (of late, with decreasing expectation) to make interesting; now, on the contrary, they inquire, into something that both for them and for their students is incontrovertibly interesting, but is something that they do not quite understand.

And yet there was a shadow across this scene. The newborn American Academy of Religion had bitten off rather more than it could chew. The spread of religious studies to the state university campuses that were proliferating in the late 1960s and the 1970s was vigorously pluralist. Jewish studies experienced an enormous growth spurt, and so did Hindu studies, Buddhist studies, Islamic studies, and so forth. Smith, a scholar of comparative religion who had made his first mark as a specialist in Islam, could only welcome this in principle. But others, writing later, would be troubled by growth that seemed to have spun out of control.

Recall that in 1971, *globalization* was not the byword that it has since become. The Hindu Diaspora in the United States was still tiny. Christian Pentecostalism, though well established, had not yet achieved critical mass in Africa. Europe's Muslim minority, if already substantial, was relatively dormant. Mainland China's population was still in Maoist lockdown. And in the United States, Americans had not yet begun to grasp the coming effects of the passage of the Immigration and Nationality Act of 1965, which removed quotas that had been in place since the 1920s; the resulting explosive growth in Hispanic and Asian immigration would by 1990 make non-Hispanic Caucasians a minority in Los Angeles, America's second-largest city. Americans still saw themselves as a colonized people who had achieved independence, rather than as a colonizing people. The rhetoric of European postcolonialism had not yet been applied to the United States, a superpower whose world hegemony was quasi-imperial in its reach and neocolonialist in its effects. Worldwide, the transformative interrogation of religious traditions by women and about women had barely begun.

While all of these changes, as they have brought about the multiplication and intensification of religious encounters, have made the study of world religions more important than ever, they have not made it easier. They have not, in particular, lent it any internal intellectual coherence. They have not created for it a new study canon to replace the narrowly Protestant study canon, as the founding of the AAR seemed in principle to require. The creation of religious studies as a field had been an academic gamble on a barely perceived religious future. Had the bet paid off? An eminent senior scholar, Jonathan Z. Smith, wrote in 1995 of the change that had taken place: "The field made a decision to give up a (limited) coherence for a (limitless) incoherence."

That limitless incoherence was the context in which we took up the challenge to produce *The Norton Anthology of World Religions*. How ever were we to begin?

There came first the recognition that we would be creating for the field of religious studies a first draft of the very canon that it lacked—a canon covering nearly four thousand years of history in a score of different languages, aspiring not to be authoritative regarding belief or practice but to be plausibly foundational for the study of the subject.

There came second the recognition that though canons, once achieved, are anonymous, they do not begin anonymously. They begin with somebody who declares this in and that out and defends his or her choice. This realization shifted the decision to be made from *What?* to *Who?*

There came third the question of whether the answer to the question *Who?* would come in the singular or in the plural and if in the plural, how multitudinously plural. For each of the traditions to be anthologized, would a large board of specialist advisers be assembled to determine what would be included? Would the selections be formally approved by some kind of plebiscite, as in the verse-by-verse ratification by translators of the language included in the King James Version of the Bible? Would the work of annotating the resulting selections be divided among committees and subcommittees and so forth? Would some governing board formulate a set of topics that each editor or team of editors would be required to address so as to confer a sturdy structure upon the whole? Would there be, for example, a different board of consultants for each period in the long history of Judaism or each language across the geographic breadth of Buddhism?

Our decision was to reject that kind of elaboration and gamble instead on six brilliant and creative individuals, each with a distinct literary style and a record of bold publication, and then to impose no common matrix of obligatory topics or categories on them, nor even a common set of chronological divisions. (Does China have its own Middle Ages? When does modernity begin in Turkey?) It was understood, however, playing to an institutional strength at W. W. Norton & Company, that the prose of these editors, formidable though they were, would be edited very heavily for explanatory clarity even as we second-guessed very lightly indeed their actual anthological choices. To what end this blend of laxity and severity? Our aim has been simply to enhance the intelligent delight of students in religious literature both as literature and as religion. "Intelligent" delight does not mean the delight of intelligent people. The reference is rather to the delight that a strange and baffling ancient text can provide when a great scholar, speaking in his or her own voice, renders it intelligible for you and you recognize, behind it, a human intelligence finally not all that unlike your own.

If that has been our aim for students, our aim for professors has been rather different. Professors of religious studies often find themselves called upon to teach insanely far beyond their area of trained academic competence. For them, we hope to have provided both an invaluable reference tool and a rich reservoir of curricular possibilities. For their graduate students, we hope to have provided breadth to complement the depth of doctoral study at its best. A student studying in depth and probably in the original language some particular religious text can discover here what *else* was being written in the same tradition at the same time. What preceded that text in the life of the religious tradition? What followed it? Who celebrated it? Who attacked it? The fine art of page flipping, crucial to the unique operating system of an ink-on-paper anthology, enables just this kind of exploratory learning. Over time, by repeated forays backward and forward in the evolution of a religious tradition, a serious student can come to know its literature like the interior of a large residence. But this is just the beginning. Comparable forays into the development of other traditions can by degrees situate the target religious tradition in the global religious context. Finally, to further aid all users, the companion website to *The Norton Anthology of World Religions* will provide, over time, both supplementary substantive content—other religious traditions, to begin with—not included in the print anthology and an array of aids for the use of teachers and students.

Beyond these conventional services, however, lies something riskier. We acknowledge that we have provided the professoriate a target to shoot at: "How could you *possibly* omit X?" some will exclaim. And others: "Why on *earth* did you ever bother with Y?" We welcome all such objections. They betray nothing more than the real, existential condition of a field still in many ways struggling to be born. Disciplines do not spring into existence overnight. They are negotiated into existence over time through trial and error. The more vigorously our colleagues find fault with this first draft of a canon for their field, the more productive will be the ensuing negotiation.

Intuition based on deep scholarship and teaching experience has surely played a role in the choices made by the six associate editors responsible, respectively, for anthologizing the six religious literatures covered: Wendy Doniger (Hinduism), Donald S. Lopez, Jr. (Buddhism), James Robson (Daoism), David Biale (Judaism), Lawrence S. Cunningham (Christianity), and Jane Dammen McAuliffe (Islam). They have all sought to include those incipiently canonical texts that few of their colleagues would dare exclude. More intuitively, they have sought to include neglected works of beauty and power whose very appearance here might help them become canonical. The editors have even included occasional attacks on the religious traditions anthologized—for example, excerpts from Kancha Ilaiah, "Why I Am Not a Hindu," in the Hinduism anthology and from Bertrand Russell, "Why I Am Not a Christian," in the Christianity anthology. As these two contrarian entries nicely demonstrate, the canon of texts regarded as permanent and irreplaceable in a religious tradition does not coincide exactly with the canon of texts arguably crucial for the study of the tradition. Coping with all these complications, the editors have coped in every case as well with the painful space limitations that we have had to impose on them even after allowing the anthology to grow to nearly twice its originally envisioned size.

One large question remains to be addressed in this brief preface: *By what criteria did you choose to anthologize these and only these six religions?* This question has a theoretical as well as a practical dimension. How, to begin with, do we distinguish that which is religious from that which is not? Is atheism a religion, or at least a "religious option"? Whatever atheism is, it is certainly no modern novelty. *The Cambridge Companion to Atheism* (2007) begins with a substantial chapter, "Atheism in Antiquity," by the distinguished Dutch classicist Jan Bremmer. Whether atheism in a given ancient or modern form should be considered a strictly religious option may depend on how a given atheist "plays" it. The novelist Alain de Botton, nothing if not playful, dreams or artfully feigns dreaming of a floridly religious enactment of atheism in his *Religion for Atheists: A Non-believer's Guide to the Uses of Religion* (2012). Meanwhile, a 2010 survey by the Pew Forum suggests that the religiously unaffiliated might actually be both more interested in and better informed about religion than the affiliated. But back to the question at hand: If we cannot clearly distinguish religion from irreligion or the "strictly" from the "casually" religious, how can we be sure that we are choosing six versions of the same thing? Arcane and obscure as this question may sound, it did bear rather directly on one of our six key choices, as will be explained below.

In the end, in making our choices, we fell back to an infra-theoretical, practical, or "working" criterion for inclusion: we required that the religions anthologized should be the six most important *major, living, international* religions, a rubric in which each of the three italicized words counted.

Because we anthologize only *living* religions, we do not anthologize the religions of ancient Mesopotamia, Greece, and Rome, despite the fact that these religious traditions loom large in the history of the study of religion in the West, thanks to the dominance of the Bible and of the Greco-Roman classics in Western higher education.

Because we anthologize only *international* religions, we do not anthologize folkloric or indigenous religions, which are typically and symbiotically confined to a single locale, despite the fascination that these religions have had for the sociological or anthropological study of religion, from Johann Gottfried Herder and Émile Durkheim in the late eighteenth and nineteenth century to Clifford Geertz in the twentieth.

Geography, except as the difference between national and international, is not the principle of organization in this anthology. One consequence, however, of our anthologizing only literary religions and then applying a mostly demographic criterion in choosing among them has been the omission of indigenous African religion. While it is true that Yoruba religion is now international and that some texts for it are now available, no such text has become canonical even for practitioners themselves. Rather than saying anything about the limitations of African or other indigenous religious traditions, notably the rich array of Amerindian religions, our decision says something about the inherent limitations of any text-based approach to the study of religion. Texts can indeed teach much, but they cannot teach everything about everybody.

As for the key criterion *major*, we apply it demographically with one glaring exception. Religious demography tends to overstate or understate the size of a religion depending on whether and how that religion counts heads. Roman Catholicism, which counts every baptized baby as a member, probably ends up with somewhat overstated numbers. Daoism, by contrast, probably ends up with its adherents undercounted because formal affiliation is not a recognized criterion for basic participation in it.

Yet even after these difficulties have been acknowledged, there can be no quarrel that Christianity and Islam are demographically major as well as living and international. The same goes at almost equal strength for Hinduism and Buddhism. The obvious exception is Judaism, whose numbers worldwide, though far from trivial, are small even when the question "Who is a Jew?" is given its most broadly inclusive answer. Too small to be reckoned major by a head count, Judaism is too important on other counts to be reckoned less than major. It is the exception that breaks the rule. Its categories, its legends, and many of its practices have been decisive not only for Christianity and Islam but also, arguably, for Western secularism.

As many readers will have noticed by now, this grid of six does not stray very far from the textbook areas of religious studies, as is only right and proper in a reference work, yet this claim of relative "normality" calls for qualification in two final regards if only to provide the occasion for a pair of disclaimers.

First, this anthology does not deal with several religious traditions that, though fully literary and indeed of great intrinsic interest, do not meet its stated criteria. Three that might be named among these are Sikhism, Jainism, and Shinto, but several other traditions commonly enough included in textbooks might easily be added to the list. No judgment of intrinsic worth or importance should be inferred from their exclusion, just as none should be inferred from the omission of indigenous African or Amerindian religion. A less ample presentation of a larger number of religious traditions would always have been possible. Our choice, and all such choices come at a cost, has been to produce ampler presentations of plausibly canonical texts for those most populous religions traditions that the world citizen is likeliest to encounter in the new religious environment that we all inhabit.

To name a second perhaps surprising choice, our grid of six, though generally familiar, has "Daoism" where most textbooks have "Chinese religion." The usual textbook grid resorts to geography or ethnicity as a naming criterion in and only in the Chinese case. Why so? Though, as noted, the designations "Eastern" and "Western" do still have some textbook currency, no one speaks of Christianity as "European religion" or of Islam as "Afro-Asiatic religion." Why proceed otherwise in the Chinese case alone?

Our decision, breaking with this practice, has been, in the first place, to anthologize Chinese Buddhism within the Buddhism anthology, allowing that sub-anthology to become, by the inclusion of its Chinese material, the longest of the six. Our decision, in the second place, has been not to anthologize Chinese Confucianism at all. We have a secondary and a primary reason for this second decision.

The secondary reason not to anthologize Confucianism is that the People's Republic of China does not regard it as a religion at all. The government recognizes only five religions: Buddhism, Daoism, and Islam plus (as separate religions) Catholicism and Protestantism. Confucianism it simply defines as altogether out of the category *religion*.

Properly so? Is Confucianism a religion, or not? This question is notoriously one that "the West has never been able to answer and China never able to ask," and we do not presume to give a definitive answer here. It is true, on the one hand, that at many points during its long history, Confucianism has seemed to be neither a religion nor quite a philosophy either but rather a code of wisdom and conduct for the Chinese gentleman scholar—or, perhaps better, the aspiring Chinese statesman. Yet at other points in Confucian history, it must be noted, Confucius has been accorded the honor of a virtual god. We choose to leave that question in abeyance.

Our primary reason, in any case, to set Confucianism aside and dedicate our limited space to Daoism is that while the Confucian canon has been widely translated and, as ancient religious texts go, is relatively accessible, the Daoist canon has only recently been rescued from near death and has never before been presented for the use of nonspecialists in an overview of any historical completeness.

While two pre-Daoist classics—the gnomic *Daode jing* of Laozi and the tart wisdom of Zhuangzi—have been endlessly translated and are in no danger of disappearance, their relationship to the Daoist canon as a whole is, to borrow from an observation quoted in James Robson's introduction to the Daoism anthology, like the real but distant relationship of Plato and Aristotle to the Christian canon. What would we know of Christianity if Paul, Augustine,

Dante, Luther, Milton, and so on down the hallowed list had all been lost and only Plato and Aristotle survived?

Such a fate did indeed very nearly befall Daoism. In the nineteenth century, leading up to the establishment of the first Republic of China in 1912, Qing dynasty authorities systematically confiscated Daoist temples and turned them into schools and factories. Having begun as an underground movement in the second century, Daoism—long out of official favor—was largely forced underground only again and more deeply so after the establishment of the Republic, which condemned it as superstition.

For the Daoist canon, the cost of this persecution was nearly outright extinction. By the early twentieth century, few copies of Daoism's canon of eleven hundred religious texts survived in all of China. But then, remarkably, circumstances eased enough to permit the reprint in 1926 of a rare surviving copy of the full 1445 Ming dynasty canon. This had been the last great effort at canon formation in Daoist history before Daoism's long decline commenced. As this reprint reached the West, scholarship on the history of Daoism and the interpretation of its texts slowly began. Nonetheless, particularly after the establishment of the Communist People's Republic of China in 1949, with its aggressive early persecution of all religions, many in the West believed that the actual practice of Daoism had finally died out in its birthplace.

They were mistaken. Over the past few decades, reliable reports have made it clear that Daoism is still alive and indeed is growing steadily stronger, having survived as if by taking Mao Zedong's advice to his guerrillas that they "move among the people as a fish swims in the sea." Just as the fish in the sea are not easily counted, so the Daoists of China escape the usual forms of Western quantification and Communist surveillance alike. But the Daoist fish are numerous, even if they have reason to swim deep.

Meanwhile, the work of translating and contextualizing the recovered texts has attracted a growing corps of Western scholars—initially in France and more recently in other Western countries, including the United States. As their work has gone forward, the world has begun to hear of Daoist messiahs and utopian dreams of peace; Daoist confession rituals and community liturgies; Daoist alchemy and proto-scientific experimentation; Daoist medicine, bodily cultivation (as distinct from asceticism), and sexual practices; Daoist prayer, including Daoist letter-writing to the gods; and Daoist pageantry, costume, magic, and music. In short, a lost religious world—the central, popular, indigenous, full-throated religious world of China—has been brought back to textual life. Our decision was to bring our readers a major sampling from this remarkable recovery.

The major religions of the world are probably better grasped, many scholars now insist, as a set of alternative customs and practices in loose organization—worship liturgies, pilgrimages, dietary restrictions, birth and burial practices, art, music, drama, dance, and so forth—than as a set of contending ideologies. Millions of men and women, even when they practice religions that we rightly regard as literary, are themselves illiterate. Yet when writing remade the world, it did remake religion as well. The major religious traditions of the world would not be major today had they not become literary traditions as well.

Because it is *written*, religious literature can be and has been shared, preserved through wars and persecutions, transmitted over time and space, and, most important of all, *taught* with ease and delight. When all else perishes, the written word often survives. The work before you is a self-contained, portable library of religious literature. You may read it on a plane, in the park, or in a waiting room and trust that every foreign or otherwise strange term will be explained on or near the page where it occurs. No foreign alphabets are used. Transliterations have been simplified to serve pedagogical utility rather than philological perfection. Diacritical marks have been kept to the absolute minimum. Though, as noted, a few of the large theoretical considerations that religion raises as a subject for human inquiry will be addressed in the general introduction, the emphasis in this work is overwhelmingly pragmatic rather than theoretical. For in this domain, more perhaps than in any other, outsiders have historically been as important as insiders, and beginners as welcome as veterans. So, to conclude where we began, whether you are an outsider or an insider, a beginner or a veteran, we welcome you to the pages of *The Norton Anthology of World Religions*.

JACK MILES
IRVINE, CALIFORNIA

Acknowledgments

The Norton Anthology of World Religions would not have been possible without the help of many generous and able friends. We are grateful for the help of those named below as well as of others too numerous to list.

From W. W. Norton & Company, we wish to thank Roby Harrington, head of the college division, who conceived this volume; Pete Simon, its first editor, who contributed its title; Carly Fraser Doria, who has managed the assembly of illustrations and ancillary materials with intelligence and taste; developmental editors Alice Falk, Carol Flechner, and Kurt Wildermuth, who have tamed its prose to the demanding Norton standard; Adrian Kitzinger, who created the beautiful maps; Megan Jackson and Nancy Rodwan, permissions experts; art directors Debra Morton Hoyt and Ingsu Liu, designer Chin-Yee Lai, and artist Rosamond Purcell; production managers Sean Mintus and Julia Druskin; managing editor Marian Johnson, whose project-editorial wisdom is quietly evident on every page; and, most of all, Julia Reidhead, editorial director, whose taste and managerial finesse have preserved and advanced this work sagaciously for fully seven years.

Wendy Doniger wishes to thank Velcheru Narayana Rao for finding "Sita Lost in Thought" for her, and for finding and translating "Kausalya in Fury"; Vasudha Naranayan and Richard Fox for the Southeast Asian materials; Eleanor Zelliot, Gail Omvedt, and Dilip Chitre for the Dalit materials; her student assistants, Jeremy Morse and Charles Preston, for assembling all the texts; and Anne Mocko for help with the pronouncing glossaries.

James Robson wishes to thank Stephen R. Bokenkamp, for helping to get this project started; Alice Falk, for helping to get it completed; and Billy Brewster, for help with the pronouncing glossaries.

David Biale wishes to thank Ariel Evan Mayse and Sarah Shectman for research assistance beyond the call of duty.

Lawrence S. Cunningham wishes to thank his beloved wife, Cecilia, and their two daughters, Sarah and Julia.

Jane Dammen McAuliffe wishes to thank her splendid research associates, Carolyn Baugh, Sayeed Rahman, Robert Tappan, and Clare Wilde, and to recognize with appreciation both Georgetown University and Bryn Mawr College for their support of this work.

For generous financial support of this project, Jack Miles wishes to thank the John T. and Catherine D. MacArthur Foundation, the Getty Research Institute, and the University of California, Irvine. He thanks, in addition, for early editorial consultation, his publishing colleague John Loudon; for generous technical assistance, Steve Franklin and Stan Woo-Sam of UCI's information technology office; for invaluable assistance with the initial enormous delivery of texts, his former student Matthew Shedd; for helpful counsel on

Asian Christianity, his colleague Tae Sung; for brilliant assistance in editorial rescue and rewrite, his irreverent friend and colleague Peter Heinegg; and for her sustaining and indomitable spirit, his irreplaceable Catherine Montgomery Crary.

This work is dedicated—in gratitude for all that they have preserved for our instruction—to the scribes of the world's great religions.

THE NORTON ANTHOLOGY OF

WORLD
RELIGIONS

DAOISM

The relation of the various peoples of the earth to the supreme interests of life, to God, virtue, and immortality, may be investigated up to a certain point, but can never be compared to one another with absolute strictness and certainty. The more plainly in these matters our evidence seems to speak, the more carefully must we refrain from unqualified assumptions and rash generalizations.

—JACOB BURCKHARDT,
*The Civilization of
the Renaissance in Italy* (1860)

GENERAL INTRODUCTION

How the West Learned to Compare Religions

BY JACK MILES

How to Read This Book: A Poetic Prelude

The Norton Anthology of World Religions is designed to be read in either of two ways. You may read it from start to finish, or you may pick and choose from the table of contents as in a museum you might choose to view one gallery rather than another or one painting rather than another.

Imagine yourself at the entrance to a large museum containing a great many strange works of religious art. If you enter, what will you do? Will you devote equal time or equal intensity of attention to every work in the huge museum? Or will you skip some works, linger over others, and shape as you go a kind of museum within the museum? In the latter case, what will be your criteria? Those, too, you may well shape as you go. You may not entirely know even your own mind as you begin. You may not know exactly what you're after. You may be detached, and yet—disinterested? No, you are not exactly disinterested. You're looking around, waiting for something to reach you, some click, some insemination, a start. Entering is sometimes enough. You do not need a briefing by the curator to begin your visit.

So it is with this anthology. Take the works assembled here as lightly as you wish. You will still be taking them properly: you will be taking them for what they are. A new path begins to open into the consideration of religion when it is regarded as unserious, un-adult—but only in the way that art, poetry, and fiction in all its forms (including the theatrical and the cinematic) are so regarded. They all deal with made-up stuff. And yet will we ever be so adult as to outgrow them?

The Western cast of mind has undeniably had an intrusive and distorting effect in many parts of the world as Western culture has become a world culture, and yet that cast of mind has also had a liberating and fertilizing effect. It has opened a space in which the once incomparable has become comparable. Looking at the religions of others even from the outside but with a measure of openness, empathy, and good will can enable those of any religious tradition or none to see themselves from the outside as well, and that capacity is the very foundation of human sympathy and cultural wisdom.

In church one morning in the eighteenth century, the poet Robert Burns spotted a louse on a proper lady's bonnet and started thinking: If only she could see herself as he saw her! He went home and wrote his wonderfully earthy and witty "To a Louse, On Seeing One on a Lady's Bonnet, at Church 1786." The fun of the poem is that it is addressed to the louse in a mock "How dare you!" tone almost all the way to the end. At that point, however, it becomes suddenly reflective, even wistful, and Burns concludes, in his Scots English:

> O wad some Pow'r the giftie gie us
> To see oursels as ithers see us!
> It wad frae monie a blunder free us,
>   An' foolish notion:
> What airs in dress an' gait wad lea'e us,
>   An' ev'n Devotion!

Burns dreams, or half-prays, that some power would "the giftie gie us" (give us the gift) to see "oursels" (ourselves) as others see us—to see, as it were, the lice on our bonnets. Our fine and flouncing airs then "wad lea'e us" (would leave us). But it might not be simply vanity that would depart. The last words in the poem are "an' ev'n Devotion!" (and even devotion). Even our religious devotions might be affected if we could see ourselves at that moment just as others see us. So many of the cruelest mistakes in religion are made not out of malice but out of simple ignorance, blunders we would willingly avoid could we but see ourselves as others see us. Looking at other traditions, you need to see the bonnet and not just the louse. Looking at your own, however you define it, you need to see the louse as well as the bonnet.

Can Religion Be Defined?

What is religion? The word exists in the English language, and people have some commonsense notion of what it refers to. Most understand it as one kind of human activity standing alongside other kinds, such as business, politics, warfare, art, law, sport, or science. Religion is available in a variety of forms, but what is it, really? What makes it itself?

Simple but searching questions like these may seem to be the starting point for the study of religion. Within the study of religion, they are more precisely the starting point for the *theory* of religion. And readers will not be surprised to learn that academic theoreticians of religion have not been content with the commonsense understanding of the subject.

The theoretical difficulties that attend any basic element of human thought or experience are undeniable. What is mathematics? What is art? What is law? What is music? Books have been written debating number theory, aesthetic theory, legal theory, and music theory. It should come as no surprise then that the theory of religion is no less actively debated than are those other theories. Some definitions of religion are so loose as to allow almost anything to qualify as a religion. Others are so strict as to exclude almost everything ordinarily taken to be a religion (prompting one recent contributor to the *Journal of the American Academy of Religion* to give his article the wry or rueful title "Religions: Are There Any?").[1]

The inconvenient truth is that no definition of religion now enjoys general acceptance. In *The Bonobo and the Atheist* (2013), the primatologist Frans de Waal writes:

> To delineate religion to everyone's satisfaction is hopeless. I was once part of a forum at the American Academy of Religion, when

someone proposed we start off with a definition of religion. However much sense this made, the idea was promptly shot down by
another participant, who reminded everyone that last time they
tried to define religion half the audience had angrily stomped out
of the room. And this in an academy named after the topic![2]

A survey of competing theories, if we were to attempt one here, could quickly
jump to twenty-three entries if we simply combined the contents of two
recent handbooks—the eight in Daniel L. Pals's *Eight Theories of Religion*
(2006) and the fifteen in Michael Stausberg's *Contemporary Theories of
Religion: A Critical Companion* (2009).[3]

Though no one writing on religion can entirely escape theoretical commitments, *The Norton Anthology of World Religions* is foremost an anthology of primary texts. By the term *primary* we understand texts produced by
the practitioners of each of the anthologized religions for their fellow practitioners. Such an anthology does not collect theories of religion, for the simple
reason that such theories are secondary texts. They belong not to the creation and practice of religion but, retrospectively, to its study and analysis.
Accordingly, they have rarely been of much interest to religious practitioners themselves.

Religious practitioners are far from unique in this regard. "Philosophy of
science is about as useful to scientists as ornithology is to birds," Richard
Feynman (1918–1988), a Caltech physicist, famously quipped.[4] The philosophy (or theory) of religion is of as little use to, say, the Buddhist as philosophy of science is to the scientist. Just as the scientist is interested in her
experiment rather than in the philosophy of science and the painter in his
painting rather than in the philosophy of art, so the Buddhist is interested
in the Buddha rather than in the philosophy of religion. The term *religion*
itself, as an academic term comprising—as indeed it does in this work—
many different religious traditions, may not be of much practical utility to
the practitioner of any one of the traditions.

And yet we who have assembled this work may not excuse ourselves
altogether from addressing the question "What is religion?" simply on the
grounds that our pages are filled with primary texts, for introducing, framing, and contextualizing these texts are the words of our six anthologizing
editors as well as the general editor. The seven of us speak in these pages not
as practitioners of the religions anthologized here but as scholars writing
about those religions. Scholarship at its most empirical cannot escape theory,
because, to quote a dictum from the philosophy of science, all data are
theory-laden. A theory of some sort will be found operative even when no
explicit theoretical commitment has been made.

If, then, some tacit theory or theories of religion must necessarily have
informed the choices made by our associate editors, given the general
editor's decision to impose no single theory, has any silent theoretical convergence occurred? Now that the results are in and the editors' choices
have actually been made, do they reflect a working answer to the question
"What is religion?"

As general editor, I believe that they do, though it would take some rather
elaborate spelling out to explain just *how* they do. Something more modest
but more readily discernible must suffice for this introduction—namely,
the claim that the choices made by the respective associate editors reflect a

common method or, more modestly still, a common approach to the task of presenting a major religious literature with some coherence. In brief, the six associate editors have approached the six religions whose texts they anthologize as six kinds of practice rather than as six kinds of belief. In common usage, religious and unreligious people are divided into "believers" and "unbelievers." The editors have departed from this common usage, proceeding instead on the silent and admittedly modest premise that religion is as religion *does*. Even when speaking of belief, as they do only occasionally, they generally treat it as embedded in practice and inseparable from practice. Monotheism in the abstract is a belief. "Hear, O Israel, the Lord is our God, the Lord alone" as sung by a cantor in a synagogue is a practice.

When religion is approached as practice, what follows? Clearly, Daoist practice, Muslim practice, Christian practice, and so on are not identical, but the substantial differences *within* each of them can loom as large as the differences from one to another among them. *The goal of this anthology is to present through texts how this variety has developed and how the past continues to shape the present.* Thus, the body of material put on exhibit here serves less to answer the question "What is religion?" in any theoretically elaborate or definitive way than to question the answers others have given to that question—answers such as those offered by, for example, the twenty-three theories alluded to above. Whatever fascinating questions a given theory of religion may have posed and answered to its own satisfaction, it must also, we submit, be able to account for the complexity of the data that these primary texts exhibit. Rather than serving to illustrate some fully developed new theory of religion, in other words, the texts gathered here constitute the empirical evidence that any such theory must cope with. In the meantime, the working focus is squarely on practice.

Each of the religions anthologized here has contained multiple versions of itself both over time and at any given time, and the anthology does not attempt to drive past the multiplicity to the singular essence of the thing. Practitioners, of course, have not always been so neutral. Many have been or still are prepared to deny the legitimacy of others as Hindu, Muslim, Christian, Jewish, and so on. But for the purposes of this anthology, those denials themselves simply become a part of the broader story.

Syncretism, moreover—namely, the introduction of a feature from one religion into the life of another—is in itself an argument that the borrower and the lender are, or can be, related even when they are not, and never will be, identical. Multiple religious belonging—double or triple affiliation—sometimes takes syncretism a step further. And while borrowings across major borders are an additive process, adjustments within borders can often be a subtractive process, as seen in many statements that take the form "I am a Buddhist, but . . . ," "I am a Catholic, but . . . ," "I am a Muslim, but . . . ," and so forth. In such statements, the speaker takes the broad term as a starting point and then qualifies it until it fits properly.

Yet we do not claim anything more than practical utility for this default approach to the subject, knowing as we do that a great many scholars of religion decline to define the essence of religion itself but do not find themselves inhibited by that abstention from saying a great deal of interest about one religious tradition or another. Rather than name at the outset the one feature that establishes the category *religion* before discussing the particular religion that interests them, they make the usually silent assumption that the full range of beliefs and practices that have been conventionally thought of as religious is vast and that each religion must be allowed to do as it does, assembling its subsets from the vast, never-to-be-fully-enumerated roster of world religious practices. Having made that assumption, the scholars take a deep breath and go on to talk about what they want to talk about.

Twenty-first-century religion scholars are prepared to acknowledge coherence when they find it but determined never to impose it. They are aware that the entries made under the heading *religion* may not all be versions of just the same thing, but they are equally aware that the overlaps, the innumerable ad hoc points of contact, are also there and also real—and so they find the continued use of the collective term *religion* justified for the enriching and enlightening comparisons that it facilitates. All knowledge begins with comparison.

In telling the life stories of six major, living, international religions through their respective primary texts, the editors of *The Norton Anthology of World Religions* have neither suppressed variability over time in service to any supposedly timeless essence of the thing nor, even when using the word *classical*, dignified any one age as truly golden. Each of the stories ends with modernity, but modernity in each case is neither the climax nor the denouement of the story. It is not the last chapter, only the latest.

How Christian Europe Learned to Compare Religions

Most people, we said earlier, understand religion as "one kind of human activity standing alongside other kinds, such as business, politics, warfare, art, law, sport, or science." Another way to say this is that they understand religion to be one domain among many, each separate from the others. Broadly compatible with this popular understanding is a widely influential definition of religion formulated by the anthropologist Clifford Geertz (1926–2006).

In "Religion as a Cultural System," first published in 1966, Geertz defined religion as

> *(1) a system of symbols which acts to (2) establish powerful, pervasive, and long-lasting moods and motivations in men by (3) formulating conceptions of a general order of existence and (4) clothing these conceptions with such an aura of factuality that (5) the moods and motivations seem uniquely realistic.*[5]

Geertz does not claim that all cultures are equally religious. In fact, toward the end of his essay he observes that "the degree of religious articulateness is not a constant even as between societies of similar complexity."[6] However, he does tacitly assume that religion is if not universal then at least extremely widespread and that it is a domain separate from others, such as—to name two that he explores—science and ideology.[7]

But just how widespread is religion, and is it truly a domain separable from the rest of culture? Can religion really be distinguished from ideology? In Geertz's terms, wouldn't Marxism qualify as a religion? In recent decades, some have argued that even a thoroughly secular anthropologist like Geertz, in whose definition of religion neither God nor Christ is mentioned, can be seen as carrying forward an ideological understanding of religion that originated in the Christian West and has lived on in Western academic life as a set of inadequately examined assumptions. That religion is a domain separate from either ethnicity or culture is one of two key, historically Christian assumptions. That religion is a universal phenomenon—in some form, a part of every human society and even every human mind—is the other key assumption.

Perhaps the most widely cited historical critique of these assumptions is Tomoko Masuzawa's revealing *The Invention of World Religions, Or, How European Universalism Was Preserved in the Language of Pluralism* (2005). Masuzawa's book is not about the invention of the world's religions themselves but about the invention of *world religions* as a phrase used in the West to talk about them, postulating their parallel existence as separable and separate realities, available as an indefinitely expandable group for academic discussion.[8]

When and how, she asks, did this omnibus-phrase *world religions* come into the general usage that it now enjoys? She concludes her influential investigation with the candid confession that the invention and, especially, the very widespread adoption of the phrase remain something of a puzzle—but her analysis traces the usage back only to the nineteenth century. Our claim below is that though the phrase *world religions* may be recent, its roots run much deeper than the nineteenth century, as deep in fact as early Christianity's peculiar and unprecedented self-definition.

To say this is not to undercut the strength of the criticism. Christian explorers, traders, missionaries, and colonists encountering non-Western societies, especially after the discovery of the Americas and the colonial expansion of the West into Asia, have often isolated and labeled as "religions" behaviors that they took to be the local equivalents of what they knew in the West as Christianity. This process of isolating and labeling was a mistake when and if the societies themselves did not understand the behaviors in question as constituting either a separate domain or merely one instance of a more general phenomenon called religion. Moreover, when those purporting to understand non-Western societies in these historically Christian terms were invaders and imperialists, a perhaps unavoidable theoretical mistake could have grievous practical consequences. And when, in turn, ostensibly neutral, secular theories of religion—not imposed by conquerors or missionaries but merely proffered by Western academics—are alleged to make the same historically Christian assumptions, the entire project of comparative religious study may be faulted as Christian imperialism.

Because the viability and indeed the enormous value of such study are premises of this anthology, the challenge calls for a significant response, one that necessarily includes substantial attention to just how Christianity influenced the study of what the West has defined as world religions. The intention in what follows, however, is by no means to make a case for Christianity as inherently central or supreme among the world's religions. We intend rather, and only, to trace how, in point of fact, Christianity began as central to the Western *study* of religions and then, by degrees, yielded its position as more polycentric forms of study emerged.

Let us begin by stipulating that Christians did indeed acquire very early and thereafter never entirely lost the habit of thinking of their religion as a separate domain. Once this is conceded, it should come as no great surprise that as a corollary of this habit, they should have adopted early and never entirely lost the habit of thinking of other religions, rightly or wrongly, as similarly separate domains. This would be simply one more instance of the human habit of beginning with the known and with the self and working outward to the unknown and to the others.

But we must stipulate further that Christians made a second assumption—namely, that theirs should become humankind's first-ever programmatically "world" religion. The idea of universally valid religious truth was not new in itself. Ancient Israel had long since been told that its vocation was to be the light of the world. In the book of Isaiah, God says to his people through the prophet (49:6):

> It is too light a thing that you should be my servant to raise up the tribes of Jacob and to restore the preserved of Israel; I will give you as a light to the nations, that my salvation may reach to the end of the earth.[9]

In the Gospel of Matthew, Jesus turns this latent potential into a radically intrusive program for action. His final words to his apostles are

> Go therefore, and make disciplines of *all nations*, baptizing them in the name of the Father and of the Son and of the Holy Spirit, teaching them to observe all that I have commanded you; and, lo, I am with you always, even to the close of the age. (Matthew 28:19–20; emphasis added)

How ever did this instruction, as the first Christians put it into practice, lead to the secular study of "world religions" as we know it today?

The Social Oddity of the Early Church

In the earliest centuries of its long history, the Christian church defined its belief as different from the official polytheism of the Roman Empire, on the one hand, and from the monotheism of Rabbinic Judaism, on the other, inasmuch as the rabbinic Jews did not recognize Jesus as God incarnate. But if the church was thus, to borrow a convenient phrase from contemporary American life, a faith-based organization, it was not just a school of thought: it was also an *organization*. As faith-based, it undeniably placed unique and unprecedented stress on belief (and indeed set the pattern by which today all those religiously active in any way are routinely called *believers*, even when not all regard belief as central to their practice). Yet as an organization, the church depended not just on a distinct set of beliefs but also on a social identity separate, on the one hand, from that of the Roman Empire (or any other empire) and equally separate, on the other, from that of the Jewish nation (or any other nation). As a faith-based, voluntary, non-profit, multiethnic, egalitarian, nongovernmental organization, the Christian church was a social novelty: nothing quite like it had ever been seen before. And as Christians, growing steadily in number, projected their novel collective self-understanding upon Roman and Jewish social reality alike, the effect was profoundly disruptive. Though many others would follow, these were the first two instances of Christian projection, and an analysis of how they worked is especially instructive.

By encouraging Roman polytheists to *convert* to Christianity while maintaining that they did not thereby cease to be Romans, the Christians implicitly invented religious conversion itself as an existential possibility. The term *religion* did not exist then in Greek, Latin, or Aramaic as a fully developed universal category containing both Roman polytheism and Christianity, but in the very action of conversion the future category was already implicit. By seeking to convert Roman polytheists to Christianity, the early Christians implied that Roman religiosity was a domain both separate from the rest of Roman life and replaceable. You could exchange your Roman religiosity for this modified Jewish religiosity, as the very act of conversion demonstrated, while bringing the rest of your Roman identity with you.

In the first century, conversion thus defined was an unprecedented and socially disruptive novelty. Until the destabilizing intrusion of Christianity, respect for the Roman gods had always been inseparable from simply being Roman: religious identity and civic identity had always constituted an unbroken whole. Christianity encouraged Romans to split that single identity into a double identity: religion, on the one hand; culture and ethnicity, on the other. In this sequestration of the religiously meaningful from the religiously neutral or meaningless was born the very possibility of secular culture, as well as religion as Western modernity has come to understand it—religion as involving some semblance of faith and some form of collective identity separable from ethnicity or culture.

In by far the most important instance of this division of social identity, the original Christian Jews, having adopted a minority understanding of Jewish tradition, denied that they were any less Jewish for that reason. Writing of his Jewish critics, St. Paul fumed (2 Corinthians 11:22): "Are they Israelites? So am I!" Much of first-century Jewry would not have disagreed with him had the matter stopped there, for there were many peacefully coexisting Jewish views about Jewish belief and practice. As no more than the latest variation on the old themes, the Christian Jews would not have created anything structurally new. But they did create something new by taking the further step of bringing themselves, with their recognizably Jewish religious views (views indeed unrecognizable as anything except Jewish), into an unprecedented social relationship with non-Jews—namely, into the Christian church. By linking themselves to non-Jews in this way, without renouncing their Jewish identity, the Christian Jews—enjoying particular success in the Roman Diaspora—demonstrated that as they conceived their own Jewish religiosity to be distinguishable from the rest of what was then the Jewish way of life, so they conceived the same two components of identity to be likewise distinguishable for all other Jews.

Rabbinic Judaism, dominant in Palestine and the Mesopotamian Diaspora, would eventually repudiate this Christian projection and reassert that Jewish religiosity and Jewish identity are one and indistinguishable. In the rabbinic view that became and has remained dominant in world Judaism, there are no "Judaists," only Jews. But this reassertion did not happen overnight: it took generations, even centuries. Neither the Romans nor the Jews nor the Christians themselves immediately understood the full novelty of what was coming into existence.

Through most of world history, in most parts of the world, what we are accustomed to call religion, ethnicity, culture, and way of life have been inextricable parts of a single whole. How did Christianity begin to become an exception to this general rule? On the one hand, it appropriated a set of Jewish religious ideas—including monotheism, revelation, covenant, scripture, sin, repentance, forgiveness, salvation, prophecy, messianism, and apocalypticism—without adopting the rest of the highly developed and richly nuanced Jewish way of life. On the other hand, it universalized these Jewish religious ideas, creating a new social entity, the church, through which non-Jews could be initiated into an enlarged version of the ancestral Jewish covenant with God. The Jews had believed for centuries God's declaration, "I am the LORD your God, who have separated you from the peoples" (Leviticus 20:24) and "you are a people holy to the LORD your God" (Deuteronomy 7:6). In effect, the Christian Jews split the idea of covenanted separateness and holiness from what consequently became the relatively secularized idea of nationality. The Jews were still a people, they maintained, but God had now revised and universalized the terms of his covenant. In the words of Jesus' apostle Peter, "Truly I perceive that God shows no partiality, but in every nation any one who fears him and does what is right is acceptable to him" (Acts 10:34–35).

The original Greek word for church, *ekklēsia*, suggests a collective understanding of church members as "called out" from other kinds of religious, ethnic, or political membership into this new—and now, in principle, universal—"people set apart as holy." The *ekklēsia* offered its members a sense of sacred peoplehood, but it tellingly lacked much else that ordinarily maintains a national identity. It had no ancestral land, no capital city, no language of its own, no literature at the start other than what it had inherited from the Jews, no distinct cuisine, no standard dress, and no political or governmental support beyond the organizational management of the church itself. Moreover, this ethnically mixed and socially unpromising group was atheist in its attitude toward all gods except the God of Israel as they had come to understand him—God as incarnate in Jesus the Messiah. Within the political culture of the Roman Empire, this rejection of the empire's gods was a seditious and rebellious rejection of Roman sovereignty itself. When, unsurprisingly, the empire recognized it as such and began intermittently to persecute the church, the Christian sense of separateness only grew.

In this form, and despite intermittent persecution, the church grew quietly but steadily for more than three centuries. At that point, with perhaps a fifth of the population of the Roman Empire enrolled in separate local Christian churches under relatively autonomous elected supervisors (bishops), the emperor Constantine (r. 312–37) first legalized Christianity and then stabilized its doctrine by requiring the Christian bishops—ordered to convene for the first time as a council at Nicaea, near his eventual capital city of Constantinople—to define it. In 381, the emperor Theodosius (r. 379–95) made this newly defined Christianity the official religion of the Roman Empire, and the new religion—no longer persecuted but now operating under a large measure of imperial control—began a fateful reversal of course. It began to fuse with the political governance and the Hellenistic culture of imperial Rome, compromising the character of the *ekklēsia* as a domain separate from nationality or culture. In a word, it began to normalize.

The establishment of Christianity as the state religion of the Roman Empire ushered in a period of rapid growth, pushed by the government, within the borders of the empire. Beyond them, however, most notably in the Persian Empire just to the east, its new status had the opposite effect.

Once relatively unhindered as a social movement taken to be as compatible with Persian rule as with Roman, Christianity now became suspect as the official religion of the enemy.

Meanwhile, in Rome itself—the "First Rome," as historically prior to the Eastern Empire's capital, Constantinople—and in the western European territories that it administered, a partial but significant return to the original separation of domains occurred just a century later. In 476, Odoacer, king of an invading Germanic tribe, deposed the last Roman emperor, Romulus Augustulus, without effectively assuming authority over the Christian church. Instead, the power of the bishop of Rome—the highest surviving official of the old imperial order—over the church in western Europe began to grow, while the power of kings and feudal lords over all that was not the church steadily grew as well. The nominally unified imperial authority over the empire and its established religion thus split apart. To be sure, for centuries the pope claimed the authority to anoint kings to their royal offices, and at certain moments this was a claim that could be sustained. But gradually, a sense that civilian and religious authority were different and separate began to set in. At the same time, the identity of the church as, once again, detached or disembedded from the state and from culture alike—the church as a potentially universal separate domain, a holy world unto itself—began to consolidate.

The Four-Cornered Medieval Map of Religion

Wealth, power, and population in the world west of India were concentrated during the sixth century in the Persian Empire and in the Eastern Roman or Byzantine Empire. Western Europe during the same century—all that had once been the Western Roman Empire—was far poorer, weaker, more sparsely populated, and culturally more isolated than the empires to its east. Then, during the seventh and eighth centuries, a third major power arose. Arabia had long provided mercenary soldiers to both of the then-dominant empires; but religiously inspired by the Islam newly preached by Muhammad (ca. 570–632) and militarily unified under his successors, it became a major world power in its own right with stunning speed. Arab armies conquered the entirety of the Persian Empire within a generation. Within a century, they had taken from the Eastern Roman Empire its Middle Eastern and North African possessions (half of its total territory) as well as the major Mediterranean islands. From what had been the Western Roman Empire, they had subtracted three-quarters of Spain and penetrated deep into France until driven back across the Pyrenees by the unprecedented European alliance that defeated them in the 732 Battle of Poitiers.

The political map of the world had been redrawn from India to the Atlantic, but what of the religious map? How did western European Christians now understand themselves among the religions of the world? The symbolic birth date of Europe as Christendom has long been taken to be Christmas Day of the year 800. On that date, Pope Leo III crowned Charles the Great, better known as Charlemagne—the grandson of Charles Martel, who had unified the European forces at Poitiers—as the first "Holy Roman Emperor." The Muslim invasion from distant Arabia had shocked an isolated and fragmented region into an early assertion of common religious and geographical identity. As a result, there was a readiness to give political expression to a dawning collective self-understanding. The lost Western Roman Empire was by no means reconstituted: Charlemagne was an emperor without much of an empire, his coronation expressing a vision more than a reality. But the vision itself mattered decisively in another way, for what came into existence at about this time was an understood quadripartite map of the world of religion that would remain standard in Europe for centuries.

There was, first and foremost for Christians, Christianity itself: the Christian church understood to be the same single, separate domain wherever it was found, with the same distinct relationship to national and cultural identity. To the extent that it rested on common faith, the church could be divided by heresy; but even heretical Christians, of whom there would be fewer in the early ninth century than there had been in earlier Christian centuries, were still understood to be Christians. They were practicing the right religion in a wrong way, but they were not practicing another religion altogether.

There was, second, Judaism: the Jews of Europe, a population living among Christians, disparaged but well known, whose relationship to Christianity was well remembered and whose religious authenticity rested on a recognized if more or less resented prior relationship with the same God that the Christians worshiped. Christian understanding of Jewish religious life as the Jews actually lived it was slender, and Christian knowledge of the vast rabbinic literature that had come into existence between the second and the ninth century, much of it in far-off Mesopotamia, was virtually nonexistent. Knowledge of Greek had been lost in Latin Europe, and knowledge of the Hebrew and Aramaic that the Jews of Europe had managed to preserve (despite recurrent persecution) was confined to them alone. Yet, this ignorance notwithstanding, Christian Europe was well aware that the Jews practiced a religion different from their own. And the implicit Christian understanding of religion as a separate domain of potentially universal extent was reinforced by the fact that from the outside, Jewish religious practice appeared to be at least as deeply divorced from national and cultural practices as was Christian religious practice: the Jews, who had lost their land and were dispersed around the world, lived in Europe much as Europe's Christians lived.

The third corner of Europe's four-cornered understanding of world religion was Islam, though the terms *Islam* and *Muslim* would not come into European usage until centuries later. Even the term *Arab* was not standard. The multinational religious commonwealth that we now call world Islam has been traditionally referred to by the Muslims themselves with the Arabic expression *dar al-islam*, the "House of Islam" or the "House of Submission" (because *islam* means "submission"—that is, submission to God). Whether it was *Saracen, Moor, Turk, or Arab*, the ethnic terms used by Christians to refer to the Muslims who faced them in the south and the east depended on time and place. Christendom as the Holy Roman Empire had become a domain geographically separate from the House of Islam. Similarly, Christianity as distinct from Christendom was evidently a domain of belief and practice separate from that of Islam. But among Christians, the further inference was that as Christian identity was separate from Bavarian or Florentine identity, so Muslim identity must be separate from Arab or Turkish identity. To some extent, this was a false inference, for obligatory Arabic in the Qur'an and obligatory pilgrimage to Mecca did much to preserve the originally Arab identity of Islam. Yet the tricontinental distribution and ethnic variability of the House of Islam fostered among Europeans an understanding of Islam as, like Christianity, a potentially universal religion separable from the ethnicity of any one of its component parts.

As Christian anxiety mounted that the year 1000 might mark the end of the world (an outcome that some Christians saw predicted in the New Testament book of Revelation), Muhammad came to be seen by some as the Antichrist, a destructive figure whose appearance during the last apocalyptic period before the end had been foretold (again in the book of Revelation). Yet gradually, albeit as "Mohammedanism," Islam came to be differentiated from Christianity in theological rather than in such floridly mythological terms. The Qur'an was translated into Latin in 1142. The High Middle Ages began to witness various forms of religious and cultural encounter—some as an unintended consequence of the Crusades; others through the influence of large Christian minorities living under Muslim rule and, over time, substantial Muslim minorities living under Christian rule, notably in Spain and Sicily. Finally, there was the mediating influence of a cross-culturally significant Jewish population residing on either side of the Muslim–Christian border and communicating across it. One result of these minglings was a gradually growing overlap in the techniques in use in all three communities for the exegesis of the sacred scriptures that for each mattered so much.

As Muslim monotheism came gradually into clearer focus, medieval Christianity came to recognize Muslims as worshippers of the same God that Jews and Christians worshipped. Meanwhile, Islam was, like Christianity, a religion that actively sought converts who were then made part of a separate quasi-national, quasi-familial, yet potentially universal social entity. The genesis of the Western understanding of religion as such—religion as a separate but expandable social category—was thus significantly advanced by Christianity's encounter with another social entity so like itself in its universalism and its relative independence from ethnic or cultural identity.

The fourth corner of the world religion square was occupied by a ghost—namely, the memory of long-dead Greco-Roman polytheism. Christianity was born among the urban Jews of the Roman Empire and spread gradually into the countryside. Even in largely rural Europe, monasteries functioned as surrogate cities and Christianity spread outward from these centers of structure and literacy. *Pagus* is the Latin word for "countryside," and in the countryside the old polytheisms lingered long after they had died out in the cities. Thus, a rural polytheist was a *paganus*, and *paganismus* (paganism) became synonymous with polytheism. In England, pre-Christian polytheism lingered in the inhospitable heath, and so *heathenism* became an English synonym for *paganism*. Though polytheism is not necessarily idolatrous (one may believe in many gods without making a single idol), polytheistic belief and idolatrous practice were generally conflated. More important for the centuries that lay ahead, the increasingly jumbled memory of what Greco-Roman polytheism—remembered as "paganism"—had been in the Christian past was projected upon the enormous and almost entirely unknown world beyond the realms occupied by Christians, Muslims, and Jews.

The quadripartite typology just sketched was only one long-lived stage in the development of the comparative study of religion in Christian Europe. We may pause to note, however, that as of the year 800 Judaism and Islam were operating under similar typologies. The Qur'an, definitive for all Islamic thought, takes frequent and explicit note of Judaism and Christianity, while the place occupied by the memory of Greco-Roman polytheism in Christianity is occupied in the Qur'an by the memory of polytheism as it existed in Arabia at the time when Muhammad began to receive his revelations. World Jewry, as a minority maintaining its identity and its religious practice in both Christendom and the House of Islam, had a richer experience of both Christians and Muslims than either of those two had of the other. Yet what functioned for Jews in the way that the memory of Greco-Roman polytheism functioned for Christians and the memory of Arabian polytheism functioned for Muslims was the memory of ancient Canaanite, Philistine, and Babylonian polytheism as recorded in the Bible and used thereafter as a template for understanding all those who were the enemies of God and the persecutors of his Chosen People.

Now, the comparison of two religions on terms set by one of them is like the similarly biased comparison of two nationalities: the outcome is a predictable victory for the side conducting the comparison. In fact, when religion and ethnicity are fused, religious comparison is commonly stated in ethnic terms rather than in what we would consider religious terms. Thus, in the Hebrew Bible, apostasy from the religion of Israel is called "*foreign worship*" ('avodah zarah) rather than simply false worship, though falsehood or worse is unmistakably implied. To the extent that ethnicity is taken to be a matter of brute fact, and therefore beyond negotiation, religion bound to ethnicity has seemed a nonnegotiable matter of fact as well.

In this regard, however, the condition of medieval Christian Europe was interestingly unstable. Demographically, the two largest religious realities it knew—Islam and Christianity itself—were consciously and ideologically multinational in character, and both actively sought converts from all nations. Judaism was not evangelistic in this way, but world Jewry was uniquely the world's first global nation: the bulk of its population was distributed internationally in such a way that Jews were accustomed in every place to distinguish their ethnicity from the ethnicity of the locale and their religion from its religion. Christian prejudice often prevented Jewish acculturation (not to suppose that Jews always wished to acculturate), but it did not always do so. And so during extended periods of Christian toleration, even the generally firm Jewish sense that religion, ethnicity, and culture were a seamless whole may have become more difficult to sustain. This three-sided—Christian, Muslim, and Jewish—embrace of the notion that religion was a separate domain set the stage in Europe for the comparison of the three on terms derived from a neutral fourth entity that was not to be equated with any one of them.

This fourth entity was Aristotelian philosophy as recovered in Europe during the eleventh and twelfth centuries. Of course, the philosophical discussions that began to be published—such as Abelard's mid-twelfth-century *Dialogue among a Philosopher, a Jew, and a Christian*, in which the philosopher of the title often appears to be a Muslim—always ended in victory for the imagined Christian. Yet Abelard (1079–1142) was eventually condemned by the church because his dialogue clearly recognized reason, mediated by philosophy, as independent of the religions being discussed and as capable of rendering judgments upon them all. Philosophy as that fourth, neutral party would be joined over time by psychology, sociology, anthropology, economics, evolutionary biology, cognitive science, and other analytical tools. But these enlargements lay centuries in the future. As the Middle Ages were succeeded by the Renaissance, philosophy had made a crucial start toward making neutral comparisons, even though Europe's quadripartite map of the world's religions was still quite firmly in place, with most comparisons still done on entirely Christian and theological terms.

The Renaissance Rehearsal of Comparative Religion

The Italian Renaissance—beginning in the fourteenth century and flourishing in the fifteenth and sixteenth—is commonly taken to be more important as a movement in art and literature than in philosophy or religion. To be sure, it did not attempt a transformation of European Christianity comparable to that of the Protestant Reformation of the sixteenth century. But the kind of religious comparison that began in the early eighteenth century, in the aftermath of Europe's devastating seventeenth-century Protestant–Catholic Wars of Religion, was foreshadowed during the Renaissance by the revival of classical Greek and Latin and by the recovery of masterpieces of world literature written in those languages.

First of all, perfected knowledge of Latin and the recovered knowledge of Greek enabled Italian scholars to publish critical editions of the texts of classical antiquity as well as philologically grounded historical criticism of such later Latin texts as the Donation of Constantine, exposed as a papal forgery by the Italian humanist Lorenzo Valla (1407–1457). It was in Renaissance Italy, too, that Christian Europe first recovered knowledge of biblical Hebrew. The earliest chair of Hebrew was established late in the fifteenth century at the University of Bologna. Despite repeated persecutions, ghettoizations, and expulsions, the Jewish population of Italy grew substantially during the Renaissance, enthusiastically embracing the then-new technology of printing with movable type. The first complete publication of the Hebrew Bible in the original, with Jewish commentaries, appeared in Venice in 1517 and proved highly instructive to Christian Europe; by the end of the following century, Italian scholars were even starting to read both the postbiblical rabbinic literature and the Kabbalah, writings in a later extra-rabbinic Jewish mystical tradition that fascinated some of them. Little by little, Christian Europe was beginning to learn from Europe's Jews.

As the Renaissance began to introduce Christian Europe by slow degrees to the critical examination of ancient texts as well as to the inner religious life of Judaism, it accomplished something similar in a more roundabout way for the lost religions of Greece and Rome. The humanists of the Renaissance did not believe in the gods and goddesses of Olympus as they believed in God the Almighty Father of Christianity, but even as they read the classical literature only as literature, they nonetheless were taken deep inside the creedal, ritual, imaginative, and literary life of another religion—namely, the lost Greco-Roman polytheism. During the Italian Renaissance, the term *humanist* (Italian *umanista*), we should recall, was not used polemically, as if in some sort of pointed contrast to *theist*. Rather, it was a declaration of allegiance to the humanizing, civilizing power of art and imaginative literature. Renaissance humanism's imaginative engagement with the religions of classical Greece and Rome thus constituted an unplanned rehearsal for the real-world, real-time imaginative engagements with non-Christian religions and cultures that lay immediately and explosively ahead for Europe. When the Spanish *conquistadores* encountered the living polytheism of Aztec Mexico, their first interpretive instinct was to translate the gods of Tenochtitlán into their nearest Greek and Roman equivalents. This was an intellectually clumsy move, to be sure, but less clumsy than interpreting them exclusively in mono-theist Christian terms would have been. Moreover, because neither classical paganism nor Aztec polytheism was taken to be true, the two could be com-pared objectively or, if you will, humanistically—and from that early and fumbling act of comparison many others would follow.

In the study of philosophy, the Renaissance added Plato and various ancient Neoplatonists to the Aristotle of the medieval universities. More important, perhaps, it began to read late-classical moral philosophies—notably Stoicism and Epicureanism—whose frequent references to the gods made them in effect lost religions. Sometimes inspiring, sometimes scandal-ous, these recovered moral philosophies introduced personality and inner complexity into the inherited category of paganism. Philosophical recover-ies of this sort could remain a purely academic exercise, but for that very reason their influence might be more subtly pervasive. Often, those who studied these texts professed to be seeking only their pro forma subordina-tion to the truth of Roman Catholic Christianity. Nonetheless, the ideas found their way into circulation. To be sure, the few who took the further step of propagating pagan worldviews as actual alternatives to Christian faith or Aristotelian cosmology could pay a high price. The wildly specula-tive Neoplatonist Giordano Bruno (1548–1600) was burned at the stake as a heretic. But others, scarcely less speculative, spread their ideas with little official interference and in response to widespread popular curiosity.

Comparative Christianity in the Protestant Reformation

Important as the Renaissance was to the development in Europe of a capac-ity for religious comparison, the Protestant Reformation was surely even more important, for it forced Europeans in one region after another to com-pare forms of Christianity, accept one, and reject the others. Frequently, this lacerating but formative experience required those who had rejected Catholi-cism to reject one or more contending forms of Protestantism as well. This was clearly the case during the English Civil War (1642–51), which forced English Christians to side either with the Anglican king or with the Puritan rebels who beheaded him; but there were other such choices, some of them much more complicated.

Tentative moves toward tolerance during these struggles were far less frequent than fierce mutual persecution and, on either side, the celebration of victims as martyrs. The Catholics tried to dismiss and suppress the Prot-estants as merely the latest crop of Christian heretics. The Protestants commonly mythologized Rome as Babylon and compared Catholics to the ancient Babylonians, viewing them as pagans who had taken the New Israel, the Christian church, into exile and captivity. The century and a half of the reformations and the Wars of Religion certainly did not seem to promise a future of sympathetic, mutually respectful religious comparison. And yet within the religious game of impassioned mutual rejection then being played, each side did develop formidable knowledge of the practices, beliefs, and arguments of the other. To the extent that the broader religious comparison initiated during the Enlightenment of the late seventeenth and the eighteenth centuries called for close observation, firsthand testimony, logical analysis, and preparatory study of all kinds, its debt to both the Protestant Reformation and the Catholic Counter-Reformation is enormous.

Particularly important was the historical awareness that the Protestant Reformation introduced into Christian thought. Protestantism took the New Testament to be a historically reliable presentation of earliest Christianity and, using that presentation as a criterion, proceeded to reject the many aspects of Roman Catholic practice that appeared to deviate from it. To be sure, the Roman church had been reading, copying, and devotedly commenting on the Bible for centuries, but it had not been reading it as history. Here the Renaissance paved the way for the Reformation, for the Bible that Rome read was the Bible in a Latin translation; and the Renaissance, as it recovered the knowledge of Hebrew and Greek, had recovered the ability to read the original texts from which that Latin translation had been made. In 1516, the Dutch humanist Desiderius Erasmus published a bilingual, Greek-Latin edition of the New Testament, correcting the received Latin to bring it into conformity with the newly recovered Greek. Armed with this new tool, the many educated Europeans who knew Latin but not Greek could immediately see that the Latin on which the church had relied for a thousand years was at many points unreliable and in need of revision. In this way, Erasmus, a child of the Renaissance, took a first, fateful step toward historicizing the Bible.

The Reformation, launched just a year later with the publication by Martin Luther of "Ninety-Five Theses on the Power and Efficacy of Indulgences," would take the further, explosive step of historicizing the church itself. To quote a famous line from Reformation polemics, Erasmus "laid the egg that Luther hatched." Thus, two epoch-making historical tools of Protestantism as it would dynamically take shape became integral parts of the later comparative study of non-Christian religions as undertaken by Christian scholars: first, the reconstruction of the composition history of the original texts themselves by scholars who had mastered the original languages; and second, the comparison of later religious practice to earlier through the study of the recovered and historically framed original texts.

In one regard, finally, Protestantism may have indirectly contributed to the comparative study of religion by setting in motion a gradual subversion of the very understanding of religion as a domain separate from ethnicity and culture that had been constitutive of Christian self-understanding almost from its start. Mark C. Taylor argues brilliantly in *After God* (2007) that what is often termed the disappearance of God or the disappearance of the sacred in modernity is actually the integration of that aspect of human experience with the rest of modern experience—a process whose onset he traces to Martin Luther's and John Calvin's sanctification of all aspects of human life as against medieval Christianity's division of the religious life of monks and nuns from the worldly (secular) life of laypeople.[10]

This progressive modern fusion of once separate domains would explain the spread in the West of the experience of the holy in ostensibly secular contexts and of the aesthetic in ostensibly religious contexts. Clearly the earlier Christian sense of religion as a separate domain has lingered powerfully in the West. Yet if Taylor is right, then post-Protestant religious modernity in the West, though deeply marked by Protestantism, may be a paradoxical correction of Christianity to the world norm. Or, to put the matter more modestly, the diffuse post-Christian religiosity of the modern West may bear a provocative similarity to the much older but equally diffuse religiosity of South and East Asia or indeed of pre-Christian world Jewry.

Toleration, Science, Exploration, and the Need for a New Map

After decades of controversy climaxing in all-out war, it became clear to exhausted Protestants and Catholics alike that neither could dictate the religious future of Europe. The Wars of Religion came to a close in 1648 with the Peace of Westphalia, which, though it by no means established individual freedom of religion, did end international religious war in Europe. Its key principle—*Cuius regio, eius religio* (literally, "Whose the rule, his the religion")—allowed the king or the government of each nation to establish a national religion, but effectively banned any one nation from attempting to impose its religion upon another. At the international level, in other words, there was agreement to disagree. Christian religious fervor itself—at least of the sort that had burned heretics, launched crusades, and so recently plunged Europe into civil war—fell into relative disrepute. The latter half of the seventeenth century saw what Herbert Butterfield (1900–1979), a major historian of Christianity in European history, once called "the Great Secularization." [11]

The old religious allegiances remained, but by slow degrees they began to matter less, even as national allegiance and national devotion—patriotism, as it came to be called—began to take on the moral gravity and ceremonial solemnity of religious commitment and the fallen soldier began to supplant the martyr. In 1689, John Locke published *A Letter Concerning Toleration*, in which he advanced the idea that a state would better guarantee peace within its borders by allowing many religions to flourish than by imposing any one of them. Locke favored a division of the affairs of religion as essentially private from the affairs of state as essentially public, capturing an attitudinal shift that was already in the air during the Enlightenment and would significantly mark the comparative study of religion as it took lastingly influential shape in the following century.

More intensely than by nascent toleration, the mood of the late seventeenth century was marked by wonder at the discoveries of natural science, above all those of Isaac Newton, whose major work establishing the laws of motion and universal gravitation was published in 1687. The poet Alexander Pope captured the popular mood in a famous couplet, written as Newton's epitaph (1730): "Nature, and Nature's Laws lay hid in Night. / God said, *Let Newton be!* and All was *Light*." Light was the master image of the Enlightenment—light, light, and "more light" (the legendary last words of Johann Wolfgang von Goethe [1749–1832]). Though the notion of natural law did not begin with Newton, his vision of the vast, calm, orderly, and implicitly benign operation of the laws of motion and gravity was unprecedented and gave new impetus to the search for comparable natural laws governing many other phenomena, including religion. Was there such a thing as a natural religion? If so, how did Christianity or any other actual religion relate to it? This idea, too, was pregnant with the promise of a future comparative study of religion.

While northern European Christianity was fighting the Wars of Religion, southern European Christianity had been transforming both the demography of Christendom and its understanding of the physical geography of the planet. The globe-spanning Portuguese and Spanish empires came into existence with speed comparable only to the Arab conquests of the seventh and eighth centuries. In evangelizing the Americas, the Portuguese and the Spaniards may have made Christianity for the first time the world's largest religion. In any case, their success in establishing colonial trading outposts along the African, Indian, Japanese, and Chinese coasts as well as founding the major Spanish colony of the Philippine Islands (named for the king of Spain) meant that European trade with India and China, above all the lucrative spice trade, no longer needed to pass through Muslim Central Asia or the Muslim Middle East.

Catholic missionaries did not have the success in Asia that they enjoyed in the Americas, yet the highly educated and culturally sophisticated Jesuit missionaries to Asia and the Americas became a significant factor in the evolving religious self-understanding of Europe itself. As extensive reports on the religions of Mexico, Peru, and above all India, China, and Japan reached Europe, they were published and read by many others besides the religious superiors for whom they had been written. Portugal and Spain had opened Europe's doors to a vastly enlarged world. The centuries-old quadripartite European division of the world's religions—Christianity, Judaism, Islam, and Paganism—was still generally in place in European minds. But from that point forward, as the sophistication of the religions of Asia and the Americas as well as the material and social brilliance of their civilizations came into focus, the inadequacy of *paganism* as a catchall term became evident, as did the need for new ways to speak of the newly recognized reality.

A New Reference Book Defines a New Field of Study

If any occasion can be singled out as the juncture when all these factors coalesced and produced a powerful new engagement with *world religions* in a way that approached the modern understanding of that phrase, it is the publication in Amsterdam between 1723 and 1737 of an epochal reference work, one that should indeed be seen as a direct ancestor of *The Norton Anthology of World Religions*. Appearing in seven sumptuous volumes comprising more than 3,000 pages with 250 pages of engravings, this encyclopedic production was *Religious Ceremonies and Customs of All the Peoples of the World* (*Cérémonies et coutumes religieuses de tous les peuples du monde*) by Jean Frédéric Bernard and Bernard Picart. Here, for the first time, was a presentation in one large work of all the religions of the world then known to Europe. Here, for the first time, was an attempt to reckon with how Europe's religious self-understanding would have to change in light of the previous two centuries of exploration, far-flung evangelization, and colonization.

It is important to note that this work, which was an immediate success and went through many editions and translations (and plagiarizations and piracies) over the next two hundred years, did not begin in the academic world and spread outward to the general public. Its address was directly to the general literate public—to the French public first, but quickly to other publics reading other languages. Jean Frédéric Bernard, brilliant but far from famous, was not just its behind-the-scenes research director, editor, and author: he was also its entrepreneurial publisher. It was a masterstroke on his part to secure the collaboration of Bernard Picart, already famous as an engraver producing reproductions of masterpiece paintings in an era before public art museums and long before photography, when what the public knew about art was limited to what they saw in church or what they acquired as engravings. By enabling the European public to see Picart's depictions of Aztec and Asian temples, costumes, and ceremonies, reconstructed from missionaries' descriptions, Bernard and Picart introduced the stimulating possibility of visual comparison. Where visual comparison led, philosophical and other critical comparison were intended to follow—and did.

As noted above, in the latter decades of the seventeenth century and the first of the eighteenth John Locke and a few other thinkers began to argue forcefully for religious toleration. Like Locke, Bernard and Picart were radical Calvinists as well as early "freethinkers," and the Netherlands was unique in their lifetimes as a haven for refugee dissidents and minorities of various kinds. Locke himself took refuge in the Netherlands during a turbulent and threatening period in England. Bernard's Huguenot (French Calvinist) family had fled to the Netherlands when Jean Frédéric was a boy. Picart, having abandoned Catholicism, moved there permanently as an adult, joining a large émigré French or French-speaking population in Amsterdam. The Peace of Westphalia, though it had imposed mutual forbearance in religious matters at the international level, had not done so at the national level. Protestants were still severely persecuted in France, as were Catholics in England. In the Netherlands, by contrast, though Calvinists were overwhelmingly dominant in public life, the private practice of Catholicism was indulged, while Jews were allowed public worship, and even deists or atheists had little to fear from the government. So it happened that though their great work was written in French, Bernard and Picart had good reason to publish it in the Netherlands.

In their magisterial account of the making of this work, *The Book That Changed Europe: Picart and Bernard's "Religious Ceremonies of the World,"* the historians Lynn Hunt, Margaret C. Jacob, and Wijnand Mijnhardt speculate about another possible consequence of its publication in the Netherlands—namely, the relative oblivion that overtook it in the twentieth century. The most populous European nations have tended to understand the intellectual history of the West through the minds of their own most influential thinkers, then through those of their major rivals, and only then through authors, however important, whose works were written or published in the smaller nations. Be that as it may, "Picart," as the work was commonly called, had two lasting effects far beyond the borders of the Netherlands. First, by discussing and illustrating the religions of Asia and of the Americas at length, it ended forever the quadripartite division of the world's religions that had structured European thought for eight hundred years. Second, it further solidified the conception of religion as a domain separable from culture and ethnicity. To quote *The Book That Changed Europe*, "This global survey of religious practices effectively *disaggregated and delimited* the sacred, making it specific to time, place, and institutions."[12]

There was now a greatly enlarged universe of religions to reckon with, to be sure, and Christian "teach ye all nations" missionary universalism had already mobilized to engage it. But also now, more strongly than ever, there was "religion" as an incipiently secular category capable of growth: it had lately been expanded by several new members and conceivably could be expanded further as further reports came in. The universalism of this emergent understanding of religion explains in part why the French Revolution, at the end of the eighteenth century, could presume to declare the "Rights of Man" rather than merely "of the [French] Citizen."

Bernard's and Picart's personal libraries suggest two favorite areas of reading: the ancient classics and travel books. The three historians note that 456 travel books were published in Europe in the fifteenth century, 1,566 in the seventeenth, and 3,540 in the eighteenth.[13] The co-creators' reading in the classics put them in touch with that pluralism of the mind made possible by the Renaissance recovery of classical moral philosophy and by the humanists' imaginative participation in the beliefs that figure so largely in classical literature. Their avid reading of travel reports gave them the enlarged geographical awareness made possible by the age of exploration.

As an early theorist of religion in this transformed mise-en-scène, Bernard blended elements of deist "natural religion" with classic Protestantism. His discussion of the religious customs of the world was scholastically Protestant in its combination of meticulous footnotes and sometimes-strenuous argumentation. More important for its later influence, Bernard's discussion was structurally Protestant in that it cast contemporary religious practice, wherever it was observed around the world, as the corruption of an earlier purity. But where sixteenth-century Protestantism had seen the purity of primitive Christianity, Bernard, writing in the full flush of eighteenth-century enthusiasm for natural science, saw the purity of an early, universal, natural, and "true" religion corrupted by the variously scheming priests of the religions reviewed. Despite this structural Calvinism in their philosophy of religion, Bernard and Picard were indebted to John Locke as well as to John Calvin; and especially when the non-Christian religions were under discussion, their manner was more often expository than forensic.

There is no doubt that Bernard discusses and Picart illustrates the religious customs and ceremonies of the world on the assumption both that each religion is, like Christianity, a separate, practice-defined domain and that these domains are all comparable. For better and for worse, the two of them contributed massively to the establishment of "religion" as a category projecting elements of Christian identity upon the vast, newly discovered worlds that lay beyond Christendom. Discussing Bernard and Picart's treatment of indigenous American religion, Hunt, Jacobs, and Mijnhardt declare:

> In short, Picart's images, especially when read alongside Bernard's text, *essentially created the category "religion."* Whereas the text sometimes wandered off on tangents about the sources of particular ceremonies, the similarities between rituals across space (Jewish and Catholic) and time (Roman antiquity and American Indian), or the disputes between scholars on the origins of different peoples, the images kept the focus on the most commonly found religious ceremonies—birth, marriage, death rituals, and grand processions—or on the most strikingly different practices,

which could range from the arcane procedures for the election of popes in Rome to human sacrifice in Mexico. Implicitly, the images transformed religion from a question of truth revealed to a select few of God's peoples (the Jews, the Catholics, and then the Protestants) to an issue of comparative social practices.[14]

The charge of Christian projection can plausibly be lodged against Picart and Bernard's interpretation of particular non-Christian rituals through their nearest equivalents in Christianity or Western antiquity. And yet if such habits of mind were limiting, they were scarcely crippling; and for Picart and Bernard themselves, they were evidently enabling and energizing. Is it true to say that between them, these two "essentially created the category 'religion'"? If they did so, we would claim, they did so largely through the convergence in their work and in themselves of the complex heritage that we have tried to sketch above.

Picart and Bernard carry forward the age-old, often suppressed, but never entirely forgotten understanding of the church as a thing in itself, not to be confounded with any nation or any set of cultural habits or practices. They carry forward the relatively subversive late medieval assumption that philosophy provides a neutral standpoint from which all religions may be compared. When considering religions remote from them in space rather than in time, they carry forward the Renaissance habit of drawing freely on classical paganism interpreted with textual sophistication and literary sympathy. They collate, as no one before them had yet done, the reports streaming into Europe about the religions of Asia and the Americas and, in their most brilliant stroke, they make these the basis for a major artistic effort to *see* what had been reported. They apply to their undertaking a distinct blend of moral seriousness, commercial enterprise, and erudite documentary attention to the particulars of religious practice that is their legacy from French Calvinist Protestantism. Finally, as sons of the Enlightenment, they bring a pioneering openness and breadth of vision to what they study.

Bernard can seem genuinely and intentionally prophetic when he writes:

> All religions resemble each other in something. It is this resemblance that encourages minds of a certain boldness to risk the establishment of a project of universal syncretism. How beautiful it would be to arrive at that point and to be able to make people with an overly opinionated character understand that with the help of charity one finds everywhere *brothers*.[15]

The place of good will—the sheer *novelty* of good will—in the study of religion has received far less attention than it deserves. Bernard's dream may seem commonplace now, when courteous interfaith dialogue is familiar enough in much of the West, but it was far from commonplace when he dreamed it.

Like *The Norton Anthology of World Religions*, Bernard and Picart's great work attended first and foremost to rituals and practices, considering beliefs only as expressed or embedded in these. Their work was path-breaking not just as a summary of what was then known about the religions of the world but also as an early demonstration of what sympathetic, participative imagination would later attain in the study of religion.

In painting their portraits of the religions of the world and in dreaming Bernard's dream ("How beautiful it would be . . . !"), Bernard and Picart were at the same time painting their own intellectual self-portrait as representative Europeans—neither clerics nor philosophers but thoughtful professionals—avid to engage in the comparison of the religions of the world on the widest possible scale. Religious comparison did not begin with them, nor had they personally created the intellectual climate in Europe that welcomed religious comparison once they so grandly attempted it. But it is not too much to say that in their day and to some significant degree because of them, Christian Europe finally learned how to compare religions.

Broadening the Foundation, Raising the Roof: 1737–1893

In 1737, when Picart and Bernard completed their work, Europe had barely discovered Australia. The peoples of the Arctic and of Oceania were living in nearly unbroken isolation. And even among peoples well-known to Europe, Japan was a forbidden kingdom, while China's first engagement with the West had only recently come to a xenophobic close. India was becoming relatively familiar, yet the doors of many smaller nations or regions remained barred. Europe had not yet lost its North and South American colonies to revolution; its later, nineteenth-century colonialist "scramble for Africa" had not yet begun. Russia had not yet expanded eastward to the Pacific. The English colonies in North America had not yet become the United States or expanded westward to the Pacific. The enlarged world that Bernard and Picart had sought to encapsulate in their illustrated reference work had many enlargements ahead, with corresponding consequences for the study of religion.

Though the intellectual framework for a global and comparative study of religion was essentially in place among an intellectual elite in Europe by the middle of the eighteenth century, much of even the known religious world remained culturally unexplored because the local languages were not understood. The accepted chronology within which Europeans situated new cultural and religious discoveries did not extend to any point earlier than the earliest events spoken of in the Old Testament. All this was to change during the century and a half that separates the publication of Picart from the convocation of the first World's Parliament of Religions at the 1893 Columbian Exposition in Chicago. That date may serve to mark the entrance of the United States of America into the story we have been telling and will bring us to the more immediate antecedents of *The Norton Anthology of World Religions*.

Broadening the Textual Base

Of special relevance for our work as anthologists is the enormous broadening of the textual foundation for religious studies that occurred during this long period. To review that transformation, we will consider the pivotal roles played by four European linguistic prodigies: F. Max Müller (1823–1900), James Legge (1815–1897), Sir William Jones (1746–1794), and Eugène Burnouf (1801–1852). One may grasp at a glance the scope of the documentary change that took place during the 150 years that followed the publication of Bernard and Picart's *Religious Ceremonies and Customs of All the Peoples of the World* by looking forward to the London publication between 1879 and 1910 of *The Sacred Books of the East* in no fewer than fifty volumes.

This enormous reference work, a superlative and in some regards still unsurpassed academic achievement, was produced under the general editorship of F. Max Müller, a German expatriate long resident in England. Müller's role in the nineteenth-century evolution of the disciplines of both comparative linguistics and comparative religious studies is large, but for the moment what concerns us is the sheer scope of the landmark reference work that he edited: two dozen volumes on Hinduism and Jainism translated into English from Sanskrit; nine on Buddhism alike from Sanskrit, from Pali (the canonical language of Indian Buddhism), and from other Asian languages; seven from Chinese on Confucianism, Daoism, and Chinese Buddhism; eight from Persian on Zoroastrianism; and two from Arabic on Islam. The range is astonishing, given that at the time when Bernard and Picart were writing and engraving, knowledge of *any* of these languages, even Arabic, was rare to nonexistent in Europe. How did Europeans learn them over the intervening century and a half? What motivated them to do so? The story blends missionary daring, commercial ambition, and sheer linguistic prowess in different proportions at different times.

Let us begin with Chinese. The first two modern Europeans known to have mastered Chinese were the Italian Jesuit missionaries Michele Ruggieri (1543–1607) and the preternaturally gifted Matteo Ricci (1552–1610), who entered China from the Portuguese island colony of Macao. Over time, as French Jesuits largely succeeded their Italian brethren in the Jesuit mission to China, the reports that they sent back to France about Qing dynasty (1644–1912) culture and the Confucian scholars they encountered stimulated French and broader European curiosity both about China itself and about the Chinese language. Though the Vatican terminated the Jesuits' Chinese mission on doctrinal grounds and though the Qing dynasty suppressed further Christian missionary work and expelled the missionaries themselves in 1724, a seed had been planted. In retirement on Macao, the French Jesuit Joseph Henri Marie de Prémare would compose the first-ever Chinese grammar in 1729. Later, during the nineteenth century, as Britain forced a weakening Qing dynasty to sign a treaty establishing coastal enclaves or "treaty ports" under British control, British Protestants commenced a new round of missionary activity in China, including the first attempt to translate the Bible into Chinese.

James Legge, originally a Scottish missionary to China, building on de Prémare's grammar and working with the help of Chinese Christians, undertook a major effort to translate the principal Confucian, Daoist, and Chinese Buddhist classics into English, always with the ultimate intention of promoting Christianity. Meanwhile, in 1814, Europe's first chair of Chinese and Manchu was established at the Collège de France. In 1822, Jean-Pierre Abel-Rémusat published in France a formal grammar of Chinese intended not for missionaries alone but for all interested European students. Legge himself became Oxford University's first professor of Chinese in 1876, and near the end of his life he was F. Max Müller's principal collaborator for Chinese texts in *The Sacred Books of the East*.

European penetration into China proceeded almost entirely from offshore islands or coastal enclaves under European colonial control; China as a whole never became a Western colony. India, by contrast, did indeed become a Western colony—specifically, a British colony—and the West's acquisition of the Indian languages and first encounter with the Indian religious classics is largely a British story. From the sixteenth through the early eighteenth century, Portuguese, Dutch, French, and British commercial interests vied for primacy in the lucrative Indian market. By late in the eighteenth century, however, Britain had overtaken all European rivals and established India, including what is now Pakistan, as its most important future colony—more lucrative at the time than the thirteen North American colonies that would become the United States of America. Britain's colonial motives were originally commercial rather than either evangelical or academic, but after British commercial and political control was firmly established in the Indian subcontinent, first cultural and linguistic explorations and then Christian missionary activity would follow.

In the launch of Sanskrit studies in the West, no figure looms larger than Sir William Jones, an Anglo-Welsh jurist in Calcutta who was at least as prodigiously gifted in language study as Matteo Ricci or James Legge. Fascinated by all things Indian, Jones founded an organization, the Asiatic Society, to foster Indian studies; and in 1786, on its third anniversary, he delivered a historic lecture on the history of language itself. In it, he expounded the thesis that Sanskrit, Greek, Latin, most of the European vernacular languages, and probably Persian were all descendants of a vanished common ancestor. Today, linguistic scholarship takes for granted the reality of "Proto-Indo-European" as a lost ancient language whose existence is the only conceivable explanation for the similarities that Jones may not have been the very first to chart but was certainly the first to bring to a large European public.

Jones's lecture detonated an explosion of European interest in studying Sanskrit and in tracing the family tree of the Indo-European, or "Aryan," languages, including all the languages mentioned in the previous paragraph but notably excluding Hebrew and Arabic—descendants of a different linguistic ancestor, later postulated as Proto-Semitic. (In the Bible, it is from Noah's son Shem—*Sēm* in Greek—that the peoples of the Middle East are descended—whence the term *Sem*-itic.) Now, the New Testament had been written in Greek rather than Hebrew or Aramaic, and Western Christianity had quickly left its Aramaic-speaking Palestinian antecedents behind and become a Greek-speaking Mediterranean religion. Did that mean that Christianity was actually Indo-European, or "Aryan," rather than Semitic, even though Jesus and Paul were Jews? This became one cultural strand within the European enthusiasm for Sanskrit studies, as further discussed below. Suffice it to say for now that it was during this period that *Semitic* and *Semitism* were coined as linguistic terms and the anti-Jewish *anti-Semitic* and *anti-Semitism* were coined as prejudicial, pseudo-anthropological counterterms.

Of greater immediate importance for the broadening of the study of religion was the window that Sanskrit opened on an almost unimaginably vast Indian literature whose most ancient and venerated texts, the Vedas, may be as old as, or even older than, the oldest strata of the Old Testament. Sanskrit is the classical language of India, no longer spoken and perhaps artificially perfected as a sacred language at some unrecoverable point in the past. But India has in addition a great many vernacular languages, more of them than Europe has, and in a number of these languages, other extensive Hindu literatures exist. These, too, gradually came to light in the nineteenth and the early twentieth century as knowledge of the relevant languages gradually spread to Europe.

India, for all its immense internal variety, did and does have a sense of itself as a single great place and of its gods as the gods of that place. Siddhartha Gautama, the Buddha, was born in India, and Indian Buddhism was the first Buddhism. Buddhist texts in Sanskrit are foundational for all students of Buddhism. But after some centuries had passed, Buddhism largely died out in India, living on in Sri Lanka, Southeast Asia, China, Korea, Japan, Mongolia, and Tibet. The linguistic and cultural variety of these countries was enormous. The Buddha was not called by the same name in all of them (in China, for example, he was called "Fo"). Western travelers, not knowing the languages of any of the countries where Buddhism was dominant, were slow to recognize even such basic facts as that the Buddha himself was a historical personage and not simply one among the many deities and demons whose statues they saw in their travels.

Donald S. Lopez, Jr., Buddhism editor for *The Norton Anthology of World Religions*, has written or edited several books telling the fascinating tale of how the puzzle of international Buddhism slowly yielded to the painstaking Western acquisition of several difficult languages and the related gradual recovery of a second, astoundingly large multilingual religious literature standing alongside that of Hinduism. In his *From Stone to Flesh: A Short History of the Buddha* (2013), Lopez allows what we might call the statue story—the gradual realization that sculptures of the Buddha represented a man, not a god—to become the human face on this much larger and less visible story of literary and historical recovery.[16]

In the story of how a broad textual foundation was laid for the study of Buddhism, a third linguistic genius stands between the Anglo-Welsh William Jones and the expatriate German F. Max Müller—namely, the French polymath Eugène Burnouf, the last of the four gifted linguists mentioned near the start of this section. Because of the enthusiasm for Sanskrit studies that Jones had touched off in Europe, copies of texts in Sanskrit began reaching European "orientalists" during the first decades of the nineteenth century. Those that arrived from India itself, as they were translated, would enable the assembly of the twenty-one volumes of Hindu texts that open Müller's *Sacred Books of the East*. Initially, however, no Sanskrit texts dealing with Buddhism were forthcoming from the Indian subcontinent. This situation would change, thanks to the fortuitous posting of an energetic and culturally alert English officer, Brian Houghton Hodgson (1801?–1894), to Nepal, where Buddhism thrived. Hodgson collected dozens of Nepalese Buddhist texts in Sanskrit, including the crucially important *Lotus Sutra*, and arranged for copies to be shipped to Europe.

Burnouf had been appointed to the Sanskrit chair at the Collège de France five years before the first shipment from Hodgson arrived. Thanks in part to earlier work he had done in the study of Pali, the Indian language in which the oldest Buddhist texts survive, Burnouf seems to have quickly grasped that what he had before him was the key to the historical roots of Buddhism in India. But this recognition was father to the further insight that Buddhism was the first true world religion (or, as he was inclined to think, the first internationally embraced moral philosophy) in human history. Burnouf was among the first, if not the very first, to see Buddhism whole. His 1844 *Introduction à l'histoire du Buddhisme indien* (*Introduction to the History of Indian Buddhism*) was the first of a projected four volumes that, had he lived to write them, would surely have been his greatest work. The one lengthy volume that he did bring to completion was already of epoch-making importance, particularly in light of his influence on his student F. Max Müller.

What the discovery and European importation of the classical religious literatures of India and China meant for the comparative study of religion in the West can be signaled concisely in the terms *Confucianism, Daoism* (earlier, *Taoism*), *Hinduism*, and *Buddhism*. They are all Western coinages, hybrids combining an Asian word at the front end and the Greek morpheme *–ism* at the back end, and each represents the abstraction of a separate domain of religious literature and religious practice from the cultural and ethnic contexts in which it originated. The coinage of these terms themselves may not coincide exactly with the recovery of the respective literatures; but to the extent that nineteenth-century Western scholarship viewed the texts as the East's equivalent of the Bible, it all but unavoidably engaged them on structurally Christian and even Protestant terms, thereby furthering the European conception of each related *–ism* as a religion in Europe's now consolidated and universalist sense of the word.

Structurally, Protestant influence was apparent again whenever, in the manner of Bernard and Picart, the great nineteenth-century linguist-historians judged the early texts to be superior to the later ones. Thus, in the interpretation of newly available Chinese texts, the earlier, more interior or "philosophical" versions of Daoism and Confucianism were often judged superior to the later, more ceremonial or "religious" versions, in which Laozi or Kongzi (Confucius) seemed to be deified or quasi-deified. Similarly, in the nineteenth-century interpretation of Hindu literature, India's British colonial rulers celebrated the supposed nobility and purity of the early Vedas and Upanishads while disparaging later Hindu religious texts and especially actual nineteenth-century Hindu practice. In the Buddhist instance, Eugène Burnouf set the early, human, historical Indian Buddha—whom he understood to have preached an ethics of simplicity and compassion—against the later, superhuman metaphysical Buddha. Consciously or unconsciously, Burnouf's contrast of the historical and the metaphysical Buddha coincided strikingly with the contrast then being drawn for a wide Christian audience between the historical Jesus of Nazareth and the divine God incarnate of Christian faith.

In short, as this new, broadened textual foundation was laid for the documentary study of Hinduism, Buddhism, and Daoism, a Christian theology of scripture and a post-Protestant philosophy of history were often projected upon it by the brilliant but Eurocentric scholars who were shaping the field. However, once primary texts are in hand, their intrinsic power can exert itself against any given school of interpretation. Thus, for example, late twentieth-century scholarship began to foreground and valorize the late and the popular over the early and the elite in several traditions, dignifying texts and practices once thought unworthy of serious scholarly attention.

Though nineteenth-century scholars might shudder at such a shift, it is essentially to them that we owe the availability of the key texts themselves. To be sure, the full recovery and the translation of these literatures are works in progress; nonetheless, knowledge of their great antiquity and their scope—barely even dreamed of by Picart and Bernard—was substantially complete by the end of the nineteenth century. The literary foundation had been put in place for an enormously enlarged effort at comparative study.

Enlarging the Chronological Frame

As already noted, Europeans as late as the early nineteenth century situated new cultural and religious discoveries, including all the texts whose recovery we have been discussing, in a chronology of religion understood to commence no earlier than the earliest events spoken of in the Old Testament. This framework led to efforts, comical in retrospect, to link newly discovered places and newly encountered legends or historical memories in Asia and the Americas to place-names in the book of Genesis, to the Noah story of Genesis 6–9, and to legends about the eastward travels of the apostles of Christ. All this would change with a discovery that might be described as blowing the roof off recorded history.

During Napoleon Bonaparte's occupation of Egypt in 1798–99, a French soldier stationed near the town of Rosetta in the Nile delta discovered a large stone bearing an inscription in three scripts: first, ancient Egyptian hieroglyphics, a script that no one then could read; second, another unknown script, which turned out to represent a later form of the Egyptian language; and finally, a third script, Greek. It took two decades of work, but in 1822, Jean-François Champollion deciphered this "Rosetta Stone." In the ensuing decades, his breakthrough enabled later scholars to translate hundreds of ancient Egyptian hieroglyphic inscriptions recovered from the ruins of ancient Egypt's immense tombs and temples and to discover, as they did so, that the Egyptians had maintained a remarkably complete chronology stretching back millennia before the oldest historical events recorded in the Bible. Decades of archaeological excavation in Egypt further enabled the construction of a chronological typology of Egyptian pottery. And then, since Egyptian pottery and pottery fragments are found all over the ancient Near East in mounds (tells) left by the repeated destruction and reconstruction of cities on the same sites, Egyptian pottery could be used to date sites far removed from Egypt. Over time, the Egyptian chronology would become the anchor for a chronological reconstruction of the entire lost history of the Near East, much of it written on thousands of archaeologically recovered clay tablets inscribed in the Mesopotamian cuneiform script that at the start of the eighteenth century was as undecipherable as Egyptian hieroglyphic.

The cuneiform (literally, "wedge-shaped") writing system was used as early as the late fourth millennium B.C.E. for the representation of Sumerian, a mysterious language without known antecedents or descendants. Sumeria, the oldest civilization of the ancient Near East—situated near the southern tip of Iraq, just north of the Persian Gulf—appears to have invented cuneiform writing. Most extant cuneiform texts, however, survive as small tablets representing several ancient Semitic languages rather than Sumerian. Starting in the mid-nineteenth century, hundreds of thousands of cuneiform tablets were recovered by archaeological excavations nearly as important as those in Egypt.

Cuneiform was deciphered thanks to the discovery in Persia in 1835 of a trilingual set of incised cuneiform wall inscriptions in Behistun (Bisitun, Iran) that, like the Rosetta Stone, included one already-known language—in this case ancient Persian—that scholars were eventually able to recognize behind the mysterious script. The challenge lay in going beyond the Persian of that inscription to decipher the language—now known to be the Mesopotamian Semitic language Akkadian—represented by one of the other two inscriptions. Though Eugène Burnouf played almost as important a role in this decipherment as he played in the recovery of Indian Buddhism, it is Henry Rawlinson, the British East India Company officer who first visited the Behistun inscriptions in 1835, whose name is usually linked to the recovery for European scholarship of the lost cuneiform literatures of Mesopotamia.

None of the now-extinct religions whose literatures survive in cuneiform is anthologized in *The Norton Anthology of World Religions*; we have chosen only major, living international religions. But the recovery of these lost literatures significantly affected the evolving historical context for all religious comparison. What these texts made clear was that recorded history had not dawned in Athens and Jerusalem. The religion of ancient Israel, in particular, was relocated from the dawn of history to a late morning hour, and thus could no longer be seen as in any sense the ancient ancestor of all the religions of the world. On the contrary, it now became possible to study the Bible itself comparatively, as a text contemporaneous with other texts, produced by a religion contemporaneous with and comparable to other ancient Semitic religions. And since the Bible is an anthology produced over a millennium, it became possible and even imperative to study each stratum within the Bible as contemporaneous with differing sets of non-Israelite religions and their respective texts.

European Protestantism, accustomed since the Reformation to employing the Bible as a historically reliable criterion for criticizing and revising the inherited practices of Christianity, was deeply affected by the discovery of both prebiblical and contemporaneous extrabiblical literatures, for they were clearly a way to deepen the historical understanding of the Bible. But the recovery of these literatures, set alongside related evidence from archaeological excavation, was a threat as well as an opportunity. It was an opportunity because it enabled illuminating comparisons of key motifs in Hebrew mythology with their counterparts in other ancient Near Eastern mythologies; it was a threat because though it corroborated the historicity of some biblical events, it undermined that of others.

Arguably, religious truth can be conveyed as well through fiction as through history. Patristic and medieval Christianity had been content for centuries to search the Bible for moral allegories rather than for historical evidence. Where history was not a central concern, comparative Semitic studies could and did enrich the linguistic and literary interpretation of the Bible without impugning its religious authority. But because Protestantism, rejecting allegorical interpretation, had consistently emphasized and valorized the historical content of the Bible, Protestant Christianity had particular trouble entertaining the notion that the Bible could be historically false in some regards and yet still religiously valid. A desire to defend the Old Testament as historically valid thus arose as a second motivation for Semitic studies. In the process, the prestige of the study of history itself as an intellectual discipline able to produce authoritative judgments about religion was significantly enhanced if not indeed somewhat inflated.

The discovery of the Rosetta Stone and the Behistun inscriptions affected the comparative study of Islam as well, though less directly. The recovery of lost Semitic languages and their lost literatures invited comparative linguistic study of the now-increased number of languages clearly related to Aramaic, Hebrew, and Arabic—the three principal languages of this family that were already known at the end of the eighteenth century. This study led to the postulated existence of a lost linguistic ancestor, Proto-Semitic, from which they were all plausibly descended. Proto-Semitic then began to play a role in the study of the religions practiced by the peoples who spoke these languages, somewhat like the role that Proto-Indo-European was playing in the study of the religions practiced by the peoples who spoke Sanskrit, Greek, Latin, German, and the other languages of that linguistic family.

As Proto-Semitic was reconstructed, moreover, it became clear to scholars that classical Arabic, the Arabic of the Qur'an, resembled it very closely and thus was an extremely ancient language that preserved almost the entire morphology of the lost ancestor of all the Semitic languages. Classical Hebrew, by contrast, was shown to be a much younger Semitic language. In an era of so much speculation about the relationship between ancient religions and ancient languages, the near-identity of classical Arabic and Proto-Semitic suggested to some that Islam might have preserved and carried forward ancient features of a Semitic proto-religion that was the lost ancestor of all the Semitic religions, just as Proto-Semitic was the lost ancestor of all the Semitic languages.

Orientalism, Neo-Hellenism, and the Quest for the Historical Jesus

The emergence of "Semitic languages" and "Semitic religions" as groups whose members were identifiable through comparison meant that biblical studies and Qur'anic studies—or more generally the study of ancient Israel and that of pre- and proto-Islamic Arabia—were more closely linked in the nineteenth century than they usually are in the twenty-first. Julius Wellhausen (1844–1918), a major German biblical scholar, reconstructed the formative stages of both. Historical linguists in Wellhausen's day who engaged in such comparative study of languages and history were called "orientalists." Orientalism is a term now associated with cultural condescension to the peoples of a region extending from Turkey through Persia to the borders of Afghanistan; but when first coined, it connoted primarily a stance of neutral comparison across that large cultural realm, a realm that the study of the languages, ancient and modern, had now thrown open for historical study as never before.

Interest in the language and history of classical Greece also grew enormously in nineteenth-century Europe, fed both by Hellenic revivalism and by Christian anxiety. The upper class generally celebrated Greek literature and thought as expressing a humane ideal distinct from and even superior to that of Christianity. In the late eighteenth century, in his *The History of the Decline and Fall of the Roman Empire* (1776–88), the English historian Edward Gibbon had already presented the emergence of Christianity as in itself the key factor in the decline of a superior classical civilization; Gibbon elevated the nobility and civic virtue of republican Rome above the faith, hope, and charity of Pauline Christianity as celebrated by classic Protestantism.

In the nineteenth century, it was Greece rather than Rome that defined the cultural beau ideal for an intellectual elite across western Europe. The German philosopher Friedrich Nietzsche (1844–1900), a classicist by training, was steeped in this philo-Hellenic tradition and drew heavily upon it for his well-known critique of Christianity. In its devout classicism, nineteenth-century European culture thus continued and intensified a celebration of an idealized and indeed a more or less mythologized Greece that had begun during the Renaissance and continued during the Enlightenment.

This European cultural identification with Greece, whether or not tinged with antipathy toward Christianity, sometimes worked symbiotically with a larger geographical/cultural identification already mentioned—namely, Europe's identification with the larger world of the Indo-European peoples as distinct from and superior to the disparaged Semitic peoples, most notably the Jews. Religiously motivated Christian prejudice against Jews had by no means disappeared, but it was now joined by a form of pseudo-scientific racism that made more of national than of religious difference. Because nationalist self-glorification linked to invidious anti-Semitism had a seriously distorting effect on the comparative study of religion in nineteenth-century Europe, the full enfranchisement of Europe's Jews as fellow scholars would have, as we will see, a comparably important corrective effect.

A second motivation for classical studies, especially in Lutheran Germany, was Christian: an urgently felt need to write the still-unwritten history of the New Testament in the context of first-century Hellenistic Judaism. The historical reliability of the New Testament had been the foundation of the Lutheran critique of sixteenth-century Catholicism. But nineteenth-century New Testament scholars now claimed to recognize adulterations by the church within the Gospels themselves. To exaggerate only slightly, the challenge that nineteenth-century Protestant scholars saw themselves facing was to recover the historical Jesus from the church-corrupted Gospels in the same way that they understood the sixteenth-century reformers to have recovered the historical practice of Christianity from the corrupted church practice of their day.

"Historical Jesus" scholarship of this sort grew enormously in scope and erudition during the first decades of the nineteenth century, fed by the growing prestige of history as a social science and climaxing with the publication in 1835–36 of David Friedrich Strauss's massive, learned, sensationally successful, but scandalously skeptical *Life of Jesus, Critically Examined*, a German work that appeared in English in 1846 in an anonymous translation by the aspiring English novelist George Eliot (Marian Evans). Decades of further scholarship followed, some of it indirectly stimulated once again by archaeology. As the excavations by Heinrich Schliemann (1822–1890) proved that there was a Troy and that a great war had occurred there, thus allegedly proving the historical reliability of the *Iliad*, so, it was hoped, further archaeological and historical research might yet demonstrate the historical reliability of the New Testament.

A denouement occurred in 1906 with the publication of the German first edition of Albert Schweitzer's epoch-making *The Quest of the Historical Jesus*.[17] Schweitzer believed that the quest for the historical Jesus had actually succeeded as history. Yet the recovered historical Jesus was more a problem for contemporary Christianity than a solution, the renowned scholar ruefully concluded. Schweitzer's work continues to haunt historical Jesus scholarship, even though fresh quests and fresh alleged recoveries of the lost historical Jesus, both learned and popular, have continued to appear.

In sum, narrowly Christian though the quest for the historical Jesus may seem, it did much to establish historical study as the default mode of religious study. Its shadow lies across studies of the historical Buddha, the historical Laozi, and the historical Muhammad, among others, stamping them all with the assumption that in the study of any religious tradition, historical truth will prove the indisputable form of truth.

The Haskalah and Its Impact on the Comparative Study of Religion

The character of the literature of religious studies is determined as much by who is writing as by what is written about. So far, we have concentrated on changes in what was available as subject matter to be written about, thanks to the recovery of religious literatures either lost in time or remote in place. We turn now to a new line of inquiry and a new question: Who was to be commissioned to conduct the study, to do the writing, to tell the story of the religions of the world? In the late eighteenth and the nineteenth centuries, above all in Germany, a Jewish religious, cultural, and intellectual movement called the *Haskalah* emerged, one of whose effects would be the historic enfranchisement of Jews as, for the first time, full participants in Europe's comparative study of religion. Before saying more about the impact of the Haskalah upon secular religious studies in Europe, we should briefly review its direct and complex impact upon the Jews of Europe themselves.

Religiously, thanks in good measure to the pathbreaking work of the Jewish-German philosopher Moses Mendelssohn (1729–1786), the Haskalah gave rise to Reform Judaism as a revised form of Jewish belief and practice more attentive to the Tanakh, or Hebrew Bible (Christianity's Old Testament), than to the Talmud. However uncontroversial it may seem in the twenty-first century for the reformers to honor the biblical prophets rather than the Talmudic sages as the ethical pinnacle of the Jewish tradition, the shift was highly disruptive in the late eighteenth and the nineteenth centuries, for the emphasis in Jewish religious practice until then had been squarely on the Talmud and on the rabbinical sages whose debates, preserved in the Talmud, had made the rabbinate the final authority in Jewish religious observance. In the rabbinic tradition, the Talmud is the heart of the "Oral Torah" that Moses, the original rabbi (teacher), received from God and conveyed in speech to his first (rabbinical) students, beginning a teacher-to-student chain that legitimated the rabbinate as authoritative. To undercut the Talmud, Rabbinic Judaism's foundational second scripture, was thus to undercut the rabbis themselves.

Reform Judaism was religiously unsettling in another way because by going back to the Bible, thereby setting aside centuries of venerable Jewish tradition and subverting established rabbinical religious authority, its founders, beginning with Moses Mendelssohn, delivered a critique that bore a striking structural resemblance to German Lutheranism's back-to-the-Bible critique of Roman Catholicism. The Jewish reformation looked rather like the Christian, to the exhilaration of many Jews at the time in Lutheran northern Germany but to the consternation of others.

Religiously disruptive in these ways, the Haskalah—often referred to as the Jewish Enlightenment—represented as well a major turning point in Jewish European cultural life, away from oppressive and once inescapable social restriction and confinement. The *Maskilim*, as the leaders of the Haskalah were called, recognized that the dawn of a culture of toleration in Christian Europe might just light the path to an escape for Jews who were willing to acculturate in certain manageable ways. Mendelssohn himself, for example, became an acknowledged master of literary German as written by the intellectual elite of Berlin. German culture was then entering its most brilliant century. In an earlier century, German Jews would have had to become Christians to exit the ghetto and take part. But absent the requirement to convert, perhaps German Jews could become Jewish Germans. Such was the tacit hope of the Haskalah.

As Reform Judaism grew in popularity, thousands of Jews gambled that the ghetto walls were indeed coming down, and ultimately they were not mistaken. Despite the murderous anti-Semitism that would rise in the later nineteenth century and the genocide that would so profoundly scar the twentieth, a page had been turned for good in Western academic life—not least in the comparative study of religion.

For this anthology, the Haskalah mattered in one further, only slightly narrower regard: while no longer deferring to the immense corpus of rabbinic literature as authoritative, the Maskilim did not ignore it. On the contrary, they began to apply to it the same techniques of critical scholarship that the Renaissance had pioneered and that Protestantism and the Enlightenment had further developed for the interpretation of the Bible and other classical texts. The process of critically editing and translating the rabbinic literature, which placed yet another major religious literature within the reach of secular study, began very slowly and approached completion only in the twentieth century. Yet were it not for the Maskilim, that great work would not have been undertaken.

Most important of all, however, was the inclusion of Christianity's original "other" in the corps of those attempting in the West to make comparative sense of the religions of the world. This inclusion was truly a watershed event, for it foreshadowed a long list of subsequent, cumulatively transformative inclusions of the previously excluded. Religious studies in the twenty-first century is open to all qualified participants, but such has not always been the case. Broadening the textual basis for religious studies and exploding the temporal frame around it were important nineteenth-century developments. Broadening the composition of the population that would engage in religious studies was even more important.

The gradual inclusion of non-Christian scholars in the Western discussion of world religions has not entailed retiring the historically Christian but now secularized concept of religion (or the related concept of world religions), but Christian or Western scholars have lost any presumptive right to serve as moderators or hosts of the discussion. The overcoming of insufferable condescension, not to speak of outright prejudice, has played a part, but so too, and more importantly, have matters of perception, perspective, and the "othering" of Christianity: the rest had long been accustomed to see themselves through the eyes of the West; now the West has begun to see itself through the eyes of the rest.

The dynamic entry of Europe's Jews not just into the European study of religion but also into many other areas of European life brought about a massive backlash in the late nineteenth century, then the Nazi genocide in the twentieth, the post–World War II triumph of Zionism, and belatedly, among other consequences, a distinct mood of remorse and repentance in late twentieth-century European Christianity.[18] Somewhat analogous emotions accompanied the end of European colonialism during the same late twentieth-century decades amid exposés of the exploitation and humiliation suffered by the colonized. The comparative study of religion has both influenced and been influenced by these ongoing revisionist shifts of mood and opinion, but, to repeat, the first steps down this long path were taken by and during the Haskalah.

Evolution and the Comparative Study of Religion

While the decipherment of Egyptian hieroglyphic and Mesopotamian cuneiform were still throwing new light on the earliest centuries of recorded history, Charles Darwin's *On the Origin of Species by Means of Natural Selection* in 1859 and *The Descent of Man, and Selection in Relation to Sex* in 1871 shone a beam into the deeper darkness of the unrecorded, biological prehistory of the human species. At the time, no one, including Darwin, knew just how old *Homo sapiens* was as a species; the technique of absolute dating by the measurement of radioactive decay would not be developed until the mid-twentieth century. What Darwin could already demonstrate from the fossil record, however, was that the human species had evolved from earlier species in a process that antedated recorded history. The implications of this discovery for all forms of scientific and historical investigation were enormous and are still being explored. For the study of religion, the discovery meant that behind the religions of recorded history, there now stood in principle all the religions of human prehistory. At what point in human evolution did religion first appear, or was that even the right question? Should the question rather be about precursors to religion—earlier behaviors that would evolve into what we now call religion? How, if at all, could the practitioners of these prehistoric proto-religions or precursors to religion be studied?

Answers to that question are still being devised, but none involves their texts, for they left none. Tempting as it would be to explore new work being done on the evolution of religion before the invention of writing, such work is not properly a part of the study of religion to which *The Norton Anthology of World Religions* contributes, for ours is, after all, a collection of texts. We know that the human species emerged some two hundred thousand years ago in southwest Africa and migrated from there eastward and then northward through the Great Rift Valley in what appear to be two noteworthy spikes. One spike proceeded by way of Lake Victoria up the Nile River to where its delta empties into the Mediterranean Sea. The other spike crossed from Africa to Arabia at the Strait of Bab el Mandeb and then proceeded along the southeast coast of Arabia to the Strait of Hormuz, where it crossed into Asia. From there, one stream of human migrants veered northward to the delta of the Tigris River at the upper end of the Persian Gulf, while the other moved southward to the delta of the Indus River. The Indus delta and the river system above it cradled the civilization that, as it moved south into the Indian subcontinent, would produce the Vedas, written in Sanskrit, the earliest scriptures of ancient India. The Nile and the Tigris deltas and the river systems that lay above them would together define the "Fertile Crescent" within which ancient Israel would produce the earliest Hebrew scriptures. The invention of writing in the Tigris delta (Sumer) and the Nile Valley (Egypt) does not antedate the late fourth millennium B.C.E. The oldest works honored as scripture by Hinduism or by Judaism may be a full millennium younger than that. As recoverable from surviving texts, the story of the world's major, living, international religions can reach no further back in time than this.

To concede this much is not to concede that the earlier evolution of religion cannot be reconstructed at all or indeed even reconstructed in a way that would link it to the story told here. It is to concede only that that reconstruction would call for another kind of book than this one, assembling very different kinds of evidence than are assembled here.

The First World's Parliament of Religions

We may close this review of the development of religious studies between 1737 and 1893 with a visit to the World's Parliament of Religions at the World's Columbian Exposition in Chicago in 1893. The vast exposition, which ran for six months and attracted millions of visitors, was a celebration of progress—scientific, political, and cultural—during the five hundred years since Columbus had discovered America. (The exposition missed its intended 1892 opening by a few months.) Though the organizers often seemed to tacitly assume that the latest and greatest chapter in world progress was the American chapter and that thriving, optimistic Chicago was the epitome of American progress, nonetheless an exuberant, generally benevolent and inclusive curiosity characterized much on display. And though there was condescension in the presentation of model villages from "primitive" societies as natural history exhibits, there was also an acknowledgment that many fascinating and once entirely unknown societies were now no longer unknown and could be presented for the instruction of the interested.

As for the World's Parliament of Religions, it seemed to reflect a contemporary, enlightened, Protestant American view that there existed—or there could come into existence—something like a generic religion whose truth all specific religions could acknowledge without renouncing their respec-

tive identities. This view may have owed something to the many translations and plagiarizations of *The Religious Ceremonies and Customs of All the
Peoples of the World* that for a century and a half had been steadily propagating Bernard and Picart's confidence that a pure, "natural" religion underlay
the variously corrupted historical religions of the world. It may have owed
something as well to the 1890 publication of James Frazer's *The Golden
Bough*, a romantic and enormously popular work that marshaled classical
mythology and selected early anthropological studies of primitive tribes in
a grand evolutionary march from magic to science.[19] It may have reflected
in addition the gradual influence on American Protestants of the Enlightenment ideas underpinning the United States Constitution. Under the Constitution, since there was no "religious test" for public office, a Muslim or even
an atheist could legally become president.[20] The legal leveling explicit in the
Constitution implicitly encouraged a comparable leveling in American society, first among Protestants but later extended to Catholics and Jews, and
gradually to the adherents of other religions. The process was slow, but its
direction was unmistakable.

What is most remarkable about the Parliament, however, is the simple fact
that when the organizers invited representatives of Hinduism, Buddhism, Daoism, Confucianism, Shinto, Jainism, Islam, and Zoroastrianism to come
together and deliberate with Christians and Jews, everyone accepted the
invitation. Swami Vivekananda (1863–1902) accepted both the invitation
and the idea behind it—namely, that Hinduism was a world religion. He did
not object that there was no such thing as "Hinduism," that the religious life
of India was not a separate province within a postulated empire named "religion," that Indians who honored the Vedas did not see themselves as en route
to any brighter collective religious future, and so forth and so on. Objections
like this are legitimate, but Vivekananda agreed to attend anyway, gave a
sensationally well-received speech, and went on to found the Vedanta Society as an American branch of Hinduism. Plainly enough, he had begun to
construe Hinduism as potentially a global religion, separable from Indian
ethnicity. The Sri Lankan Buddhist Anagarika Dharmapala (1864–1933)
did something similar. In the real world of religious practice, these were
important ratifying votes for a vision of world religious pluralism.

"How beautiful it would be," Jean Frédéric Bernard had written, "to arrive
at that point and to be able to make people with an overly opinionated character understand that with the help of charity one finds everywhere *brothers*." If the organizers of the World's Parliament of Religions thought that
they had arrived at that blessed point when Swami Vivekananda thrilled his
American audience with the opening words of his oration, "Sisters and
Brothers of America," they were mistaken. And yet something was happening. A change was taking place. In various related European and American
venues, a subtle but distinct shift of attitude was under way.

Is it possible to contemplate beliefs that one does not share and practices
in which one does not engage and to recognize in them the shaping of a life
that one can recognize as human and even good? When attitudes shift on a
question as basic as that one, novelists and poets are often the first to
notice. The novelist Marcel Proust wrote as follows about the Hindu and
Buddhist concepts of *samsara* and *karma*—though without ever using those
words—in his early twentieth-century masterpiece *In Search of Lost Time*
(1913–27):

He was dead. Dead for ever? Who can say? . . . All that we can say
is that everything is arranged in this life as though we entered it
carrying a burden of obligations contracted in a former life; there
is no reason inherent in the conditions of life on this earth that can
make us consider ourselves obliged to do good, to be kind and
thoughtful, even to be polite, nor for an atheist artist to consider
himself obliged to begin over again a score of times a piece of work
the admiration aroused by which will matter little to his worm-
eaten body, like the patch of yellow wall painted with so much skill
and refinement by an artist destined to be for ever unknown and
barely identified under the name Vermeer. All these obligations,
which have no sanction in our present life, seem to belong to a different world, a world based on kindness, scrupulousness, self-
sacrifice, a world entirely different from this one and which we
leave in order to be born on this earth, before perhaps returning
there to live once again beneath the sway of those unknown laws
which we obeyed because we bore their precepts in our hearts, not
knowing whose hand had traced them there[.][21]

   Marcel Proust was not a Hindu, he was a Frenchman of Jewish descent.
Like not a few writers of his day, he may have been influenced by Frazer's *The Golden Bough*, but *In Search of Lost Time* is in any case a novel,
not a work of science, philosophy, or theology. And yet we might say that
in the words quoted, Proust is a Hindu by sympathetic, participative
imagination and thus among the heirs of Jean Frédéric Bernard and Bernard Picart. This kind of imaginatively participant sympathy was taking
hold in a new way.
   In the United States, the World's Parliament of Religions reflected the
same *Zeitgeist* and heralded, moreover, an organizational change that would
occur in the latter third of the following century, building on all that had
transpired since Bernard dreamed his dream. That change—the decision
of the National Association of Biblical Instructors to reincorporate in 1964 as
the American Academy of Religion—reflected the emergent conviction that
some knowledge of the world's religions was properly a part of every American's education.[22]
   If American intellectual culture is distinctive in any regard, it is distinctive in its penchant for popularization or for the democratization of knowledge. The intellectual leadership of the country has generally assumed that
the work of intellectual discovery is not complete until everybody has heard
the news. But judgment about what constitutes "news"—that is, what subjects constitute the core of education for all people—has changed over
time, and knowledge of the world's religions has not always been on the list.
It was during the twentieth century that it made the list, and so for the
study of religion we may regard the World's Parliament of Religions as
opening the twentieth century.
   In the comparative study of religion, Europe was America's teacher until
the end of World War II. The secular, neutral comparative study of religion
was a European inspiration. The heavy lifting necessary to assemble linguistic and archaeological documentary materials for such study—the story
we have been reviewing here—was almost entirely a European achievement

as well. But a distinctive aspect of the American contribution to the story has been the impulse to share inspirations, achievements, and knowledge gained in the study of religion with the general public. A work like *The Norton Anthology of World Religions*, intended for the college undergraduate or the willing general reader, is a work entirely in the American grain. If you find the texts assembled in the collection that now follows surprising, if you find the editorial frame around them instructive, please know that you are cordially invited to explore the remaining five anthologies that with this one constitute the full *Norton Anthology of World Religions*.

Notes

The intellectual debts incurred in the foregoing introduction are far greater than could be registered even in a far longer list of footnotes than appears here. The subject matter touched upon could obviously command a far longer exposition than even so lengthy an introduction as this one has allowed. I beg the indulgence alike of the students I may have overburdened and of the scholars I have failed to acknowledge. JM

1. Kevin Schilback, "Religions: Are There Any?" *Journal of the American Academy of Religion* 78.4 (December 2010): 1112–38.
2. Frans de Waal, *The Bonobo and the Atheist: In Search of Humanism among the Primates* (New York: Norton, 2013), p. 210.
3. Daniel L. Pals, *Eight Theories of Religion*, 2nd ed. (New York: Oxford University Press, 2006); Michael Stausberg, ed., *Contemporary Theories of Religion: A Critical Companion* (London: Routledge, 2009). Strikingly, they do not overlap on a single entry.
4. Feynman is quoted in Dennis Overbye, "Laws of Nature, Source Unknown," *New York Times*, December 18, 2007.
5. Clifford Geertz, "Religion as a Cultural System," in *The Interpretation of Cultures: Selected Essays* (New York: Basic Books, 1973), p. 90 (emphasis his).
6. Ibid., p. 125.
7. Ibid., pp. 193–233.
8. Tomoko Masuzawa, *The Invention of World Religions, Or, How European Universalism Was Preserved in the Language of Pluralism* (Chicago: University of Chicago Press, 2005).
9. All Bible quotations in this introduction are from *The Holy Bible, Revised Standard Version* (New York: Thomas Nelson & Sons, 1952).
10. Mark C. Taylor, *After God* (Chicago: University of Chicago Press, 2007).
11. Herbert Butterfield, *The Englishman and His History* (Cambridge: The University Press, 1944), p. 119.
12. Lynn Hunt, Margaret C. Jacob, and Wijnand Mijnhardt, *The Book That Changed Europe: Picart and Bernard's "Religious Ceremonies of the World"* (Cambridge, Mass.: Belknap Press of Harvard University Press, 2010), p. 2 (emphasis added).
13. Ibid., p. 5.
14. Ibid., pp. 155–57 (emphasis added).
15. Jean Frédéric Bernard, quoted in ibid., p. 241 (emphasis in original).
16. Donald S. Lopez, Jr., *From Stone to Flesh: A Short History of the Buddha* (Chicago: University of Chicago Press, 2013).
17. *The Quest of the Historical Jesus* is the colorful title of the English translation first published in 1910; Schweitzer's sober German title was *Von Reimarus zu Wrede: Eine Geschichte der Leben-Jesu-Forschung* (From Reimarus to Wrede: A History of Research into the Life of Jesus). Hermann Reimarus and William Wrede were earlier scholars.
18. For the background in World War II and its aftermath, see John Connelly, *From Enemy to Brother: The Revolution in Catholic Teaching on the Jews, 1933–1965* (Cambridge, Mass.: Harvard University Press, 2012).
19. James Frazer, *The Golden Bough: A Study in Magic and Religion: A New Abridgment from the Second and Third Editions* (Oxford: Oxford University Press, 2009). Frazer's extravaganza eventually grew to twelve volumes, now out of print. For a more recent and more richly informed account of the evolution of religion, see Robert M. Bellah, *Religion in Human Evolution: From the Paleolithic to the Axial Age* (Cambridge, Mass.: Belknap Press of Harvard University Press, 2011).
20. See Denise A. Spellberg, *Thomas Jefferson's Qur'an: Islam and the Founders* (New York: Knopf, 2013).
21. Marcel Proust, *In Search of Lost Time*, vol. 5, *The Captive; The Fugitive*, trans. C. K. Scott Moncrieff and Terence Kilmartin, rev. D. J. Enright (New York: Random House, 1993), 5:245–46.
22. See Preface, p. xxii.

You can't discuss the ocean with a well frog—he's limited by the space he lives in. You can't discuss ice with a summer insect—he's bound to a single season. You can't discuss the Way with a cramped scholar—he's shackled by his doctrine.

—*Zhuangzi*

DAOISM

EDITED BY

James Robson

INTRODUCTION
Daoism Lost and Found

The Chinese word *dao*, which gives the religious tradition "Daoism" its name, initially meant "way" or "pathway."[1] The many primary sources assembled here will take the reader down the ways and byways that constitute the terrain of Daoism. As is true of dense religious landscapes, an accurate map of that terrain contains more detail than a single picture can convey. For most of its history in the West, the Chinese religious tradition we call Daoism—usually rendered as "Taoism" and mispronounced with a strong "T" sound—evoked exotic images of recluses in mountains living in harmony with nature's rhythms, sages living incredibly long lives, martial arts masters with esoteric powers, a "go with the flow" ethos, and a few enigmatic books containing the secrets of Eastern occult spiritual wisdom. Ideas about Daoism spread primarily through translations and interpretations of texts considered to be its sacred books: *The Scripture of the Way and Its Virtue* (*Daode jing*, or *Laozi*) and the *Book of Master Zhuang* (*Zhuangzi*). *The Scripture of the Way and Its Virtue*, often said to be the second most frequently translated text in world literature (after the Bible), has long generated tremendous transcultural appeal, its mysterious aphoristic passages suggesting an enormous range of interpretations to generations of translators, commentators, and readers. It has been connected with the individualism of Jean-Jacques Rousseau (1712–1778), Enlightenment thinkers like Immanuel Kant (1724–1804), transcendentalists like Henry David Thoreau (1817–1862) and Ralph Waldo Emerson (1803–1882), occultists like Aleister Crowley (1875–1947), Continental philosophers like Martin Heidegger (1889–1976; see "Heidegger and Our Translation of the *Daode jing*"), literary figures like Alfred, Lord Tennyson, and Oscar Wilde (see "The Ancient Sage" and "A Chinese Sage"), counterculture icons like Timothy Leary (who published a "psychedelic reading" of *The Scripture of the Way and Its Virtue*), and even Republicans espousing ideas of limited government. As president, Ronald Reagan began his final State of the Union address by weaving in a passage from chapter 60 of *The Scripture of the Way and Its Virtue*: "History records the power of the ideas that brought us here those 7 years ago—ideas like the individual's right to reach as far and as high as his or her talents will permit; the free market as an engine of economic progress. And as an ancient Chinese philosopher, Lao-tzu, said: 'Govern a great nation as you would cook a small

---

1. Daoism—pronounced "Dow-ism," like the *Dow Jones Industrial Average*—is also romanized as "Taoism," which accords with the older Wade-Giles romanization system rather than the Pinyin system that is now standard. Throughout this book "Daoism" is used in translations from the historical religious tradition; in secondary sources, the spelling is left unchanged to provide a sense of how the term entered into Western discourse.

fish; do not overdo it.'"[2] How could so many diverse people find something to value in the pages of one brief text?

Popular ideas about Daoism in the West did not spread solely through appropriations of *The Scripture of the Way and Its Virtue* and the *Book of Master Zhuang*. Vague—often misguided, but quaintly appealing—notions about Daoism are found in best-selling books like *The Secret of the Golden Flower* (1931), *The Tao of Physics* (1975), and *The Tao of Pooh* (1982), as well as lesser-known works like *The Tao of Elvis* (2002) and *The Dude De Ching* (2009),[3] a self-described publication of the Church of the Latter-Day Dude (inspired by Laozi's *Daode jing* and the 1998 cult classic movie *The Big Lebowski*). Films such as *The Tao of Steve* (2000) and *The Matrix* (1999) also spread Daoist images; and Daoist ideas are cited in social movements connected with feminists, environmentalists, peace activists, and animal rights advocates as well as in pop psychology, alternative medicine, and a variety of New Age religions. As popular knowledge about Daoism has taken these different trajectories, it has captured the imagination of Western seekers who long for access to the deep mysteries of existence, a form of spirituality without a God and the trappings of traditional religious institutions, and who question the modern valorization of instrumental rationality and technology.

It would be easy to dismiss these modern appropriations of Daoism as little more than distortions by Westerners mapping their own dreams onto an apparently distant tradition that is itself the product of an orientalist vision of the mystical East. Yet these manifestations of Daoism in the West provide effective clues to how Daoism was shaped and how its image developed. Equally important, these trends are not simply modern transformations of Daoism that arose out of nowhere: rather, they are the most recent iteration of developments that began in China's remote past and were further fueled in the sixteenth through eighteenth centuries by Jesuit missionaries who praised Confucianism and Daoist philosophy but pointedly disdained the religious aspects of Daoism.

Daoism Divided

The Western imagination of Daoism has influenced the perception of Daoism down to the present day. It has essentially created two Daoisms, imposing an artificial distinction between the "pure" (philosophy) and the "impure" (Daoist religious practices) in a process similar to the European fashioning of Buddhism as a philosophy rather than a religion. Although modern scholarship has shown that such a stark division of religion and philosophy is inaccurate and untenable, it has resulted in widespread confusion about Chinese religions in general and Daoism in particular. It was once standard to explain the division by pointing to two terms found in early Chinese writings, *daojia*

2. Ronald Reagan, "Address Before a Joint Session of Congress on the State of the Union," January 25, 1988, *The American Presidency Project*, archived by Gerhard Peters and John T. Woolley, www.presidency.ucsb.edu.
3. Richard Wilhelm, *The Secret of the Golden Flower: A Chinese Book of Life*, with a commentary by C. G. Jung (London: Routledge and Kegan Paul, 1931); Fritjof Capra, *The Tao of Physics: An Exploration of the Parallels between Modern Physics and Eastern Mysticism* (Berkeley: Shambhala; New York: Random House, 1975); Benjamin Hoff, *The Tao of Pooh* (New York: E. P. Dutton, 1982); David H. Rosen, *The Tao of Elvis* (San Diego: Harcourt, 2002); The Church of the Latter-Day Dude, *The Dude De Ching: A Dudeist Holy Book Inspired by the "Tao Te Ching" of Lao Tzu and "The Big Lebowski" of Joel and Ethan Coen* (Los Angeles: Church of the Latter-Day Dude, 2009).

(specialists of/on the Dao) and *daojiao* (teachings of/on the Dao), but only in the hands of Western polemicists did these terms have the power to separate philosophy from religion. Westerners identified *daojia* with what they called "philosophical Daoism," which was based on the writings of Laozi and Zhuangzi and included their ideas about a mystical union with the Dao; *daojiao*, or "religious Daoism," was said to refer to Daoist religious institutions that formed in the later part of the Han dynasty (202 B.C.E.–220 C.E.) and included methods to attain immortality and to use amulets and talismans for healing and protection.

In *Records of the Grand Historian* (*Shiji*)—an important historical work from the first century B.C.E.—the term *daojia* first appeared as the name of an early philosophical tradition or lineage, described there as a syncretic movement (see Sima Tan's "Essential Points on the Six Lineages of Thought"). Later in the Han dynasty, it was simply one of the bibliographic categories into which texts in the Imperial Library were sorted: it came to include the writings of Laozi and Zhuangzi, along with other works that presented alternatives to the Confucian system of social and political structuring. Similarly, the term *daojiao* initially had nothing to do the Daoist religion, which it predated. During the pre-Han period it was applied to a variety of philosophical traditions, including Confucianism, and from about the third to the fifth century C.E. the term was even used as a synonym for Buddhism (*fojiao*). Nevertheless, at some point in the fifth century *daojiao* became identified solely with organized Daoism as distinguished from Buddhism.

The fall of the Han dynasty in the third century C.E.—with the attending collapse and discrediting of the Confucian-based imperial system—was devastating to the Chinese, though it also (as discussed below) created an opening for new Daoist movements. As the Han declined, some elite court scholars retreated from imperial service, immersed themselves in the writings of Laozi and Zhuangzi, and in some cases wrote commentaries on those foundational texts that differed starkly from earlier interpretations. For example, earlier commentaries on *The Scripture on the Way and Its Virtue* had emphasized its approach to governance (see "Explaining the *Laozi*" from *The Book of Master Han Fei*), communal social organization, or self-cultivation techniques (see the "Old Man by the River [*Heshang gong*] Commentary" and the *Xiang'er Commentary on the Laozi*), but the young scholar Wang Bi (226–249 C.E.) offered a philosophically reductionist and metaphysical reading of the text. Indeed, his interpretation became so dominant that it was not necessary to anthologize his commentary here: today nearly all editions of *The Scripture of the Way and Its Virtue* base their interpretation and translation on it. Since other texts, such as the "Old Man by the River (*Heshang gong*) Commentary"—the most influential early commentary—were largely forgotten, they are excerpted here in order to illustrate the diversity of ways in which *The Scripture of the Way and Its Virtue* was understood before it became a philosophical classic.

The Lasting Influence of "Jesuit Daoism"

The elevation of *The Scripture of the Way and Its Virtue* as pure philosophy led to the portrayal of the social and religious aspects of Daoism as an egregious falling away from the pristine earlier tradition. Much of what has been written about early Daoism is colored by that pejorative view, which has proved difficult to correct. The arrival of Western missionaries in the sixteenth century helped give it lasting power; not only did they collude with the Confucian elites in advancing certain Daoist texts as the reputable philosophy of the elite and denigrating the rest of Daoism as a benighted religion pandering to the superstitious beliefs of low-class villagers, but they also spread that skewed image around the world.

When the Jesuit missionary Matteo Ricci (1552–1610) first arrived in China from Macau in the late sixteenth century he famously chose to ally himself (after a brief flirtation with Buddhism) with the elite scholar-officials whose knowledge of the Confucian classics had won them success in the official examination system and a position at court. The Jesuits saw possibilities for converting the Chinese through accommodation with Confucianism, since its main tenets—at least in the Jesuits' eyes—did not contradict or challenge Christianity. Ricci praised Confucianism as a philosophical tradition with important moral teachings befitting the wealthy and powerful, and he lambasted Daoism (as he did Buddhism) as a deviant religion based on the idolatrous and superstitious beliefs and practices of the poor and powerless. But the Jesuits were keen observers, and Ricci's descriptions of various aspects of Daoist practice are invaluable (see his "Religious Sects among the Chinese").

The Jesuits' admiration for Confucianism and disdain for Daoism persisted through the seventeenth century. Negative images of Daoist religious practices spread further after the German Jesuit scholar Athanasius Kircher published his influential *China Illustrata* (1667), a work based not on any firsthand experience but on reports sent to Europe by other Jesuits in Asia. The 1687 publication of *Confucius Sinarum philosophus, sive scientia Sinensis latine exposita* (*Confucius, Philosopher of the Chinese, or the Chinese Learning Explained in Latin*), translations and annotations written by a group of Jesuits, bolstered the image of Confucius as a paragon of Chinese philosophy. This accommodationist approach was controversial, however, and despite the Jesuits' best efforts to repackage Confucian rituals—such as the veneration of ancestors—as devoid of religious sentiment, a 1704 papal decree ruled against their interpretation in what is known as the Rites Controversy.

Yet the Jesuits' discredited position, with its artificial separation of Chinese philosophy from religion, had a profound and lasting impact on the European understanding of Daoism. The story of the foregrounding of Confucianism has been summed up nicely by John Lagerwey:

> The self-congratulatory Confucian view of its own social and political role in Chinese history, of which they were the literary guardians, was transmitted to the West by the first Christian missionaries, the Jesuits. Throughout the famous "Rites controversy" of the seventeenth century, the Jesuits tried to convince Rome that Confucianism was a rational philosophy, a rational preparation for the supernatural truths of Christianity, as Plato had been in the West. They lost the battle within the Catholic Church to their sectarian rivals the Franciscans, but they won the war in Western society at large, for their light on Chinese civilization, refracted through the prism of the Enlightenment, still shines in virtually every text on

Chinese history and thought, where China is the land of Plato's Republic come true, China is the land ruled by philosopher-kings.[4]

The Western image of Daoism conveyed by the Jesuits influenced later Enlightenment thinkers—Kant, John Locke (1632–1704), Voltaire (1694–1778), and Gottfried Wilhelm Leibniz (1646–1716) among them—who, driven by their commitment to wisdom, logic, and reason, similarly developed a deep scorn for Daoist religious practices and an admiration of Confucianism. The victory of high-minded rationality (Confucianism) over lowbrow beliefs in immortality and magic (Daoism) is a common trope in the interpretation of Western literature and religion and mirrors the Protestant notion of a pure Christian tradition that, in Roman Catholicism, devolved into mere ritual and superstitious beliefs.

James Legge and "Protestant Daoism"

The nineteenth-century figure most responsible for perpetuating the philosophy-versus-religion dichotomy was James Legge (1815–1897), a Scottish missionary perhaps best known for his translations of the Confucian classics. Legge understood his work on Daoism as a conscious extension of the Jesuits' earlier attempt to reify Daoism into a philosophical tradition transmitted in a sacred book (*The Scripture of the Way and Its Virtue*), written by that tradition's founder (Laozi). Although Legge was merely carrying forward older propositions, he had particular influence because he was tasked with translating *The Scripture of the Way and Its Virtue* and the *Book of Master Zhuang* (along with the popular *Tract of the Most Exalted on Action and Response*, anthologized here in a different translation) for Max Müller's monumental *Sacred Books of the East* series, which appeared in fifty volumes between 1879 and 1910. Legge's translation of *The Scripture of the Way and Its Virtue* (1891) presented it as the Daoist "bible." He set the content of that work against later Daoist religious practices, which he called polluted by ritual and superstition. He further described Daoist religious institutions as being headed by a figure akin to the Catholic pope. Legge's distorted framing of Daoism was significant, not least because Müller's series became an authoritative source for students and scholars of religion in the twentieth century around the world. The view of China as led by an agnostic, nonreligious Confucianism—a view that either ignored Daoism or presented it in a negative light—has until recently dominated both standard histories about China (written by Chinese as well as by Westerners) and anthologies of primary sources.[5] It has proved difficult for modern scholars to undo and revise Legge's influential interpretation.

Just two years after Legge's translations were published in Müller's series, Daoism made an appearance at the 1893 World's Parliament of Religions in Chicago as one of the world's ten great religions.[6] That a Daoist master was

4. John Lagerwey, *Taoist Ritual in Chinese Society and History* (New York: Macmillan, 1987), p. xi.
5. Norman J. Girardot, *The Victorian Translation of China: James Legge's Oriental Pilgrimage* (Berkeley: University of California Press, 2002),
pp. 443–45.
6. Richard Hughes Seager, introduction to *The Dawn of Religious Pluralism: Voices from the World Parliament of Religions, 1893*, ed. Seager (La Salle, Ill.: Open Court, 1993), p. 15.

unable to attend in person—that Daoism had to be represented by a text rather than by a living Daoist (see "Taoism: A Prize Essay")—was in a way fitting. Interacting with texts, rather than with Daoists, was precisely how the West carried on its conversation with Daoism up through the mid-twentieth century. The Daoist author, Zhang Yuanxu, was constrained by the occasion to introduce Daoism as a religion in agreement with modernity and the principles of science. His essay therefore mirrors the now-familiar view of Daoism as a tradition that had strayed far from its pristine philosophical origins as it devolved into a degenerate religion peddling magic, talismans, incantations, and beliefs about an elixir of immortality.

This negative portrayal of Daoism developed in Europe in the context of growing anti-Catholic sentiment, especially in Britain, whose manifestations included attacks on the church's superstitious practices, clerical hierarchy, and power. In the eyes of Western interpreters Daoism looked too Catholic, and many echoed Legge in describing Daoist leaders as "popes." This Protestant critique of Daoism became firmly established in scholarship when it appeared in the entry on Daoism in James Hastings's influential *Encyclopaedia of Religion and Ethics* (1908–26). That entry, which not surprisingly discussed only philosophical works, was written by P. J. Maclagan, a missionary scholar who had translated *The Scripture of the Way and Its Virtue* and published an essay with the revealing title "Taoism, Its Christian Affinities and Its Defects" (1910). Here he characterized Zhang Daoling (34–156 c.e.), the first leader of the Way of the Celestial Masters, as the pope of "popular Taoism."[7]

Daoism Adjusted for the Liberal Classroom

For some Europeans thinking about world religions, Daoist ideas, particularly those describing the Dao as universal, seemed well-suited to make a contribution to the modernizing world. In his *China and Europe* (1923), Adolf Reichwein mentioned the novel view of the German writer Rudolph Pannwitz, who saw in Daoism "the possibility, not indeed of an ideal religiosity devoid of positive content, which is not what they are seeking, but of a world-religion—a '*summa religionum mundi*'—to which the various religions might form a preparation."[8] Reichwein read Pannwitz's statement as an indictment of contemporary religion in Europe, which drove its youth to search for something different and exotic. To him, however, this searching attitude was little more than a countercultural reaction against the philosophy of eighteenth-century Enlightenment thinkers.

With Daoism now refined into its essence as a philosophy, and the rest of its history dismissed or ignored, it was ready to make a grand entrance into the general books on world religions that began to appear in the twentieth century. In those works, Daoism is presented as something rather easy to define, even if its philosophy is difficult to understand. Joseph

7. P. J. Maclagan, "Taoism," in *Encyclopaedia of Religion and Ethics*, ed. James Hastings, 13 vols. (Edinburgh: T. & T. Clark; New York: C. Scribner's Sons, 1908–26), 12:197–202. See also Maclagan, "Taoism, Its Christian Affinities and Its Defects," *Expository Times* 21.4 (January 1910): 155–57, which explicitly likens "the medley of idolatry and magic which is today called Taoism" to the "corrupt and paganized" popular religion "of one of the least enlightened Roman Catholic countries" (155).
8. Adolf Reichwein, *China and Europe: Intellectual and Artistic Contacts in the Eighteenth Century*, trans. J. C. Powell (London: Kegan Paul, Trench, Trübner, 1925), p. 9.

Gaer's *How the Great Religions Began* (1929), for example, introduces each religious tradition by presenting the same set of basic "facts" (clearly based on Western religions): date founded, founder, place founded, sacred books, total number of adherents, distribution, number of adherents in the United States, and sects. Despite titling the chapter on Daoism "The Religion Few Can Understand," Gaer with striking assurance informed his readers that the religion was founded in the sixth century B.C.E. by "Lao-tze (The Old Philosopher)" in China, and that its sacred book is "*Tao-The-King* (The Book of Reason and Virtue)."[9] By rendering Laozi as "The Old Philosopher," rather than the more literal "Old Master," and by inserting "reason" into the title of *The Scripture of the Way and Its Virtue*, Gaer betrays his debt to the lineage I have just reconstructed that deemed Daoism a philosophy—a deep and mysterious philosophy that "few can understand." The same basic picture of Daoism appears in Huston Smith's widely read *The Religions of Man* (1958; updated and republished as *The World's Religions*, 1991), which identifies Laozi as the founder of Daoism and the author of the Daoist "bible," *The Scripture of the Way and Its Virtue*.[1]

Daoism Recovered

The image of Daoism as a two-tiered tradition, composed of the "higher" teachings of philosophy and the scurrilous "lower" religious practices, did much to hinder the inception of Daoist studies in East Asia and the West. These issues received a particularly evocative articulation in Anna Seidel's analogy:

> Trying to explain the range of meanings of the term "Daoism" to a Western public would be similar to an attempt by a Chinese lecturer to elucidate to his Asian audience the elements of European culture, taking them from Greek philosophy, Christianity, the medieval church, the Vatican, to Protestant sectarian revivalism and Bavarian pilgrimage churches. If we stay for another moment with this comparison, the Asian audience of this speaker might be tempted to consider Plato and Aristotle as the founders of Christianity—an idea which is about as wrong as the view that Lao-tzu (Laozi) is the founder of Daoism. If we add the possibility that the same Asian public had learned from scholarly books that the New Testament, Augustine, Thomas Aquinas and the Church Fathers were merely a degenerate form of the high philosophy of antiquity that had sunk to the level of a primitive folk-belief and a backward and foolish form of nonsense, then we would have an analogy to what Confucian officials of the modern period, certain missionaries, and many sinologists have said about the Daoist religion.[2]

9. Joseph Gaer, *How the Great Religions Began* (1929; reprint, New York: Signet Key Books, 1954), p. 91.
1. Huston Smith, *The World's Religions* (New York: HarperCollins, 1991) p. 198.
2. Anna Seidel, "Taoism: The Unofficial High Religion of China," *Taoist Resources* 7.2 (1997): 47.

Given the legacy of Confucian, Neo-Confucian, missionary, and popular negative images of developments in Daoism after Laozi and Zhuangzi, who would ever have taken interest in such a thing or viewed it as a topic of serious academic inquiry?

It is still rather startling to consider how little was known about Daoism, the true native "high religion" of China for the past two millennia, up through the mid-twentieth century. One writer, echoing the sentiments of many others, has claimed that Daoism remains one of the least understood and the "least known of all the major religious traditions of the world."[3] We can thus sympathize with the honest reflection of a young scholar setting off to France in 1975 to study with Kristofer Schipper, a Dutch scholar of Chinese religions who became the first Westerner ordained as a Daoist priest: "I had no idea," he wrote, "that Chinese history and society had secreted its own 'higher religion.' I thought, as most Sinologists still do, that Chinese history belonged to an 'agnostic' Confucian elite, and Chinese society to the 'superstitious' masses. I loved Daoist philosophy; I believed the scornful judgment of others concerning Daoist religion. Professor Schipper's courses hit me, therefore, with the full force of revelation: 'It is not so. What you believed is false. The truth is . . .'"[4] If Daoism was not simply the philosophy condensed in Laozi's pithy maxims or expressed in Zhuangzi's intriguing stories, what were the truths of this new understanding of Daoism that were being revealed, finally, in the mid-twentieth century?

The Return of the Daoist Canon

If we were pressed to identify one watershed moment that helped unlock the secrets of Daoism and inaugurate a new generation of scholarship, it would have to be the 1926 reprinting of the Daoist canon—at that time, largely unknown to the Chinese and the world. The base text used for the reprint was a rare surviving copy of the 1445 printing housed at the White Cloud Abbey (Baiyun guan) in Beijing (see Yoshitoyo Yoshioka's "Daoist Monastic Life"). In the intervening centuries, the Daoist canon's eleven hundred texts had all but disappeared. Few copies of the collection were extant in all of China, and those held by Daoist temples were mostly off-limits to outsiders. Therefore, the main repository of Daoist texts, which contained the keys to its history, doctrines, and rituals, was unavailable for scholars' consultation. To be sure, a few intrepid scholars avoided the ideological blind spots of their contemporaries; Edouard Chavannes (1865–1918) and Paul Pelliot (1878–1945), for example, produced some admirable philological and historical works based on their studies of an incomplete woodblock edition of the Ming dynasty canon that had arrived in Paris in 1910. But the newly printed canon, circulated to libraries around the world, inspired a new generation of scholars—primarily in France, Japan, and to a lesser extent in China—to dig deeper into the sources and to uncover the riches of Daoism that had been ignored or hidden for so long.

3. Norman Girardot, "Foreword: Visualizing Taoism: Isabelle Robinet and the Mao-shan Revelations of Great Purity," in *Taoist Meditation: The Mao-shan Tradition of Great Purity*, by Isabelle Robinet, trans. Julian F. Pas and Norman J. Girardot (Albany: State University of New York, 1993), p. xvii.

4. Lagerwey, *Taoist Ritual in Chinese Society and History*, pp. xvii–xviii.

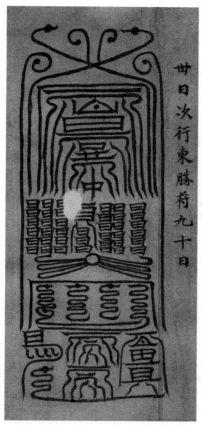

世日次行東勝荷九十日

Talisman from the Tang dynasty manuscript of a Numinous Treasure Daoist text entitled *Scripture of the Five Correspondences of the Realized One of Numinous Treasure*. This talisman was to be ingested, worn on the body, or emblazoned on stones surrounding a house to provide protection from noxious influences.

Henri Maspero (1883–1945), for example, was a formidable pioneer of Daoist studies who immersed himself in the 1926 printing. Maspero's life was cut short in the Nazi concentration camp at Buchenwald, but his publications—most of them posthumous—include a remarkable 1971 collection of essays, *Le Taoïsme et les religions chinoises* (*Taoism and Chinese Religion*, 1981), which succeed admirably in filling in the basic outlines of the historical development of Daoism as an organized religious tradition from the Han to the Tang dynasty (618–907 C.E.).[5]

Another important expansion of Daoist studies occurred in the mid-1960s, when Kristofer Schipper's studies, which focused primarily on the learning of ritual and liturgy, helped open up the study of Daoism as a living tradition. His example inspired others not just to study texts but to undertake fieldwork with Daoist priests. To the surprise of those who for years had heard pronouncements about the death of Daoism—at the hands of Confucians, missionaries, and later the Red Guards of the Cultural Revolution (1966–76)—Daoism had survived! Indeed, Schipper's research in Taiwan revealed that Daoism not only had survived but showed remarkable continuity with the tradition of earlier centuries. The handwritten ritual manuals used by contemporary Daoist priests there, passed down within their lineage from master to disciple, agreed with those printed in the Daoist canon.

Daoism Reconsidered: The "Unofficial High Religion of China"

New methodologies—including literary analysis, ritual studies, historiography, and art history—were taken up by a growing group of Daoist specialists. Once the pernicious effects of the earlier biased treatment of Daoism were recognized, scholars sought to rehabilitate Daoism and rewrite its

5. Henri Maspero, *Taoism and Chinese Religion*, trans. Frank A. Kierman, Jr. (Amherst: University of Massachusetts Press, 1981). This book includes T. H. Barrett's valuable introduction to Maspero's place within and impact on Daoist scholarship.

history as what Anna Seidel has called the "unofficial high religion of China." In this new view, Daoism is a complex, hybrid religious tradition with diverse (and continually evolving) doctrines and institutional forms. It appealed to a broad spectrum of people, from urban elites to rural villagers, whom it knit together through its communal rituals and practices. In order to assist her readers in understanding the complexities of this revised view of Daoism, Isabelle Robinet noted that Daoism "has never stopped moving, transforming, absorbing. Its history shows us how ceaselessly it has proceeded by 'recursive loops,' taking up its past like a bundle under its arm in order to travel farther toward new horizons."[6]

It is precisely the way that Daoism has proceeded by incorporating elements of the past as it innovated that has presented challenges to scholars and general readers alike. One of the unintended consequences of the flood of new scholarship on Daoism is that the earlier picture of Daoism, which was as simple as it was appealing to Western sentiments, has been replaced by one far more intricate and complex—usually expressed in exotic terminology that has tended to alienate and intimidate the general reader; the newly discovered heterogeneity of the tradition has led, as one commentator has put it, to a state of maximum chaos.[7] That perhaps helps explain why so many modern scholars continue to preface their works with some disclaimer about the difficulty of understanding Daoism. Thanks to the efforts of a dedicated group of scholars who have translated primary sources and published useful reference works, it has been possible to complete the present anthology, which ideally will begin to lessen the present chaos by providing a general picture of Daoism through a selection of its primary sources (admittedly limited to what is today available in translation). This anthology can aid readers in appreciating the breadth of Daoism and give them the tools to better assess why Daoism was an appealing religious option and understand the transformations of Daoism as it developed and as it continues to evolve. It is, after all, the recognition that everything is constantly changing and transforming that is essential to the Dao itself.

A Brief History of Daoism

Given the rich complexity and dynamism of Daoism's historical development, we should not attempt to impose a static general description on the tradition. Still, it is possible to identify a few of the elements that became significant within Daoism and to track its complicated history. This sketch of the general contours of that history will be fleshed out in more detail in the section introductions.

Many of the fundamental concepts concerning cosmology and self-cultivation that would become significant in the Han dynasty synthesis and formation of Daoism took shape during the Warring States period (403–221 B.C.E.) of the Eastern Zhou (770–256 B.C.E.), which is also when *The Scripture of the Way and Its Virtue* and the *Book of Master Zhuang* appeared. Those texts and their concepts are not exclusively Daoist—indeed, Daoism

6. Robinet, *Taoist Meditation*, pp. 2–3.
7. Catherine Bell, "In Search of the Tao in Taoism: New Questions of Unity and Multiplicity," *History of Religions* 33.2 (1993): 188.

did not yet exist as an organized religious tradition—but they would eventually take on specific (and distinctive) meanings in that tradition.

Earliest Elements of the Daoist Synthesis

Since everything can in some sense be traced back to the Dao (both the term and the concept), let us begin there. The word *Dao*, which as already noted means "Way," is found across the range of early Chinese thought. Many pre-Han philosophers proposed their own visions of the Way—usually propositions about the path to proper conduct and relations among humans. In a text like *The Scripture of the Way and Its Virtue*, however, the term *Dao*—which it famously declares cannot be captured in language—began to take on a more philosophical and metaphysical meaning, connoting that which underlies the natural state of things. That is to say, the Dao, which is indiscernible, came to designate the natural order of things both prior to and beyond human intervention or control (an unmistakable jab at the Confucian Way, which was depicted as being too meddlesome). The Dao referred to a unified universal principle preceding the origin of the universe (described as a state of primordial chaos or nothingness), which set into motion the process of creation and was the cause of its enduring transformations. The Dao is the unchanging reality behind a chaotic and ever-shifting plurality of transformations.

The Dao as universal is connected with other root concepts that also became significant within later Daoism. When the Dao was in its original unified state, the formation of *qi*—a term translated as "breath," "vapor," "pneuma," or "energy"—inaugurated a series of divisions. The first division resulted in the dyad of *yin* (the shaded side of a hill, dark, feminine) and *yang* (the sunny side of hill, bright, male); further divisions generated all things. Thus, there is no creator behind Daoist creation. This notion runs counter to dominant Western ideas, as does the concept of *qi* as something that pervades everything in different combinations (rather than supporting a dualism between spirit and matter).

The perception that the world in its natural state is the Dao itself, manifest as different transformations of *qi*, led early thinkers to further explore the implications of that view of reality: if the whole is reproduced in the parts, then there are fixed relationships between heaven, earth, and humans, which they described. They also considered how things interact in the ongoing interchange between yin/yang and the five phases (also called the five agents or five elements): wood, fire, earth, metal, and water. That complex system revealed correspondences between different aspects of reality, including directions, colors, seasons, planets, numbers, bodily organs, and sacred mountains. The south, for example, is related to fire, red, summer, Mars, the number three, the heart, and Mount Heng. The universe was perceived to be held in balance by the cyclical rise and fall of different forces that regulate the flow of nature.

Early Chinese conceptions of cyclical change and transformation were laid out in the *Book of Changes* (*Yijing*, better known in the West as the *I Ching*), a divination manual that was also important in later Daoism (see *The Seal of the Unity of the Three, in Accordance with the Book of Changes*). It is based on a set of eight trigrams—permutations of three solid (yang) or broken (yin) lines stacked up vertically—and sixty-four hexagrams, which are permutations of six solid or broken lines stacked up vertically, all named and connected with oracular statements. Within Daoism, the trigrams of the *Book of Changes*, thought to represent all the possible permutations of yin and yang, were used to symbolize cosmic directions, parts of the body, and the ingredients used in internal alchemy.

Certain sagely beings were believed able to discern the unity and patterns behind the seemingly random nature of manifest appearances and to merge themselves with the Dao. The *Book of Master Zhuang* (see "Free and Easy Wandering" and "Mastering Life") includes captivating images of a special class of beings that live in tune with the Dao (Way): they are depicted as living spontaneously, free from all constraints; as endowed with special powers (including the ability to fly); and as having incredibly long life spans. These features surfaced in the intense focus during the Han dynasty on longevity practices and on transcendent beings (*xian*, also referred to as immortals), some of whom were thought to inhabit paradisical islands just beyond the human world (see the *Record of the Ten Continents*). The images of those figures were carried forward into Daoist hagiographical collections (see *Traditions of Divine Transcendents*). But within later Daoism, these sagely types did not remain a mythic ideal; instead, they became a model of something that could be achieved. Daoists maintained that some humans, through dietary practices or alchemical pursuits, could achieve a state of transcendence and ascend to heaven in broad daylight. The basic idea was to eliminate the base forms of qi, leaving only the pure, refined qi of a perfect person.

The Birth and Spread of the First Organized Daoist Movements

From the waning days of the Han dynasty through the Six Dynasties (220–589 C.E.) period, Daoism bundled together all these earlier ideas and concepts and began to take shape as an organized religious tradition. The earliest Daoist groups were messianic movements that rose up to challenge, and hoped to replace, the discredited Han sociopolitical order. There were many such movements, but the Way of Great Peace (Taiping dao; see the *Scripture of Great Peace*) and the Way of the Celestial Masters (Tianshi dao) were the most important. The Way of Great Peace, which formed in eastern China, attracted followers with its healing techniques and the promise that its faithful would become part of a select group who would establish the kingdom of Great Peace; but the uprising it launched in 184 C.E. was quickly suppressed, and the movement soon vanished.

In western China, according to tradition, in 142 C.E. Laozi descended from heaven to a figure named Zhang Daoling, gave him the title Celestial Master (*tianshi*), and thereby inaugurated the Way of the Celestial Masters. Here we see the transformation of Laozi into an incarnation of the Dao (see "The Laozi Inscription" and the *Scripture on Laozi's Transformations*). The Dao could now take the form of a deity to disclose the Dao through a divine revelation. The Daoist universe became populated by a panoply of deities (celestial, abstract, bodily) whose roles resemble those of governmental functionaries in charge of different aspects of a bureaucracy. Daoism was heir to earlier beliefs about demons and deities. It developed specialized techniques to identify, control (usually by knowing their names), exorcize, or incorporate harmful demons (primarily those associated with local cults).

THE HISTORY OF DAOISM AT A GLANCE

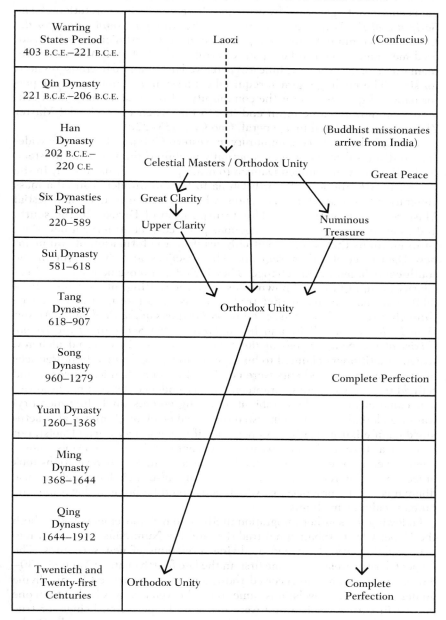

Warring States Period 403 B.C.E.–221 B.C.E.	Laozi	(Confucius)
Qin Dynasty 221 B.C.E.–206 B.C.E.		
Han Dynasty 202 B.C.E.– 220 C.E.	Celestial Masters / Orthodox Unity	(Buddhist missionaries arrive from India) Great Peace
Six Dynasties Period 220–589	Great Clarity Upper Clarity	Numinous Treasure
Sui Dynasty 581–618		
Tang Dynasty 618–907	Orthodox Unity	
Song Dynasty 960–1279		Complete Perfection
Yuan Dynasty 1260–1368		
Ming Dynasty 1368–1644		
Qing Dynasty 1644–1912		
Twentieth and Twenty-first Centuries	Orthodox Unity	Complete Perfection

This chart shows how the two officially sanctioned forms of organized Daoism that survive to this day emerged from earlier Daoist history. Much of the contemporary practice of Daoism, however, actually occurs outside these formal auspices. For more on Chinese and Daoist history, see the chronology on pages 69–72.

The Celestial Masters movement formed into a highly structured religious community governed by principles based on its interpretation of *The Scripture of the Way and Its Virtue* (see the *Xiang'er Commentary on the Laozi*). The community accepted peoples of different ethnicities and considered men and women to be equal. Central to the Celestial Masters movement was a focus on healing illnesses perceived to be caused by transgressions (or sins). The healing regimen required confession, repentance, or the performance of good works for the community. This foundational Daoist religious community came to an end in 215 C.E. when the Celestial Master Zhang Lu surrendered to a general, Cao Cao (155–220).

Although that isolated community in western China collapsed, the widespread dispersal of its members actually benefited the Celestial Masters, for it effectively introduced Daoism to other parts of China (mainly in the north). In 316, the loss of North China to foreign invaders caused a mass emigration to the south by Han elites, who carried the vestiges of Celestial Masters Daoism with them. This transposition of Daoism to the south, and its encounter there with indigenous practices, set off fervent new Daoist innovations that would eventually result in the formation of two major new Daoist scriptural movements. The practices already present in the south contributed to this change. They included a movement called Great Clarity (Taiqing) that is known to us from the writings of Ge Hong (283–343). The main focus of that tradition was on attaining transcendence through external alchemy (see the *Inner Chapters of the Book of the Master Who Embraces Simplicity* and *Instructions on the Scripture of the Divine Elixirs of the Nine Tripods of the Yellow Emperor*). In external alchemy, which practitioners claimed to be superior to the self-cultivation practices of other groups, ingredients were combined in an alchemical furnace and refined to produce a pill guaranteeing transcendence. Over time, however, it became clear that the combination of ingredients (including mercury) was often lethal: many who ingested the so-called elixir of immortality actually died of elixir poisoning. Alchemy itself was not necessarily Daoist, but alchemical texts and methods were incorporated into later Daoist movements, even as other practices developed as a result of new revelations took precedence. The religiosity of southern China also included widely diffuse dhamanistic-type practices, by which gods could be brought down into the human realm by mediums.

Following the southern migration in 316, two new movements began: both the Upper Clarity (Shangqing) tradition and the Numinous Treasure (Lingbao) tradition were launched by divine revelations of new scriptures. The Upper Clarity revelations came first, in the late fourth century. Yang Xi (330–386?), the medium who received those texts, was instructed by his divine guides that the new revelations came from a heaven that was higher than one posited in earlier Daoism and were delivered by perfected beings (or true beings) (*zhenren*) more exalted than the earlier transcendents (see the *Declarations of the Perfected*). The Upper Clarity revelations, whose florid prose was written in exquisite calligraphy, spread widely among the southern aristocracy. These new texts combined elements drawn from the Celestial Masters community, southern indigenous practices of alchemy, and Buddhism (which had entered China and begun to take root during the first century C.E.). The Upper Clarity tradition prefigured later Daoist developments by emphasizing individual meditation, visualization, and interiorization.

Following the success of the Upper Clarity revelations, another set of revelations, called Numinous Treasure, began to circulate in the same region. The Numinous Treasure texts were presented as guides to human practice superior to the Upper Clarity texts—as passed down before them, from a source in a higher heaven. The Numinous Treasure scriptures are particularly combinative, systematically incorporating Buddhist terms and practices, such as rebirth (see *The Wondrous Scripture of the Upper Chapters of Limitless Salvation*). The liturgy and communal rituals developed in the Numinous Treasure scriptures provided the template for vibrant Daoist rituals that have changed relatively little down to the present day.

There are many different types of Daoist rituals that serve different needs, but in general they are closely related to Chinese imperial rituals—the priest, in effect, has an (imperial) audience with celestial deities—and to Chinese theater (see *Zhongli of the Han Leads Lan Caihe to Enlightenment* and *The Complete Performance of Su*). Daoist rituals are replete with colorful paintings, banners, vocal and instrumental music, and a variety of documents, including some modeled on imperial communications with officials (see "Regulations for Petitioning" and the *Great Petition for Sepulchral Plaints*). Some important ritual texts are esoteric handwritten talismans. All these documents are dispatched by Daoist priests on behalf of their clients to celestial offices. Some Daoist rituals are directed at curing illnesses while others focus on confession and the demonstration of contrition (see the *Purification Rite of Luminous Perfected* and Lu Xiujing's *Five Sentiments of Gratitude*). Communal "offering" rituals are among those that aim to unite a community and renew its sense of order and purity; others, which might involve possession, exorcism, and child mediums (see Hong Mai's *Heard and Written by Yijian*), seek to drive pestilent demons away from the world of the living. Still other Daoist rituals involve elaborate visualizations of travel into the underworld to free the deceased from their suffering in hell (see *Private Tutor of the Nine Spontaneously Generating Lingbao Heavens of Primordial Commencement*).

Up through the fourth century C.E., the elements of Daoism were drawn mainly from native Chinese thought and Chinese popular religion, but beginning with the Upper Clarity and Numinous Treasure revelations the religion also reflected an active interchange of ideas and practices with Buddhism. As many of the selections in this anthology make evident, Daoist texts employed terminology and practices connected with Mahayana Buddhism, emphasizing universal salvation and the liberation of ancestors from hell and transmigration (see the *Purification Rite of Luminous Perfected*). Other Daoist texts, however, reveal competition and tension in the relationship between Daoism and Buddhism (see Xiang Kai's "Memorial to Emperor Huan concerning Buddhism and Daoism," Wang Fu's *Conversion of the Barbarians*, and the *Essay to Ridicule the Dao*).

Daoism Triumphant in the Tang, Song, and Yuan Dynasties (618–1368)

Daoism received an unprecedented level of imperial support from Li Yuan (r. 618–26 C.E.), the founder of the Tang dynasty (618–907). Since Li Yuan shared the same surname with Laozi (also known as Li Er) and considered him to be his ancestor, he felt an affinity with Daoists, and they were able to secure a privileged position at the imperial court. In turn, Daoists bolstered the emperor's position with a timely prophecy predicting his ascension to the throne. During the Tang, the earlier Celestial Masters (also called the Ortho-dox Unity [Zhengyi] tradition), Upper Clarity, and Numinous Treasure tradi-tions solidified, consolidated, and expanded. Though no new schools formed, this roughly three-hundred-year period was something of a golden age for Daoism, when important encyclopedias and hagiographic collections were produced. The Tang dynasty is also called a golden age in Chinese history more generally, in part because it increased interactions with the foreign cul-tures and amassed great wealth from long-distance trade. Not surprisingly, therefore, it was during the Tang that Daoism began to migrate out of China and into Korea and Japan (see Kukai's *Indications of the Goals of the Three Teachings* and Sŏl Ch'ong's "Inscription on an Image at Kamsan Monastery").

Daoism's period of relative doctrinal quiet was followed by renewed activ-ity and fervent innovation, differentiation, and expansion during the Song (960–1279) and Yuan (1260–1368) dynasties. Daoists maintained their imperial support during the Song, but after North China fell in 1126 to the Jurchen invaders who founded the Jin dynasty (1115–1234), Daoism trav-eled with the northern refugees to southern China, where it became deeply rooted in local society (see Hong Mai's *Heard and Written by Yijian*). These new circumstances inspired the production of new Daoist scriptures and liturgical manuals, the development of new lineages and schools, the incor-poration of local cults and their deities, and an increase in exchanges with Buddhism. One rather remarkable innovation was a sophisticated way of thinking about alchemy that became known as internal alchemy. It comple-mented the older external alchemy, but rather than produce an elixir using base minerals—a concoction that, as we have seen, could be deadly—internal alchemy interiorizes the alchemical practice using symbolic descriptions, trigrams from the *Book of Changes*, and the meditative con-junction of yin and yang. All alchemical ingredients are found in the body, and the body becomes the furnace that refines the internal elixir or immor-tal embryo (see Zhang Boduan's *Awakening to Reality* and Wang Daoyuan's *Essay on the Secret Essentials of the Recycled Elixir*). Daoist movements of the Song dynasty (960–1279) focused on new deities, newly revealed texts, and new religious associations, as well as on healing and longevity.

An important movement that began under the Jin dynasty in the north and then grew explosively during the Mongol-ruled Yuan dynasty (1260–1368) was Complete Perfection (Quanzhen) Daoism. It is the first well-attested communal form of monastic Daoism with celibate monks and nuns. Complete Perfection initiates underwent an ordination ritual involving the transmission of texts and vestments, and they also vowed to abide by a strict disciplinary code (see Wang Zhe's *Redoubled Yang's Fifteen Discourses for the Establishment of the Doctrine*). Daoist monasticism—whose emergence is difficult to date with any certainty—was a significant change and has remained an integral part of modern Daoism (see Yoshioka's "Daoist Monastic Life"). Its development was strongly influenced by Buddhism: Daoist monks, like their Buddhist counterparts, are said to "leave home" (*chujia*) to live apart in a sodality of fellow renunciates. Daoist monastics are easily identi-fied by their distinctive, and symbol-laden, clothing, hairstyle, and hats, with different garb worn in different traditions and on different occasions. Com-plete Perfection monastic clergy don simple blue or black robes for their daily activities, but their formal ritual robes are brightly colored and intricately embroidered. Nonmonastic priests, who do not leave home and can marry, dress for rituals in ornate blue or red robes. Unlike Buddhist monks, who shave their heads, Daoists wear their hair long—to symbolize longevity—and gathered up into a tight topknot that is fastened with a pin. Daoists wear a variety of hats, but during rituals the priest's topknot is covered with a metal crown. Daoists also wear special shoes marked with cloud motifs that symbolize their ability to pace the clouds and stars on their ascent to audiences with celestial deities.

The Ming Dynasty (1368–1644) and Official Chinese Syncretism

China freed itself of non-Han rule and regained its full territory during the Ming dynasty (1368–1644). Effective management of the expanded Ming domain required an elaborate official bureaucracy,

Blue-and-white porcelain vase in the shape of a gourd, a popular Daoist symbol. Ming dynasty.

which became known for its harsh rule and strict disciplinary measures. Daoism was subjected to Ming governmental oversight and control, but it also received imperial support. Daoism prospered under this arrangement, and its ideas and practices spread to intellectuals and became further integrated with popular practices (see *Journey to the North*). During the Ming, the boundaries between the "three teachings"—Buddhism, Daoism, and Confucianism—blurred as even more syncretic movements took shape. The distinctions between various Daoist lineages also grew less clear as they became more unified (see Hanshan Deqing's commentaries on the *Laozi* and *Zhuangzi*).

The Qing Dynasty (1644–1912), the West, and the Eclipse of Daoism

The Qing dynasty (1644–1912) returned China again to the control of a non-Han people, this time the Manchus. Manchu rule proved challenging for Daoists, since they were unable to win strong support from the Qing court, which was institutionalizing a largely ossified form of Confucianism. Daoism had roughly the same main features in the Qing as in the Ming, namely state control externally and consolidation and unification internally (see *Collected Statutes of the Great Qing Dynasty*). But one noteworthy aspect is the greater emphasis during the Qing on self-cultivation practices, which included internal alchemy, female alchemy (*nüdan*), and sexual self-cultivation (see *Combined Collection of Female Alchemy* and *Secret Principles of Gathering the True Essence*). Female alchemy is an outgrowth of internal alchemy, directed exclusively at women and tailored to their specific physiology and practice.

Outside of Daoism, a major shift in the Qing was in the balance of power between China and the West, which began to tilt to the West during the eighteenth and nineteenth centuries. Tensions came to a head as the Chinese attempted to control European trade—particularly the illegal trade in opium by the British. Britain's victory in the ensuing First Opium War (1840–42), and the defeat that forced China to sign a number of unequal treaties, left the Chinese feeling weak and powerless against the West. Amid these social, political, economic, and religious upheavals, Chinese peasants rose up violently in the Taiping Rebellion (1850–64), while intellectuals sought other means to strengthen the state and initiate a path toward modernization. Chinese religion in general, and Daoism in particular, fared poorly, since Daoism was equated with backward superstitions. Its temples were confiscated and repurposed as schools and factories.

As bleak as the future of Daoism looked at the end of the Qing dynasty, an even darker period of history was to follow. During the late nineteenth and early twentieth centuries, when China was inundated with foreign ideas and dominated by Western imperialists, Daoism came to be regarded as nothing more than a decrepit reminder of China's benighted and backward past—an impediment to the country's modernization and advancement. At the same time, Christianity, which came in with the wealthy and powerful Westerners, was attracting broad interest and spreading quickly. New voices began to express the need for a revived national culture based on Western science and technology. In this effort, Chinese religion was reshaped by the modernizing Chinese state through the appropriation of new terminology and categories from Japan. The Western term "religion," introduced to Japan by Portuguese missionaries, was translated by the Japanese word *shūkyō*, a term pronounced *zongjiao* in Chinese. Thus *zongjiao*, which had had other meanings in premodern Chinese, took on the meaning "religion"—with the connotation of Western religion (Christianity)—and was redefined in explicit opposition to another new term and concept, namely "superstition" (*mixin*). Because most forms of Daoism did not correspond smoothly to the new notion of religion, they were labeled superstitions.

The Twentieth Century: Daoism Meets Maoism

Throughout the early twentieth century the ideological critique of Daoism—and Buddhism and Confucianism—grew more intense, but a few decades later an even more ferocious attack would threaten its survival. It was the outgrowth of a series of events that began with the Communist victory over the Nationalists in China's civil war. After the founding of the People's Republic of China in 1949, religion was in a precarious position, but the most frenzied onslaught came during the Cultural Revolution (1966–76), which sought to eliminate all vestiges of feudal superstitions, including religion. Daoism suffered critiques, violent attacks on its institutions, the confiscation of its temples, and the suppression of rituals and self-cultivation practices (see *Why Must We Prohibit the Reactionary Daoist Cults?*). The persecution launched during the Cultural Revolution was severe and came close to achieving its goal of eradicating religion. Yet, though its case was dire, the full history of Daoism during the twentieth century is a story not merely of erasure but also of staunch resistance and persistence. Contrary to the expectations of Western observers, Daoism emerged from those traumatic times weakened but intact.

The relocation of the Nationalists to Taiwan provided a largely supportive environment for Daoism on the island. Daoism reached Taiwan during the Ming and Qing dynasties, but the arrival in 1949 of the sixty-third-generation Celestial Master, Zhang Enpu, was the catalyst for further developments and ensured the primacy of the Orthodox Unity tradition over the monastic Complete Perfection tradition. Between 1949 and the end of martial law in 1987, Daoists registered with the Taiwanese Daoist Association—which was established and headed by Zhang Enpu—were assured a safe legal status, but certain restrictions and controls came with that relationship with the state. As democracy has advanced in Taiwan since 1987, all forms of religion—including various Daoist movements—have enjoyed freedom to organize, develop, and practice as they choose.

After the excesses of the Cultural Revolution on the mainland, during the 1980s the Chinese Communist Party began to adopt a more conciliatory attitude toward Daoism. Revived Daoist sacred sites and rebuilt temples came to be seen by the government as resources that could be packaged as tourist destinations. Yet the two main surviving institutional forms of Daoism in the twentieth century—the Complete Perfection and Orthodox Unity traditions—seemed to have become the least vibrant expressions of modern Daoism.

In 1956, Joseph Needham, the British historian of Chinese science, lamented the decline of Daoism (even before the Cultural Revolution), but predicted that its philosophy would some day rise again like a phoenix from the ashes: "All in all, the Taoists had much to teach the world, and even though Taoism as an organized religion is dying or dead, perhaps the future belongs to their philosophy."[8] Needham was not entirely correct about the death of Daoism as an organized religion—recent fieldwork has discovered just how alive Daoism has remained in local society[9]—but he was right about the success of Daoist philosophy. Following the spread of interest in Daoist philosophy throughout the world, discussed above, interest in the teachings of Laozi and Zhuangzi has undergone a remarkable revival in modern China. Insofar as the contemporary Chinese Communist Party recognizes Daoism, the authorities have primarily highlighted its image as a philosophical tradition rather than a religion. In 2007, for example, the Chinese government and the Chinese Daoist Association co-sponsored a massive symposium, "The Way to Harmony: International Forum on the *Daodejing*." The title of the symposium says it all. The focus on *The Scripture on the Way and Its Virtue* reflects the continued emphasis on Daoist philosophy over religious practice. The main part of the title, "The Way to Harmony," allows

8. Joseph Needham, *Science and Civilisation in China*, vol. 2, *History of Scientific Thought* (Cambridge: Cambridge University Press, 1956), p. 152.

9. See, for example, Daniel L. Overmyer and Chao Shin-yi, eds., *Ethnography in China Today: A Critical Assessment of Methods and Results* (Taipei: Yuan-liou Publishing, 2002).

Daoism to be situated within a larger government project of marshaling the contemporary revival of religion to build a "harmonious society." That slogan, which originated in Confucianism, was embraced by the Chinese Communist Party following its utterance in 2004 by President Hu Jintao. Since that time it has been used over and over again in the context of religious conferences—including not just the Daoist symposium but also the First World Buddhist Forum, sponsored by the Chinese government and the Buddhist Association of China in 2006. These high-profile symposia, which attract important political figures, business leaders, and a nationwide television-viewing audience, provide a glimpse of how Daoist philosophy continues to represent the public face of contemporary Daoism.

What has been even more visible in contemporary China is a new form of Confucianism. Though throughout Chinese history Confucianism has had a ritual and religious side to it—including temples and other cult sites—it is not presently classified as one of China's five religions: Buddhism, Daoism, Islam, Protestantism, and Catholicism. The problems associated with adopting a facile view of Daoism and Confucianism as separable into polar opposite categories of "religion" and "philosophy" should now be clear to the reader. Religion and philosophy occupy a spectrum, and that spectrum runs through both traditions. The new Confucianism of recent years has no identifiable religious institutions or clergy, but some in China are forcefully arguing that it should be made the state religion in order to bring about a more civil and just society. This effort has made some in China rather nervous. The Chinese government's ambivalence about Confucianism—presenting it as the benign traditional face of modern China through the worldwide network of Confucius Institutes while at the same time hesitating to let it become the sixth main religion in China—recently took tangible, visible form. In January 2011, a large bronze statue of Confucius was ceremoniously erected on the eastern side of Tiananmen Square, a highly symbolic location; but in the darkness of night on April 21, 2011, the statue was unceremoniously removed. The Confucian teachings about moral and political philosophy are welcome in the public square, but worshipping the idol Confucius will have to wait. Though it is unclear what the future will be for Confucianism as a religion, it currently appears to have little international presence outside of a small group of academics hoping to revive interest in its social and ethical teachings.

Daoism in Today's China and Beyond

Renewed Chinese interest in Daoist philosophy may play some part in the broader narrative of its international appeal, but new story lines that have emerged in the past half century suggest other reasons that Daoism has thrived in those decades. In spite of, or perhaps because of, some of the challenges that Daoism faced at home in China, in the twentieth century it was flourishing around the world. We have seen that beginning at least as early as the eighth century, Daoism was spreading to other parts of East Asia (Japan and Korea). Later, Daoism reached Thailand, Vietnam, Laos, and Malaysia (see *The Dao among the Yao of Southeast Asia* and "Prayers to the Deified Laozi from Penang, Malaysia"), primarily through the movement of emigrant communities. The worldwide diffusion of Daoist ideas through its philosophical literature from the sixteenth century onward has already been noted, but in the twentieth century Daoism also began to appeal to Western- ers on the grounds of health and lifestyle.

During the early twentieth century, Chinese Daoists began to transform their older practices of internal alchemy and self-cultivation, making them more scientific and modern to avoid their being labeled superstitious (see *Explorations in Oral Secrets*). In the 1980s there was a dramatic increase in hybrid religious movements based on body self-cultivation practices, such as *qigong*. *Qigong*, which first emerged in the 1950s, combines physical posture, breathing techniques, and mental focus (drawing elements from Daoism and Buddhism), and it is just one of the variety of health- and longevity-focused movements that have tended, for better or worse, to be categorized as Dao- ist. The rapid growth of such movements in China came to a sudden halt in 1999 when the government labeled Falun Gong, a new offshoot of *qiqong*, a superstitious cult and thousands of followers expressed their displeasure by surrounding the Communist Party Headquarters in Beijing. The movement was quickly outlawed, and public *qigong* practice, which once had been such a visible part of the urban landscape in China, has almost completely disappeared.

What was perceived as a Daoist focus on health, as well as Daoist ideas about nature and ecology, spurred a new wave of interest in and populariza- tion of Daoism in the West. Centers established in the West emphasized what they called Daoist bodily self-cultivation practices, which include *qigong* and Taijiquan (better known in the West as tai chi), though what they developed were only loosely related to traditional Daoist practices. Whereas Westerners in earlier generations who engaged with Daoism stressed the interiority of the mind and philosophy, in recent years they have looked to the physicality of the body and health.

Daoist centers established in the West began to attract large followings in the 1960s and 1970s, when those rejecting the Western emphasis on materi- alism and reason turned to the "mystic East." Young seekers flocked to the centers established by the newly arrived Asian masters. Earlier, the Chinese had shunned Daoism and turned to the West for its ideas on science and rationality; now, in a remarkable reversal, Westerners were turning to China for its mystical philosophy and self-cultivation practices that some inter- preted as prefiguring the discoveries of modern science. Daoist centers have become so entrenched in North America that some Western practitioners now feel that they have surpassed the Chinese in their understanding of Daoism: "The Daoists [in China] for the most part (except Hua Shan) are far behind us 'practitioners' in the west & they don't seem to care. The Chinese people do not have any reverence for the sacred sites we visited. We went there & showed them what they could be again."[1]

Back in the days of Legge and Müller, Daoism began to earn its place in the pantheon of world religions because a particular philosophical reading of *The Scripture of the Way and Its Virtue* and *Book of Master Zhuang* had transcultural appeal. But the world is now aware of a different Daoism, brought into clearer view thanks to scholarly efforts begun in the 1950s.

1. Quoted in Elijah Siegler, "Daoism beyond Modernity: The 'Healing Tao' as Postmodern Movement," in *Daoism in the Twentieth Century: Between Eternity and Modernity*, ed. David A. Palmer and Xun Liu (Berkeley: University of Cali- fornia Press, 2012), p. 291.

It is, nonetheless, still somewhat rare to hear the name Daoism in discussions of "world religion." Daoism, it is usually reported, has not attracted the numbers enjoyed by Buddhism. Yet gaining any accurate sense of the number of Daoists in China or elsewhere in the world is a challenge because of the difficulty of deciding who counts as a Daoist. For much of its history, in the eyes of Chinese historians and Western observers, Daoism remained an invisible religion tucked away in remote villages. While their distinctive outfits might make it easy to identify certain Daoist priests, how are we to recognize other Daoists?

It is difficult to respond to that question with a single answer. Whereas, for example, a Buddhist is defined as someone who takes refuge in the "three jewels"—the Buddha, the *dharma* (the Buddha's teachings), and the *sangha* (the Buddhist community)—no one thing identifies someone as a Daoist across the past two millennia. The problem of who counts as a Daoist confounds sociologists even today. Within the first religious organization, the Celestial Masters, all members of the community were ordained by receiving registers (identifying their name and rank in the celestial hierarchy). At other times, however, Daoist priests alone take part in an ordination ritual that situates them within an esoteric transmission lineage, confers on them registers of the names of the deities with whom they are empowered, and authorizes them as the keepers of revealed manuscripts to be passed down within the tradition and kept from the uninitiated. Yet, across the sweep of history from the second century C.E. to the present, there have been many other ways of being Daoist—as demonstrated by the monastics of the Complete Perfection order, by the live-at-home ritual masters of the Orthodox Unity tradition, and by the lay followers whose commitment ranges from merely believing in the efficacy of Daoist gods to becoming a lay devotee of a particular temple, earning merit by helping out during festivals or rituals. It is these last two categories of diffused Daoists priests and practitioners that have made the Chinese state nervous, because they are impossible to detect and control (a problem also associated with more recent Chinese Christian "house churches"). In thinking about different forms of Daoists, let us also not forget the Westerners who participate in different Daoist self-cultivation practices aimed at maintaining their health and who hope to transform themselves in order to become unified with the true nature of things (the Dao).

What is it about Daoism that has appealed to emperors, literati, common villagers, and even curious Westerners? What was it about Daoism that ensured its survival even through periods that presented dramatic challenges? Daoism could attract the higher classes with its sacred symbols of royalty, depictions of the sage as akin to a perfect ruler, and liturgical texts composed in fine classical Chinese. Yet in times of imperial decline, Daoism could play the messianic upstart by offering a utopic vision of a world of Great Peace to come. Daoist texts also seduced readers, both then and now, with romantic notions of the power of passivity, the mastery of skills through effortless action, and they entertained with their stories of immortals with square pupils who breathe through their heels, gather mystical mushrooms, and can enter water without getting wet or fire without getting burned. Daoist conceptions of an interrelated universe in which everything is part of the *dao* situated humans in a natural world full of meaning and envisioned the body as a microcosm of the empire and inhabited by a pantheon of deities. One soteriological model involves a return to and integration with the undifferentiated *dao*. Other models include techniques for transcending our human condition—caught as we are in tightly woven webs of social relations. The latter model refers to a transformation of the mortal body through meditation or physiological practices to realize the status of a "perfected person" (or "true person," *zhenren*). Others sought to attain longevity through alchemical pursuits aimed at producing an elixir of immortality—akin to the "philosopher's stone" in Europe—or through an internalization of alchemy and the production of an immortal embryo. Daoism had considerable draw because of the esoteric nature of its teachings, which unlocked profound secrets of sacred time (certain moments considered most efficacious to practice) and sacred space (certain locales considered particularly numinous). Daoist texts, revealed in majestic writings by celestial beings, held out the promise of circumventing a premature death, achieving an immeasurably long life, and gaining the ability to ascend to the celestial realm in broad daylight. Daoism has also served as a key component of local village society by its ties to theatrical rituals performed in order to purify a community, reinstitute harmony, and guarantee salvation for the dead and prosperity for the living. All these facets of Daoism have helped ensure the appeal and resilience of Daoism throughout Chinese history, and some of them have also contributed to Daoism's increasingly broad appeal outside of China.

Recognizing the resurgence and spread of Daoism in all its new varieties, along with the continued worldwide allure of *The Scripture of the Way and Its Virtue* and *Book of Master Zhuang*, some have started to refer to Daoism as a world religion. Kristofer Schipper has recently written that "whereas one hundred years ago Daoism could hardly be called a world religion, it now can begin to claim this status."[2] In fact, more than one hundred years ago Daoism was already being classified as a world religion, but for rather different reasons than those that inspired Schipper's statement. What changed? The Daoist texts in this anthology can help readers form both an answer and an appreciation of how the view of Daoism has been transformed: once a philosophy represented in a few famous books, it is now seen as one of the world's major religions with a rich and complex tradition spanning thousands of years.

NOTE ON TRANSLITERATION

The Norton Anthology of World Religions employs the pinyin rather than the Wade-Giles system for representing Chinese script alphabetically in Roman (Latin) characters. Pinyin is the system of Romanization for Mandarin Chinese based on the Beijing dialect, which has become standard in both the People's Republic of China and the Republic of Taiwan. Pinyin attempts to represent Chinese sounds with phonetic English-language equivalents based on specific pronunciation rules. Since some Chinese sounds have no exact English equivalents, the correspondence between pinyin letters and Chinese sounds does not always follow phonetic English. The name of China's

---

2. Kristofer Schipper, foreword to Palmer and Liu, *Daoism in the Twentieth Century*, p. xi.

last imperial dynasty is Qing in pinyin, for example, but the word is pronounced "Ching." Pronouncing glossaries found throughout the anthology provide further guidance on the pronunciation of names and key terms. Here is a list of English-language sounds for pinyin spelling.

"b" as in "boat"
"d" as in "dog"
"f" as in "fat"
"g" as in "go"
"h" as in "hate"
"k" as in "kite"
"l" as in "law"
"m" as in "mail"
"n" as in "name"
"p" as in "picture"
"q" as in the "ch" sound in "cheap"
"t" as in "two"
"x" as in the "sh" sound in "sheet"
"z" as in the "ds" sound in "foods"

"ang" as in the "ong" sound in "song"
"ao" as in the sound of "ow" in "Dow Jones"
"ch" as in "cheese"
"en" as in the sound of "un" in "undo"
"sh" as in "sheep"
"yi" as the "ee" sound in "bee"
"zh" as in the "j" sound in "juggle"

Chronology

1600–1046 B.C.E. Shang dynasty

1046–256 B.C.E. Zhou dynasty

1045–771 B.C.E. Western Zhou dynasty

566 B.C.E. Birth of the Buddha, according to the "long chronology"

ca. 550 B.C.E. Conventional date for Laozi

551–479 B.C.E. Conventional dates for Confucius

486 B.C.E. Death of the Buddha, according to the "long chronology"

469–399 B.C.E. Life of Socrates

448 B.C.E. Birth of the Buddha, according to the "short chronology"

427–347 B.C.E. Life of Plato

403–221 B.C.E. Warring States period

384–322 B.C.E. Life of Aristotle

368 B.C.E. Death of the Buddha, according to the "short chronology"

ca. 280–233 B.C.E. Life of Han Fei

221–206 B.C.E. Qin dynasty

202 B.C.E.–220 C.E. Han dynasty

ca. 145–ca. 86 B.C.E. Life of Sima Qian, compiler of the *Records of the Grand Historian* (*Shiji*)

9 C.E. Han dynasty splits into the Western (Former) Han (206 B.C.E.–9 C.E.) and the reunified Eastern (Later) Han (25–220 C.E.), as the regent Wang Mang proclaims himself emperor of the newly founded Xin dynasty (9–23 C.E.)

ca. 50 C.E. Spread of Buddhism to China

2nd century Texts treating the divinization of Laozi begin to appear

142 Appearance of Laozi to Zhang Daoling, prompting the formation of the Celestial Masters movement.

184 Revolt of Yellow Turbans, inspired by the *Scripture of Great Peace*

215 Surrender of Zhang Lu, Zhang Daoling's grandson and third Celestial Master, to the Han dynasty general Cao Cao, who officially recognizes the Celestial Masters movement

226–249 Life of Wang Bi, who writes an influential commentary on *The Scripture of the Way and Its Virtue*

ca. 300 *Book of the Master Who Embraces Simplicity* written by Ge Hong (283–343)

316 North China seized by the "barbarian" Xiongnu invaders

364–70 Revelations of new scriptures to Yang Xi (330–ca. 386), which form the basis for the Shangqing tradition

ca. 395 Numinous Treasure (Lingbao) scriptures circulated by Ge Chaofu

406–477 Life of Lu Xiujing, who edits Numinous Treasure scriptures and compiles catalogue of Daoist scriptures

ca. 415 Title "Celestial Master" bestowed on Kou Qianzhi (365?–448), active in North China, in a revelation from Laozi

451–536 Life of Tao Hongjing, who compiles and annotates Shangqing manuscripts that had become dispersed

581–618 Sui dynasty

618–907 Tang dynasty, which claims Laozi as ancestor and divine protector of the ruling house

624 Two Daoist priests, along with a statue of a Heavenly Worthy (*tianzun*), are sent by Emperor Gaozu to the Korean kingdom of Koguryǒ

629–45 Voyage to India of Xuanzang, Chinese Buddhist monk

690–705 Reign of Wu Zetian as Empress Wu of the Zhou dynasty

731 Daoists put in charge of rituals connected to the Five Marchmounts (*wuyue*)

ca. 750 Spread of Daoist ideas to Japan begins

845 Harsh persecution of Buddhists

850–933 Life of Du Guangting, who writes hagiographies, sacred geographies, and a collection of biographies of female Daoists

902–979 Five Dynasties and Ten Kingdoms period

960–1279 Song dynasty, split in 1126 by Jurchen invasion

960–1127 Northern Song dynasty

10th century Emergence of Celestial Heart (Tianxin) traditions
Growth and development of internal alchemy (*neidan*)

ca. 994 Discovery of secret Celestial Heart texts by Rao Dongtian

998–1022 Reign of Emperor Zhenzong, who strengthens court ties to Daoism and venerates a Daoist deity, the Perfected Warrior (Zhenwu)

1101–25 Reign of Emperor Huizong, patron of Daoists

12th century Emergence of Divine Empyrean (Shenxiao) tradition

1115–1234 Jurchen Jin dynasty

1126 Jurchen invasion, driving Song out of the north

1127–1279 Southern Song dynasty

ca. 1190s Emergence of Complete Perfection (Quanzhen) Daoism, a monastic tradition

ca. 1220 Visit by Changchun (Qiu Chuji, 1148–1227), high-ranking Daoist in the Quanzhen tradition, to the Mongol leader Genghis Khan

1260–1368 Yuan dynasty, established by Mongols

1368–1644 Ming dynasty, return of Han rule

1368–98 Reign of Emperor Taizu, who strictly regulates Daoists and seeks Daoist immortals

1424–25 Reign of Emperor Renzong, who dies of elixir poisoning

1445 Ming dynasty printing of the Daoist canon

1497–98 First voyage to India, circumnavigating South Africa, by Vasco da Gama (ca. 1460–1524)

1552 Death of Saint Francis Xavier, a Jesuit missionary, while seeking admittance to China

1557 Portuguese trading offices in the port of Macao allowed by Chinese

1593 Arrival in China of Matteo Ricci (1552–1610), who dies there

1788 Presentation to the British Royal Society of the first Latin translation of *The Scripture of the Way and Its Virtue*, produced by Jesuit missionaries in China

1644–1912 Qing dynasty, established by Manchus

1646–1716 Life of Gottfried Leibniz, who criticizes Daoism

1694–1778 Life of Voltaire, who praises Confucianism and criticizes Daoism

1838 First appearance in an English publication of the term "Taouism"

1839–42 First Opium War: Britain's victory over China expands trading privileges

1842 First French translation of *The Scripture of the Way and Its Virtue*

1850–64 Taiping Rebellion, a peasant uprising that kills millions and weakens China's central government

1854–60 Second Opium War: Britain and France win more concessions for European traders and missionaries

1853 Opening of Japan by the U.S. Commodore Matthew C. Perry (1794–1858)

1861–85 Translations of the Chinese Classics by James Legge (1815–1897)

1868 First English translation of *The Scripture of the Way and Its Virtue*
Meiji Restoration, overthrowing the shogunate and returning Japan to imperial rule

1870 First German translation of *The Scripture of the Way and Its Virtue* and *Book of Master Zhuang*

1881 First English translation of the *Book of Master Zhuang*

1891 Publication of James Legge's translations of *The Scripture of the Way and Its Virtue* and *Book of Master Zhuang* in the *Sacred Books of the East* series
1893 World Parliament of Religions held in Chicago

1894–95 First Sino-Japanese War: with China's defeat, Taiwan comes under Japanese colonial rule

1898 Hundred Days of Reform, an attempt by China's emperor to follow a Western model: one of its edicts converts temples into schools

1900 Boxer Rebellion, a peasant uprising against foreigners in China

1904–05 Russo-Japanese War, Russia's failed attempt to gain control of Manchuria and Korea

1910 Version of the *Book of Master Zhuang* published by Martin Buber (1878–1965)
Annexation of Korea by Japan

1912 Abdication of the final Qing emperor
Founding of Daojioa hui, China's first national Daoist association

1912–49 Republic of China

1914–18 World War I

1916–27 Warlord era; China is fragmented into different military factions

1917 Russian Revolution, ending with Bolshevik victory

1919–21 May Fourth Movement, triggered by a mass demonstration of students in Beijing and focused on reform and Chinese nationalism

1920 Publication of Max Weber's essay on Confucianism and Daoism in *Collected Essays in the Sociology of Religion*

1921 Founding of Chinese Communist Party

1926 Printing of the modern edition of the Daoist canon

1929 Superstition (*mixin*) banned by law in China

1930 Formation of Yiguandao (Way of Pervading Unity), the most popular of the syncretic religious groups of the Republican era

1931–32 Invasion of Manchuria by Japanese, who establish puppet state of Manchukuo

1934–36 Long March, the trek by China's Communists from the southeast to the northwest (Yan'an)

1937–38 Rape of Nanjing, a massacre early in the Japanese occupation of eastern China during the Sino-Japanese War (1937–45)

1939–45 World War II, ended by the surrender of Japan

1946–49 Chinese civil war, which ends in Communist victory over the Nationalists (Guomindang)

1949 Foundation of People's Republic of China, led by Mao Zedong (party chairman, 1949–76)
Retreat of Nationalists to Taiwan (Republic of China)

1951 Establishment of China's Religious Affairs Office (later renamed Religious Affairs Bureau)

1954 First constitution of the People's Republic of China: Article 88 guarantees "freedom of religious belief"

1957 Reestablishment of China's National Daoist Association

1958–61 Great Leap Forward, a disastrously unsuccessful campaign to modernize and industrialize China

1966–76 Great Proletarian Cultural Revolution, a renewed attack on social and cultural traditions

1966 Disbanding of the National Daoist Association

1968 First international conference of Daoist studies
Ordination of Dutch scholar Kristofer Schipper (b. 1934), first Westerner to become a Daoist priest

1971 Publication of *Taoism and Chinese Religion* by Henri Maspero (1883–1945), a pioneering history of Daoism as an organized religious tradition

1973 Discovery at Mawangdui of a new manuscript of *The Scripture of the Way and Its Virtue*, which inspires new translations

1975 Abolition of China's Religious Affairs Bureau

1976 Death of Mao Zedong

1979 Reestablishment of China's Religious Affairs Bureau

1980 Reestablishment of China's National Daoist Association

1980s Boom in *qigong*, a health- and longevity-focused movement that draws elements from Daoism and Buddhism

1982 Publication of Document 19, "On the Basic Viewpoint and Policy on the Religious Question During Our Country's Socialist Period," which lays out the Chinese Communist Party's view of religion

1997 Publication of "Freedom of Religious Belief in China," white paper issued by the Chinese government

1998 Bureau of Religious Affairs renamed the State Administration of Religious Affairs

1999 Banning of Falun Gong, a popular form of *qigong*, after followers protest at Communist Party Headquarters

2007 "The Way to Harmony: International Forum on the *Daodejing*," a symposium co-sponsored by the Chinese government

Great Wall

LIAONING   JILIN
Liaoyang •

NORTH
KOREA

• Datong   ○ Beijing (Dadu)
▲ Mt.
Heng   Tianjin •
▲ Mt. Wutai

HEBEI

Taiyuan

Bo Hai

Pyongyang •

• Seoul

SOUTH
KOREA

Huang (Yellow)   Jinan •
▲ Mt. Tai   • Qingdao
SHANDONG

Yellow Sea

JAPAN

yang   Zhengzhou
○
▲ Kaifeng
Mt. Song

HENAN

CHINA

JIANGSU

Huai

Nanjing •   Yangzhou ○
ANHUI   Mt. Mao •
    Suzhou
    Tai Lake •   • Shanghai

HUBEI
• Wuhan   Hangzhou •

Shashi   Yangzi   Mt. Tiantai •

ZHEJIANG

Dongting Lake   Poyang Lake
Mt. Xiaoyao •   • Nanchang   Mt. Huagai ▲
    ◉ Mt. Longhu   Longquan •
▲ Mt. Heng   Mt. Wuyi •

JIANGXI

Xiang   FUJIAN

Pacific Ocean

Taiwan Strait

Xiamen (Amoy) •

GUANGDONG

Guangzhou •

TAIWAN

• Hong Kong

South China Sea

▲ Five sacred mountains
△ Other prominent mountains
◉ Centers of Daoism
○ Ancient capitals

DAOIST SITES
and
SACRED MOUNTAINS

The Dawn of Daoism
FROM THE ZHOU DYNASTY (1046–256 B.C.E.) THROUGH THE QIN DYNASTY (221–206 B.C.E.)

During the long era extending from the Zhou dynasty (1046–256 B.C.E.) through the Qin dynasty (221–206 B.C.E.), China was transformed from a decentralized feudal society into a unified and centralized empire. The Zhou dynasty is divided into two periods: the Western Zhou (1046–771 B.C.E.), which began when King Wu overthrew the last ruler of the Shang dynasty (ca. 1600–1046 B.C.E.) and established an age of stable rule, and the Eastern Zhou (770–256 B.C.E.), a time of internecine political strife that contains both the Spring and Autumn period (770–476 B.C.E.) and much of the Warring States period (403–221 B.C.E.). Most of the religious and philosophical texts, such as *The Scripture of the Way and Its Virtue* (*Daode jing*) and the *Book of Master Zhuang* (*Zhuangzi*), and the rich array of formative concepts that became significant within the later Daoist tradition first emerged during the

Detail from the Mawangdui Silk Texts, second century B.C.E.

Warring States period. At the same time, different philosophical groups were defining and redefining the term "Dao" (Way), while cosmological ideas and self-cultivation practices aimed at attaining longevity were being articulated and developed. The foundational texts and concepts then produced were picked up by some early religious movements, and they became important ingredients for the synthesis and formation of Daoism as an organized religious tradition during the Han dynasty (202 B.C.E.–220 C.E.).

It would seem natural for an anthology of one of the world's major religions to open with its first canonical text or a biography of its founding figure. Beginnings (founder, sacred text, creation story) are often important in narratives about the world's religious traditions, but those narratives tend to be questioned by historians. Some of the problems posed by claims about the beginnings of Daoism are particularly intractable. For example, though general writings on Chinese religions traditionally identify Laozi as the founder of Daoism and *The Scripture of the Way and Its Virtue* as its main sacred text, neither identification is accurate: Laozi did not initiate a new religion, and the first Daoist religious groups did not treat *The Scripture of the Way and Its Virtue* as a font of ineffable mystical philosophical wisdom—indeed, the text was largely ignored. To be sure, Laozi and *The Scripture of the Way and Its Virtue* would both become highly significant to Daoism, as we will soon see; but they were just anchors of that later tradition, which became attached to an august ancient sage and authoritative text that each hailed from a time in the distant past when Daoism had not yet formed as a religion.

The history of Daoism as an organized religion begins during the Han dynasty, as will be detailed in the following section, but we should note that it developed out of elements already present in the pre-Han period. Daoism, as one scholar has described it, "took shape only gradually, during a slow gestation that was actually a progressive integration of various ancient lines of thought." If the period between the Zhou and the Qin is particularly important for understanding Daoism, since the key "lines of thought" emerged at that time, then we also need to ask what elements of practice fed into Daoism and what specific historical, religious, and philosophical features of this early period were selected by later Daoists to provide themselves a heritage and distinctive pedigree.

Most pertinent here is that the roughly two hundred years of peace and stability that characterized the early Zhou was followed by division and power struggles—particularly during the Spring and Autumn and the Warring States periods—accompanied by tremendous intellectual effervescence. The early Zhou attained a symbolic importance for later generations as a time when "All under heaven," a synonym for all of China, was united and society was organized by a strict sense of ritual protocol (*li*) and hierarchical relationships; this era was glorified and idealized, even recalled as a golden age, by Confucius and others. In the chaos and ensuing metaphysical crisis brought on by the decline of the Zhou and its feudal system, important new philosophical movements arose with alternative political ideologies and social arrangements.

The intellectual ferment that occurred during the Eastern Zhou, which is often called the period of the "Various Masters and Hundred Schools/ Lineages," was part of what the German philosopher of history Karl Jaspers (1883–1969) labeled the Axial Age (800–200 B.C.E.)—when significant philosophical systems and religious traditions formed in cultures around the world. This was the time of the Greek and Indian philosophers, and of the Hebrew prophets in Israel, out of which sprang such seminal religious movements and texts as the Upanishads, Buddhism, Jainism, and Judaism.

In China, the Axial Age was the time of, among others, Kongzi (Confucius, 551–479 B.C.E.), Laozi (sixth century B.C.E.), Zhuangzi (fourth century B.C.E.), and Mozi (late fifth century B.C.E.). Confucius recommended that the scholars of his day engage with society and politics and advocated that they become persuaders, peddling their ethical and political views to aspiring rulers. Others, including Laozi and Zhuangzi, took a fundamentally different approach to reforming individuals and society. Whereas the Confucian ideal was to transform the individual by instilling certain dispositions and behaviors, Zhuangzi emphasized that humans should unlearn things and disengage from society and all its conventions.

Despite how they are commonly categorized today, neither *The Scripture of the Way and Its Virtue* nor the *Book of Master Zhuang* is specifically (or exclusively) Daoist. As the introduction to this anthology discussed, the very terms "Daoism" and "Daoist" are problematic, making the boundaries of Daoism difficult to delineate. Without ever agreeing on its content, Westerners have primarily applied the label "Daoism"—first attested (romanized as "Taouism") in the mid-nineteenth century—to texts, people, and movements connected in some way with one of a set of key Chinese terms whose meanings were themselves being defined, redefined, and contested throughout history: Dao (the Way), *daojia* (specialists of/on the Dao), *daojiao* (teachings of/on the Dao), and *daoshu* (methods of the Dao).

In the second century B.C.E., a Han court astrologer named Sima Tan (d. 110 B.C.E.) looked back over the array of texts that had been produced during the Warring States period and assessed their varying approaches to rulership and governance (see "Essential Points on the Six Lineages of Thought"). He sorted them into six groups: Yinyang (Specialists of Yin and Yang, or Naturalists), Ru (Literati, or Confucians), Mo (Mohists), Fajia (Legalists), Mingjia (Logicians, or Terminologists), and Daojia (Specialists of the Way). The Yinyang, Ru, and Mo lineages existed before Sima Tan came up with his categories, but the designations Fajia, Mingjia, and Daojia were all his coinages.

Tan used the suffix *-jia* to signal that members of each group were "specialists" or "experts," but later it acquired the meaning of "school" or "lineage." This shift has caused an inordinate amount of confusion, since writers have often misunderstood the more restrictive meaning as applying to all usages. Western scholars have become accustomed to using "Confucianism," "Mohism," "Legalism," and "Daoism" as if these labels (like other -isms) were clear references to autonomous philosophical schools that existed in antiquity. Yet that assumption is not supported by the historical record. What has come to be included under those umbrella terms were not discrete schools, at least in the way we now think of schools as being separate institutions: they were loose sodalities retrospectively grouped together according to filiations of sentiments, though the teacher–student lineages that organized them in fact had great diversity. These problems of terminology clearly do not simply reflect challenges of translation, as Sima Tan himself struggled with how to group the different writings he encountered.

For Sima Tan, Daojia were Specialists of the Way (Dao). During the second century B.C.E., those compiling collections and bibliographies applied the same term to many different schools and figures. Indeed, because many texts labeled as Daojia, such as *The Scripture of the Way and Its Virtue* and the *Book of Master Zhuang*, criticize and ridicule Confucius, scholars tended to call Daoist anything that displayed an anti-Confucian sentiment—or even merely recommended retiring to the mountains to escape from the Confucian social order.

"Daojia" is usually discussed in relation to the equally problematic term "Daojiao": an earlier generation distinguished them as "Philosophical Daoism" and "Religious Daoism," respectively. Scholars today are reluctant to draw a rigid distinction between the two, aware that doing so can lead to privileging the early texts associated with Laozi and Zhuangzi as a pure philosophy while treating all later Daoist developments as a falling away from that pure ideal and a descent into magical or superstitious practices. Nonetheless, some writers continue to employ the terms as a convenient way to discuss the Zhou philosophical movements (*daojia*) as separate from the later Han dynasty Daoist religious institutions (*daojiao*). But during the pre-Han period, the term *daojiao* was in fact applied to a variety of philosophical traditions. Mohists, for instance, used it to designate "teachings of (or on) the Way (*dao*)," which could include Confucianism. To complicate things further, from the third to the fifth century *daojiao* became a synonym for Buddhism (*fojiao*), but from some time in the fifth century onward it was used exclusively for organized Daoism to distinguish it from Buddhism. Thus Daojiao as a label (proper noun) for a unified religious tradition (now referred to as Daoism or Taoism in Western languages) dates only to about the fifth century C.E. and was applied retrospectively.

The term "Dao," the key component of "Daoism," is itself one of the most richly complicated terms in all of Chinese thought. Its basic meaning is twofold: the noun "Way" (the proper path for human conduct) and the verb "Say" (the teachings of a philosophical school). During the pre-Han period, many different philosophical schools set out their own visions of the Way, which they all called Dao—usually propositions about the path for proper conduct and relations between humans. Although most of the key philosophical texts produced in this period use the term, its meaning varies considerably within and across them.

In religious and philosophical works from the Warring States period, "Dao" has a range of meanings. In the Confucian *Analects* (*Lunyu*), for instance, it refers variously to the Way of the ancient sage-kings, the normative sociopolitical order among humans, and the Way to achieve that order (all aspects of guiding human behavior or conduct). It eventually became associated with a universal truth, or the broader natural order. In texts like *The Scripture of the Way and Its Virtue*, the Dao came to designate the natural state of things: the way things are when humans get out of the way and just let things be. This unsullied primordial state of a unified universal Dao is the goal to which humans should aim to return. Confucians may have looked back to the time of the ancient sage-kings for their ideals, but Daoists looked back even further—to the haziest time of the undifferentiated and unified Dao, before its progressive transformations and devolution into the multiplicity of things.

A number of other significant concepts, not limited to any one school or group, permeated early Chinese religious, philosophical, and cultural ideas and practices and have remained important down to the present day. There is nothing distinctly Daoist about any of them, but they were later incorporated into Daoism and took on new lives there. The Chinese universe, and all things within it, was perceived as being made up of qi, which is usually translated as "breath," "vapor," "pneuma," or "energy." The first appearance of qi (in the form of primal qi, *yuanqi*) within the Dao, which in its original form is depicted as a void of nothingness, is what puts into motion a series of divisions—the first of which is the dyad of *yin* (shaded side of a hill, dark, feminine) and *yang* (sunny side of a hill, bright, male)—that result in the formation of all that is. Thus, early Chinese texts often discuss the need for a return, or renewal: the goal is to return to the state of undifferentiated primordial qi. Qi manifests in varying degrees of density, from the ethereal to the substantial, and in physical form it can be ingested and circulated throughout the body during self-cultivation practices. Since the natural world was perceived to be the Dao itself—albeit made up of the different transformations of qi—thinkers of this period were very interested in exploring the macrocosmic–microcosmic relationships between heaven, earth, and humans and the interactions in the ongoing interchange between yin and yang and the five phases (wood, fire, earth, metal, and water). Philosophers used these notions to explore possible correspondences between seemingly disparate things (such as colors, directions, seasons, musical notes, and organs). Correlations were perceived to exist on multiple levels, including between the five planets, the five sacred mountains (*wuyue*), and a human's five viscera (the liver, heart, spleen, kidneys, and lungs). Certain exemplary figures who were well attuned to these transformations and resonances were able to discern the unity of the Dao behind manifest appearances and attempted to integrate themselves into that system of correspondences.

Pre-Han texts, such as the *Book of Master Zhuang*, discuss a category of beings that were intent on searching out transcendence or immortality, achieved through a wide variety of self-cultivation techniques, such as those depicted in *Inward Training* (*Neiye*), a text concerned with breathing meditation, and in the "Old Man by the River (*Heshang Gong*) Commentary on the Laozi," a physiological primer of self-cultivation and longevity teachings. These "transcendents" (*xian*, often translated "immortal") attained immeasurably long lives, the ability to fly, and a way of existing in the world with a natural effortless spontaneity. Such individuals have become closely associated with Daoism, but they reflect more general ideals and beliefs circulating during that period, reaching up to the emperor. Contemporary historical sources mention a category of visitors to the Zhou and Qin courts, known pejoratively as "masters of methods" (*fangshi*), who sought political patronage by peddling esoteric knowledge of magical and medical techniques, divination, and exorcism. They also regaled the emperor with stories of mystical islands inhabited by immortals. Alchemists produced golden vessels, under the theory that one who ate out of them could achieve immortality. The search for immortality would eventually drop off after the

Han dynasty emperor Wudi (r. 141–87 B.C.E.) installed Confucianism as state ideology (though it reemerged later in Daoist history). Subsequently, when imperial examinations were established as the gateway to official government positions, they were based on Confucian texts. This exclusion of Daoist texts led to their being devalued as popular religion fit only for the peasant class, a view that reinforced the new separation of Daoism and Confucianism. It has become difficult to overturn those ingrained misperceptions about early Daoism.

Daoism has traditionally been credited with furthering the development of science in China, perhaps because of the long-standing misapprehension that Daoists were nature-loving hermits engaged in alchemical pursuits. Early alchemists did seek to compound elixirs made up of minerals and metals that when ingested would confer longevity, but Chinese scientific and protoscientific ideas were widespread across different philosophical traditions. That fact has deterred neither Chinese nor Westerners from drawing such close connections between Daoism and science that anything in the past that looked scientific was retrospectively labeled Daoist.

The Qin dynasty lasted barely a generation, but it played a vital role in reshaping China (whose name derives from "Qin"). It was a turning point in Chinese history—both an ending and a beginning. Politically, the Qin unified the six warring factions that had fought for supremacy during the Warring States period and thereby conferred an imperial identity on China for the first time in 700 years. Intellectually, it imposed an ideological orthodoxy, using prodigious violence to suppress the many contending schools of philosophical and religious thought. The founding Qin emperor may have tried to suppress the writings in the Confucian canon (the "Five Classics": the Classic or Book of Changes, Classic of History, Classic of Poetry, Collection of Rituals, and Spring and Autumn Annals), but during the Han—especially during the reign of Wudi—they were rehabilitated and became Han state orthodoxy.

The historical beginning of Daoism is now generally assigned to the mid-second century C.E., during the waning days of the Han dynasty. There is much to be said for this dating as regards the formation of Daoist religious institutions. It is not possible, however, to dismiss the wealth of philosophical ideas and religious practices of the pre-Han period as completely irrelevant to later organized Daoism. It is prudent, as one scholar has aptly counseled, to view what was produced in the pre-Han period "as a heritage to be shaped rather than as an established tradition itself shaping the future." The writings in the next section will chronicle the rise and development of Daoism as an established institutional religion beginning to shape its own future.

THE BOOK OF MASTER MO
(*Mozi*)

The Book of Master Mo (*Mozi*), an important philosophical treatise, gives voice to a highly organized group of thinkers who challenged the increasing orthodoxy of the teachings of Confucius. This work is attributed to a single author named Mo Di, who allegedly lived in the late fifth century B.C.E., but scholars now view it as a composite text created by multiple authors in the fourth to third century B.C.E. An influential philosophical, social, and religious movement of the Warring States period (403–221 B.C.E.) known today as Mohism developed out of the writings of Master Mo.

In the chapter of *The Book of Master Mo* excerpted below, "Against the Confucians" ("Feiru"), the compound term "the teaching of the Dao" (*daojiao*) appears for the first time. Here, however, the term that later would be commonly applied to the Daoist religious tradition was used to refer to a Confucian teaching.

The complete text of *The Book of Master Mo* was almost entirely unknown between the Tang dynasty (618–907) and the Ming dynasty (1368–1644). A version of *The Book of Master Mo* was printed in the Ming dynasty, as part of the Daoist canon. Perhaps it was included because Master Mo is depicted in Daoist hagiographical collections such as the *Traditions of Divine Transcendents* (*Shenxian zhuan*) as an immortal-like saintly figure. Other texts, such as the *Book of the Master Who Embraces Simplicity* (*Baopu zi*), attribute characteristically Daoist practices to him.

Mozi: *mow-tzu*

From *Against the Confucians*

The Confucians say: "In treating relatives as relatives, there are gradations. In respecting the worthy, there are gradations." They speak of the differences of near and distant, honoured and lowly. Their *Rites*[1] states: "Mourning for a father or mother is three years; for a wife or eldest son it is three years; for older and younger brothers of the father, younger and older brothers, and other sons it is one full year; for other family members it is five months." If the calculation of the period of years and months is based on nearness and distance, then it should be long for near relatives and short for distant relatives. This is to take the wife or eldest son to be the same as the father [or mother]. If the calculation of the years and months is based on being honoured or lowly, then this is to honour the wife or son the same as the father or mother and to consider the father's older brothers, and older brothers to be like other sons. What greater perversity is there than this! When a parent dies, they lay out the corpse without preparation while they climb onto the roof, peer into the well, poke into rat holes and look into wash-basins seeking the person. Taking the parent to actually be alive is foolish in the extreme. To know they are dead but feel compelled to seek them is also a great hypocrisy!

TRANSLATED BY Ian Johnston. All bracketed additions are the translator's.

1. The Collection of Rituals, one of the Five Classics attributed to Confucius (551–479 B.C.E.). It discusses ritual protocol, social decorum, and court ceremonies.

[When a Confucian] takes a wife, he goes to meet her in person, correctly attired as a servant. He takes the reins of the cart himself and hands her the cord to draw herself up as if honouring a revered parent. The wedding ceremony is conducted with solemnity just like conducting a sacrifice. This is to turn high and low upside down, and is perverse conduct towards parents who are brought down to the level of the wife whilst the wife infringes on those above. In serving parents, how can something like this be called filial?

The Confucians say: "After taking a wife, she can join with you in carrying out the sacrifices whilst a son will protect the ancestral temple, therefore they are highly regarded."

In reply I say: "These are false words insofar as a man's uncles and older brothers maintain the ancestral temple for several decades, yet, when they die, he mourns them for one year whilst the wives of older and younger brothers, who assist at the sacrifices to his ancestors, are not mourned at all. Thus, mourning wives and sons for three years is certainly not because they maintain [the ancestral temple] or assist at sacrifices. Such favourable treatment of wives and sons is already excessive. They also say, 'It is the way of honouring parents.' In wishing to treat 'thickly' those towards whom they are most discriminatory, they treat 'thinly' those who are most important. Is this not a great deception?"

They also hold firmly to the doctrine that there is Fate, arguing thus: "Living to old age and dying young, poverty and wealth, peace and peril, order and disorder are determined by Heaven's decrees and cannot be decreased or increased. Success and failure, reward and punishment, good luck and bad are established [by Fate] and cannot be affected by a person's knowledge or strength." If the many officials believed this, they would be careless in their allotted duties. If the ordinary people believed this, they would be careless in following their tasks. If officials do not bring about order, there is disorder. If agricultural matters are attended to tardily, there is poverty. Poverty and disorder strike at the root of government, yet the Confucians take it [i.e. Fate] as a teaching.[2] This is damaging to the people of the world.

Moreover, they use various elaborate rites and music to delude people. They use prolonged mourning and false grief to deceive relatives. They believe in Fate and accept poverty, yet they are arrogant and self-important. They turn their backs on what is fundamental and abandon their duties, finding contentment in idleness and pride. They are greedy for drink and food. They are indolent in carrying out their responsibilities and fall into hunger and cold, but, when endangered by starvation and freezing, they have no way of avoiding these things. They are like beggars. They hoard food like field mice. They stare like billy goats. They rise up like castrated pigs. When a gentleman laughs at them, they angrily reply: "Useless fellow! What do you know of good Confucians." In spring, they beg for wheat. In summer, they beg for rice. When the five grains[3] have already been harvested, they attach themselves to large funerals with their sons and grandsons all following along, and so they get their fill of drink and food. If they are put in charge of several funerals, they have enough to live on. They depend on other people's

---

2. "A teaching" renders the term *daojiao*. A more literal translation would be "a teaching of their Dao."

3. That is, all the staple agricultural crops.

households for food and rely on other people's fields for wine. When a rich man has a funeral, they are very happy and say delightedly: "This is a source of clothing and food."

Confucians say: "A gentleman must use ancient modes of speech and dress and afterwards he is benevolent."

I say in reply: "What is called ancient in speech and dress was all once upon a time new so, if the men of old spoke this way and dressed this way, they were not gentlemen. This being so, must we clothe ourselves in the garb of those who were not gentlemen and speak the speech of those who were not gentlemen before being benevolent?"

* * *

THE SCRIPTURE OF THE WAY AND ITS VIRTUE
(*Daode jing*, or *Laozi*)

The Scripture of the Way and Its Virtue (*Daode jing*), which is also known as the *Laozi* or the *Five Thousand Character* [*Classic*] (*Wuqian wen*), is divided in two parts: Book One, the *Daojing* ("Scripture of the Way," chapters 1–37), and Book Two, the *Dejing* ("Scripture of Virtue," chapters 38–81). The passages of the text appear in different order in different versions—in one recently discovered text, the *Dejing* is placed before the *Daojing*—but their wording is remarkably consistent. *The Scripture of the Way and Its Virtue* is traditionally regarded as a form of revealed literature: according to this account, it was delivered by Laozi (the Old Master), also known as Li Er or Li Dan, an older contemporary of Confucius, to a gatekeeper named Yin Xi as he was embarking on his journey from China to the West. Few details about Laozi's biography have been passed down; most scholars now treat him as a fictional creation and believe that the work was compiled from an oral tradition that dates to about the third century B.C.E. Some sections may be even older.

The Scripture of the Way and Its Virtue contains aphoristic passages on a broad range of topics, from methods for self-cultivation (chapters 7, 10) to the arts of governance (chapters 3, 30, 37, 57, 58, 75, 80). The text is notoriously difficult to understand, in part because of its self-conscious use of negation: "The way (*dao*) that can be spoken of (*dao*) is not the constant way (*dao*); the name that can be named is not the constant name" (chapter 1). Though many of its concepts and topics became foundational within Daoism, many were also present within Confucianism and Chinese thought more generally. The term *dao* (way) in the title of the *Daode jing* originally referred to a moral social and natural order. Here, however, the Dao is presented as being indeterminate and ineffable; it came to be a referent for the source, or creative power, behind everything. In this way, the term pointed beyond any limited, or fixed, reference and toward an absolute reality. That which embodies the Dao is "De"—usually translated within Daoist texts as "virtue," though also rendered as "potency," "integrity," or "power." In the Confucian tradition the term referred to moral virtue, but its meaning in *The Scripture of the Way and Its Virtue* is more complicated: the word evokes the basic quality or character that enables a thing to be what it is and to do what it does.

One of the main concerns of *The Scripture of the Way and Its Virtue* is social and cosmic order, yet it also focuses on a perceived break with the Way. The problem is

Painting of Laozi.

apparently tied to the rise of civilization, an overemphasis on human intellect, and a tendency toward rigidly categorizing and pinning things down (usually caused by a dependence on language and naming practices) at the expense of being at one with the flow of the Dao (chapters 2, 3, 12). Artifice—exemplified in this text by the Confucian "rites" (chapter 38)—has won out over naturalness. If we can unravel the artificial fabric of the social order to return to our presocialized state, if we can eliminate all the distinctions that the exercise of human intellect imposes on us and the world, then we will be able to move without effort and in harmony with the natural rhythm of the Dao as it operates spontaneously (chapter 63). Therefore, much of *The Scripture of the Way and Its Virtue* focuses on "emptying," "undoing," and "unlearning" things in an attempt to "return" (*fan*) to the undifferentiated primordial Dao (chapters 4, 5, 19, 28, 48, 81).

The exegeses of and commentaries on *The Scripture of the Way and Its Virtue* clearly demonstrate the text's striking openness to different interpretations. Later interpreters variously read the text as being primarily concerned with self-cultivation (see the *Heshang gong* commentary, below), as offering a behavioral code for a community of religious initiates (see the *Xiang'er* commentary, below), as providing a manual for the creation of a moral and political system (the view of orthodox Confucians), and even as richly prefiguring Buddhist dialectical teachings.

The Scripture of the Way and Its Virtue is one of the most difficult and problematic texts of early Chinese thought, and (perhaps owing to its opacity) it is also one of the most frequently translated texts in all of world literature—second only to the Bible. It has had a profound impact around the world, with each translator and reader—from Alfred, Lord Tennyson and Martin Heidegger to Ursula Le Guin and the Beatles—finding a different meaning in its compressed language, nebulous philosophy, and mystical orientation. The terseness and vagueness of the text have allowed its Western interpreters and translators to make it into just about anything they wanted.

However the text and its history are interpreted, and despite the long debate among scholars over precisely how to characterize the relationship between early texts like *The Scripture of the Way and Its Virtue* and Daoism, it clearly became a seminal text in the later Daoist tradition. Most of the world's major religious traditions have a figure identified as a founder, but it would be a mistake to view Laozi as the founder and *The Scripture of the Way and Its Virtue* as the main scripture of later Daoism. It might be more accurate to understand the relationship between this work and later Daoism as an influence akin to the impact that Greek philosophy had on later Christianity.

PRONOUNCING GLOSSARY

Daode jing: *dow-duh ching*   Laozi: *lao-tzu*

From *Book One*

I

The way that can be spoken of
Is not the constant way;
The name that can be named
Is not the constant name.
The nameless was the beginning of heaven and earth;
The named was the mother of the myriad creatures.
Hence always rid yourself of desires in order to observe its secrets;
But always allow yourself to have desires in order to observe
    its manifestations.
These two are the same
But diverge in name as they issue forth.
Being the same they are called mysteries,
Mystery upon mystery—
The gateway of the manifold secrets.

II

The whole world recognizes the beautiful as the beautiful, yet this is only the ugly; the whole world recognizes the good as the good, yet this is only the bad.

Thus Something and Nothing produce each other;
The difficult and the easy complement each other;
The long and the short offset each other;
The high and the low incline towards each other;
Note and sound harmonize with each other;
Before and after follow each other.

Therefore the sage keeps to the deed that consists in taking no action and practises the teaching that uses no words.

The myriad creatures rise from it yet it claims no authority;
It gives them life yet claims no possession;
It benefits them yet exacts no gratitude;
It accomplishes its task yet lays claim to no merit.

It is because it lays claim to no merit

That its merit never deserts it.

III

Not to honour men of worth will keep the people from contention; not to value goods which are hard to come by will keep them from theft; not to display what is desirable will keep them from being unsettled of mind.
Therefore in governing the people, the sage empties their minds but fills their bellies, weakens their wills but strengthens their bones. He always keeps them innocent of knowledge and free from desire, and ensures that the clever never dare to act.
Do that which consists in taking no action, and order will prevail.

TRANSLATED BY D. C. LAU.

IV

The way is empty, yet use will not drain it.
Deep, it is like the ancestor of the myriad creatures.
Blunt the sharpness;
Untangle the knots;
Soften the glare;
Let your wheels move only along old ruts.
Darkly visible, it only seems as if it were there.
I know not whose son it is.
It images the forefather of God.

V

Heaven and earth are ruthless, and treat the myriad creatures as straw dogs;[1] the sage is ruthless, and treats the people as straw dogs.
Is not the space between heaven and earth like a bellows?

It is empty without being exhausted:
The more it works the more comes out.
Much speech leads inevitably to silence.
Better to hold fast to the void.

VI

The spirit of the valley never dies.
This is called the mysterious female.
The gateway of the mysterious female
Is called the root of heaven and earth.
Dimly visible, it seems as if it were there,
Yet use will never drain it.

VII

Heaven and earth are enduring. The reason why heaven and earth can be enduring is that they do not give themselves life. Hence they are able to be long-lived.

Therefore the sage puts his person last and it comes first,
Treats it as extraneous to himself and it is preserved.

Is it not because he is without thought of self that he is able to accomplish his private ends?

VIII

Highest good is like water. Because water excels in benefiting the myriad creatures without contending with them and settles where none would like to be, it comes close to the way.

In a home it is the site that matters;
In quality of mind it is depth that matters;
In an ally it is benevolence that matters;
In speech it is good faith that matters;
In government it is order that matters;

---

1. Effigies made to ward off evil influences; after being used, they were thrown into the street.

In affairs it is ability that matters;
In action it is timeliness that matters.

It is because it does not contend that it is never at fault.

IX

Rather than fill it to the brim by keeping it upright
Better to have stopped in time;
Hammer it to a point
And the sharpness cannot be preserved for ever;
There may be gold and jade to fill a hall
But there is none who can keep them.
To be overbearing when one has wealth and position
Is to bring calamity upon oneself.
To retire when the task is accomplished
Is the way of heaven.

X

When carrying on your head your perplexed bodily soul[2] can
     you embrace in your arms the One
And not let go?
In concentrating your breath can you become as supple
As a babe?
Can you polish your mysterious mirror[3]
And leave no blemish?
Can you love the people and govern the state
Without resorting to action?
When the gates of heaven open and shut
Are you capable of keeping to the role of the female?
When your discernment penetrates the four quarters
Are you capable of not knowing anything?
It gives them life and rears them.
It gives them life yet claims no possession;
It benefits them yet exacts no gratitude;
It is the steward yet exercises no authority.
Such is called the mysterious virtue.

XI

Thirty spokes
Share one hub.

Adapt the nothing therein to the purpose in hand, and you will have the use
of the cart. Knead clay in order to make a vessel. Adapt the nothing therein
to the purpose in hand, and you will have the use of the vessel. Cut out
doors and windows in order to make a room. Adapt the nothing therein to the
purpose in hand, and you will have the use of the room.

Thus what we gain is Something, yet it is by virtue of
Nothing that this can be put to use.

---

2. The other soul is of the spirit, which rises into
heaven at death.

3. That is, your mind.

XII

The five colours[4] make man's eyes blind;
The five notes make his ears deaf;
The five tastes injure his palate;
Riding and hunting
Make his mind go wild with excitement;
Goods hard to come by
Serve to hinder his progress.
Hence the sage is
    For the belly
    Not for the eye.
Therefore he discards the one and takes the other.

XIII

Favour and disgrace are things that startle;
High rank is, like one's body, a source of great trouble.

What is meant by saying that favour and disgrace are things that startle?
Favour when it is bestowed on a subject serves to startle as much as when it
is withdrawn. This is what is meant by saying that favour and disgrace are
things that startle. What is meant by saying that high rank is, like one's
body, a source of great trouble? The reason I have great trouble is that I
have a body. When I no longer have a body, what trouble have I?
Hence he who values his body more than dominion over the empire can be
entrusted with the empire. He who loves his body more than dominion over
the empire can be given the custody of the empire.

XIV

What cannot be seen is called evanescent;
What cannot be heard is called rarefied;
What cannot be touched is called minute.
These three cannot be fathomed
And so they are confused and looked upon as one.
Its upper part is not dazzling;
Its lower part is not obscure.
Dimly visible, it cannot be named
And returns to that which is without substance.
This is called the shape that has no shape,
The image that is without substance.
This is called indistinct and shadowy.
Go up to it and you will not see its head;
Follow behind it and you will not see its rear.
Hold fast to the way of antiquity
In order to keep in control the realm of today.
The ability to know the beginning of antiquity
Is called the thread running through the way.

---

4. Green, red, yellow, white, and black. They, like the five notes (the pentatonic scale) and the five tastes (sour, sweet, bitter, spicy, and salty), belong to a category in the Five Agents system of correspondences, a set of systematic associations between different categories (see table 2, p. 135).

XIX

Exterminate the sage, discard the wise,
And the people will benefit a hundredfold;
Exterminate benevolence, discard rectitude,
And the people will again be filial;
Exterminate ingenuity, discard profit,
And there will be no more thieves and bandits.
These three, being false adornments, are not enough
And the people must have something to which they
        can attach themselves:
Exhibit the unadorned and embrace the uncarved block,[5]
Have little thought of self and as few desires as possible.

XXI

In his every movement a man of great virtue
Follows the way and the way only.
As a thing the way is
Shadowy, indistinct.
Indistinct and shadowy,
Yet within it is an image;
Shadowy and indistinct,
Yet within it is a substance.
Dim and dark,
Yet within it is an essence.
This essence is quite genuine
And within it is something that can be tested.
From the present back to antiquity
Its name never deserted it.
It serves as a means for inspecting the fathers of the multitude.

How do I know that the fathers of the multitude are like that? By means of this.

XXII

Bowed down then preserved;
Bent then straight;
Hollow then full;
Worn then new;
A little then benefited;
A lot then perplexed.
Therefore the sage embraces the One and is a model for the empire.
He does not show himself, and so is conspicuous;
He does not consider himself right, and so is illustrious;
He does not brag, and so has merit;
He does not boast, and so endures.

It is because he does not contend that no one in the empire is in a position
to contend with him.
The way the ancients had it, 'Bowed down then preserved', is no empty saying. Truly it enables one to be preserved to the end.

5. One's original nature, before socialization.

XXVIII

Know the male
But keep to the role of the female
And be a ravine to the empire.
If you are a ravine to the empire,
Then the constant virtue will not desert you
And you will again return to being a babe.
Know the white
But keep to the role of the black
And be a model to the empire.
If you are a model to the empire,
Then the constant virtue will not be wanting
And you will return to the infinite.
Know honour
But keep to the role of the disgraced
And be a valley to the empire.
If you are a valley to the empire,
Then the constant virtue will be sufficient
And you will return to being the uncarved block.

When the uncarved block shatters it becomes vessels. The sage makes use of these and becomes the lord over the officials.

Hence the greatest cutting
Does not sever.

XXX

One who assists the ruler of men by means of the way does not intimidate the empire by a show of arms.

This is something which is liable to rebound.
Where troops have encamped
There will brambles grow;
In the wake of a mighty army
Bad harvests follow without fail.

One who is good aims only at bringing his campaign to a conclusion and dare not thereby intimidate. Bring it to a conclusion but do not boast; bring it to a conclusion but do not brag; bring it to a conclusion but do not be arrogant; bring it to a conclusion but only when there is no choice; bring it to a conclusion but do not intimidate.

A creature in its prime doing harm to the old
Is known as going against the way.
That which goes against the way will come to an early end.

XXXVII

The way never acts yet nothing is left undone.
Should lords and princes be able to hold fast to it,
The myriad creatures will be transformed of their own accord.
After they are transformed, should desire raise its head,

I shall press it down with the weight of the nameless uncarved
  block.
The nameless uncarved block
Is but freedom from desire,
And if I cease to desire and remain still,
The empire will be at peace of its own accord.

From *Book Two*

XXXVIII

A man of the highest virtue does not keep to virtue and that is why he has
virtue. A man of the lowest virtue never strays from virtue and that is why
he is without virtue. The former never acts yet leaves nothing undone. The
latter acts but there are things left undone. A man of the highest benevolence acts, but from no ulterior motive. A man of the highest rectitude acts,
but from ulterior motive. A man most conversant in the rites acts, but when
no one responds rolls up his sleeves and resorts to persuasion by force.
Hence when the way was lost there was virtue; when virtue was lost there was
benevolence; when benevolence was lost there was rectitude; when rectitude
was lost there were the rites.

> The rites are the wearing thin of loyalty and good faith
> And the beginning of disorder;
> Foreknowledge is the flowery embellishment of the way
> And the beginning of folly.

Hence the man of large mind abides in the thick not in the thin, in the fruit
not in the flower.
Therefore he discards the one and takes the other.

XLII

The way begets one; one begets two; two begets three; three begets the
myriad creatures.
The myriad creatures carry on their backs the *yin* and embrace in their
arms the *yang*[6] and are the blending of the generative forces of the two.
There are no words which men detest more than 'solitary', 'desolate', and
'hapless', yet lords and princes use these to refer to themselves.
Thus a thing is sometimes added to by being diminished and diminished by
being added to.
What others teach I also teach. 'The violent will not come to a natural end.'
I shall take this as my precept.

XLVI

When the way prevails in the empire, fleet-footed horses are relegated to
ploughing the fields; when the way does not prevail in the empire, war-
horses breed on the border.

---

6. The male principle; the term originally
referred to the sunny side of a valley, and by
extension it came to be associated with the light,
heaven, dryness, and activity. "*Yin*": the female
principle; the term originally referred to the
shady side of a valley, and by extension it came to
be associated with the dark, earth, dampness,
and passivity.

There is no crime greater than having too many desires;
There is no disaster greater than not being content;
There is no misfortune greater than being covetous.

Hence in being content one will always have enough.

XLVII

Without stirring abroad
One can know the whole world;
Without looking out of the window
One can see the way of heaven.
The further one goes
The less one knows.
Therefore the sage knows without having to stir,
Identifies without having to see,
Accomplishes without having to act.

XLVIII

In the pursuit of learning one knows more every day; in the pursuit of the
way one does less every day. One does less and less until one does nothing
at all, and when one does nothing at all there is nothing that is undone.
It is always through not meddling that the empire is won. Should you meddle,
then you are not equal to the task of winning the empire.

LVI

One who knows does not speak; one who speaks does not know.

Block the openings;
Shut the doors.
Blunt the sharpness;
Untangle the knots;
Soften the glare;
Let your wheels move only along old ruts.

This is known as mysterious sameness.
Hence you cannot get close to it, nor can you keep it at arm's length; you
cannot bestow benefit on it, nor can you do it harm; you cannot ennoble it,
nor can you debase it.
Therefore it is valued by the empire.

LVII

Govern the state by being straightforward; wage war by being crafty; but
win the empire by not being meddlesome.
How do I know that it is like that? By means of this.

The more taboos there are in the empire
The poorer the people;
The more sharpened tools the people have
The more benighted the state;
The more skills the people have

The further novelties multiply;
The better known the laws and edicts
The more thieves and robbers there are.

Hence the sage says,

I take no action and the people are transformed of themselves;
I prefer stillness and the people are rectified of themselves;
I am not meddlesome and the people prosper of themselves;
I am free from desire and the people of themselves become
simple like the uncarved block.

LVIII

When the government is muddled
The people are simple;
When the government is alert
The people are cunning.
It is on disaster that good fortune perches;
It is beneath good fortune that disaster crouches.

Who knows the limit? Does not the straightforward exist? The straightforward changes again into the crafty, and the good changes again into the monstrous. Indeed, it is long since the people were perplexed.

Therefore the sage is square-edged but does not scrape,
Has corners but does not jab,
Extends himself but not at the expense of others,
Shines but does not dazzle.

LXI

A large state is the lower reaches of a river—
The place where all the streams of the world unite.
In the union of the world,
The female always gets the better of the male by stillness.

Being still, she takes the lower position.

Hence the large state, by taking the lower position, annexes the
small state;
The small state, by taking the lower position, affiliates itself
to the large state.
Thus the one, by taking the lower position, annexes;
The other, by taking the lower position, is annexed.
All that the large state wants is to take the other under its wing;
All that the small state wants is to have its services accepted by
the other.
If each of the two wants to find its proper place,
It is meet that the large should take the lower position.

LXIII

Do that which consists in taking no action; pursue that which is not meddlesome; savour that which has no flavour.

Make the small big and the few many; do good to him who has done you an injury.
Lay plans for the accomplishment of the difficult before it becomes difficult; make something big by starting with it when small.
Difficult things in the world must needs have their beginnings in the easy; big things must needs have their beginnings in the small.
Therefore it is because the sage never attempts to be great that he succeeds in becoming great.
One who makes promises rashly rarely keeps good faith; one who is in the habit of considering things easy meets with frequent difficulties.
Therefore even the sage treats some things as difficult. That is why in the end no difficulties can get the better of him.

LXXV

> The people are hungry:
> It is because those in authority eat up too much in taxes
> That the people are hungry.
> The people are difficult to govern:
> It is because those in authority are too fond of action
> That the people are difficult to govern.
> The people treat death lightly:
> It is because the people set too much store by life
> That they treat death lightly.

It is just because one has no use for life that one is wiser than the man who values life.

LXXX

Reduce the size and population of the state. Ensure that even though the people have tools of war for a troop or a battalion they will not use them; and also that they will be reluctant to move to distant places because they look on death as no light matter.
Even when they have ships and carts, they will have no use for them; and even when they have armour and weapons, they will have no occasion to make a show of them.
Bring it about that the people will return to the use of the knotted rope,

> Will find relish in their food
> And beauty in their clothes,
> Will be content in their abode
> And happy in the way they live.

Though adjoining states are within sight of one another, and the sound of dogs barking and cocks crowing in one state can be heard in another, yet the people of one state will grow old and die without having had any dealings with those of another.

LXXXI

Truthful words are not beautiful; beautiful words are not truthful. Good words are not persuasive; persuasive words are not good. He who knows has no wide learning; he who has wide learning does not know.

The sage does not hoard.

> Having bestowed all he has on others, he has yet more;
> Having given all he has to others, he is richer still.

The way of heaven benefits and does not harm; the way of the sage is bountiful and does not contend.

THE BOOK OF MASTER ZHUANG
(Zhuangzi)

Its vibrant and shocking use of language, imaginative range, and challenging philosophical propositions have made the *Book of Master Zhuang* (*Zhuangzi*) a celebrated classic of Daoist literature—and of Chinese literature more generally. The work is attributed to a certain Zhuang Zhou who reportedly lived in the fourth century B.C.E. in southern China, and early records indicate that it originally contained 100,000 characters in fifty-two chapters: seven "inner" chapters, twenty-eight "outer" chapters, and fourteen "miscellaneous" chapters. The present version of the text, which was edited by Guo Xiang (d. 312 C.E.), has 70,000 characters in thirty-three chapters: seven inner, fifteen outer, and eleven miscellaneous. Guo Xiang apparently discarded chapters he deemed spurious or unseemly (those dealing with superstitions and shamanic practices) and felt free to reorganize the content of others. Scholars generally consider the inner chapters—from which the first three selections below are drawn—to be the oldest core of the text, perhaps even written by Zhuang Zhou himself. But the heterogeneity of the remaining materials has thwarted specialists' efforts to establish their authorship and chronology (the final selection included here is from the outer chapters). During the Tang dynasty (618–907 C.E.), the *Book of Master Zhuang* was canonized as a "classic" with the title *Authentic Scripture of Southern Florescence* (*Nanhua zhenjing*); in subsequent dynasties it received further accolades and generated numerous commentaries.

The *Book of Master Zhuang* is notable not just for its literary qualities and memorable parables but also for its numerous descriptions of the various speculative trends and spiritual practices of the late Warring States period (403–221 B.C.E.). We find, for example, several accounts of a meeting between Laozi and Confucius: Laozi is always portrayed as the elder, and his Daoist teachings confound his celebrated interlocutor. Whereas *The Scripture of the Way and Its Virtue* (*Daode jing*) can be read as largely concerned with statecraft and governance, the *Book of Master Zhuang* explicitly rejects society and politics (see "Free and Easy Wandering") and presents a philosophy centered on the individual. It also includes evocative accounts of a special class of beings that dwell apart from the quotidian human realm and live in tune with the Dao (Way). They dine on a special diet of mist and mushrooms and share none of the anxieties of ordinary humans. These ageless "perfect persons" and "transcendents," existing in the world with a natural effortless spontaneity, have the ability to fly (see "Free and Easy Wandering" and "Mastering Life"). Sages and perfected beings, they were able attain long life by appearing useless, like the gnarled old trees and crippled Shu in the chapter titled "In the World of Men."

One of Zhuangzi's signature teachings is the need to maintain a resolute attitude of equanimity toward life and death (see the account of Laozi's death in "The Secret of Caring for Life"), since they are merely two inscrutable phases in the cosmic drama of change and transformation. The *Book of Master Zhuang* is also known for its critique of both Confucians and Mohists. Zhuangzi questions the accumulation of knowledge and application of reason; specifically, he points to the possibilities and limitations of language, which rests on human-centered conceptual categories that rigidly constrain the nature of life. Through varied stories that emphasize the skills of particular people, he presents a way of being in the world in harmony with the Dao that involves maintaining a balance of control (care and focused attention) and letting go or losing oneself in the task at hand to respond spontaneously to changes and difficulties (see "The Secret of Caring for Life" and "Mastering Life").

The *Book of Master Zhuang* has confounded generations of scholars seeking to render Zhuangzi's unique vision and evocative literary style in other languages. By the late nineteenth century at least three English translations of the text—done by Frederic Henry Balfour (1881), Herbert Giles (1889), and James Legge (1891)—were circulating in Europe and attracting considerable attention. Oscar Wilde, for example, in 1890 wrote an introduction to Zhuangzi and his teachings for a general readership (see "A Chinese Sage," below) after reading Giles's translation. Martin Buber, the prominent Jewish philosopher, essayist, and translator, appears to have availed himself of both Giles's and Legge's translations in producing his German version of the work in 1910 (see his *Zhuangzi* commentary, below). Henry Miller, in a book published in 1956, mentioned that among the books in his library was *Musings of a Chinese Mystic*—selections from Giles's translation—alongside Allen Watts's *The Spirit of Zen* (1936) and the *Tibetan Book of the Dead*. In 1965, the well-known Trappist monk Thomas Merton published *The Way of Chuang-Tzŭ*, his "readings" of the *Book of Master Zhuang*; since he did not know Chinese, he based his free renderings on existing translations into English, French, and German. Though the *Book of Master Zhuang* has not achieved the same international recognition as *The Scripture of the Way and Its Virtue*, in the West it has served as a catalyst for philosophical thought—in the twentieth century, for example, Martin Heidegger seems to have been aware of Zhuangzi and his writings—and for debate, especially among those working in comparative philosophy.

PRONOUNCING GLOSSARY

Lao Dan: *lao dawn*   Zhuangzi: *chuang-tzu*
Zhuang: *chuang*

Free and Easy Wandering

In the northern darkness there is a fish and his name is Kun.[1] The Kun is so huge I don't know how many thousand li[2] he measures. He changes and becomes a bird whose name is Peng. The back of the Peng measures I don't know how many thousand li across and, when he rises up and flies off, his wings are like clouds all over the sky. When the sea begins to move, this bird sets off for the southern darkness, which is the Lake of Heaven.

The *Universal Harmony* records various wonders, and it says: "When the Peng journeys to the southern darkness, the waters are roiled for three thousand li. He beats the whirlwind and rises ninety thousand li, setting off

TRANSLATED BY Burton Watson.

1. Literally, "fish roe" (a paradox, since the fish is described as huge).

2. One li measures about 1/3 mile.

on the sixth-month gale." Wavering heat, bits of dust, living things blown about by the wind—the sky looks very blue. Is that its real color, or is it because it is so far away and has no end? When the bird looks down, all he sees is blue too.

If water is not piled up deep enough, it won't have the strength to bear up a big boat. Pour a cup of water into a hollow in the floor and bits of trash will sail on it like boats. But set the cup there and it will stick fast, for the water is too shallow and the boat too large. If wind is not piled up deep enough, it won't have the strength to bear up great wings. Therefore when the Peng rises ninety thousand li, he must have the wind under him like that. Only then can he mount on the back of the wind, shoulder the blue sky, and nothing can hinder or block him. Only then can he set his eyes to the south.

The cicada and the little dove laugh at this, saying, "When we make an effort and fly up, we can get as far as the elm or the sapanwood tree, but sometimes we don't make it and just fall down on the ground. Now how is anyone going to go ninety thousand li to the south!"

If you go off to the green woods nearby, you can take along food for three meals and come back with your stomach as full as ever. If you are going a hundred li, you must grind your grain the night before; and if you are going a thousand li, you must start getting the provisions together three months in advance. What do these two creatures understand? Little understanding cannot come up to great understanding; the short-lived cannot come up to the long-lived.

How do I know this is so? The morning mushroom knows nothing of twilight and dawn; the summer cicada knows nothing of spring and autumn. They are the short-lived. South of Chu[3] there is a caterpillar which counts five hundred years as one spring and five hundred years as one autumn. Long, long ago there was a great rose of Sharon that counted eight thousand years as one spring and eight thousand years as one autumn. They are the long-lived. Yet Pengzi[4] alone is famous today for having lived a long time, and everybody tries to ape him. Isn't it pitiful!

Among the questions of Tang to Qi we find the same thing. In the bald and barren north, there is a dark sea, the Lake of Heaven. In it is a fish which is several thousand li across, and no one knows how long. His name is Kun. There is also a bird there, named Peng, with a back like Mount Tai[5] and wings like clouds filling the sky. He beats the whirlwind, leaps into the air, and rises up ninety thousand li, cutting through the clouds and mist, shouldering the blue sky, and then he turns his eyes south and prepares to journey to the southern darkness.

The little quail laughs at him, saying, "Where does he think *he's* going? I give a great leap and fly up, but I never get more than ten or twelve yards before I come down fluttering among the weeds and brambles. And that's the best kind of flying anyway! Where does he think *he's* going?" Such is the difference between big and little.

Therefore a man who has wisdom enough to fill one office effectively, good conduct enough to impress one community, virtue enough to please

3. A large ancient Chinese state.
4. A mythical figure who lived for hundreds of years.

5. A mountain in eastern China, important in the cult of official state rituals and to Daoism.

one ruler, or talent enough to be called into service in one state, has the same kind of self-pride as these little creatures. Song Rongzi[6] would certainly burst out laughing at such a man. The whole world could praise Song Rongzi and it wouldn't make him exert himself; the whole world could condemn him and it wouldn't make him mope. He drew a clear line between the internal and the external, and recognized the boundaries of true glory and disgrace. But that was all. As far as the world went, he didn't fret and worry, but there was still ground he left unturned.

Liezi[7] could ride the wind and go soaring around with cool and breezy skill, but after fifteen days he came back to earth. As far as the search for good fortune went, he didn't fret and worry. He escaped the trouble of walking, but he still had to depend on something to get around. If he had only mounted on the truth of Heaven and Earth, ridden the changes of the six breaths, and thus wandered through the boundless, then what would he have had to depend on?

Therefore I say, the Perfect Man has no self; the Holy Man has no merit; the Sage has no fame.

Yao wanted to cede the empire to Xu Yu.[8] "When the sun and moon have already come out," he said, "it's a waste of light to go on burning the torches, isn't it? When the seasonal rains are falling, it's a waste of water to go on irrigating the fields. If you took the throne, the world would be well ordered. I go on occupying it, but all I can see are my failings. I beg to turn over the world to you."

Xu Yu said, "You govern the world and the world is already well governed. Now if I take your place, will I be doing it for a name? But name is only the guest of reality—will I be doing it so I can play the part of a guest? When the tailorbird builds her nest in the deep wood, she uses no more than one branch. When the mole drinks at the river, he takes no more than a bellyful. Go home and forget the matter, my lord. I have no use for the rulership of the world! Though the cook may not run his kitchen properly, the priest and the impersonator of the dead at the sacrifice do not leap over the wine casks and sacrificial stands and go take his place."

Jian Wu said to Lian Shu, "I was listening to Jie Yu's[9] talk—big and nothing to back it up, going on and on without turning around. I was completely dumfounded at his words—no more end than the Milky Way, wild and wide of the mark, never coming near human affairs!"

"What were his words like?" asked Lian Shu.

"He said that there is a Holy Man living on faraway Gushe Mountain, with skin like ice or snow, and gentle and shy like a young girl. He doesn't eat the five grains,[1] but sucks the wind, drinks the dew, climbs up on the clouds and mist, rides a flying dragon, and wanders beyond the four seas. By concentrating his spirit, he can protect creatures from sickness and plague and make the harvest plentiful. I thought this was all insane and refused to believe it."

6. A political philosopher (4th century B.C.E.) who advocated peace and social harmony.
7. An early Daoist philosopher (4th century B.C.E.).
8. An ancient sage; Yao was a legendary emperor of China (ca. 23rd century B.C.E.).
9. The so-called madman of Chu; he appears in the Analects of Confucius (551–479 B.C.E.).
1. That is, the staple agricultural crops.

"You would!" said Lian Shu. "We can't expect a blind man to appreciate beautiful patterns or a deaf man to listen to bells and drums. And blindness and deafness are not confined to the body alone—the understanding has them too, as your words just now have shown. This man, with his virtue of his, is about to embrace the ten thousand things[2] and roll them into one. Though the age calls for reform, why should he wear himself out over the affairs of the world? There is nothing that can harm this man. Though flood waters pile up to the sky, he will not drown. Though a great drought melts metal and stone and scorches the earth and hills, he will not be burned. From his dust and leavings alone you could mold a Yao or a Shun![3] Why should he consent to bother about mere things?"

A man of Song who sold ceremonial hats made a trip to Yue, but the Yue people cut their hair short and tattoo their bodies and had no use for such things. Yao brought order to the people of the world and directed the government of all within the seas. But he went to see the Four Masters of the far away Gushe Mountain, [and when he got home] north of the Fen River, he was dazed and had forgotten his kingdom there.

Huizi[4] said to Zhuangzi, "The king of Wei gave me some seeds of a huge gourd. I planted them, and when they grew up, the fruit was big enough to hold five piculs.[5] I tried using it for a water container, but it was so heavy I couldn't lift it. I split it in half to make dippers, but they were so large and unwieldy that I couldn't dip them into anything. It's not that the gourds weren't fantastically big—but I decided they were no use and so I smashed them to pieces."

Zhuangzi said, "You certainly are dense when it comes to using big things! In Song there was a man who was skilled at making a salve to prevent chapped hands, and generation after generation his family made a living by bleaching silk in water. A traveler heard about the salve and offered to buy the prescription for a hundred measures of gold. The man called everyone to a family council. 'For generations we've been bleaching silk and we've never made more than a few measures of gold,' he said. 'Now, if we sell our secret, we can make a hundred measures in one morning. Let's let him have it!' The traveler got the salve and introduced it to the king of Wu, who was having trouble with the state of Yue. The king put the man in charge of his troops, and that winter they fought a naval battle with the men of Yue and gave them a bad beating. A portion of the conquered territory was awarded to the man as a fief. The salve had the power to prevent chapped hands in either case; but one man used it to get a fief, while the other one never got beyond silk bleaching—because they used it in different ways. Now you had a gourd big enough to hold five piculs. Why didn't you think of making it into a great tub so you could go floating around the rivers and lakes, instead of worrying because it was too big and unwieldy to dip into things! Obviously you still have a lot of underbrush in your head!"

2. That is, everything that exists.
3. The legendary Chinese ruler who followed Yao (ca. 23rd century B.C.E.).
4. A philosopher who specialized in logic (b. 380

B.C.E.); in Chinese texts, he often symbolizes an excess of intellectualism.
5. A picul is a unit of weight (about 133⅓ lbs.).

Huizi said to Zhuangzi, "I have a big tree called a *shu*. Its trunk is too gnarled and bumpy to apply a measuring line to, its branches too bent and twisty to match up to a compass or square. You could stand it by the road and no carpenter would look at it twice. Your words, too, are big and useless, and so everyone alike spurns them!"

Zhuangzi said, "Maybe you've never seen a wildcat or a weasel. It crouches down and hides, watching for something to come along. It leaps and races east and west, not hesitating to go high or low—until it falls into the trap and dies in the net. Then again there's the yak, big as a cloud covering the sky. It certainly knows how to be big, though it doesn't know how to catch rats. Now you have this big tree and you're distressed because it's useless. Why don't you plant it in Not-Even-Anything Village, or the field of Broad-and-Boundless, relax and do nothing by its side, or lie down for a free and easy sleep under it? Axes will never shorten its life, nothing can ever harm it. If there's no use for it, how can it come to grief or pain?"

The Secret of Caring for Life

Your life has a limit but knowledge has none. If you use what is limited to pursue what has no limit, you will be in danger. If you understand this and still strive for knowledge, you will be in danger for certain! If you do good, stay away from fame. If you do evil, stay away from punishments. Follow the middle; go by what is constant, and you can stay in one piece, keep yourself alive, look after your parents, and live out your years.

Cook Ding was cutting up an ox for Lord Wenhui. At every touch of his hand, every heave of his shoulder, every move of his feet, every thrust of his knee—zip! zoop! He slithered the knife along with a zing, and all was in perfect rhythm, as though he were performing the dance of the Mulberry Grove or keeping time to the Jingshou music.

"Ah, this is marvelous!" said Lord Wenhui. "Imagine skill reaching such heights!"

Cook Ding laid down his knife and replied, "What I care about is the Way, which goes beyond skill. When I first began cutting up oxen, all I could see was the ox itself. After three years I no longer saw the whole ox. And now—now I go at it by spirit and don't look with my eyes. Perception and understanding have come to a stop and spirit moves where it wants. I go along with the natural makeup, strike in the big hollows, guide the knife through the big openings, and follow things as they are. So I never touch the smallest ligament or tendon, much less a main joint.

"A good cook changes his knife once a year—because he cuts. A mediocre cook changes his knife once a month—because he hacks. I've had this knife of mine for nineteen years and I've cut up thousands of oxen with it, and yet the blade is as good as though it had just come from the grindstone. There are spaces between the joints, and the blade of the knife has really no thickness. If you insert what has no thickness into such spaces, then there's plenty of room—more than enough for the blade to play about in. That's why after nineteen years the blade of my knife is still as good as when it first came from the grindstone.

"However, whenever I come to a complicated place, I size up the difficulties, tell myself to watch out and be careful, keep my eyes on what I'm doing, work very slowly, and move the knife with the greatest subtlety, until—flop! the whole thing comes apart like a clod of earth crumbling to the ground. I stand there holding the knife and look all around me, completely satisfied and reluctant to move on, and then I wipe off the knife and put it away."

"Excellent!" said Lord Wenhui. "I have heard the words of Cook Ding and learned how to care for life!"

When Gongwen Xuan saw the Commander of the Right, he was startled and said, "What kind of man is this? How did he come to lose his foot? Was it Heaven? Or was it man?"

"It was Heaven, not man," said the commander. "When Heaven gave me life, it saw to it that I would be one-footed. Men's looks are given to them. So I know this was the work of Heaven and not of man. The swamp pheasant has to walk ten paces for one peck and a hundred paces for one drink, but it doesn't want to be kept in a cage. Though you treat it like a king, its spirit won't be content."

When Lao Dan[6] died, Qin Shi went to mourn for him; but after giving three cries, he left the room.

"Weren't you a friend of the Master?" asked Laozi's disciples.

"Yes."

"And you think it's all right to mourn him this way?"

"Yes," said Qin Shi. "At first I took him for a real man, but now I know he wasn't. A little while ago, when I went in to mourn, I found old men weeping for him as though they were weeping for a son, and young men weeping for him as though they were weeping for a mother. To have gathered a group like *that*, he must have done something to make them talk about him, though he didn't ask them to talk, or make them weep for him, though he didn't ask them to weep. This is to hide from Heaven, turn your back on the true state of affairs, and forget what you were born with. In the old days, this was called the crime of hiding from Heaven. Your master happened to come because it was his time, and he happened to leave because things follow along. If you are content with the time and willing to follow along, then grief and joy have no way to enter in. In the old days, this was called being freed from the bonds of God.

"Though the grease burns out of the torch, the fire passes on, and no one knows where it ends."

In the World of Men

Yan Hui[7] went to see Confucius and asked permission to take a trip.

"Where are you going?"

"I'm going to Wei."

"What will you do there?"

"I have heard that the ruler of Wei is very young. He acts in an independent manner, thinks little of how he rules his state, and fails to see his

6. That is, Lao Tzu or Laozi, who is credited with writing *The Scripture of the Way and Its Virtue* (*Daode jing*; see above).

7. The favorite student of Confucius. He, like many of the figures named in this chapter, appears in the *Analects*.

faults. It is nothing to him to lead his people into peril, and his dead are reckoned by swampfuls like so much grass. His people have nowhere to turn. I have heard you say, Master, 'Leave the state that is well ordered and go to the state in chaos! At the doctor's gate are many sick men.' I want to use these words as my standard, in hopes that I can restore his state to health."

"Ah," said Confucius, "you will probably go and get yourself executed, that's all. The Way doesn't want things mixed in with it. When it becomes a mixture, it becomes many ways; with many ways, there is a lot of bustle; and where there is a lot of bustle, there is trouble—trouble that has no remedy! The Perfect Man[8] of ancient times made sure that he had it in himself before he tried to give it to others. When you're not even sure what you've got in yourself, how do you have time to bother about what some tyrant is doing?

"Do you know what it is that destroys virtue, and where wisdom comes from? Virtue is destroyed by fame, and wisdom comes out of wrangling. Fame is something to beat people down with, and wisdom is a device for wrangling. Both are evil weapons—not the sort of thing to bring you success. Though your virtue may be great and your good faith unassailable, if you do not understand men's spirits, though your fame may be wide and you do not strive with others, if you do not understand men's minds, but instead appear before a tyrant and force him to listen to sermons on benevolence and righteousness, measures and standards—this is simply using other men's bad points to parade your own excellence. You will be called a plaguer of others. He who plagues others will be plagued in turn. You will probably be plagued by this man.

"And suppose he is the kind who actually delights in worthy men and hates the unworthy—then why does he need you to try to make him any different? You had best keep your advice to yourself! Kings and dukes always lord it over others and fight to win the argument. You will find your eyes growing dazed, your color changing, your mouth working to invent excuses, your attitude becoming more and more humble, until in your mind you end by supporting him. This is to pile fire on fire, to add water to water, and is called 'increasing the excessive.' If you give in at the beginning, there is no place to stop. Since your fervent advice is almost certain not to be believed, you are bound to die if you come into the presence of a tyrant.

"In ancient times Jie[9] put Guan Longfeng to death and Zhou[1] put Prince Bi Gan to death. Both Guan Longfeng and Prince Bi Gan were scrupulous in their conduct, bent down to comfort and aid the common people, and used their positions as ministers to oppose their superiors. Therefore their rulers, Jie and Zhou, utilized their scrupulous conduct as a means to trap them, for they were too fond of good fame. In ancient times Yao attacked Congzhi and Xu'ao, and Yu[2] attacked Yuhu, and these states were left empty and unpeopled, their rulers cut down. It was because they employed their armies constantly and never ceased their search for gain. All were seekers

---

8. *Zhenren*, a concept that first appears in this work and becomes important in later Daoism.
9. The last, ruthless king of the legendary Xia dynasty (ca. 21st–16th century B.C.E.); he came to symbolize evil rulers.

1. A king during the Shang dynasty (ca. 1600–1045 B.C.E.).
2. A legendary Chinese ruler, credited with founding the Xia dynasty.

of fame or gain—have you alone not heard of them? Even the sages cannot cope with men who are after fame or gain, much less a person like you!

"However, you must have some plan in mind. Come, tell me what it is."

Yan Hui said, "If I am grave and empty-hearted, diligent and of one mind, won't that do?"

"Goodness, how could *that* do? You may put on a fine outward show and seem very impressive, but you can't avoid having an uncertain look on your face, any more than an ordinary man can. And then you try to gauge this man's feelings and seek to influence his mind. But with him, what is called 'the virtue that advances a little each day' would not succeed, much less a great display of virtue! He will stick fast to his position and never be converted. Though he may make outward signs of agreement, inwardly he will not give it a thought! How could such an approach succeed?"

"Well then, suppose I am inwardly direct, outwardly compliant, and do my work through the examples of antiquity? By being inwardly direct, I can be the companion of Heaven. Being a companion of Heaven, I know that the Son of Heaven[3] and I are equally the sons of Heaven. Then why would I use my words to try to get men to praise me, or try to get them not to praise me? A man like this, people call The Child. This is what I mean by being a companion of Heaven.

"By being outwardly compliant, I can be a companion of men. Lifting up the tablet, kneeling, bowing, crouching down—this is the etiquette of a minister. Everybody does it, so why shouldn't I? If I do what other people do, they can hardly criticize me. This is what I mean by being a companion of men.

"By doing my work through the examples of antiquity, I can be the companion of ancient times. Though my words may in fact be lessons and reproaches, they belong to ancient times and not to me. In this way, though I may be blunt, I cannot be blamed. This is what I mean by being a companion of antiquity. If I go about it in this way, will it do?"

Confucius said, "Goodness, how could *that* do? You have too many policies and plans and you haven't seen what is needed. You will probably get off without incurring any blame, yes. But that will be as far as it goes. How do you think you can actually convert him? You are still making the mind your teacher!"

Yan Hui said, "I have nothing more to offer. May I ask the proper way?"

"You must fast!" said Confucius. "I will tell you what that means. Do you think it is easy to do anything while you have a mind? If you do, Bright Heaven will not sanction you."

Yan Hui said, "My family is poor. I haven't drunk wine or eaten any strong foods for several months. So can I be considered as having fasted?"

"That is the fasting one does before a sacrifice, not the fasting of the mind."

"May I ask what the fasting of the mind is?"

Confucius said, "Make your will one! Don't listen with your ears, listen with your mind. No, don't listen with your mind, but listen with your spirit. Listening stops with the ears, the mind stops with recognition, but spirit is empty and waits on all things. The Way gathers in emptiness alone. Emptiness is the fasting of the mind."

3. That is, the emperor.

Yan Hui said, "Before I heard this, I was certain that I was Hui. But now that I have heard it, there is no more Hui. Can this be called emptiness?"

"That's all there is to it," said Confucius. "Now I will tell you. You may go and play in his bird cage, but never be moved by fame. If he listens, then sing; if not, keep still. Have no gate, no opening, but make oneness your house and live with what cannot be avoided. Then you will be close to success.

"It is easy to keep from walking; the hard thing is to walk without touching the ground. It is easy to cheat when you work for men, but hard to cheat when you work for Heaven. You have heard of flying with wings, but you have never heard of flying without wings. You have heard of the knowledge that knows, but you have never heard of the knowledge that does not know. Look into that closed room, the empty chamber where brightness is born! Fortune and blessing gather where there is stillness. But if you do not keep still—this is what is called sitting but racing around. Let your ears and eyes communicate with what is inside, and put mind and knowledge on the outside. Then even gods and spirits will come to dwell, not to speak of men! This is the changing of the ten thousand things, the bond of Yu and Shun, the constant practice of Fu Xi and Ji Qu.[4] How much more should it be a rule for lesser men!"

Zigao,[5] duke of She, who was being sent on a mission to Qi, consulted Confucius. "The king is sending me on a very important mission. Qi will probably treat me with great honor but will be in no hurry to do anything more. Even a commoner cannot be forced to act, much less one of the feudal lords. I am very worried about it. You once said to me, 'In all affairs, whether large or small, there are few men who reach a happy conclusion except through the Way. If you do not succeed, you are bound to suffer from the judgment of men. If you do succeed, you are bound to suffer from the yin and yang.[6] To suffer no harm whether you succeed or not—only the man who has virtue can do that.' I am a man who eats plain food that is simply cooked, so that no one ever complains of the heat in my kitchens. Yet this morning I received my orders from the king and by evening I am gulping ice water—do you suppose I have developed some kind of internal fever? I have not even gone to Qi to see what the situation is like and already I am suffering from the yin and yang. And if I do not succeed, I am bound to suffer from the judgment of men. I will have both worries. As a minister, I am not capable of carrying out this mission. But perhaps you have some advice you can give me . . ."

Confucius said, "In the world, there are two great decrees: one is fate and the other is duty. That a son should love his parents is fate—you cannot erase this from his heart. That a subject should serve his ruler is duty—there is no place he can go and be without his ruler, no place he can escape to between heaven and earth. These are called the great decrees. Therefore, to serve your parents and be content to follow them anywhere—this

4. Two mythological rulers, renowned for their wisdom.
5. A high minister in Qu's government.
6. That is, an imbalance within the body. "Yin" is the female principle; the term originally referred to the shady side of a valley, and by extension it came to be associated with the dark, earth, dampness, and passivity. "Yang" is the male principle; the term originally referred to the sunny side of a valley, and by extension it came to be associated with the light, heaven, dryness, and activity.

is the perfection of filial piety. To serve your ruler and be content to do anything for him—this is the peak of loyalty. And to serve your own mind so that sadness or joy do not sway or move it; to understand what you can do nothing about and to be content with it as with fate—this is the perfection of virtue. As a subject and a son, you are bound to find things you cannot avoid. If you act in accordance with the state of affairs and forget about yourself, then what leisure will you have to love life and hate death? Act in this way and you will be all right.

"I want to tell you something else I have learned. In all human relations, if the two parties are living close to each other, they may form a bond through personal trust. But if they are far apart, they must use words to communicate their loyalty, and words must be transmitted by someone. To transmit words that are either pleasing to both parties or infuriating to both parties is one of the most difficult things in the world. Where both parties are pleased, there must be some exaggeration of the good points; and where both parties are angered, there must be some exaggeration of the bad points. Anything that smacks of exaggeration is irresponsible. Where there is irresponsibility, no one will trust what is said, and when that happens, the man who is transmitting the words will be in danger. Therefore the aphorism says, 'Transmit the established facts; do not transmit words of exaggeration.' If you do that, you will probably come out all right.

"When men get together to pit their strength in games of skill, they start off in a light and friendly mood, but usually end up in a dark and angry one, and if they go on too long they start resorting to various underhanded tricks. When men meet at some ceremony to drink, they start off in an orderly manner, but usually end up in disorder, and if they go on too long they start indulging in various irregular amusements. It is the same with all things. What starts out being sincere usually ends up being deceitful. What was simple in the beginning acquires monstrous proportions in the end.

"Words are like wind and waves; actions are a matter of gain and loss. Wind and waves are easily moved; questions of gain and loss easily lead to danger. Hence anger arises from no other cause than clever words and one-sided speeches. When animals face death, they do not care what cries they make; their breath comes in gasps and a wild fierceness is born in their hearts. [Men, too,] if you press them too hard, are bound to answer you with ill-natured hearts, though they do not know why they do so. If they themselves do not understand why they behave like this, then who knows where it will end?

"Therefore the aphorism says, 'Do not deviate from your orders; do not press for completion.' To go beyond the limit is excess; to deviate from orders or press for completion is a dangerous thing. A good completion takes a long time; a bad completion cannot be changed later. Can you afford to be careless?

"Just go along with things and let your mind move freely. Resign yourself to what cannot be avoided and nourish what is within you—this is best. What more do you have to do to fulfill your mission? Nothing is as good as following orders (obeying fate)—that's how difficult it is!"

Yan He, who had been appointed tutor to the crown prince, son of Duke Ling of Wei, went to consult Qu Boyu.[7] "Here is this man who by nature is

---

7. A high government minister of Wei (fl. ca. 500 B.C.E.). "Yan He:" a noted scholar.

lacking in virtue. If I let him go on with his unruliness I will endanger the state. If I try to impose some rule on him, I will endanger myself. He knows enough to recognize the faults of others, but he doesn't know his own faults. What can I do with a man like this?"

"A very good question," said Qu Boyu. "Be careful, be on your guard, and make sure that you yourself are in the right! In your actions it is best to follow along with him, and in your mind it is best to harmonize with him. However, these two courses involve certain dangers. Though you follow along, you don't want to be pulled into his doings, and though you harmonize, you don't want to be drawn out too far. If in your actions you follow along to the extent of being pulled in with him, then you will be overthrown, destroyed, wiped out, and brought to your knees. If in your mind you harmonize to the extent of being drawn out, then you will be talked about, named, blamed, and condemned. If he wants to be a child, be a child with him. If he wants to follow erratic ways, follow erratic ways with him. If he wants to be reckless, be reckless with him. Understand him thoroughly, and lead him to the point where he is without fault.

"Don't you know about the praying mantis that waved its arms angrily in front of an approaching carriage, unaware that they were incapable of stopping it? Such was the high opinion it had of its talents. Be careful, be on your guard! If you offend him by parading your store of talents, you will be in danger!

"Don't you know how the tiger trainer goes about it? He doesn't dare give the tiger any living thing to eat for fear it will learn the taste of fury by killing it. He doesn't dare give it any whole thing to eat for fear it will learn the taste of fury by tearing it apart. He gauges the state of the tiger's appetite and thoroughly understands its fierce disposition. Tigers are a different breed from men, and yet you can train them to be gentle with their keepers by following along with them. The men who get killed are the ones who go against them.

"The horse lover will use a fine box to catch the dung and a giant clam shell to catch the stale.[8] But if a mosquito or a fly lights on the horse and he slaps it at the wrong time, then the horse will break the bit, hurt its head, and bang its chest. The horse lover tries to think of everything, but his affection leads him into error. Can you afford to be careless?"

Carpenter Shi went to Qi and, when he got to Crooked Shaft, he saw a serrate oak standing by the village shrine. It was broad enough to shelter several thousand oxen and measured a hundred spans around, towering above the hills. The lowest branches were eighty feet from the ground, and a dozen or so of them could have been made into boats. There were so many sightseers that the place looked like a fair, but the carpenter didn't even glance around and went on his way without stopping. His apprentice stood staring for a long time and then ran after Carpenter Shi and said, "Since I first took up my ax and followed you, Master, I have never seen timber as beautiful as this. But you don't even bother to look, and go right on without stopping. Why is that?"

8. Urine.

"Forget it—say no more!" said the carpenter. "It's a worthless tree! Make boats out of it and they'd sink; make coffins and they'd rot in no time; make vessels and they'd break at once. Use it for doors and it would sweat sap like pine; use it for posts and the worms would eat them up. It's not a timber tree—there's nothing it can be used for. That's how it got to be that old!"

After Carpenter Shi had returned home, the oak tree appeared to him in a dream and said, "What are you comparing me with? Are you comparing me with those useful trees? The cherry apple, the pear, the orange, the citron, the rest of those fructiferous[9] trees and shrubs—as soon as their fruit is ripe, they are torn apart and subjected to abuse. Their big limbs are broken off, their little limbs are yanked around. Their utility makes life miserable for them, and so they don't get to finish out the years Heaven gave them, but are cut off in mid-journey. They bring it on themselves—the pulling and tearing of the common mob. And it's the same way with all other things.

"As for me, I've been trying a long time to be of no use, and though I almost died, I've finally got it. This is of great use to me. If I had been of some use, would I ever have grown this large? Moreover you and I are both of us things. What's the point of this—things condemning things? You, a worthless man about to die—how do you know I'm a worthless tree?"

When Carpenter Shi woke up, he reported his dream. His apprentice said, "If it's so intent on being of no use, what's it doing there at the village shrine?"

"Shhh! Say no more! It's only *resting* there. If we carp and criticize, it will merely conclude that we don't understand it. Even if it weren't at the shrine, do you suppose it would be cut down? It protects itself in a different way from ordinary people. If you try to judge it by conventional standards, you'll be way off!"

Ziqi of Nanbo was wandering around the Hill of Shang when he saw a huge tree there, different from all the rest. A thousand teams of horses could have taken shelter under it and its shade would have covered them all. Ziqi said, "What tree is this? It must certainly have some extraordinary usefulness!" But, looking up, he saw that the smaller limbs were gnarled and twisted, unfit for beams or rafters, and looking down, he saw that the trunk was pitted and rotten and could not be used for coffins. He licked one of the leaves and it blistered his mouth and made it sore. He sniffed the odor and it was enough to make a man drunk for three days. "It turns out to be a completely unusable tree," said Ziqi, "and so it has been able to grow this big. Aha!—it is this unusableness that the Holy Man makes use of!"

The region of Jingshi in Song is fine for growing catalpas, cypresses, and mulberries. But those that are more than one or two arm-lengths around are cut down for people who want monkey perches; those that are three or four spans around are cut down for the ridgepoles of tall roofs; and those that are seven or eight spans are cut down for the families of nobles or rich merchants who want side boards for coffins. So they never get to live out the years Heaven gave them, but are cut down in mid-journey by axes. This

9. Fruit-bearing.

is the danger of being usable. In the Jie sacrifice,[1] oxen with white fore-heads, pigs with turned-up snouts, and men with piles cannot be offered to the river. This is something all the shamans know, and hence they consider them inauspicious creatures. But the Holy Man for the same reason consid-ers them highly auspicious.

There's Crippled Shu—chin stuck down in his navel, shoulders up above his head, pigtail pointing at the sky, his five organs[2] on the top, his two thighs pressing his ribs. By sewing and washing, he gets enough to fill his mouth; by handling a winnow and sifting out the good grain, he makes enough to feed ten people. When the authorities call out the troops, he stands in the crowd waving good-by; when they get up a big work party, they pass him over because he's a chronic invalid. And when they are dol-ing out grain to the ailing, he gets three big measures and ten bundles of firewood. With a crippled body, he's still able to look after himself and fin-ish out the years Heaven gave him. How much better, then, if he had crip-pled virtue!

When Confucius visited Chu, Jie Yu, the madman of Chu, wandered by his gate crying, "Phoenix, phoenix, how has virtue failed! The future you cannot wait for; the past you cannot pursue. When the world has the Way, the sage succeeds; when the world is without the Way, the sage survives. In times like the present, we do well to escape penalty. Good fortune is light as a feather, but nobody knows how to pick it up. Misfortune is heavy as the earth, but nobody knows how to stay out of its way. Leave off, leave off—this teaching men virtue! Dangerous, dangerous—to mark off the ground and run! Fool, fool—don't spoil my walking! I walk a crooked way—don't step on my feet. The mountain trees do themselves harm; the grease in the torch burns itself up. The cinnamon can be eaten and so it gets cut down; the lacquer tree can be used and so it gets hacked apart. All men know the use of the useful, but nobody knows the use of the useless!"

Mastering Life

He who has mastered the true nature of life does not labor over what life cannot do. He who has mastered the true nature of fate does not labor over what knowledge cannot change. He who wants to nourish his body must first of all turn to things. And yet it is possible to have more than enough things and for the body still to go unnourished. He who has life must first of all see to it that it does not leave the body. And yet it is possible for life never to leave the body and still fail to be preserved. The coming of life can-not be fended off, its departure cannot be stopped. How pitiful the men of the world, who think that simply nourishing the body is enough to preserve life! Then why is what the world does worth doing? It may not be worth doing, and yet it cannot be left undone—this is unavoidable.

---

1. Apparently a sacrifice related to the expiation of sins.
2. The eyes, tongue, mouth, nose, and ears.

He who wants to avoid doing anything for his body had best abandon the world. By abandoning the world, he can be without entanglements. Being without entanglements, he can be upright and calm. Being upright and calm, he can be born again with others. Being born again, he can come close [to the Way].

But why is abandoning the affairs of the world worth while, and why is forgetting life worth while? If you abandon the affairs of the world, your body will be without toil. If you forget life, your vitality will be unimpaired. With your body complete and your vitality made whole again, you may become one with Heaven. Heaven and earth are the father and mother of the ten thousand things. They join to become a body; they part to become a beginning. When the body and vitality are without flaw, this is called being able to shift. Vitality added to vitality, you return to become the Helper of Heaven.

Master Liezi said to the Barrier Keeper Yin,[3] "The Perfect Man can walk under water without choking, can tread on fire without being burned, and can travel above the ten thousand things without being frightened. May I ask how he manages this?"

The Barrier Keeper Yin replied, "This is because he guards the pure breath—it has nothing to do with wisdom, skill, determination, or courage. Sit down and I will tell you about it. All that have faces, forms, voices, colors—these are all mere things. How could one thing and another thing be far removed from each other? And how could any of them be worth considering as a predecessor? They are forms, colors—nothing more. But things have their creation in what has no form, and their conclusion in what has no change. If a man can get hold of *this* and exhaust it fully, then how can things stand in his way? He may rest within the bounds that know no excess, hide within the borders that know no source, wander where the ten thousand things have their end and beginning, unify his nature, nourish his breath, unite his virtue, and thereby communicate with that which creates all things. A man like this guards what belongs to Heaven and keeps it whole. His spirit has no flaw, so how can things enter in and get at him?

"When a drunken man falls from a carriage, though the carriage may be going very fast, he won't be killed. He has bones and joints the same as other men, and yet he is not injured as they would be, because his spirit is whole. He didn't know he was riding, and he doesn't know he has fallen out. Life and death, alarm and terror do not enter his breast, and so he can bang against things without fear of injury. If he can keep himself whole like this by means of wine, how much more can he keep himself whole by means of Heaven! The sage hides himself in Heaven—hence there is nothing that can do him harm.

"A man seeking revenge does not go so far as to smash the sword of his enemy; a man, no matter how hot-tempered, does not rail at the tile that happens to fall on him. To know that all things in the world are equal and

---

3. The gatekeeper who persuaded Laozi to transmit his knowledge, which became *The Scripture of the Way and Its Virtue.*

the same—this is the only way to eliminate the chaos of attack and battle and the harshness of punishment and execution!

"Do not try to develop what is natural to man; develop what is natural to Heaven. He who develops Heaven benefits life; he who develops man injures life. Do not reject what is of Heaven, do not neglect what is of man, and the people will be close to the attainment of Truth."

When Confucius was on his way to Chu, he passed through a forest where he saw a hunchback catching cicadas with a sticky pole as easily as though he were grabbing them with his hand.

Confucius said, "What skill you have! Is there a special way to this?"

"I have a way," said the hunchback. "For the first five or six months I practice balancing two balls on top of each other on the end of the pole and, if they don't fall off, I know I will lose very few cicadas. Then I balance three balls and, if they don't fall off, I know I'll lose only one cicada in ten. Then I balance five balls and, if they don't fall off, I know it will be as easy as grabbing them with my hand. I hold my body like a stiff tree trunk and use my arm like an old dry limb. No matter how huge heaven and earth, or how numerous the ten thousand things, I'm aware of nothing but cicada wings. Not wavering, not tipping, not letting any of the other ten thousand things take the place of those cicada wings—how can I help but succeed?"

Confucius turned to his disciples and said, "He keeps his will undivided and concentrates his spirit—that would serve to describe our hunchback gentleman here, would it not?"

Yan Yuan said to Confucius, "I once crossed the gulf at Goblet Deeps and the ferryman handled the boat with supernatural skill. I asked him, 'Can a person learn how to handle a boat?' and he replied, 'Certainly. A good swimmer will get the knack of it in no time. And, if a man can swim under water, he may never have seen a boat before and still he'll know how to handle it!' I asked him what he meant by that, but he wouldn't tell me. May I venture to ask you what it means?"

Confucius said, "A good swimmer will get the knack of it in no time—that means he's forgotten the water. If a man can swim under water, he may never have seen a boat before and still he'll know how to handle it—that's because he sees the water as so much dry land, and regards the capsizing of a boat as he would the overturning of a cart. The ten thousand things may all be capsizing and turning over at the same time right in from of him and it can't get at him and affect what's inside—so where could he go and not be at ease?

"When you're betting for tiles in an archery contest, you shoot with skill. When you're betting for fancy belt buckles, you worry about your aim. And when you're betting for real gold, you're a nervous wreck. Your skill is the same in all three cases—but because one prize means more to you than another, you let outside considerations weigh on your mind. He who looks too hard at the outside gets clumsy on the inside."

Tian Kaizhi went to see Duke Wei of Zhou. Duke Wei said, "I hear that Zhu Xian is studying how to live. You are a friend of his—what have you heard from him on the subject?"

Tian Kaizhi said, "I merely wield a broom and tend his gate and garden—how should I have heard anything from the Master?"

Duke Wei said, "Don't be modest, Master Tian. I am anxious to hear about it."

Tian Kaizhi said, "I have heard the Master say, 'He who is good at nourishing life is like a herder of sheep—he watches for stragglers and whips them up.'"

"What does that mean?" asked Duke Wei.

Tian Kaizhi said, "In Lu there was Shan Bao—he lived among the cliffs, drank only water, and didn't go after gain like other people. He went along like that for seventy years and still had the complexion of a little child. Unfortunately, he met a hungry tiger who killed him and ate him up. Then there was Zhang Yi—there wasn't one of the great families and fancy mansions that he didn't rush off to visit. He went along like that for forty years, and then he developed an internal fever, fell ill, and died. Shan Bao looked after what was on the inside and the tiger ate up his outside. Zhang Yi looked after what was on the outside and the sickness attacked him from the inside. Both these men failed to give a lash to the stragglers."

Confucius has said, "Don't go in and hide; don't come out and shine; stand stock-still in the middle." He who can follow these three rules is sure to be called the finest. When people are worried about the safety of the roads, if they hear that one traveler in a party of ten has been murdered, then fathers and sons, elder and younger brothers will warn each other to be careful and will not venture out until they have a large escort of armed men. That's wise of them, isn't it? But when it comes to what people really ought to be worried about—the time when they are lying in bed or sitting around eating and drinking—then they don't have sense enough to take warning. That's a mistake!"

The Invocator of the Ancestors, dressed in his black, square-cut robes, peered into the pigpen and said, "Why should you object to dying? I'm going to fatten you for three months, practice austerities for ten days, fast for three days, spread the white rushes, and lay your shoulders and rump on the carved sacrificial stand—you'll go along with that, won't you? True, if I were planning things from the point of view of a pig, I'd say it would be better to eat chaff and bran and stay right there in the pen. But if I were planning for myself, I'd say that if I could be honored as a high official while I lived, and get to ride in a fine hearse and lie among the feathers and trappings when I died, I'd go along with that. Speaking for the pig, I'd give such a life a flat refusal, but speaking for myself, I'd certainly accept. I wonder why I look at things differently from a pig?"

Duke Huan was hunting in a marsh, with Guan Zhong[4] as his carriage driver, when he saw a ghost. The duke grasped Guan Zhong's hand and said, "Father Zhong, what do you see?"

"I don't see anything," replied Guan Zhong.

When the duke returned home, he fell into a stupor, grew ill, and for several days did not go out.

A gentleman of Qi named Huangzi Gao'ao said, "Your Grace, you are doing this injury to yourself! How could a ghost have the power to injure you! If the vital breath that is stored up in a man becomes dispersed and does not return, then he suffers a deficiency. If it ascends and fails to descend again, it causes him to be chronically irritable. If it descends and does not ascend again, it causes him to be chronically forgetful. And if it neither ascends nor descends, but gathers in the middle of the body in the region of the heart, then he becomes ill."

Duke Huan said, "But do ghosts really exist?"

"Indeed they do. There is the Li on the hearth and the Chi in the stove. The heap of clutter and trash just inside the gate is where the Leiting lives. In the northeast corner the Bei'a and Guilong leap about, and the northwest corner is where the Yiyang lives. In the water is the Gangxiang; on the hills, the Xin; in the mountains, the Gui; in the meadows, the Panghuang, and in the marshes, the Weituo."

The duke said, "May I ask what a Weituo looks like?"

Huangzi said, "The Weituo is as big as a wheel hub, as tall as a carriage shaft, has a purple robe and a vermilion hat and, as creatures go, is very ugly. When it hears the sound of thunder or a carriage, it grabs its head and stands up. Anyone who sees it will soon become a dictator."

Duke Huan's face lit up and he said with a laugh, "*That* must have been what I saw!" Then he straightened his robe and hat and sat up on the mat with Huangzi, and before the day was over, though he didn't notice it, his illness went away.

Ji Xingzi was training gamecocks for the king. After ten days the king asked if they were ready.

"Not yet. They're too haughty and rely on their nerve."

Another ten days and the king asked again.

"Not yet. They still respond to noises and movements."

Another ten days and the king asked again.

"Not yet. They still look around fiercely and are full of spirit."

Another ten days and the king asked again.

"They're close enough. Another cock can crow and they show no sign of change. Look at them from a distance and you'd think they were made of wood. Their virtue is complete. Other cocks won't dare face up to them, but will turn and run."

Confucius was seeing the sights at Lüliang, where the water falls from a height of thirty fathoms and races and boils along for forty li, so swift that no fish or other water creature can swim in it. He saw a man dive into the water and, supposing that the man was in some kind of trouble and intended to end his life, he ordered his disciples to line up on the bank and pull the man out. But after the man had gone a couple of hundred paces, he came out of the water and began strolling along the base of the embankment, his hair streaming down, singing a song. Confucius ran after him and said, "At first I thought you were a ghost, but now I see you're a man. May I ask if you have some special way of staying afloat in the water?"

"I have no way. I began with what I was used to, grew up with my nature, and let things come to completion with fate. I go under with the swirls and come out with the eddies, following along the way the water goes and never thinking about myself. That's how I can stay afloat."

Confucius said, "What do you mean by saying that you began with what you were used to, grew up with your nature, and let things come to completion with fate?"

"I was born on the dry land and felt safe on the dry land—that was what I was used to. I grew up with the water and felt safe in the water—that was my nature. I don't know why I do what I do—that's fate."

Woodworker Qing carved a piece of wood and made a bell stand, and when it was finished, everyone who saw it marveled, for it seemed to be the work of gods or spirits. When the marquis of Lu saw it, he asked, "What art is it you have?"

Qing replied, "I am only a craftsman—how would I have any art? There is one thing, however. When I am going to make a bell stand, I never let it wear out my energy. I always fast in order to still my mind. When I have fasted for three days, I no longer have any thought of congratulations or rewards, of titles or stipends. When I have fasted for five days, I no longer have any thought of praise or blame, of skill or clumsiness. And when I have fasted for seven days, I am so still that I forget I have four limbs and a form and body. By that time, the ruler and his court no longer exist for me. My skill is concentrated and all outside distractions fade away. After that, I go into the mountain forest and examine the Heavenly nature of the trees. If I find one of superlative form, and I can see a bell stand there, I put my hand to the job of carving; if not, I let it go. This way I am simply matching up 'Heaven' with 'Heaven.' That's probably the reason that people wonder if the results were not made by spirits."

Dongye Ji was displaying his carriage driving before Duke Zhuang. He drove back and forth as straight as a measuring line and wheeled to left and right as neat as a compass-drawn curve. Duke Zhuang concluded that even Cao Fu[5] could do no better, and ordered him to make a hundred circuits and then return to the palace. Yan He happened along at the moment and went in to see the duke. "Dongye Ji's horses are going to break down," he said. The duke was silent and gave no answer. In a little while Dongye Ji returned, his horses having in fact broken down. The duke asked Yan He, "How did you know that was going to happen?" Yan He said, "The strength of the horses was all gone and still he was asking them to go on—that's why I said they would break down."

Artisan Chui could draw as true as a compass or a T square because his fingers changed along with things and he didn't let his mind get in the way. Therefore his Spirit Tower[6] remained unified and unobstructed.

You forget your feet when the shoes are comfortable. You forget your waist when the belt is comfortable. Understanding forgets right and wrong

5. A famous chariot driver.   6. A Daoist term for the mind [translator's note].

when the mind is comfortable. There is no change in what is inside, no following what is outside, when the adjustment to events is comfortable. You begin with what is comfortable and never experience what is uncomfortable when you know the comfort of forgetting what is comfortable.

A certain Sun Xiu appeared at the gate of Master Bian Qingzi to pay him a call. "When I was living in the village," he said, "no one ever said I lacked good conduct. When I faced difficulty, no one ever said I lacked courage. Yet when I worked the fields, it never seemed to be a good year for crops, and when I served the ruler, it never seemed to be a good time for advancement. So I am an outcast from the villages, an exile from the towns. What crime have I committed against Heaven? Why should I meet this fate?"

Master Bian said, "Have you never heard how the Perfect Man conducts himself? He forgets his liver and gall and thinks no more about his eyes and ears. Vague and aimless, he wanders beyond the dirt and dust; free and easy, tending to nothing is his job. This is what is called 'doing but not looking for any thanks, bringing up but not bossing.'[7] Now you show off your wisdom in order to astound the ignorant, work at your good conduct in order to distinguish yourself from the disreputable, going around bright and shining as though you were carrying the sun and moon in your hand! You've managed to keep your body in one piece, you have all the ordinary nine openings,[8] you haven't been struck down midway by blindness or deafness, lameness or deformity—compared to a lot of people, you're a lucky man. How do you have any time to go around complaining against Heaven? Be on your way!"

After Master Sun had left, Master Bian went back into the house, sat down for a while, and then looked up to heaven and sighed. One of his disciples asked, "Why does my teacher sigh?"

Master Bian said, "Just now Sun Xiu came to see me, and I described to him the virtue of the Perfect Man. I'm afraid he was very startled and may end up in a complete muddle."

"Surely not," said the disciple. "Was what Master Sun said right and what my teacher said wrong? If so, then wrong can certainly never make a muddle out of right. Or was what Master Sun said wrong and what my teacher said right? If so, then he must already have been in a muddle when he came here, so what's the harm?"

"You don't understand," said Master Bian. "Once long ago a bird alighted in the suburbs of the Lu capital. The ruler of Lu was delighted with it, had a Tailao sacrifice[9] prepared for it to feast on, and the Nine Shao music performed for its enjoyment. But the bird immediately began to look unhappy and dazed, and did not dare to eat or drink. This is what is called trying to nourish a bird with what would nourish you. If you want to nourish a bird with what will nourish a bird, you had best let it roost in the deep

---

7. See *The Scripture of the Way and Its Virtue*, chapters 10, 51.
8. The eyes, ears, nostrils, and mouth, plus either the urethra and anus or the tongue and throat.
9. An elaborate sacrifice, consisting of an ox, a sheep, and a pig.

forest, float oh the rivers and lakes, and live on snakes—then it can feel at ease.

"Now Sun Xiu is a man of ignorance and little learning. For me to describe to him the virtue of the Perfect Man is like taking a mouse for a ride in a carriage or trying to delight a quail with the music of bells and drums. How could he help but be startled?"

MASTER OF HUAINAN
(Huainan-zi)

The *Master of Huainan* (*Huainan-zi*) is a work that was compiled at the court of Liu An, the king of Huainan, in the second century B.C.E. following a series of scholarly debates; it was presented to the emperor in 139 B.C.E. The text's twenty-one chapters—or twenty-eight, in an alternate division of the same text—include a sophisticated philosophy of statecraft as they seek to provide the monarch with information about various forms of knowledge and rich accounts of self-cultivation practices, all aimed at bringing about and maintaining a harmonious sociopolitical order. This highly syncretic text is valuable today due to its encyclopedic inclusion of material on Confucian, Daoist, and Mohist philosophies. But despite the eclecticism of its material, the *Master of Huainan* is fundamentally Daoist in orientation. An edition dating to the Northern Song dynasty (960–1127) or earlier was later included in the Daoist canon, though many other versions circulated.

The *Master of Huainan* is a fascinating compilation that synthesizes many of the important teachings found in *The Scripture of the Way and Its Virtue* (*Daode jing*; see above) and the *Book of Master Zhuang* (*Zhuangzi*; see above), which are both frequently quoted or paraphrased. For example, the chapter titled "Originating in the Way"—which is traditionally understood as laying out the work's overall framework and fundamental principles—presents a cosmology of the Way (Dao) that is clearly indebted to *The Scripture of the Way and Its Virtue.* "Activating the Genuine," on the other hand, offers a picture of human perfection that is indebted to the *Book of Master Zhuang.*

The overarching emphasis in the *Master of Huainan* is on the Dao as creative power, the basis for the potency in all things that enables them to be naturally what they are. Moreover, an important feature of the work's comprehensive vision is its stress on the resonance between all levels of reality—especially between the level of the ethereal, undifferentiated Dao and the level of phenomenal existence, with its particular affairs and manifestations. "The myriad things definitely accord with what is natural to them, so why should sages interfere with this?" ("Originating in the Way"). In place of a Confucian supreme ruler, supported by laws, hierarchies, and institutions, the *Master of Huainan* highlights an ideal type of sage who—having realized the Way—fulfills what is his authentic nature and lives harmoniously with the world, without thought of accumulating wealth, reputation, or other external things.

PRONOUNCING GLOSSARY

Huainan: *hwai-nawn*   Qi/qi: *chi*
Huainan-zi: *hwai-nawn-tzu*

From *One. Originating in the Way*

1.3

The most exalted Way
      generates the myriad things but does not possess them,
      completes the transforming images[1] but does not dominate them.
Creatures that walk on hooves and breathe through beaks, that fly through
the air and wriggle on the ground,
    depend on it for life, yet none understands its Potency;
    depend on it for death, yet none is able to resent it.
Those who attain it and profit are unable to praise it;
those who use it and lose are unable to blame it.
      It gathers and collects yet is not any richer for it.
      It bestows and confers yet it not diminished by it.
      It cycles endlessly yet cannot be fathomed.
      It is delicate and minute yet cannot be exhausted.
      Pile it up, but it will not get higher;
      Collapse it, but it will not get lower.
      Add to it, but it will not increase.
      Take away from it, but it will not decrease.
      Split it, but it will not get thinner.
      Kill it, but it will not be destroyed.
      Bore into it, but it will not deepen.
      Fill it in, but it will not get shallower.
      Hazy! Nebulous! You cannot imagine it.
      Nebulous! Hazy! Your use will not exhaust it.
      Dark! Obscure! It responds formlessly.
      Deep! Penetrating! It does not act in vain.
It rolls and unrolls with the firm and the pliant.
It bends and straightens with the yin and the yang.

1.7

    Plants like duckweed take root in water.
    Plants like trees take root on land.
    Birds beat their wings in the air in order to fly.
    Wild beasts stomp on solid ground in order to run.
    Serpents and dragons live in the water.
    Tigers and leopards live in the mountains.
This is the nature of Heaven and Earth.
    When two pieces of wood are rubbed together, they make fire.
    When metal and fire are pushed together, the metal becomes
      molten.
    Round things always spin.
    Hollow things excel at floating.
This is their natural propensity.
Therefore, when spring winds arrive, then sweet rains will fall; they vitalize
    and nurture the myriad things.

TRANSLATED BY John S. Major, Sarah A. Queen, Andrew Seth Meyer, and Harold Roth, with contributions by Michael Puett and Judson Murray.

1. The eight trigrams of the *Book of Changes* (*Yijing* or *I Ching*, traditionally dated to the 12th century B.C.E.), a volume of divination and cosmology.

Those with wings sit on their nests and hatch eggs.
Those with hair gestate and give birth to their young.
Grasses and trees become lush and flowering.
Birds and wild beasts have eggs and embryos.
No one sees what effects these things, but these achievements are
completed.
The autumn winds cause frost to descend,
  and the living things [that are reached by the frost] are snapped and
    injured.
Eagles and falcons hawkishly seize [their prey];
swarming insects hibernate;
grasses and trees die back to their roots;
fish and tortoises plunge together into the deep.
No one sees what effects these things; they just disappear into the
Formless.
Tree dwellers nest in the woods;
water dwellers live in caves.
Wild beasts have beds of straw;
human beings have houses.
Hilly places are suitable for oxen and horses.
For travel by boat, it is good to have a lot of water.
The Xiongnu[2] produce rancid animal-skin garments,
The Gan and Yue [peoples] make thin clothes of *pueraria*[3] fabric.
Each produces what it urgently needs
in order to adapt to the aridity or dampness.
Each accords with where it lives
in order to protect against the cold and the heat.
All things attain what is suitable to them;
things accord with their niches.

From this viewpoint, the myriad things definitely accord with what is
natural to them, so why should sages interfere with this?

1.8

To the south of the Nine Passes,[4] tasks on dry land are few, while tasks on
water are many. So the people cut their hair and tattoo their bodies in order
to resemble scaly creatures. They wear short pants, not long trousers, in
order to make swimming easier. And they have short sleeves in order to
make poling their boats easier. In doing this, they are adapting [to their
natural environment].

To the north of the Yanmen Pass, the Di[5] tribes do not eat grain. They
devalue the aged and value the strong, and it is a custom to esteem those
with strength of vital energy. People there do not unstring their bows, nor do

---

2. Pastoral nomads who ruled much of Central
Asia and often threatened the northern border of
the Chinese imperium. Chinese sources depict
them as the uncultured opposite of the cultured
Han Chinese.
3. A plant with fine fibers. "Gan and Yue": two
linguistic groups, primarily located in southern
China.

4. Dafen, Min'ou, Jingruan, Fangcheng, Yaoban,
Jingxing, Lingci, Gouzhu, and Juyong Passes,
which are scattered across China. The cosmology of the *Master of Huainan* is based on the
number nine; in addition to the passes, there are
Nine Continents, Nine Provinces, Nine Mountains, and Nine Rivers.
5. An ethnic group in northern China.

they remove the bridles from their horses. In doing this, they are adjusting [to their natural environment].

Thus when Yu[6] went to the Country of the Naked, he removed his clothes when he entered and put them back on when he left. In doing this he was adapting [to his natural environment]. Nowadays, if those who transplant trees neglect the yin and the yang aspects of their natures, then none will not wither and die. Thus if you plant a mandarin orange tree north of the Yangzi, it will transform into an inedible orange. A mynah bird cannot live beyond [i.e., to the north of] the Qi River, and if a badger crosses [to the south of] the Min River, it will die. Physical form and innate nature cannot be changed, and propensity and locale cannot be shifted.
Therefore,

> those who break through to the Way return to clarity and tranquillity.
> Those who look deeply into things end up not acting on them.
> If you use calmness to nourish your nature,
> and use quietude to transfix your spirit,
> then you will enter the heavenly gateway.

What we call "Heaven"

> is pure and untainted,
> unadorned and plain,

and has never begun to be tainted with impurities.
What we call "human"

> is biased because of wisdom and precedent.
> Devious and deceptive,

it is what looks back to past generations and interacts with the vulgar.
Thus,

> that the ox treads on cloven hooves and grows horns
> and that the horse has a mane and square hooves,

This is heavenly [i.e., natural].

> Yet to put a bit in a horse's mouth
> and to put a ring through an ox's nose,

This is human.

> Those who comply with Heaven roam with the Way.
> Those who follow the human interact with the mundane.

Now,

> you cannot talk to a fish in a well about great things because it is confined by its narrow space.
> You cannot talk to a summer bug about the cold because it is restricted to its season.
> You cannot talk to petty scholars about the Utmost Way because they are confined by the mundane and bound up by their teaching.

---

6. The mythological hero who reputedly founded China's first dynasty, the Xia (ca. 21st–16th century B.C.E.).

Thus sages

>   do not allow the human to obscure the heavenly
>   and do not let desire corrupt their genuine responses.
>   They hit the mark without scheming;
>   they are sincere without speaking;
>   they attain without planning;
>   they complete without striving.

Their vital essence circulates into the Magical Storehouse,[7] and they become human along with what fashions and transforms them.

1.10

Thus those who attain the Way:
>   Their wills are supple, but their deeds are strong.
>   Their minds are empty, but their responses are dead on.

What we mean by a supple will is
>   being pliant and soft, calm, and tranquil;
>   hiding when others do not dare to;
>   acting when others are unable to;
>   being calm and without worry;
>   acting without missing the right moment;
>   and cycling and revolving with the myriad things.
>   Never anticipating or initiating
>   but just responding to things when stimulated.

Therefore,
>   the honored invariably take their titles from the base,
>   and those of high station invariably take what is below as their foundation.
>   They rely on the small to embrace the great;
>   they rest in the inner to regulate the outer;
>   they act pliantly to become firm;
>   they utilize weakness to become strong;
>   they cycle through transformations and push where things are shifting;
>   they attain the Way of the One and use the few to correct the many.

What we mean by strength of deeds is
>   responding with alacrity when encountering alterations;
>   pushing away disasters and warding off difficulties;
>   being so strong that there is nothing unvanquished;
>   facing enemies, there are none that are not humiliated;
>   responding to transformations by gauging the proper moment
>   and being harmed by nothing.

Therefore,
>   if you wish to be firm, you must guard it by being pliant.
>   If you wish to be strong, you must protect it by being supple.
>   When you accumulate pliability, you become firm.
>   When you accumulate suppleness, you become strong.
>   Keep a close watch on what you are accumulating
>   in order to know the tendencies toward fortune or misfortune.

---

7. Also called the Numinous Storehouse, as later in this selection: a location in the body identified with the heart (xin) or Central Cinnabar Field (dantian). It is depicted as a storehouse for spirits and emotions that enables the practitioner to pursue the Way without distractions.

Strength defeats what is not its equal. When it encounters its equal, it is neutralized. Pliability defeats what exceeds itself. Its power cannot be measured.

Thus when an army is strong, it will be destroyed.
When a tree is strong, it will be broken.
When leather armor is hard, it will split open.
Because teeth are harder than the tongue, they wear out first.
Therefore, the pliant and weak are the supports of life,
and the hard and strong are the disciples of death.

1.13

Emerging into life, entering into death;
from Nothing treading into Something;
from Something treading into Nothing,
we thereby decline into lowliness.
Therefore,
clarity and tranquillity are the perfections of Potency;
pliancy and suppleness are the essentials of the Way.
Empty Nonexistence and calm serenity are the ancestors of the myriad things.
To quickly respond when stimulated,
to boldly return to the Root,
is to be merged with the Formless.
What we call "the Formless" is a designation for the One. What we call "the One" is that which has no counterpart in the entire world.
Majestically independent,
immensely solitary;
above, it permeates the Nine Heavens;
below, it threads through the Nine Regions.[8]
Though round, it does not fit within the compass;
though square, it does not fit within the carpenter's square.
Multifarious, yet constituting a unity;
proliferating, yet without a root.
It envelops Heaven and Earth like a sack;
it closes the gates to the Way.
Mysterious and vague, hidden and dark,
its whole Potency is preserved in its solitude.
Spread it out: it never ceases;
utilize it: it is never exhausted.
Therefore,
though you look for it, you will never see its form;
though you listen for it, you will never hear its sound;
though you hold it, you will never feel its contours.
It is a formlessness from which forms are generated;
It is a soundlessness from which the five tones[9] call out.
It is a tastelessness from which the five flavors take shape.
It is a colorlessness from which the five colors develop.

---

8. That is, all of China.
9. The pentatonic scale; the first note is *gong.* These tones belong to a category in the Five Agents system of correspondences, as do the five flavors (sour, sweet, bitter, spicy, and salty) and five colors (green, red, yellow, white, and black).

Therefore,

    the Existent arises from the Nonexistent;

    the Real emerges from the Empty.

    Because the entire world is encircled by it,

    names and realities converge.

    The number of the tones does not exceed five, yet their variations cannot be fully heard.

    The harmony of the flavors does not exceed five, yet their transformations cannot be fully savored.

    The number of the colors does not exceed five, yet their variations cannot be fully seen.

Thus,

    as for tone: when the *gong* note is established, the five tones all take shape;

    as for flavor: when sweetness is established, the five flavors all become fixed;

    as for color: when white is established, the five colors all develop;

    as for the Way: when the One is established, then the myriad things all are born.

Therefore,

    the guiding principle of the One

    spreads throughout the Four Seas.

    The diffusion of the One

    extends throughout Heaven and Earth.

    In its wholeness, it is pure like uncarved wood.

    In its dispersal, it is jumbled like murky water.

    Although it is murky, it gradually becomes clear;

    although it is empty, it gradually becomes full.

    Still! It resembles a deep pool.

    Buoyant! It resembles floating clouds.

    It seems to be nonexistent yet it exists;

    it seems to be absent yet it is present.

    The myriad things in their totality

    all pass through this one portal.

    The roots of the hundred endeavors

    all emerge from this one gateway.

    Its movements are formless;

    its alterations and transformations are spiritlike [i.e., unfathomable];

    its actions are traceless;

    it constantly anticipates by following after.

Therefore, in the governing of the Perfected,[1]

    they conceal their mental acuity;

    they extinguish their literary brilliance.

Relying on the Way, they set aside wisdom and, toward the people, act impartially.

    They limit their possessions

    and reduce their needs.

    They cast off their ambitions,

    discard lusts and desires,

---

1. The *zhenren*, a concept that first appears in the *Book of Master Zhuang* (*Zhuangzi*; see above) and becomes important in later Daoism.

and abandon worries and anxieties.
Limiting their possessions, they see things clearly;
reducing their needs, they attain them.

Now those who rely on their ears and eyes to hear and see, tire out their bodies, and are not clear. Those who use knowledge and deliberation to govern afflict their minds and achieve no success.

Therefore, sages make use of the one measure to comply with the tracks of things.

They do not alter its suitability;
they do not change its constancy.

Applying it as their level, relying on it as their marking cord, through the meanderings [of life], they follow it as their benchmark.

1.18

The world is my possession, but I am also the possession of the world. So how could there even be the slightest gap between me and the world?

Why must possessing the entire world consist of grasping power, holding onto authority, wielding the handles of life and death, and using them to put one's own titles and edicts into effect? What I call possessing the entire world is certainly not this. It is simply realizing it [the Way] yourself. Once I am able to realize it [the Way], the entire world will also be able to realize me. When the entire world and I realize each other, we will always possess each other. And so how could there be any gap between us to be filled in? What I call "to realize it yourself" means to fulfill your own person. To fulfill your own person is to become unified with the Way.

Thus roaming along riverbank or seashore, galloping with Yao Niao[2] or riding a chariot beneath a kingfisher-feathered canopy, the eyes seeing the "Plumes of the Pheasant" dance or the performance of the "Emblems of King Wu" music, the ears listening to lavishly clear, elegant, and rousing melodies or being stimulated by the licentious music of Zheng and Wei or getting wrapped up in the stirring traditional ballads of Chu or shooting at high-flying birds along the lakeshore or hunting wild beasts in hunting preserves: all these are things that average people find alluring and intoxicating. Sages experience them but not so much as to dominate their Quintessential Spirit or to disrupt their vital energy and concentration or cause their minds to be enticed away from their true nature.

To reside in a remote village on the side of a deep gorge hidden amid dense vegetation in a poor hut with a thatched roof on which grass sprouts up, whose door is overgrown by vines and which has small round windows like the mouth of a jar and a mulberry staff for a hinge, a hut whose roof is leaky and whose floor is damp, whose sleeping quarters are drafty and blanketed by snow and frost so that the grass mats are soaked; to wander in a vast marsh and ramble on the side of mountain slopes: these are things that would make average people develop dark moods and make them anxious and sad and unable to concentrate on anything. Sages live in places like this, but they do not make them worried or angry or make them lose what makes them content

---

2. A legendary horse, renowned for speed and endurance [translators' note].

on their own. What are the reasons for this? Because they intrinsically have the means to penetrate to the Mechanism of Heaven, and they do not allow honor or debasement, poverty, or wealth to make them weary and lose their awareness of their Potency. Thus, the cawing of the crow, the squawking of the magpie: has cold or heat, dryness or dampness ever altered their sounds?

Therefore when the realization of the Way is secure, it does not depend on the comings and goings of the myriad things. It is not because of a momentary alteration or transformation that I have secured the means to realize it myself. What I am calling "realization" means realizing the innate tendencies of nature and destiny and resting securely in the calmness that it produces.

From Two. Activating the Genuine

2.1

[1] There was a beginning.
[2] There was not yet beginning to have "There was a beginning."
[3] There was not yet beginning to have "There was not yet beginning to have 'There was a beginning.'"
[4] There was Something.
[5] There was Nothing.
[6] There was not yet beginning to have "There was Nothing."
[7] There was not yet beginning to have "There was not yet beginning to have 'There was Nothing.'"

[1] What is called "There was a beginning":

> Pell-mell: not yet manifest;
> buds beginning, sprouts emerging;
> not yet having shape or outline.

Undifferentiated, wriggling, it is on the verge of desiring to be born and flourish but not yet forming things and categories.

[2] [What is called] There was not yet beginning to have "There was a beginning":

> The qi[1] of Heaven beginning to descend;
> the qi of Earth beginning to ascend;
> yin and yang mixing and meeting;

mutually roaming freely and racing to fill the interstices of time and space,

> enveloping Potency and engulfing harmony;
> densely intermingling;

desiring to connect with things but not yet having formed boundaries and bodies.

---

1. Vital energy, breath (pneuma).

[3] [What is called] There was not yet beginning to have "There was not yet beginning to have 'There was a beginning'":

> Heaven engulfing harmony but not yet letting it fall;
> Earth embracing the vital energy but not yet letting it rise;
> empty and still,
> inert and isolated,

Nothing and Something were a matched pair.
The vital energy pervaded and greatly penetrated Dark Obscurity.

[4] [What is called] "There is Something":
Speaks of the flourishing of the myriad things. The roots, trunks, branches, and leaves were verdant and abundant, bountiful and brilliant. [Insects] wriggled and moved, crawled and walked, crept and gasped. [All these things] could be touched, grasped, and enumerated.

[5] [What is called] "There is Nothing":

> Look at it; you do not see its form;
> listen to it; you do not hear its sound.
> Reach for it, and you cannot grasp it;
> gaze at it, and you cannot fathom it.
> Collected and fused,
> floodlike and expansive,

It is something whose brilliance cannot be penetrated by any instrument.

[6] [What is called] There was not yet beginning to have "There was Nothing":

> Encloses Heaven and Earth,
> smelts the myriad things,
> greatly penetrates the chaotic and obscure.
> Deeply impenetrable, vast and great, it can have no exterior;
> as fine as the tip of a hair, as sharp as a point, it can have no interior.

A space without containment, it generated the root of Something and Nothing.

[7] [What is called] There was not yet beginning to have "There was not yet beginning to have 'There was nothing'":

> Heaven and Earth had not yet split apart;
> yin and yang had not yet been carved out;
> the four seasons had not yet differentiated;
> the myriad things had not yet been generated.
> Enormously peaceful and tranquil,
> silently clear and limpid,
> none saw its form.

It was like Resplendent Light asking Not Something, who was withdrawn and had lost himself: "I can [conceive of] having Nothing, but I cannot [conceive of] not having Nothing. If I could reach [the state of] Not Nothing, how could even the most marvelous surpass this?"

2.3

Among the people of antiquity were some who situated themselves in the chaotic and obscure. Their spirit and vital energy did not leak out to their exteriors. The myriad things were peaceful and dispassionate and so became contented and tranquil. The *qi* of [baleful comets such as] "magnolias," "lances," "colliders," and "handles"[2] was in every case blocked and dissipated so that they were unable to cause harm. At that time, the myriad peoples were wild and untamed, not knowing East from West;

> they roamed with their mouths full,
> drummed on their bellies in contentment.
> In copulation they followed the harmony of Heaven;
> in eating they accorded with the Potency of Earth.

They did not use minute precedent or "right and wrong" to surpass one another. Vast and boundless, this is what we call "Grand Order." And so those in high station

> directed [ministers] on their left and right and did not pervert their natures;
> possessed and pacified [the people] and did not compromise their Potency.

Thus,

> Humaneness and Rightness were not proclaimed, and the myriad things flourished.
> Rewards and punishments were not deployed, and all in the world were respected.

Their Way could give rise to great perfection, but it is difficult to find a quantitative measure for it. Thus,

> calculating by days there is not enough;
> calculating by years there is surplus.
> Fish forget themselves in rivers and lakes.
> Humans forget themselves in the techniques of the Way.

The Genuine of antiquity stood in the foundation of Heaven and Earth, were centered in uninterrupted roaming, embraced Potency, and rested in harmony. The myriad things were to them like smoke piling higher. Which of them would willingly create discord in human affairs or use things to trouble their nature and destiny?

---

2. Names given to the shapes of comets portending ill.

INWARD TRAINING
(Neiye)

Inward Training is a fourth-century B.C.E. text composed of poetic verses that had an important impact on later Daoist self-cultivation practices, but its significance was recognized by Western scholarship only in the early twentieth century. Although significant new texts often have been excavated by archaeologists from the ground or tombs, this little document was discovered within another work that had never been lost—the *Writings of Master Guan* (*Guanzi*), which is primarily concerned with politics and economics.

Within its pages, *Inward Training* contains reflections on the nature of the Dao as the primordial creative power behind everything; it also offers instructions on self-cultivation practices—in particular, a form of breathing meditation—as well as on mystical practices aimed at joining the individual with the Dao. Some scholars therefore claim that it is the oldest mystical text in China. Its title underscores its orientation toward the inner life of human beings. These inner practices are necessary to counteract the propensity of human beings to fritter away their great potential, thereby harming their bodies and minds, and in the process leading to a break with the Dao. *Inward Training* provides precisely the type of teachings that will both kindle new vitality and vigor and improve physical and mental health, on the way to the ultimate goal: a reunion with the Dao. As chapter 5 of *Inward Training* puts it:

> When the mind is tranquil and the vital breath is regular,
> The Way can thereby be halted [i.e., be made to "abid[e] within
>   the excellent mind"].
> That Way is not distant from us;
> When people attain it they are sustained.
> That Way is not separated from us;
> When people accord with it they are harmonious.
> . . . .
> Cultivate your mind, make your thoughts tranquil,
> And the Way can thereby be attained.

Those who successfully cultivate their bodies and minds to become attuned to the Dao become "sages," in the language of *Inward Training*. They will manifest physical signs—"their skin will be ample and smooth, their ears and eyes will be acute and clear"—and live fulfilling and harmonious lives. Much of what is presented in the verses of *Inward Training* closely echoes concepts found in *The Scripture of the Way and Its Virtue* (*Daode jing*), the *Book of Master Zhuang* (*Zhuangzi*), and the *Master of Huainan* (*Huainan-zi*; for all three works, see above).

PRONOUNCING GLOSSARY

Neiye: *neigh-yeh*

I

> The vital essence of all things:
> It is this that brings them to life.
> It generates the five grains[1] below

TRANSLATED BY Harold D. Roth. Bracketed additions are the translator's.

1. That is, the staple agricultural crops.

And becomes the constellated stars above.
When flowing amid the heavens and the earth
We call it ghostly and numinous.
When stored within the chests of human beings,
We call them sages.

IV

Clear! as though right by your side.
Vague! as though it will not be attained.
Indiscernable! as though beyond the limitless.
The test of this is not far off:
Daily we make use of its inner power.
The Way is what infuses the body,
Yet people are unable to fix it in place.
It goes forth but does not return,
It comes back but does not stay.
Silent! none can hear its sound.
Suddenly stopping! it abides within the mind.
Obscure! we do not see its form.
Surging forth! it arises with us.
We do not see its form,
We do not hear its sound,
Yet we can perceive an order to its accomplishments.
We call it "the Way."

V

The Way has no fixed position;
It abides within the excellent mind.
When the mind is tranquil and the vital breath is regular,
The Way can thereby be halted.
That Way is not distant from us;
When people attain it they are sustained.
That Way is not separated from us;
When people accord with it they are harmonious.

Therefore: Concentrated! as though you could be roped together
    with it.
Indiscernable! as though beyond all locations.
The true state of that Way:
How could it be conceived of and pronounced upon?
Cultivate your mind, make your thoughts tranquil,
And the Way can thereby be attained.

VI

As for the Way:
It is what the mouth cannot speak of,
The eyes cannot see,
And the ears cannot hear.
It is that with which we cultivate the mind and align the body.
When people lose it they die;

When people gain it they flourish.
When endeavors lose it they fail;
When they gain it they succeed.
The Way never has a root or trunk,
It never has leaves or flowers.
The myriad things are generated by it;
The myriad things are completed by it.
We designate it "the Way."

IX

Those who can transform even a single thing, call them "numinous";
Those who can alter even a single situation, call them "wise."
But to transform without expending vital energy; to alter without
    expending wisdom:
Only exemplary persons who hold fast to the One are able
    to do this.
Hold fast to the One; do not lose it,
And you will be able to master the myriad things.
Exemplary persons act upon things,
And are not acted upon by them,
Because they grasp the guiding principle of the One.

XI

When your body is not aligned,
The inner power will not come.
When you are not tranquil within,
Your mind will not be well ordered.
Align your body, assist the inner power,
Then it will gradually come on its own.

XIII

There is a numinous [mind] naturally residing within;
One moment it goes, the next it comes,
And no one is able to conceive of it.
If you lose it you are inevitably disordered;
If you attain it you are inevitably well ordered.
Diligently clean out its lodging place
And its vital essence will naturally arrive.
Still your attempts to imagine and conceive of it.
Relax your efforts to reflect on and control it.
Be reverent and diligent
And its vital essence will naturally stabilize.
Grasp it and don't let go
Then the eyes and ears won't overflow
And the mind will have nothing else to seek.
When a properly aligned mind resides within you,
The myriad things will be seen in their proper perspective.

XIV

The Way fills the entire world.
It is everywhere that people are,
But people are unable to understand this.
When you are released by this one word:
You reach up to the heavens above;
You stretch down to the earth below;
You pervade the nine inhabited regions.[2]
What does it mean to be released by it?
The answer resides in the calmness of the mind.
When your mind is well ordered, your senses are well ordered.
When your mind is calm, your senses are calmed.
What makes them well ordered is the mind;
What makes them calm is the mind.
By means of the mind you store the mind:
Within the mind there is yet another mind.
That mind within the mind: it is an awareness that precedes words.
Only after there is awareness does it take shape;
Only after it takes shape is there a word.
Only after there is a word is it implemented;
Only after it is implemented is there order.
Without order, you will always be chaotic.
If chaotic, you die.

XVI

If people can be aligned and tranquil,
Their skin will be ample and smooth,
Their ears and eyes will be acute and clear,
Their muscles will be supple and their bones will be strong.
They will then be able to hold up the Great Circle [of the heavens]
And tread firmly over the Great Square [of the earth].[3]
They will mirror things with great purity.
And will perceive things with great clarity.
Reverently be aware [of the Way] and do not waver,
And you will daily renew your inner power,
Thoroughly understand all under the heavens,
And exhaust everything within the Four Directions.
To reverently bring forth the effulgence [of the Way]:
This is called "inward attainment."
If you do this but fail to return to it,
This will cause a wavering in your vitality.

XVIII

When there is a mind that is unimpaired within you,
It cannot be hidden.
It will be known in your countenance,
And seen in your skin color.

2. That is, the nine regions into which China was traditionally thought to have been divided.

3. According to traditional Chinese cosmology, heaven is round and the earth square.

If with this good flow of vital energy you encounter others,
They will be kinder to you than your own brethren.
But if with a bad flow of vital energy you encounter others,
They will harm you with their weapons.
[This is because] the wordless pronouncement
Is more rapid than the drumming of thunder.
The perceptible form of the mind's vital energy
Is brighter than the sun and moon,
And more apparent than the concern of parents.
Rewards are not sufficient to encourage the good;
Punishments are not sufficient to discourage the bad.
Yet once this flow of vital energy is achieved,
All under the heavens will submit.
And once the mind is made stable,
All under the heavens will listen.

XX

Deep thinking generates knowledge.
Idleness and carelessness generate worry.
Cruelty and arrogance generate resentment.
Worry and grief generate illness.
When illness reaches a distressing degree, you die.
When you think about something and don't let go of it,
Internally you will be distressed, externally you will be weak.
Do not plan things out in advance
Or else your vitality will cede its dwelling.

In eating, it is best not to fill up;
In thinking, it is best not to overdo.
Limit these to the appropriate degree
And you will naturally reach it [vitality].

XXV

The vitality of all people
Inevitably comes from their peace of mind.
When anxious, you lose this guiding thread;
When angry, you lose this basic point.
When you are anxious or sad, pleased or angry,
The Way has no place within you to settle.
Love and desire: still them!
Folly and disturbance: correct them!
Do not push it! do not pull it!
Good fortune will naturally return to you,
And that Way will naturally come to you
So you can rely on and take counsel from it.
If you are tranquil then you will attain it;
If you are agitated then you will lose it.

THE SEAL OF THE UNITY OF THE THREE, IN ACCORDANCE WITH THE BOOK OF CHANGES
(Zhouyi cantong qi)

Although *The Seal of the Unity of the Three, in Accordance with the Book of Changes* is not well known in the West—perhaps because its mysterious language and wide-ranging symbolism, metaphors, and allusions are so difficult to translate—few other Daoist works have attracted as much attention and commentary within the Chinese tradition. This text was lauded by such famous Chinese poets as Li Bo (701–762) and Bo Juyi (772–846), inspired a Buddhist monk to compose a work with the same title (see below), was commented on by the influential Confucian thinker Zhu Xi (1130–1200)—who in his dotage thought it contained the secrets to immortality—and today is available in more than one hundred editions with commentaries.

The Seal of the Unity of the Three is difficult to date with any certainty, and the modern consensus is that it grew by accretion over several centuries. It is traditionally attributed to Wei Boyang, a legendary immortal of the Han dynasty (202 B.C.E.–220 C.E.), though some scholars believe that the text was fabricated in the Tang dynasty (618–907). The main body of the text consists of rhymed verses full of metaphors; its final section appears to have been composed separately.

The Seal of the Unity of the Three is significant for being the primary scripture of both the "external" and "internal" alchemical traditions. "External alchemy" (*waidan*) entails a set of practices aimed at compounding an elixir, made out of minerals and metals, whose ingestion will guarantee longevity or immortality. The beliefs and practices that make up "internal alchemy" (*neidan*), most often referred to as the Way of the Golden Elixir, involve internalizing the alchemical processes via methods of body cultivation—meditation, gymnastics, sexual hygiene, breathing exercises, and so on. The ultimate goal is to form the inner elixir, which is depicted as a small immortal embryo that lives on after the human body is sloughed off: the practitioner thereby attains immortality and is reunited with the primordial Dao.

Modern readers may struggle with this text's cosmological symbolism, grounded in a series of correspondences that are based on Han dynasty interpretations of the ancient *Book of Changes* (*Yijing*, or *I Ching*). As the scholar and translator Fabrizio Pregadio explains in his copious notes on this text (which form the basis for this summary), the cosmological portion of the text, which is primarily concerned with the Dao and its relation to the cosmos, describes the ruler who uses the *Book of Changes'* trigrams and hexagrams—sixty-four permutations of solid (yang) or broken (yin) lines in vertical stacks of three and six, respectively—to comprehend the world and thereby maintain the proper relations between heaven, earth, and humankind (see table 1). It also assumes that all phenomena can be classified into five types, dependent on the Five Agents, whose relationships represent the basic relationships between all things (see table 2).

The opening poem of *The Seal of the Unity of the Three*, whose first two lines are adapted from the *Book of Changes*, introduces the trigrams Qian ☰, Kun ☷, Kan ☵, and Li ☲: these are the fundamental principles that generate the world of phenomenal things. The interaction between the precosmic aspects of the yang (active, male, heavenly) principle of Qian ☰ and yin (passive, female, earthy) principle of Kun ☷ generates the cosmic essences that are represented graphically and symbolically in the trigrams Kan ☵ and Li ☲. Kan ☵ is produced by the active principle (yang, represented by the unbroken line) of Qian ☰ moving into the heart of the passive principle (yin, represented by the broken lines) of Kun ☷, and Li ☲ is produced by passive principle of Kun ☷ moving into the heart of the active principle of Qian ☰. Qian ☰ and Kun ☷ can best be understood as the essence of the undifferentiated

Dao, which generates Li ☲ and Kan ☵, through which it functions in phenomena. The two metaphors at the end of the poem—hub and axle, bellows and nozzle—draw on images from *The Scripture of the Way and Its Virtue (Daode jing)*, underscoring that it is the void in the middle (of the wheel hub, a vessel, etc.) that brings forth existence and gives things their function (see chs. 5 and 11, above).

The second poem, concerning the artisan and charioteer, introduces the main tools—marking cord, plumb line, compass, and square—that enable the ruler to harmonize his rule with the patterns of the world and thus reign effortlessly (*wuwei*) from the center ("Abide in the Center to control the outside"). Like the charioteer who successfully drives his vehicle by following preexisting tracks, the ruler heeds the makeup of the cosmos. The notion of getting things done without doing anything returns in section 20 in the context of superior virtue, which is based on "not-doing," and inferior virtue, which is based on "doing." These concepts, too, draw on a passage in *The Scripture of the Way and Its Virtue*: "A man of the highest virtue does not keep to virtue and that is why he has virtue. A man of the lowest virtue never strays from virtue and that is why he is without virtue. The former never acts yet leaves nothing undone. The latter acts but there are things left undone" (chapter 38).

As *The Seal of the Unity of the Three* unfolds, especially in sections 22–25, the discussion turns to alchemy, which is presented as emblematic of the way of inferior virtue. Section 22, "The Principles of Alchemy," mentions a "man who 'wears rough-hewn clothes but cherishes a piece of jade in his bosom,'" capturing the alchemical idea that hidden at the heart of the cosmos is a principle that generates everything. The poem begins with another quotation from *The Scripture of the Way and Its Virtue*, "know the white, keep to the black" (chapter 28), and continues: "and the Numinous Light will come of its own." Black, the poem explains, is equivalent to water (yin) and white is equivalent to metal (yang). Within the tradition of external alchemy, black signifies native lead, symbolizing the phenomenal world; white refers to true lead or the "Original Pneuma" (*yuanqi*)—the state of the cosmos before differentiation into yin and yang occurs. By knowing the white and keeping to the black, one can produce the elixir of immortality (here called the Numinous Light).

The symbolism of metal and water continues into the next section, "Metal and Water, Mother and Child," which can be understood only through the prism of two distinct concepts related to the movement from the postcelestial (*houtian*, water/son) to the precelestial (*xiantian*, metal/mother) and the reverse direction (see table 3). External alchemy's way of inferior virtue is concerned with the return to the precelestial (from water/son to metal/mother), and the way of superior virtue refers to the movement from the precelestial to the postcelestial (from metal/mother to water/son). Sections 24 and 25 refer to the compounding (see also section 78) and completion of the alchemical elixir, here referred to as vermilion, inside the alchemical furnace or tripod (see section 82)—possible only if one attains a state of "not-doing" and avoids toiling or becoming distraught. Once the elixir is attained, then "it constantly stays with you" (section 25).

Section 78 uses evocative images to describe the process of compounding the elixir. Here the White Tiger refers to lead (yang), "the green liquid" to mercury (yin). Put inside the tripod, the product of their conjunction is transmuted into the Golden Elixir through an elaborate process that requires the meticulous control of fire (the Vermilion Sparrow, yang) as it succumbs to water (the "thin net," yin). In the order of the succession of elements within the system of Five Agents, fire must be conquered by water and water will be conquered by soil (see table 3).

Section 82, "The Song of the Tripod," is a sweeping composition that moves through the particulars of the alchemical process to the rewards of attaining the elixir. The first two stanzas, using a series of highly symbolic numbers, refer to the alchemical tripod itself; the following two allude to the sequence of the firing process and the relationship of water (yin) to fire (yang); and the next four describe the gradual formation of the elixir. The remainder of the poem shifts to a discussion of the importance of the mental state of the practitioner during this process, the need to maintain alchemy's secrets, and the fundamental changes undergone by the practitioner, who becomes a True Man or immortal ("Your name will be inscribed in the Heavenly Charts").

The last composition in *The Seal of the Unity of the Three*, "Wei Boyang's Final Words," contains an autobiographical statement by the purported author, appar-

Table 1. The eight trigrams (*bagua*) and their main associations*

☰ 乾 QIAN	☱ 兌 DUI	☲ 離 LI	☳ 震 ZHEN	☴ 巽 XUN	☵ 坎 KAN	☶ 艮 GEN	☷ 坤 KUN
heaven	lake	fire	thunder	wind	water	mountain	earth
father	youngest daughter	second daughter	eldest son	eldest daughter	second son	youngest son	mother
south	southeast	east	northeast	southwest	west	northwest	north
northwest	west	south	east	southeast	north	northeast	southwest

From top to bottom: elements in nature, family relations, and directions in the cosmological configurations "prior to Heaven" (*xiantian*) and "posterior to Heaven" (*houtian*).

Table 2. The five agents *wuxing* and their associations

	WOOD	FIRE	SOIL	METAL	WATER
DIRECTIONS	east	south	center	west	north
SEASONS	spring	summer	(midsummer)	autumn	winter
COLORS	green	red	yellow	white	black
EMBLEMATIC ANIMALS	green dragon	vermilion sparrow	yellow dragon	white tiger	snake and turtle
NUMBERS	3,8	2,7	5,10	4,9	1,6
YIN-YANG-1:	minor Yang	great Yang	balance	minor Yin	great Yin
YIN-YANG-2:	True Yin	Yang	balance	True Yang	Yin
STEMS	jia yi	bing ding	wu ji	geng xin	ren gui
BRANCHES	yin mao	wu si	xu, chou wei, chen	you shen	hai zi
PLANETS	Jupiter	Mars	Saturn	Venus	Mercury
RELATIONS	father	daughter	forefather	mother	son
VISCERA	liver	heart	spleen	lungs	kidneys
BODY ORGANS	eyes	tongue	mouth	nose	ears

* These tables are based on those in Fabrizio Pregadio, *The Seal of the Unity of the Three: A Study and Translation of the Cantong qi* (2011), pp. 250, 247, 249.

Table 3. "Generation" (*xiangsheng*) and "conquest" (*xiangke*) sequences of the five agents (*wuxing*)

	GENERATES	IS GENERATED BY	CONQUERS	IS CONQUERED BY
WATER	Wood	Metal	Fire	Soil
WOOD	Fire	Water	Soil	Metal
FIRE	Soil	Wood	Metal	Water
SOIL	Metal	Fire	Water	Wood
METAL	Water	Soil	Wood	Fire

ently an immortal who transcends time and space. Like the sages of the past, he deigns to descend into the human world every so often to transmit his teachings—among them, *The Seal of the Unity of the Three*. Those who simply follow the teachings encapsulated in his text will be able to face adversity, "steady and serene, and ready to live a long life."

Many of the late commentaries on *The Seal of the Unity of the Three* read it as a text of internal alchemy, despite its apparent references to external alchemy. In fact, its multivalent and highly symbolic language is not consistent with any distinct *neidan* or *waidan* methodology, though subsequent commentaries do impose such readings on the text.

PRONOUNCING GLOSSARY

Cantong qi: *tsawn-tung chi*　　　Li: *lee*
Dao: *dow*　　　Qian: *chien*
Kan: *kawn*　　　Wei Boyang: *way bow-yawng*
Kun: *koon*　　　Zhouyi: *chou-yee*

1　Qian and Kun, Kan and Li

"Qian ☰ and Kun ☷ are the door and the gate of change,"
the father and the mother of all hexagrams.[1]
Kan ☵ and Li ☲ are the inner and the outer walls,
they spin the hub and align the axle.
Female and male, these four trigrams
function as a bellows and its nozzles.

2　The Artisan and the Charioteer

Enfolding and encompassing the Way of Yin and Yang[2]
is like being an artisan and a charioteer

TRANSLATED BY Fabrizio Pregadio.

1. Lines adapted from the *Book of Changes* (*Yijing* or *I Ching*, traditionally dated to the 12th century B.C.E.), a volume of divination and cosmology. On the hexagrams and trigrams, see the introduction to this selection.
2. The male principle; the term originally referred to the sunny side of a valley, and by extension it came to be associated with the light, heaven, dryness, and activity. "Yin": the female principle; the term originally referred to the shady side of a valley, and by extension it came to be associated with the dark, earth, dampness, and passivity.

who level the marking-cord and the plumb-line,
hold the bit and the bridle,
align the compass and the square,[3]
and follow the tracks and the ruts.

Abide in the Center to control the outside:
the numbers are found in the system of the pitch-pipes and
the calendar.

20   Superior Virtue and Inferior Virtue

"Superior virtue has no doing":[4]
it does not use examining and seeking.
"Inferior virtue does":
its operation does not rest.

21   Non-Being and Being, the "Two Cavities"

Closed above, its name is Being;
closed below, its name is Non-Being.
Non-Being therefore rises above,
for above is the dwelling of the virtue of Spirit.

These are the methods of the two cavities:
Metal and Breath thus wait upon one another.

22   The Principles of Alchemy

"Know the white, keep to the black,"[5]
and the Numinous Light will come of its own.

White is the essence of Metal,
Black the foundation of Water.
Water is the axis of the Dao:
its number is 1.

At the beginning of Yin and Yang,
Mystery holds the Yellow Sprout;[6]
it is the ruler of the five metals,[7]
the River Chariot[8] of the northern direction.

That is why lead is black on the outside
but cherishes the Golden Flower[9] within,

3. Used to lay out the (square) earth; the compass was used to lay out the (round) heavens.
4. See *The Scripture of the Way and Its Virtue* (*Daode jing*, or *Laozi*; see above), chapter 38.
5. See *The Scripture of the Way and Its Virtue*, chapter 28.
6. A substance concocted by Daoist alchemists by firing quicksilver and lead together, in a preliminary step in the making of an elixir.
7. Wood, fire, earth, metal, and water. These elements are the foundation of the Five Agents system of correspondence, a set of systematic associations between different categories.
8. That is, the circulation of breath.
9. A chamber at the top of the head, which can emit a bright light or flames from the brain.

like the man who "wears rough-hewn clothes but cherishes
    a piece of jade in his bosom,"[1]
and outwardly behaves like a fool.

23   *Metal and Water, Mother and Child*

Metal is the mother of Water—
the mother is hidden in the embryo of her son.
Water is the child of Metal—
the child is stored in the womb of its mother.

24   *Born before Heaven and Earth*

The True Man[2] is supremely wondrous:
sometimes he is, sometimes he is not.
Barely perceptible within the great abyss,
now he sinks, now he wafts.

Receding, they part and distribute themselves,
and each keeps to its sector.
When collected, it is of the white kind,
when compounded, it turns to vermilion.

To refine it make an outer protection,
so that the White lies sheltered within.
"Square and round, one inch is its diameter";[3]
the two are indistinct, each seizes the other.

"Born before Heaven and Earth,"[4]
it is eminent, venerable, and exalted.

25   *The Elixir in the Tripod*

On its sides are ramparts and portals,
and in shape it resembles Penghu;[5]
round and enclosed, shut and sealed off,
it is interwoven at every turn.

Guarded, defended, solid, and firm,
it reverts all misdoing and evil;
its meanders and towers are intertwined
in order "to prevent the unforeseen."[6]

---

1. See *The Scripture of the Way and Its Virtue*, chapter 70.
2. The *Zhenren*, or "Perfect Man," a concept that first appears in the *Book of Master Zhuang* (*Zhuangzi*; see above) and becomes important in later Daoism.
3. Quoted from the *Most High Jade Scripture on the Internal View of the Yellow Court* (*Taishang huangting neijing yujing*); see below.
4. See *The Scripture of the Way and Its Virtue*, chapter 25.
5. A mythical island in the Eastern Sea where immortals were believed to live; also, in internal alchemy—the internalizing of the alchemical processes—the lower Cinnabar Field, the seat of essence (located in the abdomen).
6. See *The Scripture of the Way and Its Virtue*.

You can do this if you are free from all cares,
but hardly you can if you are toiled and distraught:
when Spirit and Breath fill the house,
no one can detain them.

Those who guard it will shine,
those who neglect it are lost.
In movement and quiescence, in rest and activity,
it constantly stays with you.

78 *Compounding the Elixir*

So that its heat may go up to Mount Zeng,
a blazing fire is made below;

the White Tiger[7] leads the song ahead,
the green liquid joins after.

The Vermilion Sparrow[8] soars into play,
flying upward in the hues of its five colors;

then it encounters the spread of a thin net—
caught, it can rise no more.

It screams deep in agony, "Wah! Wah!,"
like an infant who yearns for its mother,

as it enters the boiling pot on its head,
its feathers ripped off.

Before the water clock's notches have gone past the half,
fish scales appear throughout;

the sheen of its five colors[9] are dazzles and gleans,
their transformations proceed without pause.

As the bubbling tripod stirs and seethes,
ceaselessly gurgling and burbling,

coalescing continuously, one after the other,
the dog's teeth form a lattice.

Their shape looks like ice in the winter's middle month,
like stalactites issued forth from *langgan*:[1]

---

7. The guardian animal of the West.
8. The guardian animal of the South.

9. Green, red, yellow, white, and black.
1. An important elixir.

they tower in tangles and jumbles,
piling up upon one another.

82   *Song of the Tripod*

3 and 5 around,
an inch and one part,
4 and 8 the mouth,
the lips a pair of inches.

A foot and 2 tenths high,
evenly thick and thin;
its belly on the third day
sits beneath the descending warmth.

Yin stays above,
Yang rushes below;
fierce are the head and the tail,
gentle in between.

Seventy at the beginning,
thirty days at the end;
and for two hundred and sixty
the balance well kept.

The whiteness of the Yin Fire,
the lead of the Yellow Sprout:
the Two Sevens assemble
to support and assist man.

This suffices to order the brain
and to make steady the ascent to the Mystery:
the infant dwells within,
gaining security and stability.

Roaming in its coming and going,
it never exits the gates;
gradually does it grow,
until its qualities and nature are pure.

Then it returns to the One
and reverts to the origin,
as courteously and respectfully
as a minister is to his lord.

At the end of each cycle,
laboriously and assiduously
protect it with utmost attention
—let there be no lapse.

Long is the path
to return to the Abyssal Mystery,
but if you do arrive there,
you will comprehend Qian and Kun.

Moisten one knife-point,
and it will cleanse the *hun* and the *po*;[2]
you will obtain a long life
and find a home in the town of the Immortals.

Lovers of the Dao
should seek out its root:
look into the five agents[3]
to settle the scruples and mils.[4]

Think about this carefully;
it need not be discussed.
Hide it deep and guard it,
do not transmit it in writing.

Riding a white crane,
harnessing a scaly dragon,
you will roam through Great Emptiness
and pay homage to the Lord of the Immortals.

Your name will be inscribed in the Heavenly Charts,
and you will be called a True Man.

86   *Wei Boyang and the* Cantong qi

A lowly man born in Kuaiji,
I rust my life away in an obscure valley.
I cherish plainness and simplicity,
and find no joy in power or fame.

At leisure in a secluded place,
unconcerned with profit or name;
upholding calm and tranquility,
I seek quietness and serenity alone.

Unhurried, dwelling at ease,
I wrote this book
to sing and tell of the great *Book of Changes*
and of the words that the three sages[5] handed down.
I have examined their import and meaning
and the principle that runs through them all.

88   *Wei Boyang's Final Words*

Forsaking the times, avoiding harm,
I have entrusted myself to mountains and hills.
I have wandered and roamed through the Unbounded,
with demons as my neighbors.
Transmuting my form, transcending the world,
I have entered the depths of the Inaudible.

2. The cloud souls and the white souls; there are three of the former and seven of the latter.
3. A set of systematic associations between different categories, including five directions, five colors, five organs, and five tastes.
4. That is, the minute weights and lengths.
5. Variously identified in different texts.

Once in a hundred generations I descend
to roam in the human world;
spreading my wings,
I bend east, west, and south.

In times of adversity like those met by Tang,[6]
when flood is compounded by drought,
when the stems and leaves shrivel and fade,
losing their luster and glow,
the good-natured man braves and endures the turn of events:
steady and serene, and ready to live a long life.

6. The first ruler of the Shang dynasty (1600–1045 B.C.E.).

THE BOOK OF MASTER HAN FEI
(Han Feizi)

Of the seven hundred or more commentaries that have been written on *The Scripture of the Way and Its Virtue* (*Daode jing*; see above), the earliest, dating to the third century B.C.E., is found in the *Book of Master Han Fei* (*Han Feizi*). Two chapters, titled "Explaining the *Laozi*" (*Jielao*) and "Illustrating the *Laozi*" (*Yulao*), contain exegesis of specific lines from the work. Han Fei was born around 280 B.C.E. into a noble family, but their state was rather small, hampered by a lack of natural resources, and constantly threatened by its neighbors. Han Fei studied with key thinkers of his day, including the Confucian writer Xunzi, and because he had a speech impediment he set his own ideas down in a book. His work eventually gained the attention of the king of Qin (who would go on to conquer and unify China as the first emperor of the Qin dynasty), but the king's chief minister—Li Si, a former schoolmate of the philosopher—warned that Han Fei could never be trusted; as a result, he was imprisoned and, in 233, drank poison on Li Si's order.

Han Fei is traditionally understood as a representative Legalist thinker, belonging to a school of political philosophy concerned with establishing and maintaining the state and its authority. Legalism emphasized that the ruler should command the respect and obedience of the people by instituting clear rules and threatening strong punishment for their breach. Why, then, does the *Book of Master Han Fei* discuss a Daoist text that seems antithetical to the theories of active governance propounded by Legalists? Moreover, Legalists were known for disparaging everyday issues that were particular concerns of Confucians and Mohists, such as morality, rites and ritual, and anything related to religion. In its Legalist reading of *The Scripture of the Way and Its Virtue*, "Explaining the *Laozi*" therefore provides an especially important piece of evidence that Daoist and Legalist thought were more closely aligned during this period that we might have expected.

In that chapter, Han Fei argues that the ruler—here depicted as akin to sage figures within the Daoist tradition—who follows the Way (Dao) can govern through "non-action" (*wuwei*), since his laws are so perfectly in harmony with the natural way of things that people spontaneously fall into line and behave well. Just as the Daoist sage retreats into the solitude of the mountains to live a simple reclusive life, so the ideal Legalist ruler retreats into the solitude of the imperial palace to live an unadorned life endued with mystery and enhanced by the symbolic aura of his office.

But not all monarchs measure up to the ideal: "if the ruler of men does not uphold Dao, at home he will misgovern the people and abroad he will offend the neighboring states." He seems most likely to govern poorly when his desires for wealth and sexual gratification become excessive. In explaining a line from *The Scripture of the Way and Its Virtue* concerning avarice, Han Fei declares: "When a man has wild desires, his inferences become confused."

PRONOUNCING GLOSSARY

Dao: *dow*

De: *duh*

Han Feizi: *hawn fei-tzu*

Jielao: *jieh-lao*

Laozi: *lao-tzu*

From *Explaining the* Laozi (*Jielao*)

CHAPTER XXXVIII. DISCOURSE ON VIRTUE[1]

Superior virtue is unvirtue. Therefore it has virtue. Inferior virtue never loses sight of virtue. Therefore it has no virtue.

Superior virtue is non-assertion and without pretension. Inferior virtue asserts and makes pretensions.

Superior benevolence acts but makes no pretensions. Superior righteousness acts and makes pretensions.

Superior propriety acts and when no one responds to it, it stretches its arm and enforces its rules.

Thus one leaves Dao and then De[2] appears. One leaves Virtue and then Benevolence appears. One leaves Benevolence and then Righteousness appears. One leaves Righteousness and then Propriety appears. The rules of Propriety are the semblance of loyalty and faith, and the beginning of disorder.

Foreknowledge is the flower of Dao, but of ignorance the beginning.

Therefore a great sportsman abides by the solid and dwells not in the superficial. He abides in the fruit and dwells not in the flower.

Therefore he discards the latter and chooses the former.

Virtue is internal. Acquirement is external. "Superior virtue is unvirtue" means that the mind does not indulge in external things. If the mind does not indulge in external things, the personality will become perfect. The personality that is perfect is called "acquirement". In other words, acquirement is the acquirement of the personality. In general, virtue begins with non-assertion, develops with non-wanting, rests secure with non-thinking, and solidifies with non-using. If it acts and wants, it becomes restless; if restless, it is not perfect. If put into use and thought about, it does not solidify; if it does not solidify, it cannot work successfully. If it is not perfect and cannot work successfully, it will become self-assertive virtue. If it becomes self-assertive virtue, it is non-virtue. Contrary to this, if unvirtue,

TRANSLATED BY W. K. Liao.

1. These chapter numbers, and the text quoted immediately after them, are from *The Scripture of the Way and Its Virtue* (*Daode jing*; see above), attributed to Laozi; they have been added by the translator.

2. Virtue (also translated "potency," "integrity," or "power").

it has virtue. Hence the saying: "Superior virtue is unvirtue. Therefore it has virtue."

The reason why men value non-assertion and non-thinking as emptiness is that by remaining empty one's will is ruled by nothing. Verily, tactless people purposely regard non-assertion and non-thinking as emptiness. To be sure, those who purposely regard non-assertion and non-thinking as emptiness, never forget emptiness in their minds. They are thus ruled by the will to emptiness. By "emptiness" is meant the status of the will not ruled by anything. To be ruled by the pursuit of emptiness is *ipso facto* not emptiness. When he who rests empty does not assert, he does not regard non-assertion as having a constant way. If he does not regard non-assertion as having a constant way, he is then empty. If he is empty, his virtue flourishes. The virtue that flourishes is called "superior virtue". Hence the saying: "Superior virtue is non-assertion and without pretension."

By "benevolence" is meant the love of men in a pleasant mood in one's innermost heart. It is to rejoice in the good luck of others and to lament on their bad luck. It is born of the sense of sheer necessity, but not of the want of reward. Hence the saying: "Superior benevolence acts but makes no pretensions."

"Righteousness" covers the manners of ruler and minister, superior and inferior, the distinction between father and son, high and low, the contact between intimate acquaintances, between friends, and the difference between the close and the distant, the internal and the external. The minister ought to serve the ruler aright; the inferior ought to comfort the superior aright. The son ought to serve the father aright; the low ought to respect the high aright. Intimate acquaintances and good friends ought to help each other aright. The close ought to be taken in while the distant ought to be kept off. In short, "righteousness" implies whatever is done aright. Anything right ought to be done aright. Hence the saying: "Superior righteousness acts and makes pretensions."

"Propriety" refers to the mode in which one's feelings are expressed. It is concerned with the cultural embellishments of all righteous acts, such as the mutual relations of ruler and minister, father and son. It is the way whereby high and low, worthy and unworthy, are differentiated. For instance, when one pines after someone else but cannot make himself understood, he runs fast towards the person and bows low in front of him so as to express his attachment to that person. Similarly, when one loves someone from one's innermost heart and cannot make himself known, he uses pleasing words and beautiful phrases to convince the person loved. Thus, propriety is the outer embellishment whereby the inner heart is understood. Hence "propriety" refers to the mode in which one's feelings are expressed.

In general, when a man responds to external things, he does not know that the response reveals the propriety of his personality. The masses of the people practise propriety only to show respect for others, wherefore propriety is now cordial and again simple. The superior man practises propriety on purpose to cultivate his personality. Since it is practised on purpose to cultivate his personality, it is intrinsic in mind and forms superior propriety. Since superior propriety is intrinsic in mind and popular propriety changes from time to time, they do not respond to each other. Since they do not respond to each other, hence the saying: "Superior propriety acts and no one responds to it."

Though the masses of the people change propriety from time to time, yet the saintly man is always courteous and respectful, practising the rules of propriety which bind him hand and foot. In so doing he never slackens. Hence the saying: "Superior virtue stretches its arm and enforces its rules."

Dao accumulates; accumulation accomplishes an achievement; and De is the achievement of Dao. Achievement solidifies; solidity shines; and Ren[3] is the shining of De. Shine has gloss; gloss has function; and Yi[4] is the function of Ren. Function has propriety; propriety has embellishment; and Li[5] is the embellishment of Yi. Hence the saying: "One leaves Dao and then De appears. One leaves Virtue and then Benevolence appears. One leaves Benevolence and then Righteousness appears. One leaves Righteousness and then Propriety appears."

Propriety is the mode expressive of feelings. Embellishment is the decoration of qualities. Indeed, the superior man takes the inner feelings but leaves the outer looks, likes the inner qualities but hates the outer decorations. Who judges inner feelings by outer looks, finds the feelings bad. Who judges inner qualities by outer decorations, finds the inner qualities rotten. How can I prove this? The jade of Bian He[6] was not decorated with the five bright colours. The bead of Marquis Sui[7] was not decorated with yellow gold. Their qualities are so good that nothing is fit to decorate them. Verily, anything that functions only after being decorated must have poor qualities. For this reason, between father and son propriety is simple and not brilliant. Hence the saying: "Propriety is superficial semblance only."

In general, things that do not flourish together are Yin and Yang.[8] Principles that mutually take and give are threat and favour. What is substantial in reality but simple in appearance, is the propriety between father and son. From this viewpoint I can see that whoever observes complicated rules of propriety is rotten in his innermost heart. Nevertheless, to observe the rules of propriety is to comply with the naïve minds of people. The masses of the people, when observing the rules of propriety, rejoice imprudently if others respond, and resent it with blame if not. Now that the observers of the rules of propriety with a view to complying with the naïve minds of people are given the opportunity to blame each other, how can there be no dispute? Where there is dispute, there is disorder. Hence the saying: "The rules of propriety are the semblance of loyalty and faith, and the beginning of disorder."

To act before affairs take place and move before principles are clear, is called foreknowledge. The foreknower makes arbitrary guesses with no special cause. How can I prove this? Once upon a time, Zhan He[9] was seated and his disciples were waiting upon him. When an ox mooed outside the gate, the disciples said, "It is a black ox but white is on its forehead." In

---

3. Benevolence.

4. Righteousness.

5. Ritual or propriety.

6. A man of the ancient state of Chu; according to Han Fei, he was punished by two successive kings before a third finally recognized his unpolished stone as precious.

7. A pearl; this famous treasure is mentioned in both *The Book of Master Mo* (*Mozi*) and the *Master of Huainan* (*Huainan-zi*), in passages not included in the selections above.

8. The male principle; the term originally referred to the sunny side of a valley, and by extension it came to be associated with the light, heaven, dryness, and activity. "Yin": the female principle; the term originally referred to the shady side of a valley, and by extension it came to be associated with the dark, earth, dampness, and passivity.

9. A Daoist adept also called Zhanzi, mentioned in early texts such as the *Book of Master Zhuang* (*Zhuangzi*), in a passage not included in the selection above.

response to this, Zhan He said, "True, it is a black ox but the white is on its horns." Accordingly, they sent men out to investigate it and found the ox was black and its horns were wrapped with white cloth. To bewilder the minds of the masses with the accomplished tact of Zhanzi is almost as brilliant as any gay flower. Hence the saying: "Foreknowledge is the flower of Reason."

Supposing by way of trial we discarded the foresight of Zhanzi and sent out an ignorant boy less than five feet tall to investigate it, then he would know the ox was black and its horns were wrapped with white cloth, too. Thus, with the foresight of Zhanzi, who had afflicted his mind and exhausted his energy in order to attain it, was accomplished this same merit which an ignorant boy below five feet tall can do. Therefore, it is said to be "the beginning of ignorance". Hence the saying: "Foreknowledge is the flower of Reason, but of ignorance the beginning."

"A great sportsman" is so called because his wisdom is great. To "abide by the solid and dwell not in the superficial", as is said, means to act upon inner feelings and realities and leave aside outer rules of propriety and appearance. To "abide in the fruit and dwell not in the flower", as is said, means to follow causes and principles and make no arbitrary guesses. To "discard the latter and choose the former", as is said, means to discard outer manners and arbitrary guesses, and adapt causes, principles, inner feelings, and realities. Hence the saying: "He discards the former and chooses the latter."

CHAPTER LVIII. ADAPTATION TO CHANGE

Whose government is unostentatious, quite unostentatious, his people will be prosperous, quite prosperous. Whose government is prying, quite prying, his people will be needy, quite needy.

Misery, alas! is what happiness rests upon. Happiness, alas! is what misery is hidden in. But who foresees the catastrophe? It will not be prevented.

What is ordinary becomes again extraordinary. What is good becomes again unpropitious. This bewilders people, and it happens constantly since times immemorial.

Therefore the saintly man is square but not sharp, strict but not obnoxious, upright but not restraining, bright but not dazzling.

Man encountered by misery feels afraid in mind. If he feels afraid in mind, his motives of conduct will become straight. If his motives of conduct are straight, his thinking processes will become careful. If his thinking processes are careful, he will attain principles of affairs. If his motives of conduct are straight, he will meet no misery. If he meets no misery, he will live a life as decreed by heaven. If he attains principles of affairs, he will accomplish meritorious works. If he can live a life as decreed by heaven, his life will be perfect and long. If he accomplishes meritorious works, he will be wealthy and noble. Who is perfect, long-lived, wealthy, and noble, is called happy. Thus, happiness originates in the possession of misery. Hence the saying: "Misery, alas! is what happiness rests upon" for accomplishing its merit.

When one has happiness, wealth and nobility come to him. As soon as wealth and nobility come to him, his clothes and food become good. As soon as his clothes and food become good, an arrogant attitude appears. When an arrogant attitude appears, his conduct will become wicked and his action unreasonable. If his conduct is wicked, he will come to an untimely end. If his action is unreasonable, he will accomplish nothing. Indeed, to meet the disaster of premature death without making a reputation for achievement, is a great misery. Thus, misery originates in the possession of happiness. Hence the saying: "Happiness, alas! is what misery is hidden in."

Indeed, those who administer affairs by following reason and principle never fail to accomplish tasks. Those who never fail to accomplish tasks, can attain the honour and influence of the Son of Heaven[1] for their best or at least easily secure the rewards and bounties of ministers and generals. Indeed, those who discard reason and principle and make arbitrary motions, though they have the honour and influence of the Son of Heaven and the feudal lords on the one hand and possess ten times the wealth of Yi Dun and Tao Zhu,[2] will eventually lose their subjects and ruin their financial resources. The masses of the people who discard reason imprudently and make arbitrary motions easily, do not know that the cycle of misery and happiness is so great and profound and the way is so wide and long. Hence Laozi taught men by saying: "Who foresees the catastrophe?"

Everybody wants wealth, nobility, health, and longevity. Yet none can evade the disaster of poverty, lowliness, death, or untimely end. To have the want in mind for wealth, nobility, health, and longevity, and meet poverty, lowliness, death, or untimely end, in the long run, means the inability to reach what one wants to reach. In general, who misses the way he seeks and walks at random, is said to be bewildered. If bewildered, he cannot reach the place he wants to reach. Now the masses of the people cannot reach the place they want to reach. Hence the saying of "bewilderment".

That the masses of the people cannot reach the place they want to reach, has been true since the opening of heaven and earth till the present. Hence the saying: "The people have been bewildered from time immemorial."

By "square" is implied the correspondence of the internal with the external, the agreement of word with deed. By "strictness" is implied the determination to die in the cause of fidelity, to take matters of property and money easy. By "uprightness" is implied the sense of duty to stand by the just, the frame of mind to be impartial. By "brightness" is implied the honour of official rank and the excellence of clothes and fur garments. Now, the upholders of the right way of life, though earnest in mind and adaptable outside, neither slander the defamed nor debase the fallen. Though determined to die a martyr to fidelity and not be covetous of money, they neither insult the fickle nor put the greedy to shame. Though righteous and impartial, they neither spurn the wicked nor accuse the selfish. Though their influence is great and their clothes excellent, they neither show off before the humble nor look down upon the poor. What is the cause of this? Well, suppose those who have lost the way are willing to listen to able man and ask knowers of the way. Then they will not be bewildered. Now, the masses of the people want successes but meet failures because they were born ignorant of reason

---

1. That is, the emperor.   2. Two often-cited exemplars of excessive wealth.

and principle and are still unwilling to ask the knowers and listen to the able. The masses of the people being thus not willing to ask the knowers and listen to the able, if saintly men reproach their misery and failure, they show resentment. The masses are many, the saintly men are few. That the few cannot prevail upon the many, is natural. Now, to make enemies of All-under-Heaven habitually is not the way to keep oneself intact and enjoy a long life. For this reason, the saintly men follow the four standards of conduct and exalt them in solitude. Hence the saying: "The saintly man is square but not sharp, strict but not obnoxious, upright but not restraining, bright but not dazzling."

CHAPTER XLVI. MODERATION OF DESIRE

When All-under-Heaven follows Dao, race-horses are reserved for hauling dung. When All-under-Heaven does not follow Dao, war horses are bred in the suburbs.

No greater crime than submitting to desire. No greater misery than not knowing sufficiency. No greater fault than avarice.

Therefore, who knows sufficiency's sufficiency is always sufficient.

The ruler who upholds Dao incurs no hatred from the neighbouring enemies outside and bestows beneficence upon the people at home. Verily, who incurs no hatred from the neighbouring enemies, observes the rules of etiquette when dealing with the feudal lords; who bestows beneficence upon the people, emphasizes primary works when administering the people's affairs. If he treats the feudal lords according to the rules of etiquette, then warfare will rarely take place. If he administers the people's affairs by emphasizing their primary works, then indulgence in pleasures and extravagant livelihood will stop. Now, horses in general are greatly useful because they carry armour and weapons and facilitate indulgence in pleasures and extravagant livelihood. However, inasmuch as the ruler who upholds the true path rarely employs armour and weapons and forbids indulgence in pleasures and extravagant livelihood, the sovereign does not have to use horses in warfare and drive them back and forth and the masses of the people never have to employ horses for transporting luxuries between distant places. What they devote their strength to, is farms and fields only. If they devote their strength to farms and fields, they have to haul dung for fertilizing the land and water for irrigating it. Hence the saying: "When All-under-Heaven follows Dao, race-horses are reserved for hauling dung."

On the contrary, if the ruler of men does not uphold Dao, at home he will misgovern the people and abroad he will offend the neighbouring states. If he misgoverns the people, the people will lose their property; if he offend the neighbouring states, warfare will frequently take place. If the people lose their property, the cattle will decrease; if warfare takes place frequently, officers and soldiers will be exhausted. If cattle decrease, war horses will become few; if officers and soldiers are exhausted, the army will be jeopardized. If war horses are few, then even mares will have to appear on the battlefield; if the army is jeopardized, then even courtiers will have to march to the front line. After all, horses are of great use to troops, and "suburb" means "neighbourhood at hand". Since they have to replenish the army with mares and courtiers, hence the saying: "When All-under-Heaven does not follow Dao, war horses are bred in the suburbs."

When a man has wild desires, his inferences become confused. When his inferences are confused, his desire becomes intense. When his desire is intense, the crooked mind rules supreme. When the crooked mind rules supreme, affairs go straight to a deadlock. When affairs go straight to a deadlock, disasters take place. From this viewpoint it is clear that disasters are due to the crooked mind, which is in its turn due to submission to desire. As regards submission to desire, the positive kind would lead obedient citizens to villainy, the negative kind would lead good persons to misery. When culprits appear, the ruler will be violated and weakened. When misery comes, most people will be harmed. Thus, all sorts of submission to desire either violate and weaken the ruler or harm the people. To violate and weaken the ruler and harm the people is, indeed, a great crime. Hence the saying: "No greater crime than submitting to desire."

Therefore the saintly men are never attracted to the five colours[3] nor do they indulge in music; the intelligent ruler treats lightly amusement in curios and rids himself of indulgence in beauties. By nature man has neither wool nor feather. If he wears no clothes at all, he cannot resist cold. Above he does not belong to the heavens. Below he is not stuck to the earth. And the stomach and intestines are what he takes as roots of his life. Unless he eat, he cannot live. Therefore he cannot avoid having an avaricious mind. The avaricious mind, unless banished, would cause one worries. Therefore, the saintly men, if they have sufficient clothes to resist cold and sufficient food to fill their empty stomachs, have no worry at all. The same is not true of the ordinary man. Whether they are feudal lords or only worth a thousand pieces of gold, their worry about what they want to get is never shaken off. It is possible for convicts to receive special pardons; and it happens occasionally that criminals sentenced to death live on for some time. Since the worry of those who know no sufficiency is life-long and inevitable, hence the saying: "No greater misery than not knowing sufficiency."

Therefore, if avarice is intense, it causes worry. If one worries, he falls ill. If he falls ill, his intelligence declines. If his intelligence declines, he loses the ability to measure and calculate. If he loses the ability to measure and calculate, his action becomes absurd. If his action is absurd, then misery will befall him. If misery befalls him, the illness will turn from bad to worse inside his body. If the illness turns from bad to worse inside his body, he feels pain. If misery hangs over him from without, he feels distressed. The pain and distress that ply out and in would hurt the invalid seriously. Hurt seriously, the invalid retires and finds fault with himself. It is due to the avaricious mind that he retires and finds fault with himself. Hence the saying: "No greater fault than avarice."

CHAPTER XIV. PRAISING THE MYSTERIOUS

What we look at and is not seen is named Colourless. What we listen to and is not heard is named Soundless. What we grope for and is not grasped is named Bodiless.

---

3. Green, red, yellow, white, and black.

> *These three things cannot further be analysed. Thus they are com-*
> *bined and conceived as a unity which on its surface is not clear and*
> *in its depth not obscure.*
> *Forever and aye it remains unnamable, and again and again it*
> *returns home to non-existence.*
> *This is called the form of the formless, the image of the imageless.*
> *This is called the transcendentally abstruse.*
> *In front its beginning is not seen. In the rear its end is not seen.*
> *By holding fast to the way of the antiquity control the present. And*
> *thereby understand the origin of the antiquity. This is called the rule*
> *of Dao.*

Dao is the way of everything, the form of every principle. Principles are the lines that complete things. Dao is the cause of the completion of everything. Hence the saying: "It is Dao that rules everything."

Things have their respective principles and therefore cannot trespass against each other. Inasmuch as things have their respective principles and therefore cannot trespass against each other, principles are determinants of things and everything has a unique principle. Inasmuch as everything has its unique principle and Dao disciplines the principles of all things, everything has to go through the process of transformation. Inasmuch as everything has to go through the process of transformation, it has no fixed frame. Since everything has no fixed frame, the course of life and death depends upon Dao, the wisdom of the myriad kinds conforms to it, and the rise and fall of the myriad affairs is due to it. Heaven can be high because of it, earth can hold everything because of it, the Polar Star can have its majesty because of it, the sun and the moon can make constant illumination because of it, the five constant elements[4] can keep their positions constant because of it, all the stars can keep their orbits right because of it, the four seasons can control their diverse expressions because of it, Xianyuan,[5] could rule over the four directions at his discretion because of it, Master Red Pine[6] could live as long as heaven and earth because of it, and sages can compose essays and elaborate institutions because of it. It was manifested in the wisdom of Yao and Shun,[7] in the rampancy of Jieyu,[8] in the destruction of Jie and Zhou,[9] and in the prosperity of Tang and Wu. Near as you might suppose it to be, it travels to the four poles of the world. Far as you might suppose it to be, it always abides by the side of everybody. Dim as you might suppose it to be, its gleam is glittering. Bright as you might suppose it to be, its body is obscure. By its achievement heaven and earth are formed. By its harmony thundering is transformed. Thus everything in the world owes it its formation. By nature the inner reality of Dao is neither restrained nor embodied. It is either soft or weak according as the occasion is, and is always in correspondence with principles. Because of it everything dies. Thanks to it everything lives. Because of it every affair fails. Thanks to it every affair

4. Wood, fire, metal, water, and earth.
5. The personal name of the Yellow Emperor (Huangdi), one of the Three Sovereigns and Five Emperors (Sanhuang Wudi).
6. A Daoist who achieved transcendence and immortality.
7. The legendary Chinese ruler who followed Yao (ca. 23rd century B.C.E.).
8. Alias of Lu Tong, a native of the Chu State, who feigned himself mad [ca. 490 B.C.E.] to escape being importuned to engage in public works [translator's note].
9. Two notoriously despotic Chinese kings; they were overthrown by Tang and Wu, respectively, who ruled wisely.

succeeds. Dao can be compared to water. Who is drowning, dies as he drinks too much of it. Who is thirsty lives on as he drinks a proper amount of it. Again, it can be compared to a sword or a spear. If the stupid man uses it for wreaking his grudge upon others, calamities will happen. If the saintly man uses it for punishing the outrageous, good luck will ensue. Thus, people die of it, live owing to it, fail because of it, and succeed on account of it.

Men rarely see living elephants. As they come by the skeleton of a dead elephant, they imagine its living according to its features. Therefore it comes to pass that whatever people use for imagining the real is called "image". Though Dao cannot be heard and seen, the saintly man imagines its real features in the light of its present effects. Hence the saying: "It is the form of the formless, the image of the imageless."

CHAPTER I. UNDERSTANDING DAO

The Dao that can be traced as a way is not the eternal Dao. The name that can be defined as a name is not the eternal name. What has no name is the beginning of heaven and earth. What has a name is the mother of the myriad things. Therefore it is said:

> *"He who desireless is found*
> *The spiritual of the world will sound.*
> *But he who by desire is bound*
> *Sees the mere shell of things around."*

These two things are the same in source but different in name. Their sameness is called a mystery. Indeed, it is the mystery of mysteries. Of all subtleties it is the gate.

In general, principles are what distinguish the square from the round, the short from the long, the coarse from the fine, and the hard from the brittle. Accordingly, it is only after principles become definite that things can attain Dao. Thus, definite principles include those of existence and extinction, of life and death, and of rise and fall. Indeed, anything that first exists and next goes to ruin, now lives and then dies, and prospers at the beginning and declines afterward, cannot be said to be eternal. Only that which begins with the creation of heaven and earth and neither dies nor declines till heaven and earth disappear can be said to be eternal. What is eternal has neither a changing location nor a definite principle and is not inherent in an eternal place. Therefore the eternal cannot be traced as a way. The saintly man, looking at its mysterious emptiness and dwelling upon its universal course, forcibly gave it the name Dao. Only thereafter it can be talked about. Hence the saying: "The Dao that can be traced as a way is not the eternal Dao."

THE OLD MAN BY THE RIVER COMMENTARY
(*Heshang gong*)

The "Old Man by the River" commentary is the earliest complete interpretation of *The Scripture of the Way and Its Virtue* (*Daode jing*; see above) and, along with the equally esteemed commentary by Wang Bi (226–249 C.E.), the most influential for later Daoist interpreters of that work. In the Tang dynasty (618–907 C.E.), it came to be used as part of initiation rituals, while others argued for the primacy of Wang Bi's commentary. Eventually, a series of edicts and a commentary written by the emperor himself, all indicating a preference for the "Old Man by the River," resolved disputes about which text should be used for imperial examinations. Today, however, most modern editions of *The Scripture of the Way and Its Virtue* rely on Wang Bi, who offers a more pronounced metaphysical reading of the text focused on the ideas of "being" and "nonbeing."

According to tradition, the "Old Man by the River" commentary was written by Heshang gong, a legendary figure (second century B.C.E.) of the Han dynasty who is said to have presented it to the emperor Wen (r. 179–157 B.C.E.). An avid reader of *The Scripture of the Way and Its Virtue*, the emperor asked Heshang gong to explicate some of the text's difficult sections. His refusal angered the emperor, who set off to berate him. When the emperor arrived at Heshang gong's location "by the river" he was awed when he saw "the old man" levitate and reveal himself as a deity. After this display, the emperor humbly received the commentary. This legend was later attacked by critics who claimed that it was a fabrication intended to confuse the masses.

The body of the "Old Man by the River" commentary is a line-by-line exegesis of *The Scripture of the Way and Its Virtue* that emphasizes the mystery at the origin of the universe, self-cultivation, and state governance. This reading explains the origin of heaven and earth: it is the Way (Dao) that issues forth—in the form of breath or pneuma (*qi*)—from the void of nothingness to form all that is. Once heaven and earth have taken shape and been populated, it is the responsibility of people and other living things to maintain an ideal harmonious order, thereby fending off chaos and illness. The commentary on chapter 3 of *The Scripture of the Way and Its Virtue* explicitly correlates governing the state with governing the body. Principles such as simplicity, non-action, and purity are essential to establishing and maintaining the ruler's virtue (De), which is sufficient for keeping harmony in the realm. Conversely, the text warns against the dangers of excessive desire for wealth and of sexual indulgence, emphasizing that males need to retain semen since that is their life essence. The "Old Man by the River" commentary situates such concerns within the context of other practices of bodily cultivation, such as breathing exercises and dietary control. Through effective governance the sage ruler's guidance of a peaceful country will last a long time, and through proper self-cultivation he will become an immortal. Indeed, this dual cultivation of the sage ruler may be one of the most distinctive features of this particular commentary on *The Scripture of the Way and Its Virtue*.

PRONOUNCING GLOSSARY

Dao: *dow*

De: *duh*

Heshang gong: *huh-shawng kung*

Chapter 3. How to Pacify the People[1]

Not to exalt the worthies

> By the worthies the average worthies of the world are meant. They exchange opinions, make themselves intelligible, detach themselves from Dao, adapt themselves to circumstances, avoid reality and effect appearance. Those who are not commendable may not be honoured with functions nor endowed with posts.

does not cause the people to contend.

> Do not contend for merit and glory but return to nature.

Not to praise treasures difficult to gain

> This means that a prince ought not to rule with a love for precious treasures. He should cast the money [back] to the mountains [where it came from] and throw the pearls and jewels into the lakes.

causes people not to become thieves.

> If the superiors turn towards purity, the inferiors are not greedy.

Not to show things desirable

> One ought to banish the songs of Zheng[2] and to keep away adulators.

does not lead the mind into confusion.

> Do not be bad and excessive nor unstable and confused.

Therefore the government of the saint

> This means to govern the country together with the body.

empties their minds and fills their bellies,

> Abandon desire and flee from confusion and trouble. Enclose Dao in your bosom, embrace unity and retain the five spirits.[3]

weakens their will

> Side with the weak and supple and do not stay with the powerful.

and strengthens their bones.

> Save the semen and make its extension difficult. Then the marrow will become filled and the bones firm.

He always induces the people not to know and not to desire.

> Return to simplicity and retain purity.

He causes the knowing ones not to dare to act.

> Think with awe of the depth and do not take words easy.

If one acts non-action,

> To do nothing sets inertness in motion.

then nothing is not governed.

> If De[4] is changed to fulness, then the people are pacified.

Translated by Eduard Erkes.

1. These chapter numbers, and the lines on which the indented text comments, are from *The Scripture of the Way and Its Virtue (Daode jing*, or *Laozi*), attributed to Laozi; see above.
2. Attacked in the *Analects* of Confucius (551– 479 B.C.E.) as licentious.
3. That is, the spirits of the five viscera (liver, heart, spleen, kidneys, and lungs); see the commentary to chapter 6, below.
4. Virtue or Power.

ESSENTIAL POINTS ON THE SIX LINEAGES
OF THOUGHT
(*Lun liujia yaozhi*)

SIMA TAN

Sima Tan (d. 110 B.C.E.) is far less well known than his son Sima Qian (145?–86? B.C.E.), who followed him in the post of grand historian at the Han court and composed the most important early Chinese history, *Records of the Grand Historian* (*Shiji*), in which he included (and wrote an introduction to) his father's essay, "Essential Points on the Six Lineages of Thought" ("Lun liujia yaozhi"). Yet Sima Tan's brief account did much to distinguish and thus define six early philosophical traditions: Yinyang (called Naturalist in this translation), Confucian (Ru), Mohist (Mo), Legalist (Fajia), Sophist (Mingjia, called Terminologist in this translation), and Daoist (Daojia or Daode). The final three labels were Sima Tan's neologisms, all containing the difficult-to-translate suffix -*jia*. The term refers to some type of collectivity, but perhaps something closer to a family or lineage than to a well-defined school.

Sima Tan, a court astrologer, set out to address what he perceived as confusions among the scholars of his day by clarifying the main tenets of those different lineages. He goes beyond introducing the different schools to critically evaluate their teachings. "The Confucians," for instance, "are erudite yet lack the essentials. They labor much yet achieve little." Sima Tan is clearly partial to Daoism, which he rates the most highly of the different traditions; indeed, he tried to persuade the Han emperor to embrace it as his ruling ideology. Sima Tan notes that while the Daoists derive many of their teachings from the best aspects of the other traditions, unlike the Confucians "their tenets are concise and easy to grasp; their policies are few but their achievements are many." He emphasizes that "the Daoists do nothing, but they also say that nothing is left undone," and stresses the importance of joining with the Dao. His essay primarily demonstrates that Sima Tan portrayed the category of "Daoism" as a largely syncretic intellectual system.

Sima Qian's Introduction

The Grand Historian [Sima Tan] studied astronomy with Tang Du, received instruction in the *Classic of Changes*[1] from Yang He, and mastered Daoist discourse under Master Huang. The Grand Historian held office from the Jianyuan to the Yuanfeng periods (between 140 and 110 B.C.E.). Because he sympathized with scholars who did not understand his purpose and teachers who were confused about it, he discoursed on the essential tenets of the six lineages and stated the following:

TRANSLATED BY Harold Roth and Sarah Queen.

1. The *Yijing* or *I Ching* (traditionally dated ca. 12th century B.C.E.), a book of divination and cosmology.

Sima Tan's Lecture

The Great Commentary[2] to the Classic of Changes says: "All-under-Heaven share the same goal, yet there are a hundred ways of thinking about it; they return to the same home, yet follow different pathways there." The Naturalists (yin yang jia), Confucians, Mohists, Terminologists (ming jia), Legalists,[3] and Daoists all strive to create order [in the world]. It is just that, in the different routes they follow and in what they say, some are more perceptive than others.

I once observed that the techniques of the Naturalists magnify the importance of omens and proliferate avoidances and taboos, causing people to feel constrained and to fear many things. Nonetheless, one cannot fault the way they set out in order the grand compliances of the four seasons.

The Confucians are erudite yet lack the essentials. They labor much yet achieve little. This is why their doctrines are difficult to follow completely. Nonetheless, one cannot detract from the way they set out in order the various rituals between ruler and minister and father and son and enumerate the various distinctions between husband and wife and elder and younger.

The Mohists are frugal and difficult to follow. This is why it is not possible fully to conform to their doctrines. Nonetheless, one cannot disregard the way they strengthen the foundation [agriculture] and economize expenditures.

The Legalists are harsh and lacking in compassion. Nonetheless, one cannot improve upon the way they rectify the distinctions between ruler and minister and superior and subordinate.

The Terminologists cause people to be strict [with words], yet they outdo themselves and lose sight of the truth. Nonetheless, one cannot disregard the way they rectify names and their realities.

The Daoists enable the numinous essence within people to be concentrated and unified. They move in unison with the Formless and provide adequately for all living things. In deriving their techniques, they follow the grand compliances of the Naturalists, select the best of the Confucians and Mohists, and extract the essentials of the Terminologists and Legalists. They shift [their policies] in accordance with the seasons and respond to the transformations of things. In establishing customs and promulgating policies, they do nothing unsuitable. Their tenets are concise and easy to grasp; their policies are few but their achievements are many.

The Confucians are not like this. They maintain that the ruler is the exemplar for all-under-Heaven. For them, the ruler guides and the officials harmonize with him; the ruler initiates and the officials follow. Proceeding in this manner, the ruler labors hard and the officials sit idle.

The essentials of the Great Way are simply a matter of discarding strength and avarice and casting aside perception and intellect. One relinquishes these and relies on the techniques [of self-cultivation]. When the numen (shen, "spirit") is used excessively it becomes depleted; when the physical

---

2. The most influential part of the exegetical material included in the Classic of Changes itself.
3. On the Legalists, see the introduction to the Book of Master Han Fei (Han Feizi), above; they espoused the strict application of laws that rigidly prescribed punishments. "Mohists": followers of Mo Di (see The Book of Master Mo, or Mozi, above).

form labors excessively it becomes worn out. It is unheard of for one whose physical form and numen are agitated and disturbed to hope to attain the longevity of Heaven and Earth.

Sima Tan's Self-Commentary

According to the Naturalists, the four seasons, eight positions, twelve limits, and the twenty-four seasonal nodes[4] each have their instructions and commands. Those who comply with them will flourish; those who defy them, if their own person does not perish, will lose [their states]. Yet it does not necessarily have to be this way. Therefore I said, "They cause people to feel constrained and to fear many things." In the spring, living things are generated, in the summer they mature, in the autumn they are harvested, in the winter they are stored away: this is the Great Norm of Heaven's Way. If you do not comply with it, then you lack the means to become the guiding basis for all-under-Heaven. Therefore I said, "One cannot fault the way they prioritize the grand compliances of the four seasons."

The Confucians take the Six Arts[5] as their standards. The scriptures and commentaries on the Six Arts are innumerable. Successive generations have not been able to master their scholarship, while the present generation is not able to penetrate their rituals. Therefore I said, they "are erudite yet lack the essentials; they labor much yet achieve little." Yet even the hundred lineages cannot modify how they enumerate the various rituals between ruler and minister and father and son and how they prioritize the distinctions between husband and wife and elder and younger.

The Mohists indeed esteem the Way of Yao and Shun.[6] When they speak of their virtuous conduct they say: "The ancestral altar should be three and one half feet high. It should have three earthen steps and should have a thatched roof that is not trimmed and should use rafters that are not cut. Food should be presented in square earthenware vessels and should be sipped using earthenware utensils and should consist of coarse millet and a soup of assorted greens. In the summer one should wear clothes made of linen and in the winter one should wear garments made of deer[skin]." In their funerals they insist on a coffin of only three inches in thickness and raise their voices in mourning tones that do not exhaust their feelings of grief. In their teachings about the rites of mourning, they insist that all people follow these practices. By making all-under-Heaven follow these methods, they lose the distinction between honorable and humble. Generations differ and times change, so one's policies and undertakings do not necessarily remain the same. This is why I said they "are frugal and difficult to obey." In essence because they claim to "strengthen the foundation and economize expenditures," theirs is a way by which people can provide enough for their families. This is what Mozi excelled in; even a hundred lineages cannot disregard it.

---

4. The division of the year into twenty-four 15-day periods (this 360-day year of the folk or astrological calendar required adjustment to match the astronomical year). "Eight positions": the four cardinal directions and the four intermediary directions. "Twelve limits": the twelve sections of the sky delineated by the movement of Jupiter.

5. Rites, music, archery, chariot racing, calligraphy, and mathematics—the core of Chinese education.
6. Two legendary Chinese emperors who ruled in succession (ca. 23rd century B.C.E.), praised by Confucius for their integrity and virtue.

The Legalists do not distinguish between close and distant relations and do not differentiate between noble and base. All are one before the law. They therefore destroy the compassion that comes from cherishing one's close relations and honoring the honorable. While one can implement their schemes for a single season, they cannot be used for longer than that. Therefore I said they "are harsh and lacking in compassion." Nonetheless, even the hundred lineages cannot improve upon the way they honor the ruler and humble the ministers and the way they distinguish official duties so that they do not overstep one another.

The Terminologists chase around in circles over petty details and cause people to be unable to return to their basic meaning. They become obsessed with names, yet they lose sight of the genuine basis of human beings. Therefore I said they "cause people to be strict [with words], yet they outdo themselves and lose sight of the truth." However, their methods of selecting names and demanding a corresponding reality and of the three [tests to determine a minister's merit] and the five [tests to determine a minister's faults] do not err and cannot be ignored.

The Daoists do nothing, but they also say that nothing is left undone. Their substance is easy to practice, but their words are difficult to understand. Their techniques take emptiness and nothingness as the foundation and adaptation and compliance as the application. They have no set limits, no regular forms, and so are able to penetrate to the genuine basis of living things. Because they neither anticipate things nor linger over them, they are able to become the masters of all living things.

They have methods that are no methods:
They take adapting to the seasons as their practice.
They have limits that are no limits:
They adapt to things by harmonizing with them.
Therefore they say:
The sage is not clever:
The seasonal alternations are what the sage preserves.
Emptiness is the constant in the Way.
Adaptation is the guiding principle of the ruler.

When the various ministers arrive together [for an audience], the ruler makes each clarify himself. When their accomplishments have matched their appraisal, the ruler calls this scrupulous. When their accomplishments have not matched their appraisal, the ruler calls this deceptive. When deceptive speech is not heard, traitors do not arise, the worthy and worthless will differentiate themselves, and white and black will then take shape. Among those whom one desires to employ, what endeavor will not succeed? This is, then, how the ruler unites with the Great Way, obscure and dark, illuminates all-under-Heaven, and reverts to the Nameless.

What gives life to all human beings is the numen (spirit), and what they rely upon is the body. When the numen is used excessively it becomes depleted; when the body toils excessively it wears out. When the body and numen separate we die; when we die we cannot return to life; what separates cannot return to how it was. Therefore the sage attaches great importance to this. From this we observe that the numen is the foundation of life, and the physical form is the vessel of life. How could anyone say, "I possess the means to rule all-under-Heaven" without first stabilizing the numen?

Classical Daoism Takes Shape

FROM THE HAN DYNASTY (202 B.C.E.–220 C.E.) THROUGH THE SIX DYNASTIES PERIOD (220–589 C.E.)

The roughly eight centuries from the beginning of the Han dynasty (202 B.C.E.–220 C.E.) through the end of the Six Dynasties (220–589 C.E.) was the period when Daoism emerged as an organized religious tradition; the sage Laozi was refashioned as a deity; pantheons of deities developed, including some who resided in the human body; and a series of divine revelations inaugurated new Daoist movements in different regions within the Chinese empire. Among the religious and philosophical developments that resulted in the new Daoist schools were some new elements, which melded with formative concepts, beliefs, and practices from the pre-Han period. Some knowledge of the rise and fall of different dynasties and kingdoms during this period is necessary

This bronze statue depicts Laozi in his deified form. During the Tang dynasty, Laozi (also known as Li Er) achieved new importance for the imperial clan based on the claim that he shared their same surname of Li.

to understand the history of Daoism, since its main developments are keyed to those historical events.

As the Han dynasty declined—losing, in the eyes of its rivals, the mandate of heaven to rule—Daoist movements began to take shape, asserting themselves as its proper successors both politically and religiously. An equally momentous change came a century later when the loss of North China to the "barbarian" Xiongnu invaders in 316 C.E. caused a mass emigration of Han Chinese elites to the south, the relocation of the capital to Jiankang (also known as Jianye, present-day Nanjing), and the move of Daoism to the south. The arrival of Han Chinese in the south, which up to that point had been inhabited largely by non-Chinese tribal populations, became the catalyst for fervent new Daoist innovations.

Meanwhile, in the north, from the fourth century through its sixth-century reunification during the Sui dynasty (581–618 C.E.), a succession of kingdoms ruled by Sinicized non-Han Chinese were amenable to the arrival of Buddhism from India. In this period, we begin to see evidence that Buddhism and Daoism appropriated elements from each other. That the Buddhist tradition thrived in China also resulted in conflicts, as these two major religions each sought the support of the people and the patronage of the emperor.

As Buddhism spread and Daoism became organized, Confucianism gradually lost its purchase as a key structuring element of Chinese society, with its ideas discredited and its leadership politically marginalized after the fall of the Han dynasty. Daoism, now its chief rival, attempted with considerable success to acquire textual legitimacy as well as political influence by claiming that its scriptures supersede Confucian and Buddhist texts because they are nothing less than pure emanations from the Dao itself.

THE HAN DYNASTY AND THE BIRTH
OF ORGANIZED DAOISM

The Han dynasty was founded by Liu Bang, who later became Emperor Gaozu (r. 202–195 B.C.E.), out of the chaos created by the fall of the short-lived Qin dynasty (221–206 B.C.E.). The Han has been described as a prosperous dynasty that expanded the geographic reach of the Chinese empire, and its name came to denote the largest of China's fifty-six different ethnicities. In 9 C.E. the regent Wang Mang proclaimed himself the emperor of the newly founded Xin dynasty (9–23 C.E.), an act that split the Han dynasty into the Western (Former) Han (206 B.C.E.–9 C.E.) and the reunified Eastern (Later) Han (27 C.E.–220 C.E.).

Daoism, as an organized religious movement, began during the Eastern Han, but there is no overarching consensus on precisely when; by convention, 142 C.E. is usually taken as a plausible starting point. In that year, the visitation of Zhang Daoling (34–156 C.E.) by the divinized Laozi inaugurated the Way of the Celestial Masters (Tianshi dao), also known as the Covenantal Authority of Correct Unity (Zhengyi mengwei). The group was scornfully labeled by outsiders the Way of the Five Pecks of Rice (Wudoumi dao), because each household provided 5 pecks (40 quarts) of rice as an offering to sustain the clergy and perhaps be distributed to those in need. But in 142 C.E. Daoism was neither a fully formed tradition, nor an apparition. The various elements that came together in its formation during the Eastern

Han dynasty had existed in nascent form earlier—some going back to the Western Han and many others deeply rooted in the pre-Han period. Daoism thus emerges into view during the second century C.E. at the confluence of old and new elements. Their fusion took concrete form in the first Daoist religious community, at a time of great political flux.

One of the important ingredients carried over from the pre-Han period into the Han was the nebulous group referred to by outsiders as the "masters of methods" (*fangshi*), who specialized in medical techniques, divination, and exorcism. They also attempted to win the patronage of rulers with their stories of paradisical realms inhabited by transcendents (*xian*)—who are sometimes represented as birdlike figures—and they are best known for using various techniques to pursue immortality. It is within this group that we find the first instances of alchemical experimentation (the transmuting of cinnabar into gold) aimed at extending life and hopes of communing with the transcendents, who live on island paradises in the sea.

Another significant movement behind the historical development of Daoism was the Huang-Lao tradition, which combined the veneration of the legendary Yellow Emperor (Huangdi, hence "Huang") with the veneration of Laozi ("Lao") as a sage of governance. This movement arose on the eastern seaboard in the state of Qi (part of present-day Shandong)—connected with a figure claiming descent from Laozi—but its teachings quickly spread and found their way to the capital, where they inspired some Han leaders to rule by the principle of non-action (*wuwei*) that *The Scripture of the Way and Its Virtue* (*Daode jing*) proposed for governing. In addition to governmental reform, the Huang-Lao tradition also focused on military strategy, the renunciation of wealth, healing, the use of medicinal recipes to attain longevity, and divination. Its ideas and practices are still not entirely understood, but when Confucianism was installed as the ruling ideology early in the Han dynasty the Huang-Lao movement left the halls of political power and spread among the common people. It is therefore possible to discern the impact of the Huang-Lao tradition on the two main new movements that will be discussed below, the Yellow Turbans and Celestial Masters.

Han imperial religion was also an important conduit for ideas and practices that shaped Daoism. The best evidence for its influence is found in the surviving remnants of the Han apocrypha. These texts, which are quasi-Daoist addenda to the imperially sponsored Confucian Classics, are filled with various divination methods and keys for understanding omens, prophecies, and portents. By insisting that heaven monitored human affairs, the apocrypha emphasized that humans would be rewarded or punished, according to their good or bad behavior. While those addenda claimed to be merely revealing esoteric aspects of the Confucian Classics, they were nonetheless deemed suspicious, banned by imperial authorities, and ultimately burned at the end of the Han dynasty—creating a significant gap in the early history of Daoism. The surviving fragments reveal many similarities both with ideas and practices connected to the masters of methods and to what we find in later organized Daoism. Not only are apocryphal texts cited by name in Daoist works, but they mention deities and spirits that would later become prominent in Daoism and detail the powers that accrue to those who can learn the names of those spirits.

Organized Daoism drew as well on popular elements of pre-Han and Han religion. The humble inscriptions of commoners' tombs provide physical evidence that key ideas and beliefs that would surface in the Celestial Masters tradition—and would be essential features within subsequent Daoist movements—were already circulating in the lower strata of village society during the first century C.E. Among these beliefs and practices are precursors of the demonological tradition that would be absorbed into Daoism (see *Demon Statutes of Lady Blue*, or *Nüqing guilü*) and conceptions of a bureaucratized heaven and netherworld, which include bookkeepers who maintain the registers of life and death that dictate each person's life span. These excavated sources frequently document communication with the other world, always through written texts; many of these early examples were addressed to the Yellow Emperor. During the Warring States period (403–221 B.C.E.), stories circulated about those who retreated from society into the mountains. During the Han dynasty, by contrast, the earliest true Daoist communities mirrored that dynasty's secular bureaucracy in their organization.

THE DEIFICATION OF LAOZI AND THE RISE OF DAOIST MESSIANISM IN THE EASTERN HAN

One of the more striking Daoist developments of the Eastern Han dynasty is the transformation of the sagely Laozi into a supreme deity, who is an incarnation of the Dao itself and is described with many of the same attributes as the Buddha. Laozi's apotheosis would have a profound impact on subsequent Daoist history, since he appears again and again as the one who reveals the teachings that initiate new Daoist schools. In the *Laozi Inscription* (*Laozi ming*) and *Scripture on Laozi's Transformations* (*Laozi bianhua jing*), Laozi is depicted as a cosmic being who was also the teacher of the great legendary sages of the past, including Confucius. Those mid-second-century texts also portray him as accessible to adepts, taking the form of deities inside their bodies. The deified Laozi often appears in messianic contexts. Acknowledging the decline of the Han ruling house, Laozi sought worthy followers to bring it to a final end. This image of Laozi continued to emerge throughout Chinese history as a messianic figure helping humans to make political changes when necessary. Because he was allegedly surnamed Li, he often appeared in that guise (most commonly as Li Hong).

Thus a broad array of elements gradually came together during the later Eastern Han dynasty. The first Daoist organizations were messianic movements that challenged, and presented an alternative to, the contemporary Han sociopolitical order, which had all but collapsed. Its decline was accompanied by the widespread production of messianic literature. During the first century C.E., for instance, someone named Gan Zhongke paid a visit to the Han court and presented the emperor with a work that he claimed would help to restore the Han dynasty: the *Scripture of Great Peace* (*Taiping jing*). "Great Peace" (Taiping), a general concept predating Daoism, refers to the good government, political harmony, and good health for the masses that characterized a golden age that existed in the past but will not be restored to the empire until the ruling ideology is based on a return to the Dao. Though this idea is found in earlier Chinese political thought, movements and writings of the Han now were directing it against the ineffective political leaders who subscribed to Confucian teachings and who, they believed, had lost heaven's mandate to rule.

Gan Zhongke merely sought to renew the Han with his utopian message, but he was seen as a challenge and executed. Indeed, the threat implicit in the idea of Great Peace would become explicit as movements connected with books of the same title became increasingly radical, calling not to improve and restore the ailing regime but to overthrow it.

THE WAY OF GREAT PEACE (TAIPING DAO) AND THE WAY OF THE CELESTIAL MASTERS (TIANSHI DAO)

The best known of the various regional politico-religious movements that arose as the Han dynasty spiraled into decline were the Way of Great Peace (Taiping dao) and the Way of the Celestial Masters (Tianshi dao). The Great Peace uprising emerged out of the Yellow Turban Rebellion, which was inspired by the *Scripture of Great Peace*. The Yellow Turbans, under the leadership of Zhang Jue (d. 184 C.E.), rose up in the eastern part of China in 184 C.E., believing that in that year the new Yellow Heaven would replace the old regime of the Blue Heaven. They sought to bring about a more equal distribution of wealth and resources and made conversions through healing practices that included ingesting talisman water (mixed with ashes from paper emblazoned with powerful diagrams and then burned) and confessing one's transgressions. The *Scripture of Great Peace* proposed that following the collapse of the Han dynasty, a certain elect—called "seed" people—would populate the newly established kingdom of Great Peace. The Yellow Turbans attracted a large following that weakened the dynasty and ultimately hastened its collapse, though the movement itself was suppressed in a violent crackdown within a year of its appearance.

The other main center of rebellion was in western China, in the kingdom of Shu (which corresponds to the western part of modern Sichuan Province). It was there that the first enduring Daoist religious organization took shape. According to tradition, in 142 C.E. the newly deified Laozi visited a certain Zhang Daoling at Crane Call Mountain (Heming shan). Laozi granted him the title of Celestial Master (*tianshi*), from which this movement takes its name; he also bestowed on Zhang his Covenantal Authority of Correct Unity (Zhengyi mengwei fa). This introduced a new set of precepts intended to replace popular practices, which were also part of the state cult, based on blood sacrifices. The title "Celestial Master" was, the tradition later claimed, passed down within the Zhang family, from Zhang Daoling to his son Zhang Heng to Zhang Heng's son Zhang Lu and so on—reportedly without interruption down to the present day.

Though more is known about the Celestial Masters movement than about the Great Peace movement, the historical record for the period immediately after Lord Lao descended to Zhang Daoling is thin. It is most complete for the thirty-year span when Zhang Daoling's grandson, Zhang Lu, led a religious community in the remote Hanzhong Valley, in modern-day Sichuan. That highly structured community—which had some key resemblances to the Way of Great Peace—was organized into twenty-four administrative districts or parishes and took Daoist ideas as its official doctrine. Some have even referred to this theocratic community as a "Daocracy." The community was surprisingly inclusive; it was open to non-Han Chinese ethnicities, and the sexes were treated as equals. Administratively, the Way of the Celestial Masters mirrored the Han regime, keeping precise records and circulating considerable paperwork—in its case, religious dispatches sent to the offices of Heaven (burned), Earth (buried), and Water (submerged). Its highly structured religious hierarchy similarly took its titles from Han bureaucracy, including "libationer" for the parish head, an office open to men and women alike. The libationer was charged with a number of responsibilities, foremost among them to lead the study and recitation of *The Scripture of the Way and Its Virtue*, which was for the first time treated as a sacred scripture.

This community—with its emphasis on teaching to the masses—was the source of an important commentary on *The Scripture of the Way and Its Virtue*, called the *Xiang'er Commentary on the Laozi* (*Laozi xiang'er zhu*). It is significant for providing not just innovative interpretations of that text, which often run counter to the intent of the original, but also a religious charter for Celestial Masters and thus an intimate look inside the community. One of the primary concerns of the Celestial Masters movement, like the Way of Great Peace, was healing, because illness was tangible proof that one had committed a transgression. Illness could be cured by confession, repentance, good works performed for the community, or time spent reflecting on one's transgression in isolation in a "pure chamber." Members of the Celestial Masters community also gathered for communal meals and other rituals, including the notorious sexual rite known as "merging pneumas" (*heqi*). That highly controlled and choreographed ritual—often misunderstood, and wrongly attacked by Buddhists and others as nothing more than an orgy—was filled with meaningful hidden symbolism. Merging pneumas was a way for adepts to fortify their bodies and double the number of registers of divinities or divine generals that they commanded.

The Celestial Masters community existed in the Hanzhong Valley in relative isolation for about thirty years. Then, in 215 C.E., the third Celestial Master—Zhang Lu, who was Zhang Daoling's grandson—capitulated to Cao Cao (155–220), a general of the Wei kingdom (220–265), who officially recognized the Way of the Celestial Masters tradition and offered Zhang a position at court. This event was an important moment in Daoist history since it would lead, as the Wei kingdom disintegrated, to the dispersal of the organized Daoist community to other parts of China, particularly to the north and west. It is not entirely clear what happened to its members in Sichuan after 215, but the *Commands and Admonitions for the Family of the Great Dao* (*Dadao jia lingjie*), dated to 255, portrays a fractured group, in dire need of renewal. Apparently, the Celestial Masters community descended into chaos in tandem with its sponsor, as the Wei kingdom declined and ultimately collapsed in 265.

THE FURTHER DEVELOPMENT OF DAOISM IN SOUTH CHINA: THE UPPER CLARITY (SHANGQING) AND NUMINOUS TREASURE (LINGBAO) MOVEMENTS

The early fourth century was another important historical moment, as its events transformed the history of Daoism and catalyzed new developments. Throughout the period of disunion, northern China was ruled by a succession of foreign dynasties, and, as noted above, the fall of the Western Jin dynasty (265–316) to the nomadic Xiongnu in 316 spurred a mass migration to the south. It also divided China for the next two hundred years. The capital of the Eastern Jin dynasty (317–420) was established in the south in Jiankang in 317.

When followers of the Celestial Masters tradition reached the south in the early fourth century, they encountered an indigenous religion with deep roots in the Chinese past and its own particular local practices of sorcery and spirit mediumship. One of the key figures who provides insight into the local religious practices, as well as a bridge to the next major Daoist developments, is Ge Hong (283–343 C.E.), an aristocratic scholar and writer (see his *Inner Chapters of the Book of the Master Who Embraces Simplicity*, or *Baopu zi neipian*). His wide-ranging eclectic pursuits included an interest in the alchemical tradition of producing elixirs known as the Great Clarity (Taiqing) tradition, and he wrote a comprehensive history of various transcendent figures. Thanks to his interest in bibliography, he also chronicled some of the main texts and traditions that later made their way into the next Daoist synthesis.

The fourth and early fifth centuries witnessed the rise of two major new Daoist movements in eastern China. Both the Upper Clarity (Shangqing) tradition and the Numinous Treasure (Lingbao) tradition began with revelations of new scriptures and developed into full-blown religious organizations.

The Upper Clarity (Shangqing) Movement

From 364 to 370 C.E. a certain figure named Yang Xi (330–ca. 386) had a series of nocturnal visitations by a host of perfected beings who granted him revelations of striking new scriptures that formed the basis for the Upper Clarity tradition. Little historical information about Yang survives. He was a visionary employed by an aristocratic family—principally Xu Mi (303–373), who was a court official, and his son Xu Hui (341–ca. 370)—living near the southern capital, Jiankang. The Xu family was closely related to Ge Hong's family through marriage.

When large numbers of northern aristocrats fled the Xiongnu to southern China, they displaced the southern aristocracy. The development of the Upper Clarity tradition has therefore been understood in part as a reaction by the dispossessed southerners to the influx of northern elites. The new Upper Clarity Daoist movement provided them with what one writer has called "celestial compensation" for their social decline. Indeed, the perfected (*zhenren*) who descended into Yang Xi's meditation chamber between 364 and 370 came down from the Heaven of Upper Clarity (Shangqing tian), a higher and more ethereal heaven than that occupied by transcendents (*xian*), the Heaven of Great Clarity (Taiqing tian). The southern aristocrats were also assured of being appointed to high offices by their perfected visitors.

The Upper Clarity tradition, also known as the Maoshan tradition (from Mount Mao, the place to which a number of Daoist hermits retired to study the newly revealed scriptures), had an apocalyptic outlook. According to the revelations from the Daoist gods, a catastrophe in a *dinghai* year (in the sixty-year cycle) would wipe out all but a few, like the seed people of the earlier Celestial Masters. This small elect would survive in the caverns on Maoshan as they awaited the descent of the savior Li Hong, the deified Laozi. Several *dinghai* years passed while life carried on as usual for another two hundred years, until another rebellion began to form around a figure who took the name Li Hong.

Yang Xi delivered to the Xu family not just visions but what came to include an entirely new corpus of beautifully written sacred texts—replete with talismans and poems—that were the foundation of the evolving Upper Clarity tradition. The Upper Clarity scriptures would eventually occupy the first of the three divisions of the Daoist canon. In the decades after Yang Xi's death, the Upper Clarity revelations spread throughout the still influential circles of the southern aristocracy, but during the mid-fifth century forgeries also began to circulate as the manuscripts became more widely disseminated.

In response, a series of Daoists tried to codify the original Upper Clarity manuscripts. It was finally Tao Hongjing, a prolific historian related to both the Xus and Ges, who sorted through, verified, and organized the extant revealed scriptures and manuscript fragments. Tao Hongjing was a quintessential bibliophile who used his knowledge of Yang Xi's distinctive calligraphic style to judge the authenticity of manuscripts. The high literary quality of the new canon inspired later writers and poets.

The Upper Clarity texts combine Celestial Masters Daoism with religious traditions indigenous to the south as well as Buddhist concepts and terminology. Notably, the Upper Clarity tradition emphasizes individual meditation—as opposed to the communal practices of the Celestial Masters—and interiorizes what had been external rituals. For example, the Celestial Masters' rite of merging pneumas (*heqi*) became a visualization exercise. Other visualization exercises in Upper Clarity texts and practices include visionary journeys based on microcosmic and macrocosmic connections, whereby distant celestial deities are described as also being present in one's body and nourished through the ingestion of qi. There may be nothing truly novel in the Upper Clarity revelations, but in repurposing the practices and pantheon that it inherited, it created a new blend.

In addition to producing a separate textual corpus, the Upper Clarity movement developed a multifaceted religious tradition with its own institutions, distinct rituals and liturgies, lineage of patriarchs, and sacred geography, which centered on Mount Mao but incorporated the existing set of five sacred mountains (*wuyue*, the Five Marchmounts). The Upper Clarity tradition was the main school of Daoism in the Tang dynasty; it was well received by the imperial court, and the emperor granted titles to Upper Clarity patriarchs.

The Numinous Treasure (Lingbao) Movement

The second new Daoist movement that emerged during the fifth century, following the success of the Upper Clarity, was the Numinous Treasure (Lingbao) tradition, which similarly produced a substantial body of new scriptures. These new revelations began to be circulated by Ge Chaofu, Ge Hong's grandnephew, around 397 C.E.: he claimed that they had originally been received in the third century by Ge Xuan (164–244 C.E.), who was Ge Hong's uncle. Ge Xuan, like Yang Xi, repeatedly played host to divine instructors. These visitors belonged to a new category of beings referred to as Celestial Worthies and were led by the Celestial Worthy of Original Commencement (Yuanshi tianzun)—a figure clearly modeled on the Buddha—who revealed some of the Numinous Treasure texts. Tracing the origin of other Numinous Treasure scriptures to Ge Xuan was strategic, since it dated them to a time before the Upper Clarity revelations. In addition, the Numinous Treasure scriptures were said to have issued from a heaven higher than the Heaven of Upper Clarity.

The Numinous Treasure tradition synthesized earlier elements, including the masters of methods, apocrypha from the Han dynasty—in particular the *Array of the Five Numinous Treasure Talismans of the Most High* (*Taishang lingbao wufu xu*), which became highly influential in the Numinous Treasure movement—and the southern indigenous traditions that shaped Ge Hong's writings. It also drew liberally from Upper Clarity texts, on which it claimed to have improved. At the same time, the Numinous Treasure scriptures show the pronounced influence of Mahayana Buddhist sutras (discourses of the Buddha), both in structure and substance; specifically, they focus on universal salvation and the liberation of ancestors' souls from transmigration, displaying an emphasis on compassion that recalls that of bodhisattvas (those who have vowed to achieve buddhahood for the welfare of all beings). Although some Buddhist terms had crept into Upper Clarity works, the Numinous Treasure were the first to systematically incorporate Buddhist terminology and concepts into Daoism. Numinous Treasure practices include employing talismans, praying aloud, and chanting texts (such as the important *Wondrous Scripture of the Upper Chapters of Limitless Salvation,* or *Lingbao wuliang duren shangpin miaojing*).

The new revelations were later cataloged by Lu Xiujing (406–477), who is also credited with dividing the Daoist canon into three different sections—the Three Caverns—and thereby establishing the categories employed by all subsequent writers. In addition to his bibliographic work, Lu Xiujing gave Daoist rituals the shape that they would retain to the present day. Numinous Treasure liturgy is characterized by theatricality, repetition, and insistence on symbolic correlations between heaven, earth, and humans. Numinous Treasure rituals focus mainly on the salvation of the dead (primarily one's own ancestors) and the purification of communities.

NORTHERN DAOISM AT THE TOBA WEI COURT

Concurrent with the powerful Daoist innovations and developments in southern China were revelations in the north that urged Kou Qianzhi (365?–448) to control the Daoist clergy and limit new teachings. He took strong actions against grassroots movements, after he received messages from the deified Laozi about the need to suppress the imposters who were using his name to gather followers. This conservative posture enforcing orthodoxy and supporting the regime served Kou Qianzhi well in winning Daoism official recognition from the foreign Toba Wei dynasty (386–534) in the north. In 415, the deified Laozi revealed to Kou Qianzhi his title, "Celestial Master," and he in turn invested the Toba Wei ruler with title "Perfect Ruler of Great Peace."

THE ARRIVAL AND SPREAD OF BUDDHISM: RIVALRY AND RAPPROCHEMENT

During the Han dynasty Buddhism entered China from India and other Central Asian outposts. As Buddhism eventually succeeded in taking root—aided to some extent by its partial incorporation into the Lingbao Daoist tradition—an ongoing interchange of ideas between Buddhists and Daoists began. Traces of Buddhist terms and ideas appear in later Daoist texts, and Buddhist elements can also be discerned in Daoist iconography. But tensions also arose, and we can find evidence for the early stages of what came to be called the "Conversion of the Barbarians" (Huahu) controversy. According to a story fabricated by the Daoists, the Buddha was none other than a manifestation of Laozi, who, after leaving China through the western gate, had gone off to India and converted the barbarians there to Buddhism. The notion of Laozi incarnating as a teacher in a different time and place fits well with the account of him included in the *Scripture on Laozi's Transformations*. The Buddhists, not surprisingly, pushed back against this attempt to cast Buddhism as merely a foreign version of Daoism; one scathing response was their *Essay to Ridicule the Dao* (Xiaodao lun), which circulated in the early fifth century.

The *Essay to Ridicule the Dao* may have been effective in its critique of Daoism, since Buddhism became the dominant religion under the subsequent Sui dynasty (581–618). Nonetheless, by the dawn of the Tang dynasty Daoism was positioned to displace it. With the help of a new prophecy about the messiah Li Hong (i.e., Laozi), Li Yuan, the founder of the new dynasty, claimed descent from Laozi, using as evidence their shared surname (Laozi's other name was Li Er). The Tang dynasty not only reunified China in the early seventh century but made possible a high point in the history of Daoism, as it flourished with state support.

THE SCRIPTURE OF GREAT PEACE
(*Taiping jing*)

Though the *Scripture of Great Peace* (*Taiping jing*) is preserved only in a sixth-century C.E. version, it may date to the late second century C.E., making it one of the earliest Daoist scriptures. Its connection to Daoism is mainly retrospective, however—its ideas strongly influenced later Daoism, but at its creation it seems not to have been associated with any Daoist lineage or particular author. Because of its connection with peasant culture and the revolutionary spirit of peasant uprisings, the *Scripture of Great Peace* was the focus of renewed interest by Chinese scholars following the Communist ascent to power in 1949.

As can be seen in the brief sections included here, this lengthy work takes the form of a dialogue between a Celestial Master (a Tianshi)—a figure tantamount to a heavenly envoy who transmits heaven's message and the promise of salvation to the world—and six of the Perfected, a category of Daoist saintly types that can be traced back to the *Book of Master Zhuang* (*Zhuangzi*; see above). The text's most significant message is that an era of Great Peace (Taiping) will return to the empire only when the ruling ideology is based on the Dao—reverting to a condition that existed in the past but has been lost. The *Scripture of Great Peace* asserts that no matter how benighted the present world is, the cyclical patterns of heaven point to an opportunity for salvation.

This text is therefore aimed at political leaders. It reflects a period of Chinese history when the Han dynasty was in decline and facing social problems, widespread despair, and the threat of uprisings. In the section titled "How to Distinguish between Poor and Rich," the Celestial Master advises the Perfected: "Now if you, Perfected, were to give my book to a lord in possession of *dao* and virtue and he implemented what it says energetically, he would reach a position that would correspond to that of heaven. Thus he would achieve great peace." One meaning of "Great Peace," therefore, is the good government and political tranquillity that lead to happiness, fulfillment, and good health for the people. A diffuse concept, it predates Daoism as an organized religious tradition and later spread far wider than the limited domain of Daoism. The earlier ideal state of Great Peace is to be reestablished by creating harmony between heaven, earth, and humans.

The term "Great Peace" was also associated with the Taiping (Great Peace) movement, which led to the Yellow Turban Rebellion. The Yellow Turbans, who focused on the equal distribution of wealth and resources and the healing of illnesses, rose up throughout the empire in 184 C.E. under the leadership of Zhang Jue. Though this movement, with its large following, was violently suppressed, it weakened the empire and hastened the collapse of the dynasty.

Around the same time, Zhang Daoling—the first to have the title Celestial Master—was initiating the Celestial Masters movement in the Hanzhong Valley in modern-day Sichuan Province, the far western part of the empire. The community that developed there produced a commentary on *The Scripture of the Way and Its Virtue* (*Daode jing*; see above) titled the *Xiang'er Commentary on the Laozi* (*Laozi xiang'er zhu*; see below). That movement, too, focused on the healing of illness, since ailments were perceived to be a result of the patient's immoral actions: it viewed them as crimes that were akin to sins that required confession.

One particularly striking section of the *Scripture of Great Peace* addresses the status of women and the problem of infanticide. The text argues that women should be treated like men and allowed to earn a living, so that they not be considered an economic burden and therefore dispensable. In addition to warning against the dangers of maltreating females, the text also stresses the importance of males' having sufficient wives (ideally two, reflecting the idea that there should be two units of yin for every unit of yang) and sexual partners.

The *Scripture of Great Peace* emphasizes that those who follow the Dao (called the "true doctrine" in this text) will receive benefits and long life (here, "gai[n] points in the accounts kept by heaven" by the Controller of Fate). Conversely, those who do not follow the Dao, and thus act contrary to heaven's way, cause evil "to be inherited and passed on." That the effects of transgressions are passed down from one generation to the next—the notion of "inherited burden" (*chengfu*)—is an important concept in the *Scripture of Great Peace*.

PRONOUNCING GLOSSARY

dao: *dow* Taiping jing: *tai-ping ching*
qi: *chi*

Section 41. How to Distinguish between Poor and Rich

✻   ✻   ✻

Step forward, Perfected![1] You have been coming to study the doctrine (*dao*) for such a long time. You have really learned it all by now, don't you think?

If you had not again spoken to me, I might have thought so. But as soon as I hear your words, I know it is not so. Now I would like to reach the end but I can't think of another question. If the Celestial Master would only reveal my shortcomings once again!

All right, come here. What do we mean by "rich" and "poor"?

Well, those who own a lot are rich and those who own little are poor.

What you have said appears to be true but is in fact false.

What do you mean?

Take someone who often cheats, deceives, flatters, steals, and robs. How could we call him "rich"? Or take a situation where the people in general own a lot while the sovereign owns but little. How could we call him "poor"?

TRANSLATED BY Barbara Hendrischke. All bracketed additions are the translator's.

1. That is, a Perfect Man, or *zhenren*, a concept that first appears in the *Book of Master Zhuang* (*Zhuangzi*; see above) and becomes important in later Daoism.

Foolish and stupid as I am, I felt I had to speak up when the Celestial Master set out to instruct me. I am not good enough; I am at fault.

If *you* say you are not good enough, how shall the common people know the meaning of poor and rich?

If only you would think of my ignorance as being as that of a small child who must be instructed by its father and mother before it gains understanding.

True. Modest as you are, you don't go amiss.

Yes.

Collect your thoughts. I will tell you all. We speak of "rich" when there is sufficient supply. By making everything grow, heaven provides enough wealth. Thus we say that there is enough wealth when supreme majestic qi^2 arises and all twelve thousand plants and beings are brought to life. Under the influence of medium majestic qi, plants and beings are slightly deficient in that it cannot provide for all twelve thousand of them. This causes small poverty. When under the influence of lower majestic qi, plants and beings are again fewer than under the influence of medium majestic qi, and this causes great poverty. When there are no auspicious portents [signifying the approach of majestic qi] at all, the crops won't grow, which is extreme poverty. Take a look at a peasant family if you wish to know what this amounts to. Should they not possess any rare and valuable objects, they are considered a poor family. Should they not be supplied with what they need, they must be seen as an extremely poor family.

The problem lies in the poverty of heaven and earth. Once all twelve thousand plants and beings come forth and are nurtured by earth without detriment, earth becomes rich. If it can't nurture them well, it becomes slightly poor as long as injuries remain small, and quite poor should they be large. If crops were to shy away from being seen and fail to grow, injured by earth's body, this would lead to extreme poverty. Without jade and other valuables and with half the yields damaged, great distress and poverty would come about. Such complete damage would eradicate a poor family.

Now think of heaven as father and earth as mother. Should father and mother be in such extreme poverty all their children would suffer from poverty. The king's government is a replica of this. Thus the wise kings of antiquity, whose reign reached out to all twelve thousand plants and beings, became lords of great wealth. Harvests that reach two-thirds of their potential provide a lord with medium wealth. When they amount to only one-third, he has but little wealth. With neither valuables nor crops, he becomes a lord of great poverty. Once half of his harvests are damaged, his house is in decline. If all are damaged, he becomes a man of great poverty.

The wise and worthy of antiquity reflected deep in their dark chamber on the question of how poverty and wealth were achieved through [adhering to] *dao* and virtue. Why should anyone ask about this? Through meditation, men will find out for themselves.

---

2. Vital energy, breath.

Excellent! If the Celestial Master would only show kindness to emperors and kings! They have suffered bitterly and for a long time, and have been frustrated in their ambition. Whereby does one achieve such poverty and such wealth?

Yes, fine! Your question touches upon the crucial point of certain subtle sayings. Well, how they are put into practice brings about gain or loss. Once someone follows the true doctrine (*dao*) with all his might, heaven's life-giving spirits will help his mission. So spirits sent by heaven and good harvests will be plenty. If a man enacts virtue, earth's nourishing spirits will come forth to assist his conduct of affairs. Thus, he will gain half of his potential wealth. Once someone enacts humaneness, the humane spirits of the harmony that prevails in the realm between heaven and earth will step forward to help him conduct his affairs and achieve a small measure of wealth. Someone who attempts cultural refinement is on the way to intrigues and deceit, so that deceitful spirits will come forth to help him. Thus his conduct will be in some disorder. But if he were to undertake military action, bandit spirits would be bound to appear in his support. Government would thus be directed against the will of heaven. It would injure and harm even good men.

Dao sets the rule for heaven's conduct. Since heaven is the highest of all spirits, true spirits come forth to assist its mission. Since earth nurtures, virtuous spirits step forward to assist its mission. Humane spirits come forth to help a man's mission if he is humane. Cultured men are preoccupied with deceiving each other by means of culture.[3] They have lost their root. Thus deceitful spirits appear to assist them. Once superiors and inferiors deal with each other by means of culture, their affairs are in disorder. Soldiers subdue others through punishment, murder, and injury. Bandits do the same. Any man who in subduing others is guided by anger, joy, violence, and severity is a bandit. So, large numbers of bandits step forth to threaten his reign. Since they often damage people's belongings, such a way of government entails a loss of property.

Thus antiquity's supreme lords, who subdued others through *dao*, largely accorded with the will of heaven. They governed as if they were spirits. They subdued others through true *dao* without causing distress. Lords of middle rank exert control through virtue, and lords of lower rank through humaneness. Lords of chaos subdue others through cultural refinement, and those of disaster and defeat rule by punishing, murdering, and injuring others. Thus the supreme lords of antiquity ruled over others through *dao*, virtue, and humaneness instead of inflicting injuries by means of culture or through punishing and murdering others. Since this is the case, the use of such means is despicable.

However, a supreme lord resembles heaven and earth. Since heaven is prone to giving life rather than to inflicting injuries, we call it lord and father. Since earth likes to nurture the ten thousand plants and beings, we call it honest official and mother. Since man thinks in a humane manner and shows the same concern and care as heaven and earth do, we call him

---

3. The author is here showing his contempt for governance based on culture (*wen*) and military pursuits (*wu*) rather than rule by the Dao, criticizing the Confucian focus on ceremony, hierarchy, and decorum (all forms and artifice and all harmful to the people).

humane. Through their goodness these three manage to govern and to lead the ten thousand plants and beings. But one cannot govern by deceiving and punishing, [for then] disasters grow in number and make it impossible for emperors and kings to achieve great peace. So this must stop.

Now if you, Perfected, were to give my book to a lord in possession of *dao* and virtue and he implemented what it says energetically, he would reach a position that would correspond to that of heaven. Thus he would achieve great peace. There is no doubt that we would call his house rich. In this case nothing would cause emperors and kings to suffer distress. In the opposite case we would speak of a poor house.

Nowadays people sometimes call each other "rich families." Why is this so?

This is what they do, but the common people talk nonsense. When we use the word "rich" we mean that everything is provided for. If one single item is lacking, [supplies] are incomplete. For this reason the wise and worthy of old did not demand perfection from individuals, since they did not see them fit for it. Today goods are in short and incomplete supply in all eighty-one territories. It is impossible to achieve any long-term sufficiency, so goods are obtained from other territories. Now to what degree can one individual family be rich? Would you like to go along with the nonsense that common people put forth?

No, I would not dare to.

You have learned to watch your words, so don't utter nonsense, or you might bring disorder to the standard patterns of heaven and earth and they won't serve as a model for men. Be careful.

Yes, I will. Now the Celestial Master has shown himself to be merciful and loving. He has a kind regard for emperors and kings who on their thrones suffer distress and fail to be in favor with heaven.

Since it has all been explained to them they should be able to find the path that leads to the great peace of supreme majesty.

Foolish as I am, I have received a large amount of writings. I feel dizzy and confused as if I was a youngster and I don't know what to ask next. Since you are heaven's enlightened teacher, do convey all its warnings!

Yes, fine. Well, according to the model set by heaven, Yang's cipher is one and that of Yin[4] two. So Yang is single and Yin is a pair. Therefore, lords are few and subordinates are many. Since Yang is honored and Yin is humble, two Yin must jointly serve one Yang. Since heaven's cipher is one and that of earth is two, two women must jointly serve one man.

Why should it be necessary that two persons care for one?

The place next to someone in an honored position must never be left empty. When one is employed the other must remain standing or sitting next to the

---

4. The female principle; the term originally referred to the shady side of a valley, and by extension it came to be associated with the dark, earth, dampness, and passivity. "Yang": the male principle; the term originally referred to the sunny side of a valley, and by extension it came to be associated with the light, heaven, dryness, and activity.

person in the center to look after his needs. So the one resembles heaven while the two are similar to earth. Since men are children of heaven and earth, they must imitate both. The world has nowadays lost *dao*, so girls are often despised and even maltreated and murdered, which has caused there to be fewer girls than boys. So Yin's *qi* is reduced, which does not agree with the model of heaven and earth. Heaven's way establishes the model that a solitary Yang without a partner will bring drought and cause heaven not to rain when it should. Women correspond to earth: Should one single woman be despised, it is as if all in the world despise their true mother. Should they maltreat, hurt, or murder earth's *qi*, it will be cut off and cease to give life. In great anger the earth would then turn hostile, so that a plethora of disasters would make it impossible for the king's government to achieve peace.

Why?

The male is heaven's vital spirit; the female is earth's. Things influence each other within their own kind. It is not only the king's fault that his government is not at peace. Instead, men have in general lost *dao* and become negligent. They are all wrong. Since there is not just one mistake but ten thousand, it is difficult to conduct government affairs peacefully and they tend to go wrong. It is the nature of heaven and earth that among all twelve thousand plants and beings human life is the most important. Thus maltreating and murdering women brings profound disorder to a king's government. This is a great offense.

Now the Celestial Master has opened to kings the ascent to great peace. The true scripture on great peace has appeared. Thus they need only at their leisure to go on long spiritual journeys. How can it be that to violate women entails so much calamity for them?

This is a good question. You understand what heaven wants. Truly, the whole world despises and hates women because they condemn their conduct.

What do you mean? I wish to hear it. I will try to take notes on bamboo and silk so that for ten thousand times ten thousand generations no one will dare to depart from it.

Fine. Now that you can put it down in writing, the world will in the future never again murder women.

Yes, I want to write it down in order to free emperors and kings from calamities. I take pleasure in saving the lives of women [stricken with] grief.

Good. Now you have gained points in the accounts kept by heaven.

What do you mean?

Indeed, to give life to others means giving life to oneself, and to kill others means to kill oneself. Heaven's concern for you may already have increased your account with heaven. So the Controller of Fate[5] will make alterations in your personal records.

---

5. The celestial bureaucrat responsible for keeping a precise record of the years allotted to each individual's life.

This I would never dare to accept.

One must not turn this down; it lies within the model of heaven being the way it is. Well, women are murdered all over the world [for the following reason]: A father and mother suffer distress as long as a human being is young and small. They skimp on their own clothes and food in order to rear it. It is not only human beings who behave like this; all things that crawl and run behave like this. Everyone, big or small, must when grown up put all their energy into the search for clothes and food. Thus the ten thousand beings all leave their father and mother to clothe and feed themselves. If they are worthy they meet with happiness; if they are not they are in distress. Furthermore, when young, a child gains daily more strength until it has ample, while its father and mother are daily more wasted by old age. Their strength diminishes until it no longer suffices. But, with its surplus of knowledge, worthiness, and strength, a child, whether male or female, must nourish its father and mother in return for their exertion and kindness on its behalf. So its father and mother must no longer clothe and feed it or we say "the weak is nourishing the strong." We speak about "adverse policy" should someone with insufficient muscle power nourish those who have more than they need. This is the reason young ones who are bound to bring distress to those who are older without providing any gains for their father and mother are often killed by them. Now their father and mother murder them because clothes and food are scarce. Wouldn't it be better to rear them and let everyone find their own clothes and food? Perfected, this is really a grievous interruption of earth's dispensation. People are so foolish!

Now that I have heard this, I feel sad and alarmed. I understand that there are many grievances. What should be done?

Well, someone who likes to study but does not get clothes and food is stopped on his way (*dao*) since his studies are interrupted. But if he gets clothes and food, the worthy does not cease to learn. We should let everyone be of some use. If not they would instead cause distress and misery.

What do you mean?

Now a woman has no abode. She must get clothes and food by attending to her husband as a man does by attending to his office. When a woman attends to her husband's house, they must support each other and lead their life in unison. Together they continue the dispensation of heaven and earth, until in death their bones and flesh are returned to the same place. They get clothes and food from supporting each other. If they are worthy, they will be happy; if not, they will suffer. Take soil as an example: heaven will add its share to the rich produce of fertile soil. It does exactly the same for the poor produce of meager soil. It certainly does not deprive soil of giving growth. Heaven and earth would never deprive a woman of her achievement. How much more so should this be men's axiom! If it were, men would never again kill their women!

Excellent indeed! As soon as this one great and severe damage has been averted, great peace will come about for emperors and kings.

How do you know, Perfected?

Well, the affection a father and mother feel for their child is the most solid there is in this world. If the child did not make them miserable and distressed, there would be no reason to kill it. They must not kill it or else their qi becomes that of bandits and in their great contrariness they are thoroughly devoid of dao. *For this reason it throws the reign of emperors and kings into deep disorder. Now if women were to live without being maltreated, murdered, and violated, there would be great joy.*

Yes, what you have said is true. We may assume that you have understood. Now if one family kills one female: how many hundreds of thousands of families are there all over the world? Sometimes one family kills dozens of females or a fetus is injured before birth. Grief-stricken *qi* rises up to move heaven. How can these acts not be disorderly? So I truly want you to know more about it.

Should every human being through her own effort provide her own clothes and food, no wife would be of two hearts. She would concentrate on her activities and never again harbor any doubts. Those who lack achievement are forever deprived of a balance of mind.

So much for the methods that nature, being as it is, suggests. Pay attention, Perfected, that you don't lay this book aside, but give it to a lord who is humane and worthy, so that he can free [men] from all the grief they are stricken with and from the calamities that injure them. Pay attention to what my book says so that you can explain it to everyone. It must never again be permissible to do away with females.

Furthermore, this rule agrees with the model of heaven and earth according to which one man should have two wives because heaven has arranged that Yang is single and Yin is a pair. Since the height of middle antiquity men have forgotten what heaven's way intends and have often maltreated and murdered females, which has in turn caused men to be numerous and women to be so few that there are not enough. This is grossly opposed to heaven's way. By making the killing of females a common practice, men have caused even more [evil] to be inherited and passed on. Later generations have multiplied the world's trespasses, so that it has become completely devoid of *dao.*

Man is heir to heaven's dispensation and woman to that of earth. If we were to cut off earth's dispensation we would no longer be able to reproduce ourselves, and then many of us would die without progeny. What an awful crime! Thus all must reproduce themselves and continue their kind. But if we were to interrupt earth's dispensation and exterminate humankind, heaven would forever put an end to the species populating this world.

Moreover, when human beings come to life, heaven's *qi* shines forth in all of them: their head is round like heaven, their feet are square like earth, the four limbs resemble the four seasons, the five internal organs the five phases,[6] while ears and eyes, mouth and nose are like the seven regents or three luminaries.[7] I cannot explain to you all of this, but wise men know about it. The life of human beings is all Yin and Yang. Once the number of

6. The theory involving five agents, or five basic elements that move from one phase to another—a set of systematic associations between different categories, including the five directions, five colors, and the five internal organs, or viscera: the liver, heart, stomach, kidneys, and lungs.
7. The sun, moon, and stars. "Seven regents": the sun, moon, and five planets (Jupiter, Mars, Mercury, Saturn, and Venus).

days and months is completed, they open the womb and step outside. In sight of heaven and earth, they grow up. Together they continue the dispensation of their ancestors. They assist heaven in giving life to plants and beings and assist earth in nourishing what has taken shape.

Since the spirits of heaven and earth put their trust in a certain family, their dispensation comes to live in a certain human being. That men damage it, heaven sees as a grave misdeed. But men won't keep each other in check. Therefore heaven has sent me to make this book known to the generations to come. Although these matters are quite manifest, they are still continued, consciously. We must say that this is to consciously act against the model set by heaven. It is a crime of many layers and will no doubt put an end to humankind. Beware, Perfected, be on your guard.

Yes, I will.

Now that you have understood these issues, you and not others will be put on trial should you neglect these writings.

I would not dare to do so!

You may go now, and may each of you follow your own device.

Yes, we will.

THE LAOZI INSCRIPTION
(*Laozi ming*)

One of the important stages on the way to fully developed religious Daoism was the divinization of Laozi during the Han dynasty (202 B.C.E.–220 C.E.), when a number of texts on his biography began to appear. The earliest of them were still unclear as to whether there was such a historical personage named Laozi, and their accounts of when he was active and what he did varied widely. The stone inscription printed below, which is attributed to the scholar-official Bian Shao, is no longer extant, but if its internal dating to about 165 C.E. is accurate, then it is one of the first to present Laozi as divine. Rather than dismissing the other biographies as inaccurate, this inscription boldly asserts that all of them are true and that Laozi interceded in history at different important junctures.

The text opens by introducing Laozi and his written works from a historical perspective, describing him as an archivist from the state of Chu. It then hints at his longevity, suggesting that when he was more than two hundred years old he was the instructor of a young Confucius; as a final rhymed section declares, "Those in the world cannot trace him back to his origins, and look up to him as an immortal." The claim that Laozi could transcend time, coming into and out of existence, is grounded in the cosmological teachings of his own text, *The Scripture of the Way and Its Virtue* (*Daode jing*; see above): "Laozi separates from and joins with the undifferentiated pneumas, and so he cycles through beginnings and endings along with the three Brightnesses. . . . He undergoes nine transformations in accordance with the day and waxes and wanes along with the seasons. . . . [H]e has acted as the teacher of many generations of sages." This inscription also attests that by the mid-second century C.E. Laozi was being eulogized and was receiving imperial sacrifices at court, after he appeared in a dream to the Han emperor Huandi (r. 146–68).

PRONOUNCING GLOSSARY

Lao Dan: *lao dawn*   Laozi ming: *lao-tzu ming*

Laozi had the surname Li [Plum], with the style name Boyang, and was a native of the state of Chu and the county of Xiang. After the Spring and Autumn period,[1] Zhou was divided into two parts, their lords called the "Eastern" and the "Western." The six noble ministers of the state of Jin carried out military expeditions on their own authority and, together with the states of Qi and Chu, usurped the title of "king."

As large states took possession of small ones, Xiang County became empty and deserted, and today it is part of Bitter. The old outer walls of the city are still there, east of the village of Lai, occupying the north side of the Guo River. The earth there is rich and fecund, high and broad, and so it was suitable for raising a gentleman possessed of virtue.

Laozi was a scribe in the Zhou archives. During the reign of King You,[2] when the region of the Three Rivers was shaken by an earthquake, he thought it reflected on the sitting king in the same way that the displacements of *yin* and *yang*[3] did at the end of the ages of the Xia and Yin.[4]

Kongzi[5] was born in year 20 of King Ling of Zhou [552 B.C.E.]. In the year 10 of King Jing [535 B.C.E.], when he was seventeen, he studied the rites with Lao Dan.[6] Calculating his age, at the time Dan was already over two hundred years old. He looked droopy in his old age. Some have claimed that, 129 years after Kongzi's death, Grand Scribe Dan of the Zhou was Laozi, although no one knows where he ended up.

In his book, which consists of two chapters, [Laozi] says that "the reason that the Cosmos and the Earth are able to last long and endure is that they do not nourish themselves."[7] In the beginning, when the Cosmos and the Earth created the people, they provided them bodies that they might continue uninterrupted across the generations. From this their understanding of life and death may be understood. [The book] also has the phrase: "the spirit of the valley never dies; this is called the mysterious female."[8] On this basis, people today who are fond of the Way touch on these kinds [of words] and infer, based on like categories, that Laozi separates from and joins with the undifferentiated pneumas, and so he cycles through beginnings and endings along with the Three Brightnesses.[9] He observes astronomical phenomena and makes prophecies, rising and descending from the stars of the Dipper. He undergoes nine transformations in accordance with the day and waxes and wanes along with the seasons. He measures and delineates the paths of

---

TRANSLATED BY Mark Csikszentmihalyi. All bracketed editions are the translator's.

1. 770–481 B.C.E., during the Zhou dynasty (1046–256 B.C.E.).
2. Reigned 781–771 B.C.E.
3. The male principle; the term originally referred to the sunny side of a valley, and by extension it came to be associated with the light, heaven, dryness, and activity. "Yin": the female principle; the term originally referred to the shady side of a valley, and by extension it came to be associated with the dark, earth, dampness, and passivity.

4. The Xia and Shang dynasties, respectively (ca. 2070–ca. 1600 B.C.E.; ca. 1600–1046 B.C.E.).
5. That is, Confucius.
6. That is, Laozi.
7. *The Scripture of the Way and Its Virtue* (*Daode jing*, or *Laozi*; see above), chapter 7.
8. *The Scripture of the Way and Its Virtue*, chapter 6.
9. The sun, moon, and planets (or the sun, moon, and Big Dipper).

the Three Brightnesses, the Four Luminaries[1] at his sides. He visualizes and imagines his "Cinnabar Fields,"[2] and Great Unity in the Purple Chamber. When the Way is accomplished and his body has transformed, he is reborn like a cicada shedding its skin and transcends the world. Since the time of [Fu] Xi and [Shen] Nong, [. . .] he has acted as the teacher of many generations of sages.

One account of Laozi's "cutting off the sage and abandoning wisdom" and "the rites are the beginning of chaos,"[3] and his opposition to Kongzi's Way, when Ban Gu wrote his "Table of Figures Both Ancient and Modern" he evaluated him according to set criteria, and so belittled and lowered him. Laozi was placed in the same rank as Chuzi, and his natural endowments were compared unfavorably with [those of Confucian writers such as Xun Qing [Xunzi] and Meng Ke [Mengzi].[4]

The evaluations of these two [i.e., people who are fond of the Way and the historian Ban Gu] are far apart! This is certainly a case of "their Ways being different, they cannot plan together."[5]

Today is the *jiazi* day [i.e., day 1 of the sexagenary cycle] in the eighth month of year 8 of the Yanxi reign period [165 C.E.]. The August Ruler esteems virtue and broadens the Way, contains a huge capacity and expands on it, and preserves his spirit and nourishes physical nature, keeping his aim of reaching into the clouds. This is why he concentrated his mind with the Yellow [Emperor] Xuan [Yuan], shared a talisman with the Highest Ancestor, and dreamed he saw Laozi, and reveres and makes sacrifices to him.

As chancellor of Chen, I, Bian Shao, supervise the state rites. My abilities are thin and my thinking shallow, and I can neither take the measure of the ultimate man nor distinguish right from wrong. So I rely on past books and documents when I relate the following:

Laozi was born in the last age of the Zhou. Mysterious and empty, he preserved his quiescence, took pleasure in namelessness, preserved the not virtuous, and took high office to be dangerous and lower positions to be safe. He bequeathed his words on benevolence to Kongzi, and withdrew from the world to live in seclusion. He changed his name, only fearing that he might be recognized. Just as the sun alternates light and dark, and the moon has natural waxing and waning, so increase and decrease is the wellspring of flourishing and decline, and the basis of entry into good and bad fortune.

"The Human Way is to hate fullness and like modesty,"[6] and it is the case that Laozi's work did not settle the state and his merit was not directed to the people, so the reason that he is exalted and that he receives sacrifice from the people of this time is that he is still enjoying the leftover merit from his past rejection of an official salary and maintaining a low position, and so "decreasing and decreasing again."[7] He showed emptiness and quiescence,

---

1. The guardians of the four cardinal directions (Blue Dragon, White Tiger, Red Sparrow, and Dark Warrior).
2. Three places in the human body—abdomen, heart, and brain—important for different self-cultivation practices involving breathing and meditation and for internal alchemy (*neidan*).
3. *The Scripture of the Way and Its Virtue*, chapters 19, 38.
4. The early Chinese philosopher known in the

West as Mencius (ca. 371–ca. 289 B.C.E.). Xunzi (ca. 300–ca. 230 B.C.E.) systematized the work of Confucius and Mencius.
5. Confucius, *Analects*, chapter 15.
6. A quotation from the *Commentary on the Judgments* (Tuanzhuan) to the *Classic of Changes* [translator's note].
7. *The Scripture of the Way and Its Virtue*, chapter 48.

and so says he "was born before the Cosmos and the Earth."[8] This is a result of preserving the genuine, nourishing long life, and attaining the five boons.[9]

> I reverently eulogize him [in the following terms]:
> His Mysterious Virtue is to embrace the empty and preserve
>   the pure.
> He takes pleasure in occupying the lower position, not seeking to
>   attain salary and influence.
> Applying the plumb line he make things straight; tangling it he warps
>   them.
> His response at the Three Rivers vented anger and dispersed
>   indulgence.
> As long as *yin* does not engulf *yang*, what can be obstructed or
>   opened?
> He looks at "emergence" and then acts, "waiting in the suburbs" or
>   going to the country.
> Auspicious! Flying and fleeing, withdrawing from the world and
>   hiding his fame.
> The words he left after being pressed were the *Classics of the*
>   *Way and Virtue.*[1]
> In it, he censured his age with subtle metaphors, searching the visible
>   to infer the obscure.
> He "preserved the one"[2] without fail, and so served as exemplar for
>   the people of the world.
> He "accepts the thick and not the thin, lives in the real and dispenses
>   with ornament."[3]
> He values "consistent models," but treats "gold and jade" as trifles.
> Cutting off his appetites and eliminating his desires, he "returns to
>   infancy."[4]
> Radiantly bright, he rides over the ages; no one knows his affective
>   dispositions.
> To model sayings he is somewhat opposed, placing the forms of the
>   people first.
> In essentials he uses nonaction; for great virtue he utilizes sincerity.
> He has no constant rule on advancing and retreating; for multiplying
>   options he divines.
> He takes knowledge to be stupidity, is "empty and yet not exhausted."[5]
> A great man's measure is not always what the multitude can
>   explain.
> Collecting each of the nine ranks,[6] how could this be the criterion
>   for piling up fame?

8. *The Scripture of the Way and Its Virtue*, chapter 25.
9. Longevity, wealth, pleasure, virtue, and living out the full allotment of one's life.
1. That is, *The Scripture of the Way and Its Virtue.*
2. A meditation and visualization technique: the adept visualizes gods inside the body in his or her Cinnabar Fields and then ascends to the Dipper or descends from the Dipper into the Cinnabar Fields.
3. An echo of *The Scripture of the Way and Its Virtue*, chapter 28.
4. *The Scripture of the Way and Its Virtue*, chapter 28.
5. An echo of *The Scripture of the Way and Its Virtue*, chapter 4.
6. Of civil and military offices.

He is equally bright as the Sun and the Moon, and joins with
the Five Planets.[7]
Entering and exiting the "Cinnabar Hut," ascending and descending
to the "Yellow Court."[8]
He abandons popular customs and dwells in the shadows and hides
his physical form.
Embracing original pneuma and becoming a spirit, he inhales and
exhales the most essential.
Those in the world cannot trace him back to his origins, and look up
to him as an immortal.
The Cosmic and the Human have a system to their offerings in order
to illuminate his numinousness.

In admiration of his long life, I engrave this tablet with these commendations.

7. Jupiter, Mars, Mercury, Saturn, and Venus.
8. The lower Cinnabar Field, in the abdomen.

"Cinnabar Hut": the upper Cinnabar Field, in the brain.

SCRIPTURE ON LAOZI'S TRANSFORMATIONS
(Laozi bianhua jing)

This messianic text, which probably dates to the end of the second century c.e.,
focuses on the newly deified Laozi, now known as Lord Lao (Laojun), as a creator,
teacher, and savior. The *Scripture on Laozi's Transformations* provides an introduction
to Lord Lao's cosmic origins, miraculous powers, and his various manifestations during different historical epochs. It is best understood as part of a larger movement—to
which the "Laozi Inscription" (see previous selection) also belonged—to elevate
Laozi to the status of an exalted sage and supreme deity within the Daoist pantheon. The *Scripture on Laozi's Transformations* emphasizes Lord Lao's divine status by precisely describing his special physical attributes, which recall those of the
Buddha: long ears (with three openings, no less), prominent eyes, long eyebrows,
prominent nose (with four nostrils), square mouth, auspicious signs on his hands
and feet, and so on. Evidence of Laozi's deification is also found in his presence,
albeit under different names, in the rebel movements of the Yellow Turbans in the
East (who refer to him as Huang Laojun) and the Celestial Masters in the West
(who refer to him as Taishang Laojun).

Repeatedly, Laozi is depicted as returning to the world from his heavenly perch
in order to instruct all the great sages and leaders of Chinese antiquity. He is cast
in increasingly strong terms as the people's savior; in an apocalyptic age, believers
are urged to follow Lord Lao and thus avoid calamity:

> When the planet Venus leaves its orbit,
> Come quickly, join with me!
> . . . .
> And you will be saved from danger.

The rather surprising preservation of this messianic text—emanating from the
lower strata of society—down to the present day is due largely to its chance survival
among a large cache of texts discovered at the beginning of the twentieth century in
a sealed-up cave at Dunhuang, an oasis in western China.

PRONOUNCING GLOSSARY

Bao Xi: *pao hsi*
Chi Jingzi: *chih ching-tzu*
Dao: *dow*
Fu Xi: *fu hsi*
Guang Chengzi: *gwawng chung-tzu*
Laozi: *lao-tzu*
Laozi bianhua jing: *lao-tzu bien-hwa ching*

Tianlao: *tien-lao*
Wen Shuangzi: *when shu-awng-tzu*
Zhong Yi: *chowng yee*
Zhu Rong: *chu rowng*
Zhuanxu: *chuan-hsu*

He is the sublime essence of spontaneity, the root of the Dao.
He is father and mother of the doctrine,
The root of Heaven and Earth,
The top and bottom of the ladder of life,
The sovereign of all deities,
First ancestor of Yin and Yang,[1]
The *hun* and *po* souls of the ten thousand beings[2]
Potter and founder of the [primordial] Void,
He creates by changing and adjusting to what is required
Encircling the eight poles,[3]
He supports the Earth and hangs up the Sky. . . .
In his hands he holds the staff of the immortals
And the jade tablets with golden writing.

When he comes forth, he is the master of emperors and kings.
At the time of the August Bao Xi (=Fu Xi), his name was Wen Shuangzi. . . .
At the time of the August Zhu Rong, his name was Guang Chengzi;
At the time of the Emperor Zhuanxu, he was Chi Jingzi; . . .
At the time of the Yellow Emperor, he was Tianlao

In the first year of the era Yangjia (A.D. 132) he was seen for the first time on Mount Bian (?) jueming in the area of Chengdu.
In the first year of Jiankang (144) he transformed himself (= appeared) on the White Deer Mountain. . . .
In the first year of Dachu (146) he came forth again in the temple of the White Deer [Mountain] . . . and his name was Zhong Yi.
In the second year of Jianhe (148) . . . he manifested himself at the gate of the east quarter of Chengdu . . . and had the appearance of a Perfect Man (*zhenren*). . . .
In the first year of Yongshou (155) he returned once more to the White Deer Mountain and his name was "Great Sage of the Slaves" (*puren daxian*). When questioned, he shut his mouth and did not speak. [Then] he trans-

---

TRANSLATED BY Anna K. Seidel. All bracketed additions are the translator's.

1. The female principle; the term originally referred to the shady side of a valley, and by extension it came to be associated with the dark, earth, dampness, and passivity. "Yang": the male principle; the term originally referred to the sunny side of a valley, and by extension it came to be associated with the light, heaven, dryness, and activity.
2. That is, all the beings that exist.
3. That is, the entire world.

formed himself (= disappeared) and thirty years later a temple was constructed on the White Deer [Mountain] for the Celestial Teacher (*tianfu*).[4]

My followers are numerous.
Outwardly I look like a homeless menial
While my inward [nature] is perfect (*zhen*). . . .
If you have your minds turned to me night and day,
I will not suddenly abandon you;
If you think of me even in your dreams,
I will appear to you as a token of confidence.

In order to launch the Han dynasty[5]
I changed my own appearance.
Only fools dance and make merry,
While wise men receive instructions!
Since [now] the actions of Heaven and Earth are disturbed,
I myself will change destiny.
In this present age I will choose the good people.
You must not select yourself; By [your] upright behavior and self control
I will recognize you.

I have instructed all of you five or six times.
When the planet Venus leaves its orbit,[6]
Come quickly, join with me!
Search for me on the Southern Peak(?)
And you will be saved from danger. . . .

The people are in deep distress,
Epidemics and famine are everywhere.
(In order to) turn your destiny
I will shake the Han reign.

On hearing this, my people
Get determined to chase away all viciousness. . . .
[Only] upright minds and sincere hearts
Will know about my deeds. . . .
The saints practice my thought
While perverse hearts ask who I am.

I have manifested myself many times in order to save [mankind],
[Following] the junctures of time I have transformed myself.
Few are those who understand me,
Numerous those who disapprove.

4. A concept that first appears in the *Book of Master Zhuang* (*Zhuangzi*; see above) and becomes important in later Daoism.

5. 202 B.C.E.–220 C.E.
6. A sign of impending war.

TWO POEMS ON TAISHAN

CAO ZHI

Cao Zhi (192–232 C.E.), the son of a Chinese emperor by his consort, was an imaginative and talented poet who became known for works that described mystical travels to far-off places and meetings with fantastic transcendent beings. The two poems included here feature Mount Tai, or Taishan—a sacred mountain located in modern-day Shandong Province that for millennia was important for the imperial cult and for Buddhists as well as for Daoists—for whom it was the site of encounters with transcendents and immortals. It was one among a set of five sacred peaks (*wuyue*), called in the first poem below the Five Marchmounts: four were located at the four cardinal directions, with one at the center. Mount Tai, the Eastern Sacred Peak, is often regarded as the most revered of the five. It has long been the location for the performance of imperial rituals for the protection of the state (the *feng* and *shan* sacrifices), and it was believed to lie over the Yellow Springs, the resting place for the souls of the dead. This connection between Mount Tai and the dead carried over into later Daoism, since the deity of the sacred peak came to be the figure responsible for judging dead souls in a purgatorial realm.

Mount Tai has been celebrated by many poets who focused on its lofty heights, proximity to heaven, numinous air, and awe-inspiring natural presence. In these two poems, however, Mount Tai is portrayed with an explicitly Daoist vocabulary. For example, the sky is referred to as "Grand Clarity," the name of the first of three levels of Daoist heavens; "Upper Clarity" and "Jade Clarity" are located above it. Moreover, Cao Zhi presents Mount Tai as the perfect spot to cultivate Daoist immortality. Indeed, the poet is himself transported to paradise, where two "Realized Persons" (i.e., "Perfected Ones"), the highest form of Daoist beings, instruct him in the drugs and self-cultivation techniques that produce immortality.

PRONOUNCING GLOSSARY

Cao Zhi: *cao chih*   Tai Shan: *tai shaun*

[*Urge on the Carriage*]

Urge on the carriage, shake up the worn-out steeds,
Eastward to arrive at the enceinte of Fenggao.[1]
Divine, oh, is Mount Tai in that place!
Among the Five Marchmounts[2] its name is special.

Arched and high—threading the clouds and rainbows:
Upborne and abrupt—emerging into Grand Clarity.[3]

TRANSLATED by Paul W. Kroll. All bracketed additions are the translator's.

1. Located about 6 miles northeast of modern Tai'an, in Shandong Province on China's northern coast.
2. Five sacred peaks: one each at the four cardinal directions and one in the center.
3. A term with multiple meanings within Daoism. In early texts, "Grand Clarity" referred to the inner state of a practitioner. It then became the name of a heaven that was the source of new revelations related to external alchemy (the sense here), and later was applied to one section of the Daoist canon.

Detail from *The Kangxi Emperor's Southern Inspection Tour* by Wang Hui. This detail features Mount Tai, preeminent among the set of five sacred mountains, and shows the pilgrimage route to the summit and the many pavilions that dot the path. Near the beginning of the Manchu Qing dynasty (1644–1912), the Kangxi (r. 1662–1722) emperor traveled to Taishan in a symbolic effort to gain legitimacy for his rule, since this site was traditionally where Chinese rulers went to perform rituals when they consolidated their authority.

Coursing round about it are twice six watch-mounds,
And placed atop them are kiosks ten and two.

Above and below are springs of gushing ale,
With stones of jade displaying their floriate blooms.
To the southeast one gazes on the countryside of Wu;
Looking west, one observes the germ of the sun.

It is where cloud-soul and spirit are tethered and attached—
In the passage away [of time], one feels this ongoing march.
They who are kings, in returning their allegiance to Heaven,
Devote to it (i.e., Tai Shan) the completion of their principal deeds.

In successive ages there are none who have not paid it honor,
For the rites and litations have their gradings of quality.
If one probes the divining slips, some are long-lived, others short;
It is only virtue that "succeeds and furthers through perseverance."

Those that offered the *feng* were seven tens of thearchs,[4]
But Xuan the August[5] was the primary, unmatched numen.
He partook of the aurorae, rinsed his mouth with cold-night damps,
And fur and feathers then mantled the form of his person.

Rising up and away, he trod the outskirts of emptiness;
Aloof and afar, he ascended to sequestered tenebrity.
Equal in span of years to the Father in the East,
He wastes the ages now in perpetual prolongation of life!

[*In the Morn I Wandered*]

In the morn I wandered to Mount Tai;
Clouds and fog were comely and coy.
Of a sudden I came upon two lads—
The beauty of their features fresh and fine.

They were mounted on that deer of white,
Their hands were masked by polypore[6] plants.
I deemed that they were Realized Persons,[7]
And I knelt down long and inquired of the Way.

We ascended westward to a hall of jade—
Loft-buildings of gold, streets of mallotus trees!
To me they transmitted drugs of transcendence
That had been fashioned by their divine radiances.

They instructed me in their ingestion and eating,
And in the cycling of sperm to supplete the brain.[8]
With a life-span now equal to metal or stone,
For generations everlasting, it is impossible to age!

4. Divine sovereigns. "*Feng*": an imperial sacrifice to heaven held at the top of Taishan.
5. Huangdi, the mythological Yellow Emperor (27th century B.C.E.).
6. A fungus.
7. That is, Perfected Ones (*zhenren*); the concept of the Perfect Man first appears in the *Book of*

Master Zhuang (*Zhuangzi*; see above) and becomes important in later Daoism.
8. In this self-cultivation practice, a man refrains from ejaculation during sexual intercourse so that his semen (considered his life essence) will supplement his brain.

MEMORIAL TO EMPEROR HUAN CONCERNING BUDDHISM AND DAOISM

XIANG KAI

In 166 c.e., Emperor Huan (r. 147–67) performed a sumptuous ritual sacrifice to Laozi and the Buddha in the imperial palace. Xiang Kai wrote a memorial criticizing the practices, warning that inauspicious portents were showing the disapproval of heaven. This work is closely related to the *Scripture of Great Peace* (*Taiping jing*; see above), whose antecedent text is here mentioned as the "spirit book" presented to the throne, and to the *Scripture on Laozi's Transformations* (*Laozi bianhua jing*; see above), which included a reference to the same portent involving the planet Venus.

In the section of the memorial printed below, Xiang Kai criticizes the emperor for behaviors and other foibles that have caused problems for him and the empire, including the employment of eunuchs in the palace. More significantly, this text contains the first allusion to the Conversion of the Barbarians (Huahu) theory. According to Daoists, the Buddha—here called "Futu"—was a manifestation of Laozi, who had left China for India and converted the barbarians there. In this telling, what the Indians called Buddhism was merely a foreign version of Daoism, the teaching that was fit for the Chinese. In texts from the second to the fourth century C.E., this early theory became the basis for polemics and fueled a dispute that arose between Buddhists and Daoists that became known as the Conversion of the Barbarians controversy. The development of this controversy in later Daoist literature can be traced in the texts included in the next selection.

PRONOUNCING GLOSSARY

Xiang Kai: *hsiang kai*

When the Son of Heaven[1] is unfilial in his service to Heaven, then there are solar eclipses and stellar or planetary intrusions. This year there was a solar eclipse on the first day of the first month. The Three Brightnesses are dim, and the Five Planets[2] are in retrograde motion. The spirit book that my predecessor Gong Chong presented [to the throne] specially takes an appreciation of the bounty of the Cosmos and the Earth and following the five phases[3] as its basis. It also contains techniques to bring prosperity to the state and broaden your hereditary line. Its style is easy to understand and it matches with the classical records, yet Emperor Shun [r. 125–144 C.E.] did not put it into practice, and so the heirs to the state did not prosper. Filial Emperor Chong [r. 144–145 C.E., the son of Emperor Shun] and Filial Emperor Zhi [r. 145–146 C.E.] died after short reigns in consecutive years.

I have also heard that, having gained what he likes, if the ruler acts against the Correct Way, the spirits act on this by creating calamities. Thus the Zhou[4] declined and the feudal lords used their strength campaigning to supplant one another. Thereupon that age gave rise to [strongmen] like Xia Yu, Shen Xiu, Wan from Song, Master Peng, and Ren Bi. The Yin-period [despot] Zhou loved sex, and so [a consort like] Da Ji emerged. The Duke of She liked dragons, and a real dragon wandered into his court. Today, there are the men who have suffered the "punishment of Heaven" [i.e., eunuchs], the Yellow Gates [the private apartments of the emperor] regular attendants. Your majesty looks after and supports them, showing them constant favor. That you are suffering the bad luck of not having any heirs, how could it but be because of this?

TRANSLATED BY Mark Csikszentmihalyi. All bracketed additions are the translator's.

1. That is, the emperor.
2. Jupiter, Mars, Mercury, Saturn, and Venus. "The Three Brightnesses": the sun, moon, and stars.
3. The theory involving five agents, or five basic elements that move from one phase to another—a set of systematic associations between different categories (five directions, five colors, five organs, etc.).
4. The Zhou dynasty (1046–256 B.C.E.).

The stars of the Eunuchs among the Cosmic offices are not in the Purple Palace sector but rather in the Cosmic Market sector [of the night sky].[5] This clearly shows that [the Eunuchs] should have employment in the markets and alleys. Today, however, it is just the opposite, since they reside in place of the High Ministers of Old. This truly contradicts Heaven's intent.

I have heard that in the palace you have erected shrines to Huang-Lao and Futu.[6] Their Ways are those of clarity and emptiness, and they value the promotion of nonaction. They love life and hate death, reduce desires and eliminate excess. Now your majesty's predilections and desires have not been eliminated, and the death penalty has overstepped its principled application. Once one has turned one's back on the Way, how is it possible to obtain heirs?

Some have said that Laozi entered the Yi and Di nations[7] and became Futu. Futu did not spend three nights under a mulberry tree—he did not desire to stay there long, because this would give birth to kindness and caring for it. This is the epitome of essence. A heavenly spirit gave him a gift of beautiful women, and Futu said: "These are only leather sacks suffused with blood!"

Then he did not give them an interested look. Those who can "preserve the one" like this are then capable of realizing the Way.

Now, your majesty rapes girls and covets wives and so will soon exhaust all the beauties of the world. You savor the best food and drink the best beverages so as to consume all the good tastes of the world. In what sense do you desire to be like Huang-Lao?

5. Chinese astronomers and astrologers saw the sky as containing three "enclosures," each made up of numerous constellations. The Purple Palace was related to the court; the Cosmic Market was related to the economy in general.
6. The Buddha. "Huang-Lao": a word that combines the names Huangdi (the mythological Yellow Emperor, 27th century B.C.E.) and Laozi; their worship was popular among the ruling class of the Han dynasty (202 B.C.E.–220 C.E.).
7. Barbarian groups in eastern and northern China, respectively.

THE CONVERSION OF THE BARBARIANS

WANG FU

The Conversion of the Barbarians (Huahu) theory, first mentioned in Xiang Kai's second-century C.E. "Memorial to Emperor Huan" (see the previous selection), initially was the claim that "Buddhist" teachings were in fact the preaching of Laozi, after he left China for India. The idea that Laozi was incarnated in different times as a renowned teacher corresponds well with the image of the deified Laozi presented in the *Scripture on Laozi's Transformations* (*Laozi bianhua jing*; see above). Though its earliest mention is neutral in tone, the theory changed in scope and tenor over the next few centuries: eventually, the Daoist propagation of increasingly anti-Buddhist and anti-foreign sentiments sparked a major controversy.

The controversy heated up as the different accounts of Laozi's conversion of the barbarians in India began to take on a more polemical tone and critics sought to denigrate the Buddha's teachings. Unfortunately, the main source for the earliest phase of the dispute, the fourth-century *Scripture on the Conversion of the Barbarians*

(*Huahu jing*) by a certain Wang Fu, was proscribed and ordered destroyed at several points in China's history; it today survives only in fragments cited in other texts. In the textual fragments presented here, the increasing vitriol is palpable. We witness Laozi taking the form of the sun's rays to enter into the mouth of Qingmiao (the Buddha's mother) to impregnate her and ultimately issue forth from her right armpit in a birth story that echoes that of the Buddha. We also find Laozi teaching that the Indians must embrace asceticism "to restrain their cruel and obstinate hearts," that Buddhist robes are ochre (like those of criminals), and that the bodies of Buddhist monks are damaged just like those of criminals. One of the better-known, and perhaps most salacious, of the story's narrative elements is the claim that Laozi taught Buddhist monks to be celibate to put "an end to their rebellious seed" and thereby bring about the foreigners' eventual extinction.

The Conversion of the Barbarians controversy was just one element within the broader set of debates and confrontations between Buddhists and Daoists. Buddhists in China did not let the Daoists' attacks go unanswered, and they began to retaliate in texts of their own. In one account they reversed the Daoist narrative, claiming that Laozi was none other than an incarnation of a disciple of the Buddha who was sent to China to introduce a version of Buddhism to China via *The Scripture of the Way and Its Virtue* (*Daode jing*; see above). Buddhists also produced their own polemical critique of Daoism, the *Essay to Ridicule the Dao* (*Xiaodao lun*), which is included in this anthology, below.

PRONOUNCING GLOSSARY

Daode jing: *dow-duh ching*   Laozi: *lao-tzu*
Huahu jing: *hwah-hu ching*   Wang Fu: *wang foo*

When the barbarian king did not believe in Laozi('s teachings), Laozi subdued him by his divine power. Then (the king) begged for mercy and repented his sins. He personally shaved (his head) and cut (his beard), and acknowledged his errors and faults. Master Lao in his great compassion had pity on his foolish delusion and expounded to him an expedient doctrine, providing him with prohibitive and restrictive rules according to circumstances. He ordered all (barbarian converts) to practise ascetism (read *dhuta*[1]) and alms-begging in order to restrain their cruel and obstinate hearts; to wear (like criminals) reddish-brown garments and an incomplete dress in order to crush their fierce and violent nature; to cut and damage their complexion in order to show how their bodies (like those of criminals) have tattooed faces and amputated noses; to abstain from sexual intercourse in order to make an end to their rebellious seed. This is why a grave disease is said to need a violent therapy, for (in such a case) one has to split open the belly and to wash the intestines, and why great crimes must be restrained by a severe punishment, for (in such a case) one must necessarily exterminate the clan and destroy all descendants of the criminal.

●

It is said in the *Chuji*:[2] Laozi, because the virtue of the Zhou[3] king Yu (trad. 781–771 BC) was waning, wished to go through the (frontier-)pass to the

TRANSLATED BY Erik Zürcher.

1. Literally, "abandoned" (Sanskrit), a set of twelve Buddhist ascetic practices.

2. *Record of Beginnings.*
3. The Zhou dynasty (1046–256 B.C.E.).

West. He agreed with Yin Xi that they would see each other after three years inside the liver of a black sheep on the market at Chang'an. Laozi was then (re)born in the womb of the empress. At the agreed date (Yin) Xi saw that (on the market at Chang'an) there was one who sold livers of black sheep, and through (this trader) he inquired for and saw Laozi . . . (there seems to be a hiatus in the text here) . . . coming forth from his mother's body. He had (long) hairs on the temples and his head was hoary; his body was sixteen feet tall; he wore a heavenly cap and held a metal staff. He took Yin Xi with him to convert the barbarians. (Once arrived in India) he withdrew to the Shouyang mountains, covered by a purple cloud. The barbarian king suspected him of sorcery. He (attempted) to boil him in a cauldron, but (the water) did not grow hot. . . .

It is said in the *Wenshi zhuan*:[4] In the first year of *shanghuang* (an imaginary *nianho*[5]) Laozi descended and became the teacher of the Zhou (court). In the first year of *wuji* he went through the pass, riding a car of thin boards (drawn by) a black ox. He spoke the five thousand words (of the *Daode jing*[6]) for Yin Xi and said: 'I am roaming between Heaven and Earth, (but) as you have not yet obtained the Way you cannot follow me. You must recite the five thousand words (of the *Daode jing*) ten thousand times; your ears must (develop the faculty of) penetrating hearing, your eyes must (develop the faculty of) penetrating sight. Then your body will be able to move by flying, (endowed with) the six supernatural powers and the four attainments.[7] They agreed to a date (to meet each other) at Chengdu. (Yin) Xi followed up his words and obtained the (Way). When he had sought for and met (Laozi), they went into the Tante (Dandaka) mountains in Kashmir. And afterwards the king attempted to burn or drown him with fire and water. . . .

It is said in the *Guangshuo pin*:[8] At the beginning, when the king had heard the Heavenly Worthy expound the doctrine, he obtained together with his wife and children the fruit of *srota-apanna*.[9] The king of Qing Heguo, having heard about this, betook himself together with all his courtiers to the place where the Heavenly Worthy was dwelling, and all of them ascended to Heaven in broad daylight. The king (who had obtained the fruit of *srota-apanna*) became the head of the Brahma-gods, with the appellation of 'the master of the doctrine Xuanzhong.' His wife, who had (also) listened to (the exposition of) the doctrine, ascended together with (the king) and became the *devaraja*[1] Miaofan. Later she was (re)born in Kashmir as a king with the name of Fentuoli. (This king) was killing and murdering (people) and (in all respects) destitute of right principles. The master of the doctrine Xuanzhong wanted to convert him; he transformed himself and was born in the womb of a woman named Li. After eighty-two years he ripped open her left arm-pit. At birth he had (already) a hoary head. Three months later he travelled to the West together with Yin Xi riding a white deer. He retired into the Tante (Dandaka) mountains.[2] After three years the king Fentuoli

---

4. *Biography of Wenshi.*
5. Reign name (the Chinese system of dating).
6. *The Scripture of the Way and Its Virtue* (see above).
7. The four stages on the path to enlightenment: Stream Enterer (or Stream-Winner), Once Returner, Never Returner, and Arhat (one who will enter nirvana at death). "The six supernatural powers": clairvoyance, clairaudience, telepathy, memory of one's past lives, yogic powers,

and freedom from rebirth.
8. A chapter in the *Collection of Important Odes of the Law* (*Faji yasong jing*), a Chinese translation of the Sanskrit *Udanavarga* (literally, "chapters of utterances").
9. Stream Enterer (Sanskrit).
1. God-king (Sanskrit).
2. Said to be located in what is now Pakistan, near Kashmir.

(who in a former existence had been his wife) met him when hunting, and (tried to kill him) by burning and drowning, but Laozi did not die.

•

Laozi entered the (frontier)-pass and went to the country of Weiwei (Kapilavastu)[3] in India. The wife of the king of this country was named Qingmiao. Laozi, taking advantage of the fact that she was sleeping in the daytime, used the essence of the sun to enter into Qingmiao's mouth. On the eighth day of the fourth month of the next year, at midnight, he ripped open her right arm-pit and was born. As soon as he had come down on the ground he walked seven paces, raised his hand and said, pointing to Heaven:

> (Among all beings) above and under Heaven
> I alone am venerable.
> All the Three Worlds[4] are full of pain—
> What is there enjoyable (in them)?

From that (moment onward) Buddhism took its rise.

•

[Laozi, after the Indian king had repented his sins,] chose Yin Xi to be their master, and said to the king: "My master is called the Buddha; the Buddha (in turn) served the Supreme Way". The king followed Yin Xi and was converted by him; men and women shaved their heads and observed celibacy. Thus the Supreme Way, by the grace of the Buddha, commissioned Yin Xi to be a Buddha in Kashmir with the appellation of Mingguang rutong.

•

At the time of king Huan, in the year *jiazi* (which would be 716 BC), in the month with the one *yin* (*i.e.*, the fifth month of the lunar calendar), I shall order Yin Xi to use that essence of the moon (as a vehicle) to descend in Central India. (There) he will enter into the mouth of the wife of (king) Baijing (Shuddho[dana]); (thus) he will be born, availing himself of (the queen's body) as a shelter. He will be named Siddharta.[5] He will abandon the position of a crown-prince, and go into the mountains in order to cultivate the Way. (Finally) he will realize the unsurpassed Way, and obtain the appellation of Buddha. . . .

•

It is said in the *Huahu jing*:[6] Buddhism arose in a barbarian region. In the West the metallic fluid prevails; therefore (people of that quarter) are hard and without decorum. The gentlemen of Shenzhou (China) have imitated their manners as a model and have erected Buddhist temples. Everywhere they treat the Buddhist scriptures with special veneration, and so they turn their back on what is essential and apply themselves to secondary matters. Their words are extravagant and do not agree with the wonderful

---

3. The kingdom of the Shakya tribe, on the border of India and Nepal, where the Buddha—also called Shakyamuni, "Sage of the Shakyas"— grew up.
4. The Realm of Desire (inhabited by beings who desire objects of the senses), the Realm of Form (inhabited by gods who possess physical form),
and the Formless Realm (inhabited by gods who do not have physical form).
5. The birth name of the historical Buddha was Siddhartha Gautama.
6. *Conversion of the Barbarians Sutra* (*Huahu jing*).

doctrine (of Daoism). They adorn the sutras and carve statues in order to deceive the ruler and his subjects. As a result, the world suffers from floods or drought, the weapons are (incessantly) used in mutual attacks. Within only ten years calamities have happened everywhere: the five planets have deviated from their fixed course, mountains have collapsed, rivers have dried up. That the transforming influence of royal (government) has not been peacefully (realized) is in all respects the result of the disorder (brought about by) Buddhism. Emperors and kings do not occupy themselves with their ancestral temples, and common people do not sacrifice to their ancestors: that is why the spirits of Heaven and Earth, the Way (of nature) and the fluids cannot be (propitiated or) restored to order.

•

It is said in the *Laozi xu:*[7] The Way of *yin* and *yang*[8] by transformation creates the myriad things Dao(ism) has originated in the East and corresponds to (the element) of wood and to *yang*; Buddhism has originated in the West and corresponds to (the element) of metal and to *yin*. (Thus) Daoism is the father, Buddhism the mother; Daoism is Heaven, Buddhism Earth; Daoism is birth (or: life), Buddhism death. Daoism is the primary cause (*yin* = *hetu*), Buddhism the secondary cause (*yuan* = *pratyaya*). Together they form (a couple of) one *yin* and one *yang* which (can)not be separated. Thus Buddhism has been produced by Daoism, whereas Dao(ism) spontaneously exists and has not been produced by anything. The Buddhist assembly has large seats which are square in imitation of Earth; the Daoist assembly has small seats which are round in imitation of Heaven. That the Buddhist monk does not wear arms is because the *yin* fluid is symbolized by the woman: therefore (the priest, associated with West = *yin* = woman) is not made to perform military or corvee duties. (In view of this) it is understandable why the Daoist (is allowed) to be a soldier. That the Buddhist monk does not bow when seeing the Son of Heaven[9] or a king or a marquis symbolizes (that he is like) the woman who remains in the deep (seclusion) of the harem and does not interfere in government affairs. That the Daoist when seeing the Son of Heaven observes (the emperor's commands and bows down is because he does engage in government matters and is active as a subject and as an official. In the Daoist assembly the drinking of wine is not a sin; that in the Buddhist assembly it is not drunk is because a woman by drinking wine commits one of the seven (sins warranting) repudiation. That the Daoist assembly knows no fasting is because (Daoism) is primarily concerned with life, and life requires food; that the Buddhist assembly observes fasting is because (Buddhism) is primarily concerned with death, and death is (the result of) abstinence from food, and also because the woman is moderate in eating. That the Buddhist priest sleeps alone is because women (have to) guard their chastity; the Daoist spends the night in company and has therefore no restrictive rules (to observe in these matters).

•

7. *Preface to the Laozi,* attributed to the legendary Ge Xuan (164–244 C.E.).
8. The male principle; the term originally referred to the sunny side of a valley, and by extension it came to be associated with the light, heaven, dryness, and activity. "*Yin*": the female principle; the term originally referred to the shady side of a valley, and by extension it came to be associated with the dark, earth, dampness, and passivity.
9. That is, the emperor.

Daoism is primarily concerned with life, Buddhism with death. Daoism eschews what is dirty, Buddhism does not. Daoism belongs to *yang*, to life, to the avoidance of what is dirty, Buddhism does the opposite. In this way pure and impure are as wide apart as Heaven (is from Earth), and (the doctrines pertaining to) life and to death are widely separated. Why then do you not observe the great Way of purity and emptiness instead of wishing to (follow) Buddhism, the dirty and evil doctrine of birth-and-death?

THE XIANG'ER COMMENTARY ON THE LAOZI
(*Laozi xiang'er zhu*)

The *Xiang'er Commentary on the Laozi* (*Laozi xiang'er zhu*) is the first commentary on *The Scripture of the Way and Its Virtue* (*Daode jing*; see above) that was the product of—and written for—an organized Daoist community: the Celestial Masters. This movement had arisen in Sichuan Province in 142 C.E. after the deified Laozi appeared to Zhang Daoling (34–156), and its members formed their own state in the Hanzhong Valley (in present-day Sichuan Province, in western China). It lasted from about 190 until 215, when Zhang Daoling's grandson, Zhang Lu, surrendered to the Han general Cao Cao and they were dispersed throughout China.

The *Xiang'er Commentary*, one of the only extant texts from the community's formative days that may have been written by Zhang Lu himself, provides insight into how the group functioned. The text had long been lost, and its newly discovered portions amount to only about half of the original. The commentary seems to have been largely intended to provide a charter for a society modeled on the Dao. The *Xiang'er Commentary*, like the *Laozi Inscription* and the *Scripture on Laozi's Transformations* (for both, see above), refers to a deified Laozi—but here he is none other than the Dao itself, and the teachings of the Dao come through his voice. Other groups' teachings, labeled in this text "perverse" or "deviant"— including the ethical teachings of Confucius—are warned against and criticized. Indeed, such criticism underlies the *Xiang'er Commentary*'s novel interpretation of a line in chapter 3 of *The Scripture of the Way and Its Virtue* on which interpreters have long focused: "He always keeps them innocent of knowledge and free from desire" (in the following translation, "He constantly causes the people to be without knowledge, without desire"). According to this commentary, the leader keeps people not ignorant of facts but rather innocent of knowledge *about the deviant teachings*.

The *Xiang'er Commentary* also reveals the moral injunctions provided by the Celestial Masters' community to all people (including the ruler). These took the form of an influential set of precepts that, if followed properly, enable the practitioner to attain longevity or escape death altogether. The text explicitly sets forth Daoist physiological and sexual practices, for the individual body should retain its life essence, should avoid being moved by excesses of emotion, and, like the body of the state, should be unified with the undifferentiated Dao. As the *Xiang'er Commentary* notes, "When one's emotions are unmoved and one's joy and anger do not issue forth, the five viscera harmonize and are mutually productive. This is to be of one radiance and of one dust with the Dao. . . . One who is still in this fashion endures perpetually without perishing."

PRONOUNCING GLOSSARY

Dao: *dow*
Laozi xiang'er zhu: *lao-tzu shee-ang-erh chu*

———————

. . . then the people will not contend, nor will they steal.

Not seeing that which is desirable will make your heart unruffled.[1]

. . . Not desiring to see something is like not seeing it at all. Do not allow your heart to be moved. If it is moved, restrain it. [If you do so,] though the Dao departs, it will return again. But if you follow the wild promptings of your heart, the Dao will leave for good.

The Sage regulates through emptying his heart and filling his belly,

The heart is a regulator. It may hold fortune or misfortune, good or evil. The belly is a sack for the Dao; its pneumas constantly wish to fill it. When the heart produces ill-omened and evil conduct, the Dao departs, leaving the sack empty. Once it is empty, deviance enters, killing the person. If one drives off the misfortune and evil in the heart, the Dao will return to it and the belly will be filled.

through weakening his will and strengthening his bones.

The will follows the heart in possessing both good and evil. The bones follow the belly in accommodating pneuma. When a strong will produces evil, the pneumas depart and the bones are desiccated. If one weakens the evil will, the pneumas return and marrow fills the bones.[2]

He constantly causes the people to be without knowledge, without desire;

When the Dao is cut off and does not circulate, deviant writings flourish and bribery arises. Then the people contend in their avarice and in their desire to study these writings. Consequently, their bodies are placed into grave danger. Such things should be prohibited. The people should not know of deviant writings; nor should they covet precious goods. Once this is accomplished, the kingdom will be easy to rule. The transformative influence of those above over those below will be like a wind through the slender grasses. If you wish this, the essential thing is that you should know to keep faith with the Dao.

and causes the knowledgeable not to dare inaction.

If his highness tirelessly keeps faith with the Dao, the knowledgeable, even though their hearts have been perverted, will still outwardly mark right and wrong. Seeing his highness acting reverently, they will dare not act otherwise.

Then all is regulated.

———————

TRANSLATED BY Stephen R. Bokenkamp. All bracketed additions are the translator's.

1. The italicized text quotes chapters 3–11 and 35–36 of *The Scripture of the Way and Its Virtue* (*Daode jing*; see above).

2. In physiological practice, the bones were important as storehouses of blood and essence [translator's note].

In this manner, the kingdom will be regulated.

Employ the Dao as it rushes in. Further, do not allow it to overflow.

The Dao values the centrally harmonious. You should practice it in inner harmony. Your will should not flood over, for this is a transgression of the precepts of the Dao.

Be deep, resembling the primogenitor of the myriad things.

This refers to the Dao. When one practices the Dao and does not transgress the precepts, one is deep like the Dao.

Blunt its sharp edges; release its vexations.

The "sharp edge" refers to the heart as it is plotting evil. "Vexations" means anger. Both of these are things in which the Dao takes no delight. When your heart wishes to do evil, blunt and divert it; when anger is about to emerge, forgive and release it. Do not allow your five viscera[3] to harbor anger and vexation. Strictly control yourself by means of the precepts of the Dao; urge yourself on with the [hope of] long life. By these means you will reach the desired state. The stirring of vexations is like the rapid vibrations of lute strings; this is why it leads to excess. You should strive to be slow to anger, for death and injury result from these violent urges. If the five viscera are injured by anger, the Dao is not able to govern. This is why the Dao has issued such heavy injunctions against anger and why the Dao teaches about it so diligently.

The five viscera are injured when the five pneumas [which fill them]—those of metal, wood, water, fire, and earth[4]—are rendered inharmonious. When these are harmonious, they give birth to one another; when they clash, they attack one another. When you give vent to anger or follow your emotions, one of these pneumas will always issue forth. It issues from one of the viscera and then attacks the others. The victorious pneuma will then form an illness and kill you. If you are strong in yang,[5] a declining pneuma will emerge to attack an ascendant pneuma and there will be no injury from the anger. Even so, in this way you are only a hair's breadth from death. If you are weak, an ascendant pneuma will emerge to attack a declining pneuma and disaster will result.

Harmonize your radiances; unify your dust.

When one's emotions are unmoved and one's joy and anger do not issue forth, the five viscera harmonize and are mutually productive. This is to be of one radiance and of one dust with the Dao.

Be deep and still and so perpetually present.

One who is still in this fashion endures perpetually without perishing.

Do you not yet know whose child I am? My image preceded the Thearchs.[6]

---

3. Liver, heart, spleen, lungs, and kidneys.
4. The five elements that are the foundation of the theory of five phases—a set of systematic associations between different categories, including the five directions, five colors, and five viscera (see table 2, p. 135).
5. The male principle; the term originally referred to the sunny side of a valley, and by extension it came to be associated with the light, heaven, dryness, and activity.
6. In Daoism, emperors in heaven. More generally, the term was applied first to deified kings and later to living emperors.

"I" refers to the Dao, as does the phrase "preceded the Thearchs." The ten thousand things[7] all alike originated in it, the nameless. It is not yet known which children from which families will be able to practice this Dao. Those who are able to practice it will pattern themselves on the Dao and will be as if they existed before the Thearchs.

Heaven and earth are inhumane; they treat the myriad things as straw dogs.[8]

Heaven and earth are patterned on the Dao. They are humane to all those who are good, inhumane to all those who do evil. Thus, when they destroy the myriad things, it is the evil whom they hate and whom they view as if they were grass or domestic dogs.

The Sage is inhumane; he treats the common people as if they were straw dogs.

The Sage models himself on heaven and earth. He is humane to good people, inhumane toward evil people. When kingly governance turns to destruction and evil, [the Sage] also views the king as a straw dog. Thus people should accumulate meritorious actions so that their essences and [internal] spirits communicate with heaven. In this way, when there are those who wish to attack and injure them, heaven will come to their aid. The common run of people are all straw dogs; their essences and spirits are unable to communicate with heaven. The reason for this is that, as robbers and thieves with evil intentions dare not be seen by government officials, their essences and spirits are not in touch with heaven, so that when they meet with dire extremities, heaven is unaware of it.

The Yellow Thearch[9] was a humane sage and knew the inclinations of later generations, so he plaited straw to make a dog and hung it above the gate, desiring thereby to indicate that within these gates in later generations, all would be straw dogs. But people did not understand what the Yellow Thearch meant to imply. They merely copied this practice without reforming their evil hearts. This is certainly a great evil.

The space between heaven and earth, is it not like a bellows?

The pneumas of the Dao reside in this space—clear, subtle, and invisible. All blood-bearing beings receive them in reverence. Only the ignorant do not believe this. As a result the space is here compared to a bellows. When the smelter works the bellows, air moves through the tube—that is, the hollow bamboo pipe—with a sound. [Although there is something there,] it cannot be seen. This is why it is here taken as a metaphor, meant to explain the matter for the ignorant.

Void, it cannot be exhausted. The more movement there is, the more it emits.

The clear pneumas are invisible, as if they were void. Yet their breathing never is exhausted. The more they move, the more it is that emerges.

Those with great learning are again and again depleted; best maintain the middle.

---

7. That is, all the things that exist.
8. Effigies made to ward off evil influences; after being used, they were thrown into the street.

9. That is, the mythological Yellow Emperor, Huangdi (27th century B.C.E.).

Those possessing great knowledge are superficial and ornate. They do not know how to hold to the Dao or to perfect the body. Once they live out their span of years, they will invariably be "depleted" [i.e., die]. "Again and again" means [that this has happened] more than once. It is better to study life, to maintain the centrally harmonious Dao.

Desiring that one's spirits do not die—this is called the mysterious feminine.

Gu [valley] means desire. Essence congeals to form [internal] spirits. If you desire to keep these spirits from perishing, you should congeal your essences and maintain them. The "feminine" is earth. The inborn nature of its body is stable. Women are patterned on it; therefore [their sexual organs] do not become rigid. If a man wishes to congeal his essence he should mentally pattern himself on earth and be like a woman. He should not work to give himself priority.

The gate of the mysterious feminine is the root of heaven and earth—

The "feminine" refers to the earth. Women are patterned after it. The vagina is the "gate," the comptroller of life and death. It is the very crux [of existence] and thus is called "the root." The penis is also called "the root."

attenuated and so enduring.

The Dao of yin[1] and yang is therefore similar to congealing the essences to produce life. At the age of fifty, having filled one's [productive] role, one should stop. Even when one is young, though one possesses [the capabilities for reproduction], one should rest [from intercourse] and preserve [these potencies]. "Attenuated" means slight. If one from youth follows the path of lessening, one will endure for a long time. At present, this matter [i.e., sexual intercourse] is the cause of great injury. Why did the Dao create it? The Dao places great emphasis on the continuation of ancestral sacrifice and the survival of the species. Desiring humanity to join their essences and so produce life, the Dao teaches the youthful to preserve their essences but not to cut them off. It does not teach humanity to labor [at intercourse]. This scheme of laboring [at intercourse] was thought up by the ignorant. The Dao cannot be held responsible for it. Those of higher virtue possess iron wills and are able to stop coupling for the purpose of reproducing. Thus they cut off the flow [of their essences] when they are young. Moreover, in this way they are sooner able to form beneficent [internal] spirits. These are called "essences of the Dao." This is why heaven and earth lack ancestral shrines, dragons lack offspring, Transcendents lack wives, and Jade Maidens[2] lack husbands. This is the highest way of keeping faith with the Dao!

Employ it without belaboring it.

If one is able to practice this Dao, one ought to obtain the longevity of a Transcendent. But one should absolutely not labor [at intercourse].

---

1. The female principle; the term originally referred to the shady side of a valley, and by extension it came to be associated with the dark, earth, dampness, and passivity.

2. Goddesses who serve as attendants in heaven. "Transcendents": *xian*, Daoists who have achieved extraordinary powers and a higher form of existence (often translated "immortals").

Heaven endures and earth is longevous; they are able to last long because they do not themselves give birth.

They are able to model themselves on the Dao and consequently are able to endure for a long time by not giving birth.

This is why the Sage, though he places lowest priority on his body, finds his body given priority.

Those who seek long life do not squander their essence and thoughts in pursuit of wealth for the maintenance of their bodies, nor do they try to coerce their lord, seeking emoluments to glorify themselves without merit, nor do they become gluttonous through eating the five flavors. Clothed humbly, they do not contend with the vulgar in fine shoes and clothes. In all of this, they place lower priority on their own bodies and by this means achieve the longevity of the Transcendents. They thus obtain good fortune greater than that achieved by all those vulgar persons. This is what is meant by "finding the body given priority."

Regarding his body as something external, he finds his body preserved.

The meaning of this phrase is the same as that above.

Because he is without a corpse, he is able to perfect his corpse.

The bodies of those who do not know the Dao of long life are but mobile corpses. It is not the Dao that they practice, but merely the way of the corpses. The reason the people of the Dao are able to achieve the longevity of Transcendents is that they do not practice the way of the corpses. They differ from the vulgar and thus are able to perfect their corpses, allowing them to enter the ranks of the Transcendent nobility.

✱   ✱   ✱

Thirty spokes join at a single hub, yet the utility of the cart resides where they are not.

In ancient times, before there were carts, [the people] were passive. The Dao sent Xi Zhong[3] to create carts. Once the ignorant obtained the cart, they used it only to satisfy their avarice. They did not contemplate practicing the Dao, nor were they aware of the spirits of the Dao. When the wise saw [the cart], they understood the beneficence of the Dao. Without uttering a sound, they were strictly self-regulated and put great emphasis on preserving the perfection of the Dao.

Clay is molded to make vessels, yet the utility of the vessel resides where it is lacking.

The explanation is the same as that for carts.

Doors and windows are hollowed out to make a room, yet the utility of the room resides where they are not.

The Dao caused the Yellow Thearch to invent dwellings. The explanation is the same as that for carts.

---

3. The culture hero credited with the invention of the wheeled vehicle [translator's note].

Therefore, [those who] have something regard its profit; [those who] lack it regard its utility.

These three objects were originally difficult to create. Without the Dao, it could not have been done. When the profane obtained these objects, they merely coveted the profit to be gained and did not know of the objects' origin. When the wise saw this, they returned to and embraced [the source of the objects'] utility. This utility finds its basis in the Dao. The hearts of the wise and the foolish are as distant from one another as north is from south. The significance of the above three sentences points to this.

Those who regularly practice false arts in the mortal world have established glib and deceptive arguments, basing themselves on this perfected text. They say that the Dao possesses a "celestial wheel-hub" and that human beings likewise have a hub that, through concentration of breath, can be made supple. The "spokes," they claim, refer to the human body for which this "hub" is the central point. They say that nurturing the [transcendent] embryo and refining the physical form should be like making clay into pottery. Moreover, they say that there are doors and windows for the Dao in the human body. All of these glosses are false deceptions and should not be adopted. To act upon them is the height of delusion.

*   *   *

Grasp the great image and all under heaven will proceed to you.

If the king grasps the correct law and models himself on the great Dao, all under heaven will take refuge in him. Vast territories requiring numerous post stations will arrive as if borne on the wind. The transformative influence of the Dao proceeds down from the top. When it designates a king, it values the "one man." In its rule there are no "two lords." This is why the thearchical king should constantly practice the Dao—so that it will spread to his officers and to the populace. It is not the case that only Daoists can practice it and the ruler is cast aside. A lord of great sageliness who makes the Dao his master and perfects the practice, transforming all with the teaching, will find the world in order. The auspicious omens betokening Great Peace will accumulate in response to human merit. One who achieves this is truly a Lord of the Dao.

A lord of middling worthiness, whose aspiration and faith are not pure, will find his rule supported and will be able to employ worthy officials. These ministers will aid him by means of the Dao. Though in this way the kingdom will be preserved and will remain unshaken, it will exhaust his essences and belabor his body. If his excellent adjutants depart one morning, the kingdom will be in danger of toppling by evening. This is because order came not from above but from those departed ministers, and in this way the transformative influence of the Dao was subverted.

Just as water cannot flow to the west, so is it difficult to achieve lasting order even with the most excellent of ministers. How much more difficult it is when all sorts of deviant influences are mixed in governance! [How much more difficult it is] when the ruling lord transgresses the Dao, belittling the perfected texts in the belief that the human world will persist in following him and in the belief that, as king, he can continue to discard the Dao!

The Dao is both exalted and spiritual. It will never obey humans. Thus, it releases sprites and perversities and causes all sorts of transformed oddities to spread as an admonition and warning. The Dao then hides away to observe. When disorder reaches its apex, order invariably returns; the will of the Dao inevitably prevails. This is why the thearchical king and the great ministers have no choice but to earnestly and carefully investigate the Dao.

When they proceed to you, there will be no harm.

When the king practices the Dao, the people will proceed to him. They will all delight in the Dao. Knowing that the spirit luminaries cannot be deceived, they will fear the celestial spirits, not laws and regulations, and will not dare to commit wrong. The loyalty of ministers and the filiality of children will proceed spontaneously from their perfected hearts. The king's law will no longer cause harm to anyone. Corporal punishments—mutilations, floggings, stocks, and jails—will be no more. Thus the people will be easily ruled and the king will enjoy happiness.

There will be peace and great happiness,

When the king rules in this fashion, there will be great happiness.

and parhelia and passing comets will cease.

All harm associated with disastrous celestial transformations and anomalies—light halos around the sun and moon, encroachments of the stellar officers, and unpropitious alignments of the heavenly bodies—is brought about through human transgression. [Under the good king,] the five planets[4] will follow their appointed courses and invading "guest stars" [i.e., comets] will not flare forth. Pestilential pneumas of all sorts will cease.

When the Dao speaks, its words are insipid and lacking in flavor.

The words of the Dao run counter to the craftiness of common speech, and so the profane find them extremely flavorless. Within this flavorlessness there is the savor of life; thus the Sage savors the savor of the flavorless.

To look at—it is not worth seeing; to hear—it is not worth listening to; but in use it cannot be exhausted.

The Dao delights in simplicity. Its words are not excessive. Looking at the words of the Dao or hearing the precepts of the Dao, some feel that they are so hard to carry out that they are not worthy of regard. But those who are able to practice them and use them will receive blessings without end.

That which will be made to shrink must have been enlarged.

Good and evil follow the same pattern; fortune and misfortune have the same root. Where they first extend, they will later shrink.

That which will be made weak must have been strengthened.

What is at first strong is later weak.

That which will be destroyed must have been flourishing.

What at first flourishes will later certainly be weakened and destroyed.

---

4. Jupiter, Mars, Mercury, Saturn, and Venus.

That which can be taken must have been increased.

What is first gained will later be taken away.

This is called "subtle wisdom."

The four things [listed above] are the "four grievances" or the "four thieves." Those who know them are subtle and wise. Knowing them, you may aid the Dao. Daoists fear shrinking, weakness, destruction, and loss. Thus, in framing their actions, they first make themselves shrink, make themselves weak, make themselves useless, and make themselves depleted so that later they may obtain propitious results. Now, as for the destructive words of the profane, they advocate the benefits of first becoming extended, strong, exalted, and well endowed, so they later face the resulting inauspicious results. This is why you are admonished to know sufficiency and why humans in the world are enjoined to diminish themselves. They should concentrate on spreading benevolence, distributing their wealth, and eradicating misfortune and not dare to seek more for themselves. Those who revere the precepts of the Dao may sit in auspiciousness forever, for it is not an empty saying that those who do not know how to stop with sufficiency will reap the opposite of their excess. Daoists do not dare to transgress this command, for, in truth, they possess this subtle wisdom.

The pliant and weak excel over the unbending and strong.

The pneumas of the Dao are subtle and weak; thus they endure and overcome everything. Water is like the Dao in its pliancy and weakness and so is able to dissolve or bore through massive rocks and cliffs. Daoists should make water their model.

Fish may not overcome the watery depths.

The precepts might be compared to the depths, the Dao to water, and the people to fish. Once fish lose the depths and are taken from the water, they die. If people do not practice the precepts and maintain the Dao, the Dao departs from them and they die.

When the kingdom possesses an advantageous implement, it should not be shown to the people.

Treasure your essences and do not squander them. If you allow them to move, you will experience lack. Another explanation says: the people of the Dao should rather act upon others than allow people to act upon them. They should rather avoid others and not be avoided by others. They should instruct others in the good and not be taught by others. They should be angered at others, not anger others. With impartiality they should give much to others, not receive much from others. Those who act contrary to this advice are showing others the advantageous implement.

COMMANDS AND ADMONITIONS
FOR THE FAMILY OF THE GREAT DAO
(*Dadao jia lingjie*)

Commands and Admonitions for the Family of the Great Dao (ca. 255 C.E.), like the *Xiang'er Commentary on the Laozi* (the previous selection), was written to the followers of the Celestial Masters community. Its authorship is unknown, but the work is traditionally attributed to the last leader of the Celestial Masters, Zhang Lu—the "I" of the text—who either wrote it toward the end of his life or transmitted it posthumously through a spirit medium (sources suggest that he died in 215/16 or perhaps 245). The social and historical context for this address is the community's dispersal from the Hanzhong Valley to different parts of the Chinese empire after Zhang Lu's surrender to the Han general Cao Cao in 215.

Commands and Admonitions begins with a cosmogony, as the Dao emanates through three pneumas (mystic, inaugural, and primal). Following a discussion of the times when the Dao was present in the world—including a brief allusion to the evolving Conversion of the Barbarians story (see above), which here contains an interesting interpretation of Buddhist tonsure practices—the text succinctly describes the establishment of the Celestial Masters community and its administrative structure of twenty-four parishes. *Commands and Admonitions* then tracks the increasingly sorry state of the Celestial Masters group after "the kingdom of the righteous toppled": "Since the exile, we have been scattered over the entire kingdom. The Dao has often saved your lives. Sometimes it has broken through the pneumas to speak to you; sometimes a minister or magistrate of the earlier days [in Hanzhong] has tried to reform you, but still you do not keep faith. This is extremely regrettable." The text clearly reflects its politically troubled times. The short-lived Wei kingdom that had patronized the dispersed Celestial Masters community was on the brink of collapse by the mid-third century (it fell in 266), and its problems and tensions further undermined the Celestial Masters' coherence and continuity.

Composed in an apocalyptic age, *Commands and Admonitions* provides the Celestial Masters community with a series of injunctions so that members can correct a wide range of problematic behaviors, particularly those involving excessive sexual desire, greed, and bribes. They are now "muddled and benighted": "Although you have heard the speech of the divine Transcendents and the words of long life, your hearts are confused and your thoughts led into deception, so that once again you do not preserve your faithfulness."

The *Xiang'er Commentary* also provides a social charter and precepts to regulate the Celestial Masters community, but in responding to the new need for order and rules *Commands and Admonitions* proposes solutions not found in that earlier text. Strikingly, it overtly calls for instilling Confucian-style ethics to reform the family and society: "All of our households should transform one another through loyalty and filiality, so that fathers are magnanimous and sons filial, husbands faithful and wives chaste, elder brothers respectful and the younger obedient." As *Commands and Admonitions* draws to a close, it insists that one must be a good citizen, even if one's good actions remain hidden and leave no trace. Such behavior is required to achieve the status of "seed people"—the elect who will lead the faithful through the troubling times and inaugurate a new age free of evil, calamity, and disease.

PRONOUNCING GLOSSARY

Dadao jia lingjie: *da-dow chia ling-*
 chieh
Dao: *dow*

Zhang Daoling: *chawng dow-ling*
Zhang Jue: *chawng jew-eh*

The great Dao is that which encompasses heaven and earth, is joined with and nourishes all forms of life, and controls the myriad initiatory mechanisms. Without shape or image, it is undifferentiated and yet spontaneously gives birth to the million species. Though it is something to which humans cannot put a name, from heaven and earth on down everything is born and dies through the Dao.

The Dao bestows itself by means of subtle pneumas. There are three colors, associated with the mystic, the primal, and the inaugural pneumas. The mystic is azure and formed heaven. The inaugural is yellow and formed earth. The primal is white and formed the Dao. Within the three pneumas, the Dao controls all above and below and is the father and mother of the myriad things. Thus it is most revered and most holy. From heaven and earth on down, there is nothing that is not born through receiving these pneumas. All longevous creatures are able to preserve the Dao, holding in its pneumas. Thus possessed of essence and [internal] spirits, they breathe in and out and have yin and yang[1] natures.

The Dao gave birth to heaven. Heaven gave birth to earth. The earth gave birth to humans. All were born of the three pneumas. Three threes are nine. Thus people have nine orifices[2] and nine pneumas. When these nine pneumas flow without obstruction, the five viscera[3] are untroubled. When the five viscera are untroubled, the six storehouses[4] are settled. When the six storehouses are settled, the corporeal spirits are luminous. When the corporeal spirits are luminous, one approaches the Dao. So, humans who practice good and maintain the Dao are cautious not to lose the Dao of life. Not losing it, they receive the triple [pneumas]. Since they are not separated from the triple pneumas, they are able to change together with heaven and earth.

The *Yijing*[5] says: "After heaven and earth came into existence, there were the myriad things. After the myriad things, there were male and female. After male and female, there were husband and wife. After husband and wife, there were father and son." Now, the mention of "father and son" indicates the desire to continue through a hundred generations, so one's seed and family name can continue. But in lower antiquity, lineages are short-lived and the people are largely ignorant and shallow. Delighting only in sensual pleasure, they indulge their ears and eyes in deviant practices.

TRANSLATED BY Stephen R. Bokenkamp. All bracketed additions are the translator's.

1. The complementary forces that unite to form the Dao: yin, a term that originally referred to the shady side of a valley, by extension came to be associated with the dark, earth, dampness, and passivity—the female principle; yang, a term that originally referred to the sunny side of a valley, by extension came to be associated with the light, heaven, dryness, and activity—the male principle.

2. The eyes, ears, nostrils, and mouth, plus either the urethra and anus or the tongue and throat.
3. The liver, heart, spleen, lungs, and kidneys.
4. The throat, stomach, large intestine, small intestine, bladder, and gallbladder.
5. The *Book of Changes* (or *I Ching*, traditionally dated to the 12th century B.C.E.), a volume of divination and cosmology.

They are infatuated with feminine beauty and so their essence and spirits spurt forth chaotically. They covet material things and bribes. As a result, miasmic pneumas rise up and foster all sorts of illness.

Ever since the time of the Yellow Thearch,[6] the people have been crafty. They make oxen serve them and they ride horses. They pass bribes to become officials. During the time of the Five Thearchs,[7] there was a gradual decrease in longevity. The three eras—Xia, Shang, and Zhou[8]—saw a turn to desire for worldly profit. Then the Inaugural Thearch of the Qin and the Five Hegemons[9] attacked and injured one another and banditry arose. Millions died—more than can be counted. All of this occurred through loss of faith with the Dao.

Generation after generation, the Dao acted as the teacher of the thearchical kings, but they were unable to revere and serve it. As a result, when there were troubles such as social upheaval or the fall of dynasties, though the Dao was there to aid in the crisis, not one in ten thousand survived.

The Dao values human life. At the end of the Zhou, one emerged to uphold the Dao in Langye. Thereupon the Dao bestowed upon that man, Gan Ji, the "Dao of Great Peace." The revival began in the east. In the east he began to save the populace from mud and ashes. Although there were those who inclined to belief in the Dao, the first transformative influence was slight. The people obeyed only when it came to matters of dietary regimen and sexual practice. Gradually, this [influence] widened to include their parents, siblings, and the spirits to whom they performed sacrifice. Eventually, the pneumas of the Dao would spread to cover the entire land within the four seas.[1]

The Dao was then born again through transformation [and came to] the western pass. This came about because the teachings of Great Peace were not complete. There was need of an enlightened master's verbal instructions and of rectification through talismanic orders. The Dao further created the five-thousand-character text, which emanated from the essentials of the divine Transcendents.[2] In it, the prohibitions became more severe and the people were instructed in the essentials of regulating the body, nurturing life, and in the explanations of the divine Transcendents. It was entrusted to the commander of the pass, Yin Xi. These transmissions were fairly complete, but most of the people of that generation were ignorant and their hearts were moreover closed. Masses of people died, and of ten thousand, not one was preserved.

The Dao then went westward into the land of the barbarians to transmit the practices of the Dao.[3] In this case, the prohibitions were extremely severe. There were no provisions for yin and yang. They were neither to

---

6. That is, the mythological Yellow Emperor, Huangdi (27th century B.C.E.). A thearch was originally a deified king, but the term was later applied to the emperor. In Daoism, thearchs are emperors in heaven.
7. That is, Chinese prehistory, before the legendary Xia dynasty (ca. 2070–ca. 1600 B.C.E.). The five are variously identified but include Huangdi.
8. The Shang (ca. 1600–1046 B.C.E.) and Zhou (1046–256 B.C.E.) are historical dynasties.
9. Rulers of the five major states who vied for power and control during the Zhou dynasty. "The Inaugural Thearch": the Qin emperor who unified China in 221 B.C.E.

1. That is, the entire world; the four seas are the metaphorical boundaries of China.
2. *Xian*, Daoists who have achieved extraordinary powers and a higher form of existence (often translated "immortals"). "The five-thousand-character-text": that is, *The Scripture of the Way and Its Virtue* (*Daode jing*, or *Laozi*; see above).
3. A reference to the "Conversion of the Barbarians" story; see Xiang Kai's "Memorial to Emperor Huan Concerning Buddhism and Daoism" and "The Texts on the Conversion of the Barbarians," above.

take life, nor to eat living things. The barbarians were unable to place their faith in the Dao, and so the Dao transformed into a perfected Transcendent. This Transcendent intermingled with the people of Heaven. They floated in the air, disporting themselves among the clouds. When they came to soar along the banks of the Weak Waters, the barbarians bowed down to them, knocking their heads millions of times, [so that the crowns of their heads were like] real mirrors reflecting into Heaven.[4] Since then, the barbarians have shaved their heads and cut off their sidelocks to seal their determination to keep faith with that Perfected Person.[5] Thus the Way of Perfection flourished there. It was not the case that the Dao acted only for the barbarians and not for the people of the Qin dynasty. The people of the Qin just did not accept the perfect Dao.

When the generations of the Five Hegemons became weak, the red Han house[6] received the mandate of Heaven. The Dao aided them in restoring order from chaos. It revealed the writings of Master Yellow Stone and bestowed them upon Zhang Liang.[7]

But the Dao also transforms its shape. Who is there that is able to perceive its perfection? Though the Han house was thus established, its last generations moved at cross-purposes to the will of the Dao. Its citizens pursued profit, and the strong fought bitterly with the weak. The Dao mourned the fate of the people, for were it once to depart, its return would be difficult. Thus did the Dao cause Heaven to bestow its pneuma, called the "newly emerged Lord Lao,"[8] to rule the people, saying, "What are demons that the people should only fear them and not place faith in the Dao?" Then Lord Lao made his bestowal on Zhang Daoling,[9] making him Celestial Master. He was most venerable and most spiritual and so was made the master of the people.

You should all know this. He was ennobled above heaven and earth, and yet your hearts are closed. Each day, each month, each year, you increasingly desire to please your mouths and bellies and give free rein to your ears and eyes. You do not keep faith with the Dao. Those who have died are numbered in the tens of thousands. Is this not lamentable?

On the first day of the fifth month in the first year of the Han Peace reign period [11 June 142 C.E.], the Dao created the Way of the Covenantal Authority of Correct Unity at Red-Stone Wall at Quting of Lin'ang County,[1] the Commandery of Shu. Binding tallies were formed with heaven and earth, and the twenty-four parishes[2] were established to promulgate the primal, original, and inaugural pneumas to rule the people.

You do not know even the basics of the Dao, nor can you distinguish its true revelations from the false. You only strive with one another for high status in the world and worry about assigning one another a social standing.

---

4. "Weak waters" is the name of a mythical river believed to be in the western regions. . . . This is a fanciful explanation for the tonsures Buddhist monks receive on ordination [translator's note].
5. The zhenren, a concept that first appears in the Book of Master Zhuang (Zhuangzi; see above) and becomes important in later Daoism.
6. The Han dynasty (202 B.C.E.–220 C.E.); the color red (fire) represented its rule.
7. An adviser (d. 189 B.C.E.) to the Han dynasty rulers. "Master Yellow Stone": Laozi.

8. The deified Laozi.
9. Founder of the Way of the Celestial Masters movement (34–156 C.E.).
1. According to the translator, Lin'ang corresponds to present-day Dayi and Pujiang Counties, suggesting that "Red Stone Wall" was Crane Call Mountain (Heming shan), where the deified Laozi visited Zhang Daoling.
2. The administrative units of the Celestial Masters community.

In so doing, you turn your backs on the Dao and rebel against its powers. You wish to follow human understanding, but the human understanding delights in chaos!

It was precisely this that caused Zhang Jue with his Yellow Turbans[3] to foment insurrection. Do you know who Zhang Jue was? From his time the dead have been numbered in the tens of millions. His deviant Dao caused the pneumas [of the correct Dao] to be divided during the last generations [of the Han].

The parish people remained in Hanzhong for over forty years. The prohibitions of the Dao, the origins of the True and Correct, the explanations of the divine Transcendents—all were promulgated to you by the Dao. This is the extent to which the Dao thinks of you!

How regrettable, how injurious it is to consider the *Seven-Character Verses of the Wondrous Perfected on the Three Numina*[4] to be not True and not Correct, and on this basis to proclaim that the Dao deceives its people.

Coming to the time when the kingdom of the righteous toppled, those who fled into exile and those killed were numbered by the tens of thousands. This injured the will of the people. Since the exile, we have been scattered over the entire kingdom. The Dao has often saved your lives. Sometimes it has broken through the pneumas to speak to you; sometimes a minister or magistrate of the earlier days [in Hanzhong] has tried to reform you, but still you do not keep faith. This is extremely regrettable.

If you wish morning, you must first have evening. If you desire Great Peace,[5] you must first experience chaos. Since the evil of humanity could not be rooted out, you must first pass through war, illness, flood, drought, and even death. Your life spans have been depleted, and so it is appropriate that you must come up against these things. Though this is so, the favored will be without injury, since such persons have practiced the Dao in the past in order to prepare against such things as have come upon us today. Even if you die without reaching the age of Great Peace, your children and grandchildren will be blessed with Heaven's favor.

* * *

When Libationers cure the ill, they should do so at the onset of the illness. But, once the illness is cured, if it returns again, that person is evil. Do not again treat or cure them.

All of our households should transform one another through loyalty and filiality, so that fathers are magnanimous and sons filial, husbands faithful and wives chaste, elder brothers respectful and the younger obedient. Mornings and evenings you should practice "clarity and stillness."[6] Root out all covetousness, abandon the pursuit of personal profit, and rid yourself of desire. Reform your evil cravings. Pity the poor and cherish the old. Be liberal in supplying others and in giving way to them. Drive from your heart excesses of jealousy, joy, and anger so that your emotions are constantly harmonious and your eyes and belly in accord. Aid the kingdom in strength-

---

3. Members of a secret society led by the Daoist Zhang Jue (d. 184 C.E.); their revolt helped bring down the dynasty.
4. The *Scripture of the Yellow Court* (*Huangting jing*, 3rd century C.E.), a work on immortality that describes the human body as housing numerous divine beings.

5. A golden age of good government, political harmony, and good health, which was believed to have existed in the past and which would be restored when the ruling ideology is based on a return to the Dao.
6. A specific meditation practice.

ening its mandate. Abandon all of your past evil pursuits. Those who, from today on, practice good actions will find that disaster and disease melt away from them, and will become seed people of the later age.

The people should not complain of their poverty and suffering or covet riches, happiness, and high position. You have seen with your own eyes and heard with your own ears: From ancient times, have the rich and honored ever endured? Their possessions are abandoned on the ground and their bodies perish in the marketplace. Looked at in this way, the old proverb is correct: "A dead prince is not worth a live rat." What you achieve will be life, and the Dao is where you should seek it.

You should remember that the Dao conceals itself and is nameless. Name is an axe that hacks at the body. "Good actions leave no trace." If they wish to make it so that others do not see their "traces," those who practice the Dao should regulate their bodies and nurture their lives to seek blessing. Instead of which you teach others to give free rein to the self. If the self is given free rein, people will see its traces and the axe will be keen. If the axe that hews down the body is keen, good fortune departs and bad arrives. Should you not be cautious? Should you not be fearful? "The reason heaven and earth endure" is because they lack willfulness. And that which "does not act falsely, leaves nothing left undone."[7] Only when one does not allow others to see one's traces can one truly accomplish wonders.

You vulgar people are truly comical: When you do some small good deed, you always want others to know of it, and when you differ by so much as a grain of rice from others, you expect to be considered worthy. These are the sorts of benefit derived from what is not the Dao. In all cases, such behavior is a violation of the proscriptions of the Dao.

Now I transmit my teachings so that you people [of the Dao], both those who joined previously and new members, shall know my heart. Do not forsake it.

7. This entire passage, a pastiche of extracts from the *Laozi*, depends for its logic on the *Xiang'er* commentary [translator's note; for the *Xiang'er* commentary, see above].

REGULATIONS OF THE DARK CAPITAL
(*Xuandu lüwen*)

An important section in *Regulations of the Dark Capital* (*Xuandu lüwen*) sets out the rules for presenting the "petitions" that were part of the early Celestial Masters community. Some have commented that throughout its history China has been a "paperwork empire," noting the important role of documents within the functioning of the bureaucracy. Ritual practices within the Daoist tradition are similarly bureaucratic, and these petitions clearly illustrate how documents used for the official communication between officials and the imperial bureaucracy came to be the model for the ritual documents used by Daoist priests to communicate with the celestial bureaucracy made up of divine officials.

We learn from "Regulations for Petitioning" that Daoists could submit three petitions per month, that the priest submitted the petition during a formal ritual that required deep meditative concentration and proper comportment, that petitions had to be submitted on the correct day and at the proper time, that petitions could be forwarded only on behalf of others who were upright members of the community, and that petitions could request health, wealth, rank promotion, and relief for ancestors in purgatory. Petitions were to be submitted by the priest on behalf of others and not for his own personal gain. This text also stipulates the specific punishments meted out to a priest who violated ritual protocol when submitting petitions. Much as the merit gained from proper behavior can earn one a longer life and a position as a transcendent in the celestial bureaucracy, so, conversely, transgressions cause one to lose rank, be fined, suffer a certain number of days of illness, or, in the worst case, have one's allotted life span reduced by a certain number of years and lose one's guaranteed position in the celestial bureaucracy at the time of death.

PRONOUNCING GLOSSARY

Dao: *dow*   Xuandu lüwen: *hsuan-du lew-when*

Regulations for Petitioning

Regulation: From his meditation chamber in Loyang the Heavenly Master[1] followed the immortals westward to Shu, to the Chi and Cheng mountains. Since "people were corrupt and unclean and it was a disorderly and unsettled age," the Heavenly Master scaled the Pillar of Heaven and strode across the celestial threshold in order to produce for the first time the Way of the Authoritative Covenant of Orthodox Unity [i.e., the Way of the Heavenly Masters[2]]. Hoping to purify and enlighten the cosmos and mankind, to punish the unrighteous, and to nurture all living things, he established twenty-four parishes.[3] For each parish he established male and female officers, a total of twenty-four [per parish]. He made use of the grace of the Dark Origin,[4] opening the way to reform in later generations, so that all [believers] will repent of their errors and be ranked as Realized Immortals.[5]

Offerings may be submitted to the celestial offices three times a month, to repent of sins, reform conduct, cut oneself off from undesirable companions, and escape calamities, diseases, and hazards. Each month three petitions may be submitted.

Regulation: When an officiant enters the parish temple to present a petition, he must conduct himself formally. Wearing formal Daoist vestments, he is to sit quietly and visualize in meditation the vital *qi* (energy or vital force) of the Five Directions [east, south, west, north, center] and the Inspector of Merits, officials, and soldiers within his own body. In order of their hierarchic positions, they reverently come to him, wait on him, and surround him [i.e., in his meditation he becomes the center of the configuration]. When one enters the parish temple and submits a petition, one stops outward thoughts and concentrates, calling up the gods from one's memory.

TRANSLATED BY Nathan Sivin. All bracketed additions are the translator's.

1. Celestial Master.
2. That is, the Way of the Celestial Masters.
3. The administrative units of the Celestial Masters community.
4. That is, the deified Laozi.

5. That is, Perfected Ones, or *zhenren*, a concept that first appears in the *Book of Master Zhuang* (*Zhuangzi*; see above) and becomes important in later Daoism.

Regulation: A petition to the celestial offices is not to be presented in the parish temple on sexagenary day 5 or 35.[6] Pollution, according to the law, does not extend beyond the last day of the month, but one may still not submit a petition on the first of the [next] month. The uninitiated may not, when polluted, visit the parish temple and have an audience with the Master in charge. When this regulation is violated, [the priest's] allotted life span will be reduced by a year, for the crime will revert to him.

[Note in text: According to the regulations, each violation will be assessed by the Director of Errors and the Director of Investigations.]

Regulation: Those who enter the temple to present petitions must do so with upright carriage and quickened step. During the rites they are to keep to their places without men and women intermingling, looking idly about, speaking falsely, or moving too quickly or too slowly. Violators in positions of authority will be reduced one grade in rank. Those who cannot be demoted will be fined three ounces of jade and six hundred days of life.

Regulation: The ordained may not in an undisciplined fashion submit a petition on behalf of a perverse person. A perverse person is defined as one who is disrespectful or lewd; one who takes goods forcibly; one who is wicked and does not embody the Dao; one who does not act filially toward his parents or masters; one who does not act in accordance with obligation toward his rulers and elders, female [as well as male]; one who does not reverently uphold the morality of the Dao; one who is disrespectful toward the gods; one who steals or harms another, or acts treacherously; one who vilifies the worthy or slanders another as a result of envy; one who turns his back upon his parents; one who rebels against his master; or one who is uncompliant and will not do good. Until a full year has elapsed [since one of these infractions], one may not submit a petition for such a person. [An officiant] who does so will be punished by a deduction of five years from his allotted life span. Then, upon his death, he will be handed over to the Earl of the River[7] for banishment. Furthermore, he will be fined eight ounces of jade and demoted two ranks.

Regulation: Petitions are to be phrased in simple rather than polished language. They may be clumsy but not artful; simple but not flowery; truthful and not false; straightforward and not convoluted; precise but not vexatious; weak (delicate) but not corrupt; pure and unsullied; straightforward but disciplined; compendious but sincere. Such petitions will move Heaven and Earth and arouse the sympathy of the spirits and gods. They will be forwarded to the celestial offices, and a response will come immediately. Violations will be prosecuted by the Director of Wrongs. Parish officials and under-officials will be held responsible.

Regulation: Petitions to cure illness shall be delivered with the officiant facing the Gate of the Spirits (northeast). Petitions seeking longevity should be delivered facing the Gate of Heaven (northwest). Petitions seeking monetary gain or worldly honor should be delivered facing the Gate of Earth.[8] Petitions seeking to end disputes or annul curses should be delivered facing the Gate of the Human.[9] Those to control the movements of tigers should

---

6. The Chinese marked time by pairing one by one the members of a cycle of ten denary "stem" characters with one of twelve duodenary "branch" characters in succession to form sixty possible unique day designations [translator's note; "den- ary" and "duodenary" mean based on ten and on twelve, respectively].
7. The god of the Yellow River.
8. In the southeast.
9. In the southwest.

be delivered facing in the tiger direction (slightly north of east) and those to control the movements of snakes facing in the snake direction (slightly east of south). This supplements one's spiritual powers with those of the cosmic meridians and secures great good fortune.

Regulation: To present a petition seeking wealth and honor, use the "celestial granary day," sexagenary day 25. To ask for rank, use the "celestial storehouse day." Don't use "self-punishing" days, duodenary days 7, 10, 12, or 5. In the duodenary terrestrial branch cycle, 3 punishes 6, 11 punishes 8, 1 punishes 4, 9 punishes 3, 4 punishes 1, and 6 punishes 9.[1] Violations will incur 50 days of illness.

Regulation: A request to petition for relief with respect to judgments enacted by the purgatorial authorities against one's deceased ancestors or with respect to sickness, calamity, or bad luck enacted as a sentence on account of one's own transgressions, must be made to one's parish. If one is far from one's master, one is permitted to proceed as the law permits. Petitions will not reach the celestial offices unless they are submitted by one's own master, a grade-A libationer,[2] or an officer directly responsible for one's household or parish. Libationers below grades A through D must petition upward. Those responsible are [defined as] parish officials who lead three hundred or more households and those holding appointment as disease officer for three or more households.

---

1. The meaning of "punish" (*ting*) in early medieval China is not clear, but it is one of a number of technical terms for unfavorable astrological relationships [translator's note].

2. Priest in the Celestial Masters movement.

THE MOST HIGH JADE SCRIPTURE ON THE INTERNAL VIEW OF THE YELLOW COURT
(*Taishang huangting neijing yujing*)

The *Most High Jade Scripture on the Internal View of the Yellow Court* (*Taishang huangting neijing yujing*), usually called simply the *Scripture of the Yellow Court* (*Huangting jing*), is difficult to assign to any particular Daoist group and is of uncertain date (perhaps third century C.E.), but it became a central scripture within the later Daoist Upper Clarity (Shangqing) tradition. There are actually two works with almost the same title, designated the "inner scripture" and the "outer scripture": the first is an esoteric version of the second, exoteric text.

The Yellow Court was literally a central courtyard, and in this context the term refers to the center of the human body. The center is variously identified as the spleen, as an area between the eyes, or as the lowest of the three "Cinnabar Fields" (*dantian*), locations important for internal alchemy; the upper Cinnabar Field is in the brain, and the middle Cinnabar Field is the heart. The text is written in verse, and its rather cryptic language makes it challenging to translate and difficult to comprehend. In order to unpack some of the embedded esoteric meanings, the translator has provided a paraphrase of each poem. The language and structure of the text suggest that it was meant to be memorized and recited: "Chant it over ten thousand times, and ascend to the Three Heavens." Indeed, this document was clearly intended to give practitioners a guide for visualizing (or actualizing), through an inner vision, the divinities that inhabit the microcosmic realm of the body and that have their correlates in the macrocosmic realm. Primary among these gods in the *Scripture of the Yellow Court* are the spirits of the five viscera: the liver, heart, spleen, lungs, and kidneys. The viscera are related to a variety of macrocosmic correlates (directions, seasons, planets, colors, etc.) through the systematic correspondences entailed in the Five Agents system (see table 2, p. 135).

The selections below provide a number of visualization practices involving the practitioner's organs and their gods. Those practices include precise visions of the body gods and their vestments as well as the instructions on circulating rays of light, pneumas, saliva, and other bodily essences. The overarching goal of this text is to aid one in fixing the body gods in their proper locations, to nourish one's organs and spirits, and thereby to transform one's mundane body into a spiritualized body that will live forever.

PRONOUNCING GLOSSARY

Dao: *dow*

Shangqing: *shawng-ching*

Taishang huangting neijing yujing: *tai-shawng huang-ting nei-ching yu-ching*

First Stanza

In the purple aurora of Highest Clarity, before the Resplendent
    One of the Void,
The Most High, Great Dao Lord of the Jade Source of Light,
Dwelling at ease in the Stamen-Pearl Palace, composed verses of
    seven words,
Dispersing and transforming the five shapes of being, permutating
    the myriad spirits:
This is deemed the *Yellow Court*, known as the *Inner Book*.
The triple reprise of a concinnate[1] heart will set the embryo's
    transcendents dancing;
Glinting and luminous, the nine vital breaths[2] emerge amidst the
    empyrean;
The young lads under the Divine Canopy will bring forth a
    purple haze.
This is known as the *Jade Writ*, which may be sifted to its essence—
Chant it over ten thousand times, and ascend to the Three Heavens;[3]
The thousand calamities will thereby be dispelled, the hundred
    ailments healed;
You will not then shrink from the fell ravagings of tiger or of wolf,
And also thereby you will hold off age, your years extended forever.

FIRST STANZA—PARAPHRASE

In the light of perpetual morning, in the Shangqing heaven, in the
    realm of the cosmocrat who puts all of space in order,
The great deity whose seat is in the ultimate illumination of dawn,
Who resides in a palace symbolic of perigynous jewels, wrote a poem
    in seven-word lines,

TRANSLATED BY Paul W. Kroll.

1. Skillfully put together.
2. The stars of the Big Dipper (according to Daoists, there are two invisible stars in addition to the seven easily seen in the constellation).

3. The three benevolent and pure heavens, as opposed in Upper Clarity cosmology to the corrupt Six Heavens.

Having the power to affect all entities, from fish, birds, men, mammals,
    and invertebrates to the multitudinous gods.
That poem was this very text, the *Inner Scripture of the Yellow Court.*
Once the three "cinnabar fields"[4] are brought into harmony through it,
    the spirits of one's immortal embryo will respond with delight,
And the pneumata of the Nine Heavens,[5] conducted through the three
    "cinnabar fields," will shine forth from the chambers of one's brain,
As the deities of one's eyes, beneath the eyebrows' arch, emit a
    vaporous aura of supernatural purple.
This text, also called the *Jade Writ*, deserves the closest study,
For, after ten thousand recitations of it, one may be translated to the
    highest heavens,
Immune to earthly misfortune, impervious to disease,
Proof against attacks from savage beasts,
And able to enjoy perpetual life.

Second Stanza

Above there are ethereal souls, below is the junction's origin;
Left serves as lesser yang, the right as greatest yin;[6]
Behind there is the Secret Door, before is the Gate of Life.
With emergent sun and retreating moon, exhale, inhale,
    actualizing them.
Where the Four Breaths are well blended, the arrayed mansions
    will be distinct;
Let the purple haze rise and fall, with the clouds of the Three
    Immaculates.
Irrigate and spray the Five Flowers, and plant the Numinous Root.
Let the channeled course of the Seven Liquors rush into the span
    of the hut;
Circulate the purple, embrace the yellow, that they enter the
    Cinnabar Field;
Make the Shrouded Room bright within, illuminating the Gate of Yang.

SECOND STANZA—PARAPHRASE

The spirits of the liver, lungs, and spleen are above, representing
    Heaven, as contrasted with the navel (or, alternatively, a spot three
    inches below the navel), representing the underworld of matter and
    generation.
The left and right kidneys are yang and yin.
The Secret Door of the kidneys is at the back of one's body, while the
    Gate of Life, located below the navel (equivalent either to the lower
    cinnabar field or to the "junction's origin" where semen is stored), is
    in front.
Sun and moon, imaged in one's left and right eyes, respectively, are to
    be made sensibly present in concentrated visualization, so that they
    will shed their light on one's internal organs, while one conducts the
    breath carefully through the body.

---

4. See the introduction to this selection.
5. A finer subdivision of the Three Heavens mentioned above.
6. The female principle; the term originally referred to the shady side of a valley, and by extension it came to be associated with the dark, earth, dampness, and passivity. "Yang": the male principle; the term originally referred to the sunny side of a valley, and by extension it came to be associated with the light, heaven, dryness, and activity.

Bringing together the pneumata of the four seasons in oneself will
    render distinct the astral lodgings and somatic dwellings of sun,
    moon, and Dipper.

As the purple vapor of the divinities of the eyes infuses one's body, it is
    joined by clouds of purple, yellow, and white, symbolic of the Primal
    Mistresses of the Three Immaculates—goddesses who preside over
    the three major divisions of the body and the twenty-four major
    corporeal divinities.

One should swallow the saliva that nourishes one's internal organs,
    especially the essential "flowers" of the five viscera,[7] taking care to
    cultivate the "Numinous Root" of the tongue, which activates and
    gathers in the saliva.

The humoral juices of the the body's seven orifices[8] are channeled
    throughout the body and into the bridge of the nose, the "hut"
    between the eyebrows.

The spreading purple vapor from the eyes and the rising yellow
    pneuma from the spleen are brought into the upper cinnabar field
    located three inches behind the sinciput,

While, below, the "Shrouded Room" of the kidneys is bathed in light,
    as is the Gate of Yang (the Gate of Life) in front.

Third Stanza

The mouth is the Jade Pool, the Officer of Greatest Accord.

Rinse with and gulp down the numinous liquor—calamities will not
    encroach;

One's body will engender a lighted florescence, breath redolent as
    orchid;

One turns back, extinguishes the hundred malignities—one's features
    refined in jade.

With practice and attention, cultivate this, climbing to the Palace of
    Ample Cold.

Not sleeping either day or night, you will achieve then full perfection;

When thunder sounds and lightning spurts, your spirits are placid,
    impassive.

THIRD STANZA—PARAPHRASE

The mouth is the reservoir of the jade liquor of saliva, controlling in
    this capacity the nourishing and harmonizing of the body's organs.

Drinking down the spiritually potent saliva and circulating it in
    prescribed fashion will enable you to avoid misfortune;

Your body will be lit from within like a luminous flower, and your
    breath will acquire a sweet fragrance;

All debilitating influences will be opposed, and your skin will become
    pure as snow, white as jade.

Through repeated exercises you will become expert in this practice and
    be able to ascend to the celestial palace where the white moon itself
    is bathed when at apogee, at the winter solstice.

Unstinting concentration will lead to complete spiritual realization,

Such that your corporeal spirits will remain serenely fixed when
    confronted by any outer startlements.

---

7. Liver, heart, spleen, kidneys, and lungs.   8. Eyes, ears, nostrils, and mouth.

Fourth Stanza

The person within the Yellow Court wears a polychrome-damask
jacket,
A volant skirt of purple flowering, in gossamer of cloudy vapors,
Vermilion and azure, with green withes, numinous boughs of
halcyon-blue.
With the jade cotter of the Seven Panicles, shut tight the two
door-leaves;
Let the golden bar of the layered panels keep snug the door-post and
catch.
The shrouded barrier of the murky freshets will be lofty, tall and
towering;
In the midst of the Three Fields, essence and breath will become more
subtle.
The Delicate Girl, winsome but withdrawn, screens the empyrean's
radiance;
The tiered hall, shiningly iridescent, illumines the Eight Daunters.[9]
From the celestial court to the earthly barrier, arrayed be the axes and
bills;[1]
With the numinous terrace hardy and firm, forever one will not
weaken.

FOURTH STANZA—PARAPHRASE

The "Mother of the Dao," one of the spleen's indwelling divinities, is
clothed in a rich coat with the symbolic colors of all Five Viscera;
Her buoyant skirt, made of the silky gauze of cloud-breaths, is
decorated in the purple hues of the deepest heavens and the celestial
pole,
With tints of red, green, and blue, in sylvan designs, embellishing her
other garments.
One must keep one's gaze focused within, concentrating on the interior
gods, oblivious of the outside world, letting nothing escape through
the doors of one's eyes, turning the key of one's seven orifices.
Barring the exits at all bodily levels, keeping the portals shut fast.
Then the shrouded barrier of the kidneys, source of bodily juices, will
grow in strength;
Elemental essence and vital breath will become rarefied, less carnal,
within the three "cinnabar fields."
The shy divinity of the ears turns away from the brilliant lights of the
heavens,
While the layered chamber of the throat—passageway for the saliva—
now gleams with a splendor that shines out to the divinities of the
eight directions.
All the inner spirits are stalwart as arrayed weapons, from the celestial
hall between the eyebrows to the earthly barrier of the feet,
And the sacred estrade[2] of the heart will prove an everlastingly
impregnable structure.

9. Vanquishers.
1. Weapons (a blade set on a staff).
2. Platform.

THE ARRAY OF THE FIVE NUMINOUS TREASURE TALISMANS OF THE MOST HIGH
(*Taishang lingbao wufu xu*)

The *Array of the Five Numinous Treasure Talismans of the Most High* (*Taishang ling-bao wufu xu*), compiled around the fourth century, is a text from the formative stage of the Daoist religion that apparently incorporates earlier material connected with apocryphal traditions. The link to Numinous Treasure (Lingbao) texts signaled in the title was added later, and the present version of the text concerns much more than the transmission of five talismans. In addition to a rich body of mythical lore and a description of a ritual (*jiao*) involving the summoning of the Five (celestial) Emperors, who are feted and then dispatched back to their celestial abodes, it presents a variety of longevity techniques (dietetics, visualizations, the circulation of pneuma to nourish the five viscera, and the use of talismans) based on microcosmic and macrocosmic correlations.

The excerpt below is on "body gods" that dwell in different organs. According to the tour of the body provided in "Absorption of Solar and Lunar Essences," the human body incorporates the entire universe, from the sun, moon, stars, and topography of the realm to the gods and the imperial bureaucracy and administrative system. Indeed, "There is nothing that [the body] does not emulate." Only at the end of this largely descriptive passage do we learn why it is necessary to know the names and correspondences of all of these spirits. Such knowledge is used to heal pain in the body: moreover, one who visualizes and summons the spirits on the full and new moon, or on the nights of the solstices and equinoxes, may be able to ascend to heaven as an immortal.

PRONOUNCING GLOSSARY

Dao: *dow*
Taishang lingbao wufu xu: *tai-shawng ling-pao wu-fu hsu*

Absorption of Solar and Lunar Essences

Central Yellow Lord of the Dao says: "Of the myriad creatures produced by heaven the most valued are humans. A single human body incorporates heaven and earth, sun and moon, the northern dipper and the Jade Astrolabe of the Dipper;[1] the five Marchmounts[2] and four waterways, the mountains, streams, rivers and seas; the Thunder Lord and Rain Master, numinous asterisms and communal earth altars; the male and female unicorns and male and female phoenix, the dragon, tiger and Dark Warrior;[3] the five grains,[4] mulberry and hemp; the six domestic animals,[5] cattle and horses, birds and beasts, fish, crabs, and turtles; bamboo, woods and the hundred grasses.

TRANSLATED BY Gil Raz. All bracketed additions are the translator's.

1. That is, stars within the Big Dipper.
2. A group of five sacred mountains—one in each of the four cardinal directions and one at the center.
3. All of these are protectors of the cardinal directions.
4. That is, the staple agricultural crops.
5. Pigs, dogs, chickens, horses, cattle, and sheep.

There is nothing that [the body] does not emulate. Also, [the body] establishes an emperor, appoints three Dukes, nine ministers, twenty-seven grand officials, and eighty-one fine officers. Also, [it] lays out the nine provinces, one hundred and twenty commanderies, one thousand and two hundred counties, eighteen thousand localities, thirty-six thousand neighborhoods, and hundred and eighty thousand guard towers. Also, [within the body] are halls and towers, houses and cottages, gates and doors, wells and stoves, cauldrons and rice cookers, glutinous rice and grain, corn and millet. All these spirits can eat and drink; if you know this, then you can lengthen your life.

Man's head is round in the image of heaven; his feet are square in the model of earth. The hair constitutes the asterisms, the eyes are the sun and moon, the brows are the northern dipper, the ears are the communal earth altars, the nose constitutes hills and mountains, the mouth constitutes rivers and streams, the teeth are jade and stones, the four limbs constitute the four seasons.

The five viscera are modeled on the five phases;[6] they also are the five Thearchs and the five Registrars.[7] Above they constitute the five planets,[8] and below they constitute the five Marchmounts. Internally they are the five kings, and externally they are the five virtues.[9] When ascending they constitute five clouds and when transforming they constitute the five dragons. The five viscera are lungs, heart, liver, spleen, and kidneys. The six storehouses are: the gall is the storehouse of the liver, the stomach is the storehouse of the spleen, the large intestine is the storehouse of the lungs, the small intestine is the storehouse of the heart, the bladder is the storehouse of the kidneys, the navel is the storehouse of the towns and localities. The gall is the Child of Heaven, Great Lord of the Dao, the spleen is the Imperial Consort Cherished Woman, the heart is the Supreme Commander, the left kidney is the Minister over the Masses, the right kidney Minister of Works.

The spirits of the eight trigrams[1] are eight. Along with the Great One in the navel they constitute the nine ministers. The twelve spirits of the twelve ringed towers, and the twelve Grand Official Censors who dwell in the liver, along with the three spirits of the Triple Burner,[2] together constitute the twenty-seven Grandees. The spirits of the four limbs are the eighty-one officers. The pneuma of Upper Prime is the Official Envoys; the pneuma of the Lower Prime was the Superintendent of State Visits.

In the upper section there are nine transformations, in the middle section are nine orifices, in the lower section are nine names; these model themselves after the nine continents.[3] The bureaus of the three Ministers, the bureaus of the nine counselors, the bureaus of the twenty-seven Grandees, and the bureaus of the eighty-one primal gentlemen constitute the hundred and twenty bureaus. Inside each bureau there are five registrars and out-

6. The theory involving five agents, or five basic elements that move from one phase to another—a set of systematic associations between different categories, including the five directions, five viscera, and five colors (see table 2, p. 135).
7. Heavenly monarchs and judges.
8. Jupiter, Mars, Mercury, Saturn, and Venus.
9. Humaneness, duty, ritual or propriety, knowl-

edge, and trust or integrity.
1. On the trigrams, see the introduction to *The Seal of the Unity of the Three, in Accordance with the Book of Changes* (*Zhouyi cantong qi*), above.
2. An organ that has no counterpart in Western conceptions of the body.
3. According to Chinese cosmography, there are nine continents in the world.

side there are five officers, in total there are ten officers. These are the twelve hundred counties. The eighteen thousand middling spirits are the eighteen thousand districts. The thirty-six thousand upper spirits are the thirty-six pavilions. In each pavilion there are five beacon mounds for a total of a hundred and eighty thousand beacon mounds.

Moreover the lungs are the Jade Hall Palace, bureau of the Secretariat. The heart is the Scarlet palace, bureau of Primal Yang.[4] The liver is the Green Yang Palace, bureau of the Orchid Terrace. The gall is the Palace of Purple Tenuity, Bureau of the Limitless. The spleen is the Central Palace, office of Grand Simplicity. The kidneys are the Palace of Abysmal Flourishing, Bureau of Grand Harmony.

If you wish to act in accordance with the Dao, live long and not die, you should first visualize these spirits, nourish their roots, and cause their pneuma to circulate, and call out their names. The spirits of the hair are seven; they are styled "searching for length." The spirits of the nape of the neck are three; they are styled "King Father of the East."[5] The spirit in the brain chamber is Lord of the Southern Culmen,[6] styled "Primal First." The spirit between the eyebrows is the Heavenly Numinous Lord. The spirits of the ears are four, styled "Elegant Maidens." The spirits of the eyes are six, styled "Blossoming Brightness." The spirit within the nose has the byname "Hut of Passage." The mouth spirit is styled "Cinnabar Bead." The tongue spirit is styled "Cinnabar and Sulfur." The tooth spirits are thirty-six, styled "The Bodyguards." The spirit in the throat is styled "Tiger Charger." The two eyebrow spirits are styled "Pitcher Spirits." The spirits of the two hands are styled "Cloud-soul Yin."[7] The lung spirit is styled "Great and Vast." The heart spirit is styled "Roar!" The liver spirit is styled "Look Down Upon." The gall spirit is styled "Hunting Game." The stomach spirit is styled "Seeping Marsh." The spleen spirit is styled "Lowly and Base." The spirits of the two kidneys are styled "Drifting and Floating." The spirit in the navel is styled "Jade Numinous Child." The spirit inside the Cinnabar Field[8] is styled "Store Essence." The spirit in the large intestine is styled "Pure and Simple." The spirit in the small intestine is called "The Bridge." The spirit of the pubic region is styled "Exhausted Blossoms." The woman's spirit (of the pubic region) is styled "Essence of Cinnabar." The spirits of the two cavities are styled "Yin Yin." The spirits of the two knees are styled "Lord of the Region." The spirit of the two shins is styled "Following Confucius." The spirit of the two feet is styled "Powerful Gentleman of the Pillars of Heaven."

When you shut your eyes and are about to lie down, from the top, thrice call out to them. When you are finished, stop. If there are any points of intense pain in your body, always call out its name nine times according to the location of the pain and order the spirit to cure it. Then lie straight out and close your eyes. Visualize the spirit at the location of the pain, and it will immediately be healed.

4. The male principle; the term originally referred to the sunny side of a valley, and by extension it came to be associated with the light, heaven, dryness, and activity.
5. The consort of the Queen Mother of the West, one of the most important goddesses in ancient China and in the Daoist pantheon.
6. A collection of stars.

7. The female principle; the term originally referred to the shady side of a valley, and by extension it came to be associated with the dark, earth, dampness, and passivity.
8. On the Cinnabar Field, see the introduction to the *Most High Jade Scripture on the Internal View of the Yellow Court (Taishang huangting neijing yujing)*, above.

Regularly visualize these spirits on nights of the full and new moon and on the nights of the solstices and equinoxes. Look within, call out and summon the names of the spirits of the body. Order them to restrain the cloud-soul and control the white-soul.[9] The Perfected Person[1] says: "If you wish to ascend as an immortal, you should summon the spirits of the body."

9. The animal soul, linked to the body; in contrast, the cloud-soul or spiritual soul rises up at death.

1. The *zhenren*, a concept that first appears in the *Book of Master Zhuang* (*Zhuangzi*; see above) and becomes important in later Daoism.

INSTRUCTIONS ON THE SCRIPTURE OF THE DIVINE ELIXIRS OF THE NINE TRIPODS OF THE YELLOW EMPEROR
(*Huangdi jiuding shendan jing*)

Instructions on the Scripture of the Divine Elixirs of the Nine Tripods of the Yellow Emperor (*Huangdi jiuding shendan jing*) opens by detailing the circumstances of its revelation and the promise of elixirs to cause salvation. This teaching was transmitted from the Mysterious Woman (Xuannü) to the Yellow Emperor (the legendary Huangdi), who then compounded the elixir, ingested it, and rose to heaven as an immortal. The special nature of this divine elixir is set against other practices, such as breathing exercises and the use of herbs, which are criticized because they merely extend life—they do not convey immortality.

Chinese alchemy involved the ingestion of various mineral compounds in pursuit of physical transcendence. *Instructions on the Scripture of the Divine Elixirs of the Nine Tripods of the Yellow Emperor*, one of the earliest texts on external alchemy (*waidan*), offers a rare description of the complete alchemical process. There are detailed rules regarding the transmission of the text itself—one must undergo purification, bathe ritually, invoke the Mysterious Woman, and cast golden images into a stream; following these rules both demonstrates one's commitment and preserves the ritual's secrecy. One must find a secluded location, observe the proper rituals to obtain the ingredients, and pay attention to auspicious and inauspicious days for compounding the elixir. These commands are followed by precise instructions on preparing the ingredients, sealing the crucible, firing its contents, and consuming the final product: "When you want to ingest the Medicine, undertake the purification practices, observe the precepts, and perform the ablutions for five times over seven days. At dawn, burning some incense, kneel down and pay obeisance facing east. Ingest the Medicine in pills the size of large grains of millet, or of small beans." If the practitioner fails to observe the precepts or execute the proper steps, then the elixir will not form. If the practitioner succeeds and is able to complete and ingest the elixir, then—after a period of practice that varies with rank—he or she is assured of joining the ranks of the immortals in heaven.

PRONOUNCING GLOSSARY

Huangdi jiuding shendan jing: *huang-dee chiu-ting shun-dawn ching*

Taiqing: *tai-ching*

The Yellow Emperor (Huangdi)[1] received the Culminant Way of the Reverted Elixirs from the Mysterious Woman, who is a celestial woman. The Yellow Emperor compounded and ingested them, and thereby rose to heaven as an immortal.

The Mysterious Woman announced to the Yellow Emperor:

All those who want to live a long life, but do not obtain the Divine Elixirs and the Golden Liquor, merely bring suffering upon themselves. Practicing breathing and *daoyin*,[2] exhaling the old and inhaling the new breath, and ingesting medicines of herbs and plants can extend the length of one's life, but do not allow one to escape death. When a man ingests the Divine Elixirs, he becomes a divine immortal and transcends the generations [of mortals]. He will be coeternal with Heaven and Earth, and as luminous as the Sun and the Moon; seated, he will see ten thousand miles away, and will have gods and demons at his service. He will rise into the Void with his whole family, and will fly even though he has no wings. Mounting the clouds and steering a chariot pulled by dragons, he will roam in the Great Clarity (Taiqing) and in one instant will tour the eight poles[3]. He will not halt in front of a river, and will not fear the hundred poisons (*baidu*).

The Yellow Emperor transmitted this Way to the Mysterious Master, and admonished him saying:

This Way is of supreme importance, and can be transmitted only to those who are worthy of it. Let it not be disclosed to those who are not fit to receive it, even if they collect heaps of gold as high as mountains, or if they own ten thousand miles of land. Obtaining just one of these elixirs is enough to become an immortal: it is not required to obtain all nine of them.

Rules for the transmission. Throw a golden figurine of a man weighing nine ounces and a golden figurine of a fish weighing three ounces into an east-flowing stream, and utter an oath. Both should be provided by the one who receives this Way. Before this, undertake the purification practices and perform the ablutions. On the banks of the stream, in a place unfrequented by other people, arrange a seat for the Mysterious Woman. Burn some incense and announce to Heaven: "I wish to transmit the Way to obtain a long life to (*name of the recipient*)!" Lay the *Scripture of the Elixirs* on a stand, and place the seat [for the Mysterious Woman] there. When you are ready to transmit the Way, face north and do not disclose it for one [double] hour. If the sky is clear and there is no wind, the Way can be transmitted. [Master and disciple] seal their covenant by drinking together some blood of a white chicken. Transmit the oral instructions and the essentials of the compounding of the elixirs, and throw the golden figurines of the man and the fish into the stream. This is done so that the multitudes of those who are not suited for becoming a divine immortal never see this Way.

The Yellow Emperor said:

When you want to compound the Divine Elixirs you should dwell in the depths of a mountain, in a wide moorland, or in a place deserted and

TRANSLATED BY Fabrizio Pregadio. All bracketed additions are the translator's.

1. A legendary Chinese emperor (27th century B.C.E.).
2. Stretching exercises.

3. The totality of the world as well as its farthest reaches [translator's note]. "The Great Clarity": one of the three heavens.

uninhabited for endless miles. If you compound them among other people you should stay behind thick, high walls, so that nothing can be seen between the inside and the outside. Your companions should not number more than two or three. First undertake the purification practices for seven days, and increase your purity with ablutions and the five fragrances. Do not pass by filth and dirt, or by houses where mourning is being observed, or by houses inhabited by women of the age of marriage.

The Yellow Emperor said:

When you want to purchase the Divine Medicines for the elixirs, first undertake the purification practices for seven days, and perform the ablutions on a day marked by the character *zi* or *chou*. You should buy the ingredients on an appointed day and in a place governed by the Virtue of the Month. Do not bargain over their price.

The Mysterious Woman said:

To prepare the Medicines, the fifth day of the fifth month is most auspicious, followed by the seventh day of the seventh month. It is good to start on a *jiazi* or a *dingsi* day,[4] or on a day of Opening (*kai*) or Removal (*chu*). The next best are the *jiashen, yisi,* or *yimao* days. The days on which the preparation of the Medicines is forbidden are:

> in spring, *wuchen* and *jisi*;
> in summer, *dingsi, wushen, renchen,* and *jiwei*;
> in autumn, *wuxu, xinhai,* and *gengzi*;
> in winter, *wuyin, jiwei, guimao,* and *guiyou*.

The day of the Killer of the Month, the days in which the Branch and the Stem are in opposition, the day of Receiving, as well as the *renwu, bingxu, guihai,* and *xinsi* days in the first, second, and third months of each season, the day of Establishment, and those of new and full moon, are all inauspicious and cannot be used for starting the fire.

When you compound the Divine Medicines, beware of intercourse with common and dull people. Do not let the envious, those who talk too much, and those who do not have faith in this Way hear or know about it. If they do, the compounding of the Divine Medicines would not be successful.

When you achieve success in making the Medicines you will become a Perfected. You will rise to heaven and enter the abyss, you will transform yourself and be "vague and indistinct". You will become an immortal with your family: how could you do that alone?

The common people are fond of wealth, and do not compound the alchemical Medicines. They believe in medicines obtained from herbs and plants, but these putrefy when buried, decompose when boiled, and burn when heated. If those medicines cannot keep themselves alive, how could they do so for humans? They can heal illnesses and increase the pneuma but cannot make one escape death. Only a few can hear the essentials of the Culminant Way of the Reverted Elixirs.

The Yellow Emperor said:

When you start the fire you should perform a ceremony beside the crucible. Take five pints of good quality white liquor, three pounds of dried ox

4. These names reflect the Chinese calendar system. Days and (later) years were designated with two characters drawn from a set of ten "celestial stems" and twelve "earthly branches," resulting in a cycle of sixty days/years. Certain combinations are considered auspicious and others inauspicious.

meat, the same amount of dried mutton, two pints of yellow millet and rice, three pints of large dates, one peck of pears, thirty cooked chicken's eggs, and three carp, each weighing three pounds. Place them on three stands, and on each stand burn incense in two cups. Pay obeisance twice and utter the following invocation:

> This petty man, (*name of the officiant*), verily and entirely devotes his thoughts to the Great Lord of the Dao, Lord Lao, and the Lord of the Great Harmony. Alas, this petty man, (*name of the officiant*), covets the Medicines of Life! Lead him so that the Medicines will not volatilize and be lost, but rather be fixed by fire! Let the Medicines be good and efficacious, let the transmutations take place without hesitation, and let the Yellow and the White be entirely fixed! When he ingests the Medicines, let him fly as an immortal, have audience at the Purple Palace,[5] live an unending life, and become an accomplished man!

Offer the liquor, rise, and pay obeisance two more times. Finally offer kaya[6] nuts, mandarins, and pomelos. After that, the fire may be started according to the method.

The Yellow Emperor said:

When you want to make the Divine Elixirs, you should always first prepare the Mysterious and Yellow.

[First Elixir: Flower of Cinnabar]

The First Divine Elixir is called *Flower of Cinnabar*. To prepare it, use one, two, or ten pounds of Real Powder (cinnabar), in the desired amount according to your wealth. Place it in a crucible

(NOTE: Someone says that the Powder should be covered with pounded lake salt.)

and smear the mouths [of the two halves] with the Mud of the Six-and-One. Make the joints tightly fit together so that there is no loss [of pneuma]. Carefully examine the crucible, and make sure that there are no cracks, even as thin as a hair. The Medicine would otherwise entirely volatilize and lose its Essence and Flower, and the ingestion of the mere residue would be of no benefit. You can use the crucible after you have smeared it and left it to dry for ten days.

(NOTE: If it is not dry it cannot be placed over the fire.)

First keep the crucible five inches above a fire of horse manure or chaff, and heat it for nine days and nine nights. Then increase the fire so that it touches the crucible, for nine more days and nights. [Then put the crucible over the fire, for nine more days and nights.] Finally let the fire cover the lower [half of the] crucible for nine more days and nights. After thirty-six days altogether, you can extinguish the fire and let the crucible cool for one day. The Medicine will have entirely sublimated, and will adhere to the

5. The Purple Palace is in the constellation of the Northern Dipper, at the center of the cosmos [translator's note].
6. An evergreen tree native to Japan.

upper crucible. It will be similar to the five-colored *langgan*,[7] to shooting stars, or to frost and snow. Sometimes it will be of a vivid scarlet color like cinnabar, sometimes it will be azure and sometimes purple. Collect it by brushing it off with a feather. One pound will have reduced to only four ounces.

If the Medicine has not been fixed by the fire, it must be sublimated again. Add it to Liquor of the Mysterious Water and to Grease of Dragons. Mix to make the compound moist, and put it again in the red earthenware crucible of the Mysterious and Yellow. Seal the joints as in the initial method. Sublimate the compound over an intense fire for thirty-six days, and the Medicine will form after altogether seventy-two days.

When you want to ingest the Medicine, undertake the purification practices, observe the precepts, and perform the ablutions for five times over seven days. At dawn, burning some incense, kneel down and pay obeisance facing east. Ingest the Medicine in pills the size of large grains of millet, or of small beans. A superior man will rise to heaven after he ingests it for seven days, an ordinary man will obtain immortality after he ingests it for seventy days, and a dull man will obtain immortality after he ingests it for one year. After you have prepared it, it will be good to use the crucible of the *Flower of Cinnabar* to sublimate the Second Elixir and all the Nine Divine Elixirs.

The Mysterious Woman said:

After you prepare the *Flower of Cinnabar*, you should test it by making gold with it. If gold forms, the making of the Medicine has been successful. If it does not form, it has not been successful: the Medicine has not been fixed by fire, and cannot be ingested. This is because you have not luted the crucible hermetically, or because you have transgressed against the precepts.

She [also] said:

Sublimate the Medicine again as in the previous method. To test it, add to it some Grease of Dragons, and make it into pills the size of small beans. Place them over an intense fire and blow the fire with a bellows. Gold will form in the time it takes to have a meal.

Gold also will form by projecting twenty-four scruples[8] of *Flower of Cinnabar* onto one pound of powdered mercury. When gold has formed, make it into a cylinder and store the Medicine in it. Similarly, if you pour one scruple of *Flower of Cinnabar* onto one pound of mercury or lead, put it over a fierce flame, and blow to make the fire increasingly intense, the whole will form gold. Be careful not to use excessive amounts [of the ingredients], or the gold will be hard; but if there is not enough, the gold will be soft. Neither would be malleable.

The Mysterious Woman also said:

> If you prepare gold, you can transcend the generations [of mortals]
> If you do not prepare it, you can hardly secure your destiny.
> Doing nothing but harm to yourself,
> Where would you find repair?

---

7. A powerful elixir produced through alchemical processes (originally, a blue-green gemstone and a special substance that grew on magical trees in the land of the transcendents).

8. Twenty-four scruples (*zhu*) correspond to one ounce (*jin*) [translator's note].

THE INNER CHAPTERS OF THE BOOK OF THE MASTER WHO EMBRACES SIMPLICITY
(*Baopu zi neipian*)

GE HONG

The selections below are taken from the *Inner Chapters of the Book of the Master Who Embraces Simplicity* (*Baopu zi neipian*). The larger *Book of the Master Who Embraces Simplicity* (*Baopu zi*), whose "outer chapters" (*waipian*) address Confucianism, was completed about 320 C.E. by Ge Hong (283–343), an aristocratic scholar-official and religious practitioner who had received some Daoist training and is often himself labeled an (unsuccessful) alchemist. He was from a family in southern China that played a central role in the transmission of an important body of texts. The *Inner Chapters of the Book of the Master Who Embraces Simplicity* treats a variety of topics and themes such as "immortals," "alchemy," and "meditation techniques," emphasizing the vast superiority of meditation and the compounding of elixirs to other forms of self-cultivation and to what Ge Hong calls "minor arts" (e.g., various longevity techniques) in circulation in his day. Although it is often viewed as a significant source for early medieval Daoism, the text covers—and sought to elevate the status of—a much wider range of practices then current in southern China.

"Climbing [Mountains] and Fording [Rivers]" ("Dengshe") focuses on the proper years, days, and times for entering into mountains; the need for proper ritual preparation; and specific practices for avoiding the dangers (mountain sprites, poisonous animals, and demons) one might encounter when venturing or retiring into mountains to escape the troubles of a chaotic age. We learn, for example, about the efficacy of using mirrors to discern the "true" form of any possible threat and the power of talismans and incantations to summon mountain deities, to repel noxious spirits and animals (snakes, tigers, wolves, etc.), and to confer on the practitioner magical powers (such as the ability to walk on water or breath under it). One of the recurring themes in this section is that to know the name of a spirit is to control that spirit.

Even though Ge Hong's work should not be interpreted as exclusively Daoist, the *Inner Chapters of the Book of the Master Who Embraces Simplicity* does occupy an important position in the wider history of Daoism. It provides a comprehensive picture of the religious landscape of South China before the dispersed Celestial Masters tradition arrived there, on the cusp of the new Upper Clarity and Numinous Treasure revelations that would inexorably transform later Daoism.

PRONOUNCING GLOSSARY

Baopu zi neipian: *pao-poo tzu naye-pien* Ge Hong: *guh hong*
Dengshe: *deng-shuh* Lingbao jing: *ling-bao ching*

Climbing [Mountains] and Fording [Rivers] (Dengshe)

One asked about the way of climbing mountains. The Master Who Embraces Simplicity replied: Whoever proceeds with the way, compounds elixirs, and those who avoid disorder and seek reclusion; all these enter the mountains. But those who do not know the methods of entering mountains often encounter misfortune and harm. Hence there is a saying: "Below Mount Hua white bones are scattered." All claim that they have knowledge of one thing only and cannot know everything, yet although they may have the intention to seek life, they conversely end up dying violently. All mountains, regardless whether great or small, have spirits and divinities. If the mountain is great, then so is its spirit; if the mountain is small, then so is its spirit. If one enters the mountains without the proper devices, then one will surely be harmed. Some may be inflicted with illness, wounded by weapons, or terrified and alarmed; some may see lights and shadows or hear strange sounds. Entering mountains without proper devices may cause large trees to spontaneously break and topple, even when there is no wind; cliff faces may collapse without cause, striking and crushing people. Others may be caused to lose their way and madly push on, finally falling into crevices, while others may be caused to encounter tigers, wolves, or poisonous vermin who will harm them. One may not lightly enter mountains!

First, one must wait to the third or ninth lunar months, as these are months when the mountains open. In addition one must choose a lucky day and auspicious time during these months. If one's business is of long duration, and one cannot patiently wait for these months, then one may just select a day and time. All those who enter mountains must first abstain and purify for seven days, they must not pass by dirt and defilement, they must carry Ascending Mountain Talismans as they leave their gate, and perform the Whole Body Three-Five Method. There are years when the Five Marchmounts[1] suffer calamities, just as all places in the Nine Continents[2] have their periods of decline and prosperity. When a place suffers from the killing pneumas of flying-talismans, then for a long time a lord cannot arise at this place. According to *Duke of Zhou's Register of City Names*,[3] disasters that befall specific locations in accord with the system of allotted fields, may be evaded but not averted by ritual means. This is also the case with homes, as well as mountains and Marchmounts.

In addition, there are important taboos: in the first and second months of *jia, yi, yin, mao* years[4] one cannot enter the Eastern Marchmount; on the fourth and fifth months of *bing, ding, si, wu* years one cannot enter the Southern Marchmount; on the seventh and eighth months of *kang, xin, shen, you* years one cannot enter the Western Marchmount; on the Four Seasonal

TRANSLATED BY Gil Raz. All bracketed additions are the translator's.

1. A group of sacred mountains, one in each of the four cardinal directions and one at the center. They are most often identified as Mount Heng (north), Mount Tai (east), Mount Heng (south), Mount Hua (west; mentioned above), and Mount Song (center); variants include Mount Huo (south) and Mount Taihua (west).
2. According to Chinese cosmography, there are nine continents in the world.
3. The Duke of Zhou, or Zhougong (d. 1094

B.C.E.), helped consolidate the Zhou dynasty; he was traditionally admired as a statesman and administrator.
4. These names reflect the Chinese calendar system. Days and (later) years were designated with two characters drawn from a set of ten "celestial stems" and twelve "earthly branches," resulting in a cycle of sixty days/years. Certain combinations are considered auspicious and others inauspicious.

months of *wu* and *ji* years one cannot enter the Central Marchmount; on the tenth and eleventh months of *ren, gui, hai, zi* years one cannot enter the Northern Marchmount. Unless obliged to enter Taihua (W), Mount Huo (S), Mount Heng (N), Mount Tai (E), or Mount Songgao (C), one must obey the taboos of these months. These restrictions apply equally to all sides of the Marchmounts.

The spirits of old creatures are able to borrow human form, thereby confusing people's vision and constantly testing them. It is only when they are viewed in a mirror that their true form cannot be altered. Therefore, since ancient times all Masters of the Dao who enter mountains have carried bright mirrors some nine inches or more in diameter, suspended on their back so that ancient demons dare not approach them. If a creature comes to test one, then one should peer back at the mirror. If that creature is an immortal or a good spirit of the mountain, then the figure in the mirror will be of human form. But if the creature is a bird, beast, or deviant demon, then its form and shape will appear in the mirror. If an ancient demon comes to you, you must walk backwards while turning the mirror towards it. Then you should observe it. If it is an ancient demon it will surely have no heels, and if it has heels then it is a mountain god.

In the past, Zhang Gaita and Ou Gaocheng together meditated in a stone chamber on Mount Yuntai in Shu;[5] suddenly a person wearing a single layer of yellow silk and a cap of kudzu approached them and said: "Exhausted masters of the Dao, you are suffering bitterly because of your reclusion." Then the two men observed him in a mirror, realizing it was a deer. They then asked him: "You are an old deer of the mountain, how dare you pretend to have human form?" Before completing their words, the person changed back into a deer and departed.

Below Mount Linlü there is a pavilion in which dwells a ghost. Whenever someone spent the night there they either died or became ill. Dozens of people dressed in yellow, white, or black, both male and female, were there every night. Once, Zhi Boyi spent a night there. He lit bright lamps and chanted scriptures. In the middle of the night some dozen persons arrived, sat across from Boyi, and proceeded to play cards and *go*. Boyi secretly shone a mirror on them—they were a bunch of dogs. Boyi then grasped a candle and stood up. Pretending that the candle was burning their clothes, he raised a smell of singed hair. Boyi held a short blade. He grabbed one person and stabbed it. At first it screamed like a human, but at its death it became a dog. The remaining dogs all fled, and hence this problem was resolved. That is the power of mirrors.

Superior masters who enter mountains carry the *Inner Writ of the Three Luminaries* and the *Charts of the True Forms of the Five Marchmounts*.[6] Wherever they are they can summon the mountain gods and in accord with the register of spirits they can summon the spirits of the local earth altars, mountain officers, and home officials, in order to question them. Then the perversities of wood and stone, the sprites of mountains and rivers will not dare come and test them. Next, they put up the seventy-two sprite-securing

---

5. An important mountain in the Celestial Masters' tradition, located in present-day Sichuan Province.

6. Daoist works, as are the other texts mentioned in this selection.

talismans, and deploy the Petitions for Controlling the Hundred Sprites, red official seals, and twelve Embracing the Primordial seals blocking the four directions of their dwelling, so that the various deviances do not dare approach it. Next, they grasp the Staff of Eight Awes and wear Laozi's Jade Switch; then the mountain spirits can be commanded. Who would then dare cause them harm?

The words I heard from Master Zheng[7] were like these, but in truth I cannot fully know all such matters. My teacher regularly told his disciples: "If in seeking the Dao a person is as anxious as he would be about a wealthy family becoming poor or as he would be about his exalted position being reduced, would he not attain it? But I fear that your intent in this is insincere, that you concern yourself with the near at hand and neglect the remote. When you hear about it then you rejoice, and though you may be fixed in the front seat[8] before long you will suddenly feel abandoned. Before the slightest benefit may be had there will be mountains of losses without cease. Indeed, how can one attain the marvelous subtlety of the ultimate words, and reach the highest peaks of the limitless?"

✳　✳　✳

According to the *Scripture of the Jade Seal* (*Yuqian jing*) if one wishes to enter the famous mountains, one must know the secret arts of Hidden *jia*,[9] but it does not provide a detailed explanation of the ins and outs of it. The *Scripture of the Numinous Treasure* (*Lingbao jing* states: "One should select a Protective Day or a Duty Day [to enter the mountains]. If it is a Focus Day it is greatly auspicious. If one uses a Control Day or an Attack Day one would inevitably die." This text too does not elaborate on each item in detail.

When I was young I had the intention to enter the mountains, so I traveled and studied the writings of the Hidden *jia*, and now have over 60 scrolls. As these matters cannot be completely understood, I summarized and collated the essentials and kept it near at hand in my robes; but as it is not proper for textual transmission, I now discuss it only briefly, thinking that those who cherish these matters and wish to enter mountains should seek those who are experts, who are not lacking in the world.

According to the *Central Scripture of the Hidden Jia* (*Dunjia zhongjing*) one who wishes to seek the Dao should on Celestial days and hours exorcize ghosts and goblins and lay out talismanic writings. If you enter mountains on Celestial-Beast days and hours and wish to command the hundred deviances, tigers, leopards, poisonous insects, robbers and bandits, then none will dare approach you. You should exit at Heaven's Treasure and enter at Earth's Door.[1] All six-*gui* days are Heaven's Treasure, six-*ji* days are Earth's Door.

It also says: "Those who wish to avoid disorder in the world, obliterate their traces in the mountains, and have no anxieties and worries, should choose an Upper Primordial *dingmao* day; this is called the time of Hidden Virtue, and also Heaven's Heart. On this day it is possible to hide and sink, as is said 'Sink into the ground in broad daylight.' The sun and moon will not shine on you, and men and ghosts will not be able to see you." It also

---

7. Zheng Yin (ca. 215–ca. 302), Ge Hong's teacher.
8. That is, receive attention.
9. A technique for becoming invisible that relies

on finding the effective periods in the calendrical system.
1. Both names of nodes of time.

says: "One who seeks the transcendent Way and enters the famous mountains, if he does so on the days and hours of the six-*gui*, which are also called Heaven's Duke days, he will certainly attain crossing the generations." It also says: "Heading into mountains and forests, you should pick with your left hand the superior Azure Dragon grass. Break it, and place half under Meeting Star, cross Bright Hall and enter Yinzhong. You should proceed with Yu's Pace,[2] and incant the following three times: 'Generals Nuogao and Taiyin, open the path solely for me, your great-grandson [add name], do not open it for anyone else. Cause that if anyone sees me, they will be considered as bound firewood; if they do not see me, they will be considered not men.' Then, break the blade of grass that you were holding and place it on the ground, with your left hand pick up earth and apply to the first man. With your right hand grasp the grass and cover yourself, with your left hand stretched forward proceed with Yu's Pace. When you reach the position of six *gui* hold your breath and stop. Men and ghosts would then be unable to see you." In general, the six *jia* times are the Azure Dragon, the six *yi* are the Meeting Star, the six *bing* are the Bright Hall, and the six *ding* are the Yinzhong.

As you proceed in Yu's Pace you will complete the hexagram[3] "Already Completed": "Initial one, initial two, the prints are incomplete, nine prints is the full number, finally relying on each other." One step is seven feet, in total twenty-one feet. As you look behind you will see nine prints.

The method of Yu's Pace: stand upright, right foot in front, left foot behind. Then, advance with the right foot, and drag the left foot alongside the right foot. This is the first step. Next, again place your right foot in front, and then move your left foot forward. Drag your right foot alongside your left foot. This is the second step. Next, again place your right foot in front, drag your left foot alongside the right foot. This is the third step. Thus, the way of Yu's Pace is complete. All those in the world who practice the various techniques must know Yu's Pace, not merely the recipes alone."

The *Lingbao jing* says: So-called Protective Days refer to days in which the combination of "branches and stems" is one in which the first element generates the second.[4] If you use the days *jiawu* (31) and *yisi* (42) that is correct. *Jia* is wood; *wu* is fire. *Yi* is also wood, *si* is also fire. These combinations are fire produced from wood. As for what are called Duty Days: these refer to days in which the combination of "branches and stems" is one in which the second element generates the first, such as the days *renshen* (9) and *guiyou* (10). *Ren* is water, *shen* is metal; *gui* is water, *you* is metal; hence these combinations are water produced from metal. The so-called Control Days refer to days in which the combination of "branches and stems" is one in which the first element vanquishes the second, such as the days of *wuzi* (25) and *jihai* (36). *Wu* is earth, *zi* is water; *ji* too is earth, *hai* too is water. In the scheme of the Five Phases earth vanquishes water. Attack Days refer to days in which the combination of "branches and stems" is one in which the second element vanquishes the first, such as the days *jiashen* (21) and *yiyou*

---

2. A form of ritual walking or dancing that follows celestial patterns mapped onto the ground. This ritual is used to purify the ritual arena and also prepares the ritual master for ascent to heaven to transmit the ritual documents.

3. On hexagrams, see the introduction to *The Seal of the Unity of the Three, in Accordance with the Book of Changes (Zhouyi cantong qi)*, above.
4. On the generation of elements in the theory of five phases, see table 2, page 135.

(22). *Jia* is wood, *shen* is metal, *yi* too is *wood, you* too is metal. Hence these combinations are metal vanquishes wood. As all other combinations are in the same form as these, you can extrapolate and know them all."

The Master Who Embraces Simplicity says: When entering famous mountains do so on *jiazi* days of opening and expulsion. Take strips of pentachromatic silk,[5] each of five inches, and hang them on large rocks. You will attain whatever you seek. I also say, when entering mountains one must know the secret incantations of the six-*jia*. Incantation: "All approaching military fighters serve as vanguard before me." These nine words must always be incanted in secret. It means "Everything will be avoided; the essential Way cannot be troubled."

The Master Who Embraces Simplicity says: The form of mountain sprites is like a small child with one foot; walking back and forth it enjoys striking people. When entering a mountain, you may hear a human voice talking loudly at night. The name of this spirit is *qi*.[6] If you know this and call it by name then it will not dare strike. Another name for it is Hot Innards. You can use both names to call it. There is also a mountain sprite shaped like a drum with red skin. It too has one leg, and one of its names is *hui*. There is another shaped like a man, nine feet tall and wearing a coat and cap. Its name is Golden Rope. Another is shaped like a dragon with a pentachromatic horn. Its name is Fly-fly. If you see them, call them by their names and they will not dare harm you.

The Master Who Embraces Simplicity says: In the mountains are huge trees that can talk; however, it is not the tree that can talk but its spirit, named Yunyang. If you call its name, you will have luck. If while in a mountain you see a fire glowing in the middle of the night, it is a long-dead tree producing it. Do not be alarmed. If while in a mountain you see a barbarian in the middle of the night, it is the spirit of copper and iron. If you see a man from Qin, it is the spirit of a hundred-year-old tree. Do not be alarmed by them, they cannot cause harm.

If you see an official in a mountain stream, its name is Sijiao. Call out its name, and you will have luck. If you see a great snake wearing a cap, its name is Shengqing. Call out its name, and you will have luck. If you encounter an official in the mountain, but just hear its voice without seeing its shape, and it calls you incessantly, throw a white stone at it and it will cease. Another method is to make a spear from reeds and prick it; you will then have no harm. If in the mountains you see a ghost calling you asking for food incessantly, throw a white reed at it, and it will die. The ghosts in the mountains always confuse people, causing them to lose their way; but if you throw a reed staff at them, they will die.

If on a *yin* day in the mountain there is someone styling itself an official, it is a tiger; if it styles itself a Lord of the Road, it is a wolf; if it styles itself a Commander, it is a fox. On a *mao* day in the mountain there is someone styling itself an Elder, it is a hare; styling itself King Father of the East, it is an elk; styling itself Queen Mother of the West,[7] it is a deer. On a *chen* day, styling itself Rain-master, it is a dragon; styling itself River Elder, it is a fish; styl-

---

5. The five colors are green, red, yellow, white, and black.
6. *Qi* is usually vital energy or breath (pneuma).
7. One of the most important goddesses in ancient China and in the Daoist pantheon; she

was believed to live on the mythical Mount Kunlun in the west, and she governed all other female deities. Her consort was the King Father of the East.

ing itself Duke Without Intestines, it is a crab. On a *si* day, styling itself Poor, it is a snake of the local altar; styling itself Lord of the Season, it is a turtle. On a *wu* day styling itself Three Dukes, it is a horse; styling itself Immortal, it is an old tree. On a *wei* day styling itself Master, it is a goat; styling itself an official, it is a roebuck. On a *shen* day styling itself a Lord of Men, it is a monkey; styling itself Nine Officers, it is an ape. On a *you* day styling itself General, it is a rooster; styling itself bandit-catcher, it is a pheasant. On a *xu* day styling itself with human name and surname, it is a dog; styling itself Lord Chengyang, it is a fox. On a *hai* day styling itself a Spirit Lord, it is a pig; styling itself Wife, it is gold or jade. On a *zi* day styling itself Lord of the Altar, it is a rat; styling itself a spirit, it is a bat. On a *chou* day styling itself a scholar, it is an ox. But if you know the names of these creatures, then they cannot harm you.

Someone asked about the way for recluses in the mountains and swamps to avoid snakes. The Master Who Embraces Simplicity says: Anciently, there were many snakes on Round Hill, which also produced good medicinal herbs. The Yellow Emperor planned to climb this mountain, so Guangcheng zi[8] instructed him to carry realgar at his belt so that the snakes departed. Now, if you carry five ounces or more of Wudu realgar, red as a chicken's comb, when you enter mountains, forests, or bush then you will not fear snakes. If a snake bites you, you should rub a little realgar in the wound, and it will heal immediately. Although there are many types of snakes, only the bites of the viper and of the Azure-gold snake are dangerous. If you do not heal them, you will die within a day. If you do not know the methods to heal these bites, and you are bit by any of these two snakes, then you should cut out the flesh of the wound with a knife and throw it to the ground. While the wound is still bubbling with burnt flesh you should cauterize it immediately, and you will survive. The venom of these snakes is at its peak during the seventh and eighth months. At this time, even if the snake does not bite anyone and its venom is not secreted, if its fangs bite a bamboo or small tree it would shrivel up and die. Now, when masters of the Dao enter mountains, though they may know the great methods if they do not know the ways of avoiding snakes, that is no small matter.

Before entering mountains you must prepare at home, studying the taboos and methods, consider the sun, moon, Red Bird, Dark Warrior, Azure Dragon, and White Tiger,[9] in order to protect your body. Then, when proceeding into mountains, forests, or bush, you must first inhale three breaths on your left and hold them in order to blow on the plants in the mountain. Visualize this breath like a red fog spreading out for several dozen leagues. If there are people accompanying you, whether many or few, you should line them up before you and exhale the held air on them. Then, though they may tread on a snake, the snake will not dare move. In general, you will not encounter snakes after this procedure. In case you do meet a snake, you should face the sun and inhale three breaths from the left and hold them. Press your tongue against the roof of your mouth, and with your hand rub the Capital Barrier. Then, shut Heaven's Gate, block Earth's Door, and using something to press the snake's head down circle it with

8. A Daoist immortal and the Yellow Emperor's teacher.

9. The animals and their characteristic colors associated with the four cardinal directions.

your hand and draw a jail on the ground to capture it. You can also pick up and play with it. Even if you wrap it around your neck it will not dare bite you. As this interdiction cannot be undone by itself, once you blow your exhalation on the snake it will forever be unable to leave the prison.

If another person is bit by a snake, inhale three breaths from your left and blow on him. He will immediately be healed and have no more pain. If you and the patient are separated by dozens of leagues, you can do this procedure at a distance by calling out the patient's name and surname; for a male incant over your left hand, for a female incant over your right hand. The person will surely be healed.

Master Jie's Method: Before arriving in the mountain, you must visualize five snakes, in each of the five colors. Then, holding your breath, twist and stab them with a green bamboo or short tree branch. Proceed with Yu's Pace and circle them from the left. Visualize making several thousand centipedes with which to dress the members of your group. You may then depart, and to the end you will not encounter snakes.

Some carry dried ginger and wolfsbane at their elbows. Others smoke their bodies by burning horns of oxen, goats, or deer. Some carry Wang Fangping's[1] realgar pills, while others place boar's cerumen and deer-musk pills between their toenails. All these methods are efficacious. Because both the musk deer and wild boar eat snakes, they can be used to suppress them.

Secretary birds and *Ying* turtles also eat snakes. Hence, when southerners enter mountains they all carry *Ying* turtles tails and beaks of secretary birds in order to evade snakes. If a snake bites a person, they scrape these things to make a salve for the wound, which is healed immediately.

When southerners enter mountains they also carry bamboo tubes filled with live centipedes. Recognizing when they are in a region inhabited by snakes, the centipedes begin moving in the tube. When this occurs the people should carefully inspect the grass, and they will certainly find snakes. If a snake is over ten feet long and it emerges from the encircling hex you made, the centipede will see it and will constrain it using its breath. The snake will immediately die. When snakes see centipedes on cliffs or river banks crannies, even large ones will flee to hide in deep waters of the river. When a centipede merely floats on the water it is invisible, as people will only see something perfectly blue as large as a ceremonial cap. But it will directly enter the water and reach the snake. Immediately the snake will float to the surface and die. Therefore, southerners make a powder from centipedes to treat snake bite; all will be healed.

Someone asked: "In the mountains and rivers of the region south of the river are numerous poisonous beasts. Are there ways to avoid them?" The Master Who Embraces Simplicity replied: The local climate of the high plateaus in the central provinces is clear and moderate, you must realize that the famous mountains of the south are different. Now, in the wilds of Wu and Chu the climate is hot, wet, odorous, and humid. Although Mount Heng and Mount Huo are official Marchmounts, they are inhabited by numerous poisonous insects, such as the Short Fox, which is in fact an aquatic insect that resembles the cicada and is as large as a three-gill cup.

---

1. A Daoist who is mentioned in several Celestial Masters texts.

It has wings and can fly; it lacks eyes, but has acute ears. In its mouth there is a horizontal thing, like a horn or crossbow. When it hears a human voice, using this thing like a horn or crossbow, it makes an arrow of its breath and shoots it at the person from the water. The person hit immediately develops an infection. Those who were in the shadow of this person will also become ill, but will not develop an infection. Not knowing how to treat this they will die. This illness is like a mortal fever, and all infected will die within ten days.

In addition there are chiggers in this region, both on land and in the water. After sudden rain, before dawn and sunset, they are sure to attach themselves to you as you walk through grass or cross streams. Only in blazing sun or in burning grass are they less abundant. Their size is as the tip of a hair, and when they first attach themselves to a person they enter the skin, making a mark like a small barb, small yet painful. They can be removed with a needle, and they will be as red as cinnabar and wriggle when placed on the tip of your finger. If you do not remove them, the worms will bore through to the bone and then travel through your entire body. Chiggers, kill people. Upon returning home from a trip through an area infested with chiggers, you should pass a flame along your body, then the chiggers will fall to the ground. Chiggers and Short Fox can be avoided if one carries pellets of Eight-animal musk, "Crossing-Generations" pellets, "Protecting Life" pellets, "Jade-amphora" pellets, Rhinoceros-horn pellets, Seven-star pellets, and *Adenophora*. If you cannot obtain these various medications, you may be fine by simply carrying "Love life" musk. It is also good if you carry a chicken-egg-sized pellet of realgar and shallots pestled together or separately. If you have already been infected, you can rub this medicine on the scar, and you will be healed. Drinking or rubbing masticated red amaranthus juice will also cure it. Also, the three ingredients, root of *acanthopanax*, Uncaria roots, and *futeng*, can be ground either separately or together into a juice, and one or two quarts ingested.

Further, the *shegong* hibernates in the valleys. If you search for it during the big-snow period, there is little snow accumulation above its location as its pneuma rises like steam, so that you can catch it by digging no more than one foot. After drying it in the shade and pulverizing it, you can carry it on your body to avoid the *shegong* in summer. However, if a Master of the Dao knows the one taboo method—the Cavern hundred taboos, and the Constant-Contemplate Taboos, and Preserves Perfect Unity—then the many toxins will not dare approach him. He will not need to use the various medicines.

Someone asked: "When a Master of the Dao dwells in the mountains, nesting in crags or hiding in caves, he does not require the warmth of cushion and ornaments, but he must beware of wind and dampness. May I ask about the methods for this?" The Master Who Embraces Simplicity replied: Ingesting [any of the following] for no more than fifty days will allow you not to fear wind and dampness for ten years: Golden-Bottle Powder, Triple-Yang Solution, Changxin pills, decoction of leeks and *camellia japonica*, paste of *Gastrodia elata* root, powdered *skimmia* and *xuanhua*, Pills of Fall Rehmania sap. If you ingest the great alchemical medicines, even before rising lightly and ascending into the void your body will not suffer from illness even if you encounter wind or lie down in damp places. Anyone who ingests these seven medicines is called Initiate Student of the Dao. Master

Yao once ingested Triple-Yang Solution and could immediately lie on ice without shivering. Ingesting all these medicines, Master Jie and Liang You-dao could lie on rocks facing wind and cold during autumn and winter, through this text verifying the efficacy of these secret methods.

Someone asked about methods for evading krakens and dragons when fording rivers and crossing oceans. The Master Who Embraces Simplicity replied: A master of the Dao who despite himself must cross great rivers should first stop at the water's edge, then break an egg into a container with water and mix and pound it with a little rice powder and assorted aromatic powders in a small vessel. After washing himself with this mixture, he will not fear wind, waves, krakens, or dragons. Also, one should wear at one's belt Talismans of Little Lad of the Eastern Ocean, Talismans for Controlling Water, and Penglai[2] staff; these devices all exorcise all harmful things that are in waters. There are also the Talismans of the Six-jia and Three-metals, and the Five-wood taboos. Another method: approaching the water first incant: "*Juanfeng, juanfeng*! River Count is to lead the way, and expel krakens and dragons; The myriad calamities will dissolve, and heaven will be clear and bright."

The *Record of the Golden Tablets* says: "On a *bingwu* (#43) day in the fifth month, at noon, pound the five minerals to obtain a compound. The five minerals are realgar, cinnabar, orpiment, alum, and malachite. When these have all been powdered, wash them in Golden Flower solvent and place inside a Six-One divine crucible,[3] and heat it over cinnamon wood using a bellows. When the compound is complete, refine it with hard charcoal, while having young boys and girls approach the fire. Use a male compound to produce a male blade, and a female compound to produce a female one, each five and half inches long. By using earth's number (5), one can suppress the watery sprites. If you carry these blades while traveling in water then the krakens, dragons, giant fish, and water spirits will not dare approach you. If you wish to distinguish between the male and female compounds, you should have the young boys and girls sprinkle water on the compound while it is on the fire and turning red. Then the compound will split in two: the part that rises and protrudes is the male compound, the part that sinks and forms a hole is the female compound. You should inscribe the proper label on each, so that you recognize them. When you wish to enter water, wear the male one at your left and the female one at your right. If you are riding in a boat and not crossing a river in person, then you should carry the male blade on *yang* days and the female blade on *yin* days. Also, you can inscribe Emperor of the North in large characters in celestial script on a silk cloth and carry it; this too will protect you from wind, waves, krakens, dragons, and water insects."

Someone asked about methods for avoiding the various ghosts at the shrines in the mountains and by rivers. The Master Who Embraces Simplicity replied: A master of the Dao should regularly carry Talismans of Heaven and Water, and the Bamboo Envoy Talismans of the Supreme Luminary, Laozi's Left Tally, while Preserving the Perfect-One and medi-

2. In esoteric Daoism, the Isles of Penglai were the home of the immortals. "Little Lad of the Eastern Ocean": an important deity in the High-est Clarity (Shangqing) tradition.
3. That is, a crucible made with a divine mud (Six-One).

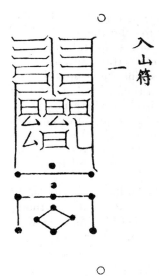

This talisman is, as the text describes, one of a set that can be worn for protection when entering mountains or hung up to ward off noxious influences around the house.

tating on the Generals of the Three Sections, then the ghosts will dare not approach. The next best method is to study the registers of the various ghosts so as to know the names of the ghosts in the world, as well as the *Chart of the Boze*[4] and the *Record of the Nine Tripods*, and then all the ghosts will depart of themselves. The next method is to ingest pills of quail-egg and hematite, malachite torch powder, onion-seed crow-eyes pills, and swallow powder of white-stone-quartz praying-mother; all these will allow one to see ghosts, so that the ghost will fear him.

The Master Who Embraces Simplicity says: There are the forty-nine perfect secret talismans of Lord Lao, the Yellow Court, and the Fetus.[5] When entering mountains, choose a *jiayin* (#51) day to inscribe them using cinnabar ink on white silk. At night place them on a table, and revere them while facing the Northern Dipper, offer then each of them a little liquor and dried meat and tell them your name and surname. Bow twice and, picking them up, place them inside your clothes at your neck. This will dispel the hundred ghosts, myriad sprites, tigers, wolves, and venomous insects. These methods are not restricted to masters of the Dao. They are appropriate to anyone who seeks refuge in the mountains to avoid the troubles of this chaotic age.

Talismans for Entering Mountains

The Master Who Embraces Simplicity says: The above five talismans are Lord Lao's Talismans for Entering Mountains. Use cinnabar to inscribe them on peach-wood tablets, use large script so that they fill the entire tablet. Hang them above the door, on the four walls, and at the four corners of your house, and at critical points along the paths to your home, about fifty paces from your dwelling. This will dispel mountain sprites, ghosts, and goblins. You can also hang them on the beams and pillars inside your home. All those who dwell in mountains and forests, or who are about to enter them, should employ these devices and the various anomalies will dare not harm them. You may inscribe three talismans together on a single tablet. This is not by Master Ge.[6]

The Master Who Embraces Simplicity says: These talismans are also Lord Lao's Talismans for Entering Mountains. They may be hung on the

4. The record of revelations to the Yellow Emperor by the boze, an auspicious animal.
5. A deity within the adept. "Lord Lao": the deified Laozi. On the Yellow Court, see the introduction to the *Most High Jade Scripture on the Internal*

View of the Yellow Court, above.
6. This line is clearly a comment by an unknown author that was interpolated into the main text [translator's note].

beams and pillars in your home. They are appropriate for all those who dwell in mountains and forests, or who are about to enter them.

The Master Who Embraces Simplicity says: These are talismans for entering mountains and evading tigers and wolves transmitted by the transcendent[7] Chen Anshi. Use cinnabar to inscribe them on silk, and keep the two talismans separately. Regularly wear them, and hang four of them in your dwelling. You should take them with you wherever you go. They are a secret of the great spirits. Mountain-opening Talismans are made from thousand-year-old *vitis flexuosa*, and placed at the gateways to famous mountains. They are precious writs, written in ancient script on gold or jade; they must be kept secret. This applies to all the above methods.

The Master Who Embraces Simplicity says: This talisman is carried by Lord Lao, it is a divine seal [to control] the hundred ghosts, snakes, pythons, tigers, and wolves. Inscribe it on a two-inch-wide tablet made of the pith of jujube wood. Twice bow, and then wear it. It has divine efficacy. It is a talisman [transmitted by] the transcendent Chen Anshi.

7. *Xian*, a Daoist who has achieved extraordinary powers and a higher form of existence (often translated "immortal").

TRADITIONS OF DIVINE TRANSCENDENTS
(*Shenxian zhuan*)

Traditions of Divine Transcendents (*Shenxian zhuan*) is a collection of immortals' biographies ascribed to Ge Hong (283–343 C.E.), the author of *Book of the Master Who Embraces Simplicity* (*Baopu zi*; see the previous selection). The complete text has not survived, and most modern editions contain only about 90 of the original 190 biographies and hagiographies. These provide precise information on the ways in which certain transcendents, or immortals, achieved their exalted state and exhibited a range of exceptional powers and capabilities—the ability to see into the future, fly, and so forth.

Traditions of Divine Transcendents includes a striking hagiography of Mozi (or Mo Di), the influential philosopher who allegedly lived in the late fifth century B.C.E. and gave his name to Mohism, a philosophical, social, and religious movement of the Warring States period (403–221 B.C.E.; see *The Book of Master Mo* [*Mozi*], above). In this text, however, he is instead presented as a transcendent and alchemist in the process of successfully learning how to concoct an elixir.

Traditions of Divine Transcendents contains some of the earliest biographies or hagiographies of important Daoist figures, including Zhang Daoling (or Zhang Ling, 34–156 C.E.), the founder of the Celestial Masters (Tianshi) tradition. Zhang Daoling's record provides a review of some of the main features of the Celestial Masters community in Sichuan, such as its administrative structure and the connection between proper behavior and healing.

The collection also contains stories of figures whose deaths are described as cases of "corpse liberation" (*shijie*)—a kind of feigned death and transformation, as a base human body is sloughed off like a cicada sheds its shell, leaving behind nothing or some small relic (a piece of clothing, sword, staff, or bamboo stave) in the coffin. Usually, after a long period of time, the "dead" individual will return home or be sighted in a far-off location, looking young and as vibrant as ever.

Ge Hong: *guh hung*

Ge Xuan: *guh hsuan*

Li Changzai: *lee chawng-tsai*

Mozi: *mow-tzu*

Shenxian zhuan: *shun-hsien chuan*

Zhang Daoling: *chawng dow-ling*

Zhang Ling: *chawng ling*

Li Changzai

Li Changzai (Li Ever-Present) was a native of Shu commandery.[1] <He trained in arts of the Dao while still young.>[2] For successive generations, commoners <served him,> and they calculated his age at four hundred or five hundred years; yet he did not visibly age, <seeming to be around fifty>. Whenever he treated those who were seriously ill, they would recover within three days; lesser cases would recover in a single day. Those whom he could not cure he did not go to treat at all.

<At home he had two sons and one daughter. After they left home to be married, he took in one son each from the families of [some of] his disciples, the Zeng household and the Kong household. Each of the boys was seventeen or eighteen. The families did not know where Li Changzai intended to go, but they sent their sons anyway. Li gave each of the boys a green bamboo stave and sent them back home with instructions to place them at the spot where they slept at home, and not to speak to any family members on their way in or out. The two boys did as told and took the staves to their homes. No one in the families saw the boys, but after they had gone, they saw on the beds the boys' dead bodies. Each family mourned and buried its dead member.

Over a hundred days later, some of his disciples were going to Pi district[3] when they met Li Changzai, who was traveling with these two boys. The boys and the disciples wept and talked for a long time. Each of the boys wrote a letter home to his family; their coffins were opened and inspected, and only a green bamboo stave was found in each. So the families realized that the boys had not died.

Some twenty years later, Li Changzai [and disciples] dwelled on Earth's Lungs Mountain. At this time he took another wife. But his former wife and one of his sons went searching for him. When they were ten days away, Li told his second wife, "My son will come here looking for me. I must go. Give him this golden disk." The son indeed arrived, asking where his father was. The second wife gave him the gold piece, to which the son responded, "My father abandoned me several decades ago. Night and day I have been thinking of him. Having heard that he was here, I traveled a long distance to investigate. I am not seeking money." He stayed there thirty days, but his father did not return. The son then said wistfully to the wife, "My father is not coming back. I am leaving." When he got outside he hid in some brush.

Li Changzai returned and said to his wife, "My son spoke falsely. He will come back. When he does, tell him that, since he is grown, he no longer

TRANSLATED BY Robert Ford Campany. All bracketed additions are the translator's.

1. Modern Sichuan Province.
2. The translator uses angle brackets to mark text that is unattested before the end of the Tang

dynasty (907 C.E.); most of the material is earlier.
3. Near the city of Chengdu.

needs me, and that according to the procedures I am not to see him any-more." Then he left. Soon the son did indeed return, and the woman told him what Li had said. Knowing he would not see his father again, the son wept, then departed.

More than seventy years after this, Li Changzai suddenly left [again]. [Afterward] some of his disciples found him living on Tiger Longevity Mountain, where he had taken yet another wife and had had sons. Genera-tions of people kept seeing him, always the same as before, so they called him Ever-Present.>

Mozi

<Master Mo, whose given name was Di, served in the kingdom of Song as a Grand Master. At the age of eighty-two years he sighed and said, "From the affairs of the world, it is already quite evident that honor and rank cannot be long preserved. I will withdraw from the common run of humanity and follow Master Red-pine in his wanderings." So he entered Mount Zhoudi and meditated. He suddenly saw a man, whereupon he asked him, "How could you not be the numinous pneuma of the mountain, or else a divine transcendent[4] who is about to escape from the world? Stay a while, I pray you, and instruct me in the teachings of the Dao."

The divine man replied, "Knowing that you have determination and love the Dao, I have come to attend you." The man then bestowed on Mo a silk text and esoteric methods and charts [for making] "efflorescence of vermil-ion" [pills]. Master Mo did obeisance and received these. He synthesized and produced [the elixir] and so confirmed [the method's] effectiveness, whereupon he selected and assembled its essentials and from these fash-ioned the *Treatise on the Five Phases* (*Wuxing ji*).[5] Afterward, he obtained the status of earthbound transcendent and secluded himself so as to avoid the wars among the states.>

Zhang Ling

Zhang Ling[6] was a native of the Pei kingdom. <Originally he was a student in the Imperial Academy, where he became well versed in the Five Classics. After this, however, he sighed and said, "None of this is of any benefit to one's years or allotted life span." So he studied the Way of long life. He obtained the Yellow Thearch's Method of the Elixirs of the Nine Tripods,[7] and he wished to synthesize these elixirs, but the necessary medicinal ingredients cost much in cash and silk. Zhang's family was simple and poor, but, desiring to establish his hold on life, he worked the fields and raised animals incessantly. However, even after a long time he had still failed to reach his goal.

4. A *xian*, a Daoist who has achieved extraordi-nary powers and a higher form of existence (often translated "immortal").
5. A treatise on esoteric arts of transformation [translator's note]. The theory of the five phases involves five agents, or five basic elements that move from one phase to another—a set of sys-tematic associations between different catego-ries, including the five directions, five viscera, and five colors (see table 2, p. 135).

6. The translator notes that although the text on which he primarily draws uses the name Zhang Daoling, "earlier *Traditions* sources usually write it as Zhang Ling." Zhang (34–156 C.E.) was the founder of the Celestial Masters movement.
7. See *Instructions on the Scripture of the Divine Elixirs of the Nine Tripods of the Yellow Emperor,* above; the Yellow Thearch is the mythological Yellow Emperor, Huangdi (27th century B.C.E.).

Having heard that many of the people of Shu were pure and generous, easy to teach and transform, and that, moreover, that country was full of noted mountains, he entered Shu with his disciples. He took up residence on Crane Cry Mountain,[8] where he composed a work on the Dao in twenty-four sections. Then he concentrated his thoughts and refined his will. Suddenly> a celestial personage descended, <with a train of one thousand carriages and ten thousand cavalrymen, golden chariots with feathered canopies, dragons and tigers in the harnesses—so many they could not be counted. One in the party announced himself as Archivist, another as the Young Lad of the Eastern Sea,[9] and these two bestowed on Zhang Ling the newly promulgated Way of the Covenant of Correct Unity.

Once Zhang had received this, he became able to cure illnesses. And so the common people flocked to him, hailing and serving him as their master. His disciples numbered several myriad households. He therefore established [the office of] Libationer, so as to divide and lead their households; a system of offices and supervisors and administrative sectors was established. He arranged for rice, fabric, tools, utensils, paper, brushes, lumber, firewood, and other supplies to be distributed as needed. He directed some people to repair certain roads, and those among them who failed to do so he caused to become ill. [From then on,] whenever a district had a bridge or stretch of road that needed repairs, the commoners there without exception cut down the brush and removed the debris. It all happened according to Zhang's plan, but the ignorant did not realize that these things were all his doing; rather, they took them as due to the scriptural text which had descended from Heaven above.

Zhang Ling wanted to rule the people by means of honesty and shame and avoid using punishments. So, once he had set up administrative sectors, whenever people in any sector became ill, he had them compose an account of all the infractions they had committed since their birth; then, having signed this document, they were to cast it into a body of water, thereby establishing a covenant with the spirits that they would not violate the regulations again, pledging their own deaths as surety. Because of this practice, the common people were extremely mindful. When they happened to become ill, they always reflected on their transgressions, [thinking that] if there was only one, they might obtain a recovery, and that if there were [as many as] two they would be mortified. Thus they did not dare to commit serious infractions but reformed themselves out of awe for Heaven and Earth; and, from this time forward, anyone who did commit infractions reformed himself to become a good person.

On account of all this, Zhang Ling obtained much wealth, which he used to buy the necessary medicinal ingredients for synthesizing elixirs.> When the elixirs were completed, he ingested <only half the dosage, not wishing to ascend to Heaven immediately.> As a result, he gained the ability to divide himself <into several dozen persons. Now, there was a pond outside the gate of Zhang's residence, on which he frequently went boating to amuse himself. Meanwhile, however, many Daoist guests would be going

8. An important mountain for the Celestial Masters tradition, located in modern Sichuan. Here the deified Laozi is said to have appeared to Zhang Daoling and proclaimed him a "celestial master."

9. An important deity in the Upper Clarity tradition. "Archivist": a title for the deified Laozi.

and coming in his courtyard. There would always be one Zhang Ling in the courtyard, conversing, eating, and drinking with these guests, while the real Zhang was out on the pond.

As for his methods of curing illness, they were selected from both esoteric and ordinary sources and were modified only slightly. Of those methods that proved most effective he altered some details, but in the main his methods still conformed to the others. As for his circulation of pneumas and dietetic regimen, he relied on [standard] methods of transcendence; here, too, he made no significant changes.

Zhang told most everyone, "You and your ilk have not yet been able to expunge the vulgar elements from your disposition, and so you are unable to leave the world behind. It is therefore appropriate that you obtain my procedures for circulating pneumas and arts of the bedchamber. Perhaps you will prove yourself capable of a special herbal diet, but even that is only a formula for living several hundred years." But as for the most essential of his Nine Cauldrons teachings, he entrusted these only to Wang Zhang,[1] who later synthesized the elixirs.

And [Zhang predicted that] there was one other person who would receive these teachings—one who would come from the east. This man, [he predicted], would certainly arrive at noon on the seventh day of the first month. He went on to describe the man's height and physical appearance. At the time specified, a man named Zhao Sheng[2] did indeed show up; he arrived from the east, and once others got a look at him, they saw that his form and features were exactly as Zhang had predicted.>

Zhang then put Zhao through a series of seven trials, and after Zhao had passed them all, Zhang bestowed the scripture on elixirs on him. <The seven trials were as follows. The first trial: when Zhao arrived at his gate, he was denied entry, and Zhang had others curse and berate him. He did not leave, in daylight or at night, for over forty days. Zhang then let him in.

The second trial: Zhang had Zhao watch over some livestock out in pasturelands. One evening Zhang sent a woman of extraordinary beauty, who pretended to be traveling far from home and asked to spend the night there and share Zhao's bed. The following day she further feigned a foot injury and said she was unable to leave; she stayed several days, during which she repeatedly flirted with him. Through all of this, Zhao never strayed from proper decorum.

The third trial: once while Zhao Sheng was walking on a road, he suddenly noticed thirty catties[3] of gold that someone had left behind. He walked past it and did not pick it up.

The fourth trial: Zhang sent Zhao into the mountains to collect firewood. Three tigers approached him at once and bit through his clothing without, however, injuring his body. Zhao remained fearless. Without changing the expression on his face, he told the tigers, "I am a practitioner of the Dao, and since my youth I have been nothing else. That is why I did not consider a thousand *li* far to travel to come and serve my divine teacher here, seeking the way of long life. What do you mean by this? Isn't it the spirit of this mountain who has caused you to come and test me like this?" Soon the tigers rose and departed.

---

1. A disciple of Zhang Daoling.
2. A disciple of Zhang Daoling.

3. About 40 pounds.

The fifth trial: while in the market, Zhao Sheng bought a dozen or so bolts of fabric, paying the price that was asked. But the fabric merchant falsely stated that Zhao had not paid him. Zhao removed his own clothes and gave them to the merchant as compensation without a trace of regret.

The sixth trial: while Zhao was on duty guarding grain from [public] fields, there came a man knocking his head on the ground begging for food. His clothes were in tatters, his face was caked with dirt, his body was filthy, and he stank terribly. Zhao was moved to sorrow at his condition. He removed his own clothes and clothed the man in them; he set out a meal for the man from his own private provisions; and he sent him off with grain from his personal supply.>

The seventh trial: with his disciples, Zhang Ling climbed up to the top of the cliff face of Cloud Terrace Mountain. Below the top of the cliff, there was a peach tree about the [thickness of a] man's arm growing out from the rock face; the depths beneath it were unfathomable, and it was thirty or forty feet down from the top of the cliff. The tree was loaded with peaches. Zhang said to his disciples, "I will declare the essentials of the Way to whoever can obtain those peaches." The disciples all broke out in a sweat, and none dared even to look down at the tree. But Zhao Sheng said, "With the divine personage protecting me, how could there be any danger in it?" He then threw himself off the top of the cliff, landing in the tree. He picked an armful of peaches, but the cliff face was sheer and he had no way to get back up. So he threw the peaches up to the top, obtaining two hundred of them. These Zhang Ling divided, giving one to each of his disciples and reserving two; of these, he himself ate one, and one he saved for Zhao. Zhang then extended his hand as if to pull Zhao up, and at once Zhao appeared back with them. Zhang gave him the last peach. <When he had eaten it, Zhang laughed beside the clifftop and said to him, "Zhao Sheng, your heart is naturally correct; that is what enabled you to throw yourself off and not to slip. I was testing you just now by sending you down after the peaches. Now I think I'll try throwing myself off, to see if I can get a bigger peach." Everyone protested this; only Zhao Sheng and Wang Zhang remained silent. Zhang then threw himself off into space. But he did not land on the peach tree, and the disciples lost sight of him. They looked everywhere—up toward Heaven, down to the ground, they searched where there were no paths. All of them were shocked and sorrowful and shed tears except for Zhao and Wang, who, after a while, said to each other, "Our master was like our father. How can we find peace when he has thrown himself off into the abyss?" So they both threw themselves off. And they landed directly in front of Zhang Ling, who was seated on a mat inside a screen. When he saw them, he smiled and said, "I knew you both would come. After I have finished transmitting the Way to you two, I will return to arrange things at my former residence; then, in three days, I shall return." The [other] disciples remained stricken with shock and grief.

Afterward, Zhang Ling, together with Zhao Sheng and Wang Zhang, rose up into the heavens in broad daylight and so departed. A crowd of disciples watched them from below as they gradually vanished into the clouds.>

THE DEMON STATUTES OF LADY BLUE
(*Nüqing guilü*)

When the *Demon Statutes of Lady Blue* (*Nüqing guilü*) was compiled—likely at the end of the fourth century C.E.—the world was believed to have fallen into such a dire state that demons were running amok, putting humans at risk of harm and even death. This work, a systematic demonology connected with earlier Chinese texts that describe the dangers of the unseen world, also offers a prescient glimpse of the new Daoist specialists who were to oversee the relationship between humans and spirits. It provides a formal code of conduct for demons: they are kept at bay by those who attain knowledge of their names, attributes, and dress, and can thereby control them.

The *Demon Statutes of Lady Blue* contains one of the earliest formulations of Daoist precepts, which are presented as a revelation by the deified Laozi (Taishang Laojun) to the Celestial Master. One of the major emphases of these rules is on keeping the community tightly organized: "You must not proclaim that Heaven has no gods, nor discuss the instructions of your teacher, subvert justice and disrupt the government, argue that you yourself are correct and the words of a man of the Dao are wrong. All contravene the demon statutes and laws." Another is on discouraging deviant sexual behavior. To be sure, sexual activity is essential for procreation, and sexual energy can have a positive effect as long as the male does not dissipate it through ejaculation; but the text warns specifically against the dangers of overindulgence and other sexual transgressions (which apparently include adultery, statutory rape, and homosexuality or transvestism). Anything that contravenes the Dao leads to the subtraction of a certain number of years, or "counters"—precisely how many varies with the severity of the infraction—from one's allotted life span.

PRONOUNCING GLOSSARY

Dao: *dow*   Nüqing guilü: *new-ching gwei-lew*

From *Chapter 1*

Man is born into the world for a period of less than a hundred years, uncertain of his safety from morning until evening, with death preponderating over life and the dead far outnumbering the living. Refractory murderous demons circulate everywhere among mortals, randomly causing all manner of ailments. There are the pathogenic influences of the five types of refractory beings bringing chills and hot sensations, headache, hard spots in the stomach, retching and shortness of breath, feelings of fullness and distension of the five viscera,[1] dazed vision, gulping and gasping, extremities palsied, so that one cannot be aware or think, and one's life hangs by a thread from morning until night.

Evil demons come to obtain control over all the men and women of the world. Your priestly officers should therefore consult my writings and discover there the names of the demons. Put into practice my lowermost talismans of Grand Sublimity with their vitalizing breaths of the Three

TRANSLATED BY Michel Strickmann.

1. Liver, heart, spleen, kidneys, and lungs.

Heavens,[2] the vitalization of the Three, Five, Seven, and Nine,[3] and bestow them on heaven's people. If heaven's people have died, they will be brought back to life.

Ever since the Great Commencement, I have observed how men and women have been tricked and deluded by the machinations of demons and so lacked faith in my Perfect Ones.[4] For that reason I kept this book secret, and as a consequence countless deaths have occurred. This causes me great sorrow whenever I think of it. For this reason I am now sending down these Statutes afresh, to make known throughout the world the names of the demons, the color of their clothing, and their strong and weak points.

The Statutes bring with them the qi[5] of True Unity (i.e., Daoism). You can thus name the relevant demons according to the various days, and none of them will dare to attack you. If, in your ignorance, however, you claim that I am without supernatural power, you will offend the Great Dao on high and incur guilt among men down below in the world of mortals. Beware of this, for you will thereby only injure yourself. In the year of the three calamities and the five evils, you will yourself observe those people who have no faith in the vital breaths of Perfection mockingly revert to consorting privily with demons. Take care that you separate yourself from such as they—otherwise, on that day, how can you hope to achieve life everlasting? Ponder this carefully again and yet again; do not transgress the rules. Pay heed!

From *Chapter 3*

You must not come and go, entering and exiting from north, south, east or west, without announcing when you leave or reporting when you return, in accordance with your own wishes and desires. All this contravenes the statutes and laws. 32 counters[6] will be subtracted.

You must not proclaim that Heaven has no gods, nor discuss the instructions of your teacher, subvert justice and disrupt the government, argue that you yourself are correct and the words of a man of the Dao are wrong. All contravene the demon statutes and laws. Heaven will deduct 13 counters.

You must not, bearing the truth, enter into falsity, defiling and disrupting your saintly luminaries, drinking wine and eating meat, lamenting that the world does not possess the Dao. 1,300 counters will be deducted.

You must not spread evil words, discuss other people, recklessly establish your own religion, disbelieve the Heavenly Dao, or speak groundless lies. Heaven will deduct 1,200 counters.

You must not spread lies, speak hypocritically or recklessly, have no constancy of emotion, devote yourself to defiance and slaughter without regard for *yin* and *yang*.[7] Heaven will deduct 132 counters.

TRANSLATED BY Terry F. Kleeman. The bracketed addition is the translator's.

2. The heavens of Great Clarity (Taiqing), Jade Clarity (Yuqing), and Upper Clarity (Shangqing).
3. These total 24, representing 24 deities as 24 breaths in the human body.
4. The Perfected, or *zhenren*, a concept that first appears in the *Book of Master Zhuang* (*Zhuangzi*; see above) and becomes important in later Daoism.
5. Vital energy, breath (pneuma).
6. The units that measure one's life span; one counter is equivalent to three days.

7. The complementary forces that unite to form the Dao: *yin*, a term that originally referred to the shady side of a valley, by extension came to be associated with the dark, earth, dampness, and passivity—the female principle; *yang*, a term that originally referred to the sunny side of a valley, by extension came to be associated with the light, heaven, dryness, and activity—the male principle.

You must not treat the aged with contempt or disparage your relatives, nor should husband and wife curse each other and cause each other harm, nor foster evil with a poisonous heart, be unfilial, or com mil the five contraventions.[8] Heaven will deduct 180 counters.

You must not, having received the Dao, transmit it to an inappropriate person with no regard for the gravity of this act, or accept a profit because of a desire for wealth, taking from others to benefit yourself, or borrow things then keep them as your private treasure rather than return them. Heaven will deduct 1,800 counters.

You must not battle with words, or indulge in sex while under the influence, or, pretending to speak for the Great Dao, recklessly pronounce the words of demons, or insistently assemble men and women to drink wine and eat meat. Heaven will deduct 300 counters.

You must not roam about, east and west, everywhere uniting with men and women. Though you seek to dispel the disaster, you will not gain liberation and this will result in deviant disorder. Heaven will deduct 13,000 counters and the deadly curse will flow down for seven generations.

You must not transmit the Dao to adolescent girls, taking this opportunity to enter their "gate of life,"[9] harming their gods and transgressing against their pneumas. This is refractory, evil, and unprincipled (literally, Dao-less). You will die and leave no posterity. You must not turn men into women (turn men over so that they become women) so that yin and yang are inverted and confused. Heaven will deduct 300 counters.

You must not have sexual congress in the open, offending against the Three Luminaries,[1] or visit people in order to drink, relying upon your authority to meet (gain contact with) them. Heaven will deduct 300 counters.

You must not cause the pneumas of one person to live while those of another person die, imposing upon and transgressing against the Perfected. Heaven will deduct 33 counters.

The sons of the same father must not live separately, leading to the scattering and dissolution of the home and family. Heaven will deduct 32 counters.

You must not become attached to that which you desire and hate to lose it, so that you gather together men and women to recklessly speak deviate words. Heaven will deduct 120 counters.

You must not be jealous of your co-religionists, gossip about each other, or put no faith in the Three and Five,[2] or comment on the strengths and weaknesses of the heavenly pneumas. Heaven will deduct 823 counters.

You must not flee from your parents, roaming to the four corners of the earth in order to establish your perfected pneumas and gather together a group. Heaven will deduct 320 counters.

You must not destroy that which Heaven has created, wantonly killing fleeing beasts or shooting flying birds; nor should you proclaim south to be north, according to the dictates of your heart. This is not is accordance with the demon statutes. Heaven will deduct 3000 counters.

---

8. That is, the five deadly offenses in Buddhism: killing one's father, killing one's mother, killing an arhat (someone who has destroyed all causes for future rebirth and will enter nirvana at death), wounding a buddha, or causing schism in the sangha (the Buddhist community).

9. That is, their vagina.
1. The sun, moon, and planets.
2. In Daoist texts, this phrase has many possible referents, including sets of rulers in antiquity, elements within the body, or the cosmos generally; it is unclear which sense is intended here.

You must not interfere in the affairs of others or make public the matters of other families, concealing their good deeds while calling attention to their evil actions, or violate the wives of others and plot to steal their sons-in-law, or rebel against the Three Luminaries, secretly harm or curse, or act unfilially, committing the Five Contraventions. Heaven will deduct 1220 counters.

You must not, on a day when you will perform a ritual to the Dao, lust after sex with a lascivious heart, circulate the pneumas too long, indulging ceaselessly in self-gratification, or enter into a secret pact. You will thereby give birth to an unfilial son, who harbors an evil heart among his five viscera and does not possess the Dao. Heaven will take away 30,000 counters.

You must not visualize a [profane] god and not report it, then circulate living pneumas, seize and bring down primordial pneumas, and spend all day in a mutual embrace of lust and sexual desire. Such a person has no Dao. Heaven will take away 342 counters.

You must not carelessly transmit the red pneumas to profane persons, so that mouth, hand, breast, and heart each come into contact in turn. This is to abandon the Dao and rebel against one's one master; to be without religion. Heaven will take away 300 counters.

You must not carelessly transmit a scriptural document to the profane, speak the taboo names of your mother or father, or reveal to the profane the essentials of the Perfected or the secret oral instructions. Heaven will take away 300 counters.

THE RECORD OF THE TEN CONTINENTS
(Shizhou ji)

The *Record of the Ten Continents* (*Shizhou ji*), which began to be compiled around the fourth century and was added to through the fifth century, describes the paradisical lands of immortality—located on the periphery of our human world—where the Daoist transcendents reside. Asked by the Han emperor Wu about the ten continents and their inhabitants, the courtier Dongfang Shuo (ca. 160–93 B.C.E.) begins with a grand tour of the cosmos, from locations in the stars down to earthly realms. In detailing each continent, he inventories all of its special plants, fungi, animals, and waters. The continent called Zuzhou, for example, supplies "death-preventing plants" that can confer longevity to those who eat it; the plant can also bring the dead back to life, if a corpse is covered by it. On the continent of Yanzhou lives a certain beast, similar to a wildcat but almost impossible to kill; eating its brain mixed with chrysanthemum blossoms will increase one's life span to five hundred years. The highly specific images of the immortals' paradises provided in the *Record of the Ten Continents* were important in shaping the ideas about those locales that were influential within Daoism and Chinese culture more generally.

PRONOUNCING GLOSSARY

Dongfang Shuo: *tung-fawng shu-oh*   Shizhou ji: *shih-chou chee*

After the Han Emperor Wu heard the Royal Mother say that there are ten continents—Zuzhou, Yingzhou, Yanzhou, Changzhou, Yuanzhou, Liuzhou, Shengzhou, Fenglinzhou, and Jukuzhou—in the Immense Sea in Eight Directions and that these were places where there were no human signs, he then began to realize that Dongfang Shuo was no ordinary man. Thereupon he invited him into a secret chamber and personally inquired about the ten continents' locations and the names of all their creatures, which he then wrote down.

Dongfang Shuo said, "I am a man who only emulates the immortals, not one who has attained the Dao. On account of your country's prosperity and beauty, your invitation of renowned Confucians and Mohists[1] into the civil order, your suppression of vulgar practices and extirpation of the remnants of hypocrisy, therefore, putting concealment aside I hasten to the imperial court; leaving the cultivation of life, I serve at the vermilion towers. I come, moreover, because Your Highness loves the Dao, yet your compound desires inhibit its ritual practices.

"I once followed my teacher on a walk, and we reached Fusang, the Vermilion Mound, the Serpent Sea, the Hill of Gloomy Night, and the tumulus of Chunyang.[2] [We walked] under the Primeval Blue and among the Moon Palaces. Internally we wandered among the Seven Hills and at the middle circled the Ten Continents. Tramping through Red District,[3] we rambled on the Five Peaks;[4] proceeding through lakes and marshes, we then rested at famous mountains. From my youthhood to the present, I have completely roamed the Six Heavens[5] and have fully ascended to the heavenly luminaries, where I reached my limit. I do not compare to the masters who ascend into the void, the dignitaries who soar in perfection, who rise and descend through the Nine Heavens[6] and clearly perceive the hundred territories. At Hooked Array by the North Celestial Pole they assemble under the Flowered Canopy;[7] southward they soar to the Supreme Cinnabar and rest at Great Summer; in the east they approach clouds of pervasive yang,[8] westward they brave the wilderness of the chilly caves. They cannot be reached by the sun and moon or be matched by the Milky Way. There is nothing covering them above and nothing grounding them below. This is the extent of my knowledge, and I am ashamed that it is not sufficient to answer your broad inquiry!

"Zuzhou (the Ancestral Continent) is near the middle of the Eastern Sea. It is five hundred square li[9] in area, and it lies seventy thousand li from the western shore [of the Eastern Sea]. Death-preventing plants that resemble

TRANSLATED BY Thomas E. Smith. All bracketed additions are the translator's.

1. Followers of Mo Di (see *The Book of Master Mo*, or *Mozi*, above).
2. All names of mythical locales.
3. A general term for China.
4. That is, the Five Marchmounts, a group of sacred mountains, one in each of the four cardinal directions and one at the center. They are most often identified as Mount Heng (north), Mount Tai (east), Mount Heng (south), Mount Hua (west), and Mount Song (center); variants include Mount Huo (south) and Mount Taihua (west).

5. Different sections of the sky.
6. The sky in the four cardinal directions, the four diagonals, and at the zenith [translator's note].
7. The name of a constellation composed of sixteen stars.
8. The male principle; the term originally referred to the sunny side of a valley, and by extension it came to be associated with the light, heaven, dryness, and activity.
9. A unit of distance, equivalent to about 1/3 mile.

the sprouts of marsh-reeds and grow to a height of three or four feet are found there. People already dead for three days, if covered with this plant, all return to life immediately. Eating it confers everlasting life."

Long ago, when the First Qin Emperor's[1] Great Garden was filled with [the bodies of] unjustly executed people, birds which resembled crows traversed the route [from Zuzhou] carrying this plant in their beaks and covered the faces of the dead with it. They sat up immediately, spontaneously coming to life. An official heard about this and reported it. The First Emperor despatched envoys to present the plant to Master Guigu[2] at the north city wall and inquire about it. Master Guigu said, "This is a death-preventing plant that grows on Zuzhou in the Eastern Sea. Grown in fields of rose-gem, some call it Spirit-Cultivating Fungus. Its leaves resemble those of marsh-reed sprouts, it grows in clusters, and one stalk is sufficient to revive a man." The First Emperor then asked eagerly, "Can it be harvested?" He then had his envoy Xu Fu send out five hundred boys and girls, lead them aboard storied ships and other vessels, and go to sea in search of Zuzhou. They did not return.

Xu Fu was a Daoist master whose style was Junfang.[3] Later he did indeed attain the Dao.

"Yingzhou (the Oceanic Continent) is in the Eastern Sea. It is four thousand square *li* in area, and it is located on the same level as Kuaiji, approximately seven hundred thousand *li* from the western shore. Divine fungi and immortal plants grow there. There is also a jade rock one thousand *zhang* [ten thousand feet] high from which gushes a spring named Sweet Jade Spring, whose water is as sweet as wine. One must drink several pints of it before becoming drunk, and it confers longevity. Many immortals make their homes on this continent, and their customs are like those of the people of Wu. The landscape is like that of the Middle Kingdom.[4]

"Xuanzhou (the Mysterious Continent) is in the northwest of the Northern Sea. It is seven thousand two hundred square *li* in area and lies three hundred sixty thousand *li* from the southern shore. The Mystery Metropolis there is governed by transcendent worthies and perfected gentlemen.[5] There are many hills and mountains, and there is also Wind Mountain, whose many winds and vapors resound like thunder and lightning. It faces the Northwest Gate of Heaven. On this continent there are many mansions of the immortal officials of the Great Mystery; each palace and chamber is unique. There is an abundance of golden fungi and jade plants. Moreover this falls under the lower jurisdiction of the Lords of the Three Heavens.[6] It is very majestic indeed.

1. Shi Huangdi (ca. 259–210 B.C.E.), creator of the short-lived Qin dynasty (221–206 B.C.E.) and the first unified Chinese empire.
2. A legendary master of divination who is supposed to have lived in the late Zhou dynasty [translator's note].
3. Style names were used in place of given names later in a person's life as a respectful form of address.
4. That is, China.

5. The *zhenren*, a concept that first appears in the *Book of Master Zhuang* (*Zhuangzi*; see above) and becomes important in later Daoism. In the Upper Clarity (Shangqing) tradition they are more exalted than the transcendents or *xian*, Daoists who have achieved extraordinary powers and a higher form of existence (often translated "immortals").
6. The heavens of Great Clarity (Taiqing), Jade Clarity (Yuqing), and Upper Clarity (Shangqing).

"Yanzhou (the Blazing Continent) is in the Southern Sea. It is two thousand square *li* in area and lies ninety thousand *li* from the northern shore. On this continent are Wind-Suscitated Beasts which resemble wildcats, are blue in color, and are the size of foxes. Spread a net, capture one, and pile several cartloads of firewood to cook it, and though the firewood will be consumed, the beast will not catch fire but stand amidst the ashes with its fur unsinged. Axes and knives will not penetrate its flesh, and if struck it is just like a leather bag. It must be hit over the head several dozen times with an iron hammer before it dies. Spread its mouth open to the wind, however, and it will revive in a moment. Stuff its nose with calamus [wrapped on] a stone, and it will die instantly. Remove its brain and eat it mixed with chrysanthemum blossoms. If you eat a full ten catties[7] of it, you will obtain a life-span of five hundred years.

"There is also the Fiery Forest Mountain, on which lives the Fiery Radiance Beast. It is the size of a rat, and its fur, which has red and white hairs, grows three or four inches long. The mountain is more than three hundred *li* high. If you can see this mountain forest at night, that is because these animals shine on it with a radiance like that of fire. Pluck its fur to weave it into cloth—this is what the people of our time call 'fire-washed linen.' The people of that country wear it. If it becomes soiled, they do not use ashes and water to clean it, for it would never become clean. They burn it instead with fire for the length of time it takes to eat two bowls of rice, then shake off the dirt, which falls off easily, so that the cloth becomes as white as snow.

"Many immortals also make their homes there."

          ✳   ✳   ✳

"What you are writing now are all the places that I have seen. As for the various spirit concourses that were mentioned by the Royal Mother, [since] these were not visited by Yu,[8] he wrote only about the famous mountains of central China.

"My former teacher, Master Guxi, is a most exalted perfected official. He once gave me the maps of the true topographies of Kunlun, Mount Zhong, Mount Penglai, and the Spirit Continent.[9] Long ago he came to China and lingered on here to transmit his knowledge to his friends. These writings are even more important than *The Maps of the True Topography of the Five Peaks*.[1] The years of their transmission are limited, just as they were in the past. If Your Majesty loves the Dao and meditates on subtlety, examines your heart and turns inward, the Heavenly Worthies will descend and also pass on their precious secrets. I am a mere trifle—how could I ever begrudge something and not offer you everything I have? The magicians, however, regard their deeds as mysterious and habitually keep their teachers secret. I say that if their teachers' techniques are revealed, then their deeds will be subject to much suspicion, and that if their teachers are exposed, then their

7. About 33 pounds.
8. Yu the Great (21st century B.C.E.), a legendary figure who quelled floods and allegedly founded the Xia dynasty.
9. Locations all associated with Daoist deities

and immortals.
1. These talismanic charts were supposed to confer immortality, wealth, etc., to the bearer [translator's note].

subtle principles will become widely known. I hope that for now you will not reveal my opinion."

Emperor Wu joyfully listened to [Dongfang Shuo's] most perfect descriptions. The next year he received as a sequel numerous true topographic maps, which he always kept close at hand. On the Eight Festivals[2] he always paid official respects to the spiritual writings and also petitioned for salvation. [Dongfang] Shuo spoke in jests, [but] knew in advance that the Emperor in his heart still manipulated ten thousand chariots and tyrannized the nobility. The Emperor could not help but make distinctions between friends and teachers; he could not help but show joy and anger. Consequently Emperor Wu could not completely adhere to the perfect principles [presented to him] by this man.

2. Celebrated on the first day of each season, the solstices, and the equinoxes [translator's note].

THE 180 PRECEPTS SPOKEN BY LORD LAO
(*Laojun shuo yibai bashi jie*)

The 180 Precepts Spoken by Lord Lao (*Laojun shuo yibai bashi jie*) supplies a full set of precepts revealed by the deified Laozi both for the "libationers" (*jijiu*), who were the religious leaders of the early Daoist Celestial Master communities, and for lay believers. The present version of the text begins with a prefatory section that briefly mentions Laozi's trip to the "West" to convert the barbarians and his return to the Hanzhong Valley in Sichuan, the home of the early Celestial Masters community. Dismayed at what he finds there, he sharply criticizes the state of affairs: "All the male and female libationers base themselves on the prestige of Laozi and covet wealth and love sensual pleasure." This Daoist community is wanton because members do not know the rules for governing the community; and so the deified Laozi issued an order to the libationers on regulating conduct and the need to follow the proper path laid out by the precepts.

The second section of the text lists all 180 precepts, beginning with 140 prohibitions. These rules range from the seemingly innocuous ("You should not write to other people in cursive script" and "You should not eat alone") to the more serious ("You should not bully others using your position of power," "You should not kill anybody from hatred," etc.). Some of the remaining precepts are phrased positively: "You should exert yourself to seek long life," "You should provide offerings within your abilities," and so on. The text is difficult to date with any certainty, but the rules display Buddhist influence—especially the injunctions against stealing, lying, eating meat, engaging in sexual misconduct, or drinking alcohol.

PRONOUNCING GLOSSARY

Laojun shuo yibai bashi jie: *lao-chun*   Laozi: *lao-tzu*
   shu-oh yee-pai baw-shih chieh

I. Formerly, towards the end of the Zhou[1] in the time of King Nan (314–255 B.C.E.) there first appeared the Dao of Great Peace and the teachings of Great Purity. Laozi arrived in Langye and passed on the Dao to Lord Gan.[2] Lord Gan received the methods of the Dao, proceeded to attain the Dao and was honoured with the title of Realized Man.[3] He also transmitted the *Taiping jing*[4] in 170 chapters, divided into ten sections using the ten stems.[5]

II. Later, when Lord Bo[6] became seriously ill, he received the Dao from Lord Gan, and was healed. When his illness had been eradicated, he also attained the Dao and was honoured with the title of Realized Man. Today in Langye there is a large magnolia tree marking where the Two Lords, Gan and Bo, propagated the doctrine.

III. In the time of King You (781–770 B.C.E.) Laozi went west and started teaching in the barbarian countries where he passed on the Buddha Dao.[7] "Buddha" in barbarian language is "Dao" in the language of the Han. The two are both transformative *qi*.[8] If one cultivates the Buddha Dao, long life will be obtained. Its path follows stillness.

IV. When he returned to Hanzhong after teaching the barbarians he passed through Langye. Lord Gan of Langye was granted an audience. Laozi upbraided and scolded Lord Gan: "Previously I gave you the commission of helping the state and saving lives. Grieving over the ten thousand people,[9] I gave you permission to appoint men and women to the office of libationer so that they would widely convert the ignorant and spread disciples everywhere. Above, this would cause a response from the Heart of Heaven and below, set in action the Spirits of Earth, causing rulers to be joyful. From that instant on, I have been watching from a million *li*[1] away. All the male and female libationers base themselves on the prestige of Laozi and covet wealth and love sensual pleasure. Daring to put themselves in this position they dispute over what is right and wrong, each one declaring, 'My opinion is correct' and saying, 'His is untrue.' They make profits from offerings and desire that others serve them. They despise their fellow Daoists, are envious of the worthy and jealous of the talented. They boastfully consider themselves great and put prohibitions on the hundred families: 'You ought to come and follow me! My Dao is most correct and his is untrue.' None of this is in order. This is why I have come to speak with you."

TRANSLATED BY Barbara Hendrischke and Benjamin Penny.

1. The Zhou dynasty, 1046–256 B.C.E.
2. Gan Ji, a figure of Daoist hagiography.
3. That is, a Perfected Person, or *zhenren*, a concept that first appears in the *Book of Master Zhuang* (*Zhuangzi*; see above) and becomes important in later Daoism.
4. *The Scripture of Great Peace* (see above).
5. The ten "celestial stems," the names of the ten days of the week (these combine with the twelve "earthly branches" to form the sixty elements of the traditional Chinese calendar).
6. Bo He, founder of a Daoist lineage.
7. A reference to the "Conversion of the Barbarians" story (see *The Conversion of the Barbarians*, above).
8. Vital energy, breath (pneuma).
9. That is, all the people in the world.
1. A unit of distance, equal to about 1/3 mile.

V. Gan Ji knocked his head on the ground, bowed repeatedly, prostrated himself on the ground and kowtowed one hundred times in agreement. He said, "Most High, I do not know how the heavy crimes of all the male and female libationers can be eradicated from now on, and allow them to maintain their livelihood and enjoy the protection of the Dao. In this way they would attain immortality after their span is exhausted and would not have to descend below the nine lands for punishment in the nine hells. It is not simply the libationers. The libationers have also infected the common people with error so that the common people are without knowledge of the laws. Thus the crimes of the libationers are the result of my transgression and truly the blame for all of this rests with me. My only wish is that the Most High pardon my past punishable errors and examine how I might cultivate future morality. I, Gan Ji, deserve death, I deserve death."

VI. Laozi said, "Be seated quietly and settle your mind. I fear that once the Great Dao is destroyed, the common people will all lose their loves. That one or two libationers would, upon their deaths, descend below the nine lands is insufficient to cause me pain. But I am mindful of the common people's pain. You should listen well. Listen well and record it in your heart so that you can be a model for later generations. Issue orders to all the male and female libationers. Command them to reform their past conduct and from now on follow the right path."

VII. Lord Lao said, "Unless the precepts and regulations are held to, even if a human life lasts 10,000 years, how is it different from an old tree or an ancient rock? It is better to hold to the precepts for a single day and to die as a virtuous man, living without committing evil. If you hold to the precepts, you will serve as a heavenly official, ascending to immortality through corpse-liberation.[2] Although the people of this generation may attain the status of emperors and lords, as they die having committed serious crimes, it is of no advantage to their hun-souls.[3] As hun-souls they will be punished. The libationers should clearly put the precepts into practice."

VIII. "When it is time to take possession of the precepts, disciples bathe, do not eat the five flavourful foods or the five pungent roots,[4] and they change their dress. The disciples should conduct rituals to their master and the teachings, prostrate to the ground and receive the prohibitions and admonitions. When they have received the prohibitions and admonitions, they should write them out once, chant them and put them into practice."

IX. He then said, "All the worthies should listen carefully. Among the ten thousand things of this world[5] none live endlessly. As people are born, they will die. Things that mature will decay. The sun rises so it will set. The moon waxes so it will wane. From ancient times until today, for anybody to have been able to attain length of life, it has been made possible only through long holding to morality. Now the month is the right month, the

2. A type of liberation or transformation in which one feigns one's own death, leaving behind nothing or some relic, and ascends to heaven.
3. Cloud souls or spiritual souls, which rise up at death.

4. Garlic, leeks, onions, scallions, and chives. "Five flavourful foods": that is, the five flavors (sweet, sout, salty, spicy, and bitter).
5. That is, all things that exist.

day the right day and the time the right time. All the worthies are good, the masters are good and the disciples are good. The ten thousands spirits have all assembled and the officials and soldiers have arrived. Now for the sake of all the worthies, for the lives of the ten thousand people as well as the good intentions of the disciples, I transmit the precepts of prohibition and the important regulations."

X. Lord Lao said, "Unless the precepts and regulations are held to, even if a human life lasts 10,000 years, how is it different from a tile or rock? It is better to hold to the precepts for a single day and to die ending one's days as a virtuous man than it is to live without opposing evil. If you die holding to the precepts, you will transit through extinction and your body will be transformed. You will serve as a heavenly official, ascending to immortality through corpse-liberation. If the people of this generation do not hold to the precepts and the regulations, they die having committed serious crimes, they cannot improve on becoming a spirit. Good men and good women should clearly put the precepts into practise.

XI. "Yes, yes. We praise them three times!" Later, he explained the precepts.

The Precepts say:

1. You should not keep too many male servants or concubines.
2. You should not debauch the wives and daughters of other men.
3. You should not steal other people's property.
4. You should not kill or harm anything.
5. You should not improperly take one cash[6] or more of anyone else's things.
6. You should not improperly burn or destroy anything worth one cash or more.
7. You should not throw food into the fire.
8. You should not keep pigs and sheep.
9. You should not seek anyone else's things for an evil purpose.
10. You should not eat garlic or the five pungent roots.
11. You should not write to other people in cursive script.
12. You should not trouble others too often with written enquiries.
13. You should not use herbal medicine to perform abortions.
14. You should not set fire to uncultivated fields and mountain forests.
15. You should not eat off gold or silverware.
16. You should not seek to know of state or military events or to prognosticate whether they will come to a lucky or unlucky conclusion.
17. You should not improperly have contact with armed rebels.
18. You should not improperly fell trees.
19. You should not improperly pick flowers.
20. You should not meet frequently with Emperors or court officials or improperly enter into marriage relations with them.
21. You should not treat disciples with contempt or maliciously show them favour and upset their purity.
22. You should not covet or begrudge wealth.

---

6. A Chinese coin of small value.

23. You should not lie, use ornate speech, create divisions, or show envy.
24. You should not drink alcohol or eat meat.
25. You should not hoard wealth or despise the orphaned, widowed and poor.
26. You should not eat alone.
27. You should not traffic in male or female slaves.
28. You should not seek knowledge about the marriages of other people.
29. You should not cause jealousy and ill will through exploiting the strengths and weaknesses of other people.
30. You should not perform as a musician.
31. You should not speak of the evil acts of others and suspect all manner of things.
32. You should not speak about the dark secrets of others.
33. You should not speak about good and evil in the lives of other people's parents.
34. You should not praise others to their face and speak evil of them behind their backs.
35. You should not play tricks on people with foul things.
36. You should not throw poison into deeps and pools or into rivers and seas.
37. You should not show partiality to members of your clan.
38. You should not make light of those honoured by others.
39. You should not participate in killing.[7]
40. You should not urge others to kill.
41. You should not separate other families.
42. You should not kill anybody from hatred.
43. You should not present petitions that slander others.
44. You should not consider yourself to be superior.
45. You should not place yourself in an honoured position.
46. You should not be arrogant.
47. You should not improperly dig the earth or spoil mountains and rivers.
48. You should not use bad language or curse.
49. You should not kick the six kinds of domestic animals.[8]
50. You should not deceive others.
51. You should not refuse to heal disease.
52. You should not covet other people's things.
53. You should not drain rivers and marshes.
54. You should not criticize teachers.
55. You should not go naked or bathe in the open.
56. You should not take lightly or show contempt for the teachings of the scriptures and sacred teachings.
57. You should not treat the old without proper respect.
58. You should not watch domestic animals having sexual intercourse.
59. You should not play tricks on people.
60. You should not bully others using your position of power.
61. You should not show favour to those with whom you are close.
62. You should not carry a sword or staff. Commentary: If you are in the army you need not follow this rule.

---

7. Perhaps a reference to suicide. 8. Pigs, dogs, chickens, horses, cattle, and sheep.

63. You should not live separately.
64. You should not show anger or displeasure.
65. You should not abuse others as slaves.
66. You should not urinate while standing.
67. You should not tattoo the faces of slaves.
68. You should not cause others death or misfortune by casting spells.
69. You should not rejoice at someone's death or misfortune.
70. You should not travel impulsively and recklessly.
71. You should not stare at other people.
72. You should not poke your tongue out at other people.
73. You should not forcibly seek other people's things.
74. You should not annoy the common folk through aggressive begging.
75. You should not collect taxes on behalf of lay people.
76. You should not organise a group to send presents to someone with yourself as leader.
77. You should not design graves, erect tombs or raise buildings for other people.
78. You should not read the stars or prognosticate the seasons.
79. You should not harm or kill any living thing through fishing or hunting.
80. You should not separate husband and wife through debauchery.
81. You should not show favouritism to your disciples. Commentary: Regard them as the equal of your sons.
82. You should not snatch other people's night-fires.
83. You should not hasten to offer condolences to recently bereaved lay people. Commentary: It is right to be privately sympathetic.
84. You should not join lay people in gangs or factions that abuse each other.
85. You should not demean the achievements of others and claim it was due to your own effort.
86. You should not select the best lodgings or the best bed for your rest.
87. You should not slander other people's things as bad.
88. You should not commend your own things as good.
89. You should not cause alarm and make people tremble with fear.
90. You should not select your food and drink from what others offer on the basis of your opinion as to its worth.
91. You should not go around speaking evil on behalf of other people.
92. You should not harm others through your position in or connections with the local administration.
93. You should not participate in mundane discussions concerning right and wrong actions.
94. You should not seize other people's things and give them away to show your kindness.
95. You should not dig up the hibernating and the hidden in winter.
96. You should not travel frivolously or charge about for days and months on end.
97. You should not improperly climb trees to search for nests and destroy eggs.
98. You should not cage birds or animals.
99. You should not bore holes in the walls of other people's houses to spy on the women and girls inside.
100. You should not throw foul things into wells.

101. You should not block up ponds and wells.
102. You should not deceive the old and the young.
103. You should not improperly open and read other people's letters.
104. You should not entice free men or women into slavery.
105. You should not pile up riches as it will attract bad luck and misfortune.
106. You should not become overly attached to your dwelling place.
107. You should not bury utensils underground.
108. You should not damage coins.
109. You should not light fires on open ground.
110. You should not spread thorns and spikes on the road.
111. You should not speak excessively or chatter.
112. You should not throw anything away that has writing on it or bury it near the toilet.
113. You should not pay ritual homage to the ghosts and spirits of other religions.
114. You should not possess the prognosticatory writings of the lay people or the Chart of the Eight Spirits.[9] Also, you should not practice any of them.
115. You should not associate with soldiers.
116. You should not urinate on living plants or in water that people will drink.
117. You should not become intimate with widows.
118. You should not make sacrifices to ghosts and spirits in order to seek good fortune.
119. You should not create too many taboos for other people.
120. You should not observe too many taboos yourself.
121. You should not improperly make light of entering a river or the sea to bathe.
122. You should not improperly suggest someone for promotion to gain presents or bribes.
123. You should not go guarantor for bonds or in buying and selling land and houses or slaves for other people.
124. You should not have regular contact with families of loose morals.
125. You should not distil poisons and medicines and put them in vessels.
126. You should not make loud and harsh sounds but always show a smile.
127. You should not write legal plaints or settle lawsuits for other people.
128. You should not show interest in or seek books of secret plots or read them.
129. You should not improperly flog any of the six kinds of domestic animals.
130. You should not ride a horse or drive a cart without cause.
131. You should not lump the leftovers from your meal together with your hands in order to eat all the delicacies.
132. You should not frighten birds and animals.
133. You should not judge whether the food and drink of other families is good or bad.
134. You should not breach levee walls.

---

9. The deified spirits of the Eight Trigrams (see the introduction to *The Seal of the Unity of the Three, in Accordance with the Book of Changes* [*Zhouyi cantong qi*], above).

135. You should not recommend yourself to heal a sick person. Commentary: You should only go when invited by the family of the sick person themselves.
136. You should not travel alone. Commentary: Travel in company.
137. You should not give people counsel on profit making schemes.
138. You should not seek widely for precious things.
139. You should not accompany women into the mountains. They should all be in separate lodgings on a different trail.
140. You should not violate the root and pursue the branches.
141. You should provide offerings within your abilities. Do not put yourself in difficulty.
142. You should always think on the methods of purity and frugality. Longing for purity and worthiness, eat like deer and drink like cattle.[1]
143. You should always take care of where you lodge for the night. Commentary: Inspect it first. Do not charge in.
144. You should take refuge in the Orthodox Unity. You should not practise vulgar cults.
145. You should possess the grand plan and grasp the purport. You should not mix up, transgress, turn your back on or avoid the teachings of the Three Venerables.[2]
146. You should exert yourself to avoid suspicion. Do not seek serve the Ruler through relying on your parents' influence.
147. You should exert yourself to seek long life. Day and night do not slacken.
148. You should exert yourself to avoid difficulties. Do not covet salary or illicit honour.
149. You should exert yourself to ingest *qi* and eliminate cereals from your diet practising the Dao of No Death.
150. You should exert yourself to avoid violent people. Do not discard friends.
151. Whenever you eat or drink, start from one side. Do not hurry to pronounce judgement on what is good and what is bad.
152. Each time you burn incense you should pray on behalf of the ten thousand families and that the empire should attain Great Peace.[3] Do not do it simply for yourself.
153. Whenever someone addresses you as Libationer, be careful to move them to awe. Do not act frivolously and hastily or make yourself laughable.
154. Whenever someone offers you a meal, you should always pray for the donor to be blessed and that all people will eat their fill.
155. Do not excessively and without cause have people gather together, leaving the remains of the meal in a mess.
156. Do not without cause improperly or too often receive the reverence of other people.

---

1. That is, live in an ascetic way [translators' note].
2. According to the translators, the Three Venerables are likely equivalent to the Three Treasures of Buddhism: "the Dao, the Scriptures, and the Teachers."

3. A golden age of good government, political harmony, and good health, which was believed to have existed in the past and which would be restored when the ruling ideology is based on a return to the Dao.

157. When you enter another state you must first enquire after the worthies and noble scholars. You should have contact with them and rely on them.
158. When you enter another state you must first enquire after that country's prohibitions.
159. When you enter someone's house you must first enquire after the taboo names of their elders and ancestors.
160. When you arrive at someone's house do not hope to be fed by your host if he is a common man.
161. Women should not walk together with men.
162. Men should not converse with women in a dark room.
163. Men's and women's clothing should not exceed three sets.
164. Men and women should not sit together to eat or touch hands to give or receive things.
165. Whenever there are calamities in Heaven or when there is flood, drought, or disharmony in the weather, do not grieve or become desperate.
166. In this generation, evil people are numerous and good ones are few. Do not be depressed. The Dao itself protects its law.
167. If others abuse you, you should simply hear it through. Do not respond.
168. If others slander you, you should simply cultivate yourself and gain enlightenment from the Great Dao. Do not do injury to your essence or spirit through distress.
169. If others wrong you, repay it repeatedly with kindness. Commentary: Being kind destroys evil as water extinguishes fire.
170. If someone gives something special to A, B should not resent that it was not given to him.
171. If someone flatters you do not show happiness. If someone abuses you do not show displeasure.
172. If someone kills birds, animals, fish, etc. for you, do not eat them.
173. If something has been killed do not eat it.
174. If food smells of mutton, do not eat it.
175. If you do not know where your food has come from, it is permissible to eat it. It is not permissible to think it delicious.
176. To be able to exclude all meat of living beings and the six domestic animals from the diet is considered best. If you cannot then you will transgress the precepts.
177. To be able to eat vegetables is excellent. If you cannot, follow the ruling phase.[4]
178. If you are able to honour the worthy, pay high regard to the sages and practise worthiness, I will cause you to transcend and you will meet with the perfected immortals.
179. If you are travelling where there are no houses it is permissible to set up lodgings among the trees or rocks. If you chant the text of the *180 Precepts*, three rings of spirits will defend you. Armed rebels, ghosts and tigers will not dare to approach you.

4. A reference to the theory of the five phases, which involves five agents, or five basic elements that move from one phase to another—a set of systematic associations between different categories, including the five directions, five viscera, and five colors (see table 2, page 135).

180. In practising the precepts do not transgress. If you do transgress, you are able to repent. Reform your past conduct and mend your ways in future. Urging others to accept the *Precepts*, thinking on the *Precepts* and not thinking on evil, you will widely save all people. If I appoint you a Spirit Perfected, the Spirit Perfected will make you complete.

On the right are the *180 Precepts* of the essential regulations for prolonging existence.

Lord Lao made this announcement to his disciples: "In the past all worthies, immortals and sages followed the *180 Precepts* and attained the Dao. The Dao is formless. By following a teacher you can attain completion. The Dao cannot be transcended, the teacher cannot be taken lightly." The disciples knocked their heads on the ground, bowed repeatedly, received their commands and withdrew.

THE SPIRIT SPELLS OF THE ABYSS
(*Dongyuan shenzhou jing*)

The *Spirit Spells of the Abyss* (*Dongyuan shenzhou jing*), composed mainly in the early fifth century (with later additions), is an apocalyptic text presented as revealed from the mouth of the deified Laozi himself. The overarching narrative concerns demonology and therapeutic healing. Like the *Demon Statutes of Lady Blue* (*Nüqing guilü*; see above), this work was written at a time when the world seemed to be falling apart, increasingly beset with evil demons and natural disasters. "The Great Kings of Malignant Wraiths of the Three Heavens," it warns, "lead a troop of forty-eight myriads that specialize in spreading red swellings."

After the world as we know it comes to a cataclysmic end, a period of Great Peace will follow; at the inauguration of the new age, the divinized Laozi will descend into the world and rule it. This world will be repopulated by an elect of the faithful—literally, "seed-people"—who, because they had come into possession of the *Spirit Spells of the Abyss*, had their names inscribed on the registers of immortality. The poor souls who do not possess this book bear the brunt of the demonic attacks: to avoid them, warns the text, "you must first receive this scripture and make offerings to the Master; only after doing this will you be able to ascend on high as an immortal." Further evidence that a "cult of the book" surrounds the *Spirit Spells of the Abyss* is its self-description as a "scripture-talisman." A similar cult is also present within Buddhism during this period. Moreover, the apocalyptic eschatology presented in the *Spirit Spells of the Abyss* closely resembles the Buddhist notion of the kalpa, a cosmic cycle that lasts from the beginning of a given world to its destruction.

PRONOUNCING GLOSSARY

Dongyuan shenzhou jing: *tung-yuen shun-chow ching*

[Selection 1]

The Dao said, "In the year of the snake and the year of the horse,[1] the demon armies will flood forth and the devil-kings will afflict mankind with their toxic infestations. I am now sending forty-nine million constables to arrest the devil-kings of the Thirty-Six Heavens, to subdue them and bind them by oath. According to the oath, from now on, should any people of this land die before the appointed time, or suffer from grievous ailments, prison, or forced labor, this will all be due to the devil-kings not having kept the lesser demons from afflicting and harming the people. From this time forth, the golden mouth of the Most High decrees that should there be any devil-kings who do not place those demons under restraint, and who allow them to cause the land's people to perish without due cause, through pestilence, war, suffering, prison, or forced labor, because these devil-kings are guilty of not having controlled the lesser demons, they shall be beheaded without mercy."

The Dao said, "From Fu Xi's time [in the distant mythological past] down to the end of the Han dynasty [220 c.e.], the people were vastly happy. Most of them did not have faith in the Dao; they all simply received the influences of heaven. They knew nothing about the Dao, the Law, or the scriptures—there was no need for such things in those happy days, when everyone was naturally good and naturally healthy. During the reign of the Jin dynasty [third/fourth centuries c.e.], though, as the secular order approached its end, people lost their original purity, and a race of degenerate rulers arose to lord it over mankind. The people suffered; the rulers were oppressive, and their subjects were harried. But in time, in the region south of the Yangzi, the people of heaven began to assemble and the Dao influence started to manifest itself."

The Dao said, "The Great Kings of Malignant Wraiths of the Three Heavens lead a troop of forty-eight myriads that specialize in spreading red swellings. The eighty myriad Great Kings of Malignant Wraiths of the Six Heavens lead troops of seven hundred myriads that specialize in spreading white swellings. The Great Kings of Malignant Wraiths of the Nine Heavens and the Great Kings of Malignant Wraiths of the Three Heavens, sixty myriads of each, lead followers to the number of thirty-nine thousand that specialize in spreading black swellings. The Great Kings of Malignant Wraiths of Thirty-Six Heavens head seventy myriads that specialize in spreading yellow swellings. The Great Kings of Malignant Wraiths of the Seven Heavens lead nine million myriads that specialize in spreading blue swellings. They attach themselves to people's bodies and inundate their four limbs; their faces turn blue, red, yellow, white, or black. They are now cold, now hot, now coming, now going. As the days drag on, they sink ever deeper into misery. The miasmas come and pain their hearts; beneath their hearts they become indurated and full. They do not wish to eat or drink. As

---

TRANSLATED BY Michel Strickmann. All bracketed additions are the translator's.

1. Two consecutive years in the Chinese zodiac, a twelve-year cycle that relates each year to a different animal. This cycle is part of the larger sixty-year (sexagenary) calendar system, in which days and (later) years were designated with two characters drawn from a set of ten "celestial stems" and twelve "earthly branches."

they eat and drink less and less, they vomit up everything or else, rebel against eating, and find everything flavorless. Sometimes the curses of dead ancestors reach to living persons; when there is guilty karma of this sort, it brings about troubles with officials, imprisonment, and resentment and blame. If you wish to eliminate such afflictions, you must first receive this scripture and make offerings to the Master; only after doing this will you be able to ascend on high as an immortal."

The Dao said, "O you Great Kings of Malignant Wraiths! In previous lives you accomplished no acts of merit; you did not have faith in the Great Tao; you heaped up mountains of guilt. Now you are among the malignant wraiths that specialize in spreading fevers and toxic infections among mankind. Some suffer from cold and heat in their bodies, in others the whites and blacks of their eyes are reversed, some run madly about, speaking without sense; others sing and howl, sob and wail. For some, their four limbs are sore and swollen and their vital breaths contend wildly within them. Ailments of these kinds fill the entire world; they may confuse people's minds, causing them to get involved in lawsuits and be cast unjustly into prison. Thus are the people bitterly afflicted. And all ailments of these sorts are the doing of you Kings of Malignant Wraiths. From this time on, you are to aid and protect those who do honor to this scripture-talisman. Do not let them suffer any evil. The place where this scripture is read is to be avoided by demon-soldiers and protected by the Good Spirits. If you do not have faith in the Great Law and so come once more to attack these Masters of the Law, you Kings of Malignant Wraiths will enter the Abyss, you Kings of Malignant Wraiths will enter the water! You Kings of Malignant Wraiths will enter the fire! You Kings of Malignant Wraiths will be decapitated ten thousand times! You Kings of Malignant Wraiths will have your heads broken into eighty pieces! Swiftly they will seize your vital essence! Swiftly they will seize your souls! Then you will not be able to attack and harm and plague and torment the good, just people of the world! Swiftly, swiftly, in accordance with the Statutes and Ordinances!"

[Selection 2]

The Dao says: Sexagenary year 21 is about to arrive. The flood is not far off. Now, epidemic demons are killing people. The world abounds in vice and lacks goodness. The people do not recognize the truth. The Three Caverns (Sandong)[2] revelations have been spreading for a long time, but the people are benighted and fail to seek out and accept them. They bring suffering on themselves. What can be done? The people are to be pitied. I will now send eight units of palace guards to annihilate the epidemic ghosts and dispatch an order to banish [the epidemic ghosts]. Let Daoist priests convert people and make them accept the Three Caverns revelations.

The Dao says: From now on, for those who accept this *Divine Incantations Scripture*, thirty thousand celestial elite troops will protect you. Convert all

---

TRANSLATED BY Nathan Sivin. All bracketed additions are the translator's.

2. The three traditions of divine revelation that came together to produce the body of Daoist scriptures. The text writes further on of the "divine protectors of the Three Caverns," gods dedicated to enforcing the prescriptions of the sacred writings [translator's note].

the unenlightened day by day on behalf of all the living. If the unenlightened persist in their confusion and ridicule people who do good, Heaven will send epidemic ghosts to kill these people. Souls of such people will enter the three evil paths of rebirth,[3] with no prospect of egress.

The Dao says: In sexagenary years 18 and 19, eighty million great ghosts will come to annihilate bad people. As for those with forked tongues, those who slander the law of the Dao, those who refer to their masters by their taboo-names, those who dispute the scriptures, those who have no faith in the Three Caverns revelations, and those who are unwilling to accept the Dao, the great ghost king will come and annihilate all of them.

The Dao says: From now on, if there is a place where Daoist priests obediently follow the Three Caverns revelations, practice the Dao, and teach the people, I will send a multitude of ninety billion great soldiers to come all at once and protect you. If there is one ghost that won't leave, the divine protectors of the ten regions will come down immediately to arrest it.

The Dao says: From now on, wherever there are Daoist priests who recite this scripture, Heaven will order four hundred ninety thousand divine protectors of the Three Caverns, eight hundred thousand divine protectors from the six-fold heaven and ninety billion from the thirty-six-fold heaven to come and in unison kill those epidemic ghosts. Heaven will allow those among the living who are ill and those with official entanglements to obtain release.

Illnesses will lighten or remit. A pleasant disposition will be brought about in all the gods, and there will be household felicity. Within and without, god of the locality and god of the stove will be made clearly distinguishable [i.e., will not intrude upon one another's responsibilities]. They will not act against the rules and make trouble for the living. Those ghosts that do not belong to the household cult will be exiled forever to other places. If there are ghost troops who disobey my orders and do not depart, each and every one will be executed by the demon kings, without lenience. Take heed! The sages do not speak empty words.

The Dao says: In this *Divine Incantation Scripture* there are the names of the demon kings of the thirty-six-fold heaven as well as of seven billion minor kings. Wherever a Daoist priest recites this scripture, the demon king of the thirty-six-fold heaven, Ju Penzi, and seventy-two minor kings will come together and offer submission. Thus, in the cases of those who can recognize the impending end of the world age, accept this scripture, and make offerings in their households, no evil ghost will be able to come in an undisciplined way. Why? Because all the demon kings send divine protectors to guard this scripture. One hundred billion Celestial Men, Jade Women,[4] and immortals also come to guard it. Ghost troops will not dare come against the rules, either in front of you or behind your back.

The Dao says: From now on, if, wherever the scriptures are recited, there are evil ghosts or vicious spirits who still dare to perpetrate bad deeds and intentionally confront the living and [even] practitioners, eight billion ghost kings and demon kings take an oath to have their [own] heads cut off three

---

3. In Buddhism, rebirth into one of the three evil realms (those of animals, ghosts, and the denizens of hell); it was also possible to be reborn into the realms of gods, of demigods, and of humans.

4. Low-ranking members of the bureaucracy of immortals [translator's note].

times and split into thirty thousand pieces [since they will have permitted a breach of discipline].

A demon king says: From now on, if there is a Daoist priest who heals illness, recites the scripture, and brings on prosperity, then I will allow everything he does to find fulfillment, all his wishes to be granted, and every plan to have its fruition. If I go back on my oath, I, your disciple Jumin, will suffer dismemberment ten thousand times.

The Dao says: From now on, the Three Caverns revelations will be disseminated far and wide. The Realized Ones[5] [i.e., adepts] will accept it and the unenlightened [who need it] still more. Henceforth, ghost troops will help those who accept the Three Caverns revelations. Every action will reach completion and all that is done will be harmonious. The great demon kings will protect them. You Daoists must assiduously convert the unenlightened. If a master who has received the Three Caverns scriptures journeys to save people when there is acute illness, and a Daoist priest recites the *Divine Incantations Scripture,* the demon kings of the threefold heaven will summon the lesser kings to shore up the disciple's power.

The Dao says: When Daoist priests receive the *Divine Incantations Scripture* they may not receive other scriptures at the same time. They must receive and practice this book separately. Why is this? Because there is so much divine power of the great demon kings in this scripture. It must not be received or copied alongside the others. It should also be stored in a separate case. When traveling, if you carry it on your person, the multitudes of ghosts can't come near. Those performing the communal rituals may also use its countless invocatory rites.

The Dao says: In this *Divine Incantations Scripture* are the names of all the demon kings. Therefore the Most Exalted considers it especially important. Where the scripture is recited, evil ghosts will not dare approach the living. Those that are not ghosts of ancestors will not approach them in violation of the rules. The great spirits of inside and outside, spirits infesting dwellings and tombs, spirits of the living and dead, and male and female spooks are henceforth banished ten thousand *li*[6] away. If you do not obey this order you will be truncated ten thousand times, with no leniency.

The Dao says: In the world there are eighty thousand drowned people. The ghosts are about three feet high. They move about in immense groups. They kill people in water. Those who do not believe in the Dao will not be protected by good spirits and will also drown there. Furthermore, there are nine hundred eighty thousand kinds of water illness. There are thirty-two black illnesses, white illnesses, red illnesses, virid illnesses, and yellow illnesses that cannot be cured. There are ninety-six varieties of sudden death. All these happen to criminals and to the worldly who do not follow the law of Dao and who plunge the country into disorder. This is because when bad people are unwilling all their lives to consider what is good, Heaven sends divine guardians with ten thousand illnesses to annihilate them. From now on, wherever a Daoist offers his meritorious good works and carries out communal rituals to save the people, you demon kings are to help this master of

5. That is, Perfected Ones, or *zhenren*, a concept that first appears in the *Book of Master Zhuang* (*Zhuangzi*; see above) and becomes important in later Daoism. They are described as beings that

have moved beyond earthly corruption and are often identified with stellar deities.
6. A unit of distance, equal to about 1/3 mile.

the law. I order you to ensure that when he treats illness the patients recover. If they do not recover, the head of the demon king Gao Linzi is to be broken into ninety pieces.

THE DECLARATIONS OF THE PERFECTED
(*Zhen'gao*)

The *Declarations of the Perfected* (*Zhen'gao*) was the product of a significant new Daoist movement, known as the Upper Clarity (Shangqing) tradition, that revised and ultimately supplanted the previously dominant Celestial Masters. To understand this new movement, we must situate it in the context of the history of the Celestial Masters movement. The Celestial Masters had formed in Sichuan Province in 142 C.E. following the deified Laozi's appearance to Zhang Daoling; after living in a quasi-theocratic kingdom for about sixty years (from about 190 until 215), they ultimately scattered throughout China following the surrender of Zhang Daoling's grandson, Zhang Lu, to the general Cao Cao.

Many Celestial Masters Daoists had settled in the north, but they moved en masse to southern China—particularly to the area of the new southern capital in present-day Nanjing—in 316, after the northern Chinese capital Chang'an (present-day Xian) fell to "barbarian" invaders. This southern migration of northern elites became a catalyst for major social and religious changes in the south, as the old southern aristocracy was displaced and popular southern religious practices were constrained and suppressed. The dispossessed southerners responded to these radical social and religious upheavals by producing a new form of Daoism that sought to trump the old Celestial Masters movement: it claimed access to revelations from deities from more ethereal celestial heights (the Perfected) than those available to the Celestial Masters. The revelations received from those high deities in the Heaven of Upper Clarity (Shangqing) succeeded in defining a new Daoist movement known as the Upper Clarity tradition, thereby helping to restore some of the southern gentry to a higher social position.

The *Declarations of the Perfected* consists of a series of notes on revelations—mostly of minor rites—given between the years 363 and 370 to a spirit medium named Yang Xi (330–386), and to his patrons the father and son Xu Mi (303–376) and Xu Hui (331—ca. 370); they transcribed what the deities wished to relate but would not themselves transmit in base (and impure) human language. As Tao Hongjing (456–536) describes it, in the first passage from the *Declarations of the Perfected* included here, the texts had become corrupt: widely dispersed, poorly copied, and even fabricated. He later gathered those materials, and also added some of his own writing at the end of the text. Tao, a polymath and an important figure in the social and political scene, explains how his detective work enabled him to track certain collections of manuscripts as they moved through different social strata in the region and how his familiarity with the calligraphy of Yang Xi and the Xus helped him distinguish the authentic materials from the numerous spurious works. Because of its exceptional literary value, the *Declarations of the Perfected* has been highly influential within Daoism and Chinese literature more generally.

A particularly evocative section of the *Declarations of the Perfected*, included below, describes the descent of the Highest Clarity deities to Yangxi; it contains a fascinating account of the descent of female deities that is framed as a spiritual marriage. This section is also significant as an example of the Upper Clarity tradition's movement away from certain Celestial Masters practices. In this passage, we find Yang Xi being introduced in proper fashion to the Perfected Consort An by an intermediary named Lady Wang of Purple Tenuity, who instructs him: "The Way of the Yellow and the Red is a method for joining the pneumas of male and female that was taught by Zhang Ling to convert people. It is only one method of joining the Elect. It is not something that the Perfected practice." The rejection of the Celestial Masters' "merging of pneumas" (heqi) sexual rite is obvious here, but perhaps less noticeable is that the highest goal of the Celestial Masters tradition—namely, to become a "transcendent" (xianren, a term often mistranslated "immortal")—is replaced with an emphasis on the "perfected ones" (zhenren), the class of deities highlighted in the title of this work: Zhen'gao, the Declarations of the Perfected. According to the Upper Clarity tradition, the transcendents are at a lower level and ultimately die (one of the reasons why "immortal" is a problematic translation). The perfected, on the other hand, are incorruptible and are described here and elsewhere as (often female) stellar deities who may or may not manifest in human form. Thus, Yang Xi's betrothal and joining of spirits with the Consort An is a "spiritual marriage" devoid of any physical contact, beyond a few teasing touches of the hand.

In passages not included here, the Declarations of the Perfected provides information on various drugs, explains lesser rites, describes Mount Mao (an important mountain both in Upper Clarity history and in religious geography) and supplies hagiographies of the Daoist practitioners who lived there, and describes the realm of the dead (Fengdu); there are records of dreams kept by Yang Xi and the Xus, and transcriptions of Xu Mi's questions to the high deities and their answers. Although the Declarations of the Perfected does not itself rise to the level of revealed sacred scriptures, its explanations are extremely valuable for those seeking to understand the Upper Clarity scriptures.

PRONOUNCING GLOSSARY

Ge Chaofu: *guh chao-fu*   Xu Mi: *hsu mee*
Wei Huacun: *wei hwa-tsoon*   Yang Xi: *yawng hsi*
Xu Mai: *hsu mai*

The Diffusion of the Corpus

The first appearance among men of the Scriptures of the Perfected of Shangqing is to be found in the second year of the Xining reign-period of the Jin Emperor Ai, the first year of the sexagesimal cycle[1] [364]. It was then that the Lady Wei of the Southern Peak, Grand Sovereign of the Purple Void and Superior Perfected-Immortal Directress of Destinies[2] descended and bestowed them upon her disciple Yang,[3] Household Secretary to the King of Langye [who was concurrently] Minister of Instruction. She had him transcribe them in standard script for transmission to Xu [Mi] of Jurong, Senior Officer to the Defensive Army, and his third son Xu Hui,[4] Assistant for Submission of Accounts. The two Xus in their turn set to work at transcribing them over again, put them into practice, and obtained the

TRANSLATED BY Michel Strickmann. All bracketed additions are the translator's.

1. In the Chinese calendar system, days and (later) years were designated with two characters drawn from a set of ten "celestial stems" and twelve "earthly branches," creating a cycle of sixty days/years.
2. The full title of this important female deity in the Upper Clarity (Shangqing) tradition. She is

the deified Wei Huacun (252–334), a libationer in the earlier Celestial Masters movement.
3. Yang Xi (330–386), a spirit medium; see the introduction.
4. Xu Mi (303–376) and Xu Hui (331–ca. 370), Yang's patrons.

Dao. Of all the manuscripts in the handwriting of these three gentlemen extant at the present time, there are over ten individual scriptures and biographies of greater or lesser length, mainly transcripts made by the younger Xu, and more than forty scrollfuls of oral instructions dictated by the Perfected, the larger part of which are in Yang's hand.

"The King of Langye" was the Emperor Jianwen, at the time he was living in the Eastern Palace and serving as Regent.

The elder and younger Xu built a retreat to the northwest of Leiping Shan, behind little Mao Shan.[5] There the younger Xu occupied himself with transcription and practice; he died in the fifth year of the Taihe reign-period [370]. The elder Xu passed away in the first year of Taiyuan [376]. At that time the son of the younger Xu, Huangmin was seventeen years old. He spent several years in assembling the scriptures, talismans and secret registers that had been transcribed. It was at this time that several scrollfuls were dispersed among friends and relatives, and these are the texts that I acquired in Jurong.

In the third year of the Yuanxing reign-period [404], when the capital district was in turmoil, Huangmin took the Scriptures and went to Shan.[6]

Xu Mi's father was once prefect of Shan, where he performed many good works, and his elder brother [Xu Mai] had lived there as well. It is on that account that Huangmin took refuge there.

He was supported by the family of Ma Lang, of Dongchan.

Lang is also known Wengong.

Lang's younger cousin on his father's side, named Han, also provided for his needs. Everyone at that time knew that [Huangmin's great-uncle] Xu Mai had obtained the Dao, and his great-grandfather [the former Prefect] was also much admired, so he was accorded considerable respect. Du Daoqu of Qiantang.

Father of the retired scholar Jingchan

was most enthusiastic concerning the Work of the Dao, and often gave him hospitality. At that time all these people were merely given the scriptures and kept them, without knowing the proper way to study them.

During the Yixi reign-period [405–418], Kong Mo, of the Principality of Lu, who had faith in the teachings of the Dao, was governor of Jin'an. He gave up his post, and in the course of returning [to the capital] reached Qiantang. There he heard of a young master Xu whose father had obtained the Dao, and who had all his sacred texts and other manuscripts. He went to call, but Xu would not receive him. For weeks and months Kong crawled on his knees and beat his forehead on the ground, was assiduous in sending gifts and exerted himself to such an extent that at length Xu had no choice but to transmit them to him. Kong had them transcribed by Wang Xing, an under-official of Jin'an Commandery.

---

5. *Shan* means "mountain."
6. In present-day Zhejiang [a southern coastal province; translator's note].

Xing had faith, and was an able calligrapher and painter as well. It was on that account that he was entrusted with the work.

Kong, when he got back to the capital, only hoarded them up, without ever putting them into practice. During the Yuanjia reign-period [424–453] he was Governor of Guangzhou. After his death, his two sons, Xixian and Xiuxian, very able and diligent scholars, took them and looked them over. They saw that the *Perfect Book of the Greater Cavern* (*Dadong zhenjing*) says, "He who recites this through ten thousand times can become an Immortal." They greatly ridiculed this, considering it to be entirely false. They thought that the Dao of the Immortals demanded elixirs and pharmaka[7] to refine the body as a prerequisite for elevation on high; how could the mere amassing of sound produce [an Immortal's] feathered garb? There were also several Buddhist monks who joined them in denigrating that practice. One said that such things ought not to be preserved, and so they burnt them all then and there. Not a single one survived.

> This was doubtless due to the Other World's not wanting them to be diffused among the uninitiated. Xixian and the others were subsequently executed for conspiring with Fan Ye.[8]

Now when Wang Xing was transcribing for Kong, he had all along been making himself a set as well. Later he started back to the Eastern Region with the intention of studying them. But just as he was crossing the River Zhe he ran into a storm, and only the *Book of the Yellow Court*[9] (*Huangting jing*) was saved. Xing reproached himself severely. He took up residence in the Shan Mountains and had only just begun his recitations when the mountain spirits burnt down his house. He then started to chant it at his open-air altar, but there suddenly came a rain-squall that soaked the paper and blurred the ink, and he was consequently unable to achieve the specified number of complete recitations.

Xing was profoundly conscious of his offense. He broke off all contact with others and wrote out almanacs, which he exchanged for provisions to keep himself alive. His son, Daotai, was Superintendent of the Maritime Bureau at Jin'an, and very well-off. He would frequently come to pay his respects to his father and bring him presents; he also brought two menials to wait on him. But Xing would accept nothing, and ended his days in the Shan Mountains. Thus both Kong's and Wang's transcriptions of the Scriptures of the Perfected were completely destroyed in turn, and as a result never came to be circulated.

> This was doubtless because Xing had not first received them from a Teacher. Such, then, was the consequence of his unauthorised transcription and employment of them.

Then again, there was one Wang Lingqi, a man of talent and refinement, who had his heart set on spreading the Dao. He observed the great influence attained by the Lingbao Scriptures[1] that Ge Chaofu had produced,

---

7. Drugs, potions.
8. Compiler of the History of the Later Han (398–445) [translator's note].
9. The *Most High Jade Scripture on the Internal*

View of the Yellow Court (*Taishang huangting neijing yujing*); see above.
1. The *Numinous Treasure Scriptures* (*Lingbao jing*, ca. 397 C.E.), credited to Ge Chaofu.

and was consumed with envy. Calling on Huangmin, he asked to be given the Supreme Scriptures, but Xu would not consent. Wang then stayed out in the frost and snow until it nearly cost him his life, whereupon Xu, moved by the extent of his devotion, transmitted them once again, to him. Having obtained the Scriptures, Wang returned home leaping for joy. Yet after due consideration he realized that it would not do to publish abroad their most excellent doctrine, and that [the form of] their cogent sayings would not lend itself to wide diffusion. Therefore he presumed to make additions and deletions, and embellished the style. Taking the titles [of scriptures] in the Lives of [Lord] Wang and [the Lady] Wei as his basis, he began to fabricate works by way of furnishing out those listings. On top of that, he increased the fees for transmission, in order that his Dao might be more worthy of respect. There were in all more than fifty such works. When the eager and ambitious learned of this great wealth of material, they came one after another to do him honour and receive them. Once transmission and transcription had become widespread, the branch and its leaves were commingled. New and old were mixed indiscriminately, so that telling them apart is no easy task. Unless one has already seen the Scriptures of the Perfected, it is really difficult to judge with certainty.

> A fair number of such elaborated texts in Wang's hand leaked out, and are still in existence at the present time. Further, when Zhu Sengbiao was studying with Chu Boyu, Chu told him, "Among men of talent in the Empire he was certainly in a class by himself. Once I set out from the capital in the same boat as Wang Lingqi. By time we reached the end of the earthworks at Dunpo Cliff, he had already finished two scrollfuls of "Supreme Scriptures": it was really amazing!" But the Supreme Scriptures had already suffered some adulteration before Lingqi's activities. In the fourth year of the Longan reign-period, the 37th of the cycle [400], Yang Xihe of Hongnong twice chanced to obtain, by Concealed Covenant, more than twenty pieces of Supreme Scripture at Hailing. Of these, several scrollfuls were not authentic. He said that he had then already been searching twelve years for scriptures, which means that his activities began directly after Master Yang's death." Thus not all the admixtures from the Lingbao Scriptures were the work of Wang Lingqi. But his fabrications are certainly in the majority.

These have now come into wide circulation, so that in the capital and the commanderies of Jiangdong there is hardly anyone that does not possess some of them. Beyond the [Yangzi] River, though, they are still not too numerous.

> This must be because, though the Doctrine of the Dao is destined to be promulgated, it is not fitting that its true subtleties be widely diffused. For this reason Wang was made to fabricate these things and put them into circulation.

Once Wang had ventured to undertake these singular innovations, everyone did him honour. He subsequently claimed that they had been bestowed on him by the Perfected themselves, and no longer based himself upon the earlier texts. Xu Huangmin saw the scrollfuls and wrapperfuls burgeon forth and noted the substantial rates of his fees for transmission, the great number of his disciples and his accumulation of gold and silk-goods—and he did not fathom how all this had really come about. He looked on the manuscripts in his own possession as commonplace, locked them away and went to Wang to transcribe *his*. Thereupon both sorts of writings were promulgated together and praised in identical tones. The result was that the Xus and Wang were made each other's peers, and true and false put on an equal footing. "Float with the current, sail with the wind, and you will go a thousand leagues."

Later on there was a certain Cai Mai [?], who also received these ten-odd scrollfuls from Xu. They included a good proportion of autograph manuscripts. He divided them up and transmitted them, and they no longer survive intact.

> Cai Mai preferred to practise lesser teachings, and did not pass on much of the Supreme Scriptures.

When Ma Lang saw how the list of scriptures [supposedly] transmitted by Xu to Wang had grown, he wanted to receive them over again [this time from Wang]. He arranged the fee he was to pay for them and fixed the day it was to be handed over. But all at once he dreamt he saw a jade bowl fall down from heaven and shatter on the earth. When he awoke, he began to wonder if it were not that these scriptures must have been a treasure when in heaven, but when once come down to earth were no longer serviceable. Thereupon he straightaway desisted from his project.

> We may judge that although Ma Lang did not practise or study them, he was nonetheless most diligent in doing the Scriptures honour. His was no ordinary dream, and the interpretation he gave it was excellent. He was doubtless one who obtained the Dao.

In the sixth year of the Yuanjia reign-period [429], Xu Huangmin decided to remove to Qiantang. He sealed up his father's authentic scriptures in a chest, which he deposited in Ma Lang's oratory. He told Lang, "All these scriptures are the relics of my late forbears; you must keep them until I myself return to get them. Even should a letter from me come, take care you do not give them up!" Apart from those, he took with him some ten-odd scrollfuls of scriptures, lives and miscellaneous autograph manuscripts and went to the house of Du [Daoqu, in Qiantang]. He had stayed there some months when he fell ill. Concerned lest he should not recover, he sent someone to get the scriptures. But Lang was enamoured of their calligraphy, and held fast to his previous instructions, [saying] "When a close friend has received strict orders, how should he dare give up such texts without due care?" And so he did not send them. Xu passed away abruptly, and the texts he had taken with him consequently remained in Du's possession. These are the various [autograph manuscripts of] scriptures and other writings [still] in private hands at the present time.

Xu Huangmin's eldest son, Rongdi, returned to the family home [in Jurong] for the period of mourning. When it was over, he travelled up to Shan and approached Ma to get the scriptures. But Ma handled him skilfully, and did not give them up. After this humiliation, Xu took no further pains to obtain them. He stayed on in Shan, and subsequently taught and promoted Wang Lingqi scriptures, as well as transcribing authentic texts. He further added a note at the end of each scripture, stating that "in such a month, of such a year, the Perfected-Immortal N. bestowed this on Xu Yuanyu [i.e. Xu Mai]."

The reason for this was that although many ordinary people at that time knew that Xu Mai had practised dietetics, gone into the mountains and obtained the Dao, they were not familiar with the activities of Xu Mi and his son.

At first no one had any suspicions or realized what he was doing. Over a period of several years, he only got two or three scrollfuls of authentic scriptures from Ma, which for the most part he also divulged.

It is these Wang Huilang and others now have.

In the twelfth year of the Yuanjia reign-period [435] he died in Shan, and was buried at White Mountain.

While Rongdi was in Shan he gave himself over to great luxury and extravagance and had no mind for the study of the scriptures at all. That is why Master He, when staying with Ma, had the good fortune of being able to examine and transcribe them.

Ma Lang and Ma Han revered their treasure of scriptures even more than they would have their father of lord. They always had two young menials, who had faith,

One was named Boshou, the other Pingtou

to wait in constant attendance on them, burn incense, sprinkle, sweep and dust. When supernatural lights and emanations appeared in the room, Lang's wife could generally perceive them. She said there were often Jade Maidens clothed in blue who came and went in the air, like birds in flight.[2] The Ma family subsequently became very wealthy; their property was worth a fortune, and they died at a great age. Lang's sons Hong and Zhen, and Han's sons, Zhi and the others, all continued to keep up the practice. But eventually they came to worship the Buddha, and so let it lapse.

This was probably brought about by the Scriptures' being destined to come forth.

He Daojing of Shanyin was not interested in an official career, and was a skilled calligrapher and painter. When young he wandered about the Shan Mountains, and was hospitably received by the Ma family. They entrusted him with all their scriptures and other manuscripts and things pertaining to the Doctrine. He observed that the calligraphy of the talismans, in its splendour, differed from the usual style. In the eleventh year of the Yongjia reign-period [434] he began to make some traced facsimile copies of them. Ma Han was at that time already living apart in a house of his own, and he too had He do several items for him. That is why the Two Registers remained in Han's possession. Afterwards He took many of the originals, replacing them with his own copies, and returned to live at Qingtan Shan in Dongshu, Shan Commandery. There he set down an account of matters relating to the Scriptures of the Perfected, some two or three pages in length. But He's nature was mean and obstinate; he was unable to devote himself fully to the practice of the Lofty Work, and later on a great deal was either lost or

---

2. These were of course the scriptures' guardian spirits [translator's note].

dispersed. A few remaining scrollfuls are still extant in the possession of his woman disciple, Zhang Yujing, at Houtang Shan in Shifeng.

> He constantly occupied himself with sexual techniques and was, besides that, vulgar enough by nature. The retired scholar Gu Huan heard that he had obtained scriptures and so went to call on him. The first person he saw on arrival was He coming home with a hoe over his shoulder. Taking him for a menial or household servant, Gu asked if Master He were at home. He answered that he did not know and went inside, so they never made one another's acquaintance. Gu stayed there day after day, making every effort, but was still not received. People at the time all thought that He could not free himself from shame at his low estate, and so missed this chance of recognizing the right man.

Now that He had made off with a portion of the scriptures and divulged their contents besides, Ma Lang was furious. He had molten copper poured over the lock of the chest, and made his household swear that it would never again be opened.

In the seventh year of the Daming reign-period [463], when there was famine in the three commanderies of Wu, Shan Commandery had a harvest. The retired scholar Lou Huiming had at one time lived in Shan, and now went back there, taking with him the Master of the Doctrine Zhong Yishan of Yanguan and several of his family, to live off that region. Lou was already accomplished in the writing of petitions[3] and talismans, and he understood both the workings of the Five Elements[4] and the operations of destiny. Ma Hong, for his part, treated him with respect, and he frequented Ma's hall and oratory, where he saw the chest of scriptures. Being already acquainted with the account of the subject that He had written, he would dearly have liked to see its contents. But they were solidly locked up, and he had no way of examining them. In the first year of the Jinghe reign-period [465] he went to the capital. There he had Shu Jizhen of Jiaxing memorialize the emperor to the effect that the texts should be confiscated. But since "Jinghe" was already insane, Lou felt it was not right that the Supreme Scriptures should be divulged to him. He therefore examined the texts and picked out the authentic scriptures and lives and over ten scrollfuls of assorted instructions, and left them in Zhong's keeping. To the capital he only took the *Huoluo Talismans* and twenty-odd short pieces of the instructions of the Perfected, together with the facsimile copies of the Two Registers and other pieces that had been made by Master He. There Shu presented them straightaway to "Jinghe", who glanced them over at the Hualin [Park], and then entrusted them to the Daoists of his household. At the beginning of the Taishi reign-period [465–471] Shu memorialized, that they be removed to his own establishment.

When Lu Xiujing[5] came down to the capital from the South and founded the Chongxu guan, he obtained them and kept them there. After Lu's death they went to [his disciple] Xu Shubiao at Lu Shan, who later brought them

3. The ritual documents used by Daoist priests to communicate with the celestial bureaucracy made up of divine officials.
4. Metal, wood, water, fire, and earth, which are the foundation of the theory of five phases—a set of systematic associations between different categories, including the five directions, five colors, and five viscera (see table 2, p. 135).
5. The scholar who edited the revealed Numinous Treasure scriptures (406–447).

back down to the capital with him. At Xu's death they came into the possession of Lu's nephew, Lu Guiwen.

> Among them were instructions transmitted by the Perfected, in
> the handwriting of Yang and the two Xus, which some later person
> had mounted together in confused sequence, divided into twenty-
> four separate items. In the third year of the Qianyuan reign-period
> [481], the emperor ordered Dong Zhongmin to go to Lu Shan and
> accumulate merit. Dong was interested in discovering unusual
> things of spiritual portent, and so Xu Shubiao divided one of the
> pieces written by Yang into two parts, which he gave him, and
> which Dong on his return presented to Emperor Gao. The emperor
> entrusted them to Dai Qing, Curator of Manuscripts in the Bureau
> of the Five Classics, who took them with him when he left the
> court. After the death of Xu Shubiao, his disciple, Li Guozhi, went
> off with yet another item and the Huo [-lo Talismans?]. Of the mere
> twenty-one pieces that then remained, all have been recovered and
> deposited in the Zhao Tai.[6]

When Lou returned from the capital, he stopped in Shan and went to
Zhong Yishan to ask for the scriptures that had been left in his keeping. But
Zhong would not give them up, and so he began to make transcriptions of
them. Only after a very long time did he obtain a few pieces [of the original
MSS]. As he had incurred Ma Hong's resentment, he removed to Chang Shan
in Dongyang. Ma later went there to recover the scriptures by stealth, but
mistakenly took others instead. It would appear that there were subsequent
losses from Lou's material; at present one or two items may still remain.

> Two scrollfuls have been recovered and deposited in the Zhao Tai.

At a time when Kong Cao still occupied a lowly position, the retired
scholar Du Jingchan went to live at Daxu in Nanshu, Shan Commandery,
bringing with him various scriptures and other writings. It was then that he
studied them with several persons that included Gu Huan, Ji Jingxuan and
Zhu Sengbiao. Gu had already transcribed the scriptures in Lou Huiming's possession, and could more or less recognise the calligraphy of the
Perfected. He thereupon sorted them and selected [as being authentic] a
total of four or five scrollfuls of scriptures and lives and seven or eight
individual pieces of the instructions; these are still in the possession of the
Du family.

> Two scrolls of scriptures, which are authentic, together with the
> instructions of the Perfected, have been recovered and deposited in
> the Zhao Tai. At the end of the Daming reign-period of the Song
> [457–464], Dai Yanxing, the elder brother of Dai Faxing, was Prefect
> of Shan. He, too, loved the Dao, and together with Zhu Xuanxiu of
> Tianmu Shan in Wuxing, was able to transcribe a large part of Du's
> scriptures. Lou Huiming's younger cousins, Daoji and Fazhen, as
> well as Zhong Xing's daughter, Fuguang, were all able to transcribe
> the scriptures owned by Lou and Zhong, and all were on friendly

---

6. Tao's special repository for the manuscripts of Yang and the Xus, at his Hua-Yang Hermitage on Mao
Shan [translator's note]

terms with one another. All traced facsimile copies of the talismans, but these are very poorly done. They tried to prettify them, and added arbitrary embellishments, but in no way did they reproduce the precision and incisiveness of the originals. They committed even more faults in transcribing the scriptures. By the seventh year of the cycle (490), when I set out for Dangyang, several younger scholars were becoming able to make transcriptions of high quality. Pan Wensheng of Shanyin, Du Gaoshi of Qiantang, Jiang Hongsu, of Yixing, and Xu Lingzhen of Jurong, are all accomplished at it. People nowadays know about tracing facsimiles of the two Wangs' model autographs, but have no notion of thus copying the Scriptures of the Perfected. This has in fact begun with me. Nor is it always necessary to outline first and then fill in; one has only to use the full brush in each stroke, and the result will hardly differ in form from the originals. But talismans, no matter what their dimensions, should first be outlined and then filled in.

In the fourth year of the Taishi reign-period [468], [Ma Han] died in Shan. [Zhong Yishan] moved to Tiao Shan in Shining. When [Ma Han's son] Ma Zhi eventually came under the monks' influence and changed his allegiance to the Doctrine of the Buddha, he sent all his Daoist scriptures, some ten scrollfuls, to Zhong. These included all the transcriptions which He Daojing had made for his father, and also some of Wang Lingqi's adulterated scriptures. Only four or five items, together with six or seven pieces of the instructions of the Perfected, were authentic and not included among those that Lou Huiming had already obtained.

> Two scrollfuls of these scriptures and the instructions of the Perfected, etc., have all been recovered and deposited in the Zhao Tai. The remaining texts not recovered after Zhong's death are probably in the possession of his niece and Qi Jingxuan.

Earlier there had been one Chen Lei of Dongyang, who was a dependent of the elder Xu. He was diligent and had faith, and Xu used to let him read the scriptures and other writings, a number of which he explained and transmitted to him. Chen also took autograph manuscripts which he replaced with his own transcriptions; among them was Xu's own *Diagram for Walking the Seven Primary Stars*. After Xu's death he returned to Dongyang. In the thirteenth year of the Yixi reign-period [417], he and two nephews of Wei Xin of Rencheng, the Prefect of Dongyang, compounded an elixir. On its completion, the three of them consumed it one after another, and they all then experienced preternatural effects: presenting the appearance of momentary death, they transformed themselves and vanished away. There is a certain descendant of Chen Lei's, whose byname is Changle, living at present to the north of the Heng River Bridge in Yongkang. The Daoist Fan Xian of Jing Shan frequented him and obtained the transcriptions of scriptures and other writings [that had been made by Chen Lei. But the *Diagram for Walking the Dipper*[7] is still there with him. This text is the one in use at the present time.

---

7. A form of ritual walking, used to purify the ritual arena and the Daoist master; here, it follows the pattern of the Great Dipper, mapped onto the ground.

I have composed a separate list, enumerating the individual scriptures and other writings that are stated above to have been in private hands. Herewith I shall set down the particulars of a few odd items still remaining. One scroll of the *Five Talismans of Lingbao* written by Yang. This was originally in the possession of Ge Can of Jurong. Sometime during the Taishi reign-period [465–471], Ge showed it to Master Lu [Xiujing]. Lu had already propagated the *Red Writing in the Script of the Perfected* and the *Five Manbird Talismans*, etc., in his teaching, and they had by then achieved a wide circulation. He did not want this divergent text to be revealed in addition. Accordingly he got it from Ge by giving him silk-goods, and kept it in the greatest secrecy. It came to the attention of Master Gu [Huan], and he made a great effort to examine it, but Lu would not let it be seen. He transmitted it only to Sun Yuyue of Dongyang, and to his [own] woman disciple, Mei Lingwen. On Lu's death, it too went to Xu Shubiao of Lu Shan. Later Xu brought it with him when he came to the capital. At his death it passed into the possession of Lu Guiwen.

It has been recovered and deposited in the Zhao Tai.

The *Life of Lord Wang*, one scroll, in Yang's writing. This first belonged to Ge Yongzhen of Jurong,[8] then to Wang Wenqing, and finally to the *daoshi* Ge Jingxian of Mao Shan.

It has been recovered and deposited in the Zhao Tai.

The *Flying Steps Scripture*, one scroll, written by the younger Xu. This was in the possession of Yan Qiu of Jurong. Wang Wenqing, of the same locality, obtained it from Yan by giving him money and foodstuffs during the dearth in the seventh year of the Daming reign-period [463], when provisions were scarce. It was subsequently kept in Wang's family.

It has now been recovered and deposited in the Zhao Tai.

Talisman of the Duke of the Western Peak for Interdicting Mountains, Zhao Tai written by the younger Xu, and *Talisman of [Him of] the Yellow Centre for Mastery Over Tigers and Leopards,* written by Yang; together, two short scrolls. Wu Tanba of Shangyu had originally got a gourdful of assorted Daoist writings from Xu Huangmin. Wu gave these two scrolls to Master Chu Boyu. Boyu kept them with him at all times when he was living at Huo Shan of the South[9] and wandering about the mountains. At his death [in 479] they were left in the possession of his disciple, Zhu Sengbiao. Later on, a grandson of Chu's fifth younger brother, named Zhongyan, went to Zhu and obtained them.

They have been recovered and deposited in the Zhao Tai. Wu Tanba was a native of Jumi in Shangyu Commandery, and a man of some ability. He was at first a *daoshi*, and Xu Huangmin gave him a gourdful of writings, all of them very short, assorted practical instructions written by Yang and the Xus. Later he worshipped the Buddha, was ordained a monk, and gave them away to anyone who asked until they were all gone. He subsequently abandoned

---

8. A Daoist practitioner.
9. Huo Shan, sacred peak of the South for Mao

Shan Taoists, was the seat of Lord Mao and the Lady Wei [translator's note].

Buddhism, too, and once more became a layman. He died, finally, while sojourning in Dang. I have not discovered the whereabouts of any of those other writings and instructions.

Scripture of the Great Simplicity on the Five Spirits and the Twenty-four Spirits, together with the *Scripture of the Hidden Way of the Recurrent Prime*, a single scroll, and the *Songs of Yin and Yang of the Eight Simplicities*, one scroll, both written by the younger Xu. Zhang Lingmin of Dongyang chanced to acquire both these scrolls once when on the way to the capital. At that time Zhang was not yet acquainted with the calligraphy of the Perfected, and simply took them for ordinary Daoist scriptures. On his return to Dongyang he showed them to Gu Huan. Gu did not immediately inform him about them, and so Zhang left them there with him. Gu divided [the scroll containing] the *Recurrent Prime* into two scrolls. Only later, when he had realized what they were, did Zhang go and get them back. They are now in Zhang's possession. The *Songs of Yin and Yang* Zhang gave to Master Sun Yuyue.

> They have been recovered and deposited in the Zhao Tai. Zhang says, "At that time there were also several scrolls containing the texts of the *Qusu Jinzhen* and *Jinhua*, among others, stained and torn. Not then realizing that they were in the hand of the Perfected, I did not know enough to make exact tracings of the characters; I merely transcribed the wording, and buried all the original texts of these scriptures."

The *Annals*, one short scroll written on yellow silk by the younger Xu, which he wore on his person. This was originally given by Xu Huangmin to his disciple, Su Daohui. Daohui bestowed it on He Faren of Shangyu. Faren transmitted it to Zhu Sengbiao, who presented it to the *fashi*[1] Zhong Yishan. The retired scholar Lou Huiming saw it and acquired it, and it is probably still in his possession.

Several pages of the *Book of the Yellow Court*, transcribed by the younger Xu from the *Life of the Lady Wei*, together with supplementary instructions of the Perfected. These were formerly owned by Wang Huilang, in the Shan Mountains. Now that he is dead, they must be in the possession of his woman disciple, and his fellow-student, Zhang Lingmin.

There was in Yongxing a family named Xie who at one time gave hospitality to Xu Huangmin. They too obtained a few assorted writings. Later the woman Daoist Fan Miaoluo of Jing Shan was destined to acquire their text of the "Account of the Palaces of Fengdu", a single scroll, in Yang's writing. After Fan's death it came into the possession of her woman disciple, Shen Ou. Shen in her turn gave it to Kong Zong of the Siming Mountains.

> It has been recovered and deposited in the Zhao Tai.

The remainder of the Xie family's texts have now disappeared without trace. It is said that several families in Shanyin and Qiantang possess old scriptures, and I would suppose that they might include autograph manuscripts of the Perfected. Not yet having had occasion to examine them, I hope that such persons as are fond of study and resolute of character may

---

1. Master of Techniques.

seek them out with all diligence. Should such a man chance to discover any, he will know the jade from the shingle at a single glance.

Further, when the younger son of the Lady Wei, [Liu] Xia, went to serve as Prefect of Guiji, he took with him her scripture box and religious robe. He also took scriptures and other writings, which he revered. These later remained in Shanyin, where they must still exist today. But I have not yet had the opportunity to search for them.

Betrothal

On the night of the twenty-fifth day of the sixth month (July 26, 365), Lady Wang of Purple Tenuity[2] descended to me. A divine woman came along with her. This goddess was wearing a blouse of cloud-brocade and outer garments of cinnabar red above and blue below with multicolor patterns that glistened brightly. At her waist was a green embroidered belt from which were suspended more than ten tiny bells. These bells were green or yellow and hung irregularly spaced around the belt. To the left of her belt hung a jade pendant just like those of our world, but a bit smaller.

Her garments flashed with light, illumining the room. Looking at her was like trying to discern the shape of a flake of mica as it reflects the sun. Her billowing hair, black and long at the temples, was arranged exquisitely. It was done up in a topknot on the crown of her head, so that the remaining strands fell almost to her waist. There were golden rings on her fingers and jade circlets on her arms. Judging by her appearance, she must have been about thirteen or fourteen.

To her left and right were two maids. One of these wore a vermilion robe and carried slung on a sash a bag with blue insignia. In her hand, she held another brocade bag about eleven or twelve inches in length and filled with some ten scrolls. A white jade tag closed the mouth of the bag. I saw inscribed upon the tag the words: "Cinnabar Seal of Purple Primordiality for the Jade Clarity Heaven[3] *Divine Tiger Text of Inner Perfection.*"

The other maid was dressed in blue and held in both her hands a white casket bound with a scarlet sash. The casket appeared to be made of ivory. The two maids seemed to be about seventeen or eighteen years of age. The decorations of their clothing were quite out of the ordinary.

Both the divine maiden and her maids had complexions as bright and as freshly translucent as jade. Their five-fragrance perfume filled the room with a delightful scent as if I had lit incense. When they first entered the room, they followed behind Lady Wang of Purple Tenuity. Just as she entered the door, the Lady said to me: "Today an honored guest has come to see you. She wishes to form a relationship with you."

At this, I immediately rose to my feet. The Lady said: "O but you need not arise. You may sit facing each other to make your courtesies." She then sat in the position of master, facing south. On that night I had previously taken up a position on the lower end of the bed platform, facing west. The divine

TRANSLATED BY Stephen R. Bokenkamp. All bracketed additions are the translator's.

2. The circumpolar constellation that surrounded the star that represented the celestial emperor, according to Daoists.

3. The highest heaven (Yuqing), in which the gods dwell.

maiden, noticing this, sat down beside me on the bed platform facing east. Each of us then made our greeting to one another with our left hands.

When we had finished, Lady Wang of Purple Tenuity said: "This is the youngest daughter of the Upper-Perfected Primal Sovereign of the Grand Void, Lady Li of Golden Terrace. Long ago the Primal Sovereign sent her to Tortoise Mountain to study the Way of Highest Clarity. Once she had achieved the Way, she received the writ of the Most High appointing her as Perfected Consort Nine Blossoms of the Upper Palaces of Purple Clarity. She was given the surname An, the name Yubin (Densecloud Dame) and the byname Lingxiao (Spirit Syrinx)."

Lady Wang of Purple Tenuity also asked me whether I had ever seen such a person as this in the world. I responded: "She is numinous! Illustrious! Exalted! Outstanding! I have nothing with which to compare her!"

Hearing this, the Lady laughed out loud and said: "And how do you feel about her?"

I did not venture any further response.

The Perfected Consort sat for a long time without saying anything. In her hands she held three jujubes—at least they looked like dried jujubes, but they were larger, had no pits, and did not taste like jujube, but like pear. First she gave one to me, then one to Lady Wang, keeping one for herself, and said we should eat them. After we had eaten, some more time passed in silence.

After a while the Perfected Consort asked me my age and in what month I was born. I immediately answered: "I am thirty-six. I was born in the *gengyin* year (330 C.E.), ninth month."

The Perfected Consort then said: "Your master is that Perfected Lady of the South Mount[4] (Wei Huacun) who holds power as the Director of Destinies. Her Way is exalted and wondrously complete. In truth, yours is a lineage of great virtue. I have long heard of your own virtues, but I never expected that one day I would be able to discuss with you our predestined affinities. I take delight in the fact that the conjunction of our hidden destinies in fact betokens the intertwining intimacy of kudzu and pine."

Then, using my name for the first time,[5] I responded, saying: "Sunken in this inferior baseness, dust staining my substance, I regard you as distant as the clouds. There is no affinity that would allow me to receive your respect; in fact, I fear for my deficiencies whenever the spirits descend. Now I leap in joy, forgetting my limitations, in the hope that you might instruct me and dispel my ignorance, thereby saving this human, Yang Xi. This is my only wish, night after night."

The Perfected Consort said: "My lord should not speak deferentially. Deferential speech is really not appropriate to this occasion."

There was another long pause. Then the Perfected Consort commanded me, saying: "I wish to present you with a page of writing, so I must trouble you to take up the brush to convey my humble sentiments. Is this possible?"

---

4. Also referred to as Lady Wei of the Southern Sacred Peak.
5. In polite speech, Chinese avoid using the first-person pronoun. One might simply drop the pro- noun altogether or, at a slightly more intimate level (as Yang adopts here), refer to oneself by one's given name [translator's note].

"I obey your commands," I responded. Forthwith, I smoothed out a sheet of paper, dipped my brush, and copied verbatim the following poem:

A Cloud-swathed gate stands above in the emptiness;
Then red-gem tower rises into the densecloud Net.
The Purple Palace[6] rides on green phosphors,
Its spirit-observatories shadowed among jagged peaks.
Within vermilion chambers roofed in malachite,
Upper potencies flash their scarlet auroras.
Looking down, I rinse my mouth with liquid from a cloudvase;
Looking up, I pluck a deep-blue blossom from a crabapple tree.
Bathing my feet in heaven's jade pool (stars in our Sagittarius),
Striking oars in the ox-herder's river (the Milky Way),
I urge on the carriage of effulgent clouds (exteriorized spirits of my
    own body)
And rein in the descending dragons on the Slopes of Mystery.
Shaking out my garments on the borders of this world of dust and
    dregs,
I lift my skirts and stride over the turbid waves.
My desire is to make a bond between mountain and marsh,
To let the rigid and the yielding conform to one another in
    harmony.
Hand in hand, paired in matched purity:
Our Way of supreme perfection will not be depraved.
In Purple Tenuity we have met a fine matchmaker.
I sing that we may receive blessings in abundance.

When I had finished writing, she took the paper and looked it over, then said: "I present this to you to reveal the sincerity of my intentions. You need utter no thanks. If there is something that you do not understand, please just ask."

Lady Wang of Purple Tenuity then said: "I would also like you to transcribe a text to ensure that you understand and to set forth this auspicious event." So I again spread out paper and wet my brush. Then the Lady bestowed upon me the following poem:

Two images—one inside, one outside—melt together;
Like the primal breath which indeed split in two.
This mystic union requires no wedding carriage,
It only awaits your elevation to perfection.
[Lady] of the South Mount has smelt forth shining gold—
Her wondrous perceptions fill your book-bag.
Now your fine virtue reflects into the flying auroras
And, as a result, you have moved a person of the holy heavens.
Riding whirlwinds, companions in quilt-wrapped repose;
When you match her in durability, she will lead you into the crimson
    clouds.

6. One of the three "enclosures," each containing numerous constellations, that made up the sky, according to Chinese astronomers and astrologers; the Purple Palace is at the center of the cosmos.

Enlightened, you protest the barriers between Heaven and humanity,
But the fated numbers already hold your predestined affinities.
The Highest Way, in truth, is not depraved;
It is something unheard of in the world of dust.
Now, with mortal eye, you observe the signs betokening eternal
    union;
I sing forth boldly—this is your fate!

Once I had finished writing, Lady Wang of Purple Tenuity took it and looked it over. When she was finished, she said: "I present this to you. Today it has fallen to me to act both as overseer of your predestined relationship and as the matchmaker who sings your unspoken intentions."

She also said: "Tomorrow, Lady of the South Mount is to return from her journey. The Perfected Consort and I should go to greet her at Cloud-kiln. If we do not return tomorrow, it will be several days before you see us again."

After a long interval, Lady Wang announced: "I am leaving. The Perfected Consort and I should be able to come and see you tomorrow after all."

I sensed her descending from the bed platform, but she had already disappeared. The Perfected Consort remained behind for a moment and said to me: "You have not expressed your deepest sentiments, but I have not failed to notice your intentions. I wish you would give voice to all you feel. Tomorrow I will come again." With these words, she took my hand and pressed it. Then she descended from the bed platform. She had not even reached the door when suddenly I could no longer see her.

Marriage

On the night of the twenty-sixth of the third month [July 27], a host of Perfected came as listed below:

Lady Wang of Purple Tenuity;
The Perfected Consort Nine Blossoms of the Upper Palaces of
    Purple Clarity;
My Teacher, Lady of the South Mount, Director of Destinies of
    the Upper Perfected;
The Perfected One of Purple Solarity;
The Middle Lord of Mount Mao;
The Perfected One of Pure Holiness;
The Younger Lord of Mount Mao;
[and a youth I learned was Wang Ziqiao, the Perfected of Mount
    Tongbo.]

After each had been seated for a long while, the Perfected Consort of Purple Clarity said: "I wish again to tire your hand in writing out a matter that I might clear my mind and forget speech."

I spread out paper and awaited her transmission. The Perfected Consort then spoke, slowly and in a soft voice: "I am the youngest daughter of the Primal Sovereign; the beloved child of Lady Li of the Grand Void. Long ago I began my study of transcendence at Tortoise Terrace [on Kunlun Moun-

TRANSLATED BY Stephen R. Bokenkamp. All bracketed additions are the translator's.

tain[7]] and received my jade insignia from the Most High [Lord Lao]. I accepted the Tiger spirit-registers from the Purple Sovereign and the rose-gem halberd from the Thearch[8] of Heaven. Having received documentation as a Consort of the Highest Perfected, I traveled the heavens of Jade Clarity. Frequently I

> Opened the gates into the Nine Nets with my own hands,
> Tread with my own feet the chambers of mystery.
> Taking celestial form in that holy Void,
> I raised my head to sip from the solar root,
> Joined in feasts at the Seven Watchtowers,
> Emerging to rein on my cloudy chariot.
> Controlling the three celestial timekeepers (sun, moon, and stars)
> I ascended with them.
> Dispersing the effulgent spirits of my own body as rosy mists to
> serve as my flying conveyance.
> It is not that I am unable
> To pick and choose among the highest chambers,
> Search among the scarlet lads,
> Seek a fine match in the palaces of kings,
> Or mate myself to some exalted spirit.
> I could touch the mysterious and draw out a counterpart;
> I could befriend some gentleman in the court of the Thearch.

"It is just that I grasp the crux of things and so seized this rare opportunity, thereby responding to cosmic rhythms and numerological fate. In lowering my effulgent corporeal spirits into the dust and evanescence of your world, I have harnessed them as dragons to plunge below. This was done expressly to summon to me the male who pursues the mysterious and to pursue with him an association wherein I might gain a suitable counterpart. We came together because of predestination. As a result

> Our records were compared, our names verified;
> Our immaculate tallies joined in the jewelled realms—
> Our dual felicity has been arranged:
> We will travel as wild geese supporting one another.
> We will share sips from a single gourd-goblet,
> Toasting the nuptial quilt and knotting our lower garments.
> When you look to your mate for the food she will prepare—
> It is the Perfected drugs she holds inside herself. . . .

"If, from this moment wherein we achieve the Way, we fasten the inner and the outer as securely as metal or stone, intertwining our emotions in shared affection and joining our hearts within the bed curtains, then what need is there to embrace beneath the quilts? If we were to engage in such meaningless contact, would not it only defile your corporeal spirits, bring to grief your cloud-souls, and give free rein to your white-souls?[9]

"It is I who have come to seek familial ties with you, noble lord. There is nothing depraved in what I propose.

---

7. The mythical location of the paradise of the Queen Mother of the West; Daoists view it as the place where the Dao congealed as Lord Lao (the deified Laozi).

8. In Daoism, an emperor in heaven.
9. Seven heavy souls, linked to the earth; the three cloud-souls are linked to heaven and its pneumas.

"Now it can be said that we have achieved our dearest ambitions. Our true feelings are already one. We are about to

> Yoke our team together in the gemmy Void,
> To travel together in the dark mysteries.
> We will together pluck scarlet fruit in the groves of jade;
> Together pick cinnabar blossoms in Wildwind Garden;
> Share with each other the waters of Vermilion Stream;
> Side-by-side bathe on the banks of the Cyan River.
> Clothed in feather capes with purple flowers,
> You in solar cap, I in Lotus crown,
> We will roam carefree the Heaven of Highest Clarity,
> Together joining in audience the Three Primes.[1]
> The eight effulgent-spirits of our bodies will then emerge,
> Bearing us through phoenix portals and cloudy gates.
> We will raise our heads to sup marrow of gold,
> Then sing songs of jade mystery.
> Floating in the emptiness, we'll sleep and feast,
> And meet on high the grand dawn.
> As the music of the spheres issues all around,
> The incense-mother will present us with pleasing vapors.
> Side-by-side, we will observe all as one,
> Taking each other's sashes in our hands, binding together our
>   skirts—

"Will this not be the highest joy? Will this not be the fulfillment of our aspirations?

"If you, noble lord, will only comply with fate and consent to this marriage, I will certainly not decline. Moreover, you should not turn your back on the true and the unseen merely to give free rein to your baser human emotions."

Once she had completed transmitting this to me, she once more took it and looked it over. Then she said: "I present this writing to you in the hopes that it will relieve your hesitations and doubts." As she finished speaking, she smiled.

After a long while, Lady Wang of Purple Tenuity said: "The Perfected Consort's declaration is now complete. The predestined relationship we have discussed is now evident to all. You should no longer harbor any doubts, your mystic apportionment of fate has brought this about."

Then Lady of the South Mount, my teacher, presented writings to me that said: "You have repeatedly moved the unseen to meet with you. It is this mystic fate that brings the two of you together. In response to your destiny, I have come to betroth you and to construct for the first time this destined match. This joining of Perfected persons is a joyous event.

"Though you are announced as mates, this only establishes your respective functions as inner and outer. You must not recklessly follow the filthy practices of the world by performing with her base deeds of lewdness and impurity. You are to join with the holy consort through the meeting of your

1. The three registers of the human body, centered on the head, the heart, and the area just below the navel. The "eight effulgent spirits" refer to the glowing, etherealized spirits created in each of these three areas through Shangqing meditation practice [translator's note].

effulgent inner spirits. I betroth this daughter of a noble Perfected being to you so that, in your intimate conjoinings, there will be great benefit for your advancement and no worries that you will injure or deplete your spiritual forces. Hereafter, you may command the myriad spirits. There will be no further trials of your mystic insight. Your banner of perfection will now overcome all in its path and you may together pilot a chariot of the clouds.

"Long ago, at the suggestion of Lady Wang of Purple Tenuity, I worked out this intention for you. Now all has gone as we had hoped. I am greatly pleased.

"Be cautious that doubts do not again swell in your heart. Yesterday I met with Lady Li of Golden Terrace in the clear void. She said that you still harbor in your heart doubts concerning the correctness of all of this and that there is a trace of regret in your expression. If you go contrary to this action, you will greatly wrong us.

"The Perfected Consort possesses the precious *Divine Tiger Text of Inner Perfection* written in cinnabar and blue. This is far finer than the sort of thing you now own. If, with your fine talent, you seek to copy it, I am certain she will not keep it secret from you. But the joining of your hands in wedlock is not just a matter of texts. You two will ride your effulgent inner spirits into the gem-filled heavens. If there are further matters about which you remain unenlightened, might you not simply ask me in private?"

The Perfected Consort, observing what the Lady had written, smiled and said:

> "We will join hands at the Paired Terraces—
> All sigh in delight at this fine match!
> The twin-yoked conveyance formed of our effulgent spirits,
> With this is accomplished."

The Perfected of Pure Holiness then presented me with a writing that said: "The Way of the Yellow and the Red is a method for joining the pneumas of male and female that was taught by Zhang Ling[2] to convert people. It is only one method of joining the Elect. It is not something that the Perfected practice. I have often seen people practice this and succeed in cutting off their seed, but I have never seen anyone sow this seed and thereby reap life. Among the millions who have practiced this way, none has succeeded in avoiding whippings and interrogations after death in the Three Bureaus.[3] If, among ten million, one person happens to achieve the Way this way, he or she still has far to go to avoid death. Zhang Ling received this practice only for the purpose of instructing mortals. He himself did not practice this method to achieve his own transformation and elevation.

"Be cautious lest you speak of this lower way which pollutes life, or you will injure the correct pneumas bestowed upon you by the perfected heavens. One whose thoughts harbor overflowing desires, whose heart preserves sexual fantasies, and who at the same time practices the higher Way

---

2. Zhang Daoling (34–156 C.E.), the founder of the Celestial Masters tradition; the "method" refers to sexual practices.
3. The Bureaus of Heaven, Earth, and Water.

will have cause to know the punishments of the Three Bureaus. This sort of behavior is as misguided as 'jumping into a fire while holding a piece of jade, in hopes that it will save you' or 'burying a dog in a golden casket.'" . . .

Lady Wang of Purple Tenuity presented me with a writing that said: "As to the joining of effulgent spirits among the Perfected, what is most important is that the mating and love occur between the effulgent spirits of the two parties. Though we call them husband and wife, they perform none of the acts of mortal husbands and wives. It is simply an accessible way to speak about the ineffable. If one harbors thoughts of the Yellow and the Red in one's heart, one will not be able to see the Perfected or join with a spiritual mate. Such a one would in vain labor at the task of self-perfection and would, moreover, be taken to task in the Three Bureaus."

When the cock crowed, Lady of the South Mount presented me with a writing that said: "Now that the cock has crowed, the marriage that we have discussed is confirmed." . . .

[The Perfected of Purple Solarity and the Middle Lord of Mount Mao were the last to offer their words of felicitation and advice. Once they were done speaking] the host of Perfected departed. The Perfected Consort remained behind for awhile. She said to me: "Again I must trouble the noble Lord with a few words." Then she bestowed upon me the following writing:

"You should dissolve your cares in fragrant purity and let your heart be bright at our joining of tallies. Only then will we enjoy constant intimacy in piety and clarity, so that our hidden potencies and flowing effulgences join appropriately. For our joyous meetings, you should arrange your hair. Bind it up high according to the proprieties. You, noble lord, are elevated and of dazzling spirituality. Clear away all further obstructions and forget the base ways of the world."

When she was done speaking, she grasped my hand and descended from the bed platform. Before even reaching the door, she suddenly disappeared.

MASTER ZHOU'S RECORDS OF HIS COMMUNICATIONS WITH THE UNSEEN
(Zhoushi mingtong ji)

Master Zhou's Records of His Communications with the Unseen (*Zhoushi mingtong ji*) records some of the visions received by a young adept named Zhou Ziliang (497–516) between 515 and 516 C.E. In a detailed preface to the work, Tao Hongjing (451–536) describes how he met Zhou and identified him as a precocious young Daoist who enjoyed painting and calligraphy. Zhou became Tao's disciple and assistant in compiling and editing the *Declarations of the Perfected* (*Zhen'gao*; see above). The preface traces the various stages of Zhou's gradual separation from society and his family, as he was drawn ever more deeply into the world of the Upper Clarity Perfected. It includes a touching account of his death after consuming a medicinal elixir that he had concocted following the instructions imparted by one of his divine visitors. As Tao makes clear, this was a precisely calculated death: Zhou's intentions were spelled out in "suicide" notes that he left behind and in a batch of documents that Tao found concealed in a cavern among the peaks on Mount Mao.

Master Zhou's Records of His Communications with the Unseen chronicles how Zhou, like Yin Xi before him, began in 515 to receive his own entourage of important Upper Clarity (Shangqing) "Perfected Ones"—along with a host of lower-level transcendents and functionaries associated with Mount Mao, located southeast of Nanjing. These divine visitors instructed and guided Zhou, and after praising him for the purity of his practice they informed him of his appointment to an important celestial position. According to a couple of the Perfected, who have just returned from a visit to the Palace of Eastern Florescence, his "name was already inscribed on the green tablets." His title, they tell him, is "Overseer, Guarantor of Dawn." Although his registers of life indicated that he still had forty-six years of his allotted life span left, Zhou took his own life on December 6, 516, at the age of nineteen. This "transformation" enabled him to assume his exalted celestial position early, as the Perfected wished.

Dao: *dow*
Laozi: *lao-tzu*
Tao Hongjing: *tao howng-ching*

Zhou Ziliang: *chou tzu-liang*
Zhoushi mingtong ji: *chou-shih ming-tong gee*

From *Tao Hongjing's Preface*

In the seventh year of the reign-period "Celestial Confirmation" (508 c.e.), I was roaming the mountains and seas of the eastern seaboard when I was persuaded to make for Qingzhang Mountain of Yongning. [It happened in this way:]

When I came to the east, I boarded an ocean-going catamaran bound for Mount Huo of Jin'an. Just at dusk, we set sail on the Zhejiang [River], but the ocean tides swept the boat straight for a large island at the mouth of the river with such force that human strength could no longer guide it [and we ran aground]. As a result of this near catastrophe, I headed instead upriver to Dongyang, wishing to proceed from there [overland to the mountain]. While in Dongyang, I happened upon a person of Yongjia Commandery who described the mountain scenery of that area as exceedingly beautiful. I thus changed my plans.

I accompanied this person through the mountain defiles to Yongjia Commandery, where I took lodging with the prefect of Yongning, Lu Xiang. Lu personally accompanied me to stay for a while in the hall of the local Celestial Master parish which, by chance, Zhou Ziliang had just entered as a novitiate. This is how we came to know one another. Contemplating now this predestined meeting, it seems as if the gods had mandated that we be brought together. Were it not so, there is no way to explain how we both happened to come to Qingzhang Mountain.

At this time, Zhou Ziliang was still twelve years of age and was in the process of formally requesting to "enter the mountain and submit to the discipline" as a disciple [of Celestial Master Daoism]. He first received a register of personal Transcendent Powers, the five-thousand-word text of

TRANSLATED BY Stephen R. Bokenkamp. Most bracketed additions are the translator's, but the bracketed "notes" are by Tao Hongjing.

the *Laozi*, and the "Talisman of the Elder of the Western Marchmount[1] for Interdicting Tigers and Leopards" and then devoted himself assiduously to the menial tasks assigned him of tending the incense burners and lamps in the temple. Zhou loved to practice calligraphy and paint as well as to practice other minor skills. Anything he applied himself to he was able to accomplish.

After this, he accompanied me to the Southern Marchmount[2] Huo and later on to Muliu Island (modern Yuhuan Island), serving me day and night with the utmost respect. In the eleventh year (512), he returned with me to Mount Mao.[3] There I bestowed on him the *Charts of the Five Marchmounts* and the *Inner Texts of the Three Luminaries*,[4] formally accepting him as my disciple. In the autumn of the next year, his family and close relations came to the mountain to live, establishing themselves together with Zhou in a temple outbuilding on the westernmost of the three peaks.

On the day of the summer solstice of the fourteenth year (June 20, 515), Zhou suddenly retired to recline in his chamber before noon. He conferred with the spirits for a long time and then emerged. His aunt did not know what he had been doing and questioned him closely about his strange behavior. Zhou told her a bit of what he had seen, as recorded below in his transcripts.

For the next forty or fifty days, Zhou was seen to act very strangely indeed. He would habitually close the curtains and bar the door to his chamber, not letting anyone enter. Alone in his room, he burned incense. Each day, he ate only a single cup-measure of honey-sweetened rice.

Now the Zhou family had originally served profane gods, so the family elders all feared that Ziliang might have been bewitched by some of these deities taking on the guise of Daoist spirits. Some family members even announced that they themselves were in danger of contamination by these perverse energies. They thus interrogated Ziliang closely. He would only answer: "It might after all be a false dream, you have no way of knowing for sure. If you are all so worried about it, you can break relations with me." At this, none of the family members could decide what to do. They determined to let the matter go for the present and wait to see how things would develop.

In the seventh month (August 515), Ziliang received a mandate from the Perfected[5] to mingle in the affairs of the world so that people would no longer be suspicious. From this time on, Ziliang was more active than ever before, bustling about and managing temple affairs.

Several months later, he moved to the Hermitage of Scarlet Solarity, where I was in residence. When I later went in reclusion to the eastern mountain, Ziliang lived alone in the western hall of Scarlet Solarity, managing the affairs of the temple and contacts with outsiders. He entertained both Daoists and laity, all of whom loved and respected him. He was the perfect gentleman by nature, slow of speech and quick of action. It could truly be said that he aided others wordlessly, with uprightness, impartiality, and not a trace of selfishness.

---

1. The Five Marchmounts are a group of five sacred mountains—one in each of the four cardinal directions and one at the center (the Western Marchmount is most often identified with Mount Hua). For the *Laozi* or *Daode jing* (*The Scripture of the Way and Its Virtue*), see above.
2. Also called the Southern Sacred Peak.
3. A significant sacred mountain for the Upper Clarity (Shangqing) Daoist tradition.

4. The Three Luminaries are the sun, moon, and planets.
5. *Zhenren*, a concept that first appears in the *Book of Master Zhuang* (*Zhuangzi*; see above) and becomes important in later Daoism; they are described as beings that have moved beyond earthly corruption and are often identified with stellar deities.

Last winter, in secret accord with the Perfected's instructions, he suddenly required a separate residence. On the pretext of convenience, he requested that he be allowed to build and subsequently set up a rough, three-chambered hut. It took a long time for him to complete this structure. It was not until the tenth month of this year (November 516) that he secretly completed the door and window coverings, the bed platform and curtains.

On the nineteenth (November 28, 516), his uncle came to visit and to present him with fruits [left over from the Lower Prime rites].[6] The uncle noticed that Ziliang stayed in the shadows and averted his face during the visit. No one could explain the reasons for this behavior.

On the twenty-sixth (December 5), Ziliang sealed all of the doors to the western and eastern halls [of Scarlet Solarity]. In his hut, he bathed and massaged himself to circulate the pneuma within his body in preparation for meditation. Then he entrusted his ledgers and ritual implements to his assistant He Wenxing. During the evening, Ziliang carried his quilt and pillows out of his temple residence, saying that he must perform purification rituals or, to others, that he was going on a short trip.

On the morning of the next day, he was alone in his hut. When he later returned to the hermitage, his appearance and speech were as usual. No one noticed anything extraordinary. Again he bathed himself with scented water and put on clean clothes. Then he played chess with Wenxing and read, repeatedly glancing out at the sundial. When the *die* hour had passed (about 3:00 P.M.), he arose, saying, "It is time." He immediately fastened his belt, lit incense, and went to the main hall of Scarlet Solarity where he did obeisance in turn to all of the powers of the Dao. He then returned straight to his hut. Everyone thought that he was preparing to perform the purification rituals he had mentioned.

About the *bu* hour (5:00 P.M.), Ziliang's younger brother Ziping found him in the meditation chamber of his hut burning incense. Ziliang came out to the door and asked Ziping why he had come. Ziping said, "Auntie has become ill. She wants you to come and fix a medicinal broth for her."

Ziliang replied: "I am also feeling a little ill. I was just about to take some medicine. You should go back now. If she is not feeling better, you can come back again." Ziping saw that there was a half-cup measure of liquor heating in a kettle in Ziliang's hut.

Ziping hastily returned to their aunt and repeated Ziliang's message to her. She was greatly alarmed. She immediately ordered Ziping to run back to Ziliang's hut. When he reached the hut, Ziping saw Ziliang lying prone on the floor and did not dare enter. Within a few moments, Ziliang's mother and aunt reached the hut as well and, seeing Ziliang prostrate on the floor, began to wail mournfully: "What have you done? What have you done?"

Ziliang only closed his eyes, raising his hand to snap his fingers three times, and said: "Don't cry out. Don't cry out. You will ruin everything."

Ziliang's mother, in trying to raise his head, stepped on his headcloth. He rolled over, his hand still raised, and repeatedly fumbled with his headcloth, setting it straight. In a moment, his breathing ceased.

Ziliang had ignited in his censer a sliver of frankincense about the size of a cowhage bean. When he died, it had not yet stopped burning. Judging

6. A ritual of confession.

from this, we can estimate that only about half the time it takes to eat a meal had elapsed since he took the elixir. He was only twenty years old.[7]

He had clothed himself only in his undergarments, his sleeping robes and his Daoist ritual robes, the sash of which was tightly tied. He had removed his everyday outer garments and folded them. His face and body were fresh and unblemished, as if he were still alive. Everyone who heard of the event or who saw him was shocked and dismayed.

On the twenty-ninth (December 8), Zhou Ziliang was prepared for burial and a mound was readied on the easternmost ridge. At the *die* hour (around 2:00 P.M.) on the third day of the eleventh month (December 12, 516), Ziliang's coffin was lowered into the ground and earth was carried to form his grave mound.

From this time forward Zhou Ziliang was remote from me in both voice and form—he appeared to me in neither vision nor dream. Such is the gulf of separation between humans and the spirits. But should I not await the proper moment to meet with him again?

The means by which Ziliang achieved the Dao as well as his present rank and style in the spirit world are all layed out in his records. Here I have simply summarized some of his earthly activities as well as what I observed of him to form a preface to his own records.

Four letters, their seals still damp, were found on the bookshelf in Ziliang's lodgings. One was addressed to me, one to his aunt and mother, one to his uncle, and the lengthiest one, of four sheets in length, to the Daoists of the Southern Hall and the eastern mountain. All were farewell letters dated the twenty-seventh. Judging from these facts, Ziliang probably had written them after his return from Scarlet Solarity and before he began to burn the incense. In addition, the kettle was checked. It seemed to smell only of ordinary liquor. Ziliang's earthenware basin had been washed out and was odorless. No traces of drugs were found anywhere. There was really no evidence as to which drug he had used to achieve the Dao. [Note: In Ziliang's *Records* there was a recipe for the "Ninefold Perfected Jade-Liquor Elixir." Presumably this is what he used.]

I am full of remorse about this affair. I regret that I did not earlier look into Ziliang's activities. His letter causes me to blame myself.

I sent people to inspect all of Ziliang's chests and book boxes, hoping to find any records he might have left behind, but not a scrap was ever found. He Wenxing said that on the sixteenth (November 25) Ziliang had burnt two bundles of writings—over a hundred pages—and had not heeded when Wenxing had tried to stop him. Hearing that so many of his writings had gone up in smoke, I was even more aggrieved.

On the morning of the first day of the eleventh month (December 10), I personally went to the cavern of Yankou peak to see what I could find. I saw a large sealed letter-case that had been thrown inside. Climbing to an overhanging precipice, I was able to snag and retrieve it. I then did obeisance, respectfully requesting permission [of the spirits to whom it had been entrusted] and returned with it.

When I opened it, I saw that it was indeed a record of the instructions Zhou Ziliang had received from the Perfected. For the fifth month there were only

---

7. That is, 19; in the traditional Chinese calculation of age, an individual is 1 at birth.

four entries dating from the summer solstice forward. The records for the sixth and seventh months were complete. From the eighth month to the end of the seventh month of this year, there were only scattered entries, briefly outlining what had occurred and what was said. I could not fathom how Zhou Ziliang could have experienced further events such as those of the sixth and seventh months and still not recorded them. But it must be that he purposely abbreviated things in this manner. As I think of these things now, I fear that we will never know more. How could we?

During those weeks when the Perfected first began descending to him, Ziliang had both leisure and quiet. Later, all was hustle and bustle for him and he was forever involved in various duties so that he could not manage to get away by himself much. As a result, when he came to write out his visions, he was only able to record brief entries. I do not think that the instructions and admonitions he received from the Perfected during that period of over ten months could really have been as sparse as this. It is a shame. Not looking into this properly was the fault of his master—my fault.

Also, from the eighth to the tenth month of this year, there is not a single entry. I even looked at the remains of those writings he had burnt, but there was nothing.

That which Ziliang confided to his aunt or to me was in fact only a few items from his records. These items were as follows: (1) On that day when everyone blamed him for sleeping during the day on the summer solstice, he could not but tell something. (2) When he was blamed for ceasing to eat meat, he was forced to state his reasons. (3) That time when he helped me to prepare incantations for summoning rain and the Perfected commanded him to write them out in black ink rather than red, he could not but tell me why he suggested this. (4) When he was told by the Perfected of the divine order canceling my summons to fill a celestial position, the Perfected instructed Ziliang to tell me.

Other than these four occasions, even when questioned he would answer briefly or evasively so as not to reveal the directives of the Perfected. Because of this, I simply stopped asking after awhile.

After we moved to Scarlet Solarity Temple, I would ask him to direct appropriate questions to the Perfected. Later I would repeatedly inquire as to whether he had received an answer and he would always say "not yet," thus keeping the words of the Perfected secret. Looking at his records now, I see that he did indeed receive answers. It must have been that he was afraid to relay responses to such questions because people would give him thank-you presents and then everyone would come to rely on him for information. Then, if he did not ask the Perfected, he would be blamed by people; but if he did ask, he would violate the instructions of the Perfected. This is why he was so secretive about the whole thing.

[Note: The *Records* contain many secret names of the Perfected and Transcendents[8] as well as their precepts and teachings, just like scripture. Just as with scripture, it is required that one purify the scripture table on which the *Records* are placed and the cloth with which they are touched. One must bathe oneself and burn incense before reading them. If one wants to copy them for transmission to others, one must also make appropriate

---

8. *Xian*, Daoists who have achieved extraordinary powers and a higher form of existence (often translated "immortals"); in the Upper Clarity tradition, they are on a lower level than the Perfected.

announcements to all of the gods and to the mysterious possessors of these texts. It is not permissible haphazardly to write out their contents.]

From *Zhou's Records, Annotated by Tao Hongjing*

On the day of the summer solstice (June 20, 515), slightly before noon, I was sleeping on the bed on the south side of my residence. I awoke and ordered Shansheng [note: his aunt's seven-year-old brother] to lower the curtains of my bed. I had not quite fallen back asleep when I suddenly saw a man about six feet in height. His mouth and nose were small and he had sternly knit eyebrows and bushy sideburns that were speckled with white. He looked to be about forty years old. He wore a scarlet robe and a red headcloth topped with cicada-wing decorations and trailing extremely long ribbons. His purple leather belt was about seven inches wide and carried a pouch decorated with a dragon's head. On his feet were purple sandals that made a whistling sound as he walked.

There were twelve persons in attendance upon him. Two held up his trailing robes as he walked. They had their hair in double buns like those of the old women of Yongjia and wore purple blouses and green trousers under skirts. The trousers restricted their steps so that they walked extremely slowly. Three others wore purple trousers, tunics, and flat headcloths. Each bore a jade slip, but I could not make out the writing. The final seven all had white cloth trousers and tunics and white leather boots. Each carried something. One had a rolled mat under his arm, one carried a scepter and a five-colored feather fan, one carried a large scroll, one carried paper, a writing brush and a large black inkstone, another one grasped an umbrella.

This umbrella was shaped like a feather, but it seemed to be made of various colors of silk, so that it was wondrously variegated. It was round and deep, and the black handle was extremely long. After they had entered the room, this person propped the umbrella under the eaves by the door.

The other two dressed in white both carried bags that seemed to be as big as small posts and looked as if they were stuffed with writings. The person carrying the mat unrolled it and put it on my reading couch. It was white and glowing and woven of a grass like a calamus rush mat, though the weave was larger. Six of these servants first entered the room and leaned against Ziping's bed.

As soon as the head-man entered the room, he knitted his brows and said to them, "He is living too close!"

Then he sat down on the mat and leaned his forearm on my bookstand, where my brush and ruler were laid. He grabbed the brush and ruler, placed them in my brush holder, and moved the brush holder to the north side of the stand. He turned to his attendants and said, "Why didn't you bring my writing table?"

"When your lordship set out, you were not planning on coming here," they replied.

That person then addressed me, saying: "I am a deputy in the administrative offices of this mountain. I came to greet you because your conduct is without flaw."

I rose and staightened my tunic but did not answer. He continued: "Today is an auspicious day. It is almost noon; have you performed the purification rituals?"

"I performed the normal morning obeisances and ate. I have not yet learned the purification rites."

"It is permissible to eat at noon on such days, but sleeping on the summer solstice is not beneficial. You should not always be such a sleepyhead," he said.

"I seem to be coming down with something and feel fatigued. I was so tired I could not help but sleep."

"Well, there's no real harm in a little rest," he said.

Just then a wind arose and was about to blow over the umbrella, so he ordered his assistants to see to it.

The youngster Chidou was playing in the courtyard. He came running by and was about to bump the umbrella, but an attendant pushed him lightly to the side with his hands. At the same time, Langshan came to fetch a cup from the shelf and, in so doing, knocked into the attendant and almost fell over, but other attendants caught him in time.

"Who was that youngster?" the deputy asked.

"His family is from Qiantang and is surnamed Yu," I said. "He was sent to this place [by his Buddhist father] to stay for a while."

"Well, do not allow him to run around naked like that or the spirits will see him," said the deputy. He also asked about Langshan.

"His family is in Yongjia. He came to live with Master Tao," I replied.

"Your Master Tao is a person of perfect aspirations. That is why others throw themselves under his protection." The deputy then turned his attentions to me: "Your father was not without minor transgressions during his life. He only resolved these matters some three years ago. For the time being he is in a place where he is no longer troubled by his past misdeeds. He told me that his tomb is in the state of Yue and, even if you were personally to urge him to move it, he would not be willing. You should fill up that trench you have been digging south of here.

"Your father wanted to come with me today but could not because the proper documents have not yet been filled out. In the spring of next year, he will be reborn into a prince's family—you see, he must reemerge into the world since his former transgressions have not been entirely redeemed."

[Note: In the *jiawu* year (514), Ziliang had wanted to fetch his father's casket, but nothing came of it. . . . I went to look and there is indeed a pit that had been filled in.]

"Now your own past lives are a source of blessing for you, so you have come to know the true doctrine. In this life as well you have lost faith with neither god nor man. According to your registers of life, you have yet another forty-six years to live. It is so that 'Just as those born as humans cling to life, those who die and become spirits cherish the mysterious and dark,' but, speaking truthfully, the 'mysterious and dark' is by far superior.

"At present, our office has an open position. We desire that you fill it. The protocols are nearly settled so there is no need for me to say more about that. You are to be summoned in the tenth month of next year. I came to notify you so that you may begin making preparations ahead of time. If you choose to disobey this order, your records will be charged over to the Three Bureaus[9] where the fate of mortals is decided. Do not be imprudent!"

9. The Bureaus of Heaven, Earth, and Water.

My face showed my fear. The deputy continued: "Should you remain in this world, sowing transgressions, how will you ever repay them all? On the other hand, by taking up an official position in my grotto, you will come face to face with heavenly Perfected and roam freely through the administrative centers of the sages. Just consider! There is no better spot below the heavens!"

I said, "I only desire to follow your instructions."

"It is not," he went on, "that you have been without your minor faults. You should meditate on these and repent of them, for if you do not, they may obstruct your progress. Those who practice the Dao do not go about naked or reveal their topknots. [In Chinese belief, ghosts always appeared with disheveled hair. Mediums, when possessed by the spirits of the dead, would thus loosen their hair. To distinguish their visionary practice from that of popular mediums, Daoists always wore their hair in a topknot, which was to be kept covered. Nakedness, too, was to be avoided out of fear of spirit incursion through the unprotected nether orifices of the body.] Nor are they reckless and unrestrained toward the innocent. In all of your actions, as well as in what you eat and drink, you should strictly adhere to the regulations. I will speak with you again shortly, but this is all I want to tell you now. I am returning to my post. If you have any hesitations or doubts, I will not be far. Guard my words and do not reveal them to the uninvolved—this does not, of course, include your fellow aspirants on this mountain."

With that, he arose from his mat. He had not yet gone out the door when he saw beyond the gate several children playing. At this, he turned and added: "Do not allow the children to draw near to the ritual area or the meditation chamber. The meditation chamber contains scriptures. It is positioned on the foundations of a former temple which burned down. There are spirit soldiers still guarding the spot. Your residence is too near to this area. [This is the reason for the deputy's comment ("He is living too close!") on first entering Ziliang's chamber.] Do not enter it lightly. These children are yet innocent, so their actions will be the responsibility of the family heads.

"Further, the cause of your aunt's illness is deep-rooted. Although it will not kill her, it will be difficult to heal."

"Once we seem to have healed her, the illness arises again in her stomach. How can this be removed?" I asked.

"You cannot remove it immediately. I do not know if it can be done in months or even years. If it is possible to determine the blockage in her stomach, I will tell you." The children departed and he descended the steps and disappeared.

NIGHT OF THE SIXTH MONTH, FOURTH DAY [JUNE 30, 515]

The Huayang[1] lad came and bestowed on me the following words:

"If you wish to free your thoughts and join with the spirits, you must not mix in worldly affairs. The person constantly in your thoughts right now only desires to seek her own benefit. If you are unable to aid her, she will be displeased. Though you now serve the honored ones, she bitterly upbraids

1. A center Upper Clarity Daoism.

you. When you are scolded, you should envision the gods within your body. Though you hear, your heart should not receive such words, nor should your mouth respond. It should be as if she were cursing an animal or a bird. After such incidents, you should immediately bathe, since anger is a great defilement which robs the body. Once you are so defiled, the Perfected spirits will not descend to you and perverse pneuma will enter into your body.

"Of old there was one named Liu Wenchang whose master, Li Shaolian, was violent and abusive. Shaolian beat and cursed his disciple without restraint. Whenever this happened, Wenchang would verbally respond. After eleven years, the mountain spirits invaded Wenchang and put him to the test. He thereupon fell prey to perverse influences and was infected with illness. Today he is a common runner in the offices of the Guarantor of Human Destinies. He is able to serve the correct spirits solely due to his loyalty and simplicity in his former life. Li Shaolian is still in the world, where he suffers day and night and may not even see the spirits. Let this be a lesson to you. You must be cautious."

[Note: Last year I heard from members of Ziliang's family that his aunt often practiced by ingesting various talismans (a common Celestial Master practice). She always ordered Ziliang to write these talismans for her. Once Ziliang began to have communications with the spirits, he would be late in writing the talismans or slack off in other ways. His aunt would then scold him bitterly, saying such things as "when one raises a dog, it should bark and chase off rats—no one would bother to raise sand! You only write talismans and copy texts! And now you don't even work at that. What good are you?!?" Each time this happened, Ziliang would get angry. The instructions here probably are the result of these incidents. Now his aunt feared that he was slacking off in his required services to others and often punished him during that period of time. After this, Ziliang, whenever he was scolded, would always just smile contentedly and then go to bathe. Everyone, young and old, thought this very strange.

As to his relationship to his master, I never had an angry word with him or scowled at him. The comparison to Liu Wenchang and Li Shaolian must only be a metaphor for his relationship to his aunt.]

NIGHT OF THE NINTH DAY, SEVENTH MONTH (AUGUST 4, 515)

The Two Perfected Zhou and Wang of Ziyang and the Certifier of Registers, Lord Mao, appeared. Their dress was as before. About a dozen attendants accompanied them, among whom was the lad of Ziyang. They spoke together for a long time and then the Certifier of Registers said to me:

"We have been very busy lately. The affairs of Heaven are many and troublesome for us gods. On the sixth, I went to the Palace of Eastern Florescence and saw that your name was already inscribed on the green tablets. Your position is 'Overseer, Guarantor of Dawn.' You are now my underling. Is this not an exalted position? It corresponds perfectly with your hidden destiny. Though this is not your rank here in the world, you should begin to comport yourself accordingly. . . .

Wang Ziyang said: "This is a great achievement, but I fear that the trials will be difficult."

I then made bold to ask: "How many trials will there be? No matter if the trials are great or small, I fear that this mortal may try to avoid them. How could I not be afraid?"

"There should be two small trials," Wang responded, "perhaps wolves and wild dogs, or strange noises and shapes such as would frighten a mortal. When you see such things you should merely settle your emotions and act with determination. Do not be afraid. If you do not pass these trials, it will only temporarily delay your progress."

The Certifier of Registers went on: "All of the Directors of Destiny and the gods of various localities, together with their scribes, were assembled at the Palace of Eastern Florescence to check the registers of life. Of all people in the world, not one in fifty had a praiseworthy record; not to mention achieving the status of divine Transcendent—those were only two or three in a hundred million! There were also quite a few who had achieved Transcendence and later been dropped from the ledgers. I am beginning to worry that there will be no names left on the registers of Transcendence. This is especially worrisome in that the era is fast drawing to a close and the world is increasingly troubled by calamities. Those whose names were dropped from the registers this month must be reported to the Palace of the Grand Bourne at the turn of the seasons and further have their registers of death reinstated at Mount Tai.[2] Such as these are really pitiable! Some were dropped because they lacked diligence in their practice or because someone who preceded them in death implicated them in the practice of perverse religion. Others were diligent at first but became lax and lost all they had achieved. What a pity!

"On the other hand, there are those who are about to ascend into the cloud-filled heavens; those for whom the sun and moon do not shine in vain. The Perfected descend to such as these and bestow the teachings upon them. Some dwell deep in the mountains; others have studied the Dao for years. No one knows about them. We Perfected often descend to instruct such as you— and who now knows about you?"

"Certifier of Registers Mao is only telling you this by way of exhortation," added Lord Zhou. "Do not slack off while you are here on Earth. You are already approaching the status of a lower Transcendent. You will eventually rise to the rank of middle-level Transcendent and will be able to travel to the Grand Bourne, piloting a chariot drawn by dragons and kirin.[3] Will that not be joyous?"

Lord Wang said: "The exhortations of the Certifier of Registers Mao and of Zhou Ziyang are profound indeed. You should take note of them. On this mountain there are three or four people who have already reached the status of lower-level Transcendent. Do you want to know who they are?"

I then inquired as to the status of my Master, Elder Tao [Hongjing]. He responded: "If you only model yourself on him, your pursuit of Transcendence will be easy. Tao long ago reached the top rank of lower-level Transcendence."

[Note: Originally Ziliang had written "middle of the middle ranks of Transcendence," but this had been crossed out in dark ink and "top rank of lower-level Transcendence" had been written in instead. I do not know the reason for this. Since it says "long ago reached," perhaps I have recently

2. On the significance of Mount Tai, or Taishan, the Eastern Sacred Peak, see the introduction to "Two Poems on Taishan," above.

3. A creature in Chinese mythology, compounded of different animals, that has no Western equivalent.

been dropped two ranks for negligence. Lord Wang said that there were four people on this mountain who had already gained Transcendence, but Ziliang did not ask who they were. I wish that he had.]

So then I asked about my aunt. He replied: "She has no major transgressions, but she must be more diligent. She might achieve Transcendence in a later life, but for this one there is nothing to report."

[Note: Ziliang's aunt was originally from Qiantang and was surnamed Zhang. When she was three, her father died and she returned with her mother to Yongjia. Her mother remarried into the Xu family and the aunt took this surname. When she was ten, she left the family and began to study the Dao with a master in Yuyao, where they set up a meditation hall. She was by nature extremely upright and so was eventually given charge over the son of her younger sister, Ziliang. When she was thirty-five, Daoist officials, in response to governmental restrictions, urged her to leave the order for the sake of convenience and to marry into the Zhu family of Shangyu. (This refers to the 504 edict of Liang Wudi, on the occasion of his conversion to Buddhism, that Daoists all return to lay life.) With this, she fell into the ways of the world (an oblique reference to the fact that she had sexual intercourse with her husband) and, out of shame and remorse, developed her stomach illness. After four years, she took her newborn son and returned to Yongjia. Still, her illness has not been cured. Now, eleven years later, she tells me "since I was young I have never harmed an ant or needlessly broken the stem of a flower. I eat only once each day. Still I regret that my disposition is too stern and that I am harsh with those under me." As Lord Wang says, there is really no grave transgression here, but she is not without her minor flaws. It is probably due to the fact that she was not able to follow the destiny she had given herself to. She has been wronged by the spirits and demons, but since her studies were broken off, how can she achieve Transcendence in this life? Perhaps in two or three more lifetimes she will be more fortunate.]

Then Lord Zhou asked me my name. I was flustered and unable to respond with the name that I had previously been bestowed. I only responded without thinking, "Zhou Ziliang."

"How could you be so negligent?" Lord Zhou angrily shouted. "You are the Daoist Zhou Taixuan (Grand Mystery), with the byname Xuling (Spirit of the Void)! Your worldly name is Ziliang. As written on the jade slips of all the celestial records, your name is Taixuan! Do not reveal this secret name to the profane."

THE MARVELOUS SCRIPTURE IN PURPLE CHARACTERS OF THE LORD EMPEROR OF THE GOLD PORTAL
(Huangtian shangqing jinque dijun lingshu ziwen shangjing)

The two passages below—focused on methods for ingesting solar and lunar pneumas, respectively—are drawn from the *Marvelous Scripture in Purple Characters of the Lord Emperor of the Gold Portal* (*Huangtian shangqing jinque dijun lingshu ziwen shangjing*), one of the key texts that form the larger *Marvelous Scripture in Purple Characters* (*Lingshu ziwen*). The latter is an important example of one of the original Upper Clarity (Shangqing) Daoist texts that were revealed to the spirit medium Yang Xi (330–386) by deities from the highest reaches of the heavens, and it includes instructions on methods for securing the three *hun* souls ("cloudsouls") and controlling the seven *po* souls ("whitesouls"). Because by nature the *hun* souls want to rise up and float away, they need to be restrained. The seven *po* souls, in contrast, are of the earth and rejoice in death, and therefore are considered malevolent; one must surround them with intimidating deities to keep them in check. Other parts of the text discuss elixirs and the figure Li Hong, Sage of the Latter Age; he will appear at the end of the world to rescue the "seed people," a group of elect who have distinguished themselves through their upright practice and their respect for the *Marvelous Scripture in Purple Characters* itself.

In the first section below, the adept is directed to face the rising sun, mentally invoke specific spirits, and visualize the rays of the sun penetrating his or her body through the mouth. The text promises that those practitioners in the sacred mountains who perform this rite "will immediately notice their bodies exuding jade fluids and their faces emitting flowing light." Those still enmeshed in the quotidian world who take up this practice and pursue it for eighteen years are assured that their bodies will be transformed into glowing entities and that they will receive promotion to a high rank in the celestial bureaucracy.

The second section, on swallowing the lunar essence, tells the adept to visualize the new moon and silently intone the secret names of the spirits of the moon. What follows is modeled on the practice related to the sun, just described. After the practitioner ingests the lunar rays, his or her body will also begin to emit light. Both of these texts include instructions for ingesting the proper talisman and stipulate how to practice these rites on cloudy days and nights.

PRONOUNCING GLOSSARY

Huangtian shangqing jinque dijun lingshu ziwen shangjing: *huang-tien shawng-ching chin-chueh dee-chun ling-shu tzu-when shawng-ching*

Ingesting Solar and Lunar Pneumas

THE METHOD FOR COLLECTING AND INGESTING THE FLYING ROOT AND SWALLOWING THE SOLAR PNEUMAS FROM THE PURPLE TEXTS INSCRIBED BY THE SPIRITS OF THE PALACE OF GOLDEN PORTE IN THE HEAVEN OF UPPER CLARITY

Of old, [I] received this method from the Celestial Thearch, Lord of Grand Tenuity.[1] One name of this text is the *Scripture of Red Cinnabar, Essence of Metal, Mineral Phosphorescence, and the Jade Placenta of the Mother of Water.*

You should regularly observe the precise moment of the first emergence of the sun at sunrise. Face the emerging sun in the east and knock your teeth together nine times.[2] This complete, you should in your mind secretly invoke the spirits, calling the names of the cloudsouls of the sun and the bynames of the Five Thearchs[3] of the sun and saying:

> Cloudsouls of the Sun, Orbed Phosphors,
> Envelope of Reflectivity, Green Glare,
> Red lads of the Revolving Auroras,
> Dark Blaze, Whirlwind Simulacra.

Having invoked the spirits in your mind, calling these sixteen words, then close your eyes and seal your fists. Visualize the flowing auroras in five colors[4] from within the sun all approaching to receive your body down to your feet. Then envision these five pneumas rising to the top of your head. With this, the five-colored flowing auroras of sunlight will enter into your mouth. Moreover, within the sunlight auroras there will be also a purple pneuma, as large as the pupil of your eye, but wrapped in several tens of layers and flashing brilliantly within the five-colored rays of sun. This is called the flying root of solar efflorescence, the jade placenta, mother of water. Together with the five pneumas it will enter into your mouth.

Facing toward the sun, you should swallow these auroras, gulping breath forty-five times. Once you have completed this, swallow liquid [saliva] nine times, then knock your teeth together nine times and incant softly:

> Cinnabar pneumas of the vermilion furnace,
> Nurturing germs of the orbed heavens:
> The brittle accepts the pliant,
> Blazing liquids and shadowy blossoms.
> The primal phosphors of the solar chronogram
> Are called the Grandly Luminous.
> Their ninefold yang[5] coordinates transformation,

TRANSLATED BY Stephen R. Bokenkamp. All bracketed additions are the translator's.

1. The name of a constellation that was the administrative locale of the Celestial Thearch, one of the most important deities in the Upper Clarity (Shangqing) tradition.
2. A self-cultivation technique for attaining long life; it also involves ingesting one's own saliva.
3. Heavenly emperors. "Cloudsouls": light souls, linked to heaven and its pneumas.
4. The five colors are green, red, yellow, white, and black.
5. The male principle; the term originally referred to the sunny side of a valley, and by extension it came to be associated with the light, heaven, dryness, and activity.

As the two smoky vapors[6] issue forth,
To congeal my cloudsouls, harmonize my whitesouls.[7]
From within the germs of the five breaths,
The Five Thearchs emerge,
Riding on beams, controlling my bodily form.
I grasp the flying by means of its emptiness;
Pluck the root to achieve fullness.
Heads wrapped in dragon flowers,
Caped in vermilion, belted in green,
Reining on the raven-black, flowing darkness,
Their auroras reflect in Upper Clarity.
I will be presented a writ on jade slats;
The Golden Porte will inscribe my name.
Consuming the flowers of dawn,
I will join in spirit with the Perfected,
Will fly in transcendence to Grand Tenuity,
Will rise above to the Purple Court.

Having completed this incantation, face the sun and bow repeatedly.

Even among Transcendents and Perfected,[8] not one in a million knows the names of the cloudsouls of the sun. This is a mystic and wondrous Way—not one of which those blood eaters[9] with their rotting skeletons might have heard.

When the day is overcast and without sun, you may perform this rite by retaining the sun in vision within a secret room where you lay yourself to rest, so long as the spot is clean. This is because those Daoists who practice in purity and whose essential natures move sympathetically the spirits on high are able to practice this method without even seeing the sun.

Those Daoists who have renounced grain and live in the mountains and forests, who conduct lengthy purification rites on the Five Marchmounts,[1] who have cut themselves off from the dust of the mortal world, or whose far-ranging meditations reside only in clarity and perfection, should daily swallow the auroras of solar root and swallow the essences of Grand Solarity. They will immediately notice their bodies exuding jade fluids and their faces emitting flowing light.

For those who are still involved in external human affairs, who have not yet achieved stillness of body, who float aimlessly along the byways of the world, or whose hearts are bound by ropes and fetters, it is essential that this practice be carried out as described above on the first, third, fifth, seventh, ninth, thirteenth, fifteenth, seventeenth, nineteenth, and twenty-fifth of each month.[2] Each month, you should practice ten times. These are the days on which the cloudsouls of the sun might descend to join with you, when the flying root is overflowing and full, and the Mother of Water might

6. Unidentified; perhaps visualizations related to the sun and moon.
7. Animal souls, linked to the earth.
8. *Xian* and *zhenren*; in the Upper Clarity tradition, the Transcendents—Daoists who have achieved extraordinary powers and a higher form of existence (often translated "immortals")—are on a lower level than the Perfected, who are incorruptible and are often identified with stellar deities.
9. Those connected to popular cults.
1. A group of five sacred mountains—one in each of the four cardinal directions and one at the center.
2. Odd days, and therefore linked with yang.

ward off [your] dreams. If you practice this for eighteen years, Upper Clarity will refine [your form] to golden perfection, so that you reflect a gemmy light. Your rank will reach that of Jade Sovereign and you will fly through the Grand Void, mounted on the efflorescences of the Three Elementals,[3] exalted over all below heaven.

The talisman above is to be written in red on blue paper at midnight on the last night of each month. Face east and swallow it to provide prior notification to the cloudsouls of the sun. Just before you swallow it, block your breath and, grasping the talisman in your left hand, incant silently:

> Cinnabar writ of Grand Tenuity,
> Entitled "Opening Luminescence,"
> Bring to me the cloudsouls of the sun on high,
> To come and transform (so-and-so's) shape.
> Just at dawn, carefully garbed,
> They issue from the Round Court:
> Mother of water as a flying efflorescence;
> The golden essence, solar root.
> Their purple reflections flow within its beams,
> Which are called the Five Numens.

Having completed the incantation, swallow the talisman.

THE METHOD FOR COLLECTING AND SWALLOWING THE YIN[4] FLOWER AND SWALLOWING LUNAR ESSENCE FROM THE PURPLE TEXTS INSCRIBED BY THE SPIRITS OF THE PALACE OF GOLDEN PORTE IN THE HEAVEN OF UPPER CLARITY

Of old, I received this method from the Celestial Thearch, Lord of Grand Tenuity. One name of this text is the *Scripture of Yellow Pneuma, Essence of Yang, and Fetal Germ Stored in Heaven and Hidden in the Moon.*

You should envision the moon, at the time when it is newly emerged. Then, facing the moon in the west, knock your teeth together ten times. This complete, secretly incant, calling the names of the whitesouls of the moon and the bynames of the five Ladies within the Moon, saying:

> Whitesouls of the moon, shadowed artemisia;
> Scented Loveliness, shrouded and scattered;
> Pliant Vacuity, holy orchid;
> Mottled Flower, joined tail feathers;
> Pure Gold, clear and glittering;
> Glowing Visage, displayed atop the estrade.[5]

Having invoked the spirits in your mind, calling these twenty-four words, then close your eyes and seal your fists, visualizing the flowing essences in five colors from within the moon all approaching to receive your body down to your feet. Then envision these five pneumas rising to

---

3. Three colored clouds, made up of different combinations of the five colors.
4. The female principle; the term originally referred to the shady side of a valley, and by extension it came to be associated with the dark, earth, dampness, and passivity.
5. Platform.

the top of your head. With this, the five-colored flowing essences of moonlight will enter into your mouth. Moreover, within the moonlight essences there will also be a yellow pneuma, as large as the pupil of your eye, wrapped about several tens of times and arriving within the five-colored rays of lunar essence. This is called the flying yellow of lunar efflorescence, the germ of the jade fetus. Together with the five pneumas it will enter into your mouth.

Facing toward the moon, you should swallow these essences, gulping breath fifty times. Once you have completed this, swallow saliva ten times, then knock your teeth together ten times and incant softly:

> Mystic gleam, yellow and clear,
> Highest pneumas of primal yin,
> Scatter in profusion your chill whirlwinds,
> Ordering numinous spirits and gathering them in my stomach.
> Empty waves swell over the strand,
> Immediately cleansing and purifying the vessel.
> Moon essences, phosphors of the night,
> Exalted on high in the Dark Palace—
> The Five Sovereign Ladies
> Each maintain the position of mother.
> May the fetus fly in;
> May the newborn babe gradually emerge.
> The circling yin joins thrice,
> Its beams mystically darkening in all directions.
> Pacify my cloudsouls, control the whitesouls;
> May the five embryos circulate.
> As flying essence mounted on auroras,
> They depart the barrens in the east.
> The hair of their heads knotted in numinous clouds,
> Their glowing efflorescence summons the wind.
> With dragon talismans belted on the left,
> Tiger insignia tied on the right,
> They wear vermilion cloaks of phoenix feathers,
> Jade pendants, gold medallions.
> Soaring trees, roots knotted to the slope—
> These are called the Wood Kings.
> The divine toad draws at their roots,
> So that the moon now wanes, now waxes.
> The luminous essence glows within,
> Then spurts forth as a bridge across dark waters.
> Present me with writings and jade slips,
> Inscribe my name in the cloudy chambers.
> I now feed on the lunar efflorescences,
> Joining thereby with the Perfected.
> I will fly as a transcendent to Purple Tenuity,
> There to pay court to the Grand Luminaries.

Having completed this incantation, face the moon and bow repeatedly.

For retaining in vision the sun and the moon, you may either sit or stand as is more convenient.

Among Transcendent officials, not one knows the bynames of the white-souls of the moon. Only those about to become Perfected know them.

When the sky is overcast or there is no moon, you may perform this rite within doors. Carry out the essential instructions just as in the method for swallowing the beams of the sun. Those who daily practice this method will immediately notice their bodies exuding gleaming beams of light and their eyesight filled with flying essences.

In its most essential form, this practice should be carried out on the second, fourth, sixth, eighth, tenth, fourteenth, sixteenth, eighteenth, twentieth, twenty-second, and twenty-fourth of each month.[6] Each month, you should practice eleven times. This is enough to achieve transcendence. These are the nights on which the yin essences fly and merge, when the three pneumas overflow, the lunar waters form efflorescences, and their yellow spirits might descend to join with you. If you practice this for eighteen years, Upper Clarity will refine your cloudsouls and change your white-souls, so that you reflect a gemmy light. You will mount mystically reined phosphors to fly through the Grand Void.

The talisman above is to be written in yellow on blue paper at midnight on the last night of each month. Face east and swallow it to provide prior notification to the whitesouls of the moon after first swallowing the Numinous Talisman for Opening Luminescence. Just before you swallow the lunar talisman, block your breath and, grasping the talisman in your right hand, incant silently:

> Yellow writ of Purple Tenuity,
> Entitled "Grand Mystery,"
> Bring to me the waters of lunar efflorescence,
> To nurture my whitesouls, harmonize my cloudsouls.
> This austere practice of the secret prescriptions
> Issues from the Mystic Pass.[7]
> Stored in heaven, concealed in the moon,
> The Five Numinous Ladies
> Let fly their beams of light in nine paths,
> To illumine my Muddy Pellet.[8]

Having completed the incantation, swallow the talisman.

---

6. Even days, and therefore linked with yin.
7. This is the spot where spirit embryos are to be engendered in the human body [translator's note].
8. Niwan, the central of the nine palaces inside a person's head.

SCRIPTURE OF THE THREE PRIMORDIAL PERFECTED ONES,[1] BY THE IMPERIAL LORD OF THE GOLDEN PORTAL
(Jinque dijun sanyuan zhenyi jing)

Scripture of the Three Primordial Perfected Ones, by the Imperial Lord of the Golden Portal (Jinque dijun sanyuan zhenyi jing) is a fourth-century meditation and visualization manual associated with the Upper Clarity (Shangqing) tradition. The main focus of the text is on the "Three Ones": this supreme trinity exists simultaneously in the universe (macrocosm), as Heaven, Earth, and Humanity, and in the body (microcosm), both as Essence, Pneuma, and Spirit and as deities that reside in the three Cinnabar Fields (*dantian*). Specifically, it teaches a method for maintaining, or holding, them and describes how each divine entity is ingested and settles into its proper place inside the body.

Maintaining these divinities within the body through meditation and visualization is essential to survival: the practitioner is ominously warned, "If you have concentration, but without endurance, or if it endures but is not essential, then The Three Ones will depart. Your body will be an empty house without a master. In this disastrous condition, how could you endure for long?" But if they are held firmly in mind, "then The Three Ones can be seen. If The Three Ones can be seen, then the thousand chariots and the ten thousand horsemen will arrive. The feather-canopied cloud chariots can be mounted. You ascend to heaven in the full light of day and rise up to Taiwei." Taiwei, or Great Tenuity, is both one of the nine palaces located inside one's head and a celestial palace inhabited by the Perfected—the spiritual masters.

PRONOUNCING GLOSSARY

Jinque dijun sanyuan zhenyi jing: *chin-chueh dee-chun san-yuen chun-yee ching*

Jiu ting sheng jing ju: *chiu ting shung ching jew*

Juanzi: *chu-en-tzu*

Shangqing: *shawng-ching*

Transmitted to Juanzi by the Green Youth of the Eastern Sea[2]

It is through these that the Perfected venerates Unity and becomes Perfected: The Upper One, being The Celestial Emperor of the entire body; The Middle One, being The Cinnabar Sovereign of The Crimson Palace; The Lower One, being The Primordial King of The Yellow Court. Together they supervise the twenty-four breaths of the body and bring them in accord with The Twenty-four Perfected of Taiwei.[3]

TRANSLATED BY Poul Andersen. All bracketed additions are the translator's.

1. The Three Primordial Ones (*sanyuan*), a rich term with many associations within Daoism. Here it refers to three divinities in the body that reside in the upper, middle, and lower Cinnabar Fields (*dantian*), explained later in this passage. The Perfected (*zhenren*), emphasized in the Upper Clarity (Shangqing) tradition, are beings that have moved beyond earthly corruption and are often identified with stellar deities.
2. Also known as the Azure Lad of the Eastern Sea. He is a key deity in the Upper Clarity tradition who reveals sacred scriptures. Juanzi, also known as Xuanzi, was a master connected with transmitting a teaching on immortality.
3. Great Tenuity, a heavenly palace.

Breath is that which binds together the insubstantial vapour and produces spirit.

Each of The Three Primordial has a thousand chariots, ten thousand horsemen and a cloud chariot with a feather canopy. With this [entourage] they enter Zigong[4] and ascend to Shangqing.[5] They are recorded in the primordial registers; their rank is Perfected and they fly through the nine skies.

If you can hold them firmly, then The Three Ones can be seen. If The Three Ones can be seen, then the thousand chariots and the ten thousand horsemen will arrive. The feathers-canopied cloud chariots can be mounted. You ascend to heaven in the full light of day and rise up to Taiwei.

In Taiwei there are twenty-four breaths. They commingle in Hunhuang[6] in order that the breath may be bound together and transformed. At a certain time they suddenly disperse. In the breath there are twenty-four Perfected. It is in this way that the breath of the Imperial Sovereigns, The Three Ones, achieves division and transformation.

When you are able to hold The Three Ones of the body [here below], then the Imperial Sovereigns, The Three Ones of Taiwei above will descend and appear outside [your body] in order to speak with you.

In the body there are also twenty-four Perfected. They are also created through the division and transformation of the refined light and clear breath of the body. If the cloud chariots come to meet them and they ascend to Taiwei, then The Twenty-four Perfected of Taiwei, and the gods of the body, will feast together in Hunhuang. Their combined radiance diffuses and soars up; they bring the inner and outer powers in harmony. They go in and out of Shangqing; they stop and rest in Taiwei.

At the same time you should also cultivate Dongfang.[7] Separately situated in Dongfang are The Yellow Portal, The Purple Door and The Chamber of The Mysterious Essence. These are common places of repose of the Venerable Lords, The Three Ones of the body. The reason for cultivating this palace at the same time is that you then more quickly will perceive The Ones. [Those who seek to become] Perfected [by virtue] of Dongfang must have Holding The Ones as their basic practice. [Those who seek to become] Perfected [by virtue] of Holding The Ones must have the cultivation of Dongfang as supplementary practice. Thus The Three Ones are necessary for both, and Dongfang does service for both. Though their abodes are different, yet each is equally indispensable in the practice of the other. If you individually obtain only one of these methods and persistently concentrate on it, then you can no more than enter Taiqing;[8] your rank will be no higher than King of Immortals of Taiqing; you will not be able to roam to Taiwei nor float up to Shangqing.

This is a mark of the ultimate realization of the Perfected Emperor, The Upper One; of the complete realization of the Perfected Sovereign, The Middle One; and of the wondrousness of the Perfected King, The Lower One. The Celestial Sovereign attained ultimate realization and therefore above became The Sovereign Ultimately Realized. The Terrestrial Sovereign attained

---

4. Purple Palace, a celestial domain and the center of the cosmos; Zigong is also the name for a location inside the body (in the chest).
5. Upper Clarity, the high heaven that is the source of the revealed scriptures associated with Shangqing tradition.
6. Probably as allusion to Primordial Chaos.

7. The Palace Chamber, a palace in the head.
8. Great Clarity, the lowest heaven. The source of the teachings and practices of alchemists and the Celestial Masters, in the Upper Clarity tradition it was superseded by the Upper Clarity heaven.

complete realization and therefore above became The True and Only. The Sovereign of Man attained wondrousness and therefore above became The Lord of the Multitudinous Wonders.

The Three Sovereigns[9] came to share in Perfection through Holding The Ones; therefore The Ones did not keep themselves hidden. This was the ultimate realization of their [i.e. The Three Sovereigns'] perfection. The Three Ones were all clearly visible. [The Three Sovereigns] attained Unity and were born. Therefore those mortals who learn from The Three Sovereigns emphasize Holding The Perfected Ones.

When you seek to hold The Perfected Ones your mind must be open and simple, your spirit fixed, absorbed in the exertion of a mysterious influence. Therefore the hundred thoughts are not born, and the meditation is not dispersed. Once you look inward for three months, concentrating on The Ones, then their divine light will be transformed and born, and you will roam together with them outside your body. This is attained from the starting point of simplicity through guiding the thoughts so that they do not disperse, and concentrating on the breath so that it becomes perfectly harmonious. It is the fastest way of reaching the goal. But after simplicity has dispersed and Perfection has departed, then the trivial and false gradually arise, the contentious heart is born in disorder.

Thus The Ones do not appear straight away, the spirits do not respond immediately. It is not that they do not wish to stay, but that he who seeks to fixate them is not concentrated, he who seeks to contemplate them is not discerning. It is only after years of effort that it begins to resemble [the ideal]. If you can purify your heart and hold the world at a distance, concentrate your mind and be without plans, then you will still need three months of exertion before you stand face to face with The Ones.

The Three Primordial are The Noble Perfection of The Nine Heavens, The True Way of The Most High. Thus The True and Only Great Way by means of them [i.e. The Three Primordial] brought forth The Perfected Emperors, The Mysterious Perfection of The True Way by means of them gave birth to the great gods. As for the separation and transformation of The Three Primordial, they were born out of Unity. Therefore the multitude of the Perfected return to Unity, and in this way their mysterious work is accomplished. This [i.e. Unity] is the ancestor of The True Way, the source of The Primordial Breath.

The method of The Three Ones is to be found complete in The Three Primordial. They embrace the sacred books, they treasure the divine scriptures.

The first instruction is *Dadong zhenjing.*[1]

The second instruction is *Dayou miaojing.*

The third instruction is *Taishang suling.*[2]

---

9. Mythical emperors of the ancient past. The term can also refer to the sovereigns of Heaven, Earth, and Humanity.

1. *Authentic Scripture of the Great Cavern*, a central Upper Clarity scripture that teaches the adept how to join the deities in his or her body with the corresponding celestial deities. It also contains a variety of meditation and visualization techniques.

2. The *Marvelous Scripture of Vast Possessions* (*Dayou miaojing*) and *Most High Unadorned in Spirituality* (Taishang suling), fundamental Upper Clarity scriptures, have not survived intact to the present. Parts of each are found combined in the *Scripture [of the Celestial Palaces] of the Immaculate Numen and Great Existence* (*Dongzhen taishang suling dongyuan dayou miaojing*), a collection of scriptures that became significant within the Upper Clarity movement. It apparently was treated as two separate teachings, one focusing on the Vast Possessions (*dayou*) and the other (the third instruction) on the Unadorned Spirituality (*suling*).

Therefore the Imperial Lord, The Upper One, treasures *Dadong zhen-jing*. The Cinnabar Sovereign, The Middle One, treasures *Dayou miaojing*. The Primordial King, The Lower One, treasures *Taishang suling*. These three texts are the quintessential part of The Way to Perfection, the supreme documents of The Three Ones. Moreover they are the 'forbidden instructions' of Shangqing. Truly wondrous and indescribable! This way is not distant! Holding The Ones brings about the appearance of The Three Ones. When you see them, you can ask for these scriptures. You will surely also be entrusted with The Method of Holding The Three Ones, being the first part of The Writings of Perfection of The Imperial Lord of The Golden Portal of The August Heaven of Shangqing, the most wondrous instruction of the multitudinous Perfected.

If you can hold The Ones, The Ones will also hold you. If you can see The Ones, The Ones will also see you. Whether you are coming or going, in all circumstances and during all activities, you must constantly think of The Ones. Eating and drinking, think of The Ones. Happy and rejoicing, think of The Ones. Sad and grieving, think of The Ones. Afflicted and suffering, think of The Ones. In danger and distress, think of The Ones. Crossing fire and water, think of The Ones. Travelling by carriage or on horseback, think of The Ones. In times of crisis think of The Ones.

There are those who think of The Ones, but from start to finish merely gaze; their thoughts are still many. The thoughts must be concentrated.

Ill-fated persons, their will is not firm! Or if it is firm, it cannot endure. They know the names of The Ones but cannot hold them. Or if they can hold them, they cannot be resolute. They boast and bluster but cannot constantly hold [The Ones]. Therefore The Three Ones depart, and then the true breath disappears. If you have lost the true breath, then your breath will be corrupt. If your breath is corrupt, then the day of your death will be near.

When ordinary people study The Way, they seek but the transitory and trivial and have no faith in the worth of The Perfected Ones. At the start they may have the will, but later they will surely go to ruin. This is because their intentions are not united so that the corrupt breath penetrates into them.

The precepts of Holding The Ones warn against lack of concentration. If you have concentration, but without endurance, or if it endures but is not essential, then The Three Ones will depart. Your body will be an empty house without a master. In this disastrous condition, how could you endure for long?

Breath cleaves together and becomes essence; essence is set in motion and becomes spirit; spirit is transformed and becomes The Child. The Child rises and becomes The Perfected. The Perfected ascends and becomes The Infant. These are The Perfected Ones.

Heaven has Three Luminaries, namely the sun, the moon and the stars. They are also The Three Essential. By means of these long life is achieved. Man has Three Treasures. These are the three cinnabar-fields. They are also The Three Perfected. By means of them eternal life is achieved. *Lingbao jing*[3] says: "The Celestial Essential, The Terrestrial Perfected, these three treasures endure forever"; this refers to the above-mentioned.

---

3. *Scripture of the Numinous Treasure.*

The upper cinnabar-field is situated between the two eyebrows.
The middle cinnabar-field is The Crimson Palace of the heart.
The lower cinnabar-field is situated three inches below the navel.
In all, three cinnabar-fields.
The Infant dwells in the palace of the upper cinnabar-field.
The Perfected dwells in the palace of the middle cinnabar-field.
The Child dwells in the palace of the lower cinnabar-field.

Starting from above the space between the two eyebrows and going one inch inward, one comes to Mingtang.[4] Two inches inward one comes to Dongfang. Three inches inward one comes to the palace of Dantian, also called Niwan.[5] Here 'inward' refers to the direction toward the back of the neck. The palace of Dantian Niwan is perfectly square, each side measuring one inch. The purple breath surges up to heaven and shines out to a distance of ninety thousand miles.

[The palace] is covered by the seven stars of The Big Dipper, the bowl of The Dipper is the cover, and the handle points forward and outward. It waxes large and small, a welter of flying forms—it is fixated in the mind. The Upper Primordial, The Infant dwells here, covered by The Dipper. The taboo name of The Infant is Xuanningtian, his cognomen is Sanyuanxian. His rank is Celestial Emperor of Niwan. To his right, facing him, is an Imperial Minister. He is born through the ascent and transformation of the refined spirit of the teeth, tongue and brain. His taboo name is Zhaolejing, his cognomen is Zhongxuansheng. Above he is invested as Imperial Minister.

Together these two rule in Niwan. Both are dressed in scarlet, embroidered robes. They look like newborn infants. The Celestial Emperor holds The Divine-Tiger-Talisman of Shangqing. The Imperial Minister holds *Dadong zhenjing*. They sit either both facing outwards or facing each other. Inwardly they watch over Niwan and the face, eyes, mouth, tongue, teeth, ears, nose and hair. Outwardly they frighten off the manifold demons and evil spirits of The Six Heavens.[6] Once every five days the three *hun*-souls[7] come to pay hommage to them and receive instructions.

The heart is the middle cinnabar-field. It is called The Crimson Palace and protects the center of the heart. It is perfectly square, each side measuring one inch. Its red vapours reach up to heaven and shine out to a distance of thirty thousand miles. It transforms itself in confusion—it is fixated in the mind. The Middle Primordial, The Perfected dwells here. His taboo name is Shenyunzhu, his cognomen is Zinandan. His rank is Cinnabar Sovereign of The Crimson Palace. To his right is a minister. He is formed through the cleaving together and transformation of the refined spirit of the four viscera,[8] whereafter he is invested as a minister in The Crimson Palace. His taboo name is Guangjian. His cognomen is Siling.

Together these two rule in The Crimson Palace. Both are dressed in robes of red brocade. They look like newborn infants. The Cinnabar Sovereign holds in his left hand the planet Mars, in his right hand *Taibao jing*.[9] The minister holds *Dayou miaojing* and The Eight Luminaries.[1] They sit

---

4. Hall of Light; as a location in the body, the term usually designates one of the palaces in the head.
5. Muddy Pellet, one of the nine palaces in the head.
6. A concept connected with the impure demons of popular traditions, which are opposed to the pure deities of the Dao of the Three Heavens.
7. Cloud souls or light souls, linked with heaven and its pneumas.
8. The liver, spleen, lung, and kidneys (the heart itself is the fifth viscera).
9. Nothing is known about this scripture; later texts identify it as the *Scripture of Great Clarity* (*Taiqing jing*).
1. Deities resident in the Cinnabar Fields.

either both facing outwards or facing each other. Inwardly they watch over the muscles, bones, five viscera, blood and flesh. Outwardly they frighten away and dispel the harmful effects of the manifold evil influences. They nurture the light and pacify the spirit, so that one may obtain eternal life and perpetual youth and become a winged immortal in Taixiao.[2] Once every three days the three *hun*-souls and the seven *po*-souls[3] come to pay homage to them and receive instructions.

The place three inches below the navel is called The Gate of Destiny, The Palace of The Cinnabar-field. The Lower Primordial, The Child dwells here. Each side measures one inch. The white breath surges up to heaven and shines out to a distance of seventy thousand miles. It waxes large and small, a welter of flying forms—it is fixated in the mind. The taboo name of The Lower Primordial, The Child is Shimingjing, his cognomen is Yuan-yangchang. His rank is Primordial King of The Yellow Court. To his right is a Guardian Minister. He is born through the binding together of vapour, ascent and transformation of the spirit of the essence, breath and spittle, whereafter he is invested as minister in The Palace of The Cinnabar-field. His taboo name is Guishangming, his cognomen is Guxiaxuan.

Together these two rule in The [Palace of The] Cinnabar-field in the lower division of the body. Both are dressed in robes of yellow, embroidered gauze. They look like newborn infants. The Primordial King of The Yellow Court holds in his left hand, the planet Venus, in his right hand *Yuchen jinzhen jing*. The minister holds *Taishang suling jing* and *Jiuting shengjing fu*. They sit either both facing outwards or facing each other. Inwardly they watch over the four limbs, the juices and blood, and the receptacles: intestines, stomach and bladder. Outwardly they dispel calamity and disaster and repel the manifold evil influences. Three times each day the three *hun*-souls and the seven *po*-souls come to pay homage and receive instructions from The Primordial King.

The method of Holding The Ones:

On the day *lichun*[4] at midnight one sits upright, facing east, exhales nine times and swallows the spittle thirty-five times.[5] Then one fixates the seven stars of The Big Dipper. It comes slowly downward until it rests above one's head, receding toward heaven [i.e. upright], with the handle pointing directly forward toward the east. One fixates it in such a way that the two stars Yinjing (Essence of Yin)[6] and Zhenren (The Perfected) are just above the top of the head, while the two stars Yangming (Brightness of Yang)[7] and Xuanming (Mysterious Darkness) are placed further up. Yangming and Yinjing are behind, Xuanming and Zhenren are in front. At this the thoughts are as if fixated.

When these positions are established one further meditates on the Venerable Lords, The Three Ones. Suddenly they are transformed and emerge; they

2. One of the nine divisions of the celestial sphere [translator's note].
3. White souls, linked to the earth.
4. The names of days reflect the Chinese calendar system, in which days and (later) years were designated with two characters drawn from a set of ten "celestial stems" and twelve "earthly branches"; these combine to create a cycle of 60 days/years.
5. A self-cultivation technique for attaining long life.
6. The female principle; the term originally referred to the shady side of a valley, and by extension it came to be associated with the dark, earth, dampness, and passivity.
7. The male principle; the term originally referred to the sunny side of a valley, and by extension it came to be associated with the light, heaven, dryness, and activity.

appear together in the bowl of The Dipper. After a short while the three ministers are also born in the same way as The Three Venerable. Again after a short while one sees these six ascend together to Xuanming, go east, passing Gangxing, until they reach Tianguan (The Gate of Heaven), where they stop. They all turn toward one's mouth, and further one fixates the vision of them.

The Upper Primordial leans with his hand on the upper minister, The Middle Primordial leans with his hand on the middle minister, and The Lower Primordial leans with his hand on the lower minister.

Thereupon one breathes in once, very deeply. The Upper Primordial and his minister follow with the breath and enter the mouth. They ascend and return to the Niwan palace. Thereafter one breathes in once more, very deeply. The Middle Primordial and his minister follow with the breath and enter the mouth. They descend and return to The Crimson Palace. Thereafter one breathes in once more, very deeply. The Lower Primordial and his minister follow with the breath and enter the mouth. They descend and return to the lower cinnabar-field.

One fixates the star Tianguan and brings it down before the mouth at a distance of seven feet. The Three Ones make their entrance into one's three palaces.

When all this is completed then one meditates to determine that The Perfected Ones are at rest in their respective palaces. Sitting or lying down one meditates on them in the mind. If one has some desires, then one states them inwardly point by point. If one has a request, it can also be presented here. Meditation requires only peace and solitude. One can also meditate in the daytime in a quiet bedchamber.

When one fixates The Three Ones on the day *lixia*, one faces south and meditates as before, on the day *lichun*.

When one fixates The Three Ones on the day *liqiu*, one faces west and meditates as on the day *lixia*

When one fixates The Three Ones on the day *lidong*, one faces north and meditates as on the day *liqiu*.

Having determined through meditation that The Three Ones are at rest in their respective palaces, one very quietly recites the following invocation:

> The five directions are governed by The Dipper,
> spirit brings down the seven stars.
> The Three Venerable emerge and are transformed,
> above they summon The Purple Court.
> The Six Gods come and go
> in the three palaces and at the cinnabar walls.
> Mysteriously they communicate with The Great Emperor,
> below they penetrate to The Yellow Quiescence.
> The Celestial Perfected watch over them
> and summon forth The Six Ding.[8]
> The immortals drift up together with them
> and ride the vapours of The Three Pure [Celestial Regions].
> The four limbs become firm and imperishable,
> the five viscera are born of themselves.

---

8. Protective deities associated with the Chinese calendar system; each has a name containing the character *ding*.

THE WONDROUS SCRIPTURE OF THE UPPER CHAPTERS OF LIMITLESS SALVATION
(Lingbao wuliang duren shangpin miaojing)

The Wondrous Scripture of the Upper Chapters of Limitless Salvation (*Lingbao wuliang duren shangpin miaojing*), usually called simply the *Scripture of Salvation*, was a product of the Numinous Treasure (Lingbao) movement. It is associated with Ge Chaofu (fl. early fifth century C.E.), the central figure in the early Numinous Treasure textual revelations and a descendent of Ge Hong (283–343), who wrote the *Inner Chapters of the Book of the Master Who Embraces Simplicity* (*Baopu zi neipian*; see above). Perhaps because he observed the success of the Upper Clarity (Shangqing) revelations, Ge Chaofu claimed to have access to a corpus of manuscripts that had been revealed to Ge Hong's great-uncle, Ge Xuan. Though this textual pedigree may seem fairly trivial, its implications were profound, since it placed the origin of the Numinous Treasure scriptures before the Upper Clarity revelations granted to Yang Xi (330–386). The Numinous Treasure tradition claimed a provenance not just earlier than the Upper Clarity scriptures but more lofty—a higher heaven. Such self-promotion quickly won the Numinous Treasure scriptures a wide following, and in the years and generations after their appearance they have remained popular and influential, forming the foundation and liturgical core for Daoism down to the present day.

If the Upper Clarity revelations are understood as bringing together the southern religious movements and the Way of the Celestial Masters, then the Numinous Treasure tradition can be seen as going a step further—adding Chinese Buddhism into that mix, while subordinating all those elements to its own doctrine. The Numinous Treasure scriptures therefore represent a body of writings that responded to, incorporated, and modified Buddhist ideas to create an amalgam that appealed to Chinese cultural sensibilities. The most important and best known of them is the *Scripture of Salvation*, which was included on official exams, was later greatly expanded from one chapter to sixty-one chapters, and was chosen to be the opening text in the Ming edition of the Daoist canon.

Like other Numinous Treasure scriptures, the *Scripture of Salvation* shows a palpable Buddhist impact, with Buddhism-tinged vocabulary and ideas throughout. The text also recalls Buddhist scriptures in its form, style, and emphasis on frequent recitation. Perhaps in response to the bodhisattva ideal within Mahayana Buddhism, it repeatedly offers "universal, unending salvation" for all beings. Readers of the *Scripture of Salvation* will no doubt recognize a Daoist version of the Buddha in the main Numinous Treasure deity, the Celestial Worthy of Primordial Commencement. So popular did this deity become within Daoism that the Buddhists eventually had to forfeit the very epithet of the Buddha—Celestial Worthy—that the authors of the Numinous Treasure scriptures had taken from them. The *Scripture of Salvation* also borrows more subtle specific details from Buddhism, such as the opening description of the perfect land being "uniform and flat," just like the Buddhist Pure Lands. Moreover, the name of the bodily location of the spirit Grand Unity is a palace in the head called the "Muddy Pellet" (*niwan*), which is also the transliteration from Sanskrit of the Buddhist term *nirvana*.

The *Scripture of Salvation* opens with the divinized Laozi—Taishang laojun, referred to simply as the Dao—relating the circumstances of its entrance into the world in its present form and its marvelous powers. After he received the *Scripture of Salvation*, the Celestial Worthy of Primordial Commencement undertook an extraordinary ordination ritual, which ended in the gathered multitudes of high deities of the pantheon following him into a pearl suspended in the air. It was from inside this pearl that the Celestial Worthy expounded the scripture.

The first part of the *Scripture of Salvation* emphasizes oral recitation as a means to activate the transformative powers of the text. Upon the first recitation, all those who were deaf regained their hearing; upon the second, the blind regained their sight. Different forms of miraculous healing continued through ten recitations; on the final recitation, the dead—namely, the ancestors—were revived and "All achieved long life." We see here the central claim of this text: the goal of reciting this scripture is, like that of Buddhist Mahayana scriptures, salvation for all.

In the second part of the *Scripture of Salvation* we learn that the text is efficacious because it contains the "inner," or hidden, names of deities and "the sounds of the secret rhymes of all the heavens." The salvific power of the text is based, therefore, on its use of a special kind of language: this "Hidden Language of the Great Brahma" is the language of the gods. Its wide-ranging talismanic powers ("there is no evil that they do not expel and cleanse; there are no mortals that they do not save and complete") are all available to the one who is able to pronounce it correctly when chanting the text.

PRONOUNCING GLOSSARY

Lingbao wuliang duren shangpin miaojing: *ling-pao wu-liang doo-run shawng-peen miao-ching*

Preface

The Dao[1] said:

Of old, in the *Biluo kongge dafuli* land in the midst of the Inaugural Azure Heavens, I received the *Boundless Upper Chapters of the Scripture of Salvation of Primordial Commencement.*[2] When the Celestial Worthy of Primordial Commencement pronounced this scripture, he made ten complete recitations to summon in the ten directions[3] the Great Spirits of Heavenly Perfection, the Most Honored of the Exalted Sages, and the Perfected of Wondrous Deeds in all their countless multitudes who might attend his throne. These beings came, mounted on air. They arrived in flying clouds and cinnabar-red cirrus wisps, in green chariots with rose-gem wheels. Their feathered canopies shrouded the land, while their streaming essences glittered with gemmy light, so that the five colors billowed forth, flashing penetratingly throughout the Grand Void.

For the space of seven days and seven nights, the suns and moons, stars and lodgings, even to the Cogs, Armils, and Jade Transverses[4] of all the Dippers of all the heavens, stopped at once in their rotations. The spirit-driven winds were still and silent. The mountains and seas hid away their cloudy emanations. The heavens lacked even floating haze; the air was perfectly clear in all directions. Throughout the whole kingdom, the earth—all mountains and rivers, forests and groves—became uniform and flat, so that

TRANSLATED BY Stephen R. Bokenkamp.

1. Laozi.
2. Another name for the present work. "*Biluo kongge dafuli*": the name of a heaven in the northeast, written as if it were the transliteration of a Sanskrit name.
3. A common expression in Buddhist texts,

meaning "everywhere": north, south, east, west, northeast, northwest, southeast, southwest, the nadir, and the zenith.
4. The three stars that form the handle of the Dipper. "Cogs, Armils": the four stars that form its bowl.

there were no longer high and low places. All became as cyan jade; there were no other colors. As the multitude of Perfected[5] attended his throne, the Celestial Worthy of Primordial Commencement sat suspended in the air, floating above a pentachromatic[6] lion. When he spoke the scripture through for the first time, all of the assembled great Sages voiced their approval. At once all those in the kingdom afflicted with deafness, both male and female, were able to hear again. When he expounded the scripture a second time, the eyes of the blind were opened to the light. When he expounded the scripture for the third time, the mute were able to speak. When he expounded the scripture for the fourth time, those long lame or paralytic were able to arise and walk. When he expounded the scripture for the fifth time, those with chronic illnesses or diseases were immediately made whole. When he expounded the scripture for the sixth time, white hair turned black again and lost teeth were regrown. When he expounded the scripture for the seventh time, the aged were restored to youth and the young were made strong. When he expounded the scripture for the eighth time, wives became pregnant, while birds' and beasts' wombs were quickened. Not only were those already born made whole, but the unborn as well came whole into life. When he expounded the scripture for the ninth time, the stores of earth were leaked forth; gold and jade lay revealed. When he expounded the scripture for the tenth time, desiccated bones were revivified; all rose up to become human beings again. At once the whole kingdom, both male and female, inclined their hearts to the Dao. All received protection and salvation. All achieved long life.

The Dao said:

At that time, when the Celestial Worthy of Primordial Commencement spoke the scripture for the first time, the innumerable grades of completely perfected Great Spirits in countless numbers from the limitless realms of the east arrived, mounted on air. When he spoke the scripture for the second time, the innumerable grades of the completely perfected Great Spirits in countless numbers from the limitless realms of the south arrived, mounted on air. When he spoke the scripture for the third through the tenth times, the Great Spirits of the west, the north, the northeast, the southeast, the southwest, the northwest, the zenith, and the nadir all arrived in their turn, mounted on air.

When the ten recitations were completed, the Celestial Perfected and Great Gods of the illimitable realms of all ten directions had assembled as one. The entire kingdom, male and female, inclined their hearts and took refuge in the Dao. Those assembled were like droplets of mist or dense fog, countless in their multitudes. They crowded into one-half of the area of the kingdom, so that it tipped to the side, but still they would not be stopped.

At this, the Celestial Worthy of Primordial Commencement suspended a precious pearl, as big as a grain of millet, in the empty darkness fifty feet

5. The *zhenren*, a concept that first appears in the *Book of Master Zhuang* (*Zhuangzi*; see above) and becomes important in later Daoism. Described as beings that have moved beyond earthly corruption and often identified with stellar deities, they are more exalted in the Upper Clarity (Shangqing) tradition than the Transcen-

dents or *xian*, Daoists who have achieved extraordinary powers and a higher form of existence (often translated "immortals," and the status sought by members of the Celestial Masters movement).
6. The five colors are green, red, yellow, white, and black.

above the ground. Then he rose to lead the countless assembly of the celestially perfected Great Gods, the Highest Sages, and the Most Honoured Perfected of Wondrous Deeds of all the innumerable realms in the ten directions into the middle of the precious pearl. When the celestial citizens of the kingdom raised their eyes to look, they saw only the swelling multitudes following into the opening of the precious pearl. Once these had entered the pearl, they disappeared. The inhabitants of the kingdom then dispersed and the land returned to level, so that it no longer tipped to one side.

Straightaway the Celestial Worthy of Primordial Commencement, within the precious pearl, expounded this scripture to the end and, with the host of Perfected overseeing the ordination, transmitted the scripture to me. At this, my rejoicing was beyond description. Once the ceremony was over, all of the heavens returned to their normal positions. With a rush of wind, all was still and without reverberation.

The inhabitants of this heaven, having encountered this scripture and its ritual practice, at once universally achieved salvation and lived out their originally allotted spans of life. None of them died before their time from any injury. Those of the entire land were inclined to the Way and practiced only goodness. They neither killed nor harmed. They were neither envious nor jealous. They were neither lascivious nor thieving. They did not covet or desire. They did not hate or act selfishly. Their words were not frivolously ornate, nor did evil sounds emerge from their mouths. They were benevolent and loving to all equally, so that they treated as family even those not of their own blood. The kingdom was harmonious and the people flourished, in joy and Great Peace.

When this scripture first emerged, it instructed an entire kingdom by means of the Dao. Those with the intention of wholeheartedly revering it as the source of their practice will without fail transcend their generation.[7]

The Dao said:

The scripture that the Celestial Worthy of Primordial Commencement pronounced speaks the inner names of the Thearchs[8] and the sounds of the secret rhymes of all the heavens, as well as of the taboo names of the Demon Kings and the secret names of the myriad spirits. These are not common words of the world. Only the highest sages, those who have already become Perfected beings, who communicate with the mysterious and comprehend the subtle, will be able to completely comprehend these stanzas. When they intone it ten times, the ten heavens will sound forth in the distance, the ten thousand Thearchs will all do obeisance. The rivers and seas will become still and silent; the mountains and marchmounts will hide their clouds. The sun and moon will hold back their refulgence and the Cog and Armil will stop moving. The myriad demons will be physically restrained and spectral essences will be destroyed. Corpses will return to life and the dead will be raised, their white bones forming again into human beings.

When those mortals who have mastered the study recite this scripture, the Five Thearchs will stand guard over them and those in the three realms[9] will bow their heads. Demonic sprites will lose their sight; spectral

7. That is, live beyond their allotted life span.
8. Heavenly emperors; the Five Thearchs are variously identified.

9. Heaven, hell, and the earthly realm of the living.

incursions will be destroyed. Salvation will extend even to the dead, and though they be cut off, they will achieve life. The reason for this is that the polluted pneumas of those still engaged in study are not yet completely dispelled, so that their bodies have not yet become completely Perfected. When they summon spirits of the ten directions, their might is not yet such as to control the celestial governors. Yet they may overcome and control chthonic powers, binding both demons and spirits. Such as these may fend off death, but they are not yet able to revivify the dead.

> Disrespectful chanting of these stanzas
> Brings disaster for the individual.
> Respectfully carrying out the revered rites
> Causes one's family to prosper.
> Generation after generation, these latter will flourish—
> Granted good karmic causes.
> The myriad calamities will not block them;
> Spirit luminaries will guard their gates.
>
> This scripture, venerable and wondrous,
> Alone allows one to walk the Jade Capitoline.[1]
> It provides salvation limitlessly—
> Primogenitor of the myriad ways!
> Lofty and towering, this grand model—
> Its potencies are not to be excelled.

The Dao said:

Whenever anyone chants this scripture ten times, it reaches alike all the various heavens. The myriad generations of ancestors, those souls suffering in darkness as well as those bitterly departed—all alike will be saved and ascend on high to the Vermilion Palace.[2] After the regulation nine years' detainment, they will receive rebirth as honored personages who delight in studying the highest scriptures. Once their achievements and virtues on earth are accomplished, they will all attain the rank of divine Transcendent. Flying up, they will ascend through the Golden Porte[3] to roam and feast in the Jade Capitoline.

When those with higher attainments in the Learning recite and practice this scripture, they will immediately fly up to the Southern Palace on high. When ordinary mortals receive and recite it, they will extend their years and live long lives. At the end of their lives, they will achieve the way of release from the corpse.[4] Their cloudsouls[5] and bodily spirits will be obliterated for only an instant and will not pass through the earth-prisons, but will be immediately returned to the body so that they might roam the Grand Void.

Subtle and wondrous is this scripture. It provides universal, unending salvation. All those of heaven receive its benefits. Its blessings are without count, its grace bestowed on the living and the dead alike. Treasured in the highest heavens, it was not transmitted to the world below. Now, when

---

1. A sacred celestial mountain in a high heaven, according to the Numinous Treasure (Lingbao) tradition.
2. The place where dead spirits are refined in preparation for their next rebirth.
3. A palace in the Upper Clarity tradition.

4. A type of liberation or transformation (also called "release by means of a corpse") in which one feigns one's own death, leaving behind nothing or some relic, and ascends to heaven.
5. Light souls, linked with heaven and its pneumas.

those of highest attainment proffer gold and valuables, binding their hearts in a covenant with heaven, it is to be transmitted to them. If they treat it lightly, leak its contents, or are dilatory with respect to its injunctions, disaster will reach even to their nine generations of ancestors and they will all do hard labor with the demon officers.

Attendant on this scripture are twenty-four Jade Lads and twenty-four Jade Maidens of the Five Thearchs. They guard the spirit text and protect the persons of those who have received it.

The Dao said:

If in the first month you conduct a long retreat and chant this scripture, it will end the detention within the earth of the departed cloudsouls of those of previous generations, transferring them above to the Southern Palace.

If in the seventh month you conduct a long retreat and chant this scripture, you will attain the status of divine Transcendent. Where your name is inscribed in all the various heavens on the white slips of the Yellow Registers, "death" will be scratched out and "life" written over it.

If in the tenth month you conduct a long retreat and chant this scripture on behalf of your thearchs and princes, rulers of the kingdom, your lords and ministers, fathers and sons, then the mandate of the kingdom will be secure. Preserved by heaven, it will long endure, not dying out for generation after generation. For the lords of humanity, it will secure their region; for the citizens it will ensure Great Peace.

If on the days of the eight seasonal nodes[6] you chant this scripture, you will become a Perfected being in the Nine Palaces.

If on the days of your natal destiny[7] you chant this scripture, your cloudsouls and bodily spirits will be purified, and the myriad pneumas will preserve you. You will not encounter vexations, and your body will become luminous. The Three Realms will stand guard over you and the envoys of the Five Thearchs will be sent to receive you. With the myriad spirits in ritual attendance, your name will be written in the highest heavens so that, once your merit making is complete, your virtues fulfilled, you may fly above to Upper Clarity.[8]

The Dao said:

On the days on which you practice this Dao, you should bathe in perfumed water. Then, having purified and observed the prohibitions, enter your chamber. Facing east, knock your teeth thirty-two times to alert the thirty-two heavens on high. Then mentally bow thirty-two times. Shutting your eyes, in stillness imagine your body seated in the midst of tricolored clouds of green, yellow, and white.[9] Both within and without it is obscure and dark. To the left and the right, arrayed closely beside you, are the green dragon, the white tiger, the vermilion sparrow, the murky warrior, the lion,

6. The equinoxes, the solstices, and the first days of the four seasons [translator's note].
7. [Those days] bearing the cyclical designation of the year of one's birth. On these days, which occur six times a year, the Director of Destinies was believed to check one's deeds and enter them in the books of life [translator's note]. In the Chinese calendar system, days and years were named by pairing characters drawn from a set of ten "celestial stems" and twelve "earthly branches," which formed a cycle of 60 days or years.
8. That is, the Heaven of Upper Clarity (Shangqing).
9. These are the colors of the three pneumas: the mysterious pneuma is green, the primal pneuma yellow, and the inaugural pneuma white [translator's note].

and the white crane.[1] The sun and moon, in full luminescence, shine penetratingly into the chamber. From the back of your neck emerges a round image[2] that, with its beams, shines into the ten directions.

When all of this appears clearly before you as described, secretly incant as follows:

> Most High Lord of the Dao of the ultimate Mysterious and Primordial pneumas, summon from this servant's body the official envoys of the left and right from the three and the five Merit Sections, the thirty-two Jade Lads who attend the incense, the thirty-two Jade Maidens who transmit messages, and the thirty-two incense officers, talisman bearers of the Five Thearchs who correspond to this day. They are to inform those on high of what I say. Today is a day of blessings. I now hold a long retreat in the pure hall to practice the ultimate scripture for limitless salvation. Your servant, for the sake of (so-and-so), recites the scripture repeatedly to receive life. I vow that my entreaties should penetrate above to the daises of the most revered High Thearchs of Primordial Commencement who control the highest thirty-two heavens.

Once you have completed this, draw the pneumas into your body thirty-two times. Then face east and chant the scripture.

* * *

Postface 1

The Dao said:

The above two sections contain the secret intonations of the Highest Thearchs of the various heavens and the most holy Demon Kings. They contain the words of the Grand Brahma,[3] which are not the ordinary terms of this world. This language lacks resonance and ornamentation; its melodies lack artful fluidity. Thus it is said that the deepest mysteries are difficult to understand.

These words are treasures of the highest heavens, hidden in the upper palaces of Purple Tenuity[4] in the Mystic Metropolis. According to the Mystic Statutes, they are to be transmitted only once in every forty thousand kalpas.[5] One of higher attainments who contributes gold and valuables as a token of belief and who, in accord with the old statutes, makes a covenant with the ten heavens may then be granted this text.

The Dao said:

The cyclical movements of heaven and earth have their depletion and end. The sun, moon, and five planets[6] have their times of fullness and eclipse. The highest sages and spirit beings, in like fashion, have their times of growth and decay, and those who come late to the Study have their

1. The animals and their characteristic colors associated with the four cardinal directions and the center (above and below).
2. Like the halo that appears on Buddhist and Daoist images of deities in this period [translator's note].
3. In Hinduism, Brahma is the creator god; in Buddhism, he is the god who persuaded the Buddha to teach.
4. The Daoist heaven in which the celestial emperor lives.
5. A kalpa is the Buddhist term (adopted by Daoists) for an aeon, a complete cosmic cycle from the creation to the destruction of a particular world.
6. Jupiter, Mars, Mercury, Saturn, and Venus.

time of illness and injury. Whenever such calamities occur, you should in the same fashion purge your heart and practice the retreats. When you conduct a retreat, you should offer incense and recite the entire scripture ten times at six points during the day. Then fortune-giving power will immediately descend to you, dissolving all unpropitiousness. The boundless script provides universal salvation without end.

The Dao said:

Those who come to the Study late and whose grasp of the Dao is shallow in some cases do not possess Transcendent rank sufficient to have overcome the cycles of rebirth. Such as these must pass through oblivion, passing bodily through Grand Darkness.[7] As they are about to pass through, their fellow adepts and persons of attainment may offer incense and recite the scripture ten times for the salvation of their physical forms in accordance with the law. Their cloudsouls and spirits will then ascend directly to the Southern Palace, where a date will be fixed in accord with their studies and merit so that they might receive rebirth. Through cycles of birth and death they will not perish and will eventually attain the state of divine Transcendence.

The Dao said:

Whenever the cycles of heaven and earth come to their end, you should practice retreats, presenting incense and reciting this scripture. When the stars and lunar lodgings depart from their paths or the sun and moon are darkened by eclipse, you should also practice retreats, presenting incense and reciting this scripture. When the four seasons lose their measure or yin and yang[8] are inharmonious you should also practice retreats, presenting incense and reciting this scripture. When the ruler of the kingdom meets with disaster and the rebellious take up arms in the four quarters you should also practice retreats, presenting incense and reciting this scripture. When pestilential disease spreads and mortals die or fall ill you should also practice retreats, presenting incense and reciting this scripture. When master or companion come to the ends of their lives you should also practice retreats, presenting incense and reciting this scripture. The merit of practicing retreats, keeping the precepts, and reciting this scripture is indeed great. Above, it dissolves celestial disasters and provides surety for the thearchs and kings who rule on earth; below, it drives off pestilential injuries and provides salvation for the masses. It provides a security in both life and death; its propitiousness is unequaled. This is why it is said to provide universal and limitless salvation for the people of heaven.

The Dao said:

Whoever possesses this scripture is able to mobilize its powerful merit on behalf of heaven and earth, the thearchical rulers, and the masses of people. When, in times of calamity, you arouse your faith and practice retreats,

---

7. The Palace of Grand Darkness, where the bodies and souls of the dead are refined and transformed so that they attain long life.
8. The complementary forces that unite to form the Dao: yin, a term that originally referred to the shady side of a valley, by extension came to be associated with the dark, earth, dampness, and passivity—the female principle; yang, a term that originally referred to the sunny side of a valley, by extension came to be associated with the light, heaven, dryness, and activity—the male principle.

burning incense and reciting this scripture ten times, your name will in all cases be recorded in the various heavens and the myriad spirits will guard you. In contradistinction to the aforementioned whose grasp of the Dao is shallow, those who excel in its study will serve as ministers of the Sage Lord[9] in the Golden Porte.

In recording peoples' merits and transgressions, the various heavens do not miss even the slightest event. The Demon Kings of the various heavens will also protect your body and cause you to ascend. Those who are to achieve the Dao in this way must have penetrating insight into the ultimate teachings.

[The Hidden Language of the Great Brahma appears in the text at this point.]

Postface 2

The Dao said:

Above are the Illimitable Tones of the Hidden Language of the Grand Brahma of All the Heavens. The ancient graphs were all one *zhang*[1] square. Of old, the Heavenly Perfected Sovereign wrote out this script in earthly graphs in order to reveal the correct pronunciations. The various heavens will send down spirit kings who fly through the heavens to keep watch over the bodies and record the meritorious strivings of all those who know these pronunciations and are able to chant them during retreats. These things will be reported back to the heavens. The myriad spirits will reverentially honor such persons; chthonic spirits will guard their households. The Demon Kings who render service to the Dao will ensure their elevation to the status of higher Transcendent. When their Dao is complete, they may roam freely throughout the Three Realms, rising to enter the golden portals.

As for these sounds, there is no evil that they do not expel and cleanse; there are no mortals that they do not save and complete. They are the self-actualizing sounds of the Celestial Perfected. As a result, chanting them causes:

> Those who fly through the heavens to look down;
> The highest thearchs to sing afar;
> The myriad spirits to ritually honor one;
> The Three Realms to assemble on one's behalf;
> The masses of evil sprites to be bound and decapitated;
> The demonic essences to disappear of their own accord.

> Chiming and resounding, its reverberating echoes
> Cause all in the ten directions to be reverential and clear.
> Rivers and seas cease moving and are silent;
> The mountains and marchmounts hold back their mists.
> The myriad numinous spirits, trembling, bow down
> As it calls to assembly the massed Transcendents.
> > In heaven, no miasmic vapors;
> > On earth, no ill-omened dust.
> > Wisdom of the hidden leads to full clarity,
> > Illimitable, the mystery of mysteries!

9. Li Hong, figure in the Upper Clarity tradition whose attributes are based on those of the dei- fied Laozi.

1. A unit of length equal to about 10 feet.

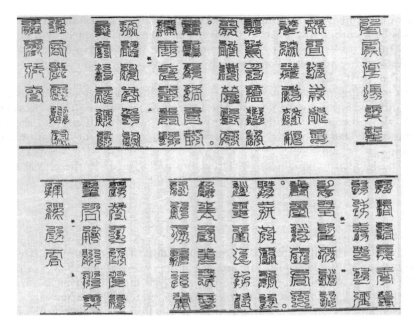

This image of a portion of *The Wondrous Scripture of the Upper Chapters of Limitless Salvation* is written in an esoteric script—referred to as the Hidden Language of the Great Brahma—that is unintelligible to the human reader. This language of the deities in the high heavens contains the "secret rhymes of all the heavens" and is considered to hold talismanic powers.

PURIFICATION RITE OF LUMINOUS PERFECTED
(*Mingzhen zhai*)

The *Purification Rite of Luminous Perfected* (*Mingzhen zhai*) is the product of the original Numinous Treasure (Lingbao) revelations and, like the *Scripture of Salvation* (*Duren jing*; see the previous selection), was revealed by the Celestial Worthy of Primordial Commencement. The text begins with a miraculous, though ominous, vision by the deified Laozi of the Celestial Worthy, who illuminates both the celestial heavens and the earth-prisons (hells), and a short description of karmic causality (good leads to joy, bad leads to pain). Its primary focus on the netherworld and the redemption there of the souls of the damned is thus immediately clear, as it poses the question: What act of merit can save all the souls of the dead? The *Purification Rite of Luminous Perfected* then provides one of the earliest examples of a purification ritual for "universal salvation" (*pudu*), aiding those unfortunate enough to have fallen into the horrible hells as a consequence of their bad past deeds. Although this rite—performed with numerous lamps, copious incense, and some penitential acts of contrition (such as banging one's head on the ground more than 600 times!)—is carried out in the courtyard of one's own home, over a period of some eighty ritually potent days per year, its soteriological benefits flow broadly and universally to others ranging from the heavenly emperor and the ancestors to those creatures "that creep or fly, that wriggle or crawl." Therefore, in this text we see the influence of Buddhist notions of karma and merit transfer, since in this ritual the living can impart some of their own good merit to the suffering dead to aid them in the netherworld.

Mingzhen zhai: *ming-chun chai*
Zuifu yuandui badu shangpin jing:

tsuei-fu yuen-dwei bah-doo shawng-peen ching

The Most High Lord of the Dao advanced, bowed, and said to the Heavenly Worthy: "Today, in attendance on your throne, I was privileged to see the Celestial Youths of the various heavens receive your awesome illumination which lighted not only the Halls of the Blessed of all the heavens but also the earth-prisons of the innumerable worlds. Everywhere the reward of good is joy, the reward of evil, pain. The good enjoy blessings and wander freely and limitlessly. The evil, smeared with soot, are dragged endlessly through the eight sorts of difficulty[1] and no longer enjoy human shape.

"These latter are extremely pitiful. They suffer the results of their evil karma for millions of *kalpas*,[2] never recognizing the root cause of their fate. Is there not some act of merit that might redeem the souls of these dead from the Nine Dark Regions of Everlasting Night so that they might physically enter into the light and achieve rebirth in a fortunate family? If they receive your mercy, they will enjoy grace in life and in death. The departed will know carefree joy and flourish when they come back into the world, enjoying fortune, fame, and a longevity in years. Then, in truth, your mercy will be as clouds that shade the eight reaches of the realm and as breezes that spatter dew on fragrant orchards, so that all men and women yet to be born will come to hear the sounds of the law. I beg that you, O Heaven-honored one, might expound such a method, bestowing on us the proper explanations that all will see the light and achieve peace."

The Heavenly Worthy announced to the Most High Lord of the Dao: "Listen attentively to my words. Seal these good thoughts and right understandings in your heart and ponder them day and night so that you do not forget. I will now expound for you the wondrous sounds of the true law which you may use to redeem the souls of transgressors, releasing them from the Nine Dark Regions of Everlasting Night and the eight sorts of difficulty, eradicating from their hearts the imbedded evil to plant the roots of faith. In both life and death they will know joy. This karma will extend from generation to generation.

TRANSLATED BY Stephen R. Bokenkamp. All bracketed additions are the translator's.

1. That is, the eight forms of rebirth that, according to Buddhist texts, block one's ability to see or hear a buddha: being reborn in hell, as a hungry ghost, as an animal, as a god, in a barbaric area, without vision or hearing, as a devotee of a heretical teacher, or in a time without a buddha.

2. A kalpa is the Buddhist term (adopted by Daoists) for an aeon, a complete cosmic cycle from the creation to the destruction of a particular world. Karma, in Buddhism, is the positive and negative deeds that bear fruit as either happiness or suffering in the future.

"This is an exalted and wondrous method that might be transmitted only once every 400,000 *kalpas*. If there is in the world one worthy and enlightened, then bind that person by oath and transmit it. If this method is kept secret, then good fortune will descend to the possessor; but if it is improperly leaked to others, then misfortune will follow. This is an injunction of wind-borne swords, announced to the Luminous Perfected.[3] One who breaks these regulations has no cause to complain to the heavens."

Thereupon, the Heavenly Worthy commanded the Heaven-soaring Spirit to recite the *Upper Chapters of Salvation through Counteracting the Sources of Blessing and Blame (Zuifu yuandui badu shangpin)*. When he recited this scripture, the sun, moon, and stars in all of the heavens shone dazzlingly into the Nine Dark Regions and the Courts of Everlasting Night in all the illimitable worlds. The bodies of the hungry ghosts and of the dead in penal servitude there were illumined so that they all saw the root causes of their various fates. At this, they were all enlightened. At once, their hearts were fixed on goodness and within them arose the desire to return to the gates of the blessed. They were released from the five sorts of suffering and the three paths of unfortunate rebirth[4] and their karmic guilt was cleansed. At this, the earth-prisons were quiet and vacant. All of the inhabitants, male and female, heard the sounds of the law. Those who responded in their hearts became divine Transcendents.[5]

This is what the Heaven-soaring Spirit said:

According to the *Upper Chapters of Salvation through Counteracting the Sources of Blessing and Blame*, you should regularly practice this purification rite in the six odd-numbered months of each year. In those months, you should observe ten days—the 1st, the 8th, the 14th, the 15th, the 18th, the 23rd, the 24th, the 28th, the 29th, or the 30th—as well as the eight seasonal nodes (the days beginning each of the four seasons, the solstices, and the equinoxes) and the *jiazi* and the *gengshen* days (the 1st and 57th days of each sixty-day cycle).[6]

In the central courtyard of your house, set up a large lamp with nine flames. Light them so that their luminescence will above penetrate to the halls of the blessed in all of the nine mysterious regions of the heavens and will below shine into the Nine Dark Regions of Everlasting Night.

Then, according to the old methods of the awesome rites, perform the ritual calling forth the officials of your body to communicate with and report to the officials of Heaven [in the following manner:] Face toward the east and knock your teeth three times. Then, while holding incense in your fingers, utter the following incantation:

> Most High Lord Lao of the three pneumas—the mystic, the primordial, and the inaugural—of the Three Heavens, call forth from

---

3. *Mingzhen*, deities that are stellar emanations and spirits associated with the four cardinal directions.

4. In Buddhism, rebirth into one of the three evil realms (those of animals, ghosts, and the denizens of hell); it was also possible to be reborn into the realms of gods, of demigods, and of humans. "The five sorts of suffering": identified by the translator as "the representative punishments of the earth-prisons: (1) embracing the fiery bronze pillar, (2) impalement on the moun-

tain of swords, (3) climbing the tree of blades, (4) being boiled in a pot, and (5) swallowing coals and ashes."

5. *Xian*, in the Upper Clarity (Shangqing) tradition on a lower level than the Perfected (*zhenren*).

6. In the Chinese calendar system, days and (later) years were designated with two characters drawn from a set of ten "celestial stems" and twelve "earthly branches," creating a cycle of sixty days or years.

my body the merit officers of the three and the five:[7] the official envoys of the left and right, the runners mounted on dragons of the left and right, the incense-bearing golden lads, the message-bearing jade maidens, and those directly commissioned by the Five Thearchs,[8] thirty-two persons of each class. Issuing forth, they are to inform the Perfected officers of this area that I am now burning incense to communicate with the spirits. I vow that the correct and perfected breaths of the ten directions[9] might enter into my body to bear all of my vows swiftly and directly to those above.

Above you should call from the myriad armed and mounted warriors of the Celestial Transcendents, the Earth-bound Transcendents, the Perfected Ones, the Flying Transcendents, the sun and moon, the planets and constellations, the Nine Palaces, the Five Thearchs, the Five Marchmounts, the Three Rivers, and the four seas,[1] thirty-two riders of each class. Also call on the attendants of the thirty-two heavens who oversee purification rituals, the incense-bearing golden lads, the flower-strewing jade maidens, and those directly commissioned by the Five Thearchs, thirty-two persons from each class. Together with the envoys mounted on flying dragons who announce affairs, these deities should all descend en masse to oversee the purification ritual and the ritual hall. In this manner, your incense fumes and your vows will both penetrate immediately to those above. Once your practice of the Dao is complete, these spirits and powers will all return forthwith to the palaces of the heavens to report.

During the day you should burn incense and at night light the lamps, so that the fires are never extinguished.

Once the scriptures are exposed in the center of the courtyard below the nine lamps and you have circled the lamps to present incense and to deliver the above vows, you should then make nine bows to the east and say:

Now I [fill in your name] take refuge in the Heavenly Worthy of the Numinous Treasure, overseer of the illimitable realms of the east, in all of the great sages who have already achieved the Dao, in all of the supreme Perfected lords, in the venerable ones, in the celestial lords of the nine pneumas, and in all of the spiritual officers of the east. As a result of this bond of trust, I now perform this purification ritual, burning incense and lighting lamps that the merit of this rite will illuminate all of the heavens and universally provide salvation for the emperor and princes, rulers of our kingdom, their officials, envoys, and subjects, all Masters of the Law who have received the Dao, my father and mother and venerable ancestors, my fellow students of the Way, the members of my household, Daoists studying in reclusion in the mountains and forests, and all worthies, even unto all forms of life that creep or fly, that wriggle or crawl, and which are endowed with breath. May they all alike obtain release from the ten

7. There are many different combinations of "the three and the five" in Daoist texts. "The Three Heavens": the heavens of Great Clarity (Taiqing), Jade Clarity (Yuqing), and Upper Clarity (Shangqing).
8. Heavenly emperors. "Jade maidens": goddesses who serve as attendants in heaven.
9. A common expression in Buddhist texts,

meaning "everywhere": north, south, east, west, northeast, northwest, southeast, southwest, the nadir, and the zenith.
1. The four major oceans known to the ancient Chinese. "The Five Marchmounts": a group of five sacred mountains—one in each of the four cardinal directions and one at the center.

sorts of suffering[2] and eight sorts of difficulty. May they reside in inaction and all come to experience self-realization.

Let the brilliance also shine on the millions of ancestors of the [*insert your surname*] family whose departed souls now serve as captive laborers in the earth-prisons that they all might find release and be implanted with the roots of faith. May they depart forever from the five roads leading to suffering[3] and may their karma from previous lives be erased. In death may they enjoy extended bliss and in life blessings. May all realms below the heavens enjoy great peace! May the Way and its power flourish!

Now therefore, I burn incense, taking refuge of my own accord in the virtue of the master, the Heavenly Worthy, in the great sages, and in the highest Perfected. Once I have achieved the Way, I will rise into the formless to join in perfection with the Dao.

Having completed this vow, remove your headcloth and kowtow, knocking your forehead on the ground eighty-one times.

Next face south and bow three times, saying:

Now I [*fill in name*] take refuge[4] in the Heavenly Worthy of the Numinous Treasure, overseer of the illimitable realms of the south, in all of the great sages who have already achieved the Dao, in all of the supreme Perfected lords, in the venerable ones, in the celestial lords of the three pneumas, and in all of the spiritual officers of the south. . . .

The rest of the vow is the same as that above. When you are finished, remove your headcloth and kowtow, knocking your forehead to the ground twenty-seven times.

Next face west and bow seven times, saying:

Now I [*fill in name*] take refuge in the Heavenly Worthy of the Numinous Treasure, overseer of the illimitable realms of the west, in all of the great sages who have already achieved the Dao, in all of the supreme Perfected lords, in the venerable ones, in the celestial lords of the seven pneumas, and in all of the spiritual officers of the west. . . .

The rest of the vow is the same as that above. When you are finished, remove your headcloth and kowtow, knocking your forehead to the ground sixty-three times.

Next face north and bow five times, saying:

Now I [*fill in name*] take refuge in the Heavenly Worthy of the Numinous Treasure, overseer of the illimitable realms of the north, in all of the great sages who have already achieved the Dao, in all of the

2. The five sufferings of the dead listed above as well as five more kinds of torment afflicting the living. These are: (1) serving as a slave and thus suffering the bitterness of separation from the family; (2) to remain in ignorance, never meeting a teacher, and thus never coming to know the Dao; (3) to be orphaned and alone; (4) being imprisoned for some offense; (5) constant illness throughout one's life [translator's note].

3. The paths of behavior that lead to the five sorts of suffering in the hells: (1) jealousy, (2) murder, (3) stealing, (4) lust, and (5) untruthfulness [translator's note].

4. Buddhist terminology; the formal definition of a Buddhist is someone who takes refuge in the Buddha, takes refuge in the dharma (the doctrine or discourses of the Buddha), and takes refuge in the sangha (the Buddhist community).

supreme Perfected lords, in the venerable ones, in the celestial lords of the five pneumas, and in all of the spiritual officers of the north. . . .

The rest of the vow is the same as that above. When you are finished, remove your headcloth and kowtow, knocking your forehead to the ground forty-five times.

Next face northeast and bow one time, saying:

> Now I [*fill in name*] take refuge in the Heavenly Worthy of the Numinous Treasure, overseer of the illimitable realms of the northeast, in all of the great sages who have already achieved the Dao, in all of the supreme Perfected lords, in the venerable ones, in the celestial lords of the Brahma breath, and in all of the spiritual officers of the northeast. . . .

The rest of the vow is the same as that above. When you are finished, remove your headcloth and kowtow, knocking your forehead to the ground nine times.

Follow the same procedure for the southeast, the southwest, and the northwest, in that order. For all of the four corners, you should bow once and knock your head nine times. The deities in whom you take refuge for each of the four corners will all be the same as in the case of the northeast.

Next face northeast and make thirty-two bows toward the upper direction, saying:

> Now I [*fill in name*] take refuge in the Heavenly Worthy of the Numinous Treasure, overseer of the illimitable realms of the thirty-two heavens, in all of the great sages who have already achieved the Dao, in all of the supreme Perfected lords, in the venerable ones, in the celestial lords of the thirty-two heavens, and in all of the Perfected Beings, jade maidens, divine Transcendents, and spiritual officers of the Mystic Metropolis of the Jade Capital[5] and the upper palaces of Purple Tenuity.[6] . . .

The rest of the vow is the same as that above. When you are finished, remove your headcloth and kowtow, knocking your forehead to the ground 288 times.

Next face toward the southeast and make twelve bows toward the lower direction, saying:

> Now I [*fill in name*] take refuge in the Heavenly Worthy of the Numinous Treasure, overseer of the illimitable realms in the lower direction, in all of the great sages who have already achieved the Dao, in all of the supreme Perfected lords, in the venerable ones, in the high luminaries of the nine regions of the Earth, in the four overseers, the Five Thearchs, the twelve Transcendent superintendents, in the Perfected persons, divine Transcendents, and jade maidens of the Five Marchmounts, the Four Watercourses, and the nine palaces, and in all of the spiritual officers of the nine realms of Earth in the illimitable worlds.

---

5. A sacred celestial mountain in a high heaven in the Numinous Treasure (Lingbao) tradition.

6. The Daoist heaven in which the celestial emperor lives.

Now, therefore, I burn incense and light lamps that, through the merit of these actions, I might illumine the nine stygian regions of the courts of eternal night in the subterranean realms of the illimitable worlds. I do this universally for the Thearch and kings, rulers of the kingdom, their officials and subjects, all Masters of Law who have received the Dao, my father and mother and honored ancestors, my fellow students of the Dao, those within my gates, those Daoists studying perfection in seclusion in the mountains and forests, and all worthies, even unto my ancestors of the millionth generation. I do this for all departed souls in the halls of eternal night; to redeem all they have done in former lives, breaking the laws of Heaven and the prohibitions of Earth, so that they are bound about by their transgressions and receive the recompense of their hidden deeds at death. They return again and again to be smeared with soot since their fated destinies cannot be broken. They are dragged through the five sorts of suffering and have no way to depart the courts of eternal night.

Now, through burning incense, lighting lamps, and through the forgiveness that comes of confession, I hereby redeem and rescue them. May the brilliant light universally shine throughout the halls of everlasting night and the earth-prisons of the nine stygian regions to eradicate the roots of transgression of these benighted souls and to release them from the Three Bureaus[7] and the nine suboffices. May they not be shackled or locked up. May they receive salvation to ascend to the halls of the blessed. Departing from the paths of evil, may they be reborn to live forever in blessed households, in the families of princes or nobles. May there be rejoicing at their rebirth; peace and prosperity throughout the heavens.

Now, therefore, I burn incense, taking refuge of my own accord in the virtue of the master, the Heavenly Worthy, in the great sages, and in the highest Perfected. Once I have achieved the Way, I will rise into the formless to join in perfection with the Dao.

When you have finished, kowtow, knocking your forehead to the ground 120 times.

---

7. Those of Heaven, Earth, and Water, thought to have ultimate charge of the records of life and death of all living beings [translator's note].

THE ABRIDGED CODES OF MASTER LU FOR THE DAOIST COMMUNITY
(Lu xiansheng daomen kelüe)

LU XIUJING

The *Abridged Codes of Master Lu for the Daoist Community* (*Lu xiansheng daomen kelüe*) is an apocalyptic text that addresses the (dis)organization of the Daoist religious community and makes an impassioned plea for the need to reform its general social organization and specific ritual practices. It is attributed to Lu Xiujing (406–477), the principal codifier of the Numinous Treasure (Lingbao) corpus of scriptures and a central figure in medieval Buddho-Daoist debates, who is said to have felt that the Daoists of his day had abandoned the practices of the earlier Celestial Masters tradition. This text provides not just an outline of the community's religious organization and rules but also a precious glimpse into how this community of Daoists was not operating as it should. In its articulation of normative behavioral standards, the *Abridged Codes of Master Lu for the Daoist Community* is similar to other contemporaneous works aimed at reforming the Daoist community, such as the *Scripture of the Inner Explanations of the Three Heavens* (*Santian neijie jing*; see below).

The text opens on a dire note, observing that before the Celestial Masters tradition arose, the world had fallen into such decline that "the cosmic order had lost its balance, and men and demons mingled chaotically." Thanks to the interventions of the deified Laozi, order was restored as a system of twenty-four parishes (*zhi*), petitions, talismans, and regular meetings, or assemblies, was established. During the reign of the Celestial Masters all the proper rites were performed without money being given to priests, all the faithful were registered on the parish records, the sick were healed by ingesting talismans and confessing their sins, and people lived long lives.

The *Abridged Codes of Master Lu for the Daoist Community* offers an intimate view of strains in the Daoist community after the kingdom of the Celestial Masters ceased to exist. People no longer attended the assemblies, the records and registers of the faithful were no longer kept current, the ritual masters demanded payment, the people were misled by fraudulent teachers selling registers, and the "quiet rooms" (*jingshe*)—required of all households, since they were where the Daoist master communicated with the celestial deities—were being misused and polluted. The priests are assessed with particular harshness—lacking compassion, greedy for money, and obsessed with food and drink: "Then they end up sleeping on the Quiet Room's altar and vomiting beside the petition table."

The text insists that the proper forms of worship must be revived—namely, the keeping of accurate records, the offering of "pledges" to the Daoist master, the wearing of vestments, and the maintenance and appropriate use of the "quiet room." Though offering few specifics on what precisely needs to be done and how rituals are to be carried out, it sheds light on a Daoist world that has come apart at the seams, exposing unscrupulous Daoists at whose existence most canonical texts barely hinted.

PRONOUNCING GLOSSARY

Lu xiansheng daomen kelüe: *lu Hsien-shung tao-men kuh-lew-eh*   Zhang Daoling: *chawng tao-ling*

Now the Way is empty and quiescent, beyond forms and appearances; [but] the Greatest Sage applies his character and actions to his teachings. The Most High Lord Lao [the deified Laozi] saw that Lower Antiquity was decrepit and full of malice. The pure had become insipid and the simple broken up. The cosmic order had lost its balance, and men and demons mingled chaotically. The stale vapors of the Six Heavens[1] took on official titles and appellations and brought together the hundred sprites and the demons of the five kinds of wounding, dead generals of defeated armies, and dead troops of scattered armies. The men called themselves "Generals"; the women called themselves "Ladies." They led demon troops, marching as armies and camping as legions, roving over Heaven and Earth. They arrogated to themselves authority and the power to dispense blessings. They took over people's temples and sought their sacrificial offerings, thus upsetting the people, who killed the three kinds of sacrificial animals [ox, sheep, and pig], used up all their prospects, cast away all their goods, and exhausted their produce. They were not blessed with good fortune but rather received disaster. Those who died unjustly or early and violently could not be counted.

The Most High was appalled that things were like this and therefore gave to the Celestial Master [that is, to Zhang Daoling, traditionally in 142] the Way of Correct Unity and the Covenant with the Powers [i.e., Daoism], with its prohibitions, vows, statutes, and codes, in order to regulate and instruct the myriad people.[2] As for contrariness and obedience, calamities and blessings—he made them know what was good and what was evil. He set up twenty-four parishes and thirty-six chapels, with female and male priests numbering 2,400. He sent down 10,000 sets of the petitions[3] to the 1,200 Celestial Officials, and talismans of punishment for attacking temples [of the popular religion]. He killed demons and gave life to men. He washed the universe clean and made the cosmic order bright and correct. All around Heaven and all over Earth, there were no longer any wanton, wicked demons. Putting an end to the people's obsession with [divinatory and geomantic] prohibitions, he governed them with a Pure Bond.

The spirits did not eat or drink [i.e., receive sacrificial offerings], and Daoist Masters did not accept money. The people were made to cultivate compassion and filiality within, and to practice respect and yielding without, thus aiding the times and regulating change, assisting the state and supporting its mandate. Only the Son of Heaven[4] sacrificed to Heaven; only the Three Dukes sacrificed to the five sacred peaks;[5] only the feudal lords sacrificed to the mountains and rivers; and the people gave cult to their ancestors only on the auspicious days of the Five La [in the first, fifth, sev-

---

TRANSLATED BY Peter Nickerson. All bracketed additions are the translator's.

1. A concept connected with the impure demons of popular traditions, which are opposed to the pure deities of the Dao of the Three Heavens.
2. What follows is a summary of the founding and (improper) functioning of the Celestial Masters movement in Sichuan.
3. The ritual documents used by Daoist priests

to communicate with the celestial bureaucracy made up of divine officials.
4. That is, the emperor.
5. The Five Marchmounts, one in each of the four cardinal directions and one at the center. "The Three Dukes": the three highest officials in ancient China, beneath the emperor.

enth, tenth, and twelfth months] and sacrificed to the Soil God and the Stove God only in the second and the eighth months. Beyond this, no sacrifices were allowed. If one gave cult to one's ancestors other than on the auspicious days of the Five La, or sacrificed to the Soil God or the Stove God other than on the days of the Soil God in the second and eighth months, this was to commit the offense of giving excessive cult.

The ill were not to take medicines or use the acupuncture needle or moxa. They were only to ingest talismans, drink water [into which the ashes of the burnt talismans had been mixed], and confess all their sins from their first year of life. Even all those who had committed capital crimes were pardoned, and of those whose symptoms had accumulated and were distressed by major illnesses, none was not healed. Thus those of the highest virtue attained divine transcendence;[6] those of medium virtue doubled their lifespans; and those of the lowest virtue extended their years.

But now the people who worship the Way turn these matters upside down; in everything they rebel. I respectfully request that I might expose these maladies, as follows:

When the Celestial Master set up parishes and established offices, they were like the offices of the daylight world in the commanderies, counties, cities, and prefectures that govern the people's affairs. Those who worship the Way all list their households and are entered in the records, each having a place to which he or she belongs. Now on the seventh day of the first month, the seventh day of the seventh month, the fifth day of the tenth month—the annual Three Assemblies—each of the people assembles in his or her own parish. The Master should revise the registers—removing the dead and adding births, checking and tabulating the population figures, and correcting the roster of names. Promulgating this and ordering that, he makes the people know the Rituals (*fa*, also "Law"). On that day the Celestial Officials and the Terrestrial Spirits all assemble at the Master's parish and collate the documents. Master and people both ought to be quiet and serious; they may not drink wine, eat meat, or chatter and joke. When the Assembly is over and the people have returned home, they should instruct old and young in the codes and prohibitions and the rituals and encourage them reverently to practice them. If this sort of transformation through the Way is propagated, then there will be Great Peace for family and state.

But the people who worship the Way nowadays mostly do not go to the Assemblies. Some use distance as an excuse, while some, refusing to leave home, turn their backs on their original Masters and go over to closer parishes. They only appreciate wine and meat, and they egg each other on in corruption. The bright codes and upright teachings they cast away and do not continue to spread. The canons of the Rituals and the old petitions thereupon are sunk into oblivion. Once the main net-cord has been abandoned, the myriad meshes all come loose in disorder. Not knowing the codes and constitutions, they are partial only to pledge-offerings. The people of the Way cannot tell contrariness from obedience and have a nose only for food and drink. Above and below are both lost and can no longer

6. That is, achieved extraordinary powers and a higher form of existence—the goal of the Celestial Masters but lower than becoming a Perfected One, according to the Upper Clarity movement.

rely on one another. Instead, people decide things arbitrarily and stab each other in the back; once they act they are lost in conflict. They take the true as false and the false as true, right as wrong and wrong as right. A thousand branches and ten thousand strands—in what matter are they not obstreperous? Upside-down, disordered, muddled—they remain forever unaware. A Master like this will have his descendants extinguished and his seed cut off. People like this will have Heaven destroy them before their time. Although the future is all dark, once this has come to pass it will be exceedingly clear. Can the understanding, noble person afford not to reflect on this?

The household registers of the Daoist codes are the auxiliary registers of the people. The male and female population both should be entered in them. The Celestial Officials who Guard the House will take these registers as correct, and the household members, whether moving or resting, will always be protected. In each of three seasons (the Three Assemblies in Spring, Autumn, and Winter), one revises the entries in the registers; for this there is a constant rule. If the population numbers increase or decrease, the records should always be changed. If a boy is born and survives his first month he should be given a hundred sheets of paper and a pair of writing-brushes. Hold a kitchen-feast of superior quality for ten people. If a girl is born and survives her first month she should be given one each of a broom, a dustpan, and a mat. Hold a kitchen-feast of medium quality. When taking a wife, hold a kitchen-feast of superior quality for ten people. The owners of the registers [i.e., the heads of the bride's and groom's families] should take the registers of both households to their own parishes in order that [the Masters of those parishes] may exchange registers and edit the Records of Destiny [to show that the bride has joined the groom's family's household].

On the days of the Three Assemblies, the myriad spirits of the Three Offices [of Heaven, Earth, and Water, which keep records on each individual's behavior] check all their records against each other. If a new person has been added but the news is not sent up, the Celestial Bureaus will not have the name. If a person has been lost but is not removed from the record, then the roster of names will not be correct. As for the people who worship the Way nowadays, sometimes one person is converted in the beginning, and down to his grandchildren's time the registers are not revised. On the days of the Three Assemblies, they also do not make a report. Since neither root nor branch has been attended to, the original Master has no way to find out about the true situation and thus fills in his records in accordance with the previous year. Sometimes the dead bones have been scattered, and still their owner is listed. Or someone is born and lives to have a hoary head and yet still has not been registered. Sometimes someone marries a wife and does not send up the news. Sometimes a woman is given in marriage but is not removed from the records of her natal household. Thus one ends up with hundred-year-old boys and centenarian virgins. In this way present and departed are mixed up; existence and nonexistence are not genuine. Then when the day comes that one is ill, one does not go to one's original Master but instead solicits another priest. The new priest makes no inquiries about the past and simply writes a petition. The ailing person was not previously registered, yet the present petition suddenly appears. It will not be under the jurisdiction of the Celestial Officials who Guard the House, nor will the first Three Celestial Masters take charge. The Three Heavens[7] will lack a record, and the Directorate of Destiny will not have the name. In vain one shatters one's skull on the ground [from vigorous kowtowing]—though there be a profusion of documents, since it was not done according to the Rituals, the Way will not assist. How can one help but to give thought to a principle like this?

As for the codes for worship of the Way, the Master takes the Records of Destiny as the root, and the people take pledges as the chief matter. The Master sets out the pledges for them and sends the pledges up to the Three Heavens. He asks the Celestial Officials who Guard the House to protect, ward off disaster, and dispel calamities in accordance with the population records. Although there are three Assemblies in one year, the donation of pledges is entirely restricted to the fifth day of the tenth month. Once having arrived at the parish, if one's household is safe and well, one should hold a kitchen-feast of the highest quality for five people. If one's household has decreased, then one does not hold the kitchen-feast but does donate the pledges as usual. If one's Destiny-Pledges do not arrive, then one's Record of Destiny is not sent up. Although one might later make bountiful offerings and gain blessings through kitchen-feasts, this cannot absolve the lack of the annual pledge. Therefore the Teachings say: "Although a thousand pieces of gold are precious, they do not compare to one's original Pledge-Destiny". If a household that worships the Way does not offer its Destiny-Pledges for years repeatedly, the Three Heavens will excise their names from the records. The Officials who Guard the House will return to the Celestial Bureaus and the Emanations of the Way will no longer shade them. The injuries of demon-bandits will bring them illness and early death. These discouraged families remain forever unaware and instead blame the Master and resent the Way. Is it not pitiful!

For the household that worships the Way, the Quiet Room is a place of utmost reverence. The structure should be separate, not joined with other buildings. Inside it should be pure and empty, not cluttered with extra things. When coming and going, do not go crashing in and out recklessly. The room should be sprinkled and swept and kept immaculate and austere, like a dwelling for gods. Place in it an incense burner, an incense lamp, a petition table, and a scholar's knife—these four things only. Plain and unadorned, expenses for it should amount to just one hundred or so cash.[8] Nowadays those who mix with the profane have altars, icons, banners, and all manner of ornament. Is there no longer a distinction between elaborate and simple, or a difference between ostentatious and plain?

Yet the people who worship the Way nowadays mostly do not even have a Quiet Room. Some mark and fence off an area and make a parish altar without even clearing it first, so that the weeds and underbrush stick up into the heavens. Or, even if they put up a building, it has no door, so that the domestic animals all wander in, and the excrement and filth piles up knee-deep. Some call it a Quiet Room but store miscellaneous household items in it. They blunder in and out, while rats and dogs take up residence there. Is not praying in such a place to the venerated and marvelous Way far from the mark?

7. The heavens of Great Clarity (Taiqing), Jade Clarity (Yuqing), and Upper Clarity (Shangqing).

8. A Chinese coin of small value.

The ritual vestments of the Daoists are like the court clothing of the secular world. Lords, literati, and commoners each have rank and order: a system of five grades in order to distinguish noble and base. Therefore the *Classic of Filial Piety* (*Xiaojing*) says: "If they are not the ritual vestments of the former kings, one dare not wear them." The old ritual vestments were the single-layered robe and the lined turban, with trousers and coat for the novices. As for the pledges made when receiving a parish, a man gives a single-layered robe and a black turban, and a woman gives a deep purple robe. This clear statement should be sufficient to put confusion to rest.

The turban and the robe of coarse cloth, as well as the cape, come from the Supreme Way. When making ritual prostrations one wears the coarse cloth; when chanting scriptures one wears the cape. How could the models of the Three Caverns of Daoist scripture[9] have anything to do with the lesser ways? Recently, even those who merely receive the rituals of a small parish or of a novice usurp the prerogative of the robe and coarse cloth. This is already greatly mistaken. Then moreover to match a hat and coat with a skirt, or wear trousers with the cape or robe of coarse cloth—how can one even discuss this sort of muddle and disorder?

There are standards for the turban, the robe of coarse cloth, the skirt, and the cape, as well as their lengths and the numbers of stitches. This is why they are called ritual vestments [lit. also "legal/regulated clothing"]. The vestments all have powerful gods that attend on and protect them. The Perfected of the Grand Ultimate[1] said: "If they are not made in accordance with the Rituals, then the spirits will punish the wrongdoer." Since by dressing contrary to the codes one oversteps one's bounds and indulges in excess, can one escape calamities?

The teachings of the codes say that if a person (*min*, a Daoist "commoner") has three diligences, this makes a merit. Three merits make a virtue. If a person has three virtues, then he or she becomes different from ordinary people and may be appointed with a register. After receiving the register, one must have merit in order to advance from the Register of Ten Spirit-Generals by steps to the Register of One Hundred Fifty Spirit-Generals. If among the novices (lit. "Clerks of the Registers") there are those who are loyal and good, simple, careful, and prudent, loving the Way and surpassing in diligence, steeped in the old and knowledgeable about the present, capable in proselytizing—they may be appointed as Priests who Disperse the Emanations of the Way. If among the Dispersers of Emanations there are those who are pure in cultivation of the Way, they may be promoted to posts in Detached Parishes. If in the Detached Parishes there are those who are even more refined and sincere, they may be promoted to posts in Traveling Parishes. . . . [And so on through eight more grades.] One ought to seek offices through perspicaciously spreading merit and virtue. Neither let the person dominate the office, nor the office the person.

If one learns without a Master this becomes like a plant growing without a root. Something that grows severed from its basis is called a "rootless weed" (commentary omitted). . . . Yet people today receive registers without such virtues and receive parishes without such talents (commentary omitted). . . . Some are without both a teacher and documentary records.

---

9. That is, the texts in the Daoist canon; they were divided into three "caverns," or collections, by Lu Xiujing in 471.
1. A lofty class of deities.

Such a person first worshiped the Way, but then lost his or her Master for some time and did not reaffiliate. Or first the person was an ordinary layperson, living alone away from home, fickle and false of faith. The priest did not first convert the person in accordance with the rituals, but instead immediately conferred a register and a parish. This kind of practitioner is entirely a fraud, a priest in vain. Even if the person additionally cultivates diligently and submits to the good, his or her name will not be in the records of the Three Heavens. Therefore there will be no escape from a premature demise. How much more dismal will things be in the case of the licentious and disobedient!

Some have a Master but no records (commentary omitted). . . . Some, although they have a Master and records, are without virtues. When they receive registers, they cross over to another Master, thus neither returning to the basis nor following the proper sequence of grades. The appointments are made recklessly without the selection of qualified people. In carrying registers these lax Daoists care only for quantity; in receiving parishes they care only for quantity and size. They compete to be first and struggle to be victorious, each trying to be ascendant over the other. (More details on the parish system omitted.)

Without the Precepts and the Statutes, inferior priests do not follow the commands of the teachings. They overstep the codes and break the Prohibitions, slight the Way and debase the Rituals.

Now those who receive the Way keep to to the Precepts and Statutes within and hold to the Mighty Rituals. Observing avoidances and prohibitions in accordance with the Codes, they follow the commands of the teachings. Therefore the Scripture says: "If the priest does not receive the 180 Precepts of Lord Lao, he is without virtue." Then, if one is not a real priest, one does not deserve the obeisance of the common people and cannot control spirits. Being so obtuse, lax priests do not know that the Way and Virtue are venerable, and whether acting or at rest they are guilty of shortcomings, thus debasing their rituals and techniques.

They let free their covetous natures, drowning themselves in wine and lusting after food.

When they propagate the Rituals of the Way, they do not look for merit and virtue. When they perform healing rituals, they lack any compassionate or humane intent. They hope only for gain, and their thoughts are all on wine and meat. Never do they instruct the people in the Codes and Prohibitions. They only collect substantial offerings and seek for good food—dishes flavored with the five pungent roots, and the meat of the six kinds of domestic animals.[2] The things that in the Way are most tabooed, they eat! Then, having violated the prohibitions themselves, they then go on to butcher chickens, pigs, geese, and ducks. They drink wine until they are

2. Pigs, dogs, chickens, horses, cattle, and sheep. "The five pungent roots": garlic, leeks, onions, scallions, and chives.

awash in it, then in that condition go to send up petitions (lit. to "memorialize" in a communication to an emperor). Then they end up sleeping on the Quiet Room's altar and vomiting beside the petition table. There are always those of this sort.

They turn their backs on the upright teaching of the Pure Bond of the Covenant with the Powers

> The Ritual Master of the Covenant with the Powers does not take money; the spirits neither eat nor drink. This is called the Pure Bond. In curing illness one does not use acupuncture, moxa, or hot liquid medicines. One only ingests talismans, drinks [talismanic] water, confesses one's sins, corrects one's behavior, and sends a petition—and that is all. When choosing a site for a dwelling-place, installing a sepulcher, or moving house—when moving, coming to rest, or in all the hundred affairs—not divining for a lucky day or making inquiries concerning auspicious times, simply following one's heart, avoiding or inclining toward nothing is called the Bond [or "is called restraint"]. Casting out the thousand sprites and ten thousand numena—all the profane gods—as one takes up the worship of the Lord Lao and the first Three Celestial Masters is called the Upright Teaching.

and resort to the upside-down rites of perverse and calamitous spirit-mediumism.

> Making sacrifices to demons and gods and praying for blessings is called Perverse. Weighing the words of demons and gods in order to divine auspiciousness and inauspiciousness is called Calamitous. Irresponsibly creating taboos and avoidances that are not in the codes and teaching of the Celestial Masters and Laozi is called Spirit-mediumism. As for writing charts, and thus divining the baneful geomantic influences of the sites of sepulchers and dwellings, one ought instead to send up a petition to exorcise those influences. To persist in using calendars to pick days and choose times is even more stupidly obstreperous. That which is illumined by the upright codes, they are forever unwilling to follow. That which the rituals prohibit, they compete in reverently employing. Thus turning one's back on the true and turning toward the false is called Upside-down.

They take up their scholars' knives and brushes [the basic tools for writing petitions] and travel among the villages.

> The Rituals of the Way are incorrupt and retiring, responding rather than singing their own praises. Quietly one refines one's techniques on one's own, waiting for the one who will seek one out and make a sincere claim of his or her need, after which one will extend one's succor. If one goes about promoting oneself, this is prohibited by the Rituals.

When they meet up with fugitive disobedient people, inquisition weighs them down, and disasters descend upon them.

Although they are people of the Way, for long they have had no Master. The parish has no record of their Destinies, and their families have no household registers. Or they have a Master, but on the Three Auspicious Days they do not attend the Assemblies and offer their pledges. Then, when they have some emergency, they set down offerings and make vows to give kitchen-feasts, not understanding how grace is bestowed. This is called Fugitive. Although they worship the Way and its Rituals, they do not follow the prohibitions in the codes, committing excesses and killing living beings, believing in perversities and making divinatory inquiries, doing evil in a hundred ways, malefic and rebellious beyond description. This is called Disobedient. All fugitive and disobedient people will have their Reckonings (i.e., their predetermined lifespans) shortened and their names excised from the records. The Three Offices will send out the Lords and Clerks of Summoning for Inquisition secretly to keep watch on their households, afflict their members with inquisitorial punishments, and call disasters down upon them. If their sins are heavy, then they will meet with the Six Calamities; if their sins are light, then the Five Disasters descend upon them. Thus they are made to suffer from death, disease, state officials, imprisonment, floods, fire, thieves, and bandits.

In the case of people like this, if in emergencies they wish to be instructed in the Way, the Master should always dispel the inquisition and the sin-produced affliction in accordance with the codes. If the people can be persuaded gently and will return to the good, spit out evil, and take an oath with the Three Offices, then once they confirm this faith they may be delivered following the sequence prescribed by the codes. Yet stupid, false Priests have no codes or precepts to go by and no way of distinguishing the empty from the substantial. They only have decrepit, old petitions, and talismans with parts missing. The beginnings of these documents do not fit with the ends; they cannot be used in worship. And still these priests follow their own opinions and edit the documents as they wish, recklessly making emendations. With filthy turbans, foul ink-stones, shameful paper, dirty brushes, and cursive writing with wild strokes, stinking of wine and meat, they follow their appetites and seek whatever their minds fasten on. With substanceless words and false speech, they ignore the facts. They go against the source and turn their backs on principle, offending the [otherworldly] Officials of Inquisition. Sometimes they go overboard and arrest innocent demons, or unjustly charge spirits that are causing no affliction. Sometimes they bind spirits they should loose, or promote the ones they should attack. Upside-down and jumbled, affairs thus have no standard.

When they enter the Quiet Room to memorialize the Celestial Bureaus, these inferior priests cannot tell where one sentence of the petition ends and the next begins. What they recognize, with a torrent of a voice and a roll of drums they broadcast to neighbors in all directions. What they cannot understand, they skip over—coughing, sputtering, and bellowing. The Celestial Clerks and Soldiers will not serve people such as this, and the Emanations of the Way will not descend upon them. Inquisitorial afflictions will become more urgent daily, and illnesses will keep taking turns for the worse. Vainly increasing one's rich offerings in the end produces no results. Guest and host [i.e., client and priest] are lost together and cannot see that they are wrong. This then gives rise to slander: resentment against the Way and blame toward the spirits. Sometimes things get to the point that people burn their registers, destroy their Quiet Rooms, and make over their chapels—serving demon-kind in all possible ways—and then disaster entirely destroys their families. A loss such as this!—can one afford to be unaware?

THE FIVE SENTIMENTS OF GRATITUDE
(Dongxuan lingbao wugan wen)

LU XIUJING

This fifth-century c.e. text, attributed to Lu Xiujing (406–477), is part of the Numinous Treasure (Lingbao) textual corpus that he helped codify. It focuses primarily on the moral purification and rectification necessary to effectively perform a specific ritual known as the Mud and Soot Retreat (Tutan zhai). As the translator Franciscus Verellen notes, this severe rite of penance was undertaken by those hoping for a remission of sins accrued by themselves and by others (especially their parents) who had acted on their behalf. Because sins were believed to cause sickness and premature death, they needed to be repented, and the penitent's relative success was determined by the degree of suffering sustained. In the *Five Sentiments of Gratitude* the practitioner is directed to cultivate specific sentiments of gratitude toward his or her parents, master, and the great sages of the past. The strong Buddhist influence on this text is palpable both in its vocabulary (dharma, eight hardships, five ways of reincarnation, kalpas) and in its larger conceptual systems (karma and rebirth).

PRONOUNCING GLOSSARY

Dongxuan lingbao wugan wen: *tung-hsuen ling-pao wu-gwan when*   Lu Xiujing: *loo hsiu-ching*

First Sentiment: Father and mother engendered me and gave me life, nourished me and nurtured me. Coming and going, they cradled me in their arms, soothed and comforted me, caressed and tended me. They damaged their health with anxiety and wore themselves out with worry. When I was unwell or fell ill, they were distressed and preoccupied on my account, their hearts burning as if on fire. Apprehensive day and night, they forgot their food and gave up their sleep; with growing agitation, they became emaciated. Shedding ceaseless tears they yearned for my growth and development. Enabled to become as I am now, I am mindful of their great, their immeasurable kindness. I sincerely vow to repay the boundless beneficence of my parents!

TRANSLATED BY Franciscus Verellen. All bracketed additions are the translator's.

Second Sentiment: Father and mother provided for my education in adolescence and arranged for my marriage. They accumulated property and acquired the foundations of my livelihood. When it came to wanting more for me, they did not notice their greed. Contending with others engenders envy and avarice, which lead to transgressions and misdemeanors. In disobedience against Heaven and Earth, they caused injury to men and creatures. Without, they broke the king's law, and, within, offended against the rites of the nether world. They incurred increasing sanctions to the point of forfeiting their lives. And I am at the origin of it all, having invited this misfortune. Now they have fallen into the Three Paths (of retribution)[1] encountering numerous hardships. They are subjected to the Tree of Swords and fall upon the Mountain of Knives; they walk the Fire of Flames, hot as a boiling cauldron, and are submerged in the Night of Darkness, cold as icy frost. Suspended in the flogging cage, their thousand pains and ten thousand sufferings are unbearable under the rod. Vexed and distraught, and ever hard-pressed to endure it, they hope for release but are unable to deliver themselves by their own effort. Thinking of this, I collapse and choke, my liver and heart break down in confusion, and my whole body trembles. My body and soul confounded and oblivious, I prostrate myself and with mud and coal beg for mercy.

Third Sentiment: In the whole world, noble and lowly, men and women, all alike receive a human body, and the burdens of the body and mouth. All alive prize the five flavors in food and five-colored silks in clothing.[2] Even when already satisfied and warm, they can no longer restrain themselves. They use clothing and precious objects recklessly and delight in dissipation and the pursuit of schemes. Never feeling satiety, they harm the spirit and hurt the body, mindless that their vitality is already withering, their bodies decrepit. A lifetime of handling things, and to what use in the end? The orphaned soul dies alone and fully undergoes all its sufferings. Truly benighted, the world does not understand this! Once the excess wealth is distributed, it becomes the bane of posterity, engendering treachery and giving rise to thievery. Disputed by children and grandchildren, the strong grasp much, while the weak obtain little. Giving and taking, loss and gain increase their mutual rancor. If they take their plaints to the tribunal, they suffer chastisement and execution; if they appeal to spirits and demons, they incur occult calamities. The kinship with one's closest is contrived to create mutual enmity. Esteem for one's natural kin is discarded like dirt. [Under these conditions even the natural] love between brothers becomes war to the knife. The body perishes and the family is destroyed. Such feuds proceed from cupidity and extravagance. Altogether they sink and go under forever. Either they have not yet seen the light or, if they have understood, they are incapable of renunciation. The departed were thus, as those to come shall be again. They are content to accept this as the norm, without regret. I understand this is wrong and therefore turn my back on the world. Taking leave of my Six Kin[3] and putting aside all cares and ambitions, I seek the Dao and strive for life, accumulate learning, and work for my salvation.

---

1. Rebirth as animals, hungry ghosts, or denizens of hell.
2. The five flavors are sour, bitter, sweet, acrid, and salty; the five colors are green, red, yellow, white, and black.
3. Apparently a reference to close family members.

If I can attain some usefulness, I shall first repay the kindness of my parents, who raised and nurtured me day after day. If I now obtain the divine elixir with which to rescue them from submersion, may they ascend the Dharma Bridge[4] and cross over to the distant shore. Leaping with joy, the five emotions[5] exalted, my heart soars and my spirit wanders. Suddenly I become oblivious of my four limbs. Unconscious, I abandon myself and take refuge in the Three Treasures[6] I pour out my possessions and make everything over to the dharma, fearing only that it will not suffice and that I have not yet relinquished all avarice. I wish that my father and mother shall ascend to the Hall of Felicity, forever escape the Eight Hardships,[7] and never again suffer distress. May my small sincerity afford them sustenance.

Fourth Sentiment: All the Venerables on High, the great Sages, and the Perfected brought forth this great civilization and issued the wonderful dharma to deliver us from the Three Paths (of retribution) and save us from the Five Ways (of reincarnation).[8] Once the calamitous grievances of myriads of generations of great-grandfathers and grandfathers through the accumulated *kalpas*[9] are resolved, the souls of the departed are relieved and rise up to the Hall of Felicity. The elect of karmic causation all at once receive their recompense. My body attains the Way, and felicity is bestowed on succeeding generations. This rare grace occurs once in ten thousand *kalpas*. I shall faithfully carry out the ritual with all my heart and utmost devotion, and resolve to be remiss in nothing.

Fifth Sentiment: If I obtain this blessing, it will not happen without reason. Causation illumines salvation. It is the kindness of my teacher that caused me to see. My veneration for him knows no bounds, exceeding Heaven and Earth. Therefore, each day we carry out the rites I pray with utmost sincerity, hoping that I may possess some small merit with which to repay his benevolence. Even as I suffer bodily hardship and physical fatigue, I shall not dare spare myself.

4. In Buddhism, *dharma* is a term notoriously difficult to translate, most commonly understood as doctrine or discourses of the Buddha.
5. Anger, joy, compassion, grief, and fear.
6. By definition, a Buddhist is someone who "takes refuge in" the Three Jewels or Treasures—the Buddha, the dharma, and the sangha (the Buddhist community).
7. That is, the eight forms of rebirth that, according to Buddhist texts, block one's ability to see or hear a buddha: being reborn in hell, as a hungry ghost, as an animal, as a god, in a barbaric area, without vision or hearing, as a devotee of a heretical teacher, or in a time without a buddha.
8. As gods, humans, animals, hungry ghosts, or denizens of hell. The Buddhist goal is to escape the endless cycle of birth, death, and rebirth.
9. A kalpa is the Buddhist term (adopted by Daoists) for an aeon, a complete cosmic cycle from the creation to the destruction of a particular world.

SCRIPTURE OF THE OPENING OF HEAVEN BY THE MOST HIGH LORD LAO
(Taishang laojun kaitian jing)

The *Scripture of the Opening of Heaven by the Most High Lord Lao*, a sixth-century cosmogonic text, is quite similar to the Dunhuang manuscript of the *Scripture on Laozi's Transformations* (*Laozi bianhua jing*; see above). Along with many references to traditional Chinese mythology, it contains an account of the divinized Laozi's creation of the universe, describes his descent down to the earth to give political support and instruction to ancient rulers in different epochs, and also evinces some Buddhist influence. Laozi is depicted as being present at the font of creation—before the differentiation of the Dao, which led to the separation of heaven and earth and then the creation of the manifest world of beings. The *Scripture of the Opening of Heaven by the Most High Lord Lao* chronicles a number of the key phases and incarnations of Laozi, down to the Zhou dynasty.

PRONOUNCING GLOSSARY

Taishang laojun kaitian jing: *tai-shahng lao-chun kai-tien ching*

This is made known:
In that interval when Heaven and Earth did not yet exist,
Incalculably far beyond grand clarity,[1]
Inside of barren nullity,[2] was
Silent, unoccupied—there was nothing beyond.
Neither sky nor earth; neither yin nor yang;[3]
Neither sun nor moon; neither scintilla nor radiance;
Neither East nor West; neither blue nor yellow;
Neither South nor North; neither tender nor tough;
Neither covering nor carrying; neither spoiling nor preserving;
Neither competent nor incomparable; neither loyal nor estimable;
Neither going nor coming; neither living nor passing away;
Neither before nor after; neither round nor square;
A hundred lacs[4] of conversions and mutations; shoreless and unconfined;
Neither forms nor simulacra; spontaneous, empty, and obscure;
Explore it—its end is hard to reach:
Neither measure nor bounds;
Neither high-up nor down-below;
Neither equivalence nor disparity;
Neither left nor right.
High-up or low-down—spontaneous.

Only our Lord Lao[5] dwelt all the while in the empty and obscure,
[Even] beyond the silent outerworld and within the obscure barrens.
Look for him—he is not visible; listen for him—he is not audible.
You may say "he exists"—(but) one does not see his form;
You may say "he does not exist"—(but) the myriad creatures are born
      from him.
Beyond the Eight Outsides; very gradually [it/he] began to divide;
Formed below [something] tenuous and subtle from which was created
      a dimensional world.
Thus "Vast Prime"[6] came to be.

Translated by Edward H. Schafer. All bracketed additions are the translator's.

1. Within the Upper Clarity (Shangqing) tradition, the Grand Clarity was the lowest of three heavens; Upper Clarity and Jade Clarity were above it.
2. The source of the Dao and being.
3. Yin and yang are the complementary forces that unite to form the Dao: yin, a term that originally referred to the shady side of a valley, by extension came to be associated with the dark, earth, dampness, and passivity—the female principle; yang, a term that originally referred to the sunny side of a valley, by extension came to be associated with the light, heaven, dryness, and activity—the male principle.
4. That is, lakhs; one lakh is 100,000.
5. The deified Laozi.
6. The primordial period before there were beings.

In the time of Vast Prime, neither Heaven nor Earth yet existed.
Barren Emptiness had not separated;
Clear and turbid had not divided.
Within the obscure barrens of silent outworld,
Vast Prime, once put in order, went on for a myriad of kalpas.[7]
After the division of Vast Prime, "Encompassing Prime" came to be:

Encompassing Prime, once put in order, was for a myriad of kalpas, going on into a hundred fulfillments, which is also eighty-one myriads of kalpas. Thus "Grand Antecedence" came to be.

In the time of Grand Antecedence, Lord Lao descended from Barren Emptiness and became the teacher of Grand Antecedence. His mouth emitted the entire set, in forty-eight myriads of scrolls, of the scripture of the opening of heaven. A single scroll had forty-eight myriads of characters. A single character was a square with sides of one hundred *li*.[8] With it he taught "Grand Antecedence."

Grand Antecedence first separated Heaven and Earth
And parted clear and turbid,
Split apart the boundless fog and vast haze;
Set forms and simulacra in place;
Planted South and North securely;
Constrained East and West correctly;
Opened the covert and revealed the luminous;
Light involved the Four Ligatures.[9]
Above and below, inside and outside;
Exterior and interior, long and short;
Coarse and fine, feminine and masculine;
White and black, great and small;
Honorable and humble—[all were] constantly operating as if in the
    night.

When Grand Antecedence obtained this scripture on the opening of Heaven by Lord Lao, clear and turbid were now parted. Clear pneuma rose above and became the sky; turbid pneuma sank below and became the earth. With the Three Holdfasts[1] now parted, from this [point] Heaven and Earth began their existences. Sun and Moon did not yet exist. Heaven inclined toward the mutation of creatures, [but] there was no procedure by which they could be evolved. So then it established life. Sun and Moon were situated in its midst. They illuminated the occluding tenebrity below.

In the time of Grand Antecedence, although Sun and Moon existed,
    human folk did not yet exist.
With the gradual onset of primary life,
Above the germ of Heaven was taken;
Below the germ of Earth was taken;
In the middle space between these joined in concordance.
From this was formed a single spirit, which is called by the name
    "human."

---

7. A kalpa is the Buddhist term (adopted by Daoists) for an aeon, a complete cosmic cycle from the creation to the destruction of a particular world.

8. A unit of distance, equal to about 1/3 mile.
9. The cables that attach the earth to the heavens.
1. Cables or mainstays.

Since Heaven and Earth were empty, life first came to exist by a triple
    parting. The kinds of life were simulacra lacking forms. Each came
    to life on receiving a single pneuma.
Some came to life by the pneuma of crudity; such are mountains and
    rocks.
Or came to life by the pneuma of mobility; such are the fliers and the
    treaders.
Or came to life by the pneuma of vitality; such are the humans.
Among the myriad creatures, humans were the most noble.
Grand Antecedence, once put in order, was for a myriad of kalpas.
The antecedence of human folk is therefore called Grand Antecedence.

At that time there were only Heaven and Earth.
Sun and moon and human folk—none had distinguishing names;
After the extinction of Grand Antecedence, Grand Initiation came
    to be.

In the time of Grand Initiation, Lord Lao descended and became its teacher.
His mouth emitted the entire set of the Scripture of Grand Initiation. He
taught this "Grand Initiation," setting under-heaven in place for ninety-one
kalpas. Ninety-one kalpas extended to a hundred fulfillments: A hundred
fulfillments also eighty-one myriads of years.

Now Grand Initiation was the initiation of the myriad beings. Therefore
it is called "Grand Initiation." Streaming and revolving, it formed a shim-
mering white texture, with the simulacra visible in its midst. Pneuma and
substance evolved spontaneously and secured the formation of yin and
yang: After the extinction of Grand Initiation, Grand Simplicity came to be.

In the time of Grand Simplicity, Lord Lao descended and became its
    teacher. He taught and demonstrated Grand Simplicity, by which
    he systematized under-heaven for eighty-one kalpas,
Extending to a hundred fulfillments, also eighty-one myriads of years.

Now Grand Simplicity was the simplicity of the myriad beings. Therefore
    it is called "Grand Simplicity."

Coming down from Grand Antecedence until the coming of Grand Simplicity,
Heaven generated sweet dew; earth generated springs of ale.[2] When human
folk partook of them they gained long life. Dying, they did not know funeral
or interment. Their corpses were discarded in the distant countryside. This
was named "High Antiquity." After the extinction of Grand Simplicity,
Encompassed Potentiality came to be.

In the time of Encompassed Potentiality, mountains and rivers first came
to be. Lord Lao descended and became its teacher. He taught and demonstrated Encompassed Potentiality, by which he put under-heaven in order for
seventy-two kalpas.

2. Like "sweet dew," a term for saliva.

Encompassed Potentiality streamed into motion and formed those mountains and rivers as the "Five Marchmounts" and the "Four Conduits."[3] High-up and down-below, honorable and humble now arose for the first time. Following upon Encompassing Potentiality, distinguishing names first existed. Encompassing Potentiality bore two sons; the greater one was Hu Chen; the lesser one was Hu Ling. Hu Chen died and became god of the marchmounts; Hu Ling died and became god of the waters. So, they made the Five Marchmounts and the Four Conduits, mountains and rivers, high-up and low-down, in conformity with their names."

3. Four sacred rivers. "The 'Five Marchmounts'": a group of five sacred mountains—one in each of the four cardinal directions and one at the center. They are most often identified as Mount Heng (north), Mount Tai (east), Mount Heng (south), Mount Hua (west), and Mount Song (center); variants include Mount Huo (south) and Mount Taihua (west).

BIOGRAPHIES OF STUDENTS OF THE DAO
(Daoxue zhuan)

Biographies of Students of the Dao (*Daoxue zhuan*) is a lost hagiographical collection—existing today only as fragments preserved in other sources—that features a variety of individual practitioners associated with the Upper Clarity (Shangqing) and Numinous Treasure (Lingbao) Daoist traditions. The first compilation of Daoist biographies based on contemporary figures, whose lives spanned the fourth to sixth centuries, it was also the first such Daoist collection to contain a chapter dedicated to the lives of female Daoists. Most of the accounts are of individuals attested in secular biographical texts, whereas in other Daoist biographical/hagiographical collections, accounts tend to end with the figures' becoming immortal. Given its this-worldly focus, *Biographies of Students of the Dao* has also become an important resource for studying early Daoist monasticism, which seems to have been a particular focus of the author.

PRONOUNCING GLOSSARY

Daoxue zhuan: *dow-hsueh chuan*
Ji Huiyuan: *chee hway-yuen*
Li Lingcheng: *lee ling-chung*
Qian Miaozhen: *chien miao-chun*

Song Yuxian: *song yu-hsien*
Wang Daolian: *wawng dow-lien*
Xu Daoyu: *hsu dow-yu*
Zhang Yuanfei: *chawng yuen-fay*

From *Chapter 20*

57. JI HUIYAN

The twentieth *juan*[1] [of the *Daoxue zhuan*] says:
Ji Huiyan was a native of Xuhang in Wuxing. She was a child [when] she left [her] family and became a Buddhist nun. Later she abandoned the

---

TRANSLATED BY Stephen Bumbacher. All bracketed additions are the translator's.

1. Roll or scroll.

nun[nery] and became a female Daoist. Subsequently she went up onto and dwelt on Mount Tianmu and stopped [eating] cereal food. [Whenever] someone had an ailment and it became serious, she bestowed a single charm, and nobody was not immediately cured.

[The *Daoxue zhuan* says:]
Ji Huiyan dwelt on Mount Tianmu in Yuqian and learned the *dao*. After [she had left behind] the mortal frame,[2] [people] buried her according to lay ceremonies. Several years later, one could suddenly hear the sound of the crash of a mountain canopy, and it was like the sound of thunder. Villagers went to look [and] saw the coffin planks flying into the sky; [while] the upper plank fell on the southern hamlet—today it is 'Upper-plank-hamlet'—, and the bottom board fell on the northern hamlet—today it is 'Lower-board-hamlet'—, both side planks [fell] together on the same place, [which therefore] today is 'Planks-together-hamlet'. As a consequence of that, [she] ascended to Heaven.

58. LI LINGCHENG

The twentieth *juan* [of the *Daoxue zhuan*] says:
[When] Liang Emperor Yuan's[3] crown prince's, [Xiao] Fangdeng's ailment became serious, consort Xu controlled her mind and purified [her] self, and dispatched people to the female official Li Lingcheng's Flowering Forest Convent [to] do meritorious [deeds]. The consort in a nighttime dream [then] saw two young serving lads, [their] appearance and garments being different [from the] common ones, and they declared [themselves to be] Flowering Forest's serving lads, and [said that] they had been sent [to] inform her that the illness was because he had taken stones from the altar of the convent, and that he ought to hand [them] over, [and] then [he would be] cured. [When the consort] woke up, she immediately questioned the crown prince. The crown prince said: "[Since I] was recently constructing a mountain pond, [I] took and used [them]." [When they] sent [someone] to return [them], [and they] also sent a Reader-in-attendance, Wang Xiaosi, [with him], who entered the mountain and repeatedly performed a fast, regret, and confession [ritual], the crown prince was immediately cured [of the illness].

* * *

59. XIAO LIANZHEN

The twentieth *juan* [of the *Daoxue zhuan*] says:
The female official Xiao [Lian]zhen was a native of Dantu in Donghai. [When] she was young, she parted from [her] family and entered Mount Yi, learned the *dao* and only ate cypress leaves.

[The *Daoxue zhuan* says:]
Xiao Lianzhen entered Mount Yi and learned the *dao*. [When] aged forty,[4] she only ate cypress leaves, plucked the various flowers and made pills.

---

2. A reference to "release by means of a corpse," a type of liberation or transformation in which one feigns one's own death, leaving nothing or some relic, and ascends to heaven.

3. Reigned 552–54.
4. That is, 39; in the traditional Chinese calculation of age, an individual is 1 at birth.

Moreover, she took leaves of mulberry trees, mixed [them with] *polygenatum giganteum, atractylis,*[5] and so on, and simmered and ate [them], [When] aged eighty, [her] white hair [became] black [again] and [her] teeth, which had fallen out, grew [again]. She regularly recited the *Scripture of the yellow court.*[6] She always had a tiger. It crouched and stayed in front of [her] bed. [Whenever] she wanted to rise, she first with a dog-stick urged the tiger forward, [and] like a dog it went on ahead [of her].

60. SONG YUXIAN

The twentieth *juan* [of the *Daoxue zhuan*] says:
The nun Song Yuxian was a native of Shanyin in Kuaiji. When she was in puberty, her determination was not wholly devoted to herself. [As her] years advanced and she was about to be marriageable,[7] and [her] father and mother were about to give [her] in marriage to the Xu clan, she secretly prepared the 'garments of the law,'[8] and mounted the carriage, [and] when she reached [her] husband's gate [and] the time came for the 'six ceremonies [of marriage],' she changed [her clothing] and put on a yellow linen skirt and very coarse woollen [clothes], held a 'magpie-tail' incense burner in [her] hands, and did not attend in person the wife's ceremonies. Guests and hosts were startled. [As] the husband's family was not able to bend [her will] by their efforts, [they] abandoned [her] and let [her] go and return to [her] own family. She subsequently achieved leaving [her] family.

61. ZHANG YUANFEI

The twentieth [*juan*] of the *Daoxue zhuan* says:
Zhang Yuanfei, styled Jingming, resided in Caipo hamlet in Qu'a. At the age of eleven she was able to [perform] long fasts with ease.

[The *Daoxue zhuan* says:]
Zhang Yuanfei, styled Jingming, dwelt in Caipo hamlet in Qu'a. Later she left the capital [Jiankang] and built the Convent of the Highest Virtue north of Dongfucheng. [This was during] the time of Liang Wu[di]. Moreover, she sought permission to afterwards be allowed to 'screen [her] traces' [on] Mao Shan.[9] [When] she returned to [Mao Shan's] Southern Grotto, she set up the Convent of the Mysterious Brightness, broke off [the consumption of] cereals, ceased [eating] grain, and devoted [herself] to undertake 'spewing out and inhaling' [breath]. In the third year of the Eternal Arrangement [period][1] she went to Mount Haiwu. In the Nanshaqiu Convent she informed [the others that she was going to be] transformed. [Subsequently,] she was brought back [to be] buried [on] Mao Shan.

✳   ✳   ✳

---

5. Giant Solomon's seal and thistle, both plants used in herbal medicine.
6. See the *Most High Jade Scripture on the Internal View of the Yellow Court* (*Taishang huangting neijing yujing*), above.
7. Fifteen years old [translator's note].

8. Buddhist ceremonial clothes [translator's note].
9. That is, Mount Mao, a significant sacred mountain for the Upper Clarity (Shangqing) Daoist tradition. "To 'screen [her] traces'": to live in seclusion.
1. According to the translator, 559 C.E.

63. XU DAOYU

Xu Daoyu, female perfected.[2]
Xu Huangmin's[3] daughter, Daoyu, died on Mount Dai in the first year, [the year] *jiawu* [of the sexagenary cycle], of the Establishment of Filiality [period] of the Song [dynasty].[4] The world called her 'Paternal Aunt Xu.' [When people] laid down [her] corpse on top of a stone, the corpse decayed, [as] it was not put into a coffin, [but] it always had a fragrant smell.

(Apparent commentary:) "[This] is also taken from the second *juan* of the *Daoxue zhuan*."

64. WANG DAOLIAN

[The *Daoxue zhuan*] also says:
Wang Daolian was a woman from Pengcheng. [As] she had made it her ideal to leave the family, she accordingly entered Mount Long, sold and traded clothes and valuables, and herself set up a convent living quarter and called [it] [Convent] of the Mysterious Glory. [Since] the storied pavilions and connected chambers were finished before long, and [although] they were sturdy they were very quick[-ly made], it was somewhat as if she had supernatural assistance.

* * *

The *Daoxue zhuan* [says]:
[When] the female perfected Wang Daolian [was aged] seven years, she knew the *dao*. [Later] she marketed incense, oil, provisions, sweets, and vegetables. She did not wear silken fabrics or coloured [clothes]. [When] she received the *Scripture of the three grottos* (*Sandong jing*),[5] she day and night practiced reciting [it]. [When,] before that, she entered the Long Shan and set up a convent living quarter and called [it] [Convent] of the Mysterious Glory, it had a supernatural-like [power]: South-east of the three altars there suddenly grew a tree, [and its] appearance was like a basket lid and it encircled and sheltered a whole altar, five leaves being opposite to each other. [Since] none of [her] contemporaries recognised [the tree], they called [it] 'shell-leaf' [-tree]. There was also a jade box. [When] it descended [from heaven (?)] on the top of the altar, it had a nimbus. [After] her reciting the scripture ten thousand [times], there was a cloud carriage [which] came to collect [her], and [there was] a sudden [clap of] thunder and a violent wind, and a fragrant scent filled the sky.

65. QIAN MIAOZHEN

The *Daoxue zhuan* [says]:
[When] the female perfected Qian Miaozhen was [still] a child, she studied the *dao*. [Later she] dwelt in the grottos and mountains of Juqu. [When she was] aged eighty-three, she recited the *Scripture of the yellow court*. [Having] completed [the requisite number of times], she then bade farewell to

---

2. *Zhenren*, a concept that first appears in the *Book of Master Zhuang* (*Zhuangzi*; see above), is emphasized in the Upper Clarity tradition; the perfected are beings that have moved beyond earthly corruption and are often identified with stellar deities.
3. The possessor of many Upper Clarity texts (361–429); he inherited them from his father

and grandfather, Xu Hui and Xu Mi, who received the scriptures revealed to Yang Xi (see the introduction to the *Declarations of the Perfected* [*Zhen'gao*], above).
4. According to the translator, 454 C.E.
5. A general term for the Daoist canon or texts in the Daoist canon.

relatives and friends, ate yellow and white coloured drugs, [and when she had] finished, entered Swallow Grotto and stayed [there] the whole night, and the next morning, [when] Daoist nuns and [male ordained] Daoists vied to go and ask after her, they suddenly heard that in the grotto there was a sound of thunder and saw a carriage [drawn by] a dragon and a phoenix. [It] came from the north-west and bore [her] ascending to Heaven.

*   *   *

[The *Laoshi shengji*] also says:
Qian Miaozhen was a native of Jinling. [When] she was a child, she was fond of the *dao*. [When] she wished to separate [herself] from secular [life], [but her] parents and clan pressed [her] to marry a man, she wept and shed tears and mourned bitterly. Subsequently, she dwelt [on] both the Bigger and Lesser Mao Shan. Later she went to Swallow Mouth Grotto. [With her own] hands she wrote a letter and a seven-stanza *shi*-poem[6] and gave [them] to Tao 'The Recluse' (*s.c.* Tao Hongjing).

6. Prominent Daoist in the Upper Clarity tradition (451–536). "*Shi*-poem": a form of regulated poetry in five or seven verses whose meaning relies heavily on the juxtaposition of ideas in parallel positions.

THE SCRIPTURE OF THE INNER EXPLANATIONS OF THE THREE HEAVENS
(*Santian neijie jing*)

The *Scripture of the Inner Explanations of the Three Heavens* (*Santian neijie jing*) is a product of the southern Celestial Masters, dating to roughly the mid-fifth century. In presenting a partisan history of Daoism, it emphasizes the cosmology of the Three Heavens (*santian*) and the role of people's behavior in maintaining cosmic harmony. The details of its cosmology are important, since, as Stephen Bokenkamp has noted, many of Daoism's internecine struggles played out as battles over competing cosmologies.

Because the *Scripture of the Inner Explanations of the Three Heavens* postdates the new Upper Clarity and Numinous Treasure revelations, its own cosmology is best understood as a critique of—and attempt to supplant—their cosmological conceptions. It decries the Six Heavens, which it regards as corrupt. Here, the Celestial Masters deploy a complicated cosmogonic theory—according to which the cosmic Laozi in essence gives birth to himself from the undifferentiated Dao—in their efforts to restore the heaven of Grand Clarity (or Greatest Purity) to the highest status. It was merely one of three heavens, the others being Upper or Highest Clarity and Jade Clarity, and those in the Upper Clarity tradition had displaced it and the Celestial Masters as they arrogated to themselves the heaven of Upper Clarity. The heaven of Jade Clarity was envisioned as being the residence of deities so ethereal that they do not commune with humans; the Numinous Treasure scriptures, revealed later, made the audacious claim that those texts emanated from a realm even more exalted.

The short selection below opens with an account of the mysterious birth of the cosmic Laozi out of nothing and the origin of all the myriad things (including the three pneumas—mystic, primal, and inaugural, or in this translation "the *qi*-energy of mystery, principle, and beginning"—that Lord Lao divided and distributed) and the population of the world. The text goes on to describe the three teachings that Laozi used to instruct people in different times and places: first, the Great Dao of Non-Assertion (or Great Way of Nonacting); second, the Dao of the Buddha (or Way of the Buddha); and third, the Great Dao of the Pure Covenant (or Great Way of the Pure Covenant). It also alludes to the story of Laozi converting the barbarians and describes the cosmic Laozi's descent to install Zhang Daoling as the Master of the Three Heavens.

What is perhaps most significant about this text is its redefinition of the earlier Celestial Masters (Tianshi) Daoist tradition, made necessary by the successful revelations of other Daoist lineages and the new pressures brought on by the spread of Buddhism. Although the *Scripture of the Inner Explanations of the Three Heavens* purports to narrate a history of early Daoism, it is better understood as a snapshot account of Celestial Masters Daoism at a particular point in its history during the Liu Song dynasty (420–479).

PRONOUNCING GLOSSARY

Laojun: *lao-choon*
Laozi zhongjing: *lao-tzu chong-ching*
Santian neijie jing: *sahn-tien nay-jieh ching*

Yinxi: *yin-hsi*
Zhang Daoling: *chawng dow-ling*

The Dao originally sprang from what had nothing before it, from that infinite misty [Chaos] in which there was nothing that caused it to be. From that void something whole was produced spontaneously and through transformation: the Great Being of the Way and its Power, which was born before the Original *qi*-energy.[1] This is the Venerable in the center of the Dao, and thus it is called "the Great Being of the Way and Power." From it are derived all the True Beings as they are addressed in our petitions today to the [Heavens] of Greatest Purity: "Their Highnesses the Limitless Great Dao of the Supreme Three Heavens[2] of the Mysterious Origin of Greatest Purity, the Most High Old Lord, the Most High Great Being, the Ancestral Sovereigns of Heaven, the Nine Ancient Lords of the Capital of the Immortals, the Great Beings of the Nine *qi*-energies, etc., [ending with] the hundred and thousand energy layers of the Dao, [which produce] the Twelve Hundred [Cosmic] Officials." After this, in the midst of obscure darkness appeared the Empty Cavern, and in the midst of the Empty Cavern appeared the Great Non-Being, and this Great Non-Being transformed and became the *qi*-energy of mystery, principle, and beginning. These three *qi*-energies mingled in chaotic coalescence and through transformation produced the Jade Maiden of Dark Mystery. When the Jade Maiden was born, the chaotic *qi*-energy coalesced again and through transformation produced Laozi. He was born through the left armpit of the Jade Maiden of Dark Mystery.[3] At his birth his hair was [already] white, and thus he was called Laozi (the Old

---

TRANSLATED BY Kristofer Schipper. All bracketed additions are the translator's.

1. *Qi* is vital energy or breath (pneuma).
2. The heavens of Great Clarity (Taiqing), Jade Clarity (Yuqing), and Upper Clarity (Shangqing).

3. In contrast to the Buddha, who was born through the right armpit of Queen Maya [translator's note].

Infant). Laozi is Laojun (the Old Lord). Through transformation he achieved the qi-energy [creating] Heaven, Earth, and humankind. . . . The Old Lord disseminated the [three] qi-energies of mystery, principle, and beginning. . . . The qi-energy of mystery, clear and limpid, rose and created Heaven; the qi-energy of beginning, dense and turbid, coalesced and descended to form the Earth; the qi-energy of principle, being light and subtle, streamed forth and became water. Sun and moon, stars and constellations then were expanded and scattered [through the sky]. The Old Lord then harmonized the [different] qi-energies and transformed them into nine countries, in which he placed nine human beings: three men and six women. At the time of Fu Xi and Nüwa,[4] each of these adopted family and personal names. Thereupon [the Old Lord] produced three Dao, in order to instruct the Heavenly people [i.e., the elect]: in China (the Middle Kingdom) the qi-energy of yang[5] being pure and correct, he made (the people) venerate the Great Dao of Non-Assertion [i.e., ancient Daoism]; in the lands of the foreigners with their eighty-one regions, where the qi-energy of yin[6] predominates, he made the people venerate the Dao of Buddha with its severe rules and commandments in order to counter the yin-energy. In the lands of Chu and Yue,[7] where yin and yang qi-energies are weak, he made the people venerate the Great Dao of the Pure Covenant. At that time, the reign of the Six Heavens[8] flourished.

The text continues by describing the repeated manifestations of Laozi as the teacher of kings in each major period of the history of ancient China. At last, during the Zhou,[9] he was incarnated again, becoming first Mother Li (Mother Plumtree) and her "old child," who lived in her womb and there recited scriptures during eighty-one years. Born again through her left armpit, he lived in China until the time of King You.[1] Then, observing the growing decadence of the dynasty, he "let down his hair and raved like a madman; he took leave of the Zhou and departed." Next follows the well-known story of his journey through the mountain pass and transmission of the *Daodejing,* here coupled with another book, the *Middle Scripture of the Laozi* (*Laozi zhongjing*).[2] Finally he departed with Yin Xi, the guardian of the pass, for the western regions, where he was reincarnated as the Buddha, "and from these times on, Buddhism [which had already existed before] flourished again." However, in later times, decline and corruption set in. Buddhism, which originally was meant for non-Chinese, was introduced into the Middle Kingdom,[3] and the Three Ways became confused:

The more things went wrong in the world of men, the more the qi-energy of Heaven became greatly troubled. When Heaven's qi-energy had become troubled and impure, the people lost their Fundamental Truth. Thereupon, in the years of Emperor Shun of the Han dynasty (r. 125–144 C.E.), the Most High (Laojun) chose a personal emissary in order to rectify the reign

---

4. The legendary divine founder of the Chinese people and his wife, credited with creating living beings.
5. The male principle; the term originally referred to the sunny side of a valley, and by extension it came to be associated with the light, heaven, dryness, and activity.
6. The female principle; the term originally referred to the shady side of a valley, and by extension it came to be associated with the dark, earth,

dampness, and passivity.
7. An ancient state on the southeastern coast of China; Chu adjoined it to the north and west.
8. The demonic heavens, which were surpassed by the pure Three Heavens system of the Daoists.
9. The Zhou dynasty, 1046–256 B.C.E.
1. Reigned 781–771 B.C.E.
2. For this text, as well as *Daode jing* (*The Scripture of the Way and Its Virtue*), see above.
3. That is, China.

of the Six Heavens, to separate the true from the false and to reveal the *qi*-energy of the Highest Three Heavens. Thus, in the first year of the Han'an period, [the cyclical year being] *renwu* (142 C.E.), on the first day of the fifth moon, Laojun met with Zhang Daoling,[4] the Daoist, in the cave of the Quting mountain in the district of Shu . . . and appointed him Master of the Three Heavens, of the One Correct *qi*-energy of Peace of the Great Mysterious Capital.

4. The founder of the Celestial Masters movement (34–156 C.E.); see the *Xiang'er Commentary on the Laozi* (*Laozi xiang'er zhu*), above.

THE GREAT PETITION FOR SEPULCHRAL PLAINTS
(*Dazhong songzhang*)

The *Great Petition for Sepulchral Plaints* (*Dazhong songzhang*), most likely dating to the sixth century, is an example of a particular type of "petition" text used by medieval Daoists. Such texts, modeled on imperial communications with officials—the documents that enabled what some have called the Chinese "paperwork empire" to function—were used during rituals to address those in the underworld. They were dispatched (through vocalization and visualization) to celestial offices by contrite Daoist priests on behalf of their clients. As the example below makes clear, petition texts provided templates: the pertinent individual information would be supplied to fill in the blank spaces. Some modern scholars have seen them as demonstrating the bureaucratic nature of Daoist ritual itself.

One of the main functions of such texts was to solicit help in treating illnesses, especially those inflicted on the living by the resentful dead. Thus the *Great Petition for Sepulchral Plaints* opens by identifying the petitioner, who has attested to the "disastrous decline" of "the auspices of his house" and to the "successive illnesses" burdening "the members of his household."

PRONOUNCING GLOSSARY

Daozhong songzhang: *dow-chong sung-chawng*

Wei Huacun: *wey hua-tsoon*

Zhang Daoling: *chawng dow-ling*

Complete religious title [of the priest]
We address our superiors:

Now (so-and-so), of (such-and-such) region, district, township, and village, has provided a full statement in which he has said that the auspices of his house are in disastrous decline, and the members of his household have been burdened with successive illnesses. Their activities are unprofitable; their dwelling is unquiet. Thus he has pleaded for a petition for the dispersal and elimination of a sepulchral plaint.[1]

TRANSLATED BY Peter Nickerson. All bracketed additions are the translator's.

1. A lawsuit initiated by the spirit of a dead person.

Now, judging by the appearance of the situation, one might seek out the [plaint's] roots in a rough fashion. One must suspect that, among his ancestors to the seventh generation, or his forebears to the ninth, among his close relatives or his near kin, [there was someone who,] since when alive his or her trespasses were excessive, after death became subject to all manner of inquisitions and punishments. His descendants having yet to redeem him, in the darkness he is crying out bitterly.

Perhaps it is a plaint over burial on a spring, or over a funeral's having encroached on a god's temple. Perhaps it is a plaint over a grave having been dug into a cavern, or over a coffin having been damaged. Perhaps it is a plaint over old sepulchers lying atop one another, or new sepulchers striking against one another. The months and years having passed long away, the heirs would be unaware [of the problem]. Perhaps it is a plaint over drowning in water, or being burned by fire, or wounding with vermin, or poisoning with drugs. Perhaps it is a plaint over weapons and imprisonment, or plague and ulcers. Perhaps there are paternal uncles or brothers, or paternal aunts, nieces, nephews, or sisters, infecting each other in succession and causing calamities and harm.

Once there is deception and calumny and [the culprit] is not called to account, the Mansions of Feng[du][2] will make their indictment arbitrarily. However, the Mysterious Statutes may yet send down their beneficence, and [the issue of responsibility for] the trespass may still be pursued.

Your servant, relying completely on the *Protocols of the Twelve Hundred Officials* and the rituals for curing illness and extinguishing evil bestowed on the Southern Marchmount's[3] Primal Suzeraine of the Purple Void [Wei Huacun] by the Perfected of Upright Unity, the Ritual Master of the Three Heavens [Zhang Daoling],[4] respectfully invites his superiors:

The Lord of Celestial Glory and his hundred thousand troops dressed in yellow to apprehend these demons in (so-and-so's) household—the hundred and twenty harmful anomalies, the violent harmers within and without, and the twelve punishing killers[5]—and annihilate them all.

Also we invite the Supreme Lord of the High Storehouse and his ten thousand troops. On behalf of (so-and-so's) household they are to apprehend and place under their control those demons of the five tombs that come and go, wounding and killing, attaching themselves to the descendants and causing harmful anomalies and calamitous injuries, making (so-and-so) ill to the point that his deadly wounds are unceasing. Annihilate them all.

Also we invite the Lord Who Revolves Pneumas and Disperses Disasters and his army of ten thousand. On behalf of (so-and-so) they are to disperse and eliminate the contrary infusions[6] in his household, the twelve punishing killers in (so-and-so's) body that inflict distress, and the hundred and twenty harmful inquisitors. Let them all be dissipated, so that infusional

---

2. The place where the dead were judged.
3. The Five Marchmounts are a group of five sacred mountains—one in each of the four cardinal directions and one at the center. The southern mountain is often identified as Mount Heng, a important site in the veneration of Lady Wei, a Daoist born Wei Huacun (252–334).
4. The founder of the Celestial Masters movement (34–156 C.E.); see the *Xiang'er Commentary on the Laozi* (*Laozi xiang'er zhu*), above.

5. "Harmers" (*yang*), as well as killers (*sha*), unite fears about wandering spirits of dead ancestors—the killer-demons are the spirits of the recently deceased who return to their old homes and attack their surviving kin—with worries relating to the spirits of astro-geomancy and taboos on burials and funerals [translator's note].
6. Pestilential vapors "infused" or poured (*zhu*) into the bodies of humans [translator's note].

obstructions may be brought under control, demons extinguished, and calamities brought to an end. Dispel the vapors of the Six Heavens.[7]

Also we invite the Great General Who Benefits Heaven and his great army of ten thousand, the five Lords of Ten Thousand Blessings and their hundred and twenty civil and military officials, the Lord of Lapideous Peace and his hundred and twenty civil and military officials, and the Lord of Shuoping and his hundred and twenty civil and military officials who govern the Mansion of Mysterious Beginnings. Together on behalf of (so-and-so) they are to drive off stale vapors and arrest the world's demon bandits that are lording it up, eating and drinking [i.e., receiving sacrifices], creating all kinds of spirit afflictions, and disturbing (so-and-so) and young and old in his household. Let them all be apprehended and severed, immediately pulverized, and directly destroyed. Dispel death and send life; extinguish calamities and bring blessings.

Also we invite the Lord of Lapideous Transcendence and his hundred and twenty civil and military officials. On behalf of (so-and-so's) household they are to dispel the demons of violent harm and suppress spirit afflictions so that they may do no injury.

Also we invite the five Lords of the Four Ministers and their hundred and twenty civil and military officials. On behalf of (so-and-so) they are to dissipate the demonic afflictions of inquisitions and plaints in the household and all incorrect pneumas that disturb the dwelling, bringing disquiet. Directly apprehend and execute them all. Dissolve the plaint's inquisitions; separate the clear from the turbid.

Also we invite the Lord of the Vermilion Heaven Who Imbibes Pneumas and his hundred and twenty civil and military officials. On behalf of (so-and-so) they are to drive off the arrests resulting from plaints [instigated by] near and distant relatives and those of other surnames, as well as all manner of the malignant and rancorous accusations with which [souls] disturb one another, unwilling to withdraw. Bring under control, sever, and annihilate all the affliction and injury thereby caused.

Also we invite the Lord of Highest Illumination Who Receives Divinity and his hundred and twenty civil and military officials. On behalf of (so-and-so) they are to disperse and eliminate derangements brought on by evil dreams, dispossessions of souls, and departures of essence and spirit, making him at rest and well. Put infusions from previous generations to rest.

Also we invite the Lord of the Grand Mystery and his hundred and twenty civil and military officials who govern the Mansion without Moats. They are to take charge of any vapors of malignant infusions in (so-and-so's) household that cause the loss of essence and spirit, debilitating illnesses, and delirious fright and insensibility. Annihilate these criminal injurers so that they may never cause harm or trouble.

Also we invite the five Lords Who Control the Earth and their hundred and twenty civil and military officials, who [below] govern the Mansion of the Shady Springs. On behalf of (so-and-so) as well as old and young in his household, they are to disperse all subordinate junior demons, whether high or low [in rank], that have caused afflictions and injury owing to blows or offenses against the Motion of the Year, the Original Destiny, Great Year,

---

7. The demonic heavens, which were surpassed by the pure Three Heavens system of the Daoists.

the Kings of the Soil,[8] or the establishing or breaking influences of the chronograms of the tomb. Annihilate them all.

Also we invite the Supreme Lord of Heavenly Birth and his army of ten thousand and the Supreme *Fangxiang* Lord and his army of ten thousand. Together on behalf of (so-and-so), they are to apprehend those of his recently or long-ago deceased kin who have seized him with infusions. Let them be annihilated.

Also we invite the Marksman Lord of Distressed Districts and his hundred and twenty civil and military officials who govern the Mansion of Grand Clarity, and the Lord of Release by Petition and his hundred and twenty civil and military officials who govern the Mansion of Grand Clarity.

Also we invite the General of Assistance and Protection and his clerks and soldiers to bestow on us a True Talisman of the Grand Mystery that will bring under control the Nüqing Edicts, the subterrestrial Two Thousand Bushel Officials, and the Twenty-four Prisons of Mount Tai.[9] [Cause them] on behalf of (so-and-so) to arrest and disperse the tomb demons that seize and harm. They should subject to their orders the Officials and Chiefs in the Earth, the Assistant of the Mound and the Sire of the Tomb, the Lord of Canglin, the Lord of Wuyi, the Marksmen of the Sepulcher of Left and Right, the Director of Boundaries in the Earth, the Grave Minister's Official of the Right, the Elders of Haoli, and the powers of all earth regions. Let them together cut off the vapors of injurious inquisitions and infectious infusions, totally annihilating them.

If in the family of (so-and-so), from the time of grandparents or great-grandparents onward—whether departed earlier or dead later, male or female, old or young—someone in his or her burial has offended the establishing, breaking, ruling, or impoverishing influences of the twelve months, or the Eight Generals and the Six Opposites,[1] thus violating the prohibitions and taboos; or the orientation [of the tomb] was not correct with respect to the tone;[2] or the order of feeding was not correct; or from left or right, above or below, hidden corpses or old remains of those who died before reaching adulthood contravened the [separate?] positions of male and female—as for all these things that cause punishment and calamity and bring disquiet, causing illness among the descendants, let them be entirely dissolved and let harmony be restored. Trace [the case] to its origins and repair the situation; change the inauspicious into the auspicious. Turn calamities into blessings, so that life and death, dark and light, do not interfere with one another.

We invite the Lord Who Dwells in the Stars and his hundred and twenty civil and military officials who rule the Mansion of the Floriate Canopy, the Lord Who Executes Harmers and his hundred and twenty civil and military officials who rule the Mansion of Luminous Jupiter, and the Illuminated Lord of the Great White's [i.e., Venus's] Central Phalanx and his hundred and twenty civil and military officials. Together, on behalf of the seven generations of deceased ancestors of (so-and-so's) household—departed

8. Spirits associated with divination by means of the earth. The first three terms are linked to Chinese astronomy and astrology.
9. The Eastern Marchmount; on the significance of Mount Tai, or Taishan, see the introduction to "Two Poems on Taishan," above.

1. Astral entities. "The Eight Generals": eight menacing stars.
2. It was believed that the tone of one's surname, associated with one of the five musical tones, should determine the form of one's dwelling or tomb.

earlier or transformed later, male or female, old or young—they are to disperse the infectious ties of the Offices of the Stars, to apprehend the lingering, contrary killers of the twelve periods of the day that bring punishment and calamities, and to eliminate them all, together with their deadly influences. Cut off infectious infusions.

If stale vapors of subordinate officials assume form and lead demon troops, driving forth the demons of wounding infusions among the previously departed, [forcing them to] come and go from the family's gate to intimidate the living, seizing cloudsouls and whitesouls[3] and thereby causing illness, let them all be brought under the control of the Demon Statutes. Annihilate them all.

Also we invite the Supreme Lord of the Celestial Mystery and his army of twelve thousand. On behalf of (so-and-so) they are to apprehend and place under their control all those—be they far or near, noble or base, male or female—who might have [given rise to] pneumas of plots involving dispute, slander, or curses and oaths. Make them hide themselves away and do no injury.

Also we invite the Lord of Vermilion Cinnabar and his hundred and twenty civil and military officials who govern the Mansion of Southern Glory. On behalf of the family of (so-and-so) they are to apprehend the Five Gu-Poisons,[4] the Six Goblins, and the hundred and twenty demons of malignant disasters and impoverishment that are always causing decrement and loss in (so-and-so's) home. Annihilate them all.

Let all the twenty-four Lords, civil and military officials, and clerks and soldiers who have been invited descend all together this very day. Let each in accordance with his own office on behalf of (so-and-so) dissipate the inquisition and punishment, destroy the harmful affliction, and pacify and dissolve all the infusion-vapors that have been thus cut off. If there are demons of those who [died by] violence or injustice or were exiled and buried away from home, or who [died] without descendants—be they departed earlier or dead later, agnates or affines—and whether the affair is one of those anticipated in the eighty-one plaints named above, or any one of a hundred myriad types of inquisitory infusions, let [those troubles] be altogether laid to rest, not allowed to stir, and entirely washed away.

If there are still those who want to give vent to grudges and are lying in wait for openings whereby they can send down depletion and then stir up calamities and injury, let one and all be bound and pulverized, speedily destroyed, and so prevented from interfering with (so-and-so). Let present and departed have their separate realms, and calamities and blessings stand opposed to one another.

From now on, as for (so-and-so) and his family, let divine pneumas radiate all about them and celestial numina aid and protect them. Let their five organs be attuned and their six viscera[5] be open and clear, replete with perfected essence, with the hundred illnesses put to rest. Let their enterprises be successful and their merit be renewed daily. Let all auspicious things descend and wickedness be dissipated. Let both their public and private

---

3. Heavy souls (po-souls), linked to the earth; cloudsouls (hun-souls) or light souls are linked with heaven and its pneumas.
4. Made from toxic worms.
5. The small intestine, the gallbladder, the stomach, the large intestine, the bladder, and the triple burner (an organ that has no Western equivalent). "Five organs": liver, heart, spleen/stomach, kidneys, and lungs.

affairs flourish, with the living and the departed [beneficially] relying on one another.

As for the Celestial Officials, Lords, Generals, Clerks, and Soldiers—both civil and military officers—who have been invited, if they diligently achieve results and drive off demonic injury, and in apprehending and executing [the malefactors] establish merit, then we beg directly to state their merit and reward them with promotion, adding to their offices and advancing their rank, in order of high and low in accordance with the constant codes of the Celestial Bureaux, so that they shall be without resentment.

As for the pledges offered by (so-and-so)—forty feet of figured purple cloth, one bushel and two pecks of Destiny Rice, twelve hundred cash, one set of pure clothes[6] for wearing, one hundred and twenty sheets of deposition paper, two sticks of ink, two brushes, one ounce of cinnabar, one scholar's knife, a pure mat, and one pure turban—they are for requiting the Officials, Lords, Generals, and Clerks for their efficacious diligence.

We pray to the Most High, etc., etc. . . . . Because (so-and-so) is ill, and in order to disperse the inquisitory pneumas and seizing infusions of those departed earlier or dead later, your servant respectfully offers up this Great Petition for Sepulchral Plaints and presents himself on high, etc., etc.

6. Special clothing worn during religious services[;] . . . a common term also in Buddhism, whose laypeople wore white [translator's note]. "Cash": a Chinese coin of small value.

A NEW ACCOUNT OF TALES OF THE WORLD
(Shishuo xinyu)

LIU YIQING

A New Account of Tales of the World was compiled by Liu Yiqing (403–444) from anecdotes and conversations that he heard. Though it primarily depicts various facets of the aristocratic society of prominent families, it also provides some interesting glimpses of Buddhism and Daoism. In the selection printed below, we find a Buddhist monk ridiculing the common Daoist practice of using paper talismans for healing. In addition to offering a specific critique of that practice—a practice followed by Buddhists as well, incidentally—the passage nicely exemplifies how polemically charged the relationship between Buddhists and Daoists had become during this period.

PRONOUNCING GLOSSARY

Chi Yin: *chih yin*
Liu Yiqing: *liu yee-ching*

Shishuo xinyu: *shih-shu-oh hsin-yu*
Yu Fakai: *yu fah-kai*

[A Buddhist Critique of Daoist Talismans]

Chi Yin believed in the Daoist religion[1] with zealous devotion. Once he was suffering from an ailment in his bowels, which various Daoist physicians were unable to cure. Hearing that the Buddhist monk Yu Fakai had a good reputation, he went to consult him. After he had come, Fakai took his pulse and said, "What Your Excellency is suffering from is caused by none other than an excess of zeal, that's all." Whereupon he mixed a dose of medicine with some hot water and gave it to him. No sooner had Chi taken the medicine than immediately he had an enormous bowel movement in which he evacuated several wads of paper, each as big as a fist. When he opened them up to look, they turned out to be the Daoist paper charms (*fu*)[2] he had ingested earlier.

TRANSLATED BY Richard B. Mather. This selection has been converted from Wade-Giles to pinyin by the Norton editor.

1. He belonged to the "Heavenly Master" sect 2. Talismans.
[translator's note].

THE ESSAY TO RIDICULE THE DAO
(*Xiaodao lun*)

ZHEN LUAN

The *Essay to Ridicule the Dao* (*Xiaodao lun*) is, as its title signals, a polemical work. This critical Buddhist response to the Daoist "Conversion of the Barbarians" (*huahu*) theory—the claim that "Buddhist" teachings were in fact the preaching of Laozi, after he left China for India (see "The Conversion of the Barbarians," above)—was written by a court official named Zhen Luan (fl. 535–81) as a memorial to the emperor in 570 C.E. In attacking the Conversion of the Barbarians theory, he focuses primarily on the Numinous Treasure (Lingbao) tradition, because it borrowed Buddhist vocabulary and doctrines; he also makes many critical comments on earlier practices of the Celestial Masters.

Zhen Luan's approach is to quote a passage from a Daoist sacred scripture and then launch into a rabid critique, prefaced by "I laugh at this and say." He emphasizes the logical fallacies within the passage and sets its claims against the differing assertions of other Daoist texts, as well as invoking various other religious, historical, and scientific sources. The *Essay to Ridicule the Dao* may have convinced the emperor that Daoism was not the tradition on which he should base his rule, but it was just one among many salvos fired in the ongoing debates between Buddhists and Daoists at court. Daoists would reassert themselves in the Tang dynasty (618–907), only to be steamrolled by debates with Buddhists during the Yuan dynasty (1260–1368).

PRONOUNCING GLOSSARY

Daode jing: *dow-duh ching*
Laozi: *lao-tzu*
Luan Da: *luan dah*

Shakya: *shaw-key-yah*
Xiaodao lun: *hsiao-dow loon*
Zhen Luan: *chun luan*

Preface

Your servant, Zhen Luan, humbly offers this memorial. By imperial decree, I was ordered to examine the two teachings, Buddhism and Daoism, in order to settle their precedence, their relative value, and their differences. Because this humble servant is not sufficiently experienced to judge the quality of the teachings, I reverently present the following concrete record to gracious imperial hearing.

In private, I think there are considerable differences between the visible traces of Buddhism and Daoism. Their respective rise and decline, appearance and withdrawal, and their overall transformations are not alike at all. In either case, however, the inner subtleties and esoteric mysteries are not easily understood.

Yet upon comparing them one finds that although the Buddhists consider karma[1] and retribution as the main doctrine, the Daoists venerate natural spontaneity as their major principle. Natural spontaneity is constituted by nonaction; karma and retribution, on the other hand, are manifest in the accumulation of deeds. When one holds onto the origin, all affairs will be tranquil and principle will be well balanced. But when one deviates from the main doctrine, one's intention will go astray and the teaching will be perverted. Only with principle in perfect balance can beginning and end be in complete harmony. But when the teaching is perverted, then there is nothing that is not done.

For me, Laozi's *Wuqian wen* (Text in Five Thousand Words)[2] is venerable and lofty both in style and in meaning. It should be valued very highly. By righting the self and ordering the state, the ways of the ruler are enriched. For this purpose, the Daoists have the practices of writing talismans and reciting spells, whereas the Buddhists prohibit all arts that rely on extrasensory powers or are contrary to the ideal of compassion.

Placing the outer appearances of both side by side, the average person is easily confused about which is true and which false. How could this be the meaning of the Great Dao with its natural spontaneity, emptiness, and nonaction? It can only be explained in that later generations turned their backs on the origins and erroneously brought forth specious ideas.

Then again, there are all those Daoist magical arts by which one supposedly can ascend to the immortals as a spirit. They all brought forth nothing but deception, doubt, and betrayal. In antiquity, for example, Xu Fu[3] used such ideas to cheat [the First Emperor of the Qin] and enter the country of the eastern barbarians; later Li Shaoweng and Luan Da[4] bewitched and betrayed Emperor Wu of the Han. Then the three Zhangs[5] caused disorder in the west, in Liang, and later Sun En[6] raised the banner of rebellion in the east, in Yue.

TRANSLATED BY Livia Kohn. All bracketed additions are the translator's.

1. The positive and negative deeds that bear fruit as either happiness or suffering in the future.
2. *The Scripture of the Way and Its Virtue (Daode jing)*; see above.
3. A court diviner (fl. 219–210 B.C.E.); he persuaded the emperor, Qin Shi Huangdi (r. 221–210 B.C.E.), to support his efforts to bring back herbs of immortality from the isles of the blessed in the eastern seas. The "eastern barbarians" were the Japanese.

4. Magicians of the Han court [translator's note]. Emperor Wu (r. 141–87 B.C.E.) greatly increased Chinese influence and the dynasty's power, and instituted Confucianism as the state religion.
5. Father, son, and grandson, the first three leaders of the Celestial Masters: Zhang Daoling (34–56 C.E.), Zhang Heng (d. 179), and Zhang Lu (d. 215/16? 245?).
6. The leader (d. 402) of a messianic Daoist rebellion in southern China (399).

Terrible disturbances of this kind have always been condemned, even in antiquity. Most certainly, any government applying such behavior can only be a government of falsehood and corruption. A people guided along such lines will surely be deluded and confused.

In addition, the examination of Daoist scriptures reveals contradictions from scroll to scroll, whereas the analysis of their doctrines shows they have neither head nor tail.

Traditionally, one judged the quality of a person's filial behavior from the way he behaved toward his ruler. Seeing a man who served his lord with exhaustive ritual formality, one would honor him like a filial son caring for his parents. Seeing a man who served his lord without ritual formality, one would persecute him like an eagle chasing a sparrow.

Confucius said, "The gentleman serves his lord in such a way that, approaching him, all his thinking is of loyalty; withdrawing from him, all his concerns are about making up his shortcomings. He strives ardently to emulate his lord's good characteristics and works hard to correct his bad traits. Only thus can ruler and minister treat each other like kin."[7]

The *Zuozhuan* (Mr. Zuo's Commentary to the *Spring and Autumn Annals*[8]) says, "Whenever in what the lord says there is some part acceptable and some part unacceptable, one should relate to what he can accept and dismiss what he cannot."

Now, although I am not quite like that, having been asked for my judgment by Your Majesty, I yet do not dare to answer fully. [I will freely admit that] the *Daode jing* in two scrolls can easily be accepted by an orthodox Confucian. Still, what I consider questionable is that it does not go with the extreme other end of the Daoist teaching. I, therefore, pray you judge and evaluate my opinions.

The *Daode jing* says,

> When the highest kind of people hear of the Dao, they diligently
>   practice it.
> When the medium kind of people hear of the Dao, they half believe
>   in it.
> When the lowest kind of people hear of the Dao, they laugh heartily
>   at it.
> If they did not laugh at it, it would not be the Dao.

Your servant has taken the liberty to follow the attitude of the lowest kind and has written a treatise called "Laughing at the Dao" in three scrolls and thirty-six sections. The three scrolls laugh at the Daoist classification of the Three Caverns;[9] the thirty-six sections laugh at the thirty-six divisions of scriptures.

Cold sweat on my forehead, my heart trembling to distraction, I venture to present this to Your Majesty.

On the fifteenth of the second month, fifth year of Heavenly Harmony under the Great Zhou [570].

---

7. Quoted from the *Hanshu* (the *History of the Former Han*, ca. 90 C.E.); Confucius lived from 551 to 479 B.C.E.

8. One of the Six Classics of Confucian literature. The *Zuozhuan* is traditionally attributed to

Zuo Qinming (5th c. B.C.E.).

9. That is, the texts in the Daoist canon; they were divided into three "caverns," or collections, by Lu Xiujing in 471, and each "cavern" was divided into twelve sections.

With deepest respects,

Zhen Luan

Metropolitan Commandant
Native of Wuji District
Earl of Opening the Country

6. *Revival of the Dead through Fivefold Purification*

The *Wulian jing* (Scripture of Fivefold Purification) says:

"Bury the deceased with dyed silk. For the emperor use one bolt [14 m]; for a king or lord, one fathom [3.50 m]; for a commoner, five feet [1.75 m]. In addition, forge dragons from five pounds of pure gold, iron in the case of commoners. Then take five pieces of colored stone and inscribe them with jade writing. After leaving the body outside for one night, bury it three feet deep."

The *Nüqing wen* (Nüqing's Writ)[1] has: [Through the proper purification] the souls of one's ancestors up to nine generations can leave their abode of perpetual night and enter the heavens of radiant light. There they feast. After thirty-two years, they return to their former bodies and come back to life."

I laugh at this and say:

The *Sanyuan pin*[2] says, "In the 3 offices of heaven, earth, and water, there are 9 departments and 9 palaces with 120 offices, whose conscientious officials record all crimes, events of good fortune, and meritorious actions. There are no lacunae or errors. The life span of someone who does good is accordingly lengthened; the years of one who does evil are properly shortened."

How could one, therefore, disregard karmic retribution and just use five feet of dyed silk to make the souls of one's ancestors up to nine generations enter the heaven of radiant light, and then, after thirty-two years, return to their former bodies? Obviously, this is entirely absurd!

From this, however, one can see that the text on the fivefold purification comes from a period before the separation of heaven and earth. If it were still applicable today, then the dead would all dig open their graves and come back to life after thirty-two years. Everyone would surely notice such an event with their eyes and ears.

Why, then, is it that in all the time since Fu Xi[3] no one ever heard of any Daoist whose ancestors of nine generations have risen from the dead and stepped out of their graves? Such absurdity! One can only laugh!

These days, I hear, somewhere in the country an old mound opened. Should it not it be some Daoist's forefather coming back to life? That is worth a good laugh, too!

---

1. A text of the early Celestial Masters better known as *Nüqing guilü* [translator's note]. For the *Nüqing guilü* (the *Demon Statues of Lady Blue*), see above.
2. *Precepts of the Three Primes* (5th century C.E.),

a scripture of the Numinous Treasure (Lingbao) tradition.
3. The mythical first emperor of China, who was the legendary divine founder of the Chinese people.

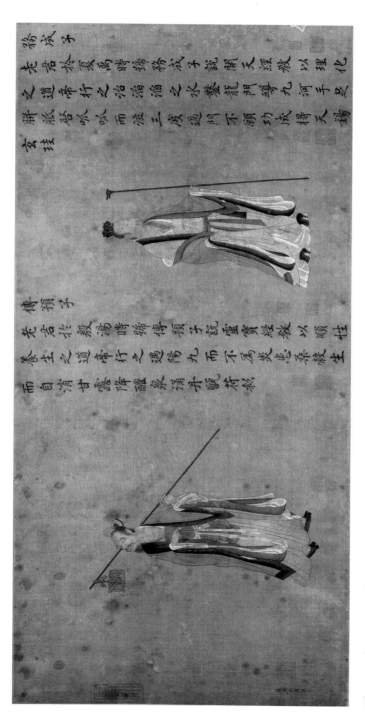

The transformations of Lord Lao, scroll, China, Song dynasty (960–1279)

This excerpt from a longer scroll by Wang Liyong (fl. 1120) shows two of the transformations of Laozi. Following his divinization in the Han dynasty (202 B.C.E.–220 C.E.), legends developed about how Laozi descended into this world to teach different Chinese emperors and reveal important scriptures. These images, the last two on the scroll, show Laozi as the teacher of the mythical emperor Yu and of the Shang emperor (the first historical dynasty, ca. 1600–1045 B.C.E.). THE NELSON-ATKINS MUSEUM OF ART, KANSAS CITY, MISSOURI. PURCHASE: WILLIAM ROCKHILL NELSON TRUST, 48-17. PHOTO: JOHN LAMBERTON

Daoist Official of Heaven, painting, China, Song dynasty (960–1279)

Here the Official of Heaven sits like a bureaucrat at his table, surrounded by attendants standing on a cloud. He is one of the Three Officials who record humans' behavior and, on the basis of those records, determine their fate. To communicate with these deities, on specific ritual days priests burned documents intended for the Official of Heaven, buried documents for the Official of the Earth, and submerged documents for the Official of Water. © 2014 MUSEUM OF FINE ARTS, BOSTON

The Perfected Warrior (*Zhenwu*), porcelain figure, China, Ming dynasty (Wanli reign, 1573–1620)

The Perfected Warrior (*Zhenwu*)—who developed from the Dark Warrior (*Xuanwu*), a Han dynasty (202 B.C.E.–220 C.E.) directional deity associated with the northern celestial region and with winter, black, and water—was made more important by emperors of the Ming dynasty (1368–1644) seeking to revive his sacred mountain, Wudang (in Hubei Province). This type of blue-and-white Ming porcelain later became quite popular in Europe and the Middle East. © 2014 MUSEUM OF FINE ARTS, BOSTON

Celestial Worthy of the Sound of Thunder Transforming All, painting, China, 1596.

This ritual painting commissioned by the Ming dynasty Wanli emperor, (r. 1572–1620) depicts the Celestial Worthy of the Sound of Thunder Transforming All (the main Daoist thunder god, 1) surrounded by functionaries he oversees: the Duke of Thunder (2), the Mother of Lightning (3), the Rain Master (4), the Earl of the Winds (5), Marshal Bi (9), Marshall Gou (14), the Four Great Celestial Lords (the Celestial Lord Xin, 6; Deng, 7; Tao, 8; and Zhang, 12), and the Four Great Marshals (Marshal Ma, 10; Wen, 11; Zhao, 13; and Guan, 15). All of the iconographic identifications and historical information about this painting have been established by Professor Poul Andersen of the Daoist Iconography Project. © THE NATIONAL MUSEUM OF DENMARK, ETHNOGRAPHIC COLLECTIONS

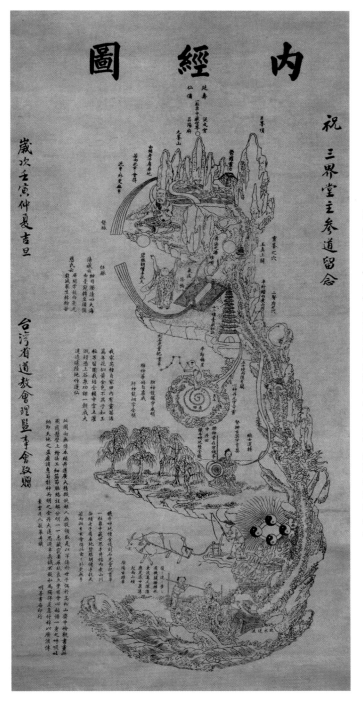

Illustration of inner circulation (*neijing tu*), China, Qing dynasty (1644–1912)

This sketch, of a lost image from Beijing's White Cloud Temple, depicts the body's pathways along which the Daoist practitioner of internal alchemy circulates internal energies (qi) to refine the elixir of immortality. The organs are shown symbolically and are correlated with the celestial realm. The Herd Boy (holding the dipper) and the Weaving Maiden (with the spinning wheel), lovers of legend who can meet only once a year, here represent the heart and kidneys.

ETHNOLOGISCHES MUSEUM, STAATLICHE MUSEEN, GERMANY/ART RESOURCE, NY

Daoist priest's robe, embroidered satin, China, Qing dynasty (1644–1912)

Ritual robes in different Daoist traditions often indicate a priest's rank and are covered with symbols: the back of this robe displays numerous deities, patterns of flowing pneuma, and trigrams (across the bottom). At the top are the Three Pure Ones: Original Commencement (Jade Clarity), Numinous Treasure (Upper Clarity), and Way and Its Virtue (i.e., the deified Laozi, Great Clarity); the central figure is the Jade Emperor, surrounded by an array of attendants. V&A IMAGES, LONDON/ART RESOURCE, NY

Meizhou zumiao talisman, Fujian Province, 1993

The title of this popular talisman for achieving peace is "*Meizhou zumiao*," which literally means the "ancestral (or original) temple" in Meizhou. Meizhou is an island in Fujian Province, the location of the main temple to Mazu. Mazu, pictured in the center of this talisman, is a popular goddess who is venerated within Daoism and Buddhism. There are many legends about Mazu; most claim that she saved someone (usually her father or brothers) following a powerful storm. Cults to Mazu developed by the eleventh century as she became known as a patron deity for fishermen, seafarers, and those who are suffering and in need of assistance. Temples dedicated to Mazu's memory have spread around the world with Chinese diaspora communities and are now found, for example, in Taiwan, Singapore, Macao, and San Francisco. MAZU MEIZHOU ZUMIAO, PUTIAN, 1992–1993/SANDER VINK

Daoist ritual performance, Jiangsu Province, 2014

Daoist rituals—large or small, wherever performed—combine singing, chanting, music, and burning of incense. This photograph captures key elements found in many Daoist rituals. The head ritual priest (standing to the left of the flames) holds an audience tablet, which signals his authority and power to command Daoist deities, while reciting sacred formulas with eyes partly closed. The burning of paper objects or documents is accompanied by music (usually drums, gongs, cymbals, flutes, and bells).

PATRICE FAVA

18. Laozi Became the Buddha

The *Xuanmiao neipian*[4] says:

"After Laozi had crossed the pass and reached the kingdom of Kapilavastu, he entered the mouth of Queen Maya. Later he ripped open her left armpit and was born.

"He then took seven steps and exclaimed: 'In heaven above, on the earth below, I alone am venerable.'

"This was the beginning of Buddhism."

I laugh at this and say:

The *Huahu jing* states: "When Laozi converted Kashmir, all its people began to worship Buddhism.

"Then Laozi said: 'One hundred years from now, there will be another, a true Buddha, who now dwells in the Tusita Heaven.[5] He will then be born in Shravasti [Kapilavastu] as a son to King Shuddhodana. At that time, I will send Yin Xi to be born and become the Buddha's disciple. His name will be Ananda. He will compile the scriptures in twelve divisions.'

"One hundred years after Laozi had left, a son was indeed born to the king of Shravasti. After six years of mortification, he perfected the Tao and was named the Buddha Shakyamuni.

"Forty-nine years later, when he was about to enter nirvana, Laozi appeared again on earth. He was then called Kashyapa.[6] Under a pair of sal trees, he asked the Tathagata[7] thirty-six questions on behalf of the great assemblies [of followers]. Then the Buddha entered nirvana.

"After cremating the Buddha's corpse, Kashyapa assembled his relics, distributed them to different countries, and erected stupas over them. Later, King Ashoka[8] also built eighty-four thousand stupas."

Following this account, Laozi cannot actually have become the Buddha. If he had indeed become the Buddha, would he not have had to cremate his own corpse and erect stupas in his own honor? What a joke!

Yet many texts assure us that Laozi, in fact, became the Buddha, just as they say that he served as the teacher of dynasties. Really, must all the dynastic teachers and buddhas of the world inevitably depend on old Boyang?[9] Must the salvation of humankind, the reform of the world, always be steered by Mr. Li Er?[1]

If you say that even the Buddha could not be himself without the Dao, does this mean that ever since the primordial beginning of things there was only one and the same Laozi? There never were any others allowed to realize the Dao and serve as dynastic teachers? If this is the case, then Laozi really puts himself ahead as the only one on earth able to perform these tasks.

At the same time, Buddhist sutras maintain that everyone can attain the fruits of Buddhahood by practicing the proper cultivation.[2] Daoist

---

4. *Esoteric Account of Mystery and Wonder* (ca. 5th century C.E.).
5. The abode of Maitreya, the buddha who will follow Shakyamuni Buddha.
6. One of the Buddha's chief disciples.
7. A title of a buddha (literally, "one who has thus come/gone"); it is the one most often used by the

historical Buddha to refer to himself.
8. Emperor of the Mauryan dynasty of India (ca. 300–232 B.C.E.), a patron of Buddhism.
9. One of the names of Laozi [translator's note].
1. Laozi's original name.
2. This is true of Mahayana (Great Vehicle) Buddhism but not of all Buddhist sects.

scriptures do not speak of this. For them, there was and is only one, the Venerable Lord. How, then, is it that Buddhism is so generous while Daoism is so mean?

In addition, Daoist words are foolish and the tradition is hollow. One cannot make head or tail of its claims: just as the *Shuji* states that Zhang Ling[3] was devoured by a snake, while the Daoists claim that he ascended to heaven in broad daylight; just like the *Hanshu*, which says that Liu An[4] was killed upon imperial order, whereas Daoist legends make him out to be an immortal who never died at all.

Is it, therefore, any wonder that Daoist accounts lie about Laozi becoming the Buddha?

Moreover, the *Zao tiandi jing*[5] says: "When he had converted the barbarians in the west, Laozi transformed his body and vanished. His left eye became the sun; his right eye became the moon." Yet, according to the *Xuanmiao jing*,[6] "Laozi strode on the essence of the sun and entered the mouth of Queen Maya." This means that Laozi strode on the essence of his very own left eye to enter her mouth.

If we now assume that [Laozi as] the all-pervasive spirit of the Great Dao is present everywhere, then why would he have to rely on one specific essence to enter the womb of the queen? If, however, he must make use of some essence, then this essence, in turn, has to depend on his head. Consequently, if he indeed strides on his own head to enter the queen, then both his eyes should be going in together.

But here he is—entering her astride on only one eye! Is there thus a single-eyed, lopsided Great Dao? How utterly ridiculous!

28. *Taking Cinnabar Brings a Golden Complexion*

The *Shenxian jinye jing* (The Spirit Immortals' Scripture on the Golden Fluid) says:

"The golden fluid and reverted cinnabar were taken by the Highest Lord to become a spirit being. When heated, cinnabar turns into mercury, then it reverts back to cinnabar.

"Taking this, one attains immortality and ascends to heaven in broad daylight. To aspire for immortality without attaining this method is to pain oneself for nothing.

"NOTE: When heated, cinnabar turns into mercury. Heat this mercury, and it will revert back to cinnabar. Thus, one speaks of reverted cinnabar.

"In antiquity, Han Zhong[7] took it and his complexion turned golden.

"In addition, the radiant golden complexion of the Buddha developed because he used this method of the Dao. Only thereby did his body, inside and out, become as solid as gold. Therefore, it was called the gold-hard [diamond] body of the Buddha."

---

3. That is, Zhang Daoling. "The *Shuji*": the *Record of Shu*, a lost text.
4. The prince of Huainan (ca. 179–122 B.C.E.). "The *Hanshu*": the History of the Former Han (ca. 90 C.E.).
5. An unidentified work, whose title could be translated as *Scripture on the Creation of Heaven and Earth*.

6. An unidentified work, whose title could be translated as *Scripture on Mystery and Wonder*.
7. An immortal in the time of the First Emperor of Qin [3rd century B.C.E.; translator's note]. A Daoist immortal or transcendent (*xian*) has reached a higher form of existence than common humans.

I laugh at this and say:

The *Wenshi zhuan* states: "The highest Lord Laozi and the Primal Lord of the Great One—these two sages join to form one body."

Yet the *Jinye jing*[8] says: "As regards the Great One, the Elder of Central Yellow and the Lord of the Great One are the true rulers of the immortals. They drank the golden fluid and ascended to heaven. There they became great gods and harmonized yin and yang."[9]

According to this, Han Zhong never took the golden fluid but was just an ordinary person. The one who took it and ascended to heaven was, in fact, the Venerable Lord. Yet he is the Highest Lord anyway, the master of the myriad perfected.[1] Why should he need to take the golden fluid and only then be able to harmonize yin and yang?

Moreover, how many have attained the high divinity of the Great One? How many must there be who are able to harmonize yin and yang? If everyone who takes cinnabar attains this high state, how numerous must they be?

Moreover, cinnabar and mercury can be found all over the earth. To heat them and obtain reverted cinnabar is not difficult at all. Why, therefore, do the Daoists not all take it and ascend to heaven in broad daylight? Why do they not all become rulers among the heavenly immortals instead of bearing hardships and knocking their teeth together,[2] thus wasting all their lives? How very deplorable!

At the same time, the very fact that Daoists do not all take it shows clearly that the whole cinnabar thing is just a hoax. It is just like trying to catch one's shadow.

They also say that the Buddha's golden complexion came about through a concoction of cinnabar. Yet the truth is that he did not need even one heated cinnabar pellet to achieve this. Such a mass of wrong notions! It is really too sad!

29. Plagiarizing Buddhist Sutras for Daoist Scriptures

The *Miaozhen ge* (Song of Wondrous Perfection) says:

> Even as many people as there are sands of the Ganges,
> Who have heard the teaching,
> Will not be able
> To measure the wisdom of the Dao,
> Try though they may with their combined efforts.

I laugh at this and say:

This text is merely a plagiate of the *Lotus Sutra*,[3] changing "wisdom of the Buddhas" to "wisdom of the Dao." Except for this minor change, the two texts are identical. Nor is this a unique example.

---

8. The *Scripture of the Golden Liquor*, a major work in the Taiqing (Great Clarity) tradition of external alchemy.

9. Yin and yang are the complementary forces that unite to form the Dao: yin, a term that originally referred to the shady side of a valley, by extension came to be associated with the dark, earth, dampness, and passivity—the female principle; yang, a term that originally referred to the sunny side of a valley, by extension came to be associated with the light, heaven, dryness, and activity—the male principle.

1. The *zhenren*, who in later Daoism are described as beings that have moved beyond earthly corruption and are often identified with stellar deities; in the Upper Clarity (Shangqing) tradition, the perfected are more exalted than the *xian*.

2. A preliminary exercise in Daoist gymnastics and meditation and a protective measure against bad luck and nightmares [translator's note].

3. *White Lotus of the True Dharma* (*Saddharma-pundarika*, later 1st–2nd century C.E.?), the most important sutra in the Mahayana tradition. "Plagiate": that is, a plagiarism.

In the old days, the Daoist Gu Huan[4] was confronted with the problem. He countered: "The *Lingbao jing* (Scripture of Numinous Treasure) is written in heavenly script and with great characters; it was brought forth directly from spontaneity and was not originally based on the *Lotus Sutra*. On the contrary, Kumarajiva and Sengzhao[5] copied our Daoist scriptures to compile the *Lotus*."

Stealing the *Lingbao jing* from the *Lotus Sutra* is an act that may deceive the eastern people of Xia [China]. But although the *Lotus Sutra* is different from the *Lingbao jing*, it is identical to the texts of the western regions. All versions produced by translators even today never deviate from the original text of the sutra. Seen from this angle, it is clear that the Daoists plagiarized the Buddhist text rather than vice versa.

In addition, Buddhist sutras are learned and concise; their words and meaning are broad and deep. Although they make up a thousand scrolls and a hundred divisions, there is no superfluous repetition—not at all like the scriptures of Laozi's followers, which entirely lack special insight and have to rely on Buddhist sutras to expand their volume.

In addition, there is not a single reference to the Buddha in the *Daode jing*. Nor do the eight collections of Buddhist texts ever talk about the Dao. All other Daoist texts were made up later, stolen from Buddhist sutras. The case really is so self-evident, there is no need to go into it any further.

One more point, though. Ever since antiquity, the wise and worthy have been chanting and reciting Buddhist sutras. To the present day, they have been handed down for generation after generation without interruption. If the Daoist teaching really were superior, why is it that their scriptures are not handed down through recital? Wherever you look throughout the whole country, who would ever recite a Daoist text?[6] Thus, we know that Daoist scriptures cannot possibly be of any authority.

---

4. A priest (421/428–183/491 C.E.).
5. A Chinese monk (384–413 C.E.), who translated and wrote Buddhist treatises. He was the disciple of Kumarajiva (344–413), a monk of Indian ancestry known for his fluent renderings of Sanskrit texts into Chinese.
6. The translator notes that in fact Daoist scriptures have always been chanted and recited.

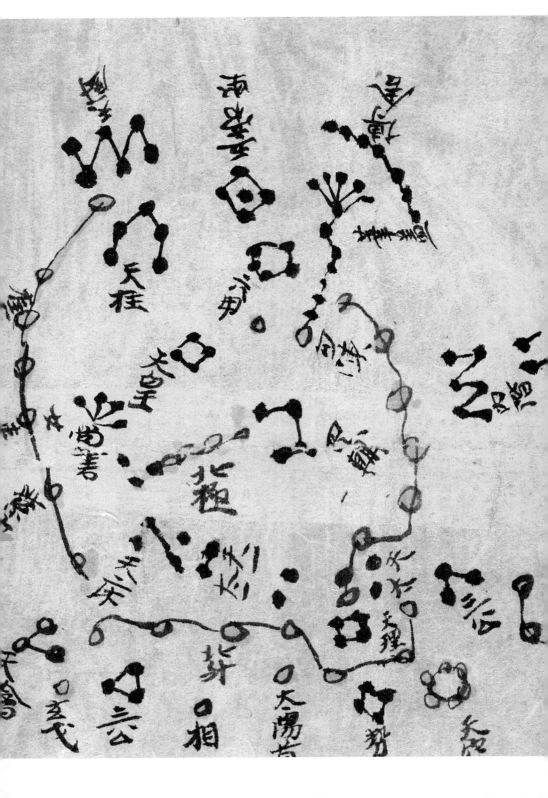

The Consolidation and Expansion of Daoism

FROM THE SUI DYNASTY (581–618 C.E.) THROUGH THE TANG DYNASTY (618–907 C.E.)

Although it was short-lived, the Sui dynasty (581–618 C.E.) reunified China after centuries of division and laid the foundations for the flourishing of Chinese culture under the subsequent Tang dynasty (618–907). The inaugural Sui emperor Wendi (r. 581–604) took Buddhism as his preferred religion, his ruling ideology (he presented himself as a Buddhist universal ruler—in Sanskrit, *chakravartin*—modeled on King Ashoka, whose third-century B.C.E. rule was based on Buddhist principles), and his method of unifying his kingdom (he undertook an ambitious campaign to distribute throughout the imperium Buddha relics, which are small fragments of the Buddha's body perceived to be "alive" and to allow access to his powers). Wendi encouraged many favorable policies toward Buddhism, but he did not entirely ignore Daoism. After a series of auspicious Daoist prophecies about him came true, he rewarded

This Tang dynasty star map depicts different asterisms—such as the Northern Dipper (Ursa Major)—that are important within Daoism as celestial locations and as the residences of deities in the Daoist pantheon.

the Daoist prophets for their support. Wendi also turned to Daoist rituals during times when he needed added divine assistance; he established many new Daoist temples; and he was a notable supporter of the Lou Abbey (Louguan), the site where Laozi was said to have written down *The Scripture of the Way and Its Virtue* (*Daode jing*; see above) on his way out of China. Daoism was more than a mere passing interest or means to political ends for Wendi, since he also underwent a Daoist ordination ceremony.

Wendi's successor, Emperor Yangdi (r. 605–17), likewise primarily supported Buddhism, but he also received counsel from the Shangqing Daoist Wang Yuanzhi (528–635). Following a dispute with the emperor, however, Wang threw his support behind a figure named Li Yuan (the future Tang dynasty founding emperor Gaozu, r. 618–26), who had his sights on the throne. While Yangdi's official posture toward Daoism was a mixture of state support and state regulation, his personal interest was strong. He ardently desired to obtain a Daoist elixir of immortality, and he summarily executed the Daoist who promised to concoct one for him and failed. The Sui dynasty came to an end after troubles caused by a series of overly ambitious projects spawned popular uprisings and new Daoist prophecies associated yet again with the divinized Laozi, indicating the imminent rise of a new dynasty.

The Tang dynasty—generally celebrated as a "golden age" because it flourished both economically and culturally—marked the beginning of a high point in Daoist history. This period, unlike the previous epoch from the beginning of the Han dynasty (202 B.C.E.) to the end of the Sui dynasty (618 C.E.), which often experienced political struggles yet fostered religious innovation, saw neither any new scriptures revealed nor any major new Daoist schools formed. At the same time, however, the Tang dynasty was significant for the further development of Daoist traditions that had emerged between the second and sixth centuries—including the Celestial Masters, Shangqing, and Lingbao traditions. This is best thought of as a period of solidifying, consolidating, and expanding the earlier Daoist schools. Indeed, during the Tang dynasty a number of synoptic works such as encyclopedias, hagiographic collections, and monastic regulations were compiled, and a hierarchically arranged canon of Daoist texts appeared.

There were also many smaller local Daoist movements. Among these local traditions were some pioneering amalgamations with Buddhism, such as the philosophical movement known as Twofold Mystery. It was inspired by Buddhist Madhyamaka philosophy, whose founding is credited to the Indian thinker Nagarjuna (second century C.E.).

One distinctive aspect of Tang Daoist history that helped boost Daoism's standing in the Chinese religious landscape was the privileged position it attained at the imperial court. This unprecedented level of imperial support for much of the dynasty, coupled with an increase in the influence of Daoism on the state religious cult, provides the main story line of Daoist history for roughly three hundred years, up to the founding of the Song dynasty (960–1279 C.E.).

While the dynasty's founder, Li Yuan—the emperor Gaozu (r. 618–26 C.E.), a name he chose in conscious emulation of the founder of the Han dynasty, who had the same imperial title—was securing his reign over the newly unified empire, he was aided by a series of auspicious Daoist prophecies. According to one millenarian prophecy, a savior surnamed Li would manifest himself and lead the world into an era of peace. This Li (clearly referring to Li Yuan) was equated with Laozi's avatar Li Hong, who had already appeared in messianic contexts during the Eastern (Later) Han dynasty (25 C.E.–220 C.E.). Later, on several occasions, Laozi manifested himself and predicted Li Yuan's success. Moreover, Laozi (also known as Li Er) proclaimed that he was related to the Tang ruling family, as demonstrated by their shared surname. This claim was important for Li Yuan: he hailed from a family of foreign stock (most likely of Turkish origin), and ties to the indigenous sage Laozi no doubt bolstered his image in the eyes of the majority Han Chinese. During the Tang dynasty Laozi was refashioned as an ancestor and divine protector of the Tang ruling house, and Daoism became part of Tang ruling ideology and state cult. Gaozu's reunification of the empire and his rule by Daoist principles were touted as fulfilling the prophesied return to an era of Great Peace (Taiping), which harked back to the ancient goal of Great Peace and the Daoist-inspired expression of that hope during the Han dynasty in the form of the *Scripture of Great Peace* (*Taiping jing*; see above) and similar works.

A later Tang ruler, Emperor Gaozong (r. 649–83), bestowed a new elevated title on Laozi (August Emperor of Mystery and Primordiality, Xuanyuan huangdi), mandated that every province establish a new imperially sponsored Daoist temple, called for the compilation of the first Daoist canon, and in 678 added *The Scripture of the Way and Its Virtue* to the imperial examinations. Other Daoist works later made their way onto a Daoist civil service exam, including the Upper Clarity (Shangqing) text titled the *Most High Jade Scripture on the Internal View of the Yellow Court* (*Taishang huangting neijing yujing*; see above)—or simply the *Scripture of the Yellow Court* (*Huangting jing*)—and the Numinous Treasure (Lingbao) tradition's main sacred text, the *Book of Salvation* (*Duren jing*; see *The Wondrous Scripture of the Upper Chapters of Limitless Salvation*, above). Those exams were structured exactly as was the examination on the Confucian classics. Gaozong had a deep understanding of Daoism; reports of his meeting with an important Shangqing patriarch, Pan Shizheng (585–682), remark on the quality and depth of his questions.

In 683, however, Emperor Gaozong became incapacitated by illness, leading to an occurrence unprecedented in Chinese history: his politically astute concubine Wu Zetian (also known as Wu Zhao, ca. 625–705) usurped his position, ascended the throne, and ruled for about fifteen years (690–705) at the head of her self-proclaimed Zhou dynasty. No other woman ever ruled as an emperor. In garnering support to justify her claim to the throne, Empress Wu received strong doctrinal and ideological backing

Wu Zetian, China's only female emperor.

from Buddhists. Thus Buddhists came to enjoy the privileged position at court that earlier in the Tang dynasty had been held by Daoists. There must also have been some pressure on Empress Wu to distance herself from Daoism because of the deep-rooted connections between the Li ruling clan and Laozi. Nonetheless, while scholars have often commented on Buddhism during her reign, she—like many emperors before her—received support from Daoists as well. She was given a report that Laozi had descended with an entourage of transcendents at a Daoist abbey; moreover, other Daoists emphasized the high position that women held within Daoism and tried to establish connections between her and the important female immortal Wei Huacun (also called Lady Wei or Wei furen, 252–334), who had been instrumental in transmitting the Shangqing manuscripts to Yang Xi between 364 and 370. During the Tang dynasty a female Daoist adept named Huang Lingwei (640–721) sought out Lady Wei's tomb in order to venerate her and, finding it in disrepair, restored and expanded it (see "Stele Inscription for the Altar of the Transcendent Lady Wei of the Jin Dynasty, the Lady of the Southern Peak, Primal Worthy of the Purple Void, Concurrently Supreme True Mistress of Destiny"). She then presented objects connected with Lady Wei to Empress Wu, seeking to strengthen their filiation, but these efforts did not have a discernible impact on the empress's official posture toward Daoists.

Following Empress Wu's reign, the next two emperors—Zhongzong (r. 705–10) and Ruizong (r. 710–12)—reinstated imperial support for Daoists. The *Short Exposition on the Transmission of the Scriptures, Rules, and Registers of the Three Caverns* (*Chuanshou sandong jingjie falu lüeshuo*), which was compiled by Zhang Wanfu (fl. 711–713), the author of many texts formalizing Daoist rituals, chronicles the Daoist ordination of two Tang dynasty imperial princesses (both of them daughters of Emperor Ruizong). Gold Immortal and Jade Perfected received their investiture in 711 and 712, respectively, at a Daoist abbey within the Inner Palace, where court women lived. This event was marked by the appearance of the deified Laozi (Lord Lao) and other auspicious signs.

Within the golden age of the Tang dynasty, no period glimmered more brightly for Daoists than the reign of Emperor Xuanzong (r. 713–56). Xuanzong maintained deeper Daoist commitments than his predecessors, attempted to make Daoism the official religion of his reign, had statues of himself and Laozi enshrined inside the network of state-sponsored Daoist temples, and even shifted jurisdiction over Daoism from the Daoist Worship Bureau to the Court of the Imperial Clan, thereby explicitly linking Daoism with the imperial family. The emperor also championed Daoism in people's homes by decreeing that every household in the empire should possess a copy of *The Scripture of the Way and Its Virtue* (a work so important to him that he wrote a series of commentaries on it). We do not know whether that goal was realized, but the spread of woodblock printing techniques during the Tang did boost literacy rates, making the text more widely accessible. Going beyond merely supporting Daoism, Xuanzong underwent a personal Daoist ordination and became a fervid practitioner of alchemy as he sought immortality. The search for immortality would preoccupy many future Tang emperors, often with fatal consequences: no fewer than five of his successors died of elixir poisoning.

During Xuanzong's reign the state supported a wide network of Daoist monasteries, and imperial support for Daoism during the Tang led to a number of eminent Daoists being invited to the imperial capital, where they received lavish state support. After Daoism gained a footing at court and among the literati, we see the emergence of Daoists who became accomplished poets—such as Wu Yun, the author of the "Cantos on Pacing the Void"—and poets who integrated Daoist ideas and themes into their works, including Li Bo (701–762) and Bo Juyi (772–846). Daoists also appropriated certain imperial rituals for themselves. For example, Sima Chengzhen (647–735), an important Daoist supported by the court, in 731 persuaded the emperor to put Daoists in charge of the rituals relating to the highly symbolic Five Sacred Peaks. Along with state support came oversight by and responsibilities to the state. Daoists were expected to perform rituals on the state's behalf, and the state also controlled the Daoist clergy and influenced their liturgy.

A violent rebellion in 755 by the Turkic general An Lushan ended Xuanzong's illustrious reign, and the later years of the Tang dynasty were wracked by crises and religious persecutions. During the ninth century, Daoists again attained a favored position at court and were granted the right to perform large-scale ordinations. They may have helped foment a particularly harsh persecution aimed at Buddhists that occurred in 845, during the Huichang reign period (841–47).

The prolific writings of Du Guangting (850–933), a celebrated court Daoist under the reign of Emperor Xizong (r. 873–88), describe the close of the Tang dynasty and the early part of the Five Dynasties and Ten Kingdoms period (902–979) from the perspective of a particular region. In 881, when the capital of Chang'an (modern-day Xi'an) was overrun by rebels, Du fled to an area that corresponds to today's Sichuan Province, in western China. There he wrote many important works, including hagiographies, such as his *Biographies of Persons Who Had Contacts and Encounters with Supernatural Beings and Immortals* (*Shenxian ganyu zhuan*); commentaries on Daoist texts, such as his massive interpretation of *The Scripture of the Way and Its Virtue*; and liturgies. He also chronicled the expansion of Daoist sacred geography, providing detailed accounts of the Daoist networks of sacred sites categorized as "Cavern Heavens" and "Blissful Realms," which were located throughout the Chinese landscape.

In addition, Du Guangting compiled an important work exclusively devoted to female Daoist immortals, *Records of the Assembled Transcendents of the Fortified Walled City* (*Yongcheng jixian lu*). Though centered on the Queen Mother of the West, the collection also contains hagiographies and biographies of other goddesses and female practitioners—primarily those associated with the Shangqing tradition. Together with the records concerning Lady Wei (a major Shangqing immortal) and the collection of poems penned by the Daoist nun Yu Xuanji (b. ca. 848), that work demonstrates the attention paid to women during this period of Daoist history.

Although we have seen how Daoism was taken up as the ruling ideology of the Tang family, Buddhism retained a powerful position, and Buddhists' temples far outnumbered those of the Daoists. Even Emperor Xuanzong, who has generally been portrayed as an ardent supporter of Daoism both institutionally and personally, also wrote commentaries and prefaces to important Buddhist and Confucian texts. Like Xuanzong, the Tang thinker Li Ao (ca. 772–836) wrote a text—the *Book of Returning to One's True Nature* (*Fuxing shu*)—difficult to label as exclusively Confucian, Buddhist, or Daoist. Indeed, during the Tang dynasty Buddhist and Daoists produced a number of hybrid texts. Among them were the *Seal of the Unity of the Three* (*Cantong qi*) by the Tang Chan (Zen) Buddhist monk Shitou Xiqian (700–790), which was related to the earlier Daoist alchemical work titled the *Seal of the Unity of the Three, in Accordance with the Book of Changes* (*Zhouyi cantong qi*; see above), and the *Sutra of the Three Kitchens, Preached by the Buddha* (*Foshuo sanchu jing*), which drew on another Daoist text, *Commentary on the Scripture of the Five Kitchens Spoken by Laozi* (*Laozi shuo wuchu jing zhu*).

In addition to the production of hybrid texts, one of the most important innovations in Daoist practice during the Tang dynasty was an emphasis on meditation and interiorization. Those new elements, which derived from Buddhist practices, influenced the later development of "internal alchemy" (*neidan*), whose precise origins remain a topic of debate. Daoist meditation practices did not form the basis of a new school, but they amounted to a discernible trend within Daoist history. One particularly good example of this change is the *Scripture on Inner Observation by the Most High Lord Lao* (*Taishang laojun neiguan jing*), a very popular, and widely cited, eighth-century text. The Daoist canon remained open, and some scriptures purported to be from the mouth of Lord Lao (Laojun) himself, just as some Chinese Buddhist pseudepigrapha were presented as the spoken words of the Buddha. During the Tang dynasty, Daoist scriptures reflect a variety of other Buddhist techniques that were adapted for Daoist purposes, such as "insight meditation" (in Sanskrit, *vipashyana*) and conceptions of rebirth.

Alongside these benign forms of borrowing and appropriation is evidence of underlying antagonism. During the Tang dynasty the infamous Conversion of the Barbarians (Huahu) theory, which presented the Buddha as inferior to Laozi, reemerged, leading to tensions that were reflected and exacerbated in oral and textual disputes. Such disputes could become physical, as seen in "An Examination of the Altar of the Transcendent Lady Wei of the Southern Sacred Peak," which details a failed attempt by a group of Buddhist monks to destroy and take over a Daoist cult site dedicated to the memory of Lady Wei. The centerpiece of that cult site, Lady Wei's altar, remained unharmed; the Buddhist monks fled; and all but one—the survivor who related the story—were killed by a ferocious tiger.

Buddhist and Daoist polemics played out more visibly in debates sponsored by the imperial court. But according to some sources, Tang Daoists focused mainly on continuing to oppose the popular practices of local cults, which they deemed profane (*su*) or illicit (*yinsi*) because spirit mediums demanded blood sacrifices. Local popular cults were to Daoists what the border cultures (which the Chinese labeled "barbaric") were to the court—and both were viewed as requiring suppression.

Nonetheless, the pronounced regional move into local society that was a key feature of late Tang Daoism rendered the oppositional relationship between Daoism and local popular cults less clear-cut. Daoism began to interact with and absorb elements of local cults (which conversely appropriated Daoist elements) in ways that would be seen again, fully developed, during the Song dynasty, when Daoism once more would experience a flurry of new activity and innovation.

Given the cosmopolitan nature of the Tang dynasty and its interactions not just with the foreign cultures on its borders but also with those encountered through long-distance trade, it is predictable that the first evidence of the spread of Daoism outside of China dates to this period. According to Chinese reports, during the Tang dynasty a copy of *The Scripture of the Way and Its Virtue* was sent to Tibet, and a Sanskrit translation of the text was produced at the bequest of the Indian king of Kashmir. Little is known about the subsequent history of Daoism in India and Tibet, but the historical record concerning the transmission of Daoism to Japan and Korea is robust.

The diaries of Japanese Buddhist monks who traveled to China during the Tang dynasty reveal the strength of Daoism on the continent. During one such Japanese embassy to China in 753, the envoys visited Emperor Xuanzong and requested that the Chinese Buddhist Vinaya master Jianzhen (Ganjin, 688–763) be allowed to accompany them back to Japan, since his expertise was needed there. Xuanzong assented, on the condition that they take a learned Daoist master back with them as well. Because the Japanese emperor disliked Daoism, he rejected the Chinese emperor's request. Despite this initial setback, a variety of Japanese sources provide ample evidence that Daoist ideas—though not organized Daoist religious institutions—were transmitted to the Japanese islands by the Nara period (710–794) at the latest. The *Chronicles of Japan* (*Nihongi*), completed in 720, includes an account of a person whose death is described as a form of Daoist "corpse liberation" (*shijie*): a feigned death and transformation in which one sloughs off one's old mortal body, like a cicada shedding its shell, and ascends to heaven—perhaps appearing in the world now and again at long intervals.

Some poems in Nara anthologies use specialized Daoist terminology; for example, one in the eighth-century *Collection of Ten Thousand Leaves* (*Manyōshū*) describes Mount Yoshino as a natural Daoist paradise where mountain deities dwell and spirits roam. This imagery also evokes what is commonly referred to as Shintō, Japan's indigenous religion, but the similarity is not surprising, given that "Shintō" (in Chinese, *shendao*) was another term for Daoism. Other Japanese works from this period portray Japanese figures as immortals who flew up to heaven in broad daylight. Kukai (774–835), the famous esoteric Buddhist polymath, evaluates Buddhism, Daoism, and Confucianism in his *Indications of the Goals of the Three Teachings* (*Sangō shīki*). He displays an intimate familiarity with Daoist practices, which he ultimately judges inferior to those of Buddhism. Further evidence of the transmission of Daoist elements to Japan can be found in material culture (the presence of Daoist talismans); in court terminology, such as the use of the title *tennō* (derived from the Daoist pantheon, *tianhuang*) for the Japanese emperor or of *shinjin* (from the Daoist term for the Perfected, *zhenren*) for the highest court rank bestowed on the emperor's descendants; in medical knowledge (ingestion of elixirs); and in the Japanese pantheon. Historians have been unable to explain why, despite this rich record of influence, organized Daoist institutions were never established in Japan.

Korea became one of the most important places outside of China for the transmission and development of Daoist ideas, practices, and organized religious institutions, though their impact on Korean history and culture is generally less familiar than that of Confucianism and Buddhism. Chinese and Korean official histories record that the first efforts to spread Daoism to Korea occurred during Korea's Three Kingdoms period (57 B.C.E.–668 C.E.). Daoism may already have been present, since there are some earlier vague references to special beings whose lives were extremely long, but its initial transmission to Korea is commonly ascribed to 624 C.E. In that year, the Tang Chinese emperor Gaozu sent two Daoist priests, along with a statue of a Heavenly Worthy (*tianzun*), to the Korean kingdom of Koguryŏ. In 643, after the Koreans appealed to the Chinese emperor to send more— ostensibly to counter the ascendant power of Buddhism in Koguryŏ—eight more Daoist priests were dispatched, and they recited *The Scripture of the Way and Its Virtue* at the imperial court. *The Scripture of the Way and Its Virtue* and *Book of Master Zhuang (Zhuangzi*; see above) circulated in Korea no later than the seventh century, when those texts begin to be cited in Korean literature and in inscriptions (such as the "Inscription on an Image at Kamsan Monastery"). Despite the early spread of Daoist texts and ideas to Korea, organized Daoist institutions would not be established until as late as the twelfth century, when the first Daoist temple was built (the Palace of the Source of Happiness—in Korean, Bokwŏn kung); Daoism, particularly internal alchemy, later flourished on the peninsula.

The dispatch of *The Scripture of the Way and Its Virtue* to Tibet, its translation into Sanskrit, and the movement of Daoist priests, statues, scriptures, terms of art, and ideas to Korea and Japan mark the beginning of the transformation of Daoism into something more than what has been called China's indigenous "high religion." During the Tang dynasty Daoism began to make its way onto the international stage and thereby also began its evolution into a world religion.

THE ESSENTIALS OF THE PRACTICE OF PERFECTION FROM THE ONE AND ORTHODOX RITUAL CANON
(*Zhengyi fawen xiuzhen zhiyao*)

Our selection from the *Essentials of the Practice of Perfection from the One and Orthodox Ritual Canon (Zhengyi fawen xiuzhen zhiyao)*, a text specifying a variety of practices related to breathing, physical exercises, and healing, focuses on the symptomology and prognosis of illnesses; its aim is to ensure that the Daoist rituals of curing will be effective. The passage below describes the use of powerful "seals"—stamps with esoteric diagrams carved onto them—and talismans in exorcisms that treat different types of diseases. It emphasizes that success in the healing ritual rests largely on the attitude and motivation of the Daoist master, whom it addresses directly: "If you act in the spirit of succor and charity, spirits will certainly assist you and the vital breaths of the Dao will definitely respond. If, however, you act in hope of gain, without concern to give help, your actions will have no efficacy; on the contrary, you yourself will be harmed by them." Another key for the master is to perfect his breathing so that he will be granted detailed visions of the spirits—both external and internal—to confirm their presence and support for the healing ritual. In addition, *Essentials of the Practice of Perfection* carefully instructs the practitioner on the seal's handling and care. It should never be carried into places that have been made tainted, and following every use it must be cleaned and stored properly.

PRONOUNCING GLOSSARY

Yijing: *yee-ching*

Zhengyi fawen xiuzhen zhiyao: *chung-yee fah-when hsiu-chen chih-yao*

If you are going to practice the cure of illness by spells, you should have the sufferer's family all perform the early morning obeisance to the Dao and purify themselves. The whole house should be quiet, and all noise and confusion should be kept away. The Daoist master then approaches the patient, burns incense, and most carefully examines the patient's state. If his physical symptoms are bad and not susceptible of cure, then the master should on his behalf visualize the spirits, circulate the breaths throughout his own body, and apply the seal[1] three times. At noon, he should once more go and examine the patient's condition to see whether or not it has improved somewhat. If it has not yet improved, he should once more use his spell. During the night he should again examine whether there has been any alteration, and if there has not yet been any, he should once more apply his spell. The following morning at dawn [after dawn worship], he should go and examine

TRANSLATED BY Michel Strickmann. All bracketed additions are the translator's.

1. A stamp with esoteric diagrams carved onto it.

his condition; if there has still been no change, it means that his life is finished and he cannot be cured.

In curing illness, it is necessary to despise material rewards. If you act in the spirit of succor and charity, spirits will certainly assist you and the vital breaths of the Dao will definitely respond. If, however, you act in hope of gain, without concern to give help, your actions will have no efficacy; on the contrary, you yourself will be harmed by them. The talismans and spells of the rites of the Dao are for helping people in sickness and suffering. The Daoist master should frequently discourse upon the venerable scriptures in the thirty-six divisions of the Daoist canon and promote the rites of talismans and spells of the sublime saints. He should, moreover, study their profound subtleties with all his might. The instructions that follow represent the arts of talismans and spells in the secret directives of the Three and the Five of the divine transcendents of Right Unity.[2] The Twelve Asterisms[3] and great conjunctions of the Three and the Five reveal the instructions of the dark invisible world. The Daoists' wondrous rites of spell-recitation are numerous and complex, obscure in their diversity, and difficult for anyone to comprehend fully. But for saving lives in peril of death, there is nothing better than seals. In ancient times, Fan Li[4] practiced this, causing mountains to crumble, rivers and seas to flow backward, spirit-powers to tremble with fear, and thunderclaps to resound. With seals one can smelt metal and polish jade, restore vital breaths and bring back the ethereal souls [to reanimate corpses]; how much more easily, then, can one heal the sick by these means! But for ordinary persons in their shallow delusion, the sublime arts are difficult to master. It is for that reason that most people at the present time are unable to achieve results in these practices. This is most likely due to their not having studied the techniques thoroughly, or else because their hearts are not fully focused. Li Daohua has said, "I do not practice this rite with the frivolous or the young."

The difficult point to understand about the seal lies in the visualizations. But if you are able to perfect the breathing and understand the timing, then the visualization will be accomplished by itself and the spirits will all be fully present. If you coif and cincture yourself with the Five Spirits, and pace out the pattern of the first *Yijing* hexagram[5] [that is, *qian* or "heaven"], rare will be those whom you cannot cure. Now we will give a terse outline of the sequence of procedures, in order to make it manifest to fellow-adepts who have not yet been able to exhaust its essential secrets.

For the sevenfold rite of the vital breaths, first one must spew forth water and eliminate impurities. In your left hand, hold a bowl filled with water, in your right, a sword. With sword and water held opposite each other, place your back to the reigning asterism of the month and face the Breaker Star.

---

2. Also referred to as "Orthodox Unity" or "Correct Unity." "The Three and the Five": there are many different combinations of three and five in Daoist texts; here, the phrase apparently refers to rulers and to elements of the cosmos. "Transcendents": *xian*, Daoists who have achieved extraordinary powers and a higher form of existence (often translated "immortals").
3. An asterism is a prominent group of stars, generally smaller than a constellation.

4. A figure of Daoist hagiography (ca. 5th century B.C.E).
5. On the hexagrams in the *Yijing* or *Book of Changes* (traditionally dated to the 12th century B.C.E.), a volume of divination and cosmology, see the introduction to *The Seal of the Unity of the Three, in Accordance with the Book of Changes* (*Zhouyi cantong qi*), above. "The Five Spirits": the deities that dwell in the five viscera (the liver, heart, spleen, lungs, and kidneys).

Visualize in front of you a celestial official in a vermilion robe; he is nineteen feet tall; on his head he wears a spirit-register; set in it is a nine-phoenix hat. In his mouth he takes water and sprays it out in front of him over the sick person and the room: It is brilliantly red, like the sun rising at dawn. Then, with sword and water held opposite each other, visualize the seven stars of the Dipper above your own head; the end star of the handle should be in the bowl of water. Recite [this spell]:

> I respectfully request the spirit-essences
> of the Northern Dipper's seven stars
> to descend into this water,
> so that all noxious demons
> quickly depart, ten thousand leagues away!
> If you do not leave, I will decapitate and kill you
> and consign you to the White Youth of the West.
> Speedily, as the Statutes and Ordinances command![6]

Spray out water in each of the five directions;[7] then spray it on the sufferer and put the seal into operation. Stand ten feet away from the patient. You press the "supervisor" phalanx [the second segment of the fourth finger] of your left hand; your right hand holds the seal against your heart. Stand facing the reigning direction.

Step One: First visualize yourself as a spirit bearing heaven on his head and stamping on the earth with his feet. A five-colored cloud[8] of vapor covers your body.

Step Two: Over your head visualize the five planets,[9] each in its proper place, a foot away from your head.

Step Three: In front of your face visualize on the left the sun, on the right the moon, nine inches away from your face.

Step Four: On top of your head visualize the vermilion bird, to the left the azure dragon, to the right the white tiger, beneath your feet the Eight Trigrams (of the *Book of Changes*) and the divine tortoise. To the left and right are the jade youths and jade maidens[1] who put the seal into action.

Step Five: Visualize five-colored vital breaths of Perfection, the size of strands of thread, proceeding from your five viscera, coming out of your mouth, and rising into the air to a height of eighteen feet above your head. They go three times around your head. Next visualize three little men in your liver, dressed in blue robes and blue caps, coming out and standing to your left. The three little men in your heart, dressed in red with red caps, come out and stand to your right. The three little men in your kidneys, dressed in black with black caps, come out and stand behind you. The three men in your spleen, dressed in yellow with yellow caps, come out and stand to the south. They all hold swords in their left hands and war hatchets in their right.

Next visualize above your head the seven stars of the Dipper, with the star at the end of the handle pointing at the spot where the sufferer feels

---

6. An echo of the command used to close official orders in the Han dynasty (202 B.C.E.–220 C.E.)
7. East, west, north, south, and center.
8. The five colors are green, red, yellow, white, and black.
9. Jupiter, Mars, Saturn, Venus, and Mercury.
1. Attendants in heaven.

pain. Then visualize the previously mentioned Perfect Official[2] wearing the nine-phoenix hat, mounted upon red vapors of the sun. Imagine that he performs the Step of Yu[3] with the seal in his hand, then brings it down once on the patient's heart. Next he presses it once on his stomach, then once again on the place where he feels pain. Visualize the toxic vapors coming out of the patient and rushing away. When this has been done, concentrate your vision on your own body. Close off your breath and perform the Step of Yu for nine paces, bringing you to the patient. Stand there, before you apply the seal, and breathe out of your mouth on the sufferer three *xi*, three *ta*, and three *chi* breaths. Next sound the bells of heaven six times, then strike heaven's stone-chimes six times: For summoning, use the bells; for subjugating, use the chimes. Then recite this spell:

> The spirit-seal of the Monarch of Heaven:
> When you seal a mountain, it turns to a lake.
> Seal a stone and it turns to earth.
> Seal a tree, the tree withers.
> Seal the earth, the earth splits.
> Seal wood, the wood breaks.
> Seal fire, the fire goes out.
> Seal water, the water dries up.
> Seal above, it penetrates below.
> Seal before, it penetrates behind.
> Seal the left, it penetrates the right.
> Seal malignant wraiths, and wraiths perish.
> Seal pain, and pain stops.
> Seal sickness, sickness disperses.
> Seal demons, demons flee.
> It overcomes the symptoms and eliminates knotted breaths,
>   banishes afflictions and punishes ghost-infection.
> May they all flee away of their own volition
>   and the True Spirits take up their abode in you.
> Swiftly, swiftly, in accordance with the Statutes and Ordinances
>   of Lord Lao[4] the Most High.

Then bring down the seal [on the patient's body]. You must close off your breaths for a good long time; only then raise the seal and step back. Then recite:

> The man or woman named so-and-so [fill in the blank], born in thus-and-such a year, month, day, and hour, in his present life is troubled by thus-and-such an ailment and has requested me, your servant, to cure it. Your servant respectfully requests the General of the Three Divisions, the General Who operates the Seal, the General Who Cures Illness, the General Who Destroys Disease-Wraiths, and the General Who Arrests Devils—requests that all of

2. That is, a Perfected One or *zhenren*, who in later Daoism is described as a being that has moved beyond earthly corruption and is often identified with a stellar deity; in the Upper Clarity (Shangqing) tradition, the perfected are more exalted than the transcendents.
3. A form of ritual walking or dancing that follows celestial patterns mapped onto the ground.
4. The deified Laozi.

you accompany the seal and cure the illness, and save that person from the ailment in his body. Swiftly, swiftly, come out! Now, with the seal of the Yellow God's Emblem of Transcendence, I seal the heart—take it out of his heart!

> Sealing his stomach, it comes out of the stomach!
> Sealing the liver, it comes out of the liver!
> Sealing the lungs, it comes out of the lungs!
> Sealing the kidneys, it comes out of the kidneys!
> Sealing the spleen, it comes out of the spleen!
> Sealing the head, it comes out of the head!
> Sealing the back, it comes out of the back!
> Sealing the breast, it comes out of the breast!
> Sealing the waist, it comes out of the waist!
> Sealing the hand, it comes out of the hand!
> Sealing the foot, it comes out of the foot!
> Quickly come forth, quickly come forth, swiftly, swiftly,
>   in accordance with the Statutes and Ordinances!

Each time you apply the seal, recite this through one more time. When that has been completed, lift the seal, hold it facing the patient's heart, and recite:

> Demons of the south,
> demons of the north,
> demons of the east,
> demons of the west,
> demons of the center,
> demons of the earth,
> demons of the spirit-demons,
> demons of the man-demons,
> demons of the woman-demons,
> demons of the sunken corpse-specters,
> toxic ghost-infestations—
> who face the seal, die!
> Who meet the seal, perish!
> Swiftly come forth, swiftly come forth!

Bring the seal down to rest and recite this two more times through; only then lift the seal. After sealing, have the sufferer swallow three or two talismans. [Note in text: a man consumes three talismans, a woman two.]

In using spells to cure illness, always visualize the perfect breaths of the ten regions [as you recite the spells]. Before taking action, you should enjoin the sufferer not to consume the five sharp-flavored herbs[5] for three days or flesh of the animals of the twelve asterisms [i.e., of the twelve earthly 'stems' of cyclical time-space computation[6]]. Indeed, all shellfish, wine, and fresh meat should be avoided. Only a very small amount of dried deer meat is acceptable. Only when this has been accomplished may you apply the seal. But if the patient is unable to carry this out, then sealing will cause him harm and not do any good at all.

---

5. Garlic, leeks, onions, scallions, and chives.
6. In the traditional Chinese calendrical system, days and (later) years were designated with two characters drawn from a set of ten Celestial Stems and twelve Earthly Branches, resulting in a cycle of sixty days/years.

After using the seal, bathe it in fragrant hot water, wipe it dry with a new cloth, and place it in a box.

This seal should not be brought into a household in mourning, into one in which a woman has just given birth, or into a place where there is blood or raw flesh or milk, or filth of the six sorts of domestic beast;[7] to none of these places may it be taken. If when asleep you should suddenly be frightened by a dream, or be unusually shaken by a sound, arise at once and call out in a loud voice: "Ye seven spirits of the house, Director of Destinies, Lord of the Hearth! How have you permitted uncouth demons to strike at a descendant of the Yellow Monarch?[8] Apprehend them and commit them to the officer of the prison, to be punished for their crime!"

When you have said this, take the seal and hang it over the door. Return to bed, and a moment later you will hear the sound of whipping and torture.

If a person is suddenly struck by flying evil cadaver-specters, demonic hereditary infestation, chronic faintness, and pains in the heart, seal him over the heart and it will stop at once. If a person talks demon-speech incessantly, seal him according to the ritual and it will stop at once. If a person is walking along a road, or has gone into the mountains or moorlands, or is crossing a river or traversing a lake, or if he sees wolves, tigers, bears, or the like, or if such animals attack any of the six sorts of domestic beast, let him seal their tracks with the seal and tigers will run thirty leagues away; if he reverses the seal, they will come back. If, while someone is in the water, dragons, fish, turtles, crawling things, poisonous snakes, or the like attack him, make a seal-impression on clean yellow clay, throw it in the water, and the beasts will die. If male or female slaves run away, press the seal in their footprints and they will return. If a person is suddenly struck by bad vapors, or 'dies' and is unconscious, or while walking feels his limbs struck as if pierced by an awl or a knife, take the seal, close off your breaths, press it on the painful spot and on the heart, and recite: "Wraith-breaths depart, right breaths remain!"

7. Pigs, dogs, chickens, horses, cattle, and sheep.
8. The mythological Yellow Emperor, Huangdi (27th century B.C.E.).

SCRIPTURAL INSTRUCTIONS OF THE PRIMORDIAL PERFECTED FROM THE HALL OF LIGHT OF HIGHEST CLARITY
(Shangqing mingtang yuanzhen jingjue)

Scriptural Instructions of the Primordial Perfected from the Hall of Light of Highest Clarity (*Shangqing mingtang yuanzhen jingjue*, fifth century C.E.) draws on the Upper Clarity (Shangqing) tradition and *Declarations of the Perfected* (*Zhen'gao*; see above). The excerpt below sets forth a visualization technique that involves ingesting plasmas of the sun and moon mixed with liquid emissions from the mouth of the Jade Woman of Great Mystery. After these instructions are followed for five years, "the Jade Women of Great Mystery will come down to you, and lie down to take her ease with you"; she can also "make several tens of Jade Women who will be responsible for your urgent errands."

PRONOUNCING GLOSSARY

Shangqing mingtang yuanzhen jingjue: *shawng-ching ming-tahng yuen-chun ching-chu-eh*

The Technique of the Mystic Realized One

Actualize sun or moon within the mouth. In the white light of day actualize the sun; in the middle of the night actualize the moon. It is also permissible to actualize [either one] when it is neither [plainly] daytime nor nighttime so that a decisive distinction can be made as to whether it is to be sun or moon. The sun's color is red. The moon's color is yellow. The sun has nine rays of purple light. The moon has ten rays of white light. Cause sun or moon to stand opposite the mouth, nine feet away from it. The light rays should be directed towards the mouth, with the rays straight as bowstrings so that they will enter into the mouth. Next, actualize a young woman as present within the sun or moon. A purple cap is placed on her head, and she has a cloak and skirt of vermilion damask. She calls herself Jade Woman of the Cinnabar Aurora of the Highest Mysteries of the Greatest Mystery. Her taboo-name is Binding Coil and her agnomen is Secret Realized One. From her mouth she exhales a red pneuma which fills the space between the light-rays from sun or moon completely. It combines with them until rays and auroral glow are both used up, then gushes into one's own mouth. One masters it and gulps it down. Actualize the woman also as exhaling it in sequence; activate it nine times ten. After these have been gulped down, actualize a conscious command to the phosphor[1] of sun or moon to press intimately close upon one's own face, and command that the Jade Woman's mouth press a kiss upon your own mouth, causing the liquor of the pneuma to come down into the mouth. One then conjures here inaudibly: "Jade Woman, Living Germ of Sun and Moon, Conserving Spirit of the Luminous Hall,[2] Purple Realized One of the Grand Aurora, Binding Coil, generated spontaneously from the Barrens in the Prior Age, whose agnomen is Secret Realized One, whose head is capped with the Numinous Crown of the Purple-flowered Lotus, and whose body is cloaked in a multicolored damask cloak and a Flying Skirt of Vermilion Cinnabar, who emerges from the sun and enters the moon. Lit by Heaven! Subtly fragrant! May your mouth emit the orange pneuma to irrigate my Three Primes.[3] May my face gaze upon the Sky Well. Make my white-souls[4] compliant. Give definition to my cloud-souls. May the mystic liquor move in streams. May the foetal germ[5] grow to completion. May the Five Stores[6] generate efflorescence. Open my pupils in reverse to my face, that I may inspect and rein the myriad numina,

Translated by Edward H. Schafer. All bracketed additions are the translator's.

1. A luminous divine projection.
2. *Mingtang*, a term that can refer to the politico-religious structures of the imperium or to a location just behind the forehead (one of the nine palaces inside the head).
3. That is, the three Cinnabar Fields (the brain, the heart, and the abdomen).

4. The heavy soul, linked to the earth (in contrast to the cloud-soul or light soul, which is linked to heaven).
5. The immortal embryo being nurtured inside the adept's body.
6. The five viscera (the lungs, heart, liver, spleen, and kidneys).

the Supervisor of Destiny, and the "flying transcendents." This done, actualize the salival liquor from the mouth of the Jade Woman, commanding it to gush into one's own mouth. Then, having rinsed it with the liquor, proceed to swallow it. Stop only after nine times ten passages. [Then], in quieting the heart, in making thoughts resonant and activating them, there need no longer be any limit set on most of one's strivings. If one is actualizing the sun, he does not actualize the moon. If one is actualizing the moon, he does not actualize the sun. It is only essential that he should actualize them both impartially. If one misses the time for taking the dose, he should actualize the two phosphors as returning to the Luminous Hall—the sun on the left, the moon on the right. Command the lights and flashes of sun and moon to radiate jointly with the pupils of the eyes, reflecting the two pneumas in the four [directions], so that they may gush freely through one. One may also actualize sun and moon regularly as in place in the Luminous Hall, without waiting for the regular taking of the dose from [one of] the two phosphors of sun and moon, and thus exploit them concurrently. Perform these things for five years and the Jade Woman of Greatest Mystery will come down to you, and lie down to take her ease with you. The Jade Woman of Greatest Mystery can also divide her shape to make several tens of Jade Women who will be responsible for your urgent errands. This is the ultimate in accumulating resonance, in knotting germinal essences together, in transmuting life, and in seeing germinal essences as simulacra. In the end, it is a miraculous response to your resonance. The Most High Realized Magistrates employ the Way of the Sun's Aurora and the Technique of Draining the Two Phosphors to bring men into communication with the numina, to summon the Realized Ones, to embody their lives in gemmy refulgence, to bind the myriad spirits in service and to command them, and finally to rise up into the chambers of the divine kings. The Way which was taught to Yu of Xia[7] long ago by the Realized Person of Mount Zhong—that was precisely the Technique of the Mystic Realized One. However, this is no more than an excerpted outline; and indeed we lack anything about the affairs of Binding Coil.

---

7. Yu the Great (21st century B.C.E.), legendary founder of the Xia dynasty.

THE SHORT EXPOSITION ON THE TRANSMISSION OF THE SCRIPTURES, RULES, AND REGISTERS OF THE THREE CAVERNS
(*Chuanshou sandong jingjie falu lüeshuo*)

ZHANG WANFU

The *Short Exposition on the Transmission of the Scriptures, Rules, and Registers of the Three Caverns* (*Chuanshou sandong jingjie falu lüeshuo*) is a theoretical treatise on ordination in the Tang dynasty, describing the ritual and discussing its symbolism. It was compiled by Zhang Wanfu (fl. 711–713), the author of many ritual and liturgical works and one of the most revered masters of the Numinous Treasure (Lingbao) tradition; he also enjoyed close ties with the imperial house. The selection below is the final part of the text, an evocative and thorough account of the Daoist ordination of two Tang dynasty imperial princesses—Gold Immortal (Jinxian) and Jade Perfected (Yuzhen)—in 711 and 712 C.E. at an abbey within the Great Inner Palace. After detailing the altar furnishings, pledges to the Daoist officiant, and all the ornamentation—from the wrappers for the scriptures to the food containers, banners, and lanterns—the passage describes the auspicious natural phenomena (snow and cloud patterns) that accompanied the arrival of Lord Lao, sanctioning their ordination.

PRONOUNCING GLOSSARY

Chuanshou sandong jingjie falu lüeshuo: *chuan-show sawn-ding ching-
  jieh fah-lu lew-eh-shu-oh*

Suqi: *sue-chi*
Zhang Wanfu: *chawng wanfoo*

Introduction

On the Tenth of February, 711, I witnessed Princess Gold-Immortal and Princess Jade-Perfected visit Reverend Preceptor Shi—

Grand Canon Preceptor of the Three Caverns[1];
Abbot of the Supreme Purity Abbey;
Grandee of Illustrious Noble Rank, Gold Signet and Purple Ribbon;
Chief of the Service for Stentorian Annunciation;
Principality-Founding Duke, Henei Commandery;
Pillar of State, First Class

—to receive investiture as Daoist priests [literally, receive the Dao], rend

the Self-Generated Tally of the Numinous Treasure,

TRANSLATED BY Charles D. Benn. All bracketed additions are by the translator, who has also supplied the subtitles.

1. That is, the texts in the Daoist canon; they were divided into three "caverns," or collections, by Lu Xiujing in 471.

and secure

> the Canon of the Central Covenant in Eight Satchels; forty-seven scrolls, two True Writ Registers[2],
> Belt Talismans and
> Staffs

in the Abbey of Refuge in Perfection at the Great Inner Palace.

Altar

So earth was excavated to form an altar, in three tiers, which was one *zhang* two *chi* (about 3.54 meters or 11.6 feet) high. Gold lotus blossom poles; purple and gold title-tablets, and a blue-green silk cordon encircled the altar.

Floor Coverings

Cushions of layered cloth were made from

> eastern blue-green brocade,
> southern cinnabar (red) brocade,
> western white brocade,
> northern purple brocade, and
> central yellow brocade

and there were also dragon whisker, phoenix pinion, and other types of mats for covering the earth.

Table Settings

Brocades were fabricated according to the colors of the directions for each of the five tables. Curly gold dragons and jade disks [were placed on the tables] to defend them.

Articles of Appeasement

In addition,

> eighteen lengths of blue-green silk net,
> six lengths of scarlet silk net,
> fourteen lengths of white silk net,
> ten lengths of black silk net, and
> twenty-four lengths of yellow silk net

were used to appease [the gods of] the five directions.[3]

---

2. The particular texts that a Daoist priest receives at each rank. True Writs are talismans marked with writing in an esoteric script that only ethereal deities can read.

3. East, west, north, south, and center.

Pledges

To bind [the ordinands] to the numinous bureaucrats

240 lengths of purple silk net,
480 lengths of pongee,[4]
240 strings of cash,[5]
200 ounces of gold,
25 lengths of five-color cloud brocade,[6]
120 catties[7] of incense,
500 ounces of continuous blue-green Seven Treasure thread,[8]
24,000 sheets of memorial paper,
240 writing brushes and 240 inksticks,
12 knives for straightening documents,
38 knives and 38 kerchiefs for preserving injunctions,
6 gold dragons, and
54 gold knobs

were employed to defend at the altar's center.

Braziers

There were also

coiled-dragon incense braziers,
dancing-phoenix incense braziers,
auspicious-leaf incense braziers,
propitious-blossom incense braziers,
lotus-blossom incense braziers, and
magic-mushroom incense braziers

together with incense caskets and incense chests, all of which were fabricated from pure gold and solid silver.

Table Cloths

There were also brocade cloths with matched cranes and paired simurghs,[9] flying dragons, and bowing phoenixes.

Canon Wrappers

There were also wrappers for covering the scriptures embroidered with Divine Diamond Kings; Immortal Lads and Jade Maids;[1] smoke-clouded landscapes; grasses, trees, insects, and fish; sacred beasts and numinous birds; and ornamented marvels and precious objects.

---

4. A thin fabric made from raw silk.
5. A Chinese coin of small value.
6. The five colors are green, red, yellow, white, and black.
7. About 160 pounds.
8. Probably thread of seven colors. In Buddhism,

the Seven Treasures are gold, silver, lapis lazuli, crystal, ruby, pearl, and carnelian.
9. Mythical large winged creatures whose appearance is auspicious.
1. Attendants in heaven.

Tables

There were also tables of carved jade, chased gold, purple sandalwood, white sandalwood, and aloeswood, all of which were made with carved or engraved ornamentations of soaring simurghs and dancing phoenixes, gold blossoms, and jade leaves.

Canon Cases

There were also

Seven Treasure cases,
Nine Immortal cases,
yellow-gold cases, and
white-jade cases,

for holding the scriptures.

Satchels

There were also

bags of blue-green brocade,
bags of scarlet brocade,
bags of plain white brocade,
bags of purple brocade,
bags of yellow brocade,
bags of cloud brocade, and
bags of polychrome brocade,

for holding the liturgical registers.

Food Containers

There were also kitchen baskets and hampers, all embellished with pearl and jade ornaments of such marvelous craftsmanship and beauty as the world has never possessed nor the eye ever seen.

Pennons

There were also

banners of the Perfected,[2]
banners of the Jade Lads and Jade Maids,
banners of the Divine Diamond Kings,
brocaded lotus-blossom banners,
brocaded magic-mushroom banners,
brocaded coiled-dragon banners,
brocaded dancing-phoenix banners,

2. Beings that have moved beyond earthly corruption and are often identified with stellar deities.

brocaded soaring-simurgh banners, and
brocaded flying-crane banners.

Some [had motifs of] brilliant suns in flying clouds, dark shadows embracing
smoke, revolving graphs and unfurling flowers, linked gold, and strung jade.
Others [had designs of] painted landscape images, birds and animals of strange
shapes, propitious grasses and auspicious blossoms, and the sun piercing the
unfolding clouds. These banners were suspended from the altar's four sides.

Lighting Accoutrements

There were also

gold-lotus lamp trees,
silver-lotus lamp trees,
Seven Treasure lamp trees, and
polychrome lamp trees.

Chiliads and myriads of them were arrayed on and below the altar as well
as within the cloister of the abbey. The illumination of their beams pierced
and penetrated [the dark]. There were also

polychrome blossom candles,
gold coiled-dragon candles,
silver soaring-simurgh candles,
thousand-petaled lotus candles,
nine-color cloud candles,
lanterns of like minds,
lanterns of split blossoms,
candles of strung pearls,
lanterns of threaded blossoms,
divine revolving lanterns,
numinous flying-terrace lanterns,
purple flaming-orchid lanterns,
blue-green beamed magic-mushroom lanterns,
thousand boughs of rosy-blossom lanterns,
moonlit thousand-leaf lanterns,
five-star lanterns,
seven planetoid lanterns,
twenty-eight asterism[3] lanterns,
thirty-six heaven lanterns,
sheathed-light lanterns, and
extinguishing-smoke lanterns

which radiated their brilliance within and without.

The Suqi

On the eve of the twenty-seventh day (February 19, 711), the officiants
performed the rites of the Dao. Just as they began to chant the retreat of

---

3. A prominent group of stars, generally smaller than a constellation.

annunciation an auspicious snow drifted down like flowers. As they were about to reveal the True Writs, a propitious cloud floated [over the altar] like a canopy. During the fourth watch (2:00 to 4:00 A.M.) of that night, Lord Lao (Lao Tzu Deified) descended to the altar and spoke to the Princesses.

The Transmission of the Procedures

On the day for the transmission of the procedures an auspicious cloud of five colors and incense smoke of the eight inhalations [appeared]. When the transmission of the procedures had concluded, both Princesses abandoned their couches to recline on armrests and cushions.

Conclusion

The value of the musical instruments and clothing [for wearing] in secular life, 500 sets of pongee for each woman; 10,000 lengths of brocade and net; cash, colored silks, and the liturgical paraphernalia exceeded 10,000 strings of cash (that is, 10,000,000 cash). And this figure does not include the liturgical objects which defended the altar.

THE SCRIPTURE AND CHART FOR THE MYSTERIOUS CONTEMPLATION OF MAN-BIRD MOUNTAIN
(Xuanlan renniao shan jingtu)

The *Scripture and Chart for the Mysterious Contemplation of Man-Bird Mountain* (*Xuanlan renniao shan jingtu*), which may be a Tang dynasty (619–907) rewrite of a Six Dynasties (220–589) scripture, is a wonderfully detailed example of a specific class of texts within Daoism. These "charts" or "diagrams" (*tu*) are potent esoteric images with talismanic powers. The passage below focuses on the sacred geography of a set of mountains, each inhabited by beings with human faces and the bodies of birds and each produced by marvelous energies that form characters in its shape. If adepts—whether Daoist ritual masters or solitary practitioners in the mountains— can visualize these characters, then they will become able to fly like a bird. A Daoist who "has a picture of this mountain and all the accompanying documents will obtain passage to immortality"; no other techniques are required of one who reads the scripture "ten thousand times. . . . Practice earnestly without ceasing, and you will in due course ascend to heaven."

PRONOUNCING GLOSSARY

Xuanlan renniao shan jingtu: *hsuan-lawn run-niao shawn ching-tu*

The Most High says: the innumerable heavens has each its mountain of the man-bird. Each has the face of a man and the body of a bird. Its soaring peaks and precipices are too many to mention. In its mysterious belvederes and precious halls dwell venerable gods. The birds and animals in its forests and ravines, the trees and rocks, the incense flowers and the mushroom grasses, all the various medicines, the fountains of youth and the saps of immortality cannot all be described, and to describe them would be of no use to study. Students must search earnestly to obtain the one and know the all: then they will truly know everything. In teaching one must show the titles; therefore I sketch an outline.

The marvelous energies form characters; the saintly craftsman writes them. He transmits them to superior students; they are not to be divulged to ordinary people. These characters of marvelous energy are the *configuration of the mountain* [italics mine]. It is strange in outward appearance, and its contours are unusual. It is entirely the product of the transformations of the marvelous energy. By mystery-penetrating visualizations, you can see it when you close your eyes. When you have completed your investigation, you will get results from its use. Once the marvelous energy has descended, your fleshly body will be able to fly. If you refine it long enough to attain to mystery, mystery will fill you and your flesh disappear. Your flight will be that of a bird's, and you will roam in the mountains beyond the Three Realms.[1] Your soul will be that of a perfect man, and you will go in to the feast in the Three Pure Heavens.[2] Its general title is "man-bird." He who studies it will go from mountain to mountain, and the Supreme Way will protect and keep him forever. If you are not in utter earnest, do not set out foolishly.

The Most High says: the body of the man-bird mountain is the living root of heaven, earth, and man, that from which emerges the primordial energy, that on which the marvellous transformation relies. Saints and perfected[3] search for this place; immortals and potentates look up to its god. Worship it with reverence; visualize it with concentration. Banquet it when you receive it, give it offerings when you wear it. Practice it earnestly; hide it prudently. If you do so without slacking for a long time, your three energies[4] will harmonize: they will give birth to a body, to an infant, and you will become one of the elect of the Way.

Whether you stay in the world (as a priest) and practice transformation or enter the mountains to study recipes, wherever you are, you will be at ease, and the demons will not dare stand up to you. Then you will be able to bring the five peaks[5] into your court and to have the eight seas do your bidding. You will be a follower of the Lord of the Three Heavens, and wear at your belt the essences of sun and moon. He who knows this will not die; he

---

TRANSLATED BY John Lagerwey. All bracketed translations are the translator's.

1. The realms of desire, form, and formlessness (a Buddhist concept).
2. Great Clarity (Taiqing), Jade Clarity (Yuqing), and Upper Clarity (Shangqing).
3. The *zhenren*, who in later Daoism are described as beings that have moved beyond earthly corruption and are often identified with stellar deities;

in the Upper Clarity tradition, the perfected are more exalted than the *xian* or transcendents (often translated "immortals").
4. Generative (*jing*), vital (*qi*), and spiritual (*shen*).
5. That is, the Five Marchmounts, a group of five sacred mountains—one in each of the four cardinal directions and one at the center.

who practices it will live forever. He who examines it will merge with Wisdom; he who understands it will be as the gods.

On top of the mountain dwells the Celestial King of the Primordial Beginning; the multitude of saints, immortals, and the perfected live at its foot. The energy of this mountain gives birth to water of five colors:[6] it is called the Flowing Sap of the Returning Soul. It forms a lard which is called the Incense of the Eastern Sandalwood. The Queen Mother of the West,[7] when she first began to study the Way, went to visit the Celestial King of the Primordial Beginning. After three thousand years, having completed the Way and attained its power, she had to go back home to Mount Kunlun.[8] Just before she left, she went to take leave of the Celestial King of the Primordial Beginning, and together they carved an inscription in the space above Man-Bird Mountain. Each of the characters they formed was a meter square, and they hung them up in space for transmission to students of after days. They have survived to this day.

The Lord of the Capital of the Immortals, Nine Times Ancient, and the Giant of the Nine Energies drew a map of the mountain and wore it at the elbow. The Emperor of Heaven wrote down the characters in space and appended them to the body of the man-bird. Once in a hundred years it appears and is then transmitted to a perfect man. A Daoist who has the picture of this mountain and all the accompanying documents will obtain passage to immortality, to roam banqueting in Kunlun. If you read this book ten thousand times and practice it without infringing its instructions, the Lord-Emperor of Heaven will dispatch a cloud-chariot with a feather canopy to come and fetch you. You need not take cinnabar liquor; it is useless to draw-and-pull, crouch-and-stretch. Practice earnestly without ceasing, and you will in due course ascend to heaven.

6. Green, red, yellow, white, and black.
7. Xi Wang Mu, one of the most important goddesses in ancient China and in the Daoist pantheon.
8. A mythical mountain supposedly located in the far western part of the Chinese empire; it was the home of the Queen Mother of the West. Kunlun was also thought to possess various plants and minerals that confer immortality.

THE REGULATIONS FOR THE ACCEPTANCE AND CULTIVATION OF DAOISM ACCORDING TO THE DONGXUAN, LINGBAO, AND SANDONG SCRIPTURES
(Dongxuan lingbao sandong fengdao kejie yingshi)

Dating from the early Tang dynasty (618–907), the *Regulations for the Acceptance and Cultivation of Daoism According to the Dongxuan, Lingbao, and Sandong Scriptures (Dongxuan lingbao sandong fengdao kejie yingshi)* has been described as the first handbook of Daoist monasticism. It addresses the life and practices of professional Daoist priests, including information on fundamental rules, on ritual vestments and ordinary clothing (included below), and on organizational principles, such as the ranks of Daoist priests and the "registers" (*lu*) that they are given at each rank. It also contains more practical instructions, such as precisely how to make and care for Daoist icons (included below) and how to copy scriptures.

One of the sections included here is a long series of warnings to those who (among other things) might defame or slander the scriptures, insult religious practitioners, defile sacred Daoist sites, or break rules on clothing or ornamentation. The text details the precise nature of the retribution incurred for each transgression—contraction of a disease; a shorter life span; birth among boars, pigs, or idiots; physical deformities—in a chain of causation much like Buddhist karma. Another selection from the *Regulations* lists the positive behaviors and meritorious acts that lead to pleasant or auspicious rebirths.

PRONOUNCING GLOSSARY

Dongxuan lingbao sandong fengdao kejie yingshi: *tung-hsuan ling-pao sawnting fung-tao kuh-jieh ying-shih*

Yuanshi tianzun: *yuen-shih tien-tsoon*

From *Crimes as Conditions for Retribution*

1: "The scripture says": Whoever destroyed icons of the Heavenly Worthies and other representations of Great Dao, after death he or she shall enter the nine abysses and eighteen hells. 10,000 *kalpas*[1] will elapse until birth occurs, with a skin disease all over the body.

2: Whoever defamed the scriptures and manuals of the great teachings of the Three Caves,[2] or she shall pass through the nine abysses and eighteen hells. 100 *kalpas* will elapse until birth occurs with the body of a wild animal. If the person returns to a life amongst human beings, the root of the tongue shall rot away.

 ✻   ✻   ✻

4: Whoever destructed divine belvederes and Daoist altars, he or she shall lose eyebrows or beard in the present life, and the physical body shall rot away. After that, birth shall occur in the body of a poisonous snake.

5: Whoever was not respectful vis-à-vis the Heavenly Worthies and Great Dao, he or she shall become dull and stupid in the present life. After that, birth shall occur amongst the six domestic animals.

 ✻   ✻   ✻

14: Whoever stole material goods which were presented by the faithful of the four grades,[3] he or she shall turn crazy in the present life. After that, birth shall occur amongst idiots.

 ✻   ✻   ✻

TRANSLATED BY Florian C. Reiter.

1. A kalpa is the Buddhist term (adopted by Daoists) for an aeon, a complete cycle from the creation to the destruction of a particular world.
2. That is, the texts in the Daoist canon; they were divided into three "caverns," or collections, by Lu Xiujing in 471.
3. The monks, nuns, male and female disciples [translator's note].

21: Whoever broke the disciplinary rules, he or she shall experience the three catastrophes[4] in the present life. After that, birth shall occur amongst poisonous wasps or the deaf and the blind.

* * *

30: The scripture says: The fact that both eyes are blind was caused by disbelieving the teachings of the scriptures and a slighting or indifferent attitude vis-à-vis the Three Treasures.

* * *

32: The fact that the tongue rots away was caused by defaming the teachings of the scriptures of the Three Caves of the Great Vehicle.[5]

* * *

From *Good Deeds as Conditions for Retribution*

1: Whoever produced scriptures and icons, established belvederes and converted people, made donations, fasted and observed the disciplinary regulations, helped the dying and converted the living, rescued and widely spread propitious activities, greatly contributing to the advantage of all living beings, such a person shall be born as Heavenly King or Ruler of State.

2: A woman who owned scriptures and accepted the disciplinary rules, recited, meditated, offered ritual veneration and widely opened fields of charity, she shall be born as empress or Mother of State.

3: Whoever supported and maintained the Three Treasures, burnt incense and lit lamps without getting exhausted day and night, who produced scriptures and cast icons, he or she thus achieved to be born amongst the entourage of the Heavenly Kings.

4: Whoever believed and rejoiced in the scriptures and the Daoist teachings, relied on the disciplinary norms, accepted and practised them, who kept to the rules for fastings and meditated on Dao, made donations and established merits, such a person shall be born as a rich and noble person.

5: Whoever kept and accepted the scriptures and the disciplinary rules, recited and meditated as an abbot, such a person shall be born to be an intelligent and bright person.

* * *

35: That there are sons and nephews in great numbers, being rich and noble in a most satisfactory way, this comes from having widely distributed donations and promoting good luck.

36: That the wife gives birth to sons, and the couple lives together in respect and love, this comes from having believed in the teachings which emanate from Daoist services.

37: That at birth there are clear and refined sounds around, this comes from having sung and recited at Daoist ritual services.

---

4. War, pestilence, and famine.
5. The teachings of Daoism. ("Great Vehicle" translates the Sanskrit *Mahayana*, a Buddhist tradition that arose in India centuries after the Buddha's death and became dominant in Central and East Asian Buddhism.)

38: That at birth there is joy and good luck and blessings which spontaneously evolve, this comes from having sincerely learned about the doctrines and listened to the scriptures at Daoist services, and also from
making donations.

The Creation of Icons

The great images do not have any form, and being utmost perfect they do
not have any colour. They are clear, void and tranquil. Neither seeing nor
hearing can reach them, but they let their bodies become visible, responding
to cosmic mutations. For a short while they may manifest themselves and
retreat again into a hidden state of existence. Those persons who behold the
perfected this way, attach their thoughts to these appearances of the saints.
For this reason they use colours, metal and jade to work out the portraits
and icons . . . All those who devote their mind in this way are the first to create icons. There are six types of representations which they properly realize.

1) They first create representations of the divinities: Wushang fawang,
   Yuanshi tianzun, Taishang xuhuang, Yuzhen dadao, Gaoshang Laozi,
   Taiyi tianzun.
2) They create representations of the immeasurable saints, perfected
   and immortals in the realm of the Three Pure Ones, below the Daluo
   Heaven and above the Taiqing Heaven.[6]
3) They create representations of the saints, "who peer into the future
   without limit".
4) They create or draw representations of the perfected and immortals of
   the astral constellations in all the heavens.
5) They create holy representations of the countless categories of saints,
   perfected and immortals.[7]
6) They create figures and representations of the infinite saints and perfected, who accord with the causation of *karma*.

When the mind is engaged like this, eighteen methods then can be used to
model the true appearances of the perfected:

1) To carve precious jade, red and green jasper, or stones of the sort of the
   Seven Jewels.[8]
2) To cast gold.
3) To cast silver.
4) To cast bronze.
5) To cast blue iron.
6) To cast pewter.
7) To carve fragrant materials, like the sandalwood from river Chen.
8) To do weaving work.
9) To do embroideries.

6. Each of the many cosmological systems within
Daoism has its own hierarchy of heavens. The
Great Clarity Heaven (Taiqing tian) would usually be below the Great Canopy Heaven (Daluo
tian), generally the highest heaven.
7. Transcendents (*xian*), Daoists who have
reached a higher form of existence than common

humans; in the Upper Clarity (Shangqing) tradition, they are less exalted than the perfected
(*zhenren*), who in later Daoism are described as
beings that have moved beyond earthly corruption and are often identified with stellar deities.
8. A Buddhist concept; the jewels are variously
enumerated.

10) To model clay.
11) To press hempen cloth.
12) To do paintings on white silk.
13) To do wall paintings.
14) To cut stone caves.
15) To engrave fine stones.
16) To set up steles.
17) To do imprints on incense clay.
18) To print paper, model mud, carve bricks, pile up earth, to engrave tiles, rub bones, carve ivory, cut wood, pile up snow, and to paint with lime.

Whoever is thus most thoughtfully engaged, earns immeasurable blessings. It may be that these icons have a size of one, two, three, four or five *zun*, up to the size of one *chi*,[9] nothing stands against any size, and there is no limit as to the quantity. There may be one location or ten, hundred, thousand and ten thousand locations. The icons may count from one piece up to ten, hundred, thousand and ten thousand pieces. There may be one, ten, hundred, thousand and ten thousand caves, scrolls, and altar figures. There may be one, ten, hundred, thousand and ten thousand chapels and temple halls, some of them are extremely huge, counting in millions and tens of millions. There may be one, two, up to ten, hundred, thousand, ten thousand, one million, tens of millions of Heavenly Worthies, and the perfected, the immortals and saints, the jade lads and girls,[1] all the heavenly emperors and kings, the Diamond Divine Kings, the incense officials who attend the incense, the dragons and tigers, the lions . . . , the temple halls, scrolls and figures, adornments and embroidered baldachins, the immortal musicians who soar in the heavens, any type of administrative and protective agents, all of this is realized according to the vigor of the mind. Supporting the religious veneration, presenting incense and meditating day and night, this results in facing the true forms. For the past and the future "immeasurable blessings will be achieved and the true Dao completed".

Any creation of icons is based on the scriptures, implementing their instructions about the identifying marks. The Heavenly Worthies have fifty million marks, Daojun has seventy-two, Laojun[2] thirty-two, and the perfected have twenty-four. Clothes, hats and adorned seats have all to accord with the rules. Heavenly Worthies wear as an upper dress a nine-coloured open gaze gown, or also a five-coloured "clouds-and-vapours" gown. They wear yellow clothes with varied embroideries of landscapes, golden or jade hats with tassels and girdles at the rim of the left and right sides. Their golden or jade hats have multicoloured ornaments. The upper dress must not be unicoloured with purple, crimson, blue, white or green or any other colour. The perfected must not have loose hair. Above the long ears and the one chignon they have to wear "hibiscus-flower" hats, or hats of the type "flying clouds" or "original beginning". On the other hand, they must not wear hats of the type "*eryi* flat cap" and hats of the sort "deer-fawn cap". The two perfected on the left and right sides (of the Heavenly Worthies) present offerings or hold

9. A unit of length, equal to about 1 foot; each *chi* is divided into 10 *zun*.
1. Attendants in heaven.

2. Lord Lao, the deified Laozi. "Daojun": Lord Dao, the incarnation of the Dao (a title also given to Laozi).

scriptures, the insignia or fragrant flowers. They all must look reverential and stern . . . The Heavenly Worthies sit upright, their fingers "grasping the Void". Their hands do not hold the *ruyi*[3] sign or the deer-tail whip. The hands are just empty.

On the left and right hand side of the Heavenly Worthies, of Daojun Laojun, there are representations of the perfected, of jade lads and jade girls who administer the incense and the scriptures. Incense officials and dragon- and tiger-lords are on the left and right sides. Official messengers and the heavenly wards and warriors, the Diamond Divine Kings, lions, the *bixie*[4] dragon and unicorn, wild beasts and flying snakes, divine tigers, phoenix and peacock, scarlet birds with golden wings, the four mighty forces and the eight potencies, the good deities which protect the doctrine, they all are to extend their protection . . . They are installed according to the available means.

The names and titles of honour of the perfected are a vast lot and cannot be told or counted. All of them had been planted in a former *kalpa*, and due to the final perfection in Dao this utmost result was reached. On the left and right side of the Heavenly Worthies, of Daojun and Laojun these perfected agents assist and keep guard and memorialize the (cosmic) mutations.

The jade lads and jade girls were born by the transmutations of the breaths of Dao. They did not come forth from a womb. All of them have administrative functions. Some of them administer the scriptures and the incense, others distribute fragrant flowers . . . Their ranking does have grades.

All the assistants for presenting the scriptures and the incense are born out of a condensation of the breaths. They are always present in the places where the Heavenly Worthies live, and the true scriptures are stored. They transmit memorials and roam freely, recording and filing the good and the bad.

The divinities of the four poles of the Diamond Heaven are positioned at its four corners and at the gates of heaven and the windows of earth. They are 1,200 *zhang* tall,[5] holding down a sword and grasping a club. Their bodies are clad with heavenly clothes. They wear precious Flying-Clouds hats. Their feet tread upon the demons, the great rocks and divine beasts of huge mountains. They are set up to wield the might of killing demons. They dominate those unlawful demons and deities "below heaven and above earth". Due to their angry eyes and biting shouts, the evil forces fearfully submit. As to the gates and windows of temples and halls at the domains of the Heavenly Worthies, the icons of these divinities are to be installed for the sake of protection on the left and right sides. Their mutations are without limit, and thus they do not have a regular appearance. This is so, because they are born by the fierce breaths of Dao. It is not that they had "attained their existence by birth from a womb". Nowadays, such icons control inside a belvedere the gates and windows of temples, halls and archives.

The divine kings are the masters of the divine forces which can be classified according to three types:

1) They are condensations of the breaths.
2) They are retributions [due to a former] life.
3) They realize the causations of *karma*.

---

3. A scepter that symbolizes power and authority (*ruyi* literally means "as one wishes").

4. Literally, "evil dispeller."

5. About 2 miles (1 *zhang* = 10 *chi*).

Those divine kings which are condensations of the breaths were not born out of a womb, but emerged due to the breaths of naturalness. Those which represent retributions obeyed all those demons and divinities, and earned merits concerning Dao. When they were born (again) they received their present bodies (as divine kings). Those which realized the causations of *karma* received on rebirth what they had positively accumulated in a preceding *kalpa*. They personally see to it, that common people complete perfectness and attain Dao. They come to supervise conversion.

The names of the divine kings are countless. They all are clad in armours and helmets, have a lance or carry knives and hold swords. Either standing or sitting they do not have any fixed outer appearances. They keep the many demons in control and expel what is unlucky and bad. "All of this is contained in the instructions of the scriptures."

The demon kings also belong to the group of the divine kings. There are three types:

1) The demon kings of the Three Heavens.[6]
2) The demon kings of the Five Emperors.[7]
3) The demon kings which roam the heavens.

They take all precautions to protect and promote those who study the practice of Dao. The great meritorious demon kings are thus the capacities, which arrange the promotion of rank.

The heavenly wards and warriors, the dragons and tigers, the incense officials on the left and right sides came into existence due to the mutations of the breaths. They appeared fitting to the causations of *karma*. They subdue demons and summon ghosts, transmit messages and go as couriers. They are the mighty officials of "the protection of the Law".

The eight mighty potencies are said to be creatures like the poisonous dragon, the fierce tiger, the flying snake, . . . Those are malignant forces which had accumulated (bad) *karma*. The Heavenly Worthies subdued them with all their might and employ them, in order to guard gates and control passways. In caves, on walls and on borders they ward off what is bad.

The four magic forces are said to be the tortoise, the dragon, the unicorn and the phoenix. They all correspond with different breaths of astral constellations and combine the fine breaths of the five elements.[8] Some recite magic formulae and have diagrams emerge on their bodies. According to the seasons they come down into the world. They are the ominous birds and auspicious animals, which live in the gardens of the Heavenly Worthies.

As to the seats of the Heavenly Worthies there are eight types:

1) The lotus flower with one-thousand leaves.
2) The five-coloured lion.
3) The golden couch with seven jewels.
4) The jade seat with nine layers.
5) The crouching nine dragons.

6. Usually, Great Clarity (Taiqing), Jade Clarity (Yuqing), and Upper Clarity (Shangqing).
7. Legendary sages of predynastic China, variously identified in different sources.
8. Metal, wood, water, fire, and earth, which are the foundation of the theory of five phases—a set of systematic associations between different categories, including the five colors, five directions, and five viscera.

6) The eight shattered poisonous snakes.
7) The seat of fleecy clouds.
8) The seat above smoke and vapours.

They become visible forms following the mutations. The Heavenly Worthies sit on them at specific occasions. For the screened seats of today only the seven jewels and the eight precious stones, pearls, jade, gold and white stone are used, in order to work out the ornamentations and to produce a likeness . . .

In the course of long years the representations of the Heavenly Worthies, of Lord Dao, Lord Lao and all the saints, perfected and immortals get soaked and injured by wind and the sprinkling and splashing of rain. In time they must be repaired or restored. One must not let them delapidate. This way one receives immeasurable blessings.

At each 15th day of a month a fasting service is held for the figures and icons of the Heavenly Worthies which were made of gold, bronze and precious jade. They are washed and adorned with well smelling liquids. In case they had been printed (as pictures) on hempen cloth or carved in wood, one has to mop them and let them shine clear and clean. "This is the best way to earn merits."

The Daoist's Clothes

The "Three-Caves clothings" of Daoist priests and nuns accord with significant regulations, all as contained in the scriptures. One should rely on the Law in order to have a system for the clothings. For this matter one can rely on the expositions in the following chapter.

All those robes with designs of mountains, with red ribbons and colourful varied ornamentations are not to be compared with the robes on the bodies of the Heavenly Worthies, which use arrangements of thin gauze in the nine colours.

When priests expound and preach the scriptures of the Great Vehicle of the Three Caves, expose and spread the mysterious Dao and ascend their elevated seats for such purposes, these "Masters of Great Virtue" don such robes.

When they perform the supreme rituals, ascend the altars, enter the retreat, announce the fasting, walk processions, act as guiding head priests, and also when they perform common services concerning the scriptures, like the transmission of scriptures and disciplinary rules, in all these cases when rituals are required, they administer their duties and wear the robes temporarily for that occasion. When the work is done they stop wearing them. Except for these [ritual] occasions, the robes must not be donned. Offenses result in a diminution of lifetime of 1,200 days.

As to the skirts of nuns, they have ornamental trimmings on the cloths. The deep yellow of the Gardenia plant is used for dying. The broad sleeves have to be arranged the same way as the priest's sleeves. They must not have brandish[9] light and varied colours. Offenses result in a diminution of lifetime of 240 days.

---

9. Probably "ostentatious."

Formerly the common work clothes of priests and nuns had not been described . . . Their upper, middle and lower clothes use a light yellow colour. As to "yellow", this is the yellow of "powdered earth (lime)", and they are made in a light colour . . . When Daoists either live in a belvedere or in residential quarters supporting a teacher-master or persons of high age and outstanding merits, they wear such clothes. They also have to wear them when they care for the maintenance and embellishment of scriptures and icons, and generally handle the operation of a belvedere. As to trousers, shirts and jackets of priests and nuns, they all show the yellow earthen colour. They must not show any other colours including "white". Offenses result in a diminution of lifetime of 360 days.

Daoist priests and nuns have caps and turbans which have many different names and shapes. All are presented in the scriptures as exposed in the following chapter. They can use shells and skin, bamboo sprouts and leaves, or black gauze and pure lacquer according to the respective regulations. They all must not use deer skin and pearls, jade and colourful ornamentations. The hairpins are made of ivory, jade, bones and horn . . . One must not air their boxes and trunks and let lay folk misuse them. Offenses result in a diminution of lifetime of 260 days.

The proper style for the shoes of priests and nuns has them styled with round "heads", perhaps with symbols of *yin* and *yang*.[1] They are made of leather or cloth with ornaments worked out in silk and in the colours yellow and black. They must not use gauze and silk, brocade and embroidery, pictorial needlework and pearls . . . , including shoes of the lay people . . . The socks must be made of plain and soft cloth or cheap silk. The boots have to have a round head and broad soles made of hemp only . . . Offenses result in a diminution of lifetime of 240 days.

Soft cloth and cheap silk is used for the beadspread and blankets of priests and nuns. They are dyed lime-yellow or with the light yellow of the Sophora Japonica.[2] As to blue or green and dark purple brocades and silk, mixed and varied colourful ornamentations, all of this must not be used. The same applies to rugs, mats and mattresses. . . . For the pillows wood is used, perhaps with some lacquer. The pillows have to be straight, rectangular and must not be bent as to have extraordinary shapes. Now, objects to bind the hair, carved adornments made of silver and gold are laid down and spread on a clean cloth. Offenses result in a diminution of lifetime of 360 days.

Generally, priests and nuns carry on their belts scriptures, disciplinary rules, amulets and registers.[3] These Heavenly Books are with the person. This way the perfected ones are close to their outer [bodily] appearance. The breath of Dao fortifies and surrounds them. The immortals and the divine forces rest on them. The clothes and hats which they don are all called "ritual garments." They all have a divine and magic might. They are

---

1. The complementary forces that unite to form the Dao (yin, a term that originally referred to the shady side of a valley, by extension came to be associated with the dark, dampness, and passivity—the female principle; yang, a term that originally referred to the sunny side of a valley, by extension came to be associated with the light, dryness, and activity—the male principle). In the *Yijing* or *Book of Changes*, yang is represented by a solid line; yin, a broken line.

2. The Japanese pagoda tree; its flowers are pale yellow or creamy white.

3. The particular texts that a Daoist priest receives at each rank.

to be protected reverentially while sitting and sleeping, and especially deserve to be kept clean. In case priests and nuns go to officiate and so enter the world of the lay folk in order to convert people, they must not let their own perfected body get mixed up with vulgar affairs. There are many dirty breaths on the beds and mats of the common people . . . Each priest has to prepare their own sitting cushion, which is four *chi* in the square . . . "The Worthy of Great Merits", the ritual masters, and those who implement the supreme methods must have cushions in purple colour. The others use the yellow of the Sophora Japonica, but must not use brocade, silk and pearls [as adornments] on the cushions. They take those cushions always along, except in the sphere of the lay folk. Offenses result in a diminution of lifetime of 360 days.

SCRIPTURE ON INNER OBSERVATION BY THE MOST HIGH LORD LAO
(*Taishang laojun neiguan jing*)

The *Scripture on Inner Observation by the Most High Lord Lao* (*Taishang laojun neiguan jing*), an eighth-century text, became highly influential in later Daoism, and passages from it are often quoted in later commentaries. Presented as coming from the mouth of Lord Lao (Laojun), the deified form of Laozi, it opens with a short discourse on the formation of human life and the development of the embryo. A detailed tour of the body follows, noting the locations of different spirits and their responsibilities. The mind—itself spirit—is in charge of the body spirits and constantly changing. Originally the mind/spirit is pure, but sensory contact with the world leads it to covet and embrace delusion. Therefore, out of compassion the sages gave people a method to purify the mind, retain the Dao, and transform themselves: the practice of inner observation.

In its descriptions of inner observation, the *Scripture on Inner Observation* displays the influence of Buddhist ideas, such as "insight meditation" (*vipashyana*), "attaining the way," and the notion that self arises "from emptiness and non-being in accordance with karma and the course of destiny." However, these ideas appear in a Daoist context that is also infused with elements drawn from ancient indigenous Chinese religious ideas and practices. To realize the Dao requires "calming the spirit and concentrating the mind." Indeed, it is by concentrating, pacifying, and emptying the mind, thereby perfecting this practice of introspection and aligning body and spirit with the Dao, that it becomes possible to fly and gain immortality.

PRONOUNCING GLOSSARY

Niwan: *knee-wawn*
Taishang laojun neiguan jing: *tie-shawn lao-chun nay-gwan ching*

The Venerable Lord said:

Heaven and earth mingle their essences; yin and yang[1] engage in interchange. Thus the myriad beings come to life each receiving a particular life: yet all are alike in that they have a share in the life-giving Dao.

When father and mother unite in harmony, man receives life.

In the first month, essence and blood coagulate in the womb.

In the second month, the embryo begins to take shape.

In the third month, the yang spirit arouses the three spirit souls[2] to come to life.

In the fourth month, the yin energy settles the seven material souls[3] as guardians of the body.

In the fifth month, the five agents are distributed to the five orbs[4] to keep their spirit at peace.

In the sixth month, the six pitches are set up in the six repositories[5] nourishing the vital energy.

In the seventh month, the seven essential stars[6] open the body orifices to let the light in.

In the eighth month, the eight phosphor spirits[7] descend with their true vital energy.

In the ninth month, the various palaces and chambers are properly arranged to keep the essence safe.

In the tenth month, the energy is strong enough to complete the image. Man's feeding on primordial harmony is never interrupted. The Lord Emperor of the Great One resides in the head. He is called the Lord of the Niwan Palace.[8] He governs the host of spirits. What makes life shine forth and lets man know of the spirits is his spirit soul. Siming,[9] the Administrator of Destiny, resides in the heart. He regulates the prime energies of life. Wuying occupies his left, from where he regulates the three spirit souls. Baiyuan occupies the right, from where he regulates the seven material souls. Taohai resides in the navel, where he preserves the root of the essence.

What makes the various joints of the body function together are the hundred manifestations of the spirit of life. As it pervades the whole of the body, spirit is not empty. When primordial energy enters through the nose

---

TRANSLATED BY Livia Kohn. This selection has been converted from Wade-Giles to pinyin by the Norton editor.

1. The complementary forces that unite to form the Dao (yin, a term that originally referred to the shady side of a valley, by extension came to be associated with the dark, earth, dampness, and passivity—the female principle; yang, a term that originally referred to the sunny side of a valley, by extension came to be associated with the light, heaven, dryness, and activity—the male principle).

2. Womb Radiance, Numen Guide, and Gloomy Essence [translator's note]. These are the three *hun* or cloud souls, linked with heaven and its pneumas.

3. "Turbid demons" in the human body[;] . . . one should strive to control them [translator's note]. These are the seven *po* or white souls, linked to the earth.

4. The lungs, heart, liver, spleen, and kidneys. "The five agents": that is, the five elements (metal, wood, water, fire, and earth) that, according to the theory of five phases, move from one phase to another as part of a set of systematic associations between different categories, including the five colors, five directions, and five viscera (or five orbs).

5. The gallbladder, bladder, stomach, large intestine, small intestine, and throat (or navel).

6. The sun, the moon, Mercury, Mars, Venus, Jupiter, and Saturn.

7. The chiefs of the twenty-four gods presiding over the contractive and defensive energies in the human body [translator's note].

8. The central of the nine palaces inside one's head. *Niwan* literally means "muddy pellet"; some have speculated that the term derives from the Sanskrit *nirvana*, a Buddhist term.

9. A deity, as are the following three inhabitants of the body named here.

and reaches the *niwan* in the center of the head, the spirit light radiates and the body is stable and at peace. For all movement and rest, however, it fully depends on the mind. This is how life first begins.

When you now observe yourself in detail and with care, beware of the mind. As the ruler of the self it can prohibit and control everything. It is responsible for the propriety of the body spirits. The mind is the spirit. Its changes and transformations cannot be fathomed. It does not have a fixed shape.

In the five orbs, the following spirit manifestations reside:
The spirit soul in the liver;
the material soul in the lungs;
the essence in the kidneys;
the intention in the spleen;
the spirit in the mind/heart.

Their appellations vary in accordance with their respective positions. The mind/heart belongs to the agent fire. Fire is the essence of the South and of greater yang. Above it is governed by the planet Mars, below it corresponds to the mind/heart. Its color is red and it consists of three valves that resemble a lotus leaf. As the light of pure spirit is rooted there, it is named accordingly.

Spirit is neither black nor white, neither red nor yellow, neither big nor small, neither short nor long, neither crooked nor straight, neither soft nor hard, neither thick nor thin, neither round nor square. It goes on changing and transforming without measure, merges with yin and yang, greatly encompasses heaven and earth, subtly enters the tiniest blade of grass. Controlled it is straightforward, let loose it goes mad. Purity and tranquility make it live, defilements and nervousness cause it to perish. When shining it can illuminate the eight ends of the universe. When darkened it will go wrong even in one single direction. You need only keep it empty and still, then life and the Dao will spontaneously be permanent. Always preserve an attitude of non-action, and the self will prosper.

The spirit is shapeless, thus it cannot be named. All good and bad fortune, all success and failure only come from the spirit. Thus the sage will always preserve a straightforward relation to the ruler and the government, to the established rewards and punishments, and to the laws and regulations of the administration. He sets an example for others. The reason why people find it hard to submit to rules and regulations is found in their minds. When the mind is pure and calm, all the many problems of misfortune don't arise.

All ups and downs, life and death, all vicissitudes and evils arise from the mind. All foolishness and delusion, love and hate, all accepting and rejecting, coming and going, all defilements and attachments, as well as all entanglement and bondage arise gradually from becoming involved in things. Madly turning hither and thither, tied up and fettered, one is unable to get free. Thus one is bound for peril and destruction.

Oxen and horses when led properly can easily wade through the marsh. When let loose, however, they will sink in deeper and deeper and can never get out again by themselves. So they have to die. People are just like this: when first born their original spirit is pure and tranquil, profound and unadulterated. But then people gradually take in shaped objects. Those will in due course defile the six senses.[1]

---

1. Sight, hearing, smell, taste, mind, and touch.

The eyes will covet color.
The ears will be obstructed by sound.
The mouth will be addicted to flavors.
The nose will always take in smells.
The mind will be intent on refusing and coveting.
The body will desire to be slimmer or fatter.

From all these ups and downs of life no one is able to wake up by himself. Thus the sages with compassionate consideration established the doctrine to teach people to reform. They made them use inner observation of the self and body in order to purify the mind.

* * *

The Venerable Lord said:

Knowing the Dao is easy, trusting the Dao is hard.
Trusting the Dao is easy, practicing the Dao is hard.
Practicing the Dao is easy, attaining the Dao is hard.
Attaining the Dao is easy, preserving the Dao is hard.
By preserving the Dao and never losing it, one will live forever.

The Venerable Lord said:

The Dao cannot be transmitted by word nor attained by hearsay. One must empty one's mind, calm the spirit, and the Dao will come to stay naturally. Ignorant people, not realizing this, labor their bodies and exhaust their minds. They exert their will and agitate their spirit. Yet thereby they push the Dao further away and make the spirit grow sadder and sadder. They oppose the Dao in search of the Dao—be warned against this!

The Venerable Lord said:

The Dao highly values long life, so guard your spirit and hold on to your root. Never let essence and energy disperse, but keep them pure white and always together. When body and spirit are aligned with the Dao you can fly to Mount Kunlun, be born in Former Heaven, continue living in Later Heaven, and forever pass in and out of the spaceless.

Yet, if you don't follow this path you will blow out your yin and radiate your yang away. You will tighten your material souls and encroach upon your spirit souls. For millions of years you will be a family man, producing offspring for thousands of generations. The yellow grime of the world will surround you while the Realized One[2] astride his ox enters the golden halls and jade chambers of heaven, always giving up the old and welcoming the new.

2. Laozi.

THE SEAL OF THE UNITY OF THE THREE
(Cantong qi)

SHITOU XIQIAN

The Seal of the Unity of the Three (*Cantong qi*) is a Chan (or Zen) Buddhist doctrinal poem written by a monk, Shitou Xiqian (700–790). It displays a number of connections to Daoism—most notably, as its title suggests, to the *Seal of the Unity of the Three, in Accordance with the Book of Changes* (*Zhouyi cantong qi*), an earlier alchemical work excerpted above. Though its dating is uncertain—some now question its traditional Han dynasty (202 B.C.E.–220 C.E.) attribution to Wei Boyang, believing instead that it was composed during the Tang dynasty (618–907)—the alchemical work clearly became popular and inspired numerous commentaries around the time that Shitou wrote his poem. The precise relationship between these two texts is difficult to pin down, however. Though one does not quote from the other, they do share a number of themes, such as the notion of "return" and the play of opposites (light and dark). Some scholars, focusing on Shitou's background as a Chan monk, see a link between the Chan practice of introspection—*neiguan*, the same term used in Daoism to refer to inner observation—and the practice of internal alchemy treated in the much longer *Seal of the Unity of the Three, in Accordance with the Book of Changes*.

PRONOUNCING GLOSSARY

Cantong qi: *tsawn-tung chi*   Shitou Xiqian: *shih-tow hsi-chien*

The mind of the great sage of India[1]
is intimately transmitted from west to east.
While human faculties are sharp or dull,
the way has no Northern or Southern Ancestors.
The spiritual source shines clear in the light;
the branching streams flow on in the dark.
Grasping at things is surely delusion;
according with sameness is still not enlightenment.
All the objects of the senses
interact and yet do not.
Interacting brings involvement.
Otherwise, each keeps its place.
Sights vary in quality and form,
sounds differ as pleasing or harsh.
Refined and common speech come together in the dark,
clear and murky phrases are distinguished in the light.
The four elements return to their natures
just as a child turns to its mother.
Fire heats, wind moves,
water wets, earth is solid.
Eye and sight, ear and sound,
nose and smell, tongue and taste.

TRANSLATED BY the Soto-Shu Liturgy Conference, with some revisions.

1. The Buddha (ca. 5th century B.C.E.).

Thus for each and every thing,
depending on these roots, the leaves spread forth.
Trunk and branches share the essence;
revered and common, each has its speech.
In the light there is darkness.
but don't take it as darkness;
In the dark there is light,
but don't see it as light.
Light and dark oppose one another
like front and back foot in walking.
Each of the myriad things has its merit,
expressed according to function and place.
Phenomena exist, like box and lid joining;
principle accords, like arrow points meeting.
Hearing the words, understand the meaning;
don't set up standards of your own.
If you don't understand the way right before you,
how will you know the path as you walk?
Practice is not a matter of far or near,
but if you are confused, mountains and rivers block your way.
I respectfully urge you who study the mystery,
don't pass your days and nights in vain.

STELE INSCRIPTION FOR THE ALTAR OF THE TRANSCENDENT LADY WEI OF THE JIN DYNASTY, THE LADY OF THE SOUTHERN PEAK, PRIMAL WORTHY OF THE PURPLE VOID, CONCURRENTLY SUPREME TRUE MISTRESS OF DESTINY

(Jin zixu yuanjun ling shangzhen siming nanyue furen xiantan beiming)

YAN ZHENQING

This loftily titled inscription is primarily a hagiography of the important noble-woman Wei Huacun (252–334). As the female immortal Lady Wei (Wei furen) she played a key role in the Upper Clarity (Shangqing) tradition, revealing some of its most important texts to the spirit-medium Yang Xi (330–386). The "Stele Inscription for the Altar of the Transcendent Lady Wei of the Jin Dynasty, the Lady of the Southern Peak, Primal Worthy of the Purple Void, Concurrently Supreme True Mistress of Destiny"—written by the prominent official, writer, and calligrapher Yan Zhenqing (709–785)—details the history of Wei Huacun, her apotheosis as the transcendent Lady Wei, and the role she played in transmitting the Highest Clarity scriptures to Yang Xi and his patrons, the Xu family (see the *Declarations of the Perfected*, or *Zhen'gao*, above). It also notes the construction of her altar and other cultic sites in Linchuan (present-day Jiangxi); the fall into ruin of those ritual sites, as nature reclaimed them; the rediscovery of the overgrown altar by Huang Lingwei

(640–721), also known as Flowery Maiden, who expanded the site and charged two female Daoists to care for the sanctuary; and finally the official restoration work carried out on the site by Yan Zhenqing himself.

PRONOUNCING GLOSSARY

Yan Zhenqing: *yan chun-ching*

Primal Mistress of Purple Barrens[1]
Is Wei, Great Lady.
Her place was in the rank of the Five Marchmounts;[2]
Her name was high—with the Seven Realized Ones.
This congelation of blossoms; with exalted [parental] assent,
Deprived of her objective, became the handmaiden of Liu.[3]
But at the radiant entreaty of the Grand Theocrat[4]
Clear Barrens let his spirit descend [to her].
As the company of transcendents[5] ended their assembly,
The jade portfolios were laid out before her.
Through submission to the Dao she wasted with the days,
But the concentration of her heart was increasingly zealous.
She divested [herself of] her form [in the semblance of] a divine sword;[6]
She assumed the steering of the tempest wheels—
Her ultimate destination was Yanglo.[7]
In haste she ascended [the Platform of] the Hidden Prime[8]
To the brilliant odes of Yellow Court[9]
Under white sun she rose into the dawn.
She descended to the Royal Mother in the west,[1]
She went by Shushen[2] in the east.
She transmitted the Laws through the attendant on the Penetralia;
Xu and Yang[3] became her neighbours.
Long ago, she had crossed over into the south,
Moved her residence far off to the shore of the Ru.[4]
Place of altar, site of arena:
Buried, submerged—a wild tangle of growth.

TRANSLATED BY Edward H. Schafer. All bracketed additions are the translator's.

1. Also Purple Void, a precinct in the sky that is beyond human perception. Some equate it with the Jade Clarity Heaven's Palace of Purple Tenuity, in which the celestial emperor lived.
2. A group of five sacred mountains—one in each of the four cardinal directions and one at the center. She is associated with the Southern Marchmount, usually identified as Mount Heng.
3. Her husband, Liu Youyan.
4. The highest deity in the universe.
5. Daoists who have achieved extraordinary powers and a higher form of existence (*xian*, often translated "immortals").
6. This is release through the sword, a type of liberation or transformation similar to release by means of a corpse: that is, the feigning of one's own death, leaving behind nothing or some relic and then ascending to heaven.
7. A sacred mountain in the far north of China.

8. The Heaven of Upper Clarity.
9. Literally, a central courtyard, but in the Shangqing (Upper Clarity) tradition the center of the human body; see the introduction to the *Most High Jade Scripture on the Internal View of the Yellow Court* (*Taishang huangting neijing yujing*), above.
1. One of the most important goddesses in ancient China and in the Daoist pantheon, who governed all other female deities.
2. That is, Mao Shushen (or Mao Ying), one of the founding deities of the Upper Clarity (Shangqing) school of Daoism; his two younger brothers were also venerated in the tradition.
3. That is, the spirit-medium Yang Xi (330–386) and his patrons, Xu Mi (303–376) and Xu Hui (331–ca. 370).
4. A river in Linchuan (present-day Jiangxi).

It lay with Miss Flower[5] to find the truth;
She took counsel with the Reverend Hu:[6]
They actually found numinous remains
On the Plateau of the Crow-black Tortoise.
Next they searched the Mount of the Well:
Actuality agreed with the precursal[7] words.
She was cheerfully released through writing slips[8]—
Her pall of gauze was left empty.
Wild elephants with lotuses-stems in mouth;
Numinous melons extruding roots!
Radiant emblems, uncanny and strange,
Not susceptible of full discussion.
Two Peerless Ones,[9] in shock and surprise,
Repeatedly showed reverence with luminous incense-rites.
But, alas, the women were weak:
The aromatics were choked off, the fires were extinguished.
When I, Zhenqing, took the 'Stimulancy' of the County,
I presented myself time after time to pay my respects;
Then I commanded a scion of the Transcendents
To enlarge and restore, to convert and renew.
Miss Flower attended by their sides:
'Different eras share the same dust'.
How could I express [the Lady's] mystic virtue?
By inscribing her exploits in halcyon-blue serpentine!
To pass them down to generations to come—
Inexhaustible variety without end!

5. Huang Lingwei (640–721).
6. That is, a Daoist priest.
7. Precursory, premonitory.
8. Another form of transformation similar to release by means of a corpse.
9. That is, two officials who paid reverence to the shrine.

CANTOS ON PACING THE VOID
(*Buxu ci*)

WU YUN

"Cantos on Pacing the Void" ("Buxu ci") is a set of ten poems written by Wu Yun (d. 778), preserved in his *Collected Works of Master Ancestral Mystery* (*Zongxuan xiansheng wenji*). A Daoist priest as well as a noted poet, he had close connections to the Tang imperial house and many famous poets of the Tang dynasty (618–907), such as Li Bo (701–762) and Jiaoran (730–799). Wu Yun is especially well regarded for his ecstatic poetry that documents astral travel using the complex symbolic language characteristic of Upper Clarity (Shangqing) texts.

In Canto One we embark on a mystical journey into the starry firmament—though the imagery suggests that it might also be an inward journey into the microcosm of the body—bathed in the light cast by shining asterisms, or small constellations. On the way to the center of the universe, the adept is refined by a fire that burns off all mortal defilements. Having harmonized yang (active, male, heavenly) and yin (passive, female, earthy) principles, he can fly high and perceive the universe as it really is.

Canto Two finds the adept, whose perfected mortal body now has "golden bones," taking flight from the highest and most exalted mountain peak. He soars up, borne and guided by light, to enjoy visions of the dazzlingly jeweled abodes of ageless transcendents.

Canto Three opens with visions of numinous light pouring down from heavenly palaces as the adept travels in a "tempest," a vehicle of winds that delivers him to the realm of the Perfected Ones. Himself now perfected, the adept is described in Canto Four as a transcendent free of all vestiges of worldly characteristics, and he continues to ascend through the levels of heaven. When the adept arrives at the heavenly palace of the Metal Mother (the Queen Mother of the West), that jeweled domain is described in spectacular detail. As the adept gazes down on the imperfect world of mere mortals, he pities their inability to perceive what is in the sky—such as the raised platform supporting the palace of the supreme deity, or the other visual, aural, and olfactory delights of the celestial abode and its perfected inhabitants, set out in the verse.

After the adept finally gains a meeting with the supreme deity, he is provided with comfortable lodging and information from the heavenly musicians about the creation of it all. The tenth and final canto reveals the adept's knowledge of the workings of the universe, emphasizing the primal unity before the initial differentiation into yin and yang.

PRONOUNCING GLOSSARY

Buxu ci: *boo-hsu tzuh*
Zongxuan xiansheng wenji: *tsowng-hsuan hsien-shung when-gee*

Canto One

The host of transcendents looks up to the Numinous Template.[1]
Dignified equipages[2]—to the Levee of the Divine Genitor.[3]
Golden phosphors[4] shed asterial light on them.
By a long, circuitous route, they ascend to the Grand Hollow.
The Seven Occults[5] have already flown high.
Refinement by fire is engendered in the Vermilion Palace.[6]
The surplus of felicity extends from sky to loam.[7]
Tranquillity and harmony infuse the Kingly Way.
The Eight Daunters[8] clarify the roving pneumas.

TRANSLATED BY Edward H. Schafer.

1. Evidently the master pattern of the cosmos [translator's note]. "Transcendents": Daoists who have reached a higher form of existence than common humans; in the Upper Clarity (Shangqing) tradition, they are less exalted than the perfected (*zhenren*), who are often identified with stellar deities.
2. Retinues (made up of horses, carriages, and attendants).
3. The creator and governor of the universe. "Levee": reception.
4. Auspicious displays of light in the sky.

5. On one level, the seven stars of the Big Dipper; on another, the seven orifices of the human body (the eyes, ears, nostrils, and mouth).
6. In the macrocosmos, a heavenly palace; also, in the Upper Clarity tradition, the heart.
7. That is, from heaven to earth.
8. Vanquishers. These are spirits of the eight trigrams of Daoist cosmology (on the trigrams, see the introduction to *The Seal of the Unity of the Three, in Accordance with the Book of Changes*, or *Zhouyi cantong qi*, above), who protect the eight directions of the compass rose.

The Ten Distinctions[9] dance in the auspicious winds.
They permit *me* to scale the font of *yang*.[1]
This comes from my *yin*[2] achievements.
Footloose and fancy-free—above the Grand Aurora.[3]
The Speculum of Truth[4] penetrates everywhere.

Canto Two

Reins relaxed, I mount to Purple Clarity;
Borne by the light—overtaking the fleet lightning.
"Wind on the Fells" is sundered from the Three Heavens;[5]
But looking aloft, they seem to be visible.
The porch of jade! whence effulgences stream out widely;
The rose-gem forest—a jungle of fresh, rich verdure.
Unless one is conspicuously golden-boned,[6]
How may one be accordant with the long-standing wish?
My realized comrades—what a dense crowd!
The paired phosphors[7] allow indulgence in picnics and parties.
Forgetful in such goodly company, I protract my stay.
A thousand ages—only an eye's wink.

Canto Three

The Three Palaces emit luminous phosphors;
So brilliant that they are equal to "Steaming Regalia."[8]
I guide the impetuous tempest[9] in motley tumult,
And pluck a panicle of hollow bice[1] from above.
It causes me to be permeated with the color of gold:
A radiant rose-gem figure in these latter-day skies.
My heart is in harmony with the quiet of the Grand Void:
Rarefied and inscrutable—in the end, how to be conceived?
Within this Mystery there is the utmost happiness;
Calm, at rest—from beginning to end, no artifice.
Only in the company of a perfectly realized friend,
A wind-born waif, I am free to ramble at pleasure.

Canto Four

My quiddity[2] is transmuted, congealing the genuine Pneuma;
I have refined my form, made myself a realized[3] transcendent.

---

9. Protective entities of the ten directions (north, south, east, west, northeast, northwest, southeast, southwest, the nadir, and the zenith).
1. The male principle; the term originally referred to the sunny side of a valley, and by extension it came to be associated with the light, heaven, dryness, and activity.
2. The female principle; the term originally referred to the shady side of a valley, and by extension it came to be associated with the dark, earth, dampness, and passivity.
3. An ethereal realm glowing with light.
4. A mirror that reflects the true state of the universe.

5. Great Clarity (Taiqing), Jade Clarity (Yuqing), and Upper Clarity (Shangqing).
6. An adept's bones turn to gold before he or she abandons a mortal body for the heavens.
7. The sun and moon.
8. A spirit that accompanies the sun in its rotation.
9. A rush of colored vapors that transports beings in heaven.
1. Blue gems, hanging in clusters (panicles) that make up the flowers of a celestial tree.
2. Inherent nature or essence.
3. That is, perfected.

My oblivious heart tallies with the Primal Genitor;[4]
I have reverted to my roots—in harmony with spontaneity.
The Thearchic Monad[5] perches in his Rose-gold Palace;
Streaming light issues from Cinnabar Murk.[6]
"Nonpareil" along with "Lord Peach,"[7]
[Sing] brilliant odes from the folios of long life.
The Six Archives[8] glitter with a luminous aurora;
The Hundred Junctions[9] are netted in purple mist.
My tempest car traverses the endless expanse;
Slowly and steadily I am transported, mounted on the phosphors.
I am unaware of the distance on the clouded road;
In an instant I journey through a myriad of heavens.

Canto Five

Fusang[1] diffuses the first phosphor-glow;
The feathered canopy grazes the dawn aurora.
Swift and sudden we attain the Western Enceinte;[2]
Joyfully I roam the house of Metal Mother.[3]
Cyan exudate[4]—fathomless in the Vast Font—
Vivid and dazzling, is spread with lotus flowers.
Resplendently glowing—the palace of blue sapphires;
Sparkling, scintillant—the arrays of jade blossoms.
The pneumas of truth overflow the Rose-gold Treasury;[5]
In Spontaneity, my mind is free of perversion.
Looking down, I pity the gentlemen in that tract:
Their sky is blurred—how very much to be regretted.

Canto Six

The Rose-gem Estrade[6]—its fathoms are by kalpas;[7]
Glinting in solitude, beyond the Great Envelope.[8]
It is constantly provided with the clouds of the Three Immaculates;[9]
Clotted light flies freely around it.
Plumed phosphors drift in the luminous auroral clouds;
Rising and falling—how haunting and ethereal.
Simurghs[1] and phoenixes pour forth courtly tunes;

4. That is, the Divine Genitor.
5. The astral version of the supreme deity.
6. One of the palaces inside the human head.
7. The spirit that controls the yin and yang in one's body. "Nonpareil": the lord of one of the stars of the Dipper (literally, "Having No Equal").
8. The gallbladder, the stomach, the bladder, the throat (or navel), and the small and large intestines.
9. Points of transition within the human body.
1. A deity's palace located beyond, and below, the eastern sea; its glow is what illuminates the dawn sky.
2. The fortification around a castle or palace.
3. The Queen Mother of the West, one of the most important goddesses in ancient China and in the Daoist pantheon.
4. Celestial water that fills a gorgeous blue lake associated with the Queen Mother of the West's palace on the legendary Mount Kunlun. Its microcosmic counterpart is human saliva, also viewed as a vital fluid.
5. On the microcosmic level, the heart.
6. Platform.
7. That is, beyond measure. A kalpa is the Buddhist term (adopted by Daoists) for an aeon, a complete cosmic cycle from the creation to the destruction of a particular world.
8. That which encloses the realm of the star deities.
9. The auroral glow of dawn colors—white, yellow (or green), and purple. These rays of light can nourish adepts.
1. Mythical large winged creatures whose appearance is auspicious.

They perch, they soar—over the Rose-gold Forest.
In the Jade Void there is neither day nor night;
The numinous phosphors—how candent[2] they shine.
One look at the all-highest capital,
Then I know how small are all the Heavens.

Canto Seven

Vividly bright—the Forest of Blue Flowers;
Numinous winds shake rose-gem branches.
The Three Lights[3] have neither winter nor spring;
The totality of pneumas is both clear and concordant.
I turn my head—I am approaching "Knotted Spangles."[4]
I turn my pupils downward—I am neighbor to the asterial net.[5]
"Free Fall" constrains the Six Heavens.[6]
"Streaming Folly-bell"[7] daunts the hundred demons.
Threaded through space and time: felicity without limit;
Who says that the seniority of the cedrela[8] is so much?

Canto Eight

In this high clarity there is neither waste nor dissipation:
The beings I meet generate florescent light.
For the ultimate music—neither syrinx nor song:
Tones of jade tinkle spontaneously.
I may ascend the Platform of Light and Truth,[9]
And feast in that Hall of Plumed Phosphors.
Obscure cumuli knot into treasure-clouds;
In thin flurries they dispense numinous aromas.
As a sky person, truly my time and space are unbounded;
My joy is grand—not possibly to be measured.

Canto Nine

I make the ascent all the way from Grand Tenuity,[1]
For an interview, finally, with His Reverence, the Resplendent
    One of the Void.[2]
The Eight Phosphor Palanquin that bears me upward
By long, circuitous ways, enters the Gate of Heaven.
Once I have mounted to the court of Jade Dawn,
In all solemnity, looking up to the Purple Balcony,
I presume to ask, "At the end of Dragon Han,[3]

---

2. Glowing white.
3. The sun, moon, and stars.
4. The spirit that accompanies the moon; it is the counterpart of "Steaming Regalia," which accompanies the sun.
5. The canopy of stars in the sky.
6. The demonic heavens that the Three Heavens system of the Daoists overcame. "Free Fall": a potent talisman that draws on the power of the stars to fend off malevolent forces.

7. A bright red light that drives away demons; when agitated, it makes a loud sound.
8. The Chinese toon tree, reputedly long-lived.
9. The source of natural celestial music.
1. An important celestial administrative center, visible as a constellation.
2. The supreme deity.
3. That is, before the unity was differentiated into the multiplicity of matter.

How was it that [He] opened the way for Potent and Latent?"[4]
Agreeably, they suspend the cloudy *ao*;[5]
And inform me with speech about the Ineffable.[6]
I am fortunate to hear the system of the Ultimate Germ;
Then to see the font of the Shaping Mutator.[7]

Canto Ten

The Two Energies[8] sow the Myriad Beings;
The transmuting motor never stops its wheels.
While it is *I* who grasp its key;
So I can go forth from the Potter's Wheel.[9]
Through inconceivable mystery I ascend the Great Silence;[1]
Everything I encounter is clear and perfect.
Limpid and hyaline, embodying the Primal Harmony,
The Pneumas are conjoined in spontaneous affinity.
Rose-gold trees crystallize cinnabar fruit;
The purple aurora lets cyan exudate flow.
My wish is to use it to conserve youth and infancy;
I shall employ it forever to transcend both form and spirit.

---

4. The universal powers of generation and preservation, respectively.
5. Stones used by Daoist divinities to make music.
6. The character of the Dao that cannot be put into words.

7. The shaper and molder of physical matter into all forms.
8. That is, yin and yang.
9. That is, the creative principle in the universe.
1. The void beyond the cosmos.

SELECTED POEMS

LI BO and BO JUYI

Li Bo (or Li Bai, 701–762) and Bo Juyi (or Bai Juyi, 772–846) are two of the most celebrated poets of the Tang dynasty (618–907). Although neither is, strictly speaking, a Daoist poet, their writings illustrate the conjoining of Daoism and the literary arts. Li Bo was more closely linked to Daoism: he is associated with the important Tang Daoist Sima Chengzhen (647–735); one tradition claimed he was brought to the Tang court to serve in the Hanlin Academy by the Daoist poet Wu Yun (d. 778); and one account includes him among the Eight Immortals (legendary Daoist *xian*, or transcendents). The poems by Li Bo and Bo Juyi presented below mix Daoist and Buddhist imagery, as they describe transcendents roaming mountains and the preparation of elixirs.

Li Bo's set of six poems on Mount Tai (Taishan), written in 742, are particularly noteworthy. The various ascents of the sacred mountain mirror his spiritual progress and entrance into the realm of the transcendents, enabling him to access new realms and receive significant objects from transcendents and other key figures. Li is also reprimanded by the Azure Lad, the male counterpart to the Queen Mother of the West, for beginning his quest for the Dao too late, but after he redoubles his efforts he makes good progress and is able to refine himself. He provides evocative descriptions of Mount Tai and the transcendent beings (some feathered) he meets at that paradisical site. In the final poem, after carrying his zither up the mountain at night, he gains a vision of perfected beings dancing; and Li now acts like a perfected being himself, able to casually swish his hand in the Heavenly River (the Milky Way). But the set of Mount Tai poems ends on a sour note, as ultimately that careless gesture forces Li's return to the mundane world of humans. For this reason, Li Bo was called the Banished Immortal.

In "The Lady of the Supreme Primordial," Li Bo offers a seductively intimate and iconographically precise portrait of the goddess and describes her ascent to heaven accompanied by phoenixes. His two poems titled "Flying Dragon Conductus"— "conductus" signifying performance to a zither—describe the Yellow Thearch's ascent to heaven astride a dragon after he successfully compounds an elixir of immortality. He is followed by his concubines, whose transformation into Daoist goddesses is chronicled in the second poem.

Bo Juyi's "Composed in Response to 'Sending Daoist Master Liu Off to Wander on Heavenly Platform Mountain'" praises the Daoist master Liu as he departs for a life of seclusion on the sacred Heavenly Platform Mountain (Tiantai shan). His journey is described in terms that recall the Daoist practice of "Pacing the Void," or ascending to heaven as a transcendent, but the poem also contains a striking number of Sanskrit words, such as *skandhas* and *gata*. Though many of these Buddhist terms had already entered the medieval Chinese religious vocabulary, their use here seems to emphasize the triumph of Daoism over Buddhism, as Bo Juyi imagines Liu taking over a mountain—already sacred to Daoists—that had long been a famous Buddhist pilgrimage site.

PRONOUNCING GLOSSARY

Anqi: *awn-chi*

Bai Juyi (Bo Juyi): *bai jew-yee (bow jew-yee)*

Li Bai (Li Bo): *lee bai (lee bow)*

Tai: *tie*

LI BO

The Ascent of Mount Tai

[POEM I]

In the fourth month I ascend Mount Tai;
Its stones flat—the autocrat's road opens out.
The six dragons traverse a myriad straths;
Ravines and races wind in due course round about.

Horses' footprints wreathe the cyan peaks
That are at present overflowing with azure lichens.
Flying streams shed their spray over steep stacks;
Waters rush, and the voice of the pine-trees is poignant.

The view to the north—singular bluffs and walls;
Canted banks toward the east topple away.

TRANSLATED BY Paul W. Kroll.

The grotto gates—closed door-leaves of stone;
From the floor of the earth—rising clouds and thunder.

Climbing to the heights, I gaze afar at Peng and Ying;[1]
The image imagined—the Terrace of Gold and Silver.
At Heaven's Gate,[2] one long whistle I give,
And from a myriad *li*[3] the clear wind comes.

Jade maidens,[4] four or five persons,
Gliding and whirling descend from the Nine Peripheries.
Suppressing smiles, they lead me forward by immaculate hands,
And let fall to *me* a cup of fluid aurora!

I bow my head down, salute them twice,
Ashamed for myself not to be of a transcendent's[5] caliber.
—But broad-ranging enough now to make the cosmos dwindle,
I'll leave this world behind, oh how far away!

[POEM II]

At clear daybreak I rode upon a white deer,
And ascended straight to the mount of Heaven's Gate.
At the mountain's edge I happened on a plumed person,[6]
With squared pupils, with handsome face and features.

Holding onto the bindweed, I would have attended to his
    colloquy;
He nevertheless concealed himself with a barrier of clouds from
    the blue.
But he let fall to me a writ formed of avian tracks,[7]
Which dropped down aflutter in the midst of the rocky heights.

Its script, it turned out, was of highest antiquity;
In construing it, I was absolutely unpracticed.
Sensible of this, I thrice breathed a sigh;
But the master I would follow has till now yet to return.

[POEM III]

In the level light I climbed to the Belvedere of the Sun,[8]
Raised my hand and opened up the barrier of clouds.
My germinal spirit lifted up four directions in flight,
As though emerging from between heaven and earth!

1. Penglai and Yingrou, islands of the immortals located in the Eastern Sea.
2. A constellation, also called the Heavenly Barrier Pass.
3. A unit of distance, equal to about 1/3 mile.
4. Heavenly attendants.
5. A Daoist who has achieved extraordinary powers and a higher form of existence (often translated "immortal").
6. That is, an immortal; the immortals were often depicted as winged.
7. The earliest form of writing was thought to have been modeled on bird tracks; some talismans are written using what is called "bird script."
8. The southeastern crest of Taishan.

The Yellow River comes here from out of the west,
Winsome but withdrawn it passes into the distant hills.
Leaning against a high bank, I scanned the Eight Culmina;⁹
Vision exhausted its limits, idling in lasting emptiness.

By an odd chance then I beheld the Azure Lad.¹
His virid hair done up in twin cloud-coils.
He laughed at me for turning late to the study of transcendence:
My unsteadiness and unsureness have brought the fading of
    ruddy features.

Halting I stood and hesitant—suddenly he was gone from sight;
So careless and uninhibited—it is hard to pursue and detain him.

[POEM IV]

Purified and purged for three thousand days,
I strip plainsilk to copy the scriptures of the Way.
Intoning and reciting I hold what I have won,
As a host of spirits guards the physical form that is mine.

Proceeding with the clouds, I trust to the lasting wind,
Wafted on as though I'd spawned plumes and wings!
Clinging now to the high bank, I ascend the Sun's Belvedere;
Bending by the railing, I peer over the Eastern Gulf,

A sheen on the sea animates the distant mountains;
The Cockerel of Heaven has already given his first call.
A silvery terrace emerges out of inverted luminescence,
Where white-capped waves roll over the long leviathan.²

—Where is one to acquire the drug of immortality?
Fly away on high toward Peng and Ying!

[POEM V]

The Belvedere of the Sun inclines north and east;
Its pair of high banks—twinned stone hemmed about.
The sea's waters drop away before one's eyes;
The sky's light spreads far in the cyan-blue of the void.

A thousand peaks, vying, throng and cluster round;
A myriad straths are cut off from traverse and transit.
Thread-thin in the distance, that transcendent on his crane—
Upon departing he left no tracks among the clouds.

Long pines enter here into the Empyreal Han,³
The "distant view" is now no more than a foot away.

---

9. The far points of the eight directions.
1. That is, the King Father of the East, the consort and counterpart of the Queen Mother of the West (one of the most important goddesses in ancient China and in the Daoist pantheon).
2. A sea monster that guards Penglai.
3. The Heavenly River (that is, the Milky Way).

The mountain's flowers are different from those in the human realm—
In the fifth month they are white amidst the snows.

—I am bound in the end to come upon Anqi,[4]
Refining at this very place the liquor of jade.

[POEM VI]

At sunup I drank from the Royal Mother's pool,
Took refuge in the gloaming by the pylons of Heaven's Gate.
In solitude I embraced the Green Tracery zither,[5]
At nighttime strode out in moonlight on the azure mountain.

The mountain was luminous—moonlit dew was white;
The night was still—the pine-tree wind had died away.
Transcendent persons were roaming the cyan peaks;
From place to place songs of reed-organs issued forth!

In subdued stillness I took pleasure in the clear leaming,
As Jade Realized Ones linked up on the halcyon heights.
The image imagined—a dance of phoenixes and simurghs;[6]
Tossing and swirling—in raiment of dragon and tiger.

Touching the sky, I plucked down the Gourd[-star];[7]
Distracted and delirious, reflecting not on my return.
Lifting my hand, I swished it in the clear shallows,
And inadvertently caught hold of the Weaving Maid's[8] loom!

—Next morning I sat in forfeit of it all;
Only to be seen—pentachrome[9] clouds floating away.

The Lady of the Supreme Primordial

The Supreme Primordial: what sort of lady is she?
She's obtained more than her fair share of the Queen Mother's[1]
    seductive beauty.
Jagged and serrated: her three-cornered topknot.
The rest of her hair, spread out, hangs down to her waist.
Cloaked in blue-furred, multi-colored damask,
She wears a red frost[2] gown next to her body.
She takes Ying Nuer[3] by the hand;
Casually accompanying them, phoenixes blow syrinxes.

TRANSLATED BY Suzanne E. Cahill, as are the following two selections.

4. Anqi Sheng, a legendary Daoist immortal; he was a sorcerer and alchemist, known for concocting an elixir of immortality.
5. A famous instrument that belonged to a well-known Han writer, Sima Xiangru (179–117 B.C.E.).
6. Mythical large winged creatures whose appearance is auspicious.
7. The small constellation Delphinus.
8. The star Vega.
9. The five colors are green, red, yellow, white, and black.
1. The Queen Mother of the West, one of the most important goddesses in ancient China and in the Daoist pantheon; she governed all other female deities.
2. The crust that builds up on an alchemist's crucible.
3. A legendary maiden who married a syrinx player; they ascended to heaven as transcendents, riding phoenixes.

With eyebrows and conversation, the two spontaneously laugh,
And suddenly whirl upward following the wind.

Flying Dragon Conductus

[POEM I]

The Yellow Thearch[1] cast tripods at Mount Jing,
To refine powdered cinnabar.
With powdered cinnabar he made yellow gold,
Then, riding astride a dragon, he ascended in flight to households
    of the Realm of Grand Clarity.[2]
Clouds grew despondent, seas thoughtful, making people sigh
Over the Selected Women[3] inside the palace, their faces like flowers.
Suddenly whirling, they waved their hands and skimmed purple auroral
    clouds,
Stretched up their bodies to follow the wind and climbed into
    simurgh-belled chariots.[4]
They climbed into simurgh-belled chariots,
To wait upon Xuanyuan.
Rambling and roaming within the blue heavens,
Their delight cannot be put into words.

[POEM II]

In the flowing waters of Tripod Lake, so pure and protected,
When Xuanyuan departed, were a bow and double-edged sword.
People of old told how these things had been left among them,
And how his bewitching charmers from the rear palace—so many
    flowery countenances,
Flew, riding simurghs on the mist: they too did not return.
Astride dragons, they climbed up to heaven and advanced to
    the Heavenly Barrier Pass.[5]
They advanced to the Heavenly Barrier Pass,
Where they heard heavenly conversation.
Assembled cloud river chariots carried the jade maidens;
They carried the jade maidens,[6]
Past the Purple Illustrious One.[7]
The Purple Illustrious One then gave them prescriptions for drugs
    pounded by the white hare,[8]
So they would not age until heaven did; they would make even the
    three luminaries[9] seem faded.
Looking down at the Turquoise Pond, they viewed the Queen Mother,
Her moth eyebrows bleak and chilly, resembling an autumn frost.

1. The legendary Yellow Emperor, or Huangdi (also called Xuanyuan, 27th century B.C.E.), who here is described as compounding the elixir of immortality in ceremonial vessels.
2. The lowest of three heavens, located below Upper Clarity and Jade Clarity.
3. Concubines.
4. A simurgh is a mythical large winged creature whose appearance is auspicious.
5. A constellation (also called the Gate of Heaven).
6. Heavenly attendants—here, the former concubines.
7. The deity who rules over the heaven of Upper Clarity.
8. An animal associated with the Queen Mother of the West, one of the most important goddesses in ancient China and in the Daoist pantheon.
9. The sun, the moon, and the stars.

BO JUYI

Composed in Response to "Sending Daoist Master Liu Off to Wander on Heavenly Platform Mountain"

I hear you've dreamed of wandering in transcendence,
Lightly lifting off and leaping over worldly miasmas.
Grasping the Honored Illustrious One's tallies,
Granting you supreme command over the guard: an army of envoys
    and armed men.
Their numinous standards—with star and moon images;
Your celestial garments—with dragon and phoenix figures.
To belt your clothes: cross-tied sash registers;
You intone and sing from a stamen-beaded text.
At the Lofty Whirlwind Palace, in the realms of the subtle and
    indistinct,
Harmonious music, thinly dispersed, is heard.
You purify your heart, to pay a formal visit to the Western Mother;[1]
Saluting with the *anjali mudra,* you go to the court of the Eastern
    Lord.[2]
Mist and smoke form Zijin's[3] apron;
Auroral clouds glisten on Magu's[4] petticoat.
Suddenly separating from your realized[5] companions,
Sadly you gaze far away, following the returning clouds.
Human life is like a great dream:
Dreaming and waking—who can distinguish between them?
How much more so this dream within a dream?
How remote! What could be adequate to express it?
You seem to be at the summit of the Golden Watchtowers;
You might suppose yourself to be at the headwaters of the Silver River.
But in fact you have not yet emerged from the triple world,[6]
And still must be residing within the five *skandhas.*[7]
Drinking and gulping down essences of sun and moon,
Eating and chewing up fragrances of mist and fog.
There still remains here the scent and flavor of form,
Of that by which the six *gata*[8] are scented.
Among transcendents, there are the greater transcendents;
They emerge ahead of the flock of dreams and illusions.
Their compassion radiates as a single illuminating candle;
Along with the impenetrable dharma,[9] they are mutually generative
    vapors of heaven and earth.

1. The Queen Mother of the West, one of the most important goddesses in ancient China and in the Daoist pantheon.
2. The King Father of the East, the consort and counterpart of the Queen Mother of the West. "*Anjali mudra*": literally, "divine offering seal/ sign" (Sanskrit), a Buddhist ritual hand gesture of respect performed by raising both hands, palms together, toward the chest or face.
3. One of Laozi's names.
4. A female transcendent with fingernails like birds' talons.
5. That is, the perfected, who in later Daoism are described as beings that have moved beyond earthly corruption and are often identified with stellar deities.
6. The Buddhist universe, divided into the Realm of Desire (inhabited by beings who desire pleasing objects of the senses), the Realm of Form (inhabited by gods that have physical form), and the Formless Realm (inhabited by gods that exist only as consciousness).
7. The five "aggregates" (Sanskrit), a standard Buddhist division of the constituents of mind and body into five groups: form, feeling, discrimination, compositional factors, and consciousness.
8. The six paths into which beings can be reborn, as a god, demigod, human, ghost, animal, or denizen of hell (*gata* literally means "gone"; Sanskrit).
9. Teaching (Sanskrit): the doctrine of the Buddha.

If one does not recognize the evening of myriad teeth [old age],
He will not see the twilight of the three radiances.[1]
If one's single nature is spontaneously clear and distinct,
The myriad karmic causes[2] will accordingly fade out.
The Sea of Bitterness[3] cannot bear him away;
The kalpa[4] fire cannot consume him.
This place, in fact, belongs to the Indian teaching,
Where the prior-born will suspend the classics and the mounds.[5]

1. The sun, the moon, and the stars.
2. Karma, in Buddhism, is the positive and negative deeds that bear fruit as either happiness or suffering in the future.
3. The world of suffering.
4. The Buddhist term (adopted by Daoists) for an aeon, a complete cosmic cycle from the creation to the destruction—usually, by fire—of a particular world.
5. According to the translator, this phrase refers to Daoist records and marks the triumph of Daoism over Buddhism on the mountain.

THE BOOK OF RETURNING TO ONE'S TRUE NATURE
(Fuxing shu)

LI AO

The Tang dynasty thinker Li Ao (ca. 772–836), the author of the *Book of Returning to One's True Nature* (*Fuxing shu*), has traditionally been derided as a Confucian figure whose work was corrupted by Chan (Zen) Buddhist ideas. Recent reconsiderations of his life and writings, however, have cast him as a forerunner to the later development of neo-Confucianism and have recognized his Daoist interests.

The volume excerpted here is a work on self-cultivation that discusses the need to transcend reality. Its content, though firmly grounded in Confucian texts, also reflects Li Ao's close familiarity with the Daoist texts, terms, and ideas of his day. The *Book of Returning to One's True Nature* can be read from a number of perspectives; some traditional commentators have discerned a Buddhist or a Daoist emphasis, tracing specific terms back to their appearance in earlier texts. One such key term, appearing in both the title and the body of the work, is "return" (*fu*), which figures importantly in the *Book of Master Zhuang* (*Zhuangzi*; see above), the Daoist *Seal of the Unity of the Three, in Accordance with the Book of Changes* (*Zhouyi cantong qi*; see above), and Chan Buddhism. If we read the *Book of Returning to One's True Nature* more closely, however, we find conventional self-cultivation language—particularly terms drawn from classics like the *Book of Changes* (*Yijing*; see above), or terms that originated within Buddhism or Daoism but had come into common parlance among Li Ao's lay contemporaries—used to criticize both Buddhism and Daoism and to fashion a new form of self-cultivation. This text is therefore a good example of the heterogeneity of late-Tang religious and philosophical thought, illustrating the challenge that faces modern scholars who seek definitive conclusions about the origins of terms they find in highly syncretic texts.

PRONOUNCING GLOSSARY

Fuxing shu: *fu-hsing shoo*   Zhuangzi: *chuang-tzu*
Li Ao: *lee ah-oh*

Part I

1.1. That whereby a man may be a sage is his true nature; that whereby he may be deluded as to this nature is emotion. Joy, anger, sorrow, fear, love, hate, and desire—these seven are the workings of emotion. When the emotions have become darkened, the nature is hidden, but this is through no shortcoming of the nature: these seven follow one another in constant succession, so that the nature cannot achieve its fullness.

1.2. When water is turbid, its flow is not clear, and when fire is smoky, its light is not bright, but this is through no shortcoming of the [basic] clearness and brightness of the water and the fire. If the sand in the water is not made turbid, then the flow is clear, and if the smoke is not cloudy, the light is bright. If the emotions are not working, then the nature achieves fullness.

1.3. Neither the nature nor the emotions exist independently of one another. None the less, without the nature the emotions would have nowhere to be born from. For the emotions are born from the nature: they are not emotions of themselves, but rely on the nature to be emotions. The nature is not a nature of itself but shows its brightness through the emotions.

2.1. The nature is the decree of Heaven: the sage is he who obtains it and is not deluded. The emotions are the movements of the nature: common folk are those who drown in them and are unable to know their basis.

2.2. Is the sage without emotions? The sage is absolutely still and without movement, arrives without travelling, shows his spirit-like power through not speaking, and gives light without shining. His conduct aligns him with Heaven and Earth, and his transformations correspond to match those of the forces *yin* and *yang*.[1] Although he has emotions, he never has emotions.

2.3. So, then, do common folk not have this nature? The nature of common folk is no different from that of the sage. However, they are darkened by the emotions and under successive attack from them, and this goes on for ever, so that even to the end of their lives they do not themselves view their true natures.

2.4. When fire lies hidden in mountain stones and forest trees it is still fire. When the Jiang, the He, the Huai, and the Ji[2] have not yet flowed forth and

---

TRANSLATED BY T. H. Barrett. The bracketed addition is the translator's.

1. The complementary forces that unite to form the Dao: yin, a term that originally referred to the shady side of a valley, by extension came to be associated with the dark, earth, dampness, and passivity—the female principle; yang, a term that originally referred to the sunny side of a valley, by extension came to be associated with the light, heaven, dryness, and activity—the male principle.
2. Major rivers.

are springs under the mountains, they are still there. If stone is not struck and wood not rubbed, the fire is unable to set light to the mountains and forests and burn the natural world. If the sources of the springs are not opened up then it is impossible for them to become the Jiang, the He, the Huai, and the Ji, swirling eastward to the Great Trench,[3] boundless and vast, to become an unfathomable deep. If the emotions are moving and becoming tranquil again without cease, then common folk are unable to return to their true natures and light up Heaven and Earth in limitless brightness.

3.1. Therefore the sage is he who is the first of men to be awakened.

3.2. After awakening one achieves brightness; if not, one is deluded, and if one is deluded, one is in darkness. Brightness and darkness are termed different. But if the nature basically does not have either brightness or darkness then it transcends both similarities and differences. We know that brightness is that whereby darkness is opposed. Once darkness is done away with, brightness for its part is not established.

3.3. Therefore it is sincerity that the sage takes as his nature, absolutely still and without movement, vast and great, clear and bright, shining on Heaven and Earth. When stimulated he can then penetrate all things in the world. In action or at rest, in speech or in silence, he always remains in the ultimate. It is returning to his true nature that the worthy man follows without cease. If he follows it without cease he is enabled to get back to the source.

3.4. The Yijing[4] says, 'The sage matches his virtue with Heaven and Earth, his brightness with the sun and moon, his order of proceeding with the four seasons, and his good and bad fortune with the ghosts and spirits. When he acts ahead of Heaven, Heaven does not go against him; when he acts following Heaven, he respects the seasons of heaven. Even Heaven does not go against him, let alone men, let alone the ghosts and spirits.' This is not something that he gains from elsewhere; it is simply because he is able to develop his nature to the full.

3.5. Zi Si[5] says, 'only the sage, possessed of the most complete sincerity in the world, is able to develop his nature to the full. Because he is able to develop his own nature he is able to develop to the full those of other men, and because he is able to develop those of other men, he is able to develop to the full the true nature of the whole natural world. Because he is able to develop the true nature of the natural world, he may assist Heaven and Earth in transforming and producing. Because he may assist Heaven and Earth in transforming and producing, he may align himself with Heaven and Earth. Next to him is the worthy man, who (by contrast) deals with small matters. Because they are small he is able to have complete sincerity in relation to them (though he has not developed his nature to the full). Because he is sincere, this becomes apparent. Having become apparent, it then becomes con-

3. The sea.
4. The Book of Changes (traditionally dated to the 12th century B.C.E.), a volume of divination and cosmology that is one of the Five Classics of the Confucian tradition.

5. The grandson (483–402 B.C.E.) of Confucius (551–479); he himself was an influential philosopher, and the quotation is from his Zhongyong (see below, n. 9, p. 413).

spicuous, and having become conspicuous, it becomes bright. Having become bright, he moves others. Moving others, he changes them, and changing, he transforms them. Only the most complete achieved sincerity in the world can transform.'

4.1. The sages know that the true nature of man is good and that it may be followed, and that if this is done without cease, one reaches sagehood, so they have set up the rites to regulate him, and introduced music to give him harmony. To be at ease through harmonious music is the basis of music, and in movement to accord with the rites is the basis of ritual. Therefore 'when in their chariots they heard the sound of the bells attached to them, and when they walked they heard the sound of the jade pendants at their belts'. 'They never laid aside their lutes and zithers without good reason.'[6] In sight, hearing, speech, and action they moved only following the pattern of the rites. By this means the sages taught men to forget their desires and return to the Way of their true natures and Heavenly destinies.

4.2. This Way is complete sincerity. If one is completely sincere without cease one becomes empty; if one is empty without cease one becomes bright; if one is bright without cease one shines upon Heaven and Earth without omission: This is nothing other than developing to the full the Way of the true nature and destiny. Alas! All men are able to achieve this and yet though no one prevents them they do not do so: are they not deluded?

5.1. Of old the sage took this Way and transmitted it to Yan Hui;[7] Yan Hui took it and clasped it tightly, never letting go. He returned before going far; his mind for three months never strayed from benevolence. Confucius said, 'Hui has nearly achieved. He is often empty.' The reason why he never became a sage was because of a single pause. It was not that his strength was insufficient, but because his decreed lifespan was short, so he died.

5.2. So Confucius's other disciples,[8] it seems, transmitted the Way. They were nourished by one and the same psychophysical stuff (*qi*), and moistened by the same rains, but those who received the Way each possessed it to a varying degree, and were not necessarily equal. When Zi Lu died, though Shi Qi and Yu Yan attacked him with a lance and cut his capstring, he said, 'When a superior man dies, he does not remove his cap.' So he tied the capstring and died. That Zi Lu should have been without fear though not given by disposition to feats of bravery was because his mind was absolutely still and unmoving. When Zengzi died he said, 'Why should I seek for anything? It is enough for me to die having done what was right.' To say this was doing right with regard to his true nature and his decreed lifespan.

5.3. Zi Si was the grandson of Confucius. He received the Way of his grandfather and wrote the *Zhong Yong*[9] in forty-seven sections, and then

---

6. The quotations are from the *Liji* (*Classic of Rites*), one of the Five Classics.
7. Confucius's favorite disciple.

8. Those named in this paragraph were disciples.
9. The *Doctrine of the Mean*, a brief essay that contains central teachings on Confucian ethics.

transmitted it to Mencius.[1] Mencius said, 'At forty I had an unmoving mind'. Among Mencius's disciples Gongsun Chou and Wan Zhang were the most accomplished, and they, it seems, passed it on. But after suffering the burning of the books under the Qin dynasty[2] only one section survived. Thereupon this Way fell into desuetude and suffered loss. Those who passed on their exposition of it taught only decorum, punctuation, ceremonials, and swordsmanship. As for the source of the true nature and the decreed lifespan, I do not know where it was transmitted. But when the Way reaches its nadir in being overthrown, it is certain to return to strength. Am I not at a time when it is about to return?

6.1. I have been reading books since I was five, but this was simply the study of words and phrases; it is only for the past four years that I have had my purpose set on the Way. But when I have spoken with others about it, there has never been anyone who has agreed with me. When I went south to see the bore on the Jiang I went into Yue, where I met Lu Can[3] of Wu Commandery. When I spoke with him of the way he said, 'Your words show the mind of Confucius. If a sage appeared in the East, he would not differ from this. If a sage appeared in the South, he would not differ from this. All you have to do, sir, is to practise this without cease.'

6.2. Alas! Although books concerning the true nature and the decreed lifespan do survive, none of those who study them can understand them, therefore they turn to Zhuangzi, Liezi, Laozi,[4] and the Buddha. The ignorant say that the followers of Confucius are unable to master thoroughly the Way of the true nature and decreed lifespan, and the believers in these other teachers all agree with them. Since I was asked about it, I passed on what I myself knew of it, and then wrote it in a book, in order to open up the source of sincerity and brightness, so that this Way, at present interrupted, discarded, and unpromoted, might be transmitted to this present age. I called it *Returning to One's True Nature*, for setting the mind in order, and for transmission to the appropriate people. Alas! If the Master were to return, he would not deny my words.

1. Mengzi (ca. 371–ca. 389 B.C.E.), a major figure in the development of orthodox Confucianism.
2. 221–206 B.C.E.
3. Li Ao's patron.
4. The first three major philosophers of Daoism, whose names are also the titles of important works: Master Zhuang (4th century B.C.E.; see above), Master Lie (fl. ca. 400 B.C.E.), and Master Lao (fl. 6th century B.C.E.; see above).

THE INQUIRY INTO THE ORIGIN
OF HUMANITY
(*Yuanren lun*)

GUIFENG ZONGMI

The Inquiry into the Origin of Humanity (*Yuanren lun*) is an early ninth-century essay
on Buddhism by the monk and scholar Guifeng Zongmi (780–841). Zongmi, regarded
as a patriarch within both the Huayen and Chan (Zen) Buddhist traditions, was a
complex figure; well educated in the Confucian Classics, he advocated a form of
Buddhism that could be reconciled with Confucianism. Daoism was also integrated
into his considerations of the different religious teachings found in China. In
Zongmi's view, the differences between Buddhism, Confucianism, and Daoism lay
primarily in the historical circumstances within which each arose.

The section of the essay included here, "Exposing Deluded Attachments," exemplifies Zongmi's effort to reconcile the native Chinese traditions of Confucianism and
Daoism to Buddhism. He directly addresses lay followers well versed in the teachings
of the first two traditions, treating them sympathetically and thoroughly despite
concluding that Buddhism should be considered the highest teaching. Zongmi's
main charge against Confucianism and Daoism is that they focus merely on embodied human existence—emphasizing moral teachings and the nurturing of life, respectively. They are thus provisional teachings, unlike Buddhism, which "investigat[es] the
ultimate source of this bodily existence." In this excerpt, Zongmi also criticizes key
Daoist concepts, including the Way (*dao*), spontaneity (*ziran*), primal pneuma (*yuanqi*),
and the mandate of heaven (*tianming*), making copious allusions to the *Scripture of the
Way and Its Virtue* (*Daode jing*; see above) and the *Book of Master Zhuang* (*Zhuangzi*;
see above). His argument focuses largely on the inability of Daoism (or Confucianism)
to offer a clear explanation and basis for ethical action.

Exposing Deluded Attachments

The two teachings of Confucianism and Daoism hold that human beings,
animals, and the like are all produced and nourished by the great Way of
nothingness. They maintain that the Way, conforming to what is naturally
so, engenders the primal pneuma. The primal pneuma engenders heaven
and earth, and heaven and earth engender the myriad things.

Thus dullness and intelligence, high and low station, poverty and wealth,
suffering and happiness are all endowed by heaven and proceed according
to time and destiny. Therefore, after death one again returns to heaven and
earth and reverts to nothingness.

TRANSLATED BY Peter N. Gregory. All bracketed additions are the translator's.

This being so, the essential meaning of the outer teachings merely lies in establishing [virtuous] conduct based on this bodily existence and does not lie in thoroughly investigating the ultimate source of this bodily existence. The myriad things that they talk about do not have to do with that which is beyond tangible form. Even though they point to the great Way as the origin, they still do not fully illuminate the pure and impure causes and conditions of conforming to and going against [the flow of] origination and extinction. Thus, those who study [the outer teachings] do not realize that they are provisional and cling to them as ultimate.

Now I will briefly present [their teachings] and assess them critically. Their claim that the myriad things are all engendered by the great Way of nothingness means that the great Way itself is the origin of life and death, sageliness and stupidity, the basis of fortune and misfortune, bounty and disaster. Since the origin and basis are permanently existent, [it must follow that] disaster, disorder, misfortune, and stupidity cannot be decreased, and bounty, blessings, sageliness, and goodness cannot be increased. What use, then, are the teachings of Laozi and Zhuangzi?[1] Furthermore, since the Way nurtures tigers and wolves, conceived Jie and Zhou,[2] brought Yan Hui and Ran Qiu[3] to a premature end, and brought disaster upon Boyi and Shuqi,[4] why deem it worthy of respect?

Again, their claim that the myriad things are all spontaneously engendered and transformed and that it is not a matter of causes and conditions means that everything should be engendered and transformed [even] where there are no causes and conditions. That is to say, stones might engender grass, grass might engender humans, humans engender animals, and so forth. Further, since they might engender without regard to temporal sequence and arise without regard to due season, the immortal would not depend on an elixir, the great peace would not depend on the sage and the virtuous, and benevolence and righteousness would not depend on learning and practice. For what use, then, did Laozi, Zhuangzi, the Duke of Zhou,[5] and Confucius establish their teachings as invariable norms?

Again, since their claim that [the myriad things] are engendered and formed from the primal pneuma means that a spirit, which is suddenly born out of nowhere, has not yet learned and deliberated, then how, upon gaining [the body of] an infant, does it like, dislike, and act willfully? If they were to say that one suddenly comes into existence from out of nowhere and is thereupon able to like, dislike, and so forth in accordance with one's thoughts, then it would mean that the five virtues and six arts[6] can all be understood by according with one's thoughts. Why then, depending on causes and conditions, do we study to gain proficiency?

---

1. See above The Scripture of the Way and Its Virtue (Daode jing) and the Book of Master Zhuang (Zhuangzi).
2. The last rulers of the Xia (ca. 2070–ca. 1600 B.C.E.) and Shang dynasties (ca. 1600–1045 B.C.E.). Notorious despots, they are often mentioned together as historical examples of rulers whose personal wickedness brought down their dynasties.
3. Two disciples of Confucius (551–479 B.C.E.) who died young.
4. Two loyal subjects of the Shang dynasty; their self-imposed exile to protest the new Zhou dynasty (1046–256 B.C.E.) ended when they starved to death.
5. The Duke of Zhou (11th century B.C.E), brother of the founder of the Zhou dynasty, was revered as a paragon of wisdom and credited with contributing to the Yijing (Book of Changes), one of the Five Classics of Confucianism.
6. Two Confucian concepts. The five virtues are benevolence, righteousness, propriety, wisdom, and trustworthiness; the six arts are rites, music, archery, chariot racing, calligraphy, and mathematics (the core of Chinese education).

Furthermore, if birth were a sudden coming into existence upon receiving the endowment of the vital force and death were a sudden going out of existence upon the dispersion of the vital force, then who would become a spirit of the dead? Moreover, since there are those in the world who see their previous births as clearly as if they were looking in a mirror and who recollect the events of past lives, we thus know that there is a continuity from before birth and that it is not a matter of suddenly coming into existence upon receiving the endowment of the vital force. Further, since it has been verified that the consciousness of the spirit is not cut off, then we know that after death it is not a matter of suddenly going out of existence upon the dispersion of the vital force. This is why the classics contain passages about sacrificing to the dead and beseeching them in prayer, to say nothing of cases, in both present and ancient times, of those who have died and come back to life and told of matters in the dark paths or those who, after death, have influenced their wives and children or have redressed a wrong and requited a kindness.

An outsider [i.e., a non-Buddhist] may object, saying: If humans become ghosts when they die, then the ghosts from ancient times [until now] would crowd the roads and there should be those who see them—why is it not so? I reply: When humans die, there are six paths;[7] they do not all necessarily become ghosts. When ghosts die, they become humans or other forms of life again. How could it be that the ghosts accumulated from ancient times exist forever? Moreover, the vital force of heaven and earth is originally without consciousness. If human beings receive vital force that is without consciousness, how are they then able suddenly to wake up and be conscious? Grasses and trees also all receive vital force, why are they not conscious?

Again, as for their claim that poverty and wealth, high and low station, sageliness and stupidity, good and evil, good and bad fortune, disaster and bounty all proceed from the mandate of heaven, then, in heaven's endowment of destiny, why are the impoverished many and the wealthy few, those of low station many and those of high station few, and so on to those suffering disaster many and those enjoying bounty few? If the apportionment of many and few lies in heaven, why is heaven not fair? How much more unjust is it in cases of those who lack moral conduct and yet are honored, those who maintain moral conduct and yet remain debased, those who lack virtue and yet enjoy wealth, those who are virtuous and yet suffer poverty, or the refractory enjoying good fortune, the righteous suffering misfortune, the humane dying young, the cruel living to an old age, and so on to the moral being brought down and the immoral being raised to eminence. Since all these proceed from heaven, heaven thus makes the immoral prosper while bringing the moral to grief. How can there be the reward of blessing the good and augmenting the humble, and the punishment of bringing disaster down upon the wicked and affliction upon the full? Furthermore, since disaster, disorder, rebellion, and mutiny all proceed from heaven's mandate, the teachings established by the sages are not right in holding human beings and not heaven responsible and in blaming people and not destiny. Nevertheless, the [Classic of] Poetry censures chaotic rule, the [Classic of]

---

7. That is, the six paths into which beings can be reborn, according to Buddhists, as a god, demigod, human, ghost, animal, or denizen of hell.

History extols the kingly Way, the [*Book of*] *Rites* praises making superiors secure, and the [*Classic of*] *Music*[8] proclaims changing [the people's] manners. How could that be upholding the intention of heaven above and conforming to the mind of creation?

8. Four of the Five Classics of Confucianism (the fifth is the *Classic* or *Book of Changes*).

RECORDS OF THE ASSEMBLED TRANSCENDENTS OF THE FORTIFIED WALLED CITY
(*Yongcheng jixian lu*)

DU GUANGTING

The following selections are from *Records of the Assembled Transcendents of the Fortified Walled City* (*Yongcheng jixian lu*), by the prolific Daoist scholar Du Guangting (850–933). The collection originally contained 109 biographies of transcendents, but many are no longer extant. The key figure in Du's text is the Queen Mother of the West, who rules over the "walled city" and had become an important guardian deity within the Upper Clarity (Shangqing) tradition; his work is also full of fascinating accounts of Tang female Daoists and their self-cultivation practices.

Two of the three narratives below are about women. Wang Fajin was entrusted as a child to a Daoist nun; she quickly attracted the attention of celestial deities, who in due course summoned her to heaven. After three months of instruction, she returned to teach the inferior people—suffering because of their waywardness—to live in accordance with the Dao. Following her work on earth, Wang Fajin rose back up to heaven accompanied by auspicious cranes, just as the Supreme Thearch had earlier predicted she would.

The second hagiography below is that of Ms. Wang, a chronic invalid who was restored to health overnight after swallowing a talisman dissolved in holy water. She therefore sought instruction from the Daoist master who had cured her, Wu Yun (d. 778), and became a skilled practitioner. Signs of her eminence included her "rare fragrance"; and, as she predicted to her daughters hours before her death, when she died she transformed "like a cicada." Clearly, Ms. Wang had attained "corpse liberation" (*shijie*)—a kind of feigned death and transformation: her base human body was sloughed off just as a cicada sheds its shell.

The long hagiography of Mao Ying (Lord Mao)—one of the key figures at the beginning of the Upper Clarity movement, who received texts and registers directly from the Queen Mother of the West—is the last one in Du's collection. Mao Ying's entry was apparently intended to serve as a model for all Daoist practitioners hoping to be transmitted texts and talismans, to obtain a divine bride (in his case, the noblewoman-become-immortal Lady Wei), and ultimately to enter the Daoist celestial bureaucracy.

PRONOUNCING GLOSSARY

Du Guangting: *doo kuang-ting*
Mao Ying: *mao ing*
Wang Fajin: *wawng fah-chin*

Yongcheng jixian lu: *yung-chung gee-hsien lu*

Wang Fajin

Wang Fajin [Dharma Progress] was a person of Linjin County in Jian Province [Sichuan]. As a young child, she naturally loved the Way. Her household was near an old belvedere [Daoist monastery]. Although no Daoist master lived there any longer, she never belittled or insulted the revered images, even in play. Whenever she saw them, she felt compelled to join her hands in prayer and do obeisance; she trembled before them as if afraid.

When [Wang] was just over ten years old, a Daoist nun from Jian Province who was traveling through other townships passed her household. [Wang's] father and mother, because of her longing for the Way, asked the Daoist nun to safeguard and protect her. The nun, [ordaining her as a novice,] bestowed upon Ms. Wang the "Register of Rectified Unity for Extending Life,"[1] and gave her the religious name Dharma Progress. She then became especially diligent at the incense fire [rituals]. She protected and assisted at fast and abstinence ceremonies. She also ate fungus and cedar seeds while cutting off [the five] grains.[2] Sometimes descents of deities took place in response [to her religious practice].

That year a famine took place in the Three Rivers region [Sichuan], with attendant shortages of food. Grain prices soared. The dead numbered five or six out of every ten. People often pulled up mountain taro and wild creepers to satisfy their hunger. Suddenly two blue lads descended into [Wang's] courtyard, proclaiming the Supreme Thearch's[3] decree.

> Because you were endowed from birth with transcendent bones, your submissive heart is essential and sincere, and you have not been negligent regarding the Way, I now summon you by means of these blue lads to receive a position in the Jade Capital [heaven].

Thereupon Fajin followed the blue lads as they soared up bodily and skimmed the void, passing through to the place where the Supreme Thearch was located. He ordered that she be given auroral broth in a jade cup. After she finished drinking, the Thearch told her:

> People's natural endowments are the great embodiment of the five phases[4] and of the harmonious breaths of Heaven and Earth. It is extremely difficult to obtain human form and in addition to dwell in the central land [China]. Moreover, Heaven causes the breaths of the four seasons to revolve, while Earth receives what is necessary for the five phases to flourish, producing the five grains and five hundred fruits to provide nourishment for the people.

> But the people have not been acknowledging the nurturing mercy of Heaven and Earth: they belittle and reject the five grains, and irritably forsake fabrics of hemp and silk. As a result, husbands

TRANSLATED BY Suzanne E. Cahill. All bracketed additions are the translator's.

1. At each rank, a Daoist priest receives a particular "register" (lu).
2. That is, abstaining from the staple foods of China.
3. One of the most important deities in the Daoist pantheon. "Blue lads": minor Daoist deities

who serve as heavenly attendants.
4. The set of systematic associations between different categories that, according to Chinese thought, explain the operation of nature; they are based on five agents, or elements (wood, fire, metal, water, and earth).

who do the tilling and farming, along with their wives who do the spinning and weaving, exhaust their bodies in labor without obtaining their fill, and exert their strength with utmost effort without avoiding the cold. They provide their labor in vain; no one spares or pities them. Thus when they are oppressed by divinely brilliant [spirits], Heaven and Earth do not protect them.

Most recently, [the deities of the] marchmounts[5] and waterways that are my earthly offices have daily produced memorials saying: "The people detest and despise rice and barley; they do not treasure the basis of their clothing and food [sericulture and agriculture]."

In response, I ordered the Bureaus of the Grand Florescence to restrain the spirits of the five grains and commanded the grain that has already been planted not to mature. I sent down famine and starvation to the people to show my criticism and punishment, in order to correct their hearts. [And yet] this generation's foolishness is so far-reaching that they still have not experienced awakening or enlightenment.

Now we have received the Grand Supreme's[6] [new] command to cherish life by means of the Great Way. We must not harm the masses of good folk on account of some evil people. Although Heaven and Earth and the divinely brilliant [spirits] find them guilty [and punish them], the ignorant people still do not understand the arising of their transgressions. Thus they do not take the road of repentant prayer or confession of original [sins]. So they receive bitter suffering in vain.

You must, acting as one of my unsurpassable attendant lads, enter and wait upon the Heavenly Storehouse Chronogram[7] [to obtain the rituals]. After that, I order you to descend to the mundane world to report and teach the inferior people how to send away their regrets and sins. Have them treasure mulberry and silkworm, value and revere agricultural matters, and love the five grains and hundred fruits. They must recognize that the Great Way nurtures the people, while the abundant earth nourishes all creation. They should elevate and honor the Rectified Way, venerating and serving the divinely brilliant [spirits].

When it comes to the use of water and fire [in ritual and daily life], they may not reject them in annoyance. When it comes to the nurturing of clothing and food, they must be frugal with themselves and restrain their bodies. If they can practice these bright prohibitions, then Heaven and Earth will love them and the divinely brilliant [spirits] will protect them. Wind and rain will prove favorable and harmonious, while family and nation will become peaceful and prosperous. [These practices] will also increase your own hidden accomplishments.

5. The Five Marchmounts are a group of five sacred mountains—one in each of the four cardinal directions and one at the center.
6. A revealer of sacred scriptures from the Heavenly Honored Ones to humanity. He is a high god originating in the Lingbao school of Daoism [translator's note].
7. A star.

Then [the Supreme Thearch] ordered his attendant girls to unroll white gemstone book bags and pearl-beaded containers, bringing out the "Method of the Pure Fast of the Numinous Treasure for Reporting to and Thanking Heaven and Earth" in one scroll. He gave it [to Wang Fajin] for transmission and practice in the world, telling her:

> The people of the world can lead one another to a high, clear place on a dark mountain. There they can establish a fast to repent and give thanks. Within one year, they can do this twice, in the spring and autumn. In the spring, let them pray for abundance in the earth's harvests; in the autumn, let them thank the strength of the Way. In this manner, their indwelling faults will be exterminated and the deities known as Grain Father and Silk Mother [ancient folk deities] will arrange overflowing riches on their behalf. In a dragon-tiger year, I will summon you again.

[The Supreme Thearch] ordered the blue lads to accompany her as she departed. When she returned home, it had already been three months. The text she received was precisely the same as today's "Method of the Pure Fast of the Numinous Treasure for Reporting to and Thanking Heaven and Earth." This method is simple and easy, belonging to the same category [of ritual] as the "Spontaneous Fast of the Great Universal from the Numinous Treasure." Whenever it is practiced among people, it produces immediate results. But if there should ever be the least display of levity, tardiness, turbidity, or dirtiness among the sets of ritual utensils, or if anyone with the least sign of an inequitable heart should be present among the people offering up the rite, then whirling wind and violent rain will destroy the altars and prayer mats, while swift thunder will roar, and lightning will destroy the utensils.

Thereafter, people of the Three Rivers, Liang, and Han River regions [Sichuan] all reverently performed this affair each year. Even officials who were fools or dolts, even crazy or violent men, all trembled equally in dread of such warnings. Grave and reverent, kneeling in awe, they learned how to carry out this method. Whenever caterpillars and locusts or droughts and floods hurt crops and harmed agriculture, the masses would sincerely and obediently exert themselves to practice [this rite] and make offerings. Then after they burned incense and sent their reports to the mysterious ones, dawn and evening they received echoes and responses, increasing their blessings to the utmost. [Even] for impious and unbelieving persons, this established proof and witness [of the efficacy of the rite]. South of Ba [eastern Sichuan], they call this rite the Pure Fast. In Shu territory [western Sichuan], they call it the Fast of Heaven's Accomplishments. It is probably the same holiday.

In the eleventh year of the Heavenly Treasure reign period [752], an I-dragon [*renchen* = dragon and tiger] year, cloud cranes welcomed Fajin and she returned to heaven. This tallies precisely with the [calendrical] revolutions of the dragon and tiger[8] as [foretold in] the words of the deity.

---

8. In the traditional Chinese calendrical system, days and (later) years were designated with two characters drawn from a set of ten "Celestial Stems" and twelve Earthly Branches, resulting in a cycle of sixty days/years.

Ms. Wang

Ms. Wang was the wife of the Resident of the Central Secretariat, Xie Liangbi. A descendent of [Xie] Yishao of the Right Army of the Eastern Jin Dynasty [317–419], he was a person from Kuaiji [Zhejiang]. When Liangbi passed his Advanced Scholar exam, he became Secretary of the Region East of the Zhe River, and [Ms. Wang] married him. Thereupon she embraced sickness, sinking into chronic invalidism. Several years passed without improvement. Liangbi attended the watchtowers [took up his office], but she was unable to accompany him. Instead, her sickness just continued, increasing in extent and gravity.

At that time Heavenly Master Wu Yun[9] was wandering through the Four Bright [Mountains] [in Zhejiang]. He passed Mount Tiantai, the Orchid Pavilion, and Yu's Caverns, and then stopped on the shady side of Whip Mountain.[1] A relative of Ms. Wang made a formal visit to him, seeking his saving powers. He prepared holy water for her and had her swallow a talismanic text [dissolved in that water as medicine]. She recovered overnight.

Moved by the power of the Way to save and protect, Ms. Wang made formal visits to the Heavenly Master [Wu Yun]. She received registers [of deities signifying initiation], purified her practice, and burned Brahman incense. She contemplated in stillness, dwelling alone in a quiet room. She intended and hoped to fly to the chronograms. Accordingly, she [fasted by] cutting off the five grains. She swallowed vapors, so that her spirits became harmonious and her body light. Sometimes there was a rare fragrance [about her], or strange clouds drew near and illuminated her residence. It seemed that realized ones descended to her and she secretly communicated with numina, but nobody knew about it.

Suddenly she said to her daughters [or disciples]:

> My former illnesses had lasted nearly ten years when I took refuge with Heavenly Master [Wu Yun], who cured me and extended my already exhausted lifespan. My entering the Way of enlightenment was already late, and I have not yet become essential in practicing what I received. When I seriously examine my past excesses, I regret them no end. For my whole life, because of the sickness inherent in ordinary behaviors of everyday life, I have inclined towards cherishing jealousy and envy. Now my heart is still obstructed, my storehouses [organ systems] black, and not circulating [vital breath] along the proper pathways. I must [visualize] my secluded interior, refine my form, wash my heart, and transform my storehouses. After twenty years [of practice], I will certainly be able [to transform] like a cicada[2] [breaks through its shell].

> When I die, do not use a coffin. You may make me a screen of cedar wood. Convey my corpse into the wilds. At the right time, you may depute someone to examine it.

9. Daoist master and poet (d. 778).
1. All locations in present-day Zhejiang Province, on the eastern China coast.
2. A reference to "release by means of a corpse," a type of liberation or transformation in which one feigns one's own death and ascends to heaven, leaving the body behind.

That very night she died. People from her household prepared her for burial as she had instructed; everything was simple and frugal. They set her up in a grove in the hunting park, reclining as if in bed. There were no changes or alterations [in her appearance]. Some twenty years later, thieves discovered her interment and abandoned her form [body] on a mound of dirt. During the cold winter months that followed, reverberations of thunder and lightening were suddenly heard beside her screen. Her whole household, finding this startling and strange, rushed to look at her. When they arrived and lifted out her corpse, her body was as light as an empty husk. Her flesh, nails, and hair were all complete, but on the right side of her rib cage a scar more than a foot long had split open. Later she was reburied with proper rites.

As the Lady of the Southern Marchmount[3] [Wei Huacun] once said:

> Members of the highest class of those who attain the Way ascend to heaven in broad daylight. Their forms and bones fly up together to fill vacancies as realized officials. Members of the next class shed their skin like cicadas. They also soar and rise up with forms and bones, their flesh and material substance climbing to heaven. In both of these cases, they become heavenly transcendents; they do not dwell in [earthly] mountains and marchmounts.

[Her husband Xie] Liangbi also grasped the rites of discipleship and in person attended the Heavenly Master [Wu Yun]. He established a transmission about [biography of] the Heavenly Master, to record in detail the traces of his affairs.

Mao Ying

Again there was the Great Lord Mao Ying who ruled over Bucklebent Mountain[4] in the south. In the second year of the Primordial Longevity reign period [1 B.C.], in the eighth month, on the F-Cock [ji yu] day, the Realized Person of the Southern Marchmount, Lord Chi and Wang Junfeng of the Western Walled City, and various blue lads followed the Queen Mother and descended together to Mao Ying's chambers. In an instant, the Celestial Illustrious Great Thearch sent his messenger in embroidered clothing, called Ling Guangzi Qi, to present Ying with a divine seal and jade emblem. The Lord Thearch of Grand Tenuity[5] sent the Autocrat's Notary of the Left Palace of the Three Heavens, Guan Xiutiao, to present Ying with an eight dragon multi-colored damask carriage and purple feathered floriate clothing. The Grand Supreme Lord of the Way sent the Dawn Assisting Grandee, Shi Shumen, to present Ying with the Veritable Talisman of the Metal Tiger and a folly bell of flowing metal. The Incomparable Lord of the Golden Watchtower commanded the Realized Person of the Grand Bourne to send the Jade Squires of the Rectified Unity and Supreme Mystery: Wang Zhong, Bao Qiu and others, to present Ying with swallow wombs of the four junctions and divine fungi of flowing brightness.

---

3. Usually identified as Mount Heng or Mount Huo. On Wei Huacan (252–334), see the *Stele Inscription for the Altar of the Transcendent Lady Wei of the Jin Dynasty*, above.

4. Maoshan, or Mount Mao, in present-day Jiangsu Province.
5. A constellation and a heavenly palace.

When the messengers from the four had finished the bestowals, they had Ying eat the fungi, hang the seal at his belt, don the clothing, straighten his crown, tie the talismans at his waist, grip the folly bell, and stand up. The messengers from the four told Ying: "He who eats concealed fungi from the four junctures takes up the position of a Steward of Realized Ones. He who eats jade fungi of the Golden Watchtowers takes up the position of Director of Destiny. He who eats metal blossoms of flowing brightness takes up the position of Director of Transcendent Registers. And he who eats the paired flying plants of extended luminosity takes up the position of a Realized Sire. He who eats the grotto grasses of night radiance will always have the responsibility of governing the autocrat's notaries of the left and right. You have eaten all of these. Your longevity will be coequal with heaven and earth. Your place will be situated as the Supreme Realized Person who is Director of Destiny and Supreme Steward of the Eastern Marchmount.[6] You will control all divine transcendents of the former kingdoms of Wu and Yue, and all the mountains and water sources left of the Yangzi River."

Their words finished, all the messengers departed together. The Five Thearchic Lords,[7] each in a square-faced chariot, descended in submission to his courtyard. They carried out the commands of the Grand Thearch, presenting to Ying a purple jade plaque, writs carved in yellow gold, and patterns of nine pewters. They saluted Ying as Supreme Steward of the Eastern Marchmount, Realized Lord Who Is Director of Destiny, and Realized Person of the Grand Primordial. The affair finished, they all departed.

The Queen Mother and Ying's master, Lord Wang of the Western City, set forth drinks and a feast from the celestial kitchen for Ying. They sang the "Tune of the Mysterious Numen." When the feast was over, the Queen Mother took Lord Wang and Ying to examine and inspect Ying's two younger brothers. Each had bestowed on him the requisite essentials of the Way. The Queen Mother commanded the Lady of the Supreme Primordial to bestow on Mao Gu and Mao Zhong the Hidden Writs of the Supreme Empyrean, the Seminal Essence of the Way of Cinnabar Elixir and the Phosphors,[8] and the like, comprising the Precious Scriptures of the Daoist Canon in Four Sections. The Queen Mother held the Hidden Writs of the Grand Empyrean and commanded her serving girl Zhang Lingzi to hold the oath of exchanging faith, while she bestowed them on Ying, Gu, and Zhong. The affair concluded, the Queen Mother of the West departed by ascending to heaven.

After this, the Primordial Ruler of the Purple Heavens, Lady Wei Huacun, purified herself and fasted on the Hidden Primordial Terrace at the Mountain of Yanglo. The Queen Mother of the West and the Incomparable Lord of the Golden Watchtower descended to the terrace. They were riding an eight-phosphor carriage. Together they had visited the Supreme Palace of the Pure Void and had received by transmission the Hidden Writs of the Realm of Jade Clarity in four scrolls in order to bestow them on Huacun. At this time, the Lady of the Three Primordials,[9] called Feng Shuang Li Zhu,

---

6. Taishan, or Mount Tai.
7. Gods of the four cardinal directions and the center.
8. Numinous divine projections.

9. A term with many associations in Daoism, including the primordial forces of heaven, earth, and humans and three divinities in the human body.

along with the Left Transcendent Sire of the Purple Yang, Shi Lucheng, the Lofty Transcendent Sire of the Grand Bourne, Yan Gai Gongzi, the Realized Person of the Western City, Wang Fangping, the Realized Person of the Grand Void, Chi Songzi of the Southern Marchmount, and the Realized Person of Paulownia-Cedar Mountain, Wang Ziqiao, over thirty realized beings, each sang the "Tune of the Yang Song and the Yin Song of the Grand Bourne."[1] The Queen Mother composed the lyrics for it:

> I harness my eight-phosphor carriage;
> Like thunder! I enter the Realm of Jade Clarity.
> Dragon pennants brush the top of the empyrean;
> Tiger banners lead vermilion-clad men-at-arms!
> Footloose and fancy-free: the Mysterious Ford separates me
>   from the human world;
> Among a myriad flows, I have no temporary resting place.
> Grievous—this alternate departing and lingering of unions.
> When a kalpa[2] is exhausted, heaven and earth are overturned.
> She must seek a phosphor with no center,
> Not dying and also not born.
> Embodying the spontaneous Way,
> Quietly contemplating and harmonizing the great stygean realm.
> At Southern Marchmount she displays her veritable trunk;
> Jade reflections shine on her accumulated essences.
> Having the responsibility of office is not your affair;
> Empty your heart—you will naturally receive numina.
> The "Scarlet River Tune" of your auspicious meeting—
> The joy you give each other is neverending.

When the Queen Mother had finished the song, and the answering song of the Lady of the Three Primordials also reached its end, the Queen Mother, along with the Lady of the Three Primordials, the Left Transcendent Sire of the Purple Yang, and the Transcendent Sire of the Grand Bourne, as well as Lord Wang of the Pure Void, departed together with Wei Huacun. They went to the southeast and all visited Mount Huo in the Heavenly Terrace Mountains. When they passed the Golden Altar on Bucklebent Mountain, they gave a feast for the Grand Primordial Realized Person Mao at the Grotto-heaven of the Floriate Yang. Leaving Huacun behind, beneath the jade eaves of the grotto palace at Mount Huo, all the flock of the realized ascended following the Queen Mother and returned to Tortoise Terrace.

1. Yin and yang are the complementary forces that unite to form the Dao. Yin, a term that originally referred to the shady side of a valley, by extension came to be associated with the dark, earth, dampness, and passivity—the female principle; yang, a term that originally referred to the sunny side of a valley, by extension came to be associated with the light, heaven, dryness, and activity—the male principle.
2. The Buddhist term (adopted by Daoists) for an aeon, a complete cosmic cycle from the creation to the destruction of a particular world.

BIOGRAPHIES OF PERSONS WHO HAD CONTACTS AND ENCOUNTERS WITH SUPERNATURAL BEINGS AND IMMORTALS
(Shenxian ganyu zhuan)

DU GUANGTING

Biographies of Persons Who Had Contacts and Encounters with Supernatural Beings and Immortals (Shenxian ganyu zhuan) is a collection of seventy-five biographies compiled by the Daoist scholar Du Guangting (850–933). The one reprinted below is representative of a type of Daoist hagiography that concerns esoteric transmissions from immortals to humans. It centers on the *Secret Talisman of the Yellow Emperor*, a mysterious military scripture that Li Quan finds, copies, and recites. From an old woman—who is actually a Daoist immortal—he learns the precise protocol surrounding the transmission of an esoteric text and the rewards that come from its proper veneration: "If a perfected man uses it, he obtains its Way; if a superior man uses it, he obtains its methods; and if the common people use it, they meet with disaster." Before he came to enjoy the ethereal rewards of a transcendent later in life, Li Quan benefited from the female transcendent's tutelage in his secular career as a master of military strategy and an accomplished statesman, though he ultimately ran afoul of a rival political faction.

PRONOUNCING GLOSSARY

Du Guanting: *doo gwan-ting*
Li Quan: *lee chu-en*

Shenxian ganyu zhuan: *shun-hsien gawn-yu chuan*

Biography of Li Quan

Li Quan, surnamed Master Daguan, lived at Mount Shaoshi [in the Song-shan range in Dengfeng county, Henan province]. An adept in the Way of the Immortals, he regularly roamed the great mountains, searching widely for esoteric methods and skills. When he came to Tiger Mouth Cliff at Song-shan, he found a copy of the *Secret Talisman of the Yellow Emperor (Huangdi yinfu)* there. The white silk scroll with vermilion script on a black lacquered roller was enclosed in a jade casket inscribed with the words "Secreted in the famed mountains by the Supreme Purity[1] Daoist master Kou Qianzhi[2] (364–448), on the seventh day of the seventh month of the second year Zhen-jun under the Great Wei dynasty (441), for transmission to fellow devotees." The copy was in a state of decay. After Quan had copied it out and recited it several thousand times he still did not understand its meaning.

Upon entering Qin (Shaanxi) and arriving at the foot of Mount Li (in Lin-tong county), he encountered an old woman. She wore a topknot, letting half her hair hang down. Clad in tattered clothes and leaning on a staff, she

---

TRANSLATED BY Franciscus Verellen. All bracketed additions are the translator's.

1. That is, Upper Clarity.
2. The religious leader who helped establish

Daoism as the state religion of the Northern Wei dynasty (386–534).

had the extraordinary air of a spiritual being. On the side of the road, he saw a burning tree in flames. Thereupon the old woman mumbled to herself: "Wood begets Fire; when calamity arises, it must needs prevail." Quan was startled and asked, "These words are from the *Secret Talisman of the Yellow Emperor*, Part One. How did the old lady come to be able to pronounce them?" The old woman said, "I already received the talisman six cycles of the three monads' sexagesimal periods[3] ago [i.e., in the mists of antiquity]. And where did the young man get it from?" Quan prostrated himself and after repeated reverences fully related how he had obtained it. The old lady said, "Young man, your cheekbones connect with your parietal bones; your wheel of fate joins a prominent forehead. Your vitality is undiminished, you have a detached disposition and a virtuous nature, and you are interested in esoteric methods; your spirit is brave and you love wisdom; truly, you are meant to be my disciple! At forty-five, however, there shall be great misfortune." Thereupon she produced a paper charm in vermilion script that was attached to the end of her staff. She bade Quan kneel and swallow it, saying, "May Heaven and Earth protect you!" Then, sitting on a rock, she proceeded to explain the meaning of the *Secret Talisman* to Quan:

"This talisman comprises three hundred characters in all. One hundred expound the Way; one hundred expound Methods; and one hundred expound Stratagems. Section one contains the Way of the immortals and of embracing the One; the middle section, methods for making the nation prosper and bringing peace to the people; and the final section, stratagems for strengthening one's arms and winning victory in battle. They each foster discernment within and correspond to human concerns without. When it comes to contemplating deeply perceived truth, the Yellow Court and Eight Effulgences[4] do not measure up to it in subtlety; as for inquiring into matters of quintessential importance, scripture, tradition, philosophy, and history are unequal to it as literature; and in exercising skillful perspicacity, Sun, Wu, Han, and Bo[5] are inferior to its ingenuity. Only gentlemen possessing the Way may be apprised of it. Thus if a perfected man[6] uses it, he obtains its Way; if a superior man uses it, he obtains its methods; and if the common people use it, they meet with disaster. Each has a different degree of understanding. To transmit it to fellow devotees, one must celebrate a pure retreat before bestowing it. The holder of the book is the master; he who does not [yet] possess it, the disciple. It is not admissible to value wealth and influence while disregarding the poor and the humble. Offenders have their life span cut by twenty years. Recite the scripture seven times on your Personal Destiny day.[7] This will benefit your intelligence and increase your longevity. On the seventh day of the seventh month of each year write out one copy and secrete it in

---

3. That is, calendrical cycles; in the Chinese system, days and (later) years were designated with two characters drawn from a set of ten Celestial Stems and twelve Earthly Branches, resulting in a cycle of sixty days/years.
4. A reference to self-cultivation practices. "The Yellow Court": the *Scripture of the Yellow Court* is a central text of the Upper Clarity (Shangqing) tradition (see the *Most High Jade Scripture on*

the *Internal View of the Yellow Court*, above).
5. Sun Wu (fl. 6th century B.C.E.), Wu Qi (440–381 B.C.E.), Han Xin (d. 196 B.C.E.), and Bo Qi (d. 257 B.C.E.) were famous ancient strategists.
6. That is, a Daoist who has achieved a higher form of existence and moved beyond earthly corruption.
7. The date of your birth.

the cliff side of a great mountain. That will earn you another increase [in longevity]."

A long time had passed. The old woman said, "It is already the hour of *bu* (3–5 P.M.). I have some wheat meal that we shall eat together." She drew a gourd from her sleeve and told Quan to fetch water from the valley. Once it was filled with water, the gourd suddenly grew heavy, weighing more than a hundred pounds. As Quan did not have the strength to hold it, it sank into the spring. When he returned, the old woman had already disappeared. All that remained were several *sheng*[8] of wheat meal. Quan served as deputy military governor of Jiangling (Hubei) and as vice president of the Censorate. A master of military strategy, he compiled the *Secret Classic of Taibo (Taibo yinjing)* in ten scrolls. An accomplished statesman, he also wrote the *Zhongtai zhi (Record of Zhongtai)* in ten scrolls. As a result of having been ostracized by [the faction of Chief Minister] Li Linfu[9] (d. 752), he did not rise to a prominent position. In the end he entered the great mountains in search of the Way. After that, his whereabouts were unknown.

8. A unit of volume, equal to about a cup.
9. A powerful figure at the Tang dynasty court of

Emperor Xuanzong; a defender of aristocratic influence, he was known for his ruthlessness.

RECORD OF MIRACLES IN SUPPORT OF DAOISM
(*Daojiao lingyan ji*)

DU GUANGTING

The stories in *Record of Miracles in Support of Daoism (Daojiao lingyan ji)*, an extensive collection by the Daoist scholar Du Guangting (850–933), often support Daoism by describing the miraculous events that occurred during some kind of desecration, sacrilege, or attack on Daoism. The tale below, "An Examination of the Altar of the Transcendent Lady Wei of Nanyue," details a failed attempt by a group of Buddhist monks to take over a local cult site dedicated to the memory of the Daoist Lady Wei (Wei furen), born Wei Huacun (252–334). As the Buddhists seek to dislodge her altar, a seemingly easy task, they hear a loud rumbling in the sky; and when they try to flee, all but one are devoured by a tiger. Like *Record of Miracles in Support of Daoism* as a whole, this text displays some of the tensions that existed between Buddhism and Daoism during the late ninth and early tenth centuries.

PRONOUNCING GLOSSARY

Daojiao lingyan ji: *dow-chiao ling-yen chi*
Nanyue: *nawn-yu-eh*

Nanyue Wei furen xiantanyan: *nawn-yu-eh way fu-run hsien-tawn-yen*

A Examination of the Altar of
the Transcendent Lady Wei of Nanyue
(Nanyue Wei furen xiantanyan)

The altar of Lady Wei is located in front of the Central Peak (Heavenly Pillar Peak) at Nanyue.[1] On the top of a great rock there is another large rock exceeding ten feet square. It has a stable appearance, with a round base and a level top. [However,] it is perched tenuously, and it seems that if it were pushed by one person, it could be toppled. Yet, when many people [push on it] it remains firm and stable. It is said that because strange and divine things happen there, spirits, transcendents[2] and other anchorites frequently come to reside there. Strange and wonderful clouds, as well as numinous qi[3] often obscure its top.

Suddenly, ten or more Buddhist monks carrying torches and staffs arrived at the altar during the night. These monks [wanting to inflict injury] waited for Transcendent Gou to return to her residence. But, Transcendent Gou was [at that time] already inside her residence on her bed, and the monks didn't see her and left. They proceeded to Lady Wei's altar and pushed on it hoping to push it over. Then there was a loud, angry-sounding rumble. Hearing this, they raised their torches to try to see what it was. The monks were unable to move in the face of this strange and supernatural intervention. [Eventually] they fled and made it to a distant village. [Then] out of the ten monks nine were devoured by tigers. One of the monks, who hadn't agreed with [the others'] evil actions at the time they attacked the altar, was spared the wrath of the tigers. When he returned to his village and told his story, people from near and far were astonished.

TRANSLATED BY James Robson. All bracketed additions are the translator's.

1. The Southern Marchmount in the system of Five Marchmounts, a group of five sacred mountains—one in each of the four cardinal directions and one at the center. Lady Wei (252–334), the title of Wei Huacan after her elevation to divine status, transmitted the Upper Clarity (Shangqing) scriptures to Yang Xi and his patrons, the Xu family (see the *Declarations of the Perfected*, or *Zhen'gao*, above).
2. Daoists who have achieved extraordinary powers and a higher form of existence.
3. Vital energy, breath (pneuma).

THE SUTRA OF THE THREE KITCHENS,
PREACHED BY THE BUDDHA
(Foshuo sanchu jing)

According to the Daoist scholar Du Guangting (850–933), *Sutra of the Three Kitchens, Preached by the Buddha* (*Foshuo sanchu jing*) was plagiarized by Buddhists from an earlier Daoist work, titled either *Commentary on the Scripture of the Five Kitchens Spoken by Laozi* (*Laozi shuo wuchu jing zhu*)—which includes the main body of the text and a commentary by Yin Yin (d. 741)—or *Method of Energy of the Scripture of the Five Kitchens* (*Wuchu jing qifa*). The term *chu*, here rendered "kitchens," can also be translated "cuisines" or "feasts." These were originally communal feasts held within the Celestial Masters movement, both to honor gods of the soil and to exorcize threats to the community, such as illness and death; kitchens bestowed merit and good fortune on the community. Preparation for these feasts required rites of purification, such as fasting and abstention from sex. As the tradition developed, the "five kitchens" followed the general pattern of Daoist practices and became internalized; they were correlated with the body's five viscera, and it was believed that practitioners would eventually be able to forgo food.

The *Sutra of the Three Kitchens, Preached by the Buddha* appeared by the beginning of the eighth century, and the version translated below was found in the cache of manuscripts discovered in caves at Dunhuang in the early twentieth century; today the work is included in the Buddhist canon. It is presented as a teaching of the Buddha and is filled with Buddhist technical terms, such as the Six Perfections (giving, ethics, patience, effort, concentration, and wisdom) and the Three Poisons (the negative emotions of desire, hatred, and ignorance), but its object is the same as the Daoist original: "Reciting this Method of the Three Kitchens allows [one] to be free from hunger, [to attain] clarity and limpidity [of the mind], and [to acquire] longevity." It similarly focuses on a series of recitations that enable practitioners to gradually give up normal food and eventually nourish themselves solely on primordial breath. In its structure and content, the *Sutra of the Three Kitchens* illustrates how a "Daoist" text can be taken over and systematically transformed into a "Buddhist" text.

PRONOUNCING GLOSSARY

Foshuo sanchu jing: *foe-show sawn-chu ching*

nirvana: *near-vah-nah*
bodhisattva: *bow-dee-saw-twah*

Reciting this Method of the Three Kitchens allows [one] to be free from hunger, [to attain] clarity and limpidity [of the mind], and [to acquire] longevity.

At the outset, one should believe devotedly in the Three Jewels,[1] respect them, and permanently honor and revere them morning and evening, and without fail contemplate them assiduously. One must [also] piously care for the masters, the monks, one's parents, and relatives, close and distant. It is recommended [besides] that one observe the Six Perfections[2] and practice self-abnegation.

One is thus fit for the conduct of this Method of the Three Kitchens: the Spontaneous Kitchen of all the buddhas and bodhisattvas[3] of the three aeons, and the Kitchen of immutability, of quietude, of non-movement, of the successive kalpas,[4] and of compassion.

This Method of the Three Kitchens was preached by the Buddha at the moment he attained *nirvana*, during an assembly of the eight categories of beings,[5] in front of all the buddhas and bodhisattvas of the ten directions,[6] to all the buddhas of the three periods, past, present and future.

* * *

TRANSLATED BY Christine Mollier. All as bracketed additions are the translator's, as are the italicized comments in parentheses.

1. The Buddha, the dharma (his doctrine), and the sangha (the Buddhist community, especially the community of monks and nuns); by tradition, a Buddhist is anyone who states that he or she takes refuge in them.
2. Giving, ethics, patience, effort, concentration, and wisdom.
3. Beings intent on enlightenment, who have vowed to achieve buddhahood—a state of perfect enlightenment for the welfare of all beings.

4. "Kalpa" is the Buddhist term for an aeon, a complete cosmic cycle from the creation to the destruction of a particular world.
5. Varieties of supernatural beings. "*Nirvana*": the state of the cessation of the accumulated causes of future suffering and rebirth (literally, "blown out," "extinguished"; Sanskrit).
6. That is, everywhere: north, south, east, west, northeast, northwest, southeast, southwest, the nadir, and the zenith.

Whoever is receptive to the words of these Heavenly Kitchens and recites them every day will know neither hunger nor thirst. Reciting them while keeping still, without moving and without thought, just like the buddha Amitabha[7] of the land of Limitless Longevity, one will have no [need] of nourishment for a period of one hundred days, for ten years or a hundred years consecutively, or for a thousand years, ten thousands years, or [even] for a small kalpa.

The Buddha informs the great assembly: It suffices that one who practices this Method be entirely predisposed to place faith in the Three Jewels and to adore them. Whoever wishes to make a retreat in the depths of the mountains to study the Way may begin by practicing and propagating this Method. Should someone manifest doubts and lack of conviction [or even formulate] criticism with respect to it, one must not in any case transmit it to him, for there is reason to fear that the blasphemer will fall into [one of the Three] Evil Ways [of rebirth].[8] This is why, in this world, one must take care not to diffuse it carelessly.

The recitation of [the poem] from the ninety repetitions to the eastern direction to the fifty repetitions to the north, constitutes a complete practice [of the Method]. If [after doing this] one still does not become satiated, one begins the recitation once more. Two recitations assuredly suffice [to put a stop to sensations] of hunger and thirst.

One must always begin the recitation of the *gatha* during the *yin* hour[9] (i.e., between three and five a.m.). Four moments [during the day] will be chosen by the adept for the recitation, whose number must conform to that which is indicated above. Prior to this silent recitation, one prepares oneself by means of movements of the mouth and rotations of the tongue. When saliva forms, one swallows it. At the outset, [one practices] for one to three days. If it so happens that the urine becomes reddish, one should not be disturbed. By the end of the third day of recitation, one's physical forces will dwindle considerably, [but,] following this period of time, at the end of the seventh day, one steadily regains energy. After a hundred days, mundane dishes of great refinement appear in each dream, and one finds oneself fully satisfied. Celestial perfumes become manifest. [At the end of a practice] of altogether three hundred days, one's forces attain a perfect plenitude. One may eat if one so wishes, [but] one will no longer [experience] hunger or thirst.

7. The buddha who presides over the Pure Land of Sukhavati, to which he vowed to lead all beings who call upon him (rebirth in Sukhavati was a common goal of Buddhist practice throughout East Asia).

8. Rebirth as an animal, a ghost, or a denizen of hell.
9. Traditionally, the Chinese day is divided into twelve named periods.

RECORDED FOR THE RITUAL OF MERIT AND VIRTUE FOR REPAIRING THE VARIOUS OBSERVATORIES OF QINGCHENG MOUNTAIN
(Xiu qingcheng shan zhuguan gongde ji)

DU GUANGTING

This account of Mount Qingcheng, in modern-day Sichuan Province (near the city of Chengdu), is from an inscription placed in a Daoist abbey at the base of the sacred mountain in 895 C.E. that praised the renovation work carried out by Duke Mo Tingyi—lauded for the merit he thereby gained as both a Daoist and a Confucian. It was written by Du Guangting (850–933), who had retired to Mount Qingcheng after serving in high positions for the emperor Xizong (r. 873–88), whose court was driven by peasant revolts out of the capital, Chang'an (present-day Xi'an), and later the new Shu dynasty.

Because Du Guangting lived on Mount Qingcheng, his essay displays both a striking sense of intimacy with and on-the-ground (even underground) knowledge about the site that extends to geography, history, biography, hagiography, mythology, and cosmology. Mount Qingcheng became significant within the nascent Daoist Celestial Masters community when, in 142 C.E., the deified Laozi descended to Zhang Daoling and installed him as the first Celestial Master, and it has remained important to Daoists ever since. Given that Du Guangting supported Daoists by recounting stories that involve miraculous interventions (especially to stop the incursions of Buddhists), such as those in his Record of Miracles in Support of Daoism (Daojiao lingyan ji; see above), it is not surprising to find narratives here about the eviction of local cults and about Buddhists who had taken over a Daoist abbey.

PRONOUNCING GLOSSARY

Mo Tingyi: *mow ting-yee*

Xiu qingcheng shan zhuguan gongde ji: *hsiu ching-chung shawn chu-gwan kung-te gee*

The Declaration of the Perfected[1] states: "Within the Great Heaven there are ten Great Cavern Heavens.[2] Inside them, the sun and moon conceal their roots. The essences of the three chronograms shine in the caverns, illuminating them, as do the two phosphors.[3] All have golden walls and jade gate-towers, which perfected transcendents[4] take as their capitols." Qingcheng Mountain contains the fifth, the Heaven of Nine Chambers of the Precious Mountain. Gentleman Ning[5] resides there. Here the Yellow Emperor rode a whirlwind chariot, received the Way of the Dragon Bridge, and com-

---

TRANSLATED BY Thomas H. Peterson.

1. See the Declarations of the Perfected (Zhen'gao), above.
2. Paradisical utopias (also called the ten major Grotto Heavens) found inside sacred mountains (the Ten Mountains).
3. The sun and the moon. "The three chronograms": the sun, the moon, and the five planets

(Mercury, Venus, Mars, Jupiter, and Saturn).
4. Daoists who have achieved extraordinary powers and moved beyond earthly corruption.
5. Ning Fengzi, according to legend the master potter of the mythological Yellow Emperor (Huangdi, 27th century B.C.E.), who was credited with receiving several Daoist scriptures.

missioned the gentleman "Elder of the Five Marchmounts,"[6] in charge of superintending these collective heavenly peaks. Traces of his wheeltracks and an altar's site still exist there today. The marchmount's spirit[7] from above the mountains' stark precipices drips down water all year long, which substitutes for a sundial or waterclock. Lord Wang,[8] Overseer of the Perfected of the Western Extremities, further directs ten thousand transcendents in controlling this cavern bureau. Self-perpetuating divine lamps shine and illumine the forests and gullies. Meeting with rain increases their brilliance. They are scattered and transformed by the wind.

The mountain's steep walls and repeating cliffs are as lofty as parapets. Their red color resembles swirling auroral clouds. It is referred to as Red Stone Wall, though it is also named Heavenly Region. Certainly these variant names specify no more than one and the same mountain.

In former times, the Han Dynasty's position deteriorated. People and spirits of the dead interrelated and mixed, rousing miasma, breathing poison, and generation after generation slaughtering the spirits of the living. The Most High[9] mandated the Perfected One of True Unity, Lord Zhang of the Three Heavens,[1] to prepare to ride from Chuting and Heming Mountains[2] to this mountain range to carry out the Law of the Awesome Covenant, cleanse and purify the forests and marshes, and repel the enemy for ten thousand li.[3]

Lord Zhang rooted out demons from their cities and markets and carved stone figures of heaven, earth, sun and moon. At the Three Teachers Altar of the Ram and Horse Pavilion he suspended pennants commanding demons to enact a vow between spirits of the dead and spirits of the living so that the latter would have charge of day and the former of night. He painted the mountain with a red brush, severing the green cliff-face, wherein remnants of his brushwork remain. This is what the scriptures and charts record.

At the extreme summit is the Palace of Upper Clarity, which caps the various peaks and blossoms out of the cloud cover. Next to it is Heaven's Pool, which remains the same in drought and downpour. Below is Joining Dragon Bridge, a stone causeway supported by suspension. Here, in truth, is the cave dwelling of divine transcendents.

The Observatory of the Constant Way was seized by Buddhist monks for a short time. In the jiazi year,[4] the twelfth year of the Opening of the Prime reign period (724 C.E.), a special imperial order moved them back to their old place in the mountains. An imperial stone tablet remains at the site of the observatory. The Emperor ordered and bestowed perfected rites making another temple the Elder Observatory. On this day, transcendent clouds formed a cover; sweet springs glistened in their holes.

---

6. The Five Marchmounts were a group of five sacred mountains—one in each of the four cardinal directions and one at the center.
7. A reference to Gentleman Ning [translator's note].
8. Wang Yuan (fl. ca. 150 C.E.), a figure of Daoist hagiography.
9. That is, Laozi.
1. Zhang Daoling (34–156 C.E.), founder of the Celestial Masters movement; the Three Heavens

are Great Clarity (Taiqing), Jade Clarity (Yuqing), and Upper Clarity (Shangqing).
2. Two mountains in modern Sichuan Province.
3. A unit of distance, equal to about 1/3 mile.
4. A reference to the Chinese calendrical system, in which days and (later) years were designated with two characters drawn from a set of ten Celestial Stems and twelve Earthly Branches, resulting in a cycle of sixty days/years.

* * *

In the xinzhou year of the Central Harmony reign period (881 C.E.), the Xizong Emperor halted on circuit at Chengdu. There he conferred the honorific title of Soundless and Colorless. He then stopped at Qingcheng Mountain to rest his entourage. Dragons chanted in the midst of rushing torrents. In search of a divine response, he repeatedly fasted and made offerings to Heaven. Spiritual bronze gongs sounded of their own accord. Transcendent torches filled the mountainside. Kirins[5] and golden snakes congregated on an altar. The withered coir palm flourished anew. The six types of grasses and trees were reborn. These auspicious omens appear thus arranged on the green bamboo slips of history.

* * *

In the midst of the mountain are the various observatories, Elder, Constant Way, Austere Ceremony and Cavern Heaven. Through long, continuous years, much has fallen into ruin. Formerly, Ministers Cui Zhenggui of Boling, and Wu Tingxiu of Bohai, both added adornments and reinforced the old foundations. These were men who made rounds by carriage to all states and divisional districts, unceasingly providing for buildings' stability. When their repairs were gradually completed and the desecration and destruction had been contained, they rushed off in a star chariot helterskelter. In the space of ten years there were no additional repairs necessary.

In the guichou year (893 C.E.), District Magistrate of the Southern Commandery, Duke Mo Tingyi received imperial commandment to conduct long libational services of Offering, and personally performed these rituals. Examining the mountain's excellence and uniqueness, he was pained by this overgrowth and neglect. He showed no concern for his private wealth and did not encroach upon public funds, but for two years concentrated on repairing the two main observatories, and renovating the ancestral temples of this mountain of favored ground. He re-established each of their sites and carved images in stone for them. He then drew charts of the temples for posterity.

5. Mythological creatures, compounded of different animals, that have no Western equivalent.

THE COLLECTION OF BOOKS NEW AND OLD
ON THE ABSORPTION OF BREATH GATHERED
BY THE MASTER OF YANLING
(Yanling xiansheng ji xinjiu fuqi jing)

The *Collection of Books New and Old on the Absorption of Breath Gathered by the Master of Yanling* (*Yanling xiansheng ji xinjiu fuqi jing*), probably compiled in the middle of the eighth century by an otherwise unknown figure, is a detailed account of the Daoist practice of "embryonic respiration" (*taixi*). In general, embryonic respiration is an attempt to gain the vitality of the fetus—in particular, to reverse the process of aging—through a set of techniques intended to re-create the breathing of an embryo in the womb. These techniques, as set out in this text, reflect the increasing emphasis within Daoism in the late Tang dynasty (618–907) on internal rather than external practices.

The "Formula for the Use of Breath by Perfect Men of Mysterious Simplicity, Expounded by the Master of Great Respect" describes a preliminary practice. Adepts must do physical exercises, calm the mind through meditation, clack their teeth, swallow their own saliva, and visualize the breath traveling properly through the body. Those who perfectly and constantly follow this method for nine years will be able to "walk upon emptiness as one walks on substance, on water as if on earth."

PRONOUNCING GLOSSARY

Da weiyi xiansheng xuanshu zhenren yongqi jue: *dah way-gee hsien-shung hsuan-shoo chun-run yung-chi chueh*
taixi: *tai-hsi*

Yanling xiansheng ji xinjiu fuqi jing: *yen-ling hsien-shung gee hsin-foo foo-chi ching*

Formula for the Use of Breath by Perfect Men of Mysterious Simplicity, Expounded by the Master of Great Respect (Da weiyi xiansheng xuanshu zhenren yongqi jue)

In all prescriptions for the use of breath, one must first do gymnastic exercises on the right and left sides of the body, so that the bones and the joints will open and connect, so that the nerves will be soft and the body relaxed. After that, sit down, the body in correct position, and exhale and inhale three times, so that there are no knots of obstruction. Calm all thought and forget the body so that the breath may be drawn in peacefully. After a while, first very gently expel the impure breath through the mouth, and inhale the pure breath through the nose. Do all this six or seven times. This is called "harmonizing the breaths."

When the harmonizing of breaths is finished, then, with both mouth and nose closed and completely empty, let the breath fill the mouth. Then beat the drum[1] in the mouth fifteen times; if it is done more, better yet. (Swallow the breath) as if a great gulp of water had been swallowed, and make it enter the belly. Concentrate your entire attention (on the breath's going) to the Ocean of Breath and remaining there for a long time. After a while, swallow again according to the above procedure and, determining (the number of times to do it by) when the belly is satisfied, but not fixing a specific number of times. After that, empty the heart and fill the belly. Close the mouth, massage both sides of the belly with the hands so that the breath will flow along; and let the respiration penetrate very gently into the nose without breathing heavily for fear of losing harmony. After that, the body lying in a correct position, place yourself on a couch with a pillow. The pillow must be such that the head is level with the body, both hands tightly closed. Extend the open hands to a distance of four or five inches from the body, the two feet likewise to a distance of four or five inches from each other. After that, breathe through the nose: with the mouth and nose both closed, let the heart concentrate itself upon the breath and make it circulate

TRANSLATED from the Chinese by Henri Maspero; translated from the French by Frank A. Kierman, Jr.

1. Twist one's tongue and grind one's teeth.

throughout the body. This is what is called "making the breath circulate." If you are ill, let the heart concentrate upon the breath and apply it to the ailing area. If the breath is rapid, (panting?), release it inside the nose (in a) very fine (current of air) so as to make the breathing communicate, without opening the mouth, and wait until the breathing is even. Then hold it closed in again according to the above methods. Move the toes of both feet, the fingers of the hands, and the bones and joints: for measure take (the moment when) perspiration appears. That is what is called the penetration of the breath.

Then very gently, lying down, bend the legs, first touching them to the ground on the left side (for the time of) ten breaths, and then touching them to the ground on the right side, also for the time of ten breaths. This is what is called "making up for the diminution."

While following these methods, at the end of one month, walking or standing (still), seated or lying down, when the belly is empty, beat the drum and swallow (the breath) without time limit, as if eating. When a meal of emptiness of one or two mouthfuls has been eaten, add to it some water which is swallowed and made to go down. This is what is called "washing the five viscera."[2] Then warm up again and rinse the mouth with pure water, empty the heart and fill the belly, so that the viscera and the receptacles have their layers dilated, swallow (the breath) so that the five viscera do not hold the breath of the five flavors[3] in.

Having finished this, (you must) first spit the impure breath out through the mouth, and inhale the pure breath through the nose without counting how many times; it has to be ejected entirely. If one soiled breath is allowed to escape by the lower orifice, set yourself again to beating the drum and refine one mouthful, joining it to the breath so as to complete it.

If you eat or drink tea in the ordinary way, those are all exterior breaths entering. When they have remained in the mouth a moment, it is closed and when it is closed, the exterior breaths which have entered it go out into the nose. But the breath which enters through the nose is the pure breath; therefore you must always eat with the mouth closed so that no breath enters through the mouth, (for) if it does, it is a deadly breath.

Whenever men speak, and the breath within the mouth goes out, it must enter through the nose. This is exhalation and inhalation as they are carried on ordinarily.

If in walking, in pausing, in sitting, or in lying down, you are always moving the toes, that is called seeing constantly that the breath succeeds in going down below. This is something to practise constantly, something you must think of while at rest as well as when moving.

If attention is not given to time, so that exterior breath suddenly penetrates into the belly and a light bloating is felt, you must massage the belly a hundred times: the breath will escape below. If the breath goes up and cannot get out, make it go down by pressing with the hand. This is called "putting things in order."

Abstain from things which interrupt the breath, and from fat things or things which stick together or which produce chill; you must not eat cold things which disturb the breath.

---

2. The liver, heart, spleen, lungs, and kidneys.   3. Sweet, bitter, sour, pungent, and salty.

If this method is followed without mistake and practised constantly for nine years, the result will be attained; you will walk upon emptiness as one walks on substance, on water as if on earth.

YU XUANJI'S LIFE AND POEMS

HUANGFU MEI

The Daoist nun Yu Xuanji (b. ca. 848) lived in the Chinese capital of Chang'an (modern Xi'an). Noted for her beauty and her intellect, in her teens she became the concubine of an official named Li Yi. As the translators Wilt Idema and Beata Grant note, it was only after he sent her away that she entered a Daoist nunnery, though her life in it was hardly cloistered. One source of her biography, as well as her verse, is *Minor Writings from Shanshui* (*Shanshui xiaodu*), a collection of anecdotes by Huangfu Mei (fl. late ninth century). In the excerpt below, he recalls her active social life and severely observes that "she was incapable of preserving her honor." According to Huangfu, she murdered her own servant girl in a jealous rage; even in prison, she continued to write poems, and despite the efforts of her powerful friends she was executed.

Yu Xuanji's Daoism-inspired poems include one addressed to Wen Tingyun (812– ca. 870), a poet who frequented the pleasure quarters and who lost his political appointment after engaging in a drunken brawl in a bar. In another poem she bemoans the fate of talented women who aspire to literary success yet are barred from taking the imperial service examination.

PRONOUNCING GLOSSARY

Huangfu Mei: *huang foo may* Yu Xuanji: *yu hsien-gee*
Shanshui xiaodu: *shawn-shuei hsiao-doo*

FROM MINOR WRITINGS FROM SHANSHUI (SHANSHUI XIAODU)

The style name of Yu Xuanji, a Daoist nun in the Xianyi Convent of the Western Capital [Chang'an],[1] was Youwei and she was the daughter of a commoner family in Chang'an. Not only was her beauty earth-shattering, but her intellectual capacities were also extraordinary. She loved to read books and compose texts, and devoted herself in particular to the writing of poetry. By the age of sixteen, her mind was focused on "the pure and empty," and in the early years of the reign period Full Communication [Xiantong, 860–873] she donned the capeline[2] and stole [of a Daoist nun] at the Xianyi Convent. Her fine verses of appreciation and enjoyment of breeze and moonlight often circulated among the forest of gentlemen.

However, possessed as she was of the weak nature of a fragrant orchid, she was incapable of preserving her honor. She allowed herself to accept the

TRANSLATED BY Wilt Idema and Beata Grant. All bracketed additions are the translators'.

1. Modern Xi'an. 2. An elaborate headdress worn by Daoist nuns.

advances of powerful bosses, and accompanied them on their excursions and elsewhere. All the men about town vied with each other to appear at their finest in the hopes of starting an affair with her. Occasionally they would come to visit her, bringing wine with them, and she would strum the zither and recite poetry, interspersing this with risqué banter. Those with insufficient learning would feel very much out of place. Her poems included lines such as the following:

> Gauze pathways: the spring outlook is distant,
> Jade zither-studs: autumnal feelings in profusion.

And:

> Filled with devotion, unable to speak,
> Red tears course down my cheeks.

And:

> Burning incense, I ascend the jade platform,
> Grasping my tablet, I bow to the golden gate.

And:

> Cloud emotions, thick and heavy—it could not be a dream:
> Fairy face, forever fragrant—far more lovely than a flower!

These several couplets were her finest.

Her servant girl, Lüqiao, was also very clever and beautiful. One day, when Xuanji had been invited by the nuns of the adjoining courtyard [in the convent], she left Lüqiao with the following instructions: "Don't go out, and if a guest should show up, just tell him that I am at such-and-such a place." Xuanji was kept longer than expected by her girlfriends and did not return to her own courtyard until evening. Lüqiao opened the gate for her, saying: "Just a moment ago such-and-such a guest showed up. When he heard that you were not in, he went away without dismounting from his horse." Now, although this guest was an old patron of hers, Xuanji suspected Lüqiao of having an affair with him.

That night she lit a lamp and, after locking the door, ordered Lüqiao to come into her bedroom so as to question her. Lüqiao said: "During all the years that I have been your servant, I have truly behaved myself properly and have never committed a transgression of the sort that would offend you. Moreover, when that guest arrived, I kept the door locked, and it was from behind the door that I informed him that you were not at home. He then went away without saying a word, spurring on his horse. You talk about love—but it has been years since I have harbored that kind of feeling in my heart! Mistress, please do not doubt me!" But Xuanji only grew more enraged. Stripping her servant naked, she lashed her hundreds of times with a cane. But Lüqiao continued to protest her innocence. She then collapsed to the ground, and requesting a cup of water, she poured it out on the ground saying: "You wish to pursue the Way of Longevity of the Three Purities,[3] but are incapable of denying yourself the pleasures of

---

3. Probably a reference to the three superior heavens or to three high deities, the Celestial Worthy of Numinous Treasure (Lingbao tian-zun), Celestial Worthy of Primordial Commence-ment (Yuanshi tianzun), and Celestial Worthy of the Way and Its Virtue (Daode tianzun); the term has many meanings in Daoism.

removing your skirts and sharing the couch. But because of your inveter-
ate suspicion you falsely accuse me, who am chaste and correct! It turns
out that I will be dying a cruel death under your brutal hands. If there is
no Heaven, I will have nowhere to lodge my complaint. But if there is, no
one will be able to thwart my stubborn soul! I swear I will not wriggle
about like a worm in deepest darkness and allow you to indulge in your
lasciviousness!" As soon as she had spoken these words, she passed away
right there on the spot. Xuanji was filled with fear and buried her in a hole
that she dug in her backyard, thinking that no one would find out. This
took place in the First Month of spring in the ninth year of Full Communication [868].

Whenever someone would ask after Lüqiao, Xuanji would say: "She ran
away after the spring rains cleared!" Once a guest who had been dining in
Xuanji's room went out into her backyard to urinate. On the spot where
Xuanji had buried Lüqiao, he noticed quite a number of green flies, which,
when he chased them away, only came back again. When he looked more
carefully, he noticed not only traces of what appeared to be blood, but a
rancid smell as well. After the guest had left, in confidence he told his
servant what he had seen. The servant, once he got home, told it in turn to
his elder brother. Now this elder brother was a patrolman. He had once asked
Xuanji for money, but she had ignored him, and so he harbored a grudge
against her. When he heard this story, he immediately went to the convent gate
to spy on her. When he overheard people speculating as to why they hadn't
seen Lüqiao coming in and out, the patrolman called together some additional
police officers, and with spades in their hands they rushed into Xuanji's
courtyard. When they dug Lüqiao up, they found that her face looked just as
it had when she was alive.

The policemen arrested Xuanji, and when she was questioned by the clerks
of Chang'an prefecture, she confessed. Many of the gentlemen at court tried
to intervene on her behalf but the prefecture submitted her name to the
emperor in a memorial and when autumn came around, she was, in fact,
executed. While in prison, she also wrote poems, the most beautiful couplets
of which are the following:

> Easy it is to find a priceless treasure,
> Difficult it is to find a steadfast lover.

And:

> A full moon shines through the dark crack,
> A clear breeze blows open my short jacket.

Feelings in the Last Month of Spring;
Sent to a Friend

The chatter of orioles startles me from my dream,
And a light makeup disguises the traces of tears.
Above the dark bamboo, a thin new moon,
On the quiet river, a heavy evening mist.
With moistened beaks, the swallows carry loam,
With perfumed beards, the bees collect their honey.

Alone in love, my longing is without end—
My poem intoned, the pine branches hang low.

On the Assigned Topic of Willows by the River

Their verdant color conjoins with the grassy bank,
Their misty forms enter into the distant towers.
Their shadows spread out over the river's face,
And their floss falls down upon the angler's head.
Their old roots conceal the holes where fishes hide,
Their low branches snare the boats of merchants.
In desolate nights of sighing wind and rain
They startle me from my dreams, adding to my sorrows.

Early Autumn

Tender chrysanthemums carry new colors,
As distant mountains idle in the evening mists.
A cool breeze startles the green trees,
And pure rhymes enter the red strings:
The longing wife: brocade on the loom,
The man on campaign: sky beyond the border.
Geese fly overhead, fish swim in the water,
But how could they ever carry any letter?

Selling Wilted Peonies

Facing the wind they evoke a sigh as their petals continue to fall,
Their fragrance fades and dissolves as yet another spring goes by.
It must be because of their high price that no one shows interest,
And because of their extreme fragrance butterflies cannot come near.
Their red flowers are fit to be grown only inside the palace,
How could their green leaves bear to be tainted by dew and dust?
But when their roots will have been transplanted to the Imperial Park,
You, my prince, will then regret that you can no longer buy them!

During a Visit to the Southern Tower of the Veneration of Truth Monastery I Saw the New Examination Graduates Writing Their Names on the Wall

Cloudy peaks fill one's eyes under a clear spring sky:
Clearly legible "silver hooks"[1] emerge from their fingers.
Oh how I hate this gauze gown for hiding my verses!
To no avail I look up with envy at the names on the list.

1. Chinese characters.

THE CHRONICLES OF JAPAN
(*Nihongi*)

Completed in 720 C.E., the *Chronicles of Japan* (*Nihongi*) is an important source for early Japanese history. The record included here, relating events of 613 C.E., presents a Daoist-like figure whose death appears to fit the pattern of *shijie*, or "corpse liberation"—a type of liberation or transformation in which one feigns one's own death, leaving behind nothing or some relic, and ascends to heaven.

PRONOUNCING GLOSSARY

Katawoka: *ka-ta-oh-ka*   Nihongi: *knee-hown-gee*

[*Corpse Liberation*]

[21st year,][1] 12th month, 1st day. The Prince Imperial took a journey to Katawoka.[2] Now a starving man was lying by the roadside. He asked his name, but there was no answer. The Prince Imperial, seeing this, gave him to eat and to drink, and taking off his own raiment, clothed with it the starving man, saying to him, "Lie in peace." Then he made a song, saying:—

> Alas! for
> The wayfarer lying
> An hungered for rice
> On the hill of Katawoka
> (The sunshiny).
> Art thou become
> Parentless?
> Hast thou no lord
> Flourishing as a bamboo?
> Alas! for
> The wayfarer lying
> An hungered for rice!

2nd day. The Prince Imperial sent a messenger to see the starving man. The messenger returned and said:—"The starving man is already dead." Hereupon the Prince Imperial was greatly grieved, and accordingly caused him to be buried at that place, a mound erected, and firmly closed.

Many days after, the Prince Imperial called for his personal attendants, and said to them:—"The starving man who was lying on a former day on the road was no ordinary man. He must have been an upright man." A messenger was sent to see. On his return he reported that when he went to the mound and made inspection, the heaped-up earth had not been disturbed, but on opening the tomb and looking in, there was no corpse. It was empty, and there was nothing but the garment folded up and laid on the coffin.

TRANSLATED BY W. G. Aston.

1. The 21st year of the regency of Prince Shōtoku (574–622), 613 C.E.
2. Kataoka, in present-day Nara Prefecture.

Thereupon the Prince Imperial sent the messenger back a second time to fetch the garment, which he continued wearing as before.

The people of that time wondered much at this, and said:—"How true it is that a sage knoweth a sage." And they stood more and more in awe of him.

POEMS COMPOSED BY KAKINOMOTO NO ASOMI HITOMARO WHEN THE SOVEREIGN WENT ON AN EXCURSION TO THE PALACE AT YOSHINO

Kakinomoto Hitomaro (fl. ca. 680–700) is one of the most celebrated poets in early Japanese literature. His surviving works are found in the eighth-century *Collection of Ten Thousand Leaves* (*Manyōshū*), the oldest imperial anthology of Japanese verse; it contains some poems that allude not just to Confucianism and Buddhism but also to Daoist beliefs and legends. Though the context is not strictly Daoist, these writings— together with other textual and material evidence, such as the numerous poems in the collection *Fond Recollections of Poetry* (*Kaifūsō*, 751) with explicit Daoist references—indicate that by the eighth century, sophisticated Japanese were famil- iar with Daoist vocabulary and cultural elements.

The poems by Kakinomoto included here celebrate a visit by Empress Jitō (r. 686– 97) to the imperial palace at Mount Yoshino, a mountainous area in central Japan. It is depicted as a natural Daoist paradise where mountain deities dwell and spirits roam.

PRONOUNCING GLOSSARY

Kakinomoto no Asomi Hitomaro: *kah-key-no-mow-tow no ah-sow-mee he-tow-maw-row*

Manyōshū: *mahn-yo-shoo*
Yoshino: *yo-she-no*

[*Where our Sovereign reigns*]

Where our Sovereign[1] reigns,
Ruling the earth in all tranquility,
    Under the heaven
Of this realm she holds in sway,
    Many are the lands,
But of their multitude,
    Seeing the clear pools
That form along this mountain stream,
    She gave her heart
To the fair land of Yoshino,[2]
    And where blossoms fall
Forever on the fields of Akizu[3]

TRANSLATED BY Edwin A. Cranston.

1. Empress Jitō (r. 686–97).
2. A mountainous area in present-day Nara Pre- fecture; it was an important center for mountain asceticism (a Japanese practice with connections to Daoist ideas and practices).
3. A specific site near the Yoshino River at the foot of the Yoshino mountains.

She planted firm
The mighty pillars of her palace halls.
  Now the courtiers,
Men of the palace of the hundred stones,
  Line up their boats
To row across the morning stream,
  Vie in their boats
To race upon the evening stream:
  And like the stream
This place shall last forever,
  Like these mountains
Ever loftier shall rise
  Beside the plunging waters
Of the torrent her august abode:
Long though I gaze, my eyes will never
    tire.

ENVOY

Long though I gaze,
Never shall I tire of Yoshino,
  Within whose stream
The water-moss grows smooth forever,
As I shall come to view these sights anew.

[Our great Sovereign]

Our great Sovereign
Who rules the land in all tranquility,
  She who is a god
In action godlike has ordained
  That by Yoshino,
Where seething waters deepen into pools,
  Lofty halls shall rise,
Lifting high above the stream;
  And when she climbs aloft
That she may gaze upon her land,
  Fold upon fold
The mountains standing in green walls
  Present as tribute
Offered by the mountain gods
  In springtime
Blossoms worn upon the brow,
  And when autumn comes
Deck themselves in yellow leaves.
  Gods of the river too,
That flows along the mountain foot,
  In order to provide
The Sovereign's table with good fare,
  At the upper shallows
Start the cormorants[4] downstream,

---

4. Birds native to Japan; partially domesticated, they were traditionally used by Japanese fishermen.

And at the lower shallows
Spread their nets from bank to bank.
Mountain and river
Join thus in fealty to serve
The god who rules this glorious age.

ENVOY

Whom mountain and river
Join thus in fealty to serve,
    She who is a god
Now sets her boat upon the stream
Where seething waters deepen into pools.

INDICATIONS OF THE GOALS
OF THE THREE TEACHINGS
(Sango shiki)

KUKAI

Kukai (774–835), a key figure in the Shingon school of esoteric Buddhism, is celebrated as one of Japan's foremost Buddhist monks. In addition to being a major Buddhist philosopher and serving in important monastic offices, Kukai was a poet and prolific writer on a range of subjects; he is noted for his work as a calligrapher and an artist and for his contributions to the development of music, civil engineering, and architecture. He traveled to China in 804 as part of an official Japanese mission and brought back many important texts, works of art, and ritual implements. Later in life Kukai settled on Mount Koya; there he began to build a large monastic center, and the site has been indelibly connected with him ever since. The tradition claims that Kukai's death was only apparent—and since his body did not corrupt, he is understood as having entered into a deep state of meditation (*samadhi*). Kukai is still considered to be alive in a sanctuary on Mount Koya—monks continue to serve him breakfast daily—as he awaits the future buddha, Maitreya. In his posthumous cult, Kukai is called Kobo daishi (Great Teacher Who Spread the Dharma), a title awarded by the Japanese emperor in 921.

In *Indications of the Goals of the Three Teachings (Sango shiki)*, Kukai evaluates the relative merits of Buddhism, Daoism, and Confucianism. His approach is unusual, as each teaching represented by a different figure: Buddhism by Mendicant X (Kamei-kotsuji), Confucianism by Tortoise Hair (Kimo), and Daoism by Nothingness (Kyobu). The discussion is hosted by Hare's Horn (Tokaku). In the preface, Kukai explains that his main audience is a nephew, here represented by Leech's Tusk (Shitsuga), "who is depraved and indulges in hunting, wine, and women, and whose usual way of life consists of gambling and dissipation." As the three spokesmen debate, they reprove the nephew.

The section on Daoism below presents Kyobu as a person who conceals his wisdom behind a pretense of foolishness. He proceeds to lay out a summary view of some of the main tenets and practices of Daoism; he stresses the ingestion of different medicinal herbs and elixirs, noting the benefits they confer on the adept (including the ability to "see through the earth and walk on water" and "fly into the sky"). Kyobu's audience at first finds his teachings attractive, but in a passage not included here he is criticized for overemphasizing longevity. Kukai concludes by judging Buddhism to be the highest teaching, thereby justifying his own entry into the priesthood, and ultimately the Confucian and the Daoist both convert to Buddhism.

PRONOUNCING GLOSSARY

Daode jing: *dow-duh ching*

Kimo: *key-mow*

Kūkai: *koo-kai*

Kyobu: *key-yo bu*

Sango shiki: *sawn-go shee-key*

Shitsuga: *she-tsu-ga*

Tokaku: *toe-kah-ku*

Preface

For any natural phenomenon or literary work there exists a cause. The sun, the moon, and the stars appear when the sky is clear. A man writes when moved. So the Eight Trigrams of Fu Xi, the *Daode jing*, the *Book of Odes*, the *Elegies of Chu*[1] were written down by men who were inspired from within. Of course, there can be no comparison between these sages of the past and a common man of the present such as I, yet somehow I feel compelled to express my innermost feelings.

At fifteen I began my studies [of Chinese classics] under the guidance of Atō Ōtari, the teacher of a prince and an uncle on my mother's side. At eighteen I entered the college in the capital[2] and studied diligently. Meanwhile a Buddhist monk showed me a scripture called the *Kokūzō gumonji no hō*.[3] In that work it is stated that if one recites the mantra one million times according to the proper method, one will be able to memorize passages and understand the meaning of any scripture. Believing what the Buddha says to be true, I recited the mantra incessantly, as if I were rubbing one piece of wood against another to make fire, all the while earnestly hoping to achieve this result. I climbed up Mount Tairyū in Awa Province and meditated at Cape Muroto in Tosa. The valley reverberated to the sound of my voice as I recited, and the planet Venus[4] appeared in the sky.

From that time on, I despised fame and wealth and longed for a life in the midst of nature. Whenever I saw articles of luxury—light furs, well-fed horses, swift vehicles—I felt sad, knowing that, being transient as lightning, they too would fade away. Whenever I saw a cripple or a beggar, I lamented and wondered what had caused him to spend his days in such a miserable

TRANSLATED BY Yoshito S. Hakeda. All bracketed additions are the translator's.

1. Four major works in Chinese culture. The first mythical emperor of China, Fu Xi, is credited with discovering the trigrams (on which see the introduction to *The Seal of the Unity of the Three, in Accordance with the Book of Changes* [*Zhouyi cantong qi*], above); the *Daode jing* (*The Scripture of the Way and Its Virtue*; see above) is credited to Laozi; the *Book of Odes* (*Shijing*, 5th century B.C.E.), usually known as the *Book* or *Classic of Poetry*, an anthology, is one of the Confucian Five Classics; and the *Songs of Chu* or *Songs of the South* (*Chuci*, 2nd century C.E.) collects poems that reflect the culture of Chu,

which before the expansion of the Han dynasty (202 B.C.E.–220 C.E.) was the southernmost part of China.
2. At that time, Nagaoka.
3. *Akashagarbha's Technique for Seeking, Hearing, and Retaining*. Akashagarbha (Kokuzo)—a bodhisattva, or one who has vowed to achieve buddhahood for the sake of all beings—was particularly important in Japanese Shingon Buddhism, which associated him with wisdom and memory.
4. The morning star, a manifestation of Akashagarbha.

state. Seeing these piteous conditions encouraged me to renounce the world. Can anyone now break my determination? No, just as there is no one who can stop the wind.

My relatives and teachers opposed my entering the priesthood, saying that by doing so I would be unable to fulfill the Five Cardinal Virtues[5] or to accomplish the duties of loyalty or of filial piety. I thought then: living beings are not of the same nature—there are birds which fly high in the sky and fish which sink low in the water. To guide different types of people, there are three teachings: Buddhism, Daoism, and Confucianism. Although their profoundness varies, they are still the teachings of the sages. If an individual chooses one, he does not necessarily repudiate loyalty and filial piety by doing so.

Now I have a nephew who is depraved and indulges in hunting, wine, and women, and whose usual way of life consists of gambling and dissipation. It is obvious that an unfavorable environment has caused him to lead this kind of life. What has induced me to write [this story] are the opposition of my relatives [to my becoming a Buddhist] and the behavior of this nephew.

Here in my writing I should like to propose Tokaku (Hare's Horn) as host, with Kimō (Tortoise Hair) as guest speaker for Confucianism, Kyobu (Nothingness) as spokesman for Daoism, and Kamei-kotsuji (Mendicant X) as representative of Buddhism. These speakers will debate over Shitsuga (Leech's Tusk), the nephew, and admonish him. The work will consist of three parts and be called the *Indications of the Goals of the Three Teachings*. Of course, I am writing just to express my own unsuppressible feelings and not in order to be read by others.

First Day of the Twelfth Month
Enryaku 16 (797)

Part Two: The Argument of Kyobu [Daoist]

Kyobu (Nothingness) had been beside them listening for some time. He was a person who concealed his wisdom by pretending to be a fool; he mingled with the people in the streets, acting as if he were mad. His hair was disheveled, more so than that of Deng Tuzi's wife,[6] and his ragged garment seemed shabbier than that of Dong Wei.[7] He had been listening, squatting with his legs far apart, and smiling arrogantly. But now he opened wide his eyes and spoke:

"How strange is your therapeutic medicine! When you started I thought your speech would be as valuable as a priceless fox coat; I was struck with awe as if I were facing a dragon or a tiger. But toward the end I felt as if I were watching a tiny snake or a rat. You are unable to cure your own dread disease, but still you have the nerve to speak about another's swollen legs; it is better not to cure at all than to cure by such a therapy."

5. The five Confucian virtues: humaneness, righteousness, propriety, knowledge, and integrity.
6. Well known for her ugliness [translator's note].

7. Reputed to care nothing about his clothes [translator's note].

Thereupon, Kimō turned around in astonishment. Quite embarrassed, he drew near to Kyobu and said:

"If you know of any other teaching, please share it with us. I may have spoken carelessly, being unable to ignore Tokaku's request. Please instruct us with your teaching, which is like the thunder in spring."

Kyobu said: "The sun is bright, but a blind man is unable to see the glittering rays. Though thunder roars violently, a deaf man does not know the sound. The secret doctrines of Emperor Huang[8] do not reach the ears of ordinary people. Why should I teach indiscriminately the divine founder's secret doctrines? In olden times people drank the blood of a sacrificial animal and made a vow before they heard the doctrines; these teachings can seldom be heard. They engraved an oath on the bones vowing that they would keep the secret. These doctrines cannot be easily transmitted. Why is this so? Ordinary people assume that the well is dry, when in actuality the bucket they lower has too short a rope and cannot reach the water; or they try to measure the depth of the ocean by dipping a finger into it and imagine that they have touched the bottom. To an unfit person, we do not open our mouths; unless a man be a proper vessel, we hide our book in a wooden box deep down in the earth. When the occasion comes, we open the box and transmit the secret to those who have been selected."

Thereupon, Kimō and the others consulted together:

"Long ago when Emperor Wu of Han went searching for the secret of longevity, he came upon Xi Wangmu [Queen of the West][9] and with her he pleaded earnestly in a most polite manner for the revelation of the secret; Fei Changfang[1] learned the secret formula from an old man in a jar. Now we have unexpectedly met this teacher; from him we can learn the method of attaining longevity. We need not exert ourselves as Bing Yuan[2] did. We may be able to live as long as Pengzi[3] did. Will it not be marvelous! How fortunate we are!"

Thus they approached Kyobu, courteously prostrated themselves again, and said, "We earnestly entreat you once more to favor us with your instruction."

Then Kyobu said, "If you build an altar and make a vow, I shall teach you."

They did as they had been told. They constructed an altar and made a vow; they also drank the blood of a sacrificial animal and read an oath in front of the hole they dug in which to bury the animal. After completing the ceremony, they asked for instruction.

"Fine," said Kyobu. "Listen with sincerity. I shall bestow upon you the divine techniques for prolonging your life and attaining immortality. You, whose term of life is as short as that of the mayflies, will be able to live as long as a tortoise or a crane; you, whose speed compares to that of a lame

---

8. The mythical Yellow Emperor (Huangdi), who was credited with receiving several Daoist scriptures; he himself became a Daoist immortal (one who has achieved extraordinary powers and a higher form of existence).
9. The Queen Mother of the West, one of the most important goddesses in ancient China and in the Daoist pantheon; her home was on the mythical Mount Kunlun. According to legend,

Emperor Wu (141–87 B.C.E.) received her teachings but did not follow them.
1. A legendary Daoist magician of the Eastern Han dynasty (25–220 C.E.).
2. Famous for his long journeys in search of the appropriate teacher.
3. A legendary figure, said to have lived from the 26th to the 7th century B.C.E.

donkey walking, will be as fast as a flying dragon. You will be everlasting like the sun, the moon, and the stars! You will be able to meet the Eight Immortals[4] who ascended to the sky. You will climb the three mystical mountains [in the Eastern Sea] in the morning, enjoy yourselves in the silver palaces all day long, and in the evening reach the five mountains[5] [in the East] and wander on the golden platform all night. I will make all these miracles possible for you."

Kimō and the others replied, "Yes, yes, we should like to hear."

"A potter's wheel when it shapes does not discriminate between earthen vessels; a large furnace, when melting metals, has neither affection nor hatred for the metals it melts. That Chi Songzi and Wang Ziqiao[6] had long lives was not because they had any unusual good fortune; that Xiang Tuo and Yan Hui[7] died young does not mean that they were unfortunate. The difference is determined by how well they maintained their given nature. The methods of nourishing nature and of maintaining longevity are many; therefore, I cannot explain them all to you. I shall teach you a little by describing things in outline.

"In olden times, Emperor Shi Huang[8] of Qin and Emperor Wu of Han longed for the art of becoming immortal, but their way of life had been the same as that of everyone else in the world. The functions of their ears were weakened by hearing music and their eyesight was dulled by the brightness of brocade and embroidery. They were unable, even for a short while, to be away from beautiful women, with their pink-colored eyelids and red lips. Dishes of fresh fish, birds, and animals appeared on their table without fail, even for the simplest meal. In battle they piled up corpses as high as a tall building, causing blood to flow like a river. Stories such as these are too numerous to tell in detail. In short, they exhausted their energies in vain; there was a gap between their aspirations and their achievements. They hoped that a round cover would fit a square container, or that fire would come from ice. How stupid they were! People in the world, however, say that, since even the noblest emperors were unable to attain immortality, how can it be possible for commoners like us to attain it. They therefore consider Daoism a fraud and call it nonsense. How confused they are! Luan Tai[9] and both the emperors I have mentioned were but the lowest scum among all those who have been attracted to Daoism; they were abominable. Since people such as they exist, when we transmit the teaching, we must choose proper persons, regardless of their social standing. You had better apply yourselves diligently to learning so that you will not be blamed by later generations. Those who study well are different from the men I have mentioned. Refrain from killing the insects that come near you and do not let sperm or saliva escape from your body. Physically, abstain from worldly pollutions; mentally, get rid of your greediness. Stop looking into the dis-

---

4. Popular Daoist figures in Chinese mythology (symbols of longevity and prosperity).
5. The Five Marchmounts, a group of five sacred mountains—one in each of the four cardinal directions and one at the center.
6. The heir of King Ling of the Zhou (r. 571–545 B.C.E.), a Daoist adept who lived in seclusion for decades and then rode a white crane into heaven. Chi Songzi (Master Red Pine) was the legendary rainmaster of the mythical Chinese emperor Shennong. The two were often mentioned together in lore about immortals.
7. The favorite disciple of Confucius (551–479 B.C.E.), who is said to have received instruction from the legendary child prodigy Xiang Tuo.
8. Qin dynasty emperor (r. 221–210 B.C.E.).
9. An alchemist who pledged to obtain the drug of immortality for Emperor Wu; unable to keep his promise, he was killed.

tance and cease listening continuously. Avoid talking nonsense; give up eating delicious food. It goes without saying, however, that you should be dutiful to your parents, faithful to your friends, benevolent and compassionate. You must surrender wealth as if it were a thorn, and an emperor's position as if you were casting off your [worn-out] straw sandals. When you see a beautiful girl with a slender waist, think of her as a devil or a ghost. Consider peerage and fiefdom as if they were dead rats. Remain quiet, doing nothing intentionally; with pride reduce your worldly affairs. Thereafter, if you study, it [to master this art] will be as easy as pointing at your own palm. What the worldly people like most, that the followers of Daoism most detest. To realize Daoism is not difficult if one stands apart from what people are fond of. Grains are poisonous to the internal organs. Spices are like a poisonous bird with a black body and red eyes—they damage your eyes. Liquors are swords that slice your intestines; pork and fish are halberds that cut your life; beautiful women are axes that chop you down; singing and dancing shorten your allotted period of time. To laugh heartily, to be overly delighted, to be extremely angry, and to be exceedingly sad all do great harm to your body. Even within our bodies are numerous enemies. Unless you overcome them, you cannot expect to have a long life. In everyday living it is extremely difficult to relinquish these enemies, but once rid of them it is very easy to realize Daoism. You should first understand the essence of it and apply the following prescriptions to yourselves:

"Medicines that cure inner diseases are *Atractylis ovata, Polygonatum stenophyllum*,[1] pine resin, the seed of paper mulberry, etc. The arrow of Rubus,[2] the halberd of reed, charms and spells, etc., prevent external difficulties. You must practice the methods for regulating your breath according to the time of day and the season. Inhale air through the nostrils and swallow your saliva. Dig the ground and drink minerals. Satisfy your hunger in the morning with *caozhi* and *ruzhi*;[3] take *fuling* and *weixi*[4] for evening fatigue. After you have followed these practices, you will be able to make your shadow vanish, even when out under the sun, and to write in darkness during the night; you will be able to see through the earth and walk on water. You will be able to make demons your slaves, dragons and one of the excellent steeds [of Mu Wang[5] of Zhou] your vehicles. You will be able to swallow swords and fire, stir winds, and produce clouds. In this way there is no magic that cannot be practiced; there are no desires which cannot be fulfilled.

"Silver and gold are the essence of heaven and earth. Divine pills and refined pills are the most miraculous of all the medicines. Certain procedures in taking them and certain techniques in compounding them must be followed. If one becomes an expert, the other members of his family will also be able to fly into the sky; by drinking only a small quantity of the elixir, one can fly to the Milky Way during the daytime. There are yet many other methods—techniques of swallowing divine amulets and inhaling air;

1. Thistle and Solomon's seal, plants used in herbal medicine and believed by Daoists to prolong life.
2. The genus of raspberries and blackberries.
3. A species of fungus [and] a dried frog [translator's notes].
4. A species of fungus that grows on the stump of a pine [and] a little plant that grows on old *fuling* [translator's notes].
5. The fifth king of the Western Zhou dynasty (r. 10th century B.C.E.), who famously traveled across his realm in a chariot drawn by eight horses.

the technique of traveling swiftly, and the magic of changing one's form—so many that I cannot enumerate them all here.

"When you realize the Way and master this art, your aged body and gray hair will be rejuvenated and life prolonged. Death will be postponed and you will live long in this world. Freely you will fly up to the sky and wander in the regions where the sun sets. Whipping the horse of your mind, you will run to the ends of the eight directions;[6] oiling the wagon of your will, you will gambol throughout the nine skies. You may roam about the palace of the sun, wander in the mansion where the Emperor of Heaven lives; you may see the weaving girl [Vega] or seek Heng'e[7] in the moon. Visiting the Yellow Emperor, you can stay in his company; seeking Wang Ziqiao, you can make him your friend. You may investigate the whereabouts of the roc (*peng*) depicted in *Zhuangzi* and see for yourself the footprints of Huai's dog.[8] You may examine the stables of the horse constellation and the residence of the star Altair. You can lie down at will anywhere and ascend and descend freely. You will be indifferent, free from desires, and at peace in solitude. You will live as long as the heaven and earth; enjoy life for an eternity together with the sun and moon. How excellent! How great! The existence of the immortal married couple, Dong Wang Gong [King of the East] and Xi Wang Mu [Queen of the West], is not a fabrication; what I have spoken of is the most mysterious art that I have ever heard of or learned.

"Now let us examine the worldly life. People are restrained by avarice and suffer bitterly. Chained by passion, their hearts burn. They are compelled to work for their morning and evening meals; they must exhaust themselves for the necessary summer and winter clothing. With the hope of gaining a wealth that is as unstable as floating clouds, they gather property that is just as foamlike. Seeking after unmerited luck, they cherish their bodies, which indeed are as transient as lightning. Given a little pleasure in the morning, they scorn the delights of heaven; but given a little worry in the evening, they agonize as if they have fallen into filthy mire, or onto a bed of burning charcoal. Before the merry music has ended, a sad tone creeps in. A prime minister today is a servant tomorrow. In the beginning men are like the cat on top of a rat, but in the end they are like the sparrow under a hawk. They rely on the dew on the grass and forget that the sun rises at dawn; they trust the leaves at the end of a branch and forget that the frost may come. What a pity! They are not different from the tailorbirds.[9] They are indeed not worthy to be mentioned. Which is better, my teacher's instruction, or what you believe in? Which is superior, what you enjoy, or the life we Daoists admire?"

At this point Kimō, Shitsuga, and Tokaku knelt in a row and said, "We have been fortunate to meet you and to hear a good speech. Now we realize the difference that exists between the foul smell of a fish store and the exquisite fragrance of mystical Mount Fanghu,[1] between the homeliness

---

6. The eight points of the compass rose; those directions and the center are the nine skies.
7. The spirit of the moon; she stole the elixir of immortality from the Queen Mother of the West or from her husband, who had himself received it from the goddess, and flew to the moon.
8. According to Daoist lore, the Prince of Huainan, a vassal of Emperor Wu, ascended to heaven as an immortal—and so did his dogs and cocks who happened to drink some of his elixir of immortality. "*Zhuangzi*": the *Book of Master Zhuang*; see above.
9. Birds that build their nests in a fragile cradle made of leaves stitched together.
1. One of the mythical islands of the immortals, traditionally thought to be located in the East China Sea.

of Chou Mi [appearing in the *Spring and Autumn of Mr. Lü*[2]] and the fairness of Zi Du [in the *Book of Odes*]. Gold is different from stone; a fragrant grass cannot be compared with an ill-smelling one. From now on we shall concentrate on refining our spirits and for a long time savor your teaching."

2. A collection of essays, compiled (ca. 240 B.C.E.) under the direction of Lü Buwei (d. 235 B.C.E.), on the teachings of several schools of philosophy as well as regional folklore.

INSCRIPTION ON AN IMAGE AT KAMSAN MONASTERY

SŎL CH'ONG

It is not clear precisely when Daoist ideas began to trickle into Korea, but references to *The Scripture of the Way and Its Virtue* (*Daode jing*; see above) begin to be found in literature produced in Koguryo, Paekche, and Silla—the Three Kingdoms that ruled Korea from 57 B.C.E. to 668 C.E.—around the seventh century. In 624 the Tang dynasty emperor sent a group of Daoist masters and a set of images to Koguryo, followed in 643 by eight more Daoist priests and a copy of *The Scripture of the Way and Its Virtue*. Apparently, the court was seeking to reduce the dominance of Buddhism. The official transmission of Daoism to Silla came in the next century: an envoy from Tang China brought a copy of the scripture to the ruler in 738.

The following inscription on an image at Kamsan Monastery, written for an eighth-century nobleman named Kim Chijŏn (d. ca. 720) by the Confucian scholar Sŏl Ch'ong (ca. 660–730), demonstrates that Daoism was spreading among the nobility in Korea. Composed on the occasion of the casting of a Buddhist image, it naturally contains copious references to Buddhist ideas and philosophical works. The inscription also informs us Kim Chijŏn read such Daoist texts as the *Book of Master Zhuang* (*Zhuangzi*; see above) and *The Scripture of the Way and Its Virtue*.

PRONOUNCING GLOSSARY

Kamsan: *kahmn-sawn*
Kim Chijŏn: *kim chee-jown*
Silla: *she-lah*

Sŏl Ch'ong: *see-ol chee-owng*
Zhuangzi: *chuang-tzu*

Buddhism is everlasting in its nature, yet it manifested itself in early Zhou.[1] Shakyamuni[2] comes and goes at will, yet he showed his form to Emperor Ming [58–75] of the Later Han in a dream. It began in the Western Regions

TRANSLATED BY Peter H. Lee.

1. The Zhou dynasty began in 1046 B.C.E.; in Japan and Korea, the traditional date of the Buddha's death (placed by most modern scholars around 400 B.C.E.) is 949 B.C.E.

2. Literally, "Sage of the Shakyas": a title of the Buddha, who was born into the Shakya clan.

and transmitted its lamp to the east. It then reached Silla.[3] The Shadow of the Buddha Sun soon illuminated Korea; its scriptures crossed the P'ae River[4] and made clear the Buddha's teaching. Monasteries rose up all jumbled together; stupas stood in rows. Silla resembled Shravasti and the Pure Land.[5]

Chungach'an Kim Chijŏn[6] was born in a blessed land and received the power of the stars. His nature was in harmony with the clouds and mist; his emotion befriended the mountains and waters. Equipped with outstanding ability, his name was known to his generation; carrying wise strategies in his heart, he assisted his time. He went to China as envoy, and the Son of Heaven bestowed on him the title of chief steward in the palace administration. Upon returning to Silla, he was granted the important post of minister of state. At age sixty-seven he withdrew and, shunning the world, lived in seclusion. He emulated the lofty magnanimity of the Four White Heads,[7] declined glory, and nourished his nature. Like brothers Shu Kuang and his nephew Shu Shou,[8] he retired at an opportune time.

Looking up with respect to the true teaching of Asanga[9] [fourth century], he read the *Stages of Yoga Practice*[1] from time to time. In addition, he loved the dark and mysterious way of Zhuangzi and read the "Free and Easy Wandering" chapter.[2] He intended to repay his parents' love thereby, but it could not match the power of the Buddha. He wanted to repay the favor of his king, but it could not equal the primary cause of the Three Jewels: the Buddha, the Dharma, and the Order.[3]

3. One of the Three Kingdoms of ancient Korea; in 668 c.e., it subsumed the other two under the Unified Silla dynasty.
4. That is, the Yalu River; it served as the border between Korea and China.
5. Sukhavati, a world that lacks the three unfortunate realms (of animals, hungry ghosts, and denizens of hell); rebirth in it was a common goal of Buddhist practice throughout East Asia. "Shravasti": the capital of Kosala, an ancient kingdom in northern India (in modern Uttar Pradesh), where the Buddha lived for twenty-five years.
6. The nobleman (d. ca. 720) who sponsored the casting of the images that this inscription commemorates.

7. Legendary hermits of the Han dynasty (202 b.c.e.–220 c.e.).
8. Figures in a poem by the great Chinese poet Tao Qian (365–427).
9. The Indian founder (5th century c.e.) of the Yogacara (literally, "practitioner of yoga") school of Buddhist philosophy, sometimes called Chittamatra (Mind Only).
1. A key treatise of the Yogacara school, attributed either to Asanga or to his younger brother Vasubandhu, whom he reportedly converted to Yogacara.
2. That is, a chapter of the *Zhuangzi* (*Book of Master Zhuang*; see above).
3. That is, the Buddhist community (sangha).

The Resurgence and Diversification of Daoism

THE SONG
(960–1279 C.E.)
AND YUAN
(1260–1368 C.E.)
DYNASTIES

During the Song (960–1279 C.E.) and Yuan (1260–1368 C.E.) dynasties, creativity and innovation in Daoism surged. As the religion produced new scriptures and liturgical manuals, developed new lineages and schools, incorporated local deities, exchanged ideas and practices with Buddhism (particularly Esoteric Buddhism), and spread much more widely throughout society, there emerged many of the key features that have remained significant within the Daoist tradition down to the present

This Yuan dynasty illustration is part of a woodblock print of the Uppermost *Highest Spirit Thunder Jade Pivot Thunderous Pearl Precious Scripture with Talismanic Seals*. It shows the Lord of Nine Heavens astride a dragon with a fierce countenance being empowered by the Highest Prince of Jade Purity. Thunder gods and other attendants help the Lord of Nine Heavens punish those who commit transgressions.

day. To fully understand and appreciate those developments requires knowing something more about the complicated and unstable history of the Song dynasty and its fall to the Mongols, who established the Yuan dynasty—the first foreign dynasty to conquer all of China.

SONG DYNASTY HISTORY: UNIFICATION AND FRAGMENTATION

The Song dynasty was a period of significant social, political, economic, technological, and religious changes and developments. A centralized bureaucratic ruling system returned, and the aristocratic families that had held power in the Tang dynasty (618–907) declined precipitously. Political and military power had already begun to fragment before the Tang dynasty fell, and localization only increased during the transitional Five Dynasties and Ten Kingdoms period (902–979). Aided by the reunification achieved under the Song, China made great advances in its mercantile economy, including growth in trade, agriculture, its monetary system, and its transportation networks, as well as in printing; as a result, urbanization increased as commercial cities formed, and literacy rates rose. The examination system that had begun in the Tang dynasty expanded and took on greater importance during the Song as a means to recruit officials. Successful aspirants to office had to spend years studying classical texts and cultivating artistic skills under the tutelage of a master. The revival of Confucianism during the Song led to reforms in the classical tradition—partially in response to Buddhism and Daoism—and the Neo-Confucian tradition that took shape in the eleventh century would have a profound impact on the next thousand years of Chinese history. For a span of roughly three centuries, China was the most advanced (and populous) society in the world.

But though the Song dynasty is rightly celebrated for its cultural achievements, it was never able to attain the preeminent position in East Asia enjoyed by the Han (202 B.C.E.–220 C.E.) and Tang dynasties. The Song managed its relationships with powerful non-Chinese states on its northern and western borders by relying on agreements and tribute offerings, while guarding against possible incursions. Ultimately, its efforts to protect the integrity of the Chinese domain failed. The Mongols, after years of attacking the Song's frontier fortifications, finally broke through and laid siege to its then-capital, Hangzhou; in surrendering, the dynasty ended.

The Song dynasty is divided into two periods, which take their names from the location of their respective capitals. The Northern Song (960–1127), whose capital was the northern city of Kaifeng (in modern Henan Province), ruled over most of North and South China. Its territory extended from the seas in the south and east to modern Sichuan in the west, excluding what is today Yunnan on the southern frontier. Two northern areas that eluded Song control, both held by non-Chinese people, were the Liao state of the Khitan (around Beijing) and, in the northwest, the Xia state of the Tangut. In 1115 the Khitan were attacked from the north by the Jurchen—yet another non-Chinese people, from eastern Manchuria. Initially the Song aided the Jurchen, but this alliance ended in 1126 when the Jurchen mounted a relentless attack on Kaifeng, forcing Song loyalists to relocate to the south. The Jurchen established their own dynasty, the Jin (1115–1234).

The Southern Song dynasty (1127–1279) established its new capital in Hangzhou (in present-day Zhejiang Province); its new northern boundary was just north of the Yangzi River. The southern and western borders remained nearly the same as they were during the Northern Song, and on the east it still stretched to the coast.

During the 1200s the Jurchen Jin dynasty and the Southern Song dynasty both fell to powerful Mongol warriors, led first by Genghis Khan (Chinggis Qan, 1162–1227) and then by his grandson Kubilai Khan (1215–1294), who completed the project of unifying China by defeating the Southern Song in 1279 and inaugurating the Yuan dynasty.

THE SONG DYNASTY RELIGIOUS LANDSCAPE: FROM IMPERIAL PATRONAGE TO LOCAL DIFFUSION

The late tenth to mid-fourteenth century can be characterized as an age of development and prosperity, despite the occasional crises caused by regular threats from non-Chinese peoples on the frontier. Its political schism and instability complicated but did not slow the growth of Daoism. Some new Daoist movements that began in the north traveled with the Song to the south, where after 1127 they were codified and elaborated on. At the same time, other Daoist schools developed under Jurchen rule in the north, while new innovations in the south also produced new schools. Indeed, in its religious renaissance during the Song, Daoism changed significantly from what it had been in the preceding Tang dynasty. The Song dynasty witnessed the birth of many new Daoist movements and textual revelations, fundamental liturgical and institutional transformations, and diffusion into local communities and a wider range of social groups—all laying the foundation for the forms of Daoism still visible in China today.

The religious landscape of the Song dynasty was populated by Buddhists, Daoists, Confucians, and a variety of popular local cults. For Buddhism, too, which already had large, thriving monastic institutions, the era was marked by doctrinal and ritual innovation. And elite scholar officials who mainly favored new forms of Confucianism—which developed into Neo-Confucianism—engaged in discussions with the learned monks of the Buddhist clergy and interacted with Daoists (see *Explanation of the Diagram of the Supreme Polarity*, or *Taijitu shuo*, and the "Biography of the Gentleman with No Name," or "Wuming jun zhuan").

Like the Tang dynasty rulers before them, some Song emperors forged connections with Daoism out of genuine conviction as well as a pragmatic belief that it could enhance their legitimacy. Although the Song's founding emperor, Taizu (r. 960–76), took a personal interest in and supported Buddhism, his successors patronized Daoism—albeit mixing in Esoteric Buddhist elements—as a means to provide religious sanction for their rule and to gain religious protection from incursions from the north. Taizu's brother, the emperor Taizong (r. 976–97), inaugurated a shift toward accepting Daoism at court. Taizong's son, the emperor Zhenzong (r. 998–1022), strengthened the rulers' ties to Daoism by asserting that the Yellow Emperor (Huangdi) was his ancestor, thereby providing himself—and the later Song emperors who echoed his assertion—with an even more venerable lineage than that of the Tang emperors, who had claimed descent from Laozi. Zhenzong venerated the Perfected Warrior (Zhenwu, also known as the Dark Warrior, Xuanwu), a Daoist deity associated with the north whom he placed at the forefront of a cult at the imperial court; he also created a vast network of temples staffed by Daoists who were designated government officials. In addition, Zhenzong established a laboratory for a court-sponsored Daoist alchemist to continue his elixir experiments (on the making of elixirs in the Song, see the *Scripture on the Golden Elixir of the Dragon and Tiger*, or *Jindan longhu jing*).

Imperial support for Daoism peaked during the reign of Emperor Huizong (r. 1101–25). Huizong's acceptance and support of Daoism was so pronounced that he, like Xuanzong in the Tang, has often been called a Daoist emperor. He sponsored the building of Daoist temples, participated in Daoist rituals, encouraged the inclusion of Daoist learning in the civil service examinations, awarded honorific court titles to Daoist priests, and oversaw the production of the first printed edition of the Daoist canon, which was completed in 1119. Huizong aided a range of Daoist traditions, from venerable schools of the past, such as the Celestial Masters (Tianshi), to those founded recently, such as the Divine Empyrean (Shenxiao). Moreover, he was openly critical of Buddhism and decreed that Buddhist monasteries be converted into Daoist abbeys. While Huizong's support for Daoism largely reflected the depth of his personal engagement with the religion, it also seems to have been part of a last-ditch effort to use religion to ward off the military advances of the Jurchens, whose conquest of the north he could not prevent. Historians—both secular and Buddhist—who are critical of Daoism have argued that its role in Huizong's regime was a significant cause of the empire's breakup.

The loss of North China did not lead to a complete collapse of the Song dynasty or its economy. On the contrary, the Southern Song dynasty prospered, with social, cultural, and economic growth fueled by trade and the development of vibrant urban centers. But as it became clear that the new government's material success would not translate into an ability to regain the north, Neo-Confucian thinkers turned their focus from large-scale social initiatives to reforms at the level of the local community, the family, and the individual. They saw a clear connection between individual behavior and the transformation of society. In the historical narrative of Daoism in the Southern Song there is a similar shift, focusing less on particular emperors and how their patronage affected Daoism than on the development of new Daoist schools and how (in ways not involving rulers) Daoism became more widely diffused through society.

A distinctive feature of the Daoist history of the Song dynasty was its varied and complex interaction with popular local cults. Some of the displaced Song viewed the south, where malaria and other diseases unknown in the north were common, as a region of pestilence, disease, and epidemics. That belief both inspired Daoists to develop rituals aimed at fending off those dangers and was used to justify the violent suppression of local gods and their spirit mediums as well as the destruction of their temples. For others, who instead saw the south as offering rich lands to support agriculture and a prosperous economy, the environment seemed less threatening. Thus some new Daoist movements developed by incorporating local cults; at the same time, some local cults tried to expand their reach and ingratiate themselves with the new rulers by assimilating imperium-wide Daoist traditions. During the Southern Song dynasty, the lines between Daoism and local cults blurred as new revelations brought local gods into the Daoist pantheon (see *Heard and Written by Yijian*, or *Yijian zhi*, and *The Scripture of the Responses and Proofs of the Divine Lord of Zitong, Expounded by the Heavenly Worthy of Primordial Beginning*, or *Yuanshi tianzun shuo Zitong dijun yingyan jing*).

DAOISM TAKES NEW FORMS

The new Daoist movements of the Song and Yuan periods centered primarily on new deities, newly revealed texts, new religious associations, and new ritual practices, and they also had a strong focus on healing. Owing to the development of printing and the concomitant rise of literacy, Daoism was better chronicled in the Song than in previous periods. Of the many new movements that arose during the Song—or developed from those nascent in the Tang and the Five Dynasties and Ten Kingdoms period—the most significant were the Divine Empyrean (Shenxiao) and Celestial Heart (Tianxin) traditions; others included Pure Tenuity (Qingwei), Youthful Incipience (Tongchu dafa), and the Pure and Luminous Way of Loyalty and Filial Obedience (Jingming zhongxiao dao). The rather exotic sounding names of movements such as Celestial Heart, Divine Empyrean, and Pure Tenuity derive from different ethereal celestial locations. During the late Song dynasty a new monastic form of Daoism known as Complete Perfection (Quanzhen) also appeared. Many older Daoist teachings were woven into the fabric of these new movements: one example is the Salvation through Refinement (*liandu*) rite (see *Great Lingbao Method of the Shangqing Heaven*, or *Shangqing Lingbao dafa*), a funerary ritual that involved fashioning an immortal body for the dead who are suffering in hell.

There are at least two further general developments across various Daoist lineages and ritual systems during the Song and Yuan dynasties that should be mentioned here. The first are Thunder Rituals (*leifa*, also called Thunder Rites), powerful exorcistic rituals intended to harness the power of thunder and summon thunder deities—usually local spirits who had been pacified and incorporated into Daoism (see *The Corpus of Daoist Ritual*, or *Daofa huiyuan*, and *A Vermilion Petition Memorializing the Thunder Court on the Matter of Deliberating Merit Titles*, or *Leifu zou shiyi xun danzhang*). The powers harnessed by the ritual master can be directed toward controlling recalcitrant demons, expelling evil, averting calamities, negotiating the labyrinthine world of the heavenly bureaucracy, or, as in later traditions, breaking open the gates of hell and setting free the dead. From the twelfth century onward Thunder Rituals spread widely: various systems developed, fused with regional exorcistic traditions (primarily during the Southern Song), and they strongly influenced the shape of later Daoism.

Daoism's second significant general development in the Song is inner alchemy (*neidan*), which complements the much older practice of external alchemy (*waidan*)—the manufacture of an elixir using base minerals. Inner alchemy interiorizes this practice, relying on highly symbolic descriptions that involve chemical terminology, the trigrams of the *Yijing* (*Book of Changes*), and the meditative conjunction of yin and yang. When successful, it can produce an inner elixir (*neidan*), the immortal embryo (*shengtai*), immortality, or, if all goes well, a state of union with the Dao itself. Thus,

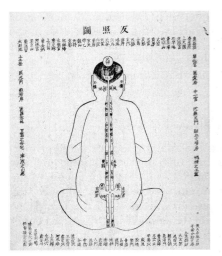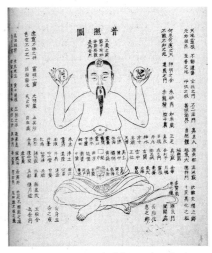

These woodblock prints from an illustrated compendium on internal alchemy (*neidan*), entitled *Directions for Endowment and Vitality* (*Xingming guizhi*), show the inside of the human body from two perspectives. In the view from the front, the three circles (one with a crow, one with a rabbit pounding the elixir of immortality, and one with an imbricated Chinese character) represent, respectively, the sun=yang (on the right), the moon=yin (on the left), and their integration (center). The internal alchemical crucible is visible in the figure's stomach. The view from the back depicts the spinal cord and the kidneys, with the right and left symbolizing yin and yang and each identified as a particular body god.

much of the esoteric vocabulary of inner alchemy scriptures relates to "reversal" and the goal of regaining the unity of the primordial Dao. Though its roots are in earlier periods, the practice achieved greater vitality, complexity, and relevance during the Song dynasty—particularly in connection with the Complete Perfection tradition—and developed further during the Ming (1368–1644) and Qing (1644–1911) dynasties, when a number of different lineages emerged. Many of the new scriptures of the Song are revealed works, but the teachings of inner alchemy are presented instead through poetry and essays (see *Awakening to Reality*, or *Wuzhen pian*, and *Essay on the Secret Essentials of the Recycled Elixir*, or *Huandan biyao lun*). Inner alchemy was closely related to forms of Buddhism in East Asia, especially their meditative tradition, and it in turn influenced the development of Neo-Confucianism (see *Explanation of the Diagram of the Supreme Polarity*, or *Taijitu shuo*).

The Rectifying Rites (or Correct Method) of the Celestial Heart (Tianxin zhengfa) Tradition

An example of a new Daoist tradition that claimed an older stratum of Daoist history as its own was the Rectifying Rites (or Correct Method) of the Celestial Heart (Tianxin zhengfa). The origin of this therapeutic and exorcistic movement, whose name refers to the Big Dipper, is unclear. Those who trace it back to the much earlier Celestial Masters give it a venerable pedigree and align it with the revival of that tradition in the Song. Others see the movement as beginning in 994, with the discoveries of secret texts by Rao Dongtian. According to a report by a later Celestial Heart adept, Rao saw a bright light emanating from one of the peaks on Mount Huagai (in present-day Jiangxi prefecture); when he dug into the earth at that spot, he found a container with the "secret formulas of the Celestial Heart." Not knowing what they were, he was advised to become a disciple of a figure named Tan Zixiao (fl. ca. 950), the founding patriarch of the Celestial Heart tradition.

Tan, when asked to interpret the relics unearthed earlier, had concluded that they were a secret set of esoteric talismans empowered by the Northern Emperor (Beidi) and his agents in the Department of Exorcism, including Heavenly Mugwort (Tianpeng), Black Killer (Heisha), and the Perfected Warrior (Zhenwu)—all members of the powerful Daoist celestial pantheon effective at warding off demons. Those talismans were said to have been passed down from Zhang Daoling himself and thus established a connection to the Celestial Masters tradition. According to Celestial Heart historians, after a hiatus that early tradition was restored by Tan and Rao and then continued and systematized by Deng Yougong (fl. late eleventh–early twelfth century), whose ritual liturgies—which he claimed were based on the secret texts found by Rao Dongtian—were incorporated into Huizong's Song Daoist canon. *Heard and Written by Yijian* (*Yijian zhi*), also known as *Record of Hearsay*, by Hong Mai (1123–1202) provides solid evidence that the Celestial Heart techniques enjoyed great popularity among scholar-officials intent on fending off the spread of "illicit cults."

The Divine Empyrean (Shenxiao) Tradition

Divine Empyrean Daoism began in the north under the reign of Emperor Huizong, who was himself initiated into the tradition and believed that its robust pantheon was incarnate in his array of court officials. He was the patron of Lin Lingsu (1076–1120), who in turn proclaimed that Huizong was the human manifestation of the aptly named Great Emperor of Long Life (Changsheng dadi), the main deity at the pinnacle of that pantheon. Lin Lingsu declared that he had received new revelations from the lofty Divine Empyrean heaven, which supplied protective rituals that clearly echoed earlier Upper Clarity (Shangqing) and Numinous Treasure (Lingbao) rites. An important Divine Empyrean text included in the Song canon—which would become the opening scripture in the Ming canon—was the voluminous *Wondrous Scripture of the Upper Chapters of the Numinous Treasure on Limitless Salvation* (*Lingbao wuliang duren shangpin miaojing*). An expanded and revised version of the Numinous Treasure tradition's *Scripture of Salvation* (*Duren jing*), it was intended to buttress the Divine Empyrean tradition and the Song imperial house.

Lin Lingsu played a key role in the movement's inception, but his influence lasted only about three years; he then mysteriously disappeared from the capital. The Divine Empyrean tradition continued without him, however, and after the fall of the Northern Song later figures like Wang Wenqing (1093–1153) ensured that it would survive and indeed flourish at the local level in the south. The Divine Empyrean tradition is a complex hybrid movement that combines new elements with features drawn from Upper Clarity, Numinous Treasure, Thunder Rites, local popular religion, and Esoteric Buddhism.

DAOISM UNDER THE YUAN DYNASTY (1260–1368): THE RISE OF THE COMPLETE PERFECTION (QUANZHEN) MONASTIC TRADITION

The Yuan was the first foreign dynasty to conquer all of China. The Yuan rulers were Mongols, a nomadic people highly skilled at war, who began to conquer and unite a vast area of Central Asia and northern China under the leadership of Genghis Khan. Under Genghis Khan's grandson Kubilai Khan, who defeated the Southern Song in 1279, the entirety of the Chinese domain was brought under Yuan control. The Mongols then began to rule and administer their large empire from a newly established capital in Dadu (modern Beijing). The expanded Yuan dynasty lasted only about a century; weakened by internal disputes, in 1368 the Yuan rulers were deposed by Zhu Yuanzhang (also known as Hongwu, 1328–1398), the future founding emperor of the Ming dynasty (1368–1644), who restored Chinese rule to a reunited country.

The religious climate under the Yuan was relatively tolerant, and the Mongol takeover had little effect on the practices of most Chinese. Representatives of all the major religions of the day (Buddhism, Daoism, Neo-Confucianism) vied for the patronage of the Mongol court, but the Mongols' main concern was to foster harmony among them. Buddhism, particularly Esoteric Tibetan Buddhism, was in an especially strong position, as the Mongols had a cultural affinity with other steppe-dwelling nomadic peoples, whom they eventually controlled.

Daoism also found a place for itself among the Yuan leaders while remaining important among the populace. Not all traditions fared equally well, however. Despite its great success in the south, the Divine Empyrean movement appeared to vanish in the late thirteenth century when Kubilai Khan ended the support for Daoism that had began under Genghis Khan and put the Celestial Masters in charge of the religion in southern China. Nevertheless, important elements of the Divine Empyrean movement deeply and permanently influenced the doctrines and rituals of Daoism.

The most significant new Daoist development of the period was the Complete Perfection (Quanzhen) tradition. Complete Perfection Daoism began slowly in the late twelfth century as an unofficial movement of Wang Zhe (also known as Wang Chongyang, 1113–1170) and his group of followers in North China (see *Redoubled Yang's Fifteen Discourses for the Establishment of the Doctrine*, or *Chongyang lijiao shiwu lun*). It started to grow under the leadership of Changchun (literally, "Perpetual Spring"; also known as Qiu Chuji, 1148–1227), who paid the Jurchens to grant it official religious status in 1197. A turning point was Qiu's trip from 1220 to 1222 to visit the Mongol leader Genghis Khan (see *Record of Perfected Perpetual Spring's Travels to the West*, or *Changchun zhenren xiyou ji*). Genghis Khan seems to have viewed Daoism as helpful to him in governing the Chinese population now under his rule. In the years following Qiu's visit, Complete Perfection religious institutions spread; some adherents saw embracing the religion as beneficial, thanks to Genghis Khan's decree exempting Daoists (as well as Nestorian Christians, Muslims, and Buddhists) from taxes and corvée labor (see "A Stele of on the Reconstruction of the Great Palace," or "Dachao chongjian Chunyang wanshou gong zhi bei"). The movement's growth was temporarily halted by Kubilai Khan, who ordered the burning of the recently compiled Daoist canon—the largest ever produced. Yet the

Complete Perfection movement continued to grow and spread throughout the Yuan dynasty and in the Qing. Today it is the primary Daoist tradition in China.

The most noteworthy innovation of the Complete Perfection Daoist order is its communal monastic structure, much like that of Buddhism: its monks and nuns take vows of celibacy and are governed in their daily lives by a disciplinary code. Nuns, and women more generally in the Yuan dynasty, played a prominent role within the movement. Sun Bu'er, one of Wang Zhe's major disciples who were known collectively as the Seven Perfected (Qizhen), was a woman, and about a third of the ordained clergy were nuns. As can be seen in Wang Zhe's *Redoubled Yang's Fifteen Discourses for the Establishment of the Doctrine*, Complete Perfection Daoism primarily incorporated inner alchemy practices aimed at immortality, which practitioners viewed as something psychological, not physical: the response of the adept's enlightened mind. The Complete Perfection tradition also drew liberally from Neo-Confucianism and Buddhism. Its canon included scriptures both Buddhist (the *Heart Sutra*) and Confucian (the *Classic of Filial Piety*), and Complete Perfection self-cultivation methods such as "seeing one's nature," "quiet sitting," and "illuminating one's mind" clearly resonate with Buddhist ideas and practices—particularly those associated with the Chan/Zen school.

During the Yuan dynasty, texts helped spread Complete Perfection. Reflecting the close relationship between Daoist ritual and theatrical performances, drama played an important role in its rising popularity (see *Zhongli of the Han Leads Lan Caihe to Enlightenment*, or *Han Zhong Li dutuo Lan Caihe*).

CANONIZING AND ANTHOLOGIZING SONG AND YUAN DYNASTY DAOISM

Texts dating from the innovative years of the Song and Yuan dynasties make up more than half of the most widely consulted Daoist canon, completed during the Ming dynasty in 1445. The invention of printing together with imperial support had aided the production of earlier canons, in which the many works created in this period were also well represented. Large ritual compendia and comprehensive reference works also appeared during the Song and Yuan dynasties, consolidating knowledge and reflecting Daoism's development into a mature tradition conscious of its own history. A good example of such works is the voluminous *Seven Lots from the Bookbag of the Clouds* (*Yunji qiqian*). This valuable anthology of writings from the early eleventh century draws together scriptures from different Daoist lineages, some with prefaces ascribed to Emperor Zhenzong. It includes not just texts on diverse subjects, such as cosmogony, rituals, breathing exercises, and elixir production, but also poetry and biography.

The Song and Yuan dynasties were remarkable epochs in Chinese history and the development of Daoism. Even as it resisted and sometimes fell to foreign invaders, China experienced unprecedented economic, agricultural, and cultural advances fueled by impressive technological innovations, and Daoism underwent a renaissance that fundamentally reshaped the tradition. Its institutional and popular success would rise and fall in the subsequent Ming and Qing dynasties, in repeated cycles of creative growth and decline, but Daoism would never regain the heights it reached in the Tang, Song, and Yuan periods.

THE SCRIPTURE ON THE GOLDEN ELIXIR OF THE DRAGON AND TIGER
(*Jindan longhu jing*)

The three excerpts below from the *Scripture on the Golden Elixir of the Dragon and Tiger* (*Jindan longhu jing*) are quoted consecutively in a collection of textual fragments in the *Divine Grades of the Elixir Methods from the Various Lineages* (*Zhujia shenpin danfa*). That anthology of alchemical texts from different periods—which is included in the Daoist canon—was compiled and edited by Meng Yaofu (Xuanzhen zi, fl. ca. 1160); it focuses on external alchemy (*waidan*), the making of elixirs that are then ingested. The passages from the *Scripture on the Golden Elixir of the Dragon and Tiger* offer valuable insights into alchemy during the Song dynasty (960–1279). At a time when alchemy had shifted largely toward internal alchemy (*neidan*)—a self-cultivation technique based on meditation, visualization, and the creation of elixirs inside one's own body—some Daoists clearly were still concerned with external alchemy and the compounding of elixirs (especially the "cyclically transformed elixir") that would enable them to attain longevity, advance up the spiritual hierarchy, and control deities.

PRONOUNCING GLOSSARY

Daode jing: *dow-duh ching*
Jindan longhu jing: *chin-dawn lowng-hu ching*

Laozi: *lao-tzu*
Shennong: *shun-noung*

Marvelous Instructions on the Inner Secrets and Real Writs of the Dragon and Tiger

The [teachings of the] Great Elixir of the Dragon and Tiger arose with the Three Sovereigns (Fuxi, Suiren, and Shennong)[1] and were continuously passed down from High Antiquity, orally transmitted and memorized by heart without ever having been written down. Since the Five Emperors (the Yellow Lord, Zhuan Xu, Yao, Shun, Yu),[2] the methods first came to circulate in the world, and in the succeeding ages multitudes attained the Way. Since not even one or two of the Utmost Men[3] personally transmitted the oral instructions, how much greater is it than the Five Thousand Character Text (i.e., the *Daode jing*) passed on by Laozi and the teachings of the Tripitaka[4] issued by the Buddha, which merely expound the principles of non-activity and seeing Buddha-nature [respectively]? To be dead while alive—just preserving your inborn nature intact or creating gods of empty brilliance—will never make you able to become as invincible as the Cyclically Transformed Elixir. [How much better] to remain undyingly alive, protecting the Soaring

TRANSLATED BY Lowell Skar.

1. Mythical rulers of predynastic China.
2. Legendary rulers who followed the Three Sovereigns; Yu was credited with founding the first dynasty, the Xia (ca. 2070–ca. 1600 B.C.E.).
3. Sometimes translated as "Accomplished Men";

this title goes back to the *Zhuangzi*, where it refers to a sage of the highest accomplishment.
4. The canon (literally, "three baskets"; Sanskrit) of Buddhism. On the *Daode jing* (*The Scripture of the Way and Its Virtue*), see above.

Transcendents without losing [your] inner constitution with these Genuine Methods in the activist mode.

Although not a few divine transcendents[5] from antiquity to the present have attained the Way, none have mentioned anything about the Cyclically Transformed Elixir. This is because This Way is of utmost greatness, and may not be carelessly divulged. If you only teach people the methods of absorbing or emitting the radiances of the sun and moon, circuiting the seminal essence and circulating the *qi*,[6] preserving unity by concentrating on spirits, retaining the seminal essence by [the ritualized sex of] riding women, or ingesting medicines of plants, the Five Metals or the Eight Minerals, even though you will temporarily extend your allotted number of years well beyond that of common people, you will ultimately lose the path of Everlasting Life. If you come upon waters, fires, swords, armies, poisonous creatures and wild beasts, poisonous medicines and evil calamities of the spirits, they will damage the inborn nature and natural endowments, and you will be unable to leave the Grand Cycles of Cosmic Creation. This being the case, none of the thousand ordinary methods will let you endure for long.

How could you not have noticed that all of the ancients whose entire families soared aloft [into the Heavens] did so through the powers of the most treasured, most revered, most valued, and most marvelous Great Cyclically Transformed Elixir? "Cyclically Transformed" means "returning back home" and "Elixir" is the name of the color crimson. This is [the process of] cinnabar exuding Realized Mercury, which, when blended with lead, becomes the Yellow Sprouts. The Yellow Sprouts once again become cinnabar. When fire subdues Cinnabar, it becomes the Cyclically Transformed Elixir. Whenever there are such wonders of cyclically reverting, the [product] is able to make the old become young, the dead revive, and the withered flourish. Sprinkling it on potsherds will turn them into most treasured [items]. With such efficacies of the Divine Sage, how could they not be great?

The Three Grades of Great Cyclically Transformed Elixir

The Superior Grade of the Nine Times Recycled, Golden Liquor, and Langgan[7] Roseate Gem are the Great Cyclically Transformed Elixirs treasured in the Supreme Heavens and have not been passed down to the world. The Middle Grade of the Great Elixir of the Dragon and Tiger and the Inferior Grade of Eight Mineral [Elixirs] that transform into Quicksilver[8] constitute the Nine Grades of the Divine Elixirs [available to human beings]. Ever since the Yellow Emperor (Huang Di) of Xuanyuan refined the elixir and soared aloft [into the Heavens], the powers of Our Great Elixir of the Dragon and Tiger have been most great! Upon entering the mouth, a single spatula [of it] will forever fix [the natural endowments] and extend the years, get rid of heteropathic and restore orthopathic[9] [vital energies],

---

5. Daoists who have achieved extraordinary powers and a higher form of existence (often translated "immortals").
6. Vital energy, breath (pneuma).
7. A growth of mythical trees (also the name of an actual lustrous blue-green gemstone).

8. Mercury.
9. Treatment to restore normal structure and health, without the use of drugs. "Heteropathic": treatment that relies on traditional medical practice.

instantly expel the [body's] Three [Deadly] Corpse-worms and Nine [Mortal] Creatures, and secure [the divinizing energies of] Essence and Spirit in the [lower] Elixir-Field without letting them escape.

The countless Divine Transcendents who attained the Way in High Antiquity completely concealed the principles of the Cyclically Transformed Elixir. Although the Elixir Scriptures in the mundane world of dust sketch out its broad outlines, its abstruse fundamentals are totally hidden in secrecy with no oral explanations. While some in later generations have hankered after the Way, they had no starting point and blindly stumbled about on their own into decrepit old age.

I will now divulge the Heavenly Key and straightforwardly write out the method's orally transmitted explanations in order to ensure determined men who want to cultivate the Way of inborn nature and natural endowments that they need not doubt they are being deluded.

Oral Instructions on the Realized Dragon and Realized Tiger

The Realized Dragon is the Quicksilver within Cinnabar, and is the product of the descent into the ground of the Solar Light of the Grand Radiance as Realized Qi called Mercury. The Realized Tiger is the White Silver within Black Lead, and is the product of the descent into the ground of the Lunar Florescence of the Grand Darkness as Realized Qi known as Lead. Because these two treasures are endowed with the Realized Qi of the Solar Essence and Lunar Florescence, Lead contains Qi and Mercury is fundamentally Formless. None of the revered seventy-two minerals surpass Lead and Mercury in their being able to produce the Dragon and Tiger. The *Scripture on the Great Cyclically Transformed Elixir* says, "There is proof that live [unfired?] Quicksilver can secure the dead, and dead [fired?] Quicksilver can secure the living right before the eyes." How could the ranks of the walking corpses who fail to seek the Great Elixir possess spiritual powers like these? Those who come upon it have a long-held Transcendent Lot as the inherited blessings of their ancestors. Those who come upon this method should keep it secret and hidden, preserving it and being careful about divulging it lightly, since anyone who so divulges it will be punished [by Heaven]. Even though you may be as close as father and son [to someone], do not speak about it. If you come upon an Utmost Man with the same ambition who is in tune with the Way, you may transmit the Oral Instructions.

AWAKENING TO REALITY
(Wuzhen pian)

ZHANG BODUAN

Awakening to Reality (*Wuzhen pian*), written by Zhang Boduan (987?–1082)—considered the first patriarch of the Southern Lineage (Nanzong) of internal alchemy—is one of the most important Daoist alchemical texts. Containing a rich array of Buddhist technical terms, this collection of eighty-one poems is also included in the Buddhist canon and in a variety of Confucian anthologies. It is widely understood as a commentary on (or elaboration of) *The Seal of the Unity of the Three, in Accordance with the Book of Changes* (*Zhouyi cantong qi*; see above), but it has also been interpreted as a manual of sexual techniques as well as other bodily cultivation practices (such as breathing and gymnastics).

Awakening to Reality appears to have been directed at fairly advanced practitioners, since it provides little introductory information. The poems are full of metaphors, allusions, and symbolic language, making them both difficult to interpret and open to many interpretations. The Dragon and Tiger, for example, symbolize True Yin (the trigram Li ☲, which is also the Golden Tripod) and True Yang (the trigram Kan ☵, which is also the Jade Pond), respectively, and thus are also associated with the two main alchemical ingredients. Those two trigrams, which represent the conditioned state of the world we live in, are the result of the union of Qian ☰, the celestial primordial unconditioned state, and Kun ☷, the alchemical laboratory.

Its textual obscurity has made *Awakening to Reality* the object of many commentaries, which have sought to draw out its meaning and provide guidelines for adepts to put into practice. Zhang Boduan's overarching concern in the sixteen poems below is with the evanescent nature of human life—"a whole lifetime is a bubble / floating on the water"—and the need to study the Golden Elixir (which the poems tell us we all already possess) in order to attain celestial immortality or transcendence. He also offers a rather trenchant critique of other Daoist practices, such as the ingestion of herbal medicines and external elixirs, techniques of exercise and breathing, and visualization methods.

PRONOUNCING GLOSSARY

Wuzhen pian: *wu-chun pien*

Poem 1

> If you do not search for the Great Dao
> and do not leave the delusive paths,
> you may be endowed with worthiness and talent,
> but would you be a great man?
> One hundred years of age
> are a spark sent forth from a stone,
> a whole lifetime
> is a bubble floating on the water.

TRANSLATED BY Fabrizio Pregadio.

You only covet profit and emolument
and search for nothing more than glory and fame,
without considering that your body
covertly withers and decays.
Let me ask you—Even if you pile up gold
as high as one of the sacred mountains,
bribing impermanence would be impossible,
wouldn't it?

Poem 2

Whilst human life may have
a span of one hundred years,
longevity or early death, exhaustion or accomplishment
cannot be known in advance.
Yesterday you were on the street
riding on horseback,
this morning in your coffin
you are already a sleeping corpse.

Your wife and wealth are cast off,
they are not in your possession;
retribution for your faults is about to come—
now you can hardly fool yourself.
If you do not search for the Great Medicine,[1]
how can you ever come upon it?
But coming upon it and not refining it,
this is truly foolish and insane.

Poem 3

If you study immortality,
you should study celestial immortality:
only the Golden Elixir
is the highest principle.
When the two things meet,
emotions and nature join one another;
where the five agents[2] are whole,
Dragon and Tiger[3] coil.

Rely in the first place on *wu* and *ji*[4]
that act as go-betweens,

---

1. According to a later commentator, this refers to finding a master and embarking on the path of self-cultivation.
2. Wood, fire, earth, metal, and water. They are the foundation of the theory of five phases—a set of systematic associations between different categories, which describe the operations of nature.
3. True Yin within yang (trigram Li ☲) and True Yang within yin (trigram Kan ☵), respectively. When they coil, each returns its essence back to the other, producing the original trigrams Qian ☰ and Kun ☷. Yin and yang are the complementary forces that unite to form the Dao: yin, a term

that originally referred to the shady side of a valley, by extension came to be associated with the dark, earth, dampness, and passivity—the female principle; yang, a term that originally referred to the sunny side of a valley, by extension came to be associated with the light, heaven, dryness, and activity—the male principle. On the trigrams and hexagrams, see the introduction to *The Seal of the Unity of the Three, in Accordance with the Book of Changes* (*Zhouyi cantong qi*), above.
4. Two of the ten Celestial Stems (elements of the Chinese calendar); they represent yang and yin and are associated with earth in the five phases system.

then let husband and wife
join together and rejoice.
Just wait until your work is achieved
to have audience at the Northern Portal,[5]
and in the radiance of a ninefold mist
you will ride a soaring phoenix.

Poem 4

This is the method of wondrous Reality
within Reality,
where I depend on myself, alone
and different from all others.
I know for myself how to invert,
starting from Li ☲ and Kan ☵:
who else can comprehend the floating and the sinking,
and determine the host and the guest?

If in the Golden Tripod you want to detain
the Mercury within the Vermilion,
first from the Jade Pond[6] send down
the Silver within the Water.
The cycling of fire in the spiritual work
before the light of dawn
will cause the whole wheel of the Moon[7] to appear
in the Deep Pool.[8]

Poem 5

The Tiger leaps, the Dragon soars,
wind and waves are rough;
in the correct position of the center
the Mysterious Pearl[9] is born.
A fruit grows on the branches
and ripens at the end of season:
could the Infant in the womb
be different from this?

Between south and north, the ancestral source
causes the hexagrams to revolve;
from daybreak to dusk, the fire times
accord with the Celestial Axis.
You should know the great concealment
while you dwell in the marketplace:
what need is there of entering the mountains' depths
and keeping yourself in stillness and solitude?

5. The gate at the center of heaven.
6. The mouth.
7. The elixir that has been produced.
8. The lower Cinnabar Field (in the abdomen).

9. The inner elixir, or Golden Elixir, which every human possesses and which represents his or her own realized state.

Poem 6

All people on their own have
the Medicine of long life;[1]
it is only for insanity and delusion
that they cast it away to no avail.
When the Sweet Dew[1] descends,
Heaven and Earth join one another;
where the Yellow Sprout[2] grows,
Kan ☵ and Li ☲ conjoin.

A frog in a well would say
that there are no dragon lairs,
and how could a quail on a fence know
that phoenix nests exist?
When the Elixir ripens, spontaneously
Gold fills the room:[3]
what is the point of seeking herbs
and learning how to roast the reeds?[4]

*   *   *

Poem 8

Desist from refining the Three Yellows
and the Four Spirits:[5]
if you seek the common medicines,
none of them is the real thing.
When Yin and Yang are of one kind,
they conjoin;
when the Two Eights match one another,
they merge.

The Sun is red at the pool's bottom,[6]
and Yin wondrously is exhausted;
the Moon is white at the mountain's peak,[7]
and the Medicine puts forth new sprouts.
The people of our times should comprehend
True Lead and Mercury:
they are not the common sand
and quicksilver.[8]

*   *   *

1. The elixir (a term used by practitioners of internal alchemy).
2. The initial stage of the production of the elixir.
3. That is, a specific location within the body, or the body as a whole.
4. Two methods used in external alchemy.
5. Cinnabar, quicksilver, lead, and saltpeter. "The Three Yellows": realgar (an orange-red mineral), orpiment (a yellow mineral), and sulfur. These are ingredients used in external alchemy.
6. The lower Cinnabar Field. "The Sun": a symbol for Pure Yang as it exists in the lower Cinnabar Field.
7. The upper Cinnabar Field (in the head). "The Moon": a symbol for Pure Yang as it exists in the upper Cinnabar Field.
8. In external alchemy, mercury (quicksilver) is refined from cinnabar (the ore of mercury).

Poem 10

Hold True Lead firmly
and seek with intention;
do not let time
easily slip by.
Just let the earthly *po*-soul[9]
seize the Mercury in the Vermilion,[1]
and you will have the celestial *hun*-soul[2] by itself
controlling the Metal in the Water.[3]

One can say that when the Way is lofty,
Dragon and Tiger are subdued,
and it may be said that when Virtue is hefty,
gods and demons are restrained.
Once you know that your longevity
equals that of Heaven and Earth,
troubles and vexations have no way
to rise to your heart.

*   *   *

Poem 12

In plants and trees, Yin and Yang
are equal to one another;
let either be lacking,
and they do not bloom.
First the green leaves open,
for Yang is the first to sing,
then a red flower blossoms,[4]
as Yin follows later.

This is the constant Dao
that everyone uses daily;
but returning to the True Origin—
does anyone know about this?
I announce to all of you
who study the Dao:
if you do not comprehend Yin and Yang,
do not fiddle around.

Poem 13

If you do not comprehend that within the Mystery
there is an inversion and then again an inversion,

---

9. The white soul, linked to the earth; in internal alchemy, it refers to True Yang that is found within True Yin.
1. True Yin within yang.
2. The light cloud soul, linked with heaven; in internal alchemy, it refers to True Yin that is found within True Yang.
3. True Yang within yin. This mutual control makes possible the conjoining that creates the elixir.
4. The colors refer to the early stage of elixir production (green) and its completion (red).

how can you know the beautiful lotus bud
within the Fire?[5]
Take the White Tiger back home,[6]
and nourish it:
you will give birth to a bright pearl
as round as the Moon.

Desist from guarding the furnace of the Medicine
and from watching over the fire times:
just settle the breathing of the Spirit
and rely on the celestial spontaneity.
When all of Yin is entirely dispelled,
the Elixir ripens:
you leap out of the cage of the mundane,
and live ten thousand years.

* * *

Poem 15

If you do not comprehend that True Lead[7]
is the proper ancestor,
the ten thousand practices[8]
will all be vain exercises:
leaving your wife and staying in idle solitude
will separate Yin and Yang,
and cutting off the grains will only cause
your stomach to be empty.

Herbs and trees and gold and silver[9]
are all dregs,
clouds and mist and Sun and Moon[1]
partake of haziness;
and as for exhaling and inhaling,[2]
or visualizing and meditating,[3]
these pursuits are not the same
as the Golden Elixir.

Poem 16

The scriptures of the Immortals, ten thousand scrolls,
all tell one thing:
only the Golden Elixir
is the ancestor, the root.

5. A reference to the movement of the True Yang line (the lotus bud) at the heart of the trigram Kan ☵ (water) to its place within the trigram Li ☲ (fire).
6. That is, into the trigram Kan ☵.
7. True Yang within True Yin; it is therefore the key ingredient in completing the internal elixir.
8. Ingesting herbs and alchemical elixirs, prac-

tices followed earlier (as were celibacy and abstaining from staple foods).
9. That is, herbal medicines and alchemical elixirs.
1. That is, the practice of ingesting the essences of the Sun and Moon.
2. Breathing practices.
3. The practice of visualizing internal body gods.

Relying on the other in the position of Kun ☷,
it comes to life and acquires a body,
then it is planted within the house of Qian ☰,
in the Palace of Conjunction.[4]

Do not marvel that the mechanism of Heaven
is now entirely disclosed:
it is only because students
are deluded and dull.
If you are able to understand
the central meaning of my poems,
you will behold at once the Most High Elders[5]
of the Three Clarities.[6]

4. This passage seems to be saying that the adept should add True Yang (the solid line), which is hidden in Kun ☷—as seen in the yang line within the trigram Kan ☵—to Li ☲ (the Palace of Conjunction, hidden within Kun ☷) in order to complete Qian ☰.

5. The Celestial Worthy of Primordial Beginning (*Yuanshi tianzun*), Celestial Worthy of Numi-nous Treasure (*Lingbao tianzun*), and Celestial Worthy of the Way and Its Virtue (*Daode tianzun*).

6. The three high heavens within Daoism: Great Clarity (Taiqing), Upper Clarity (Shang-qing), and Jade Clarity (Yuqing), from lowest to highest.

A SONG FOR LIU, A COMRADE OF THE DAO, OF WHITE TIGER CAVE
(*Zeng bailongdong Liu daoren ge*)

ZHANG BODUAN

A *Song for Liu, a Comrade of the Dao, of White Tiger Cave* (*Zeng bailongdong Liu daoren ge*) reiterates the main points of our previous selection, *Awakening to Reality* (*Wuzhen pian*), and it is usually attributed to that work's author, Zhang Boduan (987?–1082). This song similarly criticizes those who consume medicinal herbs in the hope of attaining longevity or immortality. Here, comrade Liu is instead exhorted to get to work compounding his internal elixir, which is described in embryological language, and to engage in meditative concentration so that he does not fall into an undesirable rebirth.

PRONOUNCING GLOSSARY

Zeng bailongdong Liu daoren ge: *zuhng bai-lung-tung liu tao-run guh*

Zhang Boduan: *chang bow-do-an*

The running of jade, the flying of gold; the two luminous bodies move hurriedly. As soon as the news of the blooming of the flowers is heard, then the frost of the autumn follows closely thereafter. It was in vain that *Jian* was proud of his long life of a thousand years. For this is only as long as the glare of lightning upon the clouds. The glare of lightning! A great speed! A hundred years (of living) amounts to about thirty thousand days, during which the cold seasons and the hot seasons fry and boil (beat, press) one another. Imperceptibly boyhood vanishes easily into the silence. Even though you have many sons and grandsons before your eyes, yet your affection for them becomes a matter of anxiety. At the time when your energy is exhausted and when your body is going to decay, who then can teach you how to continue your life and to let yourself stay for a longer while? A longer while for staying! One has no means of contriving it! Eventually you will let your life go back like the passing of water down the stream.

Look at the ancient people, the saints and the sages. How many of them could know how to maintain their lives in the world? Maintain lives in the world! Yet means are available. However, it is ungratifying that the people nowadays are unthoughtful, and attempt to search for grass and wood from the mountains.[1]

Surrendering lead, controlling mercury, and staining the *dan* (medicine, red color) of *yang*.[2] Stain the *yang dan*! It is an entirely different thing (from grass and wood). One must obtain the red blood from *kan*,[3] and must bring it over to the position of *li* for controlling the essence of *yin*.[4] The matching and the blending should have their definite time. The time must be accurately chosen, and it is necessary that a matchmaker should be present. *Jingong* (golden fellow) and *chanü* (elegant lady) will be made to marry each other. *Jingong* likes very much to ride on the white tiger's back, whereas *chanü* often drives about upon the body of the scarlet dragon.[5]

The tiger comes down from the autumn mountain while the dragon goes up swiftly from the green gulf. The waves roll and roar like water boiling in a *ding*.[6] *Huangpo* (yellow dame, the matchmaker) and *dinglao* (old fellow) then assist in striking up terror and in beating up power. *Qian* and *kun* (heaven and earth) are then shaken up and the spirits and ghosts stir about.

After a while the battle ceases. The clouds and rains withdraw. The mysterious pearl[7] is planted deeply in the soil. Its roots and sprouts grow out gradually. The *zhenjing* (true essence) is then used to irrigate it from time to time. After ten months it comes out from the womb, and is ingested by the mouth. He (the worker) then feels that his material body already possesses its efficacious properties.

TRANSLATED BY Tenny L. Davis and Chao Yün-ts'ung

1. An allusion to the earlier practice of ingesting herbs to gain longevity.
2. The male principle; the term originally referred to the sunny side of a valley, and by extension it came to be associated with the light, heaven, dryness, and activity.
3. The trigram Kan ☵; on the trigrams, see the introduction to *The Seal of the Unity of the Three, in Accordance with the Book of Changes* (*Zhouyi cantong qi*), above.
4. The female principle; the term originally referred to the shady side of a valley, and by extension it came to be associated with the dark, earth, dampness, and passivity. "*Li*": the trigram Li ☲.
5. In other words, the White Tiger (male, yang) and the Red Dragon (female, yin) are conjoined.
6. A bronze vessel with three legs and two handles; used primarily for ritual offerings and cooking food (Shang Dynasty, ca. 1600–1045 B.C.E.).
7. The elixir.

This subject is little known in the world. It is unlikely that ordinary people will hear of it. If your former life has not given you in your bones an affinity for *xian* (immortal, the qualities of *xian*, the art of immortality), how can you meet it (the medicine) easily? When you meet it, you should work on the compounding—because time passes as fast as an arrow. Whenever one desires to catch fish, he ought first to construct the net. Otherwise, he can only sigh in vain beside the pond. I have heard that you, *Liu* comrade, have studied the medicines for many years. Why don't you concentrate your mind on the compounding of mercury and lead? Do not let the candle be blown out by the wind. Otherwise, on the six-fold way of *Lunhui* (transmigration, the revolving re-union)[8] one can be called only when it is too late to murmur to heaven.

Nowadays, people are becoming unreliable. All those who dress in cotton clothes, and pretend that they are Daoists, cannot answer even a word and keep their mouths shut as if they were dumb, when you choose to inquire of them about what *jin* (gold) and *mu* (wood) are going to be. They may mean the practices of taking doses of *qi* (ethereal essence)[9] and of ceasing to eat food. But these are other doors and courts which lead one far away from success. Do you not see the teachings in the Song on Clearing Up Perplexity? The song suggests that the grand One, which contains the truth, is the best method. One should not say that the song's words are nonsense. The difficulty lies rather in the fact that the common people are unable to understand (recognize) them.

I know that you, *Liu* comrade, have the same mind (heart) as I do, and so I dare to discuss the subject with you frankly.

8. The six paths of Buddhist rebirth: as a god, demigod, human, ghost, animal, or denizen of hell.

9. For example, of the sun and moon; such practices were followed earlier.

EXPLANATION OF THE DIAGRAM OF
THE SUPREME POLARITY
(*Taijitu shuo*)

ZHOU DUNYI

The Song dynasty (960–1279) witnessed a major Confucian revival, now referred to as "Neo-Confucianism," that has come to be primarily associated with the synthesis of ideas formulated by Zhu Xi (1130–1200). Zhu Xi himself claimed that the first real Chinese sage since Mencius (ca. 371–ca. 289 B.C.E.)—who had carried forward and defended the teachings of Confucius (551–479 B.C.E.)—was Zhou Dunyi (1017–1073), whose impact on Neo-Confucianism was crucial. His influence on the brothers Cheng Hao (1032–1085) and Cheng Yi (1033–1107), on whose ideas Zhu Xi drew, was especially strong.

As the translator Joseph Adler notes, one of Zhou Dunyi's best-known contributions to the Neo-Confucian tradition is *Explanation of the Diagram of the Supreme Polarity (Taijitu shuo)*. But because the diagram it explained was attributed to Chen Tuan (906–989), a Daoist master, and because it used technical vocabulary derived from Daoist texts and practices, the work has provoked much controversy in the Confucian tradition down to the present day.

Daoist texts offer many different versions of the Diagram of the Supreme Polarity (Taijitu), also referred to as the Diagram of the Great Ultimate. There, the term "Supreme Polarity" (or "Great Ultimate") refers to the origin of the world: the first division of the primordial unity into two (yin and yang); then into the five agents (*wuxing*), or five phases (water, fire, wood, metal, and earth); and then into male and female. However, the Confucian and Daoist interpretations of the diagram differ in a crucial respect: whereas the Confucians read the diagram from the top down as describing the genesis of the world, the Daoists read it from the bottom up as capturing the process of reversal (or inversion) involved in the generation of the internal elixir (*neidan*), which enables the initiate to again grasp the undifferentiated state.

PRONOUNCING GLOSSARY

Taijitu shuo: *tai-chee-tu shu-oh*   Zhou Dunyi: *chou do-un-yee*

Non-Polar and yet Supreme Polarity![1] The Supreme Polarity in activity generates yang; yet at the limit of activity it is still. In stillness it generates yin; yet at the limit of stillness it is also active. Activity and stillness alternate; each is the basis of the other. In distinguishing yin and yang, the Two Modes are thereby established.

The alternation and combination of yang and yin generate water, fire, wood, metal, and earth.[2] With these Five [Phases of] qi[3] harmoniously arranged, the Four Seasons proceed through them. The Five Phases are simply yin and yang; yin and yang are simply the Supreme Polarity; the Supreme Polarity is fundamentally Non-Polar. [Yet] in the generation of the Five Phases, each one has its nature.

The reality of the Non-Polar and the essence of the Two [Modes] and Five [Phases] mysteriously combine and coalesce. "The Way of *qian* becomes the male; the Way of *kun* becomes the female";[4] the two qi stimulate each other, transforming and generating the myriad things. The myriad things generate and regenerate, alternating and transforming without end.

Only humans receive the finest and most spiritually efficacious. Once formed, they are born; when spirit is manifested, they have intelligence; when their fivefold natures[5] are stimulated into activity, good and evil are distinguished and the myriad affairs ensue.

The sage settles these [affairs] with centrality, correctness, humaneness, and rightness (the Way of the Sage is simply humaneness, rightness, centrality, and correctness) and emphasizes stillness. (Without desire, [he is] therefore still.) In so doing he establishes the ultimate of humanity. Thus the

---

TRANSLATED BY Joseph Adler. All bracketed additions are the translator's.

1. Here, that which causes the differentiation of the original state of primordial chaos (sometimes equivalent to the Dao) into yin and yang (the complementary forces that unite to form the Dao: yin, a term that originally referred to the shady side of a valley, by extension came to be associated with the dark, earth, dampness, and passivity—the female principle; yang, a term that originally referred to the sunny side of a valley, by extension came to be associated with the light, heaven, dryness, and activity—the male principle). Supreme Polarity is also the name of one of the Daoist heavens and one of the deities within the Daoist pantheon, among other meanings.

2. The five agents, which are the foundation of the theory of five phases—a set of systematic associations between different categories, which describe the operations of nature.
3. Vital energy, breath (pneuma).
4. The trigram Qian ☰ is made up entirely of yang lines; the trigram Kun ☷ of yin. On the trigrams and hexagrams, see the introduction to *The Seal of the Unity of the Three, in Accordance with the Book of Changes (Zhouyi cantong qi)*, above.
5. Humaneness, righteousness, propriety, knowledge, and integrity (the five Confucian virtues).

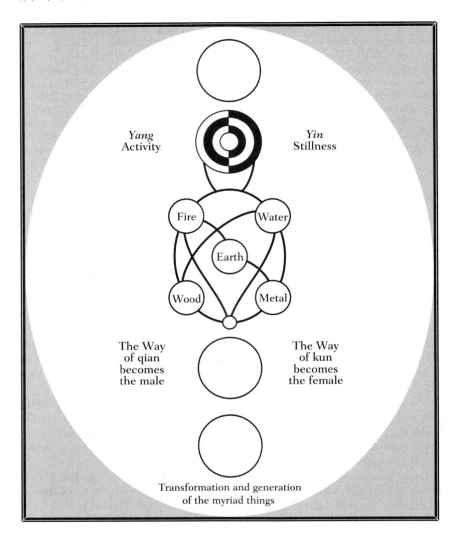

sage's "virtue equals that of Heaven and Earth; his clarity equals that of the sun and moon; his timeliness equals that of the four seasons; his good fortune and bad fortune equal those of ghosts and spirits." The superior person cultivates these and has good fortune. The inferior person rejects these and has bad fortune.

Therefore [the *Classic of Changes*[6] says], "Establishing the Way of Heaven, [the sages] speak of yin and yang; establishing the Way of Earth they speak of yielding and firm [hexagram lines]; establishing the Way of Humanity they speak of humaneness and rightness." It also says, "[The sage] investigates beginnings and follows them to their ends; therefore he understands death and birth." Great indeed is [the *Classic of*] *Changes*! Herein lies its perfection.

---

6. The *Yijing* (traditionally dated to the 12th century B.C.E.), a volume of divination and cosmology that is one of the Five Classics of the Confucian tradition; it contains the trigrams and hexagrams.

BIOGRAPHY OF THE GENTLEMAN WITH NO NAME
(*Wuming jun zhuan*)

SHAO YONG

Though Shao Yong (1012–1077) never served in an official position, preferring to live a simple life, he has been held in high esteem throughout Chinese history as a philosopher of wide learning who was also well versed in fortune-telling and prognostication. He was respected for his poetry, which tended to be colored by Chan (Zen) Buddhist images and Daoist ideas. Shao Yong considered himself a Confucian, but he was highly knowledgeable about Buddhism and Daoism. As the translator Alan J. Berkowitz notes, there are strong Daoist overtones in his "Biography of the Gentleman with No Name" ("Wuming jun zhuan"), an account—perhaps based on his own life story—of a peerless Confucian individual.

PRONOUNCING GLOSSARY

Shao Yong: *shao yung*
Wuming jun zhuan: *woo-ming choon chuan*

The Gentleman with No Name was born in the Ji area and grew old in the Yu area.[1] When he was ten he sought to learn from the people of his village, and subsequently exhausted the insights of the villagers. When he left them behind, of his dregs he had cast out one or two parts in ten. At twenty he sought to learn from the people of the district, and subsequently exhausted the insights of the district's people. When he left them behind, of his dregs he had cast out three or four parts in ten. At thirty he sought to learn from the people of the state, and subsequently exhausted the insights of the state's people. When he left them behind, of his dregs he had cast out five or six parts in ten. At forty he sought to learn from the past and the present, and subsequently exhausted the insights of the past and the present. When he left them behind, of his dregs he had cast out eight or nine parts in ten. At fifty he sought to learn from Heaven and Earth, and subsequently exhausted the insights of Heaven and Earth. When he wished to leave them behind, of his dregs there was nothing he could cast out.

At the beginning, the villagers wondered whether he was peculiar and asked the people of the district, who said, "This man is adept at keeping company with others; how can you call him peculiar?" Later, the people of the district wondered whether he was superficial and asked the people of the state, who said, "This man does not indiscriminately have relations with others; how can you call him superficial?" Later, the people of the

TRANSLATED BY Alan J. Berkowitz.

1. Present-day Henan Province (located south of the Yellow River). "The Ji area": present-day Hebei Province (located north of the Yellow River).

state wondered whether he was inferior and asked people of all four directions, who said, "This man cannot be typed and put to use; how can you consider him inferior?" Later, the people of all four directions further wondered about him and sought for an explanation of him from among the people of the past and the present. But of the people of the past and the present, there was not a single one among them who could be considered the same as him. They further took their investigation of him to Heaven and Earth, but Heaven and Earth did not respond. At that time, the people of all four directions were bewildered and in confusion, and as they could gain no further information they accordingly gave him the sobriquet of the Gentleman With No Name. "With No Name" signifies that he was unnamable.

Whenever things have a form, they then can be typed and put to use. When something can be typed and put to use, it can be named. This being so, then did this man have no body? It is said that he had a body; he was one who had a body but left no traces. Did this man have no usefulness? It is said that he was useful; he was one who was useful but had no animus. As for those who leave traces and have an animus, they can be found out about. As for those who leave no traces and have no animus, whereas even ghosts and spirits cannot be fathomed, nor can they be named, how much more is the case for men? Therefore his poem says:

> Before reflection and contemplation arose,
> Ghosts and spirits were known to none.
> If not coming from among us,
> Then from whom do they come instead?

What is capable of creating the myriad things is Heaven and Earth. What is capable of creating Heaven and Earth is the Non-Plus-Ultra.[2] As to the Non-Plus-Ultra, could it possibly be fathomed? Therefore when forced to name it, we call it the Non-Plus-Ultra. "Non-Plus-Ultra"—is that not a designation for its lack of a name? Thus, he himself once composed for it a panegyric, which says:

> I borrow from you face and appearance.
> And appropriate from you body and form.
> I calmly juggle with leisure to spare,
> Coming and going in idlesse.

When others accused him of cultivating prosperity, he replied, "I have never once not practiced goodness." When others accused him of sacrificing to avert disaster, he replied, "I have never once indiscriminately made oblation." Thus he wrote in a poem:

> If calamity permitted exemptions,
>   people would have to flatter.
> If prosperity awaited being sought,
>   Heaven could be outguessed.

---

2. *Taiji,* the Supreme Polarity or Supreme Ultimate. It is that which causes the differentiation of primordial chaos into yin (a term that originally referred to the shady side of a valley; by extension it came to be associated with the dark, earth, dampness, and passivity—the female principle) and yang (a term that originally referred to the sunny side of a valley; by extension it came to be associated with the light, heaven, dryness, and activity—the male principle).

He also wrote:

> "Inner Sincerity" brings about trust,
> so whether in peace or annoyance I pray.
> "Innocence" generates disaster,
> so I never alter my sacrifices.[3]

By nature he enjoyed drinking wine, and often called it "The Great Harmonizing Liquid." He did not drink much of it, and when slightly tipsy he would stop; he did not like to surpass his capacity. Therefore a poem of his says:

> By nature he enjoys drinking wine;
> Drinking, he enjoys being slightly flushed.
> When drinking and not yet slightly flushed,
> His mouth first chants and intones.
> When chanting and intoning is insufficient,
> He then presses into exuberant song.
> When exuberant song is insufficient,
> Then what is he left to do?

He called the house where he slept "Nest of Peace and Joy." He did not seek excessively beautiful things, he but sought to be warm in the winter and cool in the summer. If it happened that he had thoughts of dozing, then he would go to his pillow. Thus a poem of his says:

> His walls are higher than his windows,
> His room larger than a bushel container.
> His cloth coverings are warm aplenty,
> And after his coarse pottage has filled him,
> The breath and life-blood within his breast
> Fill up full the universe.

As to his relations with others, even if they were lowly, he certainly was on good terms. To the end of his life there was nothing he longed for, and he never once engaged in any affair that would cause one to knit one's brows. Thus others all were the recipients of his joyful heart. When he encountered an honored person, he never once was obsequious. When he encountered a person of bad character, he never once hurried away. When he encountered a good person whom he did not yet know, he never once hurried to ally with him. Thus a poem of his says:

> A free and easy "wind and moon" state of mind,
> A liberated "rivers and lakes" disposition;
> In a startling flight he rises up,
> After soaring about he then arrives.
> He is without poverty, without wealth,
> Without baseness, without nobility.
> There is nothing he resists, nothing he welcomes;
> He is without restraints, without cares.

When he heard of slander by others, he never once became angry. When he heard of praise by others, he never once was glad. When he heard others

---

3. "Inner Sincerity" and "Innocence" are hexagrams from the *Classic of Changes* (nos. 61 and 25), to which these lines refer [translator's note]. On the *Book of Changes* or *Yijing* (traditionally dated to the 12th century B.C.E.) and its hexagrams, see the introduction to *The Seal of the Unity of the Three, in Accordance with the Book of Changes (Zhouyi cantong qi)*, above.

speak of another's evils, he never once joined in. But when he heard others speak of another's goodness, then he went forward and joined them, and moreover found joy in doing this. Thus a poem of his says:

> He delights in meeting good people,
> He delights in hearing of good doings.
> He delights in speaking good words,
> He delights in carrying out good intentions.
> He hears the evil of others
> As though toting prickly grass.
> He hears the goodness of others
> As though girding sweet blooms.

Although his household was poor, he never once begged from others. When others offered him food, though it be little he would be certain to accept. Thus a poem of his says:

> Though distressed, he never has been grieved.
> When drinking, he doesn't reach drunkenness.
> Reaping the "springtide of the world,"
> He brings it home to his vital organs.

When the court conferred official positions on him, even though he did not vigorously decline, neither was he compelled to accede. Late in life he had two sons; he instructed them in humaneness and righteousness, and imparted to them the Six Classics.[4] Though the entire world esteemed empty talk, he never once hung onto a single word. Though the entire world esteemed strange affairs, he never once adopted strange conduct. Thus his poem says:

> He doesn't toady to Buddhist elders,
> He doesn't flatter men of arcane arts.
> Without leaving his courtyard,
> He straightaway conjoins with Heaven and Earth.

His family's longstanding calling was Confucianism, and in word and deed he never practiced anything but Confucian conduct. Thus a poem of his says:

> His mind has no reckless thoughts,
> His feet no reckless steps.
> He has no indiscriminate relations with others,
> And no indiscriminate acceptance of goods.
> When there is hot debate about something,
> He willfully keeps to his humble manner.
> But when there is calm discussion,
> None can excel him.
> The writings of Fu Xi and the Yellow Emperor[5]
> Never have left his hands;
> The words of Yao and Shun[6]

---

4. That is, the Six Classics of Confucianism: the *Classic of Poetry, Classic of Changes, Book of Documents, Book of Rites, Spring and Autumn Annals,* and lost *Classic of Music.*
5. Huangdi, a mythical ruler who was credited with receiving several Daoist scriptures. Fu Xi, the first mythical emperor of China, was credited with discovering the trigrams used in the *Yijing.*
6. A legendary emperor; he and Yao, his father-in-law and predecessor, are often mentioned together as models of integrity who ruled in a golden age.

Never have been gone from his mouth.
Keeping to the center, harmonizing with Heaven,
He shares his joy and easily makes friends.
He intones "free from trammels" poems
And drinks "pleasing and joyous" wine.
One hundred years of soaring peace
Cannot be but unexpected;
But with seventy years of health and vigor,
He cannot be but longlived.

Would not this be the conduct of the Gentleman With No Name?

SECRET ESSENTIALS OF THE MOST HIGH PRINCIPAL ZHENREN ASSISTING THE COUNTRY AND SAVING THE PEOPLE
(Taishang zhuguo jiumin zongzhen biyao)

YUAN MIAOZONG

Because he discerned gaps in the Daoist canon newly compiled under imperial sponsorship, in 1116 Yuan Miaozong presented the Northern Song emperor Huizong with *Secret Essentials of the Most High Principal Zhenren Assisting the Country and Saving the People (Taishang zhuguo jiumin zongzhen biyao)*, a comprehensive collection of ritual materials. Deriving from (and serving as a systematic introduction to) the Celestial Heart (Tianxin) Daoist movement, it mainly adds to the canon information on healing and aiding the world through the deployment of talismans, invocations, and other ritual procedures. As the title indicates, these were secret (primarily oral) instructions. The Celestial Heart tradition was founded by Tan Zixiao (fl. ca. 950) and Rao Dongtian (fl. 994) after Rao discovered a cache of texts at Mount Huagai, in what is now Jiangxi Province. It can be understood as deriving from the Orthodox Unity (Zhengyi) tradition associated with the Celestial Masters and Zhang Daoling (34–156 C.E.), since its rituals and recipes originally belonged to him.

Secret Essentials of the Most High Principal Zhenren Assisting the Country and Saving the People covers many topics. Our first selection is an example of a model ritual document dispatched to Mount Tai, announcing the transmission of the key Celestial Heart teachings to an adept and requesting that he be assigned a set of spirit officers and spirit troops; it leaves blanks in which the appropriate names, ranks, and dates can be entered. The second text below illustrates the types of rules that govern malevolent spirits and demons as well as benevolent spirits and deities. In addition to noting the punishments suffered by those who disobey the regulations, it details the rewards that should go to those who perform good deeds.

The third excerpt, "Method of the Pace of Yu via the Intercrossing of Qian," presents exorcistic methods of invoking the power of the stars of the Big Dipper. Here, the ritual foot movements of the "Pace of Yu"—a practice in which the adept drags one foot after the other while walking, in imitation of the ancient hero Yu the Great (whose exertions in taming the floodwaters that inundated China left him without control of the movement on one side of his body)—helps win access to the heavenly courts. The priest paces the Eight Trigrams, which express the cosmological system (see the introduction to *The Seal of the Unity of the Three, in Accordance with the Book of Changes,* or *Zhouyi cantong qi,* above); ascends the Three Terraces, which are three pairs of stars below the Big Dipper; and then meditatively "transforms the form" by means of a divine seal of authority, riding a white crane (a celestial symbol) to the heavenly courts to present his "memorial." Such petitions, like the first selection below, are a part of a bureaucratic procedure for communicating with the heavenly deities. The priest plays the role of an official of the celestial empire, writing a formal message to his superiors. Indeed, presenting a written document has been viewed as one of the most characteristic of Daoist ritual procedures.

Secret Essentials provides strong evidence for the popularity of the Celestial Heart techniques, as does Hong Mai's (1123–1202) *Heard and Written by Yijian* (*Yijian zhi*; see the following selection), a collection of gossip that offers insight into how its exorcistic methods were actually used in social contexts.

PRONOUNCING GLOSSARY

Qian: *chien*	Yu: *you*
Taishang zhuguo jiumin zongzhen biyao:	Yuan Miaozong: *yuen miao-tsowng*
tie-shawng chu-kuo chiu-mean tsowng-	zi: *tzu*
hun bee-yao	

A Disciple's Application

From the Omnicelestial Controller of the Perverse and Demonic for their Return to the Correct (insert ranks, surname, and given name, in full): This bureau,[1] on the (Xth) day of the (present) month, has received the application of the disciple B, of (X) prefecture, county, and ward, offered in heartfelt sincerity, requesting transmission of the Correct Rites of Celestial Heart of the Northern Bourne, in order to assist the proper and remove the perverse, to aid Heaven in its transformations, to relieve the ills and sufferings of the people, and to cut short the ambitions and strivings of evil spirits. The officiant A, above, has already personally drawn up an account of this matter and notified the Emperor on High by memorial, and has further accepted B for appointment to office (X), and further given him talisman-texts, lists of manual signs, and the printed formats of the Bureau for Expelling Perverse Forces; and has, in accordance with regulations, performed the transmission and ordination. This completed, the officiant A carefully inscribes [this] notification to his Humane Sageliness of Tianqi of the Eastern Mount [the god of Mt. Tai], begging that his sagely intelligence grant the favor of an order universally notifying the Great Kings of Walls and Moats [i.e., city gods] within the Three Regions . . . and all the spiritual intelligences of the Five Mounts,[2] of the Four Rivers, of the mountains

TRANSLATED BY Robert Hymes. All bracketed additions are the translator's.

1. The Northern Bourne Bureau for Expelling Perverse Forces, the central bureau in the Celestial Heart movement in charge of communication with the deities above.

2. That is, the Five Marchmounts, a group of five sacred mountains—one in each of the four car-

dinal directions and one at the center. The Eastern Marchmount, the most important of the five, was Mount Tai, where emperors offered sacrifices to heaven; Tianqi, its deity, was particularly revered during the Song dynasty (960–1279).

of renown and the great streams, of the temples and of the altars of the soil, and of the hills and streams and numinous marshes, and directing them to take notice that B has received the rites and undertaken an office, and that if in the future he may for others' sake treat illness or expel perverse forces, they must assist him in his rites and capture evil spirits without lapsing into laziness or sloth.

The officiant A further requests, in accordance with the precedents, the assignment of two spirit officers and a thousand spirit troops to be dispatched to the office of the new appointee, B, for him to oversee and to assist him in his rites.

Respectfully drawn up on (X) day of month of the year (X), by (insert ranks, surname, and given name).

The Code of the Celestial Heart

Any spirit who steals men's property, if the amount be a full thousand cash, shall be exiled to a distance of two thousand *li*;[3] or, if the amount be less than a thousand cash,[4] shall receive two years' penal servitude. If it is property donated to a temple, regardless of amount, he shall be destroyed. Where the chief [divinity] of one of the various geographic divisions knowingly indulges [such] perverse spiritual manifestations within his jurisdiction, it is up to the spirit clerks who accompany him daily to report it. Violators shall be beaten one hundred strokes with the heavy rod.

When any spirit secretly shuts off rain and moisture and does not relieve drought and alleviate suffering in time of emergency, and where the chief [divinity] of that water conspires in covering this up and does not expose it, they shall both be given two years' penal servitude.

Any spirit officer, spirit clerk, or spirit soldier who leaves an officiating rite officer without authorization shall be beaten one hundred strokes with the heavy rod. In case of emergency shortage of personnel, [the rite officer] is permitted to borrow spirit troops from the shrine of a neighboring deity, not to exceed five hundred persons. Once their service is done, he is to reward them with special grants and report by memorial to their superiors to record their merit.

All spirit officers, spirit clerks, and spirit troops assigned by the Eastern Mount shall complete one service rotation in three years. (One rotation each year is also permitted.) Record fully all achievements and violations, and report them to the Mount for examination and reward or punishment. Replacements shall be assigned one month in advance of the completion of and departure from a rotation. Failure to rotate or unauthorized rotation shall be punished by one hundred strokes with the heavy rod.

Any deceased person who, bearing a grievance against a living person and having made a statement of his case through the Office of Hell, prior to its resolution and without authorization causes spiritual monstrosities

---

3. A unit of distance, equal to about 1/3 mile.   4. A Chinese coin of small value.

in the person's home . . . shall be turned over to the Office of Hell to be destroyed.

Method of the Pace of Yu via the Intercrossing of Qian

With both feet on the Kan trigram pace onto the Gen trigram, matching up with the Qian trigram.[5] Pace with both feet onto the Zhen trigram, and then likewise with the Dui trigram. Pace onto the Kun trigram with one foot, and onto the Li trigram with another, having both feet together when stepping onto the Zhuan trigram. When you come back up through the Three Terraces,[6] you will then be paying homage at the celestial courts.

After walking the preceding paces, take out the seal of Purple Tenuity,[7] and while standing on the Qian coordinate transform your form so that you are riding a white crane, fluttering up till you reach the heavenly courts to pay homage to the sovereign lord, where you relate the affairs on your mind via the petition. When finished you will be able to issue summons and commands [to the demons and gods] as desired. Then, come back from the Heavenly Gate and pace back to the Xun[8] coordinate. While at the altar of your pure chamber, on the appropriate day and at the zi hour, you may ascend the altar and perform the Pace of Yu.[9] With your hair unkept and wielding a sword, pace until you are upon the Qian coordinate, and when you enter upon the altar area your heart should be firmly established. Close your eyes and intone: "The trigram Qian embodies the processes of transformation from seedling, to germination, to flowering, to fruition. May the sun and moon conceal my form. Cause it so that the myriad disasters cannot disturb me and so that I may enjoy a lifespan as long as Heaven's. Quickly, quickly according to the ordinances."

Further intone: "I am a lord among those of the Daoist lineage who perform magical methods. Floods, flames, blades, and arms cannot touch me, illness and thieves cannot harm me. I am as brilliant as the sun and moon, and all that I do is auspicious and flourishing. Quickly, quickly according to the ordinances!"

After the above pacing and invocations are finished, perform your rituals according to their proper orderings.

TRANSLATED BY Julius N. Tsai. All bracketed additions are the translator's.

5. The Eight Trigrams are the different combinations of three lines, broken (yang) and unbroken (yin); each is named (see the introduction to *The Seal of the Unity of the Three, in Accordance with the Book of Changes*, or *Zhouyi cantong qi*, above), and Qian ☰ is made up entirely of yang lines. Yin and yang are the complementary forces that unite to form the Dao.
6. Three pairs of stars below the Big Dipper.
7. The constellation in which the supreme god of the central heavens lives.
8. Another trigram.
9. A practice in which the adept drags one foot after the other while walking, in imitation of the ancient hero Yu the Great (whose exertions in taming the floodwaters that inundated China left him without control of the movement on one side of his body). "The zi hour": between 11 P.M. and 1 A.M. (the Chinese day is divided into named two-hour blocks).

Woodblock print of an early twelfth-century text entitled *Secret Essentials of the Most High Principal Zhenren Assisting the Country and Saving the People* (excerpted here), depicting the ritual steps known as the Pace of Yu (*Yubu*), which can be traced back to an ancient pre-Daoist ritual. These steps, which imitate the halting steps of Emperor Yu, depict the Daoist priest ascending to the heavens to tread on the stars of the Northern Dipper during exorcistic rituals.

HEARD AND WRITTEN BY YIJIAN
(*Yijian zhi*)

HONG MAI

Heard and Written by Yijian (*Yijian zhi*)—a work also known as *The Record of the Listener* or *Record of Hearsay*—is essentially a miscellany; the stories recorded by Hong Mai (1123–1202) about Chinese society in the late Song dynasty (960–1279) range from gossip and hagiography to records of rituals. Hong Mai was a well-regarded scholar-official, historian, and collector of oral and written accounts of strange occurrences. *Heard and Written by Yijian* includes hundreds of descriptions, spread over some two hundred chapters, of spirit possessions and exorcisms by Buddhist priests, Daoist priests, Ritual Masters, and spirit mediums. These accounts attest to the rise in the twelfth century of a new class of exorcists: referred to as "Ritual Masters" (*fashi*), they had connections with the Celestial Heart (Tianxin) movement, Thunder Rites (*leifa*), Confucian literati, and Esoteric Buddhism.

The selections below illustrate various aspects of *Heard and Written by Yijian*. For example, the story of Ritual Master Cheng is typical in mixing elements of Daoism, Buddhism, and local cults. Exorcists in this region (Jiangxi) regularly appealed to the powers of Nezha—a Buddhist guardian deity whose lethal weapon was fireballs—and availed themselves of Buddhist symbolic hand gestures (mudras) and words or phrases used as a focus of meditation (mantras). The account of Li Mingwei demonstrates that a Ritual Master, even if he is a lay practitioner, is the equal of an initiated Daoist priest. Indeed, Li not only performs a ritual with a priest resident in a Daoist abbey but corrects another on particular matters of protocol.

The diverse content that thwarts generalizations about *Heard and Written by Yijian* may also be its greatest asset. It provides a rare window onto the full complexity of the Chinese religious landscape in the twelfth century, offering glimpses of lower and upper classes alike.

PRONOUNCING GLOSSARY

Cheng: *chung*
Fuzhou: *foo-chou*
Hong Mai: *howng mai*
Li Mingwei: *lee ming-way*

Qingxi: *Ching-hsi*
Yijian zhi: *yee-chien chih*
Zhao Shandao: *chao shawn-tao*
Zhao Zujian: *chao tzoo-chien*

[*Ritual Master Cheng*]

Cheng *fashi*,[1] from Zhang village [Wuyuan, Jiangxi], practiced the "Rectifying Rites of Maoshan."[2] Many commoners in the vicinity went to his altar to entreat [his aid], and none was not completely cured. Chan Cong, a man from the neighboring village of Xinding, suddenly fell ill and summoned Cheng to save him. Cheng complied and promptly restored him to health. The time was already dusk, and Cheng desired to return home. Cong's father begged him to remain until morning, but Cheng declined and went on his way. As soon as he reached the Sun Family Hill, when the moon's color revealed a weak luminescence, a black, bell-shaped prodigy emerged directly out of the trees in front of him. It circled and turned, producing a noise as if it intended to attack him. Cheng anxiously recited a spell and walked the [Celestial] Outline. The prodigy showed not the slightest fear and gradually pressed in upon his body. Cheng realized that this was a "rock sprite." Consequently, he recited the "Spell of Nezha's Fireball" and, forming a mudra[3], recited, "Do you think that my spirit-general would permit a *wangliang* demon[4] to obstruct my forward progress! Quickly stop and pull back!" And suddenly a fireball emerged from behind his body and struggled with the black lump. After a while a noise burst out, like clashing metal, and the black lump disappeared. The fireball made several revolutions around Cheng's body and also vanished. At the time, the resident at the foot of the Sun Family Hill, Xiang Dun, as well as his entire household, had heard the clamor of metal drums atop the mountain, like the sound of a hundred thousand men at war. With his sons and nephews, Xiang Dun watched from a distance, yet they saw only Cheng, standing absolutely rigid, in stillness and in darkness. Then they called out to him, and Cheng became aware. Immediately they took him back home, and his heart and intention stabilized. From that time he didn't dare travel at night.

[*Li Mingwei*]

The *fashi* Li Mingwei was a native of Fuzhou [Fujian] who observed the precepts of the Dao with exceptional care. He sent petitions and submitted writs on behalf of the people, and the response was immediate. In 1135, the Controller-General of Jianzhou, Yuan Fuyi, had him perform an "offering"[5] together with Ye, a Daoist priest of the Tianqing Abbey. After the completion

---

TRANSLATED BY Edward L. Davis. All bracketed additions are the translator's.

1. Ritual Master.
2. Mount Mao, the center of the Shangqing (Upper Clarity) movement.
3. A symbolic hand gesture; such gestures are particularly important in tantric Buddhism, a form of practice highly influential in East Asia

that focuses on attaining all manner of supernatural powers. Nezha is a tantric deity.
4. A mountain-dwelling demon that can take on human form.
5. A large-scale ritual offering or sacrifice, sponsored by a community.

of the ceremony, Li addressed Ye: "When I was sending up the petition, I arrived before the Gate of the Three Heavens[6] and saw the Daoist priest of the commandary, named Zhang, also memorializing green writs on someone's behalf. The envelope of the memorial had been prepared very clumsily, and it was damaged a bit as well. The Celestial Master [i.e., Laozi] said, 'This cannot be offered to me (the imperial person),' and Zhang threw it away." Ye responded: "Zhang is a Daoist colleague in my abbey. However, I do not know in whose home he is spending the evening." On the following day Zhang returned from outside, and Ye asked him where he had been. Zhang said, "Last night I performed an offering at the home of the Ye family twenty miles away. The village households were crude and careless, and the paper for the green writs was not good at all. Moreover, at the point of burning the memorial, the [wooden] envelope turned over, and the writ fell upon the ground. I quickly used a calling-card to prop it up, so it was not seriously damaged. However, my feathered outer-garment was burned." Ye told Zhang what Mingwei had seen. Zhang became very frightened and immediately prepared an offering to confess his transgressions.

[Zhao Zujian]

Zhao Zujian, a Daoist priest from Heng prefecture, once practiced the Rites of the Celestial Heart and would cure demonic illness for rural folk. Suddenly he could no longer perform. Unable to control his anger, he summoned a spirit to take possession of someone so that he could interrogate him. The spirit responded, "It is unlawful to dare come without authorization. Yet because a spirit-general in the law courts received a certain bribe, this was allowed to happen." Zhao silently thought to himself: "In suppressing *chimei*-demons[7] by upholding the Rectifying Rites to make a living, I have put my trust in the spirits and employed them. Now this spirit has received a commission by bribery; in what way have I presumed upon my authority?" And Zhao intended to report this transgression to the Eastern Peak.[8]

That night, Zhao dreamed that an armored knight with a particularly fierce demeanor came before him with clasped hands and said, "I, your disciple, am the spirit-general under you, the Ritual Master. When alive, I was a soldier with awesome power, and people called me 'Chen the Iron Whip.' In death I became a god and was attached to a sacrificial altar. I was unable to control myself to such an extent that I offered a demonic bribe. Now I hear that the Ritual Master intends to inform Mount Tai, whereby I will fall into the eternal prison of Fengdu,[9] forever without salvation. I hope you will condescend to pity and forgive me, and I beseech you to purify your heart and reform yourself." Zhao replied, "I cannot bear to report your transgression and will only mention that I am no longer willing to practice these rites and that I have caused you yourself to return." The soldier then bowed in gratitude and retreated. In the end, Zhao sent up a memorial to nullify his practices. He considered changing to practice the Rites of the Five Thunder

6. The Three Heavens are Great Clarity (Tai-qing), Jade Clarity (Yuqing), and Upper Clarity (Shangqing).
7. A type of mountain demon.
8. That is, Mount Tai, the Eastern Marchmount (the Five Marchmounts are a group of five sacred mountains—one in each of the four cardinal directions and one at the center); its god is Dongyue.
9. The mountain that is the Daoist abode of the dead and their place of judgment.

[Gods], and without his spirit-general, he burned incense before an effigy of Tan the Perfected[1] and anticipated receiving admonishment.

After several years, Zhao again practiced "rites of summoning and investigating [demons]" for people. At the time he compelled a boy to investigate by illumination. Suddenly the youth jumped up, and with his hair disheveled and his feet bare, he shouted angrily, "I am Tan the Perfected. I have taken pity on your diligence and industry. Therefore I will instruct you in ritual. Have you heretofore obtained anything?" Zhao responded, "Only four talismans that were transmitted to this world by the Perfected Warrior (Zhenwu)." The spirit said, "My talismans of the Five Thunders have seventy-two manifestations. Those that you have already received are only one-eighteenth of them, so how can you possibly control demonic malignancies?! It would benefit you to take one hundred sheets of paper and place them upon the table, and I will transmit them to you." Then, planting his sword in the ground, the spirit said, "I have welcomed a Judicial Officer of the Five Thunders to quickly transmit the seventy-two talismans, and I specified that they only be completed now." From the beginning Zhao did not see what was being done, but after a mealtime had passed, the spirit said, "The talismans have already been completed," and he ordered Zhao to take them in his hands. Raising them up, Zhao examined the paper. Altogether there were sixty-eight sheets. On each was drawn a talisman, and the celestial seals were resplendent. They were not written in an earthly style. Zhao was ecstatically happy and he held them up in supplication. The youth also became conscious. From this time Zhao used the talismans with spiritual efficacy.

[The Retribution of Qingxi's Cat]

In the summer of 1192—twenty-two years since I recorded [the anecdote entitled] "The Retribution of Qingxi's Cat"—Qingxi's mistress became ill from water vermin and daily her condition became increasingly dangerous. The woman's hired servant, Wang Fu, said, "I have heard Mr. Qianyong Erlang of the teashop in Tianjing alley remark that a Mr. Pan, who resides outside the gate of Mount Gen, is good at matters that concern the other world. People call him 'Pan the Demon Seer.' I will beg him to go with me and pay my respects." Wang consequently dragged Qian to Pan's residence.

Pan burned mulberry paper money and with his hands offered up a handkerchief before the effigy of the spirit he served. At the top of a lantern, he saw a woman and a cat standing opposite each other. Pan said, "Both of you have grievances, yet I do not understand the cause." Wang and Qian took the handkerchief, returned home, and explained to the mistress what had transpired. The mistress was astonished and said, "Years ago, I was in fact angry and blamed this servant. However, her death was from injuries. It was not I who caused her death. For what reason does she cause demonic visitations like this?" And she sent them back to see Pan.

Pan [performed a rite of] summoning for investigation by compelling a boy to become possessed. The boy said, in the voice of a woman, "My name is Qingxi. I died before my allotted time. Up to now, I have not yet been reborn. Originally it was not my mistress who killed me; yet it was because

1. The spirit of Tan Zixiao (fl. mid-10th century), the founder of the Rites of the Celestial Heart. A perfected is a Daoist being that has moved beyond earthly corruption and is often identified with a stellar deity.

of her that I died. Hitherto her good fortune has not declined, and therefore I have waited and held on these many years." Pan promised to perform a fast and an offering, but there was absolutely no response. Moreover, the boy cried out several times in a cat's voice and then fell asleep. When he awakened he was unable to recall anything. Pan sent an official dispatch [a warrant] to the City God, who ordered that her spirit be placed in the Palace of Fengdu. Moreover, Pan sacralized some jujube and water, and gave it to the woman to drink. She seemed to improve somewhat, but within several days her condition became grave, and she could not get up at all. Qian went to mourn her death. That night, Qian dreamed that Qingxi arrived, saying, "I myself will avenge the injustice. Why did you interfere in this matter, hiring and ordering the Ritual Master Pan to imprison me in purgatory? It is an injustice for which you will go to purgatory to bear witness!" And she caused him to come down with a fever, and he died within a day.

[An Exorcism by Zhao Shandao]

In 1181, in the subprefecture of Fenghua, [Zhejiang,] a literatus named Dong Song summoned an exorcist to cure his wife, Lady Wang. Lady Wang had become possessed by an incubus. The exorcist, Zhao Shandao, was related to the imperial clan, bore an official title, and was also a resident of Fenghua. His Daoist career began in his youth when he received the "Great Rites of Numinous Treasure" from a certain Mr. Zhou of Mount Jiuhua [Anhui]. [I include here only the central events of Zhao's exorcism, which took place at Dong Song's home.]

On the first day, Zhao Shandao pressed a ritual seal[2] against the chest of Lady Wang. Suddenly, she acted as if she were drunk and related that, in fact, she had been drinking with a young man. At that point a sword-bearing, red-clothed emissary appeared and took away the youth.

Three days later, Zhao returned. He constructed an altar and began the ritual. First, he burned incense and danced "the steps of Yu."[3] Then he ordered the "young boys of the Dong household" to search for demonic images in the incense burner. [Hong Mai comments here that Zhao's technique enabled light to be retained in the incense smoke like a mirror and to gradually expand until ghosts, spirits, and the demonic forms of inanimate things all manifested themselves, and a person could converse with these directly.]

Dong Song's eleven-year-old nephew, Dun, saw a fierce spirit of barbarian appearance descend in a garland of flames and take a seat at the altar, surrounded by his bodyguards. Humbling himself, Dun approached the god, who declared himself to be "Commander Deng of the Celestial Prime Who Summons for Investigation." In the ensuing conversation with the nephew, Commander Deng identified the incubus as the transformation of the pollution associated with a canine corpse buried long ago behind the house by some of Dong's relatives. The corpse was located, exhumed, and brought before the altar, whereupon Commander Deng expressed his surprise that a family with pretensions to classical learning would not have been

---

2. A stamp made of wood carved with special powerful signs; it either serves as a talisman or is placed directly on the body to heal or prevent disease.
3. A form of ritual walking or dancing that follows celestial patterns mapped onto the ground; the adept drags one foot after the other while walking, in imitation of the ancient hero Yu the Great (whose exertions in taming the flood-waters that inundated China left him without control of the movement on one side of his body).

more familiar with the principles of natural transformation embodied in the *Yijing*.[4]

Dong Song then asked Zhao to get rid of the pollution. If this were an exorcism performed by one of the Daoist or Buddhist Ritual Masters examined in Chapter 6[5] and in previous sections of this chapter, the remains of the dog would simply have been boiled in oil or disposed of somewhere in the hills. But here, among the members of a literati family with official aspirations, everything must first follow bureaucratic procedure. On the following morning, the nephew witnessed the descent of a band of martial youths whom Commander Deng ordered to restore the corpse to its original canine form. Then the Commander had the nephew ask the Ritual Master to memorialize the Emperor on High. On the following evening, the nephew again witnessed the descent of a yellow-robed Daoist priest holding the Ritual Master's memorial, with four characters now written on the back: "*Chaotiao juzhan*" (Certification for Decapitation). In parallel actions, the Commander's spirit-soldiers then cut up the restored dog into three pieces while Dong Song sliced what remained of the corpse with a steel saw and threw it in the river. His wife subsequently recovered.

[A Yellow Register Retreat]

On the sixteenth day of the second month of 1198, a Yellow Register Offering[6] was held in the Tianqing Abbey in Rao prefecture. It was offered for people who wanted to summon the dead. For each person it cost 1,200 copper cash.[7] Almost a thousand people participated in the ceremony.

Just at the end of the ceremony, the merchant Fu San saw his mother, who had recently died. She was wearing the clothes that she wore when alive. She was drenched from top to bottom and had come from afar. She entered the ritual area. Watching this was so painful that Fu couldn't bear it; he cried bitterly and immediately returned home. His mother gradually followed him home. Their conversation was just as in earlier days. She said, "Because of the effort of your paying the money at the sacrifice, my voice is the same as when I was alive." Fu wanted to ask in detail about what had happened to her, but she disappeared suddenly.

The daughter of the eye doctor, Wei Sheng, was married to Zhou Si. In the first month she had died because of something related to producing milk. She also participated on the altar. When the priest summoned her, Zhou saw her distinctly. Her body was covered in white clothes. She walked through water in bare feet. He could still hear the sound of the water. After she appeared before him, both her feet were still wet. Suddenly fear came over him. He hurriedly left his wife and returned home. His wife also chased after him. Zhou hid in the bathroom, and his wife entered the kitchen. Zhou observed that his wife's facial expression was just like when she was alive. He became even more frightened. He ran to his room and immediately took off his clothes and went to bed. His wife also slept by his side. She left at dawn.

---

4. The *Book of Changes* (traditionally dated to the 12th century B.C.E.), a volume of divination and cosmology.
5. That is, the translator's chapter 6, "Tantric Exorcists and Child-Mediums" (see "Xu Jixian," above); the present excerpt is from his chapter 7, "Priests, Literati, Child-Mediums."
6. One of three Register Retreats (the other two are the Gold and Jade Register Retreats). The Yellow Register Retreat became an important, and very popular, ritual for earning merit for and summoning the dead; the term now refers to Daoist ritual generally.
7. A Chinese coin of small value.

ESOTERIC BIOGRAPHY OF QINGHE
(*Qinghe neizhuan*)

The Divine Lord of Zitong was originally a regional deity limited to the mountain area of Zitong, where he appeared in the guise of a snake, but he came to enjoy a cult across the empire as God of Literature (Wenchang) and a patron of those sitting for the civil service exams. A series of texts came to be connected to that cult; two of them appear below.

The *Esoteric Biography of Qinghe* (*Qinghe neizhuan*) is one of the first in a series of revealed documents that concern the incarnations of the Divine Lord of Zitong, produced by spirit writing—a stick guided by someone in trance—around 1170 C.E. An autobiography of the god, it mentions his first human birth millennia earlier and his seventy-three other incarnations (often as a scholar-official), but it focuses on a single lifetime in the fourth century C.E. He was no ordinary

This detail from a painting of the God of Literature (Wenchang) depicts him in scholarly garb and descending on clouds astride a mule. This deity was initially venerated as a snake, but during the Song dynasty (960–1279 C.E.) was transformed into a widely worshipped Daoist deity named the Divine Lord of Zitong who was thought to assist aspiring scholars taking civil service exams.

child; solitary and serious, he had auspicious dreams. This short autobiography became the basis for the *Book of Transformations of the Divine Lord of Zitong* (*Zitong dijun huashu*), a much longer and more detailed account that follows the Divine Lord of Zitong's full career from his start as a lowly viper up through his appointment as God of Literature and patron of literati and examination candidates. To this day, he is invoked by students trying to win admission to good universities.

PRONOUNCING GLOSSARY

Qinghe neizhuan: *tsing-huh nay-chuan*   Zitong: *tzu-tung*

I was originally a man from around Wu and Gui. Born at the beginning of the Zhou dynasty (ca. 1027–256 B.C.E.), I subsequently underwent seventy-three transformations, repeatedly becoming a scholar-official. Never have I mistreated the people or abused my clerks. I am ardent by nature but circumspect in my conduct. Like the autumn frost or the bright light of day, I am not to be disobeyed.

TRANSLATED BY Terry F. Kleeman. All bracketed additions are the translator's.

Later, at the end of the Western Jin dynasty (265–317), I incarnated west of Yue and south of Sui, between the two commanderies. I was born in a *dingwei* year on a *xinhai* day,[1] the third day of the second lunar month. An auspicious glow veiled my door and yellow clouds obscured the fields. The place where I lived was low and close to the sea. A man of the village said to the elder from Qinghe, "You are now sixty yet you have obtained a precious heir."

As a child, I did not enjoy playing games. I always longed for the mountains and marshes, and often my words seemed to have hidden meanings. I copied and recited all the books. At night I avoided the gangs of children, laughing contentedly to myself. My body emitted a radiant glow. When the local people prayed [to statues of gods] I scolded and rebuked them. Giving a long cry, I said, "These images are of wood and clay, yet they wear the clothing of men and eat the food of men. When you entertain them, they respond to your wishes. When you calumniate them, they visit upon you disaster. I am a human being, how can it be that I lack spiritual power?"

After this I had strange dreams at night. Sometimes I dreamed I was a dragon. Sometimes I dreamed I was a king. There was a heavenly talisman saying that I was an official of the Water Office. I thought this strange and did not really believe it was an auspicious omen. Later drought plagued the three classes of farmers and no enriching moisture revived the plants. The farmers danced the Yu raindance and invoked the spirits, all to no avail. I thought, "At night I dream that I am in charge of the Water Office. This has been going on for a long time and by now there should be some confirmation."

That night I went to the edge of the river to throw in a memorial to the Earl of the Sea on which I had written the name of the office which I held in my dreams, but my heart failed me and I was too embarrassed to do it. Suddenly clouds converged swiftly from the four directions and wind and thunder roared. A clerk bowed before me, saying, "The Judge of Fates should transfer his residence." I said, "That is not me. I am the son of old Mister Zhang, named Ya. Later, because I became prominent through the Water Office, I was given the sobriquet Peifu (Deluger)." The clerk said, "I have been commanded to speed you on your way." I said, "What about the members of my family?" The clerk said, "Let us first go to your headquarters." I was confused and had not yet made up my mind. The clerk with a bow bade me mount a white donkey and I was gone. When I looked down I saw the village gate, then in the midst of the roar of wind and rain I suddenly lost sight of my native place.

I arrived at a mountain in the Knife Ridge range which supports the asterism Triaster. It was shaped like a phoenix lying faceup. There was an ancient pool that led me into a huge cave, by the entrance to which there were several stone "bamboo shoots." The clerk said, "When the people pray, if they call using these stones there is a response. They are called 'thunder pillars.'" I had just lifted the hem of my robe to enter the cave when the clerk said, "Do you recall that you were incarnated during the Zhou and have up until now transmitted hidden merit to your family through seventy-three transformations?" Suddenly I was enlightened as if waking from a dream. The clerk said, "In the rolls of Heaven you have the rank of a god, but there are few in the human world who know this. Soon there will be

---

1. These names reflect the Chinese calendar system. Days and (later) years were designated with two characters drawn from a set of ten Celestial Stems and twelve Earthly Branches, resulting in a cycle of sixty days/years.

portents of a revival of the Jin dynasty. You should search out a place to manifest your transformation." I said, "Thank you, heavenly clerk, for having made this resounding report."

When I entered the cave, it was like dropping down a thousand-fathom ravine. Approaching the ground, my feet made no contact and it was as if my body could soar through the sky. There was a palace fit for a king and guards ringed about it. I entered and found that my entire family was there.

Later I assumed the form of a scholar and went to Xianyang to tell the story of Yao Chang.[2] This is the *Esoteric Biography of Qinghe*. Those who worship me with incense must remember it!

2. A Qing military leader (330–393); his story became part of the cult lore of the Divine Lord of Zitong.

THE CORPUS OF DAOIST RITUAL
(*Daofa huiyuan*)

The *Corpus of Daoist Ritual* (*Daofa huiyuan*)—likely compiled in the early fifteenth century, though most of its contents date to the twelfth century—is a massive anthology of largely anonymous writings related to rituals or methods (*fa*). It is the single largest work in the Daoist canon, which preserves the sole extant version. The ritual manuals and other texts it contains are primarily those that were in use in southern China during the Song (960–1279) and Yuan (1260–1368) dynasties. The *Corpus of Daoist Ritual* documents a rich array of ritual methods, such as exorcistic Thunder Rites (*leifa*), including the use of spirit mediums; methods for empowering and using "seals" (carved wooden stamps) and talismans; initiation and ordination rites; practices of internal alchemy; salvation of the dead through meditation; and practical rituals aimed at pacifying domestic spirits inside the house and external pests (such as locusts).

The *Corpus of Daoist Ritual* is closely related to the Pure Tenuity (Qingwei) and Divine Empyrean (Shenxiao) schools, local ritual traditions that were absorbed into Daoism during the thirteenth century. By the Ming dynasty (1368–1644), the two traditions—both influenced by developments in tantric Buddhism—were providing the main templates for most Daoist ritual liturgy. Other schools that underpin texts in the *Corpus of Daoist Ritual* include Five Thunders and Thunderclap.

"Song of the Dark Pearl" is a poem written by a famous thunder ritualist named Wang Wenqing (1093–1153), and its accompanying commentary is by the equally renowned Bai Yuchan (also known as Bo Yuchan, fl. 1194–1229). It presents a formidable synthesis of Thunder Ritual and Daoist literature going back to *The Scripture of the Way and Its Virtue* (*Daode jing*; see above) and the *Book of Master Zhuang* (*Zhuangzi*; see above). After setting forth the correlations between the macrocosm (the planets, elements, and Three Marshals) and the microcosm (the orifices and viscera of the human body), the poem uses the language of internal alchemy to describe the production of the "infant," or Perfected Person, within the adept's body.

PRONOUNCING GLOSSARY

Bo Yuchan (Bai Yuchan): *bow you-chawn* (*bai you-chawn*)
Daofa huiyuan: *dow-fah hwei-yuen*

qi: *chi*
Wang Wenqing: *wawng wun-ching*

FROM SONG OF THE DARK PEARL

The Great Dao knows no words,
    The Dao originally is wordless; speaking much will diminish your *qi*.[1]
Gather your *qi* and preserve your spirits, cherish your essences and love
yourself. If you refine your interior, your cinnabar[2] will be completed, if
you apply it externally, your rituals will be successful. If your spirits and
qi scatter and disperse, your rituals will not be efficacious.

So, lock your breath and gaze within:
    To 'lock your breath' means that nothing can enter from without, and
nothing can exit from within. 'Gaze within' means to not have one single
strain of distracted thought. Your eyes look at the Muddy Pellet,[3] your
tongue is pointed towards the palate, spirits and *qi* come and go of their
own accord. When you 'lock your breath,' your *qi* will gather; when you
'gaze within,' your spirits will concentrate.

The Celestial Guideline circulates and revolves,
    The 'Celestial Guideline' is the heart. With your heart you circulate your
various *qi*. If you move *yang* then *yang* will respond, if you move *yin* then
yin will respond.[4] If you circulate and revolve the Five Phases[5] then you
can forever visit the Celestial Emperor. If you set in motion the swirl of
creative transformations, and if you turn *yin* and *yang* upside down, then
you will be able to adjust yourself to all circumstances.

And the Seven Luminaries radiate coldly.
    The 'Seven Luminaries' refer to the Northern Bushel[6] in the sky, and in the
human body they refer to the seven orifices of the eyes, ears, nose, and
mouth. If you know to shut off the seven orifices, then the seven luminaries
will shine upon each other, and *qi* will burst forth from your entire body,
expelling sweat, and on top of your head there will also be sweaty *qi* as if it
were clouds. You begin to correspond to the creative transformations.

The Five Planets have joined together,
    The 'Five Planets' are Metal [Venus], Wood [Jupiter], Water [Mercury],
Fire [Mars], and Earth [Saturn]. In humans they are the heart, the liver,
the spleen, the lungs, and the kidneys. To 'lock your breath' and 'gaze
within' means that your Five *Qi* will gather by themselves, and that *qi*
will fill the Muddy Pellet. Only then can you visit the Celestial Emperor.

TRANSLATED BY Mark Meulenbeld. All bracketed additions are the translator's.

1. Vital energy, breath (pneuma).
2. That is, the internal elixir.
3. The central palace of the nine palaces inside a person's head.
4. Yin and yang are the complementary forces that unite to form the Dao: yin, a term that originally referred to the shady side of a valley, by extension came to be associated with the dark, earth, dampness, and passivity—the female principle; yang, a term that originally referred to the sunny side of a valley, by extension came to be associated with the light, heaven, dryness, and activity—the male principle.
5. The set of systematic associations and transformations between different categories that, according to Chinese thought, explain the operation of nature; they are based on five agents, or elements (wood, fire, metal, water, and earth), and include such categories as the five planets and five viscera.
6. The Great Bear, a constellation made up of seven stars; it controls people's destiny.

And circle around the Muddy Pellet.

The 'Muddy Pellet' is the place where the Myriad Spirits convene, and the dwelling of the Celestial Emperor. When you are about to apply your cultivated skills, recycle your *qi* from the Tailgate[7] upwards, and crossing the twofold passes of the spine, have it arrive straight at the Muddy Pellet. Only then can you topple Heaven and uproot the Earth, and attain clear skies or rain according to circumstances.

Water and fire spout towards each other,

'Water' refers to the kidneys, and 'fire' to the heart. Water is *yin* and fire is *yang*. When *yin* and *yang* collide, and when water and fire charge at each other, then thunder and lightning will occur in turn.

And metal overcomes wood.

'Metal' refers to the lungs, and 'wood' to the liver. Metal can overcome wood, wood corresponds to [the trigram[8]] 'quake,' and 'quake' is thunder. Because you overcome the 'wood' of eastern 'quake' with the 'metal' of western 'pond,' therefore thunder sounds.

Metal produces water,

'Metal' refers to the lungs, and 'water' to the kidneys. Metal can beget water, water is produced from metal. Because with metal you get water, and with water you can overcome fire, therefore with the water from metal you can support the Great *Yang*, which is the wonder of rainpraying.

And wood attains fire.

'Wood' refers to the liver and 'fire' to the heart. Wood can beget fire, fire is produced by wood. Because wood begets fire, therefore fire is the crux of praying for clear skies and praying for wind.

Earth is the spirit of the will,

Metal, wood, water, and fire—they beget and overcome each other, but the 'Earth' does not move. If the various *qi* have no 'Earth' then they cannot convene, and they cannot set forth. 'Earth' refers to the spleen; it is the will. The spirit of the spleen is the Emissary [Zhang].[9] Only during years that are associated with 'water' and months that are associated with earth, one ought not pray for rain. Otherwise you personally violate the ancestral interdictions. Those who have attained the Dao will not do this.

It begets and overcomes according to circumstance.

Without 'Earth' the various *qi* cannot creatively transform. "It begets and overcomes according to circumstance"; this is just as when, for a rainprayer, water is born out of metal, and fire attained out of wood, or, for moving thunder, metal is overcome by wood.

Wind, fire, thunder, and lightning,

'Wind' is [the trigram] *xun*, 'fire' is the heart, 'thunder' is the *qi* from the gall, and 'lightning' is also fire.

---

7. Tailbone.
8. On the trigrams, see the introduction to *The Seal of the Unity of the Three, in Accordance with*

the Book of Changes (Zhouyi cantong qi), above.
9. One of the Three Marshals of Thunder Magic.

Rain, clear skies, snow, and hail,
'Rain' is the water from the kidneys. If you exercise the *qi* from your own Ocean of Darkness,[1] and with it fill your cosmos to the brim, then there shall be rain. 'Clear skies' refers to the fire of the heart. If you imagine your cosmos to be one huge, blazing fire, and if you blast open the atmosphere of *qi* within your body, then there will be clear skies. For 'snow' and 'hail' you must exhaustively apply a reverse flow of dark *qi*. Actualize first the ascent of *yang* and then the descent of *yin*. Only then will you know that it works.

The Totality of qi flows through all.
'Qi' is the perfected *qi* of primal *yang*. If you circulate it at will, you shall produce wind, clouds, thunder, rain, and lightning.

Hundun[2] is a hodge-podge,
This means: "When the firm and the yielding displace each other, the eight trigrams succeed one another. Things are drummed up by thunder and lightning, they are moistened by wind. Sun and Moon follow their courses, and cold and hot are full to the brim."[3]

When dispersed, there will be the Myriad Beings,
"Myriad Beings" refers to the Myriad Images: "In Heaven they become images, on Earth they become shapes."[4] Everywhere it flows to produce transformations, this is the dynamic of *qi*.

When condensed, there will be an infant.
'An infant' refers to the Perfected Person within my body. Man's cultivation and sublimation requires the intermingling of spirits and *qi*. If you sublimate your interior so that your cinnabar will be completed, then your sacred womb will materialize.

When permutated, there will be Thunder Gods.
'Thunder Gods' similarly are transformations that correspond to the original spirit. If a human being understands movement as well as stillness then he can penetrate heaven and pierce the earth, call up wind and summon thunder, beheading deviant specters, and whipping demonic spirits into submission. There is nothing to which it cannot be applied. This is what is called "to apply one's original spirit."

When transformed, there will be the Self.
'The Self' refers to the Perfected Nature. It is quiet and moves not. Therefore, the meaning of "to curl it up" is when one stores it back into secrecy, "to unfold it" is when one fills the Six Dimensions[5] with it. Thousand permutations, and ten thousand transformations—can there be anything to which the "Self" cannot extend?

---

1. The fertile and productive field of *qi* in the lower abdomen [translator's note].
2. Undifferentiated primordial chaos.
3. Quoted from the "Great Commentary" to the

Book of Changes (Yijing, xici zhuan, 1.2).
4. Quoted from the "Great Commentary" to the *Book of Changes (Yijing, xici zhuan,* 1.1).
5. Top and bottom, front and back, left and right.

Before Heaven and before Earth,
All is one and nothing but one.

"Heaven attains Oneness by its purity, Earth attains Oneness by its Peace-fulness, the Spirit attains Oneness by its Efficacy."[6] As for *qi*, Heaven and Earth ascend and descend by means of *qi*, the human body can breathe in and out by means of *qi*. If you know the way of 'Maintaining Oneness,' then quietude will lead to the Golden Elixir, and movement will lead to thunder-clap. Therefore Wang Wenqing said: "If people of this world see Oneness but do not recognize it, then every actualized thought will be in vain."

The fire of the heart forms a spirit,

The heart is the chief marshal. If fire bursts forth then the spirit sets out; if the spirit comes out to roam then ritual [effects] will become manifest. Dignified and lofty, the myriad spirits will humbly obey. The spirit of the heart is [Marshal Deng] Blazing Fire. It is the red *qi*.

When the liver is angry the cloud-souls[7] are alarmed,

The liver corresponds to wood. Only when the fire of the heart erupts, then the spirit of the liver will be angry, and the cloud-souls of your own body are alarmed. When I am angry, it is the anger of the Celestial Emperor; how could demons and spirits dare not to fear? When they hear your orders they will carry them out. The spirit of the liver is Lord Xin. It is the azure *qi*.

The spirit of the spleen governs the will,

The spleen is the Earth of the Central Palace. When your thoughts are fast, each of your operations will be successful. Without hurrying they are swift, without traveling they arrive. You can move Heaven and Earth, you can influence demons and spirits. If the most sincere of human beings can achieve this, how much more so those learned men who know ritual. The spirit of the spleen is the Emissary [Zhang]. It is the yellow *qi*.

The Three Marshals transform their shapes.

The 'Three Marshals' are Deng, Xin, and Zhang. The heart is Marshal Deng, the liver is Marshal Xin, and the spleen is the Emissary [Zhang]. If the will is sincere then the Emissary will arrive, if the liver is angry then Marshal Xin will attend, and if the fire of the heart angrily bursts forth then Blazing Fire [Deng] will descend. This is how "the Three Marshals transform their shapes."

When pure and turbid first separate,

When Heaven and Earth divide, then there will be Thunderclap. The light and pure *qi* form Heaven, the heavy and turbid *qi* form Earth. Heaven is *yang*, Earth is *yin*. Thunder is *yang* and its clap is *yin*.

---

6. Chapter 39 of the *Daode jing* [*The Scripture on the Way and Its Virtue*; see above] states this about all those who want to attain oneness [translator's note].

7. Light souls, linked with heaven.

Then there will be Five Thunders.
The 'Five Thunders' are Metal, Wood, Water, Fire, and Earth. In humans they are heart, liver, spleen, lungs, and kidneys. When the Five *Qi* collide in turn, then there will be Five Thunders.

Below are the Five Peaks,[8]
Above [the Five *Qi*] correspond to the Five Heavenly Planets, in the middle they correspond to the Five Human Organs, and below they correspond to the Five Earthly Peaks.

The Five Qi *come and go.*
The 'Five *Qi* come and go,' they keep begetting and transforming. If human beings can accumulate the *qi* of the Five Phases, then their correlative transformations will be endless.

Begetting the splendid, burying the conquered,
This has a profound meaning!
It is only because of 'begetting the splendid, burying the conquered,' that one may complete the creative transformations. Like when you want to pray for rain, metal begets water, and when you want to move thunder, metal conquers wood. These principles are profoundly obscure, if you have not found the oral instructions of an enlightened teacher, then you cannot attain knowledge of this.

The Mysterious Female is the Gate of Earth,
The 'Mysterious Female' refers to the Ancestral *Qi*. It is the root of the universe, and the foundation of one's life. If a human being can know this one aperture, his practice of the Dao will be perfected and his practice of ritual will be efficacious. It is the transformation of spirit and *qi*, the essence of *kan* [water] and *li* [fire].

She is the Ancestor of the Five Qi.
The 'Mysterious Female' is the Ancestor of the Five *Qi*. If you want to apply them, you must first close off the Five *Qi*, and only then can the Ancestral *Qi* be nurtured. Whenever you open up a clear sky or make rain come down, whenever you set in motion the swirl of creative transformations, proceed on the basis of this.

The Muddy Pellet is the Gate of Heaven,
The head has nine palaces, the middle one is the Muddy Pellet. It is where the Celestial Emperor resides. If you want to make use of the Muddy Pellet, you must go upwards via the Three Passes[9] straight into its middle, and only then can you become one with the creative transformations of Heaven and Earth.

It is the mansion of the myriad spirits.
The 'Muddy Pellet' is the mansion of the myriad spirits. Moreover, there is the theory of *yin* spirits and *yang* spirits. If you can merge the myriad spirits, then they will all be present in this place waiting to be sent forth to serve.

---

8. The Five Marchmounts, a group of five sacred mountains—one in each of the four cardinal directions and one at the center.
9. That is, up the spine.

PRIVATE TUTOR OF THE NINE SPONTANEOUSLY GENERATING LINGBAO HEAVENS OF PRIMORDIAL COMMENCEMENT: ON LATENT REFINEMENT FOR TRANSCENDENT SALVATION AND VITALIZING TRANSFORMATION
(Yuanshi lingbao ziran jiutian shenghua chaodu yinlian bijue)

One of the perennial concerns of Daoist writings, beginning at least as early as the Numinous Treasure (Lingbao) *Wondrous Scripture of the Upper Chapters of Limitless Salvation* (*Lingbao wuliang duren shangpin miaojing*; see above), is the salvation of the dead who are suffering in the netherworld. The *Private Tutor of the Nine Spontaneously Generating Lingbao Heavens of Primordial Commencement: On Latent Refinement for Transcendent Salvation and Vitalizing Transformation* (*Yuanshi lingbao ziran jiutian shenghua chaodu yinlian bijue*) is a meditation text— embedded within the much longer *Great Rites of the Book of Universal Salvation* (*Lingbao wuliang duren shanjing dafa*), which focuses on methods for saving souls from hell—in which the Daoist master visualizes the path to salvation for souls lost deep in purgatory.

This text provides us with an excellent record of what kinds of transformations are perceived to be going on inside of the Daoist master's body while he is performing the ritual. It proceeds from the ingestion of pneumas to the formation of the immortal embryo (the homunculus). Then, just as in descriptions of the Buddha, the Supreme Monarch (or Celestial Worthy) of Primordial Commencement emits rays of light from the tuft of hair between his eyes—in his case, illuminating the purgatorial realm of the Nine Abysses of Fengdu. The purgatories are thereby transformed into Pure Lands, where the formerly tormented souls are "satiated" with all forms of nourishment, as they are pardoned and released from their awful fate.

PRONOUNCING GLOSSARY

Fengdu: *fung-doo*
Yuanshi lingbao ziran jiutian shenghua chaodu yinlian bijue: *yuen-shih ling-pao hzu-ran chiu-tien shung-hwa chao-doo yin-lien bee-chueh*

The practitioner lights the incense. Facing East, prostrate yourself nine times. Address the intent of your retreat and prostrate yourself nine more times. Sit quietly and tune in the rectified pneumas of the spirits by chanting the *Precious Stanzas for Vitalizing the Spirits*[1] nine times. Each time draw in one mouthful of pneuma and direct it straight down into your cinnabar field [belly]. Now visualize the nine pneumas inundating your body. Within the Water Bureau [bladder] of your body condense the radiance of the nine

---

TRANSLATED BY Judith M. Boltz. All bracketed additions are the translator's.

1. Probably a text in the Numinous Treasure (Lingbao) corpus, though the title does not match any of them exactly.

pneumas to form a homunculus.[2] Like unto you, the homunculus faces outward, sitting erect with hands clasped. His residual radiance suffuses and enshrouds heaven and earth. When body and spirit are radiant and luminescent, the five visceral [heart, spleen, liver, lungs, kidneys] pneumas of five colors,[3] within but an instant, spontaneously descend like clouds and then arise, lifting the homunculus from the Double Gates [lumbar vertebrae] of your spine in ascent to the Nirvana[4] [central cranial chamber] which is then transformed into a precious pearl the size of a grain of millet. Simultaneously, the homunculus becomes the [Supreme] Monarch

This detail from a Song dynasty painting by the celebrated artist Liang Kai (early thirteenth century) depicts the descent of a Daoist deity and his attendants to a Daoist priest performing a ritual to liberate a soul from the netherworld.

of Primordial Commencement[5] and the nebulous pneumas of the five viscera form a lion. As the [Supreme Monarch of] Primordial Commencement sits magically on the five-colored lion within the precious pearl, a hundred-, thousand-, myriad-, million radiating lumina permeate and charge all the celestial and terrestrial realms, the lumination of which penetrates inside and out. Visualize next the myriad savants and thousand perfected[6] as they come drifting through space and enter the precious pearl en masse. Each and every one, bearing a countenance in compliance with the ritual, reverently kneels outstretched before the [Supreme Monarch of Primordial Commencement. Then immediately after all of the perfected have assembled, the [Supreme Monarch of] Primordial Commencement releases the propitious rays of the white hairs between his eyebrows, casting them down to illuminate all the purgatories of the Nine Abysses of Fengdu;[7] that is, they shine down from the Nirvana to beneath the navel. Within each ray, one by one, are made manifest precious pearls and within each pearl, one by one, are made manifest the thirty-two heavens and the myriad savants and thousand perfected in protective escort to

2. The embryo created by practices of internal alchemy.

3. Green, red, yellow, white, and black.

4. That is, the *niwan*, or Muddy Pellet, one of the nine palaces inside the head.

5. The highest deity of the Lingbao tradition.

6. Daoist beings that have moved beyond earthly corruption.

7. The mountain that is the Daoist abode of the dead and their place of judgment. Here, it also refers to a location inside the body between the kidneys and lumbar vertebrae.

the [Supreme Monarch of] Primordial Commencement; [in other words,] they duplicate the initial pearl. Within each ray, one by one, are made manifest the Celestial Worthies who Relieve the Suffering and, conveyed by their radiance, they enter into all the purgatories. As all the purgatories within Fengdu sustain the brunt of the potent radiance and the force of the Dao from the Celestial Worthies, the layered shades, crushed at once by the luminescence and terminally obliterated, are transformed into Pure Lands.[8]

Visualize next your two kidneys as the [double-doored] gateway to the Palace of Fengdu, whereby you reach all the purgatories. Open wide [the gateway] from within and beneath the two kidneys, that is, the stomach, small and large intestines, are all [the places in which] the abyssal shades take form and where the potency of the perfected does not reach—these are all the purgatories. Once the gateway to the purgatories is opened, the Northern Monarch together with all the Officers of the Nether World and the Purgatory Functionaries line up and perform prostrations outside the gateway of [Feng]du behind the Water Bureau of Fengdu and in front of the lumbar vertebrae. When performance of the prostrations has been completed, the Spirit-princes of the Volatile Heavens of the Ten Directions[9] are made manifest, driving chariots. The Golden Lads stand guard alongside, holding the Talismanic Decree of Primordial Commencement in their hands. Once they personally receive instruction on the Dao from the Monarch they descend, astride the rays, directly into all the purgatories of Fengdu. [The Golden Lads] respond to all the incriminated *hun* [ouranic]-souls[1] and, in all cases, they are pardoned and forgiven, and they exit forthwith from the purgatories, assembling in front of the Palace of Fengdu.

Visualize next the Florescent Pool, making it churn to unfathomable depths.

Visualize next the thousand perfected and myriad savants within the precious pearl(s), chanting in unison the "Incantation of the Celestial River Inundating the Eastern Well."[2]

Visualize next the Supreme Monarch of Primordial Commencement commandeering the ruby-red dragon to stir up waves in the bottomless pool so that it inundates the Eastern Well like the cascade of a waterfall. Immediately visualize your tongue as the ruby-red dragon agitating the Florescent Pool [of saliva]. Wait until the divine water fills to overflowing and, shifting it leftwards, swallow it directly to the front of the Water Bureau (NOTE: This is the Celestial River).

Visualize next a Vast Sea in front of the Water Bureau, limitless and border-free, into which all the incriminated *hun*-souls enter to bathe. The propitious breezes and harmonious pneumas are springtime warm. With limbs steamed in fragrant vapors, each and every one rejoices exceedingly. Bowing their heads, [the *hun*-souls] purge all avarice and contempt and submit their hearts to the veritable Dao. Once their bathing is completed, the Supreme Monarch of Primordial Commencement summons the Golden Lads and Jade Lasses to offer forth unknown quantities of purified garments

---

8. In Buddhism, a pure land is a world that lacks the three unfortunate realms (of animals, ghosts, and denizens of hell); rebirth in such a land was a common goal of Buddhist practice throughout East Asia.
9. That is, all directions: north, south, east, west, northeast, northwest, southeast, southwest, the nadir, and the zenith.
1. Cloud or light souls, linked with heaven and its pneumas.
2. This incantation is part of the rite of purification.

and bestow them on the incriminated *hun*-souls. Having visualized them dressing, concentrate on the thousand perfected and the myriad savants within the precious pearl, chanting in unison with variant voices the grand Brahman language of the *Scripture on the Relief of the Suffering*. Visualize next the Celestial Worthy of Grand Unity who Relieves the Suffering and the Celestial Worthies of the Ten Directions who Relieve the Suffering join in chanting and descend, pacing the phosphorescent clouds. They uniformly sprinkle all the *hun*-souls with sweet dew and ritual rains, by which they are able to cool and clarify their minds and bodies, and open wide their throats. With sweet dew and jade-like unction in golden basins and jade spoons, each of the Celestial Worthies of the Ten Directions disperses nourishment throughout the dark void. Succoured by this ritual repast, each and every one of the *hun*-souls is satiated.

Visualize next your spine as the Bridge of the Grand Ritual for Ascent to Heaven, extending up to the Bureau of the Vermilion Mound (NOTE: This is the Scarlet Palace) and down to the Water Bureau. Holding banners and pennants in their hands, the Golden Lads and Jade Lasses volatilize the incense, scatter flowers, and lead forth all the *hun*-souls up the Bridge to the Fire Bureau of the Vermilion Mound. Within the Bureau are made manifest: the Grand Lord of Long Life (NOTE: in monarchial gowns), the Grand Spirit Sima (NOTE: star-cap and gown), the Elder Lord Han (NOTE: white jade cap, blue gown with black border), the Director of Destiny, the Director of the Registers, and the Worthy Spirits who Prolong Life, Extend the [Life Span] Allotment, and Save the Imperiled (NOTE: star-caps and gowns) who supervise the transfer of all the *hun*-souls into the Grand Fire-pool, the blazing fires of which provide salvation through refinement. Once all have undergone refinement by fire, they uniformly gown themselves in celestial garments. From within the Fire-pool, a hundred-thousand fire-dragons leap out astride the flames and convey all departed [souls] up the Twelve-storied Tower [trachea]. Soaring through the void, they ascend directly to the realm of Jade Clarity[3] and, bowing before the Supreme Monarch of Primordial Commencement, are assumed within the jewel-like radiance of his person. Practitioner—[you are] now deeply absorbed within the recesses of your heart; external phenomena and the self equally forgotten, [you are] quiescent and unstirring—DO NOT inquire into the [ultimate] habitation of the departed. It [their destiny, this technique?] hangs but by a single thread. If this [manual, meditation?] is not followed through to the end, there will be no means for achieving [their] salvation.

---

3. The highest of Daoism's three supreme heavens.

A VERMILION PETITION MEMORIALIZING THE THUNDER COURT ON THE MATTER OF DELIBERATING MERIT TITLES
(Leifu zou shiyi xun danzhang)

BAI YUCHAN

By the thirteenth century, Thunder Rituals (*leifa*) were well-known in China, as numerous systems had grown out of and merged with regional exorcistic traditions. Those diverse Thunder Ritual traditions had also incorporated elements of Buddhism and of imperial sacrifice. This bewildering multiplicity is addressed in *A Vermilion Petition Memorializing the Thunder Court on the Matter of Deliberating Merit Titles (Leifu zou shiyi xun danzhang)*, which was sent to the Thunder Court by the famous Daoist priest Bai Yuchan (also known as Bo Yuchan, fl. 1194–1229), who had established a Daoist monastery in the mountains of Fujian Province in the far south.

The text positions the reader as a witness to Bai's confusion about various aspects of the Thunder Court at the start of a ceremony that lasted from January 17 to March 26, 1216. What, he asks, is designated by the term Five Thunders? After providing a long list of different possible answers drawn from available celestial authorities, he notes that there are discrepancies between all of these and what had been transmitted by Lord Lao himself. These possible errors were important to Bai, since the ceremony of 1216 was intended to ensure that the proper thunder deities obtained appropriate promotions and rewards. Once he has chosen the single "correct and true" system—the one laid out in the Thunder Communiqué from the Phosphor Empyrean, which he elaborates on and "swears to practice and uphold, without the least hesitation"—Bai can submit his "Vermilion Petition": a formal administrative document that provides relevant details about a ritual, specifies its purpose, and requests blessings from the deities. He sends a long list of the deities from his system up to the celestial offices so that they can carry out "a review and grading of merit titles and heroic [achievement awards], and an evaluation for reassignment of accomplishments and meritorious services. Promote the nominees and invest them with merit-ranks. Assign those commissioned and promote those chosen." In *A Vermilion Petition Memorializing the Thunder Court on the Matter of Deliberating Merit Titles*, Bai Yuchan thus tries to impose some order on the proliferating strands of Thunder Rites—as well as on the recruitment, review, and rewards due to thunder deities.

PRONOUNCING GLOSSARY

Bai Yuchan: *bai yoo-chawn*

He Lou: *huh low*

Leifu zou shiyi xun danzhang: *kay-foo shih-yee dawn-chang*

Disciple of the Supreme Mystery Metropolis' Correct Unity Pacifying Qi,[1] and of the Clarified Tenuity Heaven's Transforming Qi of the Heavenly Master [Zhang Daoling[2]], and of the Elder Master of Heavenly Prisons and of the Perfected Scarlet Thearch's Grand Cavern of Highest Purity Precious Register,[3] Bai so-and-so,[4] lowers his head and bows repeatedly, respectfully offering up these words: Your Humble Servant, as an Assistant Clerk for Administering the Thunder of the Divine Empyrean [Heaven],[5] is generally aware of the activities administered by the Thunderclap, well-versed in the communiqués transmitted by the Thunderclap, and fully familiar with the systems practiced by the Thunderclap. However, among them transcriptions are sometimes wrong and transmissions are sometimes vague. Therefore, [your Servant] will point out mistakes in the complex parts and correct the errors. [Since] secret hand gestures are in the murky spots and incantations in the inscrutable places, the [mistakes] are hard to recognize yet easy to do, and hard to pass on but easy to learn. Whatever Your Humble Servant has learned, down to the finest details, he will completely address Your Majesty at the Unapproachable Throne. Your Humble Servant has heard that the Two [Phases of] Yin and Yang[6] Qi mingle to make Thunder, and after the Thunderclap; [this Qi] is immediately distributed among [Thunder] ministry personnel. The Thunder Ancestor of the Ninefold Heavens uses it to discriminate among the Five Subordinate [Heavenly Offices (?)], and the Perfected King of the Divine Empyrean relies on it to rule over the Three Realms.[7] Examining the Golden Portfolio and checking the Jade Register[8] has raised doubts about what are deemed the Five Thunders.

[The "Correct" System]

Now, picking up from the Thunder Communiqué from the Phosphor Empyrean [one finds that]

the Winnower asterism is in control of Heavenly Thunder;
the Chamber asterism is in control of Earthly Thunder;
the Straddler asterism is in control of the Water Thunder;
the Ghost asterism is in control of Divine Thunder;
the Harvester asterism is in control of Supernatural Thunder; [and]

TRANSLATED BY Lowell Skar. All bracketed additions are the translator's.

1. Vital energy, breath (pneuma). "The Supreme Mystery Metropolis": one of the most important administrative centers within Daoist cosmology.
2. Founder of the Celestial Masters movement (34–156 C.E.). "The Clarified Tenuity Heaven": the highest of Daoism's three supreme heavens (also called Jade Clarity); the other two are Great Clarity (Taiqing) and Upper Clarity (Shangqing).
3. At each rank, a Daoist priest receives a particular "register" (lu), and according to some accounts this one was the highest. "Perfected Scarlet Thearch": an ancient deity incorporated into Daoism.
4. That is, Bai Yuchan himself.

5. This title indicates that Bai Yuchan considered himself an initiate in the Divine Empyrean ritual system [translator's note].
6. The complementary forces that unite to form the Dao: yin, a term that originally referred to the shady side of a valley, by extension came to be associated with the dark, earth, dampness, and passivity—the female principle; yang, a term that originally referred to the sunny side of a valley, by extension came to be associated with the light, heaven, dryness, and activity—the male principle.
7. Heaven, earth, and water.
8. Two documents kept in the Heaven of Highest Clarity that list the precise rankings of deities.

Heavenly Thunder is subordinated under the Winnower asterism, which is why there are the Heavenly Crow's Heavenly Garrison, and the Heavenly Cavern's Heavenly Perfected divinities;

Earthly Thunder is subordinated under the Chamber asterism, which is why there are the Miao Aboriginal-Ruler's Blocking Patrician and Fire Patrician Wind Thunder divinities;

Water Thunder is subordinated under the Straddler asterism, which is why there are the Wood Lord's Light-Pervading and the Golden Essence's Gleaming Master divinities;

Divine Thunder is subordinated under the Ghost asterism, which is why there are the Crackling Fire's Statutes and Ordinances and the Shao-yang's Wolf-Fanged divinities;

Supernatural Thunder is subordinate to the Harvester asterism, which is why there are Ding Xin, Di Xi, He Lou, and Jia Ye divinities.

Therefore, Your Humble Servant takes these alone to be correct and true. The Thunder Ritual systems transmitted from ancient times to the present have all had numerous hierarchical ranks [of initiation]. How resplendent and awe-inspiring their revelatory power and miraculous efficacy have been to the world's later generations! Now, since a Clap of Thunder is not something that may be concealed, what human being fails to recognize Thunder? A Clap of Thunder is the means to reveal Heaven's Might and issues the Way's Powers. If Heaven's Might is not revealed, then how will the extraordinary powers of the Occult and Bright [i.e., the worlds of the living and the dead] afflict and bless? If the Way's Powers are not issued, then how will the Two [Phases of] Yin and Yang Qi produce and destroy? Issuing the Way's Powers through the Two [Phases of] Yin and Yang Qi is able to reveal Heaven's Might. Revealing Heaven's Might through the extraordinary powers of the Occult and Bright is able to issue the Way's Powers. This is the [same] reasoning [whereby] a flaw in jade does not diminish its value and [a person's] cataracts fails to hide wrongdoing. As for all the sacrifices to the interconnected temples and constellations of earth-god shrines and [as for] all the spirits of the numinous sacred spaces and ancient miracle sites, there is bound to be the benign and the baleful among them. [As for] all the competencies of wealthy gentlemen and lowly personnel, and [as for] all the noble orders of upright people and extraordinary scholars, there are bound to be good and bad among them. When spirits are culpable, how can nobles complain about them? When the nobles are guilty, how can the spirits cry out "Alas!"? Illustrious Heaven has done each of the following—constructed the Thunder Wall and laid out the Thunder Prison, founded the Thunder Offices and assigned the Thunder Administration, propagated the Thunder Civil Norms and issued the Thunder Punishments, enlisted the Thunder Deities and commanded the Thunder Troops, deployed the Thunder Might and wielded the Thunder Instruments—through managing the levers of reward and punishment, and controlling the powers of generation and destruction. This permits [Heaven, acting through the Thunder institutions] to seal off mountains and break through caverns, decapitate supernatural [apparitions] and behead malicious [things] in the Yin-Dark Realm [of spirits], and also to destroy lethal [things] and exterminate deviants, attack the wicked and extirpate the vicious in the Yang-Bright Way [of the living]. It is clear that issuing the Way's Powers and revealing

Heaven's Might are matters of adjusting to the Two [Phases of] Yin and Yang *Qi*, and of affecting the extraordinary powers of the Occult and Bright worlds. The Myriad Things standing upright in the realm of Heaven and Earth have never lacked the endowments generated by [the cycles of] Yin and Yang. Generative growth and vitality is the means by which whatever has been formed or imagined becomes human and whatever is formless or unimagined becomes spiritual. Humans dwell in the Yang-[Bright realm] and spirits dwell in the Yin-[Dark realm], which is why they come and go [respectively] from the Four [modes of] Generation and circulate throughout the Six Ways.[9] If Heaven did not have the Thunderclap, then how could it put forth the punishments and institutions for correcting the recalcitrant and criticizing the ignorant? Recalling that Your Humble Servant has been blessed in his past lives and has been graced by advancement into the Thunder Ranks, he swears to practice and uphold [this system], without the least hesitation.

[Advancing the System]

At this favorable time, prostrate upon the ground and submitting a single memorial petition for an audience before the [Personnel Evaluation] Sections of the Three [Supreme] Heavens, Your Humble Servant will respectfully dispatch from this system * * * [deities who][1] will accompany the petition and join in an audience in the Administrative Palaces for a review and grading of merit titles and heroic [achievement awards], and an evaluation for reassignment of accomplishments and meritorious services. Promote the nominees and invest them with merit-ranks. Assign those commissioned and promote those chosen. [Your Humble Servant] pledges on this, the *xingai* day of the twelfth month of the present year [17 January 1216] to order the Officers and Subfunctionaries, Generals and Army Troops of the Five Thunder [Offices] to depart for a meeting in the Supremely Illustrious Court that Responds to the Primordial[2] to register merits and record accomplishments. Then, on the first day of the first month [21 January 1216], in the *bingzi* year [1216–17] at the time of Heavenly *La* [Festival] they will forthwith ascend for an audience in the Jade Clarity [Realm] to plead for permission on the seventh day of the third month [26 March 1216] to partake in the Heavenly [Personnel Evaluation] Sections' assembly for the recruitment and selection of [meritorious] awards. On the first day of the first month, at the *jiazi* time [17 January 1216], on the day of the Grand Monad's evaluation of the divinities and earth-spirits, permit each of the Five Thunder [Offices'] Generals and Clerks to receive one [degree of] merit and await the Superior Prime [Day on the] fifteenth day of the first month[3] [4 February 1216], when the Heavenly Department's Officials, at the Blessed hour, will all proceed to the Northern Culmen [Asterism's] Purple Tenuity [Court's] Jade-Cog Pivot Palace for the issuance of new duty-assignments and a change of official rank. Your Humble Servant vows

9. The six paths of Buddhist rebirth, as a god, demigod, human, animal, ghost, or denizen of hell. "The Four [modes of] Generation": according to Buddhists, sentient beings are born variously from the womb, from the egg, from warmth and moisture, and from a miracle.
1. Editor's bracket; omitted here is a long list of deities.
2. The highest deity, the Celestial Worthy of Primordial Commencement.
3. This is the first full moon of the New Year, which has long been celebrated in China in various ways [translator's note].

here and now that the Ninefold Mysteries and Seven Ancestral Generations will join in protecting, promoting, and transferring the spirits of the Three Realms and that he will devote himself to promoting prosperity and well-being. Thereafter, Your Humble Servant vows to [perform rituals to] pray for clear skies and plead for rain, summon snow and raise up clouds, gather up lightning and call out for thunder, chase away winds and send down hail, seal off mountains and destroy caverns, attack shrines and exorcize demons, execute krakens and dragons, control wolves and tigers, drive out water and fire, send away drought and locusts, drive away disasters on behalf of the people, chase away perversities and heal disorders, practice and deploy talismans and decrees, and materialize retributions. Your Humble Servant prostrates himself expectantly at the Your Majesty's Unapproachable Throne. Pour down a flood of Qi from the Purple Numina's Mysterious Unity, circulate [it] around inside the Triple Burner and Five Systems of Function of Your Humble Servant's person, flood the core of the Three Primordials' Nine Palaces.[4] Let Your Humble Servant's heart-mind expand and his body enlarge, his spirit clarify and his Qi purify. [Let him] successfully master the Way and successfully attain transcendence. Your Humble Servant meekly and respectfully relies on all these pairs of officials, the Two Offices' Auxiliary Envoys, the Correctly Unified Personnel Officers: the Left and Right Official Envoys, the Yin and Yang Divine-Acroama[5] Clerks, the Regularly-Recruited Chariot and Scarlet Talisman Clerks, the [Dipper-]Guideline and Wind-Riding Deployed Clerks, the Postal-Horse and Petition-Submitting Clerks, and the Flying Dragon-Striding Clerks to depart under the orders of Your Humble Servant. At the present time, a single brief, the Vermilion Petition Memorializing the Thunder Court on the Deliberation of Merit-Titles, is respectfully sent up for review to the Three Heavenly [Administrative] Sections, [with the] request that it be advanced to the Palace of the Most High Empty Void Nobleman's Palace in charge of pending [administrative] business and governing the Supreme White [i.e., Venus] Palace. Prostrating himself and imploring his vow, Your Humble Servant, with genuine fear and trepidation, lowers his head and bows repeatedly, reporting to the Supreme Purity Mysterious Primordial and Most High Unbounded Great Way, the Most High Lord of the Way and Nobleman of the Void, the Most High Lord Lao and the Most High Nobleman, the Lord of the Heavenly Thearch and the Heavenly Thearch's Nobleman, and the Nine Elder Transcendent Metropolis Lords and the Nine Qi Noblemen, who multiply the Way's Qi by the hundreds, thousands, myriads, and millions to the One Thousand Two Hundred Official Lords at the Unapproachable Jade Throne in the Supreme Clarity [Heaven].

On this, the twenty-seventh day of the twelfth lunar month, in the winter of the eighth year of the Jiading reign period, in the *yigai* [period] of the Supreme Year [Cycle] of the August Song [Dynasty; i.e., 17 January, 1216], at the auspicious *xingai* time, in the southwest corner of Zhongyou Abbey in the Wuyi Mountains,[6] repeatedly bowing and offering this up, Your Humble Servant, surnamed Bai, as one of the Chosen, Elite of the Golden Pylons, presently sends up this petition to whatever awaits its fate.

4. Locations inside a person's head. "Triple Burner": an organ in traditional Chinese physiology that has no Western equivalent.
5. An oral teaching heard only by initiates.

6. An area important and sacred to Daoists, located on what is today the border between Jiangxi and Fujian Provinces.

THE GREAT LINGBAO METHOD OF
THE SHANGQING HEAVEN
(*Shangqing lingbao dafa*)

WANG QIZHEN

The *Great Lingbao Method of the Shangqing Heaven* (*Shangqing Lingbao dafa*), compiled by Wang Qizhen in the thirteenth century, is a ritual manual connected with the Numinous Treasure (Lingbao) tradition at the sacred mountain Tiantai (in present-day Zhejiang Province). It is related to another text in the Daoist canon of the same name—but critical of the Lingbao tradition transmitted at Tiantai—which was compiled by Jin Yunzhong (fl. 1225). The *Great Lingbao Method of the Shangqing Heaven* is a good example of a work that meshes the old Numinous Treasure liturgies with diverse practices drawn from Upper Clarity (Shangqing) meditation, internal alchemy, tantric Buddhism, and local shamanistic and exorcistic traditions. Thus topics discussed in the fifty-three chapters of the full manual include the liturgical calendar, rules for entering and exiting the oratory, cosmology, the pantheon, the use of talismans for healing and exorcisms, model ritual documents, and precise descriptions of various Daoist rituals.

The section of the *Great Lingbao Method of the Shangqing Heaven* printed below focuses on the production of written talismans and registers used in Daoist rituals. It provides a detailed and fascinating account of the powers of written symbols and esoteric talismanic script. The symbols' efficacy depends on their correct preparation by the ritual master, whose body is transformed in the process. He must enter the oratory to write out the talismans at a particular time and carry out specific actions (grind his teeth, hold his breath, perform visualizations, recite incantations, swallow saliva) in order to summon the right spirits and generate the numinous power captured in the written symbol. After the writing is complete, the ritual master must offer a prayer of thanks and gratitude to the celestial deities for their assistance, apologize for any infractions committed, and then put away the symbols into storage.

This passage is also useful in helping us to understand the nature of the esoteric script that it describes. The wavy lines typical of seal script and talismanic writing are said to represent clouds, thereby capturing and condensing that pristine celestial energy. It is the power that congeals in this type of script that can bring salvation to the dead suffering in hell.

PRONOUNCING GLOSSARY

Shangqing lingbao dafa: *shawng-ching*   Wang Qizhen: *wawng chee-chun*
    ling-pao dah-fah

Whenever you write seal characters, you must use symbol-orders. Enter your oratory in proper ritual manner and visualize the imperial masters of the Three Realms,[1] the Sovereign of Heavenly Perfection, the True Master of the Yellow Register, and the potent officers of the symbol-register.[2]

TRANSLATED BY John Lagerwey.

1. Heaven, earth, and water.
2. At each rank, a Daoist priest receives a particular "register" (*lu*).

When the incense, flowers, altar, brush, inkstone, and red ink are all ready, you must first do the method of "internal smelting." At the sixth *yang* hour,[3] enter your oratory and sit in the lotus position. Grit your teeth three times, hold your breath in silence, and visualize in the lower Cinnabar Field[4] a flame the size of a pill. It turns nine times toward the left (clockwise: gestation) and mounts to the Scarlet Palace (the heart), and then gradually goes up through the twelve-storied tower (the trachea) to the Jade Chamber (a womb) in the *niwan* (between the eyes), where it sits lotus style, holding the sun in its right hand and the moon in its left. Its name is Worthy Emperor, Great One of the Large Cavern. Pray:

> Let my superior souls be clean and correct
> And my myriad energies remain forever intact.
> May I avoid suffering,
> May my body be luminous.
> May [the officers of] the Three Realms wait upon me
> And the Five Emperors[5] welcome me.
> Let the myriad spirits pay their respects
> And my name be written in Highest Purity.
> When my merit is sufficient and my results perfect,
> Let me fly up to Highest Purity.

Repeat this incantation three times, draw the fire up [from the Cinnabar Field] three times, swallow it, and pray again:

> The golden liquor smelts the body:
> I join my perfection to that of the Way.
> That which lights up the Three Luminaries[6]
> Is called the Root of Heaven.
> In it is neither darkness nor crack,
> Neither beginning nor end.
> Nine Obstacles of the Prime Sovereign;
> Potent soul in the Scarlet Palace.
> Purple clouds fly in the sky,
> And I drive a team of six dragons.
> Water goes up, fire down:
> They flow into the Three Palaces.
> The spirit returns to the light,
> And the Great Way communicates spontaneously.

Repeat this incantation three times and swallow the saliva three times. After a long interval, a halo appears on top of the head, and its light illumines the ten directions.[7] Pray thus:

> Lord of the Way of the Most High, Supreme and Mysterious Origin, summon forth from within your servant's body the correct spirits of the Three Energies,[8] the directors of destiny, fortune, works, and judgment, as well as the two lords Taokang and Jingyan.[9] Your

---

3. Traditionally, the Chinese divide the day into twelve two-hour periods, each of which is divided into yin and yang hours (yin and yang being the complementary forces that unite to form the Dao).
4. The abdomen.
5. Deities of the four cardinal directions and the center.

6. The sun, moon, and stars.
7. That is, all directions: north, south, east, west, northeast, northwest, southeast, southwest, the nadir, and the zenith.
8. Generative, vital, and spiritual (*jing, qi,* and *shen*).
9. Two gods that reside within the body.

servant is sublimating the True Principle within. Rays light up the Nine Heavens, releasing the *yang*-essence and filling with light the Nine Gates. Cause the souls of the dead to be melted down and then return to the womb to be reborn. Let all the spirits of my body marvelously unite their perfection to that of the Way.

Draw up the fiery energy and swallow it nine times. Whenever you write symbols you must first do this, and gradually the divine lights will manifest themselves.

When you are [actually] writing the symbols, set up a table with incense, face the Gate of Heaven, and spread out before you all the ritual implements. Visualize the red inkstone and the dish of water as the sun and the moon respectively, the paper as golden strips, the brush as a green dragon, and the smoke of the incense as white clouds. The clerks of the symbol are atop these clouds, and the lads and lasses,[1] officers and generals of the symbolic method are arrayed to the right and left. When this is accomplished, form in your hand the sign of the Big Dipper, and visualize the dippers of the five directions[2] enveloping the body. Walk the Huolo Dipper, press the point of the Emperor on High in your hand, and visualize yourself entering the Three Terraces[3] and the Big Dipper. Do the dipper gesture with both hands, bow three times with your court tablet, present incense, grit your teeth, kneel down, and pray. (In the prayer, the master invokes the pantheon, recalls his mission to spread the "Great Teaching" even though he is unworthy of such a task, states that he has been asked to perform a fast by so-and-so and must therefore prepare the appropriate documents and symbols):

> Knowing himself to be foolish and filthy, incapable of creating the Mysterious Origin, your servant lifts up his eyes and begs Heaven for mercy: look down on me with compassion and grant to me the correct energies of the ten directions, the marvellous rays of the Great Way. Let them flow into your serrvant's body and heart, into my every pore, and also into the red ink and the implements. Cause all knots to be untied, the root of the foetus to be clear, my meditations efficacious, and my true lights to beam. One brush stroke, one opening: unite with the Way, unite with perfection. When I use them later, let the reactions be good ones. Cause them to symbolize with the marvels of the mysteries on high and so make whole the work of salvation. Your servant makes bold to presume upon the heavenly powers, I who am without merit and wait anxiously for your mandate.

After this prayer, visualize the Most High in the Terrace of the Celestial Treasure, surrounded by the perfected and the immortals.[4] The Emperor orders those in waiting to issue the signet-symbols and send them down. Next he sees the heavenly worthies of the ten directions emit a great light

---

1. That is, jade lads and lasses, or heavenly attendants.
2. North, south, east, west, and the center.
3. Three pairs of stars below the Big Dipper.
4. Daoists who have achieved extraordinary powers and a higher form of existence; in later Daoism the perfected, who have moved beyond earthly corruption, are generally viewed as higher than the immortals (or transcendents).

which flows down through space. Bearing a treasure box, surrounded by hundreds of precious rays, lads and lasses come before your table, open the box, and divulge them: *they unite with the seal characters you have written* (italics mine).

The light blinds the eyes, and you transform your body into that of the two perfect ones of the Green Mystery on the left and on the right, surrounded by lads and lasses. Only then do you [actually] enter the oratory and face east. Grit your teeth 32 times so that it is heard in the 32 heavens on high, and make 32 mental bows. Close your eyes and meditate in quiet: your body is seated on cloud-energies of three colors, green, yellow, and white. From the total darkness within and without emerge a green dragon, a white tiger, a red phoenix, and a somber warrior,[5] who take up their positions on the four sides of your person. The sun and the moon light up the chamber, and on the back of your head appears a nine-colored halo whose rays light up the ten directions. Now pray, saying:

> Lord of the Way of the Most High, Supreme and Mysterious Origin, summon forth from within your servant's body the officers of merit of the three and the five,[6] the agents on the left and right, the jade lads in charge of the incense, the jade lasses who transmit what is said, the keepers of the symbols of the Five Emperors, and the officers of the incense in charge today, 32 individuals in all, to report what I say. On this auspicious day I am [preparing] to perform a great fast for so-and-so, with the purpose of transmitting the documents, symbols, and registers which will rescue the soul of so-and-so from the darkness of hell. I pray that what I ask may penetrate directly to the throne of the Most Worthy Emperor on High of the Primordial Beginning[7] of the 32 supreme heavens.

Inhale (or, draw up the energy) 32 times, go to your seat, and write the symbols. . . . (Here follow incantations for the brush, the ink, the action of making the ink, the consecration of the symbols and their dispatch, and so on.) When you have finished writing the symbols, pray once again to the Most Worthy Saint of the Seven Treasures of the Golden Gate of the Infinitely Great Way of the Most High:

> I long for the compassion of the Way: may It deign to look down and observe. Your servant has heard that the Great Way, in Its compassion, opened the eight gates in order to save from distress; the Most Perfect One set forth his teaching and revealed the three registers by means of which to save men: whoever prays and makes an offering is certain to be granted deliverance. Your servant has just now, respectfully following the ritual method, written in seal characters the various perfect symbols and registers of the Most High. Although I have done so in accord with the proper method, I still fear there may have been something amiss in my visualizations,

---

5. The animals associated with the four cardinal directions.
6. An expression used to denote the entire cosmos and its correspondences; "the three" refers to celestial things (the three heavens) and "the five" to earthly things (the five sacred peaks).
7. The supreme deity.

514 | TRACT OF THE MOST EXALTED ON ACTION AND RESPONSE

or that I have made mistakes in my incantations or gestures; or else I have relied on the hand of another, who has made errors or omissions in his strokes or, not understanding ultimate principles, has not followed the revealed rules. Once again I beg heaven's mercy: pour down perfect energies, that they may flow, penetrate, and irrigate the symbols and registers I have written. Cause what I have left out to be filled in, so that their radiance may soar heavenward and constitute the rays of this ritual which symbolize with the marvels of the mysteries on high. When your servant announces them, let them be carried out one and all: open wide for the drowned souls, that all may leave their misery behind. Above, show the power of your love of life; below, symbolize with our sincerity in saving the dead. Your servant makes bold to importune the heavenly powers; with utmost humility he earnestly addresses you.

Bow three times, gather up the symbols, and put them in a box for storage.

TRACT OF THE MOST EXALTED ON ACTION AND RESPONSE
(Taishang ganying pian)

The *Tract of the Most Exalted on Action and Response* (*Taishang ganying pian*) is a famous morality book (*shanshu*) first published in 1164. Written by an unknown author, it presents itself as the words of the deified Laozi. Though this attribution has led to its being included in the Daoist canon, it is an eclectic work that combines aspects of Buddhism, Daoism, and Confucianism. It opens with its main point: the actions of human beings bring good and evil into their lives, not just determining their fates—most notably, their life spans—but even affecting their descendants in future generations. This simple and practical message, based largely on Buddhist notions of karmic causality and earlier Chinese notions about heaven responding (*ganying*) kindly to human morality, was extremely attractive, and the *Tract of the Most Exalted on Action and Response* was embraced by individuals and popular religious movements. As editions proliferated, the text expanded with the addition of prefaces, stories, and illustrations.

One of those expanded versions is *Illustrated Explanation of the Tract of the Most Exalted on Action and Response* (*Taishang ganying pian tushuo*, 1755). The three stories drawn from it illustrate well both the main teachings of the *Tract of the Most Exalted on Action and Response* and the added theme, common in later editions, that disseminating the tract to other readers was itself a highly meritorious act. Indeed, copying, printing, or distributing copies of the work became such a popular devotional activity that it may be the most frequently reprinted book in Chinese history.

PRONOUNCING GLOSSARY

Shan Yangzhu: *shawn yawng-chu*
Taishang ganying pian tushuo: *tai-shawng gawn-ying pien tu-shew-oh*

Zhu Jiayou: *chu chia-yo*

The grand elder [i.e., Laozi] has said that calamity and misfortune cannot gain entrance of their own into a person's life; it is the individual alone who calls them in. Good and evil are requited as automatically as shadow follows form. In keeping with this principle, Heaven and earth have spirits who judge transgressions. These spirits take into account the lightness or gravity of the evil deeds that human beings have committed and then deduct from those individuals' life spans correspondingly. After diminishing the culprits' life expectancy, they reduce them to poverty and visit upon them innumerable calamities. Everyone comes to hate them. Punishment and misfortune pursue them wherever they go; happiness and pleasure flee from them. An unlucky star torments them. When their allotted time is up, death claims them. There are also spirit rulers of the constellations of Three Towers and Northern Scoop,[1] who reside far above the heads of people and who keep track of their foul deeds and wickedness. They may shorten an individual's life a hundred days or twelve years. There are also three spirits of the body, which reside within the human organism. On each *gengshen* day [once every sixty days][2] they ascend to the heavenly ruler and inform him of the transgressions and harmful deeds of the people over whom they watch. On the last day of the month the kitchen god does likewise. When individuals have been found guilty of a serious transgression, they are punished by a loss of twelve years from their allotted life span. For minor transgressions, they suffer the loss of one hundred days of life.

There are hundreds and hundreds of occasions for transgressions, large and small. People who want to achieve immortality must first of all avoid these occasions. They must recognize the path of righteousness and enter upon it; they must recognize the way of evil and stay clear of it. They do not tread the byways of depravity, nor do they poke into the private affairs of others. They accumulate virtue and gain merit and have compassion for all living things. They exhibit loyalty to their ruler, filial obedience to their parents, true friendship to their older brothers. By conducting themselves with propriety, they influence others. They take pity on orphans and are kindly toward widows; they venerate the elderly and are warmhearted toward the young. They will not permit themselves to do any harm even to an insect, a plant, or a tree. They consider it proper to feel sorry when others suffer misfortune and to rejoice when others enjoy good fortune, to aid those in need and to assist those in danger. They look upon the achievements of others as if they were their own achievements, and they regard the failures of others as if they were their own failures. They do not dwell on the shortcomings of others, nor do they brag about their own strong points. They put a stop to what is evil and praise what is good. They give much and seek little. They accept honors only with misgivings. They show favor to people without seeking anything in return. When they share things with others, they do not regret it later. They are called good people and everyone reveres them. The Way of Heaven protects them from harm. Happiness and

TRANSLATED BY Mark Coyle. All bracketed additions are the translator's.

1. The Big Dipper. "Three Towers": the Three Terraces, three pairs of stars below the Big Dipper.
2. In the Chinese calendrical system, the ten Celestial Stems and twelve Earthly Branches combine to create a cycle of sixty individually named days (or years).

good fortune follow them everywhere; the depravities of the world keep their distance from them. The spirits watch over them; whatever they undertake results in success. Thus, they can hope to become immortal. Individuals who desire to achieve heavenly immortality should establish in themselves the thirteen hundred good qualities, and those who aim for earthly immortality should establish within themselves the three hundred good qualities.

Evil persons, on the other hand, are devoid of righteousness, as their actions reflect. . . . They extend rewards to the unrighteous and dole out punishments to the innocent. They will have some people executed to get their hands on their wealth and will have other people fired from their jobs to grab their positions. In war they kill those they have captured and slaughter those who have surrendered. They dismiss the upright, dispose of the virtuous, mistreat orphans, and harass widows. They ignore the law and take bribes. They take straight for crooked and crooked for straight, treating light crimes as grave ones and watching the resultant executions with glee. They know that they are doing wrong but refuse to change; they know what is right but refuse to act upon it. They blame others for their own wickedness. They obstruct the arts and sciences. They slander wisdom and morality, insult the Way and virtue.

Evil persons shoot creatures that fly and hunt those that run, stirring up hibernating animals and rousing roosting fowl. They block up animals' dens and overturn birds' nests, injuring hens and breaking their eggs. They hope for others' ill-fortune and ruin in order to secure advantage for themselves. They let others bear risks to preserve their own safety and fleece people to enrich themselves. They present things of poor quality as good. They disregard the public good for their own private advantage. They take credit for others' achievements. Concealing others' good points, they exaggerate their bad points. They expose people's private affairs. They squander the wealth of the nation. They break up friends and families. They insult the things people love. They lure others into doing evil. They get their way by intimidating people to seek triumphs by ruining others. They destroy crops while they are just sprouting up and flowering. They break up marriages. If they have ill-gotten wealth, they bristle with pride over it. They shamelessly shirk the responsibility for their acts. Quick to claim credit, they are equally quick to deny fault. They are like marriage brokers who wed people to misfortune and like peddlers who sell people evil.

Evil people buy themselves false reputations. Their hearts are nests of wicked intentions. They deprecate the strong points of others while covering up their own shortcomings. They use power tyrannically to intimidate others, not hesitating to inflict cruel and even fatal injury on people. They cut up cloth without cause and cook animals they have slaughtered sense- lessly, waste the five grains,[3] mistreat animals and other living creatures, wreck people's homes, confiscate their wealth, and destroy their homes by letting loose floods and starting fires. They throw the plans of others into confusion and thereby thwart their achievements. They break tools and make them worthless to workers. When they see others prosper, they desire to have them censured and exiled. If they encounter a rich and prosperous

3. That is, the staple foods of China.

man, they hope he will be brought to ruin. At the sight of a beautiful woman, their hearts brim over with lust. Having borrowed, they wish their creditors would die to avoid repaying them. If their wishes are not met, they curse and burn with hatred. When they notice others having a bit of bad luck, they say it must be recompense for their transgressions. When they see persons who are deformed and crippled, they laugh at them. They play down any praiseworthy talents they observe in others. They resort to magic to get rid of their enemies and use poison to kill trees. They fly into a rage at their teachers and are obstinate toward their elders. They go to violent extremes to satisfy their lusts and desires. They are more than happy to employ tricks and mischief to achieve their ends and gain wealth by plundering. Promotion they seek by cunning and deceit. They are unfair in rewarding and punishing. In indulging their pleasures they go beyond all moderation. They are cruel and severe to those below them, loving to instill fear in people.

*　*　*

Evil people's lustful desires go beyond all restraint. Although their hearts are poisonous, they put on a compassionate demeanor. They sell people contaminated food to eat; they deceive people by teaching falsehoods. They give a short foot, a narrow measure, a light pound, a small pint; they take the bad and mix it in with the good, trying to pass the whole lot off as top quality. In such ways they accumulate dishonest profits. They lure good people into disgraceful acts, deceiving and tricking the ignorant. Their avarice is insatiable. They curse those who seek rectitude. Their drunkenness leads them to sedition. They fight with their families.

*　*　*

For this sort of wickedness the judge of destiny shortens the culprit's life span twelve years or one hundred days, depending on the gravity of the offenses. Should sentence be passed and death occur without the complete expiation of the crimes, then retribution is extended to the sons and grandsons. In cases in which a man has swindled another person out of his money, the burden of restitution is reckoned and passed on to his wife, his children, and all his household to be made good until sooner or later death devours them all. If death itself does not take them, then they are visited by such calamities as floods, fires, robberies, disinheritance, loss of property, disease, and slander in order to make restitution for the crime. In cases in which people kill others unjustly, it is as if they were to hand over their swords so that they themselves in turn could be slain. In cases in which people have acquired ill-gotten wealth, it is just as if they had gulped down rotting meat to satisfy their hunger or had drunk poisoned wine to quench their thirst: they derive a short-lived satisfaction, but death soon ensues. But if within their hearts people rise toward goodness, even if they have not yet achieved it, the spirits of good fortune will watch over them. On the other hand, if within their hearts people wink toward evil, even if they have not yet been totally debased, the spirits of misfortune will pursue them.

A person who has been guilty of doing evil but later changes, repents, ceases to indulge in wickedness, and follows the good completely can attain happiness and success little by little. This can be called changing disaster into blessing.

Therefore, good people are of virtuous speech, virtuous demeanor, and virtuous behavior. If they maintain these three modes of virtue every day, in three years' time Heaven will definitely shower them with its blessings. Wicked people are of evil speech, evil demeanor, and evil behavior. If they maintain these modes of evil every day, in three years' time Heaven will definitely rain down disaster upon them. How then can we not but endeavor to act properly!

Stories

A. Zhu Jiayou of the Qiantang District in Zhejiang Province was employed in the salt business and fond of doing good deeds. When Mr. Lin Shaomu was the General Surveillance Commissioner for Zhejiang, Zhu begged him to write out the two morality books, *Tract on Action and Response* and *Essay on Secret Merit* (*Yinzhi wen*),[1] in handsome script in order to engrave the texts in stone. He also asked him to contribute more than ten thousand sheets of paper to make copies. All those who obtained a copy treasured the fine calligraphy. Night and day Zhu made copies. After a while, he gradually became able to understand the full meaning of the text, fortifying his body and soul. Both the one who wrote out the texts and the one who gave copies of them away received blessings in return. Zhu's son was given an eminent position in Anhui Province, while Lin was later appointed to an office with jurisdiction over the provinces of Hubei and Hunan.

B. Once there was a man from the Wu Xi District in Jiangsu, named Zou Yigui, also called Xiaoshan (Little Mountain). At the time of the provincial examinations people were contributing to the printing of morality books and wanted him to donate also. Zou declined, saying, "It is not because I am unwilling to give money. Rather I fear that people will be disrespectful to the text and that would put me at fault." That night he dreamed that the god Guandi[2] appeared to scold him, saying, "You study books and illuminate their basic principles, yet you also speak like this! If all people followed your example, virtue would practically disappear." Zou prostrated himself and begged forgiveness. He printed and circulated one thousand copies in order to atone for his fault. Moreover, by himself he painted a religious image on a board and devoutly chanted in front of it morning and night. Later, in the year 1727, he placed first in special examinations and entered the prestigious Hanlin Academy,[3] where he held a series of official positions, culminating in an appointment as Vice Minister in the Ministry of Rites. Zou always said to people, "One word is enough to incur fault. And among evil doers, no one is worse than the person who hinders the virtue of others." This story demonstrates that anyone who impedes contributions to morality books is guilty of the greatest fault and will be punished by Heaven.

C. Shan Yangzhu lived at a small Buddhist temple. When he was born, he was weak and often ill. His mother prayed for him, vowing that if her son

TRANSLATED BY Catherine Bell.

1. A work probably also written in the 12th century.
2. God of war and suppressor of demons.

3. An elite group of scholars who advised the imperial court (especially on the interpretation of the Confucian Classics).

were cured, he would be a vegetarian for his whole life. In addition, she nursed him at her breast for six full years until he began to eat rice at the age of seven. When his mother died, he continued to live at the temple for forty-one years, yet he was in constant pain and suffering for half his life. One day he read the *Tract on Action and Response* and, thinking about his parents, suddenly repented of all his bad deeds. Thereafter, he collected different editions of the *Tract* and amended them with his own understanding of its meaning—revising, distinguishing and analyzing point by point. Altogether his study came to 330,000 words, divided into eight volumes and entitled *An Exposition of the Tract of the Most Exalted on Action and Response*. He did this in order to made amends for all his misdeeds, but also as an attempt to repay some small part of the boundless loving kindness of his parents. In 1655 he organized people to donate the money for publishing it. Because of these activities, everything that was painful and unhappy in his life gradually improved.

REDOUBLED YANG'S FIFTEEN DISCOURSES FOR THE ESTABLISHMENT OF THE DOCTRINE
(*Chongyang lijiao shiwu lun*)

WANG ZHE

Redoubled Yang's Fifteen Discourses for the Establishment of the Doctrine (Chongyang lijiao shiwu lun) is a set of fifteen regulations for the newly formed Complete Perfection (Quanzhen) Daoist movement—the first Daoist celibate monastic order. Written by the movement's founding patriarch, Wang Zhe (1113–1170), it provides monks living in a communal context with rules related to doctrine, monastic practice, and self-cultivation. Beyond setting out instructions and regulations on living the cloistered life, *Redoubled Yang's Fifteen Discourses* addresses such themes as the study of books, the use of medicines, meditation, ways to transcend the three realms (of desire, form, and formlessness), and departing from the mundane world. Although the text is directed at Complete Perfection Daoists, it contains a rich amalgam of Buddhist and Confucian ideas.

In addition to offering insights into the internal workings of a Complete Perfection monastery, these excerpts from *Redoubled Yang's Fifteen Discourses* also give us a glimpse of an important facet of Complete Perfection self-cultivation practice. "On Cloud-like Wandering" and "On Book-Learning," for example, emphasize the need to shift focus from the external to the internal; in doing so, they reflect how the Complete Perfection tradition incorporated and emphasized the teachings of internal alchemy (*neidan*).

PRONOUNCING GLOSSARY

Chongyang lijiao shiwu lun: *chowng-yawng lee-chiao shih-wu loon*

Wang Zhe: *wawng zhuh*

On the Cloistered Life

All those who choose to leave their families and homes should join a Daoist monastery, for it is a place where the body may find rest. Where the body rests, the mind also will gradually find peace; the spirit and the vital energy will be harmonized, and entry into the Way (*Dao*) will be attained.

In all action there should be no overexertion, for when there is overexertion, the vital energy is damaged. On the other hand, when there is total inaction, the blood and vital energy become sluggish. Thus a mean should be sought between activity and passivity, for only in this way can one cherish what is permanent and be at ease with one's lot. This is the way to the correct cloistered life.

On Cloud-like Wandering

There are two kinds of wandering. One involves observing the wonders of mountains and waters; lingering over the colors of flowers and trees; admiring the splendor of cities and the architecture of temples; or simply enjoying a visit with relatives and friends. However, in this type of wandering the mind is constantly possessed by things, so this is merely an empty, outward wandering. In fact, one can travel the world over and see the myriad sights, walk millions of miles and exhaust one's body, only in the end to confuse one's mind and weaken one's vital energy without having gained a thing.

In contrast, the other type of wandering, cloud-like wandering, is like a pilgrimage into one's own nature and destiny in search of their darkest, innermost mysteries. To do this one may have to climb fearsome mountain heights to seek instruction from some knowledgeable teacher or cross tumultuous rivers to inquire tirelessly after the Way. Yet if one can find that solitary word which can trigger enlightenment, one will have awakened in oneself perfect illumination; then the great matters of life and death will become magnificent, and one will become a master of the Perfect Truth. This is true cloud-like wandering.

On Book-Learning

In learning from books, one who merely grasps onto the literal sense of words will only confuse his eyes. If one can intuit the true meaning behind the words and bring one's heart into harmony with it, then the books themselves can be discarded. One must therefore first attain an understanding of meanings and locate the principles behind them; then one should discard the principle and internalize the meaning into one's heart. When the meaning is understood, then the mind will withdraw from externals, and in time will naturally become responsive to reality. The light of the mind will overflow, the spirit of wisdom will become active, and no problem will be insolvable.

Thus one should diligently cultivate the inner self, never letting one's mind run wild, lest one lose his nature and destiny. If one cannot fully comprehend the true meanings of books, and only tries to read more and more, one will end up merely jabbering away before others, seeking to show off

TRANSLATED BY Whalen Lai and Lily Hwa. All bracketed additions are the translators'.

one's meager talent. This will not only be detrimental to one's self-cultivation but it may do harm to one's spirit and vital energy. In short, no matter how many books one reads, they will be of no avail in attaining the Way. To understand fully the deep meaning of books, one must incorporate them into one's mind.

On the Art of Medicine

Herbs are the treasures of the hills and the waters, the essence of the grass and the trees. Among the various herbs there are those which are warm and those which are cold; properly used, they can help in supplying elements to or eliminating them from the body. There are active and less active medicines, those that work externally and internally. Therefore people who know thoroughly the power of herbs can save lives, while those who do not will only do further harm to the body. Therefore the man of the Way must be expert in this art. But if he cannot be, he should not pursue it further because it will be of no use in the attainment of the Way and will even be detrimental to his accumulation of merits. This is because those who pride themselves in such knowledge crave after worldly goods, and do not cultivate the truth. They will pay for such transgression either in this life or the next. The Perfect Truth Daoist must pay heed to this.

On Residence and Covering

Sleeping in the open air would violate the sun and the moon, therefore some simple thatched covering is necessary. However, it is not the habit of the superior man to live in great halls and lavish palaces, because to cut down the trees that would be necessary for the building of such grand residences would be like cutting the arteries of the earth or cutting the veins of a man. Such deeds would only add to one's superficial external merits while actually damaging one's inner credits. It would be like drawing a picture of a cake to ward off hunger or piling up snow for a meal—much ado and nothing gained. Thus the Perfect Truth Daoist will daily seek out the palace hall within his own body and avoid the mundane mind which seeks to build lavish external residences. The man of wisdom will scrutinize and comprehend this principle.

On Companionship

A Daoist should find true friends who can help each other in times of illness and take care of each other's burials at death. However he must observe the character of a person before making friends with him. Do not commit oneself to friendship and then investigate the person's character. Love makes the heart cling to things and should therefore be avoided. On the other hand, if there is no love, human feelings will be strained. To love and yet not to become attached to love—this is the middle path one should follow.

There are three dimensions of compatibility and three of incompatibility. The three dimensions of compatibility are an understanding mind, the possession of wisdom, and an intensity of aspiration. Inability to understand the external world, lack of wisdom accompanied by foolish acts, and lack of high aspiration accompanied by a quarrelsome nature are the three dimensions of incompatibility. The principle of establishing oneself lies in the grand monastic community. The choice of a companion should be motivated by an appreciation of the loftiness of a person's mind and not by mere feelings of external appearance.

On Sitting in Meditation

Sitting in meditation which consists only of the act of closing the eyes and seating oneself in an upright position is only a pretense. The true way of sitting in meditation is to have the mind as immovable as Mount Tai[1] all the hours of the day, whether walking, resting, sitting, or reclining. The four doors of the eyes, ears, mouth, and nose should be so pacified that no external sight can be let in to intrude upon the inner self. If ever an impure or wandering thought arises, it will no longer be true quiet sitting. For the person who is an accomplished meditator, even though his body may still reside within this dusty world, his name will already be registered in the ranks of the immortals or free spirits and there will be no need for him to travel to far-off places to seek them out; within his body the nature of the sage and the virtuous man will already be present. Through years of practice, a person by his own efforts can liberate his spirit from the shell of his body and send it soaring to the heights. A single session of meditation, when completed, will allow a person to rove through all the corners of the universe.

※　※　※

On the Union of Nature and Destiny

Nature is spirit. Destiny is material energy. When nature is supported by destiny it is like a bird buoyed up and carried along by the wind—flying freely with little effort. Whatever one wills to be, one can be. This is the meaning in the line from the *Classic of the Shadowy Talismans*:[2] "The bird is controlled by the air." The Perfect Truth[3] Daoist must treasure this line and not reveal its message casually to the uninitiated. The gods themselves will chide the person who disobeys this instruction. The search for the hidden meaning of nature and mind is the basic motif of the art of self-cultivation. This must be remembered at all times.

※　※　※

On Leaving the Mundane World

Leaving the mundane world is not leaving the body; it is leaving behind the mundane mind. Consider the analogy of the lotus; although rooted in the mud, it blossoms pure and white into the clear air. The man who attains

---

1. A sacred mountain located in present-day Shandong Province that for millennia was important for the imperial cult and for Buddhists as well as for Daoists.
2. Also known as the *Scripture of the Hidden Accordance* (*Yinfu jing*), a text that first appeared in the 7th century; some scholars view it as a military treatise, while others (and most Daoist commentaries) interpret it as about the harmony between nature and humans.
3. That is, Complete Perfection.

the Way, although corporally abiding in the world, may flourish through his mind in the realm of sages. Those people who presently seek after nondeath or escape from the world do not know this true principle and commit the greatest folly.

THE RECORD OF PERFECTED PERPETUAL SPRING'S TRAVELS TO THE WEST
(Changchun zhenren xiyou ji)

LI ZHICHANG

The *Record of Perfected Perpetual Spring's Travels to the West* (*Changchun zhenren xiyou ji*) provides a first-person account of the meeting between Qiu Chuji—also known as Changchun, or Perpetual Spring (1148–1227)—and the Mongol leader Genghis Khan (Chinggis Qan, 1162–1227). This text, compiled by Qiu's disciple Li Zhichang (1193–1256), provides a precious glimpse into the conditions leading to the rise and development of the Complete Perfection (Quanzhen) movement as it became an officially recognized Daoist monastic tradition during the Yuan dynasty (1260–1368).

Qiu Chuji was himself a disciple of Wang Zhe (1113–1170), the founder of the Complete Perfection order, and by 1222, when as an elderly man he made his arduous journey via Central Asia to the Khan's seasonal abode (near present-day Kabul), he held a powerful position within the order's hierarchy. According to Li, word of Qiu's accomplishments had spread far and wide, attracting the attention of Genghis Khan. Though their discussions are not fully recorded, he apparently made a good impression, since the ruler became a strong financial and political benefactor of Qiu and the Complete Perfection Daoist tradition. For example, an inscription at the Palace of Eternal Joy (Yongle gong) records a decree allowing Daoists to focus solely on their religious prayers and exempting their temples and lands from taxation (see the following selection).

Some fifty years later, however, Genghis Khan's grandson Kubilai Khan (1215–1294) reversed those generous policies and ordered the burning of the Complete Perfection canon. The Complete Perfection order would survive that persecution, thanks to its hold on rural areas, and even would regain court patronage, but the effects were long lasting: branch lineages began to form, Complete Perfection literary output declined, and many Complete Perfection writings were lost. Indeed, the modern printing of the Daoist canon contains few Complete Perfection texts. Yet the tradition has had a profound historical impact. Today the Complete Perfection order, with its celibate clergy and large monasteries, is the main Daoist school in China.

PRONOUNCING GLOSSARY

Changchun zhenren xiyou ji: *chawng-choon chun-run hsi-yo gee*
Li Zhichang: *lee chih-chawng*
Qiu: *chi-oh*

Tämügä ot-chigin: *tah-moo-gah oht-chee-gihn*
Xuande zhou: *hsuan-duh-chou*

He[1] celebrated the Full Moon of mid-autumn (September 13th) at home in the temple. In the afternoon he initiated his followers into the use of various spells and also received candidates for the priesthood. The huge crowd that had collected was obliged to sit all day in the open. It comprised old people and children, many of whom were severely affected by the heat. Suddenly a cloud, shaped like an umbrella, settled over the assembly and remained there for several hours, to the extreme relief and astonishment of those who sat under it. A second miracle happened in connection with the well-water, which was sufficient for a hundred people, but not for a crowd of over a thousand. The people in charge made plans beforehand for getting water from elsewhere; but on the three days round the time of Full Moon the well brimmed with water right up to the top, and however much was drawn, remained at the same level, so great was the assistance that his virtue elicited from Heaven. At the beginning of the eighth month, in response to an invitation from his lordship Yelu Tuhua, Marshal of Xuande, he took up residence in the Zhaoyuan temple, which lies at the north-west angle of the town. Yelu, being a patron of this temple, had hastened, on receiving news of the Master's journey, to repair the main buildings, fill it with holy images and redecorate all the adjoining cells and outbuildings. During the tenth month the Memorial Hall (dedicated to the Patriarchs and Saints) was being decorated with wall-paintings; but the cold weather had put a stop to the work. The Master refused to let it be suspended, saying: "If ever the flute of such a one as Zouyan[2] could bring back the spring-time, surely you credit me with power enough over the elements to make this work possible?" Presently, in the middle of winter, the weather became as balmy as in spring; there were no dust-storms, and the painter was able to finish his work.

Shortly after this Alixian arrived from the Tent of Prince Tämügä ot-chigin (the younger brother of Chingiz[3]) with an invitation to the Master; he was followed by the Commissioner Wang Ji, who said that he had received special orders from the Prince that if the Master came to the West he was on no account to omit paying the Prince a visit. The Master moved his head in sign of assent. This month, when he was on an excursion to the Wang Mountains in the north, Yelu Tuhua returned from delivering his message to the Emperor. He bore a Command addressed "from the Emperor Chingiz to the Adept, Master Qiu". This document praised the Dao of the Master above that of the Three Philosophers (Laozi, Liezi, and Zhuangzi) and declared that his merits were recognized in the remotest corners of the earth. Further on the Emperor said: "Now that your cloud-girt chariot has issued from Fairyland, the cranes that draw it will carry you pleasantly through the realms of India. Bodhidharma,[4] when he came to the East, by spiritual communication revealed the imprint on his heart; Laozi, when he

Translated by Arthur Waley.

1. That is, Perpetual Spring, or Qiu Chuji (1148–1227).
2. The story is from Liezi [translator's note]. Liezi (fl. 4th century B.C.E.), to whom the *Liezi* is attributed, was one of the "three philosophers" who developed the basic ideas of Daoism; the others were Laozi and Zhuangzi.
3. Genghis or Chinggis Khan (1162–1127), founder of the Mongol empire.
4. The Indian monk said to have brought Chan (Zen) Buddhism to China in the late 5th century C.E.

travelled to the West perfected his Dao by converting the Central Asians.[5] The way before you, both by land and water, is indeed long; but I trust that the comforts I shall provide will make it not seem long. This reply to your letter will show you my anxiety on your behalf. Having learnt that you passed safely through the severe heat of autumn, I will not now trouble you with further friendly messages".

Such was the respect with which the Emperor addressed him! Chingiz also gave instructions to Liu Wen that the Master was not to over-exert himself or go too long without food, and was to travel in comfort, by easy stages. The Master now pointed out to Liu Wen that in the country through which they would have to pass the weather was already becoming severe; the passage across the Gobi[6] was long, and the necessities of the journey still remained to be collected. Why should they not stay at the Longyang temple till the spring, which was the most advantageous time at which to start? Liu Wen accepted this proposal and on the 18th day the Master journeyed South and once more took up residence at the Longyang. On the fourteenth day of the eleventh month (December 10th) he attended a service at the Buddhist temple Longyan si and wrote up a poem on the wall of the western gallery of the main hall.

On the 15th day of the first month (February 18th) of the next year (1221) he celebrated the Full Moon at the Zhaoyuan temple in Xuande zhou. Here he showed the people the following didactic verses.

> A little lump of foul flesh falls to the earth
> And from it shoots a demon-sprout of Good and Ill,
> Fills with its leaves and laced branches the Three Worlds;[7]
> This mighty tree whose ceaseless growth entangles Time!

The journey began on the eighth day of the second month (March 3rd) in excellent weather. His Daoist friends accompanied him to the western outskirts of the town and there standing at his horse's head they asked him, weeping, when they might expect to see him back from this immense journey upon which he was setting out. At first he would say no more than that, if their hearts remained firmly set upon the Dao, they would surely see him again. But when, with tears in their eyes, they begged him to be more particular, he told them that the goings and stoppings of Man were determined elsewhere than on earth. "Moreover", he said, "travelling thus into strange lands I cannot yet tell whether their Dao will harmonize with mine or not". But the people said: "Master, we cannot believe that you do not know these things. We beseech you to foretell them to us." He saw that there was nothing for it but to tell them, and twice he said distinctly, "I shall return in three years".

* * *

On the eighteenth day of the eleventh month (December 3rd, 1221) after crossing a great river, we reached the northern outskirts of the mighty city

---

5. A reference to the "Conversion of the Barbarians" story; see Xiang Kai's "Memorial to Emperor Huan Concerning Buddhism and Daoism" and "The Texts on the Conversion to the Barbarians," above.
6. The Gobi Desert.

7. The Buddhist universe, divided into the Realm of Desire (inhabited by beings who desire pleasing objects of the senses), the Realm of Form (inhabited by gods that have physical form), and the Formless Realm (inhabited by gods that exist only as consciousness).

of Samarkand. The Civil Governor his Highness I-la, together with the Mongol and local authorities, came to meet us outside the town. They brought wine and set up a great number of tents. Here we brought our wagons to a stop. The envoy Liu Wen, who had not been able to get far owing to the road being blocked, now said to the Master when seated with him: "I have just learnt that it is at present impossible to cross the great river which lies a thousand *li*[8] ahead of us, as native bandits have destroyed the boats and bridge. Moreover it is now the middle of winter. Would it not be better, my father and master, if your meeting with the Great Khan took place in the spring?" The Master agreed.

※　※　※

Li, who was in charge of the Observatory, and others, asked the Master to go for a walk to the west of the town. The envoy and other officials came, bringing us grape-wine. That day there was not a cloud, and the air was very clear. Wherever we went we came to terraces, lakes, pagodas and towers, with here and there an orchard or vegetable garden. We lay and rested on the grass, all of us very happy. The mysteries of Dao were discussed and from time to time wine was handed round. The sun was already setting when we returned.

The fifteenth of the second month (March 29th) was the hundred and fifth day (after the winter solstice, December 14th), and on the same day is celebrated the festival of the Great High Pure Original One.[9] The officials again invited the Master to take a walk to the west of the town. Woods and gardens stretched continuously for over a hundred *li*. There are none in China to surpass them. But here the woods are silent, for there are no songbirds.

In the first ten days of the month, Alixian arrived from the Emperor's encampment with the following message: "Adept! You have spared yourself no pains in coming to me across hill and stream, all the way from the lands of sunrise. Now I am on my way home and am impatient to hear your teaching. I hope you are not too tired to come and meet me". For the envoy Liu Wen there was a further message: "I count on you to convey my message and persuade him to come. If you are successful in this, I shall not fail one day to reward you with rich lands". Finally he sent to Chinkai the message: "By your careful supervision of the Adept's journey, you have earned my gratitude". The Commander-in-chief Bo'orju was ordered to convey him through the Iron Gate Pass with an escort of a thousand armed men. The Master asked Alixian about the route which they were about to follow, and he replied: "I myself left here on the thirteenth day of the first month (February 25th), and after travelling for three days towards the south-east I went through the Iron Gates. Then after five days I crossed a large river. On the first of the second month (March 15th), travelling towards the southeast, I crossed the Great Snow Mountains. The snow was so deep that when I plunged my riding-whip into it, I did not get near the bottom. Even the trodden snow of the roadway was about five foot deep. We then went south for three days, and arrived at the Khan's camp. I gave an account of your arrival, at the news of which he was delighted. I was there several days, and

---

8. One *li* is a unit of distance equal to about 1/3 mile. "The great river": the Amu Darya, which today marks Afghanistan's northern border with Tajikistan, Uzbekistan, and Turkmenistan.
9. That is, Laozi; the festival celebrates his birthday.

then came back to Samarkand". The Master left Yin Zhiping and two other disciples in his quarters and taking with him five or six disciples, together with Liu Wen and the rest, he set out on the fifteenth day of the third month (April 28th), and on the fourth day passed through the town of Jieshi (Kesh),[1] where the commander Bo'orju, having already received the Emperor's instructions, was waiting with a thousand Mongol and native troops to escort the Master through the Iron Gates (the modern Buzgala Defile, 55 miles south of Kesh). Proceeding in a south-easterly direction we crossed some very high mountains. The way was strewn with boulders and it took the strength of our whole escort to get our wagons along. We were two days crossing this pass. We then came out into a valley, and followed the stream southwards. Our convoy was obliged to turn back northwards into the mountains, to deal with some brigands. On the fifth day we reached a small river which we crossed in boats. The banks were thickly wooded. On the seventh day we crossed a large river called the Amu Munian (Amu Darya).

Hence we travelled south-east, and towards evening halted near an ancient canal. On its banks grew reeds of a peculiar kind not found in China. The larger ones keep green all through the winter. Some of these we took and made into walking-sticks. Some we used that night to hold up the wagon-shafts, and so strong were they that they did not break. On the small reeds the leaves fall off in winter and grow afresh in the spring. A little to the south, in the hills, there is a large bamboo with pith inside. This is used by the soldiers to make lances and spears. We also saw lizards about three feet long, blue-black in colour.

It was now the twenty-ninth of the third month (May 11th) and the Master made a poem. After four more days of travelling we reached the Khan's camp. He sent his high officer, Hela bode to meet us. This was on the fifth day of the fourth month. When arrangements had been made for the Master's lodging, he at once presented himself to the Emperor, who expressed his gratitude, saying: "Other rulers summoned you, but you would not go to them. And now you have come ten thousand *li* to see me. I take this as a high compliment".

The Master replied: "That I, a hermit of the mountains, should come at your Majesty's bidding was the will of Heaven". Chingiz was delighted, begged him to be seated and ordered food to be served. Then he asked him: "Adept, what Medicine of Long Life have you brought me from afar?" The Master replied: "I have means of protecting life, but no elixir that will prolong it". The Emperor was pleased with his candour, and had two tents for the Master and his disciples set up to the east of his own. The interpreter now said to him: "People call you 'Tängri Möngkä Kün'.[2] Did you choose this name yourself or did others give it to you?" He answered: "I, the hermit of the mountains, did not give myself this name. Others gave it to me". The interpreter subsequently came to him on the Emperor's behalf and asked another question. "What", he said, "were you called in former days?" He replied that he had been one of four pupils who studied under Zhongyang.[3] The other three had all grown wings, and only he was left in the world.

---

1. In Uzbekistan.
2. Mongol, "The Heavenly Eternal Man" [translator's note].

3. Wang Zhe (1113–1170), the founder of the Quanzhen (Complete Perfection) order.

"People", he said, "generally call me *xiansheng* ('senior')." The Emperor asked Chinkai what he ought to call the Adept. "Well, some people", said Chinkai, "call him 'Father and Master'; others, 'The Adept'; others, the holy *xian*."[4] "From now onwards", said the Emperor, "he shall be called the holy *xian*."

* * *

We followed the river up-stream and then went south-east for thirty *li*. Lack of water now compelled us to travel by night. We passed the great city of Balkh. Its inhabitants had recently rebelled against the Khan and been removed; but we could still hear dogs barking in its streets.

At dawn we breakfasted and after going eastward for twenty or thirty *li* came to a river that ran to the north. We were just able to ford it on horseback, and on the far side rested and camped for the night. On the twenty-second (September 28th) Chinkai came to meet us and we were soon in the Khan's camp.

Presently the Khan sent Chinkai to ask whether the Master wished to see him at once or to rest for a little first. The Master replied that he was ready. On this as on all subsequent occasions when Daoists interviewed the Emperor we did not kneel or bow down before him, but merely inclined the body and pressed the palms of the hands together on entering his tent. When the audience was over we were given kurmiss,[5] and as soon as it was finished took our leave. The Emperor asked whether we were properly provided for at our lodging in Samarkand. The Master replied that previously the supplies received from the Mongols, the natives and the Governor had been adequate, but that recently there had been some difficulties about food, the provision of which had fallen entirely upon the Governor. Next day the Emperor again sent his personal officers to our tent. He had asked him to suggest that the Adept should take all his meals with the Emperor. But the Master replied: "I am a mountain hermit and am only at my ease in quiet places". The Emperor said he was to be humoured. On the twenty-seventh day the Emperor set out on his return to the north. On the way he sent us repeated presents of grape-wine, melons and greens.

On the first of the ninth month we crossed a bridge of boats and went on to the north. The Master now pointed out that the time for his discourse had arrived and suggested that the Governor Ahai should be summoned.

On the fifteenth (October 1st) an imposing pavilion was erected, the women of the Khan's retinue were sent away. To left and right candles and torches flared. Only Chinkai, being a *chärbi*[6] and the envoy Liu Wen were allowed even to be in attendance at the door. The Master entered accompanied by the Governor Ahai and Alixian. After taking his seat he pointed out that Liu Wen and Chinkai had performed immense journeys on his behalf and begged that they might be admitted, so that they too could hear his discourse. This suggestion was followed. The Master's words were translated into Mongo[7] by Ahai. The Emperor was delighted with his doctrine and on the nineteenth, when there was a bright night, sent for him again. On this occasion too he was much pleased by what he heard, and sent for

4. An immortal or transcendent (a Daoist who has achieved extraordinary powers and a higher form of existence).

5. Fermented mare's milk (kumiss).
6. A chamberlain.
7. That is, Mongolian.

the Master to his tent once more on the twenty-third (October 29th). He was here treated with the same regard as before and the Emperor listened to him with evident satisfaction. He ordered that the Master's words should be recorded, and especially that they should be written down in Chinese characters, that they might be preserved from oblivion. To those present he said: "You have heard the holy Immortal discourse three times upon the art of nurturing the vital spirit. His words have sunk deeply into my heart. I rely upon you not to repeat what you have heard". During the remainder of the Imperial Progress to the east, the Master constantly discoursed to the Emperor concerning the mysteries of Dao.

INSCRIPTIONS FROM THE PALACE
OF ETERNAL JOY

The Palace of Eternal Joy (Yongle gong) is an important Complete Perfection (Quanzhen) Daoist temple in North China, in present-day Shanxi, connected with the cult to an immortal named Lü Dongbin. Most of the separate halls within this enormous complex were completed in the late thirteenth century. The Palace of Eternal Joy is a significant repository of massive painted murals—mainly of Daoist deities, together with a hagiographical account of Lü Dongbin—as well as statues and temple inscriptions. These inscriptions, written between the thirteenth and the fourteenth century, are important sources of information on the history of the site; three of them are translated below.

"A Record of the Tang Dynasty Shrine to Perfected Man Lü of Purified Yang" ("You Tang Chunyang Lü zhenren citang ji"), by a literatus named Yuan Congyi (1159–1224), focuses on the site's setting, described as sacred, as conducive to the pursuit of transcendence, and as marked with the traces of Daoist immortals, such as Lü Dongbin, which imbue the site with a further level of numinous power. "A Stele on the Reconstruction of the Great Palace of Purified Yang and Limitless Longevity [during] Our Great Dynasty" ("Dachao chongjian Chunyang wanshou gong zhi bei"), written by the well-regarded scholar-official Wang E (1190–1273), provides an evocative account of turning points in the temple's history, from its founding on the site of Lü's former residence to its expansion, later immolation, and restoration. The stele that records the final inscription, "A Stele of an Imperial Decree [Issued to] the Palace of Purified Yang and Limitless Longevity" ("Chunyang wanshou gong shengzhi bei"), was erected at the Palace of Eternal Joy in 1327. This imperial decree, issued by Genghis Khan (Chinggis Qan, 1162–1127), released Daoists—along with Nestorian Christians, Muslims, and Buddhists—from all quotidian duties so they could focus on their religious prayers. In addition, it exempted the buildings and lands of the Palace of Eternal Joy from taxation. This type of inscription, often found at Daoist and Buddhist sites, proclaimed in stone the imperial protection that a site had received in the past and hoped to continue to receive in the future.

The Palace of Eternal Joy can still be visited today, though no longer at its original site. To preserve it from flooding by a planned dam, the entire temple complex was removed in 1959 and rebuilt almost ten miles away.

Chunyang wanshou gong shengzhi bei: *choon-yawng wawn-show kung shung-chih bay*

Dachao chongjian Chunyang wanshou gong zhi bei: *dah-chao chowng-chien choon-yawng wawn-show kung chih bay*

Wang E: *wawng uh*

You Tang Chunyang Lü zhenren citang ji: *yo tawng choon-yawng lou chun-run tsuh-tawng gee*

Yongle gong: *yowng-luh gowng*

Yuan Congyi: *yuen tsowng-yee*

FROM A RECORD OF THE TANG DYNASTY SHRINE TO PERFECTED MAN LÜ OF PURIFIED YANG

(*You Tang Chunyang Lü zhenren citang ji*)
YUAN CONGYI

To the south of the Leishou mountains and to the north of the great river [the Yellow River], the terrain is lush and lovely, the soil highly fertile, and the woods fair. The pure essence of its *qi*,[1] when forming people, will surely create mighty immortals[2] and great worthies. From ancient times, there have been many traces of the sages who settled here.

If one walks one hundred paces to the northeast corner of Yongle Town, one comes to Summoning Worthies Village. To the north of the road lies the former residence of Lord Lü, who attained the Way during the Tang dynasty.[3] Because the locals admired his virtuous conduct, they transformed his residence into a temple and offered sacrifices on a strict basis every year.

* * *

In my youth I lived in a prince's palace less than one hundred *li*[4] from the Perfected One's [Lü's] rural home. Although I always revered [Lü], I never [went to his shrine] to make offerings of incense, something I always regretted. Now, in the autumn of this year [1221], having fled from the chaos of fighting in the north [resulting from Mongol incursions], I hid in the suburbs to the west of Ruicheng and finally had the chance to worship at this shrine. A Daoist friend residing at the shrine named Yuan Gongyi implored me to write a record of this shrine. Although I have no skill at writing, I dared not stubbornly refuse and have described [the shrine's] history [above].

TRANSLATED BY Paul R. Katz. All bracketed additions are the translator's.

1. Vital energy, breath (pneuma).
2. Daoists who have achieved extraordinary powers and a higher form of existence; the perfected, who have moved beyond earthly corruption, are higher than the immortals (or transcendents).
3. 618–907 C.E. "Lord Lü": Lü Dongbin.
4. One *li* is a unit of distance equal to about 1/3 mile.

FROM A STELE ON THE RECONSTRUCTION OF THE GREAT PALACE OF PURIFIED YANG AND LIMITLESS LONGEVITY [DURING] OUR GREAT DYNASTY
(Dachao chongjian Chunyang wanshou gong zhi bei)

WANG E

From the end of the Tang dynasty, the local people [worshiped Lü at] his former residence . . . named the Shrine of Lord Lü. Each spring, scholar-officials and commoners from near and far would gather in front of his shrine, performing music and making offerings all day long. . . .

In recent times, the local officials were concerned that the temple was too cramped and therefore enlarged it into a Daoist belvedere, selecting some of the area's most worthy Daoists to reside there. . . .

During the winter of 1244, a fire swept through the belvedere. In one night . . . this was taken as a sign of great renewal. In the following year, the status of the belvedere was elevated to that of palace, and Lü was promoted from perfected being to heavenly worthy.[5] Song Defang,[6] the Perfected Man Cloaked in the Clouds, was in the area at the time and said to his disciples: "Our patriarch has been promoted. His temple's status has been elevated. How can we justify our actions if we do not rebuild it?" Therefore . . . the leaders of the movement, Yin Zhiping [referred to by his Daoist name Qinghe, which means "Pure Harmony"] and Li Zhichang [referred to by his Daoist name Zhenchang (Perfect Constancy)], commanded that the Great Master of Soaring Harmony Pan Dechong, then Daoist registrar at Yanjing, be appointed to serve as chief superintendent of Daoists in the Northern and Southern Routes of Hedong and oversee the temple's reconstruction. . . .

Laborers for this project came from near and far, with Pan making the greatest efforts in instructing them on the new works to be completed. . . . The Mongol court later decreed that the blocks for the edition of the Daoist Canon compiled by Song Defang be stored in the temple, which augmented its prestige. . . .

In the year 1252, Li Zhichang stayed at the temple on his return trip to the capital after having made sacrifices to the Five Marchmounts[7] as commanded by the emperor Möngke. The next day he ascended Nine Peaks Mountain and rested at the Cave of Purified Yang. He loved the beauty of its heights, renaming it "Jade Seat." He then commanded his disciple Liu Ruoshui to take charge of the "Upper Palace." . . .

[There are] three [main buildings]: the Hall of the Limitless Ultimate, where the Three Pure ones[8] are worshiped; the Hall of Attainment of the Origin, in which [Lü] Chunyang is worshiped; and the Hall of Inherited Brightness, in which the Seven Perfected of the Perfect Realization

5. In the Lingbao (Numinous Treasure) tradition, the personification of the Dao.
6. A disciple (1183–1247) of the founder of the Quanzhen (Complete Perfection) tradition, Qiu Chuji.
7. A group of five sacred mountains—one in each of the four cardinal directions and one at the center.
8. Celestial Worthy of Primordial Commencement (Yuanshi tianzun), the Celestial Worthy of Numinous Treasure (Lingbao tianzun), and the Celestial Worthy of the Way and Its Virtue (Daode tianzun).

movement are worshiped. The Three Masters have their hall; the perfected man [Lü], his shrine. There are also places for Daoists to reside in and guests to stay at as well as vegetarian kitchens, storehouses, stables, gardens, wells, bathrooms. . . .

A STELE OF AN IMPERIAL DECREE [ISSUED TO] THE PALACE OF PURIFIED YANG AND LIMITLESS LONGEVITY
(*Chunyang wanshou gong shengzhi bei*)

An imperial decree relying on the might of everlasting heaven and the fortune of the emperor:

To all military officials and other military personnel, overseers serving in urban and rural areas, as well as other traveling civil officials, the following decree is hereby announced:

A decree issued by Cinggis Qan [r. 1206–1227] and Ogodei Qayan [r. 1229–1241]:

All members of the Buddhist *sangha*,[9] Nestorian Christians, Daoists, and Muslims are exempt from all manner of duties, their sole task being to pray to heaven and ask for blessings [for the emperor/state]; this has been decreed before. Today, based on the decrees already issued, do not force [these religious specialists] to undertake any duties, [apart from] praying to heaven and asking for blessings.

In Hezhong Prefecture there are three temples built by Pan Dechong [and his disciples]: the Palace of Purified Yang and Limitless Longevity, the Upper Palace of Nine Peaks [Mountain], and the Numinous Origin Palace to the River Gods (Hedu lingyuan gong). [These are managed] by the superintendents Wen Zhitong, Bai Zhichun, and Zhu Zhiwan, and this imperial decree is bestowed upon them.

As regards the various buildings inside these temples, you traveling officials should not stay in them, nor should you avail yourselves of the temples' horses. Do not levy any commercial or land taxes on these temples and their lands, gardens, or mills. As for the Daoists [living there], they may not use this decree to act in any way that they please. Would they dare do so?

Issued by the emperor in Dadu [the Yuan dynasty[1] capital, later known as Beijing].

9. The Buddhist community, especially the monks and nuns.
1. 1260–1368.

ESSAY ON THE SECRET ESSENTIALS OF THE RECYCLED ELIXIR
(*Huandan biyao lun*)

WANG DAOYUAN

The *Essay on the Secret Essentials of the Recycled Elixir* (*Huandan biyao lun*) is a text by Wang Daoyuan (fl. fourteenth century), a figure most likely connected with the Southern Lineage of internal alchemy. It provides a detailed account of the fundamental structure of internal alchemy (*neidan*)—the process of inner circulation by which an elixir is manufactured inside the body, rather than manufactured externally with base minerals. Alchemical writings are generally difficult for the uninitiated to comprehend, even when presented in prose as clear as Wang's *Essay*, which he describes as the leaking of a secret esoteric teaching.

In this text, which presents a complex body of correlations between the microcosm of the body and the macrocosm of Heaven and Earth, Wang tries to introduce the complex symbolism of internal alchemy as a path of meditative self-cultivation, leading to the completion of the internal elixir and, in turn, the creation of the immortal embryo (fetus). Once it is born, the initiate's spiritual powers can be realized and he or she can wander the clouds as a deity. That transformation is a return to an originally perfect inherent nature (a reverting to the source) from which humans stray because of commerce with the temptations and seductions of the quotidian external world.

After laying out his own "correct" path, Wang warns against a huge array of heretical teachings that apparently were circulating in his day. He concludes by emphasizing, as had those belonging to earlier Daoist movements, that one must study under a well-chosen master in order to avoid falling into heterodoxy.

PRONOUNCING GLOSSARY

hai: *hi*

Huandan biyao lun: *huan-dawn bee-yao loon*

Wang Daoyuan: *wawng dowayuen*

Now, the recycling of the elixir [i.e., alchemy] is the *dao* of reverting to the source and returning to the prime. You are born endowed with your father's (seminal) essence and your mother's blood. At first, when you were a ruddy infant, your primal essence, Qi,[1] and spirit were all pure and whole. But then as you gradually aged and grew into an adult, we may say that, because the four (sensory) gates—the eyes, ears, nose, and tongue—were tempted [by outside influences], therefore your single numinous, perfect, inherent nature was touched by colors, sounds, fragrances, and tastes, and became deeply tainted by bad habits. Thus, as day followed day, and one year succeeded the next, your primal essence transformed into coital essence, primal Qi transformed into respiratory qi, and primal spirit transformed into cognitive spirit.

TRANSLATED BY Clarke Hudson. All bracketed additions are the translator's.

1. Breath or pneuma, here capitalized or lowercased to differentiate between its perfect and common forms.

After these Three Primes have been split up and leaked away, it is difficult to recover your original, natural perfection. Therefore, the patriarchs have offered down their words to us, establishing [traditions of] teaching and recording them in the various elixir scriptures, to show us the methods of cultivation and replenishment. If essence has been depleted then use essence to replenish it, replenish *qi* with *qi*, and replenish spirit with spirit, recovering them all by applying the *dao* of reverting to the source and returning to the prime. Now, what is this "recovering"? This means making the essence whole in order to send down deep roots, making the *qi* whole in order to firm up the stem, and making the spirit whole in order [to achieve] a wondrous union. If a person of this generation is able to make these three things whole and complete, then these things will truly be perfected pharmaca[2] within the body.

However, even if this should be so, and yet you do not know the methods of transporting [the pharmacon], the [hot yang] firing and [cold yin] tallies,[3] and the tempering [with high heat], then you will remain in a state of yin, and to the end will not attain the *dao* of the wondrous [perfection] of physical form and spirit together. Don't you know that the *dao* of humanity tallies with Heaven and Earth? The work of a single breath [can] seize a year's worth of macrocosmic creation and transformation. Take Qian and Kun[4] as the cauldron and vessel, sun and moon as the water and fire, crow and rabbit as the pharmaca, yin and yang as the trigger of transformation, dragon and tiger as the marvelous application, the cyclical-signs *zi* and *wu*[5] as the winter and summer solstices, and the cyclical-signs *mao* and *you* as the vernal and autumnal equinoxes. All of these are just pattern-images or metaphors—actually, they are no different from the three words "body," "heart-mind," and "intention." The body is fastened to the essence, the heart-mind to the *qi*, and the intention to the spirit. "Reversion" means making these three things revert and advance against the current. "Returning" means recycling these three things and recovering your perfection. When the three things are made whole and united with perfection, we call this the recycled elixir.

I am afraid that students would cling to a biased point of view, and would not awaken to this truth. I do not quail at [the threat of] censure by the celestial [court], but must leak the secret and reveal the celestial key. Whenever you enter the chamber and make the elixir, your heart-mind must be empty, your inherent nature must be quiet and still, and your spirit and *Qi* must mix and meld within the middle *dantian*.[6] The moment when the one [bit of] yang first stirs is the moment of winter solstice within the body. At this moment, you must close the gates. Send the *wu*[-earth] flying,

---

2. Drugs, medicine.
3. Yin and yang are the complementary forces that unite to form the Dao: yin, a term that originally referred to the shady side of a valley, by extension came to be associated with the dark, earth, dampness, and passivity—the female principle; yang, a term that originally referred to the sunny side of a valley, by extension came to be associated with the light, heaven, dryness, and activity—the male principle.
4. The first two trigrams, Qian ☰ (entirely yang,

being all whole lines) and Kun ☷ (entirely yin, being all broken lines); on the trigrams, see the introduction to *The Seal of the Unity of the Three, in Accordance with the Book of Changes* (*Zhouyi cantong qi*), above.
5. Together with *mao* and *you*, the four cardinal points (north, south, east, and west); they are also "branches" in the traditional Chinese system of recording time, which involves ten Celestial Stems and twelve Earthly Branches.
6. The middle Cinnabar Field (the heart).

and jam it into the bottom of the ocean abyss.[7] The dragon cruising under-water is not easy to put to use.

Wait until you see the dragon in the field, then turn the chain-pump [reaching to] the fontanel, and slowly hoist [the pharmacon] up from the Palace of Great Mystery.[8] During the first six hours, the flying dragon directly penetrates the Three Passes. During the second six hours, it tra-verses the Southern Palace,[9] copulating [with the tiger]. This amounts to gathering the yang from within the trigram Kan (☵), then clearing out the yin within the trigram Li (☲) and filling it in [with the yang from Kan]. Starting at the cyclical sign of *zi* and lasting until the sign of *si*,[1] the six yang [lines] unite [to form] the hexagram Qian. From this point onward, yang will tend toward endlessness.

The one yin [*yao*-line] appears below the five yang [lines]. The action of the yin hexagram Kun [involves] using *ji*[-earth], which comes from the trigram Li, to withdraw the yin tallies.[2] Descend by the Golden Portal and Magpie Bridge, to enter the Storeyed Tower and Vermilion Palace,[3] and deliver [the amalgam] home to the crucible of earth. Starting at the cyclical sign of *wu* and reaching the sign of *hai*[4] (the six yin tallies), yang returns to [pure yin at] the position of Kun. The twin gates of Xun[5] open, and the perfected fire smelts and refines [the pharmaca], fusing them to form a golden fetus of empty *Qi*, which we call the recycled elixir.

In this fashion, gather the pharmaca at the proper time, and transport the tallies according to the norm. When you refine [the elixir] earnestly and cook it diligently, substance will appear from that which is insubstantial. Ten months later, when your labors are full and complete, the fetus is released through parturition, and switches to a [new] cauldron. Shift the spirit upward to dwell in the Muddy Pellet [Palace];[6] let it burst forth, break-ing the Celestial Gate; then send the spirit out [under your] nurturance and care. At this time, the most essential thing is to keep your feet on solid ground, and not miss [the mark] by so much as a hair. Wait until your spirit powers are full and complete: then you can transform spontaneously, pen-etrating stone or metal, appearing freely in response to time and circum-stance. Roaming at ease amidst the clouds [and far from the world], with limitless delight, you can be a perfected transcendent[7] who escapes the eon's [end]. Anyone who attains this state does it through his determined and ardent self-cultivation.

The alchemists' marvelous application is to take "action" as the starting point and "non-action" as the ending point. The establishment of inherent nature depends on life-endowment, and the cultivation of life-endowment must follow inherent nature. When nature and endowment are [in a state

---

7. The lower Cinnabar Field (the abdomen); it is yin, while the dragon is yang.
8. The lower Cinnabar Field (the dragon pro-ceeds up the spine).
9. The upper Cinnabar Field (the head).
1. Two of the Earthly Branches, here indicating two-hour increments of the day: 11 P.M.–1 A.M. (*zi*) and 9 A.M.–11 A.M. (*si*).
2. That is, the talismans.
3. Locations in the body, beginning with a spot between the eyes (Golden Portal) and with the tongue (the link between the base and roof of the mouth), then moving to the esophagus (the Sto-

reyed Tower) and the heart (the Vermilion Pal-ace, a name of the middle Cinnabar Field).
4. Another twelve-hour period, from 11 A.M.–1 P.M. (*wu*) to 9 P.M.—11 A.M. (*hai*).
5. The nostrils.
6. The crown of the head. "The Muddy Pellet [Palace]": the central of the nine palaces inside the head.
7. A Daoist who has achieved extraordinary pow-ers and a higher form of existence; in later Daoism the perfected (*zhenren*), who have moved beyond earthly corruption, are generally viewed as higher than the transcendents (or immortals, *xian*).

of] mixed completion, they are of one body with the great void. So what could still be binding them to [the realm of] birth and death? This is the great method that has been transmitted between sages, unchanged down through the ages. If you abandon this and seek after some other marvel instead, that would amount to [following] a heterodox path. There are various types [of heterodox practitioners]. Some cut off thoughts and maintain a state of emptiness; some abstain from eating grains; some [practice] penetrating visualization and silently visit the [celestial] court; some gulp auroras and swallow *qi*; some practice auto-massage or stretching and breathing; and some visualize fire roasting their umbilicus. Some select pretty women to be the furnace or cauldron, and take the unfailing golden spear as the sign of victory in the [boudoir] battle. Some take menses as the initial elixir-source, and take the female and male paired swords as the marvelous application. Some [overliterally] take the hours of *zi* [midnight] and *wu* [midday] as the times to enter the chamber and do seated meditation; some take the months of *mao* [fourth month] and *you* [tenth month] as the times to pause the firing process. There must be more than a thousand minor *daos* like these! These are all side-doors and little paths—how could they deserve to be called *daos*? The patriarch [Zhongli Quan[8]] said, "There are 3600 traditions of *dao*-methods, and each person takes one of them as his foundation. But, in all of this, there are very few points of mystery and subtlety, and they are not to be found among these 3600 traditions." This saying hits the nail on the head. Students must take care not to beguile themselves by grasping [at a limited perspective]. Haven't they heard this [Chan Buddhist] saying, spoken by the ancients?—"If you don't meet an expert from the get-go, then when you're old you'll be naught but an antiquated has-been instead." In cultivating perfection, the essential thing is to make a thorough study of [Confucian moral-cosmic] principle and inherent nature, investigating things and arriving at [moral] knowledge, and then return to the source and recover your life-endowment. Only then can you actualize the great Dao. If you do not seek the detailed instructions of a perfected master, then even if you have the talent of [Confucius's[9] favorite disciple] Yan Min, you still will not attain it. May all students chew on this!

---

8. By some accounts the most important of Daoism's Eight Immortals, a group of legendary *xian*; often called Zhongli of the Han because he was thought to have lived during the Han dynasty (202 B.C.E.–220 C.E.).

9. The teacher, philosopher, and political theorist (551–479 B.C.E.).

ZHONGLI OF THE HAN LEADS LAN CAIHE
TO ENLIGHTENMENT
(*Han Zhong Li dutuo Lan Caihe*)

Rituals generally have theatrical elements, for the origin of theater is in ritual. It is thus hardly surprising to find a close relationship between Daoist ritual and theatrical performances in China. Indeed, in one form of marionette theater, the puppeteer was an ordained ritual master (*fashi*). Ritual and theater can function similarly; for example, both can play a cathartic role in engaging with such concerns as the salvation of the dead in purgatory.

As the translators Stephen H. West and Wilt L. Idema note, the play *Zhongli of the Han Leads Lan Caihe to Enlightenment* (*Han Zhong Li dutuo Lan Caihe*, thirteenth–fourteenth century) belongs to a subgenre of northern dramas known as "deliverance plays." Some deliverance plays are Buddhist; others, such as this one, are Daoist. The label derives from a longer Buddhist phrase: "to be delivered by transcending the world and liberated from the cycle of transmigration." Deliverance is, in this understanding, a form of enlightenment and release. Because deliverance plays clearly mix Buddhism, Daoism, and Confucianism—and often incorporate some of the Eight Immortals—some scholars have connected them with the Complete Perfection (Quanzhen) Daoist order, which also was rooted mainly in the northern part of China. Among the characters in *Zhongli of the Han Leads Lan Caihe to Enlightenment* are three of the Eight Immortals: Lan Caihe, Zhongli Quan, and Lü Dongbin.

Its overall structure is similar to that of other Daoist deliverance plays. The play opens with the Daoist master and immortal Zhongli Quan recounting his vision of Lan Caihe (also called Xu Jian)—at this time an actor, though already halfway to immortality. Zhongli Quan decides to descend to him to lead him to final immortality. Yet, when Zhongli arrives at the theater where Lan is to perform with his family troupe, Lan—who obviously has no clue about his visitor's identity—mocks

Image of the Daoist transcendent Zhongli Quan holding a gourd, by Zhao Qi, Ming dynasty. Zhongli Quan headed the group of Eight Immortals and was also the master of the famous internal alchemist and transcendent Lü Dongbin. Both appear in *Zhongli of the Han Leads Lan Caihe to Enlightenment*.

"the reverend" and his piety, scorning the monastic life and aspirations to become an immortal. Unable to make headway alone in moving the recalcitrant Lan toward enlightenment, Zhongli calls on his fellow immortal Lü Dongbin, who appears in Act 2 in the guise of an official bent on physically punishing Lan for being too slow to perform his "official service." Terrified by the threat of receiving "forty blows," Lan Caihe eagerly accepts the alternative: leave home and become Zhongli's disciple. When he returns in Act 3, he joyously describes the freedom of his new life, in which he is still singing and dancing but now also reading *The Scripture of the Way and Its Virtue* (*Daode jing*; see above) and the *Book of Master Zhuang* (*Zhuangzi*; see above). In the final act, after he has spent thirty years with his master, the promise made by Zhongli Quan is fulfilled: the two go off together, joining the Queen Mother of the West at her fantastic Langyuan Orchard and Jasper Pool, as Lan Caihe himself enters the ranks of the Eight Immortals.

PRONOUNCING GLOSSARY

Han Zhong Li dutuo Lan Caihe: *hahn chowng-lee du-oh-tu-oh lawn tsai-huh*
Lan Caihe: *lawn tsai-huh*
Lü Dongbin: *lou tung-bin*

Xianlü: *hsien-lou*
Zhongli Quan: *chowng-lee chu-en*
Zhuangzi: *chuang-tzu*

Characters

Role type	Name, family role, or social role
Second male	Zhongli Quan
Female lead	Xiqianjin, Lan Caihe's wife
Extra female	Lan Caihe's sister
Child	Little Caihe
Clown	Bandleader Wang
Clown	Thinhead Li
Male lead	Lan Caihe
Runners	Yamen runners
Official	Lü Dongbin
Children	Children

[Act 1]

(SECOND MALE, *costumed as* ZHONGLI *enters, recites:*)

The gate of our birth is the door of our death,
Yet how many get it, how many become enlightened?
The hardest of men should ponder this when night falls—
Undying eternal life is a product of man himself!

This humble Daoist is surnamed Zhongli, named Quan, and styled Cloud House.[1] My designation in the Way is the Master of Upright Yang. I was just returning from a vegetarian banquet in Heaven when I saw a shaft of blue light from the lower realm stream up against the Ninth Empyrean.[2] I looked

TRANSLATED BY Stephen H. West and Wilt L. Idema.

1. By some accounts the most important of Daoism's Eight Immortals, a group of legendary *xian* ("transcendents" who have achieved extraordinary powers and a higher form of existence); often called Zhongli of the Han, because he was

thought to have lived during the Han dynasty (202 B.C.E.–220 C.E.).
2. The highest of the celestial spheres, where Daoist transcendents live.

for a long time then saw an actor in the Liangyuan Playhouse in Luoyang, Xu Jian, who is known by his stage name as Lan Caihe. This man already possesses half of what it takes to be an immortal. I might as well go straight down to the Liangyuan Playhouse and lead this person across. I'll see to it that

> King Yama remove Lan's life *and* his death from his Register,[3]
> In order to establish his name in the Palaces of the Purple Precinct;[4]
> I will point him toward that road to the corner of the sea at Heaven's edge,
> And guide that deluded one down the Great Way.

(*Exits.*)

(FEMALE LEAD *together with* EXTRA FEMALE, CHILD, *along with two* CLOWNS *dressed as* WANG *and* LI *enter,* WANG *speaks:*) One of us is Bandleader Wang, the other Thinhead Li, our elder brother is Lan Caihe. We all perform on the stage in Liangyuan Playhouse. This is our sister-in-law. We're going on ahead to set things up on the stage. . . . Let me open the door and see who shows up. (ZHONGLI *enters:*) I'll go straight down on my cloud to the lower realm and onto the stage in Liangyuan Playhouse. Here I am already. (*Acts out seeing the musician's bench and sits down.* CLOWN *speaks:*) Okay, Reverend, go on up to the bleachers or to the side seats to watch. This is where the women perform, not a place for you to sit. (ZHONGLI *speaks:*) Is that famous male lead Xu Jian home? (WANG *speaks:*) Old master, he'll be here by and by. Did you have something you wanted to say to him? (ZHONGLI *speaks:*) I'll wait until he gets here to talk to him personally. (WANG *speaks:*) Well, master, just sit here for a bit. Brother will be along any time.

(MALE LEAD, *dressed as* LAN CAIHE, *enters and speaks:*) I'm Xu Jian, called Lan Caihe in the theater. My wife is Xiqianjin, and we have a son. Little Caihe, whose wife is called Lanshanjing. Bandleader Wang is married to my elder sister and Thinhead Li to my younger. We all perform here on the stage of Liangyuan Playhouse. Yesterday we hung out our spangled advertisements, and my two brothers have gone on ahead to make everything ready. I'd best get to the stage. I believe that the life of an actor is no easy thing! (*Sings:*)

([XIANLÜ MODE:] *Dian jiangchun*[5])
I transmit these old texts on and on
To give face to our itinerant performers.
Practiced in the arts of the guild,
Telling my jokes like a monk seizing the moment of enlightenment,
Exhausting this meager art, I now understand the depth of its
   significance.

(*Hunjiang long*)
Just look at how I have carefully stitched together this livelihood,
And in this Liangyuan city have already passed twenty years since
   here I first set foot,
Always doing what people want,

---

3. That is, the registers of life and death; King Yama serves as a judge in the underworld.
4. Also called the Purple Tenuity: the constellation surrounding the North Star, in which the supreme god of the central heavens lives.

5. The Chinese word or phrase in this and subsequent stage directions names the tune used in the songs; and each tune in northern music belonged to one from a specific set of modes (here, *Xianlü*).

Treating every customer like a king.
For every new farce that tells of passionate love or urges virtue and
     piety,
I eke out a few coppers to keep the household comfortable and save
     us from hunger and cold.
But it surpasses any other district or county,
And studying just a portion of these meager arts
Is far better than owning a thousand acres of fine fields.

(LAN *speaks:*) Here I am at the theater. Are there spectators, brothers? Look at the time! Hurry and get things ready. (WANG *speaks:*) When I opened up the door to the stage, there was a reverend sitting there on the music bench. I said, "Reverend, go on up to the bleachers or to the side seats to watch, this is where the women who perform sit." But he cursed me instead. (LAN *speaks:*) You probably ruffled him. I'll attend to it myself. (LAN *acts out greeting him, speaks:*) Respectful greetings, old master. (ZHONGLI *speaks:*) Where have you been loitering around? (LAN *speaks:*) You're giving me a bum rap! You don't understand—some fine men in the city asked me to have a cup of tea with them. That's why I'm late. (ZHONGLI *speaks:*) Well, I've been sitting in this theater all day and you finally show up. "It's better that the music wait on the guests than the guests wait on the music!" I have come just to see you perform a comedy. Whichever piece you pick to perform, I'll watch.

                              ❅   ❅   ❅

(LAN *speaks:*) Bandleader Wang, put up the flags, valances, spirit pictures, and backdrop for me. (WANG *speaks:*) I already did. (LAN *sings:*)

     Here the flags and valance are raised,
     There the backdrops are hung.

(LAN *speaks:*) And when that audience catches sight as they arrive, they will let this be known outside: the male lead Lan Caihe is performing on stage at Liangyuan Playhouse. (*Sings:*)

     And I expect the whole world will glorify my name!

(LAN *speaks:*) Old master, go on over to the side seats to watch. This music bench is no place for you. This is where the women who perform sit. (ZHONGLI *speaks:*) No, I'll just sit here. (LAN *speaks:*) This spiteful reverend is really boorish. I see you're not from around here, but you're a cloud-roving reverend who washes in the river, sleeps in temples, lives in a dilapidated kiln, and doesn't even have a convent. I'm not laughing at you, since you've never seen a stage in your life. (ZHONGLI *speaks:*) And just what kind of oh-so-famous guild player are you? (LAN *speaks:*) And I suppose you're some kind of Master Guangcheng[6] or Zhongli of the Han? Don't take into account what you eat—just look at what you're wearing. So just "drop that sheep's skin of yours!" (*Sings:*)

     (*Nuozha ling*)
     Judging from the fact that your mouth has escaped the fate of
          eating dregs and chaff,

---

6. An ancient Daoist transcendent and the teacher of the Yellow Emperor (Huangdi, a legendary ruler who was himself a major Daoist figure).

And that your body has met its cloud conveyance and cap of thin
    rattan slips,[7]
I would say that you are sitting firmly astride the transcendent's
    crane bound for Heaven!

(ZHONGLI *speaks:*) I've been all over the world, but I've never seen a male
lead like you! (LAN *sings:*)

In perfect peace you insert yourself into the wine stalls,
And roam all over the world
Until that pair of those feet of yours silently cry out, "Mercy
    on me."

(ZHONGLI *speaks:*) The only reason that you take the stage to perform is to
swindle people out of their money. (LAN *sings:*)

(*Que ta zhi*)
You say I swindle people out of their money
And guilefully perform these dramatic scripts.

(*Speaks:*) Only officials, the high class, and the rich come to the theater to
relieve their minds; I've seen no reverend watch a play in my lifetime!
(*Sings:*)

Have you ever seen a clump of singers and dancers
Produce an arhat[8] or a spiritual transcendent?

(*Speaks:*) You go door to door to beg, and no one has anything good to give
you. (*Sings:*)

You point to believers and beg a few scraps and odds and ends.

(*Speaks:*) And from those contributions you patch together a tidy sum, and
when you see how much money it is, your desire for profit has already
begun. (*Sings:*)

And you don't even put it into Buddha's pocket, but whisk it away
    for your own use!

(ZHONGLI *speaks:*) Well, the only reason you have to perform every day is
because of your own "burning guild."[9] When will it end? You don't understand the pleasures we who have left the family[1] enjoy. (LAN *speaks:*) Well,
we of the vulgar world have a hundred flavors of the rarest foods when we
want to eat, and a thousand baskets of silks and damasks when we want
to put something on. I've seen what you who "leave the family" enjoy.
(*Sings:*)

(*Jisheng cao*)
You, not I, eat bland food and endure yellowed cabbage;
I, not you, pick out just what to put in my mouth, change from
    outfit to outfit.

---

7. Details often used in visual depictions to sig-
nify Daoist transcendents.
8. In Buddhism, someone who has destroyed all
causes for future rebirth and will enter nirvana
at death (Sanskrit, "worthy one").
9. A double entendre on the term *huoyuan:* (1)
"Your companions in the guild": the people who

rely on him as the lead performer; (2) "your
burning guild": akin to the Buddhist term "sea of
bitterness," the trials and tribulations of being in
and attached to the vulgar secular world [trans-
lators' note].
1. That is, become a monk or a nun.

Everyday you wind through teahouses, wineshops, and theaters,
Carrying an earthenware bottle, a wooden begging bowl, and a
    white ceramic can
To beg some noodle-leavings scraped from the bottom of the
    press.

(*Speaks:*) They push you out of a wineshop here, run you out of a teahouse
there. . . . (*Sings:*)

Eat just a little bit of a singsong girl's wine and food,
And you'd probably think it was a banquet of Queen Mother's
    sacred peaches from the Jasper Pool.[2]

(*Speaks:*) Look, you vile reverend, get out of here! You've spoiled a whole
day's performance. (ZHONGLI *speaks:*) I'll see the performance. I'm not leaving. (LAN *speaks:*) Since he won't get out, Bandleader Wang, lock up the
theater gates. (WANG *speaks:*) You've hit it on the head, brother. I'll lock up
the gate and see what he's going to do when he's locked inside! (LAN *speaks:*)
Listen here, you spiteful reverend, you've harassed us today so that we never
got to perform. If you show up again tomorrow and get in the way of our
livelihood, I'll pick out a few big toughs and beat you senseless. (*Sings:*)

(*Zhuansha*)
You'll never match the clever subtlety of the truly wise,
And I can't be concerned about another person's "face."
When will you get to the fairy isle of Penglai or Langyuan
    Orchard?[3]
When will you escape the six realms of recurrent incarnations?[4]
That crazy, mad behavior of yours will do no good!

(*Speaks:*) Let me lock up the stage doors and see how you get out. (*Sings:*)

Go ahead and ride your cloud chariot,
Ascend to the Heavens in broad daylight,
Will you dare "twaddle before my face again?"

(*Speaks:*) Bother me again and I'll keep the doors closed for ten days and
starve you to death. (*Sings:*)

That physical body of yours is so weak
Your body will fold over and you will not be able to see.

(*Speaks:*) And since you're already someone who has left the family, instead
of seeing a play, (*Sings:*)

Go ahead and imitate that Realized Lord Xu,[5] who ascended to
    blue Heaven in broad daylight!

(*Troupe members all exit together.*)

---

2. The pool near the home of the Queen Mother
of the West, one of the most important goddesses in ancient China and in the Daoist pantheon; she lived on the mythical Mount Kunlun,
and those who ate the peaches from her orchard
gained immortality.
3. That is, the orchard of the sacred peaches;
Langyuan is paradise. "Penglai": one of the islands
of the Immortals, located in the Eastern Sea.

4. In Buddhism, the six paths of rebirth: as a
god, demigod, human, ghost, animal, or denizen
of hell.
5. Xu Xun, a Daoist Perfected (the perfected,
who have moved beyond earthly corruption, are
higher than the immortals, also called transcendents), who is said to have ascended to heaven in
374 C.E. at the age of 136.

(ZHONGLI *speaks*:) I came here today to enlighten Lan Caihe, but his dull brows and carnal eyes did not recognize me. Do you think I can't go out just because you closed the stage doors? Gates, open! If this guy doesn't have something bad happen to him, he'll never be willing to leave his household. Tomorrow is his birthday. Quick! Dongbin,[6] come down to this lower realm. (*Recites*:)

> If I do not liberate him from his ties to dust-blown custom and
>   the world of the vulgar,
> How will he know that inside he is an immortal?
> When his practice of merit has reached its full, he can ascend
>   to the transcendents' realm,
> And then, at that time, he will rise to blue Heaven in the white
>   light of day!

(*Exits.*)

[Act 2]

(LI *and* WANG *enter, speak*:) Today is Brother Caihe's birthday. We brothers have brought along a few gifts, have prepared a banquet, and will wish him long life today. (LAN *enters with* WIFE, *speaks*:) It's my birthday today, and my fellow guild members have brought some presents to wish me long life. Hang up the portrait of the Longevity Star,[7] and make our offerings in front of him. Set up the incense, and on this happy occasion today, let us slowly drink a few unhurried cups.

*   *   *

(WANG *acts out taking up a cup, speaks*:) Drink a cup of birthday wine, brother. (ZHONGLI *enters and speaks*:) It's Lan Caihe's birthday today, and I'll lead him across to enlightenment now. Here I am at the gate already. (*Acts out sobbing three times, laughing three times.* LAN *speaks*:) Did you hear that, Bandleader Wang? Who's making all that racket at the doorway? (WANG *speaks*:) Don't bother yourself about little things, brother. Who knows? Let's just drink. (LAN *sings*:)

> (*He xinlang*)
> Who is that weeping and wailing?

(*Speaks*:) I'll just open the door. Oh, it's just that vile reverend. You are crazy. (*Sings*:)

> You've put a curse on our house!
> You really fan the flames of the common folk's suspicions.

(ZHONGLI *speaks*:) Go ahead, take me to court, I'm not afraid of you. You are crazy. (LAN *sings*:)

> Well if we did sue you in court, I'm afraid neither of us would get
>   off clean—

---

6. Lü Dongbin, a patriarch of the Quanzen (Complete Perfection) order, often described as the leader of the Eight Immortals.

7. Shouxing, worshipped in antiquity; beginning in the Ming dynasty (1368–1644), he is often pictured with the Eight Immortals.

(*Speaks*:) If I wanted to make a complaint against you, then the old folks would certainly say, "You're a leading male on the stage, but you're no wiser than that crazy old reverend." (*Sings*:)

But because it's my birthday I'm not going to quarrel with you.

(*Speaks*:) Today is my birthday, and I am under the Star of Longevity, so I'm going to let this go. (ZHONGLI *speaks*:) Who is the Star of Longevity? (LAN *speaks*:) I am. (ZHONGLI *speaks*:) You might be the Star of Longevity today, but tomorrow you'll be under the Star of Calamity. (LAN *speaks*:) You really lack any sense of decency to say such unpropitious things. (*Sings*:)

Quit this wild name-calling and crazy behavior.

(ZHONGLI *speaks*:) These words wouldn't hurt you either! (LAN *sings*:)

These aren't words you should use;
These aren't words fit to listen to.
Are you doing more than begging some blandly spiced soup
To temporarily stuff that skin sack of yours?

(ZHONGLI *speaks*:) I see you're enjoying yourself! (LAN *sings*:)

Yes I am! I'm eating big old buns and long broad noodles;
You're eating some vegetable filling and bland leek soup.

(*Speaks*:) This vile reverend is spoiling our banquet. Bandleader Wang, close up the gates. Brothers, sit down, let's just drink our wine. (ZHONGLI *speaks*:) Will anything make him see the light? If he doesn't experience some kind of awful situation, he'll never leave his family. Look, Xu Jian, if you leave your family and go away with me right now, roam about in leisure and freedom, happy and carefree, you'd really find its hidden pleasures! (LAN *speaks*:) I know about the kind of path you immortals trod! (ZHONGLI *speaks*:) Since you know all about it, let me hear it. (LAN *sings*:)

(*Dou hama*)
I've seen households set out a vegetarian feast,
Invite you reverends to recite a penitence or a sutra:
Right in front is hung a scroll of the Three Purities,[8]
And the patrons recite a sutra.
Busily they prepare a vegetarian feast,
Then take down the picture of Laozi[9]
And hang up a scroll of the Ten Kings of Hell,[1]
And that painter knew well the ways of the world,
And when he tells about how retribution fits the experience,
It's also painted out there frighteningly cruel.
Who can stand to look at these representations?
All I have to do is remember how lifelike the paintings are in
the Temple of the City God—
Boiling pots and pans of oil,
And stuck there inside

8. That is, the Three Pure Ones: the Celestial Worthy of Primordial Commencement (Yuanshi tianzun), the Celestial Worthy of Numinous Treasure (Lingbao tianzun), and Celestial Worthy of the Way and Its Virtue (Daode tianzun).
9. That is, the Celestial Worthy of the Way and Its Virtue.
1. The underworld contains ten courts, each presided over by a king who judges the dead as they are moved from one court to the next (a process described in the Buddhist *Shiwang jing*, or *Sutra of the Ten Kings*).

So many souls,
Each one of us from the secular world.
Among the lot neither a single monk
Nor a Daoist reverend, nor a Spiritual Codger Xu.[2]
It is said, "There is no clean escape,"
But this sentence is unheeded—
Either by me, this male lead, or by you, this reverend.

(ZHONGLI *speaks*:) Quick! Bring disaster on this man!

(*Exits.*)

(RUNNERS *enter and speak*:) Lan Caihe, open up! The magistrate summons you to perform your official service. (LAN *speaks*:) Who's that calling at the gate? (RUNNERS *speak*:) The magistrate is summoning you to perform your official service. (LAN *speaks*:) This is a special day for me, take Bandleader Wang. (RUNNERS *speak*:) We don't want him. You have to go. (LAN *speaks*:) Take Thinhead Li. (RUNNERS *speak*:) We don't want him either. (LAN *speaks*:) Have Bandleader Wang take some female roles along and go. (RUNNERS *speak*:) We don't want any of them. We only want Lan Caihe. (LAN *speaks*:) I have twenty people under my care, and I get stuck with it. All right! All right! I'll go fulfill my official service.

(*Exit together.*)

(LI *and* WANG *speak*:) Go ahead and get the banquet ready, when brother gets home we'll all eat together.

(*Exit.*)

(OFFICIAL, *dressed as magistrate, enters and speaks*:) I am the Daoist Lü Dongbin. I received the command of my master, Zhongli, and have disguised myself as the Prefect because of an entertainer in this place, called Xu Jian. He has a stage name of Lan Caihe and has it in his fated lot to be an immortal transcendent. Zhongli attempted to enlighten him and lead him over, but he couldn't see the light. Because he has been too slow to fulfill his official service, I've had some people go and fetch him here under arrest. Servants, bring in that Lan Caihe. (LAN *enters, speaks*:) Oh, no! What should I do? I screwed up my official service, and have been deemed guilty by the magistrate. Now I've been summoned and I'd better go see him. (*Acts out kneeling in audience.* LÜ DONGBIN *speaks*:) Are you aware of your crime? You did not respect the office. You were late in performing official service. Take him down into the courtyard and beat him forty times! Get the heavy clubs ready! (LAN *sings*:)

(*Ku huangtian*)
It scares me so much that I seem dumbstruck;
Away, away flies my sentient soul,
And all I can hear is someone calling my actor's name on the
    musician's dais.
It scares me so much that my three souls[3] have become lost far,
    far away,

---

2. The Daoist monk Xu Shouxin (1033–1108), a celebrated oracle.

3. Probably the three *hun* or cloud souls, linked with heaven and its pneumas.

And I can perceive not the slightest bit of motion.
I arrogantly missed the time of my official service,
So I'll hurry to smooth it over,
And if necessary to confess.
Those thick and thin thorns and staffs will be laid upon my body,
More painfully than the simulated fights on the stage!

(LÜ DONGBIN *speaks:*) Beat him forty times in the courtyard! Lay it on! Lay it on! (LAN *sings:*)

This is so much more thorough than a "Judge Bao,"[4]
No one has ever seen members of the guild "carrying thorns."[5]

(LÜ DONGBIN *speaks:*) Beat him forty times in the courtyard! Lay it on! Lay it on! (ZHONGLI *enters and speaks:*) He's good and scared now. (LAN *speaks:*) Who will save me? (ZHONGLI *speaks:*) Lan Caihe, have you seen through it all now? You didn't believe me when I told you, but what about now? (LAN *sings:*)

(*Wu ye ti*)
This reverend's words are truly to be believed,
Indeed he said, "The Star of Longevity will turn into the Star of
    Calamity."
My eyes wide open, I dare not move ahead,
I dare not reveal to sight or hearing what I feel.
Who dares say this is just to bear enough to get through it all?
I thought we were all in the ranks of Confucius;
I never would have said that I would break the laws of Xiao He.[6]

(*Speaks:*) It seems that none of the words spoken by the Sage are to be believed! (LAN *sings:*)

Each and every one
Is hard to rely one,
They are all wild words and lies,
Spurted out without any thought.

(ZHONGLI *speaks:*) Why are you here? (LAN *speaks:*) I missed the appointed time for my official service, and the magistrate is going to give me forty strokes in the courtyard. Save me, master. (ZHONGLI *speaks:*) If I save you, will you follow me and leave your home? (LAN *speaks:*) Save me and I will follow you with all my heart. (ZHONGLI *speaks:*) Stay here for a minute. (*Acts out seeing* LÜ DONGBIN, *speaks:*) Your Excellency. (LÜ DONGBIN *speaks:*) If I had known earlier that you, master, were coming, I would have met you at some distance. Please do not consider my lack of a proper welcome a crime. (ZHONGLI *speaks:*) What crime did Lan Caihe commit? (LÜ DONGBIN *speaks:*) He was remiss in fulfilling his official service, and he should be charged according to the law. (ZHONGLI *speaks:*) Are you willing to turn him over to me to become my disciple? (LÜ DONGBIN *speaks:*) Whenever you want him I'll gladly turn him over to you. Servants, bring him over here. You there, Lan Caihe—you really are lucky. If the master had not shown up, I would have given you forty in the courtyard. The master wants you for a disciple.

4. A Song dynasty judge who became a prominent symbol of justice in later times.
5. That is, as punishment for a crime.

6. The chief minister of the founder of the Han
dynasty (d. 193 B.C.E.); he drew up the dynasty's
law codes.

I'll forgive your crimes, and you go off with the master. (LAN *speaks:*) Thank you both, I'll leave my home today and follow the master! (*Sings:*)

> (*Shawei*)
> No longer will I lead those dozens of companions of the guild,
> But stride alone ever more on the twelve-tiered Terraces of Jasper.
> Former wealth dispersed, friends gone, I've turned my back on old feelings,
> Back where they raise a shout, start the music
> And call out my stage name in the theater.
> I'm now confused, beclouded, yet more awake.
> Lan Caihe's vile reputation runs through every prefecture and town,
> But have they ever seen a comedy-playing actor become enlightened first?

> (*Exits.*)

(ZHONGLI *speaks:*) Since Lan Caihe has had a change of heart today and will leave the family, I will wait until his merit is complete and his disciplines are finished, and then we can go off together to the Langyuan Orchard and the Jasper Pool.

> (*Exits.*)

[Act 3]

(LAN'S WIFE *enters and speaks:*) I am Lan Caihe's wife. On that day my man was celebrating his birthday with a little wine and was summoned away for his official service. He never came back, and someone said that he had gone off with a Daoist master. Nothing left to do now but summon my two younger brothers-in-law and discuss all this. (LI *and* WANG *enter and speak:*) No one knows where brother went after he was summoned for official service. If he really has left the home, what are we going to do? Let's go look for him today.

> (*Exit together.*)

(LAN *enters, playing the clappers, leading* CHILDREN, *speaks:*) Everything has been so serene since I went off with master. [(*Recites:*)]

> The old country of Jinling
> Was originally my home,
> So I went there many times
> And remonstrated once with the Princes Li,[7]
> But they did not listen,
> And I feared stirring up trouble or calling down misfortune.
> So I stayed not in Jinling,
> But went straight off to Bianliang,
> Where I was enlightened in the theater,
> And never went again into the ranks of performers.
> My gentry cap worn aslant,

---

7. Li Jing and Li Yu, the two rulers of the Southern Tang (937–46) [translator's note].

> I set loose my Yunyang clappers;
> Around my waist I tie a plaited rope
> Circling my long robe with dancing sleeves.

Ah, there is no greater serenity. (*Sings:*)

> ([ZHENGLÜ MODE:] *Duanzheng hao*)
> Around my waist I drag a hundred coppers,
> On my head I wear a gentry cap.
> I dance in my blue robe, clack the clappers, and sing out loud,
> Heading for the streets every day.
> How many can recognize my true worth?

> (*Gun xiuqiu*)
> Ai!
> Why do you little devils
> Keep on pestering me?
> I never really summoned them together—
> Those who run into me laugh happily, *ha ha ha.*

(*All of the* CHILDREN *pull at him,* LAN *sings:*)

> You snatch at my clappers,
> And I'm afraid my string of cash will loosen.
> You've nearly ripped my green gown to shreds;
> You beat and grasp as soon as you see me.
> This group of ruddy little faces covered with the stench of
>   mother's milk
> Is pestering Lan Caihe, who's just escaped from the twelve
>   links in the chain of causation![8]
> How will I ever perfect my nature through meditation?

(CHILDREN *speak:*) Master, give us a copper!

(LAN'S WIFE *enters and speaks:*) There's Lan Caihe! Where have you been? Come home! (LAN *speaks:*) Pleased to meet you. Who are the lot of you? (LAN'S WIFE, ENSEMBLE *speak:*) I am your wife! We are your brothers! This is your child! (LAN *sings:*)

> (*Tang xiucai*)
> I no longer heed the cacophony of chatter that passes my ears,
>   Sons and daughters are just golden cangues[9] and jade shackles,
> Isn't it said, "the more sons and daughters, the more karmic pain?"
> When I'm enjoying myself, I pick up my clappers;
> When I am troubled, I sing out loud.
> No one is as happy as me!

(LAN'S WIFE *enters and speaks:*) You come home! We'll get the theater ready, do a couple of performances to raise some living expenses for the family, and then you can go out again. (LAN *sings:*)

> (*Gun xiuqiu*)
> I will be alone ever after,

---

8. Ignorance, compounded formations, consciousness, name and form, the six senses, contact, feeling, attachment, grasping, existence, birth, and old age and death (a Buddhist concept).

9. Large wooden collars, used to confine the neck and sometimes the hands as punishment.

Don't think now about how I lived then.
Never again will I put on a costume, or keep the beat to the musical
performance.
I'll never open or close another performance on stage, ad-libbing
on the spot.

* * *

(LAN'S WIFE *speaks*:) I've tried to make you go home, but you won't. What have you studied with your master? (LAN *speaks*:) What my master taught me to sing was the "Song of Blue Skies," and what he taught me to dance is the "Stomping Song." (LAN'S WIFE *speaks*:) Perform them for us and let us hear them. (LAN *acts out dancing, recites*:)

Stomping Song,
Lan Caihe,
How long is a human life?
Red faces: a tree of "third spring,"[1]
Flowing light: a shuttle once thrown:
Those buried are buried,
The bearers bear them.
An adorned casket, a colorful hearse—what use are they?
Wrapped in a mat, carried by a pole—what can a person do?

Alive, before, they refused to chase after happy laughter,
Dead, afterward, they let others sing the burial dirges.
When you have a chance to drink, drink;
When you find a place to cool your heels, cool your heels.
Don't go around depressed with saddened brow,
Just laugh out loud with opened mouth.
You work and work all day long, greedy for fame and profit,
Paying no attention to mortal life—how long can it last?
How long can it last?
Stomping song,
Lan Caihe.

How incredibly serene!

(LAN'S WIFE *speaks*:) Don't leave the family! Follow me home! (LAN *sings*:)

(**Kuaihuo san**)
And if death should come, what then?

(*Speaks*:) Lady, go away! (*Sings*:)

Now I've got a place to cool my heels, and I'll cool them for
a while,
And study that song of Zhuangzi,[2] beating on the tub—
I've realized the disasters that will cause my death.

(LAN'S WIFE *speaks*:) Since you've already left home to become an immortal, how about letting me go with you? (LAN *speaks*:) You can't leave home. . . .

---

1. That is, the third month of spring.
2. On Zhuangzi, see above the introduction to the *Book of Master Zhuang* (*Zhuangzi*), the source of this story about Zhuangzi that demonstrates the foolishness of mourning the dead.

✻ ✻ ✻

(LAN'S WIFE *speaks*:) Go home! It looks like you'll never get the true rewards of becoming an immortal. (LAN *sings*:)

> (*Weisheng*)
> Even if I don't get the true rewards,
> Or lead you, my worthy wife, across,
> If you will just happily keep to your lot for me, go along with
>   what the world offers
> And wind up with a single day's peace—wouldn't that make me
>   ecstatic!

(*Exits.*)

(LAN'S WIFE *speaks*:) If you won't go home, we will.

(*Exit together.*)

[Act 4]

(LAN'S WIFE *enters with* LI *and* WANG. WANG *speaks*:) Thirty years have gone by since Lan Caihe left the family to follow his master. I'm now eighty, Thinhead Li is seventy, and sister-in-law is ninety. We're all old and incapable of making a living anymore. So now the younger ones perform, and we drum for them. I'll go and get the drums ready, and we'll see who comes along. (LAN *enters and speaks*:) Thirty years now since I left with the master. The master said my exercises are finished, and today we are going off together to Langyuan Orchard and the Jasper Pool. Oh, how serene it all is. (*Sings*:)

> ([SHUANGDIAO MODE]: *Xinshui ling*)
> The rules and rituals of the Daoist Way I have refined and to
>   them I hold fast.
> My master has now enlightened a disciple of the stage.
> Clearly and brilliantly my master exercised the law of the Way,
> Secretly explaining the workings of meditation.
> Now he wants to go to the Jasper Pool together—
> Could I have ever hoped for this day?

(*Speaks*:) I just passed the mountain pass and see a garden of fruit trees, with apricot flowers opening in their brilliance. Turning my head—a whole pond of fine water chestnuts, then the whole place filled with fine frost, and then a whole stretch covered with fine snow. Let me think—apricots are spring, water-chestnuts are summer, frost is autumn, and snow is winter. How can all of the seasons come at once?

(WANG *and* LI *enter and act out playing music.* LAN *sings*:)

> (*Qing dongyuan*)
> There's a group of noisy people there—

(*Speaks*:) Oh, it's the sound of music! (*Sings*:)

> It's a group of hick itinerant performers.
> I suppose they are in that public square
> Holding up their spears, knives, swords, and halberds,
> Gongs, clappers, drums, and flutes.

They already set up the valance and some flags.
I wonder which troupe of the guild they are?
Probably nobody famous.

(*Speaks:*) So, it turns out to be a troupe from the guild. I'll ask, "Which family troupe are you?" (LAN'S WIFE *speaks:*) Lan Caihe's. (LAN *speaks:*) Which members of Lan Caihe's troupe are you? (LAN'S WIFE *speaks:*) I am his wife. Those two are his brothers, Bandleader Wang and Thinhead Li. (WANG *speaks:*) It's been thirty years since our elder brother left, and now I'm eighty, brother here is seventy, and our sister-in-law is ninety. Boy, are we old. (LAN *sings:*)

(*Gu meijiu*)
Sigh over how unceasingly it changes from light to night,
Moan over how bitterly swift the days and months flee by,
And lament that our lives seem to pass but in a dream.
I am awakened now:
No life, no death, cut free from fame or profit.

(*Taiping ling*)
You must be my brothers,
The pack I ran with when young.
But it was nothing more than studying the arts when given
    place and opportunity,
From which comes these various years:
This one says seventy,
That one eighty,
The lady says ninety—
It may have been hard, but they have all lived to a ripe old age.

(WANG *speaks:*) And who are you? (LAN *speaks:*) Well, I am Lan Caihe. (WANG *speaks:*) You've been gone for thirty years, but you're still not old. You still look the same. (LAN *speaks:*) I've only been gone for three—how did you get so old? (WANG *speaks:*) We're all old now. You're still middle-aged. Wouldn't it be great if you'd go once more to the theater and do a day or two of comedies?

✳   ✳   ✳

(WANG *speaks:*) Brother, all of the costumes and accessories from your old comedies are still in good shape. Brother, just lift up the curtain and take a look. (LAN *sings:*)

My heart delights after hearing this,
And I unconsciously smile,
Let me just lift the curtain . . .

(*Acts out lifting the curtain,* ZHONGLI QUAN *and* LÜ DONGBIN *are sitting inside.* ZHONGLI *speaks:*) Xu Jian, your mortal mind is not completely gone! (LAN *sings:*)

That scares me so much my souls go flying far, far away,
I would have sworn they were my brothers,
My sisters and sisters-in-law—
It's just like coming back from the dream of the Southern Branch.

(*Shou Jiangnan*)
Ah, it was founder of the sect, teacher of the doctrine Zhongli
    of the Han all the time,

Accompanied by master Dongbin at his side.
I drop my Yunyang clappers and climb the steps,
You're all here—
The Eight Immortals now lead me off to the Jasper Pool together.

(ZHONGLI *speaks:*) Xu Jian, you are no mortal, but are now Lan Caihe of the Eight Immortals! Your practices finished, you can ascend to the immortal realm. Just listen:

Xu Jian, have no doubt in your heart,
Listen carefully as I explain:
Here is Dongbin, in the Dao designated Master of Pure Yang,
And I am called the Roaming and Loafing Zhongli of Han.

TITLE: Leading the children, he laughs heartily wherever he goes;
The Old Immortal claps his hands and drunkenly sings out a loud song.

NAME: Lü Dongbin transforms a traveler in the actor's world;
Zhongli of the Han leads Lan Caihe to enlightenment.

MEMORABILIA OF THE THREE KINGDOMS
(*Samguk yusa*)

The *Memorabilia of the Three Kingdoms* (*Samguk yusa*), a thirteenth-century text, records the deep interest that the Korean state of Koguryŏ was showing in Daoism as early as the seventh century. That interest attracted the attention of Gaozu, a Tang dynasty Chinese emperor. Gaozu dispatched to Koguryŏ a Daoist priest, along with images of Laozi, and instructed him to lecture on the *Scripture of the Way and Its Virtue* (*The Daode jing*; see above). After attending those lectures in 624 C.E., the Korean king Yŏngnyu sent an envoy to China for more information; his successor likewise sent an envoy.

This desire to support Daoism as well as Buddhism and Confucianism was roundly condemned by the Buddhist monk Podŏk, who predicted dire consequences and fled to a different kingdom—shortly before the collapse of Koguryŏ. The *Memorabilia of the Three Kingdoms* reflects the Buddhist sympathies of one of its compilers, a Buddhist monk named Iryeon (also spelled Iyrōn, 1206–1289).

PRONOUNCING GLOSSARY

Koguryŏ: *koh-gu-ryo*
Kyŏngbok: *key-owng bowk*
Podŏk: *poh-doek*

Pojang: *poh-jahng*
Samguk yusa: *sawm-gook yu-saw*
Ŭich'ŏn: *u-wee-chow-un*

Podŏk (Koguryŏ)

According to the basic annals of Koguryŏ,[1] toward the end of that kingdom [618–627] the Koguryŏ people strove to demonstrate their belief in Daoism. Emperor Gaozu of the Tang[2] heard of this and sent a Daoist priest to Koguryŏ with the images of Laozi to lecture on *The Way and Its Power*.[3] King Yŏngnyu and his people attended the lecture—it was the seventh year of Wude [624]. The following year the king sent an envoy to the Tang court to obtain books on Buddhism and Daoism, a wish the emperor granted.

Upon accession to the throne, King Pojang[4] [642] wished to see Buddhism, Daoism and Confucianism flourish in his country. At the time, his favorite minister, Yŏn Kaesomun, said, "Confucianism and Buddhism flourish now, but not Daoism. We should send a mission to China to seek knowledge of Daoism."

The Koguryŏ monk Podŏk of Pallyong Monastery (in Yonggang) lamented the danger to the country's fortunes if a conflict between Daoism and Buddhism arises and remonstrated with the king without success. By supernatural power he flew with his hermitage to Mount Kodae (or Kodal) in Wansan province[5] (now Chŏnju)—it was in the sixth month of the first year of Yonghui, *kyŏngsul* [650]. Soon thereafter, Koguryŏ was destroyed.[6] It is said that the flying hermitage in Kyŏngbok Monastery is Podŏk's.

In the eighth year of Da'an, *sinmi* [1092], the Chief of Clerics, Ŭich'ŏn, went to Podŏk's hermitage, bowed to his portrait, and composed a poem: "The teachings of universal nirvana[7] were transmitted to Korea by him. . . . Alas, after he flew with his hermitage to Mount Kodae, Koguryŏ was on the verge of ruin." The postscript reads: "King Pojang of Koguryŏ was deluded by Daoism and abandoned Buddhism. Hence the master flew south with his hermitage and landed on Mount Kodae. Later, a guardian of the dharma[8] appeared on Horse Ridge in Koguryŏ and said, 'Soon your country will be destroyed.'" This story is exactly like the one recorded in the national history, and the rest is in the original record and the lives of eminent monks.

TRANSLATED BY Peter H. Lee. All bracketed additions are the translator's.

1. The largest of ancient Korea's Three Kingdoms (also spelled Goguryeo); the other two, to its south, were Paekche and Silla.
2. The Tang dynasty (618–907); Gaozu was its founder and first emperor (618–26).
3. That is, *The Scripture of the Way and Its Virtue*; on the *Daode jing*, see above.
4. The last king of Koguryŏ (r. 642–68; also spelled Bojang).
5. In Paekche, the kingdom in southwestern Korea.
6. In 668, Koguryŏ fell to Silla (the kingdom in southwestern Korea), which had allied with Chinese forces from the Tang dynasty.
7. The state of the cessation of the accumulated causes of future suffering and rebirth (literally, "blown out," "extinguished"; Sanskrit).
8. Teaching (Sanskrit): the doctrine of the Buddha.

RECORDS OF THE THREE KINGDOMS
(*Samguk sagi*)

The paucity of extant sources makes it difficult to say much about the presence of Daoism in Korea during the period of Three Kingdoms (Koguryŏ, Paekche, and Silla). But from the "Inscription on an Image at Kamsan Monastery," we know that during the eighth century, Korean nobles were reading *The Scripture of the Way and Its Virtue* (*Daode jing*) and the *Book of Master Zhuang* (*Zhuangzi*; for all three works, see above). Tomb art also reveals a cult of immortality, and scattered references in written records seem to indicate an understanding of Daoist philosophy and religious ideas.

Records of the Three Kingdoms (*Samguk sagi*) is a twelfth-century history that includes an account of a certain Yŏn Kaesomun (d. 665), who began as a ruthless son of a chief. He seized power by massacring other chiefs and the king of Koguryŏ, becoming a despotic minister to the dead king's younger brother (or nephew, in some accounts) after installing him as ruler. On Yŏn's urging, the new king requested information about Daoism from China. After eight Daoists, carrying a copy of *The Scripture of the Way and Its Virtue*, were sent from China to Korea in 643, a Buddhist monastery was transformed into a Daoist abbey. By associating Daoism with the brutal Yŏn Kaesomun, the Buddhist compiler of the text casts Daoism in a negative light.

PRONOUNCING GLOSSARY

Ch'ŏn: *cho-own*
Koguryŏ: *koh-gu-ryo*
Samguk sagi: *sawm-gook saw-gee*

Yŏn Kaesomun: *yown kai-sow-mun*
Yŏngnyu: *yohng-nyu*

Yŏn Kaesomun (Koguryŏ)

The clan name of Yŏn Kaesomun [d. 665] was Ch'ŏn. He seduced the people by claiming that he was born under water. He had an imposing presence and was broad-minded. Upon the death of his father, who held the rank of chief of the Eastern Province[1] and chief minister, the people stopped Kaesomun from inheriting the position because they hated his coldbloodedness. Thereupon Kaesomun kowtowed and apologized and begged to be allowed to take over the position, saying, "You may depose me if I fail. I will not complain." The people sympathized with Yŏn and permitted him to succeed to his father's post. Since Yŏn continued to be cruel and wicked, the chiefs had a private talk with the king, asking that Yŏn be put to death. The plan, however, leaked out.

Yŏn gathered the soldiers of his own province and pretended to review them. He also spread a banquet to the south of the walled city and invited the ministers to review his troops. As soon as the guests arrived, more than a hundred strong, Yŏn had them massacred. He then rushed to the palace, killed King Yŏngnyu,[2] chopped the corpse into pieces, and threw the

---

TRANSLATED BY Peter H. Lee. All bracketed additions are the translator's.

1. That is, the Eastern Province of the kingdom of Koguryŏ, in Korea's north.   2. Died 642.

pieces into a ditch. He then set up the king's younger brother, Chang,[3] as king and appointed himself as *mangniji*, which was tantamount to being both the Minister of War and Secretariat Director in Tang China.[4] He dictated to those far away and those nearby alike and conducted state affairs despotically. Possessing extreme dignity, he wore five knives; no one dared look at him. When he mounted or dismounted from his horse, he would make an aristocrat general prostrate himself as a stepping stone. When going out, he would march in rank and file, and a guide in front would shout and send the people scurrying out of the way. Thus the people suffered greatly. . . .

Yŏn reported to the king, "I have heard that in China the three ways of thought exist side by side, but in our country Daoism is unknown. I suggest that we send an envoy to Tang China to obtain this learning for us." When the king sent a memorial to that effect, the Tang court sent a Daoist adept, Shuda, with seven other envoys and a copy of *Daode jing* (The Way and Its Power).[5] A Buddhist monastery was made into a Daoist temple.

3. Pojang (or Bojang), the last king of Koguryŏ (r. 642–68).
4. The Tang dynasty (618–907).

5. That is, *The Scripture of the Way and Its Virtue;* on the *Daode jing*, see above.

The New Standardization and Unification of Daoism

FROM THE MING DYNASTY (1368–1644 C.E.) THROUGH THE QING DYNASTY (1644–1912 C.E.)

A series of successive rebellions during the thirteenth century resulted in the collapse of the Mongol-ruled Yuan dynasty (1260–1368 C.E.) and the establishment of the Ming dynasty (1368–1644). The founding of the Ming freed China from non-Han rule; the new dynasty first regained the full territory of the Chinese empire and then expanded to borders roughly corresponding to those of modern China. To effectively rule this vast territory required a well-managed, highly centralized

Detail from *Spring Dawn at the Cinnabar Terrace* by Lu Guang (Yuan dynasty) depicting a Daoist temple tucked deep in the mountains. The term "cinnabar" in the title may refer to one of the ingredients used to produce an elixir in external alchemy or to an elixir produced through internal alchemy.

official bureaucracy. The Ming state apparatus, particularly during the early part of the dynasty, became notorious for its draconian measures of discipline. In addition to relying on cruel punishments to enforce law codes, the Ming also attempted to use moral suasion—through public lectures on ethical topics—to keep potentially recalcitrant regional officials and their subjects under control.

The notable features of Daoism during the Ming dynasty were its submission to the newly instituted strong state control, its penetration into disparate areas of philosophy and religious thought and practice, and an increase in the standardization and unification of its different schools. Ming Daoism was deeply imprinted with the features of the Ming's governmental policies and was subjected to stringent control. Despite that control, and despite the absence of any prominent new developments or innovations, the substantial support provided by Ming emperors to Daoists made the dynasty a period of relative prosperity for Daoism.

During the Ming dynasty, Daoist ideas and practices spread to intellectuals, such as the prominent official and philosopher Wang Yangming (1472–1529), and into diverse realms of popular practices, such as folk stories and festivals. This broader diffusion throughout society was made possible by new developments in the types of literature available. "A Taste of Immortality," included in this section, is a Ming tale (drawn from a larger literary collection) that demonstrates well the wide circulation of Daoist ideas. Yet, like the critique of immortality drugs in that story, popular representations of Daoism were not always positive. The selection included below from the *Journey to the West* (*Xiyou ji*)—a classic Ming dynasty novel that narrates the travels from China to India of the Chinese Buddhist pilgrim Xuanzang (ca. 596–664)—shows how Daoism was sometimes ridiculed.

Daoism was colored by the general religious environment of the time. During the entire dynasty, the boundaries between the "three teachings"—Buddhism, Daoism, and Confucianism—continued to dissolve, and Neo-Confucianism, which borrowed liberally from both Buddhism and Daoism, gained in importance and influence at court and throughout society. The commentaries by the Ming dynasty Buddhist monk Hanshan on the *Scripture of the Way and Its Virtue* (*Laozi*; see above) and *Book of Master Zhuang* (*Zhuangzi*; see above), which are also included in this section, suggest the general trend toward the amalgamation of the different religious traditions. In the Ming, the distinctions between various Daoist lineages and practices progressively blurred as they too became more unified.

MANAGING DAOISM: DAOISM AND THE MING COURT

The founder of the Ming dynasty, Taizu (whose birth name was Zhu Yuanzhang,[1] 1328–1398), was born into a poor peasant family, and stories about his rise from abject poverty to become the emperor of China abound. Many of those paeans, which contain Daoist references, are filled with pseudo-historical elements aimed at enhancing his image. For example,

---

1. For the sake of consistency, emperors at all times in their lives are referred to by their temple names, rather than by their personal names or reign-period names (Taizu was the Hongwo emperor).

some versions of Taizu's birth, which was marked by various auspicious natural signs, stress that it occurred on the evening after his mother dreamed of a Daoist who visited her and gave her a magical pill to swallow. Others focus on a prophecy that his father received from a Daoist about his destiny. Both of those birth stories hark back to the familiar theme of Daoist sages appearing to the founders of dynasties as a sign of legitimacy.

After his parents died while he was still young, Taizu became a destitute beggar and then a wandering Buddhist monk. He eventually joined a rebel group that espoused a messianic doctrine. By gaining the group's respect, he rose up through the ranks and eventually became its leader, and he made Nanjing the center of his operations. Taizu kept Nanjing as his center of operations—the capital—after he became emperor. That was an important decision, since it meant that for the first time in history a fully reunited China was to be ruled from a capital located south of the Yangzi River. From his southern throne Taizu began to launch successful attacks on the Mongols in the north.

Though he spent time in his youth as a Buddhist monk, Taizu later became closely connected with Daoists and Daoist myths, ideas, and practices. His future as an emperor was prefigured in his dream of his investiture as a Daoist celestial king, which just happened to coincide with his enthronement as the first Ming ruler (see "Taizu's Dream"). The clear message imparted in that dream was that Daoists had prophesied his reception of the heavenly mandate, thereby conferring legitimacy on his rule. Daoists came to hold official posts within the imperial bureaucracy in Taizu's administration. In his employ, for example, was a Daoist adviser named Crazy Immortal Zhou (Zhou Dianxian, fl. fourteenth century), who would go about announcing in a loud voice that the "Great Peace" had arrived and predicting the Ming emperor's chances on the battlefield against his main adversary. Zhou became so close to Taizu that the emperor eventually wrote his memorial epitaph (see "Crazy Immortal Zhou"). Another Daoist close to Taizu was "Master Ironcap" (Tieguan zi, also called Zhang Zhong; fl. fourteenth century), who also related to him a prophecy that he would found a new dynasty.

In addition, Emperor Taizu took considerable personal interest in Daoist immortals. Indeed, Taizu became known for sending out emissaries in search of a legendary Daoist immortal named Zhang Sanfeng in order to invite him to court. According to popular lore, Zhang Sanfeng was seen a number of times in the early Ming dynasty after his apparent death. Zhang Sanfeng, like the Daoist who had appeared to Taizu's own father, was a symbol of legitimacy, since such figures showed themselves only to sage rulers. Because of his associations with the Perfected Warrior (Zhenwu, also known as the Dark Warrior, Xuanwu;[2] see *Journey to the North*, or *Beiyou ji*)—a warrior deity—Zhang Sanfeng is perhaps best known today as the founder of the popular martial arts exercise called Taiji (Taijiquan; in English, tai chi). Because of his name "Sanfeng," meaning

---

2. His name changed during the Song dynasty (960–1279), because of the taboo against using the characters in an emperor's personal name: the Song dynasty emperor Huizong's personal name was Xuanlang, so "Xuan" became "Zhen."

"Three Peaks"—a term that can refer to three types of sexual practice—he is also associated with the esoteric arts of sexual self-cultivation.

Taizu's primary relationship with Daoist institutions was to bring them into uniformity and under control by standardizing ritual liturgy. The emperor himself even wrote the preface to a work that provided an orthodox template for Daoist rituals. Taizu gave preference to the Celestial Masters (Zhengyi) tradition, but seems to have found some value in the Complete Perfection (Quanzhen) tradition as well. During the Ming, Daoist institutions were overseen by administrative bureaus, monks and nuns were required to have ordination certificates, and age limits were set for men and women hoping to enter the priesthood. These constraints on Daoism, and on other religions, reined in the increasing number of disobedient groups intent on fomenting rebellion.

The second Ming dynasty emperor, Chengzu (also well-known by his reign-period name: the Yongle emperor, r. 1402–24), continued the policies aimed at controlling Daoists; for example, he issued an imperial decree that set the maximum number of Daoists in each prefecture. But Chengzu also ordered and supported the production of a new edition of the Daoist canon that contained some 1,500 works; a woodblock-printed set was eventually completed in 1445, after his death. It is this Ming edition of the canon that lies at the basis of all modern editions, and a photolithographic reproduction was published by the Commercial Press in Shanghai in the 1920s. The Ming dynasty canon was closely linked to catalogues of Daoist writings that had been compiled since at least the Tang dynasty (618–907 C.E.) and perhaps even earlier, and followed woodblock printings from the Song (960–1279) and Yuan dynasties.

Chengzu, like his father Taizu, sought the immortal Zhang Sanfeng, who continued to play an important role throughout the Ming dynasty in various popular tales. Zhang Sanfeng's connection to Mount Wudang led to a steep increase in imperial support for the Daoist institutions on that sacred mountain. Further enhancing the importance of Mount Wudang was its connection with the Perfect Warrior, for Chengzu was an ardent patron of that Daoist deity. In his veneration Chengzu seems to have again been following his father Taizu, who, among other acts of devotion, built a temple for the Perfect Warrior to express thanks for the assistance he received in the battles leading up to his founding of the Ming dynasty. Yet Chengzu went further and claimed that he was himself a manifestation of the Perfect Warrior. Chengzu sought martial support from the Perfect Warrior, and in return he sponsored some large-scale—and quite lavish—reconstructions of dilapidated temples on Mount Wudang. The Perfect Warrior became the dynastic protector of the Ming. In addition to officially supporting Daoism at court and serving as patron to sacred sites connected with the Perfect Warrior, Chengzu treated Daoism as a personal faith. Many sources report that he had a vision of a crane carrying a Daoist down from the clouds.

Some of Taizu's other sons were also engaged with Daoist ideas and practices. Taizu's seventeenth son, Zhu Quan (1378–1448), for example, was a prolific writer whose works included some wide-ranging Daoist texts. After he died, he was considered an immortal. Taizu's tenth son, Zhu Tan (1370–1390), was less fortunate in his relationship with Daoism, since he is known to have gone blind—and died young—as the result of consuming mercury, a drug associated with Daoist alchemy.

Many of the subsequent Ming dynasty emperors had short reigns and played no noticeable role in Daoist history, but Daoism was not entirely irrelevant to their lives. Renzong (r. 1424–25), for instance, ruled for only one year, his life cut short by the fatal ingestion of a Daoist drug. Emperor Yingzong, who sat on the throne twice (r. 1436–50, 1457–65), supervised the first printing of the canon and canonized the legendary immortal Zhang Sanfeng in 1459. But we know little else about him. Xianzong (r. 1465–88) had close Daoist associates, but he also died prematurely from elixir poisoning. Though Xianzong's son Xiaozong (r. 1487–1505) initially curtailed Daoism, he later came to support it and participated in Daoist rituals. Xiaozong's son Wuzong (r. 1505–21) yielded power to court eunuchs who supported Buddhism over Daoism.

But under the reign of Shizong (also known by his reign-period name: the Jiajing emperor, r. 1521–66), Daoism regained its privileged position at court. Following an assassination attempt that nearly killed him, he began to consume elixirs and participate in sexual rites aimed at prolonging life. Shizong's support for Daoists in official positions, combined with his personal interest in Daoist rituals and practices, strained his relationship with the imperial bureaucracy, since he began to absent himself from the daily functioning of the court to concentrate on his personal preoccupations. Historians speculate that he, too, may have died from elixir poisoning. After the fall of Shizong, whose shortcomings as an emperor were blamed on his engagement with Daoists and Daoist alchemy, there was a sharp backlash against Daoism: it lost imperial support, and Daoists were removed from court offices.

The story of Ming Daoism told above has focused on dynamics internal to China, from political elites to popular folklore. The Ming dynasty was also pivotal in the history of China's relations with the outside world, since it was during this period that Chinese emperors began to send out maritime emissaries in the hope of expanding their tribute system (vassal states paid tribute to the emperor, and in return the Chinese state was obligated to come to their aid in times of need). During Chengzu's reign in particular, maritime expeditions and trade grew as foreign demand for Chinese silk and porcelain increased. It was seafaring trade with the Middle East that introduced to China the cobalt blue that was used to create the signature Ming dynasty blue-and-white porcelain, which in turn caused a European craze for Chinese porcelain. Blue-and-white Ming vases, especially those produced in the Jiajing reign period (1522–66), were emblazoned with a rich array of Daoist symbols and motifs, including immortals, gourds, trigrams, and numinous mushrooms (*lingzhi*). Portuguese and Dutch traders also began to deal in tea and silk, further boosting Chinese prosperity. The early Ming leaders instituted strict regulations on foreign trade, but in 1577 the Portuguese were officially allowed to set up trading offices in the port city of Macau. Over the course of the Ming dynasty, Dutch, Japanese, and Spanish merchants would join the Portuguese, and transnational trade and intercultural exchange would increase under the subsequent Qing dynasty (1644–1912).

A RETURN TO NON-HAN RULE: QING DYNASTY (1644–1912) DAOISM AND THE MANCHUS

From the late sixteenth to the early seventeenth century, the Ming dynasty was in steady decline; when Beijing fell to a Chinese rebel leader in 1644, the emperor hanged himself inside the palace. A Ming general attempted to form an alliance with the Manchus on China's northeast borders in order to put down the rebellion, but after the insurgents were driven from the capital the Manchus took the throne for themselves and established China's last imperial dynasty, the Qing, in a return to non-Han Chinese rule. The Manchus were a farming and hunting people who saw themselves as the descendants of the Jurchens, founders of the earlier Jin dynasty (1115–1234). They actively resisted assimilation to their new cultural environment and strove to maintain their traditional identity and customs. Such efforts did not bode well for Daoism, which never came to play an important role at the Qing court or in the personal lives of its emperors. Nonetheless, Daoism in the Qing had much the same overall contours as in the Ming, enduring state control externally while further penetrating into lay life (thought, philosophy, and religious practice) and undergoing internal consolidation and unification.

The Manchus had begun to consolidate their power under the leadership of Nurhaci (1559–1626), locating their capital—modeled on Beijing—in the northern city of Shenyang (Mukden) in southern Manchuria. Nurhaci's son Hong Taiji (1592–1643) gave the empire the name Qing, but he did not live to witness the fall of the Ming and the inauguration of the dynasty in the south. It was Hong's younger brother, Prince Dorgon (1612–1650), the regent of the future Qing emperor Shunzhi (1638–1661, r. 1644–61), who completed the task of ushering in the Qing dynasty and establishing its capital in Beijing; Shenyang became a secondary capital. When Dorgon died in 1650, Shunzhi assumed his rightful place on the throne, becoming the first Manchu to rule over all of China. Before Shunzhi died of smallpox in 1661, he ensured that his third son, Xuanye (the future emperor Kangxi, r. 1662–1722), would assume the throne.

Qing rulers were efficient rulers who relied on a system of "banners"— devised by Nurhaci, and each originally identified by a different color—to divide the realm into military and administrative units. Under Qing rule the lives of the Chinese changed perceptibly; they lost land, and all men were required to cut their hair and grow a queue (a long braid at the back of the head) in order to demonstrate their loyalty to the new regime. The Manchus also developed their own script based on the Mongolian alphabet. Some Ming loyalists tried to resist the Manchus, but in the face of ruthlessly applied Qing strength they had little success. During the long reigns of the three most important early Qing emperors—Kangxi, Yongzheng (r. 1722–36), and Qianlong (r. 1736–95)—the Manchus gained the acceptance of the Chinese, and China prospered and grew. From the late seventeenth century to the early nineteenth century its territory expanded to include Taiwan, Tibet, Mongolia, and Xinjiang. Up through the eighteenth century, China outpaced the West in its technological development and standard of living, but it fell behind during the nineteenth century as the industrial revolution drove unprecedented growth in the West.

Qing rulers, like their Yuan dynasty predecessors, were partial to Tibetan forms of Buddhism, which seems to have offered an appealing model of sovereignty and helped them forge strong political ties with Tibetans and Mongolians. The name "Manchu" may itself also be related to the Chinese name "Manju," which refers to the Buddhist bodhisattva of wisdom, Manjushri. Under some emperors, such as Gaozong (Qianlong, r. 1736–95), the Tibetan Gelugpa tradition was even the official state religion. These religious developments weakened Daoists, who lost influence at court and social status more broadly.

Qing state regulation of Daoism was handled through a special office in the imperial bureaucracy. These rules, preserved in such official sources as the *Collected Statutes of the Great Qing Dynasty* (*Daqing lüli*) and *Imperially Commissioned Institutes of the Great Qing* (*Daqing huidian shili*), both excerpted in this section, detail what was forbidden and what was permitted, making clear the legal position of Daoist monasteries and clergy in relationship to the imperial government and attesting to the low status of the Daoist clergy during the Qing. The texts discuss issues of ordination, monastic offices, public preaching, the exclusion of women from Daoist monasteries, and the legal limits placed on the numbers of clergy and of religious institutions.

Qing Daoism: The Orthodox Unity (Zhengyi) and Complete Perfection (Quanzhen) Traditions

The Qing rulers tolerated Daoism, but officially recognized only two Daoist schools: Orthodox Unity (Zhengyi) and Complete Perfection (Quanzhen). The Orthodox Unity tradition was preferred, and the various Celestial Master leaders—who continued to receive their authority from the movement's headquarters on Dragon Tiger Mountain (Longhu shan)— received honorary titles and held official positions within the imperial bureaucracy. It was the Orthodox Unity leaders who were sanctioned by the emperor to oversee all Daoists, and they in turn performed rituals on behalf of the state.

At the same time, Qing leaders also recognized the potential benefits of the strict order maintained by the Complete Perfection tradition, whose monks and nuns lived in monasteries, issued moral teachings, and abided by strict regulations. During this period the Complete Perfection tradition grew considerably and its Longmen branch—which had its roots in the Ming dynasty—rose to prominence. The Longmen tradition was closely connected with Beijing's White Cloud Abbey (Baiyun guan), which became its headquarters and main training center. One of the texts included below, the "Biography of Wang Changyue (?–1680)," is a record of the seventh patriarch in the newly flourishing Longmen Daoist tradition. In Wang's day the tradition began to merge various branches of internal alchemy; it established its own institutional structure and separate patriarchal lineage, even as it absorbed much from the Orthodox Unity tradition. Written by another formidable Longmen patriarch named Min Yide (1748–1836), the biography emphasizes Wang's ascetic practice, a hallmark trait of the Longmen tradition (see also the later "Biographical Stele Inscription for the Daoist

Qing dynasty portrait of a Daoist priest. Clearly depicted in this painting are the distinctive Daoist hat, the ornate Daoist robe, and the Daoist priest's Ruyi scepter, which he holds in his hands.

Wang"). Wang later became the abbot of the White Cloud Abbey, where he earned a name for himself by attempting to revive Daoist monastic discipline. The monastic reforms that Wang introduced also pleased the Qing court, since they drew from Neo-Confucian ethics and integrated Buddhist elements.

While the clear trend within Qing Daoism was toward unification and standardization, a range of local Daoist traditions remained active, though they had to fall in line—at least nominally—with Longmen dictates. "The Hermits of Huashan" furnishes an important glimpse of a Longmen lineage that was outside of the orthodox lineage set forth in Min Yide's *Transmission of the Mind-Lamp from Mount Jin'gai* (*Jin'gai xindeng*). Before an ideal lineage of Longmen patriarchs was constructed, many branch lineages with different characteristics flourished in different regions.

The Evolution of Qing Daoism: Syncretic Movements and Lay Organizations

Two other general tendencies evident in Qing Daoism are the rise of syncretic movements that mixed together elements of Confucianism, Buddhism, and Daoism and an increase in lay groups whose activities spawned new popular Daoist movements. Qing emperors, like their predecessors in the Ming, championed the Unity of the Three Teachings (*sanjiao heyi*) outlook, which unified the three main religions: Confucianism, Buddhism, and Daoism. But the Qing rulers' attitude toward Daoism was different, because Daoism was implicated in the fall of the Ming dynasty and because they instead recognized Neo-Confucianism as their official doctrine. The primary concern of Qing officials was that the different religious traditions should assume easily controlled institutional forms and adhere to official policies. They viewed Confucian ethics and teachings on filial piety as effective instruments in making loyal subjects.

The Qing trend toward syncretism was visible not just at court but at the regional level as well. In the account below of shamanistic exorcism from the *Gazetteer for Western Hunan*, for instance, we see the overt mixing of elements that are Buddhist (clothing), Daoist (a tablet emblazoned with charms and talismans), and popular, all brought to bear on curing the sick. That text attests to the ongoing assimilation into Daoism of elements of popular religion; at the same time, different popular cults may have been incorporating aspects of Daoism for their own purposes. The Qing desire to exert control over all religious organizations, standardize them, and have them support state policies was often more aspirational than fully achieved.

Qing attempts at realizing a homogenized and controlled Daoism may in fact have been counterproductive, with the unintended effect of actually encouraging the proliferation of new movements and the production of more texts. One consequence of the low social status of the Daoist clergy in the Qing, for example, was that the prospect of becoming a Daoist monk or nun became less attractive. As Daoist institutions formerly patronized by the state grew weaker, participation in new lay and sectarian movements increased. This shift dovetailed nicely with the trend toward mixing together elements of different religious traditions; now, for instance, an official—by definition affiliated with Confucianism, since Neo-Confucianism was the state doctrine during the Qing—could also hold personal convictions about Buddhism or Daoism and participate in a variety of practices sponsored by lay organizations.

Lay organizations disseminated their teachings through various kinds of texts. These included morality books (such as the twelfth-century *Tract of the Most Exalted on Action and Response*, or *Taishang ganying pian*) and precious scrolls (*baojuan*, such as the twelfth-century *Esoteric Biography of Qinghe*, or *Qinghe neizhuan*), which may both have been produced through spirit writing—that is, text recorded by someone in a trance whose writing implement is controlled by a spirit, a common method of composing Qing religious works. The Qing government may have been suspicious of allowing dispersed groups to transmit their (potentially threatening) ideas in popular tracts, but it also saw the value in allowing them to circulate models of ideal Confucian social behavior and ethical teachings mixed with Buddhist notions of karma and Daoist ideas about health and longevity.

Popular literature also served to spread Daoist ideas to a wide range of social classes. For example, *Strange Stories from a Chinese Studio* (*Liaozhai zhiyi*), a famous collection of supernatural tales from the late seventeenth to early eighteenth century, contains numerous stories featuring Daoist priests, sages, and immortals; "The Daoist Priest of the Lao Mountains," included below, is drawn from it.

Qing Daoist Self-Cultivation Practices: Sex and (Symbolic) Drugs

Qing Daoist self-cultivation practices focus mainly on internal alchemy (*neidan*), female alchemy (*nüdan*), and sexual self-cultivation. Internal alchemy figured in Daoist thought from very early on, as seen in this anthology in many selections above, but during the Qing dynasty Daoists and sectarian groups attempted to write more clearly about its arcane theories. Internal alchemy practices became more accessible and less obscure, as they were no longer discussed only in esoteric teachings communicated from masters to disciples.

Many of the texts in this section concern female alchemy and sexual self-cultivation practices. Though the first writings on female alchemy appeared in the Ming dynasty, the practice did not become widely popular until the Qing. Whereas, as translator and scholar Elena Valussi notes, internal alchemy was not gender-specific—within that tradition women were securely positioned as goddesses and revealers of texts, as well as devout practitioners and believers—the texts of female alchemy were directed specifically to women, and its practices were specific to female physiology. In "Cutting the Red Dragon" ("Duan Honglong") and *Combined Collection of Female Alchemy* (*Nüdan hebian*), for example, we encounter teachings aimed at cutting off the menstrual flow. Success, as other texts like the *Queen Mother of the West's Ten Precepts on the True Path of Women's Practice* (*Xiwangmu nüxiu zhengtu shize*) explain, will return the adept to woman's primordial state. Some texts related to female alchemy privilege women within Daoist religious practice, while others maintain that even though they may be able to refine themselves through internal alchemy, women remain unable to ascend to heaven without the help of men.

One of the reasons that female alchemy focuses on "beheading the red dragon" is that the loss of bodily fluids was considered enervating. For men the same logic applied to semen, which was believed to be the source of their life force. Yet though the loss of semen caused depletion, sexual arousal was energizing. Thus ideally in sexual congress the male would become aroused but not ejaculate. In this form of controlled intercourse, called "subduing the white tiger," the energy-laden male life essence remains inside his body and travels up his spine to his brain (see *Combined Collection of Female Alchemy*). Sexual self-cultivation practices were not exclusively Daoist, but they have been connected with Daoism since the "merging pneumas" (*heqi*) initiation rite of the early Celestial Masters (Tianshi)—a rite largely known to us, unfortunately, through the critiques leveled at it by others.

The nineteenth-century *Secret Principles of Gathering the True Essence* (*Caizhen jiyao*) is associated with Zhang Sanfeng, the Daoist immortal who was so important to the early Ming emperors and whose name had sexual connotations. Though its language is explicitly sexual, there is little that the modern reader might consider erotic. The text's main purpose is to instruct the practitioner in how to collect key ingredients—primarily through the exchange of sexual energy in the form of qi—from his or her partner of the opposite sex. Certain forms of internal alchemy use highly symbolic sexual language to describe the adept's transformation. After a series of preliminary practices (breathing exercises and meditation), the adept is to ascend through three phases of transformation. The adept first converts essence (*jing*) into pneuma (*qi*) and then pneuma (*qi*) into spirit (*shen*). The transformation of essence into pneuma for men is "subduing the white tiger"; for women, "beheading the red dragon." This pneuma is then circulated inside the body until it becomes a drop of primordial qi (*yuanqi*), which is called the "outer medicine" (*waiyao*). Then, in a series of highly symbolic alchemical steps, the adept produces an immortal embryo, which is nurtured during its gestation period (in Chinese reckoning, ten months); finally, it is released through the crown of the adept's head as a transcendent—a spirit made up of primordial qi—in what is described as a return to the Dao itself.

Another Qing dynasty text on internal alchemy that has remained important to the present day is *The Secret of the Golden Flower* (*Taiyi jinhua zongzhi*). That seventeenth-century text, which was revealed through spirit writing, concerns the practice of generating the Golden Flower, which is the Golden Elixir. In the context of internal alchemy, the Golden Elixir refers to the transformation or return of one's spirit to the undivided primordial Dao. The *Secret of the Golden Flower* also exemplifies the type of Qing religious text that mixes together elements drawn from different religious traditions—in this case, in particular Buddhist philosophical vocabulary and practices, such as "calming and insight," rendered in the translation below as "fixating contemplation." The *Secret of the Golden Flower* was one of the main texts of Jingming Daoism, a minor sect that was connected with both the Longmen tradition and the official Zhengyi lineage. One of the key figures associated with the Jingming tradition was Fu Jinquan (b. 1765), who mixed Confucian ethical teachings into his writings on internal alchemy and also authored many texts on female alchemy.

EUROPE, MISSIONARIES, WAR, AND THE END OF IMPERIAL CHINA

As foreign trade with China increased during the late sixteenth century, the merchants were accompanied by missionaries and by new ideas about science, mathematics, cartography, and religion. Of the Europeans who set foot in China in the sixteenth century, the most important for our knowledge about the country during that period was the Italian Jesuit Matteo Ricci, who lived in China from 1583 until his death in 1610. Ricci and the other Jesuits learned Chinese well and developed a deep understanding of Chinese culture. Europeans began to gain information about China from the reports they received from these missionaries, who painted a rather positive image of the Chinese and their accomplishments.

The Jesuits initially saw great opportunities in China, since they thought that the ancient Chinese worship of the Highest Thearch (Shangdi) in fact preserved an old form of monotheism. They therefore viewed Daoism and Buddhism in a negative light, as having fallen away from monotheism, and labeled both as idolatrous. The Jesuits tended to pay more attention to Buddhists than to Daoists, whom they called "Epicureans" because of their attempts to achieve longevity. During the Qing there was little discussion in the West of Daoist philosophy—a situation that would change, as the next section on contemporary Daoism shows—but some writers attempted to better understand Daoist thoughts and beliefs so that they might more fully comprehend its appeal to the Chinese who embraced it.

Ricci made a special effort to master written and spoken Chinese so that he could engage with the Chinese literati. Not only did he learn from his Chinese counterparts, but his essays summarizing European intellectual history—written in classical Chinese—had a profound impact on late Ming intellectuals. Indeed, the Jesuits decided that their best strategy was to focus their efforts on converting the literati. They sought to find ways to reconcile the Confucian tradition, which they viewed as an ethical philosophy rather than a religion, with the teachings of Christianity and, conversely, to adapt Christianity to the Chinese cultural context. One of the central tenets of the Jesuit engagement with the Chinese was that certain ritual practices directed toward Confucius or ancestors were to be considered as cultural traditions, with implications not religious but merely moral or ethical; as such, they could be tolerated rather than forbidden as idolatrous.

This approach to the missionary effort in China—which was achieving only limited success in gaining Chinese converts—eventually ran afoul of church officials back in Rome. Problems for the Jesuits began in China in the form of conflicts with the recently arrived Dominicans and Franciscans, who reported the Jesuits to Pope Gregory XIII. Ultimately, the acrimonious debates of the so-called Rites Controversy during the early eighteenth century ended with a firm repudiation of the Jesuits' accommodationist position. Pope Clement XI sent envoys to Beijing to explain the orthodox stance to the Qing emperor, who later declared Christianity to be heterodox; in 1732 the Qing court expelled all missionaries from China and repurposed Christian churches as offices or shrines to indigenous deities.

The Jesuits' approach may have been officially banned, but their attempts to understand Chinese social and religious practices provide us with valuable insights. Indeed, Ricci's assessment of Chinese religions offers a fascinating look at how Europeans viewed Daoists in China during the late sixteenth century (see "Religious Sects among the Chinese"). Ricci, who thought that Confucianism could be synthesized with Christianity, was rather critical of Buddhism and Daoism (particularly the Daoist pursuit of immortality through alchemy). Yet his observations are rare glimpses of the institutional and religious forms of Daoism, rather than just the philosophies of Laozi and Zhuangzi. Ricci evocatively describes Daoist ritual music, Daoist priests, and their vestments, and he discusses the types of apotropaic rituals performed by Daoist priests.

Trade and commerce with Europe continued in the Qing much as they had during the Ming dynasty, but attitudes began to change from curiosity and tolerance to hostility, leading to war. From the late eighteenth to the nineteenth century the balance of power between China and the West shifted as the Europeans, especially the British, advanced beyond China both technologically and militarily. In 1793, Lord George Macartney showed up in China with more than 500 cases of goods manufactured in Britain, including the latest scientific instruments, intent on meeting with the Qing emperor to negotiate changes in trade policies. Though Lord Macartney's refusal to bow before Qianlong almost prevented their encounter from taking place, he was eventually given an audience. The emperor was not impressed with the trappings of Western material culture and made no agreements, but on his visit Lord Macartney gained priceless information: the Chinese were far behind the British in industrial and military development, they were woefully ill prepared to fight a modern war, and they were plagued by numerous domestic rebellions.

Trade in one particular commodity, opium, became a source of great tension between the British and the Chinese. The Chinese had long used opium medicinally, but as the practice of smoking the drug spread in the eighteenth century, rates of addiction rose. Although the Qing banned its importation in 1729, opium continued to be sold at ever-increasing levels by British merchants, who enjoyed high profits from the illegal trade. The Qing attempted to crack down on the traffic in the 1830s, but the 1839 blockade of the foreign community in Canton was answered with British warships. When the first Opium War (1839–42) ended, the defeated Chinese were forced to sign unequal treaties that guaranteed privileges for the British, including rights of trade and residence in five treaty ports. A second Opium War (1854–60), involving additional Western states, led to China ceding more territorial and sovereignty rights to foreign powers.

Even more damaging to the Qing during the nineteenth century was the Taiping Rebellion (1850–64), a peasant uprising whose roots were in the social, political, economic, and religious upheavals caused by interactions with the West. It began in South China, the area of China that suffered the most from the changes connected with the Opium War, and was led by a native of Guangdong named Hong Xiuquan (1813–1864). Inspired by visions that caused him to believe that he was the younger brother of Jesus and was charged with ridding China of demons, which he linked with the Manchus, Hong sought to create his own Kingdom of Great Peace in his own country and time. His teachings were filled with moralistic lessons aimed at bringing an end to prostitution and to opium and alcohol abuse, and he encouraged gender equality and large-scale social reforms. Thousands of impoverished and disaffected men and women joined the movement, becoming a disciplined and effective army. Hong and his army were eventually able to fight their way to Nanjing, which they seized and held for ten years, until their defeat in 1864 by Western and Qing forces. Historians estimate that during the uprising some twenty million people died in battle or from starvation. Although the Qing state survived, the rebellions undercut its authority and irrevocably weakened the central government's control over its subjects. The stage was set for the fall of the Qing to other revolutionaries in 1912.

Hong Xiuquan's visions and prophecies were clearly influenced by his exposure to Christian missionaries and tracts. But though he derived some teachings from Christianity and rejected traditional forms of Chinese ancestor worship as idolatrous, Christians still looked on the Taiping rebels as heretics. The Taiping Rebellion's possible connections with Daoism are indirect. As noted earlier in this anthology, from the Han dynasty (202 B.C.E.–220 C.E.) onward the term "Great Peace" referred to various forms of good government and political harmony. Though the concept predates the emergence of Daoism as an organized religious tradition, it came to be associated with the Taiping (Great Peace) movement, which is in turn connected with a rebel uprising led by a Daoist that began in 184 C.E. Those early rebels, the Yellow Turbans, stressed the equal distribution of wealth and resources and the healing of illnesses. Despite these ideological resonances, during the Taiping occupation of Nanjing the institutions of Daoism suffered greatly, and most Daoist temples were burned to the ground.

The final decades of the Qing dynasty were a time of enormous political and social stress. Spurred in part by their distress at China's defeat in the Sino-Japanese War (1894–95), some of the key intellectuals of the day—including Kang Youwei (1858–1927) and Liang Qichao (1873–1929)—urged the government to undertake modernizing reforms. After they briefly gained the ear of Emperor Guangxu, who put into practice some of their radical proposals, the Empress Dowager Cixi—the emperor's aunt and adoptive mother, who had been regent—reasserted herself, reversed the reforms, and executed many of those involved in advocating them. Kang and Liang managed to flee to Japan.

One of the reforms that Kang Youwei persuaded the emperor to implement in 1898 had particularly damaging consequences for Daoism and all Chinese religions. Kang urged that all academies and temples not listed on the registers of state sacrifices be converted into modern public schools. Though his proposal was mainly intended to help make Confucianism the state religion, it also reflected a wider movement promoting modernization that included educational and economic reforms as well as attempts to eradicate religious institutions and superstitious beliefs and practices. The suggestion was immediately adopted by the emperor, but his decree was annulled later that same year (except for a ban on improper shrines). Nonetheless, the events set in motion by the 1898 edict were not halted. Scholars have estimated that in the first few decades of the twentieth century, some 500,000 Daoist temples, Buddhist monasteries, and local shrines were either destroyed or repurposed as schools. Not all Daoist religious institutions were dissolved, but the removal of the religion's physical structures and the interruption of its ritual activities dealt a severe blow to Daoism.

As the dynasty grew weaker, foreign powers demanded more economic concessions and missionaries grew bolder. The Chinese people pushed back violently—most notably, a group from North China known as the Boxers, who joined together in the hopes of driving out the foreigners. They attacked and killed both Chinese Christians and foreign missionaries, and their efforts gained the support of local government officials and ultimately of the empress dowager. But when the Boxers pushed into Beijing and surrounded the foreign legations, the major foreign powers sent in an army of soldiers that crushed them; Cixi and Guangxu fled Beijing, and China once again was forced to accept a humiliating treaty. Some insight into the effects of these historical events is provided by the "Biographical Stele Inscription for the Daoist Wang" ("Wang daoren daoxing bei"). Wang's life became enmeshed with the traumatic history of China's loss of stability and power.

When the foreign troops entered Beijing in 1900, Wang showed his loyalty to the regime by committing suicide.

The Qing dynasty muddled on from 1900 to 1912 primarily because there was no viable alternative, but it continued to weaken. For more than a decade, Sun Yat-sen (Sun Zhongshan, 1866–1925), a Western-trained doctor turned anti-Manchu revolutionary, assiduously raised funds abroad and plotted unsuccessful attempts at overthrowing the Qing. When the regime finally collapsed, following a series of revolts in the provinces, Sun was elected provisional president; after the six-year-old Qing emperor abdicated, he voluntarily resigned and a reformist general, Yuan Shikai (1859–1916), was selected as the first president of the newly established Republic of China (1912–1949).[3] Yuan quickly transformed into something of a dictator, and even sought to proclaim himself emperor of a new dynasty—but China's last imperial dynasty had ended. The fall of the Qing and founding of the Republic of China did not improve the situation for Daoists, but instead presented them with new challenges to which they would have to respond in order to survive the turbulent century that lay ahead.

---

3. When the remnants of the Nationalists fled to Taiwan in 1949, they took the name "Republic of China" with them.

JOURNEY TO THE WEST
(*Xiyou ji*)

Journey to the West, a classic novel of the Ming dynasty generally attributed to Wu Cheng'en (ca. 1500–1582), depicts the intrepid Chinese Buddhist pilgrim Xuanzang (ca. 596–664) as he traveled overland from China to India from 627 to 644, in search of Buddhist scriptures. Although he left China in defiance of the emperor, he returned a hero and spent his final years ensconced in the capital of Xi'an translating Sanskrit texts (sutras) into Chinese. In this fictional account of his journey, which blends fantasy, adventure, satire, and humor, Xuanzang is accompanied by a colorful band of traveling companions: Sun Wukong (or Great Sage Sun), a sagacious monkey (thus, *Journey to the West* is alternatively titled *Monkey*) with supernormal powers who had converted from Daoism to Buddhism; Zhu Bajie, half-human and half-pig—a Daoist deity who had been expelled from heaven; a cannibalistic figure named Sha Wujing (or Sha Monk), who had also been exiled from heaven; and a hybrid dragon-horse that Xuanzang rides. Since the novel's publication it has become a much-beloved classic in China, where in recent decades its popularity has been enhanced by adaptations on television, in film, and in comic books. Thanks to the efforts of translators, *Journey to the West* has become popular in other parts of the world as well.

The bulk of the work concerns Xuanzang's quest to bring Buddhist scriptures back to China from India. In the chapter titled "At the Three Pure Ones Temple the Great Sage Leaves His Name; At the Cart Slow Kingdom the Monkey King Reveals His Power," Xuanzang and his companions are mistaken for statues of Daoist deities come to life. Taking advantage of the error, the traveling companions play coarse tricks on the temple's Daoist priests. After they are found out, they escape beheading and win their freedom to continue their journey to the West by defeating the priests in a rainmaking competition.

PRONOUNCING GLOSSARY

Aoshun: *ow shoon*

Sha Monk: *shah monk*

Sun: *soon*

Tripitaka: *tree-pee-daw-kah*

Xiyou ji: *see-yo chee*

Zhu Bajie: *chu ba-jieh*

At the Three Pure Ones Temple
the Great Sage Leaves His Name;
At the Cart Slow Kingdom the Monkey
King Reveals His Power

We now tell you about the Great Sage Sun, who used his left hand to give Sha Monk a pinch, and his right to give Zhu Bajie a pinch. Immediately understanding what he meant, the two of them fell silent and sat with lowered faces on their high seats. They allowed those Daoists to examine them back and front with uplifted lamps and torches, but the three of them seemed no more than idols made of clay and adorned with gold. "There are no thieves around," said the Tiger-Strength Immortal,[1] "but then, why are

TRANSLATED BY Anthony C. Yu.

1. A Daoist who has achieved extraordinary powers and a higher form of existence.

all the offerings eaten?" "It definitely looks as if humans have eaten them," said the Deer-Strength Immortal. "Look how the fruits are skinned and their stones spat out. Why is it that we don't see any human form?" "Don't be too suspicious, Elder Brothers," said the Goat-Strength Immortal. "I think that our piety and sincerity and the fact that we are reciting scriptures and saying prayers here night and day, all in the name of the Court, must have aroused the Honorable Divines. The Venerable Fathers of the Three Pure Ones,[2] I suppose, must have descended to earth and consumed these offerings. Why don't we take advantage of the fact that their holy train and crane carriages are still here and make supplication to the Honorable Divines? We should beg for some golden elixir and holy water with which we may present His Majesty. Wouldn't his long life and perpetual youth be in fact our merit?" "You are right," said the Tiger-Strength Immortal. "Disciples, start the music and recite the scriptures. Bring us our ritual robes. Let me tread the stars[3] to make our supplication." Those little Daoists all obeyed and lined themselves up on both sides. At the sound of the gong, they all recited in unison the scroll of *True Scriptures of the Yellow Court.*[4] After having put on his ritual robe, the Tiger-Strength Immortal held high his jade tablet and began to kick up the dust with dancing. Intermittently he would fall to the ground and prostrate himself. Then he intoned this petition:

"In fear and dread,
We bow most humbly.
To stir up our faith
We seek Purity.
Vile priests we quell
To honor the Way.
This hall we build
The king to obey.
Dragon flags we raise,
And off'rings display;
Torches by night,
Incense by day.
One thought sincere
Doth Heaven sway.
Chariots divine
Now come to stay.
Grant unto us some elixir and holy water,
Which we may give to His Majesty
That he may gain longevity."

When Bajie heard these words, he was filled with apprehension. "This is our fault! We've eaten the goods and should be on our way. Now, how shall we answer such supplication?" Pilgrim gave him another pinch before suddenly opening his mouth and speaking out loud: "You immortals of a younger generation, please stop your recitation. We have just returned from the Festival of Immortal Peaches,[5] and we have not brought along any golden

2. The highest deities in the Daoist pantheon.
3. That is, engage in a form of ritual walking that follows celestial patterns mapped onto the ground.
4. An early Daoist classic; see *Most High Jade Scripture on the Internal View of the Yellow*

Court (Taishang huangting neijing yujing), above.
5. The peaches of immortality were believed to grow in the garden of the Queen Mother of the West (one of the most important goddesses in ancient China and in the Daoist pantheon).

elixir or holy water. In another day we shall come to bestow them on you."
When those Daoists, old and young, heard that the image had actually spoken, everyone of them trembled violently. "O Fathers!" they cried, "the living Honorable Divines have descended to earth. We must not let them go. We must insist on their giving us some sort of magic formula for eternal youth." Then the Deer-Strength Immortal went forward also to prostrate himself and intone this supplication:

> "Our heads to the dust,
> We pray earnestly.
> Your subjects submit
> To the Pure Ones Three.
> Since we came here,
> The Way was set free.
> The king is pleased
> To seek longevity.
> This Heavenly Mass
> Chants scriptures nightly.
> We thank the Honorable Divines
> For revealing their presence holy.
> O hear our prayers!
> We seek your glory!
> Do leave some holy water behind,
> That your disciples long life may find!"

Sha Monk gave Pilgrim a pinch and whispered fiercely, "Elder Brother! They are at it again! Just listen to the prayer!" "All right," said Pilgrim, "let's give them something." "Where could we find it?" muttered Bajie. "Just watch me," said Pilgrim, "and when you see that I have it, you'll have it too!" After those Daoists had finished their music and their prayers, Pilgrim again spoke out loud: "You immortals of a younger generation, there's no need for your bowing and praying any longer. I am rather reluctant to leave you some holy water, but I fear then that our posterity will die out. If I gave you some, however, it would seem to be too easy a boon." When those Daoists heard these words, they all prostrated themselves and kow-towed. "We beseech the Honorable Divines to have regard for the reverence of your disciples," they cried, "and we beg you to leave us some. We shall proclaim far and near the Way and Virtue. We shall memorialize to the king to give added honors to the Gate of Mystery." "In that case," said Pilgrim, "bring us some vessels." The Daoists all touched their heads to the ground to give thanks. Being the greediest, the Tiger-Strength Immortal hauled in a huge cistern and placed it in the hall. The Deer-Strength Immortal fetched an earthen-ware garden vase and put it on top of the offering table. The Goat-Strength Immortal pulled out the flowers from a flowerpot and placed it in the middle of the other two vessels. Then Pilgrim said to them, "Now leave the hall and close the shutters so that the Heavenly mysteries will not be seen by profane eyes. We shall leave you some holy water." The Daoists retreated from the hall and closed the doors, after which they all prostrated themselves before the vermilion steps.

Pilgrim stood up at once and, lifting up his tiger-skin kilt, filled the flowerpot with his stinking urine. Delighted by what he saw, Zhu Bajie said, "Elder Brother, you and I have been brothers these few years but we have never had fun like this before. Since I gorged myself just now, I have been feeling the urge to do this." Lifting up his clothes, our Idiot let loose such a torrent that it sounded as if the Lüliang Cascade[6] had crashed onto some wooden boards! He pissed till he filled the whole garden vase. Sha Monk, too, left behind half a cistern. They then straightened their clothes and resumed their seats solemnly before they called out: "Little ones, receive your holy water."

Pushing open the shutters, those Daoists kowtowed repeatedly to give thanks. They carried the cistern out first, and then they poured the contents of the vase and the pot into the bigger vessel, mixing the liquids together. "Disciples," said the Tiger-Strength Immortal, "bring me a cup so that I can have a taste." A young Daoist immediately fetched a tea cup and handed it to the old Daoist. After bailing out a cup of it and gulping down a huge mouthful, the old Daoist kept wiping his mouth and puckering his lips. "Elder Brother," said the Deer-Strength Immortal, "is it good?" "Not very good," said the old Daoist, his lips still pouted, "the flavor is quite potent!" "Let me try it also," said the Goat-Strength Immortal, and he, too, downed a mouthful. Immediately he said, "It smells somewhat like hog urine!" Sitting high above them and hearing this remark, Pilgrim knew that he could no longer fool them. He thought to himself: "I might as well display my abilities and leave them our names too." He cried out in a loud voice:

> "O Daoists, Daoists,
> You are so silly!
> Which Three Pure Ones
> Would be so worldly?
> Let our true names
> Be told most clearly.
> Monks of the Great Tang[7]
> Go West by decree.
> We come to your place
> This fine night carefree.
> Your offerings eaten,
> We sit and play.
> Your bows and greetings
> How could we repay?
> That was no holy water you drank.
> 'Twas only the urine we pissed that stank!"

The moment the Daoists heard this, they barred the door. Picking up pitchforks, rakes, brooms, tiles, rocks, and whatever else they could put their hands on, they sent these hurtling inside the main hall to attack the impostors. Dear Pilgrim! Using his left hand to catch hold of Sha Monk and his right to take hold of Bajie, he crashed out of the door and mounted the cloudy luminosity to go straight back to the Wisdom Depth Monastery. When they arrived at the abbot's residence, they dared not disturb their master; each went to bed quietly and slept until the third quarter of the

---

6. A great waterfall mentioned in the *Book of Master Zhuang* (*Zhuangzi*; see above). Seeing the ferocity of the water's current, Confucius wrongly assumed that the man he saw in the waters was committing suicide rather than simply having a swim.
7. That is, Tang dynasty (618–907) China.

fifth watch. At that time, of course, the king began to hold his morning court, where two rows of civil and military officials—some four hundred of them—stood in attention. You see

Bright lamps and torches midst purple gauze;
Fragrant clouds rising from treasure tripods.

As soon as Tripitaka[8] Tang woke up, he said, "Disciples, help me to go and have our travel rescript certified." Rising quickly, Pilgrim, Sha Monk, and Bajie slipped on their clothes and stood to one side to wait on their master. They said, "Let it be known to our master that this king truly believes only the Daoists and is eager to exalt the Way and to exterminate the Buddhists. We fear that any ill-spoken word may cause him to refuse to certify our rescript. Let us therefore accompany Master to enter the court."

Highly pleased, the Tang monk draped the brocaded cassock on himself while Pilgrim took out the travel rescript; Wujing was told to hold the alms bowl and Wuneng to take up the priestly staff. The luggage and the horse were placed in the care of the monks of the Wisdom Depth Monastery. They went before the Five-Phoenix Tower and saluted the Custodian of the Yellow Gate. Having identified themselves, they declared that they were scripture pilgrims from the Great Tang in the Land of the East, who wished to have their travel rescript certified and would therefore like the custodian to announce their arrival. The official of the gate went at once into court and prostrated himself before the golden steps to memorialize to the king, saying, "There are four Buddhist monks outside who claim that they are scripture pilgrims from the Great Tang in the Land of the East. They wish to have their travel rescript certified, and they now await Your Majesty's decree before the Five-Phoenix Tower." When the king heard this, he said, "These monks have nowhere to court death and, of all places, they have to do it here! Why didn't our constables arrest them at once and bring them here?" A Grand Preceptor before the throne stepped forward and said, "The Great Tang in the Land of the East is located in the South Jambudvipa[9] Continent; it's the great nation of China, some ten thousand miles from here. As the way is infested with monsters and fiends, these monks must have considerable magic powers or they would not dare undertake this westward journey. I implore Your Majesty to invite them in and certify their rescript so that they may proceed, for the sake of the fact that they are the distant monks from China and for the sake of not destroying any goodly affinity."

The king gave his consent and summoned the Tang monk and his followers before the Hall of Golden Chimes. After master and disciples arrived before the steps, they presented the rescript to the king. The king opened the document and was about to read it, when the Custodian of the Yellow Gate appeared to announce: "The three National Preceptors have arrived." The king was so flustered that he put away the rescript hurriedly and left the dragon seat. After having ordered his attendants to set out some embroidered cushions, he bent his body to receive his visitors. When Tripitaka and his followers turned around to look, they saw those three great immortals swagger in, followed by a young acolyte with two tousled pigtails. Not daring

8. The canon of Buddhism (literally, "three baskets"; Sanskrit).

9. In Buddhist cosmology, the continent on which all humans live.

even to lift their eyes, the two rows of officials all bowed deeply as they walked by. After they ascended the Hall of Golden Chimes, they did not even bother to salute the king. "National Preceptors," said the king, "we have not invited you. How is it that you are pleased to visit us today?" "We have something to tell you," said one of the old Daoists, "and that's why we're here. Those four monks down there, where do they come from?" The king said, "They were sent by the Great Tang in the Land of the East to fetch scriptures, and they presented themselves here to have their travel rescript certified."

Clapping their hands together, the three Daoists burst out laughing and said, "We thought they had fled. So they are still here!" Somewhat startled, the king said, "What do you mean, Preceptors? When we first heard of their arrival, we wanted to arrest them and send them to serve you, had not our Grand Preceptor on duty intervened and presented a most reasonable memorial. Since we had regard for the fact that they had traveled a great distance, and since we did not wish to destroy our goodly affinity with China, we summoned them in here to verify their rescript. We did not expect you to raise any question about them. Could it be that they have offended you in some way?"

"Your Majesty wouldn't know about this," said one of the Daoists, chuckling. "Hardly had they arrived yesterday when they slew two of our disciples outside the eastern gate. The five hundred Buddhist prisoners were all released and the cart was smashed to pieces. As if that weren't enough, they sneaked into our temple last night, vandalized the holy images of the Three Pure Ones, and devoured all the imperial offerings. We were fooled by them at first, thinking that the Honorable Divines had descended to Earth. We therefore even asked them to give us some golden elixir and holy water with which we might present Your Majesty, so that you would be blessed with eternal youth. We hardly expected that they would trick us by leaving us their urine. We found out all right, after each of us had tasted a mouthful! Just when we were about to seize them, they managed to escape. We didn't think that they would dare remain here today. As the proverb says, 'The road for fated enemies is narrow indeed'!"

When the king heard this, he became so irate that he would have had the four priests executed at once. Pressing his palms together, the Great Sage Sun cried out in a loud voice, saying, "Your Majesty, let your thunderlike wrath subside for the moment and permit this monk to present his memorial." "You offended the National Preceptors!" said the king. "Do you dare imply that their words might be erroneous?"

Pilgrim said, "He claimed that we slaughtered yesterday two of his disciples outside the city. But who could be a witness? Even if we were to confess to this crime, and that would be a gross injustice, only two of us need be asked to pay with our lives, and two of us should be released so that we might proceed to acquire the scriptures. He claimed further that we wrecked their cart and released their Buddhist prisoners. Again, there is no witness, and moreover, this is hardly a mortal offense and only one of us should be punished for this if it were true. Finally, he charged us with vandalizing the images of the Three Pure Ones and caused disturbance in their temple. This is clearly a trap they set for us." "How could you say that it's a trap?" said the king.

"We monks are from the Land of the East," said Pilgrim, "and we've just arrived in this region. We can't even tell one street from another. How could we know about the affairs of their temple, and at night no less? If we could leave them our urine, they should have been able to arrest us right then and there. Why did they wait until this morning to accuse us? In this whole wide world, there are countless people who use false identities. How could they know for certain that we are guilty? I beg Your Majesty to withhold your anger and make a thorough investigation." The king, after all, had always been rather muddle-headed. When he heard this lengthy speech by Pilgrim, he became more confused than ever.

Just then, the Custodian of the Yellow Gate again came to make this announcement: "Your Majesty, there are outside the gate many village elders who await your summons." "For what reason?" asked the king. He ordered them brought in, and thirty or forty village elders came before the hall. "Your Majesty," they said as they kowtowed, "there has been no rain this year for the entire spring, and we fear that there will be a famine if it remains dry like this through summer. We have come especially to request that one of the Holy Fathers, the National Preceptors, to pray for sweet rain that will succor the entire population." The king said, "Let the village elders withdraw. Rain will be forthcoming." The village elders gave thanks and left.

Then the king said, "You, priests of the Tang court, why do you think that we honor the Dao and seek to destroy Buddhism? It was because in years past, the monks of this dynasty attempted to pray for rain, and they could not produce even a single drop. It was our good fortune that these National Preceptors descended from Heaven and saved us from our bitter affliction. Now all of you have offended the National Preceptors no sooner than you arrived from a great distance, and you should be condemned. We shall pardon you for the moment, however, and ask whether you dare to have a rain-making competition with our Preceptors. If your prayers could bring us the rain to assuage the needs of the people, we would pardon you, certify your rescript, and permit you to journey to the West. If you fail in your competition and no rain comes, all of you will be taken to the block and beheaded publicly." With a laugh, Pilgrim said, "This little priest has some knowledge of prayers, too!"

When the king heard this, he at once asked for an altar to be built. Meanwhile, he also gave the command that his carriage be brought out. "We want personally to ascend the Five-Phoenix Tower to watch," he said. Many officials followed the carriage up the tower and the king took his seat. Tripitaka Tang, followed by Pilgrim, Sha Monk, and Bajie, stood at attention down below, while the three Daoists also accompanied the king and took their seats on the tower. In a little while, an official came riding with the report: "The altar is ready. Let one of the Father National Preceptors ascend it."

Bowing with his hands folded before him, the Tiger-Strength Immortal took leave of the king and walked down the tower. "Sir," said Pilgrim, barring his way, "where are you going?" "To ascend the altar and pray for rain," said the Great Immortal. "You do have a sense of self-importance," said Pilgrim, "absolutely unwilling to defer to us monks who have come from a great distance. All right! As the proverb says, 'Even a strong dragon is no match for a local worm!' But if the master insists on proceeding first, then he must make a statement first before the king." "What statement?" said the Great Immortal. Pilgrim said, "Both you and I are supposed to ascend the altar to pray for rain. When it comes, how could anyone tell whether it's your rain or mine? Who could tell whose merit it is?" When the king above them heard this, he was secretly pleased and said, "The words of this little priest are quite gutsy!" When Sha Monk heard this, he said to himself, smiling, "You don't know that his stomach's full of gutsiness! He hasn't shown much of it yet!"

The Great Immortal said, "There's no need for me to make any statement. His Majesty is quite familiar with what I am about to do." "He may know it," said Pilgrim, "but I am a monk who came from a distant region. I have never met you and I'm not familiar with what you are about to do. I don't want us to end up accusing each other later, for that wouldn't be good business. We must settle this first before we act." "All right," said the Great Immortal, "when I ascend the altar, I shall use my ritual tablet as a sign. When I bang it loudly on the table once, wind will come; the second time, clouds will gather; the third time, there will be lightning and thunder; the fourth time, rain will come; and finally the fifth time, rain will stop and clouds will disperse." "Marvelous!" said Pilgrim, laughing. "I have never seen this before! Please go! Please go!"

With great strides, the Great Immortal walked forward, followed by Tripitaka and the rest. As they approached the altar, they saw that it was a platform about thirty feet tall. On all sides were flown banners with the names of the Twenty-Eight Constellations written on them. There was a table on top of the altar, and on the table was set an urn filled with burning incense. On both sides of the urn were two candle stands with huge, brightly lit candles. Leaning against the urn was a tablet made of gold, carved with the names of the thunder deities. Beneath the table were five huge cisterns full of clear water and afloat with willow branches. To the branches was attached a thin sheet of iron inscribed with the charms used to summon the agents of the Thunder Bureau. Five huge pillars were also set up around the table, and written on these pillars were the names of the barbarian thunder lords of Five Quarters.[1] There were two Daoists standing on both sides of each pillar; each of the Daoists held an iron bludgeon used for pounding on the pillar. There were also many Daoists drawing up documents behind the altar. Before them there were set up a brazier for burning papers[2] and several statues, all representing the messengers of charms, the local spirits, and patron deities.

The Great Immortal, without affecting the slightest degree of modesty, walked straight up to the altar and stood still. A young Daoist presented him with several charms written on yellow papers and a treasure sword. Holding the sword, the Great Immortal recited a spell and then burnt a charm on the flame of a candle. Down below several Daoists picked up a document and a statue holding a charm and had these burned also. With a bang the old Daoist high above brought down his ritual tablet on the table and at once a breeze could be felt in the air. "O dear! O dear!" muttered

---

1. North, south, east, west, and the center. Ritualists in the Five Thunders school of Daoism focus on harnessing the power of thunder and summoning thunder deities.

2. Papers are burned to convey the information on them to spirits and deities.

Bajie. "This Daoist is certainly quite capable! He bangs his tablet once and indeed the wind's rising." "Be quiet, Brother," said Pilgrim. "Don't speak to me anymore. Just stand guard over Master here and let me do my business."

Dear Great Sage! He pulled off a piece of hair and blew on it his immortal breath, saying, "Change!" It changed at once into a spurious Pilgrim, standing next to the Tang monk. His true body rose with his primal spirit into midair, where he shouted, "Who is in charge of the wind here?" He so startled the Old Woman of the Wind that she hugged her bag while the Second Boy of the Wind pulled tight the rope at the mouth of the bag. They stepped forward to salute Pilgrim, who said, "I am accompanying the holy monk of the Tang Court to go to acquire scriptures in the Western Heaven. We happen to pass through the Cart Slow Kingdom and are now waging a rainmaking contest with that deviant Daoist. How could you not help old Monkey and assist that Daoist instead? I'll pardon you this time, but you'd better call in the wind. If there's just the tiniest breeze to make the whiskers of the Daoist flutter, each of you will receive twenty strokes of the iron rod!" "We dare not! We dare not!" said the Old Woman of the Wind, and so, there was no sign of any wind. Unable to contain himself, Bajie began to holler: "You Sir, please step down! You've banged aloud the tablet. How is it that there's no wind? You come down, and let us go up there."

Holding high his tablet, the Daoist burned another charm before bringing down his tablet once more. Immediately, clouds and fog began to form in midair, but the Great Sage Sun shouted again, "Who is spreading the clouds?" He so startled the Cloud-Pushing Boy and the Fog-Spreading Lad that they hurriedly came forward to salute him. After Pilgrim had given his explanation as before, the Cloud Boy and the Mist Lad removed the clouds, so that

The sun came out and shone most brilliantly;
The sky was cloudless for ten thousand miles.

Laughing, Bajie said, "This master may deceive the king and befool his subjects. But he hasn't any real abilities! Why, the tablet has sounded twice! Why is it that we don't see any clouds forming?"

Becoming rather agitated, the Daoist loosened his hair, picked up his sword, and recited another spell as he burned a charm. Once more he brought down his tablet with a bang, and immediately the Heavenly Lord Deng arrived from the South Heaven Gate, trailed by the Squire of Thunder and the Mother of Lightning. When they saw Pilgrim in midair, they saluted him, and he gave his explanation as before. "What powerful summons," he said, "brought you all here so quickly?" The Heavenly Lord said, "The magic of five thunder exercised by that Daoist was not faked. He issued the summons and burned the document, which alerted the Jade Emperor. The Jade Emperor sent his decree to the residence of the Primordial Honorable Divine of All-Pervading Thunderclap in the Ninefold Heaven. We in turn received his command to come here and assist with the rainmaking by providing thunder and lightning." "In that case," said Pilgrim, "just wait a moment. You can help old Monkey instead." There was, therefore, neither the sound of thunder nor the flash of lightning.

In sheer desperation now, that Daoist added more incense, burned his charms, recited more spells, and struck his tablet more loudly than ever. In midair, the Dragon Kings of Four Oceans arrived all together, only to be met by Pilgrim, who shouted, "Aoguang, where do you think you're going?" Aoguang, Aoshun, Aoqin, and Aorun all went forward to salute him, and Pilgrim gave his explanation as before. He thanked the Dragon Kings moreover, saying, "I needed your help in times past, but we have not yet reached our goal. Today, I must rely on your assistance once more to help me achieve this merit right now. That Daoist has struck his tablet four times, and it's now old Monkey's turn to do business. But I don't know how to burn charms, issue summons, or strike any tablet. So all of you must play along with me."

The Heavenly Lord Deng said, "If the Great Sage gives us the order, who would dare disobey? You must, however, give us a sign, so that we may follow your instructions in an orderly manner. Otherwise, thunder and rain may be all mixed up, and that will not be to the credit of the Great Sage." Pilgrim said, "I'll use my rod as the sign." "O Dear Father!" cried the Squire of Thunder, horrified. "How could we take the rod?" "I'm not going to strike you," said Pilgrim, "all I want from you is to watch the rod. If I point it upwards once, you'll make the wind blow." "We'll make the wind blow!" snapped the Old Woman of the Wind and the Second Boy of the Wind in unison.

"When the rod points upward a second time, you'll spread the clouds." "We'll spread the clouds! We'll spread the clouds!" cried the Cloud-Pushing Boy and the Mist-Spreading Lad.

"When I point the rod upwards for the third time, I want thunder and lightning." "We'll provide the service! We'll provide the service!" said the Squire of Thunder and the Mother of Lightning.

"When I point the rod upwards the fourth time, I want rain." "We obey! We obey!" said the Dragon Kings.

"And when I point the rod upwards the fifth time, I want sunshine and fair weather. Don't make any mistake!"

After he had given all these instructions, Pilgrim dropped down from the clouds and retrieved his hair back to his body. Being of fleshly eyes and mortal stock, how could those people know the difference? Pilgrim then cried out with a loud voice, "Sir, please stop! You have struck aloud the tablet four times, but there's not the slightest sign of wind, cloud, thunder, or rain. You should let me take over." The Daoist had no choice but to leave his place and come down the altar for Pilgrim to take his turn. Pouting, he went back to the tower to see the throne. "Let me follow him," said Pilgrim, "and see what he has to say." He arrived and heard the king asking the Daoist, "We have been listening here most eagerly for the sounds of your tablet. Four times it struck and there was neither wind nor rain. Why is that?" The Daoist said, "Today the dragon deities are not home." Pilgrim shouted with a loud voice, "Your Majesty, the dragon deities are home all right, but the magic of your National Preceptor is not efficacious enough to bring them here. Allow us priests to summon them here for you to see." "Ascend the altar at once," said the king, "and we shall wait for the rain here."

Having received this decree, Pilgrim dashed back to the altar and tugged at the Tang monk, saying, "Master, please go up to the altar." "Disciple," said the Tang monk, "I don't know how to pray for rain." "He's trying to set you up," said Bajie, laughing. "If there's no rain, they'll put you on the pyre and finish you off with a fire." Pilgrim said, "Though you may not know how to pray for rain, you know how to recite scriptures. Let me help you." The elder indeed ascended the altar and solemnly took a seat on top. With complete concentration, he recited silently the Heart Sutra.[3] Suddenly an official came galloping on a horse with the question, "Why are you monks not striking the tablet and burning charms?" Pilgrim answered in a loud voice, "No need for that! Ours is the quiet work of fervent prayers." The official left to give this reply to the king, and we shall mention him no further.

When Pilgrim heard that his old master had finished reciting the sutra, he took out his rod from his ear and one wave of it in the wind gave it a length of twelve feet and the thickness of a rice bowl. He pointed it upwards in the air; when the Old Woman of the Wind saw it, she immediately shook loose her bag as the Second Boy of the Wind untied the rope around its mouth. The roar of the wind could be heard instantly, as tiles and bricks flew up all over the city and stones and dust hurtled through the air. Just look at it! It was truly marvelous wind, not at all similar to any ordinary breeze. You saw

> Snapped willows and cracked flowers;
> Fallen trees and toppled woods;
> Nine-layered halls with chipped and broken walls;
> A Five-Phoenix Tower of shaken pillars and beams;
> The red sun losing its brightness in Heav'n;
> The yellow sand taking wings on Earth;
> Alarmed warriors before the martial hall;
> Frightened ministers in the letters bower;
> Girls of three palaces with frowzy locks;
> Beauties of six chambers with tousled hair.
> Tassels dropped from gold caps of marquis and earls;
> The prime minister's black gauze did spread its wings.
> Attendants had words but they dared not speak;
> The Yellow Gate held papers which could not be sent.
> Gold fishes and jade belts stood not in rows;
> Ivory tablets and silk gowns had broken ranks.
> Colored rooms and turquoise screens were all damaged;
> Green windows and scarlet doors were all destroyed.
> Tiles of Golden Chimes Hall flew off with bricks;
> Carved doors of Brocade-Cloud Hall all fell apart.
> This violent wind was violent indeed!
> It blew till king and subjects, fathers and sons, could not meet,
> Till all streets and markets were emptied of men,
> And doors of ten thousand homes were tightly shut.

As this violent gust of wind arose, Pilgrim Sun further revealed his magic power. Giving his golden-hooped rod a twirl, he pointed it upwards a second time. You saw

---

3. One of the most famous of Buddhist texts, recited daily by Chinese, Japanese, Korean, and Tibetan monks; it is said to be the essence of all the perfection of wisdom sutras (works that set forth the wisdom by which a being intent on enlightenment becomes a buddha).

The Cloud-Pushing Boy,
The Fog-Spreading Lad—
The Cloud-Pushing Boy showed his godly power
And a murky mass dropped down from Heaven;
The Fog-Spreading Lad displayed his magic might
And dense, soaring mists covered the Earth.
The three markets all grew dim;
The six avenues all turned dark.
With wind clouds left the seas
And Kunlun,[4] trailing the rain.
Soon they filled Heav'n and Earth
And blackened this world of dust.
'Twas opaque like chaos of yore;
None could see Phoenix Tower's door.

As thick fog and dense clouds rolled in, Pilgrim Sun gave his golden-hooped rod another twirl and pointed it upwards a third time. You saw

The Squire of Thunder raging,
The Mother of Lightning irate—
The Squire of Thunder, raging,
Rode a fiery beast backward as he came from Heaven's pass;
The Mother of Lightning, irate,
Wielded gold snakes madly as she left the Dipper Hall.
Hu-la-la cracked the thunder,
Shattering the Iron Fork Mountain;
Xi-li-li flashed the scarlet sheets,
Flying out of the Eastern Ocean.
Loud rumbles of chariots came on and off;
Like fires and flames the grains and rice shot up.
Myriad things sprouted, their spirits revived.
Countless insects were from dormancy aroused.[5]
King and subjects both were terrified;
Traders and merchants were awed by the sound.

Ping-ping, Pang-pang, the thunder roared so ferociously that it seemed as if mountains were toppling and the earth was splitting apart. So terrified were the city's inhabitants that every house lighted incense, that every home burned paper money. "Old Deng," shouted Pilgrim. "Take care to look out for those greedy and corrupt officials, those churlish and disobedient sons. Strike down many of them for me to warn the public!" The peal of thunder grew louder than ever. Finally, Pilgrim pointed the iron rod once more and you saw

The dragons gave order,
And rain filled the world,
Strong as Heaven's river spilling o'er the dikes,
Quick as the clouds rushing through a channel.
It pattered on top of towers;
It splashed outside the windows.
The Silver Stream ran down from Heaven,

---

4. A mythical mountain paradise sacred to Dao-ists, and the home of the Queen Mother of the West.

5. The last four lines of the poem allude to the phenomenon of spring storm [translator's note].

And whitecaps surged through the streets.
It spurted like vases upturned;
It gushed forth like basins poured out.
With houses almost drowned in hamlets,
The water rose to rural bridges' height.
Truly mulberry fields became vast oceans,
And billows all too soon raced through the land.
Dragon gods came to lend a helping hand
By lifting up the Yangzi and throwing it down!

The torrential rain began in the morning and did not stop even after the noon hour. So great was the downpour that all the streets and gulleys of the Cart Slow Kingdom were completely flooded. The king therefore issued this decree: "The rain's enough! If we had any more, it might damage the crops and that would have made things worse." An official messenger below the Five-Phoenix Tower at once galloped through the rain to make this announcement: "Holy monk, we have enough rain." When Pilgrim heard this, he pointed the golden-hooped rod upwards once more and, instantly, the thunder stopped and the wind subsided, the rain ended and the clouds dispersed. The king was filled with delight, and not one of the various civil and military officials could refrain from marveling, saying, "Marvelous priest! This is truly that 'for the strong, there's someone stronger still!' Even when our National Preceptors were capable of making the rain, a fine drizzle would go on for virtually half a day before it stopped completely. How is it that the weather can turn fair the moment the priest wants it to be fair? Look, the sun comes out instantly and there is not a speck of cloud anywhere!"

The king gave the command for the carriage to be returned to the palace, for he wanted to certify the travel rescript and permit the Tang monk to pass through. Just as he was about to use his treasure seal, the three Daoists all went forward and stopped him, saying, "Your Majesty, this downpour of rain cannot be regarded as the monk's merit, for it still owes its origin to the strength of Daoism." The king said, "You just claimed that the Dragon Kings were not home and that was why it didn't rain. He walked up there, exercised his quiet work of fervent prayers, and rain came down at once. How could you strive with him for credit?"

The Tiger-Strength Immortal said, "I issued my summons, burned my charms, and struck my tablets several times after I ascended the altar. Which Dragon King would have the courage to absent himself? It had to be that someone else somewhere was also requesting their service, and that was the reason that the Dragon Kings along with the officers of the other four bureaus—of wind, cloud, thunder, and lightning—did not show up at first. Once they heard my summons, however, they were in a hurry to get here, and by that time it happened that I was leaving the altar already. The priest, of course, made use of the opportunity and it rained. But if you thought about the matter from the beginning, the dragons were those which I summoned here and the rain was that which we called for. How could you regard this, therefore, as their meritorious fruit?" When that dim-witted king heard these words, he became again all confused.

Pilgrim walked one step forward, and pressing his palms together, he said, "Your Majesty, this trivial magic of heterodoxy is hardly to be considered anything of consequence. Let's not worry about whether it's his merit or ours. Let me tell you instead that there are in midair right now the Dragon Kings of the Four Oceans; because I have not dismissed them, they dare not withdraw. If that National Preceptor could order the Dragon Kings to reveal themselves, I would concede that this was his merit." Very pleased, the king said, "We have been on the throne for twenty-three years, but we have never laid eyes on a living dragon. Both of you can exercise your magic power, regard-less whether you are a monk or a Daoist. If you could ask them to reveal themselves, it would be your merit; if you couldn't, it would be your fault."

Those Daoists, of course, had no such power or authority. Even if they were to give the order, the Dragon Kings would never dare show themselves on account of the presence of the Great Sage. So, the Daoists said, "We can't do this. Why don't you try?"

Lifting his face toward the air, the Great Sage cried out in a loud voice: "Aoguang, where are you? All of you brothers, show your true selves!" When those Dragon Kings heard this call, they at once revealed their original forms—four dragons dancing through clouds and mists toward the Hall of Golden Chimes. You see them

> Soaring and transforming,
> Encircling clouds and mists.
> Like white hooks the jade claws hang;
> Like bright mirrors the silver scales shine.
> Whiskers float like white silk, each strand's distinct;
> Horns rise ruggedly, each prong is clear.
> Those craggy foreheads;
> Those brilliant round eyes.
> They, hidden or seen, can't be fathomed;
> They, flying or soaring, can't be described.
> Pray for rain, and rain comes instantly;
> Ask for fair sky, and it's here at once.
> Only these are the true dragon forms, most potent and holy,
> Their good aura surrounds the court profusely.

The king lighted incense in the hall, and the various officials bowed down before the steps. "It was most kind of you to show us your precious forms," said the king. "Please go back, and we shall say a special mass another day to thank you." "All of you deities may now retire," said Pilgrim, "for the king has promised to thank you with a special mass on another day." The Dragon Kings returned to the oceans, while the other deities all went back to Heaven. Thus this is

> The true magic power, so boundless and vast;
> The side door's[6] cut down by nature most enlightened.

---

6. A metaphor for heterodoxy [translator's note].

JOURNEY TO THE NORTH
(*Beiyou ji*)

Journey to the North (*Beiyou ji*) is a little-known late Ming dynasty work of vernacular fiction that complements the other "journey" novels—*Journey to the West* (see previous selection), *Journey to the South*, and *Journey to the East*—with which it has often been published since early in the Qing dynasty (1644–1912). It tells the story of the Perfected Warrior (Zhenwu), who is also known as the Dark Warrior (Xuanwu), or Dark Emperor, and was one of four divine animals that were drawn into Daoism as powerful guardian deities. Although the Perfect Warrior was the object of widespread cultic worship throughout North China, he was primarily worshipped on Mount Wudang, a sacred mountain that became significant for Daoists; it enjoyed a steady stream of pilgrims and received lavish support from Ming dynasty emperors. Overall, the narrative of *Journey to the North* focuses not on travels (as did *Journey to the West*) but on powerful revelations that come from the north—and particularly from Mount Wudang—and their connection to a deity.

The chapter printed below, "The Dark Emperor Descends Once More into the Mortal World to Save the People from Misery," describes the protective powers of the Dark Emperor. He descends with his powerful sword in hand, or sends one of his manifestations, to help those in distress, especially those crossing rivers or lakes. As cults to the Dark Emperor spread, shrines with statues of him exhibiting his distinctive iconography—long, free-flowing hair; a sword; and a snake and turtle below his feet—were erected and became centers of devotion. This chapter also displays the close relationship between the Daoist establishments on Mount Wudang and the imperial house, as the emperor himself makes a pilgrimage to the sacred mountain to offer incense and sponsor the building of new temples.

At its close, the chapter notes that those who worship the Dark Emperor also refer to him as the Buddha of Boundless Longevity, suggesting some intriguing connections between the mythology of the Dark Emperor and that of Buddhist protector deities. Most editions of *Journey to the North* include an appendix calling on those who have received a boon or protection from the Perfect Warrior to make at least ten copies of the text and distribute them as widely as possible—an echo of the Buddhist belief that the production and transmission of texts were meritorious acts.

PRONOUNCING GLOSSARY

Beiyou ji: *bay-yo chee*   Zhang: *chawng*
Wudang Shan: *woo-dawng shawn*

The Dark Emperor Descends Once More into the Mortal World to Save the People from Misery

Taking up our story anew, the many demons which prowled the Yangzi River, such as the Water Snail Demon, the Horse Demon, the Brocade Demon, the Maonian Demon, etc., did not dare make trouble so long as the Venerable Teacher[1] was in the world. When they heard that he had returned

---

TRANSLATED BY Gary Seaman.

1. Another title of the Dark Emperor.

to heaven, they began to make waves and raise up billows in the river, which caused great harm to travelers and merchants. The clamor and conflict reached up to the heavens. The Venerable Teacher observed this from the Gate of Precious Virtue, and the sight made him very angry.

"I will exterminate them root and branch," he said. "I have been born into the world four times to sweep away these Dark Forces. I did not think that there were so many ghosts hidden in the waters of the Yangzi River. Now that they see I have returned to heaven, they are raising hell in the world below. There is an old saying: 'If you don't pluck out weeds by the root, they will push up sprouts anew!'"

The Dark Emperor made some magic and called forth his Eighty-two Manifestations. He chose one of these forms to remain with his marshals to guard the Gate of Precious Virtue. His True Manifestation left the Upper World and descended to Wudang Shan[2] to save the people. When he came to the banks of the Yangzi, he performed some magic and called forth the True Fire of the Three Colors[3] to dry up the river. When the ghosts came boiling up onto the bank, they saw the Venerable Teacher standing there making magic with his Seven Star Sword, and they all ran away when they saw him. The Dark Emperor pursued them and killed all the ghosts and demons except two. Only the Cauldron Demon and the Bamboo Hawser Demon ran away; they could not be captured, nor could their hiding place be found.

The Dark Emperor was very distressed about this, but could only return with his Celestial Officials to defend the passes into heaven. The Dark Emperor commanded one of his manifestations to descend once again into the mortal world at Wudang Shan to keep guard over the two demons and save the people. If officials met with difficulties while crossing the river, the Venerable Teacher would let down his hair and take up his sword and manifest himself in mid-air to save them. The Dragon Kings of the Five Lakes and Four Seas came to wait upon the Venerable Teacher and his court, and he frequently saved officials and their entourages, as well as travelers and merchants. These people molded a statue of the god at the foot of Wudang Shan and built a temple there to worship him.

Because of dreams the common people had about him, they also made statues of the Thirty-six Celestial Generals. He was represented as holding in his hand the Demon-destroying Seven Star Sword. Under his feet he trampled the Stinking Snake and the Bagua Turtle. When the rich and noble or the common people would cross rivers by boat, the Venerable Teacher would often manifest himself to save and protect every single one of them. Along the banks of the rivers, all who crossed them entered his temples to offer incense. The offerings continued to flow to him down to the third year of the Yongle period of our present dynasty.[4] In that year, the Yellow-haired Tatars rebelled. The emperor was greatly upset and ordered out his soldiers to engage the enemy, but they met with a serious defeat and had to retreat. Just as the imperial army was in desperate straits, a figure

---

2. That is, Mount Wudang in Hubei Province; it was sacred to Daoists.
3. Blue-green, yellow, and white, associated respectively with heaven, earth, and water/stars/humans.

4. That is, the Ming dynasty (1368–1644); the Yongle emperor (born Zhu Di), the dynasty's third, ruled from 1402 to 1424. Clashes with Mongol nomads (Tatars) continued through much of his reign.

appeared to them in mid-air, grasping a Treasure Sword. Accompanying him were Thirty-six Celestial Generals. They attacked the enemy with wind and lightning, raining down Yellow Lions and like beasts from right overhead and killing the Tatar leaders. The Yongle Emperor did not know what god had helped him win the victory, but when he returned to court, he sent envoys to the Palace of Supreme Purity to invite the Celestial Master Zhang[5] to come and visit at court.

"I fought a battle with the Tatars," said the emperor, "and met with defeat. Just when I was in greatest danger, I saw the manifestation of a god in mid-air. His long hair was disheveled and he carried a sword. His face was pale and he had a long beard. He had Thirty-six Celestial Generals at his side. The Turtle and the Snake accompanied him as he attacked from the North. He saved my life and killed Tatars without number. Now that I have returned to court, I would like to reward the god for saving my life. I do not know, however, what place the god comes from. It is because of this that I have summoned you to this audience. Do you know what god this was?"

"If the god had free-flowing locks and was accompanied by the Turtle and the Snake," said the Celestial Master Zhang, "then it can be none other than the Emperor of the Dark Heavens, the True Warrior General of the North, who has saved you."

"If you know that it is the Emperor of the Dark Heavens," said the emperor excitedly, "then you must know where he is presently being worshiped."

"This god has achieved perfection through his own efforts," replied the Celestial Master Zhang, "and is devoted to saving the people. If they meet with misfortune, then he saves them from misfortune. If they get into difficulties, then it is he who saves them from difficulties. If they meet with disaster while traveling by boat, then he is able to save them all. Travelers and merchants have voluntarily erected a temple to him at the foot of Wudang Shan."

"If even the common people know how to repay the benevolence of the god," said the emperor, "then how may I, the recipient of the benevolence of this god on behalf of all living things under heaven, forget to honor him? You have just reported that the original temple to the god is on Wudang Shan. I will personally go there on a pilgrimage in order to offer incense and to view the image of the deity. I will build a temple in order to express my gratitude."

The emperor issued orders to this effect, and together with his civil and military officials and the Celestial Master, he traveled to the Yangzi River Wudang Shan. The emperor and his entourage entered the temple and offered incense. He saw that the visage of the image of the Venerable Teacher was the same as his own, which pleased him very much. When he had made his offerings of incense, he returned to court, where he gave a great banquet of state for his civil and military ministers. There he issued an edict saying that Commander-in-Chief Jin should supervise, while the Marquis of Longping should recruit thirty thousand workers and go to

---

5. Zhang Daoling (34–156 C.E.), the first Celestial Master.

Wudang Shan. There he should build a Golden Hall. He should also make an image of the Venerable Teacher out of gold and construct thirty-six halls and seventy-two palaces.

Lu Ban[6] descended to help with the work, and in one year all of the palaces, halls, and images of the deities were completed. The Marquis of Longping, Commander of the Imperial Bodyguard, returned to court and reported this to the emperor, who promoted the marquis three ranks. The emperor selected eighteen Daoists and appointed them Daoist Officials. He also directed the Celestial Master to hold seven days and seven nights of Rites of Cosmic Renewal.[7] He himself attended the rites and offered incense to the gods at them. On this occasion, the Marquis of Longping stepped forward from the ranks of the officials and petitioned the throne: "Your Majesty has now completed the building of this temple and the making of the images of the gods. There are none who do not feel gratitude for what Your Majesty has done. I only fear that in days to come, although pilgrims may be many, they may not have the money or resources to worship the god properly. The Stellar Officials may also lack for income. There are no long-term provisions for them. I therefore beg my lord to show his true benevolence and take the income from some place and bestow it on the temple in order that offerings may continue here for ten thousand years."

The emperor was very glad to hear this request, and he gave a decree to fulfill it. He gave incense and lamps to the value of five hundred *qing*[8] of land and also fields in the amount of one hundred *qing*. If there was damage to the temple, it must all be repaired, so that the offerings could continue unabated for ten thousand times ten thousand years. Just as the emperor was entertaining his ministers at Wudang Shan in a great banquet, it was suddenly announced that a great bell had floated up out of the river. Triumphantly it was brought forward, and the emperor commanded that his soldiers should set it up on Wudang Shan. It turned out to be a Bronze Bell Cast from the Seven Treasures.[9] The emperor was greatly pleased as soon as he saw it, and he left Wudang Shan to return to court with his retinue of civil and military officials.

Indeed, the spirit of the Venerable Teacher on Wudang Shan has manifested his spiritual powers. He saves those who meet with difficulties from their difficulties. He saves those who meet with disasters from those disasters. He makes the wind gentle upon the four seas and causes the waves to ebb. In those homes where the god is worshiped, the sons are filial and the grandsons obedient. Parents who have no offspring and who pray to him will all be provided for. His renown has reached into both the capital cities and the thirteen provinces. Those who undertake pilgrimages to his temple to ask for his aid and mercy are without number. Those whose hearts are burdened with cares will see in midair a form gracefully floating towards them to succor them. This form will be wearing red satin draped on his body, and will be called Good Luck. All under heaven, whether man, woman,

---

6. Lu Ban, the patron deity of carpenters and woodworkers.
7. *Jiao* rituals; they are performed by Daoist priests to renew a community's relationship with its tutelary deities.
8. A unit of land area, equal to about 16 acres.

9. Identified both with physical aspects of human beings (essence, blood, *qi* or vital energy, marrow, brain, kidneys, and heart) and with their corresponding precious substances (quicksilver, gold, jade, quartz, agate, rubies, and carnelion).

or child, come to him in their myriads, holding incense and bowing to him, calling upon him as the Buddha of Boundless Longevity.[1] For ten thousand requests, ten thousand answers come. Thus it has continued up to the present day, some two hundred years from that time. Incense has been kept burning there, now as then, and the perpetual offerings of the imperial court have kept all under heaven at peace.

1. Amitayus, the name given to Amitabha—the buddha who presides over the pure land of Suhkavati and who was a particularly important fig- ure in East Asian Buddhism—as bestower of longevity.

A RECORD OF THE LAND OF THE BLESSED
(Sanshan fudi zhi)

"A Record of the Land of the Blessed" (Sanshan fudi zhi) tells the story of a humble farmer named Yuan Zishi who lends money to a "gentleman" named Miao. When Zishi falls on hard times, he seeks repayment from Miao, who has become a powerful regional office holder, but he is rebuffed. After months of being dismissed and at his wit's end, Zishi sets off to kill Miao, but changes his mind when he considers how Miao's family will suffer—a change of heart visible to a pious observer, Xianyuan, who sees that he is followed by evil demons when on his way to commit murder but accompanied by peaceful, dignified spirits on his return.

Though Xianyuan has explained that evil acts necessarily will be punished, the despairing Zishi attempts to commit suicide but instead finds himself in the "Land of the Blessed," an important category of Daoist sacred space. There a Daoist hermit gives him some magic fruit, enabling him to recall his past and see into his future, and teaches him valuable lessons about the effects of past deeds on this present life. Zishi also learns of the imminent collapse of the dynasty, and when he emerges from the Land of the Blessed he finds that two weeks have passed. Because he follows the Daoist's advice, he and his family are at a safe distance from the fighting that does indeed come—and he learns that ungrateful Miao has been killed in the political turmoil, just as the Daoist had predicted.

PRONOUNCING GLOSSARY

Miao: *mee-ao*
Sanshan fudi zhi: *sawn-shawn foo-dee chih*
Xianyuan: *she-an-you-an*
Yuan Zishi: *yuen tzu-shih*

Yuan Zishi was a native of Shandong. He was naturally slow-witted and a stranger to learning. The family was fairly well to do, deriving its income from its farm lands. In the same district was a gentleman named Miao who had been appointed to an office in Fujian. He lacked the money for traveling expenses and borrowed 200 ounces of silver from Zishi. Since the two

TRANSLATED BY Cyril Birch.

families lived in the same village and were on good terms, Zishi did not ask for a promissory note, but simply let him have the sum he requested. Toward the end of the Zhizheng period[1] (1367) there was civil war in Shandong and Zishi lost all his property to the rebels. At that time Chen Yuding was Governor of Fujian, which remained undisturbed by the war. So Zishi took his family and went there by boat, intending to apply to Miao for help. On his arrival he found that Miao was indeed in Chen Yuding's service, holding an important administrative position, exercising great power, and living in style. Zishi was delighted. However, after the hardships he had suffered and the long journey, his clothes were in tatters and his body emaciated, so that he did not venture to present himself for an interview directly. He rented a room in the city where he lodged his family, put his clothes in order, and chose a lucky day for his visit. He arrived just as Miao was leaving his gate, and bowed low before his carriage. At first Miao did not seem to recognize him, but when Zishi told him his name and where he had come from Miao made surprised apologies and invited him into his house, where he treated him as an honored guest. After some time tea was served and Zishi left. He returned on the morrow, when the entertainment was much more perfunctory. Miao was rather distant and inattentive, nor did he say anything about the money he owed.

Zishi went back to his bleak room, where his wife scolded him angrily, "Here you have come a thousand miles to get help from this man and what do you do? You sell out for three cups of wine and don't say a word. What are we to do now?" Zishi had no choice but to go again the next day.

Before he could open his mouth, Miao interposed, "I shall never forget the money you loaned me long ago. It's just that in this out of the way post my income is very small. But I would never think of being ungrateful to an old friend from afar. If you will give me back my note, I will pay you the full sum right now."

Zishi was horrified. "We are fellow townsmen and have been friends since childhood. When you said you needed the money I gave it to you; there never was any note. How can you talk like this?"

Miao was unperturbed. "Surely there was a note, but I suppose you must have lost it in the civil war. I don't know whether you have it or not, but I will give you more time to try to locate it."

Zishi went out mumbling assent and marveling at the deceit and ingratitude of the man. He was nonplussed and could see no way out of the impasse. Half a month later he paid Miao another visit and was received politely enough, but not a cent did he get. In this way he was put off for half a year.

In the market there was a little shop which Zishi always passed on his way to Miao's residence, anywhere he was accustomed to stop and rest. The proprietor, Xianyuan, a pious man, became quite well acquainted with him during his frequent trips. As the winter passed and it was nearly New Year's time, Zishi's plight became desperate, and weeping and bowing outside Miao's house he cried, "The New Year is about to begin, and my wife and children are starving. I have not a cent in my purse and no rice in my stores. I don't dare ask for the money I loaned you, but I do beg for a little help now

---

1. The second reign period (1341–68) of Shundi (r. 1333–68), the last emperor of the Yuan dynasty (1260–1368). Widespread rebellion during this period hastened the dynasty's collapse.

when my need is desperate, as a kindness to an old friend. On my knees I ask you, have pity, have compassion." And he crawled forward on his knees.

Miao helped him to his feet. Counting the days on his fingers he said, "Ten days from now is New Year's Eve. You wait at home and I will send you two hundred pounds of rice and two ingots of silver from my salary for your New Year's expenses. I hope you will not take offense that it is not more." And he repeatedly instructed him not to go out, but to wait for it at home. Zishi thanked him and went home to console his wife with Miao's promise.

When the appointed day came the whole household watched expectantly. Zishi sat straight in his chair and had his youngest son keep watch at the gate. In a minute he came running in, "A man is coming with a load of rice!" They all went out to wait for him, but he went right past their house without turning his head. Zishi thought the messenger did not know the house and ran after him to ask, but the man said, "His honor Zhang is sending this rice to a guest at the inn." Zishi returned in silence. In a little while his son came in to say that a man was coming with the money. They rushed out again, and again the man went past their house. Zishi also went after him and was told that this was a gift for a retainer of Prefect Li's. Ashamed and disappointed, he kept asking the messengers that passed until evening, but there was never a sign from Miao. Next day was New Year's, and he had neither food nor livelihood. His wife and children looked at him and wept. Unable to contain his rage, Zishi concealed a knife and sat waiting for the dawn. At cockcrow he went directly to Miao's gate, waiting for him to come out so that he might stab him.

Now just at that time, before it was light and while no one was abroad, old Xianyuan was sitting inside his shop door reading a sutra[2] by candle-light. He saw Zishi walk past, followed by an extraordinary mob of dozens of outlandish demons, holding knives and gouges. Their heads were split and their skeletons exposed, altogether a most evil-looking crew. In the time it takes to eat a meal, he saw Zishi coming back, and now he was followed by a hundred or more men wearing golden caps and jade ornaments, carrying banners and flags. Their appearance was dignified and composed, and the whole gave the impression of peace and harmony. Xianyuan was unable to understand what had happened and thought Zishi must have died. When he had finished reciting the sutra he went at once to his house to find out, and there was Zishi, whole and unharmed. When they had sat down Xianyuan asked, "Where were you going this morning in such a hurry and why did you return so slowly?"

Zishi did not venture to lie, but told about Miao's outrageous behavior. "I was at my wits' end, and this morning I put a dagger in my pocket and was on my way to kill him. When I got to his gate it suddenly occurred to me: although he has certainly done me an injury, of what are his wife and children guilty? What's more, his old mother is still alive. If I kill him, what will become of his family? Better that another should wrong me than that I should wrong another. So I gave up my plan and came home."

When Xianyuan heard this, he bowed to congratulate him. "You will have your reward; the spirits know what you did." Zishi asked how he knew and the old man said, "When your heart was set on evil, baleful demons

2. A discourse of the Buddha or one spoken with his sanction, usually presented in the form of a dialogue (literally, "discourse"; Sanskrit).

assembled, and when you decided on the good, beneficent spirits surrounded you. It is as certain as shadow follows form and echo sound; verily, neither in the privacy of one's room nor in the urgency of the act can evil go unpunished or good unrequited." He went on to tell what he had seen. He tried to console him and gave him enough money and rice to meet his immediate needs. But Zishi remained depressed and unhappy. That night he threw himself into the well at the foot of Sanshen Mountain.[3]

The water suddenly parted. On both sides were smooth stone walls between which led a narrow path just wide enough for him to pass. Zishi groped his way for several hundred paces, when the wall stopped and the path came to an end at a narrow opening. Once through that he found himself in another world, with its own sky and earth, sun and moon. Before him was a great palace with a sign that read "Land of the Blessed." Staring about him Zishi entered. The large hall was deserted, nothing stirred in the palace. He hesitated, looking in all directions, but no one was to be seen anywhere. Then he heard the far-off sound of a bell. Overcome with hunger and fatigue he was unable to go farther, and lay down beside a stone dais. Suddenly a Daoist priest appeared, wearing a green-cloud robe with moon-jade ornaments, and called to him to rise and asked, "Does the Academician know the taste of travel?" Zishi bowed and replied, "I have had altogether too much of the taste of travel, but how could you make such a mistake as to call me Academician?"

The Daoist said, "Don't you remember drafting the decree to the Tibetans in the Palace of Abundance?"

"I am an uneducated man from Shandong, a commoner, forty years old and illiterate. I have never in my life been in the capital; how could I have drafted any decree?"

"You have been so concerned about making a living that you have had no time to remember your past." And the priest took several dates and pears from his sleeve and gave them to him to eat, saying, "These are magic fruits. When you have eaten them you will know the past and the future."

As soon as Zishi had eaten them his eyes were opened and he could remember when he was a Hanlin official[4] and had drafted the decree to the Tibetans in the Palace of Abundance in the capital as though it were yesterday. He asked the priest, "What crime did I commit in a past life that I should be punished in this way?"

"It was no crime, but when you were an official you so prided yourself on your literary skill that you were unwilling to give a place to younger men. As a consequence in this life you were born to be stupid and illiterate. Because you were too proud of your rank and would not give lodging to a homeless wanderer, in this life you have been forced to drift about without any support."

Zishi mentioned a high minister of the time and asked, "A prime minister who is insatiably avaricious and overtly accepts bribes—what will be his recompense in the other world?"

3. A large mountain in modern-day Sichuan Province.
4. A graduate of the Hanlin Academy, an elite scholarly institution. During the Ming dynasty, only the best candidates who achieved the highest level of the examination system were admitted, and these academicians were the emperor's advisers and secretaries.

"In the underworld the king of the insatiable demons has ten furnaces to melt down his ill-gotten wealth. Today his good fortune is at its peak, but he will suffer the tortures of hell."

Zishi asked further, "There is a certain governor who does not control his soldiers but lets them kill the people; what will be his recompense?"

"The king of the murderous demons has three hundred hellish soldiers with copper heads and iron foreheads who aid him in his atrocities. Today his life span, too, is running out, and he will suffer the slicing torture."

"There is a judge who sentences unjustly, a prefect who levies taxes and corvée inequitably, an inspector who never makes a report, a military advisor who never offers a plan—what will be their recompense?"

"These will all be fettered and bound to await punishment until their flesh rots and their bones decay—they are not worth mentioning."

Then Zishi recounted the story of Miao's ingratitude. The priest said, "He is General Wang's treasurer, and is in no position to make free with his property." He went on to say, "Within three years there will be a revolution and a great disaster, much to be feared. You should choose a place to live, otherwise you will suffer like a fish in a pool when the water runs out." Zishi asked where he could go to avoid the fighting. "Fujing would do, but Funing is better." Then he said, "You have been here for a long time and your family is worried; you should go home now."

Zishi protested that he did not know the way, and the priest showed him a path to follow. Zishi bowed and left, and after he had gone about a mile he came out of a cave[5] in the mountain. When he got home he found he had been gone half a month. In all haste he moved his family to Funing, where he lived as a farmer. One day when he was wielding his hoe he struck something metallic, and on digging found four ingots of silver. After that his family was in more comfortable circumstances.

Later Zhang usurped the throne and Prime Minister Da was taken prisoner. As the revolting armies approached the city Governor Chen Yuding was captured, and few of his subordinates could preserve their heads. Miao was killed by General Wang, who confiscated all his property. When reckoned up, this occurred just three years after the priest had made his prediction.

---

5. In Daoism, caves constitute an important category of sacred space; they can be entrances to magical places that contain special objects and offer the possibility of meeting with transcendents, or Daoists who have achieved extraordinary powers and a higher form of existence.

COMMENTARIES ON THE *LAOZI* AND *ZHUANGZI*

HANSHAN DEQING

Hanshan Deqing (1546–1623), a Buddhist monk, was a leading reformer, a philosopher, and a prolific commentator on Buddhist texts. He is perhaps best known for his autobiography, which details his life up to its last year. Hanshan also wrote commentaries on Daoist and Confucian texts. He was rather critical of Confucian teachings, but felt that there were strong affinities between Buddhism and Daoism.

He was drawn to the spontaneity of Daoism and its suggestion that humans need to attune themselves to the natural functioning of the world; conversely, he disliked the Confucian tendency to specify virtues and impose rules that constrain humans in unnatural ways. Ultimately, Hanshan thought that all philosophical teachings are the same in that they derive from and lead to the truth of the Mind—his preferred term for ultimate reality. The traditions differ from one another in the extent to which they penetrate to the truth.

These excerpts from Hanshan's commentaries on *The Scripture of the Way and Its Virtue* (*Laozi*; see above) and *Book of Master Zhuang* (*Zhuangzi*; see above) provide an intriguing glimpse into how a Ming dynasty Buddhist monk felt about certain aspects of those Daoist classics. Hanshan understood these two scriptures as emphasizing how humans should transcend their phenomenal (bodily) existence in this world. He explains their teachings by referring to Buddhist teachings on the nature of emptiness—namely, the idea that the true nature of reality is empty of the characteristics that we ascribe to it—which equates the Dao with Buddhist liberation. Since Laozi taught humans how to try and transcend this world, he refers to him as a bodhisattva, or one who has vowed to achieve buddhahood for the welfare of all beings. In the summary that concludes the excerpts, Hanshan discusses both Daoism and Confucianism in relation to Buddhism: not surprisingly, he ranks the teachings of the Buddha most highly, because only they enable the adept to transcend consciousness.

PRONOUNCING GLOSSARY

Bodhisattva: *bow-dee-saw-tvah*
Hanshan Deqing: *hawn-shawn duh-ching*
Laozi: *lao-tzu*

Pratyekabuddha: *pra-tyey-kah-boo-dhaws*
samadhi: *saw-mah-dee*
Shravakas: *shraw-vah-kahs*
xuan: *hsuan*
Zhuangzi: *chuang-tzu*

[Hanshan's View of Daoism]

Thus, according to Laozi's teachings, the greatest calamity (of man) is in having a body, so he teaches the way of extinguishing the body to attain the realm of non-being. Since the greatest burden to the human form is having knowledge, he teaches the way of abandoning knowledge to enter the realm of emptiness. These teachings are similar to those of Shravakas and Pratyekabuddhas.[1] Laozi is like a Pratyekabuddha because, having lived in the time before Buddhism was taught, he realized the truth of non-being by contemplating the changing nature of the world. Since he regards emptiness, non-being, and spontaneity as the final doctrines, his philosophy is heterodox. But he is also like a Bodhisattva[2] because his heart was full of compassion for the salvation of the world, and because he had attained the realm in which man and heaven mutually penetrate each other and in which being and non-being mutually reflect each other. From the viewpoint of expediency, he was really (a Bodhisattva) appearing in the form of Brahma[3] in

TRANSLATED BY Sung-peng Hsu.

1. Followers of the Buddha (literally, "solitary enlightened ones"; Sanskrit) who preferred not to live among the community, but who practiced in solitude, often in silence. As the tradition developed, the pratyekabuddha became doctrinally defined in relation to the shravaka (Sanskrit, "listener"), a disciple of the Buddha who remained in his presence.
2. A being intent on enlightenment (*bodhi*); one who has vowed to achieve buddhahood for the welfare of all beings (literally, "one whose goal is awakening"; Sanskrit).
3. The god who persuaded the Buddha to teach.

order to teach the world. From the viewpoint of reality, he was the one who had attained the *samadhi*[4] of emptiness by means of pure living according to the vehicles of men and heaven.

[On Chapter 1 of the Laozi]

The Dao that is spoken of (by Laozi) is the Dao of true eternity. Thus, the *dao*[5] that can be talked about is still that of language. This means that the Dao of true eternity is originally without character and without name. It cannot be talked about. That which can be talked about is not the Dao of true eternity, thus not the eternal Dao. Though the Dao is originally without a name, it is now artificially called dao. It is thus known that all that can be named is only a *jiaming* (false or temporal name) and not an eternal name.

Though the essence of Dao that is without character and name is extremely empty, heaven and earth come out from it through transformation. It is therefore the beginning of heaven and earth. This means that the characterless and nameless essence of Dao completely becomes heaven and earth which have characters and names. The ten thousand things are completely produced (or born) from heaven and earth through the creative transformation of the *yin* and *yang*.[6] Thus, it is said that one produces two, two produce three, and three produce the ten thousand things.[7] It is therefore the mother of the ten thousand things.

[Hanshan interprets Laozi as saying in the fifth and sixth lines:]

> I always rest my mind on non-being in my daily life so that I can contemplate the subtlety of the Dao.
> I always rest my mind on being in my daily life so that I can contemplate the outer fringe of the Dao.

This means that the complete essence of Dao that is empty and non-being becomes the ten thousand things that have names. Therefore, the whole essence of Dao is present in every single thing. . . . This is why Zhuangzi[8] says that the Dao is found in weeds, excrement, and urine. Only after one contemplates so deeply can one see the subtlety of the Dao.

For fear that the student would regard the contemplation of being and that of non-being as two different things, Laozi explains that the two are the same. This means that when I contemplate non-being, I am not simply contemplating non-being but also the subtle process of transformation and production that takes place in the essence of emptiness and non-being. When I contemplate being, I am not simply contemplating being but also the subtle Dao of emptiness and non-being that is present in the ten thousand phenomena. In this way, being and non-being are contemplated simultaneously and seen as of one essence. Thus, it is said, "These two are the same."

---

4. A state of deep meditation (Sanskrit, "concentration").
5. The way. For chapter 1 of the *Laozi*, see above.
6. The complementary forces that unite to form the Dao: yin, a term that originally referred to the shady side of a valley, by extension came to be associated with the dark, earth, dampness, and passivity—the female principle; yang, a term

that originally referred to the sunny side of a valley, by extension came to be associated with the light, heaven, dryness, and activity—the male principle.
7. That is, everything that exists.
8. See *The Book of Master Zhuang* (*Zhuangzi*), above.

For fear that the student cannot understand why there is a difference between being and non-being if they are the same, Laozi explains that they have different names after one is produced from the other. This means that the essence of Dao that is empty and non-being gives birth to heaven and earth and the ten thousand things that have forms. Since being cannot give birth to being, it must be the case that non-being gives birth to being. Since non-being cannot be non-being by itself, it is because of being that non-being is revealed. This is what is meant by "being and non-being produce each other."[9] Therefore, the two names are not the same. Thus, it is said, "After one is produced by the other, they have different names."

Moreover, for fear that the student cannot understand the reason for the designation of subtle Dao if there is a distinction between being and non-being as if they were not of one essence, Laozi explains that the identity of being and non-being is called *xuan* (literally "darkness"), in which heaven, earth, and the ten thousand things are of one essence. Is it not very subtle when one comes to this depth in contemplation?

But for fear that the student at this stage cannot purify the spectacle of *xuan*, Laozi teaches the purification method of *xuanzhi you xuan* (literally "to *xuan* and further to *xuan*"). This means that in spite of the identity of being and non-being, the subtlety is not really subtle if the mind and its traces are not altogether forgotten. In the essence of the great Dao, there is neither the difference of being and non-being nor any trace of *xuan* and subtlety. Thus, it is said, "To *xuan* and further to *xuan*." At this stage of cultivation, one becomes forgetful of all thoughts and things. Wherever one goes, one feels nothing but subtlety. Thus, it is said, "This is the door of all subtleties."[1] This is the ultimate of cultivating the Dao.

Hanshan's interpretation of the last few lines may be paraphrased as follows:[2]

> The identity of being and non-being is called *xuan* (that which is deep and profound).
> To contemplate more deeply and profoundly on the identity of being and non-being so that even the contemplating mind is gone,
> This is the door of all subtleties.

[On the Zhuangzi]

"Free and easy"[3] means infinite self-contentment. It is similar to what in Buddhist scriptures is called the unlimited liberation. According to the Buddha, liberation is the state in which all *kleshas*[4] are extinguished. Zhuangzi explains liberation as the transcendence of the confines of the bodily form, as the stopping of intellectual games, and as the state in which one is not burdened by the achievement and fame of man's life. This is so because the realm of emptiness, non-being, and spontaneity is regarded as the home of the great Dao and the realm of free and easy wandering. . . .

9. Quoted from chapter 2 of the *Laozi*.
1. The final line of chapter 1.
2. Translator's comment.
3. The first chapter of the *Zhuangzi* is titled "Free and Easy Wandering."
4. Negative emotions (literally, "afflictions"; Sanskrit): the motivation for negative actions (karma), and therefore the cause of the cause of suffering.

Those who do not attain the realm of free and easy wandering owe their failure to the fetter of self-attachment.

[On Confucianism and Daoism]

The ancient worthies have said, "Confucianism helps man by means of precepts because it is strict in controlling the self. Daoism helps man with *ding* (tranquility, *samadhi*) because it is good at helping people forget the self." The teachings of Confucius[5] and Laozi are complementary to the Buddha's teachings in function. Are they of no use? From the viewpoint of reality, those who cling to Confucius' teachings live according to causes and conditions. Those who cling to Laozi's teachings fall into the realm of spontaneity. Basically, these teachings have not transcended the state of consciousness, because they cannot penetrate the One Mind to the utmost. The Buddha's teachings, however, transcend the realm of mental consciousness.

5. The teacher, philosopher, and political theorist (551–479 B.C.E.).

A TASTE OF IMMORTALITY

"A Taste of Immortality" is a short tale extracted from a Ming dynasty collection first published in 1632, *The Second Collection of Striking the Table in Amazement at the Wonders* (*Er'ke po'an jingji*). Behind the humorous account of a pious old man who meets a strange Daoist and misses his opportunity to become an immortal is a serious criticism of those intent on producing alchemical pills of immortality. In return for the old man's generous hospitality, a Daoist priest invites him to a meal at the Daoist's mountain retreat. Left alone while the priest goes off to invite a few more friends, the old man is surprised to find no stove or cooking implements and horrified to discover the form of a small dog in one jar and a tiny human baby in another. Though he is assured that they are vegetables, he abstains while the Daoist and his friends consume them with delight; after that meal has ended, the old man accepts some "homemade cake," which is slightly bitter but satisfies his hunger and leaves him feeling vigorous. A couple of days later, the priest returns to the old man's house and explains that the "dog" and "baby" were in fact made from magic roots that would have conferred immortality on him. His inability to see the objects clearly for what they were demonstrated that he was not destined to be an immortal; however, his consumption of the "cake" (actually a special type of fungus) guaranteed him a long life free of illness.

After coming to the end of the old man's story—he dies at an age over one hundred, without having suffered a day of sickness—the narrator emphasizes its moral: immortality comes only to those destined to receive it. Death is the more likely fate of those who are not worthy of joining the true immortals but nevertheless compound and consume elixirs in the hope of everlasting life (usually for all the wrong reasons).

PRONOUNCING GLOSSARY

Jin Chang'an: *gin chawng-awn*   Zhu Wengong: *chu when-kung*

Immortality has always been shaped by one's fate;
Struggling is vain if you're not marked for longevity.
But how many foolish dreamers in this mortal world
Stir their crucibles daily for the elixir of life?

Our story tells how once there lived an old man who was extremely devoted to Daoism. Whenever he saw a Daoist priest pass by, he would treat him with the utmost respect and courtesy.

One day, a priest with his hair bound up in a double knot came to pay him a visit. His clothing was tattered, but the expression on his face was healthy and pleasant. Surmising that this priest was someone extraordinary, the old man welcomed him into his home with considerable cordiality. The priest ate and drank great quantities, which the old man furnished him with unflagging diligence. Afterward the priest came and went several times, while the old man received each visit in exactly the same manner.

One day the priest said to him, "I've enjoyed your hospitality for some time now, and I'm very grateful that you haven't begrudged me anything. Would you please come to my place, so that I may serve you a few country dishes as an expression of my appreciation?"

"I've never asked where you live," said the old man. "May I now ask how far it is, and can an old fellow like me make it there?"

"My retreat is hidden in the mountains, but it's not too far from here. If you'll come along with me, we'll soon be there."

"In that case, I would certainly like to go."

With the priest leading and the old man behind, they left the busy streets of the village and walked carefully across the fields and rustic trails until they turned into a mountain path. The region was secluded and abounded with thick, luxuriant growth. After they had traveled over a few low mountain ridges, several thatched huts came into view within a small valley among the hills.

"That's my mountain hideaway," said the priest, pointing.

In a few more steps they were in front of his shack. He opened the door and helped the old man inside. The latter looked around and saw that:

It wasn't a mansion with a splendid red gate,
But it smelled of magic blossoms from fairyland.

After inviting him to sit down in the front room, the priest went alone to the back rooms for a time.

"The meal is ready," said the priest as he returned. "Please rest here for a few moments while I invite a few companions to join us in pleasant conversation."

The old man was delighted to learn that there were other priests close by and replied happily, "Please do as you wish, and I'll wait here by myself."

The priest went directly out while the old man sat there absent-mindedly. When after a long delay his host had still not returned, he became somewhat impatient and rose to look around. By now he was rather hungry and wanted to find something to eat. Anticipating that there would be some-

TRANSLATED BY Dell R. Hales. All bracketed additions are the translator's.

thing edible in the pantry, he went through a side door and reached the kitchen. He was not prepared to see that there was no cookstove there at all, but only a few date-wood spoons and some ladles made of coconut shells. There were also two earthenware water jars covered with bamboo lids.

When the old man walked over and looked, he was surprised to find that one jar actually contained a small white dog, with its hair plucked clean, immersed in water. "No wonder," thought the old man, "that this priest doesn't abstain from regular meats and wine; he also eats dog meat." When he lifted the other lid to look, he was even more startled to find a tiny dead baby, complete with hands and feet, submerged in water. The old man became quite suspicious now.

"This priest couldn't be a good fellow. He takes meat and wine, and lives out here in this mountain wilderness with no life in his hut, only these two things. I might forget the dog, but certainly not the dead baby. Is he some sort of murderer who sets people's houses on fire? I've been making a mistake in being friendly with him. Even to stay here is dangerous."

He wanted to leave, but he had forgotten the way home and would have to wait there patiently. At this moment of uncertainty the priest arrived with several other Daoist priests, all of whom had white hair and shaggy eyebrows. They entered the hut, greeted the guest courteously, and sat down. The old man felt strongly apprehensive and waited to see what would happen.

"I'd like all of you to know," he heard the priest say, "that this gentleman has been my benefactor, but I've been unable to repay his kind hospitality until now. To express my appreciation, I've given all of you a special invitation to come enjoy with us two delectable dishes that I've been fortunate enough to obtain today."

As the priest finished speaking, he went into the kitchen. He took the two things from the earthenware containers and set them on the table; then before each person he placed a pair of wooden spoons. He then turned toward the old man and said, "This fare is considered rather uncommon. Please try some."

The old man saw that the two dishes on the table were indeed the small dog and the baby which had been soaking in the water crocks. The crowd of priests all parted their beards and clapped their hands.

"Brother!" they cried. "Where did you get two such unusual things?" They all prepared to start eating and politely pushed the dishes first toward the old man, who became quite frightened.

"Ever since I was very young," the old man said, "I've never broken my vow to forego eating dog meat, not to mention human flesh! Now that I'm old, how could I go back on my word?"

"These are merely vegetable dishes," observed the priest, "and it's quite all right to eat them."

"Even if I were starving," said the old man, "I wouldn't dare."

"Naturally," said the other priests, "if he is so determined, we cannot force him to dine."

"Please forgive us for being so impolite," they said, bowing with their hands folded.

The priests then gathered around and ate up every bit of the meal. Even the remaining drops of juice that had spilled on the platter were also licked clean. The old man just stared at them in silence, for he had not the courage to utter a sound.

"Since you haven't eaten with us," said the priest, "you've wasted your visit. I haven't anything proper to serve, but how can I let you go hungry?" He went into the kitchen again and brought out some white pastry for the old man. "This is some homemade cake which will satisfy your hunger. Please have a piece."

The old man saw that it really was cake, and since he was rather hungry, ate it. The flavor seemed a little bitter to him, but he was so famished that he did not care how it tasted. No sooner had he finished it than he began to feel healthy, robust, and vigorous. "Although Chang'an[1] is nice," he thought, "it isn't a place I should stay in. Now that I'm no longer hungry I should leave." The priest did not try to detain him as he came to say good-bye, but only replied, "I'm sorry that I've treated you so rudely on this occasion, and I feel badly about it. Of course, I'll escort you home myself."

They went out with the other priests, who expressed their thanks and left. The priest accompanied him until they approached a busy spot where he knew that the old man could find his way alone. He then left without saying good-bye. As the old man continued on toward home, he suspected that they were a bad lot. He saw they were accustomed to eating dog meat and human flesh; it was likely that this group of priests practiced sorcery, and were wicked thieves and murderers.

After a couple of days had passed, the priest with the double knot in his hair again arrived at the old man's home.

"I offended you the other day," he said with a bow.

"After seeing such a strange meal," replied the old man, "even today I'm still afraid."

The priest laughed. "That's because it was not your destiny. I'd gone through a lot of trouble to obtain these two items and did not dare enjoy them by myself. I recalled your kindness and especially invited you to my retreat so that we could share the meal with my colleagues together. How could I have known that you were not ordained for immortality!"

"How can you consider that small dog and child as immortal food?"

"Those were potent medicinal herbs that were of extremely ancient vintage. They only looked like a small dog and baby, and were not really flesh and blood. The one with the shape of a dog was the root from an ageless medlar tree;[2] if you ingest the root, you can live for a thousand years. The tiny baby was a ginseng root that required ten thousands years to form; eating this will add thousands of years to your life. You shouldn't cook these things but eat them in their natural state. [If I were lying to you,] how could we humans consume the raw flesh of dogs and people, just like wild animals, without even spitting out a single bone?"

Only then did the old man recall the circumstances of that meal the other day. Of course, everyone had taken the food uncooked, and he had seen no bones. Then he was convinced that the priest was telling the truth.

"I was so stupid the other day," he said remorsefully. "Why didn't you explain?"

1. The Tang dynasty (618–907) capital of China, famous for its beauty.

2. A tree whose roots, like those of ginseng, were perceived as resembling specific things.

"This is a matter of one's fate. If you weren't appointed to this end, how could I reveal the secrets of Heaven? Now that the affair is over, I can talk about it."

The old man beat his breast and stamped his feet. "I missed the chance to become an immortal," he cried, "even though it was right before my eyes! But it's too late to grieve over it. If you have some more, could you give me another herb to eat?"

"Those herbs came from magic roots and cannot be found again under ordinary circumstances! But though you didn't have any of the vegetables the other day, you did taste some of the thousand-year tuckahoe.[3] From now on, you'll never be sick during your lifetime, and you'll live to be over a hundred."

"What is tuckahoe?" asked the old man.

"That was the white cake you ate. That was all that was provided for in your destiny; it's not that I don't want you to join me in immortality."

The priest left after he finished speaking and never came again. And from that time on, the old man did indeed live over a hundred years without a single illness before his death.

Obviously, some people have the good fortune to become immortals. But in spite of the fact that the elixir of life may be right before you, and someone deliberately points it out, if it isn't your lot, it will never touch your lips. There are imbeciles, however, who have heard the Daoist sermons and hope to make the pill of immortality. When the poisons they extract from deadly elements, such as arsenic and mercury, flow into their stomachs, they are soon beyond saving. This is why the ancients had the saying: "When taking drugs in search of immortality, there are many who misinterpret the prescription."

Ever since men of the Jin Dynasty[4] popularized elixirs like the "Five-Stone Powder" and the "Cold-Resisting Powder," who knows how many intelligent victims have been destroyed by these toxic potions? There have been many ministers of state, even emperors, who could not be revived from the effects of these toxins. Why were they so blind? Because the dosages they prepared always followed the directions left behind by immortals. In concocting the elixir, however, the immortals insisted on perfect harmony between mind and body, eliminating every particle of greed and lust. Therefore, when they swallowed the potions, the water and fire elements in their bodies automatically refined the ingredients evenly into a medicinal concentrate which made their physical powers firm and unyielding, enabling them to live forever.

The people who compound these elixirs nowadays are those who nourish evil thoughts about women and wealth. They use drugs precisely for the purpose of obtaining life so they can indulge in their lustful desires. This idea is wrong to begin with. Moreover, their bodies are weary and dissipated when they are exposed to the dangerous chemicals made from these powerful elements, so how can they survive them? This is why nine out of ten persons fail in their quest. There is an occasional poem by Zhu Wengong[5] which says:

---

3. A large edible fungus.
4. 265–420 C.E.

5. Zhu Xi (1130–1200), a famous Neo-Confucian scholar and philosopher.

I drifted along seeking immortality,
Left the world to dwell in mountains and clouds.
Like a thief who opens the secrets of Heaven,
Slipping past the gates of life and death.
Bright golden pot emblazoned with tiger and dragon,
Three years in making those wondrous pills.
When a pinch of elixir goes into the mouth,
You soar through the sky in bright sunlight.
To take the path I yearn to follow
Is as easy as casting off my shoes.
But I was afraid of opposing natural laws;
Even living longer will bring no peace of mind.

This verse is proof that there is such a thing as the elixir of life, but when the product was ready, the poet was apprehensive about violating the principles of creation. Therefore, he did not want to continue his study of Daoist mysticism. But how could one anticipate that people who are ignorant of these principles would indulge in the reckless preparation and consumption of these harmful mixtures? Do they think that Heaven would be so indiscriminate as to allow them to join the true immortals? Thus, even the life that is given them is snuffed out.

[This is only the preamble; it is followed by the long main story on a futile and a fatal attempt to make immortality drugs.]

RELIGIOUS SECTS AMONG THE CHINESE

MATTEO RICCI

In 1583, the Italians Matteo Ricci (1552–1610; known to the Chinese as Li Madou) and Michele Ruggieri (1543–1607) traveled to the southern Chinese city of Zhaoqing (in present-day Guangdong Province) from the Portuguese colony of Macau to set up the first Jesuit mission in China. Ricci, who had exceptional language skills, began studying Chinese while in Macau and, along with Ruggieri, published a Portuguese-Chinese dictionary—the first bilingual lexicon of Chinese and any European language. Just as important, the Jesuits quickly began to publish his translations of books in elegant literary Chinese. His abilities as a noted mathematician, geographer, and astronomer drew the attention of the Chinese court, and he in turn developed a deep respect for Chinese culture. But the policy of accommodation with Christianity that he advocated was questioned by his superiors in Europe, and after what came to be called the Chinese Rites Controversy erupted in 1742, Pope Benedict XIV censured the Jesuit's accommodationist approach. Ricci died in Beijing in 1610.

"Religious Sects among the Chinese" is drawn from Matteo Ricci's journals covering the almost thirty years he spent in China. He began by seeking links with Buddhists, but eventually realized that an alliance with the Confucians and their classic texts would be more appropriate. The selection below focuses on Daoism; the longer account examines Confucianism and Buddhism as well. Because Ricci did not view Confucianism as a religion, he believed that it could be fused with Christianity. In contrast, he was critical of Buddhism and Daoism, especially because he viewed them as idolatrous. His descriptions display, on the one hand, a late Ming tendency to blur the distinctions between Buddhism and Daoism, and on the other, Jesuit readiness to relegate both to the venerable Christian category of paganism. It is striking that in discussing Daoism, Ricci claims that Laozi (whom he identifies as the founder) left no writings and he seems unaware of *The Scripture of the Way and Its Virtue* (*Laozi*) or the *Book of Master Zhuang* (*Zhuangzi*; for both, see above). Rather, Ricci mainly considers the religious forms of Daoism. For example, he describes Laozi (and his deification), Daoist priests and their vestments, and Daoist ritual music. He also notes the magical rites performed by Daoist priests to avert evil and to accomplish other goals—among them the alchemical pursuit of immortality, which he scornfully dismisses (oddly enough, the Chinese believed that the Jesuits knew a special way to transmute base metals into silver).

The third religious sect is called Lauzu,[1] and had its origin with a philosopher who was contemporaneous with Confucius. The period of gestation anticipating his birth is supposed to have lasted for eighty years and so he is called Lauzu, or the Old Man Philosopher. He left no writings of his doctrine, nor does it appear that he desired to institute a new or separate cult. After his death, however, certain sectaries, called the Taufu,[2] named him as the head of their sect and compiled various books and commentaries from other religions, and these were written in rather elegant literary style. These enthusiasts, too, have their own religious houses and live as celibates. They buy in their disciples and are as low and dishonest a class as those already described. They do not cut their hair but rather wear it as do the people in general, but they are easily distinguished by the custom of wearing a wooden skullcap on the knot or cluster of hair worn on the top of the head. Some of the followers of this creed, who are married, profess a more religious observance in their homes, where they recite set prayers for themselves and for others. Among their many gods, the devotees of this faith claim that they worship the one lord of heaven, a corporeal being to whom, it would seem, many untoward things are continually happening.

Their books recount their ravings, which we would repeat here, were it not beside our purpose to do so. A single example will give one an idea of what the rest must be like. They tell a story of the present reigning lord of heaven, who is called Ciam and his predecessor Leu.[3] One day Leu came to earth riding on a white dragon, and Ciam, who was a diviner of dreams, invited Leu to a banquet. While the heavenly guest was enjoying himself at table, his host jumped on the white dragon and was carried back to the celestial realm, where he took possession of the throne and still excludes Leu in his efforts to return. The unfortunate outcast did, however, obtain from the usurping King permission to preside over a certain mountain in his kingdom, where they say he now lives but entirely stripped of his former dignity. And so these poor people now admit that they are venerating a false lord, a usurper, and a tyrant.

TRANSLATED BY Louis J. Gallagher.

1. That is, Laozi.
2. That is, Daufu or Daoists.
3. Leu (Liu) is not further identified, but Ricci later calls Ciam (Zhang) the sect's "original high priest"; he therefore is likely Zhang Daoling (34–156 C.E.), the founder of the Celestial Masters movement.

In addition to the Supreme Deity, this sect has fashioned three other gods, one of whom is Lauzu, himself, the founder of the faith. Thus we have the two sects, each in its own way fashioning a trinity of gods, so that it would seem as if the original parent of falsehood, the father of lies,[4] has not as yet put aside his ambitious desire of divine similitude. They also talk of places of punishment and of reward, but their ideas of such places differ not a little from those of the sectaries already mentioned. This group favors a paradise of body and of soul for its members, and in their temples they have pictures of those who have been taken bodily up into heaven. Certain exercises are prescribed in order to accomplish this phenomenon, such as definite sitting positions accompanied with particular prayers and medicines, by use of which they promise their followers the favor of the gods and eternal life in heaven, or at least a longer life on earth. From such nonsense as this one can easily conclude as to the deceit injected into their delirium.

The special duty of the ministers of this group is to drive demons from homes by means of incantations. This is done in two different ways; by covering the walls of the house with pictures of horrid monsters drawn in ink on yellow paper and by filling the house with a bedlam of uncanny yelling and screaming and in this manner making demons of themselves. Bringing down rain from heaven in time of drought, stopping it when rain is too abundant, and preventing public and private calamities in general are some of the powers they claim to possess. If what is promised really came to pass, then those who permit themselves to be attracted by the promises would have a reason for their interest. Since, however, these impostors are invariably wrong in everything they foretell, it is difficult to understand what excuse or pretext can be alleged for following them, by men who otherwise are sufficiently intelligent. Unless we include everything they say under the common designation of falsehood, it would seem that some of them had acquired the secret of a magic art.

The ministers of this sect live in the royal temples of heaven and earth, and it is part of their office to be present at all sacrifices made in these temples either by the King himself or by a magistrate representing him. This, of course, serves to increase their prestige and their authority. The orchestra for such occasions is also composed of the ministers. Every musical instrument known to the Chinese will be included in this assembly, but the music they produce sounds decidedly off key to European ears. These same musicians are frequently invited to funeral services which they attend in ornate vestments, playing upon flutes and other musical instruments. The consecration of new temples and the direction of public processions of supplicants through the streets also come within their jurisdiction. These processions are ordered by the civil authorities of the towns, at stated times, and at the expense of the local neighborhood.

This sect recognized Ciam as its original high priest, and he is supposed to have handed down his office and the dignity that accompanies it, by right of hereditary succession, through a thousand years to the present day. The office itself seems to have had its origin with a certain magician, who lived in a cave in the province of Quiamsi,[5] where his descendants still live and where the secrets of his art are handed on to his children, if there be

4. That is, Satan; Ricci suggests that the Daoist trinity is a diabolic imitation of the Christian Trinity (Father, Son, and Holy Ghost).
5. Modern-day Jiangxi Province.

any truth in the story. Their present leader spends most of his time in Pekin.[6] He is a recognized favorite of the King and is even admitted into the most secret chambers of the palace for ceremonies of exorcism, if perchance suspicion should arise that these places are infested with evil spirits. He is carried through the streets in an open palanquin, wears the paraphernalia of the highest magistrates, and receives a fat annual stipend from the crown. One of our neophytes informs us that the present-day prelates of this sect are so ignorant that they do not even know the unholy hymns and rites of their own order. They have no jurisdiction whatsoever over the people. Their authority is confined to the subministers, or the Tausus, of their cult and to their own religious residence, where their power is supreme. Like the sectaries already treated, a great number of their cenobites, in an effort to formulate precepts for a longer life, spend much time experimenting in alchemy, in imitation of their holy ones, who they say have handed down certain precepts of this double science.

These three sects embrace about all the capital superstitions of this pagan people, but the vanity of their human folly does not cease here. As time goes on, through the influence of their leaders, each of these sources of superstition gives rise to so many streams of deceit and deception, that under these three captions one could number nearer to three hundred different and disparate religious sects. The frequent innovations go from bad to worse by the daily augmentation of corrupt practices and rules, of which the members of the sects take advantage for loose and licentious living.

Humvu,[7] the founder of the present reigning family, ordained that these three laws, namely the sects, should be preserved for the good of the kingdom. This he did in order to conciliate the followers of each sect. In legislating for their continuance, however, he made it of strict legal requirement that the cult of the Literati should have preference over the others, and that they alone should be entrusted with the administration of public affairs. Thus it happens that no sect is allowed to work for the extinction of another. The rulers make it a practice to cultivate the devotion of all three of them, using them in their own interest when need be, and conciliating each in turn by renovating their old temples or by building new ones. The wives of the King are usually more devoted to the sect of the idols, conferring alms upon the ministers and even supporting a whole institution of them, beyond the palace walls, in order to profit by their prayers.

The number of idols in evidence throughout the kingdom of China is simply incredible. Not only are they on exhibition in the temples, where a single temple might contain thousands of them, but in nearly every private dwelling. Idols are assigned a definite place in a private home, according to the custom of the locality. In public squares, in villages, on boats, and through the public buildings, this common abomination is the first thing to strike the attention of a spectator. Yet, it is quite certain that comparatively few of these people have any faith in this unnatural and hideous fiction of idol worship. The only thing they are persuaded of in this respect is, that if their external devotion to idols brings them no good, at least it can do them no harm.

---

6. That is, Peking (Beijing).
7. Hongwu (r. 1368–98), the founder of the Ming dynasty.

In conclusion to our consideration of the religious sects, at the present time, the most commonly accepted opinion of those who are at all educated among the Chinese is, that these three laws or cults really coalesce into one creed and that all of them can and should be believed. In such a judgment, of course, they are leading themselves and others into the very distracting error of believing that the more different ways there are of talking about religious questions, the more beneficial it will be for the public good. In reality they finally end up by accomplishing something altogether different from what they expected. In believing that they can honor all three laws at the same time, they find themselves without any law at all, because they do not sincerely follow any one of them. Most of them openly admit that they have no religion, and so by deceiving themselves in pretending to believe, they generally fall into the deepest depths of utter atheism.

SELECTED QING DYNASTY EDICTS

The excerpts grouped here under "On Private Founding of Monastic Buildings, and Private Ordinations of Buddhist and Daoist Monks" and "Regulation of the Clergy" are found in official edicts preserved in important Qing dynasty legal codes. Increasingly tight state control was a key feature of the Qing's posture toward religion in general, and Daoism in particular: within its administration was a board specifically charged with certifying and disciplining Daoists. These documents of the imperial government shed much light on the legal position of Daoist monasteries and clergy, laying out in minute and comprehensive detail what is forbidden and what is permitted. The issues discussed include ordination, monastic offices, public preaching, and the exclusion of women from Daoist monasteries. The texts also attest to the rather low status of the Daoist clergy during the Qing.

Although these records might suggest that all Daoists were strictly policed by the Qing regulations, many small-scale local and regional Daoist movements thrived beyond the reach of imperial control.

On Private Founding of Monastic Buildings, and Private Ordination of Buddhist and Daoist Monks

Apart from the now existing places of that nature, legally established in former years, it is not allowed to erect privately (i. e. without official authorisation) any Daoist or Buddhist convent, nor to re-build any on a larger scale. Whoever offends against this rescript shall receive one hundred blows with the long stick; the monks shall return to the lay state and be banished for ever to the furthest frontiers of the empire, while the nuns shall be appropriated by the magistracy as slaves. The foundations and the building-materials shall be confiscated.

* * *

TRANSLATED BY J. J. M. de Groot.

When the Daoist and Buddhist clergy increase, the population decreases: this is a natural law. These folks do not plough, and have no trades or callings; so they dress and eat at the cost of the people; why then shall we allow them to build and thereby waste the wealth of the people? why allow them to bind up people's hair or shave their heads, and thus empty their dwellings?

* * *

If amongst the people there prevails a desire to build a Buddhist or Daoist monastery, or to erect a place of sacrifice in honour of gods, they shall send in a petition to this effect to the Viceroy or the provincial Governor, who shall draw up a detailed report about the matter. Should a favorable imperial resolution be received, these authorities may give their permission to build; but if, without awaiting the answer to the petition, the building-work is started, the matter shall be tried as a violation of the fundamental article.

* * *

If a Buddhist or Daoist monk to whom no official diploma of ordination has been awarded, takes the tonsure of his own accord, or does up his hair, he shall receive eighty blows with the long stick. If such an offence occurs under the pressure of the head of his family, the punishment shall fall upon this person. A like punishment shall be inflicted on any abbot of a Buddhist or Daoist convent, and besides, on the religious teacher and initiator who thus privately administered an ordination. And all such transgressors shall go back into secular life.

* * *

If amongst the people the number of sons or (orphan) brothers in a family is less than three, and one of them leaves it (to embrace religious life), or if any one does so who has passed the age of sixteen, then the perpetrator shall be exposed for one month in the cangue.[1] The same punishment shall be inflicted upon him by whose pressure or influence such an act was committed. If the officer charged with the control of the Buddhist or Daoist clergy or the abbot of the convent in question, was privy to the offence, and yet took no initiative for the prosecution, he shall be dismissed and sent back into secular life.

* * *

And the Buddhist or Daoist clergy who at present live in the world and others of their class, shall not be allowed to adopt pupils and disciples at their own discretion. He who has past the age of forty may take one; he also may adopt another if the first, without having committed any offence, falls (irrecoverably) sick, or dies. But he who takes a pupil before he is forty, or adopts more than one, shall for transgression of the law receive fifty blows with the short bamboo lath. If an adopted pupil commits adultery, theft, or any other serious offence, his religious teacher shall not adopt another, on penalty of the same chastisement.

If the officer charged with the control of the Buddhist or the Daoist clergy tolerates or hushes up such a crime as the above, he shall receive the

---

1. A large wooden collar, used to confine the neck and sometimes the hands as punishment.

same punishment. And the Prefect, if he does not move to investigate the matter, shall be delivered up to the Board, to be prosecuted and sentenced according to law. And the adopted disciple shall, in each of the above cases, be forced to re-embrace secular life.

* * *

If a Buddhist or Daoist monk or priest is punished on account of any crime, he shall be deprived of his consecration-diploma, and become a layman again.

Regulation of the Clergy

OFFICERS FOR THE CONTROL OF THE [DAOIST] CLERGY

Each official temple of the metropolis stands under the management of the Board (of Rites) and the Commandant of the Gendarmerie. The Yamen[2] in the same street or road, the Imperial Household Department, and the Court of Sacrificial Worship shall send out officials to inspect these buildings; and at the end of every year they shall send us a report concerning the same.

* * *

If a member of the Buddhist or Daoist clergy does not keep the rules and rescripts (of his religion), then his officers are entitled to investigate and try the case; but if any person belonging to the military or civil class is involved in his transgression, then the secular authorities are entitled to examine and to punish. And if a violation of the law is committed, falling under adultery, then shall justice be done according to the secular law, and the criminal be treated as a layman.

ISSUING OF DIPLOMAS TO THE CLERGY BY THE STATE

When a Buddhist monk or nun accepts the commandments (i. e. is consecrated), an ordination-diploma is given to that person, and to a Daoist monk or nun a certificate. And when any such person then becomes more than forty years old, he or she may adopt one pupil, to whom the diploma or certificate descends; but Buddhist monks who have not accepted the commandments, or Daoists with homes and families of their own, shall not be allowed to adopt any pupils. The diplomas and certificates shall on the death of the holders be sent up to the Board (of Rites), and there be cancelled in groups.

WHAT THE CLERGY ARE TO DO AND NOT TO DO

In Buddhist and Daoist convents, the Buddhist and Daoist clergy respectively are considered to have the charge of the temple-rites. If any Buddhist or Daoist priest or monk coming from distant parts, puts up at a convent and is found to have no diploma, the authorities shall at once be acquainted of the fact, and thus be enabled to examine him; if he be allowed to remain there secretly, prosecution shall follow. And if any female person enters a temple, or comes there to look round, the clergy in charge of the temple-

---

2. The office and residence of a local government administrator.

rites shall receive the same punishment as the woman, unless they forbid her to enter, or send her away.

The Buddhist and Daoist clergy shall not hold sutra-readings in market-squares, nor go about with alms-bowls, nor explain the fruits of salvation, nor collect moneys; and they who infringe this rescript shall be punished.

* * *

If in the family of an official person, warrior or citizen, any one of its female members be allowed or commanded to burn incense in the temple of a divinity, belonging to a Buddhist or Daoist convent, a punishment of forty strokes with the short lath shall be inflicted on the husband or the male guardian of the woman, or on herself if she has no husband or male guardian. The same punishment shall fall on the abbot of that convent-temple and on its porter, should they not forbid and stop her. Incense-worship performed by a woman in the temple of a convent is not only profanation, but also detrimental to the development of manners and customs.

THE DAOIST PRIEST OF THE LAO MOUNTAINS

"The Daoist Priest of the Lao Mountains" was first published in *Strange Stories from a Chinese Studio* (*Liaozhai zhiyi*), a famous collection of supernatural tales from the late seventeenth to early eighteenth century compiled by Pu Songling (1640–1715). They feature a varied cast of Daoist priests, immortals, exorcists, and Confucian literati, alongside ghosts and magical animals. Yet, as much as *Strange Stories from a Chinese Studio* is about the strange and the fantastic, it also captures many details of everyday life in China. The stories in this collection force the reader to question the traditional demarcations between reality and fiction. *Strange Stories from a Chinese Studio* is filled with stories that also call into question the boundaries between the magical and the possible. In 1880, a selection was made available to readers of English by Herbert Giles in his *Strange Tales from a Chinese Studio*. The entire collection has been reprinted often—it was admired and read by a general audience and by such writers as Franz Kafka and Jorge Luis Borges—and some of the stories have been made into films.

In the fabulous Daoist world of "The Daoist Priest of the Lao Mountains," small jars provide an endless supply of wine and a paper cutout of the moon serves to illuminate a room. The story, which centers on a man who wants to learn the ways of the Daoists, stresses the necessity of maintaining effort and dedication—a point underscored by its final cautionary lesson. After the would-be disciple gives up, overwhelmed by the hardships, the Daoist master teaches him one spell but warns that it will continue to work only if his heart remains pure. He returns home boastful, and fails miserably when he attempts to show off his new ability.

PRONOUNCING GLOSSARY

Liaozhai zhiyi: *lee-ao-chai chih-yee*   Wang: *wawng*

There lived in our village a man named Wang, the seventh son of an old family, who from youth had longed to take up Daoism. Hearing that in the Lao Mountains[1] there were many immortals, he shouldered a pack and set off in that direction.

At the top of a peak of the mountains, he came upon a secluded temple. A Daoist priest with white hair down to his neck and of lofty demeanor was sitting on a rush mat. Wang bowed low, spoke with him, and found the doctrines he expounded abstruse but profound. Wang asked the priest to take him as a disciple. The priest said, "I'm afraid you're too soft and spoiled to put up with the hardships." Wang assured him that he could.

The disciples of the priest were quite numerous. Toward evening they all assembled together. Wang made obeisance to all of them and then stayed on in the temple.

Early the next morning, the priest summoned Wang, gave him an axe, and sent him off with the others to gather firewood. Wang respectfully did as he was told. More than a month passed and his hands and feet had become heavily callused. Unable to endure this hardship, he had secretly made up his mind to go home.

Returning one evening to the temple, he saw two men drinking with the master. The sun had already set, but no lamps or candles had been lit. The master cut some paper in the shape of a round mirror and pasted it on the wall. In a moment, bright moonlight filled the room, by the light of which even a hair was visible. All the disciples crowded round to wait upon them. One of the guests said, "On such a lovely night, the joy should be shared by all." He then took a jug of wine from the table and gave it to the disciples, bidding them drink their fill. Wang wondered to himself how this one jug of wine could serve seven or eight people. Everyone then found himself a cup or bowl and raced to drain his cup first, fearing that the supply would soon be exhausted. But again and again wine was poured out without ever seeming to diminish. Wang marveled at this.

A moment later, one of the guests said, "You have provided us with bright moonlight, yet we drink alone. Why not call [the moon goddess] Chang'e to come?" He then threw a chopstick into the moon, and there, a beautiful girl came forth from the light. At first barely a foot high, upon reaching the ground she attained full stature. She had a slender waist and a beautiful neck, and gracefully she fluttered through the steps of the Rainbow Robe Dance. When this was over, she sang:

> Fairies! Oh, Fairies! Have you returned,
> Leaving me shut up in the Palace of the Moon?

Her voice, as beautiful as the notes of a lute, was clear and far-reaching. When the song was finished, she whirled around, jumped up on the table, and before the astonished gaze of the company, turned back into a chopstick. The three men laughed heartily.

Then the other guest said, "This has been a happy evening, and we've had enough wine. How about treating us to a feast in the Palace of the Moon?"

TRANSLATED BY Jeanne Kelly. All bracketed additions are the translator's.

1. A mountain range located in present-day Shandong Province, near the coast.

Leaving their seats, the three gradually walked into the moon, where all could see them sitting and drinking, their beards and eyebrows as plainly visible as images in a mirror.

After a while, the moon gradually dimmed, and when the disciples lit some candles, they found the priest sitting alone; the guests had disappeared. The food still remained on the table, while the moon on the wall was nothing but a piece of paper, round as a mirror. The priest asked, "Have you all had enough to drink?" "Quite enough," they replied. "In that case, you should get to bed early so that you won't be late in gathering firewood tomorrow." They all obeyed and withdrew. Wang was secretly delighted and all thoughts of returning home vanished.

Another month passed. The hardships had become more than Wang could endure, and besides, the Daoist priest had not taught him any magic skill. Unable to wait any longer, he took his leave, saying, "I came a long way to receive your instruction. Though I cannot obtain the secret of immortality, perhaps if you could impart some small skill, it would satisfy my desire for knowledge. Already I've been here two or three months, and I have done nothing but go out early in the morning to collect firewood and return in the evening. I never experienced such hardship at home."

The priest laughed and said, "Didn't I tell you that you couldn't stand the hardships? Now since this has been borne out, I'll send you on your way tomorrow morning."

Wang said, "I've worked for you for many days. If you could impart a little of your skill, I wouldn't have come in vain."

"What skill do you seek?"

Wang replied, "I've noticed that wherever you go, walls are never an obstacle in your path. If I could only learn the secret of that, it would be enough." The priest laughed and assented. Thereupon he taught Wang a magic spell which he had him recite through to the end. Then he cried, "Go on through!" Wang faced the wall, not daring to approach it. Again the priest said, "Try going through." Wang advanced cautiously, but when he reached the wall, he stopped. "Lower your head and rush through. Don't hesitate," commanded the priest. Wang accordingly stepped back several paces from the wall and rushed forward. When he reached the wall, it seemed as though there was nothing there. Turning to look back, he found he was indeed outside the wall. Overjoyed he returned to thank the priest, who told him, "When you return home, your heart must remain pure; otherwise the spell will not work." He then gave him money for traveling expenses and sent him home.

Back at home, Wang bragged that he had met an immortal and now solid walls could not obstruct his path. His wife did not believe him, so Wang prepared to repeat his performance. Stepping back several feet from the wall, he rushed forward. His head struck the hard wall, and abruptly he fell down flat. His wife helped him up and looked him over. His forehead had swollen into a lump the size of a huge egg. She made great fun of him and Wang, shameful and indignant, cursed the old priest for being a scoundrel.

THE SECRET OF THE GOLDEN FLOWER
(*Taiyi jinhua zongzhi*)

The Secret of the Golden Flower (*Taiyi jinhua zongzhi*) is a work of internal alchemy (*neidan*) traditionally attributed to the semilegendary Daoist master Lü Dongbin, who is said to have revealed the text through spirit writing. Its main focus is the internal alchemical practice of generating the Golden Flower, which is a symbol of the Golden Elixir that confers immortality (the Elixir of Life, in this translation). Within internal alchemy Daoism, the Golden Flower/Golden Elixir entails the return of one's spirit to the undivided primordial Dao; the text therefore contains a wide range of terms and images that emphasize the importance of "return," "reversal," and the "backward-flowing."

This text has been central to a variety of internal alchemy lineages from the seventeenth century to the present day. It also contains a rich array of Buddhist philosophical terms and practices. For example, it gives Buddhist contemplation—especially the Tiantai Buddhist practice of "calming and insight" (in Chinese, *zhiguan*; in Sanskrit, *shamatha-vipashyana*), which is here called "fixating contemplation"—a prominent role. *The Secret of the Golden Flower* became widely known to the Western world through Richard Wilhelm's 1929 German translation, a work that fascinated the Swiss psychologist Carl Jung (who wrote a foreword and appendix to it).

PRONOUNCING GLOSSARY

Jindan: *chin-dawn*
Lüzu: *lew-tzu*

Taiyi jinhua zongzhi: *tai-yee chin-hwa tzong-chih*

3. *Circulation of the Light and Protection of the Centre*

Master Lüzu said, Since when has the expression 'circulation of the light' been revealed? It was revealed by the 'True Men of the Beginning of Form.' When the light is made to move in a circle, all the energies of heaven and earth, of the light and the dark, are crystallized. That is what is termed seed-like thinking, or purification of the energy, or purification of the idea. When one begins to apply this magic it is as if, in the middle of being, there were non-being. When in the course of time the work is completed, and beyond the body there is a body, it is as if, in the middle of non-being, there were being. Only after concentrated work of a hundred days will the light be genuine, then only will it become spirit-fire. After a hundred days there develops by itself in the midst of the light a point of the true light-pole (yang).[1] Then suddenly there develops the seed pearl. It is as if man and woman embraced and a conception took place. Then one must be quite still and wait. The circulation of the light is the epoch of fire.

TRANSLATED from the Chinese by Richard Wilhelm; translated from the German by Cary F. Baynes.

1. The male principle; the term originally referred to the sunny side of a valley, and by extension it came to be associated with the light, heaven, dryness, and activity. Yin, in contrast, is the female principle; the term originally referred to the shady side of a valley, and by extension came to be associated with the dark, earth, dampness, and passivity.

In the midst of primal transformation, the radiance of the light is the determining thing. In the physical world it is the sun; in man, the eye. The radiation and dissipation of spiritual consciousness is chiefly brought about by this energy when it is directed outward (flows downward). Therefore the Way of the Golden Flower depends wholly on the backward-flowing method.

> Man's heart stands under the fire sign. The flames of the fire press upward. When both eyes are looking at things of the world it is with vision directed outward. Now if one closes the eyes and, reversing the glance, directs it inward and looks at the room of the ancestors, that is the backward-flowing method. The energy of the kidneys is under the water sign. When the desires are stirred, it runs downward, is directed outward, and creates children. If, in the moment of release, it is not allowed to flow outward, but is led back by the energy of thought so that it penetrates the crucible of the Creative, and refreshes heart and body and nourishes them, that also is the backward-flowing method. Therefore it is said, The Way of the Elixir of Life depends entirely on the backward-flowing method.

The circulation of the light is not only a circulation of the seed-blossom of the individual body, but it is even a circulation of the true, creative, formative energies. It is not a momentary fantasy, but the exhaustion of the cycle (soul-migrations) of all the aeons. Therefore the duration of a breath means a year according to human reckoning and a hundred years measured by the long night of the nine paths (of reincarnations).

After a man has the one sound of individuation behind him, he will be born outward according to the circumstances, and until his old age he will never look backward. The energy of the light exhausts itself and trickles away. That brings the ninefold darkness (of reincarnations) into the world. In the book *Leng Yan* it is said: 'By concentrating the thoughts, one can fly; by concentrating the desires, one falls.' When a pupil takes little care of his thoughts and much care of his desires, he gets into the path of submersion. Only through contemplation and quietness does true intuition arise: for that the backward-flowing method is necessary.

In the *Book of the Secret Correspondences*[2] it is said: 'Release is in the eye.' In the *Simple Questions of the Yellow Ruler*[3] it is said: 'The seed-blossoms of the human body must be concentrated upward in the empty space.' This refers to it. Immortality is contained in this sentence and also the overcoming of the world is contained in it. This is the common goal of all religions.

The light is not in the body alone, nor is it only outside the body. Mountains and rivers and the great earth are lit by sun and moon; all that is this light. Therefore it is not only within the body. Understanding and clarity, perception and enlightenment, and all movements (of the spirit) are likewise this light; therefore it is not just something outside the body. The light-flower of heaven and earth fills all the thousand spaces. But also the

---

2. The *Yinfu jing*, better known as the *Book of Hidden Accordance* or *Scripture of Hidden Accordance*. A very short treatise traditionally attributed to the legendary Yellow Emperor (Huangdi, 27th century B.C.E.), it became a classic Daoist text of internal alchemy.

3. The *Huangdi neijing suwen*, also known as the *Inner Scripture of the Yellow Emperor: Plain Questions*. This major section of a key text of Chinese medical theory was attributed to the Yellow Emperor.

light-flower of the individual body passes through heaven and covers the earth. Therefore, as soon as the light is circulating, heaven and earth, mountains and rivers, are all circulating with it at the same time. To concentrate the seed-flower of the human body above in the eyes, that is the great key of the human body. Children, take heed! If for a day you do not practise meditation, this light streams out, who knows whither? If you only meditate for a quarter of an hour, by it you can do away with the ten thousand aeons and a thousand births. All methods end in quietness. This marvellous magic cannot be fathomed.

But when the practice is started, one must press on from the obvious to the profound, from the coarse to the fine. Everything depends on there being no interruption. The beginning and the end of the practice must be one. In between there are cooler and warmer moments, that goes without saying. But the goal must be to reach the vastness of heaven and the depths of the sea, so that all methods seem quite easy and taken for granted. Only then have we mastered it.

All holy men have bequeathed this to one another: nothing is possible without contemplation (reflection). When Confucius says: 'Perceiving brings one to the goal'; or when the Buddha calls it: 'The vision of the heart'; or Laozi says: 'Inner vision', it is all the same.

Anyone can talk about reflection, but he cannot master it if he does not know what the word means. What has to be reversed by reflection is the self-conscious heart, which has to direct itself towards that point where the formative spirit is not yet manifest. Within our six-foot body we must strive for the form which existed before the laying down of heaven and earth. If to-day people sit and meditate only one or two hours, looking only at their own egos, and call this reflection, how can anything come of it?

The two founders of Buddhism and Daoism have taught that one should look at the tip of one's nose. But they did not mean that one should fasten one's thoughts to the tip of the nose. Neither did they mean that, while the eyes were looking at the tip of the nose, the thoughts should be concentrated on the yellow middle. Wherever the eye looks, the heart is directed also. How can it be directed at the same time upward (yellow middle), and downward (tip of the nose), or alternatively, so that it is now up, now down? All that means confusing the finger with which one points to the moon with the moon itself.

What then is really meant by this? The expression 'tip of the nose' is very cleverly chosen. The nose must serve the eyes as a guide-line. If one is not guided by the nose, either one opens wide the eyes and looks into the distance, so that the nose is not seen, or the lids shut too much, so that the eyes close, and again the nose is not seen. But when the eyes are opened too wide, one makes the mistake of directing them outward, whereby one is easily distracted. If they are closed too much, one makes the mistake of letting them turn inward, whereby one easily sinks into a dreamy reverie. Only when the eyelids are lowered properly halfway is the tip of the nose seen in just the right way. Therefore it is taken as a guide-line. The main thing is to lower the eyelids in the right way, and then to allow the light to stream in of itself; without effort, wanting the light to stream in concentratedly. Looking at the tip of the nose serves only as the beginning of the inner concentration, so that the eyes are brought into the right direction for looking, and

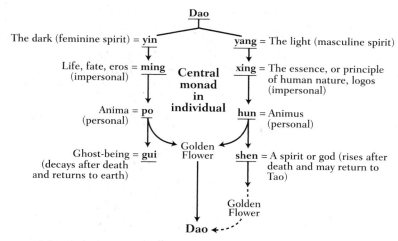

Diagram of the Chinese concepts concerned with the development of the Golden Flower, or immortal spirit body.

then are held to the guide-line: after that, one can let it be. That is the way a mason hangs up a plumb-line. As soon as he has hung it up, he guides his work by it without continually bothering himself to look at the plumb-line.

Fixating contemplation[4] is a Buddhist method which has not by any means been handed down as a secret.

One looks with both eyes at the tip of the nose, sits upright and in a comfortable position, and holds the heart to the centre in the midst of conditions. In Daoism it is called the yellow middle, in Buddhism the centre of the midst of conditions. The two are the same. It does not necessarily mean the middle of the head. It is only a matter of fixing one's thinking on the point which lies exactly between the two eyes. Then all is well. The light is something extremely mobile. When one fixes the thought on the mid-point between the two eyes, the light streams in of its own accord. It is not necessary to direct the attention especially to the central castle. In these few words the most important thing is contained.

'The centre in the midst of conditions' is a very subtle expression. The centre is omnipresent; everything is contained in it; it is connected with the release of the whole process of creation. The condition is the portal. The condition, that is, the fulfilment of this condition, makes the beginning, but it does not bring about the rest with inevitable necessity. The meaning of these two words is very fluid and subtle.

Fixating contemplation is indispensable; it ensures the making fast of the enlightenment. Only one must not stay sitting rigidly if worldly thoughts come up, but one must examine where the thought is, where it began, and where it fades out. Nothing is gained by pushing reflection further. One must be content to see where the thought arose, and not seek beyond the point of origin; for to find the heart (consciousness, to get behind consciousness

---

4. The Tiantai Buddhist practice of calming and insight (*zhiguan*).

with consciousness), that cannot be done. Together we want to bring the states of the heart to rest, that is true contemplation. What contradicts it is false contemplation. That leads to no goal. When the flight of the thoughts keeps extending further, one should stop and begin contemplating. Let one contemplate and then start fixating again. That is the double method of making fast the enlightenment. It means the circulation of the light. The circulation is fixation. The light is contemplation. Fixation without contemplation is circulation without light. Contemplation without fixation is light without circulation! Take note of that!

✻   ✻   ✻

Summary of the Chinese Concepts on Which Is Based the Idea of the Golden Flower, or Immortal Spirit-Body

The Dao, the undivided, great One, gives rise to two opposite reality principles, the dark and the light, yin and yang. These are at first thought of only as forces of nature apart from man. Later, the sexual polarities and others as well are derived from them. From yin comes *Kun*, the receptive feminine principle; from yang comes *Qian*, the creative masculine principle; from yin comes *ming*, life; from yang, *xing* or human nature.

Each individual contains a central monad, which, at the moment of conception, splits into life and human nature, *ming* and *xing*. These two are supra-individual principles, and so can be related to eros and logos.

In the personal bodily existence of the individual they are represented by two other polarities, a *po* soul (or anima) and a *hun* soul (animus).[5] All during the life of the individual these two are in conflict, each striving for mastery. At death they separate and go different ways. The anima sinks to earth as *gui*, a ghost-being. The animus rises and becomes *shen*, a spirit or god. *Shen* may in time return to the Dao.

If the life-energy flows downward, that is, without let or hindrance into the outer world, the anima is victorious over the animus; no spirit-body or Golden Flower is developed, and at death the ego is lost. If the life-energy is led through the 'backward-flowing' process, that is, conserved, and made to 'rise' instead of allowed to dissipate, the animus has been victorious, and the ego persists after death. It then becomes *shen*, a spirit or god. A man who holds to the way of conservation all through life may reach the stage of the Golden Flower, which then frees the ego from the conflict of the opposites, and it again becomes part of the Dao, the undivided, great One.

---

5. The *po* or white soul is the heavy soul, linked to the earth; the *hun* or cloud soul is the light soul, which is linked with heaven and its pneumas. *Anima* and *animus* are terms from Jungian psychology, respectively representing feminine and masculine archetypes and psychological tendencies.

CUTTING THE RED DRAGON
(*Duan Honglong*)

FU SHAN

"Cutting the Red Dragon" ("Duan Honglong") was written by the famous Chinese doctor and gynecologist Fu Shan (1607–1684). One of the first Daoist texts devoted to "female alchemy" (*nüdan*), it was revealed to Fu Shan by spirit writing. Although it is rather short, it was historically significant: it is the first concise and detailed description of the female practice and its physiological effects. As translator and scholar Elena Valussi notes, female alchemy, which is directed solely at women, developed in the seventeenth and eighteenth centuries—much later than "inner alchemy" (*neidan*), which is practiced by both men and women. Although women had always been integral to the Daoist pantheon as goddesses and revealers of texts, as well as participants in the Daoist institutional church as practitioners and believers, this was the earliest organized corpus of texts specifically targeting them and their practices. The female alchemy tradition takes into account the different physiologies of men and women in the context of meditation practices.

"Cutting the Red Dragon" provides a technique that enables a woman to stop the flow of menstrual blood (viewed as the locus of her energy and vitality) and the sublimation of the material substance of blood into *qi* (pneuma). The female practice of stopping the menstrual flow in order to retain vital essence is parallel to the male practice of stopping the spermatic flow, a topic discussed by Liu Yiming (1734–1821) in his "Questions on Female Alchemy." Since a man's sperm is the source of his energy it must be retained. Therefore, rather than ejaculating to produce offspring, men reverse the flow of sperm in order to regenerate their own bodies.

PRONOUNCING GLOSSARY

Duan Honglong: *duan howng-lowng* qi: *chi*
Fu Shan: *foo shan*

The perfected man[1] says:
All those who practice refinement for female perfection must first concentrate, then take several breaths and sit in meditation; sit until you have obtained the *qi*[2] to circulate freely within the body, then, one day before menstruation, at the hours of *zi* and *wu* (midnight and noon), start the practice. At midnight, put a robe on and sit with the legs crossed, with the two hands holding firmly to the sides of the ribs. Wait until (the *qi*) has ascended and descended within the body a few times, and then press the left heel against the vagina and the rectum, clench the teeth, close firmly the eyes, shrug the shoulders, and lift up from the perineum with great strength. Think of two red channels of *qi* rising from the womb, through the *weilü* pass and the three passes (*weilü, jiaji, yuzhen*),[3] ascending to the *niwan*,[4] descending

Translated by Elena Valussi.

1. A Daoist spiritual master; a Daoist who has moved beyond earthly corruption.
2. Vital energy, breath (pneuma).
3. These "passes" are all locations on a person's spinal column (ordered from lowest to highest).
4. Literally, "Muddy Pellet," the central of the nine palaces inside a person's head.

to the root of the tongue, and pouring into the two breasts. Practice this in this manner continuously, until the body is warm and then stop. Then use a white silk kerchief and insert it into the vagina to compare the quantity (of blood) to last month's and to see if there is any. Again, following the practice just described, use the circulation of the *qi* to scatter the blood and *qi* (in the body) in order to avoid illnesses. In less than a hundred days (the period) will be cut by itself. Check what time the period arrived the month before. Presuming it arrived on day one, you need to wait until day three to start cutting (the red dragon) the first time. The second month cut it a second time. The third month cut it a third time. It will stop within three months. The first month you will cut the tail, the second month you will cut the waist, the third month you will cut the head. This is called cutting the red dragon.

COMBINED COLLECTION OF FEMALE ALCHEMY
(*Nüdan hebian*)

HE LONGXIANG

In *Combined Collection of Female Alchemy* (*Nüdan hebian*, 1906), as Elena Valussi notes, "He Longxiang (fl. 1900) takes up large issues such as the role of women in late imperial society, female chastity, and the ever-present anxiety about the place of women in public spaces." The selections below examine the meaning of "female alchemy" (*nüdan*), explain why it rather than other practices should be followed, and describe the physiological differences between men and women relevant to Daoism. The preface opens by stating that many men have attained immortality and very few women, offering a striking analysis. He's reasoning is based largely on social factors ("women cannot leave home and find a master," few women can read, and "alchemical books for women are few and far between").

Combined Collection of Female Alchemy, Valussi further notes, "provides one of the clearest discussions of the meaning of 'female alchemy' and addresses the question of gender difference by describing male and female bodies from a cosmological as well as physiological point of view." He writes that "a woman's generative power originates from the blood"; "its color is red and its name is red dragon"; for the man, in contrast, it "is the essence, its color is white and its name is white tiger." A man's goal is to refrain from leaking his seminal essence ("subduing the white tiger"); a woman's, to refrain from releasing menstrual blood ("beheading the red dragon"). In addition, internal alchemy leads to the male practitioner's body transforming into that of a young boy, while the result of female alchemy practice is that the body of the female adept comes to resemble that of a man. "Awaiting Salvation" makes it clear that despite a female adept's successful practice and refinement, her body is still not considered purified: she is unable to ascend directly to heaven on her own, and instead must await a summons and an escort.

PRONOUNCING GLOSSARY

He Longxiang: *huh lowng-hsiang*   Nüdan hebian: *new-dawn huh-bien*

From *The Preface*

There is Heaven and there is Earth, and there are men and women. Among men, many attain immortality; among women, few attain immortality. [It is] because men can travel in search of the Dao, whereas women cannot leave home and find a master. [It is] because while there are numerous alchemical books for men, alchemical books for women are few and far between and are not transmitted. [It is also] because seven or eight out of ten men can read and understand a written text, while only one or two out of a hundred women can. If there were alchemical books for women that could be transmitted; and if women were able to read and understand them, and leave home at their convenience to seek a master and find the Dao, then the number of women attaining immortality would not necessarily be any less than the number of men.

*　　*　　*

[When discussing male and female practice,] there are three fundamental areas: the first concerns Innate Nature, the second the Shape and the Structure, the third the Methods of the Practice.

Just as the man is yang, and yang is clear, so the woman is yin, and yin is impure.[1] The male nature is hard, the female nature is soft. A man's feelings are excitable, a woman's feelings are tranquil; male thoughts are mixed, female thoughts are pure. The man is fundamentally in movement, and movement facilitates the loss of *qi*;[2] the woman is fundamentally quiet, and quietness facilitates the accumulation of *qi*. The man is associated with the trigram *Li*[3] and, like the sun, he can complete a whole circuit of the heavens in one year; the woman is associated with the trigram *Kan* and, like the moon, she can complete a whole circuit of the heavens in one month. For a man, *qi* is difficult to subdue; for a woman, *qi* is easy to subdue.

These are the differences concerning innate nature.

The man has a knot inside the windpipe (i.e., Adam's apple), the woman does not. The male breasts do not produce liquids and are small; the female breasts produce liquids and are big. A man's foundation is convex; a woman's foundation is concave.[4] In the man [the convex organ] is called the essence chamber; in the woman [the concave organ] is called the infant's palace. In men the vital force is located in the *qi* cavity; in women the vital force is located between the breasts. In the man, generative power is located in the pelvis; in the woman, generative power originates from the blood. In the man [the generative power] is the essence, its color is white and its name is white tiger; in the woman it is the blood, its color is red and its name is red dragon.[5] As for male essence, it is yin within yang; as for female blood, it is

TRANSLATED BY Elena Valussi. All bracketed additions are the translator's.

1. *Yin* and *yang* are the complementary forces that unite to form the Dao: yin, a term that originally referred to the shady side of a valley, by extension came to be associated with the dark, earth, dampness, and passivity—the female principle; yang, a term that originally referred to the sunny side of a valley, by extension came to be associated with the light, heaven, dryness, and activity—the male principle.

2. Vital energy, breath (pneuma).

3. On the trigrams, see the introduction to *The Seal of the Unity of the Three, in Accordance with the Book of Changes* (*Zhouyi cantong qi*), above.

4. The Chinese characters for "convex" (*tu*, 凸) and "concave" (*ao*, 凹) clearly depict those shapes.

5. That is, menstrual blood. "White tiger" is semen.

yang within yin. The power of male essence is more than sufficient; the power of female blood is insufficient.

These are the differences concerning Form and Structure.

A man first refines the root origin, and only subsequently does he refine the form; a woman, instead, needs to refine her form first, and only then can she refine the root origin. The male yang leaks downward, whereas the female yang moves upward. When a man has completed the practice and the seminal essence does not drip away any more, this is called "subduing the white tiger." When a woman has completed the practice and the menstrual flow does not drip away anymore, this is called "beheading the red dragon."[6] In the man, seminal essence moves against the current and he becomes immortal; in the woman, blood moves upwards, ascending towards the heart's cavity The masculine practice is called "refining the *qi* of the supreme Yang," the feminine practice is called "refining the blood of the supreme Yin." For the man we speak of "Embryo"; for the woman, we speak of "Growing." When the man has subdued the white tiger, the stem (i.e., the penis) will retract and become similar to that of a young boy; when the woman has beheaded the red dragon, the breasts will retract and become similar to those of a male body. The man progresses slowly at the moment of the manifestation of the spirit, and he is slow in achieving the Dao; the woman progresses fast at the moment of the manifestation of the spirit, and she is also fast in attaining the Dao. A man can ascend [to Heaven] on his own; a woman needs to await salvation. Men must meditate facing the wall; women who succeed in going back to emptiness are very few. The man will become an authentic man;[7] the woman will become a princess of the origin. These are the differences concerning the methods of practice.

We can say that, as for the principles that regulate Innate Nature and Vital Force, there are no differences [between men and women]. I advise the female adepts first to find out points of contiguity where there are differences, and only then to discover the differences hidden where there is similarity. In most cases, however, the contrasts are to be found before the beheading of the Red Dragon, whereas the major analogies emerge after the beheading of the Dragon. These are irrefutable and immortal arguments.

Awaiting Salvation

What is the reason why, to complete the practice that leads to feminine perfection, it is necessary to "await salvation"? The reason lies in the [female] constitution, feeble and pervaded with blood. [The woman] who practices inner refinement and sublimation is able to complete a Yang Body. But even if the formation of the Yang Body is achieved, her Yin and stagnant nature is not yet completely refined. For this reason she will not be able to fully achieve the marvelous transformations of Heaven and Earth. The primary reason why, for women, it is impossible to transcend this world [on their own], is the weakness of their constitution. The situation is different for the male constitution. After a man has practiced until the accomplishment of an adamantine and indestructible body, a Spiritual Light will pervade Heaven and Earth. Therefore a man does not need to await salvation: he will attain the

6. See "Cutting the Red Dragon" ("Duan Honglong"), above.
7. A *zhenren*, or Perfected Person—a Daoist spir-itual master; a Daoist who has moved beyond earthly corruption.

Dao and complete Authenticity, he will ascend in person to the presence of the Supreme Divinities and wander to the quiet Penglai islands.[8] For women, it is not like this. In order to complete the alchemical practice for women, it is necessary to widely cultivate merits and virtues. If the merits and virtues have been cultivated fully, then the sages from above will see it and take pity on her, and report it to the emperor. Then she will obtain an edict, (the Emperor will) send down the golden scriptures as imperial decrees, and this will be the proof of having obtained the result of the unsurpassable Dao beyond man and heaven (. . .). Only then the practice is completed.

8. Islands of the immortals (i.e., Daoists who have achieved extraordinary powers and a higher form of existence), located in the Eastern Sea.

SECRET PRINCIPLES OF GATHERING THE TRUE ESSENCE
(*Caizhen jiyao*)

ZHANG SANFENG

Although there are some early textual references to sexual alchemy (perhaps from the fourth century), it is not until the Ming (1368–1644) and Qing (1644–1912) dynasties that we find complete extant texts related to those practices. The *Secret Principles of Gathering the True Essence* (*Caizhen jiyao*), which consists of poems attributed to the legendary Daoist saint Zhang Sanfeng—together with commentaries by Fu Jinquan (fl. 1800), the author and publisher of many alchemical texts—uses the language of sexology to describe alchemical transformations. This work, which was probably written in the nineteenth century, contains little that is overtly erotic or concerned with sexual pleasure; the focus instead is on a Daoist view of biology and the need to collect or gather key elements from someone of the opposite sex. The explicitly sexual descriptions are couched in a rich variety of

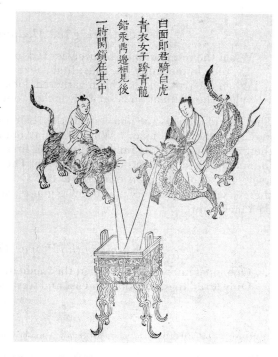

This woodblock illustration, entitled *Illustration of Marriage of the Dragon and Tiger*, depicts a girl (*yin*) riding a dragon (*yang*) and a boy (*yang*) riding a tiger (*yin*). The power of the conjoined yin and yang, a reference to the sexual nature of this image, is secreted into the alchemical crucible.

symbolic vocabulary and imagery, much of it familiar to those versed in the symbolism of internal alchemy. For example, there are terms for reversal and inversion and
for symbolic opposites, such as the dragon (male) and tiger (female) or lead (male)
and mercury (female).

PRONOUNCING GLOSSARY

Caizhen jiyao: *tsai-chun chee-yao* niwan: *knee-wawn*
dantian: *dawn-tien* qi: *chi*
Fu Jinquan: *fu chin-chu-en* Zhang Sanfeng: *chawng sahn-fung*

Establishing the Foundation

To lock the *yinjing*[1] is to establish the foundation.
Establishing the foundation consists of maintaining the feminine.
By maintaining the feminine without shaking, the lock is secure.
To lock the *yinjing* is to establish the foundation.

To establish the foundation it is most important to maintain the feminine
attitude and not the masculine. If one is able to maintain the feminine, this
is called "locking the *yinjing*". In this way we can say with certainty that the
foundation will be established. Hey! Do you not know? When the wind
rises, the sail must be lowered; when the jar is set upright, the water returns
full.

Gathering the Medicine

When the foundation is securely locked, one can study immortality.
To study immortality one must find the true lead.
When the true lead has been gathered, lock the foundation.
When the foundation is securely locked, one can study immortality.

The "foundation" is the *dantian*.[2] If the "true mercury" is not wasted, one
may seek the "true lead."[3] When one has obtained the "true lead," only
then can one hope for immortality. It is first necessary to establish the
foundation, and then gather the medicine. The medicine does not come of
itself, but depends upon our effort. Ha! Do not talk foolishness! When
there is wine, what a pity not to invite guests. Without money how can one
be a merchant?

Knowing the Proper Time

One must know the time when the medicine is produced.
Only after knowing this can east and west be matched.

TRANSLATED BY Douglas Wile. All bracketed additions are the translator's.

1. That is, the essence (*jing*) of yin, the female
principle; the term originally referred to the shady
side of a valley, and by extension it came to be
associated with the dark, earth, dampness, and
passivity. Yang, in contrast, is the male principle;
the term originally referred to the sunny side of a
valley, and by extension it came to be associated
with the light, heaven, dryness, and activity.
2. The lower Cinnabar Field, corresponding to a
location in the abdomen; it is the seat of essence.
3. In the language of Daoist alchemy, "true lead"
is true yang, and "true mercury" is true yin.

Before east and west are matched, it is difficult to produce the
medicine.
One must know the time when the medicine is produced.

"Producing the medicine" means producing the "lead." The medicine is
produced at a specific time, and only if one knows the true time can one
obtain the true medicine. Absorb your partner's lead to augment your own
mercury. When east and west are in complementary rapport, the elixir is
naturally formed. Otherwise one runs the risk of excessive *yin* or excessive
yang. Ha! Wait for the right time! The moon will come out and the "golden
flowers" appear. When the tide comes in the water covers all.

Strumming the Zither

Beat the bamboo until it opens, and then strum the zither.
Strumming the zither and beating the bamboo brings out the pure
sound.
If the pure sound has not yet arrived, the bamboo must be beaten.
Beat the bamboo until it opens, and then strum the zither.

"Beating the bamboo" empties my mind; "strumming the zither" excites my
partner's "thing." I use myself to excite my partner. When her "thing" arrives,
the "pure sound" will be loud and clear. Ha! Do you know? When the string
is slack no arrow flies. When the wind moves, one can then set sail.

Approaching the Enemy

In doing battle one must make the opponent furious.
Though the opponent is furious, I do not play the hero.
If I do not renounce heroism, there will be contention.
In doing battle, one must make the opponent furious.

"Doing battle" means approaching the battlefield. I counsel you gentlemen,
in approaching the battlefield do not underestimate the enemy. This expresses
the idea that, when having intercourse, you must allow your partner to
move on her own, while refraining from movement yourself. If I were to
move but once, I would lose my invaluable treasure. Ha! Stop going wild!
Cheating others is cheating oneself; losing to oneself is losing to others.

Upside Down

Carrying out the act upside down results in inversion.
Only when upside down do the two things achieve completion.
Completion depends on carrying out the act upside down.
Carrying out the act upside down results in inversion.

"Upside down" means earth over heaven. Upside down means going
against the normal course. The common method goes with the normal
course, but the path of immortality lies in going against it. Following the
normal course leads to the fire of hell; going against it one becomes a
"golden immortal." Upside down, upside down; only then is there completion. Hey! You ought to know this! By her occupying the superior position,
west has come to east.

Utmost Sincerity

The desire for sagehood and the true lead requires utmost sincerity.
Utmost sincerity requires that we use mercury for the meeting.
If, in meeting, one fails to converge, it is vain to hope for sagehood.
The desire for sagehood and the true lead requires utmost sincerity.

The "desire for sagehood" refers to the heart's fondest hope. The "true lead" is the prenatal monadal true *qi*.[4] Desiring that this primordial monadal true *qi* come to us requires absolute seriousness, extreme care, and utmost sincerity. It is especially important that one mobilize a bit of "true mercury" in the region of one's own anus to welcome it. Moreover, this must be done just right. Hey! Be careful! The dragon must not seek the tiger, but the tiger must find the green dragon herself.

The Water Wheel

Capturing the *yangjing* is called obtaining the lead.
After obtaining the lead, it immediately ascends to heaven.
Having ascended to heaven for a count of nine times nine, it is
    securely captured.
Capturing the *yangjing* is called obtaining the lead.

"Capturing" means that it cannot escape again. "*Yangjing*" is the prenatal true singular *qi*, the gold within water. To obtain this is to obtain the lead. Carry out the practice of ascending up the back and descending down the front. Rising to the *niwan*[5] is called "ascending to heaven." After nine times nine revolutions, the golden elixir naturally forms. Hey! One needs the secret transmissions! To ascend to heaven one must start the wheel. Only then can the water rise.

4. Vital energy, breath (pneuma).
5. Literally, "Muddy Pellet," the central of the nine palaces inside a person's head.

TRANSMISSION OF THE MIND-LAMP
FROM MOUNT JIN'GAI
(*Jin'gai xindeng*)

MIN YIDE

Transmission of the Mind-Lamp from Mount Jin'gai (*Jin'gai xindeng*), by Min Yide (1748–1836), is an extensive account of the Longmen school of Complete Perfection (Quanzhen) Daoism—the most common Daoist lineage from the Qing dynasty to the present day—focusing in particular on an orthodox view of patriarchal succession. The Longmen school traces its (mythical) origins to Qiu Chuji (1148–1227), and its name derives from that of the sacred mountain where Qiu had practiced, Mount Longmen. The line of patriarchs allegedly begins with the transmission from Qiu to Zhao Xujing (lineage name Daojian, 1163–1221), as chronicled in the

"Biography of Zhao Daojian (1163–1221), the First Patriarch." It details how Zhao received "the bowl and the robe" along with a *gatha*, or poem—precisely the objects passed down from master to disciple within the Chan/Zen Buddhist tradition. In addition to these tokens of transmission, a new patriarch also received a lineage name that was made up of two Chinese characters, the first of which was chosen from a twenty-character Longmen poem (cited in Zhao Daojian's biography but not reproducefd below).

Wang Changyue, the seventh patriarch, is a key figure in the history of the Longmen school, whose institutional structure and patriarchal lineage took separate shape during his time. Some have even called this period, when the Longmen school became an official part of the Quanzhen tradition, a Quanzhen renaissance. The "Biography of Wang Changyue (?–1680)" contains a prophecy of his arrival as a manifestation of a Perfected One named Wang Qiaoyang, charts his spiritual career, and describes his ascetic training and search for enlightened masters. Indeed, it is a hallmark of the Longmen tradition that masters undertake ascetic retreats in mountains. Wang later assumed the position of abbot of the important White Cloud Abbey (Baiyun guan) in Beijing, where he became known for reviving Daoist monastic discipline.

PRONOUNCING GLOSSARY

Jin'gai xindeng: *chin-gai hsin-teng*   Wang Changyue: wang chawng-yu-eh
Min Yide: *mean yee-duh*   Zhao Daojian: *chao dow-chien*
Qiu: *chiu*

Biography of Zhao Daojian (1163–1221), the First Patriarch

"Here is the pillar of the Mysterious Teaching, the guide of Celestial Immortals. Some day, the charge of carrying on the Lamp of Mind by transmitting the method of precepts will be in your hands."[1]

Afterwards, Zhao followed the Patriarch [Qiu] to Yan [Beijing] for spreading the teaching. He acted in the world in spontaneous harmony and without talking. At times, even when he spent entire nights [with the Patriarch Qiu], he did not utter a word. The Patriarch [Qiu] thus transmitted to him the secret of spontaneity and pure emptiness, upon which Zhao withdrew to Mount Longmen for many years.

After having come out [from this retreat], he stayed with the Patriarch [Qiu] at the Baiyun guan[2] and gathered a great number [of disciples]. The fifteenth day of the first month of the *bingchen* year of the Zhiyuan era (1280), Zhao received the Initial Precepts of Perfection as well as the Intermediate Precepts. After having practiced in accordance with the rules without losing his prodigious virtue, the Patriarch personally transmitted the "seal of mind" to Zhao and confided to him the bowl and the robe.[3] Zhao received the Precepts of the Celestial Immortals along with a four-verse *gatha*[4] amounting to twenty characters that forms the Longmen poem.

TRANSLATED BY Monica Esposito. All bracketed additions are the translator's.

1. The speaker is Qiu Chuji, on the arrival of his disciple Zhao Daojian.
2. The White Cloud Abbey in Beijing.
3. Symbols of the transmission of the dharma

(the teachings of the Buddha); traditionally, they were the sole possessions of a Buddhist monk.
4. Literally, "verse" (Sanskrit); specifically, a metrical section of Buddhist scripture.

Biography of Wang Changyue (?–1680)

Lineage name: Changyue (Perseverance for Months)
Original name: Ping
Daoist name: Kunyang
Birth-place: Lu'an (Shanxi).

During his childhood, a Daoist told him after having observed him: "Qiao-yang has been reborn" and, having made this prophecy, was no more seen.

Although his parents respected Daoism and revered Zhang Mayi, [Wang] at the outset hardly showed any interest. After Zhang Mayi had passed by and given a great demonstration of his spiritual powers by healing him of a grave illness, Wang left his home to visit him. Though still adolescent, his mind, devoted to the Dao, was already tranquil. He traveled widely, visiting the famous mountains, and braved dangers and obstacles, wind and frost: thus he was on his way for months and years, cold season after hot. Before he noticed it, more than 80 years had passed. When he reached Mt. Wangwu,[5] his heart fluttered in premonition as if he were to meet a perfect being. This turned out to be the Perfected[6] Zhao Fuyang [Zhensong], who had lived there in seclusion for a long time. [Wang] implored him to instruct him, but the Perfected one did not respond for months. Nourishing himself from pine branches and pure sources, Wang prostrated and requested [Zhao's teaching] with increasing insistence. Mayi came by especially to support Wang's demand. [So Wang] obtained the [lineage] name Changyue (Persevering for Months) and learned that Zhang [Mayi] and the Perfected [Zhao] were friends. Furthermore, [Mayi] requested that the precepts be given [to Wang], and they were handed to him in two volumes. The Perfected [Zhao] gave him the following injunction: "Achieving the Way is extremely easy and at the same time extremely difficult. Ascetic practices are a definite prerequisite since the various external affairs must be gotten rid of once and for all. Adhere to the rules and keep them with care while immersing yourself in the classics. Realize the original hidden intent of the Daode[jing]'s 'self-so' and search for the true knack of the Nanhua [jing]'s[7] 'vitality', and you will be stable: 'a great vessel, is complete only in the evening' [i.e., late in life]."

Prostrating himself again, Wang received [Zhao's] teaching. Making the rounds of the mountains, he tasted all kinds of sweetness and bitterness. Without a moment's rest he sought to peruse the classics of all Three Teachings.[8] He came by an old Daoist monastery with countless Daoist scriptures and examined them day and night. Whenever his lamp was on the verge of going out, he lighted it anew with incense; in its radiance he read for eight or nine years. He went to question masters in more than twenty places and received the seal of approval of more than fifty people.

---

5. A sacred Daoist site, located in present-day Henan Province.
6. A Daoist spiritual master; a Daoist who has moved beyond earthly corruption.
7. The Zhuangzi (Book of Master Zhuang), which received the title Nanhua zhenjing (Authentic Scripture of Southern Florescence) when it was canonized as a "classic"; for that work, as well as the Daode jing (Scripture on the Way and Its Virtue), see above.
8. Buddhism, Daoism, and Confucianism.

THE HERMITS OF HUASHAN

This short account of two Longmen school Daoist masters, Ma Zhenyi and Wang Qingzheng (fl. 1650)—of the sixth and tenth generation, respectively—provides an evocative account of their hermitage on Mount Hua (Huashan), a sacred peak in present-day Shaanxi Province that is important in Daoist history. The passage, excerpted from the *Origins and Development of the Daoist Teachings of [Qiu] Changchun* (*Changchun daojiao yuanliu*), succinctly conveys their ascetic way of life in the mountains, their divine powers of prognostication, and their irreverent attitudes toward state officials. "The Hermits of Huashan" furnishes a revealing glimpse into a Longmen lineage that was outside the one propagated in the *Transmission of the Mind-Lamp from Mount Jin'gai* (*Jin'gai xindeng*; see previous selection). Before an orthodox lineage of Longmen patriarchs was constructed, many branch lineages, each with different characteristics, flourished in different regions.

PRONOUNCING GLOSSARY

Changguang: *chawng-kuang*   Huashan: *hwa-shawn*

[In this grotto] they had only rocks as beds. There were not any books or writings, nor alchemical furnaces or ingredients [for the preparation of the elixir]. With his disciple Changguang[1] and others, like the ignorant and dull, they did not discuss alchemical processes and did not perform any purification rites or offerings or use any talismans or registers. Their teachings were simply based on complete perfection as well as on purity and tranquillity. During the winter, they would bathe themselves, and hot vapors steamed up like in summer. When they were invited by functionaries to deal with drought, they did not erect any altar nor burn any incense but went on simply drinking a lot of wine without any further consideration. While they were drinking, rain fell in a downpour. When they were asked to tell a fortune, they answered in a snap, and they were always marvellously accurate.

TRANSLATED BY Monica Esposito. All bracketed additions are the translator's.

1. Wang Qingzheng (fl. 1650), who was the disciple of Ma Zhenyi, a Longmen master of the 6th generation.

IMMORTAL'S CERTIFICATE

The "Immortal's Certificate" is an official document that a Daoist seeking the rank of Great Master receives from his initiating master during an elaborate ordination ritual (*jiao*). The abbreviated example below, quoted in a liturgical manual from the late nineteenth century, provides insight into the ordination ritual. For example, the ordinand had to supply incense and "pledges" (offerings) to the initiating master before the ritual could take place. It also asserts the primacy of Daoism and subtly criticizes Buddhism as not "admirable" and unfit to bring "glory to the country," bring "peace to the family," or "preserve oneself."

During the ordination ritual a large number of written documents are generated and then burned as a means of informing the different offices (in heaven and in hell) of the name of the new master, who receives a new rank and title as well as a new religious name. Then, based on his date of birth (which dictates his fundamental destiny), the ordinand is assigned a stellar district, and he is able to choose the name of his altar and his place set aside for meditation and reflection. These details appear in full versions of the certificate, which also provide a list of deities that accompany the newly ordained master.

Ordination is followed by the installation ceremony, during which the ordinand is dressed in an exceedingly ornate official robe, puts on special boots, has his unbound hair gathered into a top knot (fastened with a special pin and covered with a crown), and receives the key ritual instruments: a bowl, sword, and audience tablet.

PRONOUNCING GLOSSARY

khakkara: khawk-kah-rah

Immortal's Certificate conferred by the Chancellery of the Three Heavens,[1] granting admission to rank and office.

Respectfully, it is noted that the Dao is unique and venerable as the creator of the Three Heavens, that, of the ten thousand practices, keeping is the most precious.[2] Thus, neither the tin staff (*khakkara*) [of Buddhists monks] nor the white robes [of sect members] can be considered admirable; only that which is transmitted secretly between allies and is capable of forging a True Heart[3] may be considered fit to promote civilization and bring glory to the country, to bring peace to the family, and to preserve oneself.

On this day, there is in this prefecture disciple so-and-so, heir to the ritual [tradition], whose Fundamental Destiny is controlled by his birth in such and such year (full date), and controlled from above by such and such star of the Dipper constellation.[4]

Considering that the above-mentioned disciple has sought refuge with his whole heart in the Orthodox Dao, that he intends to serve the Mysteries, and that he wishes to receive the transmission of the liturgical rites, without, however, having found an Eminent Master, and fearing that his name might not be known in the Palaces of the Heavens, and that he might not have any authority in the Offices of Hell, he was fortunately able to find heads of the community (their names are inserted here) who took from their own possessions to prepare the appropriate ceremonies. They have observed that the above-named disciple has a respectful behavior, that he is fully and firmly resolved, and that, consequently, he deserves that ordination [literally: "passage"] be conferred on him.

The disciple has respectfully presented incense and pledges in order to invite so-and-so, as Initiating Master, to come into the house [of the disciple] to install a ritual area and to lead the rites of transmission there.

TRANSLATED BY Karen C. Duval and Kristofer Schipper. All bracketed additions are the translator's.

1. Great Clarity (Taiqing), Jade Clarity (Yuqing), and Upper Clarity (Shangqing).
2. Keeping the One (shouyi) is a meditation practice that evolved throughout the development of Daoism. It generally involved attaining a one-pointedness of mind or an intense focus.

3. Related to the notion of "non-knowledge" [translator's note].
4. Daoists believe that each person's life is governed by a particular star of the Northern (Big) Dipper, as determined by the date of his or her birth.

Henceforward, when the above-named disciple—who has taken the oath "to effect transformation on behalf of Heaven" and to save men and benefit all beings—performs any liturgical services, at his home or elsewhere, we hope that he will obtain an immediate response, that by the solemn rites the gods will rejoice and the demons will submit, and that by the acts of purification all will know peace.

A SHAMANISTIC EXORCISM

This short passage drawn from a Qing dynasty gazetteer, an official local history that tends to reflect a Confucian bias, defines a particular type of ritual specialist whose practice combines Daoist and shamanistic features and describes how he performs an exorcism. Spirit mediums (*wu*) have long been closely linked with Daoism, but they have also drawn much Daoist critical opprobrium. One of the perennial questions in the study of Daoism has been the nature of the relationship between Daoism and popular religion (including shamans and spirit mediums). Some scholars argue for the model of a shamanistic substrata and Daoist superstructure: that is, Daoism (and Daoist ritual in particular) provides a structure that helps organize rites and practices common in Chinese popular religion. In this account of shamanistic exorcism from the *Gazetteer for Western Hunan* we see the overt mixing of aspects that are Buddhist (e.g., clothing), Daoist (a tablet emblazoned with charms and talismans), and popular, all brought to bear on curing the sick. This passage thus attests to the ongoing assimilation into Daoism of elements of popular religion; at the same time, conversely, different popular cults may have been incorporating aspects of Daoism for their own purposes.

PRONOUNCING GLOSSARY

duangong: *doo-awn-kung*
fantan: *fawn-tawn*

guanyin: *gwan-yin*

The term *duangong*[1] appears in the Yuan code; it is an ancient title. When the country people are ill, they mostly do not believe in doctors but get *wu*[2] to imprecate for them. This is called "dancing *duangong*" or "bearing the god."

When the *wu* appears it is always night time. He puts up a small table and arranges pictures of gods, and wooden images of the *fantan*,[3] the five demons and others. The sick person's family brings one pint of rice, and places tablets and incense candles on top. The *wu* wears a *guanyin* hat or a Seven Buddha hat,[4] and a red Buddhist robe, holding in his left hand a ring

---

TRANSLATED BY Donald Sutton.

1. A master of techniques to mediate between humans, gods, and spirits (often translated "shaman").
2. Usually translated "shaman" or "spirit medium."
3. Most likely a reference to the deity Zhang Wulang (Zhang the Fifth Brother), who was also known in this area as "The Overturner of Altars

and Destroyer of Temples" (*fantan pomiao*).
4. A crown-shaped hat with seven points that is tied onto the head of the shaman. Guanyin was a female bodhisattva—a being intent on enlightenment—identified in East Asian Buddhism with Avalokiteshvara, the bodhisattva regarded as the embodiment of all the compassion of all the buddhas.

knife, popularly called the master's knife which clatters noisily, and in his right hand a Daoist tablet[5] rounded at the top and square at the base, inscribed with charms and taboo words. He blows a horn, sings and dances, rises and falls, bows and kneels, in order to please his god. He spins like lightning, whirls like the wind, and scatters and burns the paper money. During this time come the motions of beseeching the master, withdrawing the sickness, summoning the soul and "destroying the temple."[6] Earlier, reeds have been cut to make a human figure, dressed in the sick person's clothes. It is offered wine and food, carried in a reed boat through the door, and burnt. This is called "substituting the reeds." Also the *wu* bears out the mask of the dragon spirit. It is said that if it is not carried properly he will catch the disease after the substitution. Sometimes too he prays to the birth star and dipper[7] and requests thirteen men to present a guarantee before the god of the eastern mountain. This is called "insuring happiness". *Wu* all have their particular schools which differ.

5. The command tablet, a wooden Daoist ritual implement that the priest slams on the altar table when he issues orders.
6. Humans have two souls: the *po* or white soul is the heavy soul, linked with the earth; the *hun* or cloud soul is the light soul, which is linked with heaven and its pneumas.
7. An individual's destiny is controlled by the deity of the star in the Northern (Big) Dipper who is governing at the time of his or her birth.

BIOGRAPHICAL STELE INSCRIPTION FOR THE DAOIST WANG
(*Wang daoren daoxing bei*)

"Biographical Stele Inscription for the Daoist Wang" ("Wang daoren daoxing bei") was cut in stone in 1903 for the Daoist priest Wang Junfeng. It tells how his ascetic practices (his silent retreat in the mountains, his barefoot begging through the snow to raise money to reconstruct a temple, etc.) won him acceptance by the Daoist monastic establishment in the capital, Beijing (Peking). But the course of Wang's life was changed by major historical events at the end of the Qing dynasty—especially the Boxer Rebellion, an effort in 1900 to drive all foreigners from China, and the rapid urbanization of Beijing. After foreign troops captured Beijing in 1900, Wang committed suicide in order to show his loyalty to the defeated court. Wang's stele inscription represents his death and afterlife as akin to premodern Daoist forms of release from the corpse (*shijie*), emphasizing that he merely "died to this corporeal existence"; following his (apparent) death, people claimed to have seen him roaming in the mountains.

PRONOUNCING GLOSSARY

Wang daoren daoxing bei: *wawng dow-run dow-hsing bay*

Wang Junfeng: *wawng chun-fung*
Zhen Youxu: *chun yo-hsu*

The Daoist Wang Junfeng hailed from the village of Xiaoliuzhi in Qi county, Taiyuan prefecture, Shanxi province. His complexion was red and his body fat, he had little hair and mustache, and his eyes shone like lightning: [as physiognomists put it,] he was like a "suspended river." By nature he was honest and hard working. He liked to solve problems for people and arbitrated conflicts, practiced medicine and gave away drugs; he rejoiced when he saw virtuous actions but took wickedness as his own enemy. Such was his innate nature. With just a robe and two hair buns, he wandered freely and had the looks of divine immortals. Early in his life he had come to Peking[1] to study commerce, but he failed [to establish himself] and instead took to practicing Daoism in an isolated place in the Western Hills. He met Transcendent Zhen [Zhen Youxu (1819–?)] of the Namo lineage, who took him as a disciple, instructed him personally and conferred on him the secret oral instructions of alchemical training.

After Wang had thus obtained the secret oral instructions, he retreated to practice them in the area of Blue Dragon Bridge and Juyong guan [north of Peking]. There he refined himself in silence for several years until his body and soul were firmly fixed. In 1881, he came to the Mashen miao [a temple in the Inner City]. At that time, the temple's halls were in ruin, having been neglected for years. Rain and wind had destroyed everything; the place offered a desolate view and was not habitable. Wang settled down between the dilapidated rooms and the crumbled walls. During daytime, he went out and begged for his living, and he returned at night to meditate there. He was pleased with his vegetarian fare and a miserable robe. Then our Daoist solemnly vowed to raise a subscription and restore the temple. With his disheveled hair and bare feet, he walked in the snow through the freezing cold of winter, or went around under the scorching heat of spring. He endured as a routine pains that other people considered unbearable. But utmost sincerity moves people, and eventually the Peking people held him in awe. Their contributions added up like hairs woven into a cloth, and the temple was restored to its former splendor. But, although the temple was now like new, it ran the risk of falling again into ruins if nobody continued the task of managing it. Fortunately, several persons notably Li [illegible name], Yang Dajing, and Jin Dachun came one after the other to take Wang as their master, supported him generously, and thereby ensured that Wang's sustenance was guaranteed. Dajing was deeply immersed in studying Daoist mysticism, and with him, Wang's oral secret transmission was ensured. Dachun served the master with particular diligence, and thus became a reliable support for him. Although these three disciples varied in their basic orientations, they served the master with the same absolute deference and equally strove to repay his kindness to them.

When the Allied armies[2] entered Peking in 1900 and the court fled westward, our Daoist felt that, as a Daoist, he was not called to defend our

TRANSLATED BY Vincent Goossaert. All bracketed additions are the translator's.

1. Then (as now) the capital of China, Beijing.
2. An international force composed of American, Austrian, British, French, Italian, Japanese, and Russian troops.

territory and our people, and that his destiny was to travel outside this world, but, heartbroken by his feelings of loyalty, he aspired to death as the return [to his true home]. The day the Allies entered the city walls, he hanged himself to be loyal to the regime. On that day, when he died to this corporeal existence, the people all sighed with shared grief. The body may perish, but determination is indomitable; a head can roll, but righteousness cannot be bent. This suicide was truly in the style of [those of] loyal ministers and heroes of yore. After these events, some people [claimed they] saw Wang in the mountains. Whether this really happened is difficult to decide, but true loyalty shines [forever], and numinous spirits live in eternity: this at least is definitely proven by reason. Therefore, those who say that our Daoist is still living are not in the wrong. These thoughts I now entrust to the stone.

Modern Chinese History and the Remaking of Daoism

FROM THE REPUBLICAN ERA (1912–1949) TO THE EARLY TWENTY-FIRST CENTURY

A series of events in the century leading up to the end of its last dynasty, the Qing (1644–1912), left China feeling disgraced and weak. As described in the introduction to the previous section, the increasing presence of Europeans, the signing of unequal treaties, the Opium Wars, and the Taiping Rebellion all forced the Chinese to recognize the superiority of Western science, technology, and military power. They also felt outmatched closer to home. For centuries Japan had looked to China for its cultural and scientific inspiration, but after the island's rapid modernization

Female Daoist priest talking on her mobile phone as she arrives at the Jade Spring Temple at the base of picturesque Mount Hua, the site of many Daoist temples.

following the Meiji Restoration in 1868 the roles were reversed and the Japanese stood poised to make imperialist incursions into the mainland. In the face of these different forms of humiliation, China desired to catch up and secure a more respectable position for itself on the world stage by modernizing swiftly, while at the same time retaining the heights of its traditional culture. These events at the end of the Qing also had a profound impact on the shape that Daoism would take in the twentieth and twenty-first centuries.

The tragic story of religion in modern Chinese history is now quite familiar. As will be discussed in more detail below, during the early twentieth century China struggled with a choice in moving forward to science and progress—whether to take the Western liberal path, associated with materialism and Western imperialism, or the Russian communist path, deeply influenced by the writings of Karl Marx (1818–1883) on religion and revolutions and thus ideologically committed to state atheism. In 1949, civil war ended with victory by the Communists, who began to institute large-scale social and cultural changes. During the Cultural Revolution (1966–76), persecution of religions increased dramatically and came close to eradicating that irksome opiate of the people. Daoist and Buddhist temples were confiscated and repurposed, and rituals and self-cultivation practices were outlawed. Yet the full history of Daoism during the twentieth century is a story not merely of erasure but also of resilience and persistence into the twenty-first century.

Surprising as it would have seemed to someone in the early 1970s, Daoism is once again flourishing in China, and has spread to Southeast Asia, Europe, and North America. Daoist temples in China are again integral parts of local communities, and sacred sites both are visited by devout pilgrims and function as key nodes in domestic tourism. Rituals are regularly performed by ordained Daoist priests in urban and rural settings, Daoist festivals draw huge crowds, and in 2007 the Chinese government even co-sponsored a massive symposium, "The Way to Harmony: International Forum on the *Daodejing*," that drew delegates from about twenty countries.

By the late twentieth century, *The Scripture of the Way and Its Virtue* had been translated more than 300 times into many languages. The German philosopher Martin Heidegger (1889–1976) even took a crack at it one summer with the help of a Chinese assistant. What some prefer to call "versions" of Daoist classics also began to be produced by people who felt they could capture the essence of Daoism without knowing a single word of Chinese (see Ursula K. Le Guin's introduction to and selections from her *Tao Te Ching*, 1997). Elements of Daoism also found their way into the works of European writers (see Oscar Wilde's "A Chinese Sage," 1890) and the lyrics and ideas of popular musicians (see the Beatles' "The Inner Light," 1968, and works by the Wu-Tang Clan, a hip-hop group whose name is derived from Mount Wudang, sacred to Daoists). At present, American spiritual seekers can attend Daoist retreats and participate in tours to Daoist sites in China.

The recent efflorescence of Daoism in China and around the world would have been unthinkable a few decades ago, when religion was nearly erased from the Chinese landscape. But somehow Daoism found a way to survive and thrive. Indeed, contemporary Daoism has been colored by its challenges and opportunities, and in its complex response it has transformed, adapted, and reconfigured itself in a new political and cultural environment.

CHINA'S TURBULENT TWENTIETH-CENTURY HISTORY

Chinese history during the first half of the twentieth century is filled with drama and trauma. The initial optimism of the revolutionaries who helped bring down the Qing dynasty and establish the Republic of China (1912–49), with the hope of transforming China into a modern state, was short-lived. The first Chinese president, Yuan Shikai (1859–1916), unsuccessfully sought to make himself a dictator; after he died, China slipped back into disorder as battles were fought by entrenched interests vying for power in different regions. China also had to contend with threats to its sovereignty posed by imperialist foreign powers, particularly Japan. In 1931 the Japanese concocted a justification for their military invasion of Manchuria, where they established their puppet state, Manchukuo, in 1932. The Nationalists and the Communists curtailed their fighting long enough to unify the country in resisting the Japanese incursions that came later in 1937, but they rejoined their conflict immediately after Japan's defeat in 1945. That civil war ended with the Communists, under the leadership of Mao Zedong (1893–1976), in power on the mainland in the newly founded People's Republic of China, while the Nationalist government of Chiang Kai-shek (1888–1975) was sequestered on the island of Taiwan. The history of this period is intertwined with modern concerns about state formation, nationalism and anti-imperialism, liberal democracy, science, technology, education, health, gender relations, and attitudes toward religion.

To consider early twentieth-century China solely from the perspective of political and military history misses important facets of its efforts to build a strong modern country. As generals devised plans to counter the rise of local warlords and foreign imperialists—which is to say, to hold China together against internal fragmentation and external domination—a cohort of young intellectuals, many of whom had studied overseas, was pondering ways to bring China into the modern age and regain the respect of other nations. This new breed of intellectuals had witnessed the sorry condition of a failed republic. Those who spent time abroad—for example, in Japan, France, and the United States—had opportunities to witness firsthand the fruits of scientific, technological, and political development, which led them to feel embarrassed about the state of contemporary China. Those sentiments came to a head on May 4, 1919, when news reached China that the Versailles Peace Conference, which was negotiating the treaty to end World War I, was going to grant the rights in Shandong formerly held by the Germans to the Japanese. Thousands of students at Beijing University marched to Tiananmen Square to vent their anger and protests spread throughout the country, ushering in a period of Chinese nationalism founded on expressions of anti-imperialism and the need to modernize in accordance with newly introduced ideas of science and democracy. To accomplish that end, the reformers argued, China had to break free of old beliefs and traditions, which they blamed for China's backwardness.

These activists did not want to merely imitate the imperialist Western countries, for they were also reluctant to sacrifice what it meant to be Chinese. The May Fourth Movement mobilized prominent intellectuals such as Hu Shi (1891–1962), who had studied in the United States, and the famous writer Lu Xun (1881–1936), who had studied in Japan. The progressive ideas taught abroad and in newly established modern Chinese schools drove cultural transformation during this period. As the intellectuals sought to reform the Chinese educational system and Chinese literature, they also issued trenchant critiques of Confucianism, which they blamed for inhibiting Chinese progress with its pernicious conservative familial and social values. Meanwhile, world-famous intellectuals were traveling to China to give talks and share their ideas, among them the American philosopher and educational reformer John Dewey (1859–1952), the British philosopher and social critic Bertrand Russell (1872–1970), the German biologist Hans Adolf Eduard Driesch (1867–1941), the German-born American scientist Albert Einstein (1879–1955), and the Indian writer and philosopher Rabindranath Tagore (1861–1941).

At the same time, the Bolshevik Revolution of 1917 focused attention on the writings of Marx and Vladimir Lenin (1879–1924), and later the political example of Joseph Stalin (1879–1953), which proposed an evolutionary theory of society that culminated in socialism. Up until 1917, there had been much interest in anarchist thinkers and ideas, which sought to break the individual's dependence on the state and foster a sense of individual liberation. After 1917, Chinese intellectuals began to hold Marxist study meetings at the major universities: Marxist-Leninist ideas about class struggle and the need to bring down those in power, particularly capitalist exploiters and imperialists, began to spread among intellectuals and students. One student deeply influenced by those meetings was Mao Zedong. In 1921, the Chinese Communist Party was formed in Shanghai, with outside support from the Moscow-based Communist International (Comintern), whose purpose was to promote communist revolutions around the world.

From the early 1920s through 1949, the relationship between the Communists and the more numerous Nationalists shifted between strategic cooperation, especially when opposing the rise of Japan, and violent opposition. In 1934, the Nationalists drove the Communists from their base in the southeast; the troops retreated to Yan'an a year later, undertaking a 6,000-mile trek that became known as the Long March and that established Mao as the party leader. In 1937, Beijing and Tianjin fell to the Japanese, who then moved on to the south and captured the capital, Nanjing—where mass killings and rapes occurred in what came to be known as the Rape of Nanjing—and, eventually, most of eastern China. Japan's dominance in Asia grew in the 1940s. During this period popular support for the Nationalists fell while that for the Communists rose. From Yan'an, Mao consolidated his power and drew peasants under the banner of Marxist-Leninist ideology. He became known as a perceptive strategist who was merciless in eliminating his opponents. As Mao's stature grew, so did the people's hatred of Japan, as word spread of the forced prostitution of women and rampant destruction of villages. On September 2, 1945, less than a month after the United States dropped nuclear bombs on Hiroshima and Nagasaki, the Japanese formally surrendered to the Allies, ending World War II. At that time more than a million Japanese troops, and more then two million Japanese civilians, were in China. In "Daoist Monastic Life" we are afforded an intimate glimpse of this turmoil from the viewpoint of a Japanese scholar studying Daoism in Beijing's White Cloud Abbey, then the leading Daoist institution in China.

China's problems did not end with the defeat of Japan. Once their common enemy was vanquished, the Communists and Nationalists quickly turned on each other. In 1949, after years of fighting, the civil war ended and China was unified under the control of the Chinese Communist Party, who founded the People's Republic of China. The Nationalists were forced to retreat to the island of Taiwan, where they set up their government and have remained to the present day.

Reconfiguring Religion in the Modernizing Chinese State: From Dynastic China to the People's Republic of China (1912–1949)

The determination of Chinese intellectuals and political figures to modernize and establish a new national culture based on Western science and technology—even while desiring to preserve the traditional Chinese identity—put religion on shaky ground. But the Marxist-Leninist ideas that were competing with the promises of Western liberalism posed an even greater threat. For Karl Marx, religion was nothing more than an illusion that aided an oppressive state in keeping the status quo: "*Religious* suffering is at the same time the *expression* of real suffering and a *protest* against real suffering. Religion is the sigh of the oppressed creature, the sentiment of a heartless world, and the soul of a soulless condition. It is the *opium* of the people." It was noxious, so the argument went, because it kept people numb to the realities of their condition: "The abolition of religion as the *illusory* happiness of men, is a demand for their *real* happiness. The call to abandon their illusions about their condition is *a call to abandon a condition which requires illusion*."[1] Marx saw religion as an illusion that relies on the promise that heaven awaits them to keep the poor docile and content in their misery; it would naturally disappear once the social systems that cause the need for religious escape were destroyed. This view of religion's relationship to society became a cornerstone of the political systems of first the Soviets and then the Chinese. During this period, religion in China was recategorized and radically reconfigured; the upheaval affected the development of Daoism throughout the twentieth century and has deeply colored Chinese and world perceptions of Daoism to the present day.

The victory of "scientism"—the belief that everything is knowable by scientific methods, and that traditional religion is an anachronistic vestige of the past—may have been almost complete among the Communist Party elite, yet they did not call for the total suppression of religion. Rather, Chinese religion had to be reshaped into what was considered a legitimate form. Its new parameters were Western and indeed historically Christian; but for the modernizing Chinese state, what mattered was their perception as modern. The republican Chinese state had strategically appropriated the Western term "religion"—translated by the already-existing word *zongjiao*, which was redefined in explicit opposition to "superstition" (*mixin*). Both terms had acquired new meanings in Japan under the influence of Christian

---

1. Karl Marx, "Contribution to the Critique of Hegel's *Philosophy of Right*: Introduction," in *The Marx-Engels Reader*, ed. Robert C. Tucker, 2nd ed. (New York: Norton, 1972), p. 54 (emphases his).

missionaries. "Religion" now had to be something set off from other domains of society and culture. Moreover, in order to be modern, it had to include the familiar trappings of most forms of Christianity: an identifiable clergy, a church as the location of its practice, and a set canon of sacred scriptures articulating its belief system.

Chinese religious traditions, thus reconceptualized, were hemmed in by new requirements and new restrictions, and yet "freedom of religion" (similarly on the Western model) was also an innovation of this period. China's first provisional constitution from 1912 names five legitimate religions: Buddhism, Daoism, Islam, Protestantism, and Catholicism. At the same time, other religions—such as local cults and sectarian groups—were outlawed on the grounds that they were too disorganized or were plagued by superstitious beliefs and practices. Indeed, religion had to be sharply delineated from debased superstition, which was officially outlawed in 1929 following a series of violent anti-superstition campaigns.

Pressures brought on by the new conceptualization of religion and the anti-superstition campaigns affected all forms of traditional Chinese religious practice, and to find a place in the shifting Chinese religious landscape Daoists were forced to articulate a vision of themselves that was congruent with modernity and the principles of science. "Taoism: A Prize Essay," which was submitted to the World's Parliament of Religions in Chicago in 1893, offers an early view of how Daoism was to be reimagined. In that document, a member of the Chinese Daoist clergy portrays the religion as having gone astray from what he describes as the pure original teachings of Laozi in *The Scripture of the Way and Its Virtue* to become a degenerate religion focused on magic, miracles, charms, incantations, and beliefs about an elixir of immortality.

The two main lineages of Daoism that were able to secure a place as legitimate religions were the Complete Perfection (Quanzhen) and Orthodox Unity (Zhengyi) traditions, which had also defined Daoism in the final century of the Qing dynasty. Complete Perfection Daoism, with its monastic structure, had the clearest rationale for winning approval under the new conditions. It was Daoists from this lineage who became leaders of the Daoist Association (Daojiao hui), established in 1912 as Daoism's first modern national organization. Its history reveals the issues most germane to contemporary Chinese Daoism as it sought to reinvent itself as a modern religion. The Daoist Association's claim that Daoism was China's oldest native religious tradition suited the nationalist leanings of the state. Daoists also tried to make their tradition fit the new Western category of religion by attempting to institute Sunday services, and they boasted that they were a world religion with plans to launch branches worldwide. Moreover, the association was careful to distinguish Daoism from superstitious cults.

The other Daoist lineage with a venerable past was the Orthodox Unity tradition. Though it had declined in comparison to the Complete Perfection lineage, it retained some power and legitimacy because it continued to control the ordination certificates issued from its headquarters on Dragon Tiger Mountain (Longhushan). Those ordination documents were important for providing Daoist priests throughout China with a semblance of legitimacy.

While official recognition might appear to be of undeniable benefit to the five religions named by the state, the changes in the definition of religion were particularly detrimental to Daoism, as they tended to exclude its traditional forms. The early twentieth-century transformations in what it meant to be religious therefore served as a catalyst for reimagining Daoism. To present Daoism as a religion amenable to the strictures of the modernizing Chinese state required downplaying elements that might be construed as superstitious (elixirs, charms, and talismans) and highlighting the philosophy of Laozi, teachings on moral self-cultivation, and an interest in health and medicine.

Chen Yingning (1880–1969), an important Daoist of this period, exemplifies those trying to negotiate the new religious terrain by incorporating scientific thinking, along with a concern for constructing a modern state, into their teachings (see his *Explorations in Oral Secrets*). Chen established parallels between a healthy and vigorous body—which he stressed could best be achieved through Daoist internal alchemy practices, as he had reformulated them—and a strong and healthy nation. He was able to package traditional Daoist self-cultivation practices in a way congruent with science and modern medicine, thereby preventing them from being labeled superstitious religious pursuits.

Beyond the safe terrain of Daoist philosophy and science, however, other forms of Daoism suffered. Home-based ritual masters who had no unified organization, no single leader, and no set belief system articulated in sacred texts found themselves under particular threat, as their activities were reclassified as superstition and prohibited by law. Daoism faced many significant challenges as it tried to orient itself to the new political and religious realities after the fall of the Qing empire. Nonetheless, despite those difficulties and despite explicit critiques of Daoism, many Daoist beliefs and practices became infused into other newly forming religions, which helped keep those Daoist elements alive.

During the Republican period numerous spirit writing and related groups, generally called "redemptive societies" by scholars, attained adherents numbering in the millions by popularizing key aspects of Daoist practice mixed with elements drawn from other religions. They successfully presented themselves as a reformed, scientific, and more accessible form of Daoism. These redemptive societies—the Way of Pervading Unity (Yiguandao, which became the largest in China and Taiwan), Li Sect (Zailijiao), Fellowship of Goodness (Tongshanshe), and School of the Way (Daoyuan)—successfully organized in the context of a crumbling Chinese state as modern religions capable of using eclectic beliefs and practices as a means to cure the world of Western materialism. They also drew on a mix of Buddhism and Confucianism, and in their self-conscious attempt to fashion themselves as both modern and universal—in opposition to superstitious cults—they integrated elements from Protestantism, Catholicism, and Islam as well. Redemptive societies were generally concerned with self-cultivation practices aimed at universal salvation. They used modern methods of communication to spread their message widely. At times, when downplaying their religious activities was necessary, they emphasized their philanthropic and charitable activities. As successful as they were in adapting to the shifting political and religious currents from the 1910s up through the 1930s, some of the sectarian groups and redemptive societies were periodically subjected to interdictions—such as the anti-superstition campaigns of the late 1920s—until they finally were caught in the ruthless crackdowns on religion by the People's Republic of China.

The Totalitarian Ordeal (1949–1976): From the Maoist Victory through the Cultural Revolution

Following the victory of the Communists and the foundation of the People's Republic of China in 1949, religion in China—particularly the already diminished Daoist tradition—faced even graver challenges. Complicating these struggles was the state's inconsistency, as the default condition of unrelenting hostility to religion was punctuated by episodes of some variety of state support. Sometimes Buddhism and Daoism were viewed as legitimate religions, sometimes as exploitative feudal institutions. What counted as legitimate forms of religious practice was precisely specified, and the Communist government was willing to protect the people's rights to engage in them. Indeed, Article 88 of the 1954 constitution guaranteed "freedom of religious belief"—but that freedom could be exercised only among a limited set of options. The Communist leaders seemed to believe that the problem of religion would ultimately resolve itself: as class struggle played itself out and society transformed after the revolutionary victory, religion would naturally recede.

Some religious groups, like the redemptive societies, did not enjoy constitutional protection and were instead condemned as counterrevolutionary and reactionary. In "Why Must We Prohibit the Reactionary Daoist Cults?" (1953), a radio address broadcast at the height of the 1953–54 campaign against redemptive societies, we can hear the vehemence of the attack leveled at one of the most popular of them (the Way of Pervading Unity). Because the redemptive societies were closely associated with Daoism, in the campaign against them some Daoists were also rounded up and arrested.

The controls on religion could also be quite subtle. When the National Daoist Association was reestablished in 1957, with Chen Yingning as its secretary-general, it joined other national patriotic religious organizations corresponding to the official religions: the Chinese Buddhist Association, the Chinese Islamic Association, the Chinese Catholic Patriotic Association, and the Chinese Protestant "Three-Self" Patriotic Movement. Ostensibly formed to help promote and protect religious freedoms, they also aided the state in its efforts to shape and control religion.

During the Great Leap Forward (1958–61), Mao's spectacularly unsuccessful attempt to speed up China's modernization and industrialization, large-scale communes were established in the countryside and most of the remaining Daoist institutions were eliminated or abandoned. As part of the campaign, religious leaders attended political education meetings, and some Daoists expressed their acceptance of and support for the rural communes (see "Buddhists and Daoists at Mount Nanyue Welcome the People's Communes").

From 1960 until the Cultural Revolution began in 1966, Daoism was mainly ignored as irrelevant. Except for the Complete Perfection monastic movement, it was generally considered to be nothing more than a hodgepodge of debased superstitious practices. Daoism did not offer anything that could be marshaled in the service of state formation; and unlike Buddhism, it could not serve to help link China to larger transnational movements involving other postcolonial developing countries.

Just when it seemed that Daoism had passed through one of the darkest periods of its history, it was further weakened by the Cultural Revolution. One of hallmarks of that massive mobilization was an all-out attack on the four "olds" (old ideas, customs, culture, and habits), which intensified the suppression of feudal superstitions. These policies were enforced by gangs of militant youths, the Red Guards, who sought to destroy everything connected with China's venerable ancient traditions, including Daoist and Buddhist temples and images, and who publicly denounced as "bourgeois" anyone in positions of power or prestige, such as university professors, intellectuals, and priests. Yet despite the enormous destruction wrought by the Cultural Revolution, it did not—contrary to

Propaganda poster from the Cultural Revolution depicting the destruction of the old in order to build the new. This worker is smashing a variety of religious images.

common belief—completely eradicate religion from China. Daoism would reemerge with a new exuberance in the 1980s and 1990s.

The Relaxation of Controls on Religion (1976 to the Present) and the Daoist Revival

The Cultural Revolution drew to a close in 1976. Under Deng Xiaoping (1904–1997), who led the country from 1978 to 1992, religious beliefs and practices revived as the Chinese Communist Party adopted a somewhat more lenient policy toward them, which included new guarantees on religious freedoms as well as the freedom to not believe.

During the 1980s there were major efforts to reclaim and restore Daoist temples that had earlier been confiscated. At a time of intense focus on regulating which sites were officially sanctioned, the state-formed Chinese Daoist Association played a significant role: it was the body charged with issuing the permits demonstrating that temples were recognized by the state as legitimate sites of religious activity. While many famous Daoist temples were reopened under its auspices, others retained their secular repurposing as museums or schools; still others preferred to remain independent in order to preserve a modicum of autonomy. The large Daoist temples that have been reestablished since 1980 have become the outward face of contemporary Daoist culture and prime sites to display a modern Daoism refashioned to suit the twentieth and twenty-first centuries. In addition to providing a limited menu of ritual offerings, these official Daoist

People at the White Cloud Temple in Beijing rub and place coins on a stone relief of a rabbit for good luck on New Year's Day 2011, the first day of the Year of the Rabbit.

institutions focus on the dissemination of information about self-cultivation practices and ethical teachings. Increasingly they have become major tourist attractions and the main purveyors of Daoist religious objects and paraphernalia.

One of the difficulties of accurately assessing and studying Daoist movements during this period is that the greatest numbers of religious actors remained outside of the officially sanctioned form of Daoism and among the scattered traditions of live-at-home priests—non-monastic Daoists with small-scale altars at their homes and no institutional affiliation (though they are sometimes employed for rituals by the larger Daoist temples). Most recently, however, some Daoists operating from home altars have attained legitimacy and are once again performing the traditional ritual services for their communities. In addition, the name Daoism—as a label for a religious tradition—was not always used by religious groups, by ritual specialists, or by the clients of those traditions. Nevertheless, these movements do incorporate rituals, symbols, ideas, and texts from Daoism, mixed together with elements from other religions. Modern Chinese religious practice is not characterized by exclusive devotion to single religious traditions. Hybrid movements, especially those that concentrate on body cultivation, are flourishing in contemporary Chinese society; in contrast, the one unambiguously Daoist movement that enjoys state sanction, the Complete Perfection tradition, is the least vibrant.

For example, *qigong*, a practice with deep roots in Daoism and Buddhism though part of neither, became popular and spread widely throughout society in what some have called the "*qigong* boom" of the 1980s and 1990s. *Qigong* combines physical posture, breathing techniques, and mental focus, and at its emergence in the 1950s it claimed to be grounded in science and health care. From the state's perspective, this emphasis on scientific mass self-cultivation for health made the movement potentially useful in the effort to remedy China's weakened state and transform the nation into a world power. Therefore, even in the religiously volatile atmosphere after 1949, political leaders actively promoted *qigong* and its health benefits until 1964, when it was banned at the height of religious persecution. *Qigong* reemerged in the 1970s and spread like wildfire throughout China in the 1980s. Average citizens once again congregated in parks to practice breathing and other self-cultivation practices together as part of a mass movement. But later it came under attack on two fronts. As some *qigong* practitioners began making claims about supranormal powers and attempting to prove those claims, there was a backlash led by scientists who branded *qigong* "superstition." In addition, the *qigong* boom created hugely popular charismatic leaders—most notably Li Hongzhi (b. 1952), the founder of Falun Gong—who defied state control. In response, the government called Falun Gong a superstitious cult; and after thousands of followers protested the label by demonstrating at the Communist Party Headquarters in 1999, the movement was outlawed. Since that time, public *qigong* practice has almost completely disappeared.

THE GLOBALIZATION OF DAOISM

At precisely the moment when Daoism was most under fire at home and its future existence most seriously threatened, it was spreading widely to other parts of Asia and the world. This, of course, was not Daoism's first movement out of China; as we have seen, the globalization of Daoism began centuries earlier. During the eighteenth and nineteenth centuries Daoist ideas and rituals were migrating to the Yao areas of northern Thailand (see "The Dao among the Yao of Southeast Asia," above) and into Vietnam. Aided in part by an increase in Chinese emigration, by the mid-twentieth century sophisticated transnational Daoist networks linked certain Chinese regions with communities in Southeast Asia, including—in addition to Vietnam and Thailand—Malaysia (see "Two Prayers to the Deified Laozi from Penang, Malaysia"), Indonesia, and Singapore. These Daoist networks help ideas and resources flow in both directions.

One significant migration out of mainland China occurred in 1949, as the Nationalists fled to Taiwan following their defeat. They were accompanied by the 63rd Daoist Celestial Master, Zhang Enbu, and many others who had been involved with the religious modernization project. The trends that had begun on the mainland continued in Taiwan, and the transformations within Daoism boosted its appeal to an increasingly cosmopolitan Taiwanese population. As a result, Daoism has flourished in Taiwan, one of the main locations where Daoist ritual practices and temple festivals have been preserved. Much of what scholars knew about Daoism prior to the 1980s came from research and fieldwork conducted there (see "Memorial for a Communal Ritual" and "Announcement for a Communal Ritual," both from a Daoist temple in southern Taiwan). Given that Taiwan is just across the Taiwan Strait from Fujian Province (on the southern coast of the mainland), it is not surprising that some of the earliest information on the contemporary revival of Daoism on the mainland came from Fujian (see "A Daoist Ordination Certificate from Putian, Fujian").

By the sixteenth century, knowledge about Daoism had already entered Europe, albeit filtered through the interpretation of Jesuit missionaries (see Matteo Ricci's "Religious Sects among the Chinese," above). Europeans continued to learn more about Daoism during the nineteenth and twentieth centuries, primarily through translations of Daoist texts. Alfred, Lord Tennyson, for instance, wrote his poem "The Ancient Sage" (1885) after reading an English translation of *The Scripture of the Way and Its Virtue*. A few years later, the Irish writer and wit Oscar Wilde published "A Chinese Sage," which was his reflection on Herbert Giles's 1889 translation of the *Book of Master Zhuang*. While intellectuals in China were trying to present Daoism as able to contribute to the fashioning of a modern society, Wilde read Zhuangzi's words as a scathing criticism of modern life, useful for exposing the artifice of society. In the late 1800s James Legge (1815–1897), the missionary Oxford scholar who collaborated with Max Müller on *The Sacred Books of the East* series, was hard at work on inventing an image of Daoism for the Victorian age based on his philosophical interpretation of *The Scripture of the Way and Its Virtue*.

During the nineteenth and twentieth centuries Daoist beliefs and practices also started to become visible in North America. For some Westerners—philosophers, intellectuals, and others—Daoism was primarily an imaginative creation of "Eastern spirituality" or "Oriental mysticism," an understanding that was consistent with the thought of Western New Age movements. Daoists and their critics in China were attempting to shift the discourse on Daoism away from a focus on metaphysics (see Qian Zhongshu's *Limited Views: Essays on Ideas and Letters*, 1979–80) and toward the direction of science, while some scientists in the West, such as the physicist Fritjof Capra in *The Tao of Physics* (1975), were arguing that Daoism—which he understood as an Eastern metaphysical tradition—had prefigured conclusions about the physical world that modern science was just now discovering.

There have been different waves in the Western appropriation of Daoism. Not just Daoist ideas and philosophy but also some Daoist practitioners traveled to the United States, where they established Daoist temples and Daoist centers. Most of the Daoist temples that were opened in the 1960s and 1970s—in San Francisco, New York, and Toronto, for example—were extensions of Daoist temples in Hong Kong and Taiwan. Others have been initiated by Westerners, such as Liu Ming (born Charles Belyea, 1947), founder of Orthodox Daoism of America, and Alex Anatole, a Russian émigré who set up the Center for Traditional Taoist Studies in Weston, Massachusetts. Another modern Western Daoist organization that has become quite successful, with an international reach, is Healing Tao, which was begun by Mantak Chia (b. 1944) and then expanded by his disciple Michael Winn (b. 1952). Healing Tao is based on Daoist internal alchemy practice mixed with meditation, visualization, and breathing exercises.

The revival of religions in China and Daoism's spread abroad have continued into the twenty-first century. Despite earlier predictions, China has not become and shows no sign of becoming entirely secular. Daoism has survived intense religious, political, and ideological attacks on religion in modern China, and it is known to millions outside of China. Daoist institutions weathered overwhelming adversity to be restored in contemporary China and even established in other parts of the world. Nevertheless, contemporary surveys on Chinese religions show Daoism to be lagging behind

Buddhism and Christianity in its number of followers. This poor showing may say more about the difficulties of defining what counts as Daoist than about the actual state of Daoism. The officially sanctioned Daoist lineages (Complete Perfection and Orthodox Unity) represent only a minority of Daoists, far outnumbered by the Daoists of the decentralized traditions, such as priests living at home and members of groups with different names that incorporate a copious amount of Daoism. Such practitioners cannot be represented and quantified in surveys whose purview is artificially constrained by the state's refusal to acknowledge any religions other than the official five under its control. Recently, however, practitioners concerned about being on the wrong side of the divide between religion and superstition have begun registering their local cults as Daoist organizations and packaging their rituals within Daoist frameworks, hoping to thereby gain a semblance of legitimacy and avoid government censure.

Yet it appears that the real religious action in China today is taking place not within the five officially sanctioned religions but in movements outside their boundaries. There, Daoist ideas and practices are flourishing. Daoist elements pervade a variety of health-related self-cultivation practices rooted in internal alchemy, and they are also found in martial arts traditions, Taijiquan (better known in the West as tai chi)—which has largely replaced *qigong*, since it is classified as a kind of sport—local communal movements, and traditional Chinese medicine (alternative medicine), as well as on the international stage. The religious institution labeled "Daoism" may have declined, but practices derived from Daoism are thriving.

The last entry in this volume, Zhang Jiyu's "A Declaration of the Chinese Daoist Association on Global Ecology" (1995), reveals another side of Daoism. It can be understood as part of a much larger effort to formulate a "New Daoism" for the twenty-first century—a Daoism that is relevant to contemporary concerns, such as environmentalism and gender equality. Health-related body cultivation practices and Daoist ideas about nature and ecology may have spread overseas and become popular among immigrant communities and Westerners, but to most of the world the strongest associations of the name Daoism (or "Taoism," with an aspirated *t*) are with the philosophical teachings represented by Laozi and Zhuangzi. The texts and ideas of those early thinkers—especially *The Scripture on the Way and Its Virtue* (*Laozi*)—have spread around the world and are now familiar to millions, from elite intellectuals to musicians, poets, and consumers of popular culture. Even as the formal institutions of Chinese Daoism may be fading, philosophical ideas drawn from classical texts that long predate those institutions are supporting Daoism as a world religion.

THE DAO AMONG THE YAO OF
SOUTHEAST ASIA: SELECTED TEXTS

Records from northern Thailand, Vietnam, and Laos—which mostly take the form of inscriptions on the back of iconographic paintings—demonstrate the spread of Daoism among the Yao peoples of Southeast Asia. All of the texts included below date from the nineteenth and twentieth centuries. Some scholars have asserted, however, that their contents bear a striking resemblance to those of Song dynasty (960–1279) Daoist texts, suggesting that Daoists and their texts had migrated into Southeast Asia centuries earlier. It now seems clear that the Yao communities of Southeast Asia originated in Guangxi, a province in southern China. The religious practices of the Chinese Yao, which today are referred to as Plum Mountain Daoism (Meishan Daoism), can be found in a wide area encompassing parts of Sichuan, Hunan, Yunnan, Guizhou, and Guangxi. Scholars still debate whether the Yao of Southeast Asia adapted Daoism to their indigenous rituals and traditions or instead employed Daoist rituals as a kind of protective covering to shield their own practices from what might be understood as a civilizing project. In either case, the materials below testify to how a regional form of Daoism imported from China took root in Southeast Asia.

PRONOUNCING GLOSSARY

Guangxi: *gwawng-hsi*   Tang Falian: *tawng faw-leean*

The disciple of Dao, Tang Falian, decided to invite Liu Deqing, the painter from the distant hills, to paint for his major altar a quantity of holy pictures, seventeen in number, for a total price of five ounces of silver and five cash[1] of copper. In the days to come his respectful heirs, children and grandchildren in the nine branches and for a thousand generations, must make offerings without cease, and pray for the protection of this family altar, and for the prosperity and peace of all who live in this house. May husbandry increase the flocks and may the five cereals[2] give harvests in great abundance! When they aim after wealth may the profits come, and may the Fragrant Gate (of this house) prosper, so that this House of the Dao may number 1,000 souls and receive 10,000 bushels of grain, 10,000 granaries bursting with the five grains, and sons and grandsons crowding the ceremonial hall! May gold and silver accrue in quantity, may flourishing trade bring an even greater prosperity! All the foregoing was favourably received this nineteenth day of the second month in the twenty second year of Daoguang[3] (1842), in the year Renyin.

✻　✻　✻

Time: In the eighth year of the Xianfeng reign period of the Qing Dynasty,[4] Mouwu Year (1858), the ninth day of the ascending second spring moon,

---

TRANSLATED BY Jacques Lemoine, with the assistance of Donald Gibson.

1. A Chinese coin of small value.
2. That is, the staple agricultural crops.
3. The reign period of 1820–50 (the 8th Qing

emperor).
4. 1644–1912; the Xianfeng reign period was 1850–61 (the 9th Qing emperor).

the Master of the House made up his mind to invite the painter Huang Jinlong (or *Yang Chiem Luang*) to execute one full altar of gods' pictures for the reward of five ounces of silver and nine cash of copper, the 'opening of the eyes'[5] not included.

Let them protect the wealth of the House Lord, may the five cereals give him an abundant harvest, may the six animals[6] become flocks, and through this priest's gate let there pass much great good fortune, swelling in plenty through ten thousand generations!

*   *   *

On the 23rd day of the second month in the 22nd year of Jiaqing,[7] Dingzhou Year (1817), the houselord, Lei Fazhou, invited the artists, father and sons, four people altogether from the Shanglin district of the Bin department, in the Szu En Prefecture of Guangxi, the father being Yang Chiem Luang (son of) Gwin and the sons Yang Hsun Tong, Hsun Fin, Hsun Meng, to create in all sixteen pictures of the gods for which the houselord presented a price of five ounces of silver and nine copper cash.

Let them thereafter protect the houselord, so that his household may increase in numbers, his cereals crops be more abundant, the wealth of his people accumulate, his domestic animals become flocks! Let the house have five boys and two girls, seven children together, an altar full of gold and jade, the five cereals bursting from the granaries, sons and grandsons in ten directions[8] so that the incense shall burn without cease and the hooves of the horses will not flee, for the great auspiciousness. And this was done at the Dashi ("Big Stone") (tribal) settlement, in Meng La, at dawn.

*   *   *

(2)[9]   On the 5th day of the first month, Yimao day, in the 14th year of Jiaqing, Jisi Year (1809), after choosing an auspicious day, I invited Yang Chiem Hsiou and Yang Chiem Kua, Bingzhou artists, to paint (for me) until (3)   the 12th, a Renjia day, when the work was finished and the pictures dotted.[1]

(4)   I reverently hope

(5)   that the Master Ze Fuyong, endowed with the Great Dao high purity, will protect the House of his acolyte with pure propitious words for 10.000 years. May the Four Seasons be peaceful and the Ten Directions auspicious. May the six domestic animals become flocks and the people in the household increase in numbers. May the five cereals be always more abundant, and may happiness and prosperity return!

---

5. The ritual to animate an icon, image, or object, which usually involves dotting the eyes with either ink or chicken blood.

6. Pigs, dogs, chickens, horses, cattle, and sheep.

7. The reign period of 1796–1820 (the 5th Qing emperor). Note that in the Chinese calendar system, days and (later) years were designated with two characters drawn from a set of ten "celestial stems" and twelve "earthly branches," creating a cycle of sixty days/years.

8. That is, everywhere (north, south, east, west, northeast, northwest, southeast, southwest, the nadir, and the zenith).

9. So numbered by the translator (note that 1 follows 5).

1. That is, in the animation ritual; see n. 5, above.

(1)   On the 15th day of the 10th month of the 27th year of Daoguang, Ding-wei Year (1847), Pien Uen Ts'iou, Pien Uen Meng, and Pien Uen Leng hung up the lamps (the *guadeng*[2] first ordination).

(6)   Pien Fa Ho and Pien Fa Luang together, on the 19th of the 8th month of the 23rd year of Daoguang, Guimao Year (1843) at the hour of the Ox (between 1 and 3 a.m.) hung up a three stemmed candelabrum (*kwa fam toi tang*). The Instructor of Fa Ho was Pien Fa Yung, his Guarantor was Pien Fa Tong. The Instructor of Fa Luang was Pien Fa Seng, his Guarantor, Tsiou Fa Ts'ing. Their common Witness was Pien Fa Seng.

(7)   Pien Fa Heng and Pien Fa Tsoi, on the ninth day of the 10th month in the Year Dingzhou (1877), at the hour of the Ox, have together hung up a three stemmed candelabrum (*kwa fam toi tang*). Their Instructors respectively were: Lei Wai yet-long and Pien Fa Hing, their guarantors: Pien Fa Liem and Tsiou Fa Luat, and their Witness: Lei Tsun yet-long.

(8)   Pien Fa Siou on the second day of the 11th month in the Guiwei Year (1833) hung up the lamps. Pien Fa Seng was his Guarantor, and his Witness was Tang Fa Luang.

(9)   Fa Seng, on the 17th day of the 11th month, in the Ping Hsiu Year (1866), hung up the lamps (*guadeng*). His Instructor was Fa Luang.

(10) On the second day of the second month, in the Renze Year, second Year of Xianfeng (1852), at the hour of the Ox, three disciples hung up the three stemmed candelabrum (*kwa fam toi tang*) together with Fa Tsun. Fa Tsun's Instructor was Fa Luang, his Guarantor was Fa Kiem. Fa Tsing's Instructor was Falin, his Guarantor, Fa Ts'ing. Fa Tong's Instructor and Guarantor were respectively Fa King and Fa Meng. The Witness was Tsiou Luat nyi-long.

✻   ✻   ✻

[A]t the summit of the Seven Treasures Mountain grows a clump of bamboo. (The stems) are chopped up and made into a paste. Spread on a screen to dry, the paste becomes paper . . . which can equally well be used to write books, letters, invitations, and even reports to the (Divine) Administration. It can also be stamped (to make currency notes) for presentation to the Northern Dipper.[3]

> The (divine) officials are glad to receive it
> For their expenses on wine and tea.
> The old folk will use it to buy
> A prolongation of their life span.

The ritual then describes the transmutation of this paper money into Other World currency. . . . Finally, when all the paper money has been transformed into spirit currency, by burning it, there comes the lad who will carry it to the Treasuries:[4]

> The messenger in charge of transferring the money has arrived,
> (saying)
> 'The house lord determined to invite me.
> I have put on my best clothes and come to transport the money.'

---

2. "Hanging Up Lamps," a Yao ordination ritual.
3. The Big Dipper, in Daoism viewed as the pivot of the universe and associated with transformation.
4. The translator's explanation (as are the bracketed words below).

[The ritual then describes the journey to the Treasuries of the Beyond. . . .
The lad complains:]

> Carrying cash uphill makes me out of breath.
> Carrying cash downhill makes my feet ache.

[The priest addresses him as follows:]

> Lad carrying the money, lad carrying the money,
> Three sores have opened on your back.
> Your coat has been ruined by the load of strings of cash.
> Smoke comes up from the coat on your back . . .
> (On reaching your destination) you pass the first street.
> In the second street the Treasury officials stand in two lines
> on each side.
>
> The Two Treasurers come and ask you:
> 'For whom do you transport that money?'
> Lad, repeat to them exactly what I am telling you now:
> 'I come from Weiyin to bring in this money.'
> You bow your head and exchange greetings.
> The Treasurer receives the money with a salutation.
> Lad, carry the money until it crosses the threshold of the
> Treasury door.
> If there is too much, do not blame the houselord.
> If there is not enough, do not add money on his behalf.
> Too much or too little, pay it all to the Treasury as it is.

THE ANCIENT SAGE

ALFRED, LORD TENNYSON

"The Ancient Sage," first published in the collection *Tiresias and Other Poems* (1885),
was considered by its author to be one of his better late works. Alfred, Lord Tennyson
(1809–1892) wrote the "The Ancient Sage" after he read, and was inspired by, the
first English translation of *The Scripture of the Way and Its Virtue* (*Daode jing*; see
above), completed by John Chalmers in 1868—though Tennyson scholars have vigorously debated just how "Daoist" the poem is. According to Tennyson's son Hallam,
the poet himself denied that he was trying to espouse a philosophy of Daoism.

"The Ancient Sage" takes the form of a dialogue between an elderly philosopher
and a young poet on whose verse, contained within the larger poem, the philosopher
comments. The poem begins by questioning the nature of reality, as the young poet
takes a materialist stance. The old sage points out that material things can come from
nonmaterial origins. As he notes in the opening lines of "The Ancient Sage," though a
fountain's waters may seem to issue from a dark cave, its real source is from heights
beyond human perception. This resonates with the Daoist idea that things derive from
a primordial undifferentiated oneness that is transformed into the stuff of the world.

Though the many suggestive connections between ideas in "The Ancient Sage"
and Daoism are difficult to prove, Tennyson does seem to borrow specific Daoist
terms from Chalmers's translation. Most obvious is the sage's early emphasis on
the "Nameless," a concept that appears in chapter 1 of *The Scripture of the Way*

and Its Virtue: "The name which can be named is not the Eternal Name." Tennyson seems to have been attracted to the Daoist notion that one must turn inward for true knowledge—the farther one travels away from oneself, the less that one knows. It is not surprising that Tennyson quickly transitions from the "Nameless" to representing ultimate reality as the "Abysm" or the "Abysm of all Abysms," since in Chalmers's translation of chapter 1 the abyss also appears: "This sameness (of existence and non-existence) I call the abyss—the abyss of abysses—the gate of all mystery." On close reading, other ideas in the poem, such as its depiction of personal immortality, appear to echo Daoism generally and Chalmers's version of *The Scripture of the Way and Its Virtue* specifically.

———————

A thousand summers ere the time of Christ
From out his ancient city came a Seer
Whom one that loved, and honour'd him, and yet
Was no disciple, richly garb'd, but worn
From wasteful living, follow'd—in his hand
A scroll of verse—till that old man before
A cavern whence an affluent fountain pour'd
From darkness into daylight, turn'd and spoke.

This wealth of waters might but seem to draw
From yon dark cave, but, son, the source is higher,
Yon summit half a league in air—and higher,
The cloud that hides it—higher still, the heavens
Whereby the cloud was moulded, and whereout
The cloud descended. Force is from the heights.
I am wearied of our city, son, and go
To spend my one last year among the hills.
What hast thou there?   Some deathsong for the Ghouls
To make their banquet relish? let me read.

"How far thro' all the bloom and brake[1]
    That nightingale is heard!
What power but the bird's could make
    This music in the bird?
How summer-bright are yonder skies,
    And earth as fair in hue!
And yet what sign of aught that lies
    Behind the green and blue?
But man to-day is fancy's fool
    As man hath ever been.
The nameless Power, or Powers, that rule
    Were never heard or seen."

If thou would'st hear the Nameless, and wilt dive
Into the Temple-cave of thine own self,
There, brooding by the central altar, thou
May'st haply learn the Nameless hath a voice,
By which thou wilt abide, if thou be wise,
As if thou knewest, tho' thou canst not know;

———

1. Fern, bracken; thicket.

For Knowledge is the swallow on the lake
That sees and stirs the surface-shadow there
But never yet hath dipt into the abysm,
The Abysm of all Abysms, beneath, within
The blue of sky and sea, the green of earth,
And in the million-millionth of a grain
Which cleft and cleft again for evermore,
And ever vanishing, never vanishes,
To me, my son, more mystic than myself,
Or even than the Nameless is to me.
   And when thou sendest thy free soul thro' heaven,
Nor understandest bound nor boundlessness,
Thou seest the Nameless of the hundred names.
   And if the Nameless should withdraw from all
Thy frailty counts most real, all thy world
Might vanish like thy shadow in the dark.

      "And since—from when this earth began—
        The Nameless never came
          Among us, never spake with man,
           And never named the Name"—

Thou canst not prove the Nameless, O my son,
Nor canst thou prove the world thou movest in,
Thou canst not prove that thou art body alone,
Nor canst thou prove that thou art spirit alone
Nor canst thou prove that thou art both in one:
Thou canst not prove thou art immortal, no
Nor yet that thou art mortal, nay my son,
Thou canst not prove that I, who speak with thee,
Am not thyself in converse with thyself,
For nothing worthy proving can be proven,
Nor yet disproven: wherefore thou be wise,
Cleave ever to the sunnier side of doubt,
And cling to Faith beyond the forms of Faith!
She reels not in the storm of warring words,
She brightens at the clash of "Yes" and "No,"
She sees the Best that glimmers thro' the Worst,
She feels the Sun is hid but for a night,
She spies the summer thro' the winter bud,
She tastes the fruit before the blossom falls,
She hears the lark within the songless egg,
She finds the fountain where they wall'd "Mirage"!

      "What Power? aught akin to Mind,
        The mind in me and you?
        Or power as of the Gods gone blind
          Who see not what they do?"

But some in yonder city hold, my son,
That none but Gods could build this house of ours,
So beautiful, vast, various, so beyond
All work of man, yet, like all work of man.

A beauty with defect—till That which knows,
And is not known, but felt thro' what we feel
Within ourselves is highest, shall descend
On this half-deed, and shape it at the last
According to the Highest in the Highest.

"What Power but the Years that make
And break the vase of clay,
And stir the sleeping earth, and wake
The bloom that fades away?
What rulers but the Days and Hours
That cancel weal with woe,
And wind the front of youth with flowers,
And cap our age with snow?"

The days and hours are ever glancing by,
And seem to flicker past thro' sun and shade,
Or short, or long, as Pleasure leads, or Pain;
But with the Nameless is nor Day nor Hour;
Tho' we, thin minds, who creep from thought to thought
Break into "Thens" and "Whens" the Eternal Now:
This double seeming of the single world!—
My words are like the babblings in a dream
Of nightmare, when the babblings break the dream.
But thou be wise in this dream-world of ours,
Nor take thy dial for thy deity,
But make the passing shadow serve thy will.

* * *

A CHINESE SAGE

OSCAR WILDE

In February 1890, just months before his first version of *The Picture of Dorian Gray* appeared in an American magazine, the flamboyant Irish writer, philosopher, and playwright Oscar Wilde (1854–1900) published in *The Speaker: The Liberal Reviewed*, a British paper, his assessment of Herbert Giles's 1889 English translation of the *Book of Master Zhuang* (*Zhuangzi*; see above). During the late nineteenth century, the *Book of Master Zhuang* did not have the same philosophical appeal in Europe as *The Scripture of the Way and Its Virtue* (*Daode jing*; see above). But though it was not translated or referred to as often, within certain intellectual circles it attracted a substantial readership and stimulated philosophical discussion. In Zhuangzi—whom he calls Chuang Tsŭ—Wilde apparently found a thinker who corroborated his own radical impulses.

In the very first paragraph of "A Chinese Sage," Wilde declares the *Book of Master Zhuang* to be "the most caustic criticism of modern life I have met with for some time." In his view, Zhuangzi "sought to destroy society, as we know it, as the middle classes know it"; he adds, Zhuangzi "pities the rich more than the poor, if he ever pities at all, and prosperity seems to him as tragic a thing as suffering." Wilde sees

Zhuangzi as celebrating a kind of primitive agrarian utopianism: "The order of nature is rest, repetition, and peace. Weariness and war are the results of an artificial society based upon capital; and the richer this society gets, the more thoroughly bankrupt it really is." In "A Chinese Sage" Wilde interprets Zhuangzi's radical message as an indictment of Victorian systems of education, politics, ethics, and economics. He concludes his essay by noting that Zhuangzi "would be disturbing at dinner-parties, and impossible at afternoon teas, and his whole life was a protest against platform speaking." Coming from Wilde, a man intent on upending tradition and challenging the slavish embrace of old habits, this was high praise for the ancient Chinese master.

PRONOUNCING GLOSSARY

Chuang Tsŭ (Zhuangzi): *chuang-tzu*   Lao Tsu (Laozi): *lao-tzu*
Hui Tzu (Huizi): *hway tzu*

An eminent Oxford theologian once remarked that his only objection to modern progress was that it progressed forward instead of backward—a view that so fascinated a certain artistic undergraduate that he promptly wrote an essay upon some unnoticed analogies between the development of ideas and the movements of the common sea-crab. I feel sure THE SPEAKER will not be suspected of holding this dangerous heresy of retrogression even by its most enthusiastic friends. But I must candidly admit that I have come to the conclusion that the most caustic criticism of modern life I have met with for some time is that contained in the writings of the learned Chuang Tsŭ, recently translated into the vulgar tongue by Mr. Herbert Giles, Her Majesty's Consul at Tamsui.[1]

The spread of popular education has no doubt made the name of this great thinker quite familiar to the general public, but, for the sake of the few and the over-cultured, I feel it my duty to state definitely who he was, and to give a brief outline of the character of his philosophy.

Chuang Tsŭ, whose name must carefully be pronounced as it is not written, was born in the fourth century before Christ, by the banks of the Yellow River,[2] in the Flowery Land; and portraits of the wonderful sage seated on the flying dragon of contemplation may still be found on the simple tea-trays and pleasing screens of many of our most respectable suburban households. The honest ratepayer and his healthy family have no doubt often mocked at the dome-like forehead of the philosopher, and laughed over the strange perspective of the landscape that lies beneath him. If they really knew who he was, they would tremble. For Chuang Tsŭ spent his life in preaching the great creed of Inaction, and in pointing out the uselessness of all useful things. "Do nothing, and everything will be done," was the doctrine which he inherited from his great master Lao Tsŭ.[3] To resolve action into thought, and thought into abstraction, was his wicked transcendental aim. Like the obscure philosopher of early Greek speculation, he

1. Danshui, in northern Taiwan. The work reviewed is *Chuang Tzŭ: Mystic, Moralist, and Social Reformer*, translated from the Chinese by Herbert A. Giles (London: B. Quaritch, 1889); Giles (1845–1935) left the consular service in 1893 (later becoming professor of Chinese at Cambridge). For the *Book of Master Zhuang* (*Zhuangzi*), see above.
2. The second-longest river in China, which flows east from the Plateau of Tibet to the Bohai Sea (south of Beijing).
3. That is, Laozi; see *The Scripture of the Way and Its Virtue* (*Daode jing*), above.

believed in the identity of contraries;[4] like Plato,[5] he was an idealist, and had all the idealist's contempt for utilitarian systems; he was a mystic like Dionysius, and Scotus Erigena, and Jacob Böhme,[6] and held, with them and with Philo,[7] that the object of life was to get rid of self-consciousness, and to become the unconscious vehicle of a higher illumination. In fact, Chuang Tsŭ may be said to have summed up in himself almost every mood of European metaphysical or mystical thought, from Herakleitus down to Hegel.[8] There was something in him of the Quietist also; and in his worship of Nothing he may be said to have in some measure anticipated those strange dreamers of mediæval days who, like Tauler and Master Eckhart,[9] adored the *purum nihil*[1] and the Abyss. The great middle classes of this country, to whom, as we all know, our prosperity, if not our civilisation, is entirely due, may shrug their shoulders over all this, and ask, with a certain amount of reason, what is the identity of contraries to them, and why they should get rid of that self-consciousness which is their chief characteristic. But Chuang Tsŭ was something more than a metaphysician and an illuminist. He sought to destroy society, as we know it, as the middle classes know it; and the sad thing is that he combines with the passionate eloquence of a Rousseau the scientific reasoning of a Herbert Spencer.[2] There is nothing of the sentimentalist in him. He pities the rich more than the poor, if he ever pities at all, and prosperity seems to him as tragic a thing as suffering. He has nothing of the modern sympathy with failures, nor does he propose that the prizes should always be given on moral grounds to those who come in last in the race. It is the race itself that he objects to; and as for active sympathy, which has become the profession of so many worthy people in our own day, he thinks that trying to make others good is as silly an occupation as "beating a drum in a forest in order to find a fugitive." It is a mere waste of energy. That is all. While as for a thoroughly sympathetic man, he is, in the eyes of Chuang Tsŭ, simply a man who is always trying to be somebody else, and so misses the only possible excuse for his own existence.

Yes; incredible as it may seem, this curious thinker looked back with a sigh of regret to a certain Golden Age when there were no competitive examinations, no wearisome educational systems, no missionaries, no penny dinners for the people, no Established Churches, no Humanitarian Societies, no dull lectures about one's duty to one's neighbour, and no tedious sermons about any subject at all. In those ideal days, he tells us, people loved each other without being conscious of charity, or writing to the newspapers about it. They were upright, and yet they never published books upon Altruism. As

4. Heraclitus (below "Herakleitus," fl. ca. 500 B.C.E.), whose thought survives only in quoted short fragments attributed to him; he saw underlying unity in the world's constant changes.
5. Greek philosopher (ca. 427–ca. 347 B.C.E.).
6. German Lutheran theologian and mystical philosopher (1575–1624). Pseudo-Dionysius the Areopagite (fl. ca. 500 C.E.), a Christian Neoplatonist whose writings greatly influenced medieval Christian thought. John Scotus Erigena (ca. 810–ca. 877), Irish-born theologian and philosopher who attempted to reconcile Neoplatonism and Christian creationism; he also translated Pseudo-Dionysius into Latin.
7. Jewish philosopher of Alexandria (ca. 20 B.C.E.–50 C.E.), who attempted to reconcile Judaism and Greek philosophy.

8. Georg Wilhelm Friedrich Hegel (1770–1831), German idealist philosopher.
9. German Neoplatonist philosopher, Dominican theologian, and mystic (ca. 1260–ca. 1327). Johannes Tauler (ca. 1300–1361), German Dominican theologian and mystic and a student of Master Eckhart's.
1. Pure nothingness (Latin), which according to Eckhart characterizes all creatures; they depend for their existence wholly on God, who inherently possesses being.
2. Philosopher, sociologist, and social evolutionist (1820–1903); he coined the phrase "survival of the fittest." Jean-Jacques Rousseau (1712–1778), Swiss-born French political philosopher, writer, and political theorist.

every man kept his knowledge to himself, the world escaped the curse of scepticism; and as every man kept his virtues to himself, nobody meddled in other people's business. They lived simple and peaceful lives, and were contented with such food and raiment as they could get. Neighbouring districts were in sight, and "the cocks and dogs of one could be heard in the other," yet the people grew old and died without ever interchanging visits. There was no chattering about clever men, and no laudation of good men. The intolerable sense of obligation was unknown. The deeds of humanity left no trace, and their affairs were not made a burden for posterity by foolish historians.

In an evil moment the Philanthropist made his appearance, and brought with him the mischievous idea of Government. "There is such a thing," says Chuang Tsŭ, "as leaving mankind alone: there has never been such a thing as governing mankind." All modes of government are wrong. They are unscientific, because they seek to alter the natural environment of man; they are immoral, because, by interfering with the individual, they produce the most aggressive forms of egotism; they are ignorant, because they try to spread education; they are self-destructive, because they engender anarchy. "Of old," he tells us, "the Yellow Emperor[3] first caused charity and duty to one's neighbour to interfere with the natural goodness of the heart of man. In consequence of this, Yao and Shun[4] wore the hair off their legs in endeavouring to feed their people. They disturbed their internal economy in order to find room for artificial virtues. They exhausted their energies in framing laws, and they were failures." Man's heart, our philosopher goes on to say, may be "forced down or stirred up," and in either case the issue is fatal. Yao made the people too happy, so they were not satisfied. Chieh[5] made them too wretched, so they grew discontented. Then everyone began to argue about the best way of tinkering up society. "It is quite clear that something must be done," they said to each other, and there was a general rush for knowledge. The results were so dreadful that the Government of the day had to bring in Coercion, and as a consequence of this "virtuous men sought refuge in mountain caves, while rulers of state sat trembling in ancestral halls." Then, when everything was in a state of perfect chaos, the Social Reformers got up on platforms, and preached salvation from the ills that they and their system had caused. The poor Social Reformers! "They know not shame, nor what it is to blush," is the verdict of Chuang Tsŭ upon them.

The economic question, also, is discussed by this almond-eyed sage at great length, and he writes about the curse of capital as eloquently as Mr. Hyndman.[6] The accumulation of wealth is to him the origin of evil. It makes the strong violent, and the weak dishonest. It creates the petty thief, and puts him in a bamboo cage. It creates the big thief, and sets him on a throne of white jade. It is the father of competition, and competition is the waste, as well as the destruction, of energy. The order of nature is rest, repetition, and peace. Weariness and war are the results of an artificial society

---

3. Huangdi (27th century b.c.e.), a mythological Chinese emperor and an important figure in Daoism.
4. The son-in-law and successor of Yao, a legendary Chinese ruler whose reign (ca. 24th century b.c.e.) was depicted as a golden age.
5. Jie, the last ruler of the Xia dynasty (ca. 2070–

ca. 1600 b.c.e.), whose tyranny and debauchery hastened the dynasty's end.
6. Henry Mayers Hyndman (1842–1921), English author and politician; he formed Britain's first socialist party (the Social Democratic Federation, which later merged with other groups to create the British Socialist Party).

based upon capital; and the richer this society gets, the more thoroughly bankrupt it really is, for it has neither sufficient rewards for the good nor sufficient punishments for the wicked. There is also this to be remembered— that the prizes of the world degrade a man as much as the world's punishments. The age is rotten with its worship of success. As for education, true wisdom can neither be learnt nor taught. It is a spiritual state, to which he who lives in harmony with nature attains. Knowledge is shallow if we compare it with the extent of the unknown, and only the unknowable is of value. Society produces rogues, and education makes one rogue cleverer than another. That is the only result of School Boards. Besides, of what possible philosophic importance can education be, when it simply serves to make each man differ from his neighbour? We arrive ultimately at a chaos of opinions, doubt everything, and fall into the vulgar habit of arguing; and it is only the intellectually lost who ever argue. Look at Hui Tzu.[7] "He was a man of many ideas. His works would fill five carts. But his doctrines were paradoxical." He said that there were feathers in an egg, because there were feathers on a chicken; that a dog could be a sheep, because all names were arbitrary; that there was a moment when a swiftly flying arrow was neither moving nor at rest; that if you took a stick a foot long, and cut it in half every day, you would never come to the end of it; and that a bay horse and a dun cow were three, because taken separately they were two, and taken together they were one, and one and two made up three. "He was like a man running a race with his own shadow, and making a noise in order to drown the echo. He was a clever gad-fly, that was all. What was the use of him?"

Morality is, of course, a different thing. It went out of fashion, says Chuang Tsŭ, when people began to moralise. Men ceased then to be spontaneous and to act on intuition. They became priggish and artificial, and were so blind as to have a definite purpose in life. Then came Governments and Philanthropists, those two pests of the age. The former tried to coerce people into being good, and so destroyed the natural goodness of man. The latter were a set of aggressive busybodies who caused confusion wherever they went. They were stupid enough to have principles, and unfortunate enough to act up to them. They all came to bad ends, and showed that universal altruism is as bad in its results as universal egotism. They "tripped people up over charity, and fettered them with duties to their neighbours." They gushed over music, and fussed over ceremonies. As a consequence of all this, the world lost its equilibrium, and has been staggering ever since.

Who, then, according to Chuang Tsŭ, is the perfect man? And what is his manner of life? The perfect man does nothing beyond gazing at the universe. He adopts no absolute position. "In motion, he is like water. At rest, he is like a mirror. And, like Echo,[8] he only answers when he is called upon." He lets externals take care of themselves. Nothing material injures him; nothing spiritual punishes him. His mental equilibrium gives him the empire of the world. He is never the slave of objective existences. He knows that, "just as the best language is that which is never spoken, so the best action is that which is never done." He is passive, and accepts the laws of life. He rests in inactivity, and sees the world become virtuous of itself. He does not try to

---

7. Hui Shi (300 B.C.E.–?), Chinese philosopher in the school of dialecticians; his writings survive only in quotations such as Zhuangzi's.

8. In classical mythology, a nymph whose punishment was to lose all ability to speak except to repeat the last words of others.

"bring about his own good deeds." He never wastes himself on effort. He is not troubled about moral distinctions. He knows that things are what they are, and that their consequences will be what they will be. His mind is the "speculum of creation," and he is ever at peace.

All this is of course excessively dangerous, but we must remember that Chuang Tsŭ lived more than two thousand years ago, and never had the opportunity of seeing our unrivalled civilisation. And yet it is possible that, were he to come back to earth and visit us, he might have something to say to Mr. Balfour[9] about his coercion and active misgovernment in Ireland; he might smile at some of our philanthropic ardours, and shake his head over many of our organised charities; the School Board might not impress him, nor our race for wealth stir his admiration; he might wonder at our ideals, and grow sad over what we have realised. Perhaps it is well that Chuang Tsŭ cannot return.

Meanwhile, thanks to Mr. Giles and Mr. Quaritch,[1] we have his book to console us, and certainly it is a most fascinating and delightful volume. Chuang Tsŭ is one of the Darwinians before Darwin.[2] He traces man from the germ, and sees his unity with nature. As an anthropologist he is excessively interesting, and he describes our primitive arboreal ancestor living in trees through his terror of animals stronger than himself, and knowing only one parent, the mother, with all the accuracy of a lecturer at the Royal Society. Like Plato, he adopts the dialogue as his mode of expression, "putting words into other people's mouths," he tells us, "in order to gain breadth of view." As a story-teller he is charming. The account of the visit of the respectable Confucius[3] to the great Robber Chê is most vivid and brilliant, and it is impossible not to laugh over the ultimate discomfiture of the sage, the barrenness of whose moral platitudes is ruthlessly exposed by the successful brigand. Even in his metaphysics, Chuang Tsŭ is intensely humorous. He personifies his abstractions, and makes them act plays before us. The Spirit of the Clouds, when passing eastward through the expanse of air, happened to fall in with the Vital Principle. The latter was slapping his ribs and hopping about: whereupon the Spirit of the Clouds said, "Who are you, old man, and what are you doing?" "Strolling!" replied the Vital Principle, without stopping, for all activities are ceaseless. "I want to *know* something," continued the Spirit of the Clouds. "Ah!" cried the Vital Principle, in a tone of disapprobation, and a marvellous conversation follows, that is not unlike the dialogue between the Sphynx and the Chimæra in Flaubert's curious drama.[4] Talking animals, also, have their place in Chuang Tsŭ's parables and stories, and through myth and poetry and fancy his strange philosophy finds musical utterance.

Of course it is sad to be told that it is immoral to be consciously good, and that doing anything is the worst form of idleness. Thousands of excellent and really earnest philanthropists would be absolutely thrown upon

9. Arthur James Balfour (1848–1930), British conservative politician whose many posts included chief secretary for Ireland (1887–91).

1. Bernard Quaritch (1819–1899), German-born publisher and bookseller in London. He published Herbert Giles's translation of the *Zhuangzi*.

2. Charles Darwin (1809–1882), English naturalist and originator of the theory of evolution by natural selection.

3. The teacher, philosopher, and political theorist (551–479 B.C.E.).

4. *The Temptation of Saint Anthony* (*La tentation de saint Antoine*, 1874), a book in the form of a playscript by the French novelist Gustave Flaubert (1821–1880). In chapter 7, the Chimera and the Sphinx—two monstrous creatures, in classical mythology—appear, argue, and disappear.

the rates[5] if we adopted the view that nobody should be allowed to meddle in what does not concern them. The doctrine of the uselessness of all useful things would not merely endanger our commercial supremacy as a nation, but might bring discredit upon many prosperous and serious-minded members of the shop-keeping classes. What would become of our popular preachers, our Exeter Hall[6] orators, our drawing-room evangelists, if we said to them, in the words of Chuang Tsŭ, "Mosquitoes will keep a man awake all night with their biting, and just in the same way this talk of charity and duty to one's neighbour drives us nearly crazy. Sirs, strive to keep the world to its own original simplicity, and, as the wind bloweth where it listeth, so let Virtue establish itself. Wherefore this undue energy?" And what would be the fate of governments and professional politicians if we came to the conclusion that there is no such thing as governing mankind at all? It is clear that Chuang Tsŭ is a very dangerous writer, and the publication of his book in English, two thousand years after his death, is obviously premature, and may cause a great deal of pain to many thoroughly respectable and industrious persons. It may be true that the ideal of self-culture and self-development, which is the aim of his scheme of life, and the basis of his scheme of philosophy, is an ideal somewhat needed by an age like ours, in which most people are so anxious to educate their neighbours that they have actually no time left in which to educate themselves. But would it be wise to say so? It seems to me that if we once admitted the force of any one of Chuang Tsŭ's destructive criticisms we should have to put some check on our national habit of self-glorification; and the only thing that ever consoles man for the stupid things he does is the praise he always gives himself for doing them. There may, however, be a few who have grown wearied of that strange modern tendency that sets enthusiasm to do the work of the intellect. To these, and such as these, Chuang Tsŭ will be welcome. But let them only read him. Let them not talk about him. He would be disturbing at dinner-parties, and impossible at afternoon teas, and his whole life was a protest against platform speaking. "The perfect man ignores self; the divine man ignores action; the true sage ignores reputation." These are the principles of Chuang Tsŭ.

5. That is, be forced out of their jobs and onto welfare.
6. A building in London that during the 19th century was used for large-scale religious and political meetings.

TAOISM: A PRIZE ESSAY

"Taoism: A Prize Essay" is the prize-winning address delivered to the World's Parliament of Religions in Chicago in 1893. In the congress's proceedings, it was published anonymously; but when the same essay appeared in Paul Carus's magazine *The Open Court* in September 1913 under the title "An Exposition of Taoism," the author was listed as "Chang T'ien She, The Taoist Pope" (Zhang Tianshi). This "pope" was a certain Chang Yuan Hsu (Zhang Yuanxu, 1862–1924), the sixty-second Celestial Master—a hereditary title passed down for more than two millennia. The holder of the office was a distant ancestor of Zhang Daoling, the first Celestial Master, who had been visited by the divine Laozi in 142 C.E. on a mountain in Sichuan Province. His essay had been entered in a competition in China sponsored and judged by Dr. Timothy Richard (1845–1919), a British Baptist missionary there.

The winning entry provides a highly idiosyncratic history of the development of Daoism, positing Laozi and his *Scripture of the Way and Its Virtue* (*Daode jing*; see above) at the origin and then noting the division of the tradition, represented in the late nineteenth century by the Orthodox school (the Zhengyi tradition of married Daoist priests, which the author—whose lineage this is—naturally sees as leading Daoism) and the Pure Truth school (the Quanzhen order of the monastic form of Daoism). What is most striking about this account is that it baldly presents the tradition as having gone astray from the pure original teaching of Laozi, having instead become a degenerate "genii religion" focused on magic, miracles, charms, incantations, and the elixir of immortality. The author particularly criticizes *Awakening to Reality* (*Wuzhen pian*, romanized in the essay as *Wu Chin Pien*), the important Daoist alchemical text written by Zhang Boduan (987?–1082), for its excessive focus on the "germ of immortality." This view of a "religious Daoism" that branched off from the early "philosophical Daoism" of Laozi and Zhuangzi as a religious tradition developed with its own social reality and institutions is typical of the misunderstanding of Daoism found in China, and around the world, in the late nineteenth century, and it has conditioned the current reductionist understanding of Daoism as a philosophy. "Taoism: A Prize Essay" ends with a call for reform and a return to the pure philosophical teachings of the ancient sages: "If the coarse influences with which custom has obscured them were removed, the doctrines of Lao-tsze [Laozi], Chang-tsze [Zhuangzi], Yin Hi [Yin Xi] and Lie-tsze [Liezi] might shine forth brightly. Would not this be fortunate for our religion?"

PRONOUNCING GLOSSARY

Chow (Zhou): *chou*
Hwangti (Huangdi): *huang-dee*
Lao-tsze (Laozi): *lao-tzu*

Lie-tsze (Liezi): *lieh-tzu*
Tao Teh King (*Daode jing*): *dow duh ching*

Taoism and Confucianism are the oldest religions of China.[1] Taoism originated with the originator of all religions. He transmitted it to Lao-tsze, who was born in the Chow dynasty (about B.C. 604), was contemporary with Confucius,[2] and kept the records. His *Tao Teh King* treats of the origin and philosophy of nature, of the mystery behind and above the visible universe, in order to educate the ignorant. In time, Taoism divided into four schools—the Original, the Mountain, the Barrier and the Orthodox[3] schools. After ten generations these schools became one again. The Barrier school is probably represented to-day by the Pure Truth school, which really originated with Wang Chieh[4] in A.D. 1161, and has flourished all the more since the rise of the Mongol dynasty. The present head of Taoism is of the Orthodox school. At present Taoism has a northern and a southern branch. Our

1. The author's original spelling of Chinese words has been retained in this selection. Daoism appears as Taoism; Laozi appears as Lao-tsze; and Daode jing appears as Tao Teh King.
2. The teacher, philosopher, and political theorist (551–479 B.C.E.). Chow dynasty: the Zhou dynasty (1046–256 B.C.E.). This dating of Laozi, the supposed author of the *Daode jing* (*The*

Scripture of the Way and Its Virtue*, here the *Tao Teh King*; see above), is traditional.
3. The Orthodox Unity (Zhengyi) tradition.
4. That is, Wang Zhe (1113–1170), also known as Wang Chongyang, who was credited with founding the Complete Perfection (Quanzhen) tradition (the Pure Truth school).

sacred books are divided into advanced, secondary and primary classes, the advanced class discussing the question how to find truth or the eternal, the secondary class the origin of things, and the elementary class treating of spirits. There are also three secondary classes in three books—*The Great Beginning, The Great Peace, The Great Purity*. The Orthodox school also has a literature divided into three independent classes, and called the sacred literature of the three classes.

If Taoists seek Taoism's deep meaning in earnest, and put unworthy desires aside, they are not far from its original goal. But in after generations the marvelous overclouded this; Taoists left the right way, and boasted wonders of their own. Legends of gods and genii became incorporated with Taoism. In the Han dynasty[5] Taoism had thirty-seven books and the genii religion ten. These were different at first. But from the time Taoism ceased to think purity and peaceableness sufficient to satisfy men, it became the genii religion [magic and spiritualism],[6] though still called Taoism. From B.C. 206 to A.D. 220 the doctrines of Hwangti[7] and Lao-tsze flourished together. The former ones related to miracles and wonders, the latter to truth and virtue. The *Tao Teh King* had said nothing of the pellet of immortality, but about A.D. 420 this theory of a spiritual germ was read into it. Kwo Chang Keng held that what the *Tao Teh King* says about things being produced by what existed before nature, is the source of the germ of immortality. The *Wu Chin Pien,*[8] another of our orthodox books, discusses nothing except the importance of this eternal germ. The art of breathing the breath of life was practiced, and the fundamental nature of Taoism underwent change. Then the secret of the germ of life and the art of refining one's nature were sought; and its foundations experienced another change. Finally Chang Lu[9] (*circa* A.D, 385–582?) used charms in his teaching, and employed fasting, prayer, hymns and incantations to obtain blessings and repel calamities; and Taoism's fundamental doctrines had utterly disappeared.

What does Taoism mean by the phrase, Carrying out heaven's will? It means that heaven is the first cause of religion, that man is produced by two forces, Yin and Yang;[1] that heaven gave the spiritual nature; and that when this is lost he cannot carry out heaven's will nor be a man. Heaven is called the great clearness, the great space, and this clear space is heaven's natural body. Taoism regards heaven as its lord, and seeks to follow heaven's way. If men, to preserve the heaven-given soul, can premise Yin and Yang as the foundation of truth and of the spiritual nature, and can nourish the heaven-given spiritual life, what need for the medicine of immortality? But those who carry out heaven's will are able to fulfill their duties as men. Those who really study religion, cultivate their spiritual nature, preserve their souls, gather up their spiritual force, and watch their hearts. They believe that if the spiritual

5. 202 B.C.E.–220 C.E.
6. All bracketed phrases are in the original.
7. Huangdi, the Yellow Emperor (27th century B.C.E.), a mythological Chinese emperor and an important figure in Daoism.
8. *Awakening to Reality* (*Wuzhen pian*), written by Zhang Boduan (987?–1082); it is one of the most important Daoist alchemical texts.
9. Probably a reference to the Zhang Lu (d. 3rd century C.E.) who was the grandson of the founder of the Celestial Masters tradition,

Zhang Daoling, though the dates here do not match.
1. The complementary forces that unite to form the Dao: yin, a term that originally referred to the shady side of a valley, by extension came to be associated with the dark, earth, dampness, and passivity—the female principle; yang, a term that originally referred to the sunny side of a valley, by extension came to be associated with the light, heaven, dryness, and activity—the male principle.

nature be not nurtured, it daily dwindles; if the soul be not preserved, it daily dies; if the spiritual force be not exercised, it is dissipated daily; if the heart be not watched, it is daily lost. Taoism, though considering purity fundamental, adds patience to purity and holds to it with perseverance, overcomes the hard with softness, and the firmest with readiness to yield. Thus Taoism attains a state not far from man's original one of honesty and truth without becoming conscious of it.

Practice virtue in quiet and for a long time. From the unseen let something appear; afterwards let it return to the unseen. Collect your spirits till you have force. Collect your forces till you have living seeds. This is producing something where nothing existed. Sow those seeds, nourish them with your influence, exercise your influence to keep your spirits, and lead them from the seen to the unseen. When human duties are fulfilled, not a particle of the eternal intelligent germ need be lost. Space and my body are but parts of one, and will be of the same age. Without seeking immortality, the body becomes immortal. If not, this bit of divine light is Yin; extinguished by the bad influences of this life.

Comprehension of the hereafter is one of the mysteries in which no religion can equal Taoism. The living force in my body fills space, influences everything, and is one with creation. If we can in reality attain to it [life-force?], we are able to know spirits in the dark domains. In the future life there is but one principle. Ghosts are the intelligent powers of Yin; gods, those of Yang.

The benefits conferred by Taoism on the government cannot be exhausted by relating isolated instances.

Taoism and the genii-religion have deteriorated. Taoists only practice charms, read prayers, play on stringed or reed instruments, and select famous mountains to rest in. They rejoice in calling themselves Taoists, but few carry out the true learning of the worthies and the holy genii of the past. If we ask a Taoist what is taught in the *Yin Tu King*,[2] he does not know. If you kneel for explanation of the *Tao Teh King*, he cannot answer.

Oh! that one would arise to restore our religion, save it from errors, help its weakness, expose untruth with truth, explain the mysteries, understand it profoundly and set it forth clearly, as Roman Catholics and Protestants assemble the masses to hear, and to explain the doctrines that their followers may know the ends for which their churches were established! If the coarse influences with which custom has obscured them were removed, the doctrines of Lao-tsze, Chang-tsze, Yin Hi and Lie-tsze[3] might shine forth brightly. Would not this be fortunate for our religion?

---

2. It is unclear what text this title (*Yindu jing*) refers to: perhaps a mistaken transcription of the *Scripture of the Hidden Accordance* (*Yinfu jing*), a short work on the harmony between nature and humans.
3. Liezi (fl. ca. 400 B.C.E.), an ancient philosopher quoted by Zhuangzi (probably the "Chang-tsze," or Zhangzi, named here; for the *Book of Master Zhuang*, or *Zhuangzi*, see above); the *Book of Master Lie* (*Liezi*, actually written 4th century C.E.), attributed to him, is a Daoist classic. Yin Xi (Yin Hi) is a character mentioned in the *Book of Master Zhuang* and other sources who later is identified with the border guard at the Han'gu Pass who urged Laozi to teach the *Daode jing*.

COMMENTARY ON "TALKS AND PARABLES OF CHUANG TZU"

MARTIN BUBER

In 1910 the prominent German Jewish philosopher, essayist, and scholar Martin Buber (1878–1965) completed a translation of and commentary on the *Book of Master Zhuang* (*Zhuangzi*; see above) that was published as *Talks and Parables of Chuang Tzu* (*Reden und Gleichnisse des Tschuang-tse*). Around the same time, he translated a number of the tales in *Strange Stories from a Chinese Studio* (*Liaozhai zhiyi*; see "The Daoist Priest of the Lao Mountains," above); later, he completed a partial translation of *The Scripture of the Way and Its Virtue* (*Daode jing*; see above), with commentary. Martin Buber once noted that his own philosophy was "indebted a great deal" to Daoism, and all these works had a significant impact on other German intellectuals. Buber held a lectureship at the University of Frankfurt at the same time as Richard Wilhelm (1873–1930), translator of the *Secret of the Golden Flower* (*Taiyi jinhua zongzhi*; see above); Wilhelm's 1928 lectures were attended by Carl Gustav Jung (1875–1961), the Swiss psychologist who wrote the foreword and appendix to his translation. One can only wonder about what their conversations on Daoist topics must have been like in the 1920s.

Buber's translations of the *Book of Master Zhuang*, *The Scripture of the Way and Its Virtue*, and *Strange Stories from a Chinese Studio* also raise intriguing questions about rendering Chinese texts without knowing Chinese. Buber appears to have mainly based his "translations"—which some prefer to call "versions" or "redactions"—into German on works already translated from Chinese into English (using, for example, Herbert Giles's translation of the *Book of Master Zhuang*), as well as collaborating with Chinese colleagues (who remain unnamed).

Buber's wide-ranging commentary forms the heart of his *Talks and Parables of Chuang Tzu*, but it is by no means a traditional close reading of the passages; instead, he uses the translated selections from the *Book of Master Zhuang* merely to support his interpretive essay. The introduction of his commentary, despite being larded with Orientalist stereotypes, argues for the need to open up a dialogue between the religious traditions of East and West. In one section Buber's main topic of discussion is the "Dao," which he understands as being a form of mystical oneness, even the "oneness in the transformation" and in the multiplicity of things and moments. One who experiences the Dao directly and incarnates it Buber refers to as "the accomplished man," or "unified man" (his translation of the "true man," *zhenren*). Buber would later look back on this engagement with Daoism as his "mystical" period. Ultimately he would reject this collapse of everything into unitary oneness and focus more on multiplicity. As previous scholars have noted, Buber's shift in thinking about Daoism seems to mirror his philosophical development, particularly his thinking about the "I" not becoming fully lost in the "Other" in his mature "I-Thou" philosophy. His philosophy of "I-Thou" and Daoism share a paradoxical view of the nature of the relationship between unity and multiplicity.

Buber saw early philosophical Daoism as the pinnacle of the tradition and "the whole of later Taoism [as] nothing but increasing degeneration"—a view that accords well with "Taoism: A Prize Essay" (see above) and other late nineteenth- and twentieth-century writings about Daoism. And like Oscar Wilde (see above), he saw some possibilities in the radical social implications of Daoist teachings. Buber came to think that the high point of Daoism was *The Scripture of the Way and Its Virtue* and the *Book of Master Zhuang* was just the beginning of a long descent, as he became dissatisfied with its rejection of political involvement. Buber's introduction

to and commentary on the *Book of Master Zhuang* are significant primarily as a
record of how one modern Western Jewish philosopher with an interest in the medieval Hasidic mystical tradition engaged with Daoism and found an affinity with the
ideas presented in one of ancient China's most creative and lively works of literature.

Chuang Tzu (Zhuangzi): *chuang-tzu*   Lieh Tzu (Liezi): *lieh-tzu*
Lao Tzu (Laozi): *lao-tzu*

1

Across the theories of races and cultures, in our time the old knowledge has
been neglected, that the Orient forms a natural oneness, expressed in its
values and works; that across its divisions of peoples arises a commonality
that separates it from the destiny and creativity of the West in unconditioned clarity.[1] The genetic explanation for it, which is not to be expounded
here, has its foundation quite naturally in the diverse conditions not
merely in space but also in time, for indeed the spiritually determining
epoch of the Orient belongs to a moment of mankind other than that of
the West.

Here, the oneness of the Orient is only implicitly to be demonstrated in
one manifestation, which to be sure is among the most essential of all, in
the manifestation of the teaching.

In its primordial state, the Eastern spirit is what all spirit is in the primordial state: magic. This is its being, that it confronts the unrestraint of nature
that is rushing with thousandfold menace, with its restraint, the binding that
is inherent in magical power. Regulated word, ordered motion, incantation
and magic gesture compel the demonic element into rule and order. All
primitive technique and all primitive organization are magic; implement and
defense, speech and sport, custom and bond arise from magical intention
and serve in their primordial time a magical sense out of which their own life
only gradually sets itself loose and becomes independent.

This setting loose and becoming independent carries itself out much
more slowly in the Orient than in the West. In the West, the magical has
living duration only in the folk religiosity, in which the undifferentiated
wholeness of life has preserved itself; in all other domains, the loosening is
fast and complete. In the Orient, it is slow and incomplete; in the products
of separation, the magical character adheres even longer. Thus, for example,
the art of the Orient still remains in many ways, even after the attainment
of artistic freedom and might, in the magical intention, while with that of
the West, the attainment of this height confers its own right and its own
purpose.

*   *   *

TRANSLATED BY Jonathan R. Herman.

1. The author's original spelling of Chinese words has been retained in this selection. Laozi appears as
Lao Tzu and Dao appears as Tao.

6

The word "Tao" signifies the way, the path; but since it also has the sense of "speech," it is sometimes rendered with "logos." For Lao Tzu and his disciples, where it is always developed metaphorically, it is tied to the first of these meanings. Yet its linguistic atmosphere is related, in fact, to that of the Heracleitian Logos,[2] given that both transplant a dynamic principle of human life into the transcendent, but at base mean nothing other than that it is the human life itself that is the carrier and realization of all transcendence. I shall here explain this about Tao.

In the West, Tao has been understood, for the most part, as an attempt at world explanation; remarkably, the world explanation that is perceived therein continually conflates with the inclinations of the present time's philosophy; so Tao is valued first as nature, then as reason, and lately it is to be merely energy. Contrary to these explanations must be pointed out that Tao means in general no explanation of the world, but rather this: that the whole sense of existence rests in the oneness of the truthful life, will only be experienced in it, that it is precisely this oneness grasped as the absolute. If one wishes to disregard the oneness of the truthful life and consider what "lies at the foundation"[3] of it, then nothing remains left over but the imperceptible, of which nothing further is to be said but that it is imperceptible. The oneness is the only way to realize it and to experience it in such a reality. The imperceptible is naturally neither nature nor reason nor energy, but precisely the imperceptible for which no image suffices, because "in it are the images."[4] But that which is experienced is again neither nature nor reason nor energy, but rather the oneness of the path, the oneness of the truthful human way, that recovers the unified in the world and in each thing: the path as the oneness of the world, as the oneness of each thing.

But the imperceptibility of Tao cannot be so conceived as one speaks of the imperceptibility of some principles of religious or philosophical world explanations, in order to make a statement about it after all. Likewise, that which the name "Tao" states is not stated about the imperceptible: "The name that can be known is not the eternal name."[5] If one will consider Tao not as the needful whose reality is experienced in the unified life, but rather as an existence in itself, then one finds nothing for consideration: "Tao can have no existence." It cannot be investigated, cannot be explained. Not only can no truth be stated about it, but it cannot be the subject of a statement at all. What is stated about it is neither true nor false: "How can Tao be obscured so that some "truth" or some "falsity" appears in it? . . . Tao is obscured because we cannot take hold of it." When it thus appears that Tao is in some time more than in some other, then this is no reality, but only like the falling and rising of tones in music, "it belongs to the playing." We can discover it in no existence. When we seek it in Heaven and Earth, in space and in time, then it is not there, but Heaven and Earth, space and time, are founded in it alone. And when we seek it in the "mystery of the

---

2. The Greek philosopher Heraclitus (fl. ca. 500 B.C.E.) stressed what he called *logos* (a word that in Greek has a range of literal meanings, including "word," "law," and "proportion"), which is eternal and governs all experience and regulates the ceaseless conflict of opposites.

3. All quotations, unless otherwise indicated in notes or the text itself, are from the *Zhuangzi*.
4. From the *Daode jing* (*The Scripture of the Way and Its Virtue*; see above), chapter 21.
5. From the *Daode jing*, chapter 1.

essence of God," then it is not there, but rather God is founded in it alone. And nevertheless, "it can be found through the seeking:"[6] in the unified life. There it is not perceived and known, but rather possessed, lived, and done. "He who obtains it with silence and completes it with being, only he has it,"[7] it is said in the books of Lieh Tzu. And he does not have it as his own, but rather as the sense of the world: the oneness of the masculine and feminine elements that exist not for themselves but only for one another, the oneness of antitheses that exist not for themselves but only through one another, the oneness of things that exist not for themselves but only with one another. This oneness is the Tao in the world. When in a conversation narrated by Chuang Tzu, Lao Tzu says to Confucius,[8] "That Heaven is high, that the Earth is broad, that sun and moon revolve, that things thrive, this is their Tao," this dictum is thus only intelligible through an old verse adduced to Lao Tzu in his book. It reads:

> Heaven attained oneness and with it brilliance, Earth oneness and with it rest and repose.
> The spirits oneness and with it understanding, the brooks oneness and with it full banks.
> All being oneness and with it life, prince and king oneness in order to give the world the right measure.[9]

Thus the oneness of each thing decides in itself the manner and the being of this thing; this is the Tao of this thing, this thing's path and wholeness: "No thing can produce Tao and yet each thing has Tao in itself and eternally produces it anew." This means that each thing manifests Tao through the way of its existence, through its life; for Tao is the oneness in the transformation, the oneness that proves itself, just as in the multiplicity of things, so in the multiplicity of the moments that follow upon one another in the life of each thing. Therefore, the perfect manifestation of Tao is not the man whose way elapses without transformations, but rather the man who unites the purest oneness with the most vigorous transformation. There are two types of life. The one is the mere vegetative living, the wearing out until extinction; the other is the eternal transformation and its oneness in the spirit. Whoever does not let himself be consumed in his life, but rather unceasingly renews himself and just in that way, in the transformation and through it, affirms his self—which indeed is not a fixed existence, but rather simply the way, Tao—he obtains the eternal transformation and self-affirmation. For here as always in the Tao-teaching, consciousness effects existence, spirit effects reality. And as in the connection of the life moments of a thing, so Tao proves itself in the connection of the life moments of the world, in the coming and going of all things, in the oneness of the eternal, universal transformation. Thus it says in the books of Lieh Tzu, "What has no primordial source and continually engenders is Tao. From life to life therefore, though ending, not decaying, this is eternity. . . . What has a primordial source and continually dies is also Tao. From death to death therefore, though never ending, yet itself decaying, this too is eternity." Death is loosening, is transition to form, is a moment of sleep and of meditation

6. From the *Daode jing*, chapter 62.
7. Liezi (fl. 4th century B.C.E.); the book of Daoism attributed to him is the *Liezi*.
8. The teacher, philosopher, and political theorist (551–479 B.C.E.).
9. From the *Daode jing*, chapter 39.

between two worldly lives. All is becoming and transformation in the "great home" of eternity. As separation and concentration, transformation and oneness follow upon one another in the existence of things, so life and death follow upon one another in existence of the world, together proving only Tao as the oneness in the transformation. This eternal Tao, which is the negation of all apparent existence, is also called "non-being." Birth is not a beginning, death is not an end, existence in time and space is without limit and suspension; birth and death are only entrance and exit through "the invisible gate of Heaven which is called non-being. This is the abode of the accomplished man."

Here too the accomplished man, the unified man, is denoted as the one who goes through and experiences Tao directly. He looks at the oneness in the world. But this is not to be understood as if the world were a closed thing apart from him, whose oneness he penetrates. Rather, the oneness of the world is only a reflection of his oneness; for the world is nothing foreign, but rather one with the unified man. "Heaven and Earth and I came together into existence, and I and all things are one." But since the oneness of the world exists only for the accomplished man, it is thus in reality his oneness that sets oneness into the world. This also emerges from the being of Tao as it appears in things. Tao is the path of things, their manner, their proper order, their oneness; but as such it exists in them only potentially; it first becomes operative in its contact with other things: "Were metal and stone without Tao, they would produce no sound. They have the power of sound, but it does not come out of them if they are not struck. So it is with all things." Moreover, consciousness is never on the side of receiving but rather on the side of giving; "Tao is conveyed but not received." And as the Tao of the thing becomes alive and manifest only though its contact with other things, so the Tao of the world becomes alive and manifest only through its unconscious contact with the conscious existence of the unified man. This is thus expressed by Chuang Tzu that the accomplished man reconciles and brings into harmony the two primordial elements of nature, yang and yin,[1] that divide apart the primordial oneness of existence. And in a late Taoist tract, the "Book of Purity and Rest,"[2] which on this point appears to be based on an altogether limitedly held tradition, it says, "When man remains in purity and rest, Heaven and Earth return," that is, to oneness, to the undifferentiated existence, to Tao. Also in this late, degenerated literature (the whole of later Taoism is nothing but increasing degeneration), the unified man is also thus comprehended as the giving man. We may say that for the Tao-teaching, the unified man is the creating man; for all creating, seen from this teaching, intends nothing other than to evoke the Tao of the world, the Tao of things, to make living and manifest the dormant oneness.

An attempt to summarize it:

---

1. The complementary forces that unite to form the Dao: yang, a term that originally referred to the sunny side of a valley, by extension came to be associated with the light, heaven, dryness, and activity—the male principle; yin, a term that originally referred to the shady side of a valley, by extension came to be associated with the dark, earth, dampness, and passivity—the female principle.

2. More commonly known as the *Scripture of Clarity and Quiescence* (*Qingjing jing*), a Tang dynasty (618–907) work that urges the practitioner to realize that the differentiation of the originally unified Dao is ultimately not real.

Tao in itself is the imperceptible, the unknowable. "The true Tao does not declare itself." It is not to be put forward; it is not be thought, it has no image, no word, no measure. "Tao's standard of measure is itself."[3]

Tao appears in the becoming of the world as the original undifferentiation, as the primordial existence from which all elements originated, as "all beings' mother," as the "valley spirit" that bears all. "The valley-spirit is immortal; it is called the deep feminine. The deep feminine's gate which is called Heaven and Earth's root."[4]

Tao appears in the existence of the world as the constant undifferentiation, as the uniform change of the world, as its order. "It has its movement and its reality, but it has neither action nor form." It is "eternally without doing and yet without non-doing." It "perseveres and does not change."[5]

Tao appears in things as the personal undifferentiation, as the proper manner and vigor of things. There is no thing in which the whole Tao is not as this thing's self. But even here Tao is eternally without doing and yet without non-doing. The self of things has its life in the way in which things answer things.

Tao appears in man as the purposive undifferentiation, as the uniting that conquers all deviation from life's foundation, as the making whole that heals all separation and fragility, as the expiating that redeems from all disunity. "He who is in sin, Tao can expiate him."[6]

As the purposive undifferentiation, Tao has its own fulfillment as the goal. It wishes to materialize. In man Tao can become oneness so pure, as it cannot become in the world, in things. The man in whom Tao becomes pure oneness is the accomplished man. In him Tao no longer appears, but rather is.

The accomplished man is shut into himself, all secure, unified out of Tao, unifying the world, a creating man, "God's companion," the companion of the universal, creative eternity. The accomplished man has eternity. Only the accomplished man has eternity. The spirit wanders through things until it flourishes to eternity in the accomplished man.

This word of Lao Tzu means this: "Climb the height of renunciation, embrace the primordial foundation of rest. The incalculable beings all rise up. Therein I know their return. When the beings have unfurled themselves, in the expansion each returns to its root. To have returned to the root means to rest. To rest means to have fulfilled destiny. To have fulfilled destiny means to be eternal."

Tao materializes in the truthful life of the accomplished man. In his pure oneness it develops out of manifestation to direct reality. The imperceptible and the unified human life, the first and the last, touch themselves. In the accomplished man Tao returns from its world-wandering through manifestation to its self. It becomes fulfillment, becomes eternity.

---

3. From the *Daode jing*, chapter 25.
4. From the *Daode jing*, chapter 6 (the preceding quote is from chapter 1).

5. From the *Daode jing*, chapter 25 (the preceding quote is from chapter 37).
6. From the *Daode jing*, chapter 62.

FOREWORD TO "THE SECRET OF THE GOLDEN FLOWER"

CARL GUSTAV JUNG

During the early twentieth century there was a resurgence of interest in the study of Western and Chinese alchemy, which up until that point had received mostly critical attention because of its emphasis on the compounding of elixirs, or pills of immortality, intended to confer longevity. The publication of a text espousing an internalized, even spiritualized, form of Chinese alchemy changed scholars' attitude. In 1928 the German missionary and sinologist Richard Wilhelm (1873–1930) began to study and translate *The Secret of the Golden Flower* (*Taiyi jinhua zongzhi*; see above), a work of internal alchemy Daoism—heavily colored by ideas drawn from Buddhist meditation—focusing on the return of one's spirit to the undivided primordial Dao. He sent his friend Carl Gustav Jung (1875–1961) a copy of his German translation, requesting that the Swiss psychologist write a commentary on it. Their collaboration was published in German in 1929, and its English-language translation in 1931 by Cary F. Baynes, one of Jung's students, became something of a worldwide sensation.

In his foreword to *The Secret of the Golden Flower* Jung describes how this text gave him deep insight into the collective unconscious, a key concept in his own theories that he had been working on since 1913. He claims that Chinese alchemy, like Western alchemy, seeks to effect transformation—the Golden Flower, or Golden Elixir, is not unlike the West's "philosopher's stone"—and uses elixirs to return to an ideal state. Jung's foreword stands as an important example of the early twentieth-century commingling of interest in Eastern and Western alchemy that led to important publications on Daoism and alchemy by the Swiss art historian and cultural anthropologist Titus Burckhardt (1908–1984) and the Romanian historian of religion Mircea Eliade (1907–1986).

My deceased friend, Richard Wilhelm, the co-author of this book, sent me the text of *The Secret of the Golden Flower* at a time that was critical for my own work. I had been occupied with the investigation of the processes of the collective unconscious since the year 1913, and had obtained results that seemed to me questionable in more than one respect. They not only lay far beyond everything known to 'academic' psychology but also overstepped the borders of medical, strictly personal, psychology. These findings had to do with an extensive phenomenology, to which hitherto known categories and methods could no longer be applied. My results, based on fifteen years of effort, seemed inconclusive, because no possible comparison offered itself. I knew of no realm of human experience with which I might have backed up my findings with some degree of assurance. The only analogies— and these, I must say, were far removed in time—I found scattered through the reports of heresiologists.[1] This connection did not in any way ease my task; on the contrary, it made it more difficult, because the Gnostic systems[2]

Translated by Cary F. Baynes.

1. Writers against heresy.
2. The philosophies of gnostics—members of various religious groups who flourished in the early centuries of Christianity. They believed that the material world is the product of an inferior creator, whereas the world of God is eternal, transcendent, and reachable only by those with esoteric knowledge (*gnōsis*, in Greek).

672 | CARL GUSTAV JUNG

consist only in small part of immediate psychic experiences, the greater part being speculative and systematizing revisions. Since we possess only very few detailed texts, and since most of what is known comes from the reports of Christian opponents, we have, to say the least, an inadequate knowledge of the history, as well as of the contents, of this confused and strange literature, so difficult to encompass. Moreover, considering the fact that a period of not less than from seventeen hundred to eighteen hundred years separates the present from that past, support from that field seemed to me extraordinarily risky. Again, the connections were in part of a secondary character, and left gaps in the main issue which made it impossible for me to make use of the Gnostic material.

The text that Wilhelm sent me helped me out of this embarrassment. It contained exactly those pieces which I had sought for in vain among the Gnostics. Thus the text became a welcome opportunity to publish, at least in provisional form, some of the essential results of my investigations.

At that time it seemed unimportant to me that *The Secret of the Golden Flower* is not only a Taoist text of Chinese yoga but also an alchemical tract. However, a subsequent, deeper study of Latin tracts has corrected my outlook and shown me that the alchemical nature of the text is of prime significance. But this, to be sure, is not the place to go into more details about that point. I shall only emphasize the fact that it was the text of *The Golden Flower* that first put me in the direction of the right track. For we have in medieval alchemy the long-sought connecting-link between Gnosis and the processes of the collective unconscious, observable to us to-day in modern man.

I take this opportunity to point out certain misunderstandings to which even well-informed readers of this book fell victim. Not infrequently people thought that my purpose in publishing the book was to put into the hands of the public a method of achieving happiness. In total misapprehension of all that I say in my commentary, such readers tried to imitate the 'method' described in the Chinese text. Let us hope that these representatives of spiritual profundity were few in number!

Another misunderstanding gave rise to the opinion that, in the commentary, I had pictured to a certain extent my psychotherapeutic method, which, it was said, consisted in my suggesting to my patients Eastern ideas for therapeutic purposes. I do not believe that there is anything in my commentary lending itself to that sort of superstition. In any case such an opinion is altogether erroneous, and is based on the widespread conception that psychology is an invention for a definite purpose and not an empirical science. To this category belongs the equally superficial as well as unintelligent opinion that the idea of the collective unconscious is 'metaphysical'. It is a question of an empirical concept to be put alongside the concept of instinct, as is obvious to anyone who will read with some attention.

EXPLORATIONS IN ORAL SECRETS
(*Koujue gouxuan lu*)

CHEN YINGNING

Chen Yingning (1880–1969), a famous modern lay Daoist, was active in Shanghai in the early twentieth century. After suffering poor health as a child, he studied traditional medicine; he also set out in search of Buddhist and Daoist teachers. He was not afraid to criticize specific aspects of internal alchemy Daoism—he was equally critical of Buddhist views of the body—and is noted for advocating reforms to its practices in response to ideas imported from the West and revived in China within Mahayana Buddhism. Chen Yingning wrote a number of significant commentaries on Daoist alchemical texts and a general history of Daoism, and his written correspondence with female adepts brought him particular renown. He played an important role in the Chinese Taoist Association, becoming its second president in 1961.

In his writings Chen stressed the primacy of secret oral teachings regarding inner alchemy. These teachings, which he describes as being very difficult to obtain, must be procured by the disciple from a qualified teacher or master, who is to be venerated as a deity. The excerpts below, from the serialized tract *Explorations in Oral Secrets* (*Koujue gouxuan lu*, 1934–35), provide a fascinating window onto the connections Chen drew between Daoism and nationalism, science, and religious reform. An emphasis on adhering to the ancient rules of initiation to and transmission of oral secrets turned into exclusivity and eventually became tied up with Chen's nationalistic sentiments: he began to portray internal alchemy Daoism as a tradition uniquely bound to ethnic Chinese. Chen also held that the secrets passed down were an important and effective counter to Western science (especially the technologies of war).

PRONOUNCING GLOSSARY

Chen Yingning: *chun yingning*   Koujue gouxuan lu: *ko-chueh go-hsien lu*

Although Daoist books circulating in the market are numerous in titles and categories, those that discuss the theoretical principles of the practice do not address issues of the oral secrets, whereas those that discuss the oral secrets of the practice do not discuss its principles. Hence, when learners read them, either they will find them too empty and general for actually engaging in practice, or they will hold stubbornly to one particular method while remaining ignorant of [the need for] flexible adaptation. In the end, their hair turns white without their achieving anything at all. This is why Master Huang[1] stressed both principles and secrets when he was teaching the practice to people. The learner must first understand the principle clearly and then come to know the oral secrets. For the supreme wondrous secrets of the practice are quite different from those "side doors and petty techniques." Once you know the secrets, you will be able to deepen your understanding of the principle. This is the truth that unites all and differs from empty talk and general discourse. This is why I introduce his learning to those who are fond of the Way today.

TRANSLATED BY Xun Liu. All bracketed additions are the translator's.

1. The internal alchemist Huang Shang (fl. 1840), on whose work Chen Yingning based his own.

* * *

> Addressing the transmitting master, the recipient takes
> an oath to heaven.
> Silk of clouds and chiffon of phoenix are offered entwined
> with gold bands,
> Hair is cut so that the sinews and skin are preserved
> whole and sound,
> Hand in hand, ascend the mount to smear the cinnabar
> fluid on the mouth,
> Only then can the Gold Scriptures and Jade Effulgence
> be revealed.[2]

* * *

As a master, he must have sworn an oath at the time when he was taught his own oral secrets, such as "I must not casually pass it on to an inappropriate person. If I do, I will bring calamity on myself." This is just a very ordinary oath. There are more severe ones such as "If alive, condemned to die by man and Heaven; and when deceased, subject to the sufferings of the Earth's hell." Having taken all these vows, a master cannot but feel anxious at heart, apprehensive lest he breach his own vow by his lapse of caution. So he will not easily part with his secrets.

* * *

Buddhism and Christianity are world-bound religions by nature. Daoist learning and the techniques of the Immortals[3] are ethnically bound. Universal religions always welcome you to join their church organizations regardless of your ethnicity. If you don't believe, they try to persuade you to believe. Once you believe, they talk you into joining them.

As for Daoist learning and the Immortals' techniques, just the opposite position is true. If you are not a descendent of the Chinese nation and a son and grandson of the Yan and Huang emperors,[4] don't even dream of acquiring a shred of true secrets from a master.

When I was learning the Way, I also took the routine vow never to reveal the secrets for fear that foreigners may obtain them and spare nothing in putting them to practice. If they succeeded in achieving perfection, that would be just like adding wings to a tiger. We Chinese would be left further behind, only to sigh over the dust left in their trail. We would be better off preserving the little heritage bequeathed to us by our ancestors. That would still leave us with a few hopes. Perhaps, in the future, we may be able to utilize the efficacious power refined through our flesh body to overpower the deadly war machines of science and suppress into submission all the murderous fiends. Hence the unwillingness to pass on the secrets.[5]

2. According to the translator, Chen quotes this verse from the *Scripture of the Yellow Court* (*Huangting jing*), a work called in full the *Most High Jade Scripture on the Internal View of the Yellow Court* (*Taishang huangting neijing yujing*; see above).
3. Daoists who have achieved extraordinary powers and a higher form of existence.
4. That is, a Han Chinese. Yandi and Huangdi (the Yellow Emperor, 27th century B.C.E.) were two mythological emperors who battled and, after Huangdi's victory, became allies.
5. This portion of Chen's unfinished manuscript was never published in either the *Yangshan Biweekly* [*Yangshan banyuekan*] or the *Immortals' Way Monthly* [*Xiandao yuebao*, translator's note; he took the excerpt from an anthology published in 1991].

A BALLAD ON LOOKING FOR THE WAY

FANGNEI SANREN

Fangnei Sanren (born Wan Ligeng, in 1848), whose name literally means "Rambling Man of the World," was an internal alchemist who spent his life searching for Daoist masters so that they might share their oral instructions with him. His success in this endeavor enabled him to become one of the most important internal alchemists of his age. In addition to mastering many Daoist traditions, Fangnei also studied Confucianism and Buddhism. In "A Ballad on Looking for the Way," published in 1936, he looks back on all of his roaming and, as the translator Xun Liu notes, depicts it as a departure from the secular world and an entrance into a sacred realm. Far more than merely traveling, he undertook a spiritual journey to sacred mountains that was modeled on the pilgrimages of the Daoist patriarchs.

PRONOUNCING GLOSSARY

Fangnei Sanren: *fawng-naye sawn-run*   Zhongnan: *chowng-nawn*
Sanfeng: *sawn-fung*   Zu Sheng: *tsu shung*

The Great Way circulates and passes on in the world;
The threads of its Order never end in the universe.
Longing to transcend life and death, I cultivate the Gold Elixir[1]
And aspire to fraternize with the Sublime and the Perfected.[2]
Gone are the Sublime and the Perfected to the Immortals'[3] realm,
Their absence adds wrinkles daily to my worried face.
They left tomes on the elixir for us to read.
But cryptic and obscure are their subtle words and meanings.
The practice is hard without the guidance of a teacher.
Yet the bond of transcendence cannot be casual.
How dare I give up wading the rivers and scaling the mountains?
The bond is formed by traversing all the peaks and streams.
Ill at ease is my heart until I find my master.

Deviant approaches and false methods rise and rage.
The aberrant kinds may spread due to greed and depravity;
Persist diligently in your practice as if grinding down a brick.
The sagacious will never be swindled.
Peruse the Scriptures, the Ode, the Concordance, and the Treatise.[4]
The road is wider if you know the main schools;
Concealed as it may be, seek the complete truth of heaven.
Sleep exposed to the elements, and eat under the wind;
Ragged and worn may be the clothes and shoes;
But never let the heart turn cold halfway through.

TRANSLATED BY Xun Liu.

1. A substance, produced by alchemy, that confers immortality.
2. Daoist spiritual masters; Daoists who have moved beyond earthly corruption.

3. Daoists who have achieved extraordinary powers and a higher form of existence.
4. That is, the key works on internal alchemy (the precise referents are unclear).

Once upon a time there lived an immortal, the White Jade Toad.[5]
Roaming among clouds his footsteps covered mountains and rivers.
Long he journeyed before he moved Chen the Mud Ball.[6]
Yet still the Mud Ball delayed transmission for three more years.
There was also Master Sanfeng,[7] keen on intuiting the Mystery.
His ramblings led him all the way to Zhongnan Peak.[8]
He had forgotten his age of sixty or seventy,
When he met the Fire Dragon[9] who transmitted the secrets.
So many since time immemorial have learned to be immortals.
Reverent in their heart, they sought guidance from their teachers.
With Heaven silently adjudicating and controlling,
Their conundrum is solved with compassion in due time.
My quest for my master's transmission is truly pitiable.
With utmost sincerity have I beseeched heaven.
Having met my teacher, I was hampered by a lack of means.
Before long my sideburns had turned gray.
Sorrow-stricken at the mirror, I strengthened my resolve in prayer.
Year in and year out I journeyed in search' of enlightened worthies
Only to be rewarded by heaven with the fellowship united in *qi*.[1]
Enduring a hundred afflictions I sought the True Lead.[2]

With oral secrets obtained, I returned to try the refining cultivation.
Results instantly shown, I am convinced the Way does not deviate.
Now I know the True differs from the False, as heaven from earth,
And true are the Three Origin methods and the Two Schools.[3]
For those to come who will read my ballad about the search,
Each word herein is a teardrop beyond description.
Worry only about your wavering resolve
And about your unwillingness to spend.
But once the Four Requisites[4] are met,
Your true vessel of salvation is set.

I urge all of you to grab Zu Sheng's[5] staff,
And abandon your mundane passions at once.
Quickly seek the Great Way and intuit the Double Mystery[6]
So as to rub shoulders with Hong Ya the immortal.[7]

5. Bai Yuchan (also known as Bo Yuchan, fl. 1194–1229), a key figure in the southern lineage of internal alchemy; he was closely associated with the practice of Thunder Rites, intended to harness the power of thunder and summon common thunder deities.
6. Chen Niwan (d. 1213), also known as Chen Nan, the fourth patriarch of the southern lineage of internal alchemy; Bai Yuchan was his disciple.
7. Zhang Sanfeng (ca. 1320s–1410s), a (perhaps legendary) immortal who mastered internal alchemy and was believed to possess magical powers.
8. An important mountain in Shaanxi Province connected with many Daoist immortals.
9. Huo Long (usually referred to as the Perfected One Fire Dragon) was [Zhang] Sanfeng's teacher when Sanfeng was young (ca. 1250).
1. Vital energy, breath (pneuma).
2. In internal alchemy, the knowledge of the Dao with which each individual is fundamentally

endowed.
3. The southern and northern lineages of internal alchemy. "The Three Origin methods": Heavenly Origin, Earthly Origin, and Humanly Origin, different approaches to internal alchemy.
4. Food, clothing, shelter, and medicine (a Buddhist concept).
5. A general (266–321), renowned for his ability to fight using an iron staff.
6. The term "Double Mystery" (*chongxuan*) is an allusion to chapter 1 of the *Daode jing* (*The Scripture of the Way and Its Virtue*; see above), where the Dao is called "mystery upon mystery"; it can refer to the secrets of internal alchemy (as here), or to the tradition of Daoism (Twofold Mystery, which reached its height during the Tang dynasty, 618–907) that views this passage as the key to understanding the *Daode jing*.
7. It was believed that rubbing shoulders with this legendary early immortal would lead to good health, longevity, and even immortality.

THE COMPLETE PERFORMANCE OF SU
(*Dachu su*)

Chinese theater and Daoist ritual are so thoroughly interconnected that scholars often write of both ritual theater and theatrical ritual. All Daoist rituals have theatrical elements; for example, they might depict the destruction of purgatory and the release of all suffering souls. At the same time, many forms of theater—from marionette theater to opera—are exorcistic in nature. There is also a category of drama called "deliverance plays," such as *Zhongli of the Han Leads Lan Caihe to Enlightenment* (*Han Zhong Li dutuo Lan Caihe*, thirteenth–fourteenth century; see above). In the marionette theater tradition of Fujian, the puppeteers are ordained ritual masters and their main performance follows a ritual prelude.

The Complete Performance of Su (*Dachu su*) is one such ritual prelude to a marionette performance. Its transcription invites the reader into the ritual domain to hear the cacophony of the percussion instruments, smell the incense, see the vibrant colors of candles and ritual ornamentation, and taste the wine set out for the deities. The text of the play also enables us to hear the invocations that are recited, see the conflagration of burned offerings, and follow the movements of the puppets' strings as they dance.

In *The Complete Performance of Su* a host of spirits are invoked and invited to the ritual. Wishes for continued auspiciousness and thanks for boons granted to the sponsors are then transmitted to the high deities by Chief Marshall Tian. Besides being the patron deity of the theater, Chief Marshall Tian is the most important tutelary deity of the area in Fujian where this play is performed; he also holds a minor office in the heavenly bureaucracy. The performance concludes with the sending off of the deities, a wish that the people in the community will help and care for one another, and a promise that they will be watched over and will prosper.

PRONOUNCING GLOSSARY

Cai Junchao: *tsai chun-chao*   Dachu su: *dah-chu sue*
Chen Tianbao: *chen tien-bao*

A traditional libretto of the Quanzhou[1] string puppet theatre

Transcribed by the (late) Chen Tianbao and Cai Junchao[2]

The first percussion prelude

 "three prostrations" (three beats)
 "nine kowtows" (nine beats)
 "walking on knees"
"jump of the biting louse"
 "chicken picking grains"

TRANSLATED BY Robin Ruizendaal. All bracketed additions are the translator's.

1. A large city in southern Fujian Province. 2. First published by them in 1986.

"jump of the biting louse"
"noise that fills the mountains"
"jump of the biting louse"
"Suppression of the lower five"

The second percussion prelude (the same sequence as the first)

The invocation of the patron saint
(Directly after the "Suppression of the lower five" follows the beating of
the large gong, which marks the beginning of the invitation of the deity.
The beating of the large gong continues with several random beats.

The person who performs the invocation takes a cone of "opening-of-
the-eyes-paper" and bows toward the Young Lord, then bows to the
outside of the stage. He turns inside and pours out three cups of spirits
for the Young Lord, first the middle, and then to the left and to the
right. He dips the ring finger of his right hand in the wine and sprinkles
some wine upward).

The invoker:

He-cai-a! (recites the "silent spell")
A stick of incense burns on the golden altar,
The red glow of the silver candles shines in the sun,
Golden flowers are arranged in silver vases,
Fine spirits are poured in golden cups.

(The invoker dips his finger in the wine again and, sprinkles it away)

He recites:

I invoke and worshipfully invite to come to the altar: the Great King
of the Jade Tones of the Palace of Music, Chief Marshall Tian of the
Bureau of Wind and Fire of the Ninefold Heaven, the First and Second
Houseman,[3] the Judge of the Tunes; the Child-that-plays-the-Flute; the
Secretary-that-brings-Wealth; the General-of-excellent-Dance and all
36 generals and officials.

Wine is offered once, twice, three times,
I worshipfully invite the Local God of the Earth,
A sheet of burning sacrificial money turns the stage all red.

(the puppeteer burns the "opening-of-eyes-paper", and moves it inside the
stage in a circular movement; the five tones [instruments] perform *vivace*.[4]
The puppeteer makes a circular movement [with the burning paper] outside [the performance area]; drops the ashes; turns inside; offers wine, and
sprinkles it about, sprinkles the spirits while reciting the [following] spell:)

The Red Cardamom ascends to Heaven, (sprinkles upward)
The White Bird descends to Earth, (sprinkles downward)

3. Dependents of Chief Marshall Tian. "The
Ninefold Heaven": an allusion to the ancient
conception of nine heavens (Daoists usually

refer to three or six heavens).
4. Spiritedly (Italian), a marking of musical
tempo.

The Blue Dragon to the left, (sprinkles left)
The White Tiger to the right, (sprinkles right),
Excellent big screen, excellent small screen (touches the small screen three times with wine), excellent big drum, excellent small drum, excellent gong, excellent *zhong*,[5] excellent small and big clapper (when each object is mentioned, wine is sprinkled in its direction).

Recites:

He-cai-a! (pours wine again, raises the cup and offers it)
Young Lord please drink, all deities please drink (sprinkles wine).

Recites:

He-cai-a! (replaces the cup in its original position, dips [a finger] in the wine and writes in the palm of his left hand the eighteen-talisman).[6]
Eighteen unite completely, completely unite eighteen, my disciples will sing out loud. (rubs the palms of his hands together).

Recites:

He-cai-a ! (claps in his hands three times)
(Immediately the invoker takes a cup of wine and sprinkles it about. The invoker "kicks-the-foot" (*original note*: touching the ground with the tip of the right foot to indicate the end of this section). The five tones [instruments] stop, and the invoker calls out: "He-cai-a!" The five tones stop. The big gong is subsequently beaten, and the drum beats the two opening beats. The invoker solemnly stands erect and sings the melody "Da-yi-da").[7]

(After having finished the "Da-yi-da", the wine is poured back in the bottle, and the banquet is removed. First the "enter the stage" drum roll is performed, and then the "official" drum roll. At this time one of the puppeteers places the Young Lord in the "metal" position by using the puppet's strings. He makes the "kick-the-foot" sign, and drum and gong stop.

✻   ✻   ✻

Recites (whispering):

Listen to the *ding-dong* sound of drums and gongs,
One play can be performed in many different ways.
With colourful headgear
and embroidered red costume.
Where don't I go, where don't I come.
As long as you are not present, I would not dare to dance and sing;
As long as I haven't invoked the deities, I would not dare to act rashly?
(kneels)

---

5. Probably a bell or set of bells.
6. Eighteen is supposed to refer to the number of puppets of each company, before the number of puppets became thirty-six [translator's note].

7. The words that are added to the melody are the repetitions, in alternating order, of the syllables of the spell of the (marionette) theatre *luo, li* and *lian* [translator's note].

I worshipfully invite the Deities of the Three Realms.[8]
I worshipfully invite the Deities of the Upper Realm, of the Middle
Realm and the Lower Realm.

(He kowtows three times and rises. He kneels again and kowtows three
times, rises. He kneels again and kowtows three times and remains
prostrated after the last kowtow, and reads out the memorial)

Recites (whispering):

Today humble citizen xxx of xx quarter of xx du[9] of xx district of the
Quanzhou prefecture in the province of Fujian, sincerely burns incense,
worships and presents a request. He reverently understands that Heaven
has nine levels and it is touched by sincerity, the deities dwell at three
feet [above our head], and become manifest through goodness. Through
their endless transformations, we enjoy the lustre of their benevolence.
I recite the [names of the] devotees xxx *zhuming* born on xx hour of xx
day of xx month of xx year (the *zhuming* can be the members of one
family mentioned in order their birthdays, the number of persons is
unlimited). Their destiny is in the hands of the God of the Northern
Dipper.[1] May we receive:
The profound mercy of Heaven and Earth moves the three lights[2] to
shine down on their virtue. We place us of our own free will under your
protection and show our gratitude for the slightest incident. xxx Master
of the Lamps last year humbly expressed his wishes, that were rewarded.
Today we have sincerely prepared lamps and gold, a sweet pig, a grass
fed goat, string puppet theatre and opera to express our thanks. I am
afraid that members of the household have earlier on expressed wishes,
which are in their minds all the time. They are of good faith and have
prepared lamps and gold as a thanksgiving for absolution.
Today is an auspicious day; an altar of lamps has been erected; marionette theatre will be performed. Above we offer to the Heavenly Perfected, in the middle we reward the Benevolent Deity, below we say
thanks to the Tutelary Deity. We are happy with the rewarding of our
wishes, and accumulate auspiciousness. The gate and courtyard are
cleansed, our mansion is radiant. May sons and wealth be added and
strengthen our family. May the five good fortunes rise, may the three
plenties[3] all be here, and there be no disasters in the four seasons. May
the eight periods of the year be filled with happiness, may growth be
abundant as that of melon vines, and may splendour accompany a hundred generations, we reverently present the memorial.

Memorialized on (date)

(Young Lord rises and bows)

---

8. The Realm of Desire (whose inhabitants desire
pleasing objects of the senses), the Realm of Form
(inhabited by gods who have physical form), and
the Formless Realm (inhabited by gods who exist
only as consciousness); these make up the Buddhist universe.
9. A designation found in old addresses that

means something like "section."
1. The seven stars of the Big Dipper.
2. The sun, the moon, and the stars.
3. Life (i.e., longevity), children, and happiness.
"Five good fortunes": longevity, wealth, health,
virtue, and a natural death.

I worshipfully invite emperor Yama[4] of the Eastern Peak, the two Gods of the District and Prefecture, and the Guanyin Buddha,[5] Stove God, Local God of the Earth, the Gods-protecting-the-Gate, the Sergeants of the Doors, all deities that are worshipped through the incense burner of this house.

Little Su is afraid that the invitations might not be complete, if the preparations are incomplete, I request the Local God of the Earth to repeat the invitations! ("kick of the foot", and end of the *san tong* music)

[Young Lord] **Cries out**:
I have invited! (music continues with the "De sheng" melody)

In dialect:
Disciples!
All:
Hey!
Young Lord:
I have clearly invoked the deities, I will now sing about incense, flowers, lamps, candles for the deities of the Three Realms and all other deities, is that all right?"
Chorus:
All right!
Young Lord:
The Young Lord should sing well, the disciples should also harmonize well.
Chorus:
The Young Lord has to sing well, the disciples also have to harmonize well.
Young Lord:
It is said that there is a story about incense.
Chorus:
How goes the story about incense?
Young Lord:
Disciples listen:

[Offering of flowers and incense]

("Bo mei" *kun*-melody sung by the Young Lord; the chorus, in this lyric and following lyrics, is presented between parentheses)

Good incense grows on trees (good incense grows on trees)./ It is used to worship the Lords of the Three Realms./ Liu Xi, graduate of the first degree, entered a temple to burn incense./ Together with Sanniang of the Hua mountain they had a child, and called him Chenxiang ["pungent incense"]. *Lian-li lao-lao* etc. [with chorus].

Young Lord:
After incense, I have a story about flowers.

---

4. In Chinese folklore, the central judge of the dead; the Daoist underworld was near Mount Tai, the eastern of the five sacred mountains.
5. A female bodhisattva—a being intent on enlightenment—identified in East Asian Buddhism with Avalokiteshvara, the bodhisattva regarded as the embodiment of all the compassion of all the buddhas.

Chorus:
How goes the story about flowers?
Young Lord:
Disciples listen:

("Bo mei" *kun*-melody sung by the Young Lord)
Fine flowers grow on the ground (fine flowers grow on the ground)./ An immortal maiden in heaven loved flowers and descended./ Lord Huang Qiu went to the garden to enjoy the flowers and he and the Magnolia Lady fell in love.
Lian-li lao-lao etc. [with chorus].

✻　✻　✻

(The Young Lord whispers the "silent spell")
I have presented a clear invocation, and withdraw now behind the coloured screen, I have ordered my disciples to perform a play for the Deities of the Three Realms, and the Deities that are distant and close by.
Calls out:
I have invited!

("Di jin dang" melody sung by the Young Lord)
The Young Lord, the Young Lord's surname is Su (my surname is Su). My house is in Hangzhou at the head of the Iron-plated Bridge, three miles out of town (three miles). The king of the Tang was fascinated by me (fascinated), and had me roam the world (roam the world) to free the people from injustice, and to present their wishes before the heavenly officials.
Suddenly I hear, suddenly I hear a fine big drum (fine big drum) inside the coloured screen, and I also hear inside the coloured screen a fine small drum (fine small drum). The big drum is taking over from the small drum, the small drum is taking over from the big drum, the drums go *ding-dang-xiang-ding dang* (*ding-dang-xiang-ding dang*). My whole life, my whole life I have solely loved to dance (solely loved to dance), and I will dance the "yan-character" dance ("van-character" dance). Let me pace again some fine steps (some fine steps), and sing the song of Great Peace, one stanza of *lian-li lao* etc. [with chorus]

(The Young Lord enters the stage, is hung back, and this is the end of the play)
(If no altar is placed in front of the stage, the performance is called "The Young Lord Su paces the stage".

Young Lord calls out:
I have invited! (he is moved from the centre to the side of the stage, and continuous in *guanhua*). I have inspected the situation here, and I have presented a clear invocation (very clear). Do you know where I live? (Where does the Young Lord live?) Listen to me:

("Chu zhenzi" melody sung by the Young Lord)
I live in Hangzhou, I go everywhere and we come in every prefecture. Today I came here, and behind the coloured screen I hear the beating of

gong and drum. The Young Lord should dance the "yan-character" dance. My disciples will sing at the top of their voice, I shall dance and sing, sing the song of Great Peace. *Lian-li lao* etc.

(After having finished singing he whispers the "silent spell":)
I have presented a clear invocation, and withdraw now behind the coloured screen, I have ordered my disciples to perform a play for the Deities of the Three Realms, and the Deities that are distant and close by!
Calls out:
I have invited!

("Di jin dang" melody sung by the Young Lord; select one of the three lyrics below that are set to the "Di jin dang" melody)
Drum and clapper, the sound of drum and clapper makes one want to sing (makes one want to sing). A stick of fine incense offered to the Halls of Heaven (offered to the deities). The text, text can create countless marvels (countless marvels), like painting a peony with rouge. *Lian-li lao* etc.

("Di jin dan" melody sung by the Young Lord)
Purple robes, purple robes and a golden belt, in my hand I hold a peony (peony). On golden steps supported by a jade lady (jade lady). Collapsing drunk, collapsing drunk is really something to boast about. *Lian-li lao* etc.

("Di jin dan" melody sung by the Young Lord)
I see, I see the cherry-apple on the moon (cherry-apple on the moon). It makes one refrain from enjoying flowers and wine (enjoying woman and spirits). The rain hits the pear blossom. A youth of eighteen springs has arrived. *Lian-li lao* etc.

(The end of "The Young Lord Su paces the stage")

"Sending off of the gods"

("Di jin dang" sung by the Young Lord)
Lao lian etc. [with chorus].
The young have to study diligently, [the study of] texts can establish one's career (establish one's career). The dignitaries dressed in vermilion and purple that fill the court, are all men of letters. *Lian-li lao* etc. [with chorus].

(The young Lord kneels and whispers the "silent spell")
I worshipfully send off the Deities of the Three Realms: those of the Upper Realm return the Hall of Heaven; those of the Middle Realm return to the Halls of the Middle; those of the Lower Realms return to the Palace of the Earth.

(rises, bows and whispers)
I worshipfully send off the deities to their palaces, the Buddhas to their temples, the soldiers and horses of the five camps to their respective

camps, I return to my town. In my hand I hold a glowing incense burner, and three cups that will harmonize all. If there is something the matter, burn incense and invoke again; do not dare to invoke without reason. I am afraid I might not have completed the sending off, so I ask the local tutelary deity to perform the sending off again.
Calls out:
I have invited!

("Yi-dan" melody sung by the whole company)
Lao lian li etc.

(The sending off of the deities ends here) One of the songs to the tune "Di jin dang" may be selected at will to replace "the young have to study diligently", the "Yi-dan" coda remains the same.

("Di jin dang" sung by the Young Lord)
Lao li etc. [with chorus]
When spring arrives a hundred flowers bloom (a hundred flowers bloom). In summer lotus flowers in the water at the foreshore (water at the foreshore). In autumn a metal wind cuts. In winter frost and snow pile up. *Lian-li lian* etc. [with chorus]

("Di jin dang" sung by the Young Lord)
Lao lian etc. [with chorus]
The mid-autumn moon shines on the western window (shines on the western window). Melancholy baluster, I lean on it, and it makes me think of previous lovers. Suddenly I hear, suddenly I hear the *ding-ding, dang-dang, ding-ding, dang-dang* sound of the iron-horses[6] dangling from the eaves, giving Little Su a spring heartbeat. *Lian-li lao* etc. [with chorus]

("Di jin dang" sung by the Young Lord)
In the first lunar month, on the 15th day of the first lunar month we enjoy the Lantern Festival (enjoy the Lantern Festival). You still feel that it's going on when it is already Qingming[7] (it is already Qingming). When the summer, when the summer season has just finished, you can suddenly hear the autumnal cry of a lonely wild goose. *Lian-li lao* etc. [with chorus]

("Di jin dang" sung by the Young Lord)
Mounting my steed, dismounting my steed, I have come to lead the troops (lead the troops).[8] To urge you people of the world to be brothers, man and wife (man and wife), helping each other, care for each other, and get along together (get along together). Today disciples have asked me to communicate a request (communicate a request). After the communication of the request, I will protect my disciples, [and hope] that

---

6. Small pieces of metal suspended from strings that make clinking sounds when stirred by the wind or touched by a person [translator's note].
7. A festival, also known as Tomb Sweeping Day, that falls between April 4 and 6 (fifteen days after the spring equinox). On this day families pay respects to their ancestors, clean their grave sites, burn paper spirit money for them, and then enjoy a family feast outside.
8. Deities are supposed to arrive and depart on horseback, as such different types of sacrificial money depicting horses are burned during almost every ritual in Quanzhou [translator's note].

they may bring forth large and small groups of sons and grandsons (sons and grandsons). After they have graduated relatives will implore them to write, write a fine play. *Lian-li lao* etc. [with chorus]

DAOIST MONASTIC LIFE

YOSHITOYO YOSHIOKA

Yoshitoyo Yoshioka (1916–1981) was an eminent Japanese scholar of Chinese Daoism and Buddhism. From 1940 to 1946 he lived in the White Cloud Monastery (Baiyun guan)—the largest Daoist monastery in Beijing. In "Daoist Monastic Life," he vividly depicts life in a Daoist monastery in the mid-twentieth century.

After distinguishing between "hereditary" monasteries (controlled by a single lineage of Daoism) and "public" monasteries (which are open to any Daoist of any lineage and resemble the large Buddhist monasteries), Yoshioka notes that almost all Celestial Masters (Tianshi) temples are hereditary, while Complete Perfection (Quanzhen) Daoists—the other main contemporary sect—have both types. The White Cloud Monastery is public, and its residents are celibate Quanzhen clergy.

Yoshioka provides a firsthand account of the inner workings of a functioning Daoist monastery, such as the details of entry into the order, ordination (including a description of the ordination platform), clothing, hairstyle, headgear, regalia, monastic etiquette, rules and punishment, and monastic offices. He also offers a somewhat more personal reflection on the daily pulse of the monastic routine at the White Cloud Monastery and mentions by name the Daoist masters he came to know. In addition to recounting quotidian elements (such as the marking of time by the hitting of a wooden plank and the precise components of a meal), he chronicles rites that take place at particular times of year and describes special rituals and ceremonies, such as the airing of the Daoist canon. That manuscript was not only one of the monastery's treasures but also played an important role in the modern study of Daoism, since it was the basis of the first widely available print version of the canon, published in 1962 in Taiwan.

Yoshioka's account ends on a poignant note. Following Japan's defeat in World War II, he and other Japanese scholars were expelled from China and forced to leave behind all their research notes and Chinese documents. Back in Japan, he lived in extreme poverty for many years, and disturbing news from a friend in Beijing reached him: the monks of the White Cloud Monastery had burned alive their abbot—his old friend An Shilin—ostensibly because they believed he had sold off monastic property to maintain an expensive concubine. For Yoshioka this radical act, pitting monk against monk, was a sign of monastic Daoism's decline as China rushed forward into one of the most dramatic, and traumatic, revolutions in its history.

PRONOUNCING GLOSSARY

Baiyun guan: *buy-you-un gwan*
chuanjie lüshi: *chuan-chieh lew-shih*
daoshi: *dow-shih*

Quanzhen: *chu-en chun*
Tianshi Dao: *tien-shih dow*

The Daoist Equivalent of the Buddhist monastery is known as a *daoguan*. Daoist temples in general are known as *guan* "abbey," *miao* "temple," *gong* "palace," *tan* "altar," *ci* "shrine hall," *ge* "pavilion," *dong* "grotto," etc. Some of these words are also used in the names of Confucian and Buddhist temples.

Daoist temples are of two main types; "public" and "hereditary." Hereditary temples are those in which control is monopolized generation after generation by members of the same subsect. Most Daoist temples fall into this category. They are referred to as "ordinary" or "small" temples. Public monasteries are the great Daoist monastic centers which are open equally to the *daoshi* (monks or priests) of any school. They constitute a network of major monasteries very similar to the system of public Buddhist monasteries. Public monasteries do not take novices. The daoshi living in them are itinerant monks who gather from all over China to pursue their Daoist practice, or novices who have come to be ordained.

Among the special privileges accorded public monasteries the most important is the right to build an ordination platform. There the abbot, who is equivalent in status to the director of a chief monastery of a Japanese Buddhist sect, administers the vows to those daoshi ready to receive them. Since itinerant monks cannot be recognized as full-fledged daoshi until they have taken the vows at an ordination ceremony, they use the public monastery to continue their practice while awaiting ordination.

In addition to the hereditary and public categories described above, modern Daoist temples can be divided on the basis of doctrine. The two great sects are known as the Tianshi Dao, or Way of the Celestial Masters, and the Quanzhen Jiao, or Doctrine of Complete Perfection. Temples affiliated with the Celestial Masters are, almost without exception, hereditary. The headquarters of this sect are located on Longhu Shan[1] in Jiangxi, where the Celestial Master Zhang presides. His office has been hereditary from father to son for centuries, which indicates that the daoshi of this sect, although they formally renounce the world, are not strictly prohibited from wedlock.

Those who do marry, however, are not permitted to live within a proper monastery. Married daoshi are referred to by a variety of names that emphasize their domestic life or marital ties and distinguish them from daoshi who spend celibate lives in monastery cloisters. Daoshi belonging to the Celestial Master's sect do not take the ordination vows. Until the end of the Qing dynasty,[2] all that was required for their full accreditation was a registration certificate bearing the seal of the Celestial Master. After the advent of the Republican government, this system gradually died out and the Way of the Celestial Masters lost most of its sectarian cohesion.

* * *

TRANSLATED BY Holmes Welch and Anna Seidel. All bracketed additions are the translators'.

1. Mount Longhu, a sacred mountain in Jiangzi Province.   2. That is, 1911; the Qing dynasty began in 1644.

Entry into the Quanzhen Sect

There is no fixed age for admission to the life of a Daoist monk. For most daoshi, however, their religious lives begin between the ages of twelve and twenty. Motives for "leaving the world" are diverse but can be grouped under the following headings:

1. Those with a deep-seated determination to pursue the way of a Daoist immortal;
2. Those who seek a life of seclusion and tranquility;
3. Those from families so poor that they give their sons to a monastery to be brought up and become monks;
4. Those who, because of ill-health or infirmity, feel ill-equipped to cope with the problems of secular life.

Unfortunately, most Daoist monks today seem to fall into categories 3 or 4. One meets few outstanding figures; most have a deficient understanding of Daoism and seem wanting in spiritual vigor.

Anybody wishing to enter the Daoist religious life must find a suitable sponsor. Usually this means going to an ordinary small temple and requesting its daoshi to act as one's primary master. Having secured acceptance by a master, the youth becomes a novice. During the ceremony in which he does so, he first worships the deities at the altar of the Preaching Hall, then offers his respects to the spirits of earlier generations of masters of the sect in the Patriarch's Hall, and finally makes obeisances before his own master. Henceforth the novice allows his hair to grow. He learns the proper manner in which to clean the monastery buildings, to cook, and to receive visitors. At the same time he studies the Confucian *Four Books*[3] and learns to chant the morning and evening liturgy, the *Sanguan jing*, *Yankou jing*, and *Douke jing*.[4]

When the novice reaches a suitable age, his master chooses an auspicious day to perform the "rites of crown and cloth." The novice's hair is carefully combed and bound up into a top-knot. He is crowned and joins in prayers and celebrations with the daoshi and other friends of his in the community.

Shortly after "coronation" the novice enrolls in a public monastery where, when the season to take the vows comes round, he participates in the ordination ceremony. He is now a full-fledged daoshi, free to remain in the public monastery, to pursue an itinerant spiritual pilgrimage, or to return to his master. Men who enter the monastic life in middle age follow a similar course, except that they do not undergo the long novitiate. An auspicious day is chosen and the "crown and cloth" ceremony is performed almost immediately after entry. The same is true for Daoist nuns.

---

3. The *Analects*, attributed to Confucius (or Kongzi, 551–479 B.C.E.); the *Doctrine of the Mean*, attributed to Zisi, also called Kong Ji (483–402 B.C.E.), Confucius's grandson; the *Great Learning*, attributed to Zengzi (505–536 B.C.E.); and the *Mencius*, attributed to Mencius (or Mengzi, ca. 371–ca. 289 B.C.E.).
4. Literally, *Dipper Relief Scripture*, an unidentified text that probably refers to a ritual used for good luck and fortune. "*Sanguan jing*": San-kuan *ching*: the *Scripture of the Three Officials*, in full *Most High Marvelous Life-Protecting Scripture of the Three Principles Granting Happiness, Forgiving Sins, and Averting Disasters*; this text concerning the officials of Heaven, Earth, and Water is often part of modern Daoist liturgy. "*Yankou jing*:" literally, *Flaming Mouth Scripture*; there are many Buddhist texts with similar titles, which concern ritual liturgies for feeding hungry ghosts.

Ordination

For a Daoist monk the taking of the vows is a vital part of his religious life. Formerly the ordination period lasted one hundred days. It was later reduced to fifty-three days. The ceremonies held during this period are conducted at three ordination platforms and consist of:

1. Declaration of essentials
2. Midnight ordination at a "secret platform"
3. Declaration of the hundred-odd articles of the Quanzhen vows.

During the ordination season ordinands are responsible for providing their own living expenses. They must also pay for their robe and bowl, ordination certificate, and kneeling cloth.

Every ordination is presided over by a *chuanjie lüshi*[5] who holds the rank of abbot. He is assisted in administering the vows by a number of senior monks carefully selected for their spiritual insight and experience. [The titles of their offices are given.] With the exception of the ordination instructors, there is only one monk for each of the offices. The number of instructors varies with the number of ordinands and may reach as many as ten or twenty. According to the ordination register for the 1927 platform at the White Cloud Monastery, there were six instructors for the [349] ordinands and the presiding abbot was Chen Zhibin, who came from Zhili.[6] [Here follow the names, titles, and places of origin of 17 of the 31 ordination officers that year, most of whom also came from various localities in Zhili. Many of the senior ones also had the twenty-first generation name, Zhi, of the Longmen sacred verse.]

Above the ordination platform hang effigies of the Three Pure Ones,[7] the principal deities in the Daoist pantheon. Ordinands must be sixteen years of age or over. They will normally have spent at least a year in an ordinary small temple. The names of those ordained are printed in an ordination register. They are "numbered" according to the sequence of characters in the *Qianzi wen*.[8] The first four are qualified to become abbots of large public monasteries. The first two are given a religious pedigree showing their sectarian lineage. All ordinees receive ordination robes, certificates, eating bowls, and kneeling cloths.

Ordination ceremonies can only be conducted at public monasteries belonging to the Quanzhen sect. Yet daoshi of the Way of the Celestial Masters are free to participate. Large numbers of daoshi from this sect began to participate in Quanzhen ordination ceremonies after the Celestial Master ceased to issue his registration certificates. However, even if their performance in the ceremonies is excellent, there seems to be an implicit understanding that they do not have the right to become abbots of public monasteries. This is inevitable as long as sectarian lineages persist.

In the early Qing the number of legally permitted ordinands in any year was in the region of 2,000 and the ordination period was fixed at 100 days.

---

5. A precepts master.
6. A northern province constituted when China's capital was Nanjing (1368–1421), located within it; it was dissolved in 1928, after the founding of the Republic of China (1912–49) ended the Qing dynasty.
7. Variously identified at different times.
8. The Thousand Character Classic, a primer used to teach Chinese characters to children.

From about 1800 on, the numbers of those actually ordained gradually diminished, until by the late Qing some 500 daoshi were being ordained each year and the period had been reduced to 53 days. Under the Chinese Republic there was no regulation of the number of ordinands in any year.

Since 1927 the ordination platform at the White Cloud Monastery in Beijing has not been in use. Until 1949[9] this was principally due to economic factors. During the Qing dynasty generous financial assistance from the imperial court sustained the monastery and its platform. After the Republican period began, the monastery had to rely entirely on voluntary support. The ordination ceremonies held in 1927 reportedly cost some 20,000 Chinese dollars. They would have been impossible without the support of wealthy patrons. Once ordination ceased, the Quanzhen sect, like the Way of the Celestial Masters, tended to become a sect in name only, its vitality lost. [Here follows a table of the thirty-one ordinations held at the White Cloud Monastery from 1808 through 1927. In some years the number of monks ordained there exceeded the total of the number recorded at all the other Longmen monasteries together, in the chart summarized above. In 1882, for example, 264 Longmen ordinees were listed on the registers from other monasteries, whereas at White Cloud alone there were 525. At its last two ordinations (in 1919 and 1927) the White Cloud Monastery ordained 412 and 349 monks, respectively.]

The Robes and Regalia of the Daoshi

While I was staying in Beijing a group of Japanese sumo wrestlers visited China. The Chinese clerk of a bookshop asked me one day: "There are a lot of Japanese daoshi visiting Beijing these days. What are they doing here?" Puzzled by this mention of Japanese daoshi, I asked him where he had seen them. "Haven't you seen all those big fellows around the Dongtan Pailou?"[1] he said. I was struck by his description of sumo wrestlers as daoshi. He was right. With their bound-up hair and flowing robes, the wrestlers, in dress at least, truly seemed to be Japanese daoshi.

One obvious characteristic of the daoshi is that he lets his hair grow long and binds it up. Over this coil of hair he normally wears a flat cap known as a *hunyuan mao* or a *nanhua jin*. His top-knot is held in place by a hairpin made of wood or jade.

The daoshi's robes are usually blue. In Five Elements thought,[2] qing signifies the "vital spirit of the blue (or green) dragon." It is the color of the East and of the element wood. The use of this color is explained as indicating descent from Lord Donghua,[3] the founder of the Daoist religion. A daoshi's robes are not restricted to blue, however. Yellow or purple robes are also worn on ceremonial occasions, or by daoshi of the status of abbot, but not by anyone unordained. [A table gives the names and specifications of the robes and when they are worn. Many technical details of the various types of headgear follow.]

9. The year that the Communists prevailed in China's civil war and established the People's Republic of China.
1. The Eastern Decorated Archway, which stood at the eastern end of Chang'an Avenue in Beijing.
2. The five phases theory, a set of systematic associations between different categories, including the five directions and five colors; it is founded on five basic elements—metal, wood, water, fire, earth—that move from one phase to another.
3. A legendary figure viewed as the first Quanzhen patriarch.

Only with certain headgear can the crown be worn, as is customary in all ceremonies. The varieties include the Lunar Crown, Five Peaks Crown, Lotus Blossom Crown, Three Terrace Crown. Made of wood or jade, their use is carefully prescribed. They may not be used by a daoshi until he has undergone the "rites of crown and cloth" toward the end of his novitiate. The most commonly used is the Lunar Crown. The robes worn by the daoshi also vary with the kind of crown used, and both are subject to a variety of customary restrictions. The daoshi—resplendent in gorgeous robes, glittering crown and hair bindings, white stockings, and boat-shaped shoes known as "cloud shoes" or "blue shoes"—is far removed from modern taste. Yet seeing him in this raiment it is easy to believe that he is indeed unworldly, ethereal, even immortal.

The regalia of the daoshi are also subject to a variety of regulations. His "Immortal's bowls" and kneeling cloth are formally received at the ordination ceremony. The "Immortal's bowls" are made of iron, wood, and lacquer. The iron bowl is used as a cooking utensil on journeys into the mountains in search of herbs. The wood and lacquer bowls are for daily use in the monastery refectory. The kneeling cloth serves as a prayer mat. It is a piece of scarlet cloth about 1.5 meters long by 80 centimeters wide, with a black border approximately 10 centimeters wide.

The kneeling cloth is employed in three ways: (1) fully opened it is an expression of the most reverent degree of worship; (2) half-folded it is for worship of high-ranking deities; (3) fully folded it is carried over one arm on ceremonial occasions requiring reverence. Its dimensions are similar to those of the kneeling cloth used in Buddhist ceremonies and described in such Buddhist manuals as the *Pini riyong*.[4]

The above paragraphs describe the costumes of daoshi belonging to the Quanzhen sect, not those of the Celestial Masters'. In general, daoshi of the Quanzhen sect emphasize individual practice. They roam the mountains in search of medicinal herbs. To allow for their practice of austerity, their robes are light and simple. Daoshi belonging to the Way of the Celestial Masters emphasize devotional activities. They devote much of their time to magical incantations, prayers, and festivals. Their robes are correspondingly elaborate.

* * *

Punishment of Daoshi

Daoshi who break the harmony of the community or disobey the "pure rules" are punished. The code at the White Cloud Monastery provides that those who commit the offenses indicated below shall receive the following punishments:

1. Prostration for the period of the burning of one stick of incense for:
   - Anybody who does not get up immediately at the morning signal
   - Anybody who fails to attend a community assembly
   - Anybody who is ill-behaved at worship

---

4. The *Vinaya for Daily Functions*, a monastic code dating to the Ming dynasty (1368–1644).

- Anybody who leaves the monastery without permission
- Anybody who leads others into idleness or bad behavior
- Anybody who is careless about hygiene and sanitation
2. Demotion, which entails being given a lower number and more menial duties, for:
   - Anybody who gathers others about him to chat or gossip
   - Anybody who makes a mistake about signals on the bell and board
   - Anybody who is given charge of a hall and fails to keep it clean
   - Anybody who abuses the authority of his office
3. Being ordered to leave the monastery for:
   - Anybody who indulges in forbidden foods or wine
   - Anybody who neglects his duties
   - Anybody who refuses to go on an errand when dispatched
   - Anybody who is disrespectful or violent toward his seniors
   - Anybody who makes mistakes in office
   - Anybody who attacks the failings of others
   - Anybody who does not observe the rules of his office
   - Anybody who interferes with visitors
   - Anybody who engages in practical jokes, quarreling, or fighting
   - Anybody who fails to return to the monastery at night
   - Anybody who lies about why he did not return to the monastery
4. Expulsion for:
   - Anybody who does not keep the vows
   - Anybody who is lewd or immoral
   - Anybody deliberately destroying communal property, who shall be expelled, and also made to pay restitution and be beaten
   - Anybody misappropriating monastery funds, who shall, after strict examination, be expelled and also be beaten
5. Referral to the civil authorities for:
   - Anybody who instigates riots or unrest within the monastery
   - Anybody engaging in arson, who shall be referred to the civil authorities and also be beaten
   - Anybody found cheating people of their property
   - Anybody found lying in order to secure donations
   - Anybody engaging in loose talk about political matters, who shall be expelled and also be beaten
   - Anybody breaking the laws of the state, who shall be expelled and also be beaten.

At first new entrants are given such menial positions as gardener, latrine attendant, or pig-keeper. They move up to more senior positions through a series of annual promotions. Yet those who have filled such senior posts as prior, overseer, warden, or guest prefect, must, if they "erase their numbers," become itinerant monks, and upon entering another monastery, begin again there by performing the most menial tasks. This is the rule of the Quanzhen sect. In such cases, however, the time spent in menial roles may be shortened because of a daoshi's diligence in performing his duties, or simply because of his previous record.

Reminiscences of the White Cloud Monastery:
Life without Electric Lights

There were no electric lights at the White Cloud Monastery. During my initial visits to the monastery this simple fact had not struck me. I first noticed it when I entered the monastery on July I, 1940. The monastery lies only a kilometer west of the Xibianmen Gate[5] in Beijing. It is an imposing, densely roofed building, certainly not the kind that one would expect to be without electric lights.

An Shilin, then thirty-eight years old, was the daoshi in charge of the monastery. He held both the offices of head monk and prior. He was in the prime of life and full of energy. I told him that I would like to undergo all the formalities of enrollment and be treated exactly as an ordinary itinerant monk. This request was politely refused. I was told that I would always be treated as a guest of the monastery. I later learned that shortly before my arrival there had been a serious dispute within the monastery provoked by a group of daoshi who opposed the prior. It was probably because of this that they were so cautious in their treatment of a foreigner of unknown origins who had suddenly arrived.

The room to which I was assigned for my stay was the Abbot's Chamber, the innermost monastic building on the left-hand side. The similarly constructed building immediately opposite, on the right-hand side of the complex, was the Prior's Chamber. This was a complete reversal of what I had hoped for. I had wanted to experience the life of the newly entered, low-ranking daoshi, but here I found myself pressed into the chamber of the highest-ranking monk in a public monastery. Fearing that protest on my part might lead to total exclusion from the premises, however, I accepted my defeat gracefully. At that time, the White Cloud Monastery had no abbot. This chamber was therefore reserved for guests.

Li Chongyi, the guest prefect, was introduced as the monk responsible for entertaining me. He was then fifty-one years of age. With his luxuriant, flowing white hair, he seemed the very incarnation of an immortal.[6] He spoke to me with affection of Dr. Koyanagi Shikita[7] who had visited the monastery the year before. I learned in subsequent conversations that Li Chongyi had already been living for more than twenty years at White Cloud. At this time he ranked just below the prior in the monastic hierarchy, but in December of the same year he "erased his number" and became an itinerant monk again. Here was a man who could have continued to enjoy a secure and easy life but who chose to relinquish rank and office for the hard life of an itinerant monk. I was impressed. The spirit of the Quanzhen school was not yet dead. The overseer, Bai Quanyi, and the guest prefect, Li Xinlu, are two other examples of high-ranking daoshi I have known who suddenly left to return to the austere life of the lowly itinerant.

In the evening a boy lit the lamp in my room. It was only at this moment that I realized there were no electric lights in the monastery. As a product

5. The Western Gate of Expediency (Xibian Men).
6. A Daoist who has achieved extraordinary powers and a higher form of existence.
7. A scholar at the University of Tokyo who was a pioneering researcher on China (1870–1941).

of modern civilization, I regretted that I had not brought a flashlight with me. I tried to make notes on the many events of the day under the guttering wick. When eventually I looked outside, I found that every other room in the monastery was in pitch darkness. It was already midnight. Every creature, at one with nature, was sleeping. Only one solitary "unnatural" being broke the harmony of life by scribbling notes while he exhausted the flame.

I then realized that in the monastic world the scale of values was reversed, that little significance was attached to artificial, so-called cultural, activities. Taking pride in gathering scraps of knowledge, conducting surveys, doing research—these may be efforts to find some satisfaction or self-understanding in the society of men; but they end, as does life, like the flaring out of a candle. It is better to be embraced in the vastness of nature, to melt into it. Then there is no wasted resistance to life, no useless conflagration. When one's breathing is in harmony with nature, one becomes identical with its very life-flow. The life of the daoshi at the White Cloud Monastery was the perfect expression of this natural identity. I was suddenly overcome by a sense of hollowness, of humility and sadness at the sharp realization that not only was my body that of an alien but my heart as well. I doused the lamp.

I later learned that, on principle, lights were never used in the monastery. A lamp had been specially provided me as a guest. Since it was certainly odd in this quarter of Beijing to have no electricity, I raised the matter with Prior An. He first gave me an economic reason. The cost of lighting such an enormous complex (made up of dozens of buildings covering over three hectares) would be astronomical. Secondly, he explained that, as daoshi always got up at dawn, the brightening of the Heavens, and went to sleep at dusk, the darkening of the Heavens, there was no need for electric lights. The economic argument was understandable, and since I had already experienced the second reason for myself, I decided that any further comment would be superfluous and held my tongue.

The Daily Routine of the Daoshi

When light touched the eastern sky, at 5:30 A.M. in the summer, the morning stillness at the White Cloud Monastery was broken sharply by the striking of a large plank. It was struck five times, three slow then two quick. This marked the beginning of the daoshi's day. Silence was observed by those weeding the garden, fetching water, cleaning the halls, or preparing breakfast in the kitchens. The high-ranking daoshi in the meantime arose and put on formal dress: they combed their hair, washed their faces, and donned their robes, crowns, and ribbons. At 6:30, responding to signals struck on the bell and board, they made their way to the Shrine-hall of the Seven Perfect Ones[8] to perform the morning devotions.

Normally, morning devotions were attended by the prior and seven daoshi. The prior acted as celebrant and chanted the scriptures. The signals on the bell and board were fixed, and the same number of each was always given. One ring of the bell was matched by one blow on the board,

8. The seven disciples of Wang Zhe.

two rings by two blows, three rings by three blows. On special occasions the great drum might also be used, but daily signals were limited to those given on the bell and board. Never more than three rings on the bell and three blows on the board were given. The words chanted are contained in the *Quanzhen gongke jing*.[9]

[A list follows of the five texts recited at morning devotions and the four at evening devotions.]

On holidays, the first and fifteenth day of each lunar month, and on the birthdays of the various deities, the monks recited in addition the *Yuhuang jing, Sanguan jing, Zhenwu jing*,[1] and other scriptures. The first two were also recited in temples of the Way of the Celestial Masters.

After the recitation of the scriptures another signal was given on the plank (in the morning and at midday it was on the plank, in the evening on bell and board). At this signal the daoshi assembled in front of the Shrine-hall of Founder Qiu; then, in two files led by the guest prefect on duty, they entered the refectory. When they reached the entrance, a bowl-shaped gong was sounded. The morning meal began. Regulations governing behavior in the refectory were strict. Conversations and glancing at one another were absolutely forbidden. At the head of the hall was an altar for the worship of Wangling Guan.[2] On the left and right sides two long tables were placed face to face down the length of the hall.

All daoshi stood at their places while an offering was first made to Wangling Guan. A single rice bowl was placed on a small round tray. Then the cantor, who stood facing the altar on the right, struck a hand-chime and began to chant. All the monks followed him in reciting an opening and a closing grace. When these were finished, the daoshi standing to the left of the prior's seat raised the tray to eye level, set the offering down on a table before the altar, and retired to his place. The prior, guest prefect, superintendent, and cantor then left the hall. The remaining daoshi sat and began their meal. When the meal was over, they bowed once and left the hall.

The abbot's chair was set between the niche of Wangling Guan and the offering table behind the prior's seat. When an abbot was in residence he sat there. The space behind the altar was used for storing eating utensils. Inside the main part of the refectory, framed verses commemorating ordinations were hung from the ceiling at one end of the hall. These were verses written by daoshi to extol the virtues of the [former] abbots. On the eastern and western walls hung two plaques inscribed with large characters reading *Taishang ganying pian* and *Wenzhang dijun yinzhi wen*.[3] These were both originally the titles of basic texts of popular Daoism. Their presence here indicated that they were now revered by monk and layman alike.

9. The *Scripture of the Morning and Evening Services of the Quanzhen Order*, the liturgy for the performance of morning and evening rituals.
1. The *Zhenwu Scripture*, a text related to the Perfect Warrior (Zhenwu); see the introduction to *Journey to the North* [*Beiyou ji*], above). "*Yuhuang jing*": the *Scripture of the Jade Sovereign*—in full *Collected Scripture on the Deeds of the Jade Sovereign* (*Yuhuang benxing jijing*)—is a commonly recited text; the Jade Sovereign is the supreme deity of Chinese popular religion and a

deity high in the Daoist pantheon.
2. Numinous Officer Wang, or Marshal Wang, a guardian deity of Daoist monasteries.
3. The *Essay of the Imperial Lord Wenchang on Secret Virtue*, a famous 12th-century morality book (*shanshu*); Wenchang is the god of literature. "*Taishang ganying pian*": the *Tract of the Most Exalted on Action and Response*, another famous 12th-century *shanshu*, purportedly the words of the deified Laozi; see above.

After the morning meal the *Yuhuang jing* was chanted in the Lecture Hall. Daoshi then formed "education classes" to listen to a lecture. Formerly there had been no such educational provision. The morning lecture had recently been introduced by Prior An Shilin. Instruction covered such works as the *Four Books* and the *Five Classics*,[4] together with more specialized topics in the history of Daoism. There were about three hours of lectures in the morning, which were followed by the midday meal. The afternoons were allotted to the duties of the various offices and to private study or religious practice. Bell and board were sounded again at about 6:30 P.M. to signal the evening meal. After the meal the daoshi rejoined their education classes for a period of instruction in the chanting of scriptures under the direction of the cantor. (I attended one or two of these sessions. However, not only did I understand nothing that was going on, but my presence interfered with the studies of the daoshi, so I soon stopped going. Now, in retrospect, I regret that I did not persevere.)

Speaking of chanting of the scriptures I used to own a copy of the *Beidou yanming jing*[5] dating from the period 1119–25 of the Northern Song dynasty. Once, when Prior An came to visit me in my temporary residence, I showed it to him. He smiled and said, "At the White Cloud, too, we have a scripture dating from the Yuan dynasty."[6] This was news. My eyes lit up, and I asked for the name of the scripture. He pointed to a verse in the *Beidou yanming jing* and said, "Listen, I'm going to chant this," and recited it by heart. "Well, did you recognize the White Cloud's Yuan dynasty scripture?" he asked gleefully. I was nonplussed, but could not help smiling at his innocent delight. This way of chanting seems to have been handed down at the White Cloud Monastery since the Yuan dynasty. If my visit had been in these days, I would have tape-recorded it. Unfortunately, at that time, in the midst of war, all I could do was listen to it.

At nine in the evening there were more signals on the bell and board. Henceforth it was possible to loosen one's robes and relax. The tensions of the day were over. Daoshi strolled about the monastery and its environs. I sometimes persuaded Prior An to join me in a stroll. People we met whispered, "It's the old monk of the White Cloud Monastery." They stared with puzzled expressions, however, at the small bespectacled individual in Daoist robes beside him—a daoshi blessed not with flowing hair but with a balding crown!

Just in front of the White Cloud Monastery stood the thirteen-story pagoda of the Tianning Si, a famous architectural legacy from the Liao dynasty.[7] The bronze bells suspended from each of the corners of its thirteen octagonal tiers made a clear, soothing sound when touched by the wind. Heard from within the monastery, they added an elegant tone to summer evenings. One might even have been misled into thinking that this pagoda had been built for the White Cloud Monastery.

At ten there was another signal on the plank. It was a warning to make ready for bed. Continental summer evenings were long, and it was not until

---

4. The *Classic or Book of Changes, Classic of Poetry, Classic of History, Collection of Rituals, Rites (Liji),* and *Spring and Autumn Annals.*
5. Probably the *Book of the Northern Dipper of Mysterious Power Prolonging the Original Life*
Span (*Taishang xuanling beidou benming yansheng zhenjing*), a very popular work.
6. 1260–1368 C.E.
7. 907–1125 C.E.

ten that the heavens darkened. During the night, daoshi known as night wardens made the rounds of the monastery every two hours, striking their wooden clapping sticks.

The above timetable is for the summer months. Since life at the White Cloud Monastery was regulated by the sun, the daily timetable changed in the winter. Meals were then taken only twice a day, morning and evening. I have already mentioned that ordinary monks took their meals in the refectory. The food was prepared under the supervision of the monastery cook in the main kitchen. The meals of the prior, guest prefect, and other high-ranking daoshi were prepared in a separate kitchen by a "high cook." When the senior monks had guests, they would take their meals together with them. Otherwise they ate individually in their own rooms. All food within the monastery was vegetarian. The high cook of the small kitchen at the White Cloud while I was there was renowned as a master of vegetarian cooking. Unlike the other monks, senior daoshi ate only two daily meals, summer and winter, at eleven in the morning and six in the evening.

The daily menu and the amounts of ingredients to be used were carefully fixed. If any dishonesty was detected, the offender was severely punished. The morning and evening meals taken by ordinary daoshi in the refectory consisted of a bowl of congee and one plate of pickles shared by every two monks. The midday meal consisted of a portion of corn bread and fried vegetables for each, with a plate of pickles shared by two. Since this was purely vegetarian cooking, anybody not used to the diet would have had difficulty adjusting to it. On the first and fifteenth day of each month, flour was used in the bread for the midday meal, on the basis of one catty per person. It was dark, poor-quality flour. For the regular meals in the senior monks' dining room, congee or noodles were used. Vegetable dishes were only served when guests were present and were limited to a maximum of four plates. This is far removed from the luxurious Japanese image of vegetarian cooking.

The Ceremony of the Airing of the Books

July 1, 1940, the date on which I first entered the White Cloud Monastery to stay, corresponded to the first day of the sixth month according to the lunar calendar [sic]. I had a particular reason for choosing this day. I was hoping to see the ceremony of the airing of the books at the monastery. In the Beijing area, the week from the first day of the sixth month of the lunar calendar was given over to airing household items. It was said that clothes or books aired at this time would escape moths and mildew for the coming year. The White Cloud Monastery possessed the only surviving copy of the famous Ming edition of the Daoist Canon.[8] During this week the precious work was taken from its sealed repository and brought out for airing ceremonies. For anyone anxious to see the canon, to miss this opportunity would mean waiting another whole year.

It is said that these ceremonies originated in response to a request from the court during the Qing dynasty. Starting on the first day of the sixth month, the monastery used to be decorated with pennants and streamers,

---

8. A collection of almost 1,500 texts, completed in 1445 C.E.

and there was an elaborate inauguration ceremony. Throughout each of the six following days one-sixth of the canon used to be recited. This corresponded to the ceremony of reciting the long version of the *Prajnaparamita-sutra*[9] held in Buddhist monasteries. However, when I was there, the monks at White Cloud just placed long tables on the porch of the Pavilion of the Three Pure Ones, where the canon was stored, and twenty of them turned the pages of the volumes briskly with bamboo spatulas. There were a total of 5,385 *juan*.[1] Starting at seven in the morning and working for two hours or so, the monks completed the "airing" in three days.

This Daoist Canon was published between 1924 and 1926 by photocopy in 1,120 volumes by the Commercial Press in Shanghai. Xu Shichang and Fu Zengxiang were sponsors. This photocopy edition was the source of the 1962 edition, published by Yiwen Publishing Company in Taiwan. The Daoist Canon, which was formerly almost inaccessible to scholars, is now, thanks to the photographed edition, generally available. Had the original White Cloud edition been lost, the documentary study of Daoism would be virtually impossible. Here is an example of the preservation of a rare religious tradition by the White Cloud Monastery. Through this act alone the monastery has proven to be a precious cultural treasure for Daoism.

While I was in Beijing I visited the monastery whenever I had time to spare, and I stayed there at will. Prior An also visited my rooms in the city. The first time he visited me, I wondered how I was going to entertain a Daoist monk who was accustomed only to a vegetarian diet. I asked him point blank, "Can you eat meat and fish?" "Yes," he replied. I was relieved but asked, "But what about the pure rules?" He replied: "In the monastery we observe the rules strictly. When we go out, we have to be more relaxed. There are occasions when daoshi are away from the monastery on business for a fortnight or a month at a time. If one tried to stick to a vegetarian diet, without suitable eating places one might starve to death. Even on one-day visits to the city, since it isn't easy to find restaurants serving vegetarian meals, one would have to go without food all day. In practical terms it's impossible to stick strictly to the rules when outside the monastery." What he said was so obvious that I kicked myself for my stupid dogmatism.

During the Great East Asian War[2] I sometimes met White Cloud daoshi who could say "hello" or "thank you" in Japanese and who averred that they wished to learn more. I told them not to; their Japanese would sound funny and be out of character.

When the war ended everything fell apart. I vacated Beijing at the end of April 1946, leaving behind all the notes, documents, and manuscripts which I had so painstakingly gathered. Those Japanese involved in cultural activities in Beijing at the time formed a small association to negotiate with the Chinese authorities for the right to take the documents and the results of our research back to Japan. We were told that we could not take any document containing so much as a single Chinese geographical or personal name! In effect, this meant that we could take absolutely nothing: cultural

---

9. The *Perfection of Wisdom Sutra*; the "long version" is probably *Larger Perfection of Wisdom Sutra* (*Mahaprajnaparamitasutra*).
1. Volumes.

2. That is, the hostilities with China that began with the Manchurian Incident in 1931 and escalated into the Sino-Japanese War (1937–45).

documents containing no reference to Chinese people or places do not exist. I felt great affection for the Daoist robe I had worn during my stay at the White Cloud but sadly threw it away, since it was likely to provoke suspicion at the checkpoints.

In postwar Japan I lived for several years on a basic diet of potato roots and abstinence. During this period, about two years after my return, I heard from a friend who was still living in Beijing of the violent death of An Shilin. He had been burned to death in the garden in front of the Shrine-hall of Founder Qiu by a militant faction in the monastery. This report was substantiated by a photograph and clipping from a Beijing newspaper. I was shocked and saddened. I have already mentioned the dispute which had occurred just before my first stay at the monastery. In this incident Prior An and his supporters had expelled from the monastery some members of an opposing faction. These daoshi had remained in Beijing awaiting an opportunity for revenge. It is not hard to imagine that in the disturbances of the postwar period they were able to egg on militants within the monastery to accomplish their own private ends.

In the early Yuan dynasty, shortly after the death of the founder Qiu Changchun, members of the Quanzhen sect engaged in a debate with Buddhists before the Chinese emperor. The Daoists were worsted, with the result that the texts of their sect were judged apocryphal and burned. This incident put an end to attempts to establish the sect as one with roots in the general populace. From then on it developed as a docile monastic entity serving the state. This tradition was preserved at the White Cloud Monastery. The burning to death of An Shilin, ironically enough in front of the founder's hall, meant that the daoshi of the Quanzhen sect had themselves rung down the curtain on monastic Daoism—an act that coincided with the start of one of the greatest revolutions in Chinese history.

HEIDEGGER AND OUR TRANSLATION OF THE *DAODE JING*

PAUL SHIH-YI HSIAO

In 1946, just after the conclusion of World War II, the German philosopher Martin Heidegger (1889–1976) was undergoing the stressful process of "denazification"—a review by Allied authorities of his association with the National Socialists. He suggested to Paul Shih-yi Hsiao, a former student from China who had already produced a version of *The Scripture of the Way and Its Virtue* (*Daode jing*; see above) in Italian, that they spend a summer at his mountain cabin translating the work into German. Hsiao eagerly agreed, but Heidegger's persistent questions about the philosophical content of the work, his production of copious notes to the text, and Hsiao's involvement with other pursuits slowed their progress; ultimately, they completed only eight chapters (chapters 1, 15, 18, 25, 32, 37, 40, and 41). Despite Heidegger's apparent enthusiasm for this project, he evidently kept it a secret from even his closest friends and colleagues. Unfortunately, no drafts of the translated chapters have been found among Heidegger's papers.

By 1930 Heidegger had in his library a copy of Martin Buber's *Talks and Parables of Chuang Tzu* (*Reden und Gleichnisse des Tschuang-tse*, 1910; see above), which he read carefully and referred to in his writing. According to those close to Heidegger, he often discussed Daoism and Zen with his visitors and described his work as having affinities with those traditions. Heidegger's interest in the *Daode jing* was profound. In addition to beginning a translation, he included passages from the text in personal letters and referred to Laozi and the Dao directly in some of his published writings—and these allusions to Daoism increased through the 1950s, after he began his collaboration with Hsiao. In the essay included here, Hsiao describes Heidegger's particular engagement with two lines of chapter 15: "Who can, settling the muddy, gradually make it clear? Who can, stirring the tranquil, gradually bring it to life?" Rather than leave Hsiao's translation alone, in a letter to Hsiao Heidegger produced his own "version"—in the same spirit as Buber's *Chuang Tzu* and later Ursula Le Guin's *Tao Te Ching* (1997; see below): "'Who is able to be still and from and through stillness put something on the way (move it) such that it comes to light?' Who is able by making tranquil to bring something into Being? The *dao* of heaven." But many of Heidegger's direct citations of the *Daode jing* are from chapters other than those he translated with Hsiao. In 1965 he included all of chapter 47, taken from a published German translation, in a letter to a friend. Three years later the Beatles would draw on that same chapter for their song "The Inner Light" (see below).

Those searching for Daoist parallels in Heidegger's work have usually focused on the concepts of "nothingness" and "emptiness," the transcendence of opposites, and the link between language and being. The topic is still much debated, but the impact of Daoism on Heidegger's thought is perhaps seen most clearly is in his usage of the term Way (*Weg*). The Way (Dao and Weg), Heidegger explains in his collection *Woodpaths* (*Holzwege*, 1950; published in English as *Off the Beaten Track*), is that which is produced through its own doing without a sense of a predetermined destination or final outcome. As previous scholars have suggested, the Way, as Heidegger sees it, is always under way, and for Zhuangzi the "Way comes about as we walk it." Even if Heidegger may have felt little desire to deeply explore Daoist texts in order to understand their meaning more fully and precisely, he clearly viewed them as an exciting resource to provide inspiration as he developed his own ideas and philosophical positions.

PRONOUNCING GLOSSARY

Chiang Kai-shek: *chiang kai-sheck*   Laozi: *lao-tzu*
Daode jing: *dow-duh ching*

I learned of Heidegger's interest in translating the *Daode jing*[1] of Laozi in the spring of 1946, on our meeting in the Holzmarktplatz in Freiburg. At that time he suggested to me that we collaborate in the summer on translating the *Daode jing* into German in his cabin at Todtnauberg,[2] since only in the summer would he have a break from his work. I agreed gladly, being convinced that Laozi's ideas would contribute to the reflections of the German people, and indeed of the Western world, after the disastrous World War. Unfortunately we did not complete the project, but I nevertheless have the

Translated by Graham Parkes.

1. On the *Daode jing* (*The Scripture of the Way and Its Virtue*), also known as the *Laozi*, see above.

2. A village in the Black Forest, a mountainous area in southwest Germany.

impression that the work exerted a significant influence on Heidegger. Heidegger himself once said to a German friend that through this engagement with Laozi along with Confucius and Mencius he had learned more of the East.

I

I first made Heidegger's acquaintance in 1942. After completing my degree in psychology and Chinese philosophy in Peiping,[3] I went to Milan to pursue my studies further. There, accustomed to the Scholastic rigor at the University of the Sacro Cuore, I became acquainted with a no less rigorous discipline and a new depth of thought. I was permitted to attend Heidegger's seminars as an auditor. Now and then I handed him parts of my translation of the *Daode jing* into Italian, which Benedetto Croce[4] had recommended that I publish. Presumably Heidegger found something in my translation that he had not found in others, or else he would not have suggested that we collaborate on a translation into German.

On 27 November 1944, the beauty of the city of Freiburg im Breisgau, the scenic capital of the Black Forest region, was destroyed by an air raid. The air raid was unexpected, since Freiburg was supposed to have been declared exempt. Twelve hours beforehand many animals and people became uneasy. Particularly strange was the behavior of an enormous duck in the city park, which for almost twelve hours quacked and flapped around wildly. One is generally inclined to think that wild animals have premonitions of natural catastrophes, prompted by certain atmospheric changes "in the air." But air raids are not natural catastrophes, but actions decided upon and directed by human beings. The monument to the duck by the lake in the Freiburg city park (bearing the inscription: God's creature laments, accuses, and warns) offers food for thought not only for parapsychologists but also, I believe, for philosophers.

I mention these impressions from my years in Freiburg because I repeatedly discussed them in my conversations with Heidegger. For I had the same experience as many other Asians: in my attempts to understand Heidegger's ideas, I had first to learn why his thinking was so difficult for many of his Western contemporaries to understand, or appeared so sensational. What he "brought to language" has frequently been said similarly in the thinking of the Far East. For example, temporality has always been understood differently in China than in the West. For us the duck does not need any paranormal powers: everything is connected with everything else, and in each moment there is concealed the entire past and also the open future.

In the midst of the destroyed old part of the town, with debris still surrounding the cathedral, I met Heidegger again for the first time after the war in the Holzmarktplatz, a central point in the city of Freiburg. All visitors admire the cathedral there with its beautifully impressive steeple. It is held to be the most beautiful steeple of all the Gothic cathedrals in Europe. We

3. That is, Beijing (literally, "Northern Capital"); this name was used by supporters of the Nationalist government in China, who denied the legitimacy of the Communist government seated there and insisted that the genuine capital of China was Nanjing ("Southern Capital").
4. Italian historian and philosopher (1866–1952).

Chinese also find it beautiful, although not in the same way as Westerners do. We are accustomed to simple, Romanesque-looking ancestor-temples and imperial palaces, and so find this Gothic structure somewhat lacking in proportion, impressive but not harmonious. Only one who has known the piety, the yearning, and the awe for the divine loftiness of Gothic man is able to understand this magnificent structure. But now, in 1946, the city still lay devastated; nevertheless, we were glad to be there, still alive. Many of our acquaintances and friends were resuming their former activities; others had given up their lives on the battlefield, in captivity or beneath the ruins. Yet we were by no means carefree. My return to China to take up a teaching post was still uncertain. Heidegger was still undergoing the de-Nazification proceedings,[5] which could often be unpleasant, bureaucratically formal, and full of malicious resourcefulness.

"Mr. Hsiao, what would you say if people made two contradictory assertions about the same piece of writing of yours?" Heidegger surprised me with this sudden and somewhat provocative question. "How is it possible? The Nazis said of a section of my book *Being and Time*:[6] 'Herr Heidegger, from what you have written in your book here it is clear that you are not Aryan.' And now your allies, the French, have presented me with the same passage and said: 'Herr Heidegger, from what you have written in your book here it is clear that you are a Nazi.' You see, Mr. Hsiao, what different effects the same passage from the same book can produce. What do you say to that?"

I was dismayed, and could hardly dream that the Europeans could misunderstand their own languages in such a way. My confusion stemmed in part from the widespread misunderstandings of Heidegger's past. Everyone knew that in 1933 to 1934 Heidegger had been Rector of the Albert-Ludwig University in Freiburg; but he soon retired from this unfortunate position. Yet from what time was he no longer in agreement with the ideology and practices of the Nazis? And how could it have been at all possible that he wanted to collaborate with them? Without really knowing, I had assumed it as evident that Heidegger must have been not only a "hanger on" but a fully fledged National Socialist, or else he would never have become Rector in 1933. And how was one to imagine that—a Heidegger as a "hanger-on"?

I found the disappointment of Gabriel Marcel,[7] who had greatly revered Heidegger, comprehensible. When I visited him in Paris during the sixties Marcel said to me that the philosophical world's admiration for Heidegger would have doubled if after the war he had not maintained his stubborn silence and had said something about his behavior in 1933. This also gave me some inhibitions about our collaboration. It was not until after his death that I learned that Heidegger had already ten years previously said in the *Der Spiegel*[8] interview that he had been Rector for only ten months. Here Heidegger shows his wisdom and greatness!

In short, I stood there opposite Heidegger in the Holzmarktplatz with very mixed emotions. Yet at the same time I felt considerable empathy: Heidegger

---

5. After World War II, the Allies screened all former members of the National Socialist Party to determine their degree of responsibility for the Nazis' crimes. Heidegger, who had joined the party in 1933, faced a committee that was sympathetic to him.

6. Heidegger's most important book, *Sein und Zeit* (1927).
7. French philosopher connected with early existentialism (1889–1973).
8. An influential weekly German news magazine (literally, *The Mirror*).

was obviously suffering an injustice—one does not need to know the passage from *Being and Time* to be able to say with conviction that either the Nazis or the Allies must be wrong. Indeed if those responsible on either side were likewise pseudo-philosophers, they could all very well be wrong. The content of the passage had no doubt nothing to do with the accusations; that both accusers were innocent is not possible. It is a pity that I did not at that time ask Heidegger which passage was at issue.

Admittedly, after the war, China was (as a Chinese expression puts it: "with burned head and wounded brow") a pitiable victor, in reality only a "half-Ally," even if belonging to the "four great powers"[9] in the world. (France had at that time been left behind a little to the left.) In spite of this I now stood before Heidegger with something of the calm pride of the victor— even if at the same time a slightly restless conscience, since I saw clearly how unfairly and foolishly Heidegger had been treated. And with that, the spirit and strength to fight against injustice rose within me.

This was in a sense normal for a Chinese: like most Chinese I had in my youth read many novels about robbers and stories of knights and heroes. Whether robbers or heroes, they all fought against injustice: while the heroes did not rob, the robbers robbed only from the rich for the benefit of the poor. And so the Chinese generally have the need—in which they take great joy—to rebel against wrongs, and especially in the interests of others.

In actuality I was at that moment unable to do anything at all for Heidegger. Although I was a "half-Ally" I was still under the jurisdiction of the French military. I was unable to treat the officers in charge as schoolboys, even though many of them, like those in charge in other occupied zones, deserved it. As the victors they were unable to free themselves from the bad influences of soldiery, no matter how much they professed to be crusaders for democracy and humanitarianism.

In my confusion some consoling words of Mencius (372–289 B.C.), the greatest Confucian after Confucius (551–479 B.C.), occurred to me. "Professor Heidegger, you ask me what I say to the statements of the Nazis and the Allies. I can only give you a Chinese answer. I find that the surely false interpretations of the Nazis and the Allies attest to the same thing: in the future one must study your philosophy more assiduously and carefully. If it is understood properly, it will have great relevance for the future. Mencius said: 'If heaven wants to impose a difficult task on someone, it first fills his heart and will with bitterness, rots his sinew and bones, starves his frame, imposes great poverty upon his body, and confounds his undertakings, so that his heart will be inspired, his nature stimulated and his deficiencies remedied. . . . From all these things we learn that life arises out of anxiety and care, misery and privation; and that death on the other hand is the product of comforts and pleasure.'"[1]

Heidegger appeared to be quite moved by this quotation. We did not subsequently talk further about this topic. It was at this same meeting that he proposed translating the *Laozi* together. I agreed to the proposal with joy.

9. The other three were the United States, the United Kingdom, and the Soviet Union.

1. The sayings of Mencius were collected by his disciples in the *Mencius* (*Mengzi*).

II

As soon as the summer semester finished, we met regularly every Saturday in his cabin on top of Todtnauberg. Our working together provided an opportunity to counteract injustice somewhat. A friend had gladly put a motorcycle at my disposal so that it would not be commandeered. Moreover, as a "half-Ally" I received every week a priceless package full of all kinds of good things which were otherwise impossible to obtain in Germany: coffee, cocoa, noodles, sausage, butter, cigarettes, and so forth. These we shared. Also the roads to Todtnauberg were very difficult, and there was no public transportation. Mrs. Heidegger was concerned to preserve her husband's time for his intellectual work, and so tried herself to buy everything in town and bring it back to the cabin. Now I was in a position partially to relieve her of this burden. Twenty years later the farmer with whom I sometimes parked my precious Puch 200 told Heidegger with astonishment of this "Chinaman" who used to come up in those days, and who even knew how to ride a motorcycle.

At first our task of translation proceeded from the *Laozi* text of Jiang Xichang,[2] which was compiled from a comparison of over eighty-four ancient texts and could be regarded provisionally as the critical edition. We did not consult other translations and commentaries, since we wanted to offer a commentary on the *Daode jing* from Laozi own thought as far as possible.

First we worked on the chapters concerning the *dao*, which seemed to be the hardest and the most important. Because of the very thorough nature of Heidegger's thinking, we had only worked on eight of eighty-one chapters[3] by the end of the summer. According to the insightful observation of his friend Hans Fischer-Barnicol[4] on a personal visit, Heidegger was "a timid, very shy person. Not only modest in the conventional sense, but one who listened in a remarkable way, very attentive to what the other person had to say, humble. . . . Committed to thinking, and, it seemed to me, most people did not want to come without any thoughts before the presence of these eyes—these truly remarkable, astonishing eyes that listened rather than looked. Even though the nature of Heidegger's humor was not clear to me, these eyes were able to laugh."[5]

At the end of an entire summer only a tenth of the work had been completed. Presumably we would have finished in a decade or so, or perhaps somewhat sooner, since the other chapters are not nearly as obscure, and Heidegger would not have needed to question me so penetratingly and trenchantly, fixing me with that listening, inquiring gaze. Now I understand Heidegger's saying, "for questioning is the piety of thinking."[6] And it is this piety of thinking that drove Heinrich Buhr so forcefully into his engagement with the younger generation.[7]

2. Jiang Xichang, *Laozi jiaogu* [An annotated explanation of the *Laozi*] (Shanghai: Shangwu yinshuguan, 1937).
3. That is, chapters 1, 15, 18, 25, 32, 37, 40, and 41.
4. German writer and scholar of religion (1930–1999); he had close ties to China and Taiwan.
5. Hans A. Fischer-Barnicol, "Spiegelungen—Vermittelungen," in *Erinnerung an Martin Heidegger* (Pfullingen: Neske, 1977), 88 [Hsiao's note].

6. Martin Heidegger, *Die Technik und die Kehre* [Technology and the turning] (Pfullingen: Neske, 1978), 88 [Hsiao's note].
7. Heinrich Buhr and Erika Reichle, "Der Weltliche Theolog, Vor der Gemeinde as vor dem lieben Gott," in *Erinnerung an Martin Heidegger* [Hsiao's note]. Buhr, who later became a Protestant pastor, as a student in 1933 had heard Heidegger deliver a speech strongly against Christianity.

We wanted to continue our work the following summer. In the interim I was invited to give my first lecture at the University on the topic of "the encounter between China and the West." Upon this followed numerous invitations to lecture throughout Germany, also during the summer. I had to decide: should I continue this significant collaboration with Heidegger or accede to these other requests? Heidegger's *Laozi* translation with me would cause a sensation in the world of philosophy. On the other hand my lectures could afford the German people, who had suffered various injustices and privations, some kind of solace, especially through the words of General Chiang Kai-shek.[8] In contrast with the Allies in Germany, he considered the Japanese people innocent and even spoke against reparations. For according to him the decisiveness of the era of peace lies in "whether we are capable of guiding the enemy so skilfully and well that he repents in his heart and becomes an advocate of peace."[9] On the other hand—and I have to admit this—I could not during our work together get free from a slight anxiety that Heidegger's notes might perhaps go beyond what is called for in a translation. As an interpreter and mediator this tendency unsettled me.

Heidegger had essentially inquired—and asked penetratingly, tirelessly, and mercilessly—about every imaginable context of meaning in the mysterious interplay of the symbolic relations within the text. Only the complete constellation of meanings was sufficient for him to dare to determine the outline of a form of thought capable of rendering the multilayered meaning of the Chinese text into Western language in a clear and comprehensible way.

Aside from a brief communication from October of 1947 (see below), in which he wrote two lines from chapter fifteen, Heidegger unfortunately did not give me any more attempts at translation. So there remains only that the hope that his notes from the *Nachlass*[1] may come to light during my lifetime. After the summer of 1946 we did not resume our collaboration on the *Laozi* translation. Once, during the sixties, when a friend with whom I went to visit Heidegger mentioned *Laozi*, he pointed his index finger at me somewhat excitedly, but at the same time with a smile, and said: "But it was he who didn't want to do it." I smiled too, from embarrassment.

*   *   *

8. Chinese military and political leader (1887–1975), head of the Nationalist government first in China (1928–49) and then in exile on Taiwan (1949–75).
9. "Responsibility for Peace," speech by Chiang Kai-shek, translated with a commentary by Paul S.-Y. Hsiao, in *De Gegenwart*, nos. 1–2 (January 1946) [Hsiao's note].
1. Literally, "after leavings" (German): the notes and manuscripts left on the death of a scholar.

WHY MUST WE PROHIBIT THE REACTIONARY DAOIST CULTS?

XU JIANGUO

One aspect of the social and political upheaval in China after the fall of the Qing dynasty (1644–1911) was a new and severely enforced distinction between "religion" (*zongjiao*) and "superstition" (*mixin*). These categories were previously unknown, and the very understanding of the word *zongjiao* was conditioned by Christian models (the term had come back to China after it was taken up and put to new use by missionaries in Japan). What was defined as "religion" in the Republican period (1912–49) was permitted, but practices labeled as "superstition" were forbidden.

The impact of these developments on Daoism was particularly pronounced. Of the two main schools, the Complete Perfection (Quanzhen) tradition fared better: as a monastic tradition with an identifiable clergy, it shared structural characteristics with the Western churches used to define religion. The Orthodox Unity (Zhengyi) tradition, in contrast, was increasingly suppressed, because its more thorough integration into local society and the lack of monasteries for its Daoist priests made it harder for the government to control. The brunt of the new policies fell on vernacular ritual masters who performed exorcistic rituals in local communities—usually combining Buddhism and Daoism with local practices—and on the many redemptive societies and sectarian movements across the country, which were pegged as superstitious cults and targeted for eradication.

The process of cleansing religion of superstition accelerated with the founding of the People's Republic of China in 1949. Religious belief was tolerated under the law, while expression deemed to be superstitious was not. In 1957, Daoism became one of the five official religions, but as the revolution unfolded further it too suffered under new land reforms and collectivization campaigns. As the Cultural Revolution (1966–76) increased in intensity through the 1960s and into the 1970s, Daoism in all its forms, including the formerly approved Complete Perfection tradition, was heavily persecuted and on the brink of eradication. Temples and monasteries were closed and converted into schools and factories, clergy members were forced to return to lay life, and books were destroyed.

In this transcript of a radio broadcast of 1953, we hear the deputy mayor of Shanghai condemning a variety of sectarian Daoist movements as reactionary counterrevolutionary cults. Xu Jianguo focuses mainly on the Way of Pervasive Unity (Yiguan dao), the most popular sect in the country in the 1940s, though he also singles out some other high-profile movements led by women. In fiery language, he accuses these groups of having colluded with the Japanese occupiers instead of resisting their advances. After the surrender of the Japanese, according to Xu, they lent their support to the Nationalist Guomindang (which had formed as a political party in 1912 under the leadership of Sun Yat-sen) and worked with the American imperialists. In short, they were said to be engaging in counterrevolutionary practices against the People's Republic and deceiving the masses—they "swindle and injure the people." This broadcast makes clear that the forms of Daoism allied with sectarian movements, which had risen from the ashes following religious persecutions in the late nineteenth century, were accused of not being religious organizations and were labeled "reactionary cults." It thus provides a snapshot of how key elements of Daoism deemed unruly or unsavory were being purged from the tradition just at the time when Daoism was undergoing a major change: rather than a religious tradition, with institutions and practices rooted in Chinese society, it was being reformulated as a philosophical tradition and as a set of self-cultivation techniques that were now said to be rooted in science, not religion.

PRONOUNCING GLOSSARY

Daofa jiaotong: *dow-fah chiao-tung*   Yiguan dao: *yee-gwan dow*
Jiugong dao: *chiu-kung dow*   Yisheng diandao: *yee-shung duan-dow*
Laomu dao: *lao-mu dow*   Zhongde she: *chung-duh shuh*
Xijian dao: *hsi-chian dow*

Dear Listeners:

Today I propose to take a little of the time of this broadcasting station to talk to you on one problem, the problem of the prohibition of reactionary Daoist cults. A few days ago, we must all have seen in the press the notification of the Shanghai Military Control Committee on the prohibition of reactionary Daoist cults. The notification clearly ordered the prohibition of the *Yiguan dao*, the *Jiugong dao*, the *Dongshan she*, the *Longhua Shengjiao hui* of the *Yisheng diandao*, the *Xijian dao*, the *Laomu dao*, the *Daode xueshe Daofa jiaotong*, the *Zhongde she*,[1] among the scores of reactionary Daoist cults. The public security organs, in breaking up the *Yiguan dao*[2] and other reactionary organizations, placed under arrest a group of arch leaders who had committed very serious crimes and incurred the great wrath of the masses.

This decisive measure on the part of the People's Government obtained the enthusiastic support of the broad masses of the citizens. Indeed not a few members of the families of the arrested leaders of these cults, with full understanding of the cause of righteousness, had before the arrests actively given information, and after the arrests assisted the government in looking up evidences, traces, and also mobilizing their arrested relatives into speedy frank admissions of their crimes. Thus when the woman cult leader Ji Zhaodi was arrested, her daughter and her daughter-in-law both urged her to confess frankly immediately, while her son (a paper factory worker) also wrote to her saying that if she would not confess frankly, he would sever his relationships with her. When the cult leader Yu Yijing was arrested, his son also said, "In personal relationship he is my father, but from the viewpoint of class stand, he is my enemy." He proceeded to expose the crimes of the father.

These incidents are very moving, being the concrete manifestations of the further raising of the political consciousness of the people of Shanghai. However, since the backbone members of the higher ranks in the reactionary Daoist cults have been deceiving the masses under the cover of the burning of joss sticks, kowtowing before their shrines, living on vegetarian diets, and saying Buddhist prayers while in effect their organizations were actually engaged secretly in counter-revolutionary activities, there are therefore still people who do not fully understand their true nature. These people say, "There is no point in prohibiting these Daoist cults, for they all burn joss sticks and live on vegetarian diets." Some members of the families of the arrested leaders say, "It is our freedom of religion to believe in the

---

TRANSLATED BY Donald E. MacInnis.

1. Various religious movements, many led by women, that were popular in the early 20th century.

2. The Way of Pervasive Unity (Yiguan dao), the most influential sect in China in the 1940s.

Yiguan dao; why should we be arrested?" We can say that these people have their eyes blinded by the black screen of the reactionary cults. We can say definitely that reactionary cults like the *Yiguan dao* are absolutely not religious organizations, but counter-revolutionary organizations. Let us look into the facts relating to their criminal activities.

From the very beginning, these reactionary Daoist cults have been counter-revolutionary organizations employed by the imperialists and the reactionary ruling class in the country. The big chiefs of these reactionary Daoist cults have mostly been warlords, landlords, despots, collaborators and special service agents. As far back as in the days of the war against Japan,[3] these organizations acted as the abettors in crime of the Japanese imperialists, sabotaged the war of resistance, conducted propaganda among the masses to serve as loyal subjects of the Japanese invaders, supported the "Greater East Asia New Order," and assisted the enemy in investigating and reporting on the anti-Japanese elements, acting as guides to the enemy, supplying information, and persecuting the Chinese people.

On the surrender of Japan, the reactionary Daoist cults immediately colluded with the special service of the Guomindang,[4] and were exploited by the American imperialists and the Guomindang bandits for activities against the Communists and against the people, sabotaging the people's liberation war. The big chiefs of the *Yiguan dao*, Ji Mingzhou and Zhang Jinzhong, had submitted letters to the Department of Social Affairs of the Jiang bandits and the Shanghai Guomindang Headquarters pledging their loyalty to the Guomindang and their determination to oppose the Communists. Zhao Zeguang and other heads of the *Jiugong dao*[5] in coordination with the anti-people's war launched by the Jiang bandits colluded with special agents in the organization of the "China Relief Charity Association," and forced members of their cult to collect intelligence reports in the liberated areas. After the liberation, they continued to establish bases in Raining Road and other points in Shanghai, to direct the activities of leaders of their cult in Suzhou, Hangzhou and Shaoxing. The *Dongshan she*[6] established connections with Wang Shijun, special service chief of the CC Clique[7] of the Jiang bandits, and secretly organized bases with the objective of directing insurrections in Shanghai after its liberation.

After the liberation of Shanghai, the reactionary Daoist cults accepted the orders of the American-Jiang special agents, and turned to secret activities, organizing "information sections" and "liaison stations" to carry out the "single line leadership" method for continued operations. They incited members of their cults to adopt a hostile attitude toward the people's government, prevented them from cooperation with the government, sheltered counter-revolutionaries, collected intelligence reports, and plotted for opportunities to stage insurrections and enthrone themselves emperors.

In a word, they adopted a hostile stand against the masses of the people in everything. Wherever the People's Government did something for the good of the people, they would sabotage it. Thus when in 1949 there was the typhoon which damaged the sea walls, and the Shanghai Municipal People's Government called on the masses to effect repairs to them, these cult leaders spread the rumor that "the God Neptune is doing all this havoc, and we must not act against Heaven." They also incited the backward members among the masses into drowning many cadres engaged in repairs to the sea walls. When agrarian reform was introduced in the suburban areas of Shanghai, they spread the rumor that "whosoever takes the land and property of another will have generations of his descendants condemned in Hell," to sabotage the movement. When the resist-U.S. and aid-Korea campaign was launched,[8] they started spreading propaganda about the American atomic bomb and talked of the third world war, spreading the rumor that the Americans would land in Shanghai and Chiang Kai-shek would return. During the five-anti movement,[9] the *Jiugong dao* compiled a "ghost telephone directory" of six-digit numbers, and spread rumors to sow dissension in the unity of the people. After Eisenhower[1] came into power, the *Yiguan dao* fabricated the story of a baby being born out of a bitch,[2] spread ideas about a change in the universe, and impersonated gods and ghosts to threaten the masses in order to achieve their objective of sabotaging production and construction, and undermining social order.

It will be thus seen that these reactionary Daoist cults are absolutely not religious organizations, but every inch counter-revolutionary organizations. That they have succeeded in deceiving a small portion of the culturally backward masses has been due to their putting on the cloak of gods and buddhas to cover up their counter-revolutionary activities. When their crimes have not yet been fully exposed, they can for a moment blind the eyes of a small portion of the masses. This is also one of the poisonous and treacherous characteristics of the reactionary cults.

For the masses deceived by them, these reactionary Daoist cults are also organizations which swindle and injure the people. They fool the masses with superstitious practices, cheat people out of money, insult women. People who join the cults have to pay various kinds of fees, and it is claimed that only by "doing good" (that is, spending money) will one be spared from suffering. In the *Yiguan dao*, one gold bar of ten ounces will have to be spent for holding once the service known as "ferrying a believer into immortality." The *Jiugong dao* has some fifty to sixty devices of swindling its adherents on the pretext of teaching them the mysteries of the cult. The *Baoguang* chapter of the *Yiguan dao* alone held more than 600 services for "ferrying believers into immortality" and extorted sums totalling more than 12,000 silver dollars. When an adherent falls sick, he is not allowed to see a physician but is forced to pay money to the cult and seek the help of the immortals. A packet of the ashes of joss sticks is issued and is said to be the "medicine of the gods." Besides cheating one out of his money, harm is also done to his life.

---

8. Communist China intervened on the side of North Korea in the Korean War (1950–53), known in China as the War to Resist American Aggression and Aid Korea; the UN forces helping the South Koreans resist the invasion were mainly American.
9. A campaign launched in 1952 against bribery, tax evasion, theft of national resources, theft of national economic information, and cheating on government contracts; it was aimed at capitalists.
1. Dwight D. Eisenhower (1890–1969), 34th U.S. president (1953–61).
2. A female dog.

Can we thus say of the heads of these cults that they are men who believe in deities and buddhas? Absolutely no. When they talk of teaching their believers the mysteries of immortality, and hold planchette (automatic writing) sessions, everything is a secretly prepared hoax, and people are deceived by outward appearances. These people live the most debauched of lives and are most extravagant. They often drive their believers into disposing of all their property and holdings, and proceed to outside areas for "the propagation of the truth in new lands," to develop their organizations. Many people closed down their businesses, sold their land, and finally lost everything they had. . . . Only by uniting ourselves and devoting our efforts at production may we make a good job of the construction of new China. The reactionary Daoist cults fear the efforts of the people at construction. In addition to engaging directly in counter-revolutionary activities, they also produce paralyzing effects on the spirits of the people, and attempt to make people believe that their sufferings are sent down from Heaven, in the attempt to reduce the morale of the people in their fight against the enemy and their zeal in production and construction. In our determination to prohibit these anti-popular and counter-revolutionary Daoist cult organizations, we are not only taking care of the general interests of the people, but also protecting the interests of the members of the cult who have been deceived. This is very obvious. The objective of our prohibition of these cults is to destroy their organizations, purge all counter-revolutionaries, save the majority of the members who have been deceived, raise high their political consciousness, in order to remove the obstacles to production and construction of our city, and to consolidate the people's democratic dictatorship. . . .

As to the mass of members deceived or coerced into joining the reactionary Daoist cults, their treatment must be quite different from that for the chiefs referred to above. These people have been victims of deception, and have committed no crimes. Only because of their ignorance they were deceived, and we must sympathize with their ignorance, adopt the policy of patient unity and education, to assist them into awakening, call upon them to resign from the cults and to be deceived no more. We must welcome these people in taking the step of resignation from the cults, and cannot permit any action that should embarrass them. . . .

BUDDHISTS AND DAOISTS AT MOUNT NANYUE WELCOME THE PEOPLE'S COMMUNES

In this document from 1958, local Buddhists and Daoists who have gone through a "socialist learning session" sponsored by the Chinese Communist Party renounce capitalism and express their support for the movement to establish people's industrial and agricultural communes. It highlights the drastic transformation of China attempted during the Great Leap Forward (1958–61), which sought to bring about rapid industrialization and collective farming. As this text suggests, the ideological goals were divorced from any realistic methods of reaching them; the campaign failed disastrously, leading to one of the worst famines in history and tens of millions of deaths.

We also see how the normal functioning of religious activities was curtailed as Daoists and Buddhists were forced to support the party's efforts to increase production. The Buddhists and Daoists of Nanyue, a sacred mountain site in Hunan Province, pledge to help form agricultural communes as well as a steel refinery—a monastic version of the wildly unsuccessful backyard steel furnaces placed in villages and neighborhoods. This text also functions as their "challenge" to religious organizations elsewhere to extend the same support.

PRONOUNCING GLOSSARY

Nanyue: *nahn-yueh*

This year, under the correct leadership and support of the Party and the Government, we Buddhists and Daoists in Nanyue[1] have gone through a systematic socialist learning session. Through this learning session we have elevated our socialist awareness, have clearly understood the struggle between the two roads, and have completely overcome capitalism on the economic, political, and ideological fronts.

We have also expressed wholehearted support for the great movement of the people's communes, which are guaranteed to do the best job possible in the present phase of industrial and agricultural production, and we are determined to welcome the establishment of them. Now we want to present the following production pledges as a glorious salute to the establishment of the people's communes, as well as a friendly challenge to all religious followers throughout the country:

1. We will respond to the call of the Party and the Government to undertake before the establishment of the people's communes, universal propaganda within and outside the cooperatives and repeatedly explain to the masses the nature of the people's communes as well as the purpose of establishing them. We will also call meetings of various sizes to mobilize the masses to freely bloom and discuss how to establish the people's communes and learn about their superiority.

2. Through hard work during three days and three nights we will build three steel refineries and reach the goal of producing forty tons of steel by the fourth quarter of this year. We will also reach the target of letting the cooperative members contribute the basic raw materials and of letting the members themselves learn the techniques for refining steel.

3. Within five days we, the members of our cooperative, will complete the harvest of the second rice crop in the forty-nine mou[2] rice field, fertilize the field for the sixth time for the late crop of rice, and uproot the vines and weeds in the field of sweet potatoes for the third time.

4. We will organize the religious followers in our cooperative who are between forty-five and sixty-five years of age to undertake sideline produc-

---

TRANSLATED BY Donald E. MacInnis. The bracketed addition is the translator's.

1. Mount Nanyue, a sacred mountain located in Hunan Province. "The Party": the Chinese Communist Party.

2. A little more than 8 acres (1 mou is about 800 square yards).

tion and cooking according to their individual physical strength, so that they may become laborers of different degrees.

5. During the fourth season of this year we will expand supplementary production on a big scale.

6. To increase production and speed up the establishment of the people's commune, we will increase our participation in work from forty-five percent to over sixty percent of [available] manpower.

7. We guarantee that as soon as we join a people's commune we will thoroughly carry out the principle of laboring with diligence and frugality and refrain from eating expensive food and other wasteful enjoyments, so that we may accumulate production capital for the commune through centralization of material and the saving of money.

Having started our pledges, we will definitely carry out what we have pledged. We present these pledges as a congratulation to the Communist Party Committee, as a salute to the people's communes, and as a friendly challenge to religious followers throughout the nation.

> (Signed by the whole body of
> cadres and members of the
> Buddhist-Daoist Agricultural
> Cooperative in Nanyue,
> September 13, 1958.)

THE INNER LIGHT

GEORGE HARRISON

About a century after Alfred, Lord Tennyson, was inspired to write his poem "The Ancient Sage" (1885; see above) by reading the first English translation of *The Scripture of the Way and Its Virtue* (*Daode jing*; see above), the most popular rock band of the 1960s recorded a song in Bombay, India, whose lyrics are derived from chapter 47 of that work: in 1968 "The Inner Light" appeared on the B-side of the Beatles' single "Lady Madonna." The chapter came to the group's attention when Juan Mascaró (1897–1987), a noted translator of Sanskrit and Pali texts—including the *Bhagavad Gita* (a version still in print in the Penguin Classic series), the *Upanishads*, and the *Dhammapada* and other Buddhist texts—wrote to George Harrison (1943–2001).

As Harrison recalled in his autobiography, after hearing "Within You Without You" (1967), a song heavily influenced by Indian classical music, Mascaró sent the guitarist *Lamps of Fire* (1958), his anthology of inspirational religious texts from different parts of the world. Many of the selections are translated by Mascaró; a number of chapters from *The Scripture of the Way and Its Virtue* are said to be "rendered by J. Mascaró," a label indicating that—like Martin Buber, who "translated" the same text (see the introduction to Buber's *Commentary on "Talks and Parables of Chuang Tzu,"* above)—he arrived at his "version" by introducing stylistic revisions to translations by others. Mascaró himself did not read or understand Chinese. In the letter accompanying the book, Mascaró suggested that Harrison write a song using "a few words of Tao" and pointed him to chapter 47 as an example. The musician did just that, using Mascaró's rendering with only minor changes for the lyrics of "The Inner Light."

Without going out of my door
I can know all things on Earth
Without looking out of my window
I could know the ways of Heaven

The farther one travels
The less one knows
The less one really knows

Without going out of your door
You can know all things on Earth
Without looking out of your window
You could know the ways of Heaven

The farther one travels
The less one knows
The less one really knows

Arrive without traveling
See all without looking
Do all without doing

THE TAO OF PHYSICS: AN EXPLORATION OF THE PARALLELS BETWEEN MODERN PHYSICS AND EASTERN MYSTICISM

FRITJOF CAPRA

Fritjof Capra's *The Tao of Physics: An Exploration of the Parallels between Modern Physics and Eastern Mysticism*, first published in 1975, became a best-seller and something of a modern classic. It has been reprinted more than forty times and translated into more than twenty languages, selling millions of copies. Other members of the "Fundamental Fysiks Group"—an eclectic group of physicists and researchers in Berkeley, California, in the 1970s who were fascinated by possible links between the paranormal, Eastern mysticism, and quantum physics—also wrote books, but Capra's was far and away the most successful. Although *The Tao of Physics* has little to do with Daoism as a religious tradition, its presentation of Daoist mysticism as enabling a better grasp of the deepest mysteries of the universe than traditional Western science profoundly affected how "Taoist" ideas were perceived around the world. According to Capra, a mystical experience on a beach in Santa Cruz during which—apparently under the influence of psychotropic plants—he saw everything as engaged in a cosmic dance led him to write the book.

Capra's influential work, much like Gary Zukav's later and also best-selling *The Dancing Wu Li Masters* (1979), finds identities between the metaphysical teachings of Buddhism, Hinduism, and Daoism and the concepts of modern theoretical physics. Capra's thesis is that the worldviews of these Eastern forms of mysticism and of post-Newtonian physics in fact share basic elements, as he argues that both the Western mechanistic view of science and the Western Cartesian division between mind and body are inadequate to capture reality as understood in quantum theory and relativity theory. In the chapter excerpted below, "Beyond the World of Opposites," Capra cites with approval a passage about the unification of opposites from *The Scripture of the Way and Its Virtue* (*Daode jing*; see above). He points to applications of the concept in physics at the subatomic level: for example, "particles are both destructible and indestructible." Capra views advances in modern physics as reflecting the themes of many non-Western mystical traditions that emphasize holism, interpenetration, harmony, and balance. These two domains come together in their insights, according to Capra, because both reflect a reality that "repeatedly transcends language and reasoning."

Scientists have generally accepted analogies posited between the new physics and the earlier insights of Eastern mysticism—a connection famously made by Niels Bohr, one of the pioneers of quantum physics—but many physicists have criticized Capra's work for what they see as overly precise equivalencies between the two domains, as well as an inaccurate portrayal of modern physics. Nonetheless, for years *The Tao of Physics* was used in some physics classes as an accessible way to appeal to college students more interested in Eastern religions than in modern science.

The Tao of Physics also drew the attention of scholars of religion, many of whom objected to Capra's fusion of Hindu, Buddhist, and Daoist ideas into an undifferentiated "Eastern mysticism." In at least one case, the mysticism itself was attacked. In "The Insights and Myopia of Mystical Philosophies," an essay published in 1980 in his collection *Limited Views: Essays on Ideas and Letters* (*Guanzhui bian*; see the following selection), the Chinese philosopher Qian Zhongshu used the same passage celebrated by Capra—the description from *The Scripture of the Way and Its Virtue* on the unification of opposites—as an epigraph because it "evoke[s] the insights and the shortcoming of all mystical philosophies, whether Chinese or foreign." Despite its critics, *The Tao of Physics* has remained popular around the world; a fifth American edition appeared in 2010.

Long before interest in exploring parallels between Eastern mysticism (especially Daoism) and science (especially physics) emerged in the West, there was a strong movement under way in China to scientize Daoism and its self-cultivation techniques. Broad exposure to Western science began in the late Qing dynasty (1644–1911), fueling a series of important reform movements that shaped the modern development of Daoism and Buddhism and continued apace into the Republican period (1912–49). The twentieth-century remaking of Daoism as a scientific system, which was closely tied to earlier attempts to purge Daoism of elements deemed "superstitious," was part of a much larger national project aimed at constructing a rational and scientific Chinese modernity. While Daoists in China were trying to tie the tradition's metaphysics to observable laws of physics—as in Chen Yingning's critique of traditional internal alchemy practices (see above)—Westerners focusing on physics, such as Capra and Zukav, were beginning to propose that the Eastern metaphysical traditions, including Daoism, had in some ways prefigured modern science's new discoveries about the physical world.

PRONOUNCING GLOSSARY

Bhagavad Gita: *bhah-gah-vud gee-tah*
Chuang-tzu (Zhuangzi): *chuang-tzu*
Lao Tzu (Laozi): *lao-tzu*

Shiva Mahesvara: *shih-vuh maw-hesh-vah-rah*
T'ai-chi (taiji): *tai-chee*

From *Beyond the World of Opposites*[1]

When the Eastern mystics tell us that they experience all things and events as manifestations of a basic oneness, this does not mean that they pronounce all things to be equal. They recognize the individuality of things, but at the same time they are aware that all differences and contrasts are relative within an all-embracing unity. Since in our normal state of consciousness, this unity of all contrasts—and especially the unity of opposites—is extremely hard to accept, it constitutes one of the most puzzling features of Eastern philosophy. It is, however, an insight which lies at the very root of the Eastern world-view.

Opposites are abstract concepts belonging to the realm of thought, and as such they are relative. By the very act of focusing our attention on any one concept, we create its opposite. As Lao Tzu says, "When all in the world understand beauty to be beautiful, then ugliness exists; when all understand goodness to be good, then evil exists."[2] Mystics transcend this realm of intellectual concepts, and in transcending it they become aware of the relativity and polar relationship of all opposites. They realize that good and bad, pleasure and pain, life and death, are not absolute experiences belonging to different categories, but are merely two sides of the same reality; extreme parts of a single whole. The awareness that all opposites are polar, and thus a unity, is seen as one of the highest aims of man in the spiritual traditions of the East. "Be in truth eternal, beyond earthly opposites!" is Krishna's advice in the *Bhagavad Gita*,[3] and the same advice is given to the followers of Buddhism. Thus D. T. Suzuki writes:

> The fundamental idea of Buddhism is to pass beyond the world of opposites, a world built up by intellectual distinctions and emotional defilements, and to realize the spiritual world of nondistinction, which involves achieving an absolute point of view.[4]

The whole of Buddhist teaching—and in fact the whole of Eastern mysticism—revolves about this absolute point of view which is reached in the world of *acintya*, or 'no-thought,' where the unity of all opposites becomes a vivid experience. In the words of a Zen poem,

> At dusk the cock announces dawn;
> At midnight, the bright sun.[5]

The notion that all opposites are polar—that light and dark, winning and losing, good and evil, are merely different aspects of the same phenomenon—is one of the basic principles of the Eastern way of life. Since all opposites are interdependent, their conflict can never result in the total victory of one side, but will always be a manifestation of the interplay

1. The author's original spelling of Chinese words has been retained in this selection. Laozi appears os Lao Tzu and Dao appears as Tao.
2. Lao Tzu, *Tao Te Ching*, trans. Ch'u Ta-Kao (New York; Samuel Weiser, 1973), chap. 1 [Capra's note]. On the *Daode jing* (*The Scripture of the Way and Its Virtue*), see above.
3. Literally, "Song of the Lord" (Sanskrit), a section of the Hindu epic poem the *Mahabharata*; it presents a conversation between Prince Arjuna and Lord Krishna, an incarnation of the Hindu deity Vishnu.
4. D. T. Suzuki, *The Essence of Buddhism*[, rev. ed.] (Kyoto, Japan: Hozokan, 1968), 18 [Capra's note]. Suzuki (1870–1966), Japanese Buddhist scholar and popularizer of Zen Buddhism in the West.
5. Quoted in A. A. Watts, *The Way of Zen* (New York: Vintage Books, 1957), 117 [Capra's note].

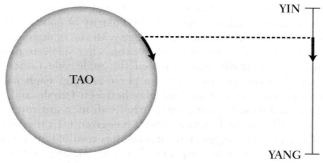

dynamic unity of polar opposites

between the two sides. In the East, a virtuous person is therefore not one who undertakes the impossible task of striving for the good and eliminating the bad, but rather one who is able to maintain a dynamic balance between good and bad.

This notion of dynamic balance is essential to the way in which the unity of opposites is experienced in Eastern mysticism. It is never a static identity, but always a dynamic interplay between two extremes. This point has been emphasized most extensively by the Chinese sages in their symbolism of the archetypal poles *yin* and *yang*.[6] They called the unity lying behind *yin* and *yang* the *Tao* and saw it as a process which brings about their interplay: "That which lets now the dark, now the light appear is *Tao*."[7]

The dynamic unity of polar opposites can be illustrated with the simple example of a circular motion and its projection. Suppose you have a ball going around a circle, if this movement is projected onto a screen, it becomes an oscillation between two extreme points. (To keep the analogy with Chinese thought, I have written TAO in the circle and have marked the extreme points of the oscillation with YIN and YANG.) The ball goes round the circle with constant speed, but in the projection it slows down as it reaches the edge, turns around, and then accelerates again only to slow down once more—and so on, in endless cycles. In any projection of that kind, the circular movement will appear as an oscillation between two opposite points, but in the movement itself the opposites are unified and transcended. This image of a dynamic unification of opposites was indeed very much in the minds of the Chinese thinkers, as can be seen from the passage in the *Chuang-tzu* quoted previously:

> That the "that" and the "this" cease to be opposites is the very essence of *Tao*. Only this essence, an axis as it were, is the center of the circle responding to the endless changes.[8]

---

6. The complementary forces that unite to form the Dao: yin, a term that originally referred to the shady side of a valley, by extension came to be associated with the dark, earth, dampness, and passivity—the female principle; yang, a term that originally referred to the sunny side of a valley, by extension came to be associated with the light, heaven, dryness, and activity—the male principle.
7. R. Wilhelm, *The I Ching or Book of Changes* (Princeton, NJ: Princeton University Press,

1967), 297 [Capra's note]. On the *Yijing*, see the introduction to *The Seal of the Unity of the Three, in Accordance with the Book of Changes* (*Zhouyi cantong qi*), above.
8. Chuang Tzu, *Genius of the Absurd*, arranged by Clae Waltham from the translation of James Legge (New York: Ace Books, 1971), chap. 13 [adapted from Capra's note]. On the *Zhuangzi* (*Book of Zhuang*), see above.

One of the principal polarities in life is the one between the male and female sides of human nature. As with the polarity of good and bad, or of life and death, we tend to feel uncomfortable with the male/female polarity in ourselves, and therefore we bring one or the other side into prominence. Western society has traditionally favored the male side rather than the female. Instead of recognizing that the personality of each man and of each woman is the result of an interplay between female and male elements, it has established a static order where all men are supposed to be masculine and all women feminine, and it has given men the leading roles and most of society's privileges. This attitude has resulted in an overemphasis of all the *yang*—or male—aspects of human nature: activity, rational thinking, competition, aggressiveness, and so on. The *yin*—or female—modes of consciousness, which can be described by words like intuitive, religious, mystical, occult, or psychic, have constantly been suppressed in our male-oriented society.

In Eastern mysticism, these female modes are developed and a unity between the two aspects of human nature is sought. A fully realized human being is one who, in the words of Lao Tzu, "knows the masculine and yet keeps to the feminine."[9] In many Eastern traditions the dynamic balance between the male and female modes of consciousness is the principal aim of meditation, and is often illustrated in works of art. A superb sculpture of Shiva in the Hindu temple of Elephanta[1] shows three faces of the god: on the right, his male profile displaying virility and willpower; on the left, his female aspect—gentle, charming, seductive—and in the center the sublime union of the two aspects in the magnificent head of Shiva Mahesvara, the Great Lord, radiating serene tranquillity and transcendental aloofness. In the same temple, Shiva is also represented in androgynous form—half-male, half-female—the flowing movement of the god's body and the serene detachment of his/her face symbolizing, again, the dynamic unification of the male and female.

In Tantric Buddhism,[2] the male/female polarity is often illustrated with the help of sexual symbols. Intuitive wisdom is seen as the passive, female quality of human nature, love and compassion as the active, male quality; and the union of both in the process of enlightenment is represented by ecstatic sexual embraces of male and female deities. The Eastern mystics affirm that such a union of one's male and female modes can be experienced only on a higher plane of consciousness where the realm of thought and language is transcended and all opposites appear as a dynamic unity.

I have already asserted that a similar plane has been reached in modern physics. The exploration of the subatomic world has revealed a reality which repeatedly transcends language and reasoning, and the unification of concepts which had hitherto seemed opposite and irreconcilable turns out to be one of the most startling features of this new reality. These seemingly irreconcilable concepts are generally not the ones the Eastern mystics

9. *Daode jing*, chapter 28.
1. An island in the harbor of modern-day Mumbai (Bombay); its famous cave temples contain many rock-cut images from Indian mythology, particularly of Shiva, one of the main Hindu deities (commonly known as the destroyer). The best-known sculpture is the one mentioned here, which shows Shiva in the roles of destroyer, pre-server, and creator.
2. A branch of Buddhism relying on texts (tantras) that set forth rituals and practices for the attainment of all manner of supernatural powers, including the power to achieve buddhahood; meant for initiates, it has been highly influential in India, Nepal, Tibet, and East Asia.

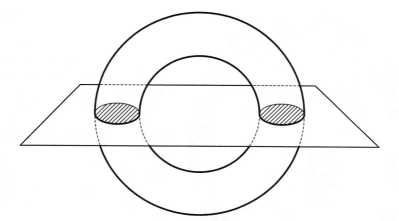

are concerned with—although sometimes they are—but their unification at a nonordinary level of reality provides a parallel to Eastern mysticism. Modern physicists should therefore be able to gain insights into some of the central teachings of the Far East by relating them to experiences in their own field. A small but growing number of young physicists have indeed found this a most valuable and stimulating approach to Eastern mysticism.

Examples of the unification of opposite concepts in modern physics can be found at the subatomic level where particles are both destructible and indestructible; where matter is both continuous and discontinuous, and force and matter are but different aspects of the same phenomenon. In all these examples, which will be discussed extensively in subsequent chapters, it turns out that the framework of opposite concepts, derived from our everyday experience, is too narrow for the world of subatomic particles. Relativity theory is crucial for the description of this world, and in the "relativistic" framework the classical concepts are transcended by going to a higher dimension, the four-dimensional space-time. Space and time themselves are two concepts which had seemed entirely different, but have been unified in relativistic physics. This fundamental unity is the basis of the unification of the opposite concepts mentioned above. Like the unity of opposites experienced by the mystics, it takes place on a "higher plane," i.e., in a higher dimension, and like that experienced by the mystics it is a dynamic unity, because the relativistic space-time reality is an intrinsically dynamic reality where objects are also processes and all forms are dynamic patterns.

To experience the unification of seemingly separate entities in a higher dimension we do not need relativity theory. It can also be experienced by going from one to two dimensions, or from two to three. In the example of a circular motion and its projection given on p. 2145 the opposite poles of the oscillation in one dimension (along a line) are unified in the circular movement in two dimensions (in one plane). The drawing above represents another example, involving a transition from two to three dimensions. It shows a "doughnut" ring cut horizontally by a plane. In the two dimensions of that plane, the surfaces of the cut appear as two completely separate discs, but in three dimensions they are recognized as being parts of one and the same object. A similar unification of entities which seem separate and irreconcilable

The coat of arms devised by Niels Bohr.

is achieved in relativity theory by going from three to four dimensions. The four-dimensional world of relativistic physics is the world where force and matter are unified; where matter can appear as discontinuous particles or as a continuous field. In these cases, however, we can no longer visualize the unity very well. Physicists can "experience" the four-dimensional space-time world through the abstract mathematical formalism of their theories, but their visual imagination—like everybody else's—is limited to the three-dimensional world of the senses. Our language and thought patterns have evolved in this three-dimensional world, and therefore we find it extremely hard to deal with the four-dimensional reality of relativistic physics.

Eastern mystics, on the other hand, seem to be able to experience a higher-dimensional reality directly and concretely. In the state of deep meditation, they can transcend the three-dimensional world of everyday life and experience a totally different reality, where all opposites are unified into an organic whole. When the mystics try to express this experience in words, they are faced with the same problems as the physicists trying to interpret the multidimensional reality of relativistic physics.

＊　　＊　　＊

For a better understanding of this relation between pairs of classical concepts, Niels Bohr[3] has introduced the notion of complementarity. He considered the particle picture and the wave picture as two complementary descriptions of the same reality, each of them being only partly correct and having a limited range of application. Each picture is needed to give a full description of the atomic reality, and both are to be applied within the limitations given by the uncertainty principle.

This notion of complementarity has become an essential part of the way physicists think about nature, and Bohr has often suggested that it might be a useful concept also outside the field of physics; in fact, the notion of complementarity proved to be extremely useful 2,500 years ago. It played an essential role in ancient Chinese thought which was based on the insight that opposite concepts stand in a polar—or complementary—relationship to each other. The Chinese sages represented this complemen-

---

3. Danish physicist (1885–1962); he received the Nobel Prize in Physics in 1922 for his work applying quantum theory to the structure of atoms.

tarity of opposites by the archetypal poles *yin* and *yang* and saw their dynamic interplay as the essence of all natural phenomena and all human situations.

Niels Bohr was well aware of the parallel between his concept of complementarity and Chinese thought. When he visited China in 1937, at a time when his interpretation of quantum theory had already been fully elaborated, he was deeply impressed by the ancient Chinese notion of polar opposites, and from that time he maintained an interest in Eastern culture. Ten years later, Bohr was knighted as an acknowledgment of his outstanding achievements in science and important contributions to Danish cultural life; and when he had to choose a suitable motif for his coat-of-arms, his choice fell on the Chinese symbol of *t'ai-chi*[4] representing the complementary relationship of the archetypal opposites *yin* and *yang*. In choosing this symbol for his coat-of-arms together with the inscription *Contraria sunt complementa* (Opposites are complementary), Niels Bohr acknowledged the profound harmony between ancient Eastern wisdom and modern Western science.

4. Literally, "great ultimate" (*taiji*); this concept of the union of yin and yang was first mentioned in the *Book of Changes.*

LIMITED VIEWS: ESSAYS ON IDEAS AND LETTERS
(*Guanzhui bian*)

QIAN ZHONGSHU

Qian Zhongshu (1910–1998) was an immensely erudite scholar of Chinese and Western literature as well as a prolific essayist and novelist. Outside of China, his best-known work is his satirical novel *Fortress Besieged* (1947), which has been recognized as a twentieth-century Chinese masterpiece and extensively translated. As a child Qian was educated in a missionary school, where instruction in Chinese and English introduced him to a wide range of foreign literature. He went on to study at Oxford and at the Sorbonne in Paris.

Qian's *Limited Views: Essays on Ideas and Letters* (*Guanzhui bian*, 1979–80) was published to wide acclaim. The English title of the work was, as the translator Ronald Egan notes, Qian's own rendering and bears little relationship to the Chinese title, which literally means "Tube and Awl Collection" and derives from a passage in the *Book of Master Zhuang* (*Zhuangzi*; see above) that mentions "using a tube to scan the sky and an awl to measure the earth." The phrase alludes to people whose field or scope of vision is limited but who try to grasp the vastness of something great; thus Qian seems to be making a self-deprecating play on his own limited ability to capture anything important about literary masterpieces.

Qian's interest in and study of Western literature and philosophy are vividly displayed in his *Limited Views*. Perhaps less immediately apparent to the contemporary reader, however, is the importance of the historical background that colors Qian's work. *Limited Views* was completed upon Qian's return to Beijing from years of reeducation in the countryside during the Great Proletarian Cultural Revolution.

A key component of that movement was its effort to destroy the old, particularly tradition and culture. Qian does not explicitly criticize the Cultural Revolution, but his thorough engagement with religious and literary classics from the deepest layers of the Chinese past obviously is intended to counter the radical attempts at erasing China's literary history.

While some have likened Qian's interdisciplinary method to that of comparative literature, he rejected that label. Though he employed a classical commentarial style of focusing on a short passage or theme within a text, he extended it in unprecedented ways by, in his phrase, "striking connections" (datong) with literature and philosophy from far outside the Chinese world. Qian's essays tend to be short and freewheeling, and he does not seek to connect them in order to build a larger systematic philosophical argument. But he does return repeatedly to certain ancient works; for example, nineteen essays in Limited Views draw on The Scripture of the Way and Its Virtue (Daode jing).

Qian opens "The Insights and Myopia of Mystical Philosophies," the selection below, with two epigraphs: a quotation from chapter 2 of the Daode jing on the transcending of dualities and of opposites, followed by a commentary on that passage by Wang Bi (226–249). Qian claims that they "evoke the insights and the shortcoming of all mystical philosophies, whether Chinese or foreign." He proceeds to cite a wide range of Chinese texts and invokes a range of Western figures—including the radical Jewish Dutch philosopher Benedict de Spinoza (1632–1677), the German mystic Johannes Tauler (1300–1361), and the French Christian mystic Madame Guyon (1648–1717)—to support his point that recognizing the dialectical interaction of opposites is an important insight, but simply erasing difference creates problems. Qian decries the writings of mystical philosophers, including Laozi, for presenting "ideas that are not intrinsically consistent" and doctrines that may sound profound but are impossible to put into practice. As a result, philosophers become entwined in such paradoxes as championing "not speaking" while nonetheless "able to speak in weighty phrases, speak with hidden meanings, . . . and speak all manner of groundless, irresponsible words." Similarly, Qian points out that "having no body," as The Scripture of the Way and Its Virtue advocates, does not prevent someone from being "able to ingratiate himself with sick ploys, to maneuver for advantage in the world, to preserve his body and protect himself, and to prolong his span in this life." The essays in Qian's Limited Views that treat Daoism-related texts reveal how for one of China's most esteemed men of letters, these topics continued to inspire thinking about larger issues that engages with more recent writings from China and the rest of the world.

PRONOUNCING GLOSSARY

Bo Juyi (Bai Juyi): bow jew-yee (bai jew-yee)
Guanzhui bian: gwan-chuei bien
Huainanzi: hwai-nahn-tzu
Qian Zhongshu: chien chong-shu
Wang Bi: wawng bee

The Insights and Myopia of Mystical Philosophies

All the world recognizes the beautiful as the beautiful, yet this is the ugly; the whole world recognizes the good as the good, yet this is the bad.

> Thus Something and Nothing produce each other;
> The difficult and the easy complement each other;
> The long and the short off-set each other;
> The high and the low incline towards each other;

TRANSLATED BY Ronald Egan.

Note and sound harmonize with each other;
Before and after follow each other.

—*Laozi*,[1] Chapter 2

Pleasure and anger have a common root, and right and wrong share a single door-way. You cannot invoke the one without the other.

—Wang Bi's[2] (226–249) commentary

These few sentences evoke the insights and the shortcomings of all mystical philosophies, whether Chinese or foreign. As Saint-Martin observed, mystical philosophers the world over seem to inhabit the same locale and speak the same language.[3] I shall elaborate on this point below.

To recognize the beautiful as beautiful is to distinguish it from what is ugly, and to perceive the good as good is to differentiate it from the bad. Even to speak of the beautiful is, implicitly, to allude to the ugly, just as to mention the good is implicitly to refer to the bad. The mention of one actually evokes both members of the complementary pair. As Spinoza observed, "To say it is 'this' is to say it is not 'that.'" (*Determinatio est negatio*),[4] "Something and Nothing," "the difficult and the easy," etc. (what Wang Bi calls the "six door-ways") may all be understood this way. There is no argument on this point.

Mystical philosophies, however, contend that the supreme truth or Way transcends such dualities and obliterates all distinctions. That is why *Laozi* is not content to say that recognizing the beautiful also involves an aware-ness of the ugly. Instead, he insists that the beautiful itself is the ugly, and that the good itself is the bad. His aim is to obliterate ordinary perception of the beautiful and good, enlarging and transforming it.

Yet the *Laozi* passage has not always been understood this way. In *Huai-nanzi*,[5] Taiqing asks, "Is it, then, that not recognizing amounts to recogniz-ing? And does recognizing amount to not recognizing?" Wushi replies by quoting *Laozi*, " 'The world recognizes the good as the good, yet this is the bad.'" Here, the passage is quoted simply by way of suggesting that people's appreciation of goodness and the Way has diminished. Wang Anshi's[6] *Explanations of Words* says, "When a sheep is full grown, it is beautiful and complete. In its beauty and completeness lies its imminent death. Does not *Laozi* say, 'All the world recognizes the beautiful as the beautiful, yet this is the ugly'?" Here, the author's goal is to equate *Laozi*'s statement with the idea that good fortune always contains misfortune hidden inside it. Actually, *Huainanzi*'s explanation is superficial, while Wang Anshi's is forced. As for the real sense of what *Laozi* means, rather than to take it as "in recognizing the beautiful your recognition also involves the ugly," it should be understood to mean "recognizing is the same as not recognizing: the beautiful that is recognized is the ugly, and the good that is recognized is the bad."

---

1. Another name for the *Daode jing* (*The Scrip-ture of the Way and Its Virtue*; see above), some-times called the *Five Thousand Words*.
2. Author of one of the most highly regarded commentaries on the *Daode jing*.
3. Quoted in Evelyn Underhill, *Mysticism: A Study in Nature and Development of Spiritual Consciousness*, 12th ed. (1930; reprint, Grand Rapids, MI: Christian Classics Ethereal Library, n.d.), 78 [adapted from Qian's note]. Louis-Claude de Saint-Martin (1743–1803), French mystic and visionary philosopher.
4. *The Correspondence of Spinoza* (Letter L),

trans. A. Wolf (London: Allen and Unwin, 1928), 270–71 [Qian's note]. Benedict de Spinoza (1632–1677), Jewish Dutch philosopher.
5. On the *Master of Huainan* (*Huainan-zi*), a work compiled in the 2nd century B.C.E., see above; it contains many quotations from the *Daode jing* and the *Book of Master Zhuang* (*Zhuangzi*; see above).
6. A government reformer (1021–1086); his lost *Zishuo* (*Explanations of Words*, or *Explanations of Characters*) provided the meanings of key words used in the Confucian Classics.

Laozi contains many restatements of this general theme of blocking perceptions and knowledge. Chapter 3 of *Laozi* says, "Therefore the sage keeps the people innocent of knowledge and free from desire." Chapter 4 says, "Soften the glare; let your wheels move only along old ruts." Chapter 18 says, "When the great Way falls into disuse there are benevolence and rectitude." Chapter 20 says, "Vulgar people are clear, I alone am drowsy. Vulgar people are alert, I alone am muddled." Chapter 49 says, "the sage muddles the mind of the empire." These repeated assertions amount to nothing more than what is referred to in *Zhuangzi* as "the arts of Mr. Primal Blob." Similarly, in *Guan Yinzi*[7] it is said that a mind that distinguishes advantage from harm or the worthy from the foolish or right from wrong or beauty from ugliness is a mind that cannot be perceptive and that this is why the sage muddles his mind. The same work says, "It is only in a muddled and confused condition that one attains to the Way." The same theme occurs in Buddhist writings. Various passages in the *Vimalakirti Sutra*[8] assert that "distinctions are all empty," "the dharma[9] permits no selecting or rejecting," "desires and greed spring from invalid distinctions," and "in the dharmas there are no distinctions." Other sutras make similar statements. The *Dharani Sutra*[1] says, "Take leave of the two sides and reside in equidistance. . . . Do not praise or blame anything . . . nor make any selections." *The Sutra of Perfect Enlightenment*[2] says, "If one attains to be free of hatred and love . . . one can then accord with enlightened nature." Monk Can's inscription on a faithful mind in *The Essence of the Five Lamps*[3] says, "The perfect Way consists of nothing other than avoidance of making choices, freedom from hatred and love, and unencumbered perception." Even the grand indifference (*von allen underscheit*) that the German mystic Tauler spoke of as well as *la sainte indifference* that Madame Guyon[4] advocated are essentially the same states.

Recognizing the beautiful as the beautiful and the good as the good causes distinctions to be drawn. These, in turn, give rise to selectivity, which sharpens distinctions even more. Love and hate ensue and engender greed and anger. *Laozi*, in seeking to clarify the true nature of the Way and Power, wants to cause the Way that has been split apart and the Carved Block[5] that has been lost to be restored to their primal unity. *The Spring and Autumn Annals of Mr. Lü*[6] says, "A man of Jing lost his bow and refused to look for it, explaining, 'A man of Jing lost the bow, but another man of Jing will find it.

---

7. A now lost work associated with Yin Xi (also known as Guanyin zi), the border guard at the Han'gu Pass who urged Laozi to teach the *Daode jing*.

8. A Buddhist text, also known as the *Instructions of Vimalakirti* (*Vimalakirtinirdesha*), composed in India (probably ca. 100 C.E.) but especially popular in East Asia. In this sutra (a discourse of the Buddha, usually presented as a dialogue), the Buddha's lay disciple Vimalakirti, who is ill, repeatedly demonstrates that his wisdom—particularly regarding the ineffable nature of nonduality—is superior to that of the monks who visit him.

9. Doctrine or discourses of the Buddha.

1. A sutra (*Da fengdeng tuoluoni jing*) featuring Guanyin, a female bodhisattva—a being intent on enlightenment—identified in East Asian Buddhism with Avalokiteshvara, the bodhisattva regarded as the embodiment of all the compassion of all the buddhas.

2. *Yuanjue jing*, a Buddhist text focused on meditation practice (probably composed in China ca. 8th century B.C.E.).

3. *Wudeng huiyuan* (also known as the *Compendium of the Five Lamps*), a Chan (Zen) work printed in 1253. "Monk Can": the third Chan Buddhist patriarch, Sengcan (d. 606); the sentence quoted appears in his doctrinal poem *Inscription on Faith in the Mind* (*Xinxin ming*).

4. The French Christian mystic Jeanne-Marie Bouvier de la Motte-Guyon (1648–1717); *la sainte indifférence* is "the holy indifference." Johannes Tauler (ca. 1300–1361), German Catholic preacher and mystic.

5. In Daoism, the uncarved block symbolizes humans' natural state.

6. *Lüshi chunqiu*, a collection of essays, compiled (ca. 240 B.C.E.) under the direction of Lü Buwei (d. 235 B.C.E.), on the teachings of several schools of philosophy as well as regional folklore.

What's the point of looking for it?' Confucius heard it and said, 'It would be better not to specify a man of *Jing*.' Laozi heard it and said, 'It would be better not to specify a *man*.'" The point is to blot out the distinction between oneself and others and to make gain and loss equivalent.

Nevertheless, the ugly cannot be invoked all by itself, just as the beautiful cannot be, and the bad must imply its opposite, just as does the good. Using its own logic, *Laozi*'s doctrine should permit this elaboration: "All the world recognizes the ugly as the ugly, yet this is the beautiful. All the world recognizes the bad as bad, yet this is the good." After all, what is west to the eastern house is east to the western house. To judge, however, from the general drift of its philosophy, *Laozi* would still say: "All the world recognizes the ugly as the ugly, and this is the ugly. All the world recognizes the bad as the bad, and this is the bad." Whether you rush to rejoin something or hurry off to avoid it, you are running in either case. To discriminate or make distinctions goes against the spirit of returning to the Uncarved Block or entering into an undifferentiated state of mind, just as it is contrary to the great principle of "equalizing all things." Still, with regard to being either "clear and alert" or "drowsy and muddled," *Laozi* certainly does make choices, preferring the latter.[7] The work does not abandon all judgment or observe everything with the same sympathetic eye. Its method too is one of making distinctions and of being selective. It claims to make no distinctions to differentiate itself from those who do, just as it claims not to be selective to separate itself from those who are. These claims follow from its doctrine that "Something and Nothing produce each other." However, Chapter 12 says, "Hence the sage is for the belly not for the eye." Chapter 38 says, "Hence the man of large mind abides in the thick not in the thin, in the fruit not in the flower. Therefore he discards the one and takes the other." Is this not "recognizing the beautiful" and "recognizing the good" and making clear-cut choices regarding them?

Yang Wanli[8] (1127–1206) deprecated *Laozi*'s statement about "not specifying a *man*" this way: "Its views certainly are lofty! Yet they are not reasonable. The bow is mentioned in the original statement for its utility. If it is not a man, then who will find the bow? And who will use it?" The problem of doctrines that cannot really be implemented or of ideas that are not intrinsically consistent is universal in mystical philosophies. *Laozi*'s shortcomings with regard to such internal consistency are many. In his "Cross-Examination of Doubtful Points in *Laozi*," Sun Sheng[9] (d. 373) fastened upon line after line and still did not exhaust all the possibilities. As Bo Juyi[1] wrote in his "Upon Reading *Laozi*":

"Those who speak do not understand, those who understand are silent,"
These words I learned from Master Lao.
But if we say that Master Lao was "one who understood,"
Why did he compose the "Five Thousand Words"?

Similarly, Chapter 13 says, "When I no longer have a body, what trouble have I?" But Chapters 7, 44, and 52 say, "Therefore the sage treats his body as extraneous to himself and it is preserved," "Your name or your body, which is dearer?" and "Bring not misfortune upon your body."

7. See *Laozi*, chap. 20 [Qian's note].
8. A poet and scholar-official; the quotation is from his *Collected Works* (*Chengzhai ji*).
9. A prolific historian.
1. A famous poet (772–846), also spelled Bai Juyi.

Now, to preserve the body and to express what one understands, these are sincere urges and pragmatic conduct. To leave one's body behind and refrain from speaking, these are arcane ideas and rarefied doctrines. Unable to free itself from what is sincere and pragmatic, *Laozi* is yet unwilling to relinquish its arcane ideas or rarefied doctrines. Left with no alternative, it intertwines the two and embellishes them. Words that were originally without substance are applied to human conduct, making them seem discriminating yet hard to pin down. And conduct that was at first quite ordinary is ornamented with words until it becomes a pretense that yet appears resolute. Consequently, while "not speaking" the philosopher is able to speak in weighty phrases, speak with hidden meanings, speak in unprincipled language tailored to the occasion, and speak all manner of groundless, irresponsible words. While "having no body," he is able to ingratiate himself with slick ploys, to maneuver for advantage in the world, to preserve his body and protect himself, and to prolong his span in this life. Doing Nothing permits him to do everything, and not to have anything to which he will not stoop. The purity and quietude of the Huang-Lao Daoists thus in practice became the cold-hearted attitude of the Legalist philosophy of Shen Buhai and Han Fei.[2]

The Uncarved Block, however, eventually loses its integrity, and the Pure finally becomes tainted, just as the Way, which is One, gives rise to Two. Things are not all equal, and so doctrines that treat them as equal are impossible to sustain. Selectivity arises from the habit of observing distinctions in the world. That is why even *Laozi* cannot help but refer to the "beautiful" and the "good" in discussing what one recognizes. Yet, irked that the world embodies such distinctions, *Laozi* tries to overcome them by developing views that admit no selectivity. This is like the youthful Kumarajiva,[3] who explained that it was only because his unenlightened mind still made distinctions that the rice bowl could feel heavy or light. It is to invert cause and consequence. Does it not resemble shutting the eyes to dispel sights or stopping up the ears to extinguish sounds? In his critical comments on Chapter 20 of *Laozi*, Yan Fu[4] (1853–1921) wrote, "When the African ostrich is being chased and has no escape, it sticks its head in the sand, thinking that if it sees no danger there is no danger. *Laozi*'s doctrine of 'eliminating learning' is precisely like this!" He appropriated a Western adage (*the ostrich policy*) to draw an apt analogy. Hegel once belittled Schelling by saying that he was like a man who "on a dark and starless night, when no mark or shape could be discerned, concluded that all the cows in the herd were black" (*sein* Absolutes *für die Nacht auszugeben, worin,* . . . , *alle Kühe schwarzs sind*).[5] This might also be said of *Laozi*.

---

2. The greatest of China's Legalist philosophers (ca. 280–233 B.C.E.; see the *Book of Master Han Fei*, or Han Feizi, above); he credited Shen Buhai (d. 337 B.C.E.) with being one of the sources on which he drew. Legalism espoused the strict application of laws that rigidly prescribed punishments; Huang-Lao Daoists revered Huangdi, the mythical Yellow Emperor, whose reign was viewed as a golden age of prosperity and harmony.
3. Buddhist monk (343/44–413) who was brought to China and became one of the most important translators of Buddhist scriptures from Sanskrit into Chinese.
4. Chinese scholar and translator of books by major Western thinkers, including Thomas Huxley, John Stuart Mill, and Herbert Spencer. The quotation is from his essay "Comments on Laozi" ("Laozi pingyu").
5. Quoted from the preface to *The Phenomenology of Mind* (1807), by the German idealist philosopher Georg Wilhelm Friedrich Hegel (1770–1831); this observation ended his friendship with Friedrich Schelling (1775–1854), another German idealist philosopher.

TWO RITUAL DOCUMENTS

China has been called a paperwork empire, a label born of the sheer volume of documents that kept the bureaucracy functioning. Daoism, modeled in part on the imperial bureaucracy, similarly depends on written texts—in its case, to communicate with the unseen world of the celestial bureaucracy—and its rituals therefore use many different types of handwritten documents. These are prepared in advance by the high priest, who holds that position by virtue of his skill and knowledge in producing the proper forms. Among the main Daoist ritual documents are a "placard," which is posted outside the temple where a ritual is being performed (allowing everyone to read it); a "memorial," which is read inside the temple (a location off-limits to most of the community); and an "announcement," which is intoned outside the temple to dispatch the priest's message to the deities above. Such rituals are referred to as "offerings" (*jiao*), and they are usually performed by Orthodox Unity (Zhengyi) Daoist priests. These elaborate rites involve the entire community and can last seven days or more.

There can be many reasons for performing a Daoist offering, but in general it serves to unite a community and renew the community's relationship with its tutelary deity. The ritual announced on the memorial translated here is a three-day offering performed when the Palace of the Rising Sun, located in southern Taiwan, was refurbished in 1980. The memorial expresses the community's thanks and gratitude to the gods for their protection and conveys wishes that they continue to bestow peace and harmony. It then goes on to describe what will transpire over the course of three days, identifying the important junctures of the ritual, the texts to be recited, and the ceremonial gifts to be made. The placard that is posted for all to read outside the temple is basically the same as the memorial, but it is formally burned at the conclusion of the offering.

The second selection is an announcement detailing the types of documents that are sent off (usually by being burned) to various celestial offices and deities. Its language is highly bureaucratic—indeed, the terminology is copied from secular governance—and it notes that all the written documents are properly stamped and sealed. The announcement also describes the messengers and the route the texts will take on their way to their destination.

PRONOUNCING GLOSSARY

Chen Dingsheng: *chun ding-shung*   Xiding: *hsi-ding*

Memorial for a Communal Ritual

Xiding Compound, Palace of the Rising Sun.

In the *gengshen* year (1980) of heaven's revolution, eleventh month.

Request for Good Fortune for the Fragrant Offering of the Golden Register[1] to Celebrate Completion and Pray for Peace.

Humble servant in charge of the various offices of thunder and lightning, the bureau of the Dipper,[2] and the Celestial Clinic, immortal minister of

---

TRANSLATED BY John Lagerwey. All bracketed additions are the translator's.

1. The Golden Register Retreat (Jinlu zhai), one of the three "register retreats" that Daoists have performed since as early as the 5th century. In contemporary Taiwan, this ritual is performed as a prayer for peace.

2. The Northern or Big Dipper, in Daoism viewed as the pivot of the universe and associated with transformation.

the canonical register of the Covenant of the Orthodox Unity of the Most High with the Powers, possessing and practicing the ritual methods of the Divine Empyrean,[3] Chen Dingshen, full of fear and trembling, does obeisance and kowtows; he bows a hundred times as he addresses himself to heaven. Respectfully, he memorializes on behalf of

All the people of the Palace of the Rising Sun in Xiding Compound, North Gate Village, district of Tainan, province of Taiwan, Republic of China. Together, they go to the Palace of the Rising Sun to worship the Way and prepare an Offering in celebration of the completion [of the temple] and to pray for peace, protection, and prosperity.

Chairman of the Assembly so-and-so;
Chairman of the Offering so-and-so;
Chairman of the Altar so-and-so;
Chairman of the Universal Salvation ritual so-and-so;
Assistant Chairman of the Assembly so-and-so;
Assistant Chairman of the Offering so-and-so;
Assistant Chairman of the Universal Salvation ritual so-and-so;
Host of the Incense Burner so-and-so;
Chairman of the Committee so-and-so;
Assistant Chairman of the Committee so-and-so;
Members of the Committee so-and-so;

together with all the faithful, having respectfully bathed and lit incense, bow humbly and address themselves to heaven:

Majestic is the temple, firmly fixed like the mountains and rivers; luminous are the gods, living forever as companions of the Father (☰) and Mother (☷).[4] It is because the people who belong to this incense burner [temple] have repeatedly experienced the protection afforded by its abundant merit that they think constantly how to show their gratitude. Seeing that the precious hall had not been cleaned up in a long time and that it was no longer very nice to look at, they engaged workers to rebuild it and to change the old to new. When the workers informed us they had finished, we rejoiced at having been able to bring it to fruition.

We pray that Sovereign Heaven will bless us and Lord Earth favor us: let the Green Dragon produce signs of approval and the White Tiger go into hiding.[5] May its broad foundations be our succor and the veins of earth our source of livelihood forever. Cause the whole area to enjoy peace and quiet and gods and men to dwell in harmony together. Allow no calamities to occur. May the students win signal honors and the farmers sing over full granaries; may the merchants make profits and the laborers obtain what they desire. Let there be abundance in fields and seas: cause the fish and crustaceans to flourish and multiply, the five grains to yield a rich harvest, and the six domestic

3. Shenxiao, an ethereal celestial locale and an organized religious movement that formed during the Song dynasty (960–1279). The Divine Empyrean movement was primarily associated with the performance of Thunder Rites, intended to harness the power of thunder and summon common thunder deities.
4. The two trigrams reproduced here, Qian and Kun, heaven and earth, are respectively pure yang (a term that originally referred to the sunny side of a valley, and by extension came to be associated with the light, dryness, and activity—the male principle) and pure yin (a term that origi-

nally referred to the shady side of a valley, and by extension came to be associated with the dark, dampness, and passivity—the female principle). On the trigrams, see the introduction to *The Seal of the Unity of the Three, in Accordance with the Book of Changes* (*Zhouyi cantong qi*), above.
5. The Green Dragon and White Tiger are two of the four directional animals, representing east and west respectively. Within internal alchemy the Green Dragon is connected with the trigram Li ☲ (fire), representing yin within yang; the White Tiger, with the trigram Kan ☵ (water), representing yang within yin.

animals[6] to increase in numbers. May all undertakings produce the desired results and every enterprise be crowned with success. We celebrate the repair, we celebrate its completion: on the land of the Way we give thanks, we pray for peace, we make our offering. We have selected by divination this month, the 11th, 12th, and 13th days, to go, leaning on the Way, to the palace in order to set up an altar and convene the great assembly of the Fragrant Offering of the Golden Register to Celebrate Completion and Pray for Peace.

For three days and nights we will execute rituals: at an auspicious hour, we will beat the drum for the first time and then flame the oil to drive away evil. First we will dispatch a whole set of documents to inform the authorities of the Three Realms[7] that we are reverently preparing a fragrant banquet. Respectfully, we will invite the Emperor in his chariot. We will raise the flag and post the placard so as to inform all the perfected[8] everywhere. We will command the generals to protect the altar and prevent the entry of nefarious energies. We will recite *The Great Litany of Confession and Homage to Heaven*, we will present our marvelous offering of nine gifts. In the evening we will make a farewell sacrifice to the earth gods of the five directions[9] so that they go far away to other regions. We will set out a libation for the Office of Earth, summon good fortune by waving the willow branch, and set in place the symbol-orders. The first night we will light precious torches so as to illumine the perfected, we will roll up the pearl screen and pay our respects to the Emperor. We will sound the golden bell so as to bring heaven and earth into harmony; we will strike the jade stone so as to bring the *yin* and the *yang* into union. Temporarily, we will close our secret canons.

The next morning, when the sky is clear and the air pure, we will add incense in the jade burner. We will mount the altar for the Land of the Way; we will present the incense three times. Again we will proclaim the scriptures; again we will make the vegetarian offering of fruit and rice and present jewels and flowers. That evening, we will light and release the water lamps so that they may illumine the paths in the darkness. We will invoke the saints and masters, worthy lords of the Great Teaching. The divine ritual of the Nocturnal Invocation[1] is the mainstay of the Teaching: we will open the cloud covers to display the True Writs, and we will hold them in place with the four treasures of the calligrapher.[2] We will memorialize the nine heavens and make confession to the ten extremities.[3] Then we will take leave of the masters and loosen our belt; for a while the divine sounds will cease.

When the third morning comes and the heavens are bright, we will clean the altar area and straighten things up. Once again we will sound the drum of the law, address ourselves once again to the most venerable ones. We will present fine teas; we will open up and intone the most perfect of the marvelous scriptures. We will mount the stage to perform our teaching, and we will respectfully forward the petition, setting it forth for imperial

---

6. Pigs, dogs, chickens, horses, cattle, and sheep.
7. The Realm of Desire (whose inhabitants desire pleasing objects of the senses), the Realm of Form (inhabited by gods who have physical form), and the Formless Realm (inhabited by gods who exist only as consciousness); these make up the Buddhist universe.
8. Daoist spiritual masters; Daoists who have moved beyond earthly corruption.
9. East, west, north, south, and center.
1. Suqi, a preparatory ritual performed near the

beginning of a larger multiday offering (*jiao*) ritual. This rite's numerous steps include lighting the incense burner, displaying talismans, chanting precepts, and completing the altar.
2. Brush, ink, ink stone, and paper. "True Writs": the writs that, in the Lingbao (Numinous Treasure) tradition, fixed the cosmic order in place.
3. That is, the ten directions: north, south, east, west, northeast, northwest, southeast, southwest, the nadir, and the zenith.

examination. At each home we will present incense, at each gate proclaim the memorial. At noon we will make the fragrant offering and strew fine flowers all around. Having finished the canonical stanzas, we will announce this in prayer to the myriad potentates of the Three Realms. The lamps of the saints aglow, the prime stars of the root destiny of the multitude will be resplendent. We will communicate our sincerity in the Orthodox Offering, welcoming all who descend from the Jade Capital.[4] We will sing the mighty texts of the great thanksgiving; we will pour the fine wine of the triple libation. Outside, we will prepare a small banquet to be distributed to all the solitary spirits. We will pray over the divine lamps of the five thunders and set forth the Pure Offering for Peace with the Pestilence (gods).[5] We will escort the ship of the immortals back to the islands in the sea; we will welcome home the felicity which enters our borders. Having completed the libations and offerings and having seen the saints off on their return journey, we will distribute by burning the money (for transmission) of the memorial to reward the officers and soldiers. We will take respectful leave of heaven's face and put the lord of this territory and the perfected back in their proper places. Having executed rituals for three days and nights, we will worship the supreme perfected on high and pray for peace and manifold blessings here below.

In the *gengshen* year of heaven's revolution, the eleventh month, the _____ day.

Your humble servant, Chen Dingsheng, bows three times and presents the memorial on high.

Announcement for a Communal Ritual

Announcement (dispatch!): Office of the Great Method of the Numinous Treasure. This office today worships the Way and prepares an Offering to give thanks and pray for peace. Being charged with maintaining the order of the Three Heavens, the office-holder is enrolled in the ranks of the five record-keeping bureaus. The antiquity of canon law ensures that sincerity penetrates the high (heaven) and the thick (earth); the luminosity of the ritual texts makes certain that the somber heavens (water) reach both the dark (earth) and the light (heaven). All our earnest petitions must be transmitted by an honorable office-holder if they are to be executed with dispatch. Those who must receive this announcement are as follows:[6]

—five box envelopes with invocations, invitations, and presentations are respectfully sent to:
the Golden Gate in the Jade Capital: respectfully invoked;
the gate of the Four Bureaus of the Three Realms: respectfully invited;
the Bureau of the Great Sovereign of the Office of Heaven: respectfully presented;
the Court of the Celestial Pivot in the Highest Purity: respectfully presented;

4. Yujing, a reference to the central Jade Capital Mountain (or Jade Capitoline) that soars into the high Grand Veil Heaven and is home to the Celestial Worthy of Primordial Commencement, the supreme deity of the Lingbao (Numinous Treasure) tradition.
5. This sentence and the next refer to another *jiao*

[offering] which may be inserted. It is addressed to the pestilence gods [translator's note].
6. The following list of bureaus and offices clearly conveys the bureaucratic nature of the Daoist priest's written communication with various deities and divine officials.

the Office of the Eastern Peak Tai:[7] respectfully presented.

—two box envelopes with letters of presentation are respectfully forwarded to:

the offices of the Six Masters of the Numinous Treasure: respectfully forwarded;

the offices of the Four Saints of the North Pole: respectfully forwarded.

—four box envelopes with missives of offering are respectfully presented to:

the officers of merit who transmit symbols,

the various gods who assist the Way,

the gods of the soil and of the walls and moats,

the gods to whom is rendered a cult recognized by law: to each, presented.

—seven letters, cards, and notes are respectfully passed on to:

the officers, generals, clerks, and soldiers of the various offices of the thunder and lightning of the Numinous Treasure in the Court of Law of the Highest Purity;

the various officers, generals, clerks, and soldiers of the altar where gather the gods of the Three Realms in the Chamber of Spontaneity for Communication with the Perfected;

the host of the immortals who bring catastrophes during the various parts of this year;

the venerable god of supreme virtue in charge of the Great Star Taisui;[8]

the venerable gods of the walls and moats of the district and the prefecture of Tainan;

the gods and keen-eared ones from above, below, far, and near who receive sacrifices in this neighborhood;

the six gods of the soil and directors of destiny of the incense burners of each family.

The above documents have all been duly stamped, sealed, and completed. We look to the divine powers on high to transmit them for us. Let the mounted gods gallop each in his own direction and give (his documents) to the right office, penetrating on high to the Golden Gate of the Jade Capital and below into the bright waters and dark earth. May our sincerity be communicated directly on high and a response be forthcoming. Let there be no delays: it must reach those concerned.

The above is announced to the jade lasses of the Three Heavens[9] charged with transmission, the messengers of the roads through the clouds of the Nine Heavens, the officers of merit of Orthodox Unity, the great generals of the molten metal and fiery bells, the potent officers in charge of memorializing on this day, the clerks mounted on the flying dragons—all the gods of transmission.

In the *gengshen* year of heaven's revolution, the 11th month, the 20th day, dispatched.

In charge of the execution of the rituals: Chen Cunxin (seal)

ANNOUNCEMENT (DISPATCH)

---

7. One of the Five Marchmounts, a group of five sacred mountains—one in each of the four cardinal directions and one at the center.

8. Jupiter, a stellar deity.

9. Great Clarity (Taiqing), Jade Clarity (Yuqing), and Upper Clarity (Shangqing). "Jade lasses": heavenly attendants.

A DAOIST ORDINATION CERTIFICATE FROM PUTIAN, FUJIAN

Many different types of ordination rituals developed within the Daoist tradition, varying over time and for different levels of investiture. The *Short Exposition on the Transmission of the Scriptures, Rules, and Registers of the Three Caverns* (*Chuanshou sandong jingjie falu lüeshuo*), excerpted above, provides a canonical ordination record from the Tang dynasty (618–907); the modern ordination certificate reprinted below comes not from a theoretical treatise but from an actual ritual carried out in Putian (in Fujian Province) in 1981.

Despite the diversity of the rituals used in different lineages throughout Chinese history, we can generalize about some of the basic characteristics of a Daoist ordination. Its liturgies are modeled in part on Buddhist ordinations. The rite signals the change in status of the ordinand into a priest who takes on important new responsibilities and commands a set of deities. Indeed, the document specifies that in the final step, the ordinand "joins the Heavenly Officials and lives in the Realm of the Immortals forever." The ordination ritual itself is preceded by rigorous preparation and training, directed and overseen by an experienced master who then vouches for the ordinand to the deities. A set of priests charged with different responsibilities, together with five to ten witnesses, participate in the ritual. The hopeful ordinand makes pledges, takes oaths, vows to uphold precepts and prohibitions, and promises to actively ward off calamities and protect the community and the state. He receives not just a new title but a considerable number of potent items that mark his newly attained rank and status—all listed in the document. Now transformed and in possession of all the necessary ritual paraphernalia, the newly ordained priest wields new powers and is ready to take up his new responsibilities and obligations.

PRONOUNCING GLOSSARY

Fujian: *foo-chien*
lingpai: *ling-pie*
Longhushan: *lowng-who-shawn*
Qingwei: *ching-way*

Shenxiao: *shun-hsiao*
Taixuan: *tai-hsuan*
Zhang Daoling: *chawng dow-ling*

The Ministry of the Most Mysterious, Taixuan, reverently receive: The order of the Dao conferring the following certificate on Huang XX, hereditary disciple who has not yet been ordained, whose name has been memorialized, who serves the Dao and thereby extends his life, who dwells in the realm of Spiritual Response of Xinxing she of the Temple of Awesome Manifestations of X *li* of X *xiang*[1] of Putian District in Xinghua, of Fujian Province, of the People's Republic of China. His ritual name is Chuanhong. His palace of destiny is [based on the moment of his birth] in the *xinmao* year [1951], the twelfth month, eighteenth day at the xu hour.[2] His Fundamental Destiny depends above on the Northern Dipper.[3] The palace of the

TRANSLATED BY Kenneth Dean. All bracketed additions are the translator's.

1. *Li* and *xiang* are old address designations without modern equivalents (the closest would be "town" and "county").
2. The traditional Chinese system of time divides the day into twelve named parts: *xu* hour is 7 to 9 P.M.
3. The Big Dipper.

Stellar Lord Wen Qu[4] illumines his [actions below]. The aforementioned Chuanhong has been fortunate to bathe in the mercy of the Mysteries. He kowtows, begging to be allowed to carry on his [family's] ancestral teachings. But he fears that he has not comprehended the marvellous meaning [of the Dao], nor comprehended the [means] of refining [himself] to perfection. He desires to enter the ranks of the Immortals.[5] [In this matter], relying upon the Emperor's strength, in the mid-autumn of the *xinyou* year [1981], the Master of Transformations, equipped with ritual staff, was ordered to proceed to Longhushan, Dragon Tiger Mountain,[6] to the Great Ancestral Altar of Ten-Thousand Ritual Methods of the Headquarters of the Perfected[7] Being, Master of the Religion, Hereditary Descendant of the Han Dynasty Heavenly Master, and received a Register of the Scriptures of a Libationer of the Officer of the Capital of the Three and the Five[8] of the Most High, Hereditary Ritual Office of the Perfect Register and Scriptures of the Pact with the Powers of True Unity. One each of silk and rings are given to him. They will always guard his body and protect his life. All this is the fruit of the actions of former generations. With all these pledges and with incense, he beseeches Master Zheng of the Temple of Chaotic Origin of the realm of Mysterious Response to be the Chief Priest of the ritual, and to memorialize his name, [transmitting] his oath to uphold the prohibitions, cultivate perfection, proclaim transformations on behalf of Heaven, dissolve disasters, save from cataclysms, lift up and save the dead, resolve their entanglements, pile up merit, perform with utmost purity the mysterious subtleties of the empty receptacle, so that family and State will be benefited. Having taken the oath, he will gladly leave the sea of bitterness, relying on the Merciful Venerables to send down their humanity and protection. Reverently, on the ninth day of the seventh month in Mingan Temple they worshipfully established a Daoist Altar of the Most High and Merciful for an Ordination ritual to prolong Life, and communicated the name [of the ordained], memorialized concerning the Registers and proclaimed the prohibitions. Both the Retreat and the Sacrifice were modeled on the Sovereign Heavens. We begged for the bestowal of good fortune and blessings for this altar. These matters, in addition to the register and reports, were clearly memorialized to all the Heavens and the Three Realms.[9] Notifications were sent to all the Officers of the Bureaus. In addition to this it was necessary to announce to Heaven the transmission of ritual methods. Before the Headquarters of the Supreme Emperor we have presented documents to the ordained [listing] the three refuges.[1] The first is to take refuge

4. Another name for the god of literature (Wenchang).
5. Daoists who have achieved extraordinary powers and a higher form of existence.
6. A mountain in Jiangxi Province important within Daoism for its associations with Zhang Daoling—the Celestial Master who received a visitation from the deified Laozi—and his family lineage; up to the formation of the People's Republic in 1949, Longhu shan was a place where Daoist priests were ordained and deities canonized. Here the priest's journey to Dragon Tiger Mountain to obtain his ordination is only symbolic.
7. A Daoist spiritual master; a Daoist who has moved beyond earthly corruption.
8. There are many different combinations of three and five in Daoist texts; in traditional Chinese cosmology, the universe is divided vertically

into three (heaven, earth, and humans) and horizontally into five (the five elements or phases: wood, fire, metal, water, and earth). "Libationer": a priest; in the Celestial Masters movement at each rank, a Daoist priest receives a particular "register" (*lu*).
9. The Realm of Desire (whose inhabitants desire pleasing objects of the senses), the Realm of Form (inhabited by gods who have physical form), and the Formless Realm (inhabited by gods who exist only as consciousness); these make up the Buddhist universe.
1. A concept from Buddhism: the definition of a Buddhist is someone who takes refuge in the Buddha, takes refuge in the dharma (the doctrine or discourses of the Buddha), and takes refuge in the sangha (the Buddhist community).

in the Ritual King of Primordial Commencement, the Perfected Heavenly Treasure. The second is to take refuge in the Most High Lord of the Dao, the Perfected Scriptural Treasure. The third is to take refuge in the Most High Lord Lao, the Perfected Treasure of the Spirit. The nine prohibitions are: (1) The initial Perfection: Respectfully behave with filial piety towards one's parents. This results in a good long life. (2) The prohibition of thoughtfulness: One should be loyal to one's kings and overlords. This results in intelligence and wisdom. (3) The upholding of perfection: Do not kill. Mercifully free animals. This results in riches and power. (4) Holding perfection: Do not tempt yourself with things. This results in good luck and happiness. (5) Protecting Perfection: Do not steal for this means harming yourself. This results in purity and a good name. (6) Cultivating perfection: Do not express anger or hatred towards people. This results in prosperity and tranquillity. (7) Completing perfection: Do not lie or harm the good. This results in satisfaction in all things. (8) Attaining perfection: Do not cheat or be tricky. This results in attaining the Correct Methods of the Great Dao. (9) Ascending to perfection: Do not turn against what one worships, uphold the prohibitions. This results in man and heaven both moving towards the good. The name of our ancestral line is True Marvel. The first ancestral Master was the Wei Yuanjun of High Prime, Purity and Perfection, of the Purple Void, the Goddess of the Qingwei (Pure Tenebrity) teachings, Lady of the Southern Sacred Mountain,[2] High Minister of the Golden Gates, [then came] Ancestral Master of the Central Alliance, True Lord Chen, Ancestral Master of Scrutiny with Penetrating Vision, True Lord Lin, Ancestral Master Great Gentleman of Great Simplicity [Taisu] . . . [the list goes on to give eleven Masters, some True Lords and others Perfected Ones, of the Western River, Suppression of Demons, Thunder Valley, Purity and Simplicity, Controller of Wind and Rain, Controller of Records. The list concludes], all the masters through time of the line that branched off from the Small Chamber of Mount Song[3] that had received the true transmission from the Southern Sacred Mountain. To memorialize on the Ritual Title [of the ordained]: Immortal Officer in Charge of the Teachings of the Jade Headquarters of the Divine Empyrean [Shenxiao], Vice-Commissioner in charge of the Powers of the North Pole for the Suppression of Demons, Attendant Censor of the Golden Gates of the Nine Heavens of the Scriptures and Registers of the Sworn Alliance of Most High Orthodox Unity, Judicial Investigator of the Jade Headquarters.

This position puts him in command of the affairs appropriately handled by all the various offices, institutes, and messengers. We memorialize on the emblems [of the ritual traditions] presented to him: The Ministry of Taixuan, the Great Ritual Office of the Spiritual Treasure, the Ministry of Thunder and Lightning, the Left Headquarters of the Yellow Register of Qingxuan, the Great Ritual Institute of Mt. Lu, the Exorcistic Institute of the North Pole. We memorialize on the seals offered as proof [of the transmission of these traditions] [There follow six, square, red-ink seals inscribed with black ink as follows: Three Treasures, Pangu, Taiji, Spiritual Treasure,

---

2. One of the Five Marchmounts, a group of five sacred mountains—one in each of the four cardinal directions and one at the center; the southern is most often identified as Mount Heng, also known as Nanyue.

3. The Central Sacred Mountain of the Five Marchmounts.

North Pole, and Seal of Office]. We memorialize concerning the bestowal of the heart-seal. [There follows the ordained priest's name and birth-date as well as his seal.] [There follows a list of thirty-five offices and institutes now under the control of the ordained priest.] We memorialize upon the ritual items presented to the ordained: The Thunder Seal and a *lingpai* [a wooden block for slapping on the altar when giving orders], a ritual measuring stick and a ritual incense burner, an "immortal sieve" and "immortal divining blocks," Daoist vestments and robes, Daoist cap and wooden sandals, a "jade court tablet" and a "golden" bell, a precious sword and a ritual whip, wooden divining blocks made from a bamboo root, a divine flag and a soul banner, a gold bell and a jade sounding-bowl, and a wooden fish [on which the tempo is beaten], a rhinoceros horn and a ritual drum, an ivory court tablet and sceptre [in a *ruyi* shape[4]]. The General Rule: Whosoever amongst the disciples who have received [training in] the rites cultivates and refines himself, piling up good deeds through his actions, will only then be qualified to receive a transmission of the ritual methods and be initiated into the Order.

The above Dispatch has been presented to the disciple cultivating perfection, Huang XX, ritual name Chuanhong. [Over the ritual name the left triangular half of a diamond-shaped seal is imprinted, the right-side half having been imprinted on the copy of the document sent to the Taixuan Ministry by transformation through burning.] Indeed, the August Emperor of the Chaotic Origin [i.e., Laozi] established the Teachings in the Zhou Dynasty.[5] The Ancestral Master of the True Unity [movement, i.e., Zhang Daoling] let shine the Fundamental Teachings in the Han Dynasty.[6] For generations these teachings have led people to cultivate perfection. Thus at the present time our ritual methods include the Mysterious Writings which show how to grasp lead and refine mercury into the elixir of ninefold transformations. [Guided by these writings] we build up the breath, visualize the spirits, and cultivate the body into pure Yang[7] [energy]. When we employ the marvellous [secret] instructions, thunder peals and lightning strikes. In the area where we pace the Mainstays of Heaven,[8] stones roll and sand flies. With perfected power we attack evil. The six demonic spirits all are annihilated. The merciful power shakes up the Underworld. The dead hun souls[9] of those in the Nine Regions [of the Underworld] all ascend, attracted by the excellent proclamation of the True Teachings, and attain a state of eternal desirelessness. The True Words [mantras[1]] pronounced secretly sweep away all sorts of disaster and difficulty. Finally one joins the Heavenly Officials and lives in the Realm of the Immortals forever.

[This document is dated the seventh month of the xinyou year [1981], and was presented by (the following five Daoist priests who all have the same basic title, although their functions in this ritual are differentiated.) The title is:]

---

4. A slender and slightly curved handle, with a round head that usually resembled a lingzhi mushroom.
5. 1046–256 B.C.E.
6. 202 B.C.E.–220 C.E.
7. A term that originally referred to the sunny side of a valley; by extension it came to be associated with the light, heaven, dryness, and activity—the male principle.

8. A practice developed from, and sometimes identified with, the Pace of Yu, a form of ritual walking or dancing that follows celestial patterns of the Big Dipper mapped onto the ground.
9. Cloud souls or light souls, linked with heaven and its pneumas.
1. Words or phrases used as a focus of meditation or worship.

Attendant Censor of the Golden Gates of the Nine Heavens of the Scriptures and Registers of the Sworn Alliance of Orthodox Unity, Commissioner (in charge) of Expanding the Way of Pure Tenebrity (Qingwei), Commissioner of the various Bureaus, Agencies, and Headquarters (or Prefectures), entrusted with the office(s) of:

The Master who Confirms the Prohibitions, Lu XX, [seal and signature].

The Master who Examines the Secret Instructions, Huang XX, [seal and signature].

The Master who Recommends and Guarantees the Initiate, Lin XX, [seal and signature].

The Master who Examines the Initiation, Huang XX, [seal and signature].

The Master who Transmits the Initiation, Zheng XX, [seal and signature].

[On the left margin, in large characters:] Ancestral Master and Founder of the Teachings of True Unity, the True Lord of Quiescent Response and Manifest Aid, Zhang.

TWO PRAYERS TO THE DEIFIED LAOZI FROM PENANG, MALAYSIA

As Daoism reached the Western world primarily through the movement of texts—translations of such iconic Daoist works as *The Scripture of the Way and Its Virtue* (*Daode jing*) and *Book of Master Zhuang* (*Zhuangzi*; for both, see above)—it was also spreading to other parts of Asia through the movement of people and Daoist ritual lineages. We know of earlier migrations: for example, Yao and Miao groups took Daoism to northern Vietnam and Thailand beginning in the fifteenth century. It is not easy to identify precisely when large-scale relocations of Daoist Chinese into Southeast Asia began, but they were certainly noticeable by the late Qing dynasty (1644–1912) and increased through the Republican period (1912–1949) and into the era of the People's Republic. The later period of migration, from the mid- to late nineteenth century through the 1970s, was intimately connected with the forces of modernity and globalization. Some Chinese groups now set off to places such as Singapore, Malaysia, and Indonesia in search of business opportunities; beginning in the 1930s, others fled Japanese incursions into southern China. These new émigrés brought cultural and religious practices with them, even as they maintained ties to their homeland.

"Limitless Longevity" ("Wanshou wuliang") is a handwritten memorial—much like the "Memorial for a Communal Ritual" (see above)—issued in the name of forty-two people "and many pious believers" living in Penang. It aptly exemplifies a Daoist rite carried out by Chinese immigrants in Peninsular Malaysia, in this case to mark the completion of repairs to the damaged main gate of their temple. Less obviously, this memorial is a sign of the religious revival taking place in Malaysia during the 1980s—though one constrained by the anxieties of the minority Chinese community, which faced an Islamic majority and new government policies taking aim at their perceived economic advantage.

The memorial is directed to the deified Laozi (Taishang Laojun) on the occasion of his birthday, in the hopes of receiving his blessing in the form of safety, good fortune, and happiness. The Daoist priests and spirit mediums undertaking the ritual seek to expel the bad and harmful and to attract the good and auspicious.

The memorial also details that the faithful have laid out a sumptuous banquet with wine and have offered flowers and incense.

"Lord Lao's Spirit Medium" records the words of a modern spirit medium working in Penang who is regularly possessed by the deified Laozi (Lord Lao). His lecture repeatedly mentions moral cause and effect and offers the possibility that people can "break the chain [and] escape from life." The spirit medium is fully aware of the teachings of Christianity and Buddhism (mentioning karma and reincarnation), and he draws on them and modern science while discussing Daoism. This document also points to the ways in which spirit mediums have played a more important role than official Daoist priests in the transnational flow of religion into Southeast Asia. Indeed, in a new development, in the 1980s spirit mediums trained in Southeast Asia (Malaysia, Singapore, or Indonesia) began flowing back into the coastal provinces of China, financing temple-building campaigns, and reviving and reconfiguring religious practices in the communities with which they maintained connections and alliances.

PRONOUNCING GLOSSARY

Penang: *peh-nawng*   Wanshou wuliang: *wahn-show woo-liang*

Limitless Longevity (Wanshou wuliang)

Now, burn incense and present a memorial.

In Penang State,[1] New Town, Jalan Rambutan, door number seventy. We respectfully prepare a festival to celebrate ten thousand autumns, to pray for peace, to plant prosperity, to pray and chant. The Keeper of the Incense Urn and the Assistant Keeper of the Incense Urn [together with] devout men and believing women [forty-two names listed] and many pious believers.

Emperor, please listen! We respectfully and sincerely present our wishes for your blessings. Please listen! We share the wish to unite the crowd together to pray for safety, and pray that all will increase their fortune and happiness. We prostrate ourselves on the ground! The longevity star is shining brightly; we gladly greet the auspicious brilliant morning sunlight of your birthday; we humbly follow the Ritual of Imperial Exaltation. Remember our gratitude for your secret blessings, even though we have not yet managed to repay your kindness.

Here we greet the Lord of the Teachings of Golden Heaven Most High Lord Lao. . . . We present wine and celebrate on the lucky fifteenth day of the month every year, we prostrate ourselves on the ground, we come to the altar and invite [the god]. . . . We offer up a meal with wine, we present fragrant flowers and humbly wish that your life will be as long as Heaven and your grace increase daily, so that the people may live in peace and safety, and old and young may enjoy pure, good luck. Send your auspicious clouds to sweep away as if by lightning all difficulty and obstruction.

Every shop shall enjoy a booming business with profits pouring in from all sides. Every family may enjoy good luck and happiness and live in health and peace. Everyone in every season shall live in peace and safety; in every season people will celebrate happiness. And so we submit a memorial to the Imperial Three Primordials,[2] proposing to offer birthday congratulations,

TRANSLATED BY Jean DeBernardi. All bracketed additions are the translator's.

1. In the northwest part of peninsular Malaysia.
2. Three deities associated with the Three Offices (heaven, earth, and water).

pray for safety, and plant blessings by means of a festive offering for which we will conduct rituals for one day.

This we humbly submit to the Lord of the Teachings of Golden Heaven, Most High Lord Lao, and all the gods. May the grace of the Way descend upon our bowed heads! Reverently composed in proper form on the fifteenth day of the second moon of the *dingsi* year of the Heavenly Revolutions [3 April 1977]. Submitted with a hundred bows.

Lord Lao's Spirit Medium

Most people are awake and active in the day. I am a man of the night. Taishang [Lord Lao] teaches that there is black and white, positive and negative. There is a dark spot in the moon. However perfect you are there will be one weak point and however bad you are there is one bright light, one good point. There is always contrast, always comparison. Satan sits next to god. . . . These are symbols. There are two forces, man and woman, love and hatred. . . .

Symbols. Law is universal. Who operates the solar system—who controls it? Christians say God. Daoism says forces that are constructive and destructive. These help the planets move, keep steady, function well. Do you pray to this? Taishang says that how it functions is due to forces which are self-regulated like molecules, small parts which are elements of life. These cannot be seen by human eyes. So science tells us that hydrogen is what? HO, H . . . H_2O? Yes. The universe operates by itself, the rotation of day and night operates by itself. From nothing comes something, which becomes nothing again. There is action and reaction, attraction and repulsion. This is universal law, it is not created, it is like god. You can call it God the Creator. It has no human form but is a system which operates by itself. [He described the five elements[3] and discussed the solar system.]

Human beings come from nothing to be something. You must cultivate and adapt yourself to be out of that system, to escape from universal law and to achieve enlightenment. That is life. Life is in a circle, the elements are in a circle, like a water cycle. If you break the chain you can escape from life. This means immortal, everlasting life. Buddhists say, to achieve enlightenment you must go through a system; the eight noble truths,[4] good actions, are intertwined in religion.

When Taishang came, in China it was a time of war, and people led a chaotic life. He came because he was merciful, and tried to tell the truth, to show the facts to society to enlighten them for a better life. He was a scholar, so he put all in a poetic form. He spoke in high-flown language, and it is hard to comprehend the actual meaning. Fifty years prior he spoke to Confucius[5] who went to him for advice. Confucius found it difficult to comprehend what was spoken to him, but couldn't contradict him. He compared Taishang to a dragon who could better the winds and thunder, but he

---

3. Wood, fire, metal, water, and earth: they are the basis of the five agents or five phases theory, as their movement from one phase to another is thought to explain the existence and development of the universe.
4. That is, the noble eightfold path of Buddhism:
right view, right intention, right speech, right action, right livelihood, right effort, right mindfulness, and right concentration.
5. The teacher, philosopher, and political theorist (551–479 B.C.E.).

couldn't understand how the dragon could survive. Confucius said, "When people want fish, they need a net. When they want to catch birds, they need a trap."[6] Confucius had problems understanding Taishang. Nothing comes from something, something from nothing. The seasons alternate, weather and so on, heat and cold. Opportunities come, but when life is over, you cannot find one. In summer the leaves are green, and good happenings will return. Life is ever living and not dead. When you die, it does not come to an end. What is left will live again. [He discussed reincarnation.]

We offer the joss stick. This signifies our life. We need to offer our sincerity to our teacher who is in a different plane, who advises us to lead a good life. The joss stick represents human beings. As it burns, it gets shorter and shorter, just as our own life gets shorter and shorter; it burns to the end to the wooden stick, just as life limits our body. When the smoke escapes it is visible to a certain stage. The significance is that our teacher is aware that we are appealing to him for guidance. He is not visible. Life is precious. As time goes by, we may not find opportunities. We don't know when life will end. The smoke escapes and it gone. We too are mortals. We think of our spiritual teacher, showing greetings, asking for sympathy, hoping for respect from them. It must have a good scent. Sandalwood is the best. We must be as pure as the joss stick, have these good qualities, and offer our sincere greetings before it is too late. All will come to a momentous halt, then will rotate over again.

The stop is only a temporary halt. It will function again, and continue until we get to enlightenment. Candles are the same. We offer lights so that they shine brightly. When we are in a bright atmosphere we are much happier. The flower is not everlasting. We will fade like the flower, but the plant we hope will grow again, will blossom again, all these things happen in a circle. You need a basis in philosophy. All prophets are saviours who try to better the life of human beings, help them to lead a happier life—to better their lives after death.

The deities are on different planes. Heaven and earth have no gates. You are welcome in both places, it is up to you to choose it, to choose good or bad habits. Heaven and hell by the right definition actually live in the heart. When the heart stops, you will know where you will be. The planets have altitudes. Heaven and hell are not visible to human eyes, but are very near to us, we are on a very close plane to heaven and hell, like two mountains coming down to a plain. This is why some people can see ghosts and demons, why they want to communicate with deities and god.

Life. Who creates you? Who creates the universe? I put it to you that life is immortal, you still live after death. After enlightenment, you can escape the world of sins and suffering. If you can escape, it is always paradise, always heaven.

This is enough for today. Study this and come back to me if you have any questions.

---

6. A story reported in *Records of the Grand Historian* (*Shiji*, 109–91 B.C.E.) by Sima Qian.

INTRODUCTION TO THE *TAO TE CHING*
and
EPILOGUE: DAO SONG

URSULA K. LE GUIN

It is often repeated that *The Scripture of the Way and Its Virtue* (*Daode jing*) is, after the Bible, the most translated book in the world. Many of these editions should be called "versions" or "renditions" but not "translations," as they have been done by those who do not know Chinese. The modernist American poet Ezra Pound once commented that poetic inspiration could enable even someone ignorant of the language to translate Chinese, and he became known for passing off what one scholar has called "stylistic revisions" of other translators' work as his own translations. Versions of *The Scripture of the Way and Its Virtue* have flowed steadily from writers who freely adapt the text, relying on other English, French, and German editions as they use the ancient work to transmit their own ideas and messages.

These authors sometimes justify their versions by claiming that they followed their intuition in rendering the text and that they understood the Chinese mind or Chinese thought even better than the Chinese themselves. Eight years after Martin Buber published *Talks and Parables of Chuang Tzu* (*Reden und Gleichnisse des Tschuang-tse*, 1910; see above), his translation of and commentary on the *Book of Master Zhuang* (*Zhuangzi*; see above), the occultist Aleister Crowley produced a translation of *The Scripture of the Way and Its Virtue* after an astral vision in which he saw its original text; he gave it a kabbalistic interpretation. A rendition of the latter work by the poet Witter Bynner, colored by Emersonian transcendentalism, was issued in 1944 with the subtitle "An American Version." In 1965 the Trappist Catholic monk Thomas Merton published his *The Way of Chuang Tzu*—a later edition added a preface by the fourteenth Dalai Lama; unable to read Chinese himself, Merton based it on his reflection on four different translations by others. Many of these versions have been almost entirely forgotten, but a 1997 take on *The Scripture of the Way and Its Virtue* by the science fiction writer Ursula K. Le Guin (b. 1929) continues to attract attention.

In the introduction to what she herself calls a version, since she does not consider her work a translation, Le Guin traces the origins of the project to her early encounter with Paul Carus's 1898 version in the library of her father, the noted anthropologist Alfred Kroeber. According to Le Guin, *The Scripture of the Way and Its Virtue* has played an important role in her life, and critics and scholars have found significant parallels between the themes of her novels and Daoist concepts.

That introduction, which defends her version and explains how it differs from translations by scholars, is included below, together with a couple of samples of her rendering of the Chinese classic and a poem she wrote in homage to the Dao. Authors of versions of Chinese classics have frequently depended on scholarly assistants, often left unnamed; unusually, Le Guin openly credited J. P Seaton, who was a professor of Chinese at the University of North Carolina at Chapel Hill, as her "collaborator." Nevertheless, Le Guin suggests that it takes a poet to capture the beauty of the work's poetry, noting that the ability of *The Scripture of the Way and Its Virtue* to "spea[k] to people everywhere as if it had been written yesterday" is what has kept it so meaningful in contemporary society.

Le Guin is thus less concerned with capturing the text's original meaning or remaining faithful to its traditional understandings as represented in the rich commentarial record than with making the text "accessible to a present-day, unwise, unpowerful, and perhaps unmale reader, not seeking esoteric secrets, but listening for a voice that speaks to the soul." In that process, masculine and authoritarian language is made more egalitarian. For example, in chapter 3, which she gives the title "Hushing," she extracts the masculine pronouns and replaces its sage who governs the people by keeping them well fed but ignorant with a wise soul who governs the people by emptying their minds of wishes and desires. Just like poets and thinkers before her, Le Guin came up with a version for a specific time—in her case, highlighting ecological responsibility, social justice, and gender equality. Her contemporary construal has not been the last, as it seems inevitable that writers in each generation will appropriate *The Scripture of the Way and Its Virtue* and provide a reading that, in varying degrees, reflects key social, cultural, aesthetic, and religious concepts and values of their time.

PRONOUNCING GLOSSARY

Lao Tzu (Laozi): *lao tzu*   Zhuangzi: *chuang-tzu*
Tao Te Ching (Daode jing): *dow-duh
   ching*

Introduction to the Tao Te Ching[1]

The *Tao Te Ching* was probably written about twenty-five hundred years ago, perhaps by a man called Lao Tzu, who may have lived at about the same time as Confucius.[2] Nothing about it is certain except that it's Chinese, and very old, and speaks to people everywhere as if it had been written yesterday.

The first *Tao Te Ching* I ever saw was the Paul Carus[3] edition of 1898, bound in yellow cloth stamped with blue and red Chinese designs and characters. It was a venerable object of mystery, which I soon investigated, and found more fascinating inside than out. The book was my father's;[4] he read in it often. Once I saw him making notes from it and asked what he was doing. He said he was marking which chapters he'd like to have read at his funeral. We did read those chapters at his memorial service.

I have the book, now ninety-eight years old and further ornamented with red binding-tape to hold the back on, and have marked which chapters I'd like to have read at my funeral. In the Notes, I explain why I was so lucky to discover Lao Tzu in that particular edition. Here I will only say that I was lucky to discover him so young, so that I could live with his book my whole life long.

I also discuss other aspects of my version in the Notes—the how of it. Here I want to state very briefly the why of it.

The *Tao Te Ching* is partly in prose, partly in verse; but as we define poetry now, not by rhyme and meter but as a patterned intensity of language, the whole thing is poetry. I wanted to catch that poetry, its terse, strange beauty. Most translations have caught meanings in their net, but prosily, letting the beauty slip through. And in poetry, beauty is no ornament; it is the meaning. It is the truth. We have that on good authority.[5]

VERSION BY Ursula K. LeGuin, with the collaboration of J. P. Seaton.

1. The author's original spelling of Chinese words has been retained in this selection. "Daode jing" appears as "Tao Te Ching." "Laozi" appears as "Lao Tzu," and "Daoism" appears as "Taoism."
2. The teacher, philosopher, and political theorist (551–479 B.C.E.).
3. German American author and editor (1852–

1919); he was the first managing editor of the Open Court Publishing Company, which published his version of the "Tao-Teh-King."
4. Alfred Kroeber (1876–1960), an influential American anthropologist.
5. That is, John Keats's "Ode on a Grecian Urn" (1820): "Beauty is truth, truth beauty."

Scholarly translations of the *Tao Te Ching* as a manual for rulers use a vocabulary that emphasizes the uniqueness of the Taoist "sage," his masculinity, his authority. This language is perpetuated, and degraded, in most popular versions. I wanted a Book of the Way accessible to a present-day, unwise, unpowerful, and perhaps unmale reader, not seeking esoteric secrets, but listening for a voice that speaks to the soul. I would like that reader to see why people have loved the book for twenty-five hundred years.

It is the most lovable of all the great religious texts, funny, keen, kind, modest, indestructibly outrageous, and inexhaustibly refreshing. Of all the deep springs, this is the purest water. To me, it is also the deepest spring.

I. TAOING

The way you can go
isn't the real way.
The name you can say
isn't the real name.

Heaven and earth
begin in the unnamed:
name's the mother
of the ten thousand things.

So the unwanting soul
sees what's hidden,
and the ever-wanting soul
sees only what it wants.

Two things, one origin,
but different in name,
whose identity is mystery.
Mystery of all mysteries!
The door to the hidden.

A satisfactory translation of this chapter is, I believe, perfectly impossible. It contains the book. I think of it as the Aleph, in Borges's story:[6] if you see it rightly, it contains everything.

3. HUSHING

Not praising the praiseworthy
keeps people uncompetitive.

Not prizing rare treasures
keeps people from stealing.

Not looking at the desirable
keeps the mind quiet.

---

6. "The Aleph" (1845), by the Argentine writer Jorge Luis Borges (1899–1986); in it, a man discovers in his cellar "an Aleph . . . one of the points in space that contains all other points" and that cannot be described in words.

So the wise soul
governing people
would empty their minds,
fill their bellies,
weaken their wishes,
strengthen their bones,

keep people unknowing,
unwanting,
keep the ones who do know
from doing anything.

When you do not-doing,
nothing's out of order.

Over and over Lao Tzu says *wei wu wei*: Do not do. Doing not-doing. To act without acting. Action by inaction. You do nothing yet it gets done. . . .

It's not a statement susceptible to logical interpretation, or even to a syntactical translation into English; but it's a concept that transforms thought radically, that changes minds. The whole book is both an explanation and a demonstration of it.

Epilogue: Dao Song

Jonathan Herman's discussion of the popular Western co-optation of Daoism (from the previous section),[1] which I found both just and provocative, brought my thoughts to an area that I've had to think about with some of the same intensity a Chinese or a sinologist might bring to this one. That is the appropriation by non-Indians of Native American religious ideas and spiritual practices. Indians have a large and legitimate problem with this. It's one I've had to take sides on, because my father, as an anthropologist, was responsible for making Native cultural elements accessible to whites and because I myself have drawn on the writings both of anthropologists and of Indians for certain models of thought and behavior that inform my books, particularly *Always Coming Home*.[2] And because when some white kid starts telling me that she's a "shawman" and knows what animal is her soul-guide and how good it makes her feel, something in me writhes in protest. To the one true shaman I knew, a Yurok,[3] being a shaman wasn't a game but the heavy burden of an undesired lifetime commitment to learning and transmitting complex knowledge, involving a profound, continual, spiritual risk.

Feeling thus, that the Indians are legitimately defensive of their religions, I feel that as an outsider to Daoism, however passionately sympathetic, I must be exceedingly conscious of possible transgression. I tried to maintain a proper wariness while working on my version of Laozi. Yet it is, to some

1. In "Daoist Environmentalism in the West: Ursula K. Le Guin's Reception and Transmission of Daoism," an essay in the same volume as this piece, Jonathan R. Herman, a professor of religious studies, criticizes what he calls the "popular Western Daoism" presented by such works as Le Guin's version of the *Daode jing* (see previous excerpts).

2. A 1985 publication that includes fiction, artwork, and music; it describes the culture of the Kesh, a people living in northern California in the distant future.

3. Native Americans whose ancestral territory was in what is now the northern part of California, along the Klamath River and the northern Pacific coastline.

degree, inevitably transgressive; and I quite expected to meet an equal degree of defensiveness here among practitioners and scholars of Daoism. Having taken upon oneself the transmission or translation of certain texts or ideas or ways of thought, one is responsible for them, protective of them. You want them to be understood rightly and respected for what they are, not trivialized and not misused. You feel toward them as the ecologist does toward a river or a desert: this is not to be abused, and if we use it we should do so very mindfully.

Defensiveness against cheapening and trivializing Daoism thus seems to me an inevitable, essential part of your work as scholars; and yet, like the ecologist, the conservationist, you don't have the luxury of being absolutely defensive. Compromise is also inevitable. People *will* use the river and the desert. Daoist texts *are* popular. The barbarians are inside the gates—here I am. I strongly support Jonathan Herman in saying that if we unscholarly types whose historical knowledge is gappy, who confuse hermeneutics with heuristics, who don't even know Chinese—if we amateurs are co-opting your texts, then perhaps your best move is to start co-opting ours. Use our efforts and our blunders, our naiveties and misunderstandings of Daoism, as signs, signals, guides to your own work: what most needs explaining, what keeps living and therefore changing in the tradition, what is translatable (in every sense of the word) and what is not. Not to declare war on foolishness and ignorance, but to use foolishness and ignorance as guides, seems quite in the spirit of Laozi.

And may I add a word here about the artist as the interpreter of religion and of thought. We have been mining our texts for ideas. But if the Laozi and Zhuangzi[4] texts were aesthetically insignificant, important only intellectually, would they matter as they do? If they were not great works of art, would they be accessible to Western popular culture? Would they have their extraordinary influence? Daoism has expressed itself most directly (and appropriately) in art. Daoist painting teaches us to see the world; Daoist poetry gives us an understanding of the world.

And, as religion has always used art to speak itself, to show, to convince, so I believe ecology can and must use art. Art is *all* turtles, all the way down.[5]

I will end with a small poem I wrote many, many years ago.

TAO SONG

O slow fish
show me the way
O green weed
grow me the way

The way you go
the way you grow
is the way
indeed

4. That is, the *Book of Master Zhuang* (see above).
5. A reference to a saying of uncertain origin that illustrates the problem of infinite regression in cosmologies. The story varies, but someone—usually a representative of an Eastern religion—claims that the world is supported ultimately on the back of a giant turtle (sometimes a tiger, elephant, or other animal stands on the turtle). When asked what is supporting the turtle, this individual responds, "It is turtles all the way down."

O bright Sun
light me the way
the right way
the one
no one can say

If one can choose it
it is wrong
Sing me the way
O song:

No one can lose it
for long

THE WU-TANG MANUAL

RZA

The Wu-Tang Clan, formed in the early 1990s, became one of the decade's most popular and influential hip-hop groups. Its name is derived from Wudang Mountain (Wudang shan), home to the Daoist deity Perfect Warrior (Zhenwu), whose story is related in the *Journey to the North* (*Beiyou ji*; see above). RZA (Robert Diggs, b. 1969), the leader of the Wu-Tang Clan, read and was profoundly moved by *The Scripture of the Way and Its Virtue* (*Daode jing*; see above). In developing his own philosophy (which he calls his path to enlightenment) and undertaking various creative projects in music, film, and writing, RZA has drawn explicitly from Daoism, Buddhism, Confucianism, Hinduism, Christianity, and Islam, as well as martial arts films. When asked by an interviewer from *Time* magazine how he brings all these disparate teachings together, RZA responded:

> First of all, the *tao* means the way. And there are many ways to get to a place as long as you stay on the path. So if you want to travel the way of Jesus, the way of the Prophet Muhammad, if you want to travel the way of Buddha or Bodhi Dharma, if you want to travel the way of a great chess master like Kasparov or Fisher—any way you can reach self-enlightenment or self-worth works. Many great men have left paths for us. In the end, we are all searching for the same thing. We're just taking different routes to the same location.

In the *Wu-Tang Manual* RZA describes meeting a master from China's Shaolin Temple in 1995 and becoming his student. Not only did he receive martial arts training but the Wu-Tang Clan learned important lessons in balance and humility as they read *The Scripture of the Way and Its Virtue*. *The Tao of Wu* (2009), RZA's sequel to the *Wu-Tang Manual*, reached the top fifty on the *New York Times* best-seller list.

PRONOUNCING GLOSSARY

Bodhidharma: *bow-dee-dhar-maw*
Ch'an (Chan): *chawn*
chi (qi): *chi*
chi gong: *chi gowng*
Da'mo: *dah-mow*

I Ching (Yijing): *yee-ching*
Sifu Shi Yan-Ming: *suh-foo shi yan-ming*
Tao Te Ching (Daode jing): *dow-duh ching*

Look to the East[1]

In '93, I saw a movie called *Zen Master*.[2] That sparked me a lot. It was the story of Da'mo, also known as Bodhidharma, the founder of Ch'an Buddhism—which became Zen Buddhism in Japan. He came around the time of Mohammed[3]—A.D. 527, to be exact. Da'mo came from India and he walked to China and when he got there they discriminated against him. He was tall and dark. In the film they say, "He's *tall*. And he's *dark*," in this dubbed "suspicious" voice. And I was watching that thinking, "Damn, black niggas is fucked everywhere! Even the Chinese niggas is against him!"

But everything Da'mo was doing was surpassing everything in that culture. When he arrived at the Shaolin Temple,[4] he created—based on yoga—the four seminal forms of chi gong, which became the foundation for the system of martial arts. At Shaolin, Ch'an Buddhism is martial arts and martial arts is Ch'an. Da'mo was basically teaching them about enlightenment.

After I saw that movie, I started reading the *Tao Te Ching* and the *I Ching*.[5] I was looking for the common thread of knowledge between what was going on then and now. I started to get more observant of what I was causing to happen and what was causing me to cause it. The lessons opened my mind up.

The "Three Ways": Taoism, Buddhism, Confucianism

The *Tao* means, basically, the "Way." It refers to the flow of life, the way nature expresses itself. Taoism teaches you to unite your actions with the flow of the universe. You want to be spontaneous and free from outside influences like social institutions. Confucianism, on the other hand, is more like a concept of government, conduct, and social order. So they seem like opposites, but in Chinese society, they—along with Buddhism—combine to form a general approach to the world.

Confucianism is about relationships. Buddhism is about release. Taoism is about balance. If your life is in turmoil and conflict, you're not living in the Tao.

I got sparked on this when I met Sifu. It was in 1995, at a record release party for GZA's *Liquid Swords*.[6] Sifu Shi Yan-Ming is a thirty-fourth-generation monk from the Shaolin Temple in China. He defected to the U.S. in 1992 and founded his own Shaolin temple in Manhattan. We became friends, and I became a student. That's when the Wu-Tang Clan became humble warriors.

We weren't humble warriors in the beginning. Before, we would always say, "We ain't about flipping and kicking, we'll flip lyrics and kick your ass." But now we started to see the truth of it. When Sifu came to us, I think

---

1. The author's original spelling of Chinese words has been retained in these selections. "Daode jing" appears as "Tao Te Ching" and "Daoism" appears as "Taoism."
2. Probably the Hong Kong movie *Master of Zen* (dir. Brandy Yuen), released in 1994.
3. The Prophet Muhammad (570–632), the founder of Islam.
4. The famous Buddhist monastery on Mount Song, in Henan Province, long associated with the martial arts (specifically, Shaolin Kung Fu).
5. The *Book of Changes* (*Yijing*), a volume of divination and cosmology traditionally dated to the 12th century B.C.E. For the *Daode jing* (*The Scripture of the Way and Its Virtue*), see above.
6. A solo album by GZA (Gary Grice, b. 1966), a founding member of the Wu-Tang Clan.

destiny brought it to us. Then we had a living example of the actual principles. I learned that kung fu was less a fighting style and more about the cultivation of the spirit.

ODB and I started to get deep into what they were saying about chi[7] energy. We got into the idea of channeling chi. It rejuvenates your body, but it's also philosophical. It's about finding balance.

Chi is the life force. It's the same thing as Prana in the Hindu religion. (My daughter's name is Prana.) Balancing your chi is in a lot of ways about putting your actions in place with the universe.

The *Tao Te Ching* teaches of three jewels, or characteristics, that man should cherish. They are Compassion, which leads to courage, Moderation, which leads to generosity, and Humility, which leads to leadership.

Confucianism was basically a wisdom of warriors. I studied Confucius[8] maybe more around 1996, I got deeper into him. It's like rules of conduct. But they both go together.

One basic element of Chinese religions is that they see all religions as part of a whole. Confucianism and Taoism are related, they're like yin and yang[9] in some ways. A lot of people see life in terms of opposites—like, good versus evil, me versus you, valuable versus worthless. Taoists believe you have to see beyond the opposites, to find the real unity among all things.

I think if you talk to everybody in the crew and ask them why they're humble now, they'd say it's because they felt the need to achieve balance. Once you have knowledge of yourself, you'll seek balance consciously. If you don't seek balance yourself, life will balance you. That's why a lot of niggas go to jail, go through hell. When Wu-Tang first came in, we were so threatening. Now you can see we've all humbled ourselves down a little. We understand you need silent weapons for quiet wars.

Today, I'm not a Muslim. I'm not a Buddhist. I'm not a soldier of any one religious sect. I realized you can never put a circle around the truth and say that it belongs to one sect. I'm a student. Like Solomon said, "He sought wisdom out from the cradle to the grave."[1]

I would say the only religion I practice now is universal love. People fight and kill each other and say they have the proper remedy to give it to you, but nobody can *give* it to you. You have to recognize it within yourself. My way of life is Islam. But there's an acronym they use for Islam which is I, Self, Lord, And Master. Or, I like to say, I Stimulate Light And Matter. You have to realize that *you* stimulate everything around you. Everything else is only a reflection.

7. That is, qi: vital energy, breath (pneuma). ODB (Russell Jones, 1968–2004), or Ol' Dirty Bastard, a founding member of the Wu-Tang Clan.
8. The teacher, philosopher, and political theorist (551–479 B.C.E.).
9. The complementary forces that unite to form the Dao: yin, a term that originally referred to the shady side of a valley, by extension came to be associated with the dark, earth, dampness, and passivity—the female principle; yang, a term that originally referred to the sunny side of a valley, by extension came to be associated with the light, heaven, dryness, and activity—the male principle.
1. Though this quotation captures the spirit of Proverbs, a book of the Hebrew Bible traditionally attributed to King Solomon (fl. 10th c. B.C.E.), these words do not appear in that book.

A DECLARATION OF THE CHINESE DAOIST ASSOCIATION ON GLOBAL ECOLOGY

ZHANG JIYU

In "A Declaration of the Chinese Daoist Association on Global Ecology" (1995), Zhang Jiyu (b. 1962)—a sixty-fifth-generation descendent of Zhang Daoling, the founder of the Celestial Masters (Tianshi) tradition—discusses how Daoism can be used to support a new ecological ethic. He draws on the philosophies found in *The Scripture of the Way and Its Virtue* (*Daode jing*) and other religious Daoist texts to propose ecological solutions for the problems of a rapidly urbanizing modern China at a time of equally rapid globalization. Through the structure of his declaration, he seeks to demonstrate that specific teachings in ancient Daoist texts have ecological ramifications for the present.

While there may indeed be important ecological resources in ancient Daoist texts, they have not helped China avoid ecological pitfalls. Indeed, other ancient texts attest to the excessive felling of trees on sacred mountains, and the damage to China's natural landscape only escalated during the twentieth century. In 1984, at an international meeting convened in Beijing, many writers and poets expressed their dismay at how estranged modern China had become from its traditional views of the natural world (as expressed in religious texts, landscape poetry, and paintings). Among them was the American poet Gary Snyder, who recited some lines from "Spring View," an old Chinese poem by Du Fu, which includes the line "Countries may be destroyed, but mountains and rivers remain." Snyder noted that the modern Japanese poet Nanao Sakaki had reversed the lines to read "When countries remain, mountains and rivers are destroyed."

In this declaration Zhang formulates his Daoist approach to China's predicament, and to the global ecological crisis more generally, by drawing on holistic Daoist teachings that treat heaven, earth, and humankind together. He proposes that "all things in the universe—including birds, animals, insects, trees, grass, and other existing entities"—are the product of the transformation of the Dao. Rather than seeing ecological problems as external to our bodies and health, he insists that self-cultivation practices can be effective only within a wholesome environment. Conversely, dealing successfully with the global ecological crisis will require a sweeping change in how people view the world.

Zhang points to some concrete actions that Daoists have taken at specific sites in China, both protecting existing trees and fostering new growth through large-scale planting of trees and grass. He calls on all Daoists to spread Daoist teachings that promote a responsible environmental ethic, to continue to plant trees and cultivate forests, and to make some Daoist sacred mountains into models of environmental engineering.

PRONOUNCING GLOSSARY

Baopuzi: *bao-poo-tzu*   Taiping jing: *tai-ping ching*
Daode jing: *dow-duh ching*

Keeping the Spontaneous (Ziran) and Natural (Benxing) Character in the World Process

Daode jing 25 says: "Humankind models itself after Earth. Earth models itself after Heaven. Heaven models itself after Dao. And Dao models itself after the natural." *Daode jing* 55 says: "To know harmony means to be in accord with the eternal [Dao]. To be in accord with the eternal [Dao] means to be enlightened." Chapter 44 says: "He who knows when to stop is free from danger. He who is contented suffers no disgrace."

As humans face an ecological crisis throughout the world, they realize increasingly that problems concerning environmental protection are not derived from industrial pollution or technological expansion alone. Rather, these problems are also derived from people's worldviews, ideas of value, or theories of knowledge. This is because the powerful industrial and technological expansion across the world has also generated systems of value and theories of knowledge affecting people's ideas about the world. These ideas have conditioned people's thought-patterns and have caused a split in their minds regarding the unity between humans and nature. These thought-patterns of contemporary people exaggerate the subjective will, causing people to think that nature can be treated as subservient to the willful desires of humans and that nature would never respond negatively to these conditions. Although these contemporary thought-patterns have achieved a high degree of social productivity throughout the world, they have also given humankind a greatly inflated image of itself. Daoists believe that this inflated image of the self is an important cause of the serious ecological crisis confronting the modern world. Today, as we face the real possibility of imminent world destruction, we should soberly examine these dominant thought-patterns associated with the contemporary worldview.

We believe that the ancient doctrines of Daoism are eminently able to remedy the deficiencies caused by contemporary ethical theories. According to Daoism, Heaven, Earth, humankind, and all things in the universe— including birds, animals, insects, trees, grass, and other existing entities— come into being through the transformation of the breath of Dao. By endowing various degrees of pure or turbid breath in the myriad things, the breath of Dao gives rise to individual things. As a result, a diversity of existing things is formed in the world. Human beings, composed of the blending of the breath of Heaven with the breath of Earth, are the most spiritual and intelligent creatures among the myriad things. They are one of the four fundamentals of the universe (Dao, Heaven, Earth, humankind). How should humankind deal with the myriad things of the universe? Let us return to the ancient *Daode jing* for the answer. Since this text asserts that Dao models itself after the natural, it follows that men or women should model themselves after the earth which they inhabit. By the same token, "Earth modeling itself after Heaven" means it must be in tune with the changes of the universe. And "Heaven modeling after the natural" means that it must follow the operations of Nature—operating spontaneously in accordance with its self-so character. This also means that human beings must not employ contrivances to coerce the self-so character of Nature to

TRANSLATED BY David Yu.

conform to human desires. Humans must nurture the spontaneous character of non-action—"Dao modeling after the natural"—in the innermost part of their hearts and practice it unceasingly. Only by so doing can humans solve the global ecological crisis. And if these problems of the natural environment are solved, then the well-being of humankind is assured.

The Lord of the Most High leaves it to us to emulate the doctrine of self-so, that is, non-action revealed in nature. Another teaching of Daoism, concerning the relationship between humans and nature is: "To be in accord with the eternal [Dao] means to be enlightened. To know the eternal is called enlightenment."[1] Closely related to this Daoist saying is: "Not to know the eternal [Dao] is to act blindly which results in disaster."[2] Now we shall attempt to apply this group of Daoist sayings to ecological considerations. Thus, "To be in accord with the eternal [Dao] means to be enlightened" denotes the fact that the myriad things of the world are mutually connected and interdependent, and that people must maintain a harmonious relationship among things in order to enhance their longevity. Daoism affirms that each of the myriad things contains the polarity of yin and yang[3] and that life is engendered only when each thing's yin-yang poles are allowed to commune with each other. In other words, the viability of life depends upon the mutual harmony of the yin-yang polarity of all things. This also means that the continuous development of world civilization depends on the harmonious relationship among all things. People who understand this principle can be called wise persons. Conversely, those who do not understand this principle or violate it—contradicting this teaching through human contrivances, breaking the laws of nature, destroying a species by artificial means, or promoting the overproduction of a certain species of things—are the violators of the principle of Dao.

The Daoist classic, *Baopuzi* (The Master Who Embraces Simplicity), a work of the fourth century C.E., makes a distinction between two kinds of people concerning their relation with nature: one type is called "those who enslave the myriad things" and the other is called "those who emulate nature." It says that the Dao, which creates the myriad things through the principle of "self-so," makes humans the most intelligent beings among all the creatures of the earth. Those who have only a superficial understanding of the relationship between people and nature are the ones who "enslave the myriad things." They subjugate nature completely to themselves. Contrariwise, people who have a profound insight into the mystery of the relationship between humans and nature are friends of nature and derive their understanding of longevity from nature by meditative observation and gazing. Because people of this kind are intimately acquainted with nature, they understand that turtles and cranes live long lives. Therefore, they try to emulate the calisthenic methods of the turtles and cranes in order to strengthen their bodies.

1. *Daode jing*, chapter 55.
2. *Daode jing*, chapter 16.
3. The complementary forces that unite to form the Dao: yin, a term that originally referred to the shady side of a valley, by extension came to be associated with the dark, earth, dampness, and passivity—the female principle; yang, a term that originally referred to the sunny side of a valley, by extension came to be associated with the light, heaven, dryness, and activity—the male principle.

From a long range perspective, the abuse of Nature will result in a disastrous destruction of our natural environment. Chapter 6 of the *Baopuzi* provides the following passages regarding this issue:

> "Flying birds are shot with bullets, the pregnant are disemboweled and their eggs are broken. When there is hunting by firearm in spring and summer. . . . Each of these destructive actions constitutes one sin, and according to its severity the Controller of Destiny will deduct a certain amount from one's life (one's natural destiny or longevity). A person dies when there are no more units of time left in one's life." Contrarily, "if one treats things with compassion, forgives others as one wishes others to forgive oneself, is benevolent even to the creeping insects . . . harms no living things. . . . In this way, one becomes a person of high virtue and will be blessed by Heaven. One's undertakings are sure to be successful, and the desire to be an immortal will be obtained." Prosperity and longevity fall upon one who extends her love to the myriad things in the natural world.

The passage, "He who knows when to stop is free from danger. He who is contented suffers no disgrace," is important for ecological ethics. "He who knows when to stop is free from danger" refers to the fact that there are limits in the natural environment as to how much abuse Nature can take from human beings. This consideration necessarily calls for human restraint against any act which might interfere with the ecological balance—even if that action might generate a huge immediate profit. In this way, we can avoid Nature's retaliation, prevent a long-term disaster for the sake of some immediate gain, or escape the predicament of losing what we have already gained. "He who is contented suffers no disgrace" means that people should have a correct understanding of what success means. One should realize that in order to avoid the overproduction of natural resources, one must not pursue material benefits in an unsatiable way. The *Taiping jing* (Scripture of Great Peace)[4] contains a passage conveying the importance of conserving natural resources for the production of wealth. It proposes that the criterion of wealth depends upon whether or not a society can protect the ability of all nature's species of things to grow and prosper. The passage says: the sage-king teaches "that people should assist Heaven to produce living things and assist Earth by giving nourishment to things to form proper shapes." Wealth requires that the living things under Heaven and of the world are all allowed to grow and flourish:

> [In antiquity], in the Higher August Period, because 12,000 species of living things grow and flourish, it is called the era of Wealth. In the Middle August Period, because the living things are less than 12,000 species, it is called the era of Small Poverty. In the Lower August Period, because the number of living species was less than that in the Middle August Period, it is called the era of Great Poverty. If the august breath keeps producing fewer species of things and if no good omens are seen to assure the growth of good things, the next era will be called Extreme Poverty.

4. See above.

According to the above passage, the reason why all things can grow in the Higher August Period is because the earth is properly nourished and is not injured by people. On the other hand, because in the Lower August Period the earth is not given proper nourishment and is greatly injured by its inhabitants, it produces fewer living things. From the perspective of the sage-ruler, if he can make the myriad living things grow and flourish, he can insure the rise of a wealthy country. On the other hand, if half of the myriad things in Nature in the sage-king's country are injured, it portends that his country is on the road to downfall. The *Taiping jing*'s insight—that the conservation of living species in the natural world is the criterion of wealth—is a real contribution to the ethics of ecological thought.

We believe that the Dao—the principle of self-so/non-action—is the fundamental Daoist teaching. This and many other Daoist concepts have positive implications for the contemporary world. We hope that the various ideas of the different world religions, which in the best sense promise to bring benefits to humankind, will attract the attention of both religious believers and nonbelievers. Given this kind of common ground, a harmonious relationship between human beings and their natural environment, between humans and society, and among diverse groups of people can be established.

Tasks and Plans

Both Daoist doctrines and disciplinary rules provide principles aimed at protecting Nature in its overall ecological context. These considerations have prompted hermitage Daoists in China both to continue and to augment their ecological concerns. For many years, China's Daoists, in the confines of their hermitages and within the limits of their capacities, have devoted themselves to the tasks of protecting trees and fruits, preserving and rebuilding forests, safeguarding the hermitage culture and ancient relics, and other ecological activities. They have also gone beyond the confines of their hermitages to establish closer relations with their lay Daoist followers. The hermitage Daoists have, therefore, taken the time to talk to their congregations of followers on the importance of protecting trees and forests in the mountains and on the relationship between Daoist doctrines and nature (including all manner of fowl, birds, and animals). They are helping their followers appreciate the oneness between the creativity of Dao and the survival of humankind. The hermitage Daoists believe that they have planted the seeds of ecological responsibility and service in the hearts of their congregations. For example, a certain Daoist master of Mount Thundergod (Leishen shan) in Baoji municipality, Shaanxi province, has spent several decades working with his followers in the voluntary maintenance of over eight hundred *mu*[5] of trees and forests. He is well recognized for his work by people in the region. There is also a Daoist congregation associated with the hermitage neighborhood of Wudang, in Yuedu county, Qinghai province, who for more than a decade has made the barren hills into green fields by planting trees and growing grass. This congregation has greatly improved the physical surroundings of the neighborhood. Then there is an

5. About 130 acres.

elderly Daoist master in Yunnan province who devoted more than sixty years of his life to the cultivation and nursing of what some international botanists call a "living fossil"—that is, the rare plant called the "Bald Pine Tree" (*tushan*). This Daoist master's work has been recognized by the staff of the Bureau of Arboriculture in Yunnan province. Deeds of this kind are too numerous to be mentioned. Environmental concern is a tradition of Daoism and deserves further promotion. For this reason, the Chinese Daoist Association in 1993 sponsored a national ecological conference that encouraged all Daoist followers to plant trees and build forests, to beautify the natural environment, and to engage in works benefiting social welfare.

The Daoist ecological agenda in the immediate future includes the promotion of the teaching of self-so or non-action for the transformation of people's lives. This is a strategy conducive to the development of environmental protection. It also involves the sacred mission of cooperating with the world community in maintaining harmony with Nature. The following are three specific tasks that all Daoists are called to perform:

- We shall spread the ecological teachings of Daoism, lead all Daoist followers to abide in the teachings of self-so or non-action, observe the injunction against killing for amusement purposes, preserve and protect the harmonious relationship of all things with Nature, establish paradises of immortals on Earth, and pursue the practice of our beliefs. In our evangelistic efforts, we shall nurture the people by teaching the importance in Daoism of maintaining harmonious relationships among things in the natural world. This means we shall promote the mutuality between valuing life and ecological concerns. We will raise the awareness regarding ecology among various social groups, resist the human exploitation of Nature and the abuse of natural environments, protect the earth upon which human survival depends, and generally make the world a better place for humans to inhabit. At the same time, we shall promote the nonviolent and pacifist ideals of Daoism—thus helping to preserve world peace and to free the world from environmental degradations due to war.
- We shall continue the Daoist ecological tradition by planting trees and cultivating forests. Using traditional hermitages as an organizational base, Daoists will conscientiously plant trees and build forests, thereby making the natural environment beautiful and transforming our hermitages into the paradise worlds of the immortals.
- We shall select some famous Daoist mountains as exemplars of the systematic task of environmental engineering. We expect to reach this goal by the early years of the new century.

Since the publication of this declaration in 1995, we have received responses from groups abroad indicating their interest in exchanging ideas with us. For example, the Religions of the World Alliance for Environmental Protection in 1996 cooperated with the China Daoist Association, in conjunction with China's State Bureau of Religious Affairs and its branch offices in Sichuan and Shaanxi, to conduct a field survey of two famous Daoist mountains: Qingcheng shan in Sichuan province; and Huashan in Shaanxi province. This survey has produced a survey report on these two sacred mountains. It deals with a critical study of these two mountains, their natural resources, famous Daoist architecture, and ancient cultural relics. The report also discusses the host hermitages' efforts to open these two mountains to the public and their work of environmental maintenance. The report concludes with some suggestions regarding the ongoing maintenance of, and public access to, these two mountains.

In sum, present-day Daoists in China have diligently worked toward disseminating Daoist teachings and in maintaining the famous Daoist mountains and hermitages, planting trees and cultivating forests, and protecting the natural environment. We believe that as the Chinese state and society today are paying greater attention to ecological problems, educational programs concerning public health issues will be further fostered and developed. We pray that tomorrow's world will be better than today's, and that, by following the principle of mutuality among all things in nature, a new harmonious world will emerge. It is this kind of harmonious natural and social environment that will be conducive to the balanced growth of the world's population.

APPENDICES

APPENDICES

Glossary

Unless otherwise indicated, italicized terms are in Mandarin Chinese. Words in SMALL CAPS are defined in their own entries.

Celestial Heart (Tianxin) tradition. A therapeutic and exorcistic movement, which began perhaps in the tenth century C.E. and claimed connections to the CELESTIAL MASTERS tradition, later referred to as the ORTHODOX UNITY TRADITION.

Celestial Masters (Tianshi). One of the most important of the early organized Daoist movements (second century C.E.), established by Zhang Daoling (34–156 C.E.) and characterized by communal practices and external rituals.

Cinnabar Fields (*dantian*). Locations in the human body important for internal alchemy: the upper is in the brain, the middle is the heart, and the lower (sometimes identified with the Yellow Court) is in the middle of the body (near the naval).

Complete Perfection (Quanzhen) tradition. A monastic form of Daoism that appeared in the late twelfth century C.E. and is today the primary official Daoist tradition in China.

corpse liberation (*shijie*). A kind of feigned death and transformation in which one sloughs off one's old mortal body, like a cicada shedding its shell, and ascends to heaven—perhaps appearing in the world now and again at long intervals.

***dantian*.** See CINNABAR FIELDS.

Dao. Literally, "way" or "pathway": a term commonly used in early Chinese thought, it came to refer to a unified universal principle preceding the origin of the universe.

***daojia*.** Literally, "specialists of/on the DAO": originally a bibliographic label, but identified by Westerners with "philosophical Daoism" (derived from the writings of Laozi and Zhuangzi).

***daojiao*.** Literally, "teachings of/on the DAO": originally applied to different teachings, but identified by Westerners with "religious Daoism" (connected with institutions and rituals).

De. Literally, "virtue" or "power": the basic quality or character that enables a thing to be what it is and to do what it does.

dharma (Sanskrit, "teaching"). A term notoriously difficult to translate, most commonly understood as doctrine or discourses of the Buddha.

Divine Empyrean (Shenxiao) tradition. A complex, hybrid movement that began in the north in the twelfth century C.E. and later flourished in the south, where it was incorporated into the CELESTIAL MASTERS tradition.

Dragon Tiger Mountain (Longhu shan). The location of the headquarters of the ORTHODOX UNITY TRADITION, in modern-day Jiangxi Province.

Eight Immortals. Legendary Daoist TRANSCENDENTS.

elixir. The product, refined via either EXTERNAL ALCHEMY or INTERNAL ALCHEMY, that enables the adept to attain longevity or even immortality and advance up the spiritual hierarchy.

embryo. The product of some forms of INTERNAL ALCHEMY, by which the adept seeks to create an immortal spirit that represents a return to the DAO.

external alchemy (*waidan*). The making of elixirs composed of base minerals, which are then ingested.

Falun Gong. A 1990s offshoot of *QIGONG*, outlawed by the Chinese government as a superstitious cult.

fangshi. See MASTERS OF METHODS.

fashi. See RITUAL MASTERS.

female alchemy (*nüdan*). INTERNAL ALCHEMY directed exclusively at women, with practices specific to female physiology.

Five Agents. Metal, wood, water, fire, and earth, the five elements that are the foundation of the theory of five phases—a set of systematic associations between different categories that, according to Chinese thought, explain the cyclical operation of nature.

Five Marchmounts. The Five Sacred Peaks (*wuyue*), a group of five sacred mountains—one in each of the four cardinal directions and one at the center—most often identified as Mount Heng (north), Mount Tai (TAISHAN, east), Mount Heng (south), Mount Hua (west), and Mount Song (center).

Grand Tenuity. The name of a constellation that was the administrative locale of the Celestial THEARCH, one of the most important deities in the UPPER CLARITY TRADITION.

Great Clarity (Taiqing) tradition. A tradition focused on attaining transcendence through EXTERNAL ALCHEMY (using elixirs).

Great Peace (Taiping). The good government, political harmony, and good health for the masses that characterized a golden age believed to have existed in the past and that would be restored when the ruling ideology is based on a return to the DAO; texts on the Great Peace inspired rebellion in the second century C.E.

Guanyin. A Chinese name of Avalokiteshvara (Sanskrit, "the lord who looks down"), the bodhisattva regarded as the embodiment of all the compassion of all the buddhas.

Heavenly Worthy of Original Commencement. Yuanshi tianzun, the being who revealed some of the LINGBAO texts (a figure modeled on the Buddha).

Hexagrams. The sixty-four permutations of solid (YANG) or broken (YIN) lines in vertical stacks of six that are listed, named, and interpreted in the *YIJING*.

Huangdi. The legendary Yellow Emperor, credited with many inventions and establishing law and revered as a patron of Daoism and medical traditions.

hun-**souls.** Cloud souls or light souls, linked with heaven and its pneumas.

inner / internal alchemy (*neidan*). A self-cultivation technique based on meditation, visualization, and the creation of elixirs inside one's own body.

jade lads / youths. Attendants in heaven.

jade maidens. Attendants in heaven.

jiao. A large-scale ritual offering or sacrifice, sponsored by a community.

kalpa (Sanskrit). An aeon; a common unit of time in Indian religions.

karma (Sanskrit, "action"). The positive and negative deeds that bear fruit as either happiness or suffering in the future.

Kunlun. A mythical mountain supposedly located in the far western part of the Chinese empire; it was the home of the QUEEN MOTHER OF THE WEST (XIWANG MU).

Libationers. Priests within the CELESTIAL MASTERS tradition.

Lingbao. See NUMINOUS TREASURE TRADITION.

Longmen tradition. A branch of the COMPLETE PERFECTION TRADITION; Beijing's White Cloud Abbey (Baiyun guan) became its headquarters and main training center.

lu. See REGISTERS.

Mahayana (Sanskrit, "Great Vehicle"). A group of sutras (discourses of the Buddha) that began to appear in India four hundred years after the Buddha's death, containing the new doctrine that all beings would one day achieve buddhahood; also, those who accepted these sutras as the word of the Buddha.

Maoshan. Mount Mao, a significant sacred mountain for the UPPER CLARITY TRADITION, located in present-day Jiangsu Province.

masters of methods (*fangshi*). Technical specialists, especially common at the Zhou and Qin courts, who sought political patronage by peddling esoteric knowledge of magical and medical techniques, divination, and exorcism.

Mohism. A philosophical, social, and religious movement of the Warring States period (403–221 B.C.E.) that takes its name from the influential philosopher Mozi (late fifth century B.C.E.?).

neidan. See INNER / INTERNAL ALCHEMY.

neiguan. In Daoism, inner observation; inner contemplation.

niwan. Literally, "Muddy Pellet," the central of the nine palaces inside a person's head; the upper CINNABAR FIELD, in the brain.

nüdan. See FEMALE ALCHEMY.

Numinous Treasure (Lingbao) tradition. A Daoist movement that emerged during the fifth century C.E., the first to systematically incorporate Buddhist terminology and concepts into Daoism; many of its texts were revealed by the HEAVENLY WORTHY OF ORIGINAL COMMENCEMENT.

Orthodox Unity (Zhengyi) tradition. A designation used especially from the Song dynasty (960–1279) onward for teachings of the CELESTIAL MASTERS: one of the two Daoist schools officially recognized by the Qing dynasty and by the Chinese government today (the other is COMPLETE PERFECTION).

Pace of Yu. A form of ritual walking or dancing (dragging one foot after the other in imitation of the ancient hero Yu the Great); specifically, it traces out cosmic patterns (such as constellations) mapped onto the ground. It is used to purify the ritual arena and also prepares the ritual master for ascent to heaven to transmit the ritual documents.

perfected (*zhenren*). A Daoist spiritual master; a Daoist who has moved beyond earthly corruption (often identified with stellar deities). *Zhenren* is sometimes translated "realized."

Perfected Warrior (Zhenwu). A Daoist warrior deity associated with the north; he became the dynastic protector of the Ming.

***po*-souls.** White souls or heavy souls, linked to the earth.

Purple Tenuity. The circumpolar constellation in which the supreme god of the central heavens lives.

qi. The basic constituent of the Chinese universe (translated as "breath," "vapor," "pneuma," or "energy"), initially undifferentiated.

qigong. A health- and longevity-focused movement that first emerged in the 1950s and became popular again in the 1980s; it combines physical posture, breathing techniques, and mental focus (drawing elements from Daoism and Buddhism).

Quanzhen. See COMPLETE PERFECTION TRADITION.

Queen Mother of the West (Xiwang mu). One of the most important goddesses in ancient China and in the Daoist pantheon; she governed all other female deities.

registers (*lu*). Records that identify a Daoist's name and rank in the celestial hierarchy and the deities and supernatural beings over which a Daoist initiate has control.

ritual masters (*fashi*). Daoist (or Buddhist) priests who perform exorcistic or healing rituals.

Shangqing. See UPPER CLARITY TRADITION.

shijie. See CORPSE LIBERATION.

Taiqing. See GREAT CLARITY TRADITION.

Taishan. Mount Tai, the Eastern Sacred Peak of the FIVE MARCHMOUNTS. This sacred mountain located in modern-day Shandong Province for millennia was important for the imperial cult and for Buddhists as well as for Daoists.

Taiyi. Literally, "Supreme Unity," an early Chinese deity.

Thearchs. In Daoism, emperors in heaven; more generally, the term was applied first to deified kings and later to living emperors.

Three Caverns (*Sandong*). The texts in the Daoist canon; they were divided into three "caverns," or collections, by Lu Xiujing in 471 C.E.

Thunder Rituals (*leifa*). Powerful exorcistic rituals intended to harness the power of thunder and summon thunder deities (usually local spirits who had been pacified and incorporated into Daoism).

transcendent (*xian*). A being who, through self-cultivation techniques, has attained an immeasurably long life, the ability to fly, and a way of existing in the world with a natural effortless spontaneity. *Xian* is often translated "immortal."

trigrams. Permutations of three solid (YANG) or broken (YIN) lines stacked up vertically, as described in the *YIJING*. The eight trigrams (*bagua*)—each with a name and distinct meaning—represent elements in nature and human society that together symbolize the entire cosmos.

Upper Clarity (Shangqing) tradition. A Daoist tradition emphasizing individual meditation and interiorized rituals, based on scriptures derived from revelations to Yang Xi (330–ca. 386).

waidan. See EXTERNAL ALCHEMY.

Wuyue. See the FIVE MARCHMOUNTS.

xian. See TRANSCENDENT.

yang. The male principle; the term originally referred to the sunny side of a valley, and by extension it came to be associated with the light, heaven, dryness, and activity. One half of the initial dyad of the universe; see YIN.

Yellow Court. In INTERNAL ALCHEMY, the center of the human body (variously identified as the spleen, as an area between the eyes, or as the lowest of the three CINNABAR FIELDS).

Yijing. The *Book of Changes,* one of the Five Classics of Confucianism. Originally used for divination, its system of TRIGRAMS and HEXAGRAMS and their interpretation in Daoism had more significance as cosmology and in INTERNAL ALCHEMY.

yin. The female principle; the term originally referred to the shady side of a valley, and by extension it came to be associated with the dark, earth, dampness, and passivity. One half of the initial dyad of the universe; see YANG.

Zhang Daoling. Founder of the CELESTIAL MASTERS tradition (34–156 C.E.).

zhenren. See PERFECTED.

Selected Bibliography*

Reference Works, General Introductions, and Anthologies

General English-language reference works on all aspects of Daoism include comprehensive works such as Fabrizio Pregadio, ed., *The Encyclopedia of Taoism*, 2008 (2 vols.); Livia Kohn, ed., *Daoism Handbook*, 2000; and Julian F. Pas, in cooperation with Man Kam Leung, *Historical Dictionary of Taoism*, 1998. More specialized reference works on Daoist texts include Kristofer Schipper and Franciscus Verellen, eds., *The Taoist Canon: A Historical Companion to the Daozang*, 2004; Judith M. Boltz, *A Survey of Taoist Literature: Tenth to Seventeenth Centuries*, 1987; and Piet van der Loon, *Taoist Books in the Libraries of the Sung Period: A Critical Study and Index*, 1984. Some entries on Daoist historical figures, texts, and terms are also included in Lindsay Jones, ed., *Encyclopedia of Religion*, 2nd ed., 2005; Michael Loewe, ed., *Early Chinese Texts: A Bibliographic Guide*, 1993; William H. Nienhauser, Jr., ed., *Indiana Companion to Traditional Chinese Literature*, 1986; and *Encyclopedia of Britannica*, 15th ed., 1974. Useful state-of-the-field reports on Daoism include Anna Seidel, "Chronicle of Taoist Studies in the West, 1950–1990," 1990, and Franciscus Verellen, "Chinese Religions: The State of the Field, Part 2, Taoism," 1995.

General introductions and surveys that discuss Daoism include Louis Komjathy, *The Daoist Tradition: An Introduction*, 2013; John Lagerwey, *China: A Religious State*, 2010; Livia Kohn, *Introducing Daoism*, 2009; Wang Yi'e, *Daoism in China: An Introduction*, 2006; Anthony C. Yu, *State and Religion in China: Historical and Textual Perspectives*, 2005; Hans-Georg Moeller,

Daoism Explained: From the Dream of the Butterfly to the Fishnet Allegory, 2004; Russell Kirkland, *Taoism: The Enduring Tradition*, 2004; James Miller, *Daoism: A Beginner's Guide*, 2003; Qing Xitai, *History of Chinese Daoism*, vol. 1, 2000; Isabelle Robinet, *Taoism: Growth of a Religion*, 1997; Laurence G. Thompson, *Chinese Religion: An Introduction*, 1995; Kristofer Schipper, *The Taoist Body*, 1993; John Lagerwey, *Taoist Ritual in Chinese Society and History*, 1987; Joseph Needham, *Science and Civilisation in China*, vol. 2, 1956 (on scientific thought) and vol. 5, 1974 (on alchemy and longevity); Henri Maspero, *Taoism and Chinese Religion*, 1981; Herrlee G. Creel, *What Is Taoism? And Other Studies in Chinese Cultural History*, 1970; Max Kaltenmark, *Lao Tzu and Taoism*, 1965; Holmes Welch, *The Parting of the Way: Lao Tzu and the Taoist Movement*, 1957; Max Weber, *The Religion of China: Confucianism and Taoism*, 1951; and Marcel Granet, *The Religion of the Chinese People*, 1922.

Essay collections that include work on Daoist history, culture, and practice include David A. Palmer and Xun Liu, eds., *Daoism in the Twentieth Century: Between Eternity and Modernity*, 2013; Florian C. Reiter, ed., *Affiliation and Transmission in Daoism*, 2012, and *Exorcism in Daoism*, 2011; Yoshiko Ashiwa and David L. Wank, eds., *Making Religion, Making the State: The Politics of Religion in Modern China*, 2009; Philip Clart and Paul Crowe, eds., *The People and the Dao: New Studies in Chinese Religions in Honour of Daniel L. Overmyer*, 2009; Florian C. Reiter, ed., *Foundations of Daoist Ritual*, 2009, and *Purposes, Means and Convictions in Daoism*, 2007; Benjamin Penny, ed., *Daoism in History: Essays in Honour of Liu*

* Much of the formative work on Daoism was published in seminal articles and in languages other than English (French, Japanese, and Chinese in particular); such works are not listed in this bibliography.

Ts'un-yan, 2006; Poul Andersen and Florian C. Reiter, eds., Scriptures, Schools and Forms of Practice in Daoism, 2005; John Lagerwey, ed., Religion and Chinese Society: Ancient and Medieval China, 2004; Daniel L. Overmyer, ed., Religion in China Today, 2003; Philip Clart and Charles B. Jones, eds., Religion in Modern Taiwan: Tradition and Innovation in a Changing Society, 2003; Livia Kohn and Harold D. Roth, eds., Daoist Identity: History, Lineage, and Ritual, 2002; Norman J. Girardot, James Miller, and Liu Xiaogan, eds., Daoism and Ecology: Ways Within a Cosmic Landscape, 2001; Mair Shahar and Robert P. Weller, Unruly Gods: Divinity and Society in China, 1996; Patricia Buckley Ebrey and Peter Gregory, eds., Religion and Society in T'ang and Sung China, 1993; Paul S. Ropp, ed., Heritage of China: Contemporary Perspectives on Chinese Civilization, 1990; Livia Kohn, ed., in cooperation with Yoshinobu Sakade, Taoist Meditation and Longevity Practices, 1989; Julian Pas, ed., The Turning of the Tide: Religion in China Today, 1989; Michel Strickmann, ed., Tantric and Taoist Studies in Honour of R. A. Stein, 1981, 1983, 1985 (3 vols.); Holmes Welch and Anna Seidel, eds., Facets of Taoism: Essays in Chinese Religion, 1979; and Arthur P. Wolf, ed., Religion and Ritual in Chinese Society, 1974.

Other anthologies of translated Daoist texts, less broad in scope than the present volume, include early works such as Frederic Henry Balfour, Taoist Texts: Ethical, Political, and Speculative, 1884; James Legge, Texts of Taoism, 1891; and Wing-Tsit Chan, A Sourcebook in Chinese Philosophy, 1963. More recent anthologies include Louis Komjathy, The Way of Complete Perfection: A Quanzhen Daoist Anthology, 2013; Stephen R. Bokenkamp, Early Daoist Scriptures, 1997; Donald S. Lopez, Jr., ed., Religions of China in Practice, 1996; Livia Kohn, ed., Taoist Experience, 1993; and William Theodore de Bary and Irene Bloom, eds., Sources of Chinese Tradition, 1960 (rev. 2000).

The Zhou Dynasty (1046–256 B.C.E.) through the Qin Dynasty (221–206 B.C.E.)

Since the first translation of the Laozi into Latin in the eighteenth century there have been so many translations of that classic into so many languages that it is now often claimed to be the second most translated book (behind the Bible). Among the transla-

tions are Robert G. Henricks, Lao-tsu's Tao-te ching: A Translation of the Startling New Documents Found at Guodian, 2000; Richard John Lynn, The Classic of the Way and Virtue: A New Translation of the Tao-te Ching of Laozi as Interpreted by Wang Bi, 1999; Michael LaFargue, The Tao of the Tao Te Ching: A Translation and Commentary, 1992; Victor H. Mair, Tao Te Ching: The Classic of Integrity and the Way, 1990; and Robert G. Henricks, Lao Tzu: Te-tao Ching: A New Translation Based on the Recently Discovered Ma-wang-tui Texts, 1989. Translations of the Zhuangzi include Victor H. Mair, Wandering on the Way: Early Taoist Tales and Parables of Chuang Tzu, 1994, and A. C. Graham, Chuang-Tzu: The Inner Chapters, A Classic of Tao, 1991. There have also been many pioneering works and collections of essays on early Chinese philosophy, religion, and history, as well as studies of the Laozi and Zhuangzi. Among these are Sarah Allan and Crispin Williams, The Guodian Laozi: Proceedings of the International Conference, Dartmouth College, May 1998, 2000; Rudolf G. Wagner, The Craft of a Chinese Commentator: Wang Bi on the Laozi, 2000; Mark Csikszentmihalyi and Philip J. Ivanhoe, eds., Religious and Philosophical Aspects of the Laozi, 1999; Michael Loewe and Edward L. Shaughnessy, eds., The Cambridge History of Ancient China: From the Origins to 221 B.C., 1999; Livia Kohn and Michael LaFargue, eds., Lao-tzu and the Tao-te-ching, 1998; Paul Kjellberg and Philip J. Ivanhoe, eds., Essays on Skepticism, Relativism, and Ethics in the Zhuangzi, 1996; Michael LaFargue, Tao and Method: A Reasoned Approach to the Tao Te Ching, 1994; Chad Hansen, A Daoist Theory of Chinese Thought: A Philosophical Interpretation, 1992; Allan K. L. Chan, Two Visions of the Way: A Study of the Wang Pi and Ho-shang Kung Commentaries on the Lao-tzu, 1991; A. C. Graham, Disputers of the Tao: Philosophical Argument in Ancient China, 1989; Benjamin Schwartz, The World of Thought in Ancient China, 1985; Norman J. Girardot, Myth and Meaning in Early Taoism: The Theme of Chaos (Hun-tun), 1983; Victor Mair, ed., Experimental Essays on Chuang-tzu, 1983; Fung Yu-lan, A History of Chinese Philosophy, Vol. 1: The Period of the Philosophers (from the Beginnings to Circa 100 B.C.), 1983; and Arthur Waley, The Way and Its Power: A Study of the Tao Te Ching and Its Place in Chinese Thought, 1958, and

Three Ways of Thought in Ancient China, 1939.

From the Han Dynasty (202 b.c.e.–220 c.e.) through the Six Dynasties Period (220–589 c.e.)
Works covering the earliest phases of Daoist history include Gil Raz, *The Emergence of Daoism: Creation of Tradition,* 2012; Ho Peng Yoke, *Explorations in Daoism: Medicine and Alchemy in Literature,* 2011; Robert Ford Campany, *Making Transcendents: Ascetic and Social Memory in Early Medieval China,* 2009; Fabrizio Pregadio, *Great Clarity: Daoism and Alchemy in Early Medieval China,* 2006; Barbara Hendrischke, trans., *The Scripture on Great Peace: The Taiping Jing and the Beginnings of Daoism,* 2007; Robert Ford Campany, *To Live as Long as Heaven and Earth: A Translation and Study of Ge Hong's Traditions of Divine Transcendents,* 2002; Qing Xitai, *History of Chinese Daoism,* 2000; Terry F. Kleeman, *Great Perfection: Religion and Ethnicity in a Chinese Millennial Kingdom,* 1998; Donald J. Harper, *Early Chinese Medical Literature: The Mawangdui Medical Manuscripts,* 1998; Stephen Eskildsen, *Early Taoist Asceticism,* 1998; Nathan Sivin, *Medicine, Philosophy and Religion in Ancient China: Researches and Reflections,* 1995; Isabelle Robinet, *Taoist Meditation: The Mao-shan Tradition of Great Purity,* 1993; John S. Major, *Heaven and Earth in Early Han Thought: Chapters Three, Four and Five of the Huainanzi,* 1993; Kenneth J. Dewoskin, *Doctors, Diviners, and Magicians of Ancient China,* 1983; Henri Maspero, *Taoism and Chinese Religion,* 1981; Michael Loewe, *Ways to Paradise: The Chinese Quest for Immortality,* 1979; Poul Andersen, *The Method of Holding the Three Ones: A Taoist Manual of Meditation of the Fourth Century A.D.,* 1979; Barbara Kandel [Barbara Hendrischke], *Taiping jing: The Origin and Transmission of the 'Scripture on General Welfare': The History of an Unofficial Text,* 1979; Jay Sailey, *The Master Who Embraces Simplicity: A Study of the Philosopher Ko Hung, A.D. 282–343,* 1978; and James R. Ware, *Alchemy, Medicine, Religion in the China of A.D. 320: The Nei-P'ien of Ko Hung,* 1967, a translation (in need of retranslation) of the *Inner Chapters of the Book of the Master Who Embraces Simplicity (Baopuzi).*

From the Sui Dynasty (581–618 c.e.) through the Tang Dynasty (618–907 c.e.)
Though the Tang dynasty was particularly important in Daoist history, few studies focus on this period. On the place of Daoism in relationship to the Tang ruling house, see T. H. Barrett, *Taoism Under the T'ang: Religion and Empire During the Golden Age of Chinese History,* 1996. On the connection between Daoism and some state rituals, see Charles D. Benn, *The Cavern-Mystery Transmission: A Taoist Ordination Rite of A.D. 711,* 1991, and Howard J. Wechsler, *Offerings of Jade and Silk: Ritual and Symbol in the Legitimation of the T'ang Dynasty,* 1985. Studies that shed light on other aspects of Tang Daoism include Livia Kohn, *Sitting in Oblivion: The Heart of Daoist Meditation,* 2010, an expansion of her *Seven Steps to the Tao,* 1987; Friederike Assandri, *Beyond the Daode Jing: Twofold Mystery in Tang Daoism,* 2009; Florian C. Reiter, *The Aspirations and Standards of Taoist Priests in the Early T'ang Period,* 1998; Timothy H. Barrett, *Li Ao: Buddhist, Taoist, or Neo-Confucian,* 1992; Edward H. Schafer, *Mao Shan in Tang Times,* 1980, and *Pacing the Void: T'ang Approaches to the Stars,* 1977. On Tang poetry and Daoism, see Jan De Meyer, *Wu Yun's Way: Life and Works of an Eighth-Century Daoist Master,* 2006, and Edward H. Schafer, *Mirages on the Sea of Time: The Taoist Poetry of Ts'ao T'ang,* 1985. On the writings of a Tang dynasty alchemist, see Nathan Sivin, *Chinese Alchemy: Preliminary Studies,* 1968.

The Song (960–1279 c.e.) and Yuan (1260–1368 c.e.) Dynasties
Most research on Song and Yuan Daoism has appeared in specialized articles, but treatment of this important period in the transformation of Daoism is found in Shin-Yi Chao, *Daoist Rituals, State Religion, and Popular Practices: Zhenwu Worship from Song to Ming (960–1644),* 2011; Robert P. Hymes, *Way and Byway: Taoism, Local Religion, and Models of Divinity in Sung and Modern China,* 2002; Edward L. Davis, *Society and the Supernatural in Song China,* 2001; and Paul R. Katz, *Demon Hordes and Burning Boats: The Cult of Marshal Wen in Late Imperial Chekiang,* 1995.

The Ming Dynasty (1368–1644 c.e.) through the Qing (1644–1912 c.e.) Dynasty
The Daoist history of the Ming and Qing dynasties has only recently begun to be extensively researched by Western scholars. On aspects of Ming Daoism, see Richard G.

Wang, *The Ming Prince and Daoism: Institutional Patronage of an Elite*, 2012, and Shin-Yi Chao, *Daoist Rituals, State Religion, and Popular Practices: Zhenwu Worship from Song to Ming (960–1644)*, 2011. On the formation of Quanzhen Daoism during the Qing dynasty, see Monica Esposito, *Facets of Qing Daoism*, 2014, and *Creative Daoism*, 2013. For a wide-ranging account of Quanzhen Daoism, see Stephen Eskildsen, *The Teachings and Practices of the Early Quanzhen Taoist Masters*, 2006. For the study of a figure who brings together Buddhism, Daoism, and Confucianism, see Judith A. Berling, *The Syncretic Religion of Lin Chao-en*, 1980. For the translation of a seventeenth-century novel full of Daoist ideas and practices, see Philip Clart's translation of Yang Erzheng's, *The Story of Han Xiangzi: The Alchemical Adventures of a Daoist Immortal* (2007). For a detailed study of Daoism at the turn of the twentieth century, see J. J. M. De Groot, *The Religious System of China*, volume 6, 1910.

From the Republican Era (1912–1949) to the Early Twenty-First Century
For studies that help to contextualize Daoism within modern Chinese religion, see Shuk-Wah Poon, *Negotiating Religion in Modern China: State and Common People in Guangzhou, 1900–1937*, 2011; Vincent Goossaert and David A. Palmer, *The Religious Question in Modern China*, 2011; Rebecca Nedostup, *Superstitious Regimes: Religion and the Politics of Chinese Modernity*, 2009; Xun Liu, *Daoist Modern: Innovation, Lay Practice, and the Community of Inner Alchemy in Republican Shanghai*, 2009; Mayfair Mei-Hui Yang, ed., *Chinese Religiosities: Afflictions of Modernity and State Formation*, 2008; Vincent Goossaert, *The Taoists of Peking, 1800–1949: A Social History of Urban Clerics*, 2007; Prasenjit Duara, *Sovereignty and Authenticity: Manchukuo and the East Asian Modern*, 2003, *Rescuing History from the Nation: Questioning Narratives of Modern China*, 1995, and *Culture, Power and the State: Rural North China, 1900–1942*, 1988. Studies of contemporary Daoist history and practice include David A. Palmer and Xun Liu, eds., *Daoism in the Twentieth Century: Between Eternity and Modernity*, 2012; Xun Liu, *Daoist Modern: Innovation, Lay Practice,* and the Community of Inner Alchemy in Republican Shanghai, 2009; Vincent Goossaert, *The Taoists of Peking, 1800–1949: A Social History of Urban Clerics*, 2007; Kenneth Dean, *Lord of the Three in One: The Spread of a Cult in Southeast China*, 1998, and *Taoist Ritual and Popular Cults of South-East China*, 1993; and Michael Saso, *The Teachings of Taoist Master Chuang*, 1978. A good review of ethnographic research on different regions of China is Daniel L. Overmyer, ed., *Ethnography in China Today: A Critical Assessment of Research Methods and Results*, 2002. On the Western reception and study of Daoism, see Norman J. Girardot, *The Victorian Translation of China: James Legge's Oriental Pilgrimage*, 2002; and J. J. Clarke, *The Tao of the West: Western Transformations of Taoist Thought*, 2000, and *Oriental Enlightenment: The Encounter Between Asian and Western Thought*, 1997.

The Culture and Practice of Daoism
For the place of Daoism in medicine and external and internal alchemy, see Isabelle Robinet, *The World Upside Down: Essays on Taoist Internal Alchemy*, 2011; Fabrizio Pregadio, *The Seal of the Unity of the Three: A Study and Translation of the Cantong qi, the Source of the Taoist Way of the Golden Elixir*, 2011; Paul U. Unschuld, *Medicine in China: A History of Pharmaceutics*, 1986, and *Medicine in China: History of Ideas*, 1985; Manfred Porkert, *The Theoretical Foundations of Chinese Medicine: Systems of Correspondance*, 1974; and the works of Nathan Sivin cited above. On Qigong practice, see David A. Palmer, *Qigong Fever: Body, Science, and Utopia in China*, 2007. Studies of Daoist art include Shih-shan Susan Huang, *Picturing the True Form: Daoist Visual Culture in Traditional China*, 2012; Stephen Little with Shawn Eichman, eds., *Taoism and the Arts of China*, 2000; Paul R. Katz, *Images of the Immortal: The Cult of Lü Dongbin at the Palace of Eternal Joy*, 1999; Stephen Little, *Realm of the Immortals: Daoism in the Arts of China*, 1988; László Legeza, *Tao Magic: The Secret Language of Diagrams and Calligraphy*, 1975; and Chang Chung-yüan, *Creativity and Taoism: A Study of Chinese Philosophy, Art, and Poetry*, 1963. Some Daoist themes and topics are found in Eugene Wang, *Shaping the Lotus Sutra: Buddhist Visual Culture*

of Medieval China, 2005. On mixed Buddho-Daoist statuary, see Stanley Abe, *Ordinary Images*, 2002. On the connections between music, theater, and Daoist ritual, see Pen-Yeh and Daniel P. L. Law, eds., *Studies of Taoist Rituals and Music of Today*, 1989, and David Johnson, ed., *Ritual Opera/Operatic Ritual: "Mu-Lien Rescues His Mother" in Chinese Popular Culture* (1989). Studies of Daoism in relation to the natural world include James Robson, *Power of Place: The Religious History of the Southern Sacred Peak (Nanyue) in Medieval China*, 2009; Robert E. Harrist, Jr., *The Landscape of Words: Stone Inscriptions from Early and Medieval China*, 2008; Norman J. Girardot, James Miller, and Liu Xiaogan, eds., *Daoism and Ecology: Ways Within a Cosmic Landscape*, 2001; Julian Ward, *Cave Paradises and Talismans: Voyages Through China's Sacred Mountains*, 1995; Susan Naquin and Chün-fang Yü, eds., *Pilgrims and Sacred Sites in China*, 1992; Munakata Kiyohiko, *Sacred Mountains in Chinese Art*, 1991; Rolf A. Stein, *The World in Miniature: Container Gardens and Dwellings in Far Eastern Religious Thought*, 1990; Aat Vervoorn, *Men of Cliffs and Caves: The Development of the Chinese Eremitic Tradition to the End of the Han Dynasty*, 1990; John Hay, *Kernels of Energy, Bones of Earth: The Rock in Chinese Art*, 1985; and Hedda Morrison and Wolfram Eberhard, *Hua Shan: The Sacred Mountain in West China: Its Scenery, Monasteries, and Monks*, 1973. Studies of female Daoist deities and female Daoist practitioners include Brigitte Baptandier, *The Lady of Linshui: A Chinese Female Cult* (2008); Suzanne E. Cahill, *Divine Traces of the Daoist Sisterhood*, 2006; Catherine Despeux and Livia Kohn, *Women in Daoism*, 2003; Suzanne E. Cahill, *Transcendence and Divine Passion: The Queen Mother of the West in Medieval China*, 1993; and Edward H. Schafer, *The Divine Woman: Dragon Ladies and Rain Maidens in T'ang Literature*, 1973. On the relationship between Daoism and the popular use of morality books, see Cynthia J. Brokaw, *The Ledgers of Merit and Demerit: Social Change and Moral Order in Late Imperial China*, 1991. On contemporary Daoist monastic practice, see Adeline Herrou, *A World of Their Own: Daoist Monks and Their Community in Contemporary China*, 2013; and on its earlier history, see Livia Kohn, *Monastic Life in Medieval Daoism: A Cross-Cultural Perspective*, 2003. On aspects of Buddho-Daoism and Buddho-Daoist conflicts, see T. H. Barrett, *From Religious Ideology to Political Expediency in Early Printing: An Aspect of Buddho-Daoist Rivalry*, 2012; Stephen R. Bokenkamp, *Ancestors and Anxiety: Daoism and the Birth of Rebirth in China*, 2009; Christine Mollier, *Buddhism and Taoism Face to Face: Scripture, Ritual, and Iconographic Exchange in Medieval China*, 2008; James Robson, *Power of Place: The Religious History of the Southern Sacred Peak (Nanyue) in Medieval China*, 2009; Michel Strickmann, *Chinese Magical Medicine*, 2002; Livia Kohn, *Laughing at the Tao: Debates among Buddhists and Taoists in Medieval China*, 1995; T. H. Barrett, *Li Ao: Buddhist, Taoist, or Neo-Confucian?* 1992; and Erik Zürcher, *The Buddhist Conquest of China: The Spread and Adaptation of Buddhism in Early Medieval China*, 2007 (1969). On Daoism among the Yao peoples, see Eli Alberts, *A History of Daoism and the Yao People of South China*, 2006, and Jacque Lemoine, *Yao Ceremonial Paintings*, 1982. On elements of Daoism in Japan, see Herman Ooms, *Imperial Politics and Symbolics in Ancient Japan: The Tenmu Dynasty, 650–800*, 2008; John Breen and Mark Teeuwen, *Shinto in History: Ways of the Kami*, 2000; and Felicia G. Bock, *Classical Learning and Taoist Practices in Early Japan: With a Translation of Books XVI and XX of the Engi-shiki*, 1985.

Permissions Acknowledgments

GENERAL INTRODUCTION

Kay Ryan: "On the Nature of Understanding," from *The New Yorker,* July 25, 2011. Copyright © 2011 by Kay Ryan. Reprinted by permission of the author.

TEXT

The Book of Master Mo (Against the Confucians): From THE MOZI: A COMPLETE TRANSLATION, translated by Ian Johnston. Copyright © 2010 by Columbia University Press. Reprinted with permission of Columbia University Press and The Chinese University Press.

The Scripture of the Way and Its Virtue (excerpts): From LAO TZU TAO TE CHING, translated and with an introduction by D. C. Lau (Penguin Classics, 1963). Copyright © 1963 by D. C. Lau. Reprinted with permission of Penguin Books Limited.

The Book of Master Zhuang (excerpts): From CHUANG TZU: BASIC WRITINGS, translated by Burton Watson. Copyright © 2003 Columbia University Press. Reprinted by permission of the publisher.

Master of Huainan (excerpts): From THE HUAINANZI: A GUIDE TO THE THEORY AND PRACTICE OF GOVERNMENT IN EARLY CHINA, translated by John S. Major, Sarah A. Queen, Andrew Seth Meyer, and Harold D. Roth. Copyright © 2010 by Columbia University Press. Reprinted with permission of the publisher.

Inward Training: From ORIGINAL TAO: INWARD TRAINING AND THE FOUNDATIONS OF TAOIST MYSTICISM by Harold D. Roth. Copyright © 1999 by Columbia University Press. Reprinted with permission of the publisher.

THE SEAL OF THE UNITY OF THE THREE: A STUDY AND TRANSLATION OF THE CONTONG QI, THE SOURCE OF THE TAOIST WAY OF THE GOLDEN ELIXIR (excerpts) by Fabrizio Pregadio. Copyright © 2001 Fabrizio Pregadio. Reprinted by permission of Golden Elixir Press.

The Old Man by the River Commentary (excerpt): From HO-SHANG-KUNG'S COMMENTARY ON LAO-TSE, translated by Eduard Erkes. Copyright © 1950. Reprinted by permission of Artibus Asiae.

Essential Points on the Six Lineages of Thought (Sima Tan): From SOURCES OF CHINESE TRADITION, SECOND EDITION, VOLUME 1, compiled by Wm. Theodore de Bary and Irene Bloom, selection translated by Harold Roth and Sarah Queen. Copyright © 1999 by Columbia University Press. Reprinted with permission of the publisher.

THE SCRIPTURE ON GREAT PEACE: THE TAIPING JING AND THE BEGINNINGS OF DAOISM (excerpts), translated by Barbara Hendrischke. Copyright © 2007 by the Regents of the University of California. Published by the University of California Press. Reprinted by permission of the University of California Press.

The Laozi Inscription: From READINGS IN HAN CHINESE THOUGHT, edited and translated by Mark Csikszentmihalyi. Copyright © 2006 Hackett Publishing Company, Inc. Reprinted by permission of Hackett Publishing Company, Inc. All rights reserved.

Scripture on Laozi's Transformations: From "The Image of the Perfect Ruler in Early Taoist Messianism: Lao-Tau and Li Hung" by Anna K. Seidel from HISTORY OF RELIGIONS 9.2/3 (1969–Feb. 1970). Copyright © 1970 by University of Chicago Press. Reprinted by permission of University of Chicago Press.

Two Poems on Taishan (Cao Zhi): From "Verses from on High: The Ascent of T'ai Shan" by Paul W. Kroll from *T'oung Pao, Second Series,* Vol. 69, Livr. 4-5 (1983). Copyright © 1983 by Koninklijke Brill NV. Reprinted by permission of Koninklijke Brill NV.

Memorial to Emperor Huan Concerning Buddhism and Daoism (Xiang Kai): From READINGS IN HAN CHINESE THOUGHT, edited and translated by Mark Csikszentmihalyi. Copyright © 2006 Hackett Publishing Company, Inc. Reprinted by permission of Hackett Publishing Company, Inc. All rights reserved.

The Conversion of the Barbarians (Wang Fu): From THE BUDDHIST CONQUEST OF CHINA: THE SPREAD AND ADAPTATION OF BUDDHISM IN EARLY MEDIEVAL CHINA, translated by Erik Zurcher. Copyright © 2006 by Koninklijke Brill. Reprinted by permission of Koninklijke Brill NV.

The Xiang'er Commentary on the Laozi (excerpts): From EARLY DAOIST SCRIPTURES by Stephen R. Bokenkamp. Copyright © 1999 by the Regents of the University of California. Published by the University of California Press. Reprinted by permission of the University of California Press.

Commands and Admonitions for the Family of the Great Dao (excerpts): From EARLY DAOIST SCRIPTURES by Stephen R. Bokenkamp. Copyright © 1999 by the Regents of the University of California. Published by the University of California Press. Reprinted by permission of the University of California Press.

Regulations of the Dark Capital (excerpt): From SOURCES OF CHINESE TRADITION, SECOND EDITION, VOLUME 1, compiled by Wm. Theodore de Bary and Irene Bloom, selection translated by Nathan Sivin. Copyright © 1999 by Columbia University Press. Reprinted with permission of the publisher.

The Most High Jade Scripture on the Internal View of the Yellow Court (translated by Paul W. Kroll; excerpts): From RELIGIONS OF CHINA IN PRACTICE, edited by Donald S. Lopez, Jr. Copyright © 1996 by Princeton University Press. Reprinted by permission of Princeton University Press.

The Array of the Five Numinous Treasure Talismans of the Most High (excerpt). Translated by Gil Raz. Reprinted by permission of W. W. Norton & Company, Inc.

Instructions on the Scripture of the Divine Elixirs of the Nine Tripods of the Yellow Emperor (excerpts): From GREAT CLARITY: DAOISM AND ALCHEMY IN EARLY MEDIEVAL CHINA by Fabrizio Pregadio. Copyright © 2006 by the Board of Trustees of the Leland Stanford Jr. University. All rights reserved. Used by permission of Stanford University Press, www.sup.org.

The Inner Chapters of the Book of the Master Who Embraces Simplicity (Ce Hong; excerpts). Translated by Gil Raz. Reprinted by permission of W. W. Norton & Company, Inc.

Traditions of Divine Transcendents (excerpts): From TO LIVE AS LONG AS HEAVEN AND EARTH: A TRANSLATION AND STUDY OF GE HONG'S TRADITIONS OF DIVINE TRANSCENDENTS, by Robert Ford Campany. Copyright © 2002 by the Regents of the University of California. Published by the University of California Press. Reprinted by permission of the University of California Press.

The Demon Statutes of Lady Blue, chapter 1: From CHINESE MAGICAL MEDICINE by Michel Strickmann, edited by Bernard Faure. Copyright © 2002 by the Board of Trustees of the Leland Stanford Jr. University. All rights reserved. Used with the permission of Stanford University Press, www.sup.org.

The Demon Statutes of Lady Blue, chapter 3, translated by Terry Kleeman: From PURPOSES, MEANS AND CONVICTIONS IN DAOISM: A BERLIN SYMPOSIUM, edited by Florian C. Reiter. Copyright © 2007. Reprinted by permission of Florian C. Reiter.

The Record of the Ten Continents (excerpts), translated by Thomas E. Smith: From *Taoist Resources* 2.2 (1990). Reprinted by permission of the *Journal of Chinese Religions*.

The 180 Precepts Spoken by Lord Lao, translated by Barbara Hendrischke and Benjamin Penny: From *Taoist Resources* 6.2 (1996). Reprinted by permission of the *Journal of Chinese Religions*.

The Spirit Spells of the Abyss, selection 1: From CHINESE MAGICAL MEDICINE by Michel Strickmann, edited by Bernard Faure. Copyright © 2002 by the Board of Trustees of the Leland Stanford Jr. University. All rights reserved. Used with the permission of Stanford University Press, www.sup.org.

The Spirit Spells of the Abyss, selection 2: From SOURCES OF CHINESE TRADITION SECOND EDITION, VOLUME 1, compiled by Wm. Theodore de Bary and Irene Bloom, selection translated by Nathan Sivin. Copyright © 1999 by Columbia University Press. Reprinted with permission of the publisher.

The Declarations of the Perfected (The Diffusion of the Corpus): From "The Mao Shan Revelations: Taoism and the Aristocracy" by Michel Strickmann from *T'oung Pao, Second Series*, Vol. 63, Livr. 1 (1977). Copyright © by Koninklijke Brill NV. Reprinted by permission of Koninklijke Brill NV.

The Declarations of the Perfected (Betrothal; Marriage), translated by Stephen Bokenkamp: From RELIGIONS OF CHINA IN PRACTICE, edited by Donald S. Lopez, Jr. Copyright © 1996 by Princeton University Press. Reprinted by permission of Princeton University Press.

Master's Zhou's Records of His Communications with the Unseen (excerpts), translated by Stephen Bokenkamp: From RELIGIONS OF CHINA IN PRACTICE, edited by Donald S. Lopez, Jr. Copyright © 1996 by Princeton University Press. Reprinted by permission of Princeton University Press.

The Marvelous Scripture in Purple Characters of the Lord Emperor of the Gold Portal (excerpts): EARLY DAOIST SCRIPTURES by Stephen R. Bokenkamp. Copyright © 1999 by the Regents of the University of California. Published by the University of California Press. Reprinted by permission of the University of California Press.

Scripture of the Three Primordial, Perfected, Ones, by the Imperial Lord of the Golden Portal: From THE METHOD OF HOLDING THE THREE ONES: A TAOIST MANUAL OF MEDITATION OF THE FOURTH CENTURY A.D., translated by Poul Anderson. Copyright © Poul Andersen 1980. Reprinted by permission of the Poul Andersen.

The Wondrous Scripture of the Upper Chapters of Limitless Salvation (excerpts): From EARLY DAOIST SCRIPTURES by Stephen R. Bokenkamp. Copyright © 1999 by the Regents of the University of California. Published by the University of California Press. Reprinted by permission of the University of California Press.

Purification Rite of Luminous Perfected, translated by Stephen Bokenkamp: From RELIGIONS OF CHINA IN PRACTICE, edited by Donald S. Lopez, Jr. Copyright © 1996 by Princeton University Press. Reprinted by permission of Princeton University Press.

Abridged Codes of Master Lu for the Daoist Community (Lu Xiujing; translated by Peter Nickerson): From RELIGIONS OF CHINA IN PRACTICE, edited by Donald S. Lopez, Jr. Copyright © 1996 by Princeton University Press. Reprinted by permission of Princeton University Press.

The Five Sentiments of Gratitude (Lu Xiujing): From SOURCES OF CHINESE TRADITION, SECOND EDITION, VOLUME 1, compiled by Wm. Theodore de Bary and Irene Bloom, selection translated by Franciscus Verellen. Copyright © 1999 by Columbia University Press. Reprinted with permission of the publisher.

Scripture of the Opening of Heaven by the Most High Lord Lao, translated by Edward H. Schafer: From *Taoist Resources* 7.2 (1997). Reprinted by permission of the *Journal of Chinese Religions*.

Biographies of Students of the Dao (excerpts): From THE FRAGMENTS OF DAOXUE ZHUAN: CRITICAL EDITION, TRANSLATION AND ANALYSIS OF A MEDIEVAL COLLECTION OF DAOIST BIOGRAPHIES, translated by Stephen Peter Bumbacher. Copyright © 2000. Reprinted by permission of Peter Lang.

Scripture of the Inner Explanations of the Three Heavens (excerpts): From SOURCES OF CHINESE TRADITION, SECOND EDITION, VOLUME 1, compiled by Wm. Theodore de Bary and Irene Bloom, selection translated by Kristopher Schipper. Copyright © 1999 by Columbia University Press. Reprinted with permission of the publisher.

The Great Petition for Sepulchral Plaints, translated by Peter Nickerson: From EARLY DAOIST SCRIPTURES by Stephen R. Bokenkamp. Copyright © 1999 by the Regents of the University of California. Published by the University of California Press. Reprinted by permission of the University of California Press.

SHIH-SHUO HSIN-YÜ, A NEW ACCOUNT OF TALES OF THE WORLD by Liu I-ch'ing (excerpts; with commentary by Liu Chün), translated and with introduction and notes by Richard B. Mather. Ann Arbor: University of Michigan, Center for Chinese Studies, 2002. Reprinted by permission. Original text in Wade-Giles, editor's conversion to Pinyin.

The Essay to Ridicule the Dao (excerpts): From LAUGHING AT THE TAO: DEBATES AMONG BUDDHIST AND TAOISTS IN MEDIEVAL CHINA, translated by Livia Kohn. Copyright © 1995 by Livia Kohn. Reprinted by permission of Livia Kohn.

The Essentials of the Practice of Perfection (excerpt): This translation first appeared in Michel Strickmann, "The Seal of the Law: A Ritual Implement and the Origins of Printing," *Asia Major* 6-2 (1996): 1.83. Reprinted with permission of *Asia Major*.

Scriptural Instructions of the Primordial Perfected from the Hall of Light of Highest Clarity (excerpt): From "The Jade Woman of Greatest Mystery" by Edward H. Schafer from HISTORY OF RELIGIONS 17.3/4 (Feb.–May 1978). Copyright © 1978 by University of Chicago Press. Reprinted by permission of University of Chicago Press.

Short Exposition on the Transmission of the Scriptures, Rules, and Registers of the Three Caverns (Zhang Wanfu; excerpt): From THE CAVERN-MYSTERY TRANSMISSION: A TAOIST ORDINATION RITE OF A.D. 711 by Charles D. Benn. Copyright © 1991 by University of Hawaii Press. Reprinted with permission.

The Scripture and Chart for the Mysterious Contemplation of Man-Bird Mountain: Excerpt from "The Presentation of the Memorial" by John Lagerwey from TAOIST RITUAL IN CHINESE SOCIETY AND HISTORY. Copyright © 1987. Reproduced by permission of John Lagerwey.

The Regulations for the Acceptance and Cultivation of Daoism (excerpts): From THE ASPIRATIONS AND STANDARDS OF TAOIST PRIESTS IN THE EARLY T'ANG PERIOD by Florian C. Reiter. Copyright © 1998. Reprinted by permission of Florian C. Reiter.

Scripture on Inner Observation (excerpt): From TAOIST MEDITATION AND LONGEVITY TECHNIQUES by Livia Kohn. Ann Arbor: University of Michigan, Center for Chinese Studies, 1989. Michigan Monographs in Chinese Studies, Vol. 61. Reprinted by permission. Original text in Wade-Giles; editor's conversion to Pinyin.

Seal of the Unity of the Three (Shitou Xiqian): BRANCHING STREAMS FLOW IN THE DARKNESS: ZEN TALKS ON THE SANDOKAI, by Shunryu Suzuki. Copyright © 2001 by the San Francisco Zen Center. Published by the University of California Press. Reprinted with permission of the University of California Press.

Stele Inscription—The Restoration of the Shrine of Wei Hua-Ts'un (Yan Zhenqing; translated by Edward H. Schafer): From *Journal of Oriental Studies* 15 (1977): 129–37. Copyright © 1977 by Hong Kong University Press. Reprinted by permission of Hong Kong University Press.

Cantos on Pacing the Void (Wu Yun; translated by Edward H. Schafer): From *Harvard Journal of Asiatic Studies* 41.2 (Dec. 1981). Reprinted by permission of Phyllis Brooks Schafer.

The Ascent of Mount Tai (Li Bo): From "Verses From on High: The Ascent of T'ai Shan" by Paul W. Kroll from *T'oung Pao, Second Series*, Vol. 69, Livr. 4-5 (1983). Copyright © 1983 by Koninklijke Brill NV. Reprinted by permission of Koninklijke Brill NV.

The Lady of the Supreme Primordial and Flying Dragon Conductus (Li Bo); **Composed in Response . . .** (Bo Juyi): From TRANSCENDENCE AND DIVINE PASSION: THE QUEEN MOTHER OF THE WEST IN MEDIEVAL CHINA by Suzanne E. Cahill, translator. Copyright © 1993 by the Board of Trustees of the Leland Stanford Jr. University. All rights reserved. Used with the permission of Stanford University Press, www.sup.org.

The Book of Returning to One's True Nature (Li Ao; excerpt): From LI AO: BUDDHIST, TAOIST, OR NEO-CONFUCIAN? translated by T. H. Barrett. Copyright © 1992 by T. H. Barrett. Reprinted by permission of Oxford University Press.

INQUIRY INTO THE ORIGIN OF HUMANITY: AN ANNOTATED TRANSLATION OF TSUNG-MI'S YÜAN JEN LUN WITH A MODERN COMMENTARY (excerpt) by Peter N. Gregory. Copyright © 1995 by Kuroda Institute. Reprinted with permission by the University of Hawaii Press.

Wang Fajin and Ms. Wang (Du Guangtin): From DIVINE TRACES OF THE DAOIST SISTERHOOD: RECORDS OF THE ASSEMBLED TRANSCENDENTS OF THE FORTIFIED WALLED CITY, translated by Suzanne E. Cahill. Reprinted by permission of Suzanne E. Cahill.

Mao Ying: From TRANSCENDENCE AND DIVINE PASSION: THE QUEEN MOTHER OF THE WEST IN MEDIEVAL CHINA by Suzanne E. Cahill, translator. Copyright © 1993 by the Board of Trustees of the Leland Stanford Jr. University. All rights reserved. Used with the permission of Stanford University Press, www.sup.org.

Biographies of Persons Who Had Encounters with Supernatural Beings and Immortals (Du Guangting; excerpts): From SOURCES OF CHINESE TRADITION, SECOND EDITION, VOLUME 1, compiled by Wm. Theodore de Bary and Irene Bloom, selection translated by Franciscus Verellen. Copyright © 1999 by Columbia University Press. Reprinted with permission of the publisher.

Record of Miracles in Support of Daoism (Du Guangting; excerpt): Reprinted by permission of the Harvard University Asia Center from James Robson, POWER OF PLACE: THE RELIGIOUS LANDSCAPE OF THE SOUTHERN SACRED PEAK (NANYUE) IN MEDIEVAL CHINA. Harvard University Asia Center, 2009, pp. 202–03. Copyright © The President and Fellows of Harvard College, 2009. Reprinted with permission.

The Sutra of the Three Kitchens, Preached by the Buddha (excerpt): From BUDDHISM AND TAOISM FACE TO FACE by Christine Mollier. Copyright © 2008 University of Hawaii Press. Reprinted with permission.

Recorded for the Ritual of Merit and Virtue for Repairing the Various Observatories of Qingcheng Mountain (Du Guangting; translated by Thomas H. Peterson; excerpt): From *Taoist Resources* 6.1 (1957). Reprinted by permission of the *Journal of Chinese Religions*.

The Collection of Books and Old New (excerpts): From TAOISM AND CHINESE RELIGION by Henri Maspero, translated by Frank A. Kierman, Jr. Copyright © 1981 the University of Massachusetts Press; copyright © 2014 Quirin Press. Reprinted by permission of Quirin Press, Melbourne, and the University of Massachusetts Press.

Zhongli of the Han Leads Lan Caihe to Enlightenment: From MONKS, BANDITS, LOVERS, AND IMMORTALS: ELEVEN EARLY CHINESE PLAYS, edited and translated by Stephen H. West and Wilt L. Idema. Copyright © 2010 by Hackett Publishing Company. Reprinted by permission of Hackett Publishing Company, Inc. All rights reserved.

Memorabilia of the Three Kingdoms (excerpt): From SOURCEBOOK OF KOREAN CIVILIZATION: VOLUME 1, FROM EARLY TIMES TO THE SIXTEENTH CENTURY, edited by Peter H. Lee. Copyright © 1993 by Columbia University Press. Reprinted with permission of the publisher.

Records of the Three Kingdoms (excerpt): From SOURCEBOOK OF KOREAN CIVILIZATION: VOLUME 1, FROM EARLY TIMES TO THE SIXTEENTH CENTURY, edited by Peter H. Lee. Copyright © 1993 by Columbia University Press. Reprinted with permission of the publisher.

THE MONKEY AND THE MONK: A REVISED ABRIDGMENT OF "THE JOURNEY TO THE WEST" (excerpt), translated by Anthony C. Yu. Copyright © 2006 by University of Chicago. Reproduced by permission of University of Chicago Press.

JOURNEY TO THE NORTH: AN ETHNOHISTORICAL ANALYSIS AND ANNOTATED TRANSLATION OF THE CHINESE FOLK NOVEL PEI-YU CHI (excerpt), translated by Gary Seaman. Copyright © 1987. Reprinted by permission of Gary Seaman.

A Record of the Land of the Blessed: From ANTHOLOGY OF CHINESE LITERATURE: VOLUME 2, FROM THE FOURTEENTH CENTURY TO THE PRESENT DAY, edited by Cyril Birch. Copyright © 1972 by Grove Press Inc. Used by permission of Grove/Atlantic, Inc. Any third party use of this material, outside of this publication, is prohibited.

The Buddhist Monk Han-Shan Te-Ch'ing's Commentaries on the Laozi and Zhuangzi (pp. 159–63) by Hanshan Deqing: From A BUDDHIST LEADER IN MING CHINA: THE LIFE AND THOUGHTS OF HAN-SAN TE-CH'ING, edited by Sung-peng Hsu. Copyright © 1979 The Pennsylvania State University. Reprinted by permission of The Pennsylvania State University Press. All rights reserved.

Erh-k'o P'o-an ching chi, A Taste of Immortality: From TRADITIONAL CHINESE STORIES: THEMES AND VARIATIONS, edited by Y. W. Ma and Joseph S. M. Lau. Copyright © 1986 Cheng & Tsui Company. Used by permission of Cheng & Tsui Company, Inc. Translated by Dell R. Hales.

Religious Sects among the Chinese: From *China in the Sixteenth Century: The Journals of Matteo Ricci, 1583–1610,* translated by Louis J. Gallagher, S.J. Copyright © 1942, 1953, and renewed 1970 by Louis J. Gallagher, S.J. Used by permission of Random House, an imprint and division of Random House LLC. All rights reserved.

The Daoist Priest of the Mountains (Liao-chai chih-i): From TRADITIONAL CHINESE STORIES: THEMES AND VARIATIONS, edited by Y. W. Ma and Joseph S. M. Lau. Copyright © 1986 Cheng & Tsui Company, Inc. Reprinted by permission of Cheng & Tsui Company, Inc. Translated by Jeanne Kelly.

THE SECRET OF THE GOLDEN FLOWER: A CHINESE BOOK OF LIFE (excerpts), translated from the Chinese by Richard Wilhelm; translated from the German by Cary F. Baynes. Copyright © 1931. Reprinted by permission of Penguin Books Ltd.

Cutting the Red Dragon (Fu Shan). Translated by Elena Valussi. Reprinted by permission of W. W. Norton & Company, Inc.

Combined Collection of Female Alchemy (He Longxiang). Translated by Elena Valussi. Reprinted by permission of W. W. Norton & Company, Inc.

Secret Principles of Gathering the True Essence (excerpts): From ART OF THE BEDCHAMBER: THE CHINESE SEXUAL YOGA CLASSICS INCLUDING WOMEN'S SOLO MEDITATION TEXTS by Douglas Wile, the State University of New York Press. Copyright © 1992 by State University of New York. All rights reserved. Reprinted by permission.

Transmission of the Mind-Lamp from Mount Jin'gai (Biography of Zhao Daojian *and* Biography of Wang Changyue) by Min Yide: From RELIGION AND CHINESE SOCIETY: VOLUME 2, TAOISM AND LOCAL RELIGION IN MODERN CHINA, edited by John Lagerwey, translated by Monica Esposito. Copyright © The Chinese University of Hong Kong and École française d'Extrême-Orient 2004. Reprinted by permission of The Chinese University Press.

Immortal's Certificate (translated by Karen C. Duval): From THE TAOIST BODY by Kristofer Schipper. Copyright © 1996 by the Regents of the University of California. Published by the University of California Press. Reprinted by permission of the University of California Press.

The Hermits of Huashan, "Origins and Development of the Dao Teachings of [Qiu] Changchun" (excerpt): From RELIGION AND CHINESE SOCIETY: VOLUME 2, TAOISM AND LOCAL RELIGION IN MODERN CHINA, edited by John Lagerwey, translated by Monica Esposito. Copyright © The Chinese University of Hong Kong and École française d'Extrême-Orient 2004. Reprinted by permission of The Chinese University Press.

A Shamanistic Exorcism: From "Pilot Surveys of Chinese Shamans, 1875–1945: A Spatial Approach to History" by Donald Sutton from *Journal of Social History* 15.1. Copyright © 1981 by Oxford University Press. Reprinted by permission of Oxford University Press.

Biographical Stele Inscription for the Daoist Wang: Reprinted by permission from Vincent Goossaert, *The Taoist of Peking 1800–1949: A Social History of Urban Clerics.* Harvard East Asian Monographs 284, Harvard University Asia Center, Cambridge, MA, 2007, pp. 131–33. Copyright © 2007 The President and Fellows of Harvard College.

The Dao among the Yao of Southeast Asia (excerpts): From YAO CEREMONIAL PAINTINGS by Jacques Lemoine. Copyright © 1982 by White Lotus Co. Ltd. Reprinted by permission of White Lotus Co. Ltd.

Commentary on "Talks and Parables" (excerpt): From I AND TAO: MARTIN BUBER'S ENCOUNTER WITH CHUANG TZU by Jonathan R. Herman, the Sate University of New York Press. Copyright © 1996 by State University of New York. All rights reserved. Reprinted by permission.

Carl Jung, Foreword to the Second German Edition of THE SECRET OF THE GOLDEN FLOWER: A CHINESE BOOK OF LIFE, translated by Richard Wilhelm. Copyright © 1931. Reprinted by permission of Penguin Books Ltd. English translation by Cary F. Baynes.

Explorations in Oral Secrets (Chen Yingning): Reprinted by permission from Xun Liu, *Daoist Modern: Innovation, Lay Practice, and the Community of Inner Alchemy in Republican Shanghai.* Harvard East Asian Monographs 313, Harvard

ILLUSTRATIONS

Index

Abridged Codes of Master Lu for the Daoist Community, The (*Lu xiansheng daomen kelüe*) (Lu Xiujing), 321, 322

Ancient Sage, The (Tennyson), 654, 655

Array of the Five Numinous Treasure Talismans of the Most High, The (*Taishang lingbao wufu xu*), 215

Ascent of Mount Tai, The (Li Bo), 404

Awakening to Reality (*Wuzhen pian*) (Zhang Boduan), 468

Bai Yuchan, 505

Ballad on Looking for the Way, A (Fangnei Sanren), 677

Baopu zi neipian (*The Inner Chapters of the Book of the Master Who Embraces Simplicity*) (Ge Hong), 223, 224

Beiyou ji (*Journey to the North*), 587

Biographical Stele Inscription for the Daoist Wang (*Wang daoren daoxing bei*), 632, 633

Biographies of Persons Who Had Contacts and Encounters with Supernatural Beings and Immortals (*Shenxian ganyu zhuan*) (Du Guangting), 426

Biographies of Students of the Dao (*Daoxue zhuan*), 336

Biography of the Gentleman with No Name (*Wuming jun zhuan*) (Shao Yong), 479

Bo Juyi,

Book of Master Han Fei, The (*Han Feizi*), 404, 405

Book of Master Mo, The (*Mozi*), 83

Book of Master Zhuang, The (*Zhuangzi*), 97, 98

Book of Returning to One's True Nature, The (*Fuxing shu*) (Li Ao), 410, 411

Buber, Martin, 667

Buddhists and Daoists at Mount Nanyue Welcome the People's Communes, 711

Buxu ci (*Cantos on Pacing the Void*) (Wu Yun), 398, 399

Caizhen jiyao (*Secret Principles of Gathering the True Essence*) (Zhang Sanfeng), 623, 624

Cantong qi (*The Seal of the Unity of the Three*) (Shitou Xiqian), 395

Cantos on Pacing the Void (*Buxu ci*) (Wu Yun), 398, 399

Cao Zhi, 184

Capra, Fritjof, 714

Changchun zhenren xiyou ji (*The Record of Perfected Perpetual Spring's Travels to the West*) (Li Zhichang), 523, 524

Chen Yingning, 675

Chinese Sage, A (Wilde), 657, 658

Chongyang lijiao shiwu lun (*Redoubled Yang's Fifteen Discourses for the Establishment of the Doctrine*) (Wang Zhe), 519, 520

Chronicles of Japan, The (*Nihongi*), 441

Chuanshou sandong jingjie falu lüeshuo (*The Short Exposition on the Transmission of the Scriptures, Rules, and Registers of the Three Caverns*) (Zhang Wanfu), 375

Chunyang wanshou gong shengzhi bei (*A Stele of an Imperial Decree [Issued to] the Palace of Purified Yang and Limitless Longevity*), 532

Collection of Books New and Old on the Absorption of Breath Gathered by the Master of Yanling, The (*Yanling xiansheng ji xinjiu fuqi jing*), 434, 435

Combined Collection of Female Alchemy (*Nüdan hebian*) (He Longxiang), 620, 621

Commands and Admonitions for the Family of the Great Dao (*Dadao jia lingjie*), 202, 203

Commentaries on the Laozi and Zhuangzi (Hanshan Deqing), 595, 596

Commentary on "Talks and Parables of Chuang Tzu" (Buber), 667, 668

Complete Performance of Su, The (Dachu su), 679

Composed in Response to "Sending Daoist Master Liu Off to Wander on Heavenly Platform Mountain" (Bo Juyi), 399

Conversion of the Barbarians, The (Wang Fu), 188, 189

Corpus of Daoist Ritual, The (Daofa huiyuan), 495, 496

Cutting the Red Dragon (Duan Honglong) (Fu Shan), 619

Dachao chongjian Chunyang wanshou gong zhi bei (A Stele on the Reconstruction of the Great Palace of Purified Yang and Limitless Longevity [during] Our Great Dynasty) (Wang E), 531

Dachu su (The Complete Performance of Su), 679

Dadao jia lingjie (Commands and Admonitions for the Family of the Great Dao), 202, 203

Dao Among the Yao of Southeast Asia, The: Selected Texts, 651

Daode jing (The Scripture of the Way and Its Virtue), 85

Daofa huiyuan (The Corpus of Daoist Ritual), 495, 496

Daoist Monastic Life (Yoshioka), 687, 688

Daoist Ordination Certificate from Putian, Fujian, A, 733

Daoist Priest of the Lao Mountains, The, 611, 612

Daojiao lingyan ji (Record of Miracles in Support of Daoism) (Du Guangting), 428, 429

Daoxue zhuan (Biographies of Students of the Dao), 336

Dazhong songzhang (The Great Petition for Sepulchral Plaints),

Declaration of the Chinese Daoist Association on Global Ecology, A (Zhang Jiyu), 343

Declarations of the Perfected, The (Zhen'gao), 261, 262

Demon Statutes of Lady Blue, The (Nüqing guilü), 240

Dongxuan lingbao sandong fengdao kejie yingshi (The Regulations for the Acceptance and Cultivation of Daoism According to the Dongxuan, Lingbao, and Sandong Scriptures), 382, 383

Dongxuan lingbao wugan wen (The Five Sentiments of Gratitude) (Lu Xiujing), 330

Dongyuan shenzhou jing (The Spirit Spells of the Abyss), 256, 257

Duan Honglong (Cutting the Red Dragon) (Fu Shan), 619

Du Guangting, 418, 426, 428, 432

During a Visit to the Southern Tower of the Veneration of Truth Monastery I Saw the New Examination Graduates Writing Their Names on the Wall (Yu Xuanji), 440

Early Autumn (Yu Xuanji), 440

Esoteric Biography of Qinghe (Qinghe neizhuan), 493

Essay on the Secret Essentials of the Recycled Elixir (Huandan biyao lun) (Wang Daoyuan), 533

Essay to Ridicule the Dao, The (Xiaodao lun) (Zhen Luan), 349

Essential Points on the Six Lineages of Thought (Lun liujia yaozhi) (Sima Tan), 154

Essentials of the Practice of Perfection from the One and Orthodox Ritual Canon, The (Zhengyi fawen xiuzhen zhiyao), 367

Explanation of the Diagram of the Supreme Polarity (Taijitu shuo) (Zhou Dunyi), 476, 477

Explorations in Oral Secrets (Koujue gouxuan lu) (Chen Yingning), 675

Fangnei Sanren, 677

Feelings in the Last Month of Spring; Sent to a Friend (Yu Xuanji), 439

Five Sentiments of Gratitude, The (Dongxuan lingbao wugan wen) (Lu Xiujing), 330

Flying Dragon Conductus [I and II] (Li Bo), 408

Foreword to "The Secret of the Golden Flower" (Jung), 673

Foshuo sanchu jing (The Sutra of the Three Kitchens, Preached by the Buddha), 429, 430

Fu Shan, 619

Fuxing shu (The Book of Returning to One's True Nature) (Li Ao), 410, 411

Ge Hong, 223
Great Lingbao Method of the Shangqing Heaven, The (Shangqing lingbao dafa) (Wang Qizhen), 510
Great Petition for Sepulchral Plaints, The (Dazhong songzhang), 343
Guanzhui bian (Limited Views: Essays on Ideas and Letters) (Qian Zhongshu), 721, 722
Guifeng Zongmi, 415

Han Feizi (The Book of Master Han Fei), 142, 143
Hanshan Deqing, 595
Han Zhong Li dutuo Lan Caihe (Zhongli of the Han Leads Lan Caihe to Enlightenment), 537, 538
Harrison, George, 713
Heard and Written by Yijian (Yijian zhi) (Hong Mai), 487, 488
Heidegger and Our Translation of the Daode Jing (Hsiao), 700, 701
He Longxiang, 620
Hermits of Huashan, The, 629
Heshang Gong (The Old Man by the River Commentary), 1432, 1433
Hong Mai, 487
Hsiao, Paul Shih-yi, 700
Huainan zi (The Master of Huainan), 117, 118
Huandan biyao lun (Essay on the Secret Essentials of the Recycled Elixir) (Wang Daoyuan), 533
Huangdi jiuding shendan jing (Instructions on the Scripture of the Divine Elixirs of the Nine Tripods of the Yellow Emperor), 218, 219
Huangfu Mei, 437
Huangtian shangqing jinque dijun lingshu ziwen shangjing (The Marvelous Scripture in Purple Characters of the Lord Emperor of the Gold Portal), 292, 293

Immortal's Certificate, 629, 630
Indications of the Goals of the Three Teachings (Sango shiki) (Kukai), 444, 445
Inner Chapters of the Book of the Master Who Embraces Simplicity, The (Baopu zi neipian) (Ge Hong), 223, 224
Inner Light, The (Harrison), 713, 714

Inquiry into the Origin of Humanity, The (Yuanren lun) (Guifeng Zongmi), 415
Inscription on an Image at Kamsan Monastery (Sŏl Ch'ong), 451, 452
Instructions on the Scripture of the Divine Elixirs of the Nine Tripods of the Yellow Emperor (Huangdi jiuding shendan jing), 218, 219
[In the Morn I Wandered] (Cao Zhi), 186
Introduction to the Tao Te Ching and Epilogue: Dao Song (Le Guin), 740, 741
Inward Training (Neiye), 128

Jindan longhu jing (The Scripture on the Golden Elixir of the Dragon and Tiger), 465
Jin'gai xindeng (Transmission of the Mind-Lamp from Mount Jin'gai) (Min Yide), 626, 627
Jinque dijun sanyuan zhenyi jing (Scripture of the Three Primordial Perfected Ones, by the Imperial Lord of the Golden Portal), 298
Jin zixu yuanjun ling shangzhen siming nanyue furen xiantan beiming (Stele Inscription for the Altar of the Transcendent Lady Wei of the Jin Dynasty, the Lady of the Southern Peak, Primal Worthy of the Purple Void, Concurrently Supreme True Mistress of Destiny) (Yan Zhenqing), 396, 397
Journey to the North (Beiyou ji), 587
Journey to the West (Xiyou ji), 573
Jung, Carl Gustave, 673

Kakinomoto Hitomaro, 442
Koujue gouxuan lu (Explorations in Oral Secrets) (Chen Yingning), 675
Kukai, 444

Lady of the Supreme Primordial, The (Li Bo), 407
Laojun shuo yibai bashi jie (The 180 Precepts Spoken by Lord Lao), 247, 248
Laozi (The Scripture of the Way and Its Virtue), 85
Laozi bianhua jing (Scripture on Laozi's Transformations), 81, 82
Laozi Inscription, The (Laozi ming), 177, 178
Laozi ming (The Laozi Inscription), 177, 178

Laozi xiang'er zhu (*The Xiang'er Commentary on the Laozi*), 193, 194
Le Guin, Ursula K., 740
Leifu zou shiyi xun danzhang (*A Vermilion Petition Memorializing the Thunder Court on the Matter of Deliberating Merit Titles*) (Bai Yuchan), 505, 506
Li Ao, 410
Li Bo, 404
Limited Views: Essays on Ideas and Letters (*Guanzhui bian*) (Qian Zhongshu), 721, 722
Limitless Longevity (*Wanshou wuliang*), 736, 737
Lingbao wuliang duren shangpin miaojing (*The Wondrous Scripture of the Upper Chapters of Limitless Salvation*), 305, 306
Liu Yiqing, 348
Li Zhichang, 523
Lord Lao's Spirit Medium, 737, 738
Lun liujia yaozhi (*Essential Points on the Six Lineages of Thought*) (Sima Tan), 154
Lu xiansheng daomen kelüe (*The Abridged Codes of Master Lu for the Daoist Community*) (Lu Xiujing), 321, 322
Lu Xiujing, 321, 330

Marvelous Scripture in Purple Characters of the Lord Emperor of the Gold Portal, The (*Huangtian shangqing jinque dijun lingshu ziwen shangjing*), 292, 293
Master of Huainan, The (*Huainanzi*), 117, 118
Master Zhou's Records of His Communications with the Unseen (*Zhoushi mingtong ji*), 280, 281
Memorabilia of the Three Kingdoms (*Samguk yusa*), 552, 553
Memorial to Emperor Huan Concerning Buddhism and Daoism (Xiang Kai), 186, 187
Mingzhen zhai (*Purification Rite of Luminous Perfected*), 314, 315
Minor Writings from Shanshui (*Shanshui xiaodu*) (Huangfu Mei), 437
Min Yide, 626
Most High Jade Scripture on the Internal View of the Yellow Court, The (*Taishang huangting neijing yujing*), 210, 211
Mozi (*The Book of Master Mo*), 83

Neiye (*Inward Training*), 128
New Account of Tales of the World, A (*Shishuo xinyu*) (Liu Yiqing), 348, 349
Nihongi (*The Chronicles of Japan*), 441
Nüdan hebian (*Combined Collection of Female Alchemy*) (He Longxiang), 620, 621
Nüqing guilü (*The Demon Statutes of Lady Blue*), 240

Old Man by the River Commentary, The (Heshang Gong), 152, 153
180 Precepts Spoken by Lord Lao, The (*Laojun shuo yibai bashi jie*), 247, 248
On the Assigned Topic of Willows by the River (Yu Xuanji), 440
[Our great Sovereign] (Kakinomoto Hitomaro), 443

Private Tutor of the Nine Spontaneously Generating Lingbao Heavens of Primordial Commencement: on Latent Refinement for Transcendent Salvation and Vitalizing Transformation (*Yuanshi lingbao ziran jiutian shenghua chaodu yinlian bijue*), 501
Purification Rite of Luminous Perfected (*Mingzhen zhai*), 314, 315

Qian Zhongshu, 721
Qinghe neizhuan (*Esoteric Biography of Qinghe*), 493

Recorded for the Ritual of Merit and Virtue for Repairing the Various Observatories of Qingcheng Mountain (*Xiu qingcheng shan zhuguan gongde ji*) (Du Guangting), 432
Record of Miracles in Support of Daoism (*Daojiao lingyan ji*) (Du Guangting), 428, 429
Record of Perfected Perpetual Spring's Travels to the West, The (*Changchun zhenren xiyou ji*) (Li Zhichang), 523, 524
Record of the Land of the Blessed, A (*Sanshan fudi zhi*), 591
Record of the Tang Dynasty Shrine to Perfected Man Lü of Purified Yang, A (*You Tang Chunyang Lü zhenren citang ji*) (Yuan Congyi), 530

Record of the Ten Continents, The (Shizhou ji), 243, 244

Records of the Assembled Transcendents of the Fortified Walled City (Yongcheng jixian lu) (Du Guangting), 418, 419

Records of the Three Kingdoms (Samguk sagi), 554

Redoubled Yang's Fifteen Discourses for the Establishment of the Doctrine (Chongyang lijiao shiwu lun) (Wang Zhe), 519, 520

Regulations for the Acceptance and Cultivation of Daoism According to the Dongxuan, Lingbao, and Sandong Scriptures, The (Dongxuan lingbao sandong fengdao kejie yingshi), 382, 383

Regulations of the Dark Capital (Xuandu liiwen), 207, 208

Religious Sects Among the Chinese (Matteo Ricci), 604, 605

Ricci, Matteo, 604

RZA (Robert Diggs), 745

Samguk sagi (Records of the Three Kingdoms), 554

Samguk yusa (Memorabilia of the Three Kingdoms), 552, 553

Sango shiki (Indications of the Goals of the Three Teachings) (Kukai), 444, 445

Sanshan fudi zhi (A Record of the Land of the Blessed), 591

Santian neijie jing (The Scripture of the Inner Explanations of the Three Heavens), 340, 341

Scriptural Instructions of the Primordial Perfected from the Hall of Light of Highest Clarity (Shangqing mingtang yuanzhen jingjue), 372, 373

Scripture and Chart for the Mysterious Contemplation of Man-Bird Mountain, The (Xuanlan renniao shan jingtu), 380, 381

Scripture of Great Peace, The (Taiping jing), 169, 170

Scripture of the Inner Explanations of the Three Heavens, The (Santian neijie jing), 340, 341

Scripture of the Opening of Heaven by the Most High Lord Lao (Taishang laojun kaitian Jing), 332, 333

Scripture of the Three Primordial Perfected Ones, by the Imperial Lord of the

Golden Portal (Jinque dijun sanyuan zhenyi jing), 298

Scripture of the Way and Its Virtue, The (Daode jing, or Laozi), 85

Scripture on Inner Observation by the Most High Lord Lao (Taishang laojun neiguan jing), 391, 392

Scripture on Laozi's Transformations (Laozi bianhua jing), 181, 182

Scripture on the Golden Elixir of the Dragon and Tiger, The (Jindan longhu jing), 465

Seal of the Unity of the Three, in Accordance with the Book of Changes, The (Zhouyi cantong qi), 133, 134

Seal of the Unity of the Three, The (Cantong qi) (Shitou Xiqian), 395

Secret Essentials of the Most High Principal Zhenren Assisting the Country and Saving the People (Taishang zhuguo jiumin zongzhen biyao) (Yuan Miaozong), 483, 484

Secret of the Golden Flower, The (Taiyi jinhua zongzhi), 614

Secret Principles of Gathering the True Essence (Caizhen jiyao) (Zhang Sanfeng), 623, 624

Selling Wilted Peonies (Yu Xuanji), 440

Shamanistic Exorcism, A, 631

Shangqing lingbao dafa (The Great Lingbao Method of the Shangqing Heaven) (Wang Qizhen), 510

Shangqing mingtang yuanzhen jingjue (Scriptural Instructions of the Primordial Perfected from the Hall of Light of Highest Clarity), 372, 373

Shanshui xiaodu (Minor Writings from Shanshui) (Huangfu Mei), 437

Shao Yong, 479

Shenxian ganyu zhuan (Biographies of Persons Who Had Contacts and Encounters with Supernatural Beings and Immortals) (Du Guangting), 426

Shenxian zhuan (Traditions of Divine Transcendents), 234, 235

Shishuo xinyu (A New Account of Tales of the World) (Liu Yiqing), 348, 349

Shitou Xiqian, 395

Shizhou ji (The Record of the Ten Continents), 243, 244

Short Exposition on the Transmission
of the Scriptures, Rules, and
Registers of the Three Caverns,
The (Chuanshou sandong jingjie
falu lüeshuo) (Zhang Wanfu),
375
Sima Tan, 154
Sŏl Ch'ong, 451
Song for Liu, a Comrade of the Dao, of
White Tiger Cave, A (Zeng
bailongdong Liu daoren ge)
(Zhang Boduan), 474, 475
Spirit Spells of the Abyss, The (Dongyuan
shenzhou jing), 256, 257
Stele Inscription for the Altar of the
Transcendent Lady Wei of the Jin
Dynasty, the Lady of the Southern
Peak, Primal Worthy of the Purple
Void, Concurrently Supreme True
Mistress of Destiny (Jin zixu
yuanjun ling shangzhen siming
nanyue furen xiantan beiming)
(Yan Zhenqing), 396, 397
Stele of an Imperial Decree [Issued to] the
Palace of Purified Yang and
Limitless Longevity, A (Chunyang
wanshou gong shengzhi bei),
532
Stele on the Reconstruction of the Great
Palace of Purified Yang and
Limitless Longevity [during] Our
Great Dynasty, A (Dachao
chongjian Chunyang wanshou
gong zhi bei) (Wang E), 531
Sutra of the Three Kitchens, Preached by
the Buddha, The (Foshuo sanchu
jing), 429, 430

Taijitu shuo (Explanation of the Diagram of
the Supreme Polarity) (Zhou
Dunyi), 476, 477
Taiping jing (The Scripture of Great Peace),
169, 170
Taishang ganying pian (Tract of the Most
Exalted on Action and Response),
514, 515
Taishang huangting neijing yujing (The
Most High Jade Scripture on the
Internal View of the Yellow Court),
210, 211
Taishang laojun kaitian jing (Scripture of
the Opening of Heaven by the Most
High Lord Lao), 332, 333
Taishang laojun neiguan jing (Scripture on
Inner Observation by the Most
High Lord Lao), 391, 392

Taishang lingbao wufu xu (The Array of the
Five Numinous Treasure Talismans
of the Most High), 215
Taishang zhuguo jiumin zongzhen biyao
(Secret Essentials of the Most
High Principal Zhenren Assisting
the Country and Saving the
People) (Yuan Miaozong), 483,
484
Taiyi jinhua zongzhi (The Secret of the
Golden Flower), 614
Taoism: A Prize Essay, 663, 664
Tao of Physics, The: An Exploration of the
Parallels between Modern Physics
and Eastern Mysticism (Capra),
714, 715
Taste of Immortality, A, 599, 600
Tennyson, Alfred, Lord, 654
Tract of the Most Exalted on Action and
Response (Taishang ganying pian),
514, 515
Traditions of Divine Transcendents
(Shenxian zhuan), 234, 235
Transmission of the Mind-Lamp from
Mount Jin'gai (Jin'gai xindeng)
(Min Yide), 626, 626

[Urge on the Carriage] (Cao Zhi), 184

Vermilion Petition Memorializing the
Thunder Court on the Matter
of Deliberating Merit Titles,
A (Leifu zou shiyi xun
danzhang) (Bai Yuchan), 505,
506

Wang daoren daoxing bei (Biographical
Stele Inscription for the Daoist
Wang), 632, 633
Wang Daoyuan, 533
Wang E, 531
Wang Fu, 188
Wang Qizhen, 510
Wang Zhe, 519
Wanshou wuliang (Limitless Longevity),
736, 737
[Where our Sovereign reigns] (Kakinomoto
Hitomaro), 442
Why Must We Prohibit the Reactionary
Daoist Cults? (Xu Jianguo), 707,
708
Wilde, Oscar, 657
Wondrous Scripture of the Upper Chapters
of Limitless Salvation, The
(Lingbao wuliang duren shangpin
miaojing), 305, 306

Wuming jun zhuan (Biography of the Gentleman with No Name) (Shao Yong), 479
Wu-Tang Manual, The (RZA), 745
Wu Yun, 398
Wuzhen pian (Awakening to Reality) (Zhang Boduan), 468

Xiang'er Commentary on the Laozi, The (Laozi xiang'er zhu), 193, 194
Xiang Kai, 186
Xiaodao lun (The Essay to Ridicule the Dao) (Zhen Luan), 349
Xiu qingcheng shan zhuguan gongde ji (Recorded for the Ritual of Merit and Virtue for Repairing the Various Observatories of Qingcheng Mountain) (Du Guangting), 432
Xiyou Ji (Journey to the West), 573
Xuandu lüwen (Regulations of the Dark Capital), 207, 208
Xuanlan renniao shan jingtu (The Scripture and Chart for the Mysterious Contemplation of Man-Bird Mountain), 380, 381
Xu Jianguo, 707

Yanling xiansheng ji xinjiu fuqi jing (The Collection of Books New and Old on the Absorption of Breath Gathered by the Master of Yanling), 434, 435
Yan Zhenqing, 396
Yijian zhi (Heard and Written by Yijian) (Hong Mai), 487, 488
Yoshioka, Yoshitoyo, 687
Youngcheng jixian lu (Records of the Assembled Transcendents of the Fortified Walled City) (Du Guangting), 418, 419
You Tang Chunyang Lü zhenren citang ji (A Record of the Tang Dynasty Shrine to Perfected Man Lü of Purified Yang) (Yuan Congyi), 530
Yuan Congyi, 530
Yuan Miaozong, 483
Yuanren lun (The Inquiry into the Origin of Humanity) (Guifeng Zongmi), 415
Yuanshi lingbao ziran jiutian shenghua chaodu yinlian bijue (Private Tutor of the Nine Spontaneously Generating Lingbao Heavens of Primordial Commencement: on Latent Refinement for Transcendent Salvation and Vitalizing Transformation), 501
Yu Xuanji, 437

Zeng bailongdong Liu daoren ge (A Song for Liu, a Comrade of the Dao, of White Tiger Cave) (Zhang Boduan), 474, 475
Zhang Boduan, 468, 474
Zhang Jiyu, 748
Zhang Sanfeng,
Zhang Wanfu, 623
Zhen'gao (The Declarations of the Perfected), 261, 262
Zhengyi fawen xiuzhen zhiyao (The Essentials of the Practice of Perfection from the One and Orthodox Ritual Canon), 367
Zhen Luan, 349
Zhongli of the Han Leads Lan Caihe to Enlightenment (Han Zhong Li dutuo Lan Caihe), 537, 538
Zhou Dunyi, 476
Zhoushi mingtong ji (Master Zhou's Records of His Communications with the Unseen), 280, 281
Zhouyi cantong qi (The Seal of the Unity of the Three, in Accordance with the Book of Changes), 133, 136
Zhuangzi (The Book of Master Zhuang), 97, 98